THE COURTS

and

THE PUBLIC SCHOOLS

THE COURTS

and

THE PUBLIC SCHOOLS

*The Legal Basis of School Organization and
Administration*

By

NEWTON EDWARDS

THIRD EDITION

WITH A PREFACE AND AN
ADDITIONAL CHAPTER BY

LEE O. GARBER

THE UNIVERSITY OF CHICAGO PRESS

CHICAGO AND LONDON

TO MY WIFE

Who Made the Writing of This Book Possible

International Standard Book Number: 0–226–18606–7
Library of Congress Catalog Card Number: 55–5122

THE UNIVERSITY OF CHICAGO PRESS, CHICAGO 60637
THE UNIVERSITY OF CHICAGO PRESS LTD., LONDON

Contents

Preface to the Third Edition

I N THE preface to the first edition of *The Courts and the Public
Schools*, which appeared in 1933, Professor Edwards stated that he
had two major purposes. He sought "(1) to make clear the fundamental
principles underlying the relation of the state to education; (2) to reduce to systematic organization the principles of the case or common
law which are applicable to practical problems of school organization
and administration." In the preface to the second edition, 1955, he
addressed himself to the same purposes. How well he succeeded in
achieving them is attested by the warm reception with which each was
greeted. They received the deserved commendation of all scholars in
the field of school law. The first edition was a pioneer effort, and the
second, like the first, was a classic.

The second edition was a complete revision of the earlier work. In
preparing it Professor Edwards followed substantially the same organization he had used earlier and included those court decisions that
had appeared in the interim. In addition he added several new chapters
which he felt were necessitated by new cases.

This third edition is not an extensive revision of the earlier work. It
was felt that little would be gained by a complete revision including
decisions of the higher courts rendered since 1955, since many of them
simply serve to reinforce the principles of law identified in the earlier
edition. Nevertheless, there are some changes in these principles, and
some new principles only recently enunciated, that should be treated
to bring the book up to date. It was decided that this new edition
would not disturb by revision the sound foundation Professor Edwards
had laid, but would reproduce it as is and add a concluding chapter
on changing principles and on those that have only recently emerged.

Because of the high standard set by Professor Edwards in the two
earlier editions, my task has not been easy. In preparing this concluding chapter I have attempted to keep in mind the major purposes that
guided him, particularly the second—"to reduce to systematic organization the principles of the case or common law which are applicable
to practical problems of school organization and administration." Until
some important new principles have gained universal acceptance, the

best one can do is treat individual cases separately, point out trends, and consider both similarities and differences in judicial thinking.

I was closely associated with Professor Edwards for a number of years, being one of his students at the time the first edition of this book was being prepared. I collaborated with him on a series of eight casebooks in school law, and he invited me to participate in the preparation of this third edition of *The Courts and the Public Schools*. I remain deeply grateful to him for his constant stimulation and encouragement.

LEE O. GARBER

ILLINOIS STATE UNIVERSITY

Preface to the Second Edition

IN THE Preface to the first edition of *The Courts and the Public Schools* the author made the following statement of the major purposes that governed his investigation and determined the structural organization of the content of the volume:

In this book the writer seeks to do two things: (1) to make clear the fundamental principles underlying the relation of the state to education; (2) to reduce to systematic organization the principles of the case or common law which are applicable to practical problems of school organization and administration. Such a book finds its justification in the fact that the maintenance and operation of our educational system has come to be one of the major public enterprises of this country. In order to deal intelligently with many of the aspects of school administration, boards of education, superintendents, and principals should be familiar with the principles of law which govern their action. Moreover, those who undertake to formulate fundamental principles of educational policy should know something of the place the school occupies in legal theory. The relation of the school to civil society, on the one hand, and to the individual, on the other, is nowhere so well defined as in the great body of decisions rendered by the highest of our state and federal courts. It would seem obvious that both the educational statesman and the practical school administrator should be familiar with the fundamental principles of law governing the operation of our system of public education.

In this revised edition the author has kept these same purposes steadily in mind. He has followed substantially the same organization, although new chapters have been added and all the material has been revised in terms of the court decisions that have appeared since the first edition. He has attempted a very thorough and painstaking revision.

For the past third of a century the author has given a course in the legal and constitutional basis of school organization and administration in the Department of Education at the University of Chicago. This volume has grown out of the material employed in that course and out of the many insights and understandings contributed by his many former students. To all these he makes a grateful acknowledgment. He is especially indebted to Dr. John M. Beck, of the Chicago Teachers College, for assistance in preparing the manuscript for the press and for many helpful suggestions with respect to content.

UNIVERSITY OF CHICAGO   NEWTON EDWARDS

Preface to the First Edition

IN THIS book the writer seeks to do two things: (1) to make clear the fundamental principles underlying the relation of the state to education; (2) to reduce to systematic organization the principles of the case or common law which are applicable to practical problems of school organization and administration. Such a book finds its justification in the fact that the maintenance and operation of our educational system has come to be one of the major public enterprises of this country. In order to deal intelligently with many of the aspects of school administration, boards of education, superintendents, and principals should be familiar with the principles of law which govern their action. Moreover, those who undertake to formulate fundamental principles of educational policy should know something of the place the school occupies in legal theory. The relation of the school to civil society, on the one hand, and to the individual, on the other, is nowhere so well defined as in the great body of decisions rendered by the highest of our state and federal courts. It would seem obvious that both the educational statesman and the practical school administrator should be familiar with the fundamental principles of law governing the operation of our system of public education.

For the last twelve years the writer has given a course in the legal and constitutional basis of school administration in the Department of Education of the University of Chicago. The present volume has grown out of the materials employed in this course and may, it is hoped, serve as a basic text for similar courses in other institutions.

The writer is deeply indebted to Professor Charles H. Judd, chairman of the Department of Education of the University of Chicago, for encouragement in the preparation of the book and for a critical reading of a large part of it while still in manuscript form. To his colleague, Professor Henry C. Morrison, he is under special obligation, not only for a critical reading of the entire manuscript, but for illuminating suggestions made while the book was in the process of being written. Miss Alma T. Edwards, of Queens College, read the entire manuscript and offered suggestions with respect to form and style. Thanks are also due to Miss Mabel C. Waltz for assistance in checking footnotes and reading proof, and to Frederick W. Schenk for making readily available the resources of the library of the Law School of the University of Chicago. To the Social Science Research Council the writer is indebted for a generous grant toward the publication of this volume. The *School Review* and the *Elementary School Journal* have given permission to publish certain portions of the book which first appeared in article form in those journals.

NEWTON EDWARDS

UNIVERSITY OF CHICAGO

CHAPTER I

Federal Relations to Education

FEDERALISM" is the term that best describes the American scheme of government. By that is meant a division of powers between the central government, on the one hand, and the governments of the several constituent states, on the other.

THE DISTRIBUTION OF POWERS

The government of the United States is one of delegated rather than inherent powers. Not only are its powers delegated, but they are expressly enumerated. And powers not expressly or impliedly conferred upon the government of the United States by the Constitution are, in the words of the Tenth Amendment, reserved to the respective states.[1] As the Supreme Court of the United States has clearly put it: "Each State has all governmental powers save such as the people, by their Constitution, have conferred upon the United States, denied to the States, or reserved to themselves. The Federal Union is a government of delegated powers. It has only such as are expressly conferred upon it and such as are reasonably to be implied from those granted."[2] It follows that the Congress at all times is under the necessity of finding express or implied authority for all its legislation in some clause or combination of clauses in the Constitution. With the states the case is different. They do not look to the federal Constitution for any grant of powers; their governmental powers are plenary unless the power in question has been delegated to the central government or unless it has been denied the states by some provision in the federal Constitution. In the words of the Supreme Court of Michigan:

When the validity of an act of Congress is challenged as unconstitutional, it is necessary to determine whether the power to enact it has been expressly or impliedly delegated to Congress. The legislative power [of a

1. Constitution of the United States, Amendment X: "The powers not delegated to the United States by the Constitution, nor prohibited by it to the States, are reserved to the States respectively, or to the people."

2. *United States* v. *Butler*, 297 U.S. 1, 56 S. Ct., 312.

state], under the Constitution of the state, is as broad, comprehensive, absolute, and unlimited as that of the parliament of England, subject only to the Constitution of the United States and the restraints and limitations imposed by the people upon such power by the Constitution of the state itself.[3]

FEDERAL AUTHORITY WITH RESPECT TO EDUCATION

Since the Constitution of the United States makes no mention of education, it follows that whatever *positive* powers the federal government may possess to support and control education in the states must grow out of some implied grant of power. Even though the federal government began to enact educational legislation before the adoption of the Constitution and has continued the practice through the years, the extent and the limits of its authority in this respect have never been clearly defined. Apparently, the positive powers of the national government with respect to education are to be found in the interpretation that has been and may be given to the general-welfare clause of the Constitution.

The general-welfare clause and the support and control of education.—The taxing clause of the federal Constitution confers upon the Congress power "to lay and collect Taxes, Duties, Imposts and Excises, to pay the Debts and provide for the common Defence and general Welfare of the United States."[4] From the very beginning of our national life, the interpretation of this clause has given rise to conflicting and long-disputed views. The debate centered around the opposing interpretations given the general-welfare clause by James Madison and Alexander Hamilton. Madison asserted that the clause had been borrowed from the Articles of Confederation, had been adopted by the constitutional convention without debate, had not been regarded by the framers of the Constitution as a phrase that would extend the area of federal authority. It conferred no substantive powers upon the national government. Madison held that the clause "amounted to no more than a reference to other powers enumerated in subsequent clauses of the same section; that, as the United States is a government of limited and enumerated powers, the grant of power to tax and spend for the general national welfare must be confined to the enumer-

3. *Young* v. *City of Ann Arbor,* 267 Mich. 241, 255 N.W. 579. See also *People* v. *Draper,* 15 N.Y. 532; *Commonwealth* v. *Hartman,* 17 Pa. St. 118.

4. Art. I, sec. 8, cl. 1.

ated legislative fields committed to the Congress."[5] Hamilton, on the other hand, maintained that the clause conferred upon the Congress power to tax and spend for purposes separate and distinct from those later enumerated, that it conferred a substantive power to tax and spend for any purpose that would promote the general welfare of the United States.

Despite the long debate with respect to the meaning of the clause and despite the fact that Congress was appropriating millions of dollars which could not be justified without reference to it, the Supreme Court was not called upon to consider it until 1936. In passing upon the constitutionality of the Agricultural Adjustment Act, the court adopted the Hamiltonian interpretation. This act provided for a processing tax, the proceeds of which would be used to regulate agricultural production. The court declared the act unconstitutional, but, in doing so, it said by way of dicta:

Each contention [the Madisonian and the Hamiltonian] has had the support of those whose views are entitled to weight. This court has noticed the question, but has never found it necessary to decide which is the true construction. Mr. Justice Story, in his *Commentaries*, espouses the Hamiltonian position. We shall not review the writings of public men and commentators or discuss the legislative practice. Study of these leads us to conclude that the reading advocated by Mr. Justice Story is the correct one. While, therefore, the power to tax is not unlimited, its confines are set in the clause which confers it, and not in those of section 8 which bestow and define the legislative powers of the Congress. It results that the power of Congress to authorize expenditure of public moneys for public purposes is not limited by the direct grants of legislative power found in the Constitution.[6]

In later cases, the Supreme Court authoritatively brought to a close the long debate over the power of Congress to tax and spend under the general-welfare clause. In *Helvering* v. *Davis*, the court upheld the Social Security Act and apparently for the first time sustained a particular use of the proceeds of taxation as an exercise of authority under the general-welfare clause. After pointing out that the scheme of benefits created by the act was not in contravention of the limitations of the Tenth Amendment and after stating categorically that Congress may spend money in aid of the general welfare, the court went on to indicate something of the criteria to be applied in determining the authority of Congress in this respect. It said:

5. *United States* v. *Butler*, 297 U.S. 1, 56 S. Ct. 312.
6. *United States* v. *Butler*, 297 U.S. 1, 56 S. Ct. 312.

Yet difficulties are left when the power is conceded. The line must still be drawn between one welfare and another, between particular and general. Where this shall be placed cannot be known through a formula in advance of the event. There is a middle ground or certainly a penumbra in which discretion is at large. The discretion, however, is not confided to the courts. The discretion belongs to Congress, unless the choice is clearly wrong, a display of arbitrary power, not an exercise of judgment. . . . Nor is the concept of the general welfare static. Needs that were narrow or parochial a century ago may be interwoven in our day with the well-being of the nation. What is critical or urgent changes with the times.[7]

While no case involving the power of Congress to tax and spend in support of education appears to be on record, the reasoning in the cases discussed and cited in the preceding paragraphs appears to be conclusive. There can be no doubt that Congress under the general-welfare clause would be accorded authority to make any reasonable appropriation for the support of education.

The constitutional authority of Congress to exercise control over education is a matter not so easily determined. It seems certain, however, that Congress cannot use its taxing and spending power for the primary purpose of regulating the fundamental educational policies of the states. That is to say, the taxing and spending power of the United States may not be employed as a means of regulating and controlling a matter outside the other enumerated powers and inside the powers retained by the states. Nor may Congress use its spending power for the primary purpose of purchasing state conformity to some policy of its own where the policy invades a subject within the jurisdiction of the states. In *United States* v. *Butler,* the court held the Agricultural Adjustment Act unconstitutional because it was a "plan to regulate and control agricultural production, a matter beyond the powers delegated to the Federal government."[8] The court went on to say: "At best, it is a scheme for purchasing with federal funds submission to federal regulation of a subject reserved to the states. . . . Congress cannot invade state jurisdiction to compel individual action; no more can it purchase such action." Thus the court took the firm position that the national government could not use the taxing power as an instrument to "enforce a regulation of matters of state concern with respect to which the Congress has no authority to interfere." That education would be considered such a concern seems reasonably certain.

7. *Helvering* v. *Davis,* 301 U.S. 619, 57 S. Ct. 904. See also *Steward Machine Company* v. *Davis,* 301 U.S. 548, 57 S. Ct. 883; *City of Cleveland* v. *United States,* 323 U.S. 329, 65 S. Ct. 280.

8. 297 U.S. 1, 56 S. Ct. 312.

It must not be assumed, however, that Congress has no regulatory powers in connection with its spending to promote the general welfare. Where regulation is not the primary purpose, the court would, no doubt, sustain regulatory measures essential to accomplish the purpose of the expenditure.

While Congress cannot use its taxing and spending power to purchase control of some matter reserved to the states, it may use this power to induce the states to co-operate with the national government in meeting some social need that is nation-wide in its scope. This was the position the court took in sustaining the system of unemployment compensation provided for in the Social Security Act.[9] Certainly education is a matter of national concern. It would seem, therefore, that the national government would not be invading the reserved powers of the states by employing its taxing and spending power to collaborate with the states in the promotion of education.

By way of summary it may be said that it seems clear that the national government may tax and spend in the support of education, it may enter into voluntary agreements with the states for the mutual support of education, it may not spend funds for the primary purpose of regulating the educational policies of the states, and it may enforce whatever control measures are incidental but essential in the accomplishment of the purposes for which federal funds are appropriated and spent.

CONSTITUTIONAL LIMITATIONS ON THE POWERS OF THE STATES

State educational policy may be profoundly affected by certain limitations on the powers of the states contained in the federal Constitution.

Impairing the obligations of contracts.—One such far-reaching limitation is the clause which prohibits any state from passing legislation impairing the obligation of contracts.[10] It is now well settled that a charter granted to a college or university is in the nature of a contract[11] and cannot be revoked or altered without the consent of those

---

9. *Steward Machine Company* v. *Davis*, 301 U.S. 548, 57 S. Ct. 883.

10. Art. I, sec. 10.

11. *Trustees of Dartmouth College* v. *Woodward*, 4 Wheaton (U.S.) 518, 4 L. Ed. 629; *Regents of the University of Maryland* v. *Williams*, 31 Am. Dec. 72; 9 Gill. & J. (Md.) 365.

to whom it was granted. In 1816 the legislature of New Hampshire passed an act materially altering the charter of Dartmouth College. The act was sustained by the Supreme Court of New Hampshire. Upon appeal to the Supreme Court of the United States, it was held that the charter was a contract between the state and the corporation and could in no manner be revoked or altered without the consent of those to whom it had been granted.[12] A later decision of the same court, however, holds that in the original charter the state may reserve the right to revoke or alter the charter at its pleasure and that such reservation becomes a part of the contract.

When a state legislature enacts a statute, the presumption is that it is no more than an expression of public policy which future legislatures may modify or revoke; each succeeding legislature, within broad limits at least, should be free and untrammeled in its right to formulate or change governmental policy. Even so, the Supreme Court of the United States has held that "a legislative enactment may contain provisions which, when accepted as the basis of action by individuals, become contracts between them and the state or its subdivisions within the protection of the clause in the federal constitution forbidding the impairment of the obligations of contracts."[13] Such was the position of the court in holding that a teacher-tenure statute in Indiana could not be amended by a subsequent legislature because it constituted a contract between the state and the teachers who were parties to it.[14] Similarly, it has been held that a contractual relation is established between teachers and the state under statutes creating a retire-

12. *Trustees of Dartmouth College* v. *Woodward*, 4 Wheaton (U.S.) 518, 4 L. Ed. 629.

13. *State* ex rel. *Anderson* v. *Brand*, 58 S. Ct. 443, 303 U.S. 95, 82 L. Ed. 685, 113 A.L.R. 1482. See also, *Faircloth* v. *Folmar*, 252 Ala. 223; 40 So. (2d) 697.

14. As a rule, however, teacher-tenure statutes are so worded as not to constitute a contract between teachers and the state. *Malone* v. *Hayden*, 329 Pa. 213, 197 Atl. 344; *Morgan* v. *Potter*, 238 Wis. 246, 298 N.W. 763; *Phelps* v. *State Board of Education*, 115 N.J.L. 310, 180 Atl. 220; *Groves* v. *Board of Education of Chicago*, 367 Ill. 91, 10 N.E. (2d) 403; *State* ex rel. *McKenna* v. *District No. 8*, 243 Wis. 324, 10 N.W. (2d) 155, 147 A.L.R. 290; *Lapolla* v. *Board of Education of New York City*, 15 N.Y.S. (2d) 149; *Taylor* v. *Board of Education of City of San Diego*, 31 Calif. App. 734, 89 Pac. (2d) 148; *Phelps* v. *Board of Education of Town of West New York*, 300 U.S. 319, 8 L. Ed. 674, 57 S. Ct. 483; *Phelps* v. *Prussia*, 60 Calif. App. 732, 141 Pac. (2d) 440; *Morrison* v. *Board of Education of City of West Allis*, 237 Wis. 483, 297 N.W. 383.

ment system which teachers voluntarily enter and to which they voluntarily contribute a percentage of their salaries.[15]

The constitutional prohibition of the impairment of the obligations of contracts must not, however, be regarded as absolute. It was not intended, nor has it been interpreted, to restrain a state from exercising its legitimate police power—the power to place on person and property whatever restraints may be reasonably necessary in the public interest. Every contract touching matters within the police power is entered into with the distinct understanding that the state reserves the right to modify the contract when and to such extent as the common good and welfare may require. The continuing supremacy of the state is not to be impaired by any contractual commitment. In South Carolina, for example, certain riparian owners had made a contract for a clear passage through a creek by the removal of existing obstructions. Later the legislature authorized the construction of a dam across the creek, a measure designed to drain certain lands and to increase their value. In sustaining the state's authority to do this, even though it did impair the obligation of a contract, the Supreme Court of the United States said:

It is the settled law of this court that the interdiction of statutes impairing the obligation of contracts does not prevent the State from exercising such powers as are vested in it for the promotion of the common weal, or are necessary for the general good of the public, though such contracts previously entered into between individuals may thereby be affected. This power, which in its various ramifications is known as the police power, is an exercise of the sovereign right of the Government to protect the lives, health, morals, comfort, and general welfare of the people, and is paramount to any rights under contracts between individuals.[16]

Following the same reasoning, some state courts have held that teacher-tenure statutes and statutes creating retirement systems for teachers do not create contractual rights which a later legislature may

15. *Raines v. Board of Trustees*, 365 Ill. 610, 7 N.E. (2d) 489; *Crawford v. Teachers Retirement Fund*, 164 Ore. 77, 99 Pac. (2d) 729; *Clarke v. Ireland*, 199 Pac. (2d) (Calif.) 965; *Driggs v. Utah State Teachers Retirement Board*, 105 Utah 417, 142 Pac. (2d) 657; *Payne v. Board of Trustees of the Insurance and Retirement Fund*, 76 N.D. 278, 35 N.W. (2d) 553. Other cases hold to the contrary. Teacher retirement systems will be discussed in detail in a later section of this volume.

16. *Manigault v. Springs*, 199 U.S. 473, 50 L. Ed. 274, 26 S. Ct. 127. Accord, *Long Island Water Supply Company v. Brooklyn*, 166 U.S. 685, 41 L. Ed. 1165; *In re Guilford Water Company*, 188 Me. 367, 108 Atl. 446; *Home Building and Loan Association v. Blaisdell*, 290 U.S. 398, 78 L. Ed. 413, 88 A.L.R. 148.

not impair if the interests of the educational system and the general public require it. In 1935 the legislature of Oregon repealed a tenure statute which had been enacted in 1913 and replaced it by a new one. The plaintiff in the case of *Campbell* v. *Aldrich*[17] contended that he had acquired vested contractual rights under the old statute which the new statute denied him. Assuming, but not deciding, that the plaintiff's contention was correct, the court nevertheless sustained the constitutionality of the new act on the ground that the sovereign power vested in the legislature to enact laws for the betterment of the state's educational system could not be bartered away. The exercise of such power at one time does not preclude its exercise by a later legislature when, in the light of experience, a different policy seems desirable. Such private rights as teachers may have acquired under the original statute "must yield to the public welfare when a different educational policy has been determined through the proper exercise of the police power."

The Supreme Court of Iowa has taken the same position with respect to a teachers' pension statute. Acting under the authority of the statute, the Board of Education of Des Moines raised the retirement age from sixty to sixty-five. A teacher who had already become eligible for retirement challenged the authority of the board to make the change, on the ground that it impaired a vested contractual right. The court held otherwise, because, in matters of government or public policy or the exercise of police power, one legislature could not be bound by another. The establishment and maintenance of a public school system is an indispensable obligation of the state, and in meeting that obligation each succeeding legislature must be free to exercise its own best judgment.[18]

Religious freedom, separation of church and state.—In the words of the First Amendment to the Constitution of the United States, "Congress shall make no law respecting an establishment of religion, or prohibiting the free exercise thereof." Before the adoption of the Fourteenth Amendment this prohibition was limited to the Congress. But the Supreme Court has held that the clause of the Fourteenth Amendment providing that "no state shall make or enforce any law which shall abridge the privileges and immunities of citizens of the

17. 159 Ore. 208, 79 Pac. (2d) 257.

18. *Talbot* v. *Independent School District of Des Moines,* 230 Iowa 949, 299 N.W. 556.

United States" makes the First Amendment applicable to the states.[19] Many cases have come before the courts, both state and federal, involving the interpretation of this amendment, and they will be discussed in some detail later in this volume. It may be pointed out here, however, that the Supreme Court of the United States has interpreted this amendment as establishing a "wall of separation" between church and state. More specifically, it has been interpreted as a denial of authority of either the national government or the government of any state to appropriate and spend moneys raised by taxation in support of sectarian institutions or instruction.

The doctrine of separation of church and state was given its strongest expression in the case of *Illinois* ex rel. *McCollum* v. *Board of Education*.[20] The case involved the constitutionality of the "released-time" plan of religious instruction in the public schools of Champaign, Illinois. It was a plan whereby the classrooms of a public school were turned over to religious instructors, who were to give sectarian instruction to such pupils as desired it. Pupils who did not desire religious instruction were required to go to some other place in the school building for pursuit of their secular studies. In holding that the program violated the First Amendment, the court gave forceful expression to the doctrine of the separation of church and state. After reviewing the facts in the case, the court said:

The foregoing facts . . . show the use of tax-supported property for religious instruction. . . . This is beyond all question a utilization of the tax-established and tax-supported public school system to aid religious groups to spread their faith. And it falls squarely under the ban of the First Amendment . . . as we interpreted it in *Everson* v. *Board of Education*, 330 U.S. 1. There we said: "Neither a state nor the Federal Government can set up a church. . . . No tax in any amount, large or small, can be levied to support any religious activities or institutions, whatever they may be called, or whatever form they may adopt to teach or practice religion." . . . In the words of Jefferson, the clause against establishment of religion by law was intended to erect "a wall of separation between Church and State."

As Mr. Justice Frankfurter pointed out in a concurring opinion in the McCollum case, agreement in the abstract that the First Amendment was designed to erect a "wall of separation between Church and

19. *Everson* v. *Board of Education of the Township of Ewing*, 330 U.S. 1, 67 S. Ct. 962; *Stromberg* v. *California*, 283 U.S. 359; *Cantwell* v. *Connecticut*, 310 U.S. 296.

20. 333 U.S. 203.

State" does not prevent a clash of views with respect to what the wall separates. Just what constitutes aid or support of a religious educational institution and just what is sectarian instruction are matters that have to be decided in terms of the facts in each particular case. As a later discussion of the relation of church and state to education will reveal, there is no unity of opinion on these matters, either in the American public or in the judicial mind.

The First Amendment reaches very far in the protection of the individual in his religious beliefs or disbeliefs. Just how sensitive the highest of our courts is to the right of the individual to be free from official censorship or control in the realm of intellect or spirit is revealed by a far-reaching decision, holding unconstitutional the action of a state in making it compulsory for children in the public schools to salute and pledge allegiance to the flag of the United States. The legislature of West Virginia enacted a statute requiring children in the public schools to salute and pledge allegiance to the flag of the United States. Refusal to salute the flag was to be regarded as insubordination, punishable by expulsion; the expelled child was to be regarded as "unlawfully absent" and subject to prosecution as a delinquent; parents of expelled children were liable to prosecution and, upon conviction, subject to fine or conviction. The plaintiff in the case was a member of the religious faith known as Jehovah's Witnesses. The ceremony of flag salute, he maintained, was violative of his religious convictions.

At the time the case came to trial, the Supreme Court of the United States itself and numerous state courts had sustained the constitutionality of similar statutes or board regulations.[21] Even so, the court reconsidered the matter and reversed its former position. It said:

> To sustain the compulsory flag salute we are required to say that a Bill of Rights which guards the individual's right to speak his own mind, left it open to public authorities to compel him to utter what is not in his mind. . . .
> We can have intellectual individualism and the rich cultural diversities that we owe to exceptional minds only at the price of occasional eccentricity and abnormal attitudes. When they are so harmless to others or to the State as those we deal with here, the price is not too great. But freedom to differ is not limited to things that do not matter much. That would be a

---

21. *Minersville School District* v. *Gobitis*, 310 U.S. 586, 846 Ed. 1375, 60 S. Ct. 1010; *Johnson* v. *Town of Deerfield*, 25 Fed. Supp. 918; *Gabrielli* v. *Knickerbocker*, 12 Calif. (2d) 85, 82 Pac. (2d) 391; *People* ex rel. *Fish* v. *Sandstrom*, 279 N.Y. 523, 18 N.E. (2d) 840, 120 A.L.R. 646; *Nicholls* v. *Mayor and School Committee of Lynn*, 297 Mass. 65, 7 N.E. (2d) 577, 110 A.L.R. 377; *State* v. *Davis*, 58 Ariz. 444, 120 Pac. (2d) 808.

mere shadow of freedom. The test of its substance is the right to differ as to things that touch the heart of the existing order. . . .

If there is any fixed star in our constitutional constellation, it is that no official, high or low, can prescribe what shall be orthodox in politics, nationalism, religion, or other matters of opinion or force citizens to express by word or act their faith therein. If there are any circumstances which permit of an exception, they do not occur to us.

We think the action of the local authorities in compelling the flag salute and pledge transcends constitutional limitations on their power and invades the sphere of intellect and spirit which it is the purpose of the First Amendment to our Constitution to reserve from all official control.[22]

Equal protection of the law.—Another limitation on the authority of the states is the clause in the Fourteenth Amendment which declares that "no state shall . . . deny to any person within its jurisdiction the equal protection of the laws." This means that no state may enforce legislation or authorize administrative agencies to enforce rules and regulations that discriminate in favor of one class of citizens as over against another. Each and every person has a right to equal treatment under the law. Moreover, the legal rights of the citizen are personal to him; in determining the rights of the individual, the courts will not rest content with ascertaining the equal treatment of different classes of citizens; whatever may be the rights of others, the individual can demand protection of his own. The courts hold, too, that rights and privileges guaranteed under the law must, in fact, be equal. And where equal protection under the law is denied, the complaining party is entitled to speedy redress. Most of the cases involving the application of this clause to educational issues have involved race segregation in the schools. These cases will be given extended treatment in a later section.

Restrictions under the due-process-of-law clause.—A clause in the Fourteenth Amendment provides that no state shall "deprive any person of life, liberty, or property, without due process of law." As this amendment is now interpreted, the Supreme Court of the United States exercises final determination of what constitutes proper exercise of the police power on the part of the states. So important and far-reaching is the exercise of the right of federal review of state legislation involving the exercise of the police power that one needs a clear conception of that power.

Judge O'Rear, speaking for the Court of Appeals of Kentucky, defined the police power about as definitely as it can be defined:

22. *Board of Education of West Virginia* v. *Barnette,* 63 S. Ct. 1178, 319 U.S. 624, 147 A.L.R. 674.

No jurist has dared to attempt to state the limit in law of that quality in government which is exercised through what is termed the "police power." All agree that it would be inadvisable to attempt it. Yet very broadly and indefinitely speaking, it is the power and obligation of government to secure and promote the general welfare, comfort and convenience of the citizens, as well as the public peace, the public health, the public morals, and the public safety (Cooley's *Constitutional Limitations,* 704). . . . It is not inaptly regarded in some of its most important features as the right of self-protection in government, the right of self-preservation in society. It inheres in every state, is fundamental in the existence of every independent government, enabling it to conserve the well-being of society, and prohibit all things hurtful to its comfort or inimical to its existence. In view of these definitions of the principle, unsatisfactory as they must be conceded to be, it is apparent that even those things reserved by the people in the Bill of Rights from the powers delegated to their magistrates are impliedly subject also to the power to preserve the State. . . . The good sense and the honest judgment of each generation must after all furnish the real limit to the police power of government. For each age must judge—and will judge—of what is hurtful to its welfare, or what endangers the existence of society.[23]

The Supreme Court of the United States has defined the police power in somewhat broader terms. Speaking of that power, the court said:

It embraces every law which concerns the welfare of the whole people of the state or any individual within it, whether it relates to their rights or duties, whether it respects them as men or citizens of the state, whether it relates to the rights of persons or property of the whole people of the state or of any individual within it.[24]

Stated in somewhat different terms, the police power is that power of the state to limit individual rights in the interest of the social group. Rights of person and of property may be restricted in any manner and to any extent reasonably necessary to promote public health, morals, comfort, and the general welfare. Even rights guaranteed by the Constitution are subject to limitation under the police power of the state.

The police power is inherent in every state, and it is a prerogative of the state legislature to determine for what purposes and in what manner it shall be exercised. There are, however, limits to the exercise of the police power; the individual has certain fundamental rights which must be respected. The state cannot arbitrarily subject person and property to all kinds of restraints and burdens. In the exercise of

23. *Berea College* v. *Commonwealth,* 123 Ky. 209, 94 S.W. 623, 124 Am. St. Rep. 344.

24. *New York* v. *Miln,* 11 Pet. (U.S.) 139, 9 L. Ed. 662.

the police power, the object to be attained must be reasonably necessary to promote the public welfare, and the measures prescribed must be reasonably necessary for the accomplishment of the end desired.

Although the police power is inherent in the legislature, the legislature itself is not the final judge of the limits to which the state may go in the curtailment of individual rights. As was said by the Supreme Court of the United States in the case of *Meyer* v. *State of Nebraska:* "Determination by the legislature of what constitutes proper exercise of the police power is not final or conclusive, but is subject to supervision by the courts."[25] The court of final jurisdiction in any state may nullify a statute as an arbitrary exercise of police power; and even when a statute is sustained by the state courts, it may be declared invalid by the Supreme Court of the United States as being in violation of the due-process-of-law clause.

If any person feels that he has been unreasonably or unjustly deprived of his liberty or his property, or if any corporation feels that it has been unreasonably deprived of its property rights,[26] and redress is not afforded by appeal to the courts of the state, an appeal may be carried to the Supreme Court of the United States. In the nature of things, that court cannot have a ready-made formula that it can apply in determining whether a person has been deprived of liberty or property without due process. Each case must be considered in terms of the particular web of facts in which it is imbedded. If, after a consideration of all the pertinent facts, the court is of the opinion that the state has exercised its police power for a purpose and in a manner reasonably necessary to protect and insure the public safety and welfare, the exercise of the police power on the part of the state will be sustained, and the statute involved will be declared constitutional. If, on the other hand, the court regards the statute as an unnecessary and unreasonable restriction upon personal liberty or an arbitrary interference with property rights, it will be declared unconstitutional as violative of due process. The important point is that the Supreme Court of the United States is the final judge as to whether a person has been unreasonably deprived of liberty or property. And since the terms "liberty" and "property" are extremely comprehensive, all manner of

25. *Meyer* v. *State of Nebraska,* 262 U.S. 390, 43 S. Ct. 625, 67 L. Ed. 1042, 29 A.L.R. 1446.

26. A corporation is considered a legal person so far as property rights are concerned.

social and economic legislation may be invalidated. Laws passed by the states to protect the life, health, and general welfare of their citizens may be set aside as arbitrary and unreasonable. Educational legislation is no exception to the general rule. Obviously, state educational policy may be profoundly affected by the decisions of the highest of our federal courts.

A few illustrations from the general field of social and economic legislation may serve to make clear the extent to which the exercise of the police power on the part of the states may be limited by the Supreme Court of the United States. A law of the state of New York prohibiting the employment of females over the age of sixteen in connection with any restaurant for more than six days or fifty-four hours a week, or earlier than six o'clock in the morning, or later than ten o'clock in the evening, was held to be an unreasonable and arbitrary interference with individual liberty.[27] Similarly, a statute of Nebraska prescribing the weight of loaves of bread offered for sale was held unconstitutional for the same reason.[28] An ordinance of the city of Milwaukee, making it unlawful for any person to circulate or distribute handbills on any sidewalk, street, or other public place, was held to be an unconstitutional abridgment of freedom of speech and press.[29] A statute of Oklahoma, making a certificate of convenience and necessity a prerequisite to the right to engage in the ice business and vesting in a state administrative body the power to regulate the price of ice, was held to violate due process because it unreasonably curtailed the right to engage in a lawful business.[30] On the other hand, the court sustained an act of Utah limiting the employment of workmen in all underground mines to eight hours a day.[31] Compulsory vaccination has been upheld as a valid exercise of the police power of the state of Massachusetts.[32] Statutes or municipal ordinances compelling the discontinuance of such businesses as the following have been sustained:

27. *Radice* v. *People,* 44 S. Ct. 325.

28. *Jay Burns Baking Company* v. *Bryan,* 264 U.S. 504, 44 S. Ct. 412, 68 L. Ed. 813, 32 A.L.R. 661.

29. *Snyder* v. *City of Milwaukee,* 308 U.S. 147, 60 S. Ct. 146.

30. *New State Ice Company* v. *Liebmann,* 285 U.S. 262, 52 S. Ct. 371.

31. *Holden* v. *Hardy,* 169 U.S. 366, 18 S. Ct. 383, 42 L. Ed. 780.

32. *Jacobson* v. *Massachusetts,* 197 U.S. 11, 25 S. Ct. 358, 49 L. Ed. 643, 3 Ann. Cas. 765.

manufacturing or selling oleomargarine,[33] selling cigarettes,[34] selling futures in grain and other commodities,[35] and keeping billiard halls.[36] Obviously, the states may go far, do very much indeed, to promote the public welfare, but in each particular instance it is for the Supreme Court of the United States to determine whether the police power has been exercised in a reasonable manner and in relation to some end within the competency of the state to effect.

The limitations upon the power of the state to formulate and execute its own educational policies may be illustrated by a few concrete cases. In 1919 the legislature of Nebraska passed an act making it unlawful to teach foreign languages to pupils in private, parochial, or public schools who had not completed the work of the eighth grade. The authority of the state to exercise the police power to the extent of prohibiting the teaching of foreign languages in private and parochial schools was promptly challenged. In holding that the act in question was a legitimate exercise of the police power, the Supreme Court of Nebraska was influenced by conditions disclosed by World War I. It was pointed out that the selective draft law revealed a condition in the body politic the evil consequences of which had not been comprehended. Thousands of men born of foreign-language-speaking parents and educated in schools taught in a foreign language were "unable to read, write, or speak the language of their country, or understand words of command given in English." It was demonstrated, too, the court pointed out, that there were local foci of alien enemy sentiment and that in those communities in which this sentiment had been strongest the instruction in private and parochial schools had been given chiefly in a foreign language. Since social and national integrity were threatened, the court was of the opinion that the challenged act was not an unreasonable interference with individual liberty:

Neither the constitution of the state nor the Fourteenth Amendment takes away the power of the state to enact a law that may fairly be said to protect the lives, liberty and property of its citizens, and to promote their health, morals, education and good order. "If the state may compel the solvent bank to help pay losses sustained by depositors in insolvent banks, if it may enact workmen's compensation laws, . . . it surely is not an

33. *Powell* v. *Pennsylvania*, 127 U.S. 678, 8 S. Ct. 992, 32 L. Ed. 256.

34. *Austin* v. *Tennessee*, 179 U.S. 343, 21 S. Ct. 132, 45 L. Ed. 224.

35. *Booth* v. *Illinois*, 184 U.S. 425, 22 S. Ct. 425, 46 L. Ed. 623.

36. *Murphy* v. *California*, 225 U.S. 623, 32 S. Ct. 697, 56 L. Ed. 1229, 41 L.R.A. (N.S.) 153.

arbitrary exercise of the functions of the state to insist" that the fundamental basis of the education of its citizens shall be a knowledge of the language, history and nature of the government of the United States, and to prohibit anything which may interfere with such education. Laws, the purpose of which are, with respect to foreign language speaking children, to give them such training that they may know and understand their privileges, duties, powers, and responsibilities as American citizens, which seek to prevent a foreign language from being used as a medium of instruction in other branches, and as the basis of their education, are certainly conducive to the public welfare, and are not obnoxious to any provision of either the state or federal Constitution.[37]

In 1921 the Supreme Court of Iowa sustained the constitutionality of an act likewise prohibiting the teaching of foreign languages to children who had not completed the eighth grade. In the opinion of this court,[38] the state of Iowa had "a right to adopt a general policy of its own respecting the health, social welfare, and education of its citizens," so long as there was no violation of constitutional prohibitions. The law in question violated no such prohibitions, for there is no inherent right to teach German to children of tender years which the legislature may not deny when, in its opinion, the exercise of such a right is inimical to the best interests of the state. The challenged legislation, therefore, was considered a reasonable exercise of the police power of the state of Iowa.

A case involving the same general issues came before the Supreme Court of Ohio in 1921.[39] The constitutionality of an act prohibiting the teaching of German to children who had not completed the eighth grade, in the opinion of the court, depended on whether the common welfare demanded such legislation. Of this the legislature is the proper judge, and the courts should not intervene unless the action of the legislature is clearly unreasonable. Such was not deemed to be the case in this instance, and the legislation was therefore upheld.

But, as has already been pointed out, it is not for the legislature of a state, or for its courts, to determine finally what constitutes a proper exercise of the police power. Under the due-process-of-law clause of the Fourteenth Amendment the Supreme Court of the United States reserves final determination to itself. Consequently, an appeal was taken, in the case previously cited, from the Nebraska court to

37. *Nebraska District of Evangelical Lutheran Synod of Missouri et al.* v. *McKelvie,* 104 Neb. 93, 175 N.W. 531, 7 A.L.R. 1688.

38. *State* v. *Bartels,* 191 Iowa 1060, 181 N.W. 508.

39. *Pohl* v. *State,* 102 Ohio St. 474, 132 N.E. 20.

the Supreme Court of the United States. The fundamental issue involved, of course, was whether the act prohibiting the teaching of foreign languages to pupils in private and parochial schools who had not completed the eighth grade deprived any person of liberty or property without due process of law. In the opinion of the court,[40] written by Mr. Justice McReynolds, the act in question was an arbitrary interference with the liberty of parents to control the education of their children and with the liberty of modern-language teachers to pursue their lawful calling.

While this court has not attempted to define with exactness the liberty thus guaranteed, the term has received much consideration and some of the included things have been definitely stated. Without doubt it denotes not merely freedom from bodily restraint but also the right of the individual to contract, to engage in any of the common occupations of life, to acquire useful knowledge, to marry, establish a home and bring up children, to worship God according to the dictates of his own conscience, and generally to enjoy those privileges long recognized at common law as essential to the orderly pursuit of happiness by free men. . . . The established doctrine is that this liberty may not be interfered with, under the guise of protecting the public interest, by legislative action which is arbitrary or without reasonable relation to some purpose within the competency of the state to effect. *Determination by the legislature of what constitutes proper exercise of the police power is not final or conclusive but is subject to supervision by the courts.*[41]

Having stated categorically that it is the function of the Supreme Court of the United States rather than of the legislature of Nebraska to pass final judgment as to the existence of facts justifying the exercise of police power, the court proceeded to point out that though "the state may do much, go very far, indeed, in order to improve the quality of its citizens, physically, mentally and morally," it cannot deprive modern-language teachers of their lawful calling or unreasonably interfere with the right of parents to control the education of their children. The right of a modern-language teacher "to teach and the right of parents to engage him to instruct their children, . . . are within the liberty of the Amendment." The statute was therefore declared to be "arbitrary and without reasonable relation to any end within the competency of the state" to effect.

The significance of the Nebraska case will be more fully appreciated when it is recalled that ten other states had in force substan-

40. *Meyer v. State of Nebraska,* 262 U.S. 390, 43 S. Ct. 625, 67 L. Ed. 1042, 29 A.L.R. 1446.

41. Italics not in the original.

tially the same kind of legislation as had Nebraska and that in two other states the supreme court had upheld the constitutionality of such legislation. In a single decision, therefore, the Supreme Court of the United States reversed an important educational policy of approximately one-fourth of the states of the Union.

Another opinion of the United States Supreme Court is informative in this connection. Acting under the initiative provision of the state constitution, the people of Oregon enacted a law in 1922 which required children between the ages of eight and sixteen to attend a public school. Obviously, the practical effect of this law would have been to prohibit private elementary schools. Two private institutions tested the constitutionality of the act before the Supreme Court of the United States. The act was declared void on the ground that it violated the due-process-of-law clause of the Fourteenth Amendment. In the opinion of the court,[42] the challenged legislation unreasonably interfered with the liberty of parents in the upbringing and education of their children:

The fundamental theory of liberty upon which all governments of this Union repose excludes any general power of the state to standardize its children by forcing them to accept instruction from public teachers only. The child is not the mere creature of the State; those who nurture him and direct his destiny have the right, coupled with the high duty, to recognize and prepare him for additional obligations.

The court held, moreover, that if the act under consideration were enforced, the two corporations concerned would be deprived of property without due process of law. Their business and property were "threatened with destruction through the unwarranted compulsion" which the state was seeking to exercise over present and prospective patrons of their schools. The maintenance of private schools, it was pointed out, is an undertaking not inherently harmful, and the court found nothing in the records of such institutions to demand extraordinary measures.

One other significant case should be mentioned. In 1914 the state of Washington adopted as an initiative measure an act which prohibited employment agencies from receiving fees for services rendered in securing employment for patrons. While it was the purpose of the law to protect industrial workers from "imposition and extortion," the

42. *Pierce* v. *Society of the Sisters of the Holy Names of Jesus and Mary,* and *Pierce* v. *Hill Military Academy,* 268 U.S. 510, 45 S. Ct. 571, 69 L. Ed. 1070, 39 A.L.R. 468.

law was obviously so worded as to apply to teachers' agencies. In the court's opinion there is nothing inherently immoral or socially dangerous in acting as the paid agent of another in securing for him a position in which he may earn a living. The law was regarded, therefore, as "arbitrary and oppressive," in that it prohibited the pursuit of a lawful business.

From what has been said, it should be clear that the Supreme Court of the United States exercises the right to review the economic and social legislation of the states and to determine whether the objects to be accomplished and the manner of their accomplishment are reasonably necessary to promote the public welfare. The state is free to formulate and to execute its own educational policies; but at any time the Supreme Court of the United States may, where the exercise of police power is involved, reverse these policies as being an arbitrary interference with either liberty or property. It should be pointed out, however, that the state legislature is primarily the judge of the necessity of all police legislation, that every possible presumption is in favor of the validity of such legislation, that the courts are never concerned with the wisdom of it. The guaranty of due process "demands only that the law shall not be unreasonable, arbitrary, or capricious, and that the means selected shall have a real and substantial relation to the object to be attained."[43]

The Supreme Court has not always exercised its present authority with respect to the police power of the states. Prior to the Civil War the states were practically unrestricted in the exercise of the police power except in two particulars: (1) they were prohibited from passing any laws impairing the obligations of contracts; (2) they were restricted in the regulation of foreign and interstate commerce. The Fourteenth Amendment made possible, therefore, a thoroughgoing revolution in our constitutional system. Although at the time of the adoption of the amendment there were those who saw and pointed out the implications of the "due-process-of-law" clause, in the minds of most people, no doubt, the chief purpose of the amendment was to restrict the southern states in their relations to the freedmen and to empower Congress to pass such legislation as would secure to the Negro his proper status as a citizen of the United States.

How far the Supreme Court went before the Civil War in refusing to interfere with the exercise of the police power on the part of the

43. *Nebbia v. New York*, 291 U.S. 502, 54 S. Ct. 505.

states is illustrated by a decision rendered in 1833. The case involved the constitutionality of a statute of the State of New York which placed certain restrictions on captains of ships bringing alien passengers into the port of New York. The court made its position clear in the following words:

We choose rather to plant ourselves on what we consider impregnable positions. They are these: That a State has the same undeniable and unlimited jurisdiction over all persons and things, within its territorial limits, as any foreign nation, where that jurisdiction is not surrendered or restrained by the Constitution of the United States. That, by virtue of this, it is not only the right, but the bounden and solemn duty of a State, to advance the safety, happiness and prosperity of its people, and to provide for its general welfare, by any and every act of legislation which it may deem to be conducive to these ends; where the power over the particular subject, or the manner of its exercise is not surrendered or restrained, in the manner just stated. That all those powers which relate to merely municipal legislation, or what may, perhaps, more properly be called internal police, are not thus surrendered or restrained; and that, consequently, in relation to these, the authority of the State is complete, unqualified and exclusive.[44]

In his first Inaugural Address, Abraham Lincoln gave presidential sanction to a concept of division of powers that would have left the ultimate control of the police power pretty much in the hands of the states. "The maintenance inviolate," he said, "of the rights of the States, and especially the right of each State to order and control its own domestic institutions according to its own judgment exclusively, is essential to the balance of power on which the perfection and endurance of our political fabric depend."[45]

For some years following the Civil War, the Supreme Court was not disposed to review cases involving the exercise of police power by the states. Soon after its adoption, the Fourteenth Amendment came before the Supreme Court for interpretation in the well-known *Slaughter-House Cases.*[46] The issue involved was the authority of the state of Louisiana to place restrictions on the slaughtering of animals in New Orleans and in certain parishes. The court refused to interfere, holding that the federal system had come out of the Civil War with its fundamental features unchanged. Justice Miller, speaking for the court, expressed impatience with any interpretation of the amendment which "would constitute this court a perpetual censor upon all legislation of

44. *New York* v. *Miln,* 11 Pet. 102, 36 U.S. 102.

45. Abraham Lincoln Association, Springfield, Illinois, *The Collected Works of Abraham Lincoln* (New Brunswick, N.J.: Rutgers University Press, 1953), IV, 263.

46. *Slaughter-House Cases,* 16 Wall. (U.S.) 36, 21 L. Ed. 394.

the states." In 1876 the position of the court was still more strongly stated in the case of *Munn* v. *Illinois.*[47] In discussing the constitutionality of a law fixing the maximum charge for the storage of grain, the court made the following significant pronouncements: "Of the propriety of legislative interference within the scope of legislative power, the legislature is the exclusive judge." "For protection against abuses by legislatures the people must resort to the polls." These and other cases indicate clearly that the Supreme Court began its interpretation of the Fourteenth Amendment by announcing the doctrine of noninterference with the social and economic legislation of the states.

The position thus taken was maintained for a number of years. Gradually, however, the position was completely reversed. This facing-about by the Court may be explained, perhaps, by the fact that in the decade from 1875 to 1885 five new justices were appointed to the Supreme Court bench. Moreover, there was going forward an unprecedented development of industry and so-called "big business," which state legislatures attempted to control through regulatory measures. There was thus brought to bear on the court a great deal of pressure to give the Fourteenth Amendment a broader interpretation. For the Supreme Court of the United States to assert its right to review the social and economic legislation of the states constituted a momentous revolution in our constitutional system. Yet that is precisely what took place, beginning about 1890 and being fully consummated by 1900.[48]

When once the Supreme Court had taken the position that, in all social and economic legislation resulting in the deprivation of some-one, including corporations, of liberty or property, the judiciary and not the legislature is the final tribunal of arbitrament, there began what has been termed a period of "judicial ruthlessness." The court seemed to have forgotten the time-honored doctrine that a law is presumed to be constitutional until proved otherwise beyond a reasonable doubt. In passing on the constitutionality of state legislation, judges did not deem it necessary to inquire into the conditions which the legislation aimed to correct. Social and economic facts were almost completely ignored in the process of judicial interpretation. The

47. *Munn* v. *Illinois,* 94 U.S. 113.

48. For a more complete discussion of the cases by which the court made the transition see "The Supreme Court and the Fourteenth Amendment," by E. S. Corwin, 7 Mich. Law Rev. 643, and "The Social and Economic Interpretation of the Fourteenth Amendment," by R. E. Cushman, 20 Mich. Law Rev. 737.

constitutionality of a law was regarded as essentially a legal matter, to be decided on the basis of abstract legal concepts.

This legalistic conception of the Fourteenth Amendment dominated the judicial mind until about 1908. In that year there came before the Supreme Court of the United States the Oregon ten-hour law for women. In this celebrated case[49] L. D. Brandeis and Pauline D. Goldmark submitted to the court a mass of data bearing on the physiological and social reasons why the law should protect women from long hours of labor. Said the court in its decision: "When a question of fact is debated and debatable, and the extent to which a special constitutional limitation goes is affected by the truth in respect to that fact, a widespread and long-continued belief concerning it is worthy of consideration. We take judicial cognizance of general knowledge."

After this decision the Supreme Court began to interpret legislation not so much in terms of abstract legal concepts as in terms of economic and social facts. Legislation which seemed necessary to protect the public welfare was sustained; otherwise it was declared unreasonable and arbitrary. Such seems to be the position which the court takes today.

49. *Muller* v. *Oregon,* 208 U.S. 412.

CHAPTER II

The School and the State

THE PUBLIC SCHOOL IN LEGAL THEORY

SINCE education in the American scheme of government is essentially a matter of state policy, the courts of the several states have been called upon repeatedly to define the function of the public school in organized society. Whatever vagaries may have been entertained by educational reformers or others, the courts have been forced by necessity to formulate a theory of education based upon what they deem to be fundamental principles of public policy. In legal theory the public school is a state institution.[1] As the Supreme Court of Minnesota has put it: "This Court so frequently has affirmed the doctrine that the maintenance of the public school is a matter of state and not local concern that it is unnecessary further to review the authorities at this date."[2] Public education is not merely a function of government; it is of government. Power to maintain a system of public schools is an attribute of government in much the same sense as is the police power or the power to administer justice or to maintain military forces or to tax.[3] The state finds its right to tax for the maintenance of a system of public schools in its duty to promote the public welfare, the good order and peace of society.[4]

1. *City of Louisville* v. *Commonwealth*, 134 Ky. 488, 121 S.W. 411; *Bissell* v. *Davison*, 65 Conn. 183, 32 Atl. 348, 29 L.R.A. 251; *Leeper* v. *State*, 103 Tenn. 500, 53 S.W. 962, 48 L.R.A. 167; *State* v. *Meador*, 284 S.W. (Tenn.) 890; *State* v. *Haworth*, 122 Ind. 462, 23 N.E. 946, 7 L.R.A. 240; *In re School District No. 6 Kent County*, 284 Mich. 132, 278 N.W. 792; *Newman* v. *Schlarb*, 184 Wash. 147, 50 Pac (2d) 36; *Thompson* v. *Board of Education*, 20 N.J. Super. 419, 90 Atl. (2d) 63; *Anderson* v. *Peterson*, 54 N.W. (2d) (N.D. 542.

2. *State* ex rel. *Board of Education of Minneapolis* v. *Erickson*, 190 Minn. 216, 251 N.W. 519.

3. *City of Louisville* v. *Commonwealth*, 134 Ky. 488, 121 S.W. 411; *Leeper* v. *State*, 103 Tenn. 500, 53 S.W. 962, 48 L.R.A. 167; *City of Edina* v. *School District of City of Edina*, 305 Mo. 452, 267 S.W. 112.

4. *Bissell* v. *Davison*, 65 Conn. 183, 32 Atl. 348, 29 L.R.A. 251; *Leeper* v. *State*, 103 Tenn. 500, 53 S.W. 962, 48 L.R.A. 167; *Scown* v. *Czarnecki*, 264 Ill. 305; *Fogg* v. *Board of Education*, 76 N.H. 296, 82 Atl. 173, 37 L.R.A. (N.S.) 1110, Ann. Cas. 1912C 758.

The primary function of the public school, in legal theory at least, is not to confer benefits upon the individual as such,[5] the school exists as a state institution because the very existence of civil society demands it. The education of youth is a matter of such vital importance to the democratic state and to the public weal that the state may do much, may go very far indeed, by way of limiting the control of the parent over the education of his child.[6] The state cannot, to be sure, prohibit private schools altogether,[7] but it can prohibit the teaching of doctrines which challenge the existence of the state and the well-being of society.[8] It may, moreover, require that children be educated in schools which meet substantially the same standards as the state requires of its own schools.[9]

The relation of the public school to the state is clearly defined by a case[10] decided by the Court of Appeals of Kentucky. By an act of the legislature of Kentucky the minimum tax levy for school purposes in cities of the first class was fixed at thirty-six cents on the one hundred dollars' valuation. The Board of Education of Louisville presented to the city council their budget, which required a levy of at least the amount provided for by statute. The council refused to make the levy, contending that the statute in question violated the following provision of the state constitution: "The General Assembly shall not impose taxes for the purpose of any county, city, town or other municipal corporation, but may by general laws confer upon the proper authorities thereof respectively power to assess and collect such taxes." In issuing a writ of mandamus which required the council to levy the tax, the court said in part:

If the maintenance of a public school is a purely municipal purpose, then the section would seem to be conclusive of the matter. But education is not a subject pertaining alone, or pertaining essentially, to a municipal

5. *Bissell* v. *Davison*, 65 Conn. 183, 32 Atl. 348, 29 L.R.A. 251; *Scown* v. *Czarnecki*, 264 Ill. 305; *Fogg* v. *Board of Education*, 76 N.H. 296, 82 Atl. 173, 37 L.R.A. (N.S.) 1110, Ann. Cas. 1912C 758; *Brown* v. *Board of Trustees of Town of Hamptonburg*, 104 N.E. (2d) (N.Y.) 866; *Orleans Parish School Board* v. *City of New Orleans*, 56 So. (2d) (La.) 280.

6. *Meyer* v. *State of Nebraska*, 262 U.S. 390, 43 S. Ct. 625, 67 L. Ed. 1042, 29 A.L.R. 1446.

7. *Pierce* v. *Society of the Sisters of the Hold Names of Jesus and Mary*, 268 U.S. 510, 45 S. Ct. 571, 69 L. Ed. 1070, 39 A.L.R. 468.

8. *People* v. *American Socialist Society*, 195 N.Y.S. 801, 202 App. Div. 640.

9. *Wright* v. *State*, 21 Okla. Cr. 430, 209 Pac. 179.

10. *City of Louisville* v. *Commonwealth*, 134 Ky. 488, 121 S.W. 411.

corporation. Whilst public education in this country is now deemed a public duty in every state, and since before the first federation was regarded as a proper public enterprise, it has never been looked upon as being at all a matter of local concern only. On the contrary, it is regarded as an essential to the preservation of liberty—as forming one of the first duties of a democratic government. The place assigned it in the deliberate judgment of the American people is scarcely second to any. If it is essentially a prerogative of sovereignty to raise troops in time of war, it is equally so to prepare each generation of youth to discharge the duties of citizenship in time of peace and war. Upon preparation of the younger generations for civic duties depends the perpetuity of this government. Power to levy taxes is an essential attribute of sovereignty. That is so because the necessity of conducting the government requires that money be raised for the purpose by some sort of taxation. So is the power to educate the youth of the state, to fit them so that the state may prosper; else the taxes raised could scarcely meet demands made upon a government in these times. Whilst the power named is older in point of adoption as a legal maxim, the other is modernly found to be of no less importance. It may be doubted if the state could strip itself of either quality of its sovereignty. Certainly it will not be deemed to have attempted it upon language open to debate.

The reasoning in the foregoing case is supported by a decision rendered by the Supreme Court of Tennessee. The legislature of that state passed an act which prescribed uniform textbooks for the schools throughout the state. A commission was to select the books to be used and to let contracts to the lowest bidder for supplying the books adopted. In sustaining the constitutionality of the act, the court identified the maintenance of a system of public schools with the exercise of the police power of the state. It was said by the court:

It is immaterial whether we consider this act as deriving validity from the police power of the state or the public character of the schools. It is evident that the basic principle of it is the power of the legislature to subserve the general welfare by prohibiting certain contracts, and throwing around others restrictions tending to promote the general welfare, and protect the citizen from oppression, fraud, and wrong. That the state may establish a uniform series of books to be taught in the schools, which it provides and controls, seems to be a proposition as evident as that it may provide a uniform system of schools, which we take it is not now an open question. . . .

We are of the opinion that the legislature, under the constitutional provision, may as well establish a uniform system of schools and a uniform administration of them, as it may establish a uniform system of criminal laws and of courts to execute them. The object of the criminal law is, by punishment, to deter others from the commission of crimes, and thus preserve the peace, morals, good order, and well-being of society; and the object of the public-school system is to prevent crime, by educating the people, and thus, by providing and securing a higher state of intelligence and morals, conserve the peace, good order, and well-being of society.

The prevention of crime, and preservation of good order and peace, is the highest exercise of the police power of the state, whether done by punishing offenders or educating the children.[11]

The relation of the school to the individual, on the one hand, and to organized society, on the other, has been clearly stated by the Supreme Court of Illinois in the following language:

The public school system of the State was not established and has not been maintained as a charity or from philanthropic motives. The first legislative expression in regard to schools in Illinois was in the ordinance of 1787, which declares that "religion, morality and knowledge being necessary to good government and the happiness of mankind, schools and the means of education shall forever be encouraged." This declaration grew, not out of philanthropic motives, but out of a consideration of the essentials of good government. The conduct and maintenance of schools by school directors, school trustees and boards of education is no less an "exercise of the functions vested in those charged with the conduct of government," is no less a part of "the science and art of government," and deals no less with the "organization, regulation and administration of a State" in its internal affairs, than the construction and maintenance of roads by the commissioners of highways; the conduct and maintenance of the charitable institutions of the State by the board of administration; the inspection of factories, and the enforcement of the laws for the protection of workmen and in regard to the employment of women and children, by the factory inspectors; the performance of the industrial board of the duties imposed upon it by law, and the performance of many other duties by public officials which, however beneficial to individuals, are not undertaken from philanthropic or charitable motives, but for the protection, safety and welfare of the citizens of the State in the interest of good government.[12]

Similarly, it was said by the Supreme Court of New Hampshire:

The primary purpose of the maintenance of the common school system is the promotion of the general intelligence of the people constituting the body politic and thereby to increase the usefulness and efficiency of the citizens, upon which the government of society depends. Free schooling furnished by the state is not so much a right granted to pupils as a duty imposed upon them for the public good. If they do not voluntarily attend the schools provided for them, they may be compelled to do so. While most people regard the public schools as the means of great personal advantage to the pupils, the fact is too often overlooked that they are governmental means of protecting the state from the consequences of an ignorant and incompetent citizenship.[13]

11. *Leeper* v. *State,* 103 Tenn. 500, 53 S.W. 962, 48 L.R.A. 167.

12. *Scown* v. *Czarnecki,* 264 Ill. 305.

13. *Fogg* v. *Board of Education,* 76 N.H. 296, 82 Atl. 173, 37 L.R.A. (N.S.) 1110, Ann. Cas. 1912C 758.

THE STATE LEGISLATURE AND EDUCATIONAL POLICY

State policy finds expression through the medium of constitutional provisions and statutory enactments. In education, as in all other matters of government, the federal and state constitutions are the fundamental law. The principle is well established, however, that the state legislature, subject to constitutional restricitons, has authority to pass any act of a legislative nature which may in its opinion seem wise.[14] While the legislature may be said to exercise delegated authority, it is authority delegated generally and not specifically. The very act of creating a legislative branch of government confers upon it all powers of a legislative nature except such as are expressly withheld. Thus it has been said by Chief Justice Denio, speaking for the Court of Appeals of New York: "The people, in framing the constitution, committed to the legislature the whole law making power of the state, which they did not expressly or impliedly withhold. Plenary power in the legislature for all purposes of civil government is the rule."[15] It follows that it is for those who challenge the constitutionality of a statute to show that it is forbidden.[16] The Congress of the United States must find constitutional authority for all its acts; a state legislature, on the other hand, may pass any act not expressly or impliedly forbidden by fundamental law.[17]

From what has been said, it is obvious that, subject to constitutional limitations, the state legislature has plenary power with respect to matters of educational policy. In the absence of constitutional prohibitions, the ends to be attained and the means to be employed are wholly subject to legislative determination. The legislature may determine the types of schools to be established throughout

14. *Fletcher* v. *Peck*, 6 Cranch (U.S.) 128, 3 L. Ed. 162; *Sill* v. *Village of Corning*, 15 N.Y. 297; *Commonwealth* v. *Hartman*, 17 Pa. St. 118; *State Female Normal School* v. *Auditors*, 79 Va. 233; *State* v. *Haworth*, 122 Ind. 462, 23 N.E. 946, 7 L.R.A. 240; *State* v. *Meador*, 284 S.W. (Tenn.) 890; *People* v. *Wood*, 411 Ill. 514, 104 N.E. (2d) 377.

15. *People* v. *Draper*, 15 N.Y. 532.

16. *People* v. *Draper*, 15 N.Y. 532.

17. *Commonwealth* v. *Hartman*, 17 Pa. St. 118; *Moseley* v. *Welch*, 209 S.C. 19, 39 S.E. (2d) 133; *People* v. *Deatherage*, 401 Ill. 25, 81 N.E. (2d) 581; *Hard* v. *Depaoli*, 56 Nev. 19, 41 Pac. (2d) 1054; *Board of Education of City of Chicago* v. *Upham*, 357 Ill. 263, 191 N.E. 876, 94 A.L.R. 813; *State* ex rel. *Gray* v. *Board of Education of City of Chetopa*, 173 Kan. 780, 252 Pac. (2d) 859; *Wheelis* v. *Franks*, 189 Ark. 373, 72 S.W. (2d) 231; *City of Manitowoc* v. *Town of Manitowoc Rapids*, 231 Wis. 94, 285 N.W. 403; *Lincoln Township School District* v. *Redfield Consolidated School District*, 283 N.W. 881, 226 Iowa 298.

the state,[18] the means of their support,[19] the organs of their administration,[20] the content of their curricula,[21] and the qualifications of their teachers. Moreover, all these matters may be determined with or without regard to the wishes of the localities, for in education the state is the unit and there are no local rights except such as are safeguarded by the constitution.

Where a state constitution requires the legislature to provide educational opportunities for certain classes of children or for persons falling in a specified age group, the mandate will not, as a rule, be interpreted as an implied limitation on the power of the legislature. The legislature must do so much; it may do more. Thus in Pennsylvania, in 1848, the constitution provided that the legislature should establish schools throughout the state in such manner that the poor might be taught gratis. The legislature enacted a statute providing for the establishment of free schools for all the children of the state between the ages of five and twenty-one. The Supreme Court ruled that the constitutional mandate to maintain schools for the poor did not forbid the legislature to provide a system of general education. Similarly, in Wisconsin, the constitution made it the duty of the legislature to provide free education for those between the ages of four and twenty. The court could not see in this mandate any implied prohibition with respect to free education for those beyond the age of twenty. So, too, in Oklahoma, a constitutional provision directing the legislature to maintain a system of free schools for all "children"

18. *State v. Freeman,* 61 Kan. 90, 58 Pac. 959, 47 L.R.A. 67; *State Female Normal School v. Auditors,* 79 Va. 233; *In re Kindergarten Schools,* 18 Colo. 234, 32 Pac. 422, 19 L.R.A. 469; *Fulton Township School District v. School District No. 4,* 302 Mich. 566, 5 N.W. (2d) 467.

19. *State v. Meador,* 284 S.W. (Tenn.) 890; *Miller v. Korns,* 107 Ohio St. 287, 140 N.E. 773; *Sawyer v. Gilmore,* 109 Me. 169, 83 Atl. 673; *Miller v. Childers,* 107 Okla. 57, 238 Pac. 204.

20. *State v. Hine,* 59 Conn. 50, 21 Atl. 1024, 10 L.R.A. 83; *State v. Haworth,* 122 Ind. 462, 23 N.E. 946, 7 L.R.A. 240; *Moore v. Board of Iredell County,* 212 N.C. 499, 193 S.E. 732; *Regional High School District No. 3 v. Town of Newton,* 134 Conn. 613, 59 Atl. (2d), 527, *Lowden v. Luther,* 190 Okla. 31, 120 Pac. (2d) 359; *Independent Consolidated School District No. 7 v. Bowen,* 199 Okla. 92, 183 Pac. (2d) 251; *Anderson v. Peterson,* 54 N.W. (2d) (N.D.) 542; *Independent School District of Danbury v. Christiansen,* 242 Iowa 963, 49 N.W. (2d) 263; *People v. Wood,* 411 Ill. 514, 104 N.E. (2d) 800; *Board of Education of City of Chicago v. Upham,* 357 Ill. 263, 191 N.E. 876, 94 A.L.R. 813.

21. *State v. Haworth,* 122 Ind. 462, 23 N.E. 946, 7 L.R.A. 240; *Associated Schools of Independent District No. 63 v. School District No. 83,* 122 Minn. 254, 142 N.W. 325, 47 L.R.A. (N.S.) 200.

was not a limitation upon its power to provide free education for those over twenty.[22]

The Supreme Court of Indiana, in the leading case of *State* v. *Haworth*,[23] expresses clearly and forcibly the authority of the state legislature to determine state educational policy. The issue involved was the constitutionality of a statute which required township trustees to distribute textbooks selected by the state board of education. The statute was assailed on the ground that it violated the right of local self-government. After pointing out that the right of local self-government could in no case be exercised except in matters of purely local concern, the court continued:

Essentially and intrinsically the schools in which are educated and trained the children who are to become the rulers of the commonwealth are matters of State, and not of local jurisdiction. In such matters, the State is the unit, and the Legislature the source of power. The authority over schools and school affairs is not necessarily a distributive one to be exercised by local instrumentalities; but, on the contrary, it is a central power residing in the Legislature of the State. It is for the law-making power to determine whether the authority shall be exercised by a State board of education, or distributed to county, township, or city organizations throughout the State. . . .

As the power over schools is a legislative one, it is not exhausted by exercise. The Legislature having tried one plan is not precluded from trying another. It has a complete choice of methods, and may change its plans as often as it deems necessary or expedient. . . . It is clear, therefore, that even if it were true, that the Legislature had uniformly intrusted the management of school affairs to local organizations, it would not authorize the conclusion that it might not change the system.

Since education is a function of the state, school officers are state officers. Consequently, they may be selected in any manner that the legislature may determine. They may be elected by the people, be appointed by the courts,[24] or be selected by any other agencies which policy may dictate. Moreover, it is not necessary that school officers reside in the district where they hold office. Such was the conclusion reached by the Supreme Court of Errors of Connecticut in a decision rendered in 1890. An act of the legislature provided that the secretary of the state board of education should be ex officio a member of

22. *Commonwealth* v. *Hartman*, 17 Pa. St. 118; *City of Manitowoc* v. *Town of Manitowoc Rapids*, 231 Wis. 94, 285 N.W. 403; *School District No. 62* v. *School District No. 17*, 143 Okla. 136, 287 Pac. 1035.

23. *State* v. *Haworth*, 122 Ind. 462, 23 N.E. 946, 7 L.R.A. 240.

24. *Minsinger* v. *Rau*, 236 Pa. St. 327, 84 Atl. 902, Ann. Cas. 1913E 1324; *Lorang* v. *High School District*, 247 Pac. (2d) (Mont.) 477.

the school committee of certain towns and districts of the state. In sustaining the act, the court made the following significant statement:

If the reasoning and the conclusions arrived at in the former part of this opinion are right, then towns in Conecticut have no inherent right to elect school committees and never had. In the absence of constitutional restriction we think the legislature may provide that school committees, whether of a town or a district or society, may be composed of any persons and chosen in any manner that it may prescribe.[25]

One other case may be cited to illustrate the freedom of the legislature in determining methods of school support. The legislature of Tennessee passed an act which required the county court of each county to provide funds for the maintenance of a four-year high school in the county. The act was challenged on the ground that it violated the right of local self-government. In holding otherwise, the court said:

The public school system is a matter of state, and not local, concern, and the establishment, maintenance, and control of the public schools is a legislative function. To promote the public schools, the state, through the Legislature, may levy taxes directly, or the state, having, as it does, full control over its agencies, the counties, may authorize them to levy a tax, or may by statute require them to levy a tax for the establishment and maintenance of public schools. . . .

The exercise of the taxing power to promote a system of public schools for all the counties does not infringe upon the right of local self-government, because a public school system, like a highway system, a penal system, or a matter of public health is not of purely local, but of state, concern. The state is a unit, and the Legislature is the state's source of legislative power, from which flows the mandate of the state.[26]

DELEGATION OF LEGISLATIVE POWER

It is a well-established principle of law that a state legislature, being itself the constitutionally established custodian of the legislative power, may not delegate its legislative powers to any other tribunal, agency, or official. In the carrying-out of its policies, however, it may create administrative boards or agencies and confer upon them broad administrative duties. That is to say, a legislature may not delegate its legislative powers, but it may delegate administrative powers. The rule is clear, but its application in specific instances may not be easy because of the difficulty in distinguishing the one power from the other. The test is: Does the act creating the administrative agency

25. *State* v. *Hine,* 59 Conn. 50, 21 Atl. 1024, 10 L.R.A. 83.

26. *State* v. *Meador,* 284 S.W. (Tenn.) 890.

contain in it some reasonably clear standard by which the discretion of the agency is to be governed?[27] Unless it does, it will be regarded as a delegation of legislative power. These standards circumscribing the discretion of the administrative agent have been referred to as "conditions, restrictions, limitations, yardsticks, guides, rules, broad outlines," and the like. It has been held that in creating administrative tribunals "the power must be 'canalized' so that the exercise of the delegated powers must be restrained by banks in a definitely defined channel."

A case decided by the Supreme Court of Kansas illustrates the application of the principle. The legislature enacted a statute setting up in each county a "school reorganization committee" with broad powers with respect to the reorganization of school districts in the county. The statute made it the duty of the committee to make a comprehensive study of various factors which should be considered in any plan of district reorganization: assessed tax valuations, size and geographical features of district, number of pupils attending school, location and condition of school buildings, centers where children attended high school, and any factors concerning adequate high-school facilities. It provided for procedures pertaining to meetings, keeping of records, hearings, and appeals. The court, however, declared the act unconstitutional as a delegation of legislative power, because, it said, "nowhere within the four corners of the act can we find a standard upon which the committees are authorized to act or not to act on the question whether a new school district shall be organized."[28]

In New York a statute provided that "no person, persons, firm, or corporation, other than the public school authorities or an established religious group" should establish or maintain a nursery school, kindergarten, or elementary school, unless the school was registered under regulations prescribed by the Board of Regents of the University of the State of New York. The act was declared to be an unconstitutional delegation of legislative power, in that it empowered an administrative agency to license private schools under regulations to be adopted

27. *State* ex rel. *Donaldson* v. *Hines,* 163 Kan. 300, 182 Pac. (2d) 865; *School District No. 5* v. *Community High School of Cherokee County,* 146 Kan. 380, 69 Pac. (2d) 1102, 113 A.L.R. 172; *Wilson* v. *School District of Philadelphia,* 328 Pa. 225, 195 Atl. 90, 113 A.L.R. 1401; *People* v. *Board of Education,* 380 Ill. 311, 43 N.E. (2d) 1012; *Packer Collegiate Institute* v. *University of the State of New York,* 298 N.Y. 184, 81 N.E. (2d) 80; *School District No. 3* v. *Callahan,* 237 Wis. 560, 297 N.W. (2d) 407.

28. *State* ex rel. *Donaldson* v. *Hines,* 163 Kan. 300, 182 Pac. (2d) 865.

with no standards or limitations of any sort.[29] And in Pennsylvania the Supreme Court has held that the delegation of an unlimited power to tax upon an appointive school board is an unconstitutional delegation of legislative power.[30] The court went on to say, however, in view of its previous decisions,[31] that it was now too late to question the power of elective boards to levy a tax.

UNIFORMITY IN THE STATE SCHOOL SYSTEM

State constitutions commonly provide for a general and uniform system of public schools, free and open to all the children of the state between certain ages. Frequently, too, legislatures are prohibited from passing special or local legislation. Often, therefore, the question arises as to what constitutes a uniform school system. Uniformity does not mean identity, a dead level of sameness, a complete lack of distinction or discrimination. Uniformity does not preclude classification. It is not necessary that every school and every district should have exactly the same course of study, the same length of term, the same items of expense, or the same qualifications for teachers. Neither is it necessary that all the children of the state be given exactly the same educational privileges. The generality of a statute is not to be tested by the uniformity of results flowing from the exercise of the powers which it confers.[32] The legislature may make classifications and confer different rights and impose different burdens upon each of the several classes. The courts seem to be unanimous in holding that the uniformity of a school system is not violated by any classification which is based upon real differences and distinctions and which operates equally upon all persons or things in the same class or situation.[33] In determining

29. *Packer Collegiate Institute* v. *University of the State of New York*, 298 N.Y. 184, 81 N.E. (2d) 80.

30. *Wilson* v. *School District of Philadelphia*, 328 Pa. 225, 195 Atl. 90, 113 A.L.R. 1401.

31. *Blair* v. *Boggs Township School District*, 31 Pa. 274.

32. *Landis* v. *Ashworth*, 57 N.J. Law 509, 31 Atl. 1017; *In re Cleveland*, 52 N.J. Law 188, 19 Atl. 17, 7 L.R.A. 431.

33. *Board of Education* v. *Lewis*, 66 N.J. Law 582, 50 Atl. 346; *Riccio* v. *Hoboken*, 69 N.J. Law 649, 55 Atl. 1109, 63 L.R.A. 485; *Ex parte King*, 157 Calif. 161, 106 Pac. 578; *In re Sugar Notch Borough*, 192 Pa. St. 349, 43 Atl. 985; *Bufkin* v. *Mitchell*, 106 Miss. 253, 63 So. 458, 50 L.R.A. (N.S.) 428; *School District No. 25* v. *Hodge*, 199 Okla. 81, 183 Pac. (2d) 575; *Dickinson* v. *Porter*, 240 Iowa 393, 35 N.W. (2d) 66; *State* ex rel. *Fisher* v. *School District No. 1*, 97 Mont. 358, 34 Pac. (2d) 522; *Malone* v. *Hayden*, 329 Pa. 213, 197 Atl. 344;

whether the basis of classification is reasonable, the courts will look at the matter from the point of view of the legislature, always keeping in mind the objects to be accomplished. They will not substitute their own discretion for that of the legislature. They will not declare statutes unconstitutional unless the basis of the classification is unreasonable, arbitrary, or unjust. Thus it was said in *Ex parte King:*

> While arbitrary discriminations by the legislature between persons standing in the same relation to the subject of legislation will not be sustained by the courts, it is firmly settled that "a law is general and constitutional when it applies equally to all persons embraced in a class founded upon some natural or intrinsic or constitutional distinction. . . . If the individuals to whom the legislation is applicable constitute a class characterized by some substantial qualities or attributes of such a character as to indicate the necessity or propriety of certain legislation restricted to that class, such legislation, if applicable to all members of that class, is not violative of our constitutional provisions against special legislation." . . . The question whether the individuals affected by a law do constitute such a class is primarily one for the legislative department of the state, and it is hardly necessary to cite authorities for the proposition that when such a legislative classification is attacked in the courts every presumption is in favor of the validity of the legislative act.[34]

Population is commonly held to be a reasonable basis for the classification of school districts.[35] As an illustration, an act of the legislature of Pennsylvania classified the school districts of the state in such a manner that Philadelphia and Pittsburgh were the only cities of the first class. The act further provided that in districts of the first class the school director should be appointed by the judges of the court of common pleas. The classification was attacked as illegal, but the court held[36] that classification based upon population had long been recognized by the law of the state. Such classification had been supported when applied to cities, counties, and townships, and the court could

---

Board of Education of Kenton County v. *Mescher*, 310 Ky. 453, 220 S.W. (2d) 1016; *Keenan* v. *San Francisco Unified School District*, 34 Calif. 708, 214 Pac. (2d) 382; *School District No. 3* v. *Callahan*, 237 Wis. 560, 297 N.W. 407, 135 A.L.R. 1081; *Benton County Council* v. *State* ex rel. *Sparks*, 224 Ind. 114, 65 N.E. (2d) 116.

34. *Ex parte King*, 157 Calif. 161, 106 Pac. 578.

35. *Minsinger* v. *Rau*, 236 Pa. St. 327, 84 Atl. 902, Ann. Cas. 1913E 1324; *Commonwealth* v. *Gilligan*, 195 Pa. St. 504, 46 Atl. 124; *State* v. *Long*, 21 Mont. 26, 52 Pac. 645; *Reynolds* v. *Board of Education*, 66 Kan. 672, 72 Pac. 274; *Bordeaux* v. *Meridan Land and Industrial Company*, 67 Miss. 304, 7 So. 286.

36. *Minsinger* v. *Rau*, 236 Pa. St. 327, 84 Atl. 902, Ann. Cas. 1913E 1324.

see no reason why it should not be sustained when applied to school districts.

Other specific instances, where classifications based upon substantial distinctions and affecting alike all within the same class or category have been sustained, will serve to illustrate the extent to which the courts will permit variation in the results of general legislation governing the public schools. A statute which provides for the consolidation of school districts and the transportation of pupils at public expense does not violate the uniformity of the school system,[37] even though school boards are vested with discretion as to whether they will afford free transportation to pupils living in isolated communities.[38] Those who live in out-of-the-way places may not actually enjoy the same school privileges as those who live in more thickly populated sections, but there is no illegal discrimination, for any member of the community, by changing his residence, may bring himself within the class afforded free transportation. The principle of uniformity is not violated by a statute applying a special tax limit to agricultural lands in all school districts. The legislature, said the court, might with reason have concluded that agricultural lands derive less benefit from school taxes than other real estate.[39] A statute which sets up certain qualifications for school-board members but which relieves incumbent members from meeting them is not class legislation.[40] The principle of uniformity is not violated by a statute which authorizes the state superintendent to attach school districts to others in case they have less than $100,000 assessed valuations.[41] The fact that a state university charges tuition fees, while the students at the state college are taught free, does not violate the uniformity of the school system.[42] "Those attending the State College are not attending the State University. It is the universality of the operation of the law on all persons of the state similarly situated with reference to the subject matter that determines its validity as a general and uniform law." Age and sex are marks of classification commonly recognized.[43] It is permissible, too, to classify school

37. *Bufkin* v. *Mitchell,* 106 Miss. 253, 63 So. 458, 50 L.R.A. (N.S.) 428.

38. *Cross* v. *Fisher,* 132 Tenn. 31, 177 S.W. 43, Ann. Cas. 1916E 1092.

39. *Dickerson* v. *Porter,* 35 N.W. (2d) 66.

40. *Commonwealth* v. *Griffin,* 268 Ky. 830, 105 S.W. (2d) 1063.

41. *School District No. 3* v. *Callahan,* 237 Wis. 560, 297 N.W. 407, 135 A.L.R. 1081.

42. *Litchman* v. *Shannon,* 90 Wash. 186, 155 Pac. 783.

43. *Hall* v. *De Cuir,* 95 U.S. 485, 24 L. Ed. 547.

districts on the basis of existing civil corporations and to extend to each class divergent regulations for the management of schools.[44]

The case of *People* v. *Weis* illustrates a classification not based upon real distinctions. An act of the legislature of Illinois authorized any township which contained a school district of more than one thousand and less than a hundred thousand population to organize as a high-school district. In holding that the classification was not based upon any rational difference of situation or condition, the court said:

Thus, two adjoining townships may have identically the same population, may be possessed of the same wealth, may have the same number of cities or villages similarly located, and yet, because of the difference in the division of the two townships into school districts, one would be entitled to organize into a township high school district under this act and the other would not. . . . We can perceive of no reason why a township which contains a school district of more than one thousand and less than one hundred thousand inhabitants can be said to differ from an adjoining township having the same population, the same wealth, the same need of a high school, the same number of cities and villages similarly located, but which has a different division of its territory into school districts.[45]

One other example of illegal classification may be cited. An act of the legislature of Arkansas appropriated forty thousand dollars of the common-school fund to the support of high schools. The state high-school board was authorized to select the particular high schools which were to be aided, and there was a general provision that no aid should be granted to a school in any city or town having over thirty-five hundred inhabitants. The court said in part:

The Legislature has no authority to select an arbitrary basis for the disbursement of the funds, but must do so upon some just basis relating either to the scholastic population or the general population of each locality or the amount of the taxes paid, or some such equal and uniform basis of distribution. . . .

The common school funds cannot be distributed in a partial manner so as to discriminate between different localities. If the Legislature has the power to take forty thousand dollars of the common school fund and use it for aiding rural high schools, it has the power to take a hundred thousand dollars of it and use it in the aid of a high school in the largest city in the State. Either constitutes an unequal distribution of the funds which prevents uniformity in the enjoyment of the funds.[46]

---

44. See, also, *Estes* v. *Jones,* 48 S.E. (2d) (Ga.) 99; *Rural High School District No. 6* v. *Board of Commissioners of Brown County,* 153 Kan. 49, 109 Pac. (2d) 154.

45. *People* v. *Weis,* 275 Ill. 581, 114 N.E. 331.

46. *Dickinson* v. *Edmondson,* 120 Ark. 80, 178 S.W. 930, Ann. Cas. 1917C 913.

VALIDATING LEGISLATION

Administrative officials not infrequently act without authority, or they may do what they have a right to do in such a manner as to render the act illegal. For example, a school board may issue bonds in excess of the statutory debt limit, sell them, and apply the proceeds. Or, again, a board may issue bonds within the statutory debt limit but may have failed to give the required notice of the election at which the bonds were voted. Moreover, state legislatures sometimes enact statutes which are later declared unconstitutional by the courts, but before this is done school officials, acting upon the assumption that the statute is valid, may do the things authorized or prescribed by it. Thus considerable embarrassment or even serious inconvenience may arise. As an illustration, a statute may authorize the establishment of high-school districts upon the fulfilment of certain conditions. A period of time elapses during which a number of districts are created, buildings erected, bonds issued, teachers employed, and the schools actually put in operation. Then a case is brought into the courts, and the statute is declared unconstitutional. Obviously, public policy demands in many instances that acts already accomplished be legalized if there is any way to do it without violating the constitution.

Within certain limitations, legislatures may enact what is known as "curative" legislation. That is, laws may be enacted with the avowed purpose of validating legal or administrative proceedings which are defective because of errors or irregularities or even because of lack of authority. The general rule is that defects in legal proceedings may be validated by subsequent legislation if the defect consists in the doing of something which the legislature might have authorized by prior statute, or if the thing not done is something which the legislature might have rendered unnecessary in the first instance. Put in other words, that which the legislature could have authorized in the first instance it can later validate.[47] Of course, curative legislation cannot disturb absolutely vested rights or impair the obligations of contracts.

A few adjudged cases may serve to illustrate this principle more fully. An act of the legislature of Illinois in 1911 authorized townships

47. *State* ex rel. *Miller* v. *Common School District No. 87*, 163 Kan. 650, 185 Pac. (2d) 677; *Hendrickson* v. *Powell County*, 112 Mont. 1, 112 Pac. (2d) 199; *People* ex rel. *Schlaeger* v. *Riche*, 396 Ill. 85, 71 N.E. (2d) 333; *Union Free School District No. 14* v. *Village of Hewlett Bay Park*, 107 N.Y.S. (2d) 858; *North Common School District* v. *Live Oak County Board of School Trustees*, 145 Tex. 251, 199 S.W. (2d) 764.

which contained a school district having a population of not less than one thousand and not exceeding a hundred thousand to organize as high-school districts. In 1917 the act was declared unconstitutional because it was regarded as special or local legislation. In the meantime, however, a number of townships had actually established high schools, and it seemed desirable to give a legal basis to these new districts. Consequently, the legislature passed a curative act which provided that where a majority of the legal inhabitants of any compact and contiguous territory had voted to establish a high-school district, such district should be regarded as legal and valid. In sustaining the curative act, the court stated clearly the principles of law governing cases of this kind:[48]

Counsel for appellees most earnestly insist that this so-called curative act can have no effect upon this suit and can not validate township high school districts organized under the law of 1911, as that law has been held unconstitutional. "A curative statute is necessarily retrospective in character and may be enacted to cure or validate errors or irregularities in legal or administrative proceedings, except such as are jurisdictional or affect substantive rights, and also to cure or give effect to contracts between parties which might otherwise fall for failure to comply with technical legal requirements. Although a retrospective statute affecting and changing vested rights is very generally considered in this country as founded on unconstitutional principles and consequently inoperative and void, this doctrine is not understood to apply to remedial statutes, which may be of a retrospective nature, provided they do not impair contracts or disturb absolute vested rights and only go to confirm rights already existing, and, in furtherance of the remedy, by curing defects add to the means of enforcing existing obligations. Such statutes have been held valid when clearly just and reasonable and conducive to the general welfare, even though they might operate in a degree upon existing rights" (6 R.C.L.320). "If the thing wanting or which failed to be done, and which constitutes the defect in the proceedings, is something the necessity for which the legislature might have dispensed with by prior statute, then it is not beyond the power of the legislature to dispense with it by subsequent statute, and if the irregularity consists in doing some act which the legislature might have made immaterial by prior law it is legally competent to make the same immaterial by a subsequent law" (Cooley's *Const. Lim.* [7th ed.] 531). "The only limitation upon the power of the legislature in this respect seems to be that the act ratified and confirmed must be one which it was lawful for the legislature to authorize in the first instance, and that the power be so exercised as not to infringe or divest property rights and vested interests of persons which are secure against such legislative action" (*People* v. *City of Rock Island*, 271 Ill. 412). . . . This doctrine as to curative statutes applies as well to laws that have been held unconstitutional as to those laws that have been held invalid for other reasons.

48. *People* v. *Stitt*, 280 Ill. 553, 117 N.E. 784.

The court concluded its opinion by holding that, since the method of establishing high-school districts prescribed in the curative act would have been constitutional as an original act, all districts which had been established under the original act in the manner prescribed in the curative act were valid and legal.

In Iowa an independent school district was organized without meeting the statutory requirement that it contain three hundred inhabitants and that ten days' notice of its organization be given the qualified electors. Later a statute was enacted for the express purpose of legalizing this district. The court held that, since the legislature might, in the first instance, have authorized the establishment of school districts having less than three hundred inhabitants and upon less than ten days' notice, it might by subsequent statute waive these particular requirements.[49]

In Kansas a statute authorizing county organization committees to reorganize the districts of the counties was declared unconstitutional because it was a delegation of legislative power. Later the legislature passed an act providing that "where the school organization committee of any county . . . has organized a new school district . . . and the order of the county committee . . . became final on or before March 1, 1947, such order organizing such new school district . . . is hereby declared to be operative and effective and validated as of March 1, 1947, even though all preliminary steps necessary to make such order operative and effective were not complied with." The court sustained the validating act, because, it said, the act did not intend to validate an unconstitutional statute but merely an act of an administrative agency which had taken the kind of action the legislature might have authorized it to take in the first instance. The matter of fixing district boundaries was within the uncontrolled discretion of the legislature; it could fix the boundaries by direct legislation, or it could do it through some designated agent. "Having power to authorize in advance or to dispense entirely with any intermediate action, it was within its competence to adopt the result of an unauthorized act, and to declare that act operative, effective, and valid."[50] In a case involving the same general principle, the statutes of Minnesota provided that bonds for

49. *State* v. *Squires*, 26 Iowa 340.

50. *State* ex rel. *Miller* v. *Common School District No. 87*, 163 Kan. 650, 185 Pac. (2d) 677.

school buildings must receive a majority of two-thirds of the voters present and voting at the election. At an election held in Minneapolis a bond issue was carried by two-thirds of those voting on the proposition but not by two-thirds of those voting at the election. At the following session the legislature passed an act making legal all bonds of this class which had been issued as the result of an election where the proposition to issue had been carried by a two-thirds majority of those voting on the proposition. This curative act was sustained by the Supreme Court of Minnesota.[51]

As previously indicated, the legislature cannot validate that which it had no authority to make legal in the first instance. Thus it has been held that a legislature cannot validate an election that is void because a dual proposition had been submitted as one.[52] Nor can a legislature validate a tax levy for building purposes, the proceeds of which are to be used for educational purposes.[53] So, too, it has been held that the legislature could not validate an election that is illegal because of want of notice of the time and place thereof. Apparently, the court took the position that lack of notice was such a serious failure to observe constitutional processes that no election was ever held.[54]

At times the question arises as to whether a curative statute is applicable to a controversy which has already been decided by the courts. Suppose a school district, for example, issues bonds without fulfilling all the statutory requirements, and a court of competent jurisdiction declares the bonds invalid. Thereupon the legislature passes an act providing that all bonds which have been issued in this particular manner shall be legal. Does the validating act legalize those identical bonds which have already been declared void? This is a question upon which the courts are sharply divided. Some hold that while the legislature may pass curative legislation applicable to defective legal proceedings in general, there is no power in the legislative branch of government to enact a curative statute which applies to a controversy already decided by the courts. The decisions which support this position rely chiefly upon the consideration that the legislative and judi-

51. *State* v. *Brown*, 97 Minn. 402, 106 N.W. 477, 5 L.R.A. (N.S.) 327.

52. *People* ex rel. *Toman* v. *Chicago Great Western Railroad Company*, 379 Ill. 594, 41 N.E. (2d) 960.

53. *People* ex rel. *Schlaeger* v. *Riche*, 396 Ill. 85, 71 N.E. (2d) 333.

54. *People* v. *McCoy*, 387 Ill. 288, 56 N.E. (2d) 393.

cial branches of government are co-ordinate and the legislature, therefore, has no authority to impair or render ineffective a judgment of a
court. As was said in the case of *People* v. *Clark*,[55] "If the existing law
had been construed and applied by the court and the rights of the
parties finally determined, it was not within the power of the General
Assembly to change the judgment or to direct the court to set it aside
and enter a different one." This is the position taken by the courts of
Illinois,[56] Indiana,[57] Maryland,[58] and Ohio.[59] In the majority of cases,
however, it is held that the legislature may enact curative statutes
applicable to proceedings already declared void by the courts as well
as to proceedings of a similar kind which have not been the subject of
controversy.[60] The reasoning upon which this line of decisions is based
is that such statutes do not impair or render ineffective the judgment
of a court but merely remove or cure the defect from which the judgment proceeded. There is no real conflict between judicial and legislative power, it is said, because the legislature does not attempt to set
aside the judgment of a court; it merely attempts to remove the cause
that made the judgment necessary.

The case of *Hodges* v. *Snyder*[61] aptly illustrates the position taken
by a majority of the courts. The Supreme Court of South Dakota declared the organization of a certain school district invalid. Thereupon
the legislature passed an act legalizing all districts organized as this
one had been organized. There was no question as to the general
validity of the curative statute, but it was claimed that the statute
could have no effect upon the status of the particular district which
had already been declared illegal. In holding that the curative statute
was applicable to the district in question, together with all other districts similarly organized, the court said:

55. *People* v. *Clark*, 300 Ill. 583, 133 N.E. 247.

56. *People* v. *Clark*, 300 Ill. 583, 133 N.E. 247; *People* v. *Wiley*, 289 Ill. 173,
124 N.E. 385.

57. *Searcy* v. *Patriot and B. Turnpike Company*, 79 Ind. 274.

58. *Baltimore* v. *Horn*, 26 Md. 194.

59. *Cowen* v. *State*, 101 Ohio St. 387, 129 N.E. 719.

60. *Hodges* v. *Snyder*, 45 S.D. 149, 186 N.W. 867, 25 A.L.R. 1128; *In re
Chester School District's Audit*, 301 Pa. St. 203, 151 Atl. 801; *North Common
School District* v. *Live Oak County Board of School Trustees*, 145 Tex. 251, 199,
S.W. 764. Note: 25 A.L.R. 1136.

61. *Hodges* v. *Snyder*, 45 S.D. 149, 186 N.W. 867, 25 A.L.R. 1128.

Why is it that the courts hold that curative legislation, enacted after suit brought, or even after judgment and pending appeal, *controls the final determination of the action?* Simply because such legislation *is not an attempted exercise of judicial power, nor an attempt to control or reverse the action of the court,* but is a proper exercise of legislative functions, and its effect is simply to remove that which otherwise must control the action of the court. As stated in 2 Lewis' Sutherland, *Stat. Constr.* 1237: "It is no objection to a curative act that it validates what has previously been declared invalid in a judicial proceeding. The judgment may furnish the occasion for the act. Of course, the Legislature can not annul or set aside the judgment of a court, but it may remove a defect from which the judgment proceeded. . . ."

In the present case, the Legislature in no manner questioned the correctness of the judgment of the court. The effect of its action is as though the Legislature had said to the courts: "You have called our attention, by your judgments, to a weakness in the law. We desired that independent districts might become parts of consolidated districts. It seems that we failed to so provide, and you have rightly held that, as long as the present law remains, defendants should be restrained. We, however, have plenary power over school corporations, and desire that, wherever independent districts have attempted, with other districts, to organize consolidated districts, such act shall be validated as of the date the abortive effort was made."

Be we ever so sensitive to legislative encroachment, we are not justified in saying that the Legislature has, in this case, encroached upon the powers of the judiciary. What the Legislature did was purely legislative in its nature. It did not overturn the judgment of any court, or question its correctness.

Where the constitution inhibits the passage of special or local legislation, the question may arise as to the authority of the legislature to enact a statute validating a single illegal proceeding. In cases of this kind, the rule seems to be that a curative statute is not special or local if it applies to all proceedings of the same class, although there may be but one illegal proceeding to be validated.[62] The city of Minneapolis, for example, held an election to determine whether bonds for school buildings should be issued. The proposition was carried by a two-thirds majority of those voting on it, but not by a two-thirds majority of those voting at the election, as the law required. The legislature at the next session passed an act that all bonds for school buildings which had been approved by two-thirds of those voting on the proposition should be considered valid. The act was challenged as

---

62. *State v. Brown,* 97 Minn. 402, 106 N.W. 477, 5 L.R.A. (N.S.) 327; *State v. Squires,* 26 Iowa 340. But see *Boyd v. Milwaukee,* 92 Wis. 456, 66 N.W. 603; *Strange v. Dubuque,* 62 Iowa 303, 7 N.W. 518; *Williams v. Boynton,* 147 N.Y. 426, 42 N.E. 184.

being special and local. The supreme court held otherwise: "It is settled, by the decisions of this court cited above and by the courts of other states, that curative statutes or remedial acts which apply to all places, things, or subjects which are affected by the conditions which are to be remedied are not special acts within the meaning of the constitutional prohibitions."[63]

STATE AUTHORITY OVER PRIVATE SCHOOLS

Education bears such a vital relation to public welfare, morals, and safety that the state may do much, may go very far indeed, by way of limitation of individual rights in order to improve the quality of its citizens, mentally and morally. But just how far the state may go in extending its control over private schools is a matter as yet not clearly determined. One thing, however, is certain: the state cannot exercise its police power to the extent of prohibiting private schools altogether. The Supreme Court of the United States reached this conclusion in a case which came before it from Oregon. The people of that state enacted a law, in 1922, which required children between the ages of eight and sixteen to attend a public school while schools of that class were in session in the district. The obvious purpose of the law was to prohibit private elementary schools. In the opinion of the court, the act violated that provision of the Fourteenth Amendment which declares that "no state . . . shall deprive any person of life, liberty, or property without due process of law":

We think it entirely plain that the Act of 1922 unreasonably interferes with the liberty of parents and guardians to direct the upbringing and education of children under their control. . . . The fundamental theory of liberty upon which all governments of this Union repose excludes any general power of the State to standardize its children by forcing them to accept instruction from public teachers only. The child is not the mere creature of the State; those who nurture him and direct his destiny have the right, coupled with the high duty, to recognize and prepare him for additional obligations.[64]

It seems clear, moreover, that the state cannot prohibit the teaching of certain well-recognized school subjects in private or parochial schools. After World War I revealed that a surprisingly large per-

63. *State v. Brown,* 97 Minn. 402, 106 N.W. 477, 5 L.R.A. (N.S.) 327.

64. *Pierce v. Society of the Sisters of the Holy Names of Jesus and Mary,* 268 U.S. 510, 45 S. Ct. 571, 69 L. Ed. 1070, 39 A.L.R. 468.

centage of the men subject to the army draft were unable to speak or understand the English language, a number of states passed legislation making it unlawful to teach German, and in some instances any foreign language, to pupils in private, parochial, or public schools who had not completed the work of the eighth grade.[65] This legislation was attacked in the courts in three states—Nebraska, Iowa, and Ohio—and in all three instances was held to be a legitimate exercise of the police power.[66] The issue was thereupon carried by certain private-school interests to the Supreme Court of the United States, where the challenged legislation was held to violate that provision of the Fourteenth Amendment which prohibits any state from depriving a person of life, liberty, or property without due process of law. In the opinion of the court:

Mere knowledge of the German language cannot reasonably be regarded as harmful. Heretofore it has been commonly looked upon as helpful and desirable. Plaintiff in error taught this language in school as part of his occupation. His right thus to teach and the right of parents to engage him so to instruct their children, we think, are within the liberty of the Amendment.[67]

In a somewhat similar case the Court of Appeals of Kentucky held that the legislature could not prohibit the establishment of a private school unless it could be shown that such institution was "in some way inimical to the public safety, the public health, or the public morals."[68] The statutes of Kentucky made the establishment of any school, college, or institute which gave instruction in farming, or in any other profession and which controlled as much as 75 acres of land, dependent upon the consent of a majority of the legal voters of the precinct in which the proposed school was to be erected and maintained. The Lincoln Institute purchased 444 acres of land and proceeded in the establishment of a normal and industrial school for colored persons without the consent of the local electors. The court

65. I. N. Edwards, "The Legal Status of Foreign Languages in the Schools," *Elementary School Journal*, XXIV (December, 1923), 270–78.

66. *Nebraska District of Evangelical Lutheran Synod of Missouri et al.* v. *McKelvie*, 104 Neb. 93, 175 N.W. 531, 7 A.L.R. 1688; *State* v. *Bartels*, 191 Iowa 1060, 181 N.W. 508; *Pohl* v. *State*, 102 Ohio St. 474, 132 N.E. 20.

67. *Meyer* v. *State of Nebraska*, 262 U.S. 390, 43 S. Ct. 625, 67 L. Ed. 1042, 29 A.L.R. 1446.

68. *Columbia Trust Company* v. *Lincoln Institute of Kentucky*, 138 Ky. 804, 129 S.W. 113, 29 L.R.A. (N.S.) 53.

held the act in question unconstitutional on the ground that it violated a provision of the Bill of Rights which guaranteed to all the right to acquire, protect, and use property in any way not inimical to the public welfare.

It is perfectly clear, on the other hand, that the state may prohibit any type of educational activity which threatens its own safety or which is subversive of public morals or the public welfare. A very pertinent case in this connection is that of *People* v. *American Socialist Society.*[69] In 1922 the New York legislature passed the following act:

No person, firm, corporation, association or society shall conduct, maintain or operate any school, institute, class or course of instruction in any subjects whatever without making application for and being granted a license from the University of the State of New York to so conduct, maintain or operate such institute, school, class, or course. . . . No license shall be granted for the conduct of any such school, institute, class or course by the regents of the University of the State where it shall appear that the instruction proposed to be given includes the teaching of the doctrine that organized government shall be overthrown by force, violence or unlawful means.

For a number of years prior to the passage of the act, the American Socialist Society had been conducting an institution known as the Rand School of Social Science. The society refused to apply for the required license, on the ground that the act violated that section of the Fourteenth Amendment which provides that no state shall deprive any person of life, liberty, or property without due process of law. The act was further attacked as being in violation of the following provision of the state constitution: "Every citizen may freely speak, write and publish his sentiments on all subjects, being responsible for the abuse of that right." In holding that the statute in question was a valid exercise of the police power of the state, the court used the following language:

The learned counsel for the defendant insists that the statute transcends any valid exercise of the police power of the state, and urges that the exercise of the police power of the state is only justified in the interests of the public when it has for its object the promotion of public health, safety, peace, order, morals, or general welfare, and that the prescribed measure must be reasonably necessary for the accomplishment of the end desired. It seems to us that every test thus laid down by counsel for the defendant is satisfied by the act under consideration. That the public interest is justified by the enactment of legislation aimed to prevent the teaching and promulga-

69. *People* v. *American Socialist Society,* 195 N.Y.S. 801, 202 App. Div. 640.

tion of doctrines aimed at the destruction of organized government seems to us to be beyond cavil. Surely the act has for its object the promotion of the safety, peace, order, morals, and general welfare of our citizens, and the prescribed measure is reasonably necessary to accomplish the desired end. So far as we know, the powers of the Legislature to pass regulatory statutes governing the activities of our citizens, requiring in some cases the adoption of certain standards and in others requiring the issuance of licenses for the purpose of carrying on lawful trades and professions, has never been successfully assailed.

There is one other very definite limitation upon state authority over private schools. The Constitution of the United States prohibits any state from passing legislation impairing the obligation of contracts,[70] and it is settled law that a charter granted to a private institution is in the nature of a contract[71] and cannot be revoked or altered without the consent of those to whom it was granted. This matter was determined once and for all in the well-known Dartmouth College case.[72] In 1816, the legislature of New Hampshire passed an act materially altering the charter of Dartmouth College. The act was sustained by the Supreme Court of New Hampshire. Upon appeal to the Supreme Court of the United States, it was held that the charter was a contract between the state and the corporation and could in no manner be revoked or altered without the consent of those to whom it had been granted. A later decision of the same court, however, holds that in the original charter the state may reserve the right to revoke or alter the charter at its pleasure and that such reservation becomes a part of the contract.

An indirect control over private schools may be exercised by the state by requiring pupils coming from nonpublic schools to take an examination in order to determine their proper assignment to grades in the public school system. For example, a board of education passed a rule that pupils from private or parochial schools would be required to pass an entrance examination in order to enter the high school. The rule was attacked as an arbitrary and unreasonable discrimination between private- and public school pupils and as a violation of the

70. Art. I, sec. 10.

71. *Trustees of Dartmouth College* v. *Woodward,* 4 Wheaton (U.S.) 518, 4 L. Ed. 629; *Regents of the University of Maryland* v. *Williams,* 31 Am. Dec. 72, 9 Gill. & J. (Md.) 365.

72. *Trustees of Dartmouth College* v. *Woodward,* 4 Wheaton (U.S.) 518, 4 L. Ed. 629.

constitutional right of all children to attend the public schools. The court ruled, however, that the assignment of pupils to the various grades of the public school system was a matter wholly within the discretion of the board and that it might adopt any reasonable means of determining the proper placement of pupils. Since private schools were not subject to inspection or visitation by public school officials, the board had no other way of determining accurately the qualifications of the graduates of such institutions and might properly require an examination of private-school graduates seeking entrance to the high school. Such a requirement was not a denial of equal educational opportunity because a pupil failing to qualify for work in the high school could find his proper place in the public elementary schools.[73] It has not been in the American tradition for the state to exercise any rigid control of private schools. There can be little doubt, however, that the state has the power to prescribe standards which the private schools must meet and to provide agencies of inspection to see that the standards are met.

73. *Creyhon* v. *Board of Education*, 99 Kan. 824, 163 Pac. 145, L.R.A. 1917C 993.

CHAPTER III

State and Church in Relation to Education

SEPARATION OF STATE AND CHURCH UNDER
THE FEDERAL CONSTITUTION

THE First Amendment to the Constitution of the United States provides that "Congress shall make no law respecting an establishment of religion, or prohibiting the free exercise thereof." It will be noted that this prohibition is directed to the Congress, but the Supreme Court of the United States has ruled that the Fourteenth Amendment makes it applicable to the several states as well.

Within the past few years the Supreme Court of the United States has rendered a number of important decisions in which it attempts to interpret this amendment as far as it affects educational policy. Previously, it had ruled that a statute of the state of Oregon, in effect prohibiting private and parochial elementary schools, violated the due-process-of-law clause of the Fourteenth Amendment.[1]

In the case of *Everson* v. *Board of Education*,[2] the court was called upon to decide whether a statute of New Jersey permitting local school boards to reimburse the cost of bus transportation to parents of children attending parochial schools was in violation of the First and Fourteenth Amendments. The court laid down the principle that the First Amendment means separation of church and state; that it requires, on the part of the state, neutrality among all religions and between "religious believers and non-believers"; and that no tax, large or small, "can be levied to support any religious activities or institutions." The First Amendment establishes a "wall of separation" between church and state which must be "kept high and impregnable." In the words of the court:

1. *Pierce* v. *Society of the Sisters of the Holy Name of Jesus and Mary*, 268 U.S. 510, 45 S. Ct. 751, 39 A.L.R. 468.

2. 330 U.S. 1.

The "establishment of religion" clause of the First Admendment means at least this: Neither a state nor the Federal Government can set up a church. Neither can pass laws which will aid one religion, aid all religions, or prefer one religion over another. Neither can force nor influence a person to go to or remain away from church against his will or force him to profess a belief or disbelief in any religion. . . . No tax in any amount, large or small, can be levied to support any religious activities or institutions, whatever they may be called, or whatever form they may adopt to teach or practice religion. Neither a state nor the Federal Government can, openly or secretly, participate in the affairs of any religious organizations or groups, and vice versa. In the words of Jefferson, the clause against establishment of religion by law was intended to erect "a wall of separation between Church and State." The First Admendment has erected a wall of separation between church and state. That wall must be kept high and impregnable. We could not approve the slightest breach.

The court went on to hold, nevertheless, that the First Amendment did not prohibit New Jersey from spending tax-raised funds to pay the bus fares of parochial-school children as a part of a general program under which it paid the fares of pupils attending public and other schools. Such an expenditure was not to be regarded as aid to parochial schools; it was, rather, to be regarded as aid to children as recipients of the benefits of public welfare legislation. Moreover, it would be a denial of the religious freedom guaranteed by the First Amendment to exclude individual Catholics, Lutherans, Mohammedans, Baptists, nonbelievers, or members of any other faith from the benefits of public welfare legislation of the kind involved here.

Attention should be called to the vigorous dissent of four of the justices in the New Jersey case. They were quite unwilling to accept the conclusion that payment of the cost of transportation of pupils to Catholic parochial schools was nothing more than the carrying-out of a legitimate social welfare program on the part of New Jersey. They regarded the reasoning of the majority opinion as inconsistent: it established an "impregnable wall of separation" between church and state and then proceeded to break it. If the state could pay the cost of transportation of pupils to parochial schools, it could, by the same logic, bear the cost of other parts of the educational program. Mr. Justice Rutledge pointed out in his dissenting opinion: "If the fact alone be determinative that religious schools are engaged in education, thus promoting the general and individual welfare, together with the legislature's decision that the payments of public moneys for their aid makes their work a public function. then I can see no possible basis, except one of dubious legislative policy, for the state's refusal to make full appropriation for support of private, religious schools, just as is done for public instruction."

In a later case the Supreme Court was called upon to decide the constitutionality of the released-time program for sectarian instruction in operation in the schools of Champaign, Illinois. This program differed from most others, in that sectarian instruction was given in the regular public school classrooms to pupils whose parents requested it. Pupils who did not want religious instruction were not released from their regular public school duties but were requested to go to other classrooms to carry on their studies. The court reaffirmed its position with respect to the "wall of separation" announced in the Everson case and held that the program in force constituted the use of tax-supported property for religious instruction. More than that, it was a close cooperation between the public school authorities and religious groups in promoting religious education; beyond all question, it was the utilization of the tax-established and tax-supported school system to aid religious groups to spread their faith. The court, therefore, found the practice squarely under the ban of the First Amendment.[3]

The issue of the constitutionality of released time came before the court later in a New York case. Here public school pupils were released during the school day so that they might go to religious centers for religious instruction and devotional exercises. Pupils were released only on the written requests of their parents, and those not released stayed on in the classrooms. The churches made weekly reports to the schools indicating the children who had been released and who had not reported for religious instruction. All costs, including application blanks, were paid by the churches. The court reasserted the principle of separation of church and state but went on to say, in holding the practice constitutional:

The First Amendment, however, does not say that in every and all respects there shall be a separation of Church and State. Rather, it studiously defines the manner, the specific ways, in which there shall be no concert or union or dependence one on the other. This is the common sense of the matter. . . . When the state encourages religious instruction or co-operates with religious authorities by adjusting the schedule of public events to

3. *McCollum* v. *Board of Education*, 333 U.S. 203.

sectarian needs, it follows the best in our tradition. For it then respects the religious nature of our people and accommodates the public service to their spiritual needs.[4]

In the case of *Cochran* v. *Board of Education*[5] it was contended that a statute of Louisiana providing for free textbooks for all children, regardless of the school they attended, violated the Fourteenth Amendment, in that it was the taking of property for a private purpose. The Supreme Court of the United States denied the contention, holding that the statute served a public purpose, in that it conferred benefits upon the pupils and not upon the schools they attended.

It may be said, then, that the First Amendment creates a "wall of separation" between church and state but that it is not very clear just what the wall separates. Although no case has come before the Supreme Court of the United States directly involving the appropriation of public funds in aid of a sectarian institution, that court has expressly said that such an appropriation would be unconstitutional. On the other hand, the court has taken the position that providing free transportation and free textbooks to parochial-school pupils is not in violation of the First or the Fourteenth Amendment. Services of this kind are to be regarded as aid to individual pupils. Just what other "services to pupils" would be permitted as a part of a state's social service program remains to be seen. It is not a violation of the First Amendment to release pupils for sectarian religious instruction, provided that the instruction is not carried on in a public school building.

TRANSPORTATION OF PUPILS TO PAROCHIAL SCHOOLS
IN VIOLATION OF STATE CONSTITUTION

Where a state legislature enacts a statute providing for free transportation of pupils to private or parochial schools and the supreme court of the state finds that the statute is not violative of the state constitution, the statute will not be declared void by the United States Supreme Court as being in violation of the First Amendment. But where such a statute is declared to be in violation of some provision of the state constitution, the matter ends there, because the Supreme Court of the United States will not take jurisdiction. A federal court will not assume jurisdiction except to protect some right guaranteed

4. *Zorach* v. *Clauson*, 343 U.S. 306. Three of the justices wrote strong dissenting opinions.

5. 281 U.S. 370.

by the federal Constitution. Nor is a state supreme court bound to follow the reasoning of the Supreme Court of the United States when it
interprets the meaning of its own state constitution.

The state of Washington passed a statute entitling all children attending school in accordance with the laws relating to compulsory
attendance to use the transportation facilities provided by the school
district in which they resided. It was contended that this statute violated the state constitution, which provided that "no public money or
property shall be appropriated for or applied to any religious worship,
exercise, or instruction, or the support of any religious establishment."
The court sustained the contention, saying:

The following paragraph, taken from Judd v. Board of Education, 278
N.Y. 200, 15 N.E. (2d) 576, 118 A.L.R. 789, . . . expresses our view
with reference to the case at bar: "The argument is advanced that furnishing transportation to the pupils of private or parochial schools is not in
aid or support of the schools within the spirit or meaning of our organic
law but, rather, is in aid of their pupils. That argument is utterly without
substance. . . . Free transportation to pupils induces attendance at the
school. The purpose of the transportation is to promote the interests of the
private school or religious or sectarian institution that controls and directs
it. It helps build up, strengthen and make successful the schools as organizations. . . . Without pupils there could be no school. It is illogical to say that
the furnishing of transportation is not an aid to the institution while the
employment of teachers and furnishing books, accommodations and other
facilities are such an aid. . . ."
Appellants have placed great reliance on the principles announced in
Everson v. Board of Education, 330 U.S. 1, 67 S. Ct. 504. . . . While that
case holds, on its facts, that the incidental furnishing of free public transportation to parochial schools is not an "establishment of religion," within the
prohibition of the First Amendment to the United States constitution, nevertheless the right of the individual states to limit such public transportation
to children attending the public schools is carefully preserved. Touching
that question, the supreme court, in the majority opinion, said: "While
*we do not mean to intimate that a state could not provide transportation
only to children attending public schools,* we must be careful, in protecting
the citizens of New Jersey against state-established churches, to be sure
that we do not inadvertently prohibit New Jersey from extending its general
state law benefits to all its citizens without regard to their religious belief"
[italics ours].
Our own state constitution provides that no public money or property
shall be used in support of institutions wherein the tenets of a particular religion are taught. Although the decisions of the United States supreme court
are entitled to the highest consideration as they bear on related questions
before this court, we must, in the light of the clear provisions of our state
constitution and our decisions thereunder, respectfully disagree with those
portions of the Everson majority opinion which might be construed, in the
abstract, as stating that transportation, furnished at public expense, to chil-

dren attending religious schools, is not *in support* of such schools. While the degree of support necessary to constitute an established religion under the First Amendment to the Federal Constitution is foreclosed from consideration by reason of the decision in the Everson case . . . we are constrained to hold that the Washington constitution, although based upon the same precepts, is a clear denial of the rights herein asserted by appellants.[6]

A similar case came before the Supreme Court of Oklahoma before the Everson case was decided. That court repudiated as "utterly without substance" the contention that the providing of free transportation to parochial-school pupils merely conferred benefits upon school children and did not result in the conferring of benefits upon parochial schools as such. An appeal was taken to the Supreme Court of the United States, but the case was dismissed for want of jurisdiction.[7]

In most instances, state courts have not accepted the "child-benefit" theory in passing upon the constitutionality of statutes providing for paying out of public funds the cost of transporting school children to private or parochial schools. They have found that such statutes are violative of some provision in their own state constitution.[8] Maryland and New Jersey courts, however, have sustained the constitutionality of such statutes.[9]

FINANCIAL AID TO SECTARIAN SCHOOLS

Practically all the states—Maine and North Carolina being exceptions—have constitutional provisions prohibiting the use of tax moneys for sectarian purposes. In a good many cases, most of them decided before 1900, the courts had held unconstitutional any attempts to provide financial aid to sectarian institutions or organizations.[10]

6. *Visser v. Nooksack Valley School District,* 207 Pac. (2d) (Wash.) 198.

7. *Gurney v. Ferguson,* 190 Okla. 254, 122 Pac. (2d) 1002; 317 U.S. 588, 63 S. Ct. 34; rehearing denied, 317 U.S. 707, 63 S. Ct. 153.

8. *Judd v. Board of Education,* 278 N.Y. 200, 15 N.E. (2d) 576, 118 A.L.R. 789; *State ex rel. Traub v. Brown,* 172 Atl. (Del.) 835; *State v. Milquet,* 180 Wis. 109, 192 N.W. 392; *Gurney v. Ferguson,* 190 Okla. 254, 122 Pac. (2d) 1002; *Sherrard v. Jefferson County Board of Education,* 171 S.W. (2d) (Ky.) 963; *Mitchell v. Consolidated School District,* 17 Wash. (2d) 61, 135 Pac. (2d) 79, 146 A.L.R. 612. See also *Hlebanja v. Brewe,* 236 N.W. (S.D.) 296; *Silver Lake Consolidated School District v. Parker,* 29 N.W. (2d) (Iowa) 214; *Costigan v. Hall,* 249 Wis. 94, 23 N.W. (2d) 495.

9. *Adams v. County Commissioners,* 180 Md. 550, 26 Atl. (2d) 337; *Board of Education v. Wheat,* 174 Md. 314, 199 Atl. 628; *Everson v. Board of Education,* 44 Atl. (2d) (N.J.) 333.

10. *Zellers v. Huff,* 55 N.M. 501, 256 Pac. (2d) 949; *Jenkins v. Andover,* 103 Mass. 94; *People v. Board of Education,* 13 Barb. (N.Y.) 400; *Otken v. Lamkin,* 56 Miss. 758; *State v. Hallock,* 16 Nev. 373; *Cook County v. Chicago Industrial School,* 18 N.E. (Ill.) 183; *Synod of Dakota v. State,* 50 N.W. (S.D.) 632.

THE HOLDING OF PUBLIC SCHOOLS IN BUILDINGS
OWNED BY RELIGIOUS GROUPS

The courts commonly hold that a board of education may use a portion of a church or other sectarian building for public school purposes and that the payment of rent for such use does not constitute aid to the church or the owners of the building.[11] In an Indiana case the parochial schools of the Roman Catholic church were closed, making it necessary for the public school system to accommodate about eight hundred additional children. The local school board assumed the administrative and instructional obligations of the Catholic parochial schools. The board used the Catholic schools—their buildings and teachers, who were members of Catholic orders and who wore the dress of their orders. These teachers were, however, regularly licensed teachers, and the schools were visited from time to time by the superintendent and director of instruction. The court held that these were not sectarian schools. The court put great stress upon the fact that these schools were under the control of the public school authorities.[12] But where a parochial school is thus taken over and incorporated into the public school system, it cannot continue to carry on sectarian instruction.[13]

11. *Millard* v. *Board of Education,* 19 Ill. App. 48, 10 N.E. 669; *Scripture* v. *Burns,* 29 Iowa 70, 12 N.W. 760; *State* ex rel. *Conway* v. *Joint School District,* 162 Wis. 482, 156 N.W. 477.

12. *State* ex rel. *Johnson* v. *Boyd,* 217 Ind. 348, 28 N.E. (2d) 256.

13. *Harfst* v. *Hoegen,* 349 Mo. 808, 163 S.W. (2d) 609, 141 A.L.R. 1136.

CHAPTER IV

District Organization and Control

SCHOOL DISTRICTS AS MUNICIPAL CORPORATIONS

CONSTITUTIONAL provisions and statutory enactments not infrequently confer certain powers or place certain restrictions upon "municipal corporations." For example, a constitution may provide that no municipal corporation shall become indebted beyond a certain percentage of its taxable wealth. It may become necessary, therefore, to determine whether school districts belong to this class of corporations. Strictly speaking, a school district is not a municipal corporation; it is a quasi-corporation.[1] A municipal corporation proper is a city or town incorporated primarily for purposes of local government. While such a corporation is in part an agency of the state established to assist in the affairs of civil government, it is created, in the main, to enable the locality to regulate and administer its own local concerns. Local interest and advantage rather than execution of state policy are its determining characteristics. In order to effectuate the purposes of their creation, it is obvious that municipal corporations must be granted considerable powers of a legislative and regulatory nature. A quasi-corporation, on the other hand, is purely a political or civil division of the state; it is created as an instrumentality of the state in order to facilitate the administration of government. While in territorial extent it may be identical with a municipal corporation proper, its duties are not essentially local. Its function is the execution of state policy. Clearly, therefore, corporations of this class possess limited powers. Their powers, duties, and liabilities are only such as are prescribed by statute.

1. *Regional High School District No. 3* v. *Town of Newton,* 134 Conn. 613, 59 Atl. (2d) 527; *Butler* v. *Compton Junior College District of Los Angeles County,* 77 Calif. App. (2d) 719, 176 Pac. (2d) 417; *Egan Independent School District No. 1* v. *Minnehaha Co.,* 65 S.D. 32, 270 N.W. 527, 108 A.L.R. 572; *Board of Education of District No. 88* v. *Home Real Estate Improvement Corporation,* 378 Ill. 298, 38 N.E. (2d) 17; *Morgan* v. *Cherokee County Board of Education,* 58 So. (2d) (Ala.) 134.

For purposes of determining their general powers and obligations, school districts are unquestionably quasi-corporations; but for purposes of constitutional or statutory interpretation, they are not infrequently held to be municipal corporations. The fact is that the term "municipal corporation" is often used as a generic term or in such a broad sense as to include quasi-corporations proper. For example, in Iowa municipal corporations were authorized to issue bonds for certain purposes. In holding that the statute applied to school districts, the court pointed out that "the word 'municipal,' as originally used in its strictness, applied to cities only. But the word now has a much more extended meaning, and when applied to corporations the words 'political,' 'municipal,' and 'public' are used interchangeably."[2] Much the same position was taken by the Supreme Court of Kansas in the case of *State* v. *Wilson*.[3] A statute provided that eight hours should constitute a day's work for all laborers employed "by the state of Kansas, or by or on behalf of any county, city, township, or other municipality of said state." The question arose as to whether a contractor who was erecting a school building could employ labor for more than eight hours a day. "Strictly speaking," said the court, "cities are the only municipal corporations in this state. We have no doubt, however, that the lawmakers by the use of the word 'municipality' in the connection in which it is employed in the eight-hour law, intended to include school districts." A statute of the state of Washington provided that the permanent school fund might be invested in national, state, county, or municipal bonds. Although the court pointed out that school districts are not, strictly speaking, municipal corporations within the definitions given in the textbooks, still it held that the school fund could be invested in school-district bonds.[4] In Illinois and New Jersey, school districts have been held to be municipal corporations within the meaning of a statute which provided that laborers and materialmen should have a lien upon the money due contractors erecting public buildings for cities, counties, townships, or other municipalities.[5] Simi-

2. *Curry* v. *District Township of Sioux City*, 62 Iowa 102, 17 N.W. 191.

3. *State* v. *Wilson*, 65 Kan. 237, 69 Pac. 172.

4. *State* v. *Grimes*, 7 Wash. 270, 34 Pac. 836.

5. *Spalding Lumber Company* v. *Brown*, 171 Ill. 487, 49 N.E. 725; *Public Instruction Commissioners* v. *Fell*, 52 N.J. Eq. 689. Accord, *Lehigh Coal and Navigation Company* v. *Summit Hill School District*, 289 Pa. St. 75, 137 Atl. 140. See also *Trustees of Schools* v. *Douglas*, 17 Ill. 209; *Rogers* v. *People*, 68 Ill. 154.

larly, a school district was held to be a municipal corporation within the meaning of a statute of the state of Washington requiring municipal corporations to take bonds of contractors to cover the cost of materials secured from materialmen.[6] A provision of the constitution of North Carolina that "no county, city, town or other municipal corporation shall contract any debt or levy any tax except by a vote of the qualified electors" was held to be applicable to school districts.[7] A constitutional debt limit applicable to counties, cities, towns, and other municipalities was held by the Court of Appeals of Kentucky to include school districts.[8] In Indiana, school townships have been held to be municipal corporations,[9] and the same is true of school districts in Michigan, New York, New Hampshire, and Wisconsin.[10]

The courts of a number of states, on the other hand, deny to school districts the status of municipal corporations.[11] A case in point is that of *Heller* v. *Stremmel*.[12] The statutes of Missouri provided that "no person shall be eligible to the office of Justice of the County Court, who at the time of his election shall hold any office under any municipal" corporation. A member of the St. Louis School Board was elected justice of the county court, and action was brought to test his right to the office. His right to the office was sustained because, in the opinion of the court, the "term municipal corporation does not in its common acceptation or its legal sense include school districts." Similarly, the Supreme Court of Arkansas held that school districts could issue bonds bearing interest coupons, although the constitution prohibited any "county, city, town, or municipality from issuing interest bearing evi-

6. *Maxon* v. *School District No. 34*, 5 Wash. 142, 32 Pac. 110.

7. *Smith* v. *Robersonville Graded School*, 141 N.C. 143, 53 S.E. 524, 8 Ann. Cas. 529.

8. *Brown* v. *Board of Education*, 108 Ky. 783, 57 S.W. 612.

9. *Davis* v. *Steuben School Township*, 19 Ind. App. 694, 50 N.E. 1.

10. *Whitehead* v. *Board of Education*, 139 Mich. 490; *Judd* v. *Board of Education*, 278 N.Y. 200, 15 N.E. (2d) 576, 18 A.L.R. 789; *Ladd* v. *Higgins*, 94 N.H. 212, 50 Atl. (2d) 89; *Iverson* v. *Union Free High School District*, 186 Wis. 342, 202 N.W. 788; *Clough* v. *Osgood*, 87 N.H. 444, 182 Atl. 169.

11. *Eaton* v. *Manitowoc*, 44 Wis. 489; *Commonwealth* v. *Beamish*, 81 Pa. St. 389; *Wharton* v. *School Directors*, 42 Pa. St. 358; *Long* v. *School District of Cheltenham*, 269 Pa. St. 472, 112 Atl. 545; *State* v. *Gordon*, 231 Mo. 547, 133 S.W. 44; *Heller* v. *Stremmel*, 52 Mo. 309; *State* v. *Powers*, 38 Ohio St. 54; *Schmutz* v. *Special School District*, 78 Ark. 118, 95 S.W. 438; *Schultes* v. *Eberly*, 82 Ala. 242, 2 So. 345; *Sheridan District Township* v. *Frahm*, 102 Iowa 5, 70 N.W. 721; *People* v. *Trustees of Schools*, 78 Ill. 136.

12. *Heller* v. *Stremmel*, 52 Mo. 309.

dences of indebtedness." The school district of Little Rock, in the opinion of the court, was not a municipality within the meaning of that provision:

The school district is, it is true, a public corporation, but the mere fact that it is a public corporation does not make it a municipal corporation or, in other words, a municipality. . . . A municipality, properly speaking, is a corporation that has the right to administer local government, as a city or incorporated town. But a school district is only an agency of the State with limited corporate powers belonging to a class of corporate bodies known as *quasi* corporations. These are not municipalities within the meaning of the constitutional provision referred to.[13]

Whether a school district is to be considered as a municipal corporation within the meaning of statutes or constitutional provisions depends very largely upon the wording of these documents. In any particular case the courts will endeavor to discover the intent of those who used the language being construed.

CREATION OF SCHOOL DISTRICTS

Legislative discretion.—Education is a state function, wholly under the control of the legislature except as that body is restricted by the state constitution or by the Constitution of the United States. Obviously, however, the legislature cannot directly administer the educational system of the state; it must employ agencies to carry out its policies and must delegate to them much of its authority. Within constitutional limits, there is no restriction on the selection or creation of such agencies.[14]

If the legislature sees fit, it may authorize or even require such subdivisions of the state as counties, townships, towns, or cities to perform certain duties with respect to the establishment and maintenance of schools.[15] The schools may be placed under the direct control of the

13. *Schmutz* v. *Special School District,* 78 Ark. 118, 95 S.W. 438.

14. *Attorney General* v. *Lowrey,* 199 U.S. 233, 26 S. Ct. 27, 50 L. Ed. 167; *City of Louisville* v. *Commonwealth,* 134 Ky. 488, 121 S.W. 411; *Pearson* v. *State,* 56 Ark. 148, 19 S.W. 499, 35 Am. St. Rep. 91; *Ward* v. *Pelton,* 176 Ark. 1062, 5 S.W. (2d) 315; *State* v. *Hine,* 59 Conn. 50, 21 Atl. 1024, 10 L.R.A. 83; *Kuhn* v. *Board of Education,* 175 Mich. 438, 141 N.W. 574, 45 L.R.A. (N.S.) 972; *Ensley* v. *Goins,* 192 Okla. 587, 138 Pac. (2d) 540.

15. *Associated Schools of Independent District No. 63* v. *School District No. 83,* 122 Minn. 254, 142 N.W. 325, 47 L.R.A. (N.S.) 200; *State* v. *Delaware Iron Company,* 160 Minn. 382, 200 N.W. 475; *State* v. *Haworth,* 122 Ind. 462, 23 N.E. 946, 7 L.R.A. 240; *State* v. *Freeman,* 61 Kan. 90, 58 Pac. 959, 47 L.R.A. 67; *State* v. *Hine,* 59 Conn. 50, 21 Atl. 1024, 10 L.R.A. 83.

municipality in much the same manner as the health or fire department is administered, or the municipal subdivision may be constituted a school district wholly independent of the municipality proper. The legislature, on the other hand, may ignore all existing corporate territories and establish school districts in such manner as policy may demand.

Consent of residents not necessary.—Since education belongs to the state, to the exclusion of all local rights except such as are delegated, the legislature may establish school districts without the consent of those residing in the territory affected, unless, of course, such consent is required by the constitution.[16] Thus the legislature, unless restrained by the constitution, may authorize the annexation of territory to a school district without the consent, or even against the remonstrance, of a majority of persons residing in the annexed territory.[17] So, too, counties, townships, or cities or any other subdivisions of the state may be required, against their consent, to perform such educational duties as the state may impose upon them.

Delegation of authority to establish school districts.—The legislature may itself create school districts or designate other agencies for the execution of its educational policies, or it may delegate its authority to establish districts to some administrative board or official.[18] While is it a generally accepted principle of law that legislative authority may not be delegated, this does not preclude the creation of administrative bodies and the vesting of them with broad discretion. In other words, the legislature may not delegate its own inherent and inalienable authority to determine what the law shall be, but it may confer

16. *Fulton Township School District* v. *School District No. 4,* 302 Mich. 566, 5 N.W. (2d) 467; *Board of Education* v. *Nickell,* 410 Ill. 98, 101 N.E. (2d) 438; *Board of Education of Fayette County* v. *Board of Education of Lexington Independent School District,* 250 S.W. (2d) 1017; *School District No. 68* v. *Hoskins,* 194 Ore. 301, 240 Pac. 949; *Regional High School District No. 3* v. *Town of Newton,* 134 Conn. 613, 59 Atl. (2d) 527; *School Board of Consolidated School District* v. *Monsey,* 198 Okla. 41, 175 Pac. 76.

17. *Wheeler School District No. 152* v. *Hawley,* 18 Wash. (2d) 37, 137 Pac. (2d) 1010.

18. *Trustees of Slaughterville Graded School District* v. *Brooks,* 163 Ky. 200, 173 S.W. 305; *Bobbitt* v. *Blake,* 25 Idaho 53, 136 Pac. 211; *Landis* v. *Ashworth,* 57 N.J. Law 509, 31 Atl. 1017; *Drouin* v. *Board of Directors,* 136 La. 393, 67 So. 191; *Norton* v. *Lakeside Special School District,* 97 Ark. 71, 133 S.W. 184; *Mitchell* v. *Directors of School District No. 15,* 153 Ark. 50, 239 S.W. 371; *Bay State Live Stock Company* v. *Bing,* 51 Neb. 570, 71 N.W. 311; *Reynolds Land & Cattle Company* v. *McCabe,* 72 Tex. 57, 12 S.W. 165; *School District No. 17* v. *Zediker,* 4 Okla. 599, 47 Pac. 482.

discretion in the administration of the law.[19] The rule is clear, but it gives rise to considerable controversy when applied to specific cases, because it is often difficult to determine whether the legislature has delegated legislative or administrative power. An Illinois case[20] is a good illustration. A statute of that state provided that a certain percentage of the legal voters residing in any compact territory might petition the county superintendent to call an election to determine whether a high-school district should be established. Before calling the election, however, the superintendent was authorized to consider the form, size, and assessed valuation of the proposed district and the number of prospective high-school pupils in the district. If, in his opinion, the proposed district was not satisfactory or likely to maintain an efficient high school, he might refer the petition back to the petitioners with recommendations as to changes, or he might deny the prayer of the petition altogether. In holding the statute unconstitutional on the ground that it delegated legislative power to county superintendents, the court said:

It attempted to confer on county superintendents a discretion as to what the law should be. That cannot be done. . . . The law as to what will constitute a satisfactory and efficient high-school district is not found in the statute itself. It does not define or specify the requisite of a satisfactory and efficient community high-school district but leaves that matter to the discretion of the county superintendent without any rules of limitation for the exercise of such discretion. Until that official acts, it cannot be known what the law is.

Other courts, however, seem to permit a larger exercise of administrative discretion. For example, the Supreme Court of Louisiana upheld a statute which gave the parish school board, in conjunction with the parish superintendent of schools, the power to divide the parish into school districts of such shape and area as would best accommodate the pupils concerned.[21] Similarly, a statute of Minnesota authorized the county commissioners to organize or change districts when the best interests of the territory affected required it. In sustaining the statute, the supreme court said: "The determination of the question of when and under what conditions school districts may be organized, or their boundaries changed, is purely a legislative one, which has been

19. 12 C.J. 840.

20. *Kenyon* v. *Moore*, 287 Ill. 233, 122 N.E. 548.

21. *Drouin* v. *Board of Directors*, 136 La. 393, 67 So. 191.

qualifiedly delegated to the respective boards of county commissioners of the state."[22]

When the legislature authorizes an administrative officer or board to establish school districts, in order that the statute may not be declared void as a delegation of legislative authority, care should be taken not to vest the officer or board with too great discretion. As indicated in the case of *Kenyon* v. *Moore*,[23] the legislature itself should prescribe the conditions to be met before districts can be established, leaving to the administrative officer the duty of determining whether the conditions have been met. This does not mean that those who are clothed with authority to establish school districts may not be permitted to exercise any discretion. It simply means that they should be governed by fundamental principles of procedure which the legislature itself has prescribed.

There is some authority, however, for the position that the establishment of school districts is not so exclusively a legislative function as to prevent their establishment by designated officials or by the people of a community, without any control whatever over their discretion. Thus, in a Wisconsin case, a statute authorized the state superintendent, by order, to attach districts with less than one hundred thousand dollars' valuation to contiguous districts. A rural-school district attached to a city district challenged the constitutionality of the act, on the ground that it was a delegation of legislative power. The court denied the contention of the plaintiff, saying:

> These contentions cannot be sustained, in view of the established rules that the formation of school districts and the power to exercise discretion in determining whether such districts shall be altered by consolidation or otherwise is not such an exclusive legislative function as may not be delegated to the state superintendent, as well as to town boards; and that this power may be delegated without any standard whatsoever to guide in the exercise of the power delegated.[24]

The court went on to point out that, from the very beginning of the state's history, the legislature had conferred upon town boards the authority to establish school districts and that it had never attempted to set up any required standard or to make the action of the boards

---

22. *Irons* v. *Independent School District No. 2*, 119 Minn. 119, 137 N.W. 303.

23. *Kenyon* v. *Moore*, 287 Ill. 233, 122 N.E. 548. See also *State* ex rel. *Donaldson* v. *Hines*, 163 Kan. 300, 182 Pac. (2d) 865.

24. *School District* v. *Callahan*, 237 Wis. 560, 297 N.W. 407, 135 A.L.R. 1081.

dependent upon any facts or circumstances. So in the present case no standard whatever need be prescribed in delegating the power in question.

The Supreme Court of Illinois appears to have taken the position that the legal voters of a territory may, through the proper statutory petition and the consent of school trustees, establish a school district without any statutory standards to govern their action. The court did not consider whether this might be regarded as a delegation of legislative power to private citizens;[25] but in an Oklahoma case this issue was pointedly met by the court. Here a statute made it the mandatory duty of the county superintendent, with no discretion in the matter, to annex territory to a school district when a majority of the voters in the territory so desired. The court held that this was not a delegation of legislative power to private individuals. It recognized the accepted canon of constitutional law prohibiting the delegation of the lawmaking power but pointed out that the rule is not applicable to municipalities or to the people of local subdivisions of the state with respect to matters concerning them alone. School districts come under this exception, said the court, because the fixing of the boundaries of school districts is a purely local affair.[26]

Authority to establish high-school and elementary-school districts embracing the same territory.—One important limitation on legislative authority in the creation of school districts should be kept in mind. It is a commonly accepted legal principle that two corporate entities performing the same functions cannot embrace the same territory at the same time.[27] It has been held, however, that the territory constituting a number of elementary-school districts may be organized as a union high-school district.[28] In the case of *Splonskofsky* v. *Minto*,[29] where a high-school district embraced the territory of a number of elementary-school districts, the court said:

25. *People* v. *Board of Education*, 380 Ill. 311, 43 N.E. (2d) 1012.

26. *Dowell* v. *Board of Education*, 185 Okla. 342, 91 Pac. (2d) 771.

27. *State* v. *Goff*, 110 Ore. 349, 221 Pac. 1057; *Clardy* v. *Winn*, 162 Ark. 320, 258 S.W. 333; *People* ex rel. *Mills* v. *Fairfield Community High School*, 397 Ill. 233, 73 N.E. (2d) 292; *Kelley* v. *Brunswick School District*, 134 Me. 414, 187 Atl. (2d) 703.

28. *Splonskofsky* v. *Minto*, 62 Ore. 560, 126 Pac. 15; *Welch* v. *Getzen*, 85 S.C. 156, 67 S.E. 294; *People* v. *Sleight*, 306 Ill. 319, 137 N.E. 829; *People* v. *Pinari*, 332 Ill. 181, 163 N.E. 385.

29. *Splonskofsky* v. *Minto*, 62 Ore. 560, 126 Pac. 15.

The plaintiffs argue that it is impossible for two corporations with like purposes to exist in the same territory. This principle, sound as it may be, does not apply to the present contention. The high school is not concerned with the primary branches of education taught in the common schools. Its field of activity is enlarged and different in scope from that of the ordinary districts. . . . The two classes of districts complement one another but do not conflict in their organization. In that they are all branches of the government, we might as well say that road districts, school districts, and drainage districts conflict with each other because they operate in the same territory.

In Illinois the supreme court has gone so far as to hold that a community high-school district is not illegal, even though it includes within its boundaries an ordinary common-school district which maintains an accredited high school.[30] If a common-school district and a high-school district embrace in part the same territory, both districts may levy the maximum taxes permitted by law.[31]

The precise question as to whether an elementary-school district and a high-school district may comprise exactly the same territory has seldom been raised. In Illinois, however, where the statutes provided that in elementary-school districts of a certain class a high-school board might also be established, the court held that two separate corporations did not exist and that the debts of the two boards would have to be considered as the debts of one district in computing the constitutional debt limit. The precise issue of the authority of the legislature to establish a high-school district and an elementary-school district in the same territory was not before the court; nevertheless, the court reasoned:

If the legislature, by authorizing a school district to establish a high school, can also authorize it to incur indebtedness beyond the constitutional limit, they could get rid of all the restrictions of the constitution by authorizing the management of each grade or department of the public school by a different board of education, with different buildings. . . . It was within the power of the legislature to provide for the establishment of a high school under the control of a board of education elected for that purpose, but they could not, by multiplying the boards of education in the same territory, authorize the district to incur indebtedness beyond the constitutional limit.[32]

30. *People* v. *Sleight,* 306 Ill. 319, 137 N.E. 829; *People* v. *Woodward,* 285 Ill. 165, 120 N.E. 496; *Schrodt* v. *Holsen,* 299 Ill. 247, 132 N.E. 424; *People* v. *Pinari,* 332 Ill. 181, 163 N.E. 385.

31. *People* v. *Henkle,* 256 Ill 585, 100 N.E. 175.

32. *Russell* v. *High School Board of Education,* 212 Ill. 327.

The Supreme Court of Arizona has held that high-school and common-school districts may be identical in territory and that property could be taxed by each district. The question as to whether or not the two corporations had different purposes was not considered.[33]

Petitions for the establishment of districts.—While the legislature may establish school districts without, or even against, the consent of the residents of the territory affected, such consent is, as a matter of policy, often, if not commonly, required by statute. A petition signed by a designated percentage of the qualified electors is frequently made a condition precedent to the calling of an election or the taking of action on the part of administrative officers with respect to the creation of districts or the change of boundaries. Where such is the case, the filing of the required petition is jurisdictional, and any election held, or any action taken, without such a petition having been filed is void.[34]

Withdrawal of names from petitions.—Not infrequently the question arises as to the right of a signer of a petition to withdraw his name therefrom. The great weight of authority supports the rule that anyone who signs a petition may withdraw his name at any time before action is taken by those to whom it is addressed.[35] The fact that the petition has been filed is, as a rule, immaterial. In the case of *People v. Strawn*,[36] where the petition had been filed before some of the petitioners sought to withdraw their names, the Supreme Court of Illinois held: "As to the third proposition, the law is that the petitioners might

33. *Glendale Union High School District* v. *Peoria School District No. 11,* 51 Ariz. 478, 78 Pac. (2d) 141.

34. *School District No 2* v. *Pace,* 113 Mo. App. 134, 87 S.W. 580; *In re School Districts Nos. 2, 3, and 4,* 122 Minn. 383 142 N.W. 723; 20 C.J. 95; *Mesquite Independent School District* v. *Gross,* 123 Tex. 49, 67 S.W. (2d) 242.

35. *Montgomery Township Board of Education* v. *Ashland County Board of Education,* 8 Ohio App. 120; *Valley Center School District No. 20* v. *Hansberger,* 28 Ariz. 493, 237 Pac. 957; *People* v. *Strawn,* 265 Ill. 292, 106 N.E. 840; *State* v. *Boyden,* 21 S.D. 6, 108 N.W. 897, 15 Ann. Cas. 1122; *Territory* v. *City Council of Roswell,* 16 N.M. 340, 117 Pac. 846, 35 L.R.A. (N.S.) 1113; *School District No. 24* v. *Renick,* 83 Okla. 158, 201 Pac. 241; *In re Mercersburg Independent School District,* 237 Pa. St. 368, 85 Atl. 467. Note: 11 L.R.A. (N.S.) 372; 15 Ann. Cas. 1125; *State ex rel. Larson* v. *Morrison,* 155 Neb. 309, 51 N.W. (2d) 626; *Zilske* v. *Albers,* 238 Iowa 1050, 29 N.W. (2d) 189. But see *State* v. *Fendall,* 135 Ore. 142, 295 Pac. 191; *Nathan Special School District No. 4* v. *Bullock Springs School District,* 38 S.W. (2d) (Ark.) 19.

36. *People* v. *Strawn,* 265 Ill. 292, 106 N.E. 840.

withdraw their names from the petition prior to any action being taken on it." The Supreme Court of Oklahoma sets forth clearly the reasons underlying this principle of law:

We do not think it is necessary for a person to give any reason why he withdraws his name from a petition thus signed by him where no action has been taken on the petition. It is not for a court to determine whether his reason for withdrawing his name is sufficient or not. He was induced to sign the petition under some representations made by the persons seeking his signature. The ingenious argument that may have been made to induce him to sign the petition was probably sufficient to satisfy his mind, and he acted upon the representations made in such argument. He may find out that he has acted on a misapprehension of the facts or that the results to be obtained are not as he understood them in his own mind. Where the petition has not been acted upon by the officers clothed with the authority to act upon it, a signer has an absolute right to withdraw his name from the petition. It is not within the province of any court to inquire into the psychology of his mind or the sufficiency of his reasons for withdrawing his name from the petition.[37]

In some states, however, the rule is that the filing or the presentation of the petition puts an end to the right to withdraw names without cause shown.[38] The act of presenting the petition, it is said, confers jurisdiction on the board or tribunal to which it is addressed, and, after jurisdiction attaches, names can be withdrawn only with the consent of the body to whom the petition is addressed.

Sometimes the statutes provide for the accomplishment of certain results by the mere act of filing a petition or remonstrance without action on the part of any board or official. In such a case, of course, names cannot be withdrawn after the petition or remonstrance has been filed.[39]

Notice of elections.—Statutes frequently provide that notices shall be posted for a certain number of days prior to the holding of an election to determine whether a school district shall be established or

37. *School District No. 24 v. Renick,* 83 Okla. 158, 201 Pac. 241.

38. *Seibert v. Lovell,* 92 Iowa 507, 61 N.W. 197; *Nathan Special School District No. 4 v. Bullock Springs Special School District No. 36,* 38 S.W. (2d) (Ark.) 19. NOTE: 15 Ann. Cas. 1126; 11 L.R.A. (N.S.) 375. See also *In re Formation and Organization of Common School District,* 235 N.W. (S.D.) 697. In Pennsylvania the rule is that jurisdiction does not attach in the case of petitions presented to municipal bodies, officers, or boards until formal action has been taken on the subject matter of the petition. The jurisdiction of a court, however, attaches as soon as the petition is filed (*In re Mercersburg Independent School District,* 237 Pa. St. 368, 85 Atl. 467).

39. *Board of Education v. Board of Education,* 112 Ohio St. 108, 146 N.E. 812.

whether the boundaries of a district shall be changed. Similarly, notice may be required of meetings of administrative officers or boards to consider the establishment of school districts. In either case it is a commonly accepted principle of law that the giving of the required notice is jurisdictional; that is, the authority to hold the election or to take official action is conditioned upon the giving of the statutory notice.[40] As the Supreme Court of Wisconsin has put it:

The giving of the notice by the municipal board constituted the first step of its authority to act. While it cannot well be said that this constituted taking jurisdiction as it is known in judicial procedure, nevertheless it is the beginning of an orderly process to carry out the authority delegated to the muncipal board by the legislature relative to school districts. The failure to give this notice of necessity constitutes a defect in procedure which deprives the board of the authority to act.[41]

Thus a statute which required that notice of a hearing on the consolidation of school districts be published once a week for two weeks was mandatory, and a notice that was published once for a period of less than two weeks did not give the county board of education jurisdiction to enter an order of consolidation.[42] So, too, where a statute required a twenty-day notice of a hearing to consider the change of district boundaries and a shorter notice was given, the order of consolidation pursuant to such notice was void.[43]

There is, however, considerable difference of opinion as to how strictly the statutes must be followed in matters of detail. Some courts hold that strict compliance with the statutory requirements is necessary.[44] Courts commonly, however, adopt the rule that a defect in the notice is immaterial where the result could not have been changed if

40. *State v. Compton*, 28 Neb. 485, 44 N.W. 660; *Huyser v. Township Boards of School Inspectors*, 131 Mich. 568, 91 N.W. 1024; *People v. Hartquist*, 311 Ill. 127, 142 N.E. 475; *Howard v. Forester*, 22 Ky. Law Rep. 843; *State v. Graham*, 60 Wis. 395, 19 N.W. 359; *Lewis v. Young*, 116 Ark. 291, 171 S.W. 1197; *Ron Consolidated School District No. 12 v. Arnett Consolidated School District No. 11*, 193 Okla. 180, 141 Pac. (2d) 998; *Sugar Grove District No. 19 v. Booneville School District*, 208 Ark. 722, 187 S.W. (2d) 339; *Oak Park School District No. 2 v. Callahan*, 246 Wis. 144, 16 N.W. (2d) 395.

41. *Oak Park District No. 2 v. Callahan*, 246 Wis. 144, 16 N.W. (2d) 395.

42. *Sugar Grove School District No. 19 v. Booneville School District*, 208 Ark. 722, 187 S.W. (2d) 339.

43. *Ron Consolidated School District No. 12 v. Arnett Consolidated School District No. 11*, 193 Okla. 180, 141 Pac. (2d) 998.

44. *Gentle v. Board of School Inspectors*, 73 Mich. 40, 40 N.W. 928; *Bowen v. Greensboro*, 79 Ga. 709, 4 S.E. 159; *Lewis v. Young*, 116 Ark. 291, 171 S.W. 1197.

the notice required had been given.[45] "It is now a canon of election law," said the Supreme Court of Oregon, "that an election is not to be set aside for a mere informality or irregularity, which cannot be said in any manner to have affected the result of the election. When it appears that no different result would have been possible in the entire district affected by the majority vote, the failure strictly to comply with the requirements of the statute in respect to giving the notice will not invalidate the election."[46] Where it is impossible, however, to ascertain with any degree of certainty what the result would have been, had the proper notice been given, the election cannot be upheld.[47]

Both reason and the pronounced weight of authority support the rule that a substantial rather than a technical compliance with the statutes is all that is necessary.[48] As a rule, the courts will not hold an election void because of a mere irregularity in the giving of notice where the purpose of giving the notice has been actually accomplished. The proper test for determining whether an election is invalidated because of a failure to give the statutory notice is: Did the electors generally have a knowledge of the election and a free opportunity to express their will? Or, on the other hand, were a sufficient number of electors deprived of the opportunity to vote to change the result of the election?[49] In the words of the Supreme Court of California, "it may be conceded to be the general rule of law that, when an election has been held in all other respects as prescribed by law, and the voters generally have knowingly had a full opportunity to express their will, such election will not be declared invalid merely be-

---

45. *State* v. *Hall*, 73 Ore. 231, 144 Pac. 475; *Sharp* v. *George*, 5 Ariz. 65, 46 Pac. 212; *People* v. *Union High School District*, 101 Calif. 655, 36 Pac. 119; *Plott* v. *Board of Commissioners*, 187 N.C. 125, 121 S.E. 190; *Parsons* v. *Batesville*, 189 Ark. 1057, 76 S.W. (2d) 83; *People* v. *Summy*, 377 Ill. 255, 36 N.E. (2d) 331; *Anderson* v. *Peterson*, 54 N.W. (2d) (N.D.) 542; *State ex rel. Mayse* v. *Goodwin*, 243 S.W. (2d) (Mo.) 353; *Lamkin Independent School District* v. *Hamilton Independent School District*, 242 S.W. (2d) 828; *Beam* v. *Wilson*, 110 N.Y.S. (2d) 94; *Wallis* v. *Williams*, 50 Tex. Civ. App. 623, 110 S.W. 785.

46. *State* v. *Hall*, 73 Ore. 231, 144 Pac. 475.

47. *State* v. *Sengstacken*, 61 Ore. 455, 122 Pac. 292, Ann. Cas. 1914B 230.

48. *State* v. *McKinny*, 146 Wis. 673, 132 N.W. 600; *Kittelson* v. *Dettinger*, 174 Wis 71, 182 N.W. 340; *State* v. *Thompson*, 260 S.W. (Mo.) 84; *In re Cleveland*, 52 N.J. Law 188, 19 Atl. 17, 7 L.R.A. 431; *State* v. *Langlie*, 5 N.D. 594, 67 N.W. 958, 32 L.R.A. 723; *State* v. *Doherty*, 16 Wash. 382, 47 Pac. 958. NOTE: 90 Am. St. Rep. 71, 18 Ann. Cas. 1137.

49. 20 C.J. 96.

cause the prescribed statutory notice has not been given."[50] In the case of *Molyneaux* v. *Molyneaux*[51] all the electors of a district were present at an election, and a clear proposition with respect to consolidation of districts was submitted to them. The court held that the action taken was not illegal simply because the notice of the election was not so specific as required. The object of the notice had been fulfilled, and that was sufficient. It has been held, too, that "failure to give notice for the full time before an election required by statute will not render the election invalid, if there were sufficient notice thereof and a full vote."[52] The court reasoned that the object of notices is to give every qualified voter a "free and fair opportunity to express his opinion on the question submitted to the people for their approval or disapproval" and that, when this is accomplished in fact, the spirit of the statutes has been carried into effect. This liberal rule is based on the theory that, when once the people have expressed their will, the courts should not set that will aside because of mere technicalities or irregularities. After all, the essential element in the procedure is the election, not the notice. Moreover, school districts are agencies of the state, created for the purpose of carrying into effect its educational policies, and the general public has too great an interest in them to permit small matters to imperil their existence.

The tacking-up of the poster, it should be kept in mind, is not the essential part of the giving of notice, the important consideration being that the notices must be posted the designated number of days before the election. In a Minnesota case,[53] Monday was the last day for posting notices of an election in proceedings for the establishment of a school district. Notices tacked up on the preceding Sunday fulfilled the requirements of the law. Said the court:

No importance attaches here to the act of tacking up the poster. This act is no part of the giving of notice. The requirement that the county superintendent shall "cause ten days' posted notice to be given" means that the notice must be up ten days before the election. No posting was necessary until Monday, February 10th. The important consideration is that these notices remained and were posted on that day. This satisfies the requirement of the statute.

50. *Odell* v. *Rihn,* 19 Calif. App. 713, 127 Pac. 802.

51. *Molyneaux* v. *Molyneaux,* 130 Iowa 100, 106 N.W. 370.

52. *Heckert* v. *Aberdeen Graded School,* 184 N.C. 475, 115 S.E. 50.

53. *In re Consolidation of School Districts 22 and 15,* 127 Minn. 84, 148 N.W. 891.

It seems, moreover, that the duty of those required to post notices is fulfilled if the notices are posted on the proper day, even though they should later become illegible or be removed by a third party. The case of *Lacock* v. *Miller*[54] is in point. Typewritten notices were posted, but some of the carbon copies later became illegible. The court ruled, nevertheless, that the requirements of the statute had been met.

Effect of irregularity of proceedings in the establishment of districts. —Officials authorized by the legislature to establish school districts or to change their boundaries must follow the procedure prescribed by statute. The courts, however, will not suffer minor irregularities to defeat the will of the people, for substantial compliance with the statutes is all that is necessary.[55]

In a Missouri case,[56] three members of a board of education met to consider the establishment of a school district; as there was not a quorum, they adjourned until the fifteenth of the month. Later it was discovered that the fifteenth fell upon Sunday, and the time of meeting was changed to the sixteenth without a formal meeting of the board. At this meeting all the persons interested were present, and action was taken establishing a new school district. The court pointed out that the action of the board was irregular, but concluded:

If all of their proceedings which are had in good faith can be set aside and treated as void in collateral proceedings, for irregularities which do not affect the substantial rights of the parties interested, the whole beneficial objects of our school system will be paralyzed and rendered inefficient. The schools must necessarily in many townships be conducted by men not accustomed to legal certainty and forms, and their action should be upheld when good faith has been exercised unless it is in very glaring cases of wrong, or where direct proceedings are instituted at the time to set their action aside.

54. *Lacock* v. *Miller*, 178 Iowa 920, 160 N.W. 291.

55. *State* v. *McKinny*, 146 Wis. 673, 132 N.W. 600; *Kittelson* v. *Dettinger*, 174 Wis. 71, 182 N.W. 340; *Clement* v. *Everest*, 29 Mich. 19; *Viktora* v. *Cressman*, 41 S.D. 159, 169 N.W. 551; *State* v. *Thompson*, 260 S.W. (Mo.) 84; *In re Cleveland*, 52 N.J. Law 188, 19 Atl. 17, 7 L.R.A. 431; *State* v. *Langlie*, 5 N.D. 594, 67 N.W. 958, 32 L.R.A. 723; *State* v. *Doherty*, 16 Wash. 382, 47 Pac. 958; *Hundley* v. *Singleton*, 23 Ky. Law Rep. 2006, 66 S.W. 279; *Lightner* v. *McCord*, 151 S.W. (2d) (Tex.) 362; *Fairfield Independent School District* v. *Streetman Independent School District*, 222 S.W. (2d) (Tex.) 651; *Lewis* v. *Woodall*, 72 Idaho 16, 236 Pac. (2d) 91; *State ex rel. Grozbach* v. *Common School District*, 54 N.W. (2d) (Minn.) 130; *State ex rel. Weatherford* v. *Hayworth*, 152 Ore. 416, 53 Pac. (2d) 1048; *Oakville Independent School District* v. *County School Trustees of Live Oak County*, 178 S.W. (2d) (Tex.) 547; *Tedder* v. *Board of Supervisors of Bolivar County*, 214 Miss. 717, 59 So. (2d) 329.

56. *Rice* v. *McClelland*, 58 Mo. 116.

Similarly, it has been held that slight inaccuracies in the description of the boundaries of a school district will not render its incorporation void.[57] Nor will the fact that qualified election officials fail to appear at an election and other persons take their place after subscribing to the oath of office invalidate the election unless it can be shown that the irregularity affected the result.[58] Even violence and intimidation will not render an election void unless it can be shown that they were sufficient to have changed the result.[59] An election held to determine whether a town should be incorporated as a school district was not declared void because the presiding officer was a candidate for the office of trustee of the proposed district.[60] Where the statutes provided that the polls should be open until seven o'clock in the evening but they were closed at five o'clock after all those entitled to vote had voted except one person who did not care to vote, the court held that under the circumstances the hour of closing the polls was not a matter of substance.[61] If the irregularity had been such as to deprive persons entitled to vote of the privilege of voting, or, if doubt could have existed as to the result, the hour of closing the polls would have been a matter of substance and the statute would have been considered mandatory. Where the statute required two polling places, one in the town and the other in the country, and there was only one provided, an election held to determine whether a school district should be established was so irregular as to render the organization of the district illegal.[62]

"The principle underlying all these decisions," says the Supreme Court of Idaho, "is that the rights of the voters should not be prejudiced by the errors or wrongful acts of the election officers, unless it be made to appear that a fair election was prevented by reason of the alleged irregularities."[63]

57. *Harbin Independent School District* v. *Denman*, 200 S.W. (Tex.) 176.

58. *Mosiman* v. *Weber*, 107 Neb. 737, 187 N.W. 109; *Collins* v. *Masden*, 25 Ky. Law Rep. 81, 74 S.W. 720; 20 C.J. 90; 15 Cyc. 311; 9 R.C.L. 1012. NOTE: 1 A.L.R. 1536.

59. *Williams* v. *Venneman*, 42 Calif. App. (2d) 618, 109 Pac. (2d) 757.

60. *State* v. *Buchanan*, 37 Tex. Civ. App. 325, 83 S.W. 723.

61. *District Township of Lincoln* v. *Independent District of Germania*, 112 Iowa 321, 83 N.W. 1068.

62. *State* v. *Alexander*, 129 Iowa 538, 105 N.W. 1021.

63. *Pickett* v. *Board of Commissioners*, 24 Idaho 200, 133 Pac. 112.

ALTERATION OF SCHOOL-DISTRICT BOUNDARIES

Since school districts are created by the state for the purpose of carrying its educational policies into effect, the legislature may create, abolish, or alter them and dispose of their property as it will, subject only to such limitations as are found in the constitution.[64] The commonly accepted rule with respect to the plenary power of the legislature over school districts has been clearly expressed by the Supreme Court of Illinois:

With or without consent of the inhabitants of a school district, over their protests, even without notice or hearing, the State may take the school facilities in the district, without giving compensation therefore, and vest them in other districts or agencies. The State may hold or manage the facilities directly or indirectly. The area of the district may be contracted or expanded, it may be divided, united in whole or in part with another district, and the district may be abolished. All this at the will of the legislature. The "property of the school district" is a phrase which is misleading. The district owns no property, all school facilities, such as grounds, buildings, equipment, etc., being in fact and law property of the State and subject to the legislative will.[65]

Effect of extension of city limits on school-district boundaries.—In cases where a school district is coextensive with the territorial limits of an incorporated city, the question may arise as to whether an extension of the city limits *ipso facto* extends the boundaries of the school district. If the statutes provide that all the territory of the city shall be embraced in the school district or that the two corporations shall be coextensive in territory, the extension of the city limits automatically works an enlargement of the school district.[66] The mere extension of the city limits, however, will not have the effect of extending the school-district boundaries unless the statutes clearly indicate

64. *Attorney General* v. *Lowrey*, 199 U.S. 233, 26 S. Ct. 27, 50 L. Ed. 167; *Connor* v. *Board of Education*, 10 Minn. 352; *Pearson* v. *State*, 56 Ark. 148, 19 S.W. 499, 35 Am. St. Rep. 91; *Pass School District* v. *Hollywood City School District*, 156 Calif. 416, 105 Pac. 122, 20 Ann. Cas. 87, 26 L.R.A. (N.S.) 485; *State* v. *Grefe*, 139 Iowa 18, 117 N.W. 13; *People* v. *Bartlett*, 304 Ill. 283, 136 N.E. 654; *State* v. *Hine*, 59 Conn. 50, 21 Atl. 1024, 10 L.R.A. 83; *Floydada Independent School District* v. *Shipley*, 238 S.W. (Tex.) 1026; *Moore* v. *Board of Education of Iredell County*, 212 N.C. 499, 193 S.E. 732; *Board of Education of Kenton County* v. *Mescher*, 310 Ky. 453, 220 S.W. (2d) 1016.

65. *People* v. *Deatherage*, 401 Ill. 25, 81 N.E. (2d) 581. See also *Norton* v. *Lakeside Special School District*, 97 Ark. 71, 133 S.W. 184.

66. *Special School District No. 2* v. *Special School District of Texarkana*, 111 Ark. 379, 163 S.W. 1164; *Winona* v. *School District No. 82*, 40 Minn. 13, 41 N.W. 539, 3 L.R.A. 46; *Weeks* v. *Hetland*, 52 N.D. 351, 202 N.W. 807; *Harrison School District No. 2* v. *City of Minot*, 48 N.D. 1189, 189 N.W. 338.

that this is the purpose of the legislature.[67] The limits of Kansas City, for example, were so extended as to include the city of Westport. Each city was a school district, although the city of Westport did not entirely coincide with the Westport school district; nor was all the Westport school district incorporated in the Kansas City municipal limits. The court held that the school-district boundaries remained unchanged because the extension of the limits of a city does not operate to change or enlarge the school district of the city; nor does the extinction of a municipality by incorporation into another city extinguish the school district of the municipality.[68] Similarly, the Supreme Court of Michigan has held that "a change in the territorial limits of the municipality of the city of Detroit of itself can have no effect upon the school districts within the annexed territory."[69] The courts reason that school districts and cities are separate and distinct legal entities,[70] that the school law itself provides a direct method of altering district boundaries,[71] and that education is wholly subject to state control and is in no sense a matter of local or municipal concern.[72]

CHANGE OF DISTRICT BOUNDARIES AS AFFECTING PRE-EXISTING ASSETS AND LIABILITIES

General legislative authority.—Education is a matter of state concern, and the legislature therefore, subject to constitutional restrictions, is free to create such agencies as it sees fit for the execution of its educational policies. School districts "are but parts of the machinery employed in carrying on the affairs of the State, and they are subject to be changed, modified or destroyed as the exigencies of the public may demand. Subject to the provisions of the national and State constitutions the Legislature has supreme power over them and may

67. *School District No. 7* v. *School District of St. Joseph,* 184 Mo. 140, 82 S.W. 1082; *State* v. *Henderson,* 145 Mo. 329, 46 S.W. 1076; *Collins* v. *City of Detroit,* 195 Mich. 330, 161 N.W. 905; *Board of Education* v. *Bacon,* 196 Mich. 15, 162 N.W. 416; *State* v. *Independent School District No. 6,* 46 Iowa 425; *Hayes* v. *City of Beaumont,* 190 S.W. (2d) (Tex.) 835.

68. *State* v. *Henderson,* 145 Mo. 329, 46 S.W. 1076.

69. *Collins* v. *City of Detroit,* 195 Mich. 330, 161 N.W. 905.

70. *School District No. 7* v. *School District of St. Joseph,* 184 Mo. 140, 82 S.W. 1082; *State* v. *Henderson,* 145 Mo. 329, 46 S.W. 1076.

71. *School District No. 7* v. *School District of St. Joseph,* 184 Mo. 140, 82 S.W. 1082; *Board of Education* v. *Bacon,* 196 Mich. 15, 162 N.W. 416.

72. *Collins* v. *City of Detroit,* 195 Mich. 330, 161 N.W. 905.

by general law define, alter, enlarge or abolish them, as in the legislative judgment the public welfare may require."[73] In the exercise of this plenary power over school districts, the legislature may provide, upon the alteration of district boundaries, for the division of property and the apportionment of debts in such manner as may be deemed just and reasonable.[74] As was said by the Supreme Court of Illinois:

> The rule is clearly established that the jurisdiction in such matters rests wholly with the legislature, and that upon the consolidation or division of one or more municipalities, or of the annexation of territory thereto or detachment of territory therefrom, the power of the legislature over the apportionment of the debts and obligations and the distribution of the property and assets of the municipalities affected, at least so far as held for governmental purposes, is absolute.[75]

In changing district boundaries, the legislature may apportion property among the new districts as it sees fit, because the public schools are state institutions and all public school property is merely held in trust for the state by the local authorities.[76] School districts have no vested rights in school property, for they merely hold title for the time being as trustees of the public at large. Territory and property may be transferred from district to district upon such principles as the welfare of the state system may demand. The only limitation, it seems, upon the authority of the legislature in this respect is

73. *People* v. *Bartlett*, 304 Ill. 283, 136 N.E. 654. See also *Attorney General* v. *Lowrey*, 199 U.S. 233, 26 S. Ct. 27, 50 L. Ed. 167; *Connor* v. *Board of Education*, 10 Minn. 352; *Pearson* v. *State*, 56 Ark. 148, 19 S.W. 499, 35 Am. St. Rep. 91; *Pass School District* v. *Hollywood City School District*, 156 Calif. 416, 105 Pac. 122, 20 Ann. Cas. 87, 26 L.R.A. (N.S.) 485; *State* v. *Hine*, 59 Conn. 50, 21 Atl. 1024, 10 L.R.A. 83; *Lincoln Township School District* v. *Redfield Consolidated School District*, 226 Iowa 298, 283 N.W. 881.

74. *Attorney General* v. *Lowrey*, 199 U.S. 233, 26 S. Ct. 27, 50 L. Ed. 167; *Mayor* v. *Sehner*, 37 Md. 180; *McCully* v. *Board of Education*, 63 N.J. Law 18, 42 Atl. 776; *Bristol* v. *New Chester*, 3 N.H. 524; *Board of Education* v. *Board of Education*, 30 W. Va. 424, 4 S.E. 640; *Pass School District* v. *Hollywood City School District*, 156 Calif. 416, 105 Pac. 122; *Coler* v. *Dwight School Township*, 3 N.D. 249, 55 N.W. 587, 28 L.R.A. 649; *School District No. 48* v. *School District No. 115*, 60 Ore. 38, 118 Pac. 169.

75. *People* v. *Bartlett*, 304 Ill. 283, 136 N.E. 654.

76. *Attorney General* v. *Lowrey*, 199 U.S. 233, 26 S. Ct. 27, 50 L. Ed. 167; *Board of Education* v. *Board of Education*, 182 Ky. 544, 206 S.W. 869; *Pass School District* v. *Hollywood City School District*, 156 Calif. 416, 105 Pac. 122, 20 Ann. Cas. 87, 26 L.R.A. (N.S.) 485; *Carson* v. *State*, 27 Ind. 465; *McGurn* v. *Board of Education*, 133 Ill. 122, 24 N.E. 529; *Prescott* v. *Town of Lennox*, 100 Tenn. 591, 47 S.W. 181; *Rawson* v. *Spencer*, 113 Mass. 40; *Board of Education* v. *Board of Education*, 147 Ga. 776, 95 S.E. 684; *In re School Committee*, 26 R.I. 164, 58 Atl. 628.

that property acquired for school purposes by local taxation or otherwise may not be seized upon by the state and appropriated for other purposes and in other ways.[77]

Transfer of property from one district to another not a violation of rights guaranteed by the federal Constitution.—The Constitution of the United States provides that no state shall impair the obligations of contracts or deprive any person of property without due process of law. Where property rights have been affected by the change of district boundaries, cases have come into the courts on the claim that these provisions of the Constitution were being violated. Such claims have no justification in the law. The Supreme Court of the United States has declared in forceful language that school districts "cannot have the least pretension to sustain their privileges or their existence upon anything like a contract between them and the legislature of the State, because there is not and cannot be any reciprocity of stipulation, and their objects and duties are utterly incompatible with everything of the nature of compact."[78] In like manner, the Supreme Court of Rhode Island has held that although district boundaries may be changed in such a way as to transfer school property from one district to another, there is no violation of contracts.[79] "Duties of a school district are obligations imposed, not a contract." Nor does the transfer of school property from district to district by annexation of territory violate the due-process-of-law clause of the Fourteenth Amendment.[80] Thus it was said by the Supreme Court of Wisconsin:

It is well established that the alteration or abolition of school districts in such manner and through such instrumentalities as the Legislature prescribes is not the taking of property nor does it deprive any person of his property within the meaning of the constitutional inhibitions in these respects; and that statutes in authorizing such changes in school districts do not deny equal protection of the laws or due process of law.[81]

77. *School District No. 48* v. *School District No. 115*, 60 Ore. 38, 118 Pac. 169; *Rawson* v. *Spencer*, 113 Mass. 40; *Pearson* v. *State*, 56 Ark. 148, 19 S.W. 499, 35 Am. St. Rep. 91; *Trustees of Schools* v. *Tatman*, 13 Ill. 28.

78. *Attorney General* v. *Lowrey*, 199 U.S. 233, 26 S. Ct. 27, 50 L. Ed. 167.

79. *In re School Committee*, 26 R.I. 164, 58 Atl. 628.

80. It has been held, too, that a statute providing for an equitable division of funds and debts on the transfer of territory from one district to another does not violate the due-process-of-law clause (*Ross* v. *Adams Mills Rural School District*, 113 Ohio St. 466, 149 N.E. 634). See also *Anderson* v. *Peterson*, 54 N.W. (2d) (N.D.) 542; *Dowell* v. *Board of Education*, 185 Okla. 342, 91 Pac. (2d) 771.

81. *School District No. 3* v. *Callahan*, 237 Wis. 560, 297 N.W. 407, 135 A.L.R. 1081.

In a California case, by way of further illustration, the School District of Hollywood was created out of territory which had theretofore been a part of Pass School District, and the school property of the latter was included in the Hollywood district. It was claimed that to deprive the old district of its buildings and to vest them in the new district would be taking property without due process of law. Said the court:

> To the contention that a transfer of ownership thus accomplished works the taking of property without due process of law, it should be sufficient to point out that in all such cases the beneficial owner of the fee is the state itself, and that its agencies and mandatories—the various public and municipal corporations in whom the title rests—are essentially nothing but trustees of the state, holding the property and devoting it to the uses which the state itself directs. The transfer of title without due process of law, of which appellant so bitterly complains, is nothing more, in effect, than the naming by the state of other trustees to manage property which it owns and to manage the property for the same identical uses and purposes to which it was formerly devoted. In point of law, then, the beneficial title to the estate is not affected at all. All that is done is to transfer the legal title under the same trust from one trustee to another.[82]

Similarly, in Missouri, a school district, at the time of its consolidation with other districts, had certain funds in its treasury which were transferred to the new corporation. This transfer, it was claimed, constituted the taking of property without due process of law. But the court held otherwise,[83] pointing out that "school districts and their property are creatures of the state which may be created and abolished at will by the Legislature, and no provision of the Constitution, either state or federal, is violated by consolidating any such school district and its property with others to form a new or consolidated district." It has been held, moreover, that the Fourteenth Amendment does not apply to governmental agencies or restrict the power of the legislature over such agencies.[84] A school district is not a "person" within the meaning of any bill of rights or constitutional limitation, and its funds are under the absolute control of the legislature.[85] It has been held,

82. *Pass School District* v. *Hollywood City School District*, 156 Calif. 416, 105 Pac. 122, 20 Ann. Cas. 87, 26 L.R.A. (N.S.) 485. To the same general effect is the case of *Trustees of Slaughterville Graded School District* v. *Brooks*, 163 Ky. 200, 173 S.W. 305.

83. *State* v. *Brooks*, 249 S.W. (Mo.) 73.

84. *Kramer* v. *Renville County*, 144 Minn. 195, 174 N.W. 101.

85. *Lincoln Township* v. *Redfield Consolidated School District*, 226 Iowa 298, 283 N.W. 881.

too, that the individuals residing in a school district have no property rights in the district.[86]

Disposition of property and debts in the absence of statutory regulation.—Where there is no statutory provision for the division of property and apportionment of debts upon the alteration of district boundaries, the general rule is that the property belongs to the district in which it is finally located, and each district is liable for the debts contracted before the change.[87] Thus it was said by the Supreme Court of West Virginia:

> Where the Legislature does not prescribe any regulations for any apportionment of the property, or that the new corporation shall pay any portion of the debt of the old, the old corporation will hold all the corporate property within its new limits, and be entitled to all the claims owing to the old corporation, and is responsible for all the debts of the corporation existing before and at the time of the division, and the new corporation will hold all the corporate property falling within its boundaries, to which the old corporation will have no claim.[88]

Thus, should a district issue bonds and build a schoolhouse with the returns and the territory embracing the schoolhouse be later incorporated in another district, the first district would still be liable for the bonds, but the second district would have title to the schoolhouse. This principle of law rests upon the theory that school districts are agencies of the state, created for the purpose of carrying into effect an important state function; they have been vested with certain powers and duties to be exercised in the interest of the state; for the more effective discharge of their powers and duties, they are given control

86. *Lowden* v. *Luther*, 190 Okla. 31, 120 Pac. (2d) 359. The Supreme Court of Nebraska, however, has held unconstitutional a statute empowering the county superintendent and county board of education to make such changes, under certain circumstances, in the boundaries of school districts as "in their judgment" would be just and equitable. The court held that the statute vested these officials with power of a judicial nature, and inasmuch as it failed to provide for the giving of notice to those whose financial burdens would be increased by the exercise of such judicial power, it violated the due-process-of-law clause of the federal Constitution. See *Ruwe* v. *School District No. 85*, 120 Neb. 668, 234 N.W. 789.

87. *Consolidated School District No. 1* v. *School District No. 24*, 33 Okla. 320, 125 Pac. 729; *Pass School District* v. *Hollywood City School District*, 156 Calif. 416, 105 Pac. 122, 20 Ann. Cas. 87, 26 L.R.A. (N.S.) 485; *Board of Education* v. *Board of Education*, 30 W. Va. 424, 4 S.E. 640; *Livingston* v. *School District No. 7*, 9 S.D. 102, 68 N.W. 167; *School District of Oakland* v. *School District of Joplin*, 340 Mo. 779, 102 S.W. (2d) 909; *Rocky Mount Independent School District* v. *Jackson*, 152 S.W. (2d) (Tex.) 400; *People* v. ex rel. *Hagler* v. *Chicago B. & L. R. Company*, 380 Ill. 120, 43 N.E. (2d) 989; *Gamble* v. *DuBose*, 215 S.C. 252, 54 S.E. (2d) 803; *Peterson* v. *Swan*, 231 Iowa 745, 2 N.W. (2d) 70.

88. *Board of Education* v. *Board of Education*, 30 W. Va. 424, 4 S.E. 640.

of the school property within their boundaries, but the beneficial ownership of the fee of school property vests in the state; the state has made them trustees of school property for the benefit of the *cestui que trust*, the public; when school-district boundaries are changed and school property is located in a different district, the only effect is that one statutory trustee has been substituted for another.[89] While it is recognized that in particular instances the application of this rule may work hardship, the courts have been able to discover no more equitable principle. "If the legislature, in making the change in the territory, directly or through authority delegated by it to a subordinate body, fails to make provision for an equitable adjustment of the assets and liabilities between the corporations affected and hardship results therefrom, it is a hardship which the legislature alone can remedy, and the courts cannot grant relief."[90]

This common-law rule has obtained in all the states with very few exceptions. But the Supreme Court of Minnesota, until the statutes provided otherwise, ruled that, upon the division of a district, the old district continued to hold the school property, even when located in the detached territory.[91] So, too, Kansas, Maine, and New Hampshire apply the rule that school property located in detached territory continues to belong to the original district.[92] Similarly, in a few states it has been held that territory detached from a district and added to another is subject to taxation to pay its proportionate share of the indebtedness of the district to which it formerly belonged.[93] And, in

89. *School District of Oakland* v. *School District of Joplin*, 340 Mo. 779, 102 S.W. (2d) 909.

90. *People* v. *Bartlett*, 304 Ill. 283, 136 N.E. 654.

91. *Winona* v. *Winona County School District No. 82*, 40 Minn. 13, 41 N.W. 539, 3 L.R.A. 46. For a later decision by this court see *Barnard and Company* v. *Polk County*, 98 Minn. 289, 108 N.W. 294, 6 L.R.A. (N.S.) 791.

92. *Union Baptist Society* v. *Candia*, 2 N.H. 20; *Troy* v. *Haskell*, 33 N.H. 533; *South Hampton* v. *Fowler*, 52 N.H. 225; *Greenville* v. *Mason*, 53 N.H. 515; *Whittier* v. *Sanborn*, 38 Me. 32; *Board of Education* v. *School District No. 7*, 45 Kan. 560, 26 Pac. 13.

93. *Walpole* v. *Wall*, 153 S.C. 106, 149 S.E. 760; *Manahan* v. *Adams County*, 77 Neb. 829, 110 N.W. 860; *Board of Education* v. *Board of Education*, 245 Mich. 411, 222 N.W. 763. For other cases not entirely in harmony with the general rule see *Abler* v. *School District*, 141 Mo. App. 189, 124 S.W. 564; *Barber* v. *Cummings*, 167 Ga. 289, 145 S.E. 443; *Colmar* v. *Alexander*, 161 Miss. 691, 137 So. 787; *Huie* v. *Morris*, 176 Ga. 562, 168 S.E. 566; *People* ex rel. *Board of Education* v. *Trustees of Schools*, 347 Ill. App. 330, 106 N.E. 892.

Kansas, attached territory is not taxable to pay the pre-existing debts of the district to which it is attached.[94]

Establishment of city systems and the adjustment of property rights. —Considerable litigation in regard to the possession of school property has grown out of the establishment of city school systems. Where an incorporated town or city is organized into a school district out of territory which formerly comprised a part of a county or township system, or common-school district, the courts commonly hold that the city district is entitled to such school property as is located within its boundaries, unless, of course, the legislature provides otherwise.[95] Public school property is merely held in trust for the state by the local school authorities, and when a city is established and vested with control of such property, there is only a change of trusteeship.[96] For example, in the case of *Board of Education of Fulton County* v. *Board of Education of College Park*,[97] the newly created school city of College Park embraced some territory which had hitherto been part of a school district in Fulton County. Within this territory were located certain school lots which had been purchased and improved by the Fulton County Board of Education. Buildings had been erected on these lots, and they were being used by the board for school purposes. Since there was no statute governing the disposition of this property, the court held that the city school district was entitled to it. The same rule applies when a city district extends its boundaries so as to include adjacent territory.[98] The school city of Louisville, for example, annexed certain territory in which was located property belonging to a county board of education. The court held that title vested in the city district, the only result in contemplation of law being a new trustee for state school property:[99]

94. *Hunziker* v. *School District No. 26*, 153 Kan. 102, 109 Pac. (2d) 115.

95. *School Township of Allen* v. *School Town of Macy*, 109 Ind. 559, 10 N.E. 578; *Carson* v. *State*, 27 Ind. 465; *Latonia Graded School District No. 12* v. *Board of Education*, 29 Ky. Law Rep. 391, 93 S.W. 590; *Board of Education* v. *Board of Education*, 147 Ga. 776, 95 S.E. 684; *Prescott* v. *Town of Lennox*, 100 Tenn. 591, 47 S.W. 181. See, however, *Board of Education* v. *Board of Education*, 46 Ohio St. 595, 22 N.E. 641.

96. *School Township of Allen* v. *School Town of Macy*, 109 Ind. 559, 10 N.E. 578; *Board of Education* v. *Board of Education*, 147 Ga. 776, 95 S.E. 684; *Board of Education* v. *Board of Education*, 182 Ky. 544, 206 S.W. 869.

97. *Board of Education* v. *Board of Education*, 147 Ga. 776, 95 S.E. 684.

98. *Vernon School District* v. *Board of Education*, 125 Calif. 593, 58 Pac. 175; *Board of Education* v. *Board of Education*, 182 Ky. 544, 206 S.W. 869.

99. *Board of Education* v. *Board of Education*, 182 Ky. 544, 206 S.W. 869.

Effect of extinction of school district upon property and debts.—In case a school district goes entirely out of existence by annexation to, or merger in, another district and no statutory provision is made in regard to apportionment of its assets and liabilities, the subsisting district is entitled to the property and funds, and answerable for the debts, of the original corporation.[100] Thus, where a district enters into a contract with a teacher but is later consolidated with another district, the new corporation is liable for the teacher's salary.[101] So, too, where a school district is dissolved by annexation to an adjoining district, it is subject to taxation to pay its share of the pre-existing debts, including bonded indebtedness, of the district to which it is attached.[102] In cases of this kind there is no violation of due process of law because the individuals residing in the district have no property rights in the district.

Some states apply somewhat different rules. The Supreme Court of Georgia holds that where part of the territory of a school district is added to another district, it is liable for its share of the pre-existing debt, but where districts are consolidated, the property in a former district having no bonded debt cannot be taxed to help liquidate the pre-existing bonded debt of the other component districts.[103] In Florida, when districts are consolidated, cash on hand in each of the com-

100. *Board of Education* v. *Board of Education,* 30 W. Va. 424, 4 S.E. 640; *Hughes* v. *School District No. 29,* 72 Mo. 643; *Thompson* v. *Abbott,* 61 Mo. 176; *Abler* v. *School District,* 141 Mo. App. 189, 124 S.W. 564; *Walker* v. *Bennett,* 125 S.C. 389, 118 S.E. 779; *Clother* v. *Maher,* 15 Neb. 1, 16 N.W. 902; *Brewer* v. *Palmer,* 13 Mich. 104; *Love* v. *Rockwall Independent School District,* 225 S.W. (Tex.) 263; *Wadsworth* v. *Menzie,* 173 N.Y.S. 620; *Nicholson* v. *Ash Flat School District,* 220 Ark. 787, 249 S.W. (2d) 983; *Board of Education* v. *Nevada School District,* 251 S.W. (2d) (Mo.) 20; *Duffee* v. *Jones,* 208 Ga. 639, 68 S.E. (2d) 699; *W. G. Schanke Company* v. *Plankington Independent School District,* 61 S.D. 164, 246 N.W. 872; *People* v. *Deatherage,* 401 Ill. 25, 81 N.E. (2d) 581.

101. *Barringer* v. *Powell,* 230 N.Y. 37, 128 N.E. 910; *Thompson* v. *Abbott,* 61 Mo. 176; *Boswell* v. *Consolidated School District No. 8,* 10 S.W. (2d) (Mo.) 665. See also *Rogers* v. *People,* 68 Ill. 154; *Adriaansen* v. *Board of Education,* 226 N.Y.S. 145. See, however, *Barber* v. *Cummings and Sons,* 167 Ga. 289, 145 S.E. 443; *Colmer* v. *Alexander,* 137 So. (Miss.) 787; *Rocky Mount Independent School District* v. *Jackson,* 152 S.W. (2d) (Tex.) 400; *People* v. *Deatherage,* 401 Ill. 25, 81 N.E. (2d) 581.

102. *Lowden* v. *Luther,* 190 Okla. 31, 120 Pac. (2d) 359; *Wheeler School District* v. *Hawley,* 18 Wash. (2d) 37, 137 Pac. (2d) 1010; *Southern Pacific Company* v. *Maricopa County,* 59 Ariz. 369, 129 Pac. (2d) 312; *Owsley County Board of Education* v. *Owsley County Fiscal Court,* 251 Ky. 165, 64 S.W. (2d) 179.

103. *Huie* v. *Morris,* 176 Ga. 562, 168 S.E. 566; *Barber* v. *Cummings,* 167 Ga. 289, 145 S.E. 443.

ponent districts must be credited on the indebtedness of that district, and the original areas of the districts that had outstanding unpaid bonds are subject to taxation to pay their respective bonded indebtedness.[104] And, in Oklahoma, when the territory of a school district is annexed, wholly or in part, to another district, the district to which the territory is annexed does not become liable for the bonded indebtedness of the annexed territory, because a constitutional provision forbids the incurring of any debt without the vote of the people concerned.[105]

When a district is legislated out of existence by the establishment of two or more new districts from its territory, the rule seems to be that each of the new districts is liable for the entire indebtedness of the original corporation; and if the debt is paid by one of these, it may have recourse against the other districts for whatever amount it may have paid in excess of its proper proportion of the debt.[106] It has been held, however, that "the remedy for a creditor is by action against the several new districts, all of which must be joined in the suit."[107] A somewhat different rule obtains where the district is dissolved by the annexation of its territory by other existing districts. In such a case, each of the subsisting corporations is liable for its proportionate share of the original indebtedness, the obligation being an individual rather than a joint one.[108]

Where a district is discontinued without having any successor, it will, in contemplation of law, continue to exist for the purpose of liquidating its obligations.[109] "It is unnecessary to cite authorities," said the Supreme Court of South Carolina, "to sustain the proposition: that neither the high school district, nor any common school

104. *Fowler* v. *Turner*, 157 Fla. 529, 26 So. (2d) 792.

105. *Protest of Missouri-Kansas-Texas Railroad Company*, 181 Okla. 229, 73 Pac. (2d) 173.

106. *Hughes* v. *School District No. 29*, 72 Mo. 643. See also *Plunkett's Creek Township* v. *Crawford*, 27 Pac. 107; *Kennedy* v. *Independent School District*, 48 Iowa 189.

107. *Welch* v. *Getzen*, 85 S.C. 156, 67 S.E. 294.

108. *Mt. Pleasant* v. *Beckwith*, 100 U.S. 514, 25 L. Ed. 699; *Board of Education* v. *Board of Education*, 30 W. Va. 424, 4 S.E. 640. In *Halbert* v. *School Districts Nos. 2, 3, & 5*, 36 Mich. 421, it was said: "Where a school district is parceled out among three other existing districts, the latter can not be held jointly liable for a debt of the former district; whatever they are bound to pay must be a several, and not a joint obligation."

109. *Welch* v. *Getzen*, 85 S.C. 156, 67 S.E. 294.

district unit thereof, by exercising its right at any time . . . to vote itself out of the high school district, can escape liability for its proportionate part of the indebtedness which it, along with other school districts, has incurred." An Illinois case is also in point. The electors of a township high-school district voted to discontinue the district. A contract had been entered into for the erection of a high-school building some time before the vote to discontinue, and the building was partly constructed at the time of the vote in favor of dissolution. The court held that the contractor was entitled to the profits he would have made on the completed contract and that such assets as the district had could be applied to meet this obligation. The obligation of contracts survived the existence of the district, and the property of the district constituted a trust fund in equity for the payments of its debts.[110]

Change of district boundaries and the collection of taxes.—When district boundaries are changed, considerable confusion may arise with respect to the collection and distribution of taxes. For example, a district may levy a tax, but before the tax is collected a part of the territory may be detached and added to another district. In such a case the general rule is that the property in the detached territory is still subject to the levy, the proceeds therefrom going to the district which levied the tax.[111] When once a tax is levied, it constitutes a lien on the property. Thus it was said in an early Massachusetts case: "If by act of the town he [a resident thereof] and his estate shall, after the assessment of the tax, be made to belong to another district by an alteration of the limits or the creation of a new district, he will still be indebted for the tax assessed before the division or alteration."[112] But the mere voting of a tax before territory is detached will not subject property in it to taxation; the levy must have been made before the detachment, or there will be no right of collection.[113] Again, taxes may

110. *Chalstran* v. *Board of Education,* 244 Ill. 470, 91 N.E. 712. See also *Rogers* v. *People,* 68 Ill. 154. But where public corporations have been dissolved without a successor and without any provision being made for the payment of their obligations, it has been held that a creditor has only the faith of the legislature to rely upon (*Barkley* v. *Levee Commissioners,* 93 U.S. 258, 23 L. Ed. 893; *Bates* v. *Gregory,* 89 Cal. 387, 26 Pac. 891).

111. *Independent District of Union* v. *Independent District of Cedar Rapids,* 62 Iowa 616, 17 N.W. 895; *Waldron* v. *Lee,* 22 Mass. (5 Pick.) 323; *Dyer* v. *School District No. 1,* 61 Vt. 96, 17 Atl. 788.

112. *Waldron* v. *Lee,* 22 Mass. (5 Pick.) 323.

113. *Hughes* v. *Ewing,* 93 Calif. 414, 28 Pac. 1067; *Richards* v. *Dagget,* 4 Mass. 534; *State* v. *Burford,* 82 Mo. App. 343; *Pierce* v. *Whitman,* 23 Vt. 626.

be voted by a district but not assessed until other territory has been annexed. It has been held that in such an instance the tax could be collected in the added portion of the district.[114] The general principle of law governing in cases of this kind is that a school district may levy a tax upon all property within its boundaries at the time of the levy, and such a tax is collectible regardless of the past or future shifting of boundary lines. To this general rule, however, there seems to be one exception. Where taxes have been levied in a district and part of the territory is detached and added to another district, the territory in question is not subject to a second levy for the fiscal year.[115]

Upon the change of boundary lines, the legislature may provide for an equitable distribution of property and debts. It is permissible, for example, to impose a tax for a certain time upon the detached territory for the benefit of the old district.[116] This is, however, a matter wholly for the legislature to determine, for detached territory is not subject, under the common law, to taxation to pay off the obligations of the old district.[117] Where districts are consolidated, the statutes sometimes provide for the appraisal of the school property, for the levy of a tax on the property of the new corporation equal to the amount of the appraisal, and for the remission of the appraised value of its property less indebtedness to the taxpayers of each original district. Such legislation has been held a constitutional mode of equalization of the burdens of the new school system.[118] On the other hand, it has been held unconstitutional on the ground that its sole purpose was to benefit one class of citizens at the expense of another and that the tax involved was not intended to meet the expenses of government.[119]

Disposition of funds.—The distribution of funds often occasions difficulty when territory is detached from school districts. In the absence of statutory provision, the general rule is that such funds belong to the

114. *Fifield v. Sweet,* 56 N.H. 432; *Grout v. Illingworth,* 131 Iowa 281, 108 N.W. 528; *Adriaansen v. Board of Education,* 226 N.Y.S. 145.

115. *Board of Education v. Givens,* 147 Ky. 837, 146 S.W. 16. But see *Waldron v. Lee,* 22 Mass. (5 Pick.) 323.

116. *Fitzpatrick v. Mt. Sterling Graded Public Schools,* 87 Ky. 132, 7 S.W. 896.

117. Contra, *Walpole v. Wall,* 153 S.C. 106, 149 S.E. 760; *Manahan v. Adams County,* 77 Neb. 829, 110 N.W. 860; *Board of Education v. Board of Education,* 245 Mich. 411, 222 N.W. 763.

118. *Rawson v. Spencer,* 113 Mass. 40; *Perry v. Town of Fitzwilliam,* 64 N.H. 289, 16 Atl. 899; *In re Town of Cranston,* 18 R.I. 417, 28 Atl. 608; *Brown v. Bunselmeyer,* 167 N.Y.S. 993.

119. *Elizabethtown Water Company v. Wade,* 59 N.J. Law 78, 35 Atl. 4.

original corporation.[120] Thus a common-school district which withdraws from a consolidated high-school district is not entitled to a proportion of the surplus bond funds in possession of the district from which is is withdrawing. Even state funds distributed upon the basis of the school census remain in the hands of the old districts.[121] For example, in a Michigan case, territory was detached from School District No. 6 and added to the school district of the city of Saginaw. The census showed that 930 of the 983 pupils in School District No. 6 had been transferred to the Saginaw district. The transfer of territory took place in April, and on the first of November the state superintendent of public instruction apportioned the primary-school money, nearly ten thousand dollars, to District No. 6 on the census showing of 983 pupils. The Saginaw district brought suit to recover a proportionate share of the money so received. In holding that District No. 6 was entitled to all the funds, the Supreme Court quoted with approval the following passage from an opinion of the Supreme Court of Missouri: "It would seem to be fair that the fund should follow the children, on whose account it was apportioned, into the new district; but the statute makes no provision for such cases, and we are not at liberty to make a law to accord to what may appear to us to be an equitable distribution."[122]

But in some jurisdictions it has been held that when a new district is created by the division of an older one, the new district is entitled to a pro rata share of the school funds.[123] So, too, it has been held that a district thus created "is entitled to a pro rata share of the state appropriation for school purposes for the current year."[124]

120. *Cooke* v. *School District No 12*, 12 Colo. 453, 21 Pac. 496; *State* v. *Northfield Township Board of Education*, 22 Ohio Cir. Ct. 224; *Morrow Company* v. *Hendryx*, 14 Ore. 397, 12 Pac. 806; *School District No. 6* v. *School District No. 5*, 18 Mo. App. 266; *School District of the City of Saginaw* v. *School District No. 6*, 231 Mich. 664, 204 N.W. 737; *Gamble* v. *DuBose*, 215 S.C. 252, 54 S.E. (2d) 803.

121. *School District of the City of Saginaw* v. *School District No. 6*, 231 Mich. 664, 204 N.W. 737; *State* v. *School Directors of District No. 15*, 90 Mo. 395, 2 S.W. 420; *Union Township* v. *Oakdale Township*, 30 Okla. 708, 120 Pac. 968, 39 L.R.A. (N.S.) 284.

122. *School District of the City of Saginaw* v. *School District No. 6*, 231 Mich. 664, 204 N.W. 737.

123. *Towle* v. *Brown*, 110 Ind. 599, 10 N.E. 628; *Porter* v. *State*, 78 Tex. 591, 14 S.W. 794; *Merrit* v. *School District No. 9*, 54 Ark. 468, 16 S.W. 287; *Cassville* v. *Morris*, 14 Wis. 440.

124. *Lower Allen Township School District* v. *Shiremanstown School District*, 91 Pa. St. 182.

Sometimes the statutes provide for an equitable apportionment of funds between old and new districts. In doing this, the legislature may even divert funds from the use for which they were raised, as, for example, the building of a schoolhouse. This can be done, for the general rule that funds cannot be diverted from the uses for which they were raised "applies to the local officers having in charge the disbursement of the money, and does not affect legislative control of the fund. . . . The legislature, having plenary control of the local municipality, of its creation, and of all its affairs, has the right to authorize or direct the expenditure of money in its treasury, though raised for a particular purpose."[125]

Not infrequently, however, there is difficulty in determining what constitutes "funds" or "assets" within the meaning of the statute. In Ohio, by way of illustration, a statute provided for an equitable division of funds and of indebtedness. A district voted and sold bonds to build a schoolhouse, but, before the contract was let, part of the territory was incorporated into another district. In holding that the funds from the sale of the bonds would have to be divided between the two districts, the court said:

"Funds" include all moneys rightfully in the possession of the board of the original district, and all moneys to which the board of the original district is entitled at the date of the transfer. . . .
"Indebtedness" includes all liabilities incurred prior to the date of the transfer, including bonded indebtedness, contractual obligations, such as building contracts, teachers' contracts, janitors' contracts, and the like, though not as yet fully performed.[126]

Similarly, where a statute required the division of all assets and moneys between the old and the new district, it was held that funds from a special tax levied and collected for the erection of a schoolhouse in the old district were assets within the meaning of the law.[127] So, too, school property has been held to be assets.[128] The proceeds of a tax voted before, but collected after, the formation of a new district have been held to be a credit of the old district within the

125. *State* v. *Board of Commissioners*, 126 Minn. 209, 148 N.W. 53.

126. *State* v. *Board of Education*, 114 Ohio St. 602, 151 N.E. 669.

127. *School District No. 61* v. *School District No. 32*, 53 Ore. 33, 98 Pac. 523. But see *Zartman* v. *State*, 109 Ind. 360, 10 N.E. 94.

128. *Williams District Township* v. *District Township of Jackson*, 36 Iowa 216; *State* v. *School District No. 21*, 6 N.D. 488, 71 N.W. 772.

meaning of a statute requiring a division of credits.[129] But where the statutes provided for an apportionment of personal property between districts and the old district had collected insurance upon the destruction of one of its buildings by fire, the court ruled that the fund did not constitute personal property. It stood in equity for the building which had been destroyed.[130] Nor is a tax collected on the property of the old and new district to meet the expenses of the current year a surplus fund within the meaning of a statute providing for the apportionment of such funds.[131]

CONTROL OF SCHOOL DISTRICTS

Whatever agencies the legislature may select as the instruments for the execution of its educational policies, these agencies are completely subject to its control within constitutional limits.[132] Since school districts are purely creatures of the state, they possess no inherent local rights—no rights at all, in fact, except those with which they are endowed by the legislature. Their powers and the mode of exercise of these powers are defined by legislative act and may be added to, diminished, or destroyed as the legislature may determine.[133] In the words of the Supreme Court of North Carolina:

> Such organizations are intended to be instrumentalities and agencies employed to aid in the administration of the government, and are always under the control of the power that created them, unless the same shall be restricted by some constitutional limitation. Hence, the legislature may, from time to time, in its discretion, abolish them, or enlarge or diminish their boundaries, or increase, modify, or abrogate their powers. It may provide that the agents and officers in them shall be elected by the electors, or it may appoint them directly, or empower some agency to appoint them, unless in cases where the constitution provides otherwise, and charge them with duties specific and mandatory, or general and discretionary in their character.[134]

129. *School District No. 9* v. *School District No. 5*, 118 Wis. 233, 95 N.W. 148.

130. *People* v. *Dunn*, 154 N.Y.S. 346.

131. *School District No. 15* v. *School District of Waldron*, 63 Ark. 433, 39 S.W. 264.

132. *Floydada Independent School District* v. *Shipley*, 238 S.W. (Tex.) 1026; *State* v. *Freeman*, 61 Kan. 90, 58 Pac. 959, 47 L.R.A. 67; *State* v. *Hine*, 59 Conn. 50, 21 Atl. 1024, 10 L.R.A. 83; *MacCormac* v. *Robeson County*, 90 N.C. 441; *State* v. *Haworth*, 122 Ind. 462, 23 N.E. 946, 7 L.R.A. 240; *Stephens* v. *Jones*, 74 S.D. 97, 123 N.W. 705; *Keime* v. *Community High School District No. 296*, 348 Ill. 228, 180 N.E. 858.

133. *Bopp* v. *Clark*, 165 Iowa 697, 147 N.W. 172, Ann. Cas. 1916E 417, 52 L.R.A. (N.S.) 493; *Honaker* v. *Board of Education*, 42 W. Va. 170, 24 S.E. 544, 32 L.R.A. 413.

134. *MacCormac* v. *Robeson County*, 90 N.C. 441.

Moreover, the state is not limited in its choice of policies. "The legislature, having tried one plan, is not precluded from trying another. It has a choice of methods, and may change its plans as often as it deems necessary or expedient." In other words, long exercise of powers on the part of local units does not give rise to vested interests, for the state does not relinquish control of the school system by delegating some of its authority to the different localities.[135]

de facto SCHOOL DISTRICTS

It frequently happens that school districts are created without complying with all the requirements prescribed by law. Or it may be that the statute itself under which a district was established is later declared unconstitutional. In either case, the legality of the acts already consummated by the district may be called into question. Bonds may have been issued, teachers' contracts entered into, and other obligations incurred. The legality of all such acts will depend upon whether or not the district is regarded as a *de facto* district.

Speaking for the Supreme Court of Minnesota, Mr. Justice Hallam lays down the following conditions as necessary to constitute a municipal corporation a *de facto* corporation:

A public or municipal corporation *de facto* exists when there is (1) some law under which a corporation with powers assumed might lawfully have been created; (2) a colorable and *bona fide* attempt to perfect an organization under such a law; (3) user of the rights claimed to have been conferred by the law.[136]

Where a public corporation, such as a school district, is organized under a valid statute authorizing its existence and its acts are acquiesced in by the public, it will be held to be a *de facto* corporation regardless of any defects or irregularities in its organization.[137] Thus in Oregon ten school districts approved a plan of consolidation at an election, the consolidated district was organized, levied taxes, began the construction of a schoolhouse, and contracted with a bank to sell bonds. The court held the district to be one *de facto*, even though it was claimed that the notice of election for consolidation did not

135. *State* v. *Haworth*, 122 Ind. 462, 23 N.E. 946, 7 L.R.A. 240.

136. *Evens* v. *Anderson*, 132 Minn. 59, 155 N.W. 1040. Accord, *Nelson* v. *Consolidated Independent School District*, 181 Iowa 424, 164 N.W. 874; *Guthrie* v. *Wylie*, 6 Okla. 61, 55 Pac. 103; *School District of Agency* v. *Wallace*, 75 Mo. App. 317.

137. *Pickett* v. *Board of Commissioners*, 24 Idaho 200, 133 Pac. 112.

indicate all the districts to be included.[138] The *de facto* character of a school district depends far more upon the general acquiescence of the public than upon compliance with the conditions precedent prescribed by the statute under which it was organized.[139]

In determining whether a public corporation is a *de facto* corporation, perhaps the most difficult problem met with is this: If a corporation is organized and operates under a statute which is later declared unconstitutional, should the corporation be regarded as a *de facto* corporation or as a mere nullity? Upon this question the courts are in sharp disagreement. One line of decisions holds that a public corporation organized under an unconstitutional statute is a corporation neither *de jure* nor *de facto*.[140] The reasoning upon which this line of decisions rests is perfectly logical. A public corporation can have no existence unless organized under a law authorizing it. An unconstitutional act is not law. As was said by the Supreme Court of the United States in the case of *Norton* v. *Shelby County:* "An unconstitutional act is not a law; it confers no rights; it imposes no duties; it affords no protection; it creates no office; it is, in legal contemplation, as inoperative as though it had never been passed."[141]

Another line of decisions holds that an unconstitutional act is a sufficient basis for a *de facto* corporation,[142] and this seems to be the better law. The opinion of the court in the case of *Speer* v. *Board of County Commissioners*[143] is such an excellent expression of the reasoning underlying these decisions that it is quoted at some length:

> Moreover, we are unable to yield our assent to the broad proposition that there can be no *de facto* corporation under an unconstitutional law. Such a law passes the scrutiny and receives the approval of the attorney general, of the lawyers who compose the judiciary committees of the state

138. *State ex rel. Hallgarth* v. *School District No. 23,* 179 Ore. 441, 172 Pac. (2d) 655.

139. *Speer* v. *Board of County Commissioners,* 88 Fed. 749; *Pickett* v. *Board of Commissioners,* 24 Idaho 200, 133 Pac. 112.

140. *Norton* v. *Shelby County,* 118 U.S. 425, 6 S. Ct. 1121, 30 L. Ed. 178; *People* v. *Wiley,* 289 Ill. 173, 124 N.E. 385. See also *Griffin* v. *Thomas,* 86 Okla. 70, 206 Pac. 604.

141. *Norton* v. *Shelby County,* 118 U.S. 425, 6 S. Ct. 1121, 30 L. Ed. 178.

142. *Ashley* v. *Board of Supervisors,* 60 Fed. 55; *Speer* v. *Board of County Commissioners,* 88 Fed. 749; *Attorney General* v. *Town of Dover,* 62 N.J. Law 138, 41 Atl. 98; *State* v. *Des Moines,* 96 Iowa 521, 65 N.W. 818, 31 L.R.A. 186; *Back* v. *Carpenter,* 29 Kan. 349. See also *State* v. *Carroll,* 38 Conn. 449, 9 Am. Rep. 409.

143. *Speer* v. *Board of County Commissioners,* 88 Fed. 749.

legislative bodies, of the legislature, and of the governor before it reaches the statute book. When it is spread upon that book, it comes to the people of a state with the presumption of validity. Courts declare its invalidity with hesitation and after long deliberation and much consideration, even when its violation of the organic law is clear, and never when it is doubtful. Until the judiciary has declared it void, men act and contract, and they ought to act and contract, on the presumption that it is valid; and where, before such a declaration is made, their acts and contracts have affected public interests or private rights, they must be treated as valid and lawful. The acts of a *de facto* corporation or officer under an unconstitutional law before its invalidity is challenged in or declared by the judicial department of the government cannot be avoided, as against the interests of the public or of third parties who have acted or invested in good faith in reliance upon their validity, by any *ex post facto* declaration or decision that the law under which they acted was void. This proposition is not without the support of eminent authority. Indeed, we believe it is founded in reason, and sustained by the great current of the decisions of the courts that have considered it.

It is well settled that the acts of a *de facto* school district, so far as third parties and the public are concerned, are as valid as the acts of a *de jure* district.[144] This principle of law is founded upon fundamental considerations of public policy. In the establishment of school districts, the law commonly requires certain preliminary steps to be taken, such as the filing of petitions, the posting of notices, and the holding of elections. One or more of these required acts may be improperly performed or neglected altogether, and yet the district be organized and accepted by the public. Bonds are issued, schoolhouses erected, teachers employed, and other contractual obligations incurred. To hold that the acts of such a corporation are void and without effect would work endless confusion and injustice. A case in point is that of *Coler* v. *Dwight School Township*.[145] An attempt was made to avoid payment of district bonds on the grounds that the district had not been legally organized, in that a petition had not been signed by a majority of the electors of the district and filed with the county superintendent as required by statute. The court held that, despite this and other defects in the organization of the district, it was nevertheless a *de facto* district and that its acts were valid with respect to third parties:

144. *Coler* v. *Dwight School Township*, 3 N.D. 249, 55 N.W. 587, 28 L.R.A. 649; *Reynolds* v. *Moore*, 9 Wend. (N.Y.) 35, 24 Am. Dec. 116; 24 R.C.L. 565.

145. *Coler* v. *Dwight School Township*, 3 N.D. 249, 55 N.W. 587, 28 L.R.A. 649.

If there cannot be a *de facto* school district, there cannot be a *de facto* city. If illegality in the proceedings to effect organization is fatal to the existence of a district, it is equally as fatal to the existence of a municipal corporation of a higher grade. Given a case where the defects in the incorporation of the city are as fatal as in this case, and then deny to that corporation any effect, although a city government is in fact inaugurated and carried on, the consequences would be intolerable. Open and acknowledged anarchy would for some reasons be preferable. In after years tax titles would be destroyed; every officer of the city would be a trespasser when the discharge of what would be his duty on the theory of the existence of the corporation led to an interference with the property or person of others. Every police or other peace officer and every magistrate acting under the supposed authority of the city government would be liable for extortion, for assault and battery, for false imprisonment, and could be prosecuted criminally for acts done in good faith in the enforcement of the criminal law. . . . All that has been done in good faith under color of law is only bare-faced usurpation, and to be treated as such for all purposes. Such a doctrine would be the author of confusion, injustice, and almost endless litigation.

Every consideration of public policy supports the principle that the acts of a *de facto* corporation are valid with respect to third parties and the public. Nor can it be claimed that such a principle works injustice. The law provides a remedy by which those whose rights are affected by the existence of an illegal corporation may attack its existence. Those who sit idly by while a school district is being illegally organized and do not question its legality while dealing with innocent third parties will not later be heard to complain. "Those who are silent, when in conscience they should have spoken, have no claim upon the equity" of the courts.[146]

MODE OF ATTACKING LEGALITY OF SCHOOL DISTRICTS

The courts are in general accord in holding that a school district acting upon color of law cannot be enjoined from acting, on the ground that it has not been legally organized.[147] While a district is being organized, an injunction will lie to restrain those who are abusing their authority or acting in excess of it.[148] Before a school district

146. *Coler* v. *Dwight School Township,* 3 N.D. 249, 55 N.W. 587, 28 L.R.A. 649.

147. *Van Wagener* v. *MacFarland,* 58 Calif. App. 115, 208 Pac. 345; *Franklin Avenue German Savings Institution* v. *Board of Education,* 75 Mo. 408; *Burnham* v. *Rogers,* 167 Mo. 17, 66 S.W. 970; *Evens* v. *Anderson,* 132 Minn. 59, 155 N.W. 1040; *Bowen* v. *Board of School Trustees,* 16 S.W. (2d) (Tex.) 424.

148. *Coler* v. *Dwight School Township,* 3 N.D. 249, 55 N.W. 587, 28 L.R.A. 649; *Lynn County School Board* v. *Garlynn,* 118 S.W. (2d) (Tex.) 1070; *Kennedy* v. *Broughton,* 70 S.W. (2d) (Tex.) 500.

has become a *de facto* district through the use of its corporate franchise, an interested party may resort to injunctive relief;[149] but, once the district is organized and obtains the status of at least a *de facto* district, its corporate existence is free from collateral attack.[150] The law provides a remedy whereby the legal existence of a school district may be brought into question, and that remedy is an action in *quo warranto*[151] brought in the name of the state by the attorney-general or state's attorney. The great weight of authority, however, is to the effect that *quo warranto* proceedings to test the legal existence of a school district cannot be brought by a private individual who shows no special interest distinct from that of the public in general.[152] To all but the state, a *de facto* public corporation has all the qualities of a corporation *de jure*.[153] The right to draw in question the legality of an existent public corporation is a prerogative of the state and not of private litigants.[154] According to some courts, this rule rests upon the consideration that public corporations, such as

149. *Fritter* v. *West*, 65 S.W. (2d) (Tex.) 414.

150. *Evens* v. *Anderson*, 132 Minn. 59, 155 N.W. 1040; *State* v. *Ryan*, 41 Utah 327, 125 Pac. 666; *Alderman* v. *School Directors of District No. 5*, 91 Ill. 179; *Coler* v. *Dwight School Township*, 3 N.D. 249, 55 N.W. 587, 28 L.R.A. 649; *Black* v. *Early*, 208 Mo. 281, 106 S.W. 1014; *Hancock* v. *Board of Education*, 140 Calif. 554, 74 Pac. 44; *Dye* v. *Brewton*, 119 Miss. 359, 80 So. 761; *Floydada Independent School District* v. *Shipley*, 238 S.W. (Tex.) 1026; *City of El Paso* v. *Ruckman*, 92 Tex. 86, 46 S.W. 25; *Brown* v. *Fouts*, 307 Ill. 430, 138 N.E. 721; *Mesquite Independent School District* v. *Gross*, 123 Tex. 49, 67 S.W. (2d) 242; *People* v. *Wood*, 411 Ill. 514, 104 N.E. (2d) 800.

151. *Griffin* v. *Thomas*, 86 Okla. 70, 206 Pac. 604; *Evens* v. *Anderson*, 132 Minn. 59, 155 N.W. 1040; *Coler* v. *Dwight School Township*, 3 N.D. 249, 55 N.W. 587, 28 L.R.A. 649; *Black* v. *Early*, 208 Mo. 281, 106 S.W. 1014; *School District of Columbia* v. *Jones*, 229 Mo. 510, 129 S.W. 705; *State* v. *Hunt*, 199 S.W. (Mo.) 944; *State* v. *Alexander*, 129 Iowa 538, 105 N.W. 1021; *School District No. 21* v. *Fremont Board of Commissioners*, 15 Wyo. 73, 86 Pac. 24, 11 Ann. Cas. 1058; *State* v. *Ryan*, 41 Utah 327, 125 Pac. 666; *Fortune* v. *Hooven*, 2 Pac. (2d) (Kan.) 142; *People* v. *Wood*, 411 Ill. 514, 104 N.E. (2d) 800.

152. *Evens* v. *Anderson*, 132 Minn. 59, 155 N.W. 1040; *Van Wagener* v. *MacFarland*, 58 Calif. App. 115, 208 Pac. 345; *Black* v. *Early*, 208 Mo. 281, 106 S.W. 1014; *Franklin Avenue German Savings Institution* v. *Board of Education*, 75 Mo. 408; *Miller* v. *Town of Palermo*, 12 Kan. 14; *State* v. *Ryan*, 41 Utah 327, 125 Pac. 666; *City of El Paso* v. *Ruckman*, 92 Tex. 86, 46 S.W. 25; *State ex rel. Smith* v. *Gardner*, 204 S.W. (2d) (Mo.) 319; *Fulton Township School District* v. *School District No. 4*, 302 Mich. 566, 5 N.W. (2d) 467; *State ex rel. Hallgarth* v. *School District No. 23*, 179 Ore. 441, 172 Pac. (2d) 655.

153. *Evens* v. *Anderson*, 132 Minn. 59, 155 N.W. 1040.

154. *Evens* v. *Anderson*, 132 Minn. 59, 155 N.W. 1040; *Fortune* v. *Hooven*, 2 Pac. (2d) (Kan.) 142; *Tilton* v. *Dayton Independent School District*, 2 S.W. (2d) (Tex.) 889.

school districts, can be created only by the state; from the state they derive all their powers, which are, in fact, a grant of sovereignty. Such corporations are brought into existence for public, and not private, purposes, for the enforcement of laws enacted for the public welfare. If the state is satisfied with its own agencies, private parties should not be heard to complain.[155] To question such corporate existence is a function of government, a function which private parties cannot directly or indirectly usurp.[156] Public rights are to be vindicated by public authority.[157] Other courts justify the rule upon considerations of public policy. Great inconvenience, confusion, and even injury would result if private parties were permitted at their pleasure to call into question the legal existence of school districts and force these agencies of the state to prove their right to exist every time they undertake to perform the duties delegated to them by law.[158] It has been held that even a school district itself cannot attack the legal existence or question the boundaries of another district.[159] There is, however, much authority for the proposition that a private individual who has some special interest distinct from that of the public in general may institute *quo warranto* proceedings to test the legality of the organization of a school district.[160] And it has been held that a taxpayer has such special interest,[161] although the weight of authority is clearly otherwise.[162]

155. *Van Wagener* v. *MacFarland*, 58 Calif. App. 115, 208 Pac. 345; *Black* v. *Early*, 208 Mo. 281, 106 S.W. 1014; *Evens* v. *Anderson*, 132 Minn. 59, 155 N.W. 1040; *Miller* v. *Perris Irrigation District*, 85 Fed. 693; *State* v. *Ryan*, 41 Utah 327, 125 Pac. 666; *State* v. *Olson*, 107 Minn. 136, 119 N.W. 799, 21 L.R.A. (N.S.) 685.

156. *City of St. Louis* v. *Shields*, 62 Mo. 247.

157. *Evens* v. *Anderson*, 132 Minn. 59, 155 N.W. 1040.

158. *Coler* v. *Dwight School Township*, 3 N.D. 249, 55 N.W. 587, 28 L.R.A. 649; *Burnham* v. *Rogers*, 167 Mo. 17, 66 S.W. 970; *School District No. 35* v. *Hodgins*, 180 Mo. 70, 79 S.W. 148; *Evens* v. *Anderson*, 132 Minn. 59, 155 N.W. 1040.

159. *School District No. 38* v. *Rural High School District No. 6*, 116 Kan. 40, 225 Pac. 732; *Willamar Independent School District* v. *Lyford*, 8 S.W. (2d) (Tex.) 239.

160. *Craft* v. *Jackson County*, 5 Kan. 313; *Wilson* v. *Brown*, 145 S.W. (Tex.) 639; *State* v. *Ryan*, 41 Utah 327, 125 Pac. 666.

161. *State* v. *Small*, 131 Mo. App. 470, 109 S.W. 1079; 22 R.C.L. 695–96. Note: 21 Ann. Cas. 1125, 21 L.R.A. (N.S.) 688. See also *People* v. *Calloway*, 329 Ill. 505, 160 N.E. 834.

162. *State* v. *Ryan*, 41 Utah 327, 125 Pac. 666. Note: 21 L.R.A. (N.S.) 685.

The rule that a *de facto* school district is not subject to collateral attack is of great practical significance. It means that a district organized under statutory authority and accepted by the public cannot be restrained from issuing bonds, collecting taxes, or doing other things authorized by law, even though its organization may have been irregular and defective.[163] The case of *Black* v. *Early*[164] illustrates the application of the rule. A school district was organized in 1902. For three years it levied and collected taxes, employed teachers, and maintained a school. In 1905 the need of a new schoolhouse was commonly recognized, but there was disagreement among the electors with respect to the amount the building should cost. Those favoring the larger expenditure succeeded in getting bonds voted and taxes levied to pay part of the interest and principal thereon. Suit was brought to restrain the collection of the taxes, on the ground that the district had been illegally organized. The court refused to grant the injunction, upon the ground that the legal organization of the district was not subject to collateral attack, the proper remedy being an action in *quo warranto* instituted by the state. In the case of *Van Wagener* v. *MacFarland*,[165] action was brought to secure an injunction restraining the issuance and sale of school-district bonds on the ground that the district had not been organized in such a manner as the law prescribed. In denying the relief sought, the court said:

The proposition that the regularity of the proceedings by which a public corporation of a municipal character has been called into existence cannot be questioned at the suit of an individual citizen or taxpayer is too well settled to admit now of any debate. The reason upon which this holding is founded is far-reaching and admits of no exception. In theory, public corporations of any character whatsoever, exercising governmental functions, do so by reason of a delegation to them of a part of the sovereign power of the state. Where they are claiming to act and are actually functioning without having complied with the necessary prerequisites, they are usurping franchise rights as against paramount authority, to complain of which it lies only within the right of the state itself. The attack by the individual is unauthorized, whether it is made in defense of a tax levied to pay existing bonded indebtedness, or whether it be by injunction to prevent the

163. *Coler* v. *Dwight School Township*, 3 N.D. 249, 55 N.W. 587, 28 L.R.A. 649; *Black* v. *Early*, 208 Mo. 281, 106 S.W. 1014; *Franklin Avenue German Savings Institution* v. *Board of Education*, 75 Mo. 408; *School District No. 35* v. *Hodgins*, 180 Mo. 70, 79 S.W. 148; *Floydada Independent School District* v. *Shipley*, 238 S.W. (Tex.) 1026; *Dye* v. *Brewton*, 119 Miss. 359, 80 So. 761.

164. *Black* v. *Early*, 208 Mo. 281, 106 S.W. 1014.

165. *Van Wagener* v. *MacFarland*, 58 Calif. App. 115, 208 Pac. 345.

issuance of bonds after an election has been held within the territory affected, authorizing such securities to be issued. . . .

It follows as a necessary conclusion that the bonds referred to may be legally issued, and that when sold they will represent binding obligations against all of the property of the *de facto* district.

Where the attorney-general or state's attorney, whose prerogative it is to institute *quo warranto* proceedings in the name of the state, refuses to act, the question may arise as to whether his discretion can be controlled by the courts. It seems clear that the courts will not require the attorney-general to bring an action in *quo warranto* against a school district on the complaint of a private party who can show no special interest distinct from that of the public in general.[166] Private citizens, many courts hold, cannot interfere with the duties of the attorney-general where the rights involved are purely public. In some jurisdictions it is held that even though a private citizen may show some special interest which would entitle him to invoke the aid of the attorney-general to bring an action on his relation, still, if the attorney-general refuses to bring the action, the courts cannot compel him to do so. The better-reasoned cases, however, hold that if the attorney-general refuses to bring an action upon the relation of a private citizen who shows some special interest in the existence of the corporation distinct from that of the public in general, the courts will entertain jurisdiction and permit the citizen to submit to it the nature of his interest. The attorney-general also may submit to the court his reasons for refusing to institute action. If the court finds that the attorney-general is justified in his refusal, the action will be dismissed. If, on the other hand, the court finds that the interest of the individual can be segregated from that of the state without injury to either, it may order the attorney-general to bring an action of *quo warranto* on the relation of the individual and, upon a hearing of the facts in the case, grant such relief as seems just and proper.[167]

166. *State* v. *Ryan*, 41 Utah 327, 125 Pac. 666; *Thompson* v. *Attorney-General*, 48 Ohio St. 552, 3 N.E. 742.

167. *State* v. *Ryan*, 41 Utah 327, 125 Pac. 666. See also *Lamoreaux* v. *Attorney-General*, 89 Mich. 146, 50 N.W. 812; *In re Bank of Mt. Pleasant*, 5 Ohio 249; *People* v. *Healy*, 230 Ill. 280, 82 N.E. 599, 15 L.R.A. (N.S.) 603.

CHAPTER V

School Districts and Municipalities

SEPARATE IDENTITY OF SCHOOL DISTRICTS
AND MUNICIPALITIES

PUBLIC education being essentially and intrinsically a state or governmental function, the state may employ whatever agencies it may see fit for the administration of its educational policies. It may establish school districts without regard to the boundaries of existing political subdivisions, or, if it seems the better policy, it may make use of such existing subdivisions as counties, townships, towns, and cities. Most states have adopted the policy of organizing cities and incorporated towns into school districts. Thus two corporate entities are superimposed upon the same territory. In such cases a good deal of confusion is likely to arise because of failure to distinguish between the city as a municipal corporation and the school district as a quasi-corporation. The two corporations have essentially different functions to perform. The city is a municipal corporation, created primarily for the purpose of local self-government; it was not created by the state as an instrument of state policy. The school district, on the other hand, is a quasi-corporation, a purely political or civil subdivision of the state. As an instrumentality of the state, it is created in order to facilitate the administration of government. In legal contemplation it is not concerned with local functions; it exists to accomplish a state purpose in the particular locality involved. The identity of the territorial boundaries in no way affects the separateness of function.[1] The

1. *People* v. *Munising Township,* 213 Mich. 629, 182 N.W. 118; *Board of Education* v. *Detroit,* 30 Mich. 505; *Kuhn* v. *Thompson,* 168 Mich. 511, 134 N.W. 722; *Heizer* v. *Yohn,* 37 Ind. 415; *City of San Diego* v. *Dauer,* 97 Calif. 442, 32 Pac. 561; *Esberg* v. *Badaracco,* 202 Calif. 110; *City of Rockdale* v. *Cureton,* 111 Tex. 136, 229 S.W. 852; *Chrestman* v. *Tompkins,* 5 S.W. (2d) 257; *Board of Education* v. *Richmond,* 137 N.Y.S. 62; *State* v. *Gora,* 195 Wis. 515, 218 N.W. 837; *Cline* v. *Martin,* 94 Ohio St. 420, 115 N.E. 37; *Follett* v. *Sheldon,* 195 Ind. 510, 144 N.E. 867; *State* ex rel. *Harbach* v. *Mayor of City of Milwaukee,* 189 Wis. 84, 206 N.W. 210; *Orleans Parish School Board* v. *City of New Orleans,* 56 So. (2d) 280; *Board of Education of City of Syracuse* v. *King,* 114 N.Y.S. (2d) 329; *Brown* v. *Bowling,* 56 N.M. 96, 240 Pac. (2d) 846; *Lansing* v. *Board of Education,* 7 Calif. App. (2d) 211, 45 Pac. (2d) 1021.

general rule governing the separate identity of school districts and municipalities has been clearly stated by the Supreme Court of Ohio:

> The Constitution of Ohio . . . authorizes the General Assembly to provide by law for the organization, administration and control of the public school system of the state supported by public funds. This does not require that the school system of the state shall be organized, administered or controlled along the lines or within the territorial limits of the political subdivisions of the state. These may be used as a convenience in the establishment of school districts throughout the state, or they may be totally disregarded, but whether the lines of the political subdivisions are, or are not, coextensive with the school district, the administration and control of schools is not vested in the officers of that political subdivision but in a board of education for each school district.
>
> Such boards are agencies of the state for the organization, administration and control of the public school system of the state, separate and apart from the usual political and governmental functions of other subdivisions of the state. The fact that certain officers of other subdivisions may be delegated some duties or authority in relation thereto does not change the status or destroy the separate identity of the school district.[2]

It is not to be assumed, however, that a state has no power to make use of its municipalities in the carrying-out of its educational policies. It may impose upon municipalities and their officers such powers and duties with respect to education as wise policy may seem to dictate. It may provide that school-board members be appointed by the mayor with the consent of the council, that the school budget be approved or even reduced by some city officer or agency, or that school-district bonds receive municipal approval before being issued and sold. It may even go so far as to make education a department of the city government, thus placing education under the complete control of the municipality.

GENERAL PRINCIPLES GOVERNING SCHOOL-DISTRICT
AND MUNICIPAL RELATIONS

In actual practice one finds the widest variations in the degree of control over education vested in municipal governments. The fact that the school district and the city comprise the same territory, together with the further fact that in many instances the city proper is charged with certain duties touching education, has occasioned much litigation to determine the limits of municipal power in the control and management of education. It is important, therefore, that

2. *Cline* v. *Martin,* 94 Ohio St. 420, 115 N.E. 37.

the principles governing school-district and municipal relations be clearly understood.

The principle is well established that education is not essentially or inherently a municipal function.[3] As the Supreme Court of Louisiana has put it: "A high school is not essential to municipal government; a system of education is not a part of municipal regulation, and the power of a corporation to establish a public school cannot be inferred from any power necessary for municipal existence."[4] It follows that a city possesses no inherent control over the public schools. Whatever powers it or its officers may possess with respect to education are necessarily conferred by statute or charter.[5] It cannot be insisted too strongly that municipal officers have only such powers with respect to education as are expressly delegated to them. Such officers draw all their power in this respect from the statutes or the city charter; they derive no authority whatever from the nature of the corporation of which they are officers. In fact, it has been held that when municipal officers perform school functions, they do not represent the city at all; they are rather ex officio officers representing the state.[6] Moreover, when interpreting statutory or charter provisions conferring powers over education on municipalities, the courts apply the rule of strict construction. That is to say, the presumption is that the state intended to confer powers over education upon its duly established educational agencies, and that presumption will be overcome only by a clear legislative intent otherwise. If there is doubt whether a particular power has been conferred upon the school corporation or the city, the doubt will be resolved against the city.

Two cases, one from Connecticut and the other from New York,

3. *Nelson v. Mayor et al. of Town of Homer,* 48 La. Ann. 258, 19 So. 271; *Board of Education v. Alton Water Company,* 314 Ill. 466, 145 N.E. 683; *Water-Supply Company v. City of Albuquerque,* 9 N.M. 441, 54 Pac. 969; *Board of Education v. Richmond,* 137 N.Y.S. 62; *National Water Works Company v. School District of Kansas City,* 23 Mo. App. 227; *Rodman v. Town of Washington,* 122 N.C. 26, 30 S.E. 118; *Board of Education v. City of Corbin,* 301 Ky. 686, 192 S.W. (2d) 951; *City of Cleveland v. Public Library Board of City School District of City of Cleveland,* 94 Ohio St. 311, 114 N.E. 247; *Board of Education of City of Minneapolis v. Houghton,* 181 Minn. 576, 233 N.W. 834.

4. *Nelson v. Mayor et al. of Town of Homer,* 48 La. Ann. 258, 19 So. 271.

5. *Van Fleet v. Oltman,* 244 Mich. 241, 221 N.W. 299; *Mayor and Council of Wilmington v. State,* 57 Atl. (2d) (Del.) 70.

6. *McDonnell v. City of New Haven,* 99 Conn. 484, 121 Atl. 824; *Kuhn v. Thompson,* 168 Mich. 511, 134 N.W. 722; *School District No. 76 v. Ryker,* 64 Kan. 612, 68 Pac. 34.

will serve to illustrate the reasoning of the courts. In the Connecticut case the comptroller of the city of Bridgeport refused to certify to the city treasurer that funds were available with which to pay teachers' salaries. In issuing a mandamus requiring that he do so, the court said:

That under our law the furnishing of education is a state function and duty is manifest from the extensive legislation relating to it. . . . Under the statutes, provision is made for the education of the inhabitants of each town through its town board of education. Accordingly, as we have stated, "A town board of education is an agency of the state in charge of education in the town; to that end it is granted broad powers by the legislature; and it is beyond control by the town or any of its officers in the exercise of those powers or in the incurring of expense, to be paid by the town, necessitated thereby, except as limitations are found in statutory provisions."[7]

In the New York case, the court held that the city of New York did not have authority to require members of the teaching staff employed by the board of education to reside within the city's corporate limits. It said:

In the delegation of the function of education, however, the Legislature has delegated the local power not to the corporation of the City of New York but to a separate corporation known as the Board of Education. To that corporation alone are the teaching and supervisory officials subject to control. While the city is custodian of the funds, for educational purposes the Board of Education has power to administer the funds and control the members of the teaching and supervisory staff without interference by the city authorities.[8]

AUTHORITY TO SPEND MUNICIPAL FUNDS
FOR SCHOOL PURPOSES

According to the weight of judicial opinion, a city cannot, in the absence of statutory authority, spend its funds for the maintenance of public schools.[9] Such is the case because public education is not a

7. *State ex rel. Board of Education of City of Bridgeport* v. *D'Aulisa*, 133 Conn. 414, 52 Atl. (2d) 636.

8. *Eriksen* v. *City of New York*, 2 N.Y.S. (2d) 280, 167 Misc. 42; Accord, *Board of Education of Syracuse* v. *Bing*, 117 N.Y.S. (2d) 674, 280 App. Div. 1033.

9. *Nelson* v. *Mayor et al. of Town of Homer*, 48 La. Ann. 258, 19 So. 271; *Board of Education* v. *Alton Water Company*, 314 Ill. 466, 145 N.E. 683; *Water-Supply Company* v. *City of Albuquerque*, 9 N.M. 441, 54 Pac. 969; *Board of Education* v. *Richmond*, 137 N.Y.S. 62; *National Water Works Company* v. *School District of Kansas City*, 23 Mo. App. 227; *Rodman* v. *Town of Washington*, 122 N.C. 39, 30 S.E. 118; *City of El Paso* v. *Carroll*, 108 S.W. (2d) (Tex.) 251; *Hamrick* v. *Special Tax School District No. 1*, 130 Fla. 453, 178 So. 406; *Board of Education* v. *City of Corbin*, 301 Ky. 686, 192 S.W. (2d) 951.

corporate or municipal function. Thus it was said by the Supreme Court of Ohio:

While it is a fact that the city of Cleveland and the City School District of the City of Cleveland are substantially the same in population and territory, yet they are nevertheless separate and distinct political subdivisions. Therefore the city of Cleveland cannot make a gift to the City School District of the City of Cleveland, nothwithstanding such a gift is for the benefit of substantially the same public.[10]

In a case decided by the Supreme Court of Louisiana, action was brought to test the authority of the town of Homer to establish a high school and to levy a tax for its support. In denying such authority to the town, it was said by the court:

The defence is that, under Art. 209 of the Constitution, municipal corporations have the power and authority to levy and collect taxes to the amount of ten mills for municipal purposes, and that an assessment for educational purposes is a municipal regulation. . . .

Corporations are the creatures of legislative will, and can do no act not authorized by their charters, unless it is by implication necessary to carry out conferred powers.

In the original charter there was no grant of any right to the corporation of Homer to erect a school building and maintain a high school. It can not by its own act usurp powers not granted. There was no authority under the act for the corporation to so amend its charter as to authorize the levying of a tax for the maintaining of a high school or for any other educational purpose. . . . The subject of education is an important matter, and it is so treated by the State, as it seems to be jealous of the exercise of the power by subordinate political corporations, as it has not granted local self-taxation for this purpose. . . . A high school is not essential to municipal government; a system of education is not a part of municipal regulation, and the power of a corporation to establish a public school can not be inferred from any power necessary for municipal existence.[11]

Similarly, in a number of cases it has been held that a city may not furnish water free of charge to public school buildings.[12] Thus it was said by the Supreme Court of Illinois, in holding that the city of Alton had no authority to furnish water free of charge to the public schools:

10. *City of Cleveland* v. *Public Library Board of City School District of Cleveland*, 94 Ohio St. 311, 114 N.E. 247.

11. *Nelson* v. *Mayor et al. of Town of Homer*, 48 La. Ann. 258, 19 So. 271.

12. *Board of Education* v. *Alton Water Company*, 314 Ill. 466, 145 N.E. 683; *Water-Supply Company* v. *City of Albuquerque*, 9 N.M. 441, 54 Pac. 969; *Board of Education* v. *Richmond*, 137 N.Y.S. 62; *National Water Works Company* v. *School District of Kansas City*, 23 Mo. App. 227.

A municipal corporation holds its property in trust for public uses, and its funds can be used only for corporate purposes. They cannot be diverted to private use. Nor can the municipal authorities or the electors give away the money or property of the municipality.

The city of Alton and the appellant board of education are separate corporate entities, each clothed with the power of taxation for its corporate purposes and for none other. They are organized under different laws, each for a specific purpose. . . . The board of education would have no power to levy a tax for the purpose of maintaining a city waterworks system or any purpose for the sole benefit of the city in its corporate capacity, nor would the city have any authority to levy a tax for the maintenance of a community high school.[13]

To the same effect are cases decided by the courts of Texas, Kentucky, and Florida. The Court of Civil Appeals of Texas held that the city council of El Paso had no authority to transfer money from the general fund of the city to the Independent School District of El Paso, whether by way of advancement or gift. The city had accumulated $54,000 from the operation of its waterworks system, and the council voted to transfer this amount to the credit of the school board. When the city treasurer refused to comply with the resolution of the council, a writ of mandamus was sought to compel him to do so. The court refused the writ, pointing out that in control of the schools the authority of the board of education was exclusive, the board was vested by statute with its own taxing power, and the city council was without power to authorize the expenditure of city funds for educational purposes.[14]

Similarly, it was held by the Court of Appeals of Kentucky that the city of Corbin had no authority by ordinance to appropriate city funds for the payment of teachers' salaries.[15] And in Florida a county has no authority to levy taxes to pay bonds issued by the county board of education for the purpose of acquiring and equipping high-school buildings,[16] and a city or town cannot levy a tax for public free-school purposes.[17]

In California, on the other hand, it has been held that a city may issue its own bonds for the construction of school buildings, notwithstanding the fact that the school district and the city are separate

13. *Board of Education* v. *Alton Water Company*, 314 Ill. 466, 145 N.E. 683.

14. *City of El Paso* v. *Carroll*, 108 S.W. (2d) (Tex.) 251.

15. *Board of Education of the City of Corbin* v. *City of Corbin*, 301 Ky. 686, 192 S.W. (2d) 951.

16. *Hamrick* v. *Special Tax School District No. 1*, 130 Fla. 453, 178 So. 406.

17. *Brown* v. *City of Lakeland*, 61 Fla. 508, 54 So. 716.

corporations and the school district has authority to issue its own bonds for building purposes. The California courts take the position that the maintenance of schools is a legitimate municipal function:

As school-houses are essential aids in the promotion of education, their erection is but incidental to the maintenance of the schools, and falls as completely within the functions of a municipal government as does the erection of a hospital for its indigent poor, or buildings for its fire engines; and the school-houses when so erected are as fully municipal buildings as are its engine-houses and hospital buildings.[18]

In Alabama,[19] Indiana,[20] and Georgia[21] it has been held that the legislature may authorize municipalities to spend municipal funds in the erection of school buildings. But, under the constitution, where the school-district indebtedness is limited to a certain percentage of the assessed valuation of the district, the legislature cannot authorize a municipal corporation coextensive with the school district to issue its bonds for school purposes after the limit of the district's indebtedness has been reached.[22]

It is permissible, however, for a city to spend municipal funds in aid of an educational institution in order to secure the location of the institution in the city.[23] Thus it was said by the Supreme Court of Massachusetts: "The establishment of a textile school in a large manufacturing city may be of such special and direct benefit to the city as to warrant the appropriation by it, under legislative sanction, of a sum of money in aid of the school."[24]

MUNICIPAL CONTROL OF SCHOOL BUILDINGS

Inasmuch as public schools are state institutions, public school buildings are state property held in trust for the state by the local school offices.[25] It has been held, therefore, in a number of instances,

18. *Wetmore v. City of Oakland*, 99 Calif. 146, 33 Pac. 769; *Los Angeles City School District v. Longden*, 148 Calif. 380, 83 Pac. 246; *Law v. San Francisco*, 144 Calif. 384, 77 Pac. 1014; *Malaley v. Marysville*, 37 Calif. App. 638, 174 Pac. 367.

19. *Carey v. City of Haleyville*, 230 Ala. 401, 161 So. 496.

20. *Follett v. Sheldon*, 195 Ind. 510, 144 N.E. 867.

21. *Mayor of Cartersville v. Baker*, 73 Ga. 686.

22. *McCullom v. State*, 195 Ind. 217, 144 N.E. 864.

23. *Hanscom v. City of Lowell*, 165 Mass. 419, 43 N.E. 196; *Burr v. City of Carbondale*, 76 Ill. 455; *Hensley v. People*, 84 Ill. 544.

24. *Hanscom v. City of Lowell*, 165 Mass. 419, 43 N.E. 196.

25. *Attorney General v. Lowery*, 199 U.S. 233, 26 S. Ct. 27, 50 L. Ed. 167; *Pass School District v. Hollywood City School District*, 156 Calif. 416, 105 Pac. 122, 26 L.R.A. (N.S.) 485; *Carson v. State*, 27 Ind. 465; *Board v. Nevada School*

that municipal officers have no authority in the control and management of school buildings.

A case[26] decided by the Supreme Court of Wisconsin illustrates the reasoning of the courts. The legislature of that state enacted a statute authorizing boards of education of cities of the first class, of which Milwaukee was one, to report to the city council the amount of money required for the next fiscal year for the repair and maintenance of school buildings. It was thereupon the duty of the city council to levy a tax equal to the amount required by the board of education, provided that the amount should not exceed one mill upon the dollar of the total assessed valuation of the city. The Board of Education of Milwaukee estimated that the amount to keep the buildings in repair for the year 1926 would be $750,000, and the board requested the mayor and city council to levy a tax for that amount. The mayor and council refused to levy the tax, on the ground that the statute violated the following provision of the state constitution: "Cities and villages organized pursuant to state law are hereby empowered to determine their local affairs and government, subject only to this constitution and to such enactments of the legislature of a state-wide concern as shall with uniformity affect every city or every village." In issuing a writ of mandamus requiring the council to levy the necessary tax, it was said by the court:

It is contended that the repair of school buildings constituted a local affair of the city of Milwaukee, and that by the constitutional provision just quoted the legislature is prohibited from legislating upon that subject except by general law which "shall with uniformity affect every city or every village"; that as ch. 285, Laws 1925, affected only cities of the first class, it was not a law which "uniformly affected every city or every village."

It is obvious that the limitation placed upon the power of the legislature with reference to laws which "shall with uniformity affect every city or every village" is confined to the "local affairs and government" of cities and villages. With reference to all subjects that do not constitute "local affairs," or relate to the government of cities and villages, the legislature has the same power of classification that it had before the adoption of the home-rule amendment. Respondents' contention, therefore, must rest upon the proposition that the repair of school buildings within the city of Milwaukee is a local affair of said city. If not, respondents' contention must fall. . . .

If the field of legislation upon the subject of education belongs to the state, it belongs to it in its entirety. If the cause of education is not a subject of municipal regulation, the municipality cannot touch it or interfere

District, 251 S.W. (2d) (Mo.) 20; *McGurn* v. *Board of Education,* 133 Ill. 122, 24 N.E. 529; *Rawson* v. *Spencer,* 113 Mass. 40.

26. *State* v. *Mayor et al. of City of Milwaukee,* 189 Wis. 84, 206 N.W. 210.

with it in the slightest degree. School buildings are an essental agency in the state's educational scheme, and to allow municipalities a voice in the construction, repair, control, or management of the school buildings within their borders is to yield to them the power to frustrate the state's plan in promoting education throughout the state. If power be granted to interfere in this respect, there would be no logical limitation to municipal interference with the district schools. . . .

These considerations lead irresistibly to the conclusion that, although the boundaries of a school district may be coterminous with the boundaries of a city, there is no merger of the school-district affairs with the city affairs. They remain separate and distinct units of government for the purpose of exercising separate and distinct powers and for the accomplishment of separate and distinct purposes. It follows that the so-called home-rule amendment imposes no limitation upon the power of the legislature to deal with the subject of education, and this applies to every agency created or provided, and to every policy adopted by the legislature, having for its object the promotion of the cause of education throughout the state.

Another Wisconsin case is in point. The city of Milwaukee adopted a minimum-wage ordinance controlling as to labor employed "in any work done by the city of *Milwaukee,* either new construction work or repair work on any roads, buildings, or any other public works whatsoever." Action was brought to restrain the city from enforcing the ordinance with respect to labor employed in constructing a public school building. In granting the injunction, the court pointed out that the school directors and not the common council had authority to make school-building contracts, notwithstanding the fact that the statutes required that such contracts should run in the name of the city, should be countersigned by the city comptroller, and should be approved by the city attorney. Since the school directors had authority to make the contract in question, they could not be interfered with or controlled by the city council. To hold otherwise would necessarily and logically permit the common council to dictate to the school board as to any and all conditions of contracts for school buildings and thereby permit the council to do indirectly the very thing that the legislature had expressly directed should be done by the school board.[27]

Municipal ordinances regulating building plans, safety, and sanitation.—A number of cases have involved a conflict in the exercise of police power by the municipality, on the one hand, and the school board, on the other. Thus a school board may refuse to conform to the building code of the city or to the regulation of a city board

27. *H. Schmitt & Son* v. *City of Milwaukee,* 185 Wis. 119, 200 N.W. 678.

of health closing the schools during a threatened epidemic of some contagious disease. Again, a school board may challenge the city's authority to inspect the heating systems in its school buildings or to inspect and regulate the conduct of its school cafeterias. The cases dealing with the exercise of police power with respect to school affairs cannot be harmonized. Some courts hold that the police power of a city must not be interpreted to extend to the control and management of public school property unless the legislature has specifically and definitely conferred that power upon the city.[28] The reasoning supporting this line of decisions is that education is a state function, public school property is state property, and the legislature must be presumed to have vested police power with respect to the state's property in the special agency charged with its control and management. This presumption can be overcome only by a specific expression of intent to the contrary. Hence the exercise of police power over school buildings is vested in the board of education, unless some statute or provision in the city charter specifically vests the power in the municipality. In other cases the court has taken the position that the police power of a city generally extends to all within its boundaries, including state agencies, unless expressly exempted by statute.[29] Still other courts hold that in particular instances, in order to insure the public safety, the police power of the board of education must be subordinated to that of the city.[30]

A case[31] decided by the Court of Appeals of Kentucky illustrates the reasoning of the courts that hold public school property exempt from the exercise of the police power on the part of a city unless specific statutory provision extends the police power of the city to it. A municipal ordinance of the city of Louisville required all buildings of a certain class to have fire escapes. A state school for the education of blind children was located in Louisville. In holding that the ordinance could not be enforced with respect to state property, the court used the following language:

28. *Salt Lake City* v. *Board of Education,* 52 Utah 540, 175 Pac. 654; *Kentucky Institution for Blind* v. *City of Louisville,* 123 Ky. 767, 8 L.R.A. (N.S.) 553, 97 S.W. 402.

29. *Bredeck* v. *Board of Education of City of St. Louis,* 213 S.W. (2d) (Mo.) 889; *Smith* v. *Board of Education of St. Louis,* 359 Mo. 264, 221 S.W. (2d) 203; *Kansas City* v. *School District of Kansas City,* 356 Mo. 364, 201 S.W. (2d) 930.

30. *Pasadena School District* v. *City of Pasadena,* 166 Calif. 7, 134 Pac. 985, 47 L.R.A. (N.S.) 892; *People* v. *Board of Education,* 224 Mich. 388, 195 N.W. 95.

31. *Kentucky Institution for Blind* v. *City of Louisville,* 123 Ky. 767, 8 L.R.A. (N.S.) 553, 97 S.W. 402.

But beyond that is the larger question, and the one upon which this decision is rested; that is, that the State will not be presumed to have waived its right to regulate its own property, by ceding to the city the right generally to pass ordinances of a police nature regulating property within its bounds. . . . The principle is that the State, when creating municipal governments, does not cede to them any control of the State's property situated within them, nor over any property which the State has authorized another body or power to control. The municipal government is but an agent of the State—not an independent body. It governs in the limited manner and territory that is expressly or by necessary implication granted to it by the State. It is competent for the State to retain to itself some part of the government even within the municipality, which it will exercise directly, or through the medium of other selected and more suitable instrumentalities. How can the city have ever a superior authority to the State over the latter's own property, or in its control and management? From the nature of things it cannot have.

The reasoning in the foregoing case is supported by a case[32] decided by the Supreme Court of Utah. Action was brought to enjoin the Board of Education of Salt Lake City from proceeding in the construction of a school building until the building ordinances of the city were complied with. The statutes did not specifically authorize the city to exercise police power with respect to school buildings, but they did provide that the city commission should have power

to prescribe the manner of constructing stone, brick, and other buildings, and the construction of fire escapes; and to cause all buildings used for public purposes to be provided with sufficient and ample means of exit and entrance, and to be supplied with necessary and appropriate appliances for the extinguishment of fire, to prevent the overcrowding thereof, and to regulate the placing and use of seats, chairs, benches, scenery, curtains, blinds, screens, or other appliances therein.

By statute the city commission also had power

to define the fire limits, and prescribe limits within which no building shall be constructed except of brick, stone, or other incombustible material, without permission, and to cause the destruction or removal of any building constructed or repaired in violation of any ordinance, and to cause all buildings and inclosures which may be in a dangerous state to be put in a safe condition or removed.

It was contended by the city that this general grant of police power was broad enough to include public school buildings. The court, however, took a contrary position. It reasoned that public school property is state property, subject to the police power of the state unless expressly made subject to the police power of the municipality:

32. *Salt Lake City* v. *Board of Education,* 52 Utah 540, 175 Pac. 654.

Under our Constitution and statutes, however, we can conceive of no distinction between what are denominated by counsel state buildings, such as the buildings of the State University, or the Capitol, and our school buildings. True, the control of the university is placed in the hands of a board of regents whose duties and powers are perhaps defined with more particularity and detail than are the powers of the boards of education. That may perhaps also be true respecting the State Capitol. Be that as it may, however, the public school buildings and their control are of as much concern to the state as are the other buildings, and a careful reading of the constitutional provisions and statutes relating to education clearly shows that the entire public school system . . . remains entirely within the control of the State Legislature, and hence within the control of the state, except where certain powers are delegated to the several boards of education as herein indicated. If it be conceded, therefore, as it is and must be, that the state has not surrendered the control over its buildings to the cities, then it necessarily follows that the terms "public buildings" and "all buildings" used in the subdivision of section 206, *supra*, which we have quoted, do not embrace all buildings within the cities. Moreover, if state buildings must be excluded, then public school buildings must likewise be excluded from those terms.

The reasoning of the courts which hold that the general police power of a city embraces the control and regulation of school buildings unless the statutes have expressly conferred the power in question on the school board is illustrated by the case of *Kansas City* v. *School District of Kansas City*.[33] Here the issue was the authority of the city to enforce an ordinance requiring the inspection of boilers, smokestacks, fuel-burning facilities, and elevators in the school buildings of the school district. In holding that the city had the authority, the court said:

The people of Kansas City have availed themselves of the privilege of local self-government. . . . The State in the exercise of the police power is discharging a governmental function. Generally, the police power affecting property and persons within the municipality's corporate limits is reposed in the City. . . . The indispensabilty of local self-government arises from problems implicit in the safety, order, health, morals, prosperity and general welfare of thickly populated areas. "Within its authorized sphere of action, a city has been termed a 'miniature state.' ". . . No constitutional or statutory restriction of City's police power as to its application to the regulation of the facilities of public school buildings has been observed by us; and, as we have seen, the State in the exercise of its own powers could have acted or could have expressly enjoined upon or delegated to School Districts board the full responsibility of taking particular measures, in connection with School District's school buildings, otherwise within the scope of City's police power. . . . Since the State itself has taken no precautionary measures, and City has been vested with regulatory and supervisory responsibilities of the exercise of the police power, and School District (having no

33. 356 Mo. 364, 201 S.W. (2d) 930.

police power) has not been expressly and specifically given full duty to attend to these responsibilities, we think the Legislature is content in the thought the measures to be taken are within the police power vested in the City.

In two other cases[34] coming before the Supreme Court of Missouri the issue involved was the power of the city to inspect and regulate the lunchrooms and cafeterias maintained by the school board. In both cases it was conceded by the school board that it had no right to exercise police power over its buildings unless that power had been expressly granted by statute. The court in neither case could find in the statutes evidence that it was the intent of the legislature to vest the police power in these matters in the board of education. This was true, even though in one case the statutes conferred on the commissioner of school buildings the responsibility for their ventilation, warming, sanitary condition, and repair.

In California, the court has held that the police power of the school district must be subordinated to that of the city when the public safety demands it. Thus the school district of Pasadena was required to obey the building code of the city of Pasadena. The court did not consider the issue as to whether school property is state property and therefore subject to the police power of the school board. It based its conclusion upon the consideration that the powers of a municipal corporation are generally broader than the powers of a quasi-corporation and upon what it deemed the necessity of subordinating the police power of the school board to that of the city in order to insure the public safety.[35] In this connection it may be pointed out, too, that in Michigan the city board of health was held to have authority to force a closing of the schools in the face of a threatened epidemic of smallpox.[36]

MUNICIPAL CONTROL OF SCHOOL FINANCE

In the exercise of its plenary control over education, the legislature may adopt any mode of financing the public schools not prohibited by the constitution. Either the board of education or the city authori-

34. *Bredeck* v. *Board of Education of City of St. Louis,* 213 S.W. (2d) (Mo.) 889; *Smith* v. *Board of Education of St. Louis,* 359 Mo. 264, 221 S.W. (2d) 203; *Kansas City* v. *School District of Kansas City,* 356 Mo. 364, 201 S.W. (2d) 930.

35. *Pasadena School District* v. *City of Pasadena,* 166 Calif. 7, 134 Pac. 985, 47 L.R.A. (N.S.) 492.

36. *People* v. *Board of Education of the City of Lansing,* 224 Mich. 388, 195 N.W. 95.

ties may be given complete control over school finance. In any particular instance the degree of control to be exercised by either school-board members or municipal officers must be ascertained by reference to statutory and charter provisions.[37] Under no circumstances, however, will municipal officers be permitted to exercise any greater degree of control[38] over school finance than that clearly intended by the legislature.

Not infrequently the statutes require that school boards submit their budgets to city councils for approval. Where such is the case, the question may arise as to whether the council may reduce the budget submitted by the school board. The answer to this question depends upon the wording of the statutes and of the charter of the city. If these documents construed together reveal that the approval of the budget and the levy of the necessary taxes is merely a ministerial duty, the council must approve the budget as submitted and levy a tax necessary to produce the required amount.[39] If, on the other hand, it appears that the council is vested with an exercise of discretion as to the amount to be raised for school purposes, the council may reduce the budget as in its opinion may seem wise.[40] Such discretionary power must be very clear, however, because, as some courts have pointed out, its exercise virtually places the control of the schools in the hands of the city council.[41]

37. *Union School District of City of Saginaw* v. *Council of City of Saginaw,* 232 Mich. 639, 206 N.W. 573; *Board of Education* v. *Townsend,* 140 Ky. 248, 130 S.W. 1105; *State* v. *Mayor et al. of City of Omaha,* 39 Neb. 745, 58 N.W. 442.

38. *George W. Shaner & Sons* v. *Board of Education,* 6 N.J. Misc. Rep. 671, 142 Atl. 425.

39. *Board of Education* v. *Mayor et al. of City of Kingfisher,* 5 Okla. 82, 48 Pac. 103; *Union School District of Bay City* v. *Board of Estimates,* 235 Mich. 323, 209 N.W. 91; *Union School District of City of Saginaw* v. *Council of City of Saginaw,* 232 Mich. 639, 206 N.W. 573; *Board of Education* v. *Townsend,* 140 Ky. 248, 130 S.W. 1105; *Mayor and Council of Wilmington* v. *State,* 57 Atl. (2d) (Del.) 70.

40. *Leonard* v. *School Committee of City of Springfield,* 241 Mass. 325, 135 N.E. 459; *Matter of Emerson* v. *Buck,* 230 N.Y. 380, 130 N.E. 584; *Reif* v. *Schwab,* 197 N.Y.S. 127; *Fleischmann* v. *Graves,* 235 N.Y. 84, 138 N.E. 745; *Fuhrmann* v. *Graves,* 235 N.Y. 77, 138 N.E. 743; *Board of Education of the City of White Plains* v. *Rogers,* 278 N.Y. 66, 15 N.E. (2d) 400; *Board of Education of Town of Stamford* v. *Board of Finance of Town of Stamford,* 127 Conn. 345, 16 Atl. (2d) 601; *Divisich* v. *Marshall,* 281 N.Y. 170, 22 N.E. (2d) 327.

41. *Union School District of City of Saginaw* v. *Council of City of Saginaw,* 232 Mich. 639, 206 N.W. 573; *Board of Education* v. *Board of Estimates of City of Saginaw,* 230 Mich. 495, 203 N.W. 68; *Board of Education* v. *Townsend,* 140 Ky. 248, 130 S.W. 1105.

A case[42] decided by the Supreme Court of Michigan is a good illustration of the position taken by the courts in holding that city councils will not be permitted to reduce school budgets unless clearly authorized to do so. The Board of Estimates of the city of Saginaw reduced a number of items in the budget submitted to it by the board of education. The court held that the board of estimates had exceeded its authority:

If defendant [the board of estimates] is right, then the legislature must have intended, in effect, to take from the school board and to give to the board of estimates the power to determine, from which no right of review or appeal is given, the length of the school year under the statute, the number and compensation of teachers, the fiscal plans and policies, and the character and quality of materials, supplies, and equipment for the district, for, if the board of estimates has power to say upon the estimate how much and for what purpose money may be raised, it is, by its absolute power of veto, virtually the master of the affairs of the plaintiff district. This was not intended. If it were, we might expect to find a clear legislative expression to that effect. The statute makes no provisions for supplying the board of estimates with facts, data, statistics, reports, etc., so that an intelligent judgment on the matter might be passed, nor does it require the school board to exhibit its affairs, its needs, its problems to the board of estimates.

The reasoning in the foregoing case is supported by a case[43] decided by the Court of Appeals of Kentucky. The Board of Education of Bowling Green submitted to the city council its estimate of the funds necessary to defray the expenses of the schools, but the council refused to make the necessary tax levy on the ground that the board had abused its discretion by employing more teachers than required and at higher salaries than were necessary. In the opinion of the court, the council had no authority to reduce the estimate of the board.

Having placed the management and control of the schools in the hands of such boards; having given them the power to employ teachers, fix the salaries, provide suitable buildings, etc.; having made it their duty to provide the buildings and teachers sufficient for the education of all children of the city between six and twenty years of age, it would certainly be an anomalous condition if the law intended that it should be dependent for its resources to carry out its contracts upon the whims or caprice of the general council, whose duty the law made it to make the necessary levy. Such a condition of affairs was not contemplated by the Legislature. It meant to make the board of education entirely independent. To that end it made the duty of the general council to levy a tax sufficient to meet the board's

42. *Board of Education v. Board of Estimates of City of Saginaw*, 230 Mich. 495, 203 N.W. 68.

43. *Board of Education v. Townsend*, 140 Ky. 248, 130 S.W. 1105.

demands, not exceeding, however, the limits prescribed by law. Where proper demand is made within the limits prescribed by law, the council will not be permitted to refuse to comply with the board's demands, unless it can show that the members of the board acted corruptly or in bad faith, or that they embraced in their expenditures items not authorized by law. That in their opinion the demands of the board are excessive or extortionate, is not sufficient.

Even though the statutes may authorize the city to fix the amount of the school budget, it does not follow that the council may direct how the gross amount shall be spent.[44] The board of education may spend the funds at its disposal in any manner and for any purposes permitted by law. In the case of *Leonard* v. *School Committee of City of Springfield*,[45] for example, the school committe requested an increase in the budget in order to raise teachers' salaries. The mayor and city council adopted an itemized budget which made no provision for an increase in salaries. The committee, in order to provide money for such increase, voted to eliminate summer schools and certain kindergarten schools. Thereupon action was brought to enjoin the committee from diverting money from the purposes for which it had been appropriated to other school purposes. The court denied the injunction. Similarly, in a number of other cases the right of the board of education to fix teachers' salaries was sustained, even though the common council had the right to determine the total amount the board could spend.[46]

The Court of Appeals of New York has expressed the rule commonly applied in cases of this kind:

The Board of Education of the City of New York must comply with formula provided in the charter of that city in making its requests or demands for necessary funds, furnishing by line items or other specified methods, the information necessary to enable the Board of Estimates to act intelligently, but otherwise it has full control over those funds when appropriated.[47]

44. *Fleischmann* v. *Graves*, 245 N.Y. 84, 138 N.E. 745; *Fuhrmann* v. *Graves*, 196 N.Y.S. 776; *Reif* v. *Schwab*, 197 N.Y.S. 127; *Brennan* v. *Board of Education*, 245 N.Y. 8, 156 N.E. 78; *Board of Education* v. *Dibble*, 240 N.Y.S. 422; *Graham* v. *Joyce*, 151 Md. 298, 134 Atl. 332; *Bailey* v. *Duffy*, 45 R.I. 304, 121 Atl. 129; *Hardy* v. *Lee*, 36 R.I. 302, 90 Atl. 383; *Leonard* v. *School Committee*, 241 Mass. 325, 135 N.E. 459.

45. 241 Mass. 325, 135 N.E. 459.

46. *Fuhrmann* v. *Graves*, 196 N.Y.S. 776; *Graham* v. *Joyce*, 151 Md. 298, 134 Atl. 332; *Hardy* v. *Lee*, 36 R.I. 302, 90 Atl. 383.

47. *Divisich* v. *Marshall*, 281 N.Y. 170, 22 N.E. (2d) 327. Accord, *Board of Education of Town of Stamford* v. *Board of Finance of Town of Stamford*, 127 Conn. 345, 16 Atl. (2d) 601.

POWERS OVER EDUCATION CONFERRED
BY HOME-RULE CHARTERS

It is the policy of a number of states, through either constitutional provision or statutory enactment, to grant to municipalities what are known as "home-rule charters." The purpose is to make such municipalities self-governing and free from legislative interference with respect to matters of local and internal concern. That is to say, cities having home-rule charters are free to determine their own local affairs and government, subject only to the constitution and to enactments of the legislature of a state-wide concern. Frequently, a city in its regulation of its "local affairs" will attempt to exercise control of some educational activity or policy.

The principle is well established that "whenever the provisions of a home-rule charter are in conflict with the constitution or the legislative policy of a state as declared in its statutes, such provision must give way to the latter."[48] And, since education is not a local or municipal affair but an affair of state-wide interest governed by constitutional and statutory provisions, a city will not be permitted to extend its control over education by virtue of its home-rule charter.[49]

In a case decided by the Supreme Court of Minnesota, the home-rule charter of Minneapolis provided that no public improvement should be authorized to be constructed in the city until its location and design had been approved by the City Planning Commission. The court held that this provision of the charter was not applicable to public school buildings, because education is a state and not a local concern. Moreover, this provision of the charter, if construed to be applicable to school buildings, would be in conflict with constitutional and statutory policy with respect to education.[50] Similarly, in Wisconsin, a home-rule

48. *Board of Education of City of Minneapolis* v. *Houghton*, 181 Minn. 576, 233 N.W. 834. In the case of a special charter for a particular city, it has been held that the charter provisions are applicable, even though they are in conflict with the general statutes on the subject (*State* ex rel. *Wallen* v. *Hatch*, 82 Conn. 122, 72 Atl. 575).

49. *State* v. *Mayor et al. of City of Milwaukee*, 189 Wis. 84, 206 N.W. 210; *Esberg* v. *Badaracco*, 202 Calif. 110, 259 Pac. 730; *Lansing* v. *Board of Education of City and County of San Francisco*, 7 Calif. App. (2d) 211, 45 Pac. (2d) 1021; *McKee* v. *Edgar*, 137 Calif. App. 462, 30 Pac. (2d) 999; *Gerth* v. *Dominguez*, 1 Calif. (2d) 239, 34 Pac. (2d) 135; *Board of Education of City of Ardmore* v. *State* ex rel. *Best*, 26 Okla. 366, 109 Pac. 563; *State* v. *Cummings*, 47 Okla. 44, 147 Pac. 161.

50. *Board of Education of City of Minneapolis* v. *Houghton*, 181 Minn. 576, 233 N.W. 834.

charter authorizing Milwaukee to determine its local affairs and government conferred no power on the mayor and the council to control policy with respect to repair of school buildings.[51] A provision in the charter of San Francisco requiring all employees of the city to reside in it was held not to be applicable to teachers. In denying a writ of mandamus to compel the board of education to dismiss teachers living outside the city limits, the court said: "The school system of the state is a matter of general concern, as distinguished from a 'municipal affair' as that term is considered in connection with chartered cities and is governed by its board of education or board of trustees."[52] The same reasoning governs a number of cases decided by the Supreme Court of Oklahoma. The city charter of Ardmore contained a provision with respect to district organization that was in conflict with the general laws of the state. The court held the provision of the charter void because it was in conflict with the statutes and also because "this important function of government" was not subject to regulation by a home-rule charter.[53] And in the case of *State* v. *Cummings,*[54] the same court said:

> The free public school system in Oklahoma is a matter of general state concern, and not a "municipal affair," and city charters can only run current with and never counter to the general laws of the state touching the free public school system; and, where a city charter fixes the terms of free public school officers in such city at three years, instead of two years as fixed by the statute, the terms of said officers will expire in two years from the date of their election.

The courts of California recognize that education is a state function, but they go further than courts in other states in holding that it is also vested with a degree of local and municipal concern. Where educational matters are not governed by a statute, it has been held that they may be subject to regulation by the municipality; and this is true, even though the charter itself is also silent on these matters. Thus in San Francisco the city established a health service, with compulsory contributions, for all its employees. Teachers were included, even though the school district was a separate corporation from the city. In holding that the city had authority to include teachers in its health service pro-

51. *State* v. *Mayor et al. of City of Milwaukee,* 189 Wis. 84, 206 N.W. 210.

52. *Lansing* v. *Board of Education of City and County of San Francisco,* 7 Calif. App. (2d) 211, 45 Pac. (2d) 1021.

53. *Board of Education of the City of Ardmore* v. *State* ex rel. *Best,* 26 Okla. 336, 109 Pac. 563.

54. 47 Okla. 44, 147 Pac. 161.

gram, the court reasoned: "The school system has been held to be a matter of general concern, rather than a municipal affair, and consequently is not committed to the exclusive control of local governments. But the cities may make local regulations beneficial to and in furtherance of the school system, provided that these provisions do not conflict with the general law."[55]

In 1953 the Supreme Court of Kings County, New York, handed down a decision in conflict with the great weight of authority in other jurisdictions and in conflict with numerous decisions in the state of New York itself. The case involved the interpretation of section 903 of the charter of the city of New York, which provided that "if any employee of the city shall refuse, before any legislative committee, to testify or answer any question regarding the official connection of any employee of the city on the ground that his answer would tend to incriminate him, his term of office or employment shall terminate and such office of employment shall become vacant, and he shall not be eligible to employment by the city." Teachers who refused to testify before the United States Senate committee investigating subversive influences, on the ground that they might incriminate themselves, were discharged by the board of education. They sought reinstatement by mandamus on the ground that they were not employees of the city and therefore the charter provision was not applicable to them. The court held otherwise. It pointed out that there is nothing in the federal Constitution that makes education an exclusive function of the state. It reasoned that school boards have a dual aspect, they are "both city and state agencies." Moreover, the board of education was appointed by the mayor of the city, and its title "indicates it is part of the city government, at least to a degree."[56]

RELATION OF SCHOOL-BOARD MEMBERS TO THE MAYOR AND CITY COUNCIL

Where members of the school board are appointed by the mayor subject to the approval of the city council, it is sometimes assumed that they are subordinated to the authority of the mayor and council. Whatever may be the facts in such a case, in contemplation of law the mayor and council have no control whatever over the policies of the school

55. *Butterworth* v. *Boyd*, 12 Calif. (2d) 140, 82 Pac. (2d) 434.

56. *Daniman* v. *Board of Education of the City of New York*, 118 N.Y.S. (2d) 487, 202 Misc. 915.

board.[57] That is, authority to control policies does not grow out of the mere act of appointment. After school-board members are appointed, the mayor has no more authority over them than does any other citizen of the school district unless such authority is conferred in express terms. Such is the case because the schools of a particular municipality are part of the state school system; they are state institutions; their officers are state officers and not officers of the municipality.[58] Since school-board members are state officers, they may be appointed in any manner the legislature may determine.[59] They may be appointed by the courts,[60] or by the state board of education,[61] or be elected by the people. Moreover, it is not necessary that they be residents of the district of which they are officers.[62] It follows, therefore, that when the mayor and council are authorized to appoint school-board members, they in no sense represent the municipality. In the performance of this function, they are merely ex officio state officers.[63] Once the appointment is made, the authority of the mayor and the council is at an end. As a general rule, the policies of a board of education are never subject to control by the municipal authorities unless such control is clearly granted by statutory enactment.

57. *Ham* v. *Mayor et al. of New York*, 70 N.Y. 459.

58. *Barnes* v. *District of Columbia*, 91 U.S. 540, 23 L. Ed. 440; *City of Louisville* v. *Commonwealth*, 134 Ky. 488, 121 S.W. 411; *Denver* v. *Spencer*, 34 Colo. 270, 82 Pac. 590, 2 L.R.A. (N.S.) 147; *Ward* v. *San Diego School District*, 203 Calif. 712, 265 Pac. 821.

59. *State* v. *Hine*, 59 Conn. 50, 21 Atl. 1024, 10 L.R.A. 83.

60. *Minsinger* v. *Rau*, 236 Pa. St. 327, 84 Atl. 902, Ann. Cas. 1913E 1324.

61. *State* v. *Haworth*, 122 Ind. 462, 23 N.E. 946, 7 L.R.A. 240.

62. *State* v. *Hine*, 59 Conn. 50, 21 Atl. 1024, 10 L.R.A. 83.

63. *McDonnell* v. *City of New Haven*, 99 Conn. 484, 121 Atl. 824; *Kuhn* v. *Thompson*, 168 Mich. 511, 134 N.W. 722; *School District No. 76* v. *Ryker*, 64 Kan. 612, 68 Pac. 34.

CHAPTER VI

School Officers

STATUS OF SCHOOL-DISTRICT OFFICERS

SCHOOL districts are, strictly speaking, quasi-corporations, created for purposes of state administration. As has been pointed out previously, however, the term "municipal corporation" is often used in constitutions and statutes to include quasi-corporations as well as municipal corporations proper. Where it is clear from an examination of the text of a constitutional provision or a statute that it was the intent to include school districts within the meaning of the term "municipal corporation," the courts, will, of course, hold them to be such.[1] But with respect to any particular municipality, school officers are not municipal officers. They are state officers.[2] The question whether officers are municipal or state officers is properly determined by the functions they perform.[3] The manner of election or appointment is of no consequence in this connection.[4] The mere fact that a school officer is appointed by the mayor does not make him a municipal officer.[5] Since education is a function of the state and not of the municipality it follows that school officers are not officers of the municipality over the schools of which they have control.

Where school-board members are appointed by the mayor or by the mayor and council, there seems to be a common belief that this mode of selection makes them municipal officers or in some way subjects them to the authority of the municipal government. Whatever may be

1. *Frans* v. *Young,* 30 Neb. 360, 46 N.W. 528, 27 Am. St. Rep. 412.

2. *City of Louisville* v. *Commonwealth,* 134 Ky. 488, 121 S.W. 411. See, however, *Boswell* v. *Powell,* 43 S.W. (2d) (Tenn.) 495.

3. *Kahn* v. *Sutro,* 114 Calif. 316, 46 Pac. 87, 33 L.R.A. 620. See also *State* v. *Bus,* 135 Mo. 325, 36 S.W. 636, 33 L.R.A. 616.

4. *Denver* v. *Spencer,* 34 Colo. 270, 82 Pac. 590, 2 L.R.A. (N.S.) 147; *Barnes* v. *District of Columbia,* 91 U.S. 540, 23 L. Ed. 440.

5. *People* v. *Metz,* 113 N.Y.S. 1007.

113

the actual facts in such a case, in contemplation of law the school board is entirely independent of the municipal authorities unless subjected to their jurisdiction by specific statutory enactment. In the case of *Ham v. New York*,[6] as an illustration, suit was brought against the city for injuries growing out of the negligence of the employees of the commissioners of education. The court refused to allow damages, on the ground that the members of the department of education were not officers of the municipality or subject to the control of the city authorities. Members of the department of education were not subject to control by the city authorities, even though they had been appointed by the mayor and a statute specifically made the education department a department of the local municipal government. In rendering its decision, the court used the following significant language:

Whether it [the education department] was a corporate body is not material, for although formally constituted a department of the municipal government, the duties which it was required to discharge were not local or corporate, but related and belonged to an important branch of the administrative department of the State government. Although the commissioners are appointed by the mayor, they are vested with full power and authority to manage and control the educational interests of the entire municipality, and to appoint all subordinate officers and employees who were subject to their government and control exclusively, and were their servants and subordinates. The commissioners, in the discharge of their functions, were not amenable to the corporation in any respect, and those who were in their employ as servants and subordinates were subject to the commissioners, bound to obey their orders and directions, and the defendant had no authority whatever either to employ, manage, control and direct their action, or to remove or discharge them for unskillfulness or neglect of duty.

STATUS OF MEMBERS OF COUNTY BOARDS OF EDUCATION, COUNTY SUPERINTENDENTS, AND CITY SUPERINTENDENTS

Where counties are used as either local or intermediate units of school administration, they are essentially agents of the state for the purpose of carrying out a state function locally. It would appear, therefore, that members of county boards of education should be regarded as state and not county officers, and such has been the conclusion reached in a number of cases.[7] Some courts, on the other hand, have

6. *Ham v. Mayor et al. of New York*, 70 N.Y. 459.

7. *Ward v. Siler*, 272 Ky. 424, 114 S.W. (2d) 516; *Benton County Council of Benton County v. State* ex rel. *Sparks*, 224 Ind. 114, 65 N.E. (2d) 116; *State v. Mason*, 133 So. (La.) 809.

held that members of county boards of education are county officers.[8]

The same lack of agreement is found with respect to the status of the county superintendent. The Supreme Court of Indiana has expressed the view entertained by a number of courts and it seems the more logical one. It said: "The office of county superintendent is not a county office, nor is the same in character local. He is a state officer, his powers and duties relate entirely to the administration of the public school system which is a function of the state government."[9]

Some courts have held that a city superintendent is a public officer.[10] Apparently, however, the better-reasoned opinions hold that a city superintendent is an employee of the board.[11] It is difficult to see how one who stands in a purely contractual relationship with a board of education can be regarded as being clothed with all the privileges and prerogatives of a public office. More important still, the true test of whether or not one occupies a public office is: Do the duties of the position require him to exercise a part of the sovereignty of the state? At present, at least, it would seem that whatever part of the sovereignty of the state is delegated, in connection with education, is delegated to the board of education.[12]

8. *Boswell v. Powell*, 163 Tenn. 445, 43 S.W. (2d) 495; *Oconto County v. Town of Townsend*, 210 Wis. 85, 244 N.W. 761; *State ex rel. Consolidated District No. 2 v. Ingram*, 317 Mo. 1141, 298 S.W. 37; *Armistead v. State ex rel. Smyth*, 41 So. (2d) (Fla.) 879.

9. *Benton County Council of Benton County v. State*, 224 Ind. 114, 65 N.E. (2d) 116. Accord, *State ex rel. Osborn v. Eddington*, 208 Ind. 160, 195 N.E. 92; *Webb County v. Board of Education of School Trustees of Laredo*, 95 Tex. 131, 65 S.W. 878; *County Court of Summers County v. Nicely*, 121 W. Va. 767, 6 S.E. (2d) 485. See, however, *Armistead v. State ex rel. Smyth*, 41 So. (2d) (Fla.) 879; *State ex rel. Consolidated School District No. 2 v. Ingram*, 317 Mo. 1141, 298 S.W. 37; *Boswell v. Powell*, 163 Tenn. 445, 43 S.W. (2d) 495.

10. *Alcorn ex rel. Hoerle v. Thomas*, 127 Conn. 426, 17 Atl. (2d) 514; *State ex rel. Brokaw v. Board of Education of St. Louis*, 171 S.W. (2d) (Mo.) 75; *Weiss v. Ziegler*, 327 Pa. 100, 193 Atl. 642; 112 L.R.A. 1021; *Bourgeois v. Orleans Parish School Board*, 219 La. 512, 53 So. (2d) 251; *Temple Independent School District v. Proctor*, 97 S.W. (2d) (Tex.) 1047; *Benson v. Inhabitants of Town of Newfield*, 136 Me. 23, 1 Atl. (2d) 227.

11. *County Court of Summers County v. Nicely*, 121 W. Va. 767, 6 S.E. (2d) 485; *State ex rel. Hill v. Sinclair*, 103 Kan. 480, 175 Pac. 41; *Baltimore v. Lyman*, 92 Md. 591, 48 Atl. 145; *Sieb v. Racine*, 176 Wis. 617, 187 N.W. 989.

12. See *County Court of Summers County v. Nicely*, 121 W. Va. 767, 6 S.E. (2d) 485; *Hartigan v. Board of Regents*, 49 W. Va. 14, 38 S.E. 698.

ELIGIBILITY AND ELECTION OF OFFICERS

The statutes usually require certain qualifications of school officers. It may be residence in the district for a prescribed period in the case of board members, or it may be educational qualifications in the case of county or state superintendents. Where such is the case, the question may arise as to when the eligibility requirements must be met. Must the officer possess the required qualifications at the time of election, or may he qualify after election and before induction into office? On this question the authorities are not in agreement. One line of decisions holds that it is sufficient if the officer is properly qualified at the time he assumes the duties of the office unless there is some provision in the statutes which clearly indicates the intent of the legislature that he should be eligible at the time of election.[13] The courts reason that the purpose of eligibility requirements is to guarantee that the duties of the office will be performed by one possessing the proper qualifications. Eligibility refers to the performance of the duties of the office, and not to the election.

In the leading case of *Bradfield* v. *Avery*,[14] the statutes of Idaho provided that no person should "be eligible to the office of county superintendent of public instruction except a first grade practical teacher of not less than two years' practical experience in Idaho, one of which must have been while holding a valid first grade certificate." In holding that the eligibility requirements prescribed in the statute might be met after election and before induction into office, the court said in part:

We are satisfied that the better reason is with the proposition that, where the word "eligibility" is used in connection with an office, and there are no explanatory words indicating that such word is used with reference to the time of election, it has reference to the qualification to hold the office, rather than the qualification to be elected to the office. . . . It will be observed that the language of the statute above quoted is "no person shall be eligible to the office" and not "eligible to be elected to the office." "Eligible to the office" clearly implies the qualification or capacity to hold the office, and clearly indicates the intent of the Legislature to use the word "eligible" in the sense that it applies to the capacity and qualification of the person to hold the office. While it is true that the word "eligible" may mean capable of being

13. *Bradfield* v. *Avery*, 16 Idaho 769, 102 Pac. 687, 23 L.R.A. (N.S.) 1228; *State* v. *Huegle*, 135 Iowa 100; *People* v. *Hamilton*, 24 Ill. App. 609; *Hoy* v. *State*, 168 Ind. 506; *Smith* v. *Moore*, 90 Ind. 294; *Brown* v. *Goben*, 122 Ind. 113, 23 N.E. 519; *Demaree* v. *Scates*, 50 Kan. 275, 32 Pac. 1123, 20 L.R.A. 97; *Kilpatrick* v. *Brownfield*, 97 Ky. 558.

14. 16 Idaho 769, 102 Pac. 687, 23 L.R.A. (N.S.) 1228.

chosen, fit to be chosen, subject to selection, and applies to the time of selection or election, yet, where such meaning is not clearly indicated by the manner in which the word is used, or by the qualifications or modifications thereof, we think it naturally applies to one's fitness or qualification to hold the office.

Most of the cases involving the question here under discussion have arisen with respect to the meaning of the term "eligible." Certain other terms prescribing qualifications for officers have, however, been interpreted to relate to the time of induction into office rather than to the time of election. Such was the case where the statutes provided that the surveyor must be a licensed land surveyor of the state.[15] In Iowa the supreme court held that an alien could not hold office until naturalized, even though there was no constitutional or statutory provision involved. But it was sufficient if naturalization was consummated after election and before induction into office.[16] Precisely the same question arose in Wisconsin, where the court held that an alien might be elected to office and hold it, provided that he became naturalized before assuming its duties. In the words of the court:

What then is the nature and effect of the disqualification under consideration? In my judgment it is not that a person who is not an elector only because of some disqualification which he has the power to remove at any time, is thereby rendered ineligible *to be elected* to a public office for a term which is to commence at a future time; but it is that a person thus disqualified shall not be eligible *to hold* such office. Such disqualification does not relate to the *election to,* but to the *holding of,* the office.[17]

While the weight of authority seems to support the rule that a public officer may meet the eligibility requirements at any time between election and induction into office, in a number of jurisdictions it is held that the candidate for office must meet the eligibility requirements at the time of election.[18] In the case of *Searcy v. Grow,*[19] for example, the constitution of California provided: "No person holding any lucrative office under the United States or any other power,

---

15. *Ward* v. *Crowell*, 142 Calif. 587, 76 Pac. 491.

16. *State* v. *Van Beek*, 87 Iowa 569, 54 N.W. 525, 19 L.R.A. 622, 43 Am. St. Rep. 397.

17. *State* v. *Murray*, 28 Wis. 96, 9 Am. Rep. 489. See also *Privett* v. *Bickford*, 26 Kan. 52; *Huff* v. *Cook*, 44 Iowa 639.

18. *Searcy* v. *Grow*, 15 Calif. 118; *Territory* v. *Smith*, 3 Minn. 164, 74 Am. Dec. 749; *Taylor* v. *Sullivan*, 45 Minn. 309, 47 N.W. 802, 11 L.R.A. 272, 22 Am. St. Rep. 729; *State* v. *Clarke*, 3 Nev. 566; *State* v. *Moores*, 52 Neb. 770, 73 N.W. 299; *State* v. *Lake*, 16 R.I. 511; *Roane* v. *Matthews*, 75 Miss. 94, 21 So. 665.

19. 15 Calif. 118.

shall be eligible to any civil office of profit under this State." While still holding the office of postmaster, Grow was elected sheriff. After the election he resigned the office of postmaster. It was his contention that the provision in the constitution only disqualified him from holding both offices at the same time and that his election was not void. The court held otherwise:

> We think the plain meaning of the words quoted is the opposite of this construction. The language is not that the Federal officer shall not *hold* a State office while he is such Federal officer, but that he shall not, while in such Federal office, be *eligible* to the State office. We understand the word eligible to mean capable of being chosen—the subject of selection or choice. The people in this case were clothed with this power of choice; their selection of the candidate gave him all the claim to the office which he has; his title to the office comes from *their* designation of him as Sheriff. But they could not designate or choose a man not eligible, i.e., not capable of being selected.

As a general rule, statutes fixing the time within which an officer shall qualify are regarded as "directory," at least to the extent that a mere delay in qualifying does not of itself cause a vacancy in the office unless there is an express provision in the statute to that effect.[20]

A number of problems of a legal nature grow out of the election of school officers. Since those who conduct such elections are not, as a rule, trained in the law, irregularities frequently occur. The statutes governing the election of school officers should be complied with strictly. It is a settled principle of law governing elections, however, that minor irregularities which do not affect the result will not render the election void. Thus it was said in the case of *Trimmier* v. *Bomar:*

> In elections the great matter is the result. When this is clearly ascertained it sweeps away all technicalities. The machinery provided should be observed, but in so far as it is not necessary to determine the result, it is directory and not mandatory. Certainly manner and form should not be allowed to defeat the undoubted will of the people clearly expressed. This would be indeed subordinating and sacrificing the substance to the shadow.[21]

Frequently, the statutes provide that an officer shall be elected on a prescribed day. Such legislation is usually regarded as directory only. If for some reason the election is not consummated on the prescribed day, those whose duty is to elect will not be estopped to elect at a later date unless the statutes expressly limit their authority to act

20. *State* ex rel. *Goodman* v. *Heath,* 345 Mo. 226, 132 S.W. (2d) 1001.
21. *Trimmier* v. *Bomar,* 20 S.C. 354.

on the prescribed date.[22] In Indiana the statutes required the township trustees to meet biennially the first Monday in June to elect a county superintendent of schools. The trustees failed to meet on the prescribed day, and it was contended that they had no authority to elect a superintendent until the same day of the next biennial period. The court refused to sustain this contention, pointing out that such an interpretation of the statute would defeat the intent of the legislalature and place the people at the mercy of unfaithful and designing officials. The duty to elect the superintendent biennially, it was said, was mandatory, but the date of election was directory.[23] In the case of *Sackett* v. *State*,[24] a statute required the common council of each city to elect one school trustee annually at the first regular meeting in June. The common council of the city of Albany, having failed to elect a trustee at the first regular meeting in June in 1880, performed this duty at the first regular meeting in July of that year. The action of the council was sustained.

The rules governing elections have been discussed elsewhere in this volume. It is only necessary here to point out that under the common law a simple majority constitutes a quorum and that an administrative board or municipal council does not, as a rule, have authority to define a quorum differently, even though it may be authorized to prescribe its own rules of procedure. Moreover, a majority of those present is not necessary to consummate an election; a majority of those voting is sufficient, provided that a quorum is present. Blank ballots are a nullity and are not to be considered in determining whether an officer has received a majority vote.

EFFECT OF FAILURE TO FILE BOND

Certain school officers are frequently required by statute to file a bond within a specified time after election or appointment. Even though the language employed in the statute may be definite and explicit, such statutes are ordinarily held to be directory and not manda-

22. *Wampler* v. *State*, 148 Ind. 557, 47 N.E. 1068, 38 L.R.A. 829; *People* v. *Allen*, 6 Wend. (N.Y.) 486; *State* v. *Smith*, 22 Minn. 218; *State* v. *Morrison*, 152 Tenn. 59, 274 S.W. 551; *Lynch* v. *Lafland*, 4 Cold. (Tenn.) 96.

23. *Wampler* v. *State*, 148 Ind. 557, 47 N.E. 1068, 38 L.R.A. 829.

24. 74 Ind. 486.

tory.[25] Failure to give the required bond within the prescribed time does not, therefore, *ipso facto*, work a forfeiture of the office.[26] As has been said by the Supreme Court of Ohio: "The law does not look with favor upon declaring a forfeiture in an office to which one has been elected in a legal manner, and where the office has not been declared vacant, and no other rights or title have intervened, such irregularities as failure to give bond, or take the oath of office within a certain time, have not generally been held to be sufficient grounds for declaring a forfeiture of the office."[27] In an Indiana case, where a county superintendent failed to give bond within the time required by statute, the court rendered the following opinion:

It is held by our own and other courts that statutes requiring official bonds to be filed within a designated time are directory, and not mandatory. Upon this question the authorities are harmonious. . . . This rule is carried very far; for it is held, without substantial diversity of opinion, that, unless the statute makes the filing of a bond within a limited time a condition precedent to the right to the office, the failure to file it within the time prescribed will not work a forfeiture of the right to the office nor create a vacancy.[28]

It has been held, moreover, that a statute requiring the giving of a bond within a prescribed time does not apply while the right to the office is being contested.[29] And even though a statute may expressly provide that failure to give bond within the prescribed time shall create a vacancy in the office, the general weight of authority is that such a failure does not work a forfeiture *ipso facto*, but is merely a ground for forfeiture.[30] In such a case it is within the discretion of the state or other power either to excuse the delinquency or to declare a forfeiture.

25. *Commissioners of Knox County* v. *Johnson*, 124 Ind. 145, 24 N.E. 148; *City of Chicago* v. *Gage*, 95 Ill. 593, 35 Am. Rep. 182; *People* v. *Holley*, 12 Wend. (N.Y.) 481; *State* v. *Falconer*, 44 Ala. 696; *State* v. *Churchill*, 41 Mo. 41.

26. *Commissioners of Knox County* v. *Johnson*, 124 Ind. 145, 24 N.E. 148; *City of Chicago* v. *Gage*, 95 Ill. 593, 35 Am. Rep. 182; *People* v. *Holley*, 12 Wend. (N.Y.) 481; *State* v. *Churchill*, 41 Mo. 41; *State* v. *Falconer*, 44 Ala. 696; *State* v. *Colvig*, 15 Ore. 57, 13 Pac. 639.

27. *State* v. *Turner*, 111 Ohio St. 38, 144 N.E. 599.

28. *Commissioners of Knox County* v. *Johnson*, 124 Ind. 145, 24 N.E. 148.

29. *Pearson* v. *Wilson*, 57 Miss. 848; *People* v. *Potter*, 63 Calif. 127.

30. *State* v. *Toomer*, 7 Rich (S.C.) 216; *Sprowl* v. *Lawrence*, 33 Ala. 674; *City of Chicago* v. *Gage*, 95 Ill. 593, 35 Am. Rep. 182; *State* v. *Ring*, 29 Minn. 78, 11 N.W. 233. Contra, *State* v. *Matheny*, 7 Kan. 327.

INCOMPATIBLE OFFICES

When the functions and duties of two offices are inherently such that one is subordinated to and controlled by the other, they are held to be incompatible under the common law.[31] Speaking in this connection in the case of *People* v. *Green,*[32] Judge Folger said:

> Where one office is not subordinate to the other, nor the relations of the one to the other such as are inconsistent and repugnant, there is not that incompatibility from which the law declares that the acceptance of the one is the vacation of the other. The force of the word, in its application to this matter is, that from the nature and relations to each other, of the two places, they ought not to be held by the same person, from the contrariety and antagonism which would result in the attempt by one person to faithfully and impartially discharge the duties of one, toward the incumbent of the other. . . . The offices must subordinate, one the other, and they must, *per se,* have the right to interfere, one with the other, before they are incompatible at common law.

Incompatibility, moreover, may arise from the fact that the constitution or a statute prohibits the holding of two offices by the same person. In such a case incompatibility in fact is not essential, for the illegality of holding the two offices is declared by positive law.[33]

It is a well-settled rule of the common law, and one that has obtained from very early times,[34] that one who, while holding a public office, accepts another office incompatible with it, *ipso facto* and without further act, resigns the first office.[35] "The law presumes that the officer did not intend to commit the unlawful act of holding both offices, and a surrender of the first is implied."[36] No shadow of title is left to the original office; and it is proper to fill it by appointment or election, as the case may require. And this is true whether the offices are incompatible at common law or by statute. In the one case, the holding of the two offices is prohibited by public policy; in the other, by positive law.

31. *State* v. *Bus,* 135 Mo. 325, 36 S.W. 636, 33 L.R.A. 616; *People* v. *Green,* 58 N.Y. 295; *Pooley* v. *Fortenberry,* 268 Ky. 369, 105 S.W. (2d) 143.

32. 58 N.Y. 295.

33. *State* v. *Bus,* 135 Mo. 325, 36 S.W. 636, 33 L.R.A. 616.

34. *King* v. *Patteson,* 4 B. & Ad. 9.

35. *State* v. *Bus,* 135 Mo. 325, 36 S.W. 636, 33 L.R.A. 616; *State* v. *Lusk,* 48 Mo. 242; *People* v. *Brooklyn,* 77 N.Y. 503; *Edwards* v. *Board of Education,* 70 S.E. (2d) 170, 235 N.C. 345; *Pruitt* v. *Glen Rose Independent School District,* 126 Tex. 45, 84 S.W. (2d) 1004, 100 A.L.R. 1158.

36. *State* v. *Bus,* 135 Mo. 325, 36 S.W. 636, 33 L.R.A. 616.

The rule as stated in the preceding paragraph is subject to one important exception. Where the statutes expressly provide that an officer shall hold office until his successor is elected and qualified, the acceptance of an incompatible office will not vacate the first office.[37] Such is the case because title to the first office is not determinable by act of the incumbent. By positive mandate of law he is required to perform the duties of the office until a successor is elected or appointed by the proper authority. An officer may not relieve himself of the responsibility of performing the duties of the office by attempting to resign, and his acceptance of the incompatible office is void and without effect.

de facto OFFICERS

Lord Ellenborough defined a *de facto* officer as "one who has the reputation of being the officer he assumes to be, and yet is not a good officer in point of law."[38] One who has color of title to an office and performs its duties with the general acquiescence of the public is at least a *de facto* officer. Ordinarily, color of title is the result of an election or appointment, however irregular or defective it may have been. A known appointment or election, however, is not necessary to constitute one an officer *de facto*, where the duties of the office have been exercised "under such circumstances of reputation or acquiescence as were calculated to induce people, without inquiry, to submit to or invoke his action, supposing him to be the officer he assumed to be."[39] In other words, acquiescence by the public in the official acts of an officer for a sufficient length of time will give rise to the implication that he must have been elected or appointed, and third parties may deal with such an officer on the assumption that he is the officer which he represents himself to be.[40] As was said by the court in *State* v. *Perkins*,[41] "the foundation stone of this whole doctrine of a *de facto* officer, as gathered from all the authorities, seems to be that of pre-

37. *Badger* v. *United States*, 93 U.S. 599, 23 L. Ed. 991; *State* v. *Nobles*, 109 Wis. 202, 85 N.W. 367; *People* v. *Supervisor*, 100 Ill. 332; *Jones* v. *City of Jefferson*, 66 Tex. 576, 1 S.W. 903.

38. *Rex* v. *Bedford Level*, 6 East 356.

39. *State* v. *Carroll*, 38 Conn. 449, 9 Am. Rep. 409. See also *Hand* v. *Deady*, 29 N.Y.S. 633, 79 Hun. 75.

40. *School Town of Milford* v. *Zeigler*, 1 Ind. App. 138, 27 N.E. 303; *School District of Kline Township* v. *McAloose*, 317 Pa. 266, 176 Atl. 435.

41. *State* v. *Perkins*, 139 Mo. 106.

venting the public or third parties from being deceived to their hurt by relying in good faith upon the genuineness and validity of acts done by a pseudo officer." It follows, therefore, that where the public or third persons are fully aware that an officer has not been duly elected or appointed, or is not qualified—if they know the true state of the case and are not deceived by color of authority—the doctrine of *de facto* officers is not applicable. Thus where a teacher knew that the board members who employed him did not possess the statutory qualifications for the office, the contract was not valid as being one made by a *de facto* officer.[42]

A volunteer is not a *de facto* officer. "A mere claim to be a public officer, and exercising the office, will not constitute one an officer *de facto;* there must be, at least, a fair color of right; or an acquiescence by the public in his official acts so long that he will be presumed to act as an officer by right of appointment or election."[43] The case of *Hand* v. *Deady*[44] is an excellent illustration of the application of this principle of law. At a district meeting someone suggested that one Buckley act as trustee. Buckley said, "No; let Dave Benjamin have it." The suggestion was seconded. Thereupon Dave Benjamin, who seemed to be intoxicated, got up and said, "All in favor of Dave Benjamin being trustee, say 'Aye.'" Someone responded "Aye." Then David Benjamin said, "I am trustee." No negative vote was called for. The meeting then proceeded in the usual manner and elected James Benjamin trustee. The behavior and claims of David Benjamin were obviously treated as a jest, for no official record was made of this part of the meeting. Three days later, however, David Benjamin called upon James Benjamin, asserted his right as trustee, and by threat and intimidation got possession of the district books. Thereupon, he assumed to act as trustee, bought lumber, brooms, locks for the doors, and employed a teacher. Soon thereafter he ceased to act as trustee. In an action on the part of the teacher to recover under the contract, the court held that David Benjamin had not been a *de facto* officer:

> It is clear that he was not a trustee *de jure;* and, to constitute a *de facto* officer, it is essential that his acts of official character be founded upon some colorable right to the office, having the form of election or appointment, or that he has acted as such, with the acquiescence of the public, for a suf-

42. *Alleger* v. *School District No. 16,* 142 S.W. (2d) (Mo.) 660.

43. *Brown* v. *Lunt,* 37 Me. 423.

44. 29 N.Y.S. 633, 79 Hun. 75.

ficient length of time to permit the presumption of an election or appointment. This assumption arises from the reputation that he acquires as an officer from such acts and acquiescence. Then, as a matter of public policy, his acts in his apparent official capacity are not subject to collateral attack to the prejudice of others, and, as to them and the public, they are deemed effectual and valid. . . . And in fact it is prima facie sufficient to establish the official character of local officers to show that they are generally reputed to be, and have acted, as such. . . . It does not appear that David Benjamin had so acted, with the acquiescence of the public, as to give him, in the district, the reputation of trustee, at the time the alleged contract was made. . . . The mere claim of a person that he is an officer does not relieve his acts from the character of usurpation, and give him the character of an officer *de facto,* unless he has notoriously performed them for such length of time, with the acquiescence of the public, as to give him the general reputation in the official district of being in that respect what he thus assumes to be.

A *de facto* officer may be one who has been duly elected or appointed but who has failed to meet some legal requirement, such as to take the oath of office or to give bond.[45] Where the oath of office, for example, is wrongly administered to school directors, by one having no authority to administer it, they are, nevertheless, *de facto* officers.[46]

Although one may be ineligible to an office, if he is duly elected or appointed and performs its duties, he will be a *de facto* officer.[47] This principle of law is well illustrated in the case of *Connine* v. *Smith.*[48] A statute of Michigan made justices of the peace ineligible to membership on a board of education and provided further that any votes cast for persons who were justices of the peace should be void. Notwithstanding this inhibition, Guernsey and Damon, justices of the peace, were elected school-board members, took the oath of office, entered upon the performance of their duties, and were recognized for nearly a year without objection. Bonds were voted in the meantime, and later, in an action to enjoin their issuance, it was claimed that Guernsey and Damon had acted without authority. The court held that Guernsey and Damon were *de facto* officers and that their acts were valid:

45. *State* v. *Carroll,* 38 Conn. 449, 9 Am. Rep. 409.

46. *State* v. *Powell,* 101 Iowa 382, 70 N.W. 592; *State* v. *Perkins,* 24 N.J. Law 409.

47. *State* v. *Hart,* 106 Tenn. 269, 61 S.W. 780; *Connine* v. *Smith,* 190 Mich. 631, 157 N.W. 450; *State* v. *Carroll,* 38 Conn. 449, 9 Am. Rep. 409; *Knight* v. *Corporation of Wells,* 1 Lutewyche 188; *Dove* v. *Kirkland,* 92 S.C. 313, 75 S.E. 503; *Rowan* v. *Board of Education,* 125 W. Va. 406, 24 S.E. (2d) 583.

48. 190 Mich. 631, 157 N.W. 450.

In the present case, Guernsey and Damon were justices of the peace. By reason of this fact, they were disqualified to become members of the board of education. Doubtless this fact was overlooked and these men were elected to that position. They filed their bond, and took the oath of office, and acted as such trustees without any question being raised, so far as the record shows, until the present time. We think it must be held that this constituted them *de facto officers*. This being so, it follows, as heretofore said, their acts as such officers cannot be questioned in this collateral proceeding.

And where school trustees were elected and performed the duties of their office, they were held to be *de facto* officers, although it was discovered later that the territory in which they resided at the time of their election was not in the district.[49] Nor is the rule modified, even though the disqualification grows out of a constitutional prohibition. The constitution of South Carolina provided that no person should hold two offices of honor or trust at the same time. A member of a township board of assessors was appointed school trustee and performed the duties of both offices. The court held that he was a *de facto* officer, despite the fact that he had been disqualified at the time of appointment.[50]

An officer may be qualified at the time of induction into office, but may later come to be disqualified. In such a case his acts, if acquiesced in by the public, will be regarded as those of a *de facto* officer. Thus a school trustee may change his residence from the district of which he is an officer and thereby create a vacancy. However, if he continues to act as trustee with the general acquiescence of the public, his acts will not later be set aside as illegal.[51] Where, for example, a teacher was employed by a board of directors, one of the members of which had moved from the district, the contract was binding and could not be repudiated.[52] And where an officer forfeits his office by accepting another incompatible with it but continues to perform the duties of the office forfeited, his acts will be valid as an officer *de facto*.[53]

Where a school officer acts with the acquiescence of the public, he will be regarded as a *de facto* officer, even though his election or appointment is void because of a lack of power in the elective or ap-

49. *Boesch* v. *Byrom*, 37 Tex. Civ. App. 35, 83 S.W. 18.

50. *Dove* v. *Kirkland*, 92 S.C. 313, 75 S.E. 503.

51. *Graham* v. *School District No. 69*, 33 Ore. 263, 54 Pac. 185; *State* v. *Hart*, 106 Tenn. 269, 61 S.W. 780; *Hardwick* v. *State*, 53 Ga. App. 299, 185 S.E. 577.

52. *Graham* v. *School District No. 69*, 33 Ore. 263, 54 Pac. 185.

53. *Privett* v. *Board of Education*, 104 W. Va. 35, 138 S.E. 461.

pointive body or because of some defect or irregularity in the exercise of power.[54] In Kentucky the statutes provided for the appointment of trustees by the city council, but the council had the trustees elected by popular vote. Their election was certified to and approved by the council. They were held to be *de facto* officers.[55] In the case of *De Loach* v. *Newton,* the election to select trustees should have been called by the county board of education; but it was, in fact, called by the ordinary, who was without statutory authority to do so. The county board, however, approved and recognized those who had been elected and issued commissions to them. They were held to be *de facto* officers and entitled to act as such until ousted.[56]

It has been frequently held that one cannot be a *de facto* officer unless he performs the functions of a *de jure* office.[57] There can be no officer, either *de jure* or *de facto,* it is said, if there be no office to fill.[58] This point of view is well expressed by the Supreme Court of the United States in the case of *Norton* v. *Shelby County.*[59] The legislature of Tennessee passed an act creating a board of commissioners for Shelby County. This board subscribed for stock in a railroad company and issued bonds of the county in payment therefor. Later the act creating the board was held unconstitutional; but it was contended, nevertheless, that the acts of the board were binding upon the county as acts of *de facto* officers. This contention the court refused to sustain. It said:

As the act attempting to create the office of commissioner never became a law, the office never came into existence. Some persons pretended that they held the office, but the law never recognized their pretensions. . . .

But the idea of an officer implies the existence of an office which he holds. It would be a misapplication of terms to call one an officer who holds no office, and a public office can exist only by force of law. . . . An unconstitu-

---

54. *Gardner* v. *Goss,* 147 Ark. 178, 227 S.W. 25; *Miller* v. *Feather,* 176 Ky. 268, 195 S.W. 449; *De Loach* v. *Newton,* 134 Ga. 739, 68 S.E. 708, 20 Ann. Cas. 342; *Howard* v. *Burke,* 248 Ill. 224, 93 N.E. 775, 140 Am. St. Rep. 159; *State* v. *Carroll,* 38 Conn. 449, 9 Am. Rep. 409; *Woodcock* v. *Bolster,* 35 Vt. 632.

55. *Miller* v. *Feather,* 176 Ky. 268, 195 S.W. 449.

56. *De Loach* v. *Newton,* 134 Ga. 739, 68 S.E. 708, 20 Ann. Cas. 342.

57. *Norton* v. *Shelby County,* 118 U.S. 425, 6 S. Ct. 1121, 30 L. Ed. 178; *People* v. *Welsh,* 225 Ill. 364, 80 N.E. 313; *Gray* v. *Ingleside Independent School District,* 220 S.W. (Tex.) 350; *Malaley* v. *City of Marysville,* 37 Calif. App. 638, 174 Pac. 367.

58. *Norton* v. *Shelby County,* 118 U.S. 425, 6 S. Ct. 1121, 30 L. Ed. 178; *Smith* v. *Morton Independent School District,* 85 S.W. (2d) (Tex.) 853.

59. 118 U.S. 425, 6 S. Ct. 1121, 30 L. Ed. 178.

tional act is not a law; it confers no rights; it imposes no duties; it affords no protection; it creates no office; it is, in legal contemplation, as inoperative as though it had never been passed.

Similarly, it has been held that where an act creating an independent school district did not go into effect until June, trustees elected in April of the same year were not *de facto* officers.[60] At the time of their election there was no office to fill. The holding of the court in the case of *People* v. *Welsh* was to the same effect. In that case the city council of the city of Rockford was authorized by special charter to appoint a board of school inspectors. A later statute provided that a board of education be appointed by the mayor. The board of inspectors continued to act in seeming ignorance of the fact that the law had been repealed. They were held not to be *de facto* officers, for, said the court, "There can be no *de facto* officer unless there could be a *de jure* officer."[61] Technically and logically, the foregoing rule is sound. That there can be no officer where there is no office is a proposition that cannot be controverted. Nor is it unreasonable to require those dealing with an officer to inform themselves with respect to the existence of the office, for all are supposed to know the law. The rule as broadly stated is, however, subject to an important modification. When an office is created by statutory enactment, but the statute is later declared unconstitutional, the acts of the incumbent of the office performed before the unconstitutionality of the act is judicially determined should be regarded as the acts of a *de facto* officer. The authorities, however, are not agreed upon this point.[62]

The authorities agree in holding that the acts of a *de facto* officer are as binding with respect to third parties and the public as are the acts of an officer *de jure*.[63] And this is true even though an action may

60. *Gray* v. *Ingleside Independent School District*, 220 S.W. (Tex.) 350.

61. *People* v. *Welsh*, 225 Ill. 364, 80 N.E. 313. See also *Griffin* v. *Thomas*, 86 Okla. 70, 206 Pac. 604.

62. *Norton* v. *Shelby County*, 118 U.S. 425, 6 S. Ct. 1121, 30 L. Ed. 178; *Griffin* v. *Thomas*, 86 Okla. 70, 206 Pac. 604; *Ashley* v. *Board of Supervisors*, 60 Fed. 55; *Speer* v. *Board of Commissioners*, 88 Fed. 749; *State* v. *Blossom*, 19 Nev. 312, 10 Pac. 430.

63. *Norton* v. *Shelby County*, 118 U.S. 425, 6 S. Ct. 1121, 30 L. Ed. 178; *Herbst* v. *Held*, 194 Iowa 679, 190 N.W. 153; *State* v. *Foxworthy*, 301 Mo. 376, 256 S.W. 466; *De Loach* v. *Newton*, 134 Ga. 739, 68 S.E. 708, 20 Ann. Cas. 342; *Howard* v. *Burke*, 248 Ill. 224, 93 N.E. 775, 140 Am. St. Rep. 159; *Gardner* v. *Goss*, 147 Ark. 178, 227 S.W. 25; *Barrett* v. *Sayer*, 12 N.Y.S. 170; *School Town of Milford* v. *Zeigler*, 1 Ind. App. 138, 27 N.E. 303; *State* v. *Warwick County*, 124 Ind. 554, 25 N.E. 10, 8 L.R.A. 607; *Graham* v. *School District No. 69*, 33 Ore. 263, 54 Pac. 185.

be pending in the courts to test the right of the officer to the office.[64] The principle which gives validity to acts of *de facto* officers despite irregularities and defects in their appointment or election is based upon considerations of public policy and necessity. For the peace and good order of society, the authority of such officers must be respected until their title has been determined in the mode prescribed by law. As was said in the case of *Buck* v. *Hawley:* "The theory and doctrine of officers *de facto* and the principles sustaining the validity of their acts are that, though wrongfully in office, justice and necessity require that their acts, done within the scope of their authority and duty, be sustained, to the end that the rights and interests of third persons be protected and preserved."[65] Thus, where school trustees continued to act after the expiration of their term of office, a contract entered into by them with a teacher was legally binding upon the town.[66] So, too, a contract made with a teacher by a director who at the time was no longer a resident of the district could not later be repudiated.[67] Where trustees, under the statutes, should have been appointed by the city council but were elected by popular vote, they could not be enjoined from issuing bonds.[68]

There cannot, however, be a *de jure* and a *de facto* officer in possession of an office at the same time.[69] Where each of two boards of education claims to be the legal board, contracts entered into with the board which does not possess title will not be enforced. Since there can be but one legal board, it is the duty of third parties to ascertain which it is. Otherwise, they contract at their own peril. In the case of *White* v. *School District of Archbald,*[70] there was a so-called "Gilroy board" and a "Miller board." The Gilroy board employed a superintendent and teachers, who later brought suit against the district to recover their salaries. The court ruled:

64. *Gardner* v. *Goss,* 147 Ark. 178, 227 S.W. 25; *Brown* v. *Tama County,* 122 Iowa 745, 98 N.W. 562, 101 Am. St. Rep. 296; *Howard* v. *Burke,* 248 Ill. 224, 93 N.E. 775, 140 Am. St. Rep. 159.

65. *Buck* v. *Hawley,* 129 Iowa 406, 150 N.W. 688.

66. *School Town of Milford* v. *Zeigler,* 1 Ind. App. 138, 27 N.E. 303.

67. *Graham* v. *School District No. 69,* 33 Ore. 263, 54 Pac. 185.

68. *Miller* v. *Feather,* 176 Ky. 268, 195 S.W. 449.

69. *Genesee Township* v. *McDonald,* 98 Pa. St. 444; *School Directors* v. *National School Furniture Company,* 53 Ill. App. 254; *School District No. 13* v. *Smith,* 67 Vt. 566, 32 Atl. 484; *White* v. *School District of Archbald,* 8 Atl. (Pa.) 443; *State* v. *Blossom,* 19 Nev. 312, 10 Pac. 430.

70. 8 Atl. (Pa.) 443.

There was no error in the court holding the Miller board to be the duly elected and qualified board of directors. They were acting as such, and performing the duties of their office. Any other *de facto* board could not bind the school-district. It follows that the plaintiff cannot compel the district to fulfill a contract made with the pretended board. When the plaintiff made a contract with it he ran the risk of its being declared to be invalid.

Where, however, a *de jure* officer fails to perform the duties of his office, there may exist a *de facto* officer whose acts are binding with respect to third parties. In Illinois, for example, two high-school boards were elected in the same district. The so-called "Hopewell board" was legally elected and was clearly the *de jure* board, but it failed to take any action pending the outcome of a controversy with the other board, known as the "town-hall board." The latter board, although it had been irregularly elected, issued bonds, employed teachers, and did other things necessary for the maintenance of the school. *Quo warranto* proceedings were brought to determine the authority of the town-hall board to act, and a judgment of ouster was issued against it. Subsequently, action was brought to enjoin the collection of taxes levied by the town-hall board. The court refused to grant the injunction:

The chief question in dispute in this case is whether the so-called town hall high school board was a *de facto* board at the time the resolution to levy such taxes was passed. It is conceded by both sides that on the record in this case the Hopewell board was the *de jure* board on that date. Counsel for appellant insist that the Hopewell board on that date was also the *de facto* board, and that therefore the town hall board could not have been a *de facto* board; that two persons cannot be officers *de facto* in the same office at the same time, as there cannot be two incumbents at once. . . .

The board of education elected at the town hall meeting was the only board of education that assumed or attempted to transact any business for said township high school district up to and after the time of making the levy in this case and the beginning of this proceeding. Its members were not mere volunteers. They were elected at an election held under notice, at which they received a much larger vote than was cast for the Hopewell board of education. They had a certificate of election from the proper officials if a proper notice for the town hall election had been given. We are disposed to hold that under the decisions they had such color of authority to act as would make them *de facto* officers under the circumstances of this case. It must be conceded on this record that there existed *de jure* offices, as to said high school board, to be filled, and that the Hopewell board were the *de jure* officers. While there can not be a *de facto* officer if a *de jure* officer is exercising the functions of the office in question, . . . such was not the case here. The Hopewell school board, after it was organized, did not attempt to act as a board. The so-called town hall board, from the time of their election until they were ousted in the *quo warranto* proceedings, assumed to act as such board of education. They were the only officials that did attempt to so act. They were in actual possession of the office. Their possession was acquiesced in and acknowledged by the public to such an extent that, so far as the public and third persons are concerned, they must be held to be the *de facto* board of education at the time this levy was made.[71]

While the acts of a *de facto* officer are valid with respect to the public and third parties, they are not valid as to himself. Accordingly, it has been held that a *de facto* officer has no legal right to the emoluments of the office. When an officer brings action for the salary of an office, he puts his legal title to it at issue and must prove that he was a *de jure* officer.[72]

RIGHT OF OFFICER TO HOLD OVER AFTER EXPIRATION OF OFFICIAL TERM

It is frequently provided by constitution or by statute that public officers shall hold office for a specified term and until their successors are elected and qualified. When such is the case, there is no question that an officer is entitled to hold over until a qualified successor has been elected or appointed;[73] and for services rendered while holding over, he is entitled to such compensation as the law provides.[74] The rule holds, even though there may be a provision in the constitution limiting the term of office to a given number of years or making the incumbent ineligible for re-election.[75]

Whether or not an officer may hold over until a successor is elected and qualified, in the absence of any constitutional or statutory provision, is a question upon which the authorities are not wholly agreed. The American courts have generally adopted the rule, however, that a public officer may hold over beyond his official term until a successor is elected and qualified, unless such holding over is expressly or

71. *Howard* v. *Burke*, 248 Ill. 224, 93 N.E. 775, 140 Am. St. Rep. 159.

72. *Edington* v. *Board of Commissioners of Martin County*, 105 Ind. App. 156, 13 N.E. (2d) 895; *State ex rel. Worrell* v. *Carr*, 129 Ind. 44, 28 N.E. 88, 13 A.L.R. 88; *Nichols* v. *MacLean*, 101 N.Y. 526, 5 N.E. 347; *Price* v. *United States*, 80 F. Supp. 542.

73. *Tuley* v. *State*, 1 Ind. 500; *State* v. *Harrison*, 113 Ind. 434, 16 N.E. 384; *State* v. *Fabrick*, 16 N.D. 94, 112 N.W. 74; *Jenness* v. *Clark*, 21 N.D. 150, 129 N.W. 357, Ann. Cas. 1913B 675; *State* v. *Tallman*, 24 Wash. 426, 64 Pac. 759; *Haymaker* v. *State*, 22 N.M. 400, 163 Pac. 248, L.R.A. 1917D 210.

74. *State* v. *Fabrick*, 16 N.D. 94, 112 N.W. 74.

75. *Jones* v. *Roberts County*, 27 S.D. 519, 131 N.W. 861, 34 L.R.A. (N.S.) 1170.

impliedly prohibited.[76] Public policy demands that there be someone to perform the duties of the office, for otherwise the public might suffer great inconvenience and hardship. Thus it was said by the Court of Appeals of Maryland: "The office being a trust created for the public good, it follows that a cessation of the benefits derived from it ought not to be sanctioned because of a failure to make an appointment by those whose duty it is to appoint. No such failure should be permitted to cause a temporary extinction of the trust."[77] Moreover, an officer who holds over after the expiration of the term for which he was appointed or elected is entitled to compensation.[78] The constitution of South Dakota provided that no person should be eligible for the office of county superintendent for more than four years in succession. A superintendent had served for four years, but the person elected as his successor was ineligible. Although there was no provision in the constitution or statutes authorizing him to hold over until a successor was elected and qualified, the superintendent continued to perform the duties of the office. Subsequently he brought action to recover his salary for services rendered after the expiration of his term of office. The court stated the rule governing such cases as follows:

The general rule seems to be that, in the absence of a statute or constitutional provision in terms prohibiting an officer from holding over after the expiration of his term, such officer may continue to retain and perform the duties of his office after the expiration of his term until his successor is elected or appointed and qualified. Mr. Mechem on *Public Officers*, § 397, says: "It is usually provided by law that officers elected or appointed for a fixed term shall hold not only for that term but until their successors are elected and qualified. . . . Where, however, no such provision is made the question of the right of the incumbent to hold over is not so clear, but the prevailing opinion in this country seems to be that, unless such holding over be expressly or impliedly prohibited, the incumbent may continue to hold until some one else is elected and qualified to assume the office"—citing numerous authorities. And in 29 Cyc. 1399, it is stated: "One who holds over after the expiration of his term, where no provision is made by statute for holding over, is, although not regarded as in most respects a de jure officer, entitled to the salary appended to the office. . . ."

In the case at bar it was determined by the adjudication of the court

76. *Tuley* v. *State*, 1 Ind. 500; *State* v. *Harrison*, 113 Ind. 434, 16 N.E. 384; *Jones* v. *Roberts County*, 27 S.D. 519, 131 N.W. 861, 34 L.R.A. (N.S.) 1170; *Thomas* v. *Owens*, 4 Md. 189; *People* v. *Oulton*, 28 Calif. 45; *Alcorn* ex rel. *Hoerle*, 127 Conn. 426, 17 Atl. (2d) 514.

77. *Robb, Register, et al.* v. *Carter*, 65 Md. 321, 4 Atl. 282.

78. *Jones* v. *Roberts County*, 27 S.D. 519, 131 N.W. 861, 34 L.R.A. (N.S.) 1170; *Robb, Register, et al.* v. *Carter*, 65 Md. 321, 4 Atl. 282; *Thomas* v. *Owens*, 4 Ind. 189; *People* v. *Oulton*, 28 Calif. 45; *State* v. *Wells*, 8 Nev. 105.

that Agnes E. Gee was ineligible to hold the office, and therefore was not an officer de jure. It necessarily follows, therefore, that the appellant was not only entitled to hold and perform the duties of the office until his successor should be elected or appointed and qualified, but that he was also entitled to the salary and emoluments of the office until the election or appointment of a successor.[79]

RESIGNATION OF SCHOOL OFFICERS

There seems to be some difference of opinion with respect to the right of a public officer to resign his office. In England under the common law a municipal office was regarded as a public duty or burden which everyone elected or appointed to such an office must bear in the interest of good government and of the community. Since anyone appointed to an office must accept and perform its duties, it naturally followed that the office could not be resigned without the consent of the appointing power. Otherwise the public interest might suffer from the want of public servants to enforce the laws.[80] In this country an officer has the right to resign, but his resignation is ineffective until accepted by the proper authority.[81] In this connection it was said by Chief Justice Ruffin, speaking for the Supreme Court of North Carolina:

> An officer may certainly resign; but without acceptance his resignation is nothing and he remains in office. It is not true that an office is held at the will of either party. It is held at the will of both. Generally resignations are accepted; and that has been so much a matter of course, with respect to lucrative offices, as to have grown into a common notion that to resign is a matter of right. But it is otherwise. The public has a right to the services of all the citizens, and may demand them in all civil departments as well as in the military. Hence there are on our statute books general acts to compel men to serve in offices. . . . Every man is obliged, upon a general principle, after entering upon his office to discharge the duties of it while he continues in office, and he cannot lay it down until the public, or those to whom the authority is confided, are satisfied that the office is in a proper state to be left, and the officer discharged.[82]

79. *Jones* v. *Roberts County*, 27 S.D. 519, 131 N.W. 861, 34 L.R.A. (N.S.) 1170.

80. *Edwards* v. *United States*, 103 U.S. 471, 26 L. Ed. 314.

81. *Edwards* v. *United States*, 103 U.S. 471, 26 L. Ed. 314; *State* v. *Ferguson*, 31 N.J. Law 107; *Townsend* v. *School Trustees*, 41 N.J. Law 312; *Clark* v. *Board of Education*, 112 Mich. 656, 71 N.W. 177; *Vaughn* v. *School District No. 31*, 27 Ore. 57, 39 Pac. 393; *State* v. *Board of Education*, 108 Kan. 101; *People* v. *Williams*, 145 Ill. 573, 33 N.E. 849, 24 L.R.A. 492; *Attorney-General* v. *Marston*, 66 N.H. 485, 22 Atl. 560, 13 L.R.A. 670.

82. *Hoke* v. *Henderson*, 15 N.C. 1, 25 Am. Dec. 677.

The foregoing passage from the opinion of Justice Ruffin has been quoted with approval by the Supreme Court of the United States[83] and seems to be supported by reason and the weight of authority. In some jurisdictions, however, it is held that a public officer has the absolute right to resign and that the mere tender of a resignation to the proper officer or body vacates the office without an acceptance of the resignation.[84]

In case the statutes do not designate the authority to whom a resignation should be tendered, the general rule is that a resignation should be made to the appointing power or, in case the office is elective, to the official authorized to call an election for the selection of a successor.[85] It is necessary, of course, that the resignation be addressed to the proper authority as provided for by statute. In Oregon, for example, a statute provided that in case there should be a vacancy in a board of school directors, the remaining members of the board should call a meeting of the district to fill the vacancy. A resignation was tendered to and accepted by the voters of the district. The court held that there had been no resignation[86] because it had not been tendered to and acted upon by the proper authorities.

One cannot resign an office to which he has not been elected or appointed, on the principle that one cannot resign what one does not possess.[87] This may seem too obvious for serious consideration, and yet there are instances where an officer has been required to sign an undated resignation and place it in the hands of the appointing power before the appointment. In Chicago, for example, certain members of the board of education were required to sign an undated resignation before receiving appointment by the mayor. After they had been per-

83. *Edwards* v. *United States,* 103 U.S. 471, 26 L. Ed. 314.

84. *Leech* v. *State,* 78 Ind. 570; *Reiter* v. *State,* 51 Ohio St. 74, 36 N.E. 943, 23 L.R.A. 681; *People* v. *Porter,* 6 Calif. 26; *State* v. *Lincoln,* 4 Neb. 260; *State* v. *Murphy,* 30 Nev. 409, 97 Pac. 391, 18 L.R.A. (N.S.) 1210; *State* v. *Fowler,* 160 Ala. 186, 48 So. 985. NOTE: 23 L.R.A. 682; 16 L.R.A. (N.S.) 1059; 13 Ann. Cas. 874.

85. *Vaughn* v. *School District No. 31,* 27 Ore. 57, 39 Pac. 393; *State* v. *Popejoy,* 165 Ind. 177, 74 N.E. 994, 6 Ann. Cas. 687; *State* v. *Huff,* 172 Ind. 1, 87 N.E. 141; *Hoke* v. *Henderson,* 15 N.C. 1, 25 Am. Dec. 677.

86. *Vaughn* v. *School District No. 31,* 27 Ore. 57, 39 Pac. 393.

87. *People* v. *Reinberg,* 263 Ill. 536, 105 N.E. 715, Ann. Cas. 1915C 343, L.R.A. 1915E 401; *In re Corliss,* 11 R.I. 638, 23 Am. Rep. 538.

forming the duties of the office for some time, the mayor accepted their resignations. In passing upon the right of the board members to continue in office, the Supreme Court of Illinois used the following language:

Respondents admit the resignations were signed by the relators and placed in the hands of the mayor before they were appointed, but it is contended that as the resignations were not recalled by the relators after their appointment but were permitted to remain with the mayor without objection, this was, in effect, a continued invitation or permission to the mayor to accept them at his pleasure, and the mayor having acted upon them, relators can not now be heard to complain. We can not agree with this contention. . . . It was never contemplated that where the law conferred the power to appoint but not to remove, the power to remove might be conferred by requiring a person, before appointment, to place his resignation in the hands of the appointing power. Such a paper is invalid when signed, and lapse of time can not render it valid.[88]

It has even been held that after election to office a person may not resign until duly qualified, and a resignation tendered to and accepted by the proper authority before induction into office is void and does not permit the officer-elect from reconsidering the matter and assuming the duties of the office.[89]

Under certain circumstances public officers have a right to withdraw resignations. In considering the right of an officer to withdraw his resignation, it is necessary to keep in mind the distinction between an unconditional resignation, one to take effect immediately, and a prospective resignation, one to take effect at some future date. The weight of authority, it seems, is to the effect that an unconditional resignation to take immediate effect cannot be withdrawn.[90] In the case of *Pace* v. *People*,[91] a county superintendent of schools addressed and presented a paper to the county court in which it was stated: "The undersigned hereby tenders his resignation as county superintendent of schools." The paper was filed with the county clerk as required. The court held the resignation was unconditional and could not be recalled. Similarly, it was said in the case of *State* v. *Hauss:* "Our conclusion is that where an officer has transmitted his written resignation of an office to, and it

88. *People* v. *Reinberg*, 263 Ill. 536, 105 N.E. 715.

89. *Miller* v. *Sacramento County*, 25 Calif. 94.

90. *State* v. *Hauss*, 43 Ind. 105; *State* v. *Clark*, 3 Nev. 566; *Pace* v. *People*, 50 Ill. 432; *State* v. *Fitts*, 49 Ala. 402; *Board of Directors of Menlo Consolidated School District* v. *Blakesley*, 240 Iowa 910, 36 N.W. (2d) 751.

91. 50 Ill. 432.

has been received by, the officer or authority appointed by law to receive it, to take immediate effect, he cannot withdraw it, and that there is a vacancy to be filled by the proper authority."[92] It has been held, too, that the transmission of a resignation to take immediate effect with the intention that it be delivered to the proper authority makes the resignation complete and effectual, and it cannot be withdrawn.[93] In some states, however, it is held that a resignation to take place at once may be withdrawn before being acted upon.[94] Where an unconditional resignation has become complete and effectual, either by transmission or by acceptance, it cannot be withdrawn. This is true, even though the power authorized to accept it may give consent to the withdrawal.[95]

A different principle of law governs the withdrawal of a prospective resignation, one to take effect at some future date. It is commonly held that such a resignation may be withdrawn at any time before acceptance.[96] Thus it was said in the case of *Biddle* v. *Willard:*

Hence, a prospective resignation may, in point of law, amount but to a notice of intention to resign at a future date, or a proposition to so resign; and for the reason that it is not accompanied by the giving up of the office possession is still retained, and may not necessarily be surrendered until the expiration of the legal term of the office, because the officer may recall his resignation—may withdraw his proposition to resign. He certainly can do this at any time before it is accepted; and after it is accepted, he may make the withdrawal by the consent of the authority accepting, where no rights have intervened.[97]

In Detroit a school-board member tendered his resignation to the mayor, who refused to accept it. Before the date on which the resignation was to take effect, the resignation was withdrawn. The court held that the office had not been vacated.[98]

The right to withdraw a prospective resignation after it has been accepted and before the date of its going into effect, without the con-

92. *State* v. *Hauss,* 43 Ind. 105.

93. *State* v. *Fitts,* 49 Ala. 402.

94. *State* v. *Strickley,* 80 S.C. 64, 61 S.E. 211. NOTE: 16 L.R.A. (N.S.) 1059.

95. *State* v. *Grace,* 113 Tenn. 9, 82 S.W. 485; *Gates* v. *Delaware County,* 12 Iowa 405. NOTE: 16 L.R.A. (N.S.) 1059.

96. *Biddle* v. *Willard,* 10 Ind. 62; *Clark* v. *Board of Education,* 112 Mich. 656; 71 N.W. 177; *State* v. *Boecker,* 56 Mo. 17; *State* v. *Clarke,* 3 Nev. 566.

97. *Biddle* v. *Willard,* 10 Ind. 62.

98. *Clark* v. *Board of Education,* 112 Mich. 656, 71 N.W. 177.

sent of the accepting authority, is a question upon which there is a difference of opinion. In the case of *Saunders* v. *O'Bannon*,[99] a school-board member tendered his resignation to become effective at the end of the school year, and it was accepted. Before the date upon which the resignation was to take effect, he attempted to withdraw it, but failed to get the consent of the board, the body which had accepted it. The court held that the failure to secure the consent of the board was fatal, and the attempted withdrawal was ineffective. In other cases, it has been held, however, that the consent of the accepting authority is not necessary where the withdrawal takes place before the date fixed for the resignation to go into effect.[100]

TEMPORARY REMOVAL FROM DISTRICT AS AFFECTING RIGHT TO OFFICE

A temporary absence from a school district on the part of one of its officers does not render the office vacant. Failure to perform the duties of an office may subject the officer to whatever penalties the law may prescribe, but it does not create a vacancy. The authorities seem to be in accord in holding that nonuser or neglect of duty does not work an abandonment of an office. Before an office will be declared vacant, it must be shown clearly that the officer intended an absolute relinquishment of the office.[101] A temporary removal from the district does not, as a rule, evidence such an intent. In the case of *School District No. 54* v. *Garrison*,[102] for example, one Walky, a school-district director, moved out of the district a mile or two to make a crop and did not move back until four or five months later. While temporarily removed from the district, Walky performed none of the duties of a director, but there was not sufficient evidence to prove that he intended to abandon or relinquish the office. In holding that Walky was still an officer of the district, the court used the following language which seems to be supported by the weight of authority:

99. 27 Ky. Law Rep. 1166, 87 S.W. 1105. Accord, *Board of Education* v. *Rose*, 285 Ky. 217, 147 S.W. (2d) 83, 132 A.L.R. 969; *State* ex rel. *Bolin* v. *Webster Parish School Board*, 150 So. (La.) 446.

100. *State* v. *Beck*, 24 Nev. 92, 49 Pac. 1035; *State* v. *Murphy*, 30 Nev. 409, 97 Pac. 391, 18 L.R.A. (N.S.) 1210.

101. *School District No. 54* v. *Garrison*, 90 Ark. 335, 119 S.W. 275. See also *State* v. *Allen*, 21 Ind. 516; 29 Cyc. 1405.

102. 90 Ark. 335, 119 S.W. 275. Accord, *Hite* v. *Irby*, 103 W. Va. 692, 138 S.E. 329.

The nonuser, or neglect of duty, or removal from the district, in order to amount to a vacation of the office, must be not only total and complete, but of such a circumstance as to make it permanent, and under such circumstances so clearly indicating absolute relinquishment as to preclude all future questions of fact. Otherwise there must be a judicial determination of the vacancy of the office before it can be so declared. . . . A vacancy in office only exists when there is no person authorized by law to perform the duties of the office. There is such authorized person, as long as the duly elected officer does not remove permanently from the district or has not intentionally and absolutely relinquished the office.

Similarly, in the case of *State* v. *Board of Education,*[103] a school-board member was absent from the district while with the army in France. In his absence a successor was elected, but upon his return he claimed title to the office. The court sustained his claim, on the ground that he had not intended to resign the office and his temporary absence did not constitute abandonment.

REMOVAL FROM OFFICE

Where the term of an appointive public officer is fixed by statute, the general rule is that the person or agency appointing the officer may not remove him without cause and without notice and hearing.[104] That is to say, the fixing of the term by statute has the effect of depriving the appointing agency of the power of removal at discretion. The rule seems to be equally well established that where an officer is appointed for an indefinite term, he may be removed by the appointing power arbitrarily and without notice and hearing.[105] In such cases the power of removal is incident to the power of appointment. And where "an appointment is during pleasure, or the power of removal is entirely discretionary, there the will of the appointing or removing power is without control, and no reason can be asked for, nor is it necessary that any cause be assigned."[106]

103. 108 Kan. 101.

104. *State* ex rel. *Rockwell* v. *State Board of Education,* 213 Minn. 184, 6 N.W. (2d) 251, 143 A.L.R. 503.

105. *Potts* v. *Morehouse Parish School Board,* 177 La. 1103, 150 So. 290, 91 A.L.R. 1093; *Oikari* v. *Independent School District,* 170 Minn. 301, 212 N.W. 598; *Ex parte Hennen,* 13 Peters (U.S.) 230; *Field* v. *Commonwealth,* 32 Pa. St. 478; *Coleman* v. *Glenn,* 103 Ga. 458, 30 S.E. 297, 68 Am. St. Rep. 108; *State* v. *Mitchell,* 50 Kan. 289, 33 Pac. 104; *Jacques* v. *Little,* 51 Kan. 300, 33 Pac. 106, 20 L.R.A. 304.

106. *Field* v. *Commonwealth,* 32 Pa. St. 478. Accord, *Johnson* v. *Ginn,* 105 Ky. 654, 49 S.W. 470.

Two cases, one from Kentucky and the other from Minnesota, will serve to illustrate the application of the rule. A Kentucky statute authorized the county superintendent to appoint examiners but prescribed no definite term of office for such appointees. The court ruled that the superintendent could dismiss them at his discretion without notice and hearing. The Minnesota case involved the authority of the state board of education to remove the state commissioner of education. The commissioner had been appointed by the board for a statutory term of six years. The court held the board had authority to remove him for due cause after notice and a hearing: "The only effect by fixing the tenure by statute is that the appointing power cannot, in such case, remove the official arbitrarily, but only for cause after due notice and hearing."[107] The fixing of the term of office could not be taken to mean that the legislature intended to deprive the appointing power of its authority to remove for cause.

In a few cases it has been held that an officer holding for a fixed term, subject to removal for cause, may be removed without notice and a hearing.[108] An Illinois statute authorized the county board to remove the county superintendent of schools "for any palpable violation of law or omission of duty." A county superintendent was removed without notice or hearing, on the ground that on a number of occasions he had been intoxicated when he should have been or was performing his duties. In holding that notice and a hearing were not necessary, the court said: "In cases where the statute is silent as to notice to the party to be removed from office, this court has had frequent occasion to say no notice will be required."[109] But when an officer is thus removed without charges preferred and an opportunity to defend, the courts, no doubt, will, in a proper action, determine whether sufficient grounds existed for removal.

The overwhelming weight of authority, however, is to the effect that an officer who holds office during good behavior or for a fixed term, subject to removal for cause, is entitled to notice of the charges pre-

107. *State* ex rel. *Rockwell* v. *State Board of Education*, 213 Minn. 184, 6 N.W. (2d) 251, 143 A.L.R. 503.

108. *People* v. *Mays*, 117 Ill. 257, 7 N.E. 660; *Hertel* v. *Boismenue*, 229 Ill. 474, 82 N.E. 298. NOTE: 12 Ann. Cas. 997.

109. *People* v. *Mays*, 117 Ill. 257, 7 N.E. 660. See also *Hertel* v. *Boismenue*, 229 Ill. 474, 82 N.E. 298.

ferred against him and an opportunity to be heard.[110] Nor does it matter that the statute conferring authority to remove an officer is silent with respect to his right to a hearing. Thus it was said by the Supreme Court of Kansas:

Nothing in the law warrants the implication that a school-district officer who has been elected and qualified and entered upon his duties may be removed at the will or pleasure of any officer. The statute prescribes the causes for which a removal may be had, and fairly implies that the cause must be shown, and that the party charged with negligence and wrong is entitled to notice and a right to be heard in his own defense. It is well established by the great weight of authority, that where an officer is elected by the people for a definite term, and provision is made for his removal for cause, the power of removal can not, in the absence of the positive mandate of statute, be exercised without notice and hearing. The mere silence of the statute with respect to notice and hearing will not justify the removal of such an officer upon a charge of misconduct and negligence, without knowledge of the charges and an opportunity to explain his conduct and defend his cause and character.[111]

In Pennsylvania a statute authorized the state superintendent of schools to remove any county superintendent "for neglect of duty, incompetency, or immorality." A county superintendent who had been elected for a period of three years was removed without charges having been preferred and without opportunity to defend. In holding that failure to give notice and a hearing was conclusive of the case, the court said: "On this question [right to be heard] the authorities in England and in this country are clear, distinct, and emphatic, and in entire accord with the spirit of our free institutions."[112] The power to remove an officer, it has been said, is essentially a judicial one, except when exercised by the appointing power, and, being such, principles of natural justice demand that no one be condemned unheard. "It is the utmost stretch of arbitrary power and a despotic denial of justice to strip an incumbent of his public office and deprive him of its emoluments and income before its prescribed term has elapsed, except for legal cause, alleged and proved, upon an impartial investigation after due notice."[113]

110. *Coleman* v. *Glenn*, 103 Ga. 458, 30 S.E. 297, 68 Am. St. Rep. 108; *Jacques* v. *Little*, 51 Kan. 300, 33 Pac. 106; *Field* v. *Commonwealth*, 32 Pa. St. 478; *Commissioners of Knox County* v. *Johnson*, 124 Ind. 145, 24 N.E. 148; *Miles* v. *Stevenson*, 80 Md. 358, 30 Atl. 646; *State* v. *Maroney*, 191 Mo. 531, 90 S.W. 141.

111. *Jacques* v. *Little*, 51 Kan. 300, 33 Pac. 106, 20 L.R.A. 304.

112. *Field* v. *Commonwealth*, 32 Pa. St. 478.

113. *Commissioners of Knox County* v. *Johnson*, 124 Ind. 145, 24 N.E. 148.

There seems to be some difference of opinion with respect to the authority of the legislature to provide for the removal of public officers without notice and an opportunity to defend. Some courts hold that such legislation is contrary to the constitutional provision that no person shall be deprived of property without due process of law. In Georgia, for example, a statute provided for the removal of members of a county board of education for certain offenses, but no provision was made for a hearing of changes against them as a condition precedent to removal. The court held the statute to be unconstitutional and void:

It may therefore be considered as settled beyond all doubt or peradventure, that a public officer who has under the law a fixed term of office, and who is removable only for definite and specified causes, can not be removed without notice and a hearing on the charge or charges preferred against him, with an opportunity to make defense. It follows necessarily that a statute providing for the removal from office of such an officer for inefficiency, incapacity, neglect of duty, or other cause, and which makes no provision for giving him notice, or for allowing him to be heard in his defense, is contrary to the constitutional guaranty which declares that no person shall be deprived of life, liberty or property without due process of law.[114]

Other courts, however, take the position that one's right to a public office is not property and that therefore a statute which provides for removal of an officer without notice and a hearing does not violate that clause of the federal constitution which prohibits any state from depriving a citizen of property without due process of law.[115] Thus in New York a statute authorized the commissioner of education to remove any school officer whenever it should be proved to his satisfaction that such officer had been guilty of wilful neglect of duty. The commissioner of education removed a school commissioner without notice or hearing, and the court sustained his action under the statute: "The office which he held as school commissioner was not property in the sense that his removal therefrom without any hearing was a taking without due process of law. . . . The Legislature has the power to authorize an officer or board to remove an appointive or

114. *Coleman* v. *Glenn*, 103 Ga. 458, 30 S.E. 297, 68 Am. St. Rep. 108. See also 6 R.C.L. 461; 22 R.C.L. Sec. 286; *Guy* v. *Nelson*, 202 Ga. 728, 44 S.E. (2d) 775.

115. *Eckloff* v. *District of Columbia*, 135 U.S. 240, 34 L. Ed. 120, 10 S. Ct. 752; *Donahue* v. *County of Will*, 100 Ill. 94; *People* v. *Draper*, 124 N.Y.S. 758; *In matter of Carter*, 141 Calif. 316, 74 Pac. 997.

elective officer without notice or hearing."[116] And in Texas a statute provided for the recall of members of a board of education. In passing upon the constitutionality of the statute, the court said:

The office of member of the board of education of Dallas is not "property" within the meaning of that word as used in the state and federal Constitutions. Offices are created for the public good, at the will of the legislative power, with such privileges and emoluments attached as are believed to be necessary to make them accomplish the purposes designed. . . . The office of member of the board of education of Dallas is property only in the sense that the incumbent is entitled to receive the emoluments of the office so long as he holds the same and until he has ceased to legally occupy the office.[117]

Even though notice and a hearing may be required before an officer can be removed from office, it is not necessary to follow all the rules of procedure of a regularly constituted court of law. A public officer who is being removed from office cannot invoke the constitutional right of trial by jury.[118] It is only necessary to follow the rules of procedure which are essential to the administration of justice. The essential thing is that the officer be notified of the charges against him and be given full and free opportunity to explain and defend his course of action.[119]

The Supreme Court of Minnesota has stated clearly the principle of law governing administrative hearings:

While proceedings by an administrative board in the exercise of its power of removal of an appointee are quasi-judicial in nature, yet such board does not, at any stage of removal proceedings, lose its identity as an administrative body and become a court. The regularity of such proceedings must be considered along with the intrinsic nature of administrative bodies, and the fundamental purposes for which they were created must be kept constantly in mind; they must not be tested by the strict legal rules which prevail in courts of law. . . .
Neither the federal nor the state constitution guarantees any particular form of administrative procedure. . . . All that is required is "adherence to the basic principles that the Legislature shall appropriately determine the standards of administrative action and that in administrative proceedings of a quasi-judicial character the liberty and property of the citizen shall be protected by the rudimentary requirements of fair play." *Morgan* v. *United States*, 304 U.S. 1, 58 Sup. Ct. 773, 82 L. Ed. 1129.[120]

116. *People* v. *Draper*, 124 N.Y.S. 758.

117. *Bonner* v. *Belsterling*, 137 S.W. (Tex.) 1154. Affirmed, 104 Tex. 432, 138 S.W. 571.

118. 26 R.C.L. 574.

119. 26 R.C.L. 572.

120. *State* ex rel. *Rockwell* v. *State Board of Education*, 213 Minn. 184, 6 N.W. (2d) 251, 143 A.L.R. 503.

It has been held that "the right to be heard" before removal includes the right to the assistance of an attorney in making appearance and defense and that witnesses must be sworn.[121]

MODE OF ATTACK UPON TITLE TO OFFICE

School officers are state officers, charged with the performance of important public duties. When such an officer is in active possession of an office, the law assumes that his title is good, and public policy demands that everyone recognize him as the officer he claims to be until such time as he shall be removed by proper proceedings instituted for that purpose.[122] Ordinarily, a school officer who is in possession of an office and actually performing its duties cannot be restrained from acting, upon the ground that his title to the office is defective. No principle of equity jurisprudence seems to be more clearly settled than that courts of equity will not attempt through the issuance of injunctions to determine disputes with respect to title to public office.[123] This is true for a number of reasons. In the first place, it is almost universally held that title to public office is not subject to collateral attack.[124] Moreover, the public has an interest in the performance of the duties of public offices; and should courts of equity interfere by granting injunctions where title is questioned, the public interest might suffer incalculable injury. Finally, from the very earliest times the law has provided a civil remedy to determine the right to title to public office. The remedy is an action in the nature of *quo war-*

121. *State ex rel. Rogers v. Board of Education of Lewis County,* 125 W. Va. 579, 25 S.E. (2d) 537.

122. *State v. Board of Commissioners of Warwick County,* 124 Ind. 554, 25 N.E. 10, 8 L.R.A. 607; *State v. Foxworthy,* 301 Mo. 376, 256 S.W. 466.

123. *Hagner v. Heyberger,* 7 Watts and Sergeant (Pa.) 104, 42 Am. Dec. 220; *Coleman v. Glenn,* 103 Ga. 458, 30 S.E. 297, 68 Am. St. Rep. 108; *Schmohl v. Williams,* 215 Ill. 63, 74 N.E. 75; *School District No. 116 v. Wolf,* 78 Kan. 805, 98 Pac. 237, 20 L.R.A. (N.S.) 358; *Miller v. Feather,* 176 Ky. 268, 195 S.W. 449; 24 R.C.L. 572.

124. *State v. Board of Commissioners of Warwick County,* 124 Ind. 554, 25 N.E. 10, 8 L.R.A. 607; *Brown v. Fouts,* 307 Ill. 430, 138 N.E. 721; *Schmohl v. Williams,* 215 Ill. 63, 74 N.E. 75; *De Loach v. Newton,* 134 Ga. 739, 68 S.E. 708, 20 Ann. Cas. 342; *Hagner v. Heyberger,* 7 Watts and Sergeant (Pa.) 104, 42 Am. Dec. 220; *Connine v. Smith,* 190 Mich. 631, 157 N.W. 450; *State v. Hart,* 106 Tenn. 269, 61 S.W. 780; *Boesch v. Byrom,* 37 Tex. Civ. App. 35, 83 S.W. 18; *Griffin v. Thomas,* 86 Okla. 70, 206 Pac. 604.

ranto.[125] This is an action brought in a court of law in the name of the state by the attorney-general or some other officer representing the state, to determine directly by what right an officer is exercising the duties of an office of which he is in possession.

The early case of *Hagner* v. *Heyberger*[126] well illustrates the principles discussed in the preceding paragraph. Action was brought for a writ of injunction to restrain a school director from exercising the duties of his office. It was claimed he had forfeited his right to the office of school director by accepting another office. Justice Sergeant, speaking for the Supreme Court of Pennsylvania, used the following language:

> On general principles, I should say that a bill for an injunction is not, in its nature, a proceeding to try the question raised here, whether the defendant, by accepting the office of commissioner of the district of Penn, vacated the office of school director. An injunction would seem to be a writ adapted to control and regulate officers in the discharge of their functions, when they are confessedly such, rather than to try their right to hold and exercise their offices. . . .
>
> In addition to this, the difficulty meets us that it would be determining collaterally the right of a person who claims the office by color of title, and exercises it *de facto*, which it has frequently been held cannot be done. To bring his right to a fair trial, you must proceed directly and frame the issue so as to try it; and in the trial of that right by *quo warranto*, the law secures to the defendant the privilege of a trial by jury in relation to contested facts, which would be taken away by the proceeding by injunction.

While it is generally considered that a *quo warranto* proceeding is the proper mode of attack upon the defective title of a public officer, such an action cannot, as a rule, be brought by private individuals who have no interest in the matter different from that of the public in general.[127] As has been said by the Supreme Court of the United States:

125. *Hagner* v. *Heyberger*, 7 Watts and Sergeant (Pa.) 104, 42 Am. Dec. 220; *Metz* v. *Anderson*, 23 Ill. 463, 76 Am. Dec. 704; *State* v. *Ladeen*, 104 Minn. 252, 116 N.W. 486, 16 L.R.A. (N.S.) 1058; *State* v. *Hart*, 106 Tenn. 269, 61 S.W. 780; *Barrett* v. *Tatum*, 66 S.W. (2d) (Tex.) 444; *State* v. *Whitford*, 233 S.W. (2d) (Mo.) 694; *Awalt et al.* v. *Beeville Independent School District*, 226 S.W. (2d) (Tex.) 913; *Board of Education of Martin et al.* v. *Cassell*, 310 Ky. 274, 220 S.W. (2d) 552; *Romine* v. *Black*, 304 Ill. App. 1, 25 N.E. (2d) 404.

126. 7 Watts and Sergeant (Pa.) 104, 42 Am. Dec. 220.

127. *Norton* v. *Shelby County*, 118 U.S. 425, 6 S. Ct. 1121, 30 L. Ed. 178; *Craft* v. *Jackson County*, 5 Kan. 313; *Connine* v. *Smith*, 190 Mich. 631, 157 N.W. 450; *Miller* v. *Feather*, 176 Ky. 268, 195 S.W. 449; *O'Brien* v. *Gassoway*, 125 Okla. 97, 256 Pac. 929.

Offices are created for the benefit of the public, and private parties are not permitted to inquire into the title of persons clothed with the evidence of such offices and in apparent possession of their powers and functions. For the good order and peace of society their authority is to be respected and obeyed until in some regular mode prescribed by law their title is investigated and determined. It is manifest that endless confusion would result if in every proceeding before such officers their title could be called into question.[128]

If the state is satisfied with the title of its officers it is not for private citizens to complain. The redress of public wrong is not committed to the hands of private citizens. It follows, therefore, that it is for the state, acting through its properly constituted officers, the attorney-general or state's attorney, to institute *quo warranto* proceedings. The rule, however, is subject to modification where a private individual is able to show some special interest in the matter distinct from that of the general public. Thus it is frequently held that one who himself claims title to an office may institute *quo warranto* proceedings to oust the incumbent.[129]

128. *Norton* v. *Shelby County,* 118 U.S. 425, 6 S. Ct. 1121, 30 L. Ed. 178.
129. Note: 21 L.R.A. (N.S.) 685.

CHAPTER VII

Legal Authority of Boards of Education

O NE of the most perplexing problems with which school officers have to deal is the determination of the legal authority which they may exercise. Statutes conferring authority on school districts and district officers must necessarily be phrased in somewhat general terms. When laws are framed, it is impossible, of course, to foresee all the specific acts which school boards may legitimately wish to undertake. Even if it were possible to foresee the specific acts, it would be impracticable to make an exhaustive enumeration of them. The result is that boards of education frequently desire to pursue particular policies but are in doubt about their authority to proceed, or, even after they have taken action, the action may be challenged in the courts and declared void. Likewise, those who deal with a board of education are confronted with the necessity of ascertaining the authority of the board to act, for acts *ultra vires,* or in excess of authority, bind neither the district nor its officers. Those who deal with a school district do so at their peril, for all are supposed to know the law. No attempt will be made in this chapter to discuss all the aspects of the authority of boards of education. For example, authority to make rules and regulations governing the conduct of teachers and pupils, to employ and dismiss teachers, to acquire and use school property, and to issue bonds and collect taxes, is treated elsewhere in this volume. The purpose of the paragraphs which follow will be to make clear the general principles which must be applied in determining whether a school board or district is acting within the scope of its authority. A sufficient number of concrete examples will be given to illustrate the practical applications of the principles involved.

School districts are quasi-corporations created by the state in order that it may more effectively administer its educational policies. They perform purely public or governmental duties.[1] Being creatures of

1. *First National Bank of Waldron* v. *Whisenhunt,* 94 Ark. 583, 127 S.W. 968.

145

the state, subject entirely to its will, they may be created or abolished at pleasure, and their powers may be added to or taken away. It follows, therefore, that they possess no inherent powers whatsoever; such authority as they may lawfully exercise is conferred upon them by statute.[2] Moreover, if there is any doubt that a school district has authority to act, the doubt will be resolved against the district and the power denied.[3] One should not, however, confuse exercise of power with exercise of discretion. The courts are slow to recognize the existence of authority in school districts and their officers; but, once authority is recognized as existing, discretion in the exercise of that authority will not be controlled unless such discretion is abused.[4]

The courts are agreed that a school district may exercise the following powers and no others: (1) those expressly granted by statute, (2) those fairly and necessarily implied in the powers expressly granted, and (3) those essential to the accomplishment of the objects of the corporation.[5] The rule governing the exercise of authority by school boards has been well expressed by the Supreme Court of Arkansas:

School directors are authorized not only to exercise the powers that are expressly granted by statute but also such powers as may be fairly implied therefrom and from the duties which are expressly imposed upon them. Such powers will be implied when the exercise thereof is clearly necessary to enable them to carry out and perform the duties legally imposed upon them. School directors are public officers, and the rules respecting their powers are the same as those that are applicable to the powers of public officers generally. "The rule respecting such powers is that, in addition to the powers expressly given by statute to an officer or board of officers, he or it

2. *Olmstead* v. *Carter,* 34 Idaho 276, 200 Pac. 134; *A. H. Andrews Company* v. *Delight Special School District,* 95 Ark. 26, 128 S.W. 361; *First National Bank of Waldron* v. *Whisenhunt,* 94 Ark. 583, 127 S.W. 968; *Honey Creek School Township* v. *Barnes,* 119 Ind. 213, 21 N.E. 747.

3. *Caldwell* v. *Bauer,* 179 Ind. 146, 99 N.E. 117; *Andrew* v. *Stuart Savings Bank,* 204 Iowa 570, 215 N.W. 807.

4. *Dahl* v. *Independent School District No. 2,* 45 S.D. 366, 187 N.W. 638; *Tufts* v. *State,* 119 Ind. 232, 21 N.E. 892; *Gemmell* v. *Fox,* 241 Pa. St. 146, 88 Atl. 426; *Lamb* v. *Redding,* 234 Pa. St. 481, 83 Atl. 362; *Venable* v. *School Committee,* 149 N.C. 120, 62 S.E. 902; *Sarratt* v. *Cash,* 103 S.C. 531, 88 S.E. 256.

5. *McGilvra* v. *Seattle School District No. 1,* 113 Wash. 619, 194 Pac. 817, 12 A.L.R. 913; *Streich* v. *Board of Education,* 34 S.D. 169, 147 N.W. 779, L.R.A. 1915A 632, Ann. Cas. 1917A 760; *Bassett* v. *Fish,* 75 N.Y. 303; *Le Couteulx* v. *City of Buffalo,* 33 N.Y. 333; *Cowles* v. *School District No. 6,* 23 Neb. 655, 37 N.W. 493; *Harris* v. *School District No. 10,* 28 N.H. 58; *State* v. *Milquet,* 180 Wis. 109, 192 N.W. 392; *Board of Education* v. *Scott,* 189 Ky. 225, 224 S.W. 860; *Honaker* v. *Board of Education,* 42 W. Va. 170, 24 S.E. 544, 32 L.R.A. 413.

has by implication such additional powers as are necessary for the due and efficient exercise of the powers expressly granted or which may be fairly implied from the statute granting the express powers."—Throop on Public Officers, § 542.[6]

The real difficulty, of course, is in determining the powers that are implied and the powers that are implicit in the very existence of the school district. It is to be assumed that the very act of creating a school district vests in it those powers indispensable to the accomplishment of its purpose. The question arises, however, as to what is indispensable. The answer to this question depends on the purposes which the school undertakes to accomplish. The school is a social institution, subject to change in purpose and function as society itself changes or as ideals and practices of education change. As the school enlarges its program, powers which were formerly unnecessary become absolutely indispensable. These are facts which the courts should, and do, take cognizance of; and yet there is danger of going too far in holding that school districts have implied powers. It is not for the courts to usurp the legislative function. If an expanded and enriched educational program demands more corporate powers, it is the duty of the legislature to bestow them. Thus it has been held that statutory authority to acquire "school lots" does not authorize a board of education to issue bonds for the purchase of a farm to be used as a laboratory in connection with instruction in agriculture;[7] that a county board of education had no implied power to pay the expenses of a county superintendent to a meeting of the National Education Association;[8] that a school board may not lease unused school property for a term as long as twenty years.[9] On the other hand, it has been held that a county board of education has the implied power to purchase membership for the board in the state school-board association.[10]

In each state, boards of education in the various classes of school districts are vested with certain fairly specifically enumerated powers.

6. *A. H. Andrews Company* v. *Delight Special School District*, 95 Ark. 26, 128 S.W. 361.

7. *Board of Supervisors of Merced County* v. *Cothran*, 84 Calif. App. (2d) 679, 191 Pac. (2d) 506.

8. *Dodge* v. *Kaiser*, 243 Wis. 551, 11 N.W. (2d) 348.

9. *Madachy* v. *Huntington Horse Show Association*, 119 W. Va. 54, 192 S.E. 128, 111 A.L.R. 1046.

10. *Schuerman* v. *State Board of Education*, 284 Ky. 556, 145 S.W. (2d) 42.

Frequently this list of enumerated powers is followed by a broader grant of power, expressed in such terms as "make all necessary provisions for the maintenance of an efficient school system," or "take such action as is necessary to promote the best interest of the schools." It is a well-established principle of statutory interpretation, known as the rule *ejusdem generis,* that the general grant of power is limited by the preceding list of specifically enumerated powers; that is, the general grant is not to be interpreted as though it stood alone; it must be taken to confer powers of the same general kind as those included in the specific enumeration. The rule has been well expressed by the Court of Appeals of Kentucky:

> Where, in a statute, general words follow an enumeration or designation of particular or specific subjects, such general words are not to be construed ordinarily in their broadest sense, but will be presumed to be restricted by the particular designations, and to apply to and include only persons or things of the same general kind or class as those specifically mentioned, unless a contrary purpose is clearly manifested.
> They are deemed to have been used not to the wide extent which they might bear if standing alone, but as related to words of more definite and particular meanings, with which they are associated.[11]

An application of the rule of *ejusdem generis* and also an illustration of the rather strict construction that courts commonly give to the implied powers of school boards are afforded by an Ohio case. The court was faced with two questions: (1) Did the Board of Education of Cleveland have authority to furnish pupils susceptible to tuberculosis free lunches and uniform sleeping garments to be used in open-air classes; and (2) did the board have the power to provide lunches without cost, at its cafeterias in its junior and senior high schools, to pupils whose parents, upon investigation, were found to be unable to pay for the lunches? The court answered both questions in the negative, even though the board, after certain specific powers had been enumerated, was authorized "to make all other necessary provisions for the schools under its control" and "to make all other provisions necessary for the convenience and prosperity of the schools." These broad grants of power, said the court, had to be interpreted in the light of the specifically enumerated grants of power, none of which conferred authority to furnish sleeping garments or free lunches.[12]

11. *Vansant v. Commonwealth,* 189 Ky. 1, 224, S.W. 367.

12. *Board of Education of City School District of Cleveland v. Ferguson,* 39 N.E. (2d) (Ohio) 196.

AUTHORITY TO MAINTAIN JUNIOR COLLEGES

There seems to be little, if any, reason to doubt the authority of the legislature to authorize local school boards to maintain junior colleges. Such is the case because the legislature, subject to constitutional restrictions, has plenary power with respect to education. The Supreme Court of Louisiana held constitutional an act which authorized the maintenance of junior colleges by parish boards of education. The act was attacked on the ground that it violated a constitutional provision requiring higher educational institutions to be under the administrative control of the state board of education. It was said by the court:

"The higher institutions of learning" . . . are in an entirely different category from the "Junior Colleges" that may be established . . . as these colleges, so called, can have no legal existence or status whatever, except in connection with a state high school, are purely local institutions, are maintained by local taxation, and are created for the sole purpose of supplementing the course of studies prescribed in the high schools of the state. A "Junior College" is permitted . . . merely to supply the place of a super-high school, in the carrying out by the Legislature of the constitutional mandate of co-ordination of the elementary and secondary schools, and the higher educational institutions of the state, so as to lead to the standard of higher education. Necessarily, these "Junior Colleges" fall within the classification of secondary schools, and occupy the same legal status as a state high school in matters of special taxes to be voted at special elections for the housing and maintenance of these institutions.[13]

There is some uncertainty with respect to the authority of a local school board to maintain a junior college where no such authority has been conferred by specific statutory enactment. In a number of states, school boards, acting on the assumption that the junior college is an integral part of the common-school system, have established junior colleges without specific statutory authority to do so. In a case which came before the Supreme Court of North Carolina, the court held that the board of commissioners of the city of Asheville "had the power . . . in the exercise of their discretion to establish, maintain and operate the junior college, as a part of an adequate and sufficient system of public schools for the City of Asheville."[14] In both Kentucky[15] and Mississippi,[16] however, the court has held that a junior college is not a part of the "common-school" system.

13. *McHenry* v. *Ouachita Parish School Board,* 169 La. 646, 125 So. 841.

14. *Zimmerman* v. *Board of Education,* 199 N.C. 259, 154 S.E. 397.

15. *Pollitt* v. *Lewis,* 269 Ky. 680, 108 S.W. (2d) 671, 113 A.L.R. 691.

16. *Wyatt* v. *Harrison, etc.,* 177 Miss. 13, 170 So. 526.

AUTHORITY TO BUILD TEACHERAGES AND
HOMES FOR SUPERINTENDENTS

The courts are divided with respect to the implied power of a school board to build residences for their teaching personnel. According to one line of decisions, authority to erect and purchase schoolhouses does not include authority to build teacherages.[17] In North Carolina the statutes authorized counties to issue bonds "for the erection of school houses" and for their "necessary equipment." The court held that this did not confer authority to erect and maintain teacherages in connection with rural consolidated schools.[18] Similarly, in Nebraska the court held a contract to purchase a house for the superintendent void, and the vendor was under obligation to restore to the district the consideration received.[19]

In other jurisdictions, however, it has been held that authority to build a "schoolhouse" or "school buildings" confers authority to build teacherages.[20] And in South Carolina a school district has been held to have the implied authority to build a home for the superintendent of grounds. In this case the schoolhouse was located outside the corporate limits, had no police protection, and was subject to constant trespass.[21]

AUTHORITY TO PROVIDE ATHLETIC FACILITIES AND
MAKE PROFITS FROM ATHLETIC ACTIVITIES

In a number of instances the courts have been called upon to decide whether boards of education, under their general power to erect school buildings, are authorized to purchase and maintain gymnasiums, athletic fields, stadiums, bleachers, and the like. The courts commonly hold that a board of education has such implied author-

17. *Denny* v. *Mecklenburg County*, 211 N.C. 558, 191 S.E. 26; *Hansen* v. *Lee*, 119 Wash. 691, 206 Pac. 927; *Fulk* v. *School District No. 8*, 155 Neb. 630, 53 N.W. (2d) 56.

18. *Denny* v. *Mecklenburg County*, 211 N.C. 558, 191 S.E. 26.

19. *Fulk* v. *School District No. 8*, 155 Neb. 630, 53 N.W. (2d) 56.

20. *Adams* v. *Miles*, 41 S.W. (2d) (Tex.) 21; *McNair* v. *School District*, 87 Mont. 423, 288 Pac. 188, 69 A.L.R. 866; *Alexander* v. *Phillips*, 31 Ariz. 503, 254 Pac. 1056, 52 A.L.R. 244; *Taylor* v. *Board of Public Instruction of Lafayette County*, 157 Fla. 422, 26 So. (2d) 180.

21. *Craig* v. *Bell*, 211 S.C. 473, 46 S.E. (2d) 52.

ity.[22] The reasoning of the Supreme Court of Arkansas is typical: "We cannot agree with appellant that the words 'school buildings' as used in [the statutes] . . . should be restricted to such buildings as are used exclusively for the mental training or for the teaching of such subjects as are ordinarily taught in the public schools. We think it is just as important that children should be developed physically and morally as it is that they should be developed mentally."[23]

It has been held, too, that a school district may make profits in the conduct of its athletic activities by the sale of tickets and concessions. Thus in a Texas case a school board granted to a broadcasting company exclusive rights to broadcast play-by-play accounts of all football games. Authority to do this was challenged by another broadcasting company. In sustaining the right of the board to make this exclusive concession, the court said: "In our opinion, even though the District is a quasi-municipal corporation, it has a right to seek to make a profit out of the games played on its premises; the profit, of course, to go for the benefit of the District. We can see no good reason why it should not have the same freedom of action as a private person or corporation putting on the games. The District owns the field and the grandstand."[24]

It has been held, too, that a school board has implied authority to provide athletic supplies to school pupils. The court reasoned that physical education is as much a part of the curriculum as are subjects of intellectual study and that athletic supplies are as necessary for school use as maps, globes, and similar objects. The court pointed out, however, that "the extent to which athletic paraphernalia should be purchased for use merely by school teams playing in competitive sports, is a matter to be answered by school boards in the exercise of a cautious discretion, with special reference to the proportionate numbers who will receive benefit of such supplies."[25]

22. *Young* v. *Linwood School District No. 17*, 193 Ark. 82; *Lowden* v. *Jefferson County Excise Board*, 190 Okla. 276, 122 Pac. (2d) 991; *Nicholas* v. *Calhoun*, 204 Miss. 291, 37 So. (2d) 313; *Moyer* v. *Board of Education of School District No. 186*, 391 Ill. 156, 62 N.E. (2d) 802; *People* ex rel. *Goodman* v. *University of Illinois Foundation*, 388 Ill. 363, 58 N.E. (2d) 33; *Juntila* v. *Everett School District No. 24*, 178 Wash. 637, 35 Pac. (2d) 78; *McNair* v. *School District*, 87 Mont. 423, 288 Pac. 188, 69 A.L.R. 866.

23. *Young* v. *Linwood*, 193 Ark. 82, 97 S.W. (2d) 627.

24. *Southwestern Broadcasting Company* v. *Oil Center Broadcasting Company*, 210 S.W. (2d) (Tex.) 230.

25. *Galloway* v. *School District of Borough of Prospect Park*, 331 Pa. 48, 200 Atl. 99.

AUTHORITY OF SCHOOL BOARD WITH RESPECT

TO HEALTH, RECREATION, AND PHYSICAL

EDUCATION FACILITIES

Authority to require physical examination of pupils.—The implied authority of boards of education to require physical examination of pupils is well illustrated in the case of *Streich* v. *Board of Education.*[26] The Board of Education of the city of Aberdeen, South Dakota, required each pupil at the beginning of each year to furnish what was known as a "Physical Record Card." One side of the card was to be filled out by the teacher; the other by a licensed physician. It was optional with parents whether the examination be made by a physician of their own choice and at their own expense or by the school physician at the expense of the school district. The card to be filled out by the physician called for such information as history of contagious diseases and condition of heart, lungs, throat, teeth, and mouth. Two pupils whose parents were members of the Christian Science church refused to provide the health cards and were denied admission to the schools of the city. A writ of mandamus was sought to compel their admission. It was contended that the board had no authority to require a physical examination as a condition of admission to school, because no such authority had been expressly conferred by statute; nor could it be implied. Moreover, it was contended that the enforcement of the rule would violate those provisions of the constitution which require a uniform school system, free and open to all; that the statutes had fixed but two qualifications for admission to school—age and residence in the district; that the police power with respect to health regulations had been conferred exclusively on the board of health; and that the rule in question "compelled the plaintiff's children either to submit to a trespass upon their most private and social rights or to yield up their right to attend the public schools." In holding that the board had the implied or inherent power to enforce the rule in question, the court rendered a decision which undoubtedly expresses correct principles of law.

Authority to employ nurses, dentists, and physicians.—A number of cases have come into the courts involving the authority of boards of education to spend school funds for the services of nurses, dentists, and physicians. The courts are in accord in holding that, even in the

26. 34 S.D. 169, 147 N.W. 779, L.R.A. 1915A 632, Ann. Cas. 1917A 760.

absence of any specific statutory grant of authority, funds may be spent for such professional services, provided that the duties performed are merely inspectorial and diagnostic.[27] In the case of *Hallett v. Post Printing & Publishing Company*,[28] an injunction was sought to restrain the Board of Education of Denver from issuing warrants for the maintenance of the school health department, in which it was employing physicians, dentists, and nurses. It was contended that the board had exceeded its lawful authority because there was no statute authorizing the expenditure of public funds for such a purpose. The court refused to issue the injunction, on the ground that the board was exercising powers necessarily implied. The court reasoned that the power of the board to exclude pupils not meeting reasonable health requirements was undoubted. Furthermore, the power to exclude such pupils implied authority to make requirements and to determine whether the requirements had been met. In both cases expert advice was necessary. Moreover, the board had the implied power to provide for the physical education of children. To provide such education, it was necessary to employ suitable persons to determine what was proper and beneficial for each pupil and to prescribe suitable exercises to overcome defects. The court was careful to point out, however, that the duties performed by the dentists and the physicians employed by the board "should not include medical or surgical treatment for disease. That would be to make infirmaries or hospitals of the schools."

To the same effect is the decision in the case of *State v. Brown*.[29] The Board of Education of Minneapolis employed a nurse for one month to make an inspection of the physical condition of the pupils in certain schools. The comptroller of the city refused to countersign the warrants for her salary, on the ground that the board had no authority to employ her. The court held that the board exercised an implied power:

The purpose of the corporaton is to maintain efficient, free public schools within the city of Minneapolis and, unless expressly restricted, necessarily possesses the power to employ such persons as are required to accomplish that purpose. Education of a child means much more than merely com-

27. *State v. Brown*, 112 Minn. 370, 128 N.W. 294; *Hallet v. Post Printing & Publishing Company*, 68 Colo. 573, 192 Pac. 658, 12 A.L.R. 919; *City of Dallas v. Mosely*, 286 S.W. (Tex.) 497.

28. 68 Colo. 573, 192 Pac. 658, 12 A.L.R. 919.

29. 112 Min. 370, 128 N.W. 294.

municating to it the content of textbooks. But, even if the term were to be so limited, some discretion must be used by the teacher in determining the amount of study each child is capable of. The physical and mental powers of the individual are so interdependent that no system of education, although designed solely to develop mentality, would be complete which ignored bodily health. And this is peculiarly true of children, whose immaturity renders their mental efforts largely dependent upon physical conditions. It seems that the school authorities and teachers coming directly in contact with the children should have an accurate knowledge of each child's physical condition for the benefit of the individual child, for the protecton of the other children with reference to communicable diseases and conditions, and to permit an intelligent grading of the pupils.

These and other considerations convinced the court that the board had the implied authority to employ the nurse for purposes of inspection.

Authority to maintain a clinic.—There seems to be but one case on record dealing with the implied authority of school boards to maintain clinics for the medical, surgical, and dental treatment of pupils. In 1914 the Board of Education of Seattle appointed a school medical inspector. At that time the city was maintaining a general clinic at the police station, where the inspector discovered certain school children were being brought into contact with criminals and other undesirable citizens. He explained the situation to a number of physicians and dentists, who volunteered to furnish their services free in the maintenance of a clinic for the treatment of pupils whose parents were unable to provide adequate medical attention for them. The board of education equipped a building to be used for the purpose. Small fees were charged those who were able to pay, and for a number of years the clinic was self-supporting. Finally, however, it became necessary to employ two full-time dentists, and there was an annual deficit of approximately two thousand dollars. Certain taxpayers sought to have the board enjoined from spending school funds for the maintenance of the clinic. In granting the injunction, the court pointed out that a school district possesses only such powers as are delegated in express words, such powers as may be implied from the powers expressly granted, or such powers as are essential for the accomplishment of the purposes for which the district was created. The court was unable to find in the statutes any express authority for the maintenance of a school clinic. The only authority vested in the board with respect to health was authority to cause inspection of buildings and premises with a view to making them sanitary and healthful and to cause inspection of persons with a view to excluding from school premises all persons infected with contagious diseases. Authority to maintain the clinic at public expense could not be implied; nor was it implicit in the existence of the district.

The rendering of medical, surgical, and dental services to pupils, however, is, and always has been, we think, so foreign to the powers to be exercised by a school district or its officers that such power cannot be held to exist in the absence of express legislative language so providing. . . .

There is much in the argument of counsel for the school officers which might be considered as lending support to the view that such power ought to be possessed by the school district and its officers, and it is probable that counsel has many well-meaning people upon his side of that question. The Legislature may give heed to such arguments, but the courts cannot do so.[30]

Authority to establish and maintain camps for school pupils.—Relatively few cases have come into the courts involving the authority of boards of education to purchase camp sites, build camps, and provide personnel for their operation. It seems clear, however, that the legislature may authorize expenditures for such purposes. In Kentucky the statutes provided that any school district might join with a city or county in "providing and conducting public playgrounds and recreational centers." The Jefferson County Board of Education spent $40,000 in co-operation with the county in providing a recreational center for school children. The statute authorizing the expenditure was attacked on the ground that it violated a constitutional requirement that taxes collected for educational purposes, common-school purposes, and the maintenance of the common-school system be applied to these and to no other purposes. In sustaining the statute, the court insisted that the terms "education," "common-school purpose," and the "common-school system" embraced recreational training. At considerable length, the court discussed the broadening meaning of these terms and concluded: "It is so well established that physical and moral training is basically important that it would be difficult to conclude that public moneys may not be expended for the purpose, and in the manner and under the circumstances here shown."[31]

In a later case the same court was called upon to decide whether, under this same statute, a county board of education had authority

30. *McGilvra* v. *Seattle School District No. 1,* 113 Wash. 619, 194 Pac. 817, 12 A.L.R. 913.

31. *Dodge* v. *Jefferson County Board of Education,* 298 Ky. 1, 181 S.W. (2d) 406.

to purchase a camp site, in another county, to be used as a recreation center for the school children and 4H club members of the county. The court held that a county board, acting *alone*, had no such implied powers. It said:

Admitting the wide scope of general powers contained in this health and welfare statute, which surely may be used as a mace of legal authority by a school board in doing many different things in the administration of its affairs for the benefit of the schools, yet it should be remembered that it is sometimes proper to inquire through court action into the arbitrariness of a particular exercise of those vested powers, however broad and untrammeled they may appear to be on their face. . . .

Everyone ought to encourage wholesome recreation for boys and girls. . . . Therefore, we yearn for an outpouring of great power into just such a program. However, it is equally appropriate to observe that the disbursement of taxpayers' dollars for the various uses of public affairs is always a very serious business, whether dollars are expended by municipalities to light the public streets or by school boards to light the individual minds of public school pupils. However laudable and worthy it might be for a Western Kentucky school board to go a few hundred miles to the east and there purchase an Eastern Kentucky mountain retreat for the health and welfare of some of its underprivileged or tubercular pupils, including its school children, yet such an undertaking would have to be considered in the nature of an arbitrary administration of public funds and therefore illegal.[32]

In a case decided by the Supreme Court of Florida, almost the identical issue was involved as in the Kentucky case. The Florida court, however, held that a county board of education had implied power to purchase a camp site in another county. In the opinion of the court:

An adequate public school system is no longer limited to exploiting the three R's and acquiring such facilities as are necessary to do so. It contemplates the development of mental, manual, and other skills that may not be derived from academic training. It is predicated on the premise that a personality quotient is just as important as an intelligence quotient and that training the character and the emotions is just as important as training the mind if the product is to be a well balanced citizen.

Eminent psychologists proclaim the doctrine that competitive sports contribute more to one's personality quotient and abilty to work with people than any other school activity.[33]

Authority to provide first aid to injured pupils.—A board of education, it has been held, has the implied authority to provide first aid for an injured pupil but no authority to pay the attending physician

32. *Wilson* v. *Graves County Board of Education*, 307 Ky. 203, 210 S.W. (2d) 350.

33. *In re Board of Public Instruction of Alachua County*, 35 So. (2d) (Fla.) 579.

after the emergency is over. In West Virginia, a pupil was severely burned at school. The superintendent immediately called a physician. At the request of the school board the physician attended the pupil for a period of several months. The board approved his bill for $380, but the county superintendent refused to countersign the order. In refusing to mandate the superintendent to sign, the court said: "*Ex necessitate rei*, boards of education must be deemed to have implied authority to assume responsibility for first aid medical or surgical services rendered to a pupil who is injured or becomes ill while engaged in school activities. Otherwise, there might be serious delay in a pupil's receiving the attention which he should have. But we are unable to justify any further extension of such implied authority."[34]

It has been held, too, that a board of education has the implied power to operate nonprofit cafeterias as a means of improving the health of pupils and that this was a governmental function.[35]

AUTHORITY TO PERMIT PRACTICE TEACHING IN THE PUBLIC SCHOOLS

Frequently teacher-college authorities find it desirable to make arrangements whereby the public schools may be used as model or practice schools for the training of prospective teachers. The legal authority of a local school board to co-operate in such an enterprise is obviously a matter of no little importance. There is not a great deal of judicial authority on the subject, but such as there is leads to the following conclusions.

Where a board of education is vested by statute with broad powers and discretion in the conduct and management of the public schools, it may, as an exercise of its authority to determine the course of study, maintain a model school for the use of teacher-college students. Students doing practice teaching in the public schools are not required to have teachers' certificates. Employment of practice teachers is merely a variation in the mode of instruction, a matter which falls wholly within the discretion of the school authorities. Control over the practice-school facilities for teacher-college students must be exercised exclusively by the school board. The law vests school boards with authority and discretion in the management and control of the public schools, and they may not divest themselves of this authority or dele-

34. *Jarrett* v. *Goodall*, 113 W. Va. 478, 168 S.E. 763.
35. *Hoskins* v. *Commissioner of Internal Revenue*, 84 F. (2d) (Tex.) 627.

gate it to others. It follows, therefore, that any contract or agreement with teacher-college authorities whereby these authorities are given the right to select the teachers of the training school, to determine the course or mode of instruction, or to decide the time the school term shall begin or end is void and without effect. It is, however, permissible for a local school board and a teachers college to pay jointly the salaries of those teachers in charge of the rooms in which practice teaching is done, provided that the local board in no way limits its discretion to employ such teachers as it may see fit.[36]

It is uniformly held that teachers colleges do not constitute a part of the common-school system.[37] It follows, therefore, that neither a local school board nor the legislature itself can apply funds which the constitution provides shall be devoted to the use of common schools to the maintenance of a model school in connection with a teacher-training institution.[38] The state of Washington, for example, passed an act authorizing the establishment of a model school in each of the teachers colleges of the state. The act made it the duty of the local school board of each district in which a teachers college was located to assign to the model school as many pupils as the authorities of that school might require. The principal of the model school had authority to reject such pupils as he deemed undesirable because of incorrigibility or mental defects. Finally, the act made it the duty of the state superintendent of public instruction to apportion to the support of the model school such part of the common-school funds as the local district would have been entitled to, had the children attending the model school attended the public school. Action was brought to restrain the superintendent from apportioning to the model schools any of the funds available for the support of the common schools. The court granted the injunction for the following reasons:

36. See *Spedden v. Board of Education*, 74 W. Va. 181, 81 S.E. 724, 52 L.R.A. (N.S.) 163; *Lindblad v. Board of Education*, 221 Ill. 261, 77 N.E. 450; *Clay v. Independent School District of Cedar Falls*, 187 Iowa 89, 174 N.W. 47.

37. *State Female Normal School v. Auditors*, 79 Va. 233; *People v. Crissey*, 45 Hun. (N.Y.) 19; *Gordon v. Cornes*, 47 N.Y. 608; *Board of Regents v. Painter*, 102 Mo. 464, 10 L.R.A. 493; *Dickinson v. Edmondson*, 120 Ark. 80, 178 S.W. 930, Ann. Cas. 1917C 913; *School District No. 20 v. Bryan*, 51 Wash. 498, 99 Pac. 28, 20 L.R.A. (N.S.) 1033; *State v. Preston*, 79 Wash. 286, 140 Pac. 350; *Turner v. City of Hattiesburg*, 98 Miss. 337, 53 So. 681.

38. *State v. Preston*, 79 Wash. 286, 140 Pac. 350; *School District No. 20 v. Bryan*, 51 Wash. 498, 99 Pac. 28, 20 L.R.A. (N.S.) 1033.

The principal of the normal school, however accomplished, is not an officer recognized by the law creating the common-school system and is in no way answerable to those who are charged with the duty of executing it. The teachers under his charge may be devoted in their pursuit of the art of teaching, but they are not teachers within the meaning of the law, which has undertaken to insure that public-school children shall be taught only by those who have met (not seeking to attain) a certain standard of proficiency. In other words, the argument of counsel emphasizes the fact that in its operation the act of 1907 would break the uniformity of the common-school system. To summarize, a common school, within the meaning of our constitution, is one that is common to all children of proper age and capacity, free, and subject to, and under the control of, the qualified voters of the school district. The complete control of the schools is a most important feature, for it carries with it the right of the voters, through their chosen agents, to select qualified teachers, with power to discharge them if they are incompetent. Under the system proposed, instead of the voters employing a teacher with proper vouchers of worthiness, they are made recruiting officers to meet a draft for material that the apprentice may be employed. . . . Nor can the legislature by any contrivance, designation, or definition make a common school a normal school, or a normal school a common school, within the meaning of the constitution.[39]

AUTHORITY TO EMPLOY LEGAL COUNSEL

Many states have statutes specifically authorizing school boards to employ attorneys; but, even in the absence of statutory grant of such authority, a board may, as a general rule, employ counsel to represent the school district whenever its legal rights and interests are involved.[40] Power to employ counsel is implied from the power to own property, to sue and be sued, and to enter into and enforce contractual obligations. In the case of *Arrington* v. *Jones*,[41] the court expressed the rule as follows:

There is no authority expressly given to trustees to employ an attorney to bring a suit in behalf of trustees against a teacher to cancel a teaching contract. But, having the power, as trustees have by the terms of the statute, to contract and to sue and be sued in the courts, the authority on the part of

39. *School District No. 20* v. *Bryan,* 51 Wash. 498, 99 Pac. 28, 20 L.R.A. (N.S.) 1033.

40. *Board of Education* v. *Thurman,* 247 Pac. (Okla.) 996; *Arrington* v. *Jones,* 191 S.W. (Tex.) 361; *Fleischmann* v. *Graves,* 235 N.Y. 84, 138 N.E. 745; *Kingsbury* v. *Centre School District in Quincy,* 53 Mass. (12 Metc.) 99; *State* v. *Aven,* 70 Ark. 291, 67 S.W. 752; *Rural Independent School District of Eagle* v. *Daly,* 201 Iowa 286, 207 N.W. 124; *Ward* v. *San Diego School District,* 265 Pac. (Calif.) 821; *Chrestman* v. *Tompkins,* 5 S.W. (2d) (Tex.) 257; *Wagner* v. *School District No. 58,* 138 Kan. 428, 26 Pac. (2d) 588; *Donna Independent School District* v. *Sanders,* 57 S.W. (2d) (Tex.) 857; *Stewart* v. *Newton Independent School District,* 134 S.W. (2d) (Tex.) 429.

41. 191 S.W. (Tex.) 361.

trustees to employ an attorney to institute and prosecute an action in their behalf would exist as a necessary incident of the powers to contract and to sue and to manage and control the affairs and interests of the public school.

It has been held, too, that a statute authorizing a school board to employ a regular attorney at an annual salary not exceeding a stipulated sum does not preclude the employment of additional attorneys.[42] The statute, the court pointed out, did not provide that the school attorney should have control of all litigation in which the school district might be interested. The statute was declaratory and not restrictive in direct terms or by fair implication of the language used.

The authority of a school district to employ counsel to represent it rests, of course, on the assumption that some legitimate right or interest of the district is involved. A school district cannot employ counsel to accomplish an unlawful act or to defend an action against private individuals. A school board in Texas, for example, employed counsel to defeat a bill pending before the state legislature. The bill, it was alleged, "would . . . deprive the district of its existing liability to raise large amounts of funds by taxation necessary to a successful continuance of the public school in the district." The attorney employed to defeat the bill did not seek to accomplish his purpose by appearing before any legislative committee but addressed letters to individual members of the legislature. The court held the contract between the district and the attorney void as *ultra vires* and as against public policy.[43] Neither private individuals nor a school district may legally contract to influence legislation through personal solicitation of individual members of the legislature. This is a principle of law on which the courts seem to be in perfect accord.[44] Contracts to procure legislation, says the Supreme Court of the United States, have been uniformly declared invalid.

The decisions have not turned upon the question whether improper influences were contemplated or used but upon the corrupting tendency of the agreements. . . . It is sufficient to observe, generally, that all agreements for pecuniary considerations to control the business operations of the government, or the regular administration of justice, or the appointments to public

42. *State* v. *Melcher*, 87 Neb. 359, 127 N.W. 241.

43. *Graves and Houtchens* v. *Diamond Hill Independent School District*, 243 S.W. (Tex.) 638.

44. *Tool Company* v. *Norris*, 2 Wall. (U.S.) 45, 17 L. Ed. 868; *Lyon* v. *Mitchell*, 36 N.Y. 235, 93 Am. Dec. 502; *Chippewa Valley and Superior Railway Company* v. *Chicago, St. Paul, Minneapolis, and Omaha Railway Company*, 75 Wis. 224, 44 N.W. 17, 6 L.R.A. 601.

offices, or the ordinary course of legislation, are void as against public policy without reference to the question whether improper means are contemplated or used in their execution. The law looks to the general tendency of such agreements; and it closes the door to temptation by refusing them recognition in any of the courts of the country.[45]

It is entirely permissible, however, for a school board to employ an attorney to represent it before a legislative committee. Such a committee exists in part for the purpose of hearing the arguments of interested parties. A school district in Georgia, for example, contracted with an attorney to appear before a committee of the legislature to secure the repeal of a bill abolishing the district. The court held the contract valid.[46]

A school board, moreover, cannot employ an attorney to enforce the rights of private individuals even though those rights may have grown out of the acts of the board itself. Where, for example, a school board issues warrants in payment of teachers' salaries and the county superintendent refuses to sign them, the board cannot employ counsel to institute mandamus proceedings to require the superintendent to sign the warrants. It was said by the Supreme Court of Florida:

The employment of attorneys to conduct litigation to require the county superintendent to countersign warrants issued by the county board of public instruction for teachers' salaries is not such a county-school purpose as will warrant payment therefor from county-school funds that by the express command of the constitution "shall be disbursed . . . solely for the maintenance and support of public free schools."[47]

The teachers' rights were involved; and, if vindicated at all, they would have to be vindicated by the teachers themselves and at their own expense. In Louisiana, however, it has been held that a board of education has authority to resist an action to garnishee teachers' salaries.[48]

Under certain circumstances a school board may spend school funds to defend a suit against the members of the board personally. To justify such an expenditure, it must be shown that the board members were acting in a matter in which the corporation had an interest, that they were acting in the discharge of a duty imposed or authorized by

45. *Tool Company* v. *Norris*, 2 Wall. (U.S.) 45, 17 L. Ed. 868.

46. *Taylor* v. *Matthews*, 10 Ga. App. 852, 75 S.E. 166. Accord, *Lyon* v. *Mitchell*, 36 N.Y. 235, 93 Am. Dec. 502.

47. *McKinnon* v. *State*, 70 Fla. 561, 70 So. 557.

48. *Bank of Winnfield* v. *Brumfield*, 124 So. (La.) 628.

law, and that they acted in good faith. In the case of *Hotchkiss* v. *Plunkett*,[49] for instance, the board of education, in purchasing school stationery, refused to consider the bid of a certain contractor. The board had purchased stationery from this contractor previously and had found it unsatisfactory. The contractor sued the members of the board personally, and later the question arose as to whether the board had authority to indemnify its individual members for losses sustained in defending the action against them. Applying the principles stated, the court held that the board did have such authority.

Where the statutes make it the duty of a state or municipal attorney to represent a school district in all legal controversies, confusion may arise with respect to the authority of the district to employ additional counsel. Are such statutes merely declaratory, or are they restrictive? According to the weight of authority, they are restrictive to the extent that a board may not ignore altogether the counsel provided by law. Where, however, the attorney provided by law refuses to act or is incapacitated or disqualified or the business of the corporation is such as to require the services of additional counsel, such additional counsel may be employed.[50] In the case of *McClintic* v. *Cavender*,[51] a statute of West Virginia provided that "it shall be the duty of the prosecuting attorney to attend to, bring or prosecute, or defend, as the case may be, all actions, suits, and proceedings in which . . . any district board of education is interested, without additional compensation." The prosecuting attorney advised the board of education of a school district that he was not required by the statute to represent the district, whereupon it employed other counsel. In passing on the authority of the district to employ additional counsel, the supreme court of appeals said:

The next and most important question is: Has the board of education of an independent school district, notwithstanding its right to be advised and represented by the prosecuting attorney and his duties in the premises, the right also to employ other counsel or counsel to assist the prosecuting attorney in extraordinary or important litigation? Mr. Dillon, than whom there is perhaps no better authority on municipal law, in the recent edition of his great work on municipal corporations, says, "If the scheme of municipal

49. 60 Conn. 230, 22 Atl. 535.

50. *Fleischmann* v. *Graves*, 235 N.Y. 84, 138 N.E. 745; *McClintic* v. *Cavender*, 75 W. Va. 36, 83 S.E. 78, L.R.A. 1917D 248, Ann. Cas. 1918A 499; *State* v. *Gage*, 107 Wash. 282, 181 Pac. 855; *Money* v. *Beard*, 136 Ky. 219, 124 S.W. 282; *Ward* v. *San Diego School District*, 265 Pac. (Calif.) 821; *Chrestman* v. *Tompkins*, 5 S.W. (2d) (Tex.) 257; *Stone* v. *School District of City of Carbondale*, 160 Atl. (Pa.) 221.

51. 75 W. Va. 36, 83, S.E. 78, L.R.A. 1917D 248, Ann. Cas. 1918A 499.

government *provides a corporation counsel or city attorney or other legal officer* for the municipality whose duty it is to appear on behalf of the municipality *in all suits* by or against the corporation and to conduct all the law business of the corporation, the municipality is deprived of its power to employ another attorney to take the place of, and perform the duties which naturally belong to, its law officers." 2 Dillon on *Municipal Corporations* (5th Ed.), Sec. 824.

This is a very clear and comprehensive statement of the law and is well fortified by the numerous decisions cited therefor in the footnote. The words italicized are so emphasized by the author. An examination of the cases cited will show that this rule is based on cases where the municipal authorities have attempted to ignore the rights, duties, and authorities of municipal-law officers, either wholly to supersede them or to waste the public funds in employing counsel not required by any exigency, as refusal, incapacity, neglect, sickness, or disqualification of the regular municipal officer to act in the premises; or where, by the terms of the charter or laws governing the municipality, legal departments have been created to transact all legal business and the implied power to employ other counsel plainly negatived thereby.

The court pointed out that the statute under consideration did not negative the right to employ other counsel to assist the prosecuting attorney and then continued as follows:

In the same paragraph Mr. Dillon says: "But the fact that an official attorney is provided for the municipality by law does not *preclude the municipality* from employing *other or additional attorneys to assist him* in prosecuting or defending suits against the municipality." The decisions cited for this proposition are numerous. Some of them do not limit the right to the employment of assistant counsel but give it whenever and wherever in the judgment of the corporate authorities the business of the corporation reasonably requires other or additional counsel.

Some courts even go so far as to held that statutes making it the duty of a district or municipal attorney to furnish free legal advice to the school board do not limit the authority of the board to the employment of assistant counsel. Other counsel may be employed, they hold, whenever, in the judgment of the corporate authorities, the business of the corporation demands such employment. Thus, in an important case,[52] the Supreme Court of Iowa said: "One of the duties of a county attorney prescribed by statute is to furnish, free of charge, legal advice to all school-board and township officers when requested so to do by such board or officers. This provision simply defines one of the duties of a county attorney, but the law does not make it mandatory upon a school board or officer to employ the county attorney." Similarly, the statutes of Washington made it the duty of the prose-

52. *Rural Independent School District of Eagle* v. *Daly*, 201 Iowa 286, 207 N.W. 124.

cuting attorney of each county to represent all school districts in all criminal or civil actions. The interests of a school district had become antagonistic to the interests of two other districts, with which a consolidation had been attempted. The prosecuting attorney advised the district officers to employ other counsel, and they did so. In sustaining this action, the court said: "The statute heretofore referred to regarding the prosecuting attorneys is merely a definition of their powers and does not attempt to restrain, modify, or define the powers of boards of school directors."[53] Likewise, in Kentucky, the statutes made it the duty of the county attorney to attend to the prosecution of all cases in which the county or commonwealth was interested. In prosecuting an action against a publisher for an alleged breach of bond, the county superintendent employed additional counsel. His action was sustained by the court of appeals: "We think the superintendent, in the exercise of a reasonable judgment, had the right to employ additional counsel, if their services were necessary under the exigencies of the case, and to pay them a reasonable fee for their services."[54]

Contrary opinion, however, has been expressed by a few courts. In the case of *Frederick* v. *Douglas County*,[55] a county board of supervisors employed an attorney, a Mr. Grace, in defense of important tax cases, because the district attorney of the county was young and inexperienced in tax litigation. The court held that the board had no authority to employ additional counsel "because they had a district attorney qualified and acting. Therefore, the employment of Mr. Grace was to the full extent an act beyond their power and hence incapable of ratification."

AUTHORITY TO INSURE SCHOOL PROPERTY
AND TEACHERS

There have been relatively few cases dealing with the authority of school boards to insure school property. There can be little doubt, however, that the power to insure school property is necessarily implied from the general power which a school board possesses to manage and control the property of the school district. To deny the officers of a school district authority to protect the district against the loss of its property by fire would be entirely unreasonable. The

53. *State* v. *Gage*, 107 Wash. 282, 181 Pac. 855.
54. *Money* v. *Beard*, 136 Ky. 219, 124 S.W. 282.
55. 96 Wis. 411, 71 N.W. 798.

Appellate Court of Indiana has said in this connection: "We are of the opinion that, under the statutory provisions placing upon the trustees the duty of caring for and managing the school property, [a township trustee] has such implied authority that, in the exercise of his discretion, he may make reasonable expenditures from the special school revenue by way of procuring insurance on such property against fire."[56] In Pennsylvania it has been held that, in the absence of legislation to the contrary, a school board may insure a building in the process of construction and embody in the building contract a provision to that effect.[57]

There is some doubt as to the authority of a school board to take out insurance in a mutual association where no fixed premium is charged, the losses being prorated among the members. A Kentucky statute authorized county boards of education to insure school property. In sustaining the right of a board to take out insurance in a co-operative or assessment association, the court reasoned as follows:

Included in these powers by implication, it would seem that the board of education is authorized to contract for insurance with any insurance corporation which the public policy of the state has by statute authorized to do an insurance business of the character of insuring public-school buildings against fire and other casualties, unless there is a statute which by express provision or necessary implication forbids the board of education to contract with it, or the provisions of its articles of incorporation are such that the nature of the contract which it can enter into is one which the board of education cannot for some valid reason effect, and is therefore necessarily excluded as an insurer.[58]

As the court indicated, there may be some constitutional or statutory provision which renders insurance in a mutual association illegal. Such was the situation in an Idaho case.[59] The constitution provided that no school district should "lend or pledge the credit or faith thereof directly or indirectly, in any manner, to, or in aid of, any individual, association, or incorporation, for any amount or for any purpose whatever, or become responsible for any debt, contract, or liability of any individual, association, or corporation." It also pro-

56. *Clark School Township* v. *Home Insurance and Trust Company,* 20 Ind. App. 543, 51 N.E. 107.

57. *Hagan Lumber Company* v. *Duryea School District,* 277 Pa. St. 345, 121 Atl. 107.

58. *Dalzell* v. *Bourbon County Board of Education,* 193 Ky. 171, 235 S.W. 360.

59. *School District No. 8* v. *Twin Falls County Mutual Fire Insurance Company,* 30 Idaho 400, 164 Pac. 1174.

hibited any school district from incurring any indebtedness exceeding in any year the income or revenue provided for it for that year. A school district took out insurance in a mutual association, incurring thereby unlimited liability. The schoolhouse was burned, and the company refused payment on the ground that the contract was void. The court sustained the position taken by the company. "To permit a school district to become a member of a county mutual fire-insurance company would be indirectly to sanction the use of public funds raised by taxation for a private as distinguished from a public purpose." It has been held, however, under constitutional provisions similar to that in the Idaho case, that the taking of insurance with a mutual company does not come within the inhibition, provided that there is a limited liability.[60] In case the liability is limited, it is said, the district does not become strictly a stockholder, nor is it loaning its credit.

There seems to be but one case dealing with the authority of school boards to carry group life insurance for teachers. In the case of *Nohl* v. *Board of Education,*[61] action was brought to enjoin the Board of Education of Albuquerque, New Mexico, from using public funds for this purpose. The statutes of New Mexico authorized boards of education to defray all expenses "connected with the proper conduct of the public schools in their respective districts." Was the expenditure in question connected with the proper conduct of schools? The court answered this question in the affirmative:

> It is admitted that the securing of group insurance for the teachers enables the Board of Education to procure a better class of teachers and prevents frequent changes in the teaching force. This is certainly desirable and conducive to the "proper conduct of the public schools." School funds are now being spent in all the school districts of the state and in many, if not all, of the other states for purposes and objects unquestionably proper, gauged by our advancing civilization, which a quarter of a century ago would have been considered highly improper. In many of the schools we have mechanical instruction in many of the trades and professions which not so many years ago would not have been tolerated. The teaching of music, arts, and science has become a recognized necessity. Many things are provided now for the comfort and convenience of both teachers and pupils which heretofore would have been prohibited by injunction as an improper expenditure of public funds. In some of the schools of the state gymnasiums, swimming pools, playgrounds, and other forms of recreation, amusement, and diversion are provided, because it is recognized by advanced public sentiment that

60. *Miller* v. *Johnson,* 4 Calif. (2d) 265, 48 Pac. (2d) 956; *Burton* v. *School District No.* 19, 47 Wyo. 462, 38 Pac. (2d) 610; *Downing* v. *School District of City of Erie,* 297 Pa. 474, 147 Atl. 239.

61. 27 N.M. 242, 199 Pac. 373, 16 A.L.R. 1085.

such instrumentalities are calculated to, and do, promote the cause of education and tend to better the schools and keep the pupils and teachers satisfied and contented. Many corporations employing large numbers of laborers throughout the country carry group insurance on such employees with the same object in view as that which evidently was in the minds of the members of the Board of Education of the city of Albuquerque when the insurance in question was purchased.

While the reasoning in this case may be convincing to many, it is very doubtful whether other courts would follow it as a precedent. Since teaching is one of the least hazardous of occupations, a school board is no more justified in purchasing insurance for teachers than it would be in purchasing various other commodities which teachers might be pleased to have. The only other case, it seems, more or less in point, is one in which it was held that a municipality may not insure employees unless authorized to do so by statute.[62]

AUTHORITY TO CARRY WORKMEN'S COMPENSATION INSURANCE

The courts are divided with respect to the constitutionality of statutes making workmen's compensation insurance applicable to the employees of boards of education. According to the weight of authority, however, such statutes are not unconstitutional, in that they authorize the expenditure of public funds for a private or nonschool purpose.[63] Thus in Maryland, the constitution limited the expenditure of state school funds to "purposes of education." It was contended that the expenditure of public school funds by a county board of education to carry workmen's compensation insurance, as provided for in the Workmen's Compensation Act, was a violation of this provision of the constitution. The court held otherwise.[64] Similarly, in Louisiana the court held a workmen's compensation act constitutional against the contention that it diverted public funds to a private use: "It is our opinion, as has often been stated, that the underlying theory and intention of compensation statutes is to shift the burden of accidental injuries incident to employment from the injured employee onto the public through the employer. The raising of funds for such purposes,

---

62. *People* v. *Dibble*, 189 N.Y.S. 29.

63. *Clauss* v. *Board of Education of Anne Arundel County*, 181 Md. 513, 30 Atl. (2d) 779; *Kroncke* v. *Caddo Parish School Board*, 183 So. (La.) 86; *School District* v. *Industrial Commission*, 66 Colo. 580, 185 Pac. 348; 53 A.L.R. 1286.

64. *Clauss* v. *Board of Education of Anne Arundel County*, 181 Md. 513, 30 Atl. (2d) 779.

where the law has provided none, becomes plainly a public purpose."[65]

A Georgia case, however, supports the contention that the expenditure of public funds to carry workmen's compensation insurance is an unconstitutional expenditure for a private purpose, or an expenditure of school funds for a purpose other than the one to which they are especially dedicated.[66]

The reasoning of the courts which permit the expenditure of school funds to pay for workmen's compensation insurance for school employees other than teachers would seem equally applicable to the expenditure of funds where teachers are included in a workmen's compensation act. There is not much authority on this specific point, but the Supreme Court of Utah has held that, where a statute authorizes it to do so, a school board may spend its funds to pay for workmen's compensation for teachers. Such an expenditure is for a school purpose.[67]

AUTHORITY TO DELEGATE BOARD'S DISCRETION

It is important that boards of education know how far they may go in delegating authority to the city superintendent or to committees of their own members. The rule seems perfectly clear that, where the law vests the exercise of judgment and discretion in a board of education or other officers of a school district, that exercise of judgment and discretion cannot be delegated to any other person or body whatsoever.[68] It is equally certain that school boards may delegate to their agents the performance of merely administrative or ministerial duties. Thus, where the law makes it the duty of a board to employ teachers, the

65. *Kroncke* v. *Caddo Parish School Board*, 183 So. (La.) 86.

66. *Floyd County* v. *Scoggins*, 164 Ga. 485, 139 S.E. 11.

67. *Woodcock* v. *Board of Education*, 55 Utah 458, 187 Pac. 181.

68. *Lindblad* v. *Board of Education*, 221 Ill. 261, 77 N.E. 450; *Taggart* v. *School District No. 1*, 96 Ore. 422, 188 Pac. 908; *Coleman* v. *District of Columbia*, 279 Fed. 990; *Harris* v. *Inhabitants of Marblehead*, 10 Gray (76 Mass.) 40; *Keeler* v. *Frost*, 22 Barb. (N.Y.) 400; *Lessin* v. *Board of Education*, 247 N.Y. 503, 161 N.E. 160; *State* v. *Jones*, 143 Tenn. 575, 224 S.W. 1041; *Mulhall* v. *Pfannkuch*, 221 N.W. (Iowa) 833; *Johnson* v. *Sabine Parish School Board*, 140 So. (La.) 87; *Bowles* v. *Fayetteville Graded School*, 211 N.C. 36, 188 S.E. 615; *Pehrson* v. *School District No. 334*, 194 Wash. 334, 77 Pac. (2d) 1022; *McGaha* v. *Curlee*, 176 Miss. 671, 169 So. 694; *O'Brien* v. *City of Pittsfield*, 316 Mass. 283, 55 N.E. (2d) 440; *Hall* v. *Delphi–Deer Creek Township School Corporation*, 98 Ind. App. 409, 189 N.E. 527; *Trustees of State Normal School* v. *Wightman*, 93 Colo. 226, 25 Pac. (2d) 193; *University Interscholastic League* v. *Midwestern University*, 250 S.W. (2d) (Tex.) 587.

board may delegate to the superintendent or to a committee the authority to ascertain proper persons to be employed and even to draw up tentative contracts, but the contracts must be ratified by the board itself, or they will not be valid. Where, on the other hand, all the terms of a contract have been definitely agreed on by the board at a legal meeting, the ministerial duty of executing the contract or reducing it to the proper form may be delegated to an agent.

An Oregon case[69] is in point. A superintendent employed a teacher to perform the duties of another teacher who had become ill. She taught for three and one-half years, after which she was discharged. At the time of her alleged employment there was a statute in force to the effect that regularly employed teachers should be put on the permanent list after two years of service. There was also in force a statute which provided that "the board, at a general or special meeting called for that purpose, shall hire teachers, and shall make contracts with such teachers which shall specify the wages, number of months to be taught, and time employment is to begin, as agreed upon by the parties, and shall file such contracts in the office of the district clerk." The discharged teacher brought action for a writ of mandamus to compel the board to restore her to her position. This the court refused to grant for the following reasons:

> The manifest purpose and spirit of the statute, and the only reasonable construction that can be given it, is that the relation of teacher cannot be created except by a written contract embodying the terms prescribed by the statute. The duty thus imposed upon the board is not delegable. The directors have been elected by the people to perform a duty requiring their judgment. It is not a ministerial function which may be performed by another. . . . The plaintiff had no right to rely upon the action of the superintendent as a basis of service in the capacity of teacher so as to become ultimately one of the permanently employed teachers. A knowledge of the law is imputed to her. There is no such thing as apparent scope of authority in one professing to act as agent for a public municipality of which the powers and their manner of exercise are so strictly and minutely defined by statute. The law prescribes the scope and extent of the authority of those acting for the district, and no one can conceal himself behind the camouflage of apparent authority. . . . At her peril she depended upon her transactions with the superintendent, who really had no authority and, if he had, could not and did not exercise it as the law requires.

Other courts have applied the same principle. In Indiana it was held that the township trustees could not delegate to the superintendent

69. *Taggart* v. *School District No. 1,* 96 Ore. 422, 188 Pac. 908.

authority to employ teachers,[70] and in Mississippi this authority could not be delegated to any third party.[71] The North Carolina court ruled that a board of education could not delegate to a subcommittee of its own members final authority to sell a vacant lot owned by the board.[72] A contract between a local school board and the board of control of a state normal school, whereby the two boards would jointly exercise control over certain schools to be used for practice teaching, was held void because the local school board could not delegate to another the powers and discretion vested by law in itself.[73] A Texas court held that a school board could not delegate to an interscholastic league authority to make rules governing any of its employees. Said the court: "The duties of an athletic director, coach, teacher, or administrator of a public school in this state can only be regulated by the officers of the school system of the state in accordance with the provisions of statutes."[74] And, finally, in Louisiana it was the custom of a parish board of education to permit the member from each ward to select the bus driver in that ward and fix his salary. After that, the parish superintendent executed the contract. A bus·driver was employed in this way for a term of two years. He served satisfactorily for one year and purchased a new bus. He was not retained for the second year. The court held the contract void and not subject to ratification.[75]

School boards may, on the other hand, delegate to their agents the performance of purely administrative or ministerial duties.[76] Where, for example, a board at a regular meeting voted to purchase a certain site for a schoolhouse at a stipulated price and authorized the presi-

70. *Hall.* v. *Delphi–Deer Creek Township School Corporation,* 98 Ind. App. 409, 189 N.E. 527.

71. *McGaha* v. *Curlee,* 176 Miss. 671, 169 So. 694.

72. *Bowles* v. *Fayetteville Graded Schools,* 211 N.C. 36, 188 S.E. 615.

73. *Lindblad* v. *Board of Education,* 221 Ill. 261, 77 N.E. 450.

74. *Interscholastic League* v. *Midwestern University,* 250 S.W. (2d) (Tex.) 587.

75. *Murry* v. *Union Parish School Board,* 185 So. (La.) 305.

76. *Looney* v. *Consolidated Independent School District of Cromwell,* 201 Iowa 436, 205 N.W. 328; *Kraft* v. *Board of Education,* 67 N.J. Law 512, 51 Atl. 483; *Schwitzer* v. *Board of Education,* 79 N.J. Law 342, 75 Atl. 447; *Ames* v. *Board of Education,* 97 N.J. Eq. 60, 127 Atl. 95; *McGaha* v. *Curlee,* 176 Miss. 671, 169 So. 694.

dent to pay the price and receive the deed for the property, there was no unwarranted delegation of discretion. The power delegated to the president was wholly ministerial.[77] Similarly, in New Jersey a committee of a board of education was delegated the duty of inviting proposals and submitting specifications with respect to school desks. Although the resolution awarding the contract was adopted in due form by the board itself, it was contended that the duties performed by the committee were of such a character as to render the final action of the board merely perfunctory. In holding otherwise, the court said:

> Where, however, the power to purchase is only ministerial or administrative, it may be delegated to a committee of the corporate body created for the purpose . . . and, even where such corporate action is necessary, the fact that the negotiations have been conducted by a committee for that purpose will not invalidate the resolution awarding the contract provided the result of such negotiation is first reported to the corporate body and there discussed and considered before final action.[78]

AUTHORITY OF SCHOOL BOARDS TO
MAKE PRIOR COMMITMENTS

It frequently happens that a board of education, by resolution or by some statement given out to the public, commits itself to a particular policy. For example, in a bond election, even though not required to do so by statute, it may represent to the public that if the bonds are voted, the proceeds will be employed to build a high-school building. Or in an election for the consolidation of school districts some announcement may be made with respect to the board's policy in regard to the transportation of pupils. Later the board may change its policy, and the question may arise as to whether it is bound by its prior commitment.

The general rule is that where a board is vested with discretion, it may not limit that discretion by any prior announcement of policy. Public policy requires that when a board is called upon to act in a matter involving discretion vested in it, it be untrammeled by any previous promises or commitments. Those to whom such promises or commitments are made are presumed to know that the board is mere-

77. *Looney* v. *Consolidated Independent School District of Cromwell,* 201 Iowa 436, 205 N.W. 328.

78. *Kraft* v. *Board of Education,* 67 N.J. Law 512, 51 Atl. 483.

ly giving expression to its present intent and that it may later change
its policy.[79]

A South Carolina case is in point.[80] There was need for a new
school building in the city of Gaffney. The board appointed a committee to make inquiries, to report as to the best location, and to
circulate a petition for an election on the question of issuing bonds to
purchase a site. It was claimed that, in circulating the petition, the
committee assured those who signed it that the new building would
be erected at the west end of the city and that, if this representation
had not been made, the bonds would not have been voted. The board
contended that, if such representation was made, it was made without
its authority. After the bonds had been voted and the money was in
hand, the board decided to erect the building near the business center
of the city. Action was brought to enjoin the board from locating the
building on the lot finally designated. The injunction was denied:

> Assuming, then, as we must for the purpose of this inquiry, that the repre-
> sentations were made with the effect alleged, the question is: Should that
> preclude the trustees from now exercising the judgment and discretion vested
> in them by law to locate the building where they believe it ought to be
> located to best subserve the educational interests of the district as a whole?
> Or, stating the proposition differently, must they now, because of those rep-
> resentations, abuse their discretion by locating the building where, in their
> judgment, it will not be for the best interests of the district? They are bound,
> under the statute and their oath of office, to exercise their discretion and
> judgment, in the language of the statute (Civ. Code, Sec. 1761) "so as
> best to promote the educational interests of their district." This power and
> duty is continuing and inalienable. They could not, therefore, bind them-
> selves by promises or representation so as to divest themselves of the right
> to a free and untrammeled exercise of their judgment and discretion for the
> best interests of their district at the time they were required to act as a
> body. They may have thought, when the representations were made, that
> it would be best to locate the building in the west end; but, upon further
> consideration of the matter, in the light of new reasons suggested by some
> of their body or others, they may have changed their minds; if so, they not
> only had the power, but it was their duty to themselves and to the district,

79. *State* ex rel. *Phillips* v. *Trent Independent School District,* 141 S.W. (2d)
(Tex.) 438; *Muehring* v. *School District No. 31,* 224 Minn. 432, 28 N.W. (2d)
655; *Hudson* v. *San Antonio,* 127 Tex. 517, 95 S.W. (2d) 673; *Conley* v. *School
Directors,* 32 Pa. St. 194; *Sarratt* v. *Cash,* 103 S.C. 531, 88 S.E. 256; *Jennings* v.
Clearwater School District, 65 Calif. App. 102, 223 Pac. 84; *State* v. *Board, of
Education,* 88 Kan. 199, 127 Pac. 623; *Lynn School District* v. *Smithville School
District,* 213 Ark. 268, 211 S.W. (2d) 641; *Wysong* v. *Walden,* 120 W. Va. 122,
196, S.E. 573.

80. *Sarratt* v. *Cash.* 103 S.C. 531. 88 S.E. 256.

to do so. It would be contrary to public policy to allow public officers who are charged with the duty of exercising their judgment and discretion for the benefit of the whole district to bind or fetter themselves by promise or representation to individuals or to electors of a section of the district so that they could not, at all times, act freely and impartially for the benefit of the whole district. The power was conferred upon them for public purposes, and it could not be lawfully bartered away to influence signatures to the petition or votes in the election. The electors are presumed to have known this. Therefore, they had no legal right to rely upon the alleged representations or to be influenced by them in signing the petition or in voting in the election.

Similarly, in a Texas case, before a common-school district was attached to an independent school district, the trustees in a pre-election agreement promised to maintain an elementary school in the old common-school district. The court held that this agreement was not a contract and that persons acting on the agreement were charged with notice that the kind of agreement here involved could not restrict the trustees in a matter of future policy.[81]

81. *State* ex rel. *Phillips* v. *Trent Independent School District*, 141 S.W. (2d) (Tex.) 438.

CHAPTER VIII

School Board Procedure and Records

NOTICE OF BOARD MEETINGS

IT IS an elementary principle of law that all members of a corporate body who are entitled to participate in the conduct of its affairs must be given actual or constructive notice of all corporate meetings. School-district meetings, therefore, are not legally constituted unless they are called in strict conformity with statutory requirements.[1] In the case of *Lander* v. *School District No. 20 in Smithfield*,[2] for example, at a district meeting held without notice, it was voted to borrow money with which to build a schoolhouse. The money was borrowed and the schoolhouse built, but the district was not held liable under its contract. The court said: "There does not appear to have been any notice of the meeting given to the inhabitants of the district. The meeting not having been legally called, the district could not be bound by its action, it was altogether inoperative and void." It has been held that a notice of six days where the law requires seven is, in effect, no notice at all.[3] The notice, moreover, must stipulate definitely the time and the place of meeting, and, if the meeting is a special one, the business to be transacted must be indicated with clearness and particularity.[4] Action at such meetings must be confined strictly to those matters

1. *Hunt* v. *School District No. 20*, 14 Vt. 300, 39 Am. Dec. 225; *Scott* v. *School District No. 9*, 67 Vt. 150, 31 Atl. 145, 27 L.R.A. 588; *Wyley* v. *Wilson*, 44 Vt. 404; *Lander* v. *School District No. 20 in Smithfield*, 33 Me. 239; *Apgar* v. *Van Syckel*, 46 N.J. Law 492; *Third School District in Stoughton* v. *Atherton*, 12 Metc. (Mass.) 105; *Rideout* v. *School District No. 5 in Dunstable*, 83 Mass. 232; *Wright* v. *North School District*, 53 Conn. 576, 5 Atl. 708.

2. *Lander* v. *School District No. 20 in Smithfield*, 33 Me. 239.

3. *Hunt* v. *School District No. 20*, 14 Vt. 300, 39 Am. Dec. 225.

4. *Wyley* v. *Wilson*, 44 Vt. 404; *Scott* v. *School District No. 9*, 67 Vt. 150, 31 Atl. 145, 27 L.R.A. 588; *Rideout* v. *School District No. 5 in Dunstable*, 83 Mass. 232; *Wright* v. *North School District*, 53 Conn. 576, 5 Atl. 708; *State* v. *Rural High School District No. 3*, 169 Kan. 671, 220 Pac. (2d) 164. In the case of *School District No. 4, Town of Campbell* v. *Baier*, 98 Wis. 22, 73 N.W. 448, a teacher was employed by two of the three members of the board at a special meeting, notice of which failed to state the place where the meeting was to be held. The teacher thus employed did not hold a valid contract.

which the electors have been called together to consider. It is not necessary, however, that the notice be drawn up in formal or technical terms. "All that is required, is that it should be so expressed that the inhabitants of the district may fairly understand the purpose for which they are to be convened."[5]

All district meetings must be held, moreover, at the time and the place provided for in the notice; if there is a change of place, all those entitled to participate must be given a reasonable opportunity to attend. By way of illustration, a town meeting in Maine was called to assemble at 1:30 P.M. in a schoolhouse. Six or eight of the inhabitants assembled at the time designated, but, as there was snow on the ground and the schoolhouse was locked and they had no key, the meeting was called to order in the road and promptly adjourned to a store about a mile away. No precaution was taken to inform any of the other inhabitants that the meeting was being held at the store. Later in the afternoon other inhabitants came to the schoolhouse but, finding no indication of a meeting, returned to their homes. The court held that the action taken at the store was without authority and therefore not binding upon the town.[6] In a very similar case, where a boy was stationed at the meeting place provided for in the notice to inform all who wished to attend that the meeting was being held a few blocks away, the court held that the action taken was legal and binding.[7] It was not shown that anyone wishing to participate in the meeting was denied the opportunity to do so.

As was said at the outset of this discussion, all those entitled to participate in school-district meetings must have actual or constructive notice. In the case of regular meetings, however, or those which are a matter of record, no special notice is required.[8] The time appointed is presumed to be known by all, and it is their duty to attend without further notification.

Formerly, school-district meetings were vested with much authority with respect to the management of the schools. As modern conditions have made it inconvenient or inadvisable for the people to conduct

5. *South School District* v. *Blakeslee*, 13 Conn. 227.

6. *Chamberlain* v. *Dover*, 13 Me. 466, 29 Am. Dec. 517.

7. *Wakefield* v. *Patterson*, 25 Kan. 709.

8. *Marchant* v. *Langworthy*, 6 Hill (N.Y.) 646; *People* v. *Batchelor*, 22 N.Y. 128; *Porter* v. *Robinson*, 30 Hun. (N.Y.) 209.

their affairs through direct participation, boards of education have commonly taken the place of the old district meetings. The same legal principles, however, which govern the calling of the district meetings are applicable to meetings of boards of education.[9] Each member of such a board must have actual or constructive notice of all meetings, for the law contemplates that all be given an opportunity to attend, not only for the purpose of voting but for the purpose of offering counsel and advice.[10] The law contemplates the combined judgment of all. It should be kept in mind, however, that board members have constructive notice of all regular meetings and that no further notification is necessary.[11]

Under certain circumstances it is not necessary to give notice of board meetings. The courts seem to hold uniformly that, if all the members of a board of education are present and consent to act, lack of notice is immaterial.[12] As was said by the Supreme Court of North Dakota, "it is no doubt the law that in such a case, and where there is a failure to give the statutory notice, if all members of the board are present and participate, the action of the board will be controlling."[13]

9. *Burns* v. *Thompson,* 64 Ark. 489, 43 S.W. 499; *State* v. *Tucker,* 39 N.D. 106, 166 N.W. 820.

10. *Aikman* v. *School District No. 16,* 27 Kan. 129; *McNolty* v. *Board of School Directors,* 102 Wis. 261, 78 N.W. 439; *Splaine* v. *School District No. 122,* 20 Wash. 74, 54 Pac. 766; *Barton* v. *Hines,* 123 Ark. 619, 185 S.W. 455; *School District No. 49* v. *Adams,* 69 Ark. 159, 61 S.W. 793; *State* v. *Tucker,* 39 N.D. 106, 166 N.W. 820; *Ward* v. *Board of Education,* 80 W. Va.. 541, 92 S.E. 741; *Hibbs* v. *Arensberg,* 276 Pa. St. 24, 119 Atl. 727. NOTE: L.R.A. 1915F 1047. See, however, *Windham* v. *Black Creek School No. 9,* 143 S.C. 511, 141 S.E. 896; *Deen* v. *Birdville Independent School District,* 138 Tex. 339, 159 S.W. (2d) 111; *Holton* v. *Board of Education,* 113 W. Va. 590, 169 S.E. 239; *Vreeland* v. *School District No. 2,* 264 Mich. 212, 249 N.W. 829.

11. *Board of Education* v. *Carolan,* 182 Ill. 119, 55 N.E. 58.

12. *Butler* v. *Joint School District No. 4,* 155 Wis. 626, 145 N.W. 180; *State* v. *Tucker,* 39 N.D. 106, 166 N.W. 820; *Lawrence* v. *Trainer,* 136 Ill. 474, 27 N.E. 197; *Capehart* v. *Board of Education,* 82 W. Va. 217, 95 S.E. 838; *Wysong* v. *Board of Education,* 86 W. Va. 57, 102 S.E. 733; *School District* v. *Allen,* 83 Ark. 491, 104 S.W. 172; *Decker* v. *School District No. 2,* 101 Mo. App. 115, 74 S.W. 390; *Johnson* v. *Dye,* 142 Mo. App. 424, 127 S.W. 413. It has been held, too, that, where all the members of a board agree to meet, no formal notice is necessary (*Olney School District* v. *Christy,* 81 Ill. App. 304); *Center Hill School District No. 32* v. *Hunt,* 194 Ark. 1145, 110 S.W. (2d) 523; *Hlavka* v. *Common School District No. 83,* 192 Minn. 169, 255 N.W. 820; *Knickerbocker* v. *Redlands High School District,* 49 Calif. App. (2d) 722, 122 Pac. (2d) 289; *Brumfield* v. *Board of Education of Logan County,* 121 W. Va. 725, 6 S.E. (2d) 238.

13. *State* v. *Tucker,* 39 N.D. 106, 166 N.W. 820.

The mere fact, however, that all the members of the board are present does not make the meeting legal. All must consent to take formal action. Where, for example, two of the three members of a board of trustees went to the home of the third to consider a contract with a teacher but the third member refused to discuss the matter, no binding contract could be entered into.[14] While all must agree to act, it is not necessary that their action be unanimous, for, once the board is convened, the usual rules of procedure apply.

There is considerable difference of opinion among the authorities as to what constitutes notice and how it may be given. In Arkansas and Michigan it has been held that written notice is necessary. "Our statute," said the Supreme Court of Arkansas, "is silent on the question whether a notice of the call meeting of a municipal corporation shall be in writing. But we are of the opinion that, when an official notice is required to be given of such a meeting, it is contemplated that it shall be in writing."[15] Similarly, in North Dakota, where a statute required a written or printed notice, it was held that notice over the telephone, which the trustee denied receiving, was not sufficient.[16] The Supreme Court of Iowa, on the other hand, has held that written notice is not necessary unless required by statute and that a message delivered over the telephone that the board will meet at a certain time and place constitutes a legal notice.[17] A statute of that state provided that special meetings might be held if a notice specifying the time and place were delivered to each member in person. One F. M. Sexton was notified by telephone of the time and the place of a meeting but failed to attend. The court held the notice sufficient.

Notice by word of mouth may be delivered quite as effectually as one in writing. What this [the statute] exacts is that it actually reach the several members, so that each shall be informed of the time and place of meeting. . . . For this purpose, oral notice would be as effective as written, and there is nothing in the context indicating that one was intended rather than the other.[18]

14. *Rice* v. *School District No. 20*, 109 Ark. 125, 159 S. W. 29.

15. *Burns* v. *Thompson*, 64 Ark. 489, 43 S.W. 499. Accord, *Vreeland* v. *School District No. 2*, 264 Mich. 212, 249 N.W. 829.

16. *State* v. *Tucker*, 39 N.D. 106, 166 N.W. 820. See also 29 Cyc. 1117.

17. *Gallagher* v. *School Township of Willow*, 173 Iowa 610, 154 N.W. 437; *Independent School District of Switzer* v. *Gwinn*, 178 Iowa, 145, 159 N.W. 687.

18. *Gallagher* v. *School Township of Willow*, 173 Iowa 610, 154 N.W. 437.

The same statute was later construed by the same court in the case of *Independent School District of Switzer* v. *Gwinn.*[19] Notice of a board meeting was given by telephone to the wife of one of the members who was sick. She delivered the message prior to the time of meeting. The court held that the character of the notice and the manner of its delivery constituted sufficient compliance with the statute. So, too, in Kentucky, where the statutes did not require written notice, oral notice given by the secretary of the board to each member in person was sufficient.[20]

Again, the question may arise as to whether the notice must be delivered in person or whether the requirements of the law are met by depositing written or printed notices in the mails. Where a statute requires that the notice shall be delivered in person, it has been held that notice by mail is not sufficient. In the case of *Barclay* v. *School Township of Wapsinonoc,*[21] for example, on the day the clerk gave notice to the other members, he was led to believe by erroneous information that one Anderson, a member, was not at home, though in fact he was. Thinking that Anderson could not be reached personally, the clerk mailed him a letter notifying him of the meeting. This letter Anderson never received. In fact, he left the state the next morning and did not return until after the meeting had been held. In the opinion of the court, the action taken at the meeting was illegal:

> The statute does not authorize a mailing of notice, and, in the absence of any such authority, we are unwilling to hold that an attempt to give notice by mail, which does not reach the member to be notified, is sufficient. . . . It is sufficient to say that the statute does not provide that reasonable effort to give notice shall be sufficient. The personal delivery of some form of a notice is required.

Ordinarily, however, it seems that notice by mail is considered good notice. In Arkansas, by way of illustration, all members of a school board were present at a special meeting except one, who had been notified by mail three days previously. The court held the meeting legal.[22] A Massachusetts statute authorized a city mayor to call a special meeting of the council by causing notice to be left at the usual place of residence of each member. Notice was given through the mail

19. *Independent School District of Switzer* v. *Gwinn,* 178 Iowa 145, 159 N.W. 687.

20. *Board of Education* v. *Stevens,* 261 Ky. 475, 88 S.W. (2d) 3.

21. *Barclay* v. *School Township of Wapsinonoc,* 157 Iowa 181, 138 N.W. 395.

22. *Schmutz* v. *Special School District,* 78 Ark. 118, 95 S.W. 438.

and received by all the members except one who had previously left the state on an extended visit to California. The court held that the requirements of the statute had been met.[23]

Where a school-board member is absent from the district and it is impracticable to give notice in the proper form, the service of the notice is waived. As has been said by the Supreme Court of New York:

> The object of notice is to give the person notified an opportunity to attend. There is no other virtue in the notice. Now when a person, elected as trustee, is at the time of his election in a distant State and continues there all the time until after the meeting in question, never having had any formal notice of his election, it would be unreasonable to say that a meeting was made invalid by a failure to give him notice thereof. Must a personal notice be served on him in Minnesota? Or if a notice left at his house is sufficient, of what use would it be to one who was beyond its reach? It cannot be necessary to do an act which, when done, would be of no use. By remaining where he could not attend the meetings of the board of education, Stone practically waived any notice of such meetings; and indeed put it beyond the power of the proper officer to give any.[24]

Whatever the form of the notice, it must, of course, be given by one having authority to call the board together. Moreover, each member of the board must be notified a reasonable time in advance.[25] What is a reasonable time will be determined by the circumstances in each case.

EFFECT OF ACTION TAKEN BY BOARD MEMBERS ACTING SEPARATELY

The rule is well settled that when school boards are authorized to perform acts involving judgment and discretion, they can act only at authorized meetings duly held. Members of such a body cannot make a determination binding upon the district by their assent individually and separately expressed.[26] As was said by the Supreme Court of Kansas, "it is an elementary principle, that when several persons are authorized to do an act of a public nature, which requires deliberation,

23. *Russell v. Wellington*, 157 Mass. 100. See also *State v. Kirk*, 46 Conn. 395.

24. *Porter v. Robinson*, 30 Hun. (N.Y.) 209.

25. *Wood v. School District No. 73*, 137 Minn. 138, 162 N.W. 1081.

26. *Third School District in Stoughton v. Atherton*, 12 Metc. (Mass.) 105; *School District No. 56 v. Jackson*, 110 Ark. 262, 161 S.W. 153; *State v. Treasurer of Liberty Township*, 22 Ohio St. 144; *Aikman v. School District No. 16*, 27 Kan. 129; *Herrington v. District Township of Liston*, 47 Iowa 11; *Honaker v. Board of Education*, 42 W. Va. 170, 24 S.E. 544, 32 L.R.A. 413; *School District No. 39 v. Shelton*, 26 Okla. 229, 109 Pac. 67, 138 Am. St. Rep. 962; *Davis v. School District No. 1*, 81 Mich. 214, 45 N.W. 989; *Townsend v. School District No. 12*, 41

they all should be convened, because the advice and opinions of all may be useful, though all do not unite in opinion."[27] Nor does it matter that all agree in the action taken, for the law contemplates that the board deliberate and counsel together.[28] Authority is vested not in a designated number of persons but in the board as a corporate body. In the case of *Herrington* v. *District Township of Liston*,[29] it was said:

> The question is here presented whether a corporation whose business is transacted by a board of directors can be bound by the assent of a majority of the directors to a contract, expressed otherwise than at a duly convened meeting. We are of the opinion that it cannot. While it is true that a majority of the board will govern in the absence of a provision by statute, or in the articles of incorporation, requiring the concurrence of a greater number, yet their determination is valid only after the minority have had an opportunity to be heard. A board must act as a unit, and in the manner prescribed. The determination of the members individually is not the determination of the board.

The same general principle of law is well stated in the case of *McCortle* v. *Bates*.[30] Members of a township board of education acting in their individual capacity agreed to purchase apparatus for the township schools and to ratify the contract at their next meeting. The court held that such an agreement had no binding force:

> The members composing the board have no power to act as a board, except when together in session. They then act as a body or unit. . . . It will not be permitted to them to make any agreement among themselves, or with others, by which their public action is to be, or may be restrained or embarrassed, or its freedom in anywise affected or impaired. The public, for whom they act, have the right to their best judgment after free and full discussion and consultation among themselves of, and upon, the public matters

N.J. Law 312; *McNolty* v. *School Directors*, 102 Wis. 261, 78 N.W. 439; *Johnson* v. *Dye*, 142 Mo. App. 424, 127 S.W. 413; *Roland* v. *Reading School District*, 161 Pa. St. 102, 28 Atl. 995; *Cooke* v. *White Common School District No. 7*, 33 Ky. Law Rep. 926, 111 S.W. 686; *State* v. *Alexander*, 130 So. (Miss.) 754; *State ex rel. Rogers* v. *Board of Education*, 125 W. Va. 579, 25 S.E. (2d) 537; *Lone Jack Graded School District* v. *Hendrickson*, 304 Ky. 317, 200 S.W. (2d) 736; *Iredell County Board of Education* v. *Dickson*, 235 N.C. 359, 70 S.E. (2d) 14; *Edwards* v. *Board of Education*, 235 N.C. 345, 70 S.E. (2d) 170; *Murry* v. *Union Parish School Board*, 185 So. (La.) 305; *American Asbestos Products Company* v. *Independent School District No. 14*, 196 Okla. 274, 164 Pac. (2d) 619.

27. *Aikman* v. *School District No. 16*, 27 Kan. 129.

28. *Midland Chemical Laboratories* v. *School District of North Little Rock*, 164 Ark. 38, 260 S.W. 726.

29. *Herrington* v. *District Township of Liston*, 47 Iowa 11. Accord, *Independent School District No. 6* v. *Wirtner*, 85 Iowa 387, 52 N.W. 243.

30. *McCortle* v. *Bates*, 29 Ohio St. 419, 23 Am. Rep. 758.

intrusted to them, in the session provided for by the statute. This can not be when the members, by pre-engagement, are under contract to pursue a certain line of argument or action, whether the same will be conducive to the public good or not. It is one of the oldest rules of the common law, that contracts contrary to sound morals, or against public policy, will not be enforced by courts of justice.

WHAT CONSTITUTES A QUORUM?

A simple majority of a school board constitutes a legal quorum unless the statutes provide otherwise.[31] Even where a statute authorizes a board of education to establish its own rules of procedure, the common-law quorum of a simple majority holds and cannot be modified.[32] The act of a majority of a quorum, whether fixed by common law or by statute, is the act of the board.[33] As was said by Mr. Justice Brewer of the United States Supreme Court: "The general rule of all parliamentary bodies is that, when a quorum is present, the act of a majority of the quorum is the act of the body. This has been the rule for all time, except so far as in any given case the terms of the organic act under which the body is assembled have prescribed specific limitations."[34] Nor does it matter that there may be a vacancy in the board, for such a body does not lose its entity so long as there exists a legal quorum.[35]

NUMBER OF VOTES NECESSARY FOR THE
PASSAGE OF A MEASURE

Under all circumstances it is necessary, of course, that a quorum be present before a board undertakes the transaction of business. In the absence of any statutory regulation, a majority of the quorum, or of those present, is not necessary for the passage of a measure. If a quorum be present, a majority of those actually voting is sufficient to

31. *Jensen v. Independent Consolidated School District No. 85,* 160 Minn. 233, 199 N.W. 911; *Decker v. School District No. 2,* 101 Mo. App. 115, 74 S.W. 390; *Collins v. Janey,* 147 Tenn. 477, 249 S.W. 801.

32. *Zeiler v. Central Railroad Company,* 84 Md. 304, 35 Atl. 932, 34 L.R.A. 469; *Heiskell v. Mayor of Baltimore,* 65 Md. 125, 4 Atl. 116, 57 Am. Rep. 308.

33. *United States v. Ballin,* 144 U.S. 1, 12 S. Ct. 507; *Jensen v. Independent Consolidated School District No. 85,* 160 Minn. 233, 199 N.W. 911; *Trustees of Slaughterville Graded School District v. Brooks,* 163 Ky. 200, 173 S.W. 305; *Attorney-General v. Bickford,* 77 N.H. 433, 92 Atl. 835, Am. Cas. 1916B 119; *Schofield v. Watkins,* 22 Ill. 66.

34. *United States v. Ballin,* 144 U.S. 1, 12 S. Ct. 507.

35. *Trustees of Slaughterville Graded School District v. Brooks,* 163 Ky. 200, 173 S.W. 305.

validate any measure under consideration.[36] The courts adhere strictly to the rule that, where a quorum is present, mere refusal to vote on the part of some members will not defeat the action of those actually voting. It is the duty of all members present to vote, and, if they fail to do their duty, they must be regarded as assenting to whatever the majority of those who do vote may determine.[37] Those who may wish to defeat a measure must vote against it, for inaction will not accomplish their purpose.

The case of *Collins* v. *Janey*[38] is an excellent illustration of this principle of law. At a full meeting of a school board a contract was discussed, and, upon motion to adopt it, three members voted "Aye," two "No," and two did not vote. The chairman of the board was directed to execute the contract but refused to do so on the ground that it had not received the assent of a majority of the board members. The court held the contract valid on the theory that the two members who refused to vote must be regarded as having given their assent to the action taken by the majority of those voting. Similarly, in the case of *Attorney-General* v. *Shepard*,[39] six of the seven members of a board of aldermen were present. Three voted for a measure, and the other three refused to vote. The court held that the measure had been carried. The same position has been taken by the Supreme Court of Indiana, where, in the election of a county superintendent of schools, three township trustees voted for one candidate and three refrained from voting.[40]

It should be kept in mind, however, that silence will not be construed as acquiescence under all circumstances. Where the statutes require affirmative action on the part of a majority of the board or a majority of those present, the measure under consideration must be positively supported by the required majority. A refusal to vote will not be considered as affirmative action.[41]

36. *Collins* v. *Janey,* 147 Tenn. 477, 249 S.W. 801; *Attorney-General* v. *Bickford,* 77 N.H. 433, 92 Atl. 835, Ann. Cas. 1916B 119; *Attorney-General* v. *Shepard,* 62 N.H. 383, 13 Am. St. Rep. 576; *Launtz* v. *People,* 113 Ill. 137, 55 Am. Rep. 405; *Rushville Gas Co.* v. *City of Rushville,* 121 Ind. 206, 23 N.E. 72, 16 Am. St. Rep. 388, 6 L.R.A. 315; *State* v. *Yates,* 19 Mont. 239, 47 Pac. 1004, 37 L.R.A. 205; 28 Cyc. 339.

37. *Collins* v. *Janey,* 147 Tenn. 477, 249 S.W. 801; *Rushville Gas Co.* v. *City of Rushville,* 121 Ind. 206, 23 N.E. 72, 16 Am. St. Rep. 388, 6 L.R.A. 315.

38. *Collins* v. *Janey,* 147 Tenn. 477, 249 S.W. 801.

39. *Attorney-General* v. *Shepard,* 62 N.H. 383, 13 Am. St. Rep. 576.

40. *State* v. *Vanosdal,* 131 Ind. 388, 31 N.E. 79, 15 L.R.A. 832.

41. *Somers* v. *Bridgeport,* 60 Conn. 521.

EFFECT OF BLANK BALLOTS

The courts have frequently been called upon to determine the effect of blank ballots cast at an election. The weight of authority is that such ballots are a nullity. They cannot be counted for or against any candidate; nor are they to be counted in estimating the total number of ballots cast at an election.[42] In its very nature a vote is an expression of a choice of candidates or measures. One who casts a blank ballot merely registers his refusal to vote, and the only importance which attaches to such a ballot is that it reveals an intent to concur in whatever measure may be determined upon by those actually voting.

In the case of *Attorney-General* v. *Bickford*,[43] as an illustration, a school committee met to elect a superintendent of public instruction for the city. The result of the ballot was: C. W. Bickford, five votes; John Smith, two votes; John Doe, one vote; and two votes were blank. The chairman declared that no election had taken place, but Bickford claimed the office. The court sustained Bickford's contention because the blank ballots were not expressive of a choice and were without effect in determining the result of the contest:

> The argument that such a ballot indicates a purpose of the voter to register his refusal to vote for the successful candidate overlooks the fact that it is just as indicative of his purpose to concur in the result which the regular ballots disclose. It is difficult to see how it has any more effect upon the result than a refusal to vote, which is regarded, so far as it is important, as an acquiescence in the result. It has no negative effect. What the voter's purpose was is not apparent.

To the same effect is the opinion of the court in the case of *Murdoch* v. *Strange*.[44] The mayor and the city council of Annapolis, Maryland, voted to elect a market master. Strange received four votes, Murdoch three, and there was one blank ballot. The court held that Strange had been elected because at common law a blank ballot is

42. *Murdoch* v. *Strange*, 99 Md. 89, 3 Ann. Cas. 66; *Attorney-General* v. *Bickford*, 77 N.H. 433, 92 Atl. 835, Ann. Cas. 1916B 119; *Hicks* v. *Krigbaum*, 13 Ariz. 237, 108 Pac. 482; *People* v. *Sausalito*, 106 Calif. 500, 39 Pac. 937; *Cashman* v. *City Clerk of Salem*, 213 Mass. 153, 100 N.E. 58; *Battle Creek Brewing Co.* v. *Calhoun County*, 166 Mich. 52, Ann. Cas. 1912D 946, 131 N.W. 160; *State* v. *Roper*, 47 Neb. 417, 66 N.W. 539; *Bonsack & Pearce* v. *School District of Marceline*, 49 S.W. (2d) (Mo.) 1085.

43. *Attorney-General* v. *Bickford*, 77 N.H. 433, 92 Atl. 835, Ann. Cas. 1916B 119.

44. *Murdoch* v. *Strange*, 99 Md. 89, 3 Ann. Cas. 66.

not to be counted in estimating the number of ballots cast. To call a blank piece of paper a ballot would be a misnomer. "It is in fact nothing; it cannot be expressive of any intention; no rule or method of interpretation can relieve it of its dumbness."

In two jurisdictions a contrary rule seems to hold. It has been held in Minnesota that where the law requires a majority of the "votes cast" in order to carry a proposition, blank ballots must be considered in determining the fact of majority.[45] So, too, in Ohio, "if it is required by law that a majority, or any certain proposition of the votes cast at the election, should be in favor of a proposition in order that it should carry, then all the votes cast at the election, including blank and unintelligible ballots, must be considered."[46]

RIGHT TO RESCIND ACTION

At any time before rights to third parties have vested, a board of education has authority to rescind any action which it may have taken. Where, for example, the inhabitants of a district voted to raise money for the erection of a schoolhouse, they had the right to rescind the vote at their discretion at any time prior to the levy of the taxes.[47] It has been held, too, that a resolution adopting a uniform system of schoolbooks may be rescinded at the same session at which the original vote was taken.[48] The Board of Education of Minneapolis passed a resolution adopting a system of shorthand as the exclusive system to be used in the school system for a period of five years. The court refused to enjoin the board from teaching any other system. The resolution was not a contract; it was nothing more than a statement of policy, which could be rescinded.[49] So, too, a resolution creating a new school district may be rescinded.[50] In Massachusetts it has been held that the election of a superintendent of schools may be rescinded at an adjourned meeting which was in legal effect a continuation of the original meeting.[51] It seems, however, that in this case the super-

45. *Smith* v. *Renville County,* 64 Minn. 16, 65 N.W. 956.

46. *Wellsville* v. *Connor,* 91 Ohio St. 28, 109 N.E. 526. See also *State* v. *Chapman,* 44 Conn. 595.

47. *Pond* v. *Negus,* 3 Mass. 230, 3 Am. Dec. 131.

48. *State* v. *Womack,* 4 Wash. 19, 29 Pac. 939.

49. *Caton* v. *Board of Education of Minneapolis,* 213 Minn. 165, 6 N.W. (2d) 266.

50. *State* v. *Carrol County Board of Education,* 129 Ohio St. 262, 194 N.E. 867.

51. *Reed* v. *Barton,* 176 Mass. 473, 57 N.E. 961.

intendent was never notified of his election. Moreover, the revocation of a former action need not be formal or done in express terms. The doing of an act wholly inconsistent with an earlier act constitutes a valid revocation.[52] And until a contract in conformity with a school board's action has been signed and delivered, it has been held, the board may rescind its action at its discretion.[53]

BINDING FORCE OF BOARD RULES
UPON BOARD ITSELF

The regulations and by-laws of a board of education made under statutory authority have the force of law and are binding even upon the board itself where rights to third parties have accrued.[54] A case in point is that of *United States* v. *Callahan*.[55] Under a rule of the Board of Education of the District of Columbia, a teacher might be granted a leave of absence for a year, provided that she filed a pledge with the superintendent to teach in the schools of the District for a period of at least two years after the expiration of the leave of absence. The board of education granted a leave of absence to one Otelia Cromwell in order that she might pursue a course of study in Yale University. She failed to file the required pledge but was assured by the assistant superintendent that she would be permitted to return to her position. The teacher next on the eligible list claimed that this failure to file a pledge as the rule required created a vacancy in the position held by Otelia Cromwell and sought a writ of mandamus requiring the board to appoint her to the place thus made vacant. The writ was granted by the Court of Appeals of the District of Columbia for the following reasons:

While it may be conceded that the board might exercise the power of appointment in any reasonable manner it might deem proper to adopt, it has in its wisdom elected to exercise this power through certain rules and reg-ulations which it has adopted and promulgated. Being empowered by the act of Congress to make such rules and regulations, they must be deemed to have the force and effect of law, unless they are in conflict with express

52. *George* v. *Second School District in Mendon*, 47 Mass. (6 Metc.) 497.

53. *Commonwealth* ex rel. *Ricapito* v. *School District of City of Bethlehem*, 148 Pa. Super. Ct. 426, 25 Atl. (2d) 786; *Ickes* v. *Costlow*, 127 Pa. Super. Ct. 180, 193 Atl. 287; *Chilli* v. *School District of McKeesport*, 334 Pa. 581, 6 Atl. (2d) 99.

54. *Montenegro-Riehm Music Company* v. *Board of Education*, 147 Ky. 720, 145 S.W. 740; *United States* v. *Callahan*, 294 Fed. 992.

55. *United States* v. *Callahan*, 294 Fed. 992.

statutory provisions. In other words, they are binding upon the respondents in the matter of appointing and promoting teachers. . . .

We think that, if the rules of the board are to be given the force of law, a teacher, obtaining a leave of absence to pursue a postgraduate course of training, must comply strictly with the letter of the rule, in order to retain her position in competition against others who would otherwise be entitled to the position vacated.

The assistant superintendent, moreover, had no authority to ignore the rules of the board, "nor indeed could the board itself abrogate its own rules, to meet the exigencies of a single case, and certainly not to the detriment of a right which had accrued."

The same position has been taken by the Court of Appeals of Kentucky.[56] The Board of Education of the city of Louisville adopted a rule that no purchase of supplies should be made in excess of five hundred dollars except upon bids previously advertised for and accepted. Notwithstanding this rule, a contract was entered into for the purchase of pianos to the amount of twenty-five hundred dollars without any bids having been received. Later the board refused to execute the contract. Said the court:

We are only concerned with the effect of the rules and by-laws adopted by public corporations to enable them to better carry out the purpose of their creation and existence, and we have no doubt that the material reasonable rules and by-laws of a public corporation made and adopted in pursuance of legislative authority and within the scope of the powers of the public corporation to aid it in the discharge of its public duties, have the same binding force and effect upon it and all persons with whom it does business as the statute under which it derives its powers.

The court pointed out, moreover, that persons dealing with a municipal corporation are bound at their peril to know that all contracts must be made in the mode appointed by the charter and ordinances. If they fail to observe the rules and regulations of a school board, for example, they must suffer the consequences.

The same principle of law was involved where a board of education refused to grant a high-school diploma to a pupil who would not wear a cap and gown at the graduating exercises, as the board required. In issuing a writ of mandamus that the diploma be granted, the court pointed out that the board had prescribed an approved course of study and had provided that the honors of graduation and diplomas should be conferred upon all who completed it. Since the

56. *Montenegro-Riehm Music Company* v. *Board of Education,* 147 Ky. 720, 145 S.W. 740.

rules established by the board became the law for the government of the school, the board, under its own rule, would be compelled to grant a diploma to any pupil who had met the requirements. It should be added, perhaps, that the rule with respect to the wearing of caps and gowns was held unreasonable and therefore void.[57]

It has been held, however, that, under certain conditions, a board may ignore its own rules and regulations. This may be done, it seems, where no rights have accrued to third parties or where the rule has to do merely with parliamentary procedure.[58] In the case of *Weatherly* v. *Chattanooga*,[59] it was held, for example, that, although a rule was in force requiring all applications for teaching positions in the schools to be made in writing, the unanimous election of a teacher who had made no such application was valid. If the board saw fit by unanimous vote to ignore the rule, it could not later repudiate the contract because the rule had not been complied with. In a somewhat similar case,[60] the Board of Education of the city of San Francisco had a regulation that any rule adopted by the board might be amended or repealed by the affirmative vote of three members, provided that notice in writing of such intended amendment or repeal had been given at a previous meeting. This regulation was ignored in amending a rule relating to teachers' absences. The court held that the rule in question was merely one of parliamentary procedure and might be suspended as occasion required. In any event, the board members alone had the

57. *Valentine* v. *Independent School District of Casey*, 191 Iowa 1100, 183 N.W. 434.

58. While the weight of authority seems to be that a municipal board may ignore its rules of procedure, there is some disagreement among the courts with respect to this rule of law. In the case of *Territory* v. *Dondero*, 21 Hawaii 19, Ann. Cas. 1914D 1192, it was said: "It is almost uniformly held that a municipal board may waive or suspend its rules of procedure. Such waiver may be brought about either by formal action on the part of the board or by ignoring of the rules without objection. If an ordinance is passed without violation of statutory requirements, but in violation merely of a rule of procedure, it will not be held invalid for that reason. 28 Cyc. 333; *Sedalia* v. *Scott*, 104 Mo. App. 595, 78 S.W. 276." To the same general effect are the following cases: *State* v. *Pinkerman*, 63 Conn. 176, 28 Atl. 110, 22 L.R.A. 653; *Wheelock* v. *Lowell*, 196 Mass. 220, 81 N.E. 977, 124 Am. St. Rep. 543, 12 Ann. Cas. 1109. In the case of *Hicks* v. *Long Branch Commission*, 69 N.J. Law 300, 55 Atl. 250, the opposite position was taken. A rule adopted to the effect that the "yeas" and "nays" should be taken on every vote relating to any special appropriation was held to be as binding upon the commission and its members as any statute or law of the commonwealth. See also *Swindell* v. *State*, 143 Ind. 153, 42 N.E. 528, 35 L.R.A. 50.

59. *Weatherly* v. *Chattanooga*, 48 S.W. (Tenn.) 136.

60. *Grosjean* v. *Board of Education*, 40 Calif. App. 434, 181 Pac. 113.

right to complain. The St. Louis Board of Education had a rule that all school-building contracts should be let to the lowest and best bidder. It advertised for bids for the erection of a schoolhouse but reserved the right to reject any or all bids. The lowest bidder was not awarded the contract; nevertheless, the court held he had no cause of action. "Whatever its rules or practices as to acceptance of bids may have been, plaintiffs' rights cannot be justly held to be greater than those conferred by the published advertisement on which their bid was made."[61] In Kansas a board rule read: "At the regular meeting in March of each year the board of education shall elect, by ballot, a superintendent of schools." At a special meeting in February a superintendent was elected on motion and not by ballot. In holding the election valid, the court said:

> It would be carrying technicalities to the extreme, however, to hold that a board of education might not by common consent waive its rule requiring an election of a superintendent to be held by ballot, and signify its choice by a call of the members and the recording of their votes. . . . Nor would it do, we think, to say that the election of a superintendent at a meeting of the board called for that purpose should be held invalid merely because the board had previously adopted a rule fixing a regular and later meeting as the time for selecting a superintendent.[62]

EFFECT OF STATUTE PRESCRIBING TIME FOR
TAKING SPECIFIC ACTION

Not infrequently a statute provides that school boards shall take certain action on or before a stipulated date. As a rule, such statutes are regarded as directory only, and, unless there is some provision expressly prohibiting the taking of the action in question after the expiration of the prescribed date, a board may act within any reasonable time.[63] A Pennsylvania statute, for example, required school directors to levy the annual tax for school purposes on or before the first Monday in May. In a case[64] testing the authority of the directors to levy

61. *Anderson v. Board, etc., of St. Louis Public Schools,* 122 Mo. 61, 27 S.W. 610, 26 L.R.A. 707.

62. *State v. Sinclair,* 103 Kan. 480, 175 Pac. 41.

63. *Walker v. Edmonds,* 197 Pa. St. 645, 47 Atl. 867; *Gearhart v. Dixon,* 1 Pa. St. 224; *Wampler v. State,* 148 Ind. 557, 47 N.E. 1068, 38 L.R.A. 829; *Sackett v. State,* 74 Ind. 486. See also *State v. Smith,* 22 Minn. 218; *People v. Allen,* 6 Wend. (N.Y.) 486. For contrary opinion see *State v. Cones,* 15 Neb. 444, 19 N.W. 682; *Willard v. Pike,* 59 Vt. 202, 9 Atl. 907; *City of Hutchinson v. Ryan,* 154 Kan. 751, 121 Pac. (2d) 179.

64. *Gearhart v. Dixon,* 1 Pa. St. 224.

the tax at a later date, the supreme court used the following language: "Here is a positive duty, enjoined by express legislative enactment. . . . The school directors of Rush township were enjoined, by law, to levy the tax on or before the first Monday in May. The act of Assembly is directory as to the time, and if by accident, or from any other cause, this duty was omitted, it could be performed in any reasonable time thereafter."

Similarly, in the case of *Hendershot* v. *State,* it was said by the Supreme Court of Indiana:

For the most excellent reason, it seems to be held by the courts everywhere that when a duty is imposed by statute upon public officers which affects the rights or duties of others, and the time of its performance designated, the officers will not be relieved of the duty by their failure to perform on the date specified, unless the language of the statute is such that the designated time must be accepted as a limitation of the officers' power. In the absence of words of limitation, the prescribed time of performance will be regarded as directory only, and the duty to perform a continuing one subject to mandamus, by the party in interest, within a reasonable period.[65]

The mandatory part of such statutes is that action be taken, whereas the time of taking the action is directory only. Obviously, public policy commonly demands that the prescribed action be taken. While the lawmaking body may desire that it be taken within certain time limits, to hold that it must be taken within those limits or not at all would often prove socially disastrous.

ADJOURNMENT OF MEETING

Like all similar bodies, a school board has the power, if unrestricted by statute, to adjourn a regular meeting to such time and place as it deems expedient, and, unless such adjournment is an abuse of power, it is not subject to review.[66] Difficulty sometimes arises, however, as to what constitutes adjournment. "An adjournment is an act, not a declaration. It is an act of separation and departure, and, until this takes place, the adjournment is not complete."[67] In the case of *Gallagher* v. *School Township of Willow,*[68] a motion to adjourn had been passed and one or two of the members may have departed, although a quorum still remained. Those remaining prepared a notice of an

65. *Hendershot* v. *State,* 162 Ind. 69, 69 N.E. 679.

66. *People* v. *Nelson,* 252 Ill. 514, 96 N.E. 1071; *Donough* v. *Dewey,* 82 Mich. 309, 46 N.W. 782.

67. *Beatle* v. *Roberts,* 156 Iowa 575, 137 N.W. 1006.

68. *Gallagher* v. *School Township of Willow,* 173 Iowa 610, 154 N.W. 437.

election, and the court sustained their action. Similarly, it has been held that, although an adjournment of court had been announced and the judges had risen to go, the court was still in session and could receive a verdict.[69] Nor does the fact that half the members of a board refuse longer to participate in the meeting constitute an adjournment if they remain in the room where the business is being transacted. In an Indiana case, six township trustees met on the first Monday in June, as provided by statute, to elect a county superintendent of schools. They balloted 236 times without consummating an election, and at midnight three of the trustees withdrew and joined the group of spectators in the room. Three votes were then cast for one candidate, and he was declared elected. The legality of the proceeding was tested in the supreme court, which held that the three trustees who attempted to withdraw were still present. They could not change from trustees to mere spectators so long as they remained in the room and had an opportunity to vote. Nor did the arrival of the hour of midnight operate *ipso facto* to work an adjournment.[70]

NECESSITY OF KEEPING RECORDS

While boards of education should keep records of their proceedings, it is not necessary that they do so in the absence of a statute to that effect.[71] It has been held, for example, that failure to keep a formal record of a board meeting at which a pupil was expelled does not render the action void.[72] Similarly, action by a school board dismissing a teacher was not void because of failure to keep a record of it.[73] In Indiana an order of a township trustee discontinuing a school was held valid, although the trustee failed to record the order at the proper time.[74] Even where a statute required a record of all orders and pro-

---

69. *Person* v. *Neigh,* 52 Pa. St. 199.

70. *State* v. *Vanosdal,* 131 Ind. 388, 31 N.E. 79, 15 L.R.A. 832.

71. *Tufts* v. *State,* 119 Ind. 232, 21 N.E. 892; *Smith* v. *Johnson,* 105 Neb. 61, 178 N.W. 835, 12 A.L.R. 231; *Bellmeyer* v. *Independent District of Marshalltown,* 44 Iowa 564; *State* v. *Cahill,* 131 Iowa 155, 105 N.W. 691; *Fleming* v. *Board of Trustees,* 296 Pac. (Calif.) 925. NOTE: 12 A.L.R. 235. In the case of *United States* v. *Dandridge,* 12 Wheat. (U.S.) 64, it was said: "We do not admit, as a general proposition, that the acts of a corporation, although in all other respects rightly transacted, are invalid, merely from the omission to have them reduced to writing, unless the statute creating it makes such writing indispensable as evidence, or to give them an obligatory force."

72. *Smith* v. *Johnson,* 105 Neb. 61, 178 N.W. 835, 12 A.L.R. 231.

73. *Holcombe* v. *County Board of Education,* 242 Ala. 20, 4 So. (2d) 503.

74. *Tufts* v. *State,* 119 Ind. 232, 21 N.E. 892.

ceedings, a board rule excluding children under seven years of age unless they entered school within four weeks after the opening of the fall term was not void because not entered upon the minutes.[75] In the case of *Russell* v. *Lynnfield,* it was said: "The school committee are required to have general charge and superintendence of all the public schools in the town, and to keep a record of their votes, orders, and proceedings. But this does not imply that all rules and orders required for the discipline and good conduct of the schools shall be matter of record."[76] Nor may a contract entered into with a school board be repudiated merely because no record of the transaction was kept;[77] this is true, even though the statutes require the clerk to keep minutes of each meeting.[78] Thus a failure to record the minutes of a meeting of a school board at which the purchase of fire insurance policies was authorized did not invalidate the policies which had been approved at delivery.[79]

SUFFICIENCY OF RECORDS

As a rule, it is not necessary that the minutes of school-board meetings be formal or technical.[80] As was said in the case of *Kinney* v. *Howard,* "too strict rules should not be adopted with reference to records of the proceedings of school boards. They are usually kept by persons not versed in the law, and are generally quite informal in character. If they show the action in fact taken, although not conveniently or formally expressed, they should be held sufficient."[81] Similarly, the Supreme Court of Nebraska has said with reference to a resolution authorizing the purchase of a schoolhouse site: "The records and proceedings of school district meetings are not to be given a narrow and technical construction, but should be construed in such a manner as to give effect to the manifest intention of the voters, if the same can be ascertained from the records."[82] Where, for instance,

75. *Alvord* v. *Chester,* 180 Mass. 20, 61 N.E. 263.

76. *Russell* v. *Lynnfield,* 116 Mass. 365.

77. *School Directors* v. *McBride,* 22 Pa. St. 215.

78. *Decker* v. *School District No. 2,* 101 Mo. App. 115, 74 S.W. 390.

79. *Columbia Insurance Company* v. *Board of Education,* 185 Okla. 292, 91 Pac. (2d) 736, 122 A.L.R. 1358.

80. NOTE: 12 A.L.R. 235.

81. *Kinney* v. *Howard,* 133 Iowa 94, 110 N.W. 282.

82. *Quisenberry* v. *School District No. 6,* 75 Neb. 47, 105 N.W. 982.

a clerk made a minute on a piece of paper but failed to transcribe it into the record-book because of sickness, the court held the minute was sufficient to indicate the action taken.[83] Sufficient, too, is a record kept on sheets of paper clipped or pinned into the record-book.[84] Even where a statute made it the duty of the secretary of the district to record all the proceedings of the board and of district meetings in separate books kept for that purpose, records kept on half-sheets and quarter-sheets of paper not bound in book form were held to be sufficient. The court was unwilling to declare void all the proceedings of the district because the statute had not been technically followed. It preferred to regard the statute as directory.[85]

As a general rule, statutes requiring that school-board records show the "yeas" and "nays" are mandatory, and a statement that a measure was carried unanimously will not suffice.[86] There are two reasons why the letter of such legislation is enforced. It is the evident policy of the state that the records show how each individual member of the board voted, so that the public may know where to place responsibility. A record showing a unanimous vote does not indicate which members were present at the time the vote was taken. Moreover, where it is merely recorded that a measure was unanimously adopted, there is no way to ascertain whether a quorum was present at the time. To illustrate, a Kentucky statute provided that boards of education could enter into contracts only with the consent of a majority of the members elected and that the "yeas" and "nays" be entered upon the record. In holding that a minute which stipulated that a certain contract had been entered into by a unanimous vote was not sufficient, the court said:

It is true the minutes show that at the opening of the board there were present a sufficient number of the members to constitute a quorum, and if they unanimously voted in favor of the acceptance of the bank's proposition

83. *Foreman* v. *School District No. 25*, 81 Ore. 587, 159 Pac. 1155.

84. *Trustees of Slaughterville Graded School District* v. *Brooks*, 163 Ky. 200, 173 S.W. 305.

85. *Higgins* v. *Reed*, 8 Iowa 298, 74 Am. Dec. 305.

86. *Board of Education* v. *Newport National Bank*, 121 Ky. 775, 28 Ky. Law Rep. 745, 90 S.W. 569; *Strathern* v. *Gilmore*, 184 Pa. St. 265, 39 Atl. 83; *Board of Education* v. *Best*, 52 Ohio St. 138, 39 N.E. 694, 27 L.R.A. 77; *Steckert* v. *City of East Saginaw*, 22 Mich. 104; *Cutler* v. *Russellville*, 40 Ark. 105; *Town of Olin* v. *Meyers*, 55 Iowa 209, 7 N.W. 509; *Morrison* v. *City of Lawrence*, 98 Mass. 219; 19 R.C.L. 889. Accord, *Potts* v. *School District of Penn Township*, 127 Pa. Super. Ct. 173, 193 Atl. 290; *Price* v. *School District of Borough of Taylor*, 157 Pa. Super. Ct. 188, 42 Atl. (2d) 99.

the requirements of the statute would be substantially complied with. . . . But it does not follow that, because there was a statutory quorum at the opening of the board, all these members remained until the proposition of the bank came up for acceptance or rejection. Common experience teaches that the contrary is usually true. The members of deliberative bodies come and go, and often, when there is not a call for the "yeas and nays," business is transacted with less than a quorum present.[87]

It has been held, however, that where the record shows that all the members of the board were present and all voted affirmatively, the "yeas" and "nays" were effectively recorded.[88] So, too, it has been held that the "yeas" and "nays" were not required by a statute which provided that "each motion, with the name of the person making it and the vote thereon, shall be entered on the record." A minute which merely stated, "Motion carried," was deemed sufficient.[89]

CONCLUSIVENESS OF RECORDS

Ordinarily, the official records of a public corporation are *prima facie* evidence of the action taken by that corporation. Such a body speaks through its records.[90] As was said by the Supreme Court of Missouri: "Where the law requires a record of the proceedings of a board to be kept, the record is not only the best evidence, but, primarily, is the only evidence by which the action of the board may be shown."[91] Few of the rules of evidence are more commonly accepted or have a wider application than that which declares that parol or extrinsic evidence is inadmissible to contradict, vary, or subtract from the official records of a public body, such as a board of education.[92]

87. *Board of Education* v. *Newport National Bank,* 121 Ky. 775, 28 Ky. Law Rep. 745, 90 S.W. 569.

88. *Burke* v. *Wilkes-Barre Township School District,* 28 Pa. Super. Ct. 16; *Tobin* v. *Morgan,* 70 Pa. St. 229; *Genesee Township* v. *McDonald,* 98 Pa. St. 444.

89. *Edwards* v. *Matthews,* 100 Ohio St. 487, 127 N.E. 462.

90. *Lawrence* v. *Trainer,* 136 Ill. 474, 27 N.E. 197; *Bartlett* v. *Kinsley,* 15 Conn. 327; *Lone Jack Graded School* v. *Hendrickson,* 304 Ky. 317, 200 S.W. (2d) 736; *Botts* v. *Prentiss County School Board,* 175 Miss. 62, 166 So. 398; *State* v. *Smith,* 336 Mo. 703, 80 S.W. (2d) 858.

91. *State* v. *Smith,* 336 Mo. 703, 80 S.W. (2d) 858.

92. *Everts* v. *District Township of Rose Grove,* 77 Iowa 37, 41 N.W. 478, 14 Am. St. Rep. 264; *Cowley* v. *School District No. 3,* 130 Mich. 634, 90 N.W. 680; *Howland* v. *Prentice,* 143 Mich. 347, 106 N.W. 1105; *Third School District in Stoughton* v. *Atherton,* 12 Metc. (Mass.) 105; *Mayhew* v. *District of Gay Head,* 13 Allen (Mass.) 129; *Cameron* v. *School District No. 2,* 42 Vt. 507; *Bartlett* v. *Kinsley,* 15 Conn. 327; *Common School District No. 50* v. *Fishback,* 20 Ky. Law Rep. 1198, 49 S.W. 29; *Brooks* v. *Franconia School District,* 73 N.H. 263, 61

If incorrect minutes are kept, the remedy lies in having them corrected at that or some subsequent meeting.[93] In the case of *Cowley* v. *School District No. 3*,[94] a teacher claimed that she had been employed by the board at a legal meeting and sought to prove it by the testimony of a majority of the members of the board. The official record of the proceedings of the meeting stated that "the application of Miss Cowley for the next term of school was presented by Mr. Wilson, but no action was taken." The court rejected such testimony as Miss Cowley was able to present, on the ground that it would contradict the official records. In Pennsylvania, the minutes of a board of school directors stated that the board had passed a resolution providing for an increase in the salary of certain designated employees. The court held that parol evidence could not be introduced to show that certain members of the board had intended by the resolution to elect one of the named employees as principal.[95] Nor may a school board, in an action for mandamus to require the state auditor to issue its bonds, introduce parol evidence to show that the proper procedures had been followed in the establishment of the district.[96] A similar conclusion was reached by the Supreme Court of Errors of Connecticut when it stated: "The intention of a corporation can be ascertained only by the language of its recorded acts; and neither the private views nor the public declarations of individual members of such corporation can, for this purpose, be enquired into."[97]

Atl. 127; *Toye* v. *Exeter Borough School District*, 225 Pa. St. 236, 74 Atl. 60; *Vaughn* v. *School District No. 31*, 27 Ore. 57, 39 Pac. 393; *Moor* v. *Newfield*, 4 Greenl. (Me.) 44; 22 C.J. 1085; 10 R.C.L. 1028. NOTE: 50 L.R.A. (N.S.) 99; 12 A.L.R. 235; *State* v. *Smith*, 336 Mo. 703, 80 S.W. (2d) 858; *Cagle* v. *Wheeler*, 242 S.W. (2d) (Tenn.) 338; *Strine* v. *School District of Upper Merion Township*, 149 Pa. Super. Ct. 612, 27 Atl. (2d) 552; *Consolidated District No. 8* v. *Hooks*, 222 S.W. (2d) (Mo.) 355; *Commonwealth* ex rel. *Hettrick*, 335 Pa. 6, 6 Atl. (2d) 279; *Potts* v. *School District of Penn Township*, 127 Pa. Super. Ct. 173, 193 Atl. 290; *People* ex rel. *Toman* v. *Chicago Heights Terminal Transfer Company*, 375 Ill. 590, 32 N.E. (2d) 161. But see *State* v. *Van Winkle*, 25 N.J. Law 73.

93. *Everts* v. *District Township of Rose Grove*, 77 Iowa 37, 41 N.W. 478, 14 Am. St. Rep. 264. An interested party may bring action for a writ of mandamus to require the proper official to correct the minutes in conformity with the truth (*Farrell* v. *King*, 41 Conn. 448).

94. *Cowley* v. *School Dostrict No. 3*, 130 Mich. 634 90 N.W. 680. Accord, *Consolidated School District No. 8* v. *Hooks*, 222 S.W. (2d) (Mo.) 355.

95. *Strine* v. *School District of Upper Merion Township*, 149 Pa. Super. Ct. 612, 27 Atl. (2d) 552.

96. *State* v. *Smith*, 336 Mo. 703, 80 S.W. (2d) 858.

97. *Bartlett* v. *Kinsley*, 15 Conn. 327.

The rule of law, however, which excludes parol or extrinsic evidence to vary or change official records is subject to a degree of flexibility and a considerable number of exceptions. It will not be taken to mean that the minutes of a board of education may not be supplemented or explained by parol evidence where such minutes are indefinite or obscure in meaning.[98] The rule has been clearly stated in the case of *Cagle* v. *Wheeler:*[98a] "The argument is . . . that the action of school boards can only be established from the minutes of such boards. Such is the general rule but it is not to be applied in a manner to exclude parol evidence which supplements, but does not contradict or vary, the terms of the minutes of such boards. Parol evidence of the latter kind is receivable unless the law expressly and imperatively requires all matters to appear of record and makes the record the only evidence."

A good example of how far the courts will go in permitting the introduction of oral evidence to clear up an ambiguous record is the case of *Westerman* v. *Cleland*.[99] The minutes of a county board of education read: "July 3d, Ukiah High School. Principal, P. B. Westerman, $1,500." Westerman acted as principal for nine months and was paid $150 a month, and then the school was closed. He brought suit to recover an additional $150. The court permitted the board of education to introduce evidence to show that it had not employed Westerman for a term of ten months or at a salary of $150 a month for the time taught. The opinion of the court is, in part, as follows:

If the minute entry of July 3, 1906, had stated what is claimed in the complaint—that plaintiff was employed for one year to be paid $1,500 for the year—the question raised by appellant that the minutes could not be impeached or contradicted might be considered. The minute entry, however, fails to import on its face such a contract as is claimed for it, or, indeed, any contract at all, and it was competent for defendants to show what the contract was—not as contradicting the minutes, but as explanatory thereof.

Parol or extrinsic evidence is admissible to supply omissions in the records of a board of education.[100] Action taken at a lawful meeting

98. *Tucker* v. *McKay*, 131 Mo. App. 728, 111 S.W. 867; *Gaston* v. *Lamkin*, 115 Mo. 20, 21 S.W. 1100; *Westerman* v. *Cleland*, 12 Calif. App. 63, 106 Pac. 606; *School District No. 2* v. *Clark*, 90 Mich. 435, 51 N.W. 529; *Gearhart* v. *Dixon*, 1 Pa. St. 224.

98a. *Cagle* v. *Wheeler*, 242 S.W. (2d) (Tenn.) 338.

99. *Westerman* v. *Cleland*, 12 Calif. App. 63, 106 Pac. 606.

100. *Kinney* v. *Howard*, 133 Iowa 94, 110 N.W. 282; *Brown* v. *City of Webster City*, 115 Iowa 511, 88 N.W. 1070; *Bigelow* v. *Perth Amboy*, 25 N.J. Law 297; *Bartlett* v. *Board of Education*, 59 Ill. 364; *Morgan* v. *Wilfley*, 71 Iowa 212, 32

will not be rendered void because of failure to make a record of it. This is especially true where rights accrue to third parties as a result of board action. If this were not the case, such corporations as cities or school districts might escape liability upon their contracts simply through failure to make a record of them.[101] A case in point is that of *German Insurance Company* v. *Independent School District of Milford.*[102] A school board authorized its president to insure the school buildings, but the clerk failed to make any record of the action. Later it was claimed that the president acted without authority, and the records of the board were offered as evidence. In holding that the facts as to what actually occurred at the meeting in question might be established by the testimony of those present, the court used the following language:

This action of the board was part of its business at that meeting, and should have been recorded. But it was the vote of the directors which gave authority to the president to act on behalf of the district, and the negligence of the clerk in failing to record the action of the board could not nullify that authority. Had the clerk made the record, it would have been competent evidence, and the best evidence, of the action of the board. But, as he failed to make such record, the fact could be proven by the persons present.

So, too, it has been held that action taken by a school board in employing a teacher may be established by parol evidence in the absence of any record.[103] And it has been held that where records have been lost or destroyed they may be established by parol evidence.[104] In the case of *Bartlett* v. *Board of Education,*[105] the Supreme Court of Illinois

---

N.W. 265; *Walker* v. *Edmonds,* 197 Pa. St. 645, 47 Atl. 867; *German Insurance Company* v. *Independent School District of Milford,* 80 Fed. 366; *Athearn* v. *Independent District of Millersburg,* 33 Iowa 105; *Pollard* v. *School District No. 9,* 65 Ill. App. 104; *Page* v. *Township Board of Education,* 59 Mo. 264; *School District No. 1* v. *Union School District No. 1,* 81 Mich. 339, 45 N.W. 993; *Roland* v. *Reading School District,* 161 Pa. St. 102, 28 Atl. 995; *Tucker* v. *McKay,* 131 Mo. App. 728, 111 S.W. 867; *Bellmeyer* v. *Independent District of Marshalltown,* 44 Iowa 564; *Jackson* v. *School Directors of District No. 85,* 232 Ill. App. 102; 22 C.J. 1014. NOTE: 74 Am. Dec. 310; *Price* v. *School District of Borough of Taylor,* 157 Pa. Super. Ct. 188, 42 Atl. (2d) 99.

101. *Brown* v. *City of Webster City,* 115 Iowa 511, 88 N.W. 1070.

102. *German Insurance Company* v. *Independent School District of Milford,* 80 Fed. 366, 25 C.C.A. 492.

103. *School Directors* v. *Kimmel,* 31 Ill. App. 537; *Pollard* v. *School District No. 9,* 65 Ill. App. 104.

104. *People* v. *Hubble,* 378 Ill. 377, 38 N.E. (2d) 38.

105. *Bartlett* v. *Board of Education,* 59 Ill. 364.

permitted the fact to be established that a board of education had approved the bond of its treasurer, although the matter was not mentioned in the minutes. A contract between a school board and an attorney has been sustained in the absence of any official record of the transaction.[106] Where the minutes of a district meeting showed that a certain motion had been adopted but did not show what motion, the court permitted parol evidence to establish the fact that the building of a new schoolhouse had been authorized.[107] In a Pennsylvania case, the secretary of a board of school directors inadvertently neglected to record the action of the board in electing a treasurer. The court permitted members of the board to testify that this action had in fact been taken.[108] That parol evidence is admissible to supply omissions in the records of school boards seems to be a common and widely accepted principle of law.

The rule as thus broadly stated, however, is subject to certain exceptions. Where the statutes require that the acts and proceedings of school boards appear of record, in some jurisdictions parol evidence is inadmissible to supply omissions, for the record is the only evidence.[109] In other jurisdictions the mere fact that a statute requires that records of acts and proceedings be kept will not preclude the introduction of parol or extrinsic evidence to supply omissions. Undoubtedly, the better principle of law is that parol or extrinsic evidence may be introduced to supply omissions in official records unless the statutes expressly provide that the records be the only and exclusive evidence of board action.[110] In the case of *School Directors* v. *Kimmel*,[111] for example, a statute provided that the school directors should appoint a clerk who should keep a "record of all the official acts of the board in a well-bound book." Nevertheless, the court ruled:

106. *Page* v. *Township Board of Education*, 59 Mo. 264.

107. *Morgan* v. *Wilfley*, 71 Iowa 212, 32 N.W. 265.

108. *Price* v. *School District of Borough of Taylor*, 157 Pa. Super. Ct. 188, 42 Atl. (2d) 99.

109. *Jordan* v. *School District No. 3*, 38 Me. 164; *Sherwin* v. *Bugbee*, 17 Vt. 337; *Broussard* v. *Verret*, 43 La. Ann. 929, 9 So. 905; *Mayhew* v. *District of Gay Head*, 13 Allen (Mass.) 129; 22 C.J. 1014. Note: 50 L.R.A. (N.S.) 105.

110. *Tucker* v. *McKay*, 131 Mo. App. 728, 111 S.W. 867; *School Directors* v. *Kimmel*, 31 Ill. App. 537; *People* v. *Lemmon*, 256 Ill. 631, 100 N.E. 200; *Jackson* v. *School Directors of District No. 85*, 232 Ill. App. 102; *Calahan* v. *Mayor of the City of New York*, 54 N.Y.S. 279; *State* v. *Scott*, 171 Ind. 349, 86 N.E. 409. Note: 74 Am. Dec. 310.

111. *School Directors* v. *Kimmel*, 31 Ill. App. 537.

The statute does not make the record kept by the clerk the only evidence of the action of the directors, and unless the law expressly and imperatively requires all matters to appear of record, and makes the record the only evidence, parol proof is admissible to prove things omitted to be stated on the record. Dillon on *Municipal Corporations,* sec. 237. While a corporation can only enter into a contract at a regular or special session of its board of directors, it does not follow that only the record of the proceedings kept by its clerk can be used as evidence to prove that a contract was entered into.

The Supreme Court of Indiana has said:

It has been a rule in this State for more than fifty years that a record is but the evidence of the fact recorded. The fact ordinarily exists independently of the record, and when there is no provision that it shall be provable only by the record, the same, upon failure of the record, may be established by parol. So in this case, if there had been no record at all, the want of it would not have invalidated the election, and the same might have been proved by parol evidence.[112]

AMENDMENT OF RECORDS

A school board may amend its records so as to make them speak the truth.[113] As was said by the Appellate Court of Illinois:

If the record truthfully states the facts and all of the facts then by this record the official acts of the board are to be determined. If the record does not state any of the facts, or does not recite all of the facts, a different rule applies. The statute does not make the record kept by the clerk the only evidence of the action of the board. If the record does not correctly state the facts, the directors have a right to amend the record to make it correctly show all of the proceedings. . . . This is the limit of the power of the board to amend their records. The board is without authority to amend their records to suit their pleasure, or convenience, or to set up a state of facts which never existed. If the record truthfully shows an employment and that a contract was entered into, the board is without authority to amend the record so as to show that no contract in fact was entered into. After an amendment, if there is any omission and the record does not show all of the facts, parol evidence is admissible to show the omission.[114]

112. *State* v. *Scott,* 171 Ind. 349, 86 N.E. 409.

113. *State* v. *Hackmann,* 277 Mo. 56, 209 S.W. 92; *Beauchamp* v. *Consolidated School Dstrict No. 4,* 297 Mo. 64, 247 S.W. 1004; *Calahan* v. *Mayor of the City of New York,* 54 N.Y.S. 279; *Board of Education* v. *Trustees of Schools of Township No. 42,* 174 Ill. 510, 51 N.E. 656; *Jackson* v. *School Directors of District No. 85,* 232 Ill. App. 102; *Kent* v. *School District No. 28,* 106 Okla. 30, 233 Pac. 431; *Harris* v. *School District No. 10,* 28 N.H. 58, *State* v. *Smith,* 336 Mo. 703, 80 S.W. (2d) 858; *Board of School Trustees of Lubbock County* v. *Woodrow Independent School District,* 90 S.W. (2d) 333.

114. *Jackson* v. *School Directors of District No. 85,* 232 Ill. App. 102. But compare *Barber* v. *Wilhelm,* 7 Pa. Co. Ct. 214.

It has been held, moreover, that a board of education may amend its minutes, even though there has been a change in its personnel. In an Illinois case,[115] a school board took action with respect to changing district boundaries, but the clerk did not accurately record the proceedings. Twice thereafter the minutes were amended, once after a change in the personnel of the board. The court sustained the amendment on the ground that authority to make it depended not on the personal recollection of the individual members but on the knowledge of the clerk as to what actually happened.

While the records of the proceedings of school boards may be amended so as to make them speak the truth, this cannot be done to the prejudice of third parties; that is, if third parties have acted in reliance on the truth of the record and private rights have accrued, the record cannot be changed,[116] or, if changed, the corporation will be estopped from taking advantage of the amendment.[117] Obviously, the fundamental attribute of a record is verity, and those who deal with a public corporation should not be required to look further than the official account of its proceedings. As was said by the Supreme Court of New Hampshire:

To permit the record to be altered or amended in accordance with facts found upon the testimony of witnesses, after individuals have dealt with the town and invested their money, or performed labor upon the faith of the vote as recorded, would produce the same mischief as if no record were required. No one could safely engage in transactions with a town, or with its special agents, without first ascertaining the accuracy of the record. In attempting to do this, the same difficulty would be met as if there were no record.[118]

In fact, a record not conclusive until proved to be right might be worse than no record at all. In many instances its only effect would be to mislead and confuse.

115. *Board of Education* v. *Trustees of Schools of Township No. 42*, 174 Ill. 510, 51 N.E. 656.

116. *New Haven M. and W. R. Co.* v. *Chatham*, 42 Conn. 465; *Sawyer* v. *Manchester and K. R. Co.*, 62 N.H. 135; *California Improvement Company* v. *Moran*, 128 Calif. 373, 60 Pac. 969; Dillon, *Municipal Corporations* (5th ed.), II, 880; *Rogers and Tracy* v. *Board of Education*, 99 Fed. (2d) 773.

117. *New Haven M. and W. R. Co.* v. *Chatham*, 42 Conn. 465.

118. *Sawyer* v. *Manchester and K. R. Co.*, 62 N.H. 135. But see *Chamberlain* v. *Dover*, 13 Me. 466, 29 Am. Dec. 517, in which the court said: "If the clerk makes an erroneous record, the town are not bound by it, merely because others confide in its correctness."

CHAPTER IX

Contractual Authority and Liability
of School Boards

THE ELEMENTS OF A VALID CONTRACT

I T IS beyond the scope of this work to treat at any length the general
subject of contracts. Under the common law, however, there are
certain essential elements common to all simple contracts, and these
cannot be ignored, of course, by boards of education or parties dealing
with them. These common prerequisites are: (1) legal capacity on the
part of the contracting parties; (2) mutual assent of the contracting
parties to the terms of the contract, or what is commonly known as a
"meeting of the minds"; (3) a valid consideration; (4) rights and liabilities sufficiently definite to be enforcible; and (5) an agreement of
such a nature as not to be prohibited by the statutes or the common
law.

The question of the legal capacity of the contracting parties does
not frequently arise in relation to school contracts. The question of
mutual assent, on the other hand, may arise in connection with any
contract. It is often difficult to determine what constitutes mutual
assent or when it has been given. It is impossible to formulate any
general principle or criterion for the determination of mutual assent;
each case must stand on its own merits. Perhaps the greatest difficulty
in this connection grows out of the fact that acts or conduct intended
by one party to constitute a mere preliminary step toward a proposal
or acceptance are relied upon by the other party as a definite proposal
or acceptance. This difficulty is well illustrated in an Iowa case. A
school district advertised for bids for the erection of a schoolhouse,
requiring a certified check to accompany each bid. Nothing was said
with respect to the purpose of such requirement. The board reserved
the right to reject all bids. One Fisher was the lowest bidder. The
board voted to award him the contract and instructed its secretary to
telegraph him to that effect. The secretary sent a telegram to Fisher
which read, "You are low bidder. Come on morning train." When
Fisher arrived, he informed the board members informally that he had

made a mistake in his bid amounting to some fifteen hundred dollars. Thereupon, the board members stated that they desired to change the specifications by providing for somewhat more expensive material. Fisher then made a corrected bid to cover the mistake and the additional cost of material. The board then went into formal session, at which the contract was awarded to a lower bidder. A resolution was also passed to the effect that Fisher had refused to contract upon the basis of his bid and that his check for five hundred dollars be forfeited to the district. The board proceeded upon the theory that there was a completed contract which Fisher refused to join in reducing to written form. To this the court would not give its assent.

The action as in fact taken by the board, considered by itself, cannot be permitted to control the situation. Until communicated to Fisher, it amounted to no more than the forming of a conclusion to accept of his bid and to enter into contracts with him. It is not enough to determine upon an acceptance, but that determination must be communicated to the other party. This is elementary; but see 9 *Cyc. Law and Proc.*, p. 270, and the cases cited. So, too, it is plain that the telegram cannot be given the effect of an acceptance of the bid of Fisher, and so give rise to contract relations, as contended by appellants. It served no other purpose than the words thereof import . . . to advise Fisher that his bid was the lowest, and that further consideration or arrangement awaited his appearance in response to the invitation to come. It has frequently been held that a message similar in wording to the one in question is not sufficient.[1]

Moreover, the court pointed out that there was no express provision for a forfeiture in the notice for bids and that the law would not imply that such was intended.

The case of *Fairplay School Township* v. *O'Neal*[2] illustrates the necessity of formulating a contract in terms sufficiently definite as to be enforcible. In that case it was held that a contract to pay a teacher "good wages" was not enforcible because of indefiniteness of consideration. Nor are teachers' contracts enforcible where the term of employment is not definitely stipulated.[3] Contracts between a board of

1. *Cedar Rapids Lumber Company* v. *Fisher*, 129 Iowa 332, 105 N.W. 595, 4 L.R.A. (N.S.) 177. See also *Erving* v. *New York*, 131 N.Y. 133, 29 N.E. 1101; *Johnston Heating Company* v. *Board of Education*, 161 N.Y.S. 867; *Leskie* v. *Haseltine*, 155 Pa. St. 98, 25 Atl. 886; *Malloy* v. *Board of Education*, 102 Calif. 642, 36 Pac. 948; *Croom* v. *Goldsboro Lumber Company*, 182 N.C. 217, 108 S.E. 735.

2. *Fairplay School Township* v. *O'Neal*, 127 Ind. 95, 26 N.E. 686.

3. *Mingo* v. *Trustees of Colored Common School District No. A*, 24 Ky. Law Rep. 288, 113 Ky. 475, 68 S.W. 483; *Atkins* v. *Van Buren School Township*, 77 Ind. 447; *State* ex rel. *Ahlstrom* v. *Bauman*, 194 Minn. 439, 260 N.W. 523; *Morris* v. *Robertson*, 189 Miss. 592, 198 So. 290.

education and one of its own members are examples of contracts which are unenforcible as contravening public policy and the principles of common law.

AUTHORITY TO CONTRACT

Boards of education are limited not alone by the general principles of the law of contracts; they must, moreover, contract within the scope of their authority. School districts are merely quasi-corporations authorized by the state to exercise limited governmental functions. They can exercise only such powers as are expressly or impliedly conferred upon them by statute, or such as necessarily grow out of the purposes of their creation. Parties dealing with school boards should keep in mind the distinction between the contractual authority of a private individual and that of a public corporation. Private parties are free to incur contractual obligations so long as they do not violate some positive mandate of law or public policy, or unless they are barred from contracting by some incapacity, such as being a minor or insane. There is, on the other hand, no inherent power to contract in such quasi-corporations as school districts. Being arms of the state, created for the purpose of exercising purely governmental functions, the measure of their contractual power is found in the laws of the state and in them alone.

MODE OF CONTRACTING

Not only is a board of education limited by the statutes with respect to the subject matter of contracts; it must follow the mode prescribed by statute.[4] The statutory mode is the measure of power. "It is a principle settled by numerous decisions," said the Supreme Court of Oregon, "that where a power is given to a corporation to do an act, and the particular method by which that power is to be exercised is pointed out by the statute, the mode is the measure of power."[5]

4. *County Board of Education of Hopkins County* v. *Dudley*, 154 Ky. 426, 157 S.W. 927; *Taylor* v. *School Town of Petersburgh*, 33 Ind. App. 675, 72 N.E. 159; *Andrews Company* v. *Delight Special School District*, 95 Ark. 26, 128 S.W. 361; *Honaker* v. *Board of Education*, 42 W. Va. 170, 24 S.E. 544, 32 L.R.A. 413; *Baumann* v. *City of West Allis*, 187 Wis. 506, 204 N.W. 907; *Johnson* v. *School District*, 67 Mo. 319; *Commonwealth* ex rel. *Ricapito* v. *School District*, 148 Pa. Super. Ct. 426, 25 Atl. (2d) 786; *Walters* v. *Topper*, 139 Pa. Super. Ct. 292, 11 Atl. (2d) 649; *Leslie County Board of Education* v. *Melton*, 277 Ky. 772, 127 S.W. (2d) 846; *Board of School Commissioners of City of Indianapolis* v. *State* ex rel. *Wolfolk*, 209 Ind. 498, 199 N.E. 569; *Gordon* v. *Trustees Tuscumbia School District*, 191 Miss. 203, 1 So. (2d) 234.

5. *Barton* v. *School District No. 2*, 77 Ore. 30, 150 Pac. 251, Ann. Cas. 1917A 252.

In the absence of statutory provision that contracts with school boards be in writing, oral contracts are as valid as written ones.[6] The only difference is that the terms of the oral contract may be more difficult to establish. Where, however, the statutes require contracts to be in writing, an oral contract is void. No recovery can be had on the contract[7] or, as a general rule, for the actual value of the goods furnished or services rendered.[8] Such is the case, too, with respect to contracts made in violation of statutory provisions which require competitive bidding.[9] Moreover, where the statutes prescribe certain procedures in the making of contracts, such as the recording of the "yeas" and "nays," such procedures must be followed, or the contract will not

6. *Robinson v. Board of Education,* 70 W. Va. 66, 73 S.E. 337; *Jameson v. Board of Education,* 74 W. Va. 389, 81 S.E. 1126; *Pearson v. School District No. 8,* 144 Wis. 620, 129 N.W. 940; *Jackson School Township v. Shera,* 8 Ind. App. 330, 35 N.E. 842.

7. *Hutchins v. School District No. 1,* 128 Mich. 177, 87 N.W. 80; *City School Corporation v. Hickman,* 47 Ind. App. 500, 94 N.E. 828; *Leland v. School District No. 28,* 77 Minn. 469, 80 N.W. 354; *Lewis v. Hayden,* 18 Ky. Law Rep. 980, 38 S.W. 1054; *Board of Trustees of Hartford Graded Schools v. Ohio County Board of Education,* 172 Ky. 424, 189 S.W. 433; *Perkins v. Independent School District of Ridgeway,* 99 Mo. App. 483, 74 S.W. 122; *Riche v. Ascension Parish School Board,* 200 So. (La.) 681; *Leslie County Board of Education v. Melton,* 277 Ky. 772, 127 S.W. (2d) 846; *Gordon v. Trustees Tuscumbia School District,* 191 Miss. 203, 1 So. (2d) 234; *Ickes v. Costlow,* 127 Pa. Super. Ct. 180, 193 Atl. 287; *Dodd v. Board of Education,* 46 Ga. App. 235, 167 S.E. 319; *Krutsinger v. School Township of Liberty,* 219 Iowa 291, 257 N.W. 797; *Michaelsohn v. Norway School District,* 63 N.D. 683, 249 N.W. 776. In a few instances it has been held that a teacher's oral contract, even though the statutes required it to be in writing, could be ratified by accepting the teacher's services. In case of partial performance, however, the ratification extended only to the period of performance. *Williamson v. Board of Education,* 189 Okla. 342, 117 Pac. (2d) 120; *Bald Knob School District v. McDonald,* 171 Ark. 72, 283 S.W. 22; *School District v. Whiting,* 52 Ariz. 207, 79 Pac. (2d) 959; *Tolleson Union High School District v. Kincaid,* 53 Ariz. 60, 85 Pac. (2d) 708.

8. *Leland v. School District No. 28,* 77 Minn. 469, 80 N.W. 354; *County Board of Education of Hopkins County v. Dudley,* 154 Ky. 426, 157 S.W. 927; *Hutchins v. School District No. 1,* 128 Mich. 177, 87 N.W. 80; *Lee v. York School Township,* 163 Ind. 339, 71 N.E. 956; *Perkins v. Independent School District of Ridgeway,* 99 Mo. App. 483, 74 S.W. 122. Contra, *Bald Knob Special School District v. McDonald,* 171 Ark. 72, 283 S.W. 22; *Williams v. Board of Education,* 45 W. Va. 199, 31 S.E. 985; *Cook v. Independent School District of North McGregor,* 40 Iowa 444; *Greeson Manufacturing Co. v. County Board of Education,* 217 Ala. 565, 117 So. 163.

9. *Reams v. Cooley,* 171 Calif. 150, 152 Pac. 293, Ann. Cas. 1917A 1260; *Strauch v. San Mateo Junior College District,* 286 Pac. (Calif.) 173; *Brady v. Mayor et al., of City of New York,* 16 How. (N.Y.) 432; *Conners v. City of Lowell,* 246 Mass. 279, 140 N.E. 742; *Rankin v. Board of Education,* 135 N.J.L. 299, 51 Atl. 194; *Seim v. Independent District of Monroe,* 70 S.D. 315, 17 N.W. (2d) 342.

be enforcible.[10] Usually, however, where there has been a substantial fulfilment of the statutory formalities, the courts will not suffer minor irregularities to invalidate the contract. Thus it has been held that where the terms of the contract have been fully agreed upon, the contract need not be signed by the members of the school board at the same time and place.[11] Nor will failure to execute duplicate copies impair the validity of a contract.[12]

ADMISSIBILITY OF PAROL EVIDENCE IN THE INTERPRETATION OF CONTRACTS

When contracts are brought into the courts for interpretation and enforcement, it frequently happens that one or both of the contracting parties may seek to introduce oral or other evidence not found in the written contract itself. It is important that boards of education and all who deal with them know to what extent and for what purposes such parol or extrinsic evidence is admissible. In courts of law, parol evidence may be introduced to prove the existence of a simple contract, that is, one not under seal, or to show that the document does not constitute a valid agreement because of mistake, fraud, illegality of object, or some other reason. But, once the existence of a legal written contract is established, the courts will not admit parol or extrinsic evidence to contradict, vary, add to, or subtract from the meaning of the written document.[13] It is assumed that all previous discussions are merged into the written agreement and that it is an expression of the intent of the contracting parties. In a South Dakota case,[14] for example, members of a school board purchased books from a publishing house,

10. *Board of Education* v. *Newport National Bank*, 121 Ky. 775, 28 Ky. Law Rep. 745, 90 S.W. 569; *Price* v. *School District of Borough of Taylor*, 157 Pa. Super. Ct. 188, 42 Atl. (2d) 99.

11. *Armstrong* v. *School District No. 3*, 28 Mo. App. 169; *Holloway* v. *Ogden School District No. 9*, 62 Mich. 153, 28 N.W. 764; *School Town of Milford* v. *Zeigler*, 1 Ind. App. 138, 27 N.E. 303; *Faulk* v. *McCartney*, 42 Kan. 695, 22 Pac. 712; *School District No. 16* v. *Barnes*, 44 Okla. 489, 144 Pac. 1046. But see *Barton* v. *School District No. 2*, 77 Ore. 30, 150 Pac. 251, Ann. Cas. 1917A 252.

12. *Marr* v. *School District No. 27*, 107 Ark. 305.

13. *Western Publishing House* v. *Murdick*, 4 S.D. 207, 56 N.W. 120, 21 L.R.A. 671; *Van Syckel* v. *Dalrymple*, 32 N.J. Eq. 233; *Board of Education* v. *American National Bank of Oklahoma City*, 294 Fed. 14; *Connor* v. *Lasseter*, 98 Ga. 708, 25 S.E. 830; *Griggs* v. *School District No. 70*, 87 Ark. 93, 112 S.W. 215; *Wing* v. *Glick*, 56 Iowa 473, 9 N.W. 384, 41 Am. Rep. 118; *Andrews* v. *Estes*, 11 Me. 267, 26 Am. Dec. 521.

14. *Western Publishing House* v. *Murdick*, 4 S.D. 207, 56 N.W. 120, 21 L.R.A. 671.

and the contract was so written as to show on its face that it was the personal contract of the individual members. In defense to an action against the members of the board personally, an attempt was made to show that, in reality, the contract was intended to bind the district. The court refused to admit parol evidence to establish the claim:

It is a well-settled rule that parol evidence is inadmissible to vary, contradict, or explain an agreement when reduced to writing, in the absence of fraud or mistake. . . . The facts alleged in the answer, and proven on the trial, under the objections of the plaintiff, could have had no other effect, and could have been offered for no other purpose, than to contradict, vary, and impair the written instrument made by the defendants with the plaintiff; and hence they were incompetent and inadmissible, and constituted no defense to the action. It may be that the defendants did not actually intend to bind themselves individually by the agreement executed by them. If so, it is unfortunate for them that they executed the instrument in its present form. This court, however, is unable to relieve them. It can only judge of the intent of the parties in executing written instruments by the form of the instrument itself, unless fraud or mistake is alleged and proven in obtaining it.

Where, however, the contract is expressed in language so indefinite as to render its meaning doubtful or where ordinary terms are used which have some special, technical, or professional meaning, parol evidence may be introduced to make the meaning clear. An English case is an excellent illustration of how far the courts will go in permitting parol evidence to be introduced in order to make clear the meaning of terms used in some special or technical sense. A lessee of a rabbit warren agreed to leave ten thousand rabbits on the warren. In interpreting the contract, it was said by the court:

But here the ordinary meaning of the word "thousand" as applied to rabbits in the place where the contract was made, was one hundred dozen. The word "hundred" does not necessarily mean that number of units, for one hundred and twelve pounds is called a hundredweight; so where that term is used with respect to ling or cod, it denotes six score; and there being no precise meaning affixed by the legislature to the word "thousand" as applied to rabbits, I think the parol evidence was admissible to show that in the county where the contract was made the word "thousand" meant one hundred dozen.[15]

The courts are slow, however, to admit parol evidence to clarify the meaning of a contract. Such evidence must tend to show the correct interpretation of the language used, or it will be excluded. Its only purpose is to enable the court or the jury to reach an understanding of the language used in the contract. Evidence which tends to create, rather than to construe, a contract will be excluded, for the law will

15. *Smith* v. *Wilson*, 3 Barn. & Adol. 728.

not do for a party that which he has not done for himself. As a man contracts, so is he bound. While the courts will seek to discover the intent of the contracting parties as that intent is expressed in the written document, they will give no heed to previous or contemporary understandings which find no expression in the contract itself.

DISTRICT LIABILITY ON *ultra vires* CONTRACTS

Frequently, boards of education misjudge their powers and attempt to enter into contracts which they have no authority to make. Such contracts are said to be *ultra vires,* that is, beyond the powers of the corporation. They may be *ultra vires* in the primary sense, that is, they are expressly forbidden by constitution or by statute, or so violative of public policy as to be illegal; they may be *ultra vires* in the secondary sense, that is, they are not expressly prohibited, but they are outside the scope of the powers expressly or impliedly conferred upon the school corporation. In either case, according to the great weight of authority, they are unenforcible and without effect.[16] The fact that the school authorities may themselves have thought that they had authority to make the contract in question and may have so represented it to the other party is of no consequence. The doctrine upon which such contracts are held to be unenforcible is based upon the consideration that school districts are quasi-corporations with very limited powers. They are mere agents of the state for the better administration of an important public policy and possess only such contractual powers as are expressly or impliedly delegated to them. All are presumed to know the law and to determine for themselves the measure of authority which the state has seen fit to confer upon its subordinate agencies. Hence one who misjudges the powers of a school district does so at his own peril. Even though the school district breach the contract

16. *Honey Creek School Township* v. *Barnes,* 119 Ind. 213, 21 N.E. 747; *First National Bank* v. *Adams School Township,* 17 Ind. App. 375, 46 N.E. 832; *Anderson* v. *Prairie School Township,* 1 Ind. App. 543, 27 N.E. 439; *Andrews Company* v. *Delight Special School District,* 95 Ark. 26, 128 S.W. 361; *Farmers' and Merchants' National Bank of Valley City* v. *School District No. 53,* 6 Dak. 255, 42 N.W. 767; *Powell* v. *Bainbridge State Bank,* 161 Ga. 855, 132 S.E. 60; *Fletcher* v. *Board of Education,* 85 N.J. Law 1, 88 Atl. 834; *Littlewort* v. *Davis,* 50 Miss. 403; *McCormick Lumber Company* v. *Highland School District,* 26 Calif. App. 641, 147 Pac. 1183; *Seaborn* v. *School District No. 42,* 149 S.C. 76, 146 S.E. 675; *Special Tax School District* v. *Hillman,* 131 Fla. 725, 179 So. 805; *Flatonia Independent School District* v. *Broesche,* 176 S.W. (2d) (Tex.) 223; *Toler* v. *Love,* 170 Miss. 252, 154 So. 711; *Seim* v. *Independent School District of Monroe,* 70 S.D. 315, 17 N.W. (2d) 342; *Craig* v. *Bell,* 211 S.C. 473, 46 S.E. (2d) 52.

and even though it retain the benefits of the performance of the contract by the other party, the courts will not permit any recovery on the express contract itself.[17] Whatever rights the other party to the contract may have, they do not grow out of the contractual relationship.

The case of *Powell* v. *Bainbridge State Bank*[18] is a good illustration of the application of the principles stated in the foregoing paragraph. In that case a school board borrowed money from a bank, despite the fact that the only statutory mode of borrowing money was by the issuance of bonds. Action was brought for a writ of mandamus to compel the board to repay the amount borrowed. The court refused the writ:

> If there is no warrant or authority of law for the trustees of a local school district, or more than one school district when consolidated, to borrow money except in the manner prescribed by law for the issuance of bonds, then the obligation cannot be treated as an official obligation, and the creditors would be remitted to an individual personal liability altogether different from liabilty on the part of the board of trustees of the local school districts or of the consolidated school district. The grant of power to public officers to borrow money which must be repaid by the taxpaying public cannot be implied. Such power rests upon an express grant, subject to such restrictions and limitations as the law making power may see fit to impose. . . .
>
> In our opinion, the board of trustees had no authority of law authorizing them to borrow money; and, though the bank doubtless acted in the utmost good faith, an examination of the law would doubtless have created in the minds of its officers such a degree of caution as would have caused them to decline to make the loan.

Similarly, where a school trustee purchased textbooks for the free use of pupils without specific statutory authority, the district was not bound to pay for them, even though they were received and used by the pupils.[19] A school township cannot be required to pay for reading-

17. *First National Bank* v. *Adams School Township*, 17 Ind. App. 375, 46 N.E. 832; *Anderson* v. *Prairie School Township*, 1 Ind. App. 543, 27 N.E. 439; *Honey Creek School Township* v. *Barnes*, 119 Ind. 213, 21 N.E. 747; *Powell* v. *Bainbridge State Bank*, 161 Ga. 855, 132 S.E. 60; *Eastern Illinois State Normal School* v. *Charleston*, 271 Ill. 602, 111 N.E. 573, L.R.A. 1916D 991; *Reams* v. *Cooley*, 171 Calif. 150, 152 Pac. 293, Ann. Cas. 1917A 1260; *McCormick Lumber Company* v. *Highland School District*, 26 Calif. App. 641, 147 Pac. 1183; *First National Bank of Waldron* v. *Whisenhunt*, 94 Ark. 583, 127 S.W. 968. There is some authority to the effect that where an *ultra vires* contract has been executed and the municipality has accepted and enjoys the benefits of it, the municipality will be estopped from denying the validity of the contract. See *Allen* v. *LaFayette*, 89 Ala. 641, 8 So. 30, 9 L.R.A. 497; *East St. Louis Gas, Light & Coke Company*, 98 Ill. 415.

18. *Powell* v. *Bainbridge State Bank*, 161 Ga. 855, 132 S.E. 60.

19. *Honey Creek School Township* v. *Barnes*, 119 Ind. 213, 21 N.E. 747.

circle books purchased by the township trustee without statutory authority. "For an act done by such school trustee not within the scope of his statutory power and where he has no authority to act at all, his township is not liable. . . . The rule is well settled in this state that persons contracting with school trustees are bound to know that their powers to contract are limited by statute, and that beyond such limit they cannot go, and bind their townships."[20]

In some jurisdictions, however, it has been held that where an *ultra vires* contract has been fully executed and the corporation retains and enjoys the benefits thereof, the corporation is estopped to deny the want of power to make the contract.[21] The doctrine of *ultra vires*, it has been said, should not be permitted to work injustice and legal wrong. This is especially true where the contract is not one prohibited by law, or *malum in se*, or tainted with bad faith or fraud.[22]

The question not infrequently arises as to whether parties dealing with a school district may invoke the doctrine of *ultra vires*. That is to say, is one who enjoys the benefits of an *ultra vires* contract estopped to deny the authority of the district to make it? Where a contract is expressly prohibited by constitution or statute or is illegal as violative of public policy, the general rule is that parties dealing with a school district may set up the defense of *ultra vires*, and this is true, even though they may have received benefits under the contract. In Idaho, for instance, a constitutional provision made it illegal for a school district to take out insurance with a county mutual fire insurance company. Nevertheless, such insurance was taken. In holding that the insurance company was not estopped to plead the invalidity of the contract and that no recovery could be had by the district when its property was destroyed by fire, the court cited Dillon on *Municipal Corporations* as follows: "Estoppel cannot be invoked to prevent the denial of power in a municipal corporation to enter a contract which is expressly prohibited by a constitutional provision or statute."[23]

Where, however, the contract is not expressly prohibited by constitution or statute but is *ultra vires*, in that it is beyond the scope of the

20. *First National Bank* v. *Adams School Township*, 17 Ind. App. 375, 46 N.E. 832. Accord, *Anderson* v. *Paririe School Township*, 1 Ind. App. 543, 27 N.E. 439.

21. 21 C.J. 1214; 19 R.C.L. 1061.

22. See *Allen* v. *LaFayette*, 89 Ala. 641, 8 So. 30, 9 L.R.A. 497; *East St. Louis* v. *East St. Louis Gas, Light & Coke Company*, 98 Ill. 415.

23. *School District No. 8* v. *Twin Falls County Mutual Fire Insurance Company*, 30 Idaho 400, 164 Pac. 1174. Contra, *Columbia Insurance Company* v. *Board of Education*, 185 Okla. 292, 91 Pac. (2d) 736, 122 A.L.R. 1358.

general powers of the district, or falls within the general powers of the district but has been made in violation of some statutory mode of making it, the general rule is that third parties, while retaining the benefits of the contract, cannot set up the defense that the school corporation was without authority to make it.[24] The reasoning of this line of decisions is that the limitations upon the contractual authority of public corporations are intended to protect the public and that private parties dealing with such corporations cannot, while enjoying the benefits of a contract, set up the defense that the corporation was without authority to make it.

There is another class of contracts which school districts have authority to make, but which cannot be made under certain conditions or until certain preliminaries have been complied with. That is to say, the legislature has conferred the power to contract but has also provided that the power cannot exist until the performance of some prior act. Or it may be that the mode of contracting has been so definitely stipulated as to exclude all other modes. While contracts made in violation of the statutory requirements are, broadly speaking, *ultra vires*, they are so only in a secondary sense, and it is perhaps best to regard them merely as invalid contracts. Whatever their proper classification, contracts of this kind cannot be enforced, nor can recovery be had upon them for benefits received. In an Arkansas case,[25] for example, the statutes limited the annual expenditure of a school district for maps and charts to a sum not to exceed twenty-five dollars unless a larger amount was authorized at the annual election. It was also provided that the maps and charts must be approved by the state superintendent as to both price and merit. Charts were purchased and used in disregard of both these requirements. The court refused to hold the district liable on warrants issued in payment of the charts, giving the following reasons:

A school district is by the statutes of this State made a body corporate, but it is intended as an agency in administration of public functions. It is a quasi public corporation, and can exercise no powers beyond those expressly conferred by statute, or which arise therefrom by necessary implication. The powers and duties of the directors of a school district are derived only from legislative authority, and they can exercise no power that is not

24. *City of Belfast* v. *Belfast Water Company,* 115 Me. 234, 98 Atl. 738, L.R.A. 1917B 908; *Baumann* v. *City of West Allis,* 187 Wis. 506, 204 N.W. 907. NOTE: 122 A.L.R. 1371.

25. *First National Bank of Waldron* v. *Whisenhunt,* 94 Ark. 583, 127 S.W. 968. See also *Farmers' and Merchants' National Bank of Valley City* v. *School District No. 53,* 6 Dak. 255, 42 N.W. 767.

thus expressly or by necessary implication granted by statute. A contract entered into by the directors, therefore, which is beyond the powers conferred on them by statute to make is null and void. . . . And all persons who deal with the school officers are presumed to have full knowledge of the extent of the powers of these officers to make the particular contract.

Similarly, where the statutes provided that a county board of education had no authority to contract with a school principal until he had been recommended by the county superintendent, a principal who had not been recommended could not recover for services rendered.[26] So, too, in Indiana, where a statute required the township trustee to secure an order from the county commissioners before contracting an indebtedness, a contract made in disregard of the statute was unenforcible and no recovery could be had on the contract.[27] In the case of *Keeler Brothers* v. *School District No. 3*,[28] the plaintiff entered into a contract with the board of education to purchase certain bonds of the district, but at the time the contract was made, the statutory proceedings necessary to be taken by the board in order to authorize it to issue and deliver bonds had not been taken. The bonds were never delivered, and the plaintiff sued for damages, claiming that it had gone to considerable expense as a result of the contract. The court held the contract invalid, inasmuch as no proceedings had been taken to authorize the issuance of any bonds. Hence no damages were allowed. Again, the statutes may require that certain contracts be in writing, and where this is so, the mode of contracting is the measure of power. Contracts made otherwise cannot be enforced.[29]

It is commonly held, also, that contracts made in disregard of a statutory provision requiring competitive bidding are unenforcible,[30] and no recovery can be had upon them, even though the district may retain the benefits conferred by performance on the part of the other party.[31] In the case of *Reams* v. *Cooley*,[32] a contract for plastering was

26. *Board of Education* v. *Watts*, 19 Ala. App. 7, 95 So. 498.

27. *Clark School Township* v. *Home Insurance and Trust Company*, 20 Ind. App. 543, 51 N.E. 107.

28. *Keeler Brothers* v. *School District No. 3*, 62 Mont. 356, 205 Pac. 217.

29. *Perkins* v. *Independent School District of Ridgeway*, 99 Mo. App. 483, 74 S.W. 122.

30. *Hibbs* v. *Arensberg*, 276 Pa. St. 24, 119 Atl. 727; *Strauch* v. *San Mateo Junior College District*, 104 Calif. App. 462, 286 Pac. 173; *Brady* v. *Mayor et al., of City of New York*, 16 How. (N.Y.) 432; *Conners* v. *City of Lowell*, 246 Mass. 279, 140 N.E. 742; *Rankin* v. *Board of Education*, 135 N.J.L. 299, 51 Atl. 194; *Seim* v. *Independent District of Monroe*, 70 S.D. 315, 17 N.W. (2d) 342.

31. *Reams* v. *Cooley*, 171 Calif. 150, 152 Pac. 293, Ann. Cas. 1917A 1260; *Brady* v. *Mayor et al., of City of New York*, 16 How. (N.Y.) 432.

32. *Reams* v. *Cooley*, 171 Calif. 150, 152 Pac. 293, Ann. Cas. 1917A 1260.

let without competitive bidding, as the law required. In holding that the school district was not liable, on the express contract, the court expressed the rule as follows:

> Under such circumstances the express contract attempted to be made is not invalid merely by reason of some irregularity or some invalidity in the exercise of a general power to contract, but the contract is void because the statute prescribes the only method in which a valid contract can be made, and the adoption of the prescribed mode is a jurisdictional prerequisite to the exercise of the power to contract at all and can be exercised in no other manner so as to incur any liability on the part of the municipality. Where the statute prescribes the only mode by which the power to contract shall be exercised the *mode* is the *measure* of the power. A contract made otherwise than as so prescribed is not binding or obligatory as a contract.

DISTRICT LIABILITY ON VOID CONTRACTS

Some contracts are so defective that they are held to be absolutely void. Such a contract cannot in any manner be ratified; it is without any force or effect whatever and cannot under any circumstance be made the basis of a cause of action. Speaking of such a contract, it was said by the Supreme Court of Pennsylvania:

> The law when appealed to will have nothing to do with it, but will leave the parties just in the condition in which it finds them. If they have fully executed their unlawful contract, the law will not disturb them in the possession of what each has acquired under it. If one has executed in whole or in part, the law turns a deaf ear when he pleads for its aid to compel the other to do as much.[33]

Contracts clearly *ultra vires*,[34] or prohibited by statute,[35] or contrary to public policy[36] are commonly held to be void.

33. *City of Pittsburgh* v. *Goshorn*, 230 Pa. St. 212, 79 Atl. 505.

34. *Fletcher* v. *Board of Education*, 85 N.J. Law 1, 88 Atl. 834; *First National Bank* v. *Adams School Township*, 17 Ind. App. 375, 46 N.E. 832.

35. *Perkins* v. *Independent School District of Ridgeway*, 99 Mo. App. 483, 74 S.W. 122; *Littlewort* v. *Davis*, 50 Miss. 403; *School District No. 89* v. *Van Arsdale*, 63 Okla. 82, 162 Pac. 741; *Myers* v. *Independent School District*, 104 Okla. 51, 230 Pac. 498; *Superior Manufacturing Company* v. *School District No. 63*, 28 Okla. 293, 114 Pac. 328, 37 L.R.A. (N.S.) 1054; *Clark* v. *School Directors of District No. 1*, 78 Ill. 474; *Moe* v. *Millard County School District*, 54 Utah 144, 179 Pac. 980; *City of Hogansville* v. *Farrell Heating and Plumbing Company*, 161 Ga. 780, 132 S.E. 436; *Shonk Land Company* v. *Joachim*, 96 W. Va. 708, 123 S.E. 444; *Riesen* v. *School District No. 4*, 189 Wis. 607, 208 N.W. 472; *Bartelson* v. *International School District No. 5*, 43 N.D. 253, 174 N.W. 78; *Goose River Bank* v. *Willow Lake School Township*, 1 N.D. 26, 44 N.W. 1002, 26 Am. St. Rep. 605; *Reams* v. *Cooley*, 171 Calif. 150, 152 Pac. 293, Ann. Cas. 1917A 1260; *Geister* v. *School District No. 1*, 243 Mich. 357, 220 N.W. 745.

36. *City of Pittsburgh* v. *Goshorn*, 230 Pa. St. 212, 79 Atl. 505.

LIABILITY OF DISTRICT FOR BENEFITS RECEIVED
UNDER ILLEGAL CONTRACT

As indicated in the preceding paragraphs, express contracts of a quasi-corporation which are *ultra vires* or void cannot be enforced, nor will the corporation be held liable on the contract, even though it be fully performed by the other party and the corporation retain the benefits of the performance. For example, it may be that the contract created an indebtedness in excess of the constitutional or statutory debt limit, or it may not have been made in writing, as the law required. A member of a school board may contract with the board of which he is a member, in violation of a statute. One may agree to transport pupils to and from school and keep his agreement and then discover that the board had no authority to make the agreement. Again, a school board may contract for goods and services which it had authority to contract for, but it may have done so in such an irregular or illegal manner as to render the contract unenforcible. In such instances the party dealing with a school board has no contract, and he cannot, therefore, recover on it in a court of law. His only recourse is to abandon the contract entirely, throw himself on the mercy of a court of equity, and seek equitable relief. In such cases the action is brought on a contract implied in law, or on what is known as a "quasi-contract." The complaining party does not seek necessarily to recover the contract price, he seeks to recover on *quantum meruit*. That is, he seeks to recover the actual value of the services or the goods furnished. The contention is that one should not in equity be permitted to take the property of another and enjoy the benefits thereof without compensation, that one should not be permitted to enrich one's self at the expense of another where it is possible that justice be done. In other words, the contention is that, although the contract is illegal and cannot be enforced, simple principles of justice and equity require that the school district be required to pay the actual value of the goods or services it retains under the executed illegal contract.

In order to understand the obligations of a school district to pay for benefits retained under an executed illegal contract, one must grasp at least the elementary principles governing what are known as "contracts implied in law," or quasi-contracts. In the case of contracts proper, whether express or implied in fact, the contract is based upon agreement. In an express contract, the agreement is evidenced by spoken or written words; in a contract implied in fact, the agreement is evidenced by conduct. Offer and acceptance are implied as a fact from the acts of the parties and from the circumstances surrounding the case. A contract implied in law, or a quasi-contract, on the other hand, is not based upon agreement. Logically, it is not a contract at all because there is present no element of agreement. In order to do justice, the courts have adopted a fiction, namely, that a promise is "implied in law." In other words, where the facts of a particular case show that it is the duty of the school district to pay, the law imputes to it a promise to fulfil its obligation. The express contract is disregarded and a fiction is created to the effect that the parties must have intended that the goods and services be paid for. The Supreme Court of Michigan has put it thus:

> But the doctrine has grown up, based upon equitable principles, that where anything has been done from which the other party has received substantial benefit and which he has appropriated, a recovery may be had upon a *quantum meruit*, based upon that benefit. And the basis of this recovery is not the original contract, but a new implied agreement deducible from the delivery and acceptance of some valuable service or thing.[37]

The liability of school districts upon contracts implied in law is a close question. Since school districts have very limited powers and the mode of their exercise is often strictly prescribed, the courts not infrequently find themselves in something of a dilemma. On the one hand, they feel the necessity of giving full force and vigor to the limitations placed upon the exercise of power by the district, because such limitations and restrictions are designed to protect the public. On the other hand, the principles of simple justice and fair dealing may make it appear that the district, having retained and enjoyed the benefits of the goods furnished or services rendered by the other party, should be required to pay their actual worth. Indeed, some courts taking this latter view seem to have gone farther than equity warrants.

Both reason and authority support the rule that where a school district is given general power to contract with respect to a subject matter, and the express contract made in pursuance of this power is invalid for some mere irregularity or invalidity in the execution thereof, the district will be held liable on a contract implied in law to pay for benefits received, provided that the form or manner of entering the contract is not violative of any statutory restriction upon the authority

37. *Allen* v. *McKibbin*, 5 Mich. 449.

of the district to contract.[38] The rule as stated, it should be noted, is not generally applicable to those contracts in which the form and manner of contracting are prescribed by statute. Neither is it applicable when the statutes prescribe or prohibit the parties to the contract.[39] The principle of law involved here is well illustrated in a West Virginia case.[40] Two members of a county court purchased from one Goshorn certain hogs for the use of the county poor farm. The court was not in session, and no record was made of the transaction. Nevertheless, the hogs were delivered and consumed. When the bill for the hogs was presented to a regular session of the county court, it was not allowed in full, but the court voted to pay a lesser sum, which it considered just compensation. The controversy was carried to the Supreme Court, which held that there could be no recovery on the express contract but that a recovery could be had upon *quantum meruit*. The original contract was invalid because not made by the court as such. It was, however, such a contract as the court could have regularly made; it was not invalid because prohibited by law, nor was the mode of entering it violative of any statutory provision.

In the case of *McCormick Lumber Company* v. *Highland School District*,[41] the notices calling for a meeting of electors to consider erecting a new building were not posted the requisite length of time, nor was there sufficient publication of notice calling for bids. Nevertheless, the board of trustees made a contract for the erection of the schoolhouse, and the building was completed and used. It was said by the court:

> The question presented is as to whether, admitting the informalities of notice in the calling of the meeting and advertising for bids for the construction of the building, the school district, having received and appropriated the benefit of the labor and materials supplied by the contractor, is estopped from maintaining a defense based upon the irregularities noted. We think, under the circumstances of the case, the contractor, or his assignee, was entitled to recover.

> Substantially, the authorities indicate no different rule in applying the doc-

38. *Goshorn's Executors* v. *County Court*, 42 W. Va. 735, 26 S.E. 452; *Reams* v. *Cooley*, 171 Calif. 150, 152 Pac. 293, Ann. Cas. 1917A 1260; *McCormick Lumber Company* v. *Highland School District*, 26 Calif. App. 641, 147 Pac. 1183; *Board of Education* v. *Watts*, 19 Ala. App. 7, 95 So. 498; *United States Rubber Products* v. *Batesburg*, 183 S.C. 49, 190 S.E. 120.

39. NOTE: 27 L.R.A. (N.S.) 1117.

40. *Goshorn's Executors* v. *County Court*, 42 W. Va. 735, 26 S.E. 452.

41. *McCormick Lumber Company* v. *Highland School District*, 26 Calif. App. 641, 147 Pac. 1183.

trine of estoppel to the acts of individuals or private corporations than is proper to be applied to the acts of municipal corporations. There is, however, a distinction suggested, and it is this: That where the contract or agreement upon which recovery is sought is one wholly without the scope of the power of the municipality to make—in other words, is *ultra vires*—then there can be no estoppel; but, where the authority exists to make the contract, but the proceedings precedent thereto have been informally taken only, then the rule of estoppel may be made to operate against a municipality as completely as it would against an individual under the same circumstances. . . . This rule of estoppel warranted the respondent in insisting upon the recovery of the reasonable value of the material furnished and services rendered by its assignor, not exceeding, we think, however, the total amount agreed upon to be paid.

According to the weight of judicial opinion, a school district will not be required to pay for benefits received under an express contract which it had no authority to make. That is, there is no implied liability to pay for benefits received under an *ultra vires* contract.[42] The law, it is said, will not imply a contract which could not have been made expressly. The law, it should be noted, is more strict in the case of *ultra vires* contracts of municipal corporations proper, or quasi-corporations such as school districts, than it is in the case of private corporations.[43] Speaking of the liability of a private corporation to pay for benefits received under an *ultra vires* contract, the Supreme Court of the United States has said:

According to many recent opinions of this court, a contract made by a corporation, which is unlawful and void because beyond the scope of its corporate powers, does not, by being carried into execution, become lawful and valid, but the proper remedy of the party aggrieved is by disaffirming the contract, and suing to recover, as on a *quantum meruit*, the value of what the defendant has actually received the benefit of.[44]

This position is taken by many courts.[45] Private corporations may be held to pay for benefits received under *ultra vires* contracts with-

42. *First National Bank* v. *Adams School Township*, 17 Ind. App. 375, 46 N.E. 832. NOTE: 27 L.R.A. (N.S.) 1117; *Bluthenthal* v. *Headland*, 132 Ala. 249, 31 So. 87; *Richland County Bank* v. *Joint School District No. 2*, 213 Wis. 178, 250 N.W. 407; *Seim* v. *Independent School District of Monroe*, 70 S.D. 315, 17 N.W. (2d) 342; *Flatonia Independent School District* v. *Broesche*, 176 S.W. (2d) (Tex.) 223. But see *Waitz* v. *Ormsby County*, 1 Nev. 370.

43. *Superior Manufacturing Company* v. *School District No. 63*, 28 Okla. 293, 114 Pac. 328, 37 L.R.A. (N.S.) 1054.

44. *Pittsburgh, Cincinnati & St. Louis Railway Company* v. *Keokuk and Hamilton Bridge Company*, 131 U.S. 371, 9 S. Ct. 770, 33 L. Ed. 157.

45. *Superior Manufacturing Company* v. *School District No. 63*, 28 Okla. 293, 114 Pac. 328, 37 L.R.A. (N.S.) 1054.

out imposing any great burden upon the public. School districts, on the other hand, are merely quasi-corporations with very limited powers. They perform purely public or governmental functions, and all their acts affect the public directly. Taxation is very nearly the exclusive source of their funds. Limitations upon their powers and upon the mode of their exercise are designed primarily to protect the public. To permit recovery for benefits received under *ultra vires* contracts might place the taxpayers of the district at the mercy of its officers. It might, in fact, enable school-district officers to set at naught many of the fundamental educational policies of the state. Nor have those who furnish goods or services under such contracts any right to complain of injustice. The constitution and statutes are the charter of the district's powers, and all are presumed to know the law. If one misjudges of the power of a school district, he will be held to pay the penalty of his error. And while this rule may seem harsh and does, no doubt, in some instances, work great hardship upon individuals, even greater public hardship and confusion would result were the rule otherwise.[46]

Two cases will serve to illustrate the reasoning of the courts that hold no recovery may be had on a *quantum meruit* where the board of education had no authority to make the contract. In Mississippi a statute provided that no interest-bearing debt could be incurred by a school board unless authorized by a majority of the electors at an election called for that purpose. Without such an election having been called, a school board borrowed money from a bank for the purchase of land for a teachers' home, the bank taking a trust deed to secure the loan. The court held that since the loan had not been authorized by the electors, the bank was accountable in a suit by taxpayers for interest collected and was without any rights against the school district. To enforce the repayment of the loan "would, in effect, defeat the policy of the law prohibiting the incurring of debts without a vote of the qualified electors of the district, and prohibiting the purchase of lands or buildings by interest-bearing bonds or obligations without a majority vote of the qualified electors voting for same as required by the foregoing statute. The equity maxim that he who seeks equity must do equity will not be applied when to do so would defeat or contravene a public policy of the state."[47]

In the second case a Texas statute prohibited a school board from

46. See, however, *Bluthenthal* v. *Headland*, 132 Ala. 249, 31 So. 87; *Waitz* v. *Ormsby County*, 1 Nev. 370.

47. *Toler* v. *Love*, 170 Miss. 252, 154 So. 711.

creating a debt or making a contract for school buildings, to be paid
for by the issuance of bonds, before the bonds had been sold and the
money was actually available. A school board contemplated a building
program, part of the cost of which was to be paid by a federal agency
(WPA). The board employed an architect to make plans and specifications and to estimate cost. These plans and specifications were submitted to the federal agency and were approved by it. The board of
education had bonds voted but did not sell them. Then the federal
agency notified the board that it could not go forward with the project
because of a shortage of materials occasioned by war. The architect
admitted he could not recover on his contract but sought recovery on
a *quantum meruit*. The court denied equitable relief. The statutes, it
said, limited the expenditures of school boards to available funds. All
persons dealing with school boards were charged with notice of this
limitation. Therefore, no equity arose in the architect's favor because
he knew that there were no available funds to pay for the services
which he rendered.[48]

By the great weight of authority a school district is not liable for
benefits received under a contract made in violation of statutory restrictions.[49] By statute, the power of the school district to contract
may be expressly or impliedly prohibited under certain circumstances,
or the mode of making the contract may be so definitely prescribed as
to prohibit all other modes. Again, the contractual power of a school
board may depend upon the taking of prior action by some other
board or official. Contracts made in violation of such statutory provisions are unenforcible, and, as a rule, recovery cannot be had upon
quantum meruit.

Contracts in excess of a constitutional or statutory debt limit belong
to that class of illegal contracts under which school districts will not

48. *Flatonia Independent School District v. Broesche,* 176 S.W. (2d) (Tex.)
223.

49. *Clark v. School Directors of District No. 1,* 78 Ill. 474; *Riesen v. School
District No. 4,* 189 Wis. 607, 208 N.W. 472; *McGillivray v. Joint School District,*
112 Wis. 354, 88 N.W. 310, 58 L.R.A. 100; *School District No. 89 v. Van Arsdale,*
63 Okla. 82, 162 Pac. 741; *Edwards v. School District No. 222,* 117 Okla. 269,
235 Pac. 611; *Superior Manufacturing Company v. School District No. 63,* 28
Okla. 293, 114 Pac. 328, 37 L.R.A. (N.S.) 1054; *Shonk Land Company v. Joachim,*
96 W. Va. 708, 123 S.E. 444; *Bartelson v. International School District No. 5,* 43
N.D. 253, 174 N.W. 78; *Kruesler v. School District of the Borough of McKees
Rocks,* 256 Pa. St. 281, 100 Atl. 821; *Moe v. Millard County School District,* 54
Utah 144, 179 Pac. 980; *City of Hogansville v. Farrell Heating and Plumbing
Company,* 161 Ga. 780, 132 S.E. 436; *Price v. School District Borough of Taylor,*
157 Pa. Super. Ct. 188, 42 Atl. (2d) 99.

be held to pay for benefits received. On this point the courts seem to be in entire accord.[50] In the case of *Superior Manufacturing Company v. School District No. 63*,[51] action was brought to secure judgment against a school district for the value of property which the district had purchased in excess of the statutory debt limit. At the time that action was brought, the district was in possession of and using the property. In denying the judgment, the court expressed the law covering such cases in a very forceful opinion, part of which was as follows:

In other words, the language [of the statute] is intended as a limitation absolute and is for the protection of the taxpayers against any liability on contracts or purchases made on behalf of the municipality by its agents or officers, beyond an amount certain. After that point is reached, they are powerless and cannot in any manner or for any purpose burden it with any greater. It is manifest at a glance that to yield to the contention of counsel for plaintiff would virtually wipe out the protection intended by this statute, because, if the district could be made liable to any extent in excess of the legal limit for the value of property received, this would be one manner of creating indebtedness, and would be the manner to which resort would always be made whenever the necessity or desire to evade the law existed. And in such cases the more the actual danger of excessive indebtedness, and the greater the need for the protection afforded by the act, the greater would be the certainty of its being evaded and an enforceable liability incurred.

An exhaustive examination of the authorities on this subject discloses that, while courts have been astute to require and compel private corporations to pay for property purchased *ultra vires* by their agents and officers, where it has been of value and retained and used, they have guarded zealously the rights of taxpayers under statutes similar to the one we are now considering, and have with practical unanimity held that persons dealing with public officers of municipalities do so at their peril and are charged with full knowledge of the rights and powers of these agents and officers to make contracts which will bind their principals. The question has arisen in almost every conceivable form; but the conclusion reached by the courts has been one, and to relieve the municipality of any liability whatsoever, either on the contract or for the actual value of the property delivered and received.

50. *Edwards* v. *School District No. 222*, 117 Okla. 269, 235 Pac. 611; *School District No. 89* v. *Van Arsdale*, 63 Okla. 82, 162 Pac. 741; *Superior Manufacturing Company* v. *School District No. 63*, 28 Okla. 293, 114 Pac. 328, 37 L.R.A. (N.S.) 1054; *Clark* v. *School Directors of District No. 1*, 78 Ill. 474; *Riesen* v. *School District No. 4*, 189 Wis. 607, 208 N.W. 472; *McGillivray* v. *Joint School District*, 112 Wis. 354, 88 N.W. 310, 58 L.R.A. 100; *Shonk Land Company* v. *Joachim*, 96 W. Va. 708, 123 S.E. 444; *Goose River Bank* v. *Willow Lake School Township*, 1 N.D. 26, 44 N.W. 1002, 26 Am. St. Rep. 605; *Bartelson* v. *International School District No. 5*, 43 N.D. 253, 174 N.W. 78; *Kruesler* v. *School District of the Borough of McKees Rocks*, 256 Pa. St. 281, 100 Atl. 821; *Moe* v. *Millard County School District*, 54 Utah 144, 179 Pac. 980; *Wayne County* v. *Hopper*, 114 Miss. 755, 75 So. 766.

51. *Superior Manufacturing Company* v. *School District No. 63*, 28 Okla. 293, 114 Pac. 328, 37 L.R.A. (N.S.) 1054.

Similarly, in a Wisconsin case[52] a contract to furnish "millwork" for a schoolhouse created an indebtedness beyond the constitutional limit. The court denied recovery on *quantum meruit:*

Appellant, however, contends that, even though the express contract to pay for the "mill-work" furnished and performed by him be void, yet, as he has alleged and proved that the district has had the benefit, it must be held liable as upon an implied contract. Obviously, if that position is to be sustained in all such cases, the constitutional prohibition . . . is ineffectual to protect the inhabitants and taxpayers against the unlawful acts of their agents, either the electors in school district assembled, or the school board, or even the individual officers. If, whenever those agents are able to cause lumber to be wrought into a school-house, or work to be done thereon, the district must be held to pay therefor, however unlawful or forbidden, the result prohibited by the constitution is accomplished, for the district becomes indebted. Nevertheless, the doctrine is not without support from remarks made in opinions of courts and from text-writers, though it is believed that all well-considered decisions stop short of holding that a municipal corporation may be held liable on implied contract to pay *quantum meruit* for property which it had no power or was forbidden to purchase. . . .
In the instant case we find the direct and positive prohibition against incurring the liability for the property and labor furnished by appellant, and that prohibition can not be evaded by the legerdemain of substituting the fiction of an implied contract on which the prohibited liability may rest instead of the void express contract.

Often the statutes confer upon school districts the power to contract with reference to certain subject matter, but prescribe the manner of making the contract. Where the statutes definitely prescribe the mode of contracting and any other mode of contracting is expressly or impliedly prohibited, the mode is the measure of power, and a school district will not ordinarily be held liable to pay for benefits received under a contract made in any other manner than that prescribed in the statutes. Thus the statutes may require that certain classes of contracts be let to the lowest responsible bidder after due notice has been given. Such requirements are usually considered mandatory, and one who furnishes labor or materials in disregard of them will not be able to recover on *quantum meruit.*[53]

52. *McGillivray* v. *Joint School District,* 112 Wis. 354, 88 N.W. 310, 58 L.R.A. 100, 88 Am. St. Rep. 969.

53. *Reams* v. *Cooley,* 171 Calif. 150, 152 Pac. 293, Ann. Cas. 1917A 1260; *Zottman* v. *San Francisco,* 20 Calif. 96, 81 Am. Dec. 96; *Brady* v. *Mayor et al., of City of New York,* 16 How (N.Y.) 432; *Strauch* v. *San Mateo Junior College District,* 286 Pac. (Calif.) 173; *Seim* v. *Independent School District of Monroe,* 70 S.D. 315, 17 N.W. (2d) 342. Contra, *Williams* v. *National Contracting Company,* 160 Minn. 293, 199 N.W. 919.

The case of *Reams* v. *Cooley*[54] illustrates the reasoning of the courts in cases of this kind. A contract for plastering was let without competitive bidding, as the law required. Action was brought to recover on *quantum meruit*. Recovery was denied:

Undoubtedly, a school board, like a municipal corporation, may, under some circumstances, be held liable upon an implied contract for benefits received by it, but the rule of implied liability is applied only in those cases where the board or municipality is given the general power to contract with reference to the subject-matter and the express contract which it has assumed to enter into in pursuance of this general power is rendered invalid for some mere irregularity or some invalidity in the execution thereof, where the form or manner of entering into a contract is not violative of any statutory restriction upon the general power of the governing body to contract nor violative of public policy. In the absence of such restriction on the mode or manner of contracting the same general rule applies to such inferior political bodies as to individuals, and the former will be held responsible on an implied contract for the payment of benefits it receives under an illegal express contract not prohibited by law. . . . But while the doctrine of implied liability applies where general power to contract in a subject exists and the form or manner of doing so is not expressly provided by charter or statute, the decided weight of authority is to the effect that, where by statute the power of the board or municipality to make a contract is limited to a certain prescribed method of doing so and any other method of doing it is expressly or impliedly prohibited, no implied liability can arise for benefits received under a contract made in violation of the particularly prescribed statutory mode. Under such circumstances the express contract attempted to be made is not invalid merely by reason of some irregularity or some invalidity in the exercise of a general power to contract, but the contract is void because the statute prescribes the only method in which a valid contract can be made, and the adoption of the prescribed mode is a jurisdictional prerequisite to the exercise of the power to contract at all and can be exercised in no other manner so as to incur any liability on the part of the municipality. Where the statute prescribes the only mode by which the power to contract shall be exercised, the *mode* is the *measure* of the power. A contract made otherwise than as so prescribed is not binding or obligatory as a contract and the doctrine of implied liability has no application in such cases. . . .

No contract, either expressly or impliedly, could be entered into by the school board except with the lowest bidder after advertisement, and, of course, no implied liability to pay upon a *quantum meruit* could exist where the prohibition by the statute against contracting in any other manner than as prescribed is disregarded.

It is urged in this case, as it invariably is in all such cases, that the application of this rule works a great hardship if the school district may retain the benefit of the work by the contractor and be relieved of liability to compensate him therefor. But the provision of the law limiting the power of school boards to validly contract, except in the prescribed mode, proceeds from a consideration of public policy not peculiar to such boards, but

54. *Reams* v. *Cooley*, 171 Calif. 150, 152 Pac. 293, Ann. Cas. 1917A 1260.

adopted as the policy of the state with reference to inferior boards and public bodies, and it would be difficult to perceive what practical public benefit or result could accrue by legislative limitation or prohibition on the power of such bodies to contract if courts were to allow a recovery where the limitation or prohibition is disregarded. In fact, the plea of harship urged here was answered in the Zottman case [*Zottman v. San Francisco,* 20 Calif. 96] by language as pertinent now as it was then, where the court said: "It may sometimes seem a hardship upon a contractor that all compensation for work done, etc., should be denied him; but it should be remembered that he, no less than the officers of the corporation, when he deals with a matter expressly provided for in the charter, is bound to see to it that the charter is complied with. If he neglects this, or choose to take the hazard, he is a mere volunteer, and suffers only what he ought to have anticipated. If the statute forbids the contract which he has made, he knows it, or ought to know it, before he places his money or services at hazard."

Again, the statutes may require that certain classes of contracts be made in writing. In most jurisdictions contracts made in disregard of such a requirement are unenforcible, and no recovery can be had for benefits received.[55] To hold otherwise would defeat the purpose the legislature had in placing safeguards around the contracting parties. The reasoning of the courts is illustrated by a Missouri case.[56] A teacher requested the president of the board of directors to employ a janitor, but no action was taken by the board. Thereupon, the teacher employed a janitor, who, at the end of the school year, sought to recover for his services. He could not recover even on *quantum meruit,* because the contract had not been reduced to writing as the law required. So, too, in Kentucky the court held that an architect could not recover on *quantum meruit* on an oral contract where the statutes required that it be in writing. Said the court:

This seems at first blush to be a harsh rule and one which no doubt works an injustice to appellant in the present case. However, the law must deal in general rules if we are to have a government of laws and not of men. That these general rules sometimes work a hardship in particular cases does not alter the fact that the principle is, on the whole, a healthy one. If school boards should be held upon implied contracts or if those who, without a contract, contribute their services and supplies should be permitted to recover upon a *quantum meruit,* the doors would be open to the most glaring raids upon the school funds. In the prevention of this contingency it is neces-

55. *Taylor v. School District No. 3,* 60 Mo. App. 372; *Perkins v. Independent School District of Ridgeway,* 99 Mo. App. 483, 74 S.W. 122; *Metz v. Warwick,* 217 Mo. App. 504, 269 S.W. 626; *Leland v. School District No. 28,* 77 Minn. 469, 80 N.W. 354; *Evansville v. Hickman,* 47 Ind. App. 500, 94 N.E. 828; *Oberwarth v. McCreary County Board of Education,* 275 Ky. 319, 121 S.W. (2d) 716; *Pfitzinger v. Johnson,* 177 S.W. (Mo.) (2d) 713.

56. *Taylor v. School District No. 3,* 60 Mo. App. 372.

sary to lay down fixed rules and more necessary still to live up to them in every case. Appellant might easily have learned at the outset how to enter into a binding contract with appellee. He must now suffer the loss resulting from this neglect.[57]

Similarly, it was held in Pennsylvania that recovery could not be had on a *quantum meruit* where the contract had been made in violation of a statutory requirement that all such contracts be entered into on the basis of a majority vote of the board with the "ayes" and "noes" recorded.[58]

Authority of a school board to contract may, by statute, be made to depend upon prior action by some other board or official or upon the existence of certain facts. Such statutory provisions are usually mandatory, and, when disregarded, no recovery can be had upon an implied contract. Where, for example, the statutes made it the duty of the county superintendent of public instruction to examine the plans for all school buildings and to issue a permit if the plans were satisfactory, and prohibited the payment of any funds for the construction of a building where such permit had not been issued, a contractor who constructed a building without the permit could not recover on *quantum meruit*.[59] "The rights of the contracting parties are in no degree altered because of the erection of the building and the consequential benefits to the district. The failure of the parties to contract strictly in accordance with the terms of the statute renders the contract itself void and precludes a recovery upon an implied contract."

Similarly, in Illinois, a statute provided that school-district authorities might appropriate to the purchase of libraries and apparatus any surplus funds after all necessary school expenses had been paid. Prior to the existence of the condition named in the statute, a library was purchased and used by the district. The contract was later repudiated, and the party who had sold the library contended that the district, having appropriated and enjoyed the use of the library, should be held to pay its value. The court denied the relief sought, pointing out that the authority given to purchase libraries after all necessary school expenses had been paid was a limitation upon the contractual power

57. *Oberwarth* v. *McCreary County Board of Education*, 275 Ky. 319, 121 S.W. (2d) 716.

58. *Price* v. *School District of Borough of Taylor*, 157 Pa. Super. Ct. 188, 42 Atl. (2d) 99.

59. *Kerbow* v. *Wooldridge*, 184 S.W. (Tex.) 746. See, however, *Sluder* v. *City of San Antonio*, 2 S.W. (2d) (Tex.) 841; *Page* v. *Harlingen*, 23 S.W. (2d) (Tex.) 829.

of the district and an implied restriction of power to purchase generally on credit. The law would not, under such circumstances, imply a
contract to pay for the articles purchased and used.[60]

In some jurisdictions, however, the courts are more liberal in granting equitable relief where an illegal contract has been executed and the
school district retains the benefit of the contract. In Indiana a township trustee borrowed money to complete a school building, although
he had no authority to borrow the money. The court permitted a recovery of the amount loaned:

> The findings show that the money received by the trustee was paid out
> by him for property actually received by the school corporation and retained
> by it. The contract for building the house was such a contract as the trustee
> was authorized to make. The money was advanced to the trustee for the
> purpose of completing a necessary and suitable school house. The trustee
> had not the means in hand to complete the building, and the money ad-
> vanced was, in fact, applied to that purpose. To permit a recovery in such
> a case is in no way recognizing the general power of the trustee to borrow
> money. There is no suggestion whatever of any fraud in the building of the
> house. Appellant has received and retains the benefit of the money so ad-
> vanced, and the simplest principles of equity and justice require that it
> should repay it.[61]

Similarly, in Florida, school trustees agreed to pay $125,000 for a
schoolhouse site, paying $5,000 in cash and giving a promissory note
for $40,000 to each of the three parties selling the land. This they had
no authority to do, unless authorized by an affirmative vote of the
qualified electors, and no such authorization had been given. Action
was brought by holders of the promissory notes to establish and fore-
close a lien on the property. The court pointed out that the purchase
of the property and the giving of the notes were done without any
authority whatever. Even so, the court held that the holders of the
notes were vested with an equitable lien to secure payment of the
actual value of the property. The court said:

> As the promise to pay the particular sum of $125,000 for the property
> was wholly *ultra vires* and void, a vendor's lien, strictly speaking, was not
> created, but in a court of conscience equity will decree and impose an equi-
> table lien in the nature of a vendor's lien to protect and secure to the ap-
> pellees the payment of their proportion of the actual property at the time
> they made the conveyance.[62]

60. *Clark* v. *School Directors of District No. 1,* 78 Ill. 474.

61. *White River School Township* v. *Dorrell,* 26 Ind. App. 538, 59 N.E. 867.
Accord, *Bicknell* v. *Widner School Township,* 73 Ind. 501.

62. *Special Tax School District* v. *Hillman,* 131 Fla. 725, 179 So. 805.

The Supreme Court of South Carolina has taken much the same position. The statutes of that state did not confer upon the trustees of a school district authority to borrow money. The trustees, believing that the statutes did confer such power upon them, borrowed money nevertheless and gave the note of the school district to secure the loan. In an action to enjoin the payment of the note and to have it declared void, the court held that the note was not a valid obligation in itself, one that could be sued on, because the trustees had no authority to borrow the money. But the court went on to hold that, under the principle of money had and received, the district was obligated. The trustees could, therefore, legally deliver a new note and substitute it for the invalid note which the lender held.[63]

In some jurisdictions it is held, too, that where a school district makes a contract which it is authorized to make but which is invalid because not executed in the manner prescribed by statute, the district will be required to pay for benefits received on the theory of an implied contract.[64] Thus it has been held that recovery may be had upon *quantum meruit* for benefits received under a contract which was made in disregard of a statutory provision requiring competitive bidding.[65] In a Minnesota case,[66] a contract was made without competitive bidding, as the law required. The supreme court held the contract void but allowed recovery on *quantum valebat* for the following reasons:

The improvement served a municipal purpose and the contract was one that the city had power to make, and, had the essential requirements of the law been complied with, the contract would have been enforceable. In such a situation the village may be compelled to pay the value of what it has received. The express contract disappears from the case. The cause of action

63. *Craig* v. *Bell*, 211 S.C. 473, 46 S.E. (2d) 52. See also *Luther* v. *Wheeler*, 73 S.C. 83, 52 S.E. 874, 4 L.R.A. (N.S.) 746.

64. *Greeson Manufacturing Company* v. *County Board of Education*, 217 Ala. 565, 117 So. 163; *Williams* v. *National Contracting Company*, 160 Minn. 293, 199 N.W. 919; *Fargo Foundry Company* v. *Village of Calloway*, 148 Minn. 273, 181 N.W. 584. NOTE: 27 L.R.A. (N.S.) 1117. See also *Chicago* v. *McKechney*, 205 Ill. 372, 68 N.E. 954; *City of Providence* v. *Providence Electric Light Company*, 122 Ky. 237, 91 S.W. 664; *Tolleson Union High School District* v. *Kincaid*, 53 Ariz. 60, 85 Pac. (2d) 708; *Sluder* v. *City of San Antonio*, 2 S.W. (2d) (Tex.) 841.

65. *Williams* v. *National Contracting Company*, 160 Minn. 293, 199 N.W. 919; *Fargo Foundry Company* v. *Village of Calloway*, 148 Minn. 273, 181 N.W. 584.

66. *Fargo Foundry Company* v. *Village of Calloway*, 148 Minn. 273, 181 N.W. 584.

arises, not from any contract on the subject, but from the general obligation to do justice which binds all persons, natural and artificial. . . . The obligation to pay is measured by the benefit which the village has received.

And in Arizona it has been held that a teacher could recover in *quantum meruit* for services rendered under an oral contract, even though the statutes required that the contract be in writing.[67]

In a number of Indiana cases recovery has been allowed on implied contracts for benefits received from the use of property suitable and necessary for school purposes, even though the express contract was made in violation of statutory provisions.[68]

In Minnesota the court permitted recovery on *quantum meruit* in a case where the contract was void because statutory requirements had not been met. A contract with an architect was illegal because the improvement to be undertaken had not been previously authorized by the voters, as required by statute. The following excerpt is from the opinion of the court: "The defendant could legally make the contract involved, had it first been authorized by the voters. As made, it was void because the requirements of the law were not met. The rule of law applicable to such a situation is that the district is obliged to pay for the reasonable value of any benefits which it receives."[69]

RIGHT TO RECOVER POSSESSION OF PROPERTY OR MONEY DELIVERED UNDER INVALID CONTRACT

While the law will not enforce an invalid contract or even allow recovery upon *quantum meruit* under certain conditions, equity and justice may demand that one who has performed his part of an invalid contract be allowed to recover possession of that which is justly his. Contracts which are *malum in se*, which are violative of public morals and public policy, are so utterly void that the law will have nothing to do with them. They cannot become the basis of any action whatsoever; the law leaves the parties where they are found. If one of the parties to the transaction suffers loss and inconvenience

67. *Tolleson Union High School District* v. *Kincaid,* 53 Ariz. 60, 85 Pac. (2d) 708.

68. *Clark School Township* v. *Home Insurance and Trust Company,* 20 Ind. App. 543, 51 N.E. 107; *Oppenheimer* v. *Jackson School Township,* 22 Ind. App. 521, 54 N.E. 145; *Clinton School Township* v. *Lebanon National Bank,* 18 Ind. App. 42, 47 N.E. 349.

69. *Olsen* v. *Independent & Consolidated School District No. 50,* 175 Minn. 201, 220 N.W. 606.

as a result of the agreement, he will be required to suffer the consequences of his illegal act. The rule is different, however, in the case of contracts which are not prohibited by law or contrary to public policy. One may recover possession of money or property delivered in the performance of such contracts, provided that such money or property can be identified and returned to the original owner without material injury to the property of the other party to the contract.[70]

In the case of *Superior Manufacturing Company* v. *School District No. 63,*[71] the district purchased furniture and supplies in violation of a statutory debt limit. In passing upon the rights of the parties to the contract, the court said: "While, under the circumstances arising in this class of cases, all the authorities deny the right of recovery either on the contract or *quantum meruit,* still all agree that the municipality cannot keep the property, and that the plaintiff is entitled to retake it. This seems to be the only remedy available."

There is, however, no right of recovery in the original owner unless the property can be recovered without working an injury to the property of the school district. A North Dakota case illustrates the rule.[72] A contract to construct a schoolhouse created an indebtedness in excess of the constitutional debt limit. After the building had been completed and was in use by the district, the contractor brought action to have the contract disaffirmed, to have the parties put *in statu quo,* and to have the property returned to him. The court denied the relief sought.

In accordance with the stipulated facts, it is impossible to restore to the plaintiff the building erected without destroying property of the municipality. It is likewise impractical to segregate or detach that portion of the building which represents the excess moneys therein owing to the plaintiff. . . . Although, in equity, recovery may be permitted in such cases, where no additional burden is thereby placed upon the municipality in excess of the

70. *School District No. 89* v. *Van Arsdale,* 63 Okla. 82, 162 Pac. 741; *Edwards* v. *School District No. 222,* 117 Okla. 269, 246 Pac. 444; *Superior Manufacturing Company* v. *School District No. 63,* 28 Okla. 293, 114 Pac. 328, 37 L.R.A. (N.S.) 1054; *Clark* v. *School Directors of District No. 1,* 78 Ill. 474; *McGillivray* v. *Joint School District,* 112 Wis. 354, 88 N.W. 310, 58 L.R.A. 100; *Moe* v. *Millard County School District,* 54 Utah 144, 179 Pac. 980; *Bartelson* v. *International School District No. 5,* 43 N.D. 253, 174 N.W. 78; *Strauch* v. *San Mateo Junior College District,* 286 Pac. (Calif.) 173.

71. *Superior Manufacturing Company* v. *School District No. 63,* 28 Okla. 293, 114 Pac. 328, 37 L.R.A. (N.S.) 1054.

72. *Bartelson* v. *International School District No. 5,* 43 N.D. 253, 174 N.W. 78.

constitutional debt limit, or where the property itself can be identified, segregated, and restored to the parties without injuring the municipality or its property by so doing, nevertheless, in upholding the contractual restrictions absolutely imposed, relief upon equitable principles can not be granted where this can not be accomplished.

In an Oklahoma case,[73] however, the plaintiff, who had built a schoolhouse at a price exceeding the debt limit, was decreed equitable ownership of the building. And in New Mexico, where a school building had been erected with funds derived exclusively from the sale of illegal bonds, the holders of the bonds were entitled to have the building sold and the proceeds distributed among themselves.[74]

In determining the right of a contractor to recover property which has been delivered under an invalid contract, the rule governing fixtures, it has been held, does not apply. This is true because in such cases no distinction should be made between real and personal property. The fundamental consideration is not whether the property is real or personal; it is, Can the property be restored to the original owner without doing injury to the property of the other party to the contract? In the case of *Moe v. Millard County School District*,[75] a contractor installed a heating plant under a contract void because in excess of the constitutional debt limit. No recovery was allowed on *quantum meruit*, but the contractor was permitted to recover the property.

We can not see how the doctrine of fixtures becomes applicable to this case so as to prevent a recovery of the property here sought. Why should not a school district be required to return real estate as readily as personal property which it has acquired under circumstances such as are shown by the facts in this case? . . . Neither can we see that it makes any difference in this case whether the property has retained its character as personal property, or has, by being affixed to the freehold, become real estate. If it has become so affixed to the building, as is admitted that some portions of it are, that its removal would cause material injury to the structure of the building itself, then it would seem to us that a recovery could not be had, not for the reason that the property had become a "fixture" in the ordinary meaning of that term, but for the reason that to permit its removal would work injustice upon the owner of the property to which it had been so affixed.

However, to deny removal of this property, which is clearly subject to

73. *Edwards* v. *School District No. 222*, 117 Okla. 269, 246 Pac. 444.

74. *Shaw* v. *Board of Education*, 38 N.M. 298, 31 Pac. (2d) 993, 93 A.L.R. 432.

75. *Moe* v. *Millard County School District*, 54 Utah 144, 179 Pac. 980. Accord, *Shaw* v. *Board of Education*, 38 N.M. 288, 31 Pac. (2d) 993, 93 A.L.R. 432.

identification, easily removable without material injury to the structure of the building, when it is conceded that the plaintiff has no other remedy, would clearly be a subversion of the purpose for which the constitutional and statutory provisions in question were framed and would permit the taxpayers of the defendant school district improperly, because unnecessarily, to shift the burden of the education of the children of the district to the shoulders of those who in good faith have furnished the material for the completion of the school building, to the extent of the value of this property, which we think they would not desire, nor should they be permitted to do.

LIABILITY ON CONTRACTS BETWEEN THE
DISTRICT AND ITS OFFICERS

In a number of states the statutes expressly prohibit a school district from entering into contracts in which one or more of its officers have a pecuniary interest. Where this is true, the courts uniformly hold that contracts made in violation of the statutory prohibition are invalid and cannot be enforced.[76] Nor will the district as a rule be held liable on an implied contract for any benefits received as a result of the performance of the contract by the other party.[77] The law, it is said, "never implies an obligation to do that which it forbids the party to do."[78] Were the courts to permit recovery on *quantum meruit* in cases where the express contract is prohibited, they would defeat the very purpose which the legislature had in mind in enacting the legislation and invite abuses of a very grave nature. As an illustration, in an Indiana case[79] the statutes made it unlawful for a school trustee to be interested in any contract with his district. The president of a plumbing and heating company was elected trustee, but

76. *Independent School District No. 5* v. *Collins*, 15 Idaho 535, 98 Pac. 857, 128 Am. St. Rep. 76; *Noble* v. *Davison*, 177 Ind. 19, 96 N.E. 325; *Poling* v. *Board of Education*, 56 W. Va. 251, 49 S.E. 148; *Bissell Lumber Company* v. *Northwestern Casualty and Surety Company*, 189 Wis. 343, 207 N.W. 697; *Kennon* v. *Adams*, 176 Ky. 618, 196 S.W. 173. NOTE: 34 L.R.A. (N.S.) 129; Ann. Cas. 1912D 1132; *Dowell* v. *School District No. 1*, 250 S.W. (2d) (Ark.) 127; *State ex rel. Ellis* v. *Ellis*, 234 S.W. (2d) (Tenn.) 817.

77. *Wilson* v. *Otoe County*, 71 Neb. 435, 98 N.W. 1050; *Antigo Water Company* v. *Antigo*, 144 Wis. 156, 128 N.W. 888; *Independent School District No. 5* v. *Collins*, 15 Idaho 535, 98 Pac. 857, 128 Am. St. Rep. 76; *Noble* v. *Davison*, 177 Ind. 19, 96 N.E. 325; *Brazil* v. *McBride*, 69 Ind. 244; *Domingos* v. *Sacramento County*, 51 Calif. 608; *West* v. *Berry*, 98 Ga. 402, 25 S.E. 508; *Dwight* v. *Palmer*, 74 Ill. 295; *Winchester* v. *Frazer*, 19 Ky. Law Rep. 1366, 43 S.W. 453; *Goodrich* v. *Waterville*, 88 Me. 39, 33 Atl. 659. NOTE: 34 L.R.A. (N.S.) 129. But see NOTE: Ann. Cas. 1912D 1132.

78. *Brady* v. *Mayor et al., of City of New York*, 16 How. (N.Y.) 432. Accord, *Reams* v. *Cooley*, 171 Calif. 150, 152 Pac. 293, Ann. Cas. 1917A 1260.

79. *Noble* v. *Davison*, 177 Ind. 19, 96 N.E. 325.

before he qualified for the office he entered into a contract with the board of trustees to instal a heating plant in a school building. In the contract it was specified that, in case the president of the company qualified as a trustee before the work was completed, the company would employ, at its own expense, an expert to be approved by the other members of the board, to act with the disinterested members in determining whether the contract had been fully performed. The court held the contract void and denied recovery for benefits received.

It is maintained by counsel for appellants that one seeking equity must do equity; that the school city holds the benefit of the labor and materials furnished by the plumbing company, and it would be inequitable to adjudge an avoidance of the contract without restoration to the plumbing company of the reasonable value of all work done and materials furnished. In answer to this contention, it is sufficient to say that an equitable right cannot be founded on a violation of law. . . . Equity follows the law, and assists no one in obtaining or holding the fruits of an illegal agreement, but, on the contrary, leaves such person where it finds him. . . . This contract reveals a palpable attempt to evade the law. "He that hath committed iniquity shall not have equity."

It has been held, however, that a statute prohibiting the employment of a board member by the board does not apply to unpaid services rendered before the board member took office. As the court put it: "An outstanding claim against the school board does not disqualify the claimant from seeking membership upon it, nor is the price of his election the loss of the claim."[80] And this was true, even though the member voted to pay his own claim.

A more difficult situation arises where contracts between the district and its officers are not prohibited by statute. In such cases, it is commonly held that the contract is contrary to public policy and therefore unenforcible.[81] At any time before the performance of the contract it may be repudiated by the district. In some jurisdictions

---

80. *In re Zeigler,* 328 Pa. 280, 194 Atl. 911.

81. *Spearman* v. *Texarkana,* 58 Ark. 348, 24 S.W. 883, 22 L.R.A. 855; *Smith* v. *Dandridge,* 98 Ark. 38, 135 S.W. 800, 34 L.R.A. (N.S.) 129, Ann. Cas. 1912D 1130; *Pickett* v. *School District No. 1,* 25 Wis. 551, 3 Am. Rep. 105; *Scott* v. *School District No. 9,* 67 Vt. 150, 31 Atl. 145, 27 L.R.A. 588; *Chicago* v. *Tribune Company,* 248 Ill. 242, 93 N.E. 757; *Ames* v. *Board of Education,* 97 N.J. Eq. 60, 127 Atl. 95; *Bornstein* v. *Louisville School Board,* 137 Ky. 108, 122 S.W. 522; *Venable* v. *School Committee of Pilot Mountain,* 149 N.C. 120, 62 S.E. 902; *Beebe* v. *Sullivan County,* 64 Hun. (N.Y.) 377, 19 N.Y.S. 629, 46 N.Y. St. Rep. 222; *School District No. 98* v. *Pomponi,* 79 Colo. 658, 247 Pac. 1056; *Youngblood* v. *Consolidated School District No. 3,* 104 Okla. 235, 230 Pac. 910; *Currie* v. *School District No. 26,* 35 Minn. 163, 27 N.W. 922. NOTE: Ann. Cas. 1912D 1132.

such contracts are held to be void,[82] and in all jurisdictions they are held to be at least voidable.[83] Even though the statutes may be silent upon the subject, public policy demands that contracts between the district and its officers be held at least voidable, because "the law will not allow an agent or trustee to place himself in such an attitude towards his principal or his *cestui que trust* as to have his interest conflict with his duty."[84] As was said in a New York case: "The illegality of such contracts does not depend upon statutory enactments. They are illegal at common law. It is contrary to good morals and public policy to permit municipal officers of any kind to enter into contractual relations with the municipality of which they are officers.[85] Nor does it matter whether the contract be entered into in good faith, for the courts will not pause to inquire whether the officer has acted fairly or unfairly. It is enough to show that his self-interest conflicts with the performance of his official duty.[86]

In the case of *Smith* v. *Dandridge*[87] the Supreme Court of Arkansas expresses forcefully the rule of law governing contracts of this kind:

As a general rule, it is unlawful for a director to enter into a contract with the school district in which he has a personal and individual interest. His relation to the school district as a director thereof is of a confidential and fiduciary nature; he represents the school district, and is its agent. On this account he cannot place himself in a position where his own personal interests might conflict with those of the school district which he must represent. The law and public policy forbid him from making a contract with the school district in which he has an individual interest; and a contract so made by a director will not be enforceable. The principle upon which this

82. *Weitz* v. *Independent District of Des Moines,* 87 Iowa 81, 54 N.W. 70; *Shakespear* v. *Smith,* 77 Calif. 638, 20 Pac. 294, 11 Am. St. Rep. 327; *Beebe* v. *Sullivan County,* 64 Hun. (N.Y.) 377, 19 N.Y.S. 629, 46 N.Y. St. Rep. 222; *Reckner* v. *School District of German Township,* 341 Pa. 375, 19 Atl. (2d) 402.

83. *Smith* v. *Dandridge,* 98 Ark. 38, 135 S.W. 800, 34 L.R.A. (N.S.) 129, Ann. Cas. 1912D 1130; *Pickett* v. *School District No. 1,* 25 Wis. 551, 3 Am. Rep. 105; *Scott* v. *School District No. 9,* 67 Vt. 150, 31 Atl. 145, 27 L.R.A. 588; *Chicago* v. *Tribune Company,* 248 Ill. 242, 93 N.E. 757; *School District No. 98* v. *Pomponi,* 79 Colo. 658, 247 Pac. 1056. Note: Ann. Cas. 1912D 659.

84. *Hornung* v. *State,* 116 Ind. 458, 19 N.E. 151, 2 L.R.A. 510.

85. *Beebe* v. *Sullivan County,* 64 Hun. 377, 19 N.Y.S. 629, 46 N.Y. St. Rep. 222.

86. *Shakespear* v. *Smith,* 77 Calif. 638, 20 Pac. 294, 11 Am. St. Rep. 327.

87. *Smith* v. *Dandridge,* 98 Ark. 38, 135 S.W. 800, 34 L.R.A. (N.S.) 129, Ann. Cas. 1912D 1130.

public policy is founded is that where one is acting in a fiduciary capacity for another he will not be permitted to make a contract with himself in his individual capacity relative to the subject-matter of such employment.[88]

There is great difference of opinion, however, as to whether a school district is liable for benefits received under a contract with one of its officers where such contracts are not prohibited by statute. According to one line of decisions, such contracts are void, and no recovery can be had for benefits received.[89] In the case of *Weitz* v. *Independent District of Des Moines*,[90] a member of the board, an experienced architect, was employed to supervise the construction of a school building. The court refused any recovery for his services, even though no statute prohibited the district from contracting with its officers. In the opinion of the court: "If the way be opened by a decision of this court by which officers of counties, cities, incorporated towns and school districts may let contracts to themselves, and recover thereon by showing that the contract was beneficial to the corporation, it would lead to the grossest abuses."

According to the weight of authority, however, contracts between a district and one of its officers, in the absence of statutory restriction, are not void but merely voidable at the option of the district.[91] It follows, therefore, that if the district elects to permit performance, it will be held to pay for benefits received either upon the principle that the voidable contract has been ratified[92] or upon the principle of an implied contract.[93]

88. See, however, *Hassett* v. *Carroll*, 85 Conn. 23, 81 Atl. 1013, Ann. Cas. 1913A 333.

89. *Weitz* v. *Independent District of Des Moines*, 87 Iowa 81, 54 N.W. 70; *Bay* v. *Davidson*, 133 Iowa 688, 111 N.W. 25, 9 L.R.A. (N.S.) 1014, 119 Am. St. Rep. 650; *Moore* v. *Independent District of Toledo City*, 55 Iowa 654, 8 N.W. 631; *Bornstein* v. *Louisville School Board*, 137 Ky. 108, 122 S.W. 522. NOTE: Ann. Cas. 1912D 1132; 24 R.C.L. 581.

90. *Weitz* v. *Independent District of Des Moines*, 87 Iowa 81, 54 N.W. 70.

91. *Smith* v. *Dandridge*, 98 Ark. 38, 135 S.W. 800, 34 L.R.A. (N.S.) 129, Ann. Cas. 1912D 1130; *Pickett* v. *School District No. 1*, 25 Wis. 551, 3 Am. Rep. 105; *Scott* v. *School District No. 9*, 67 Vt. 150, 31 Atl. 145, 27 L.R.A. 588; *Chicago* v. *Tribune Company*, 248 Ill. 242, 93 N.E. 757; *Sylvester* v. *Webb*, 179 Mass. 236, 60 N.E. 495, 52 L.R.A. 518; *Trainer* v. *Wolfe*, 140 Pa. St. 279, 21 Atl. 391; *Currie* v. *School District No. 26*, 35 Minn. 163, 27 N.W. 922.

92. *Pickett* v. *School District No. 1*, 25 Wis. 551, 3 Am. Rep. 105; *Scott* v. *School District No. 9*, 67 Vt. 150, 31 Atl. 145, 27 L.R.A. 588; *Sylvester* v. *Webb*, 179 Mass. 236, 60 N.E. 495, 52 L.R.A. 518; *Trainer* v. *Wolfe*, 140 Pa. St. 279, 21 Atl. 391.

93. *Smith* v. *Dandridge*, 98 Ark. 38, 135 S.W. 800, 34 L.R.A. (N.S.) 129, Ann. Cas. 1912D 1130; *Spearman* v. *Texarkana*, 58 Ark. 348, 24 S.W. 883, 22 L.R.A. 855; *Rowell* v. *School District*, 59 Vt. 658, 10 Atl. 754; *Concordia* v. *Hagaman*, 1 Kan. App. 35, 41 Pac. 133.

In the case of *Pickett* v. *School District No. 1*[94] the Supreme Court of Wisconsin has well expressed the position of those courts which hold that contracts of the kind here under consideration are voidable and may be ratified:

Still, there seems ground for a distinction between contracts which are held to be against public policy, merely on account of the personal relations of the contractor to the other parties in interest, and those which are void because the thing contracted for is itself against public policy. . . . But in the former, the thing contracted for being in itself lawful and beneficial, it would seem unjust to allow the party who may be entitled to avoid it, to accept and retain the benefit without any compensation at all. And it is accordingly held, in all those cases where agents or trustees empowered to sell attempt to purchase for their own benefit, not that the sales are absolutely void and pass no title, but that they may be avoided by the principal, who may have them set aside in equity, if, after a knowledge of the facts, he so elect. . . . In such cases the trustee or agent, if the sale or contract were avoided, would get his money back. The principal could not take the money and avoid the sale too.

And, perhaps, the true theory is, that, in all cases where the principle we have discussed is applicable, the contract is rather voidable in equity at the option of the principal than absolutely void at law. So that, in a case like this, the defense would be, under the present practice, an equitable one.

Undoubtedly in such cases the principal, having full knowledge of all the facts, may affirm the contract. And if he should do so, it would become binding. If it had been fully executed by the contracting party, and the principal should, knowing all the facts, elect to accept and retain the benefit of it, he might be held to have thereby ratified it according to all its terms and conditions. And where it had not been so executed, but had been partially fulfilled, and he elected to accept and retain such partial benefit, he might become liable, on a *quantum meruit,* upon the same principles as in other cases.

In other jurisdictions a district is required to pay for benefits received, not upon the theory of ratification, but upon the principle of an implied contract.[95] Equity and justice, it is said, will not permit the district to accept the property or services of its officers and then refuse to pay what they are fairly and reasonably worth. Under such circumstances the law implies a contract.[96] Thus, in the case of *Smith* v. *Dandridge,*[97] a director was employed to supervise the construction

94. *Pickett* v. *School District No. 1,* 25 Wis. 551, 3 Am. Rep. 105.

95. *Smith* v. *Dandridge,* 98 Ark. 38, 135 S.W. 800, 34 L.R.A. (N.S.) 129, Ann. Cas. 1912D 1130; *Spearman* v. *Texarkana,* 58 Ark. 348, 24 S.W. 883, 22 L.R.A. 855; *Rowell* v. *School District,* 59 Vt. 658, 10 Atl. 754; *Concordia* v. *Hagaman,* 1 Kan. App. 35, 41 Pac. 133.

96. *Spearman* v. *Texarkana,* 58 Ark. 348, 24 S.W. 883, 22 L.R.A. 855.

97. *Smith* v. *Dandridge,* 98 Ark. 38, 135 S.W. 800, 34 L.R.A. (N.S.) 129, Ann. Cas. 1912D 1130.

of a school building. A warrant was issued in payment of his services, but an injunction was sought to restrain payment of the warrant. The court denied the writ because the district could not ask for relief which would work injustice. In the opinion of the court:

A director is disabled from making a binding contract with the school district, not because the thing contracted for is itself illegal or tainted with moral turpitude, but because his personal relation to the district as its agent requires that he should have no self-interest antagonistic to that of the district in making a contract for it. The contract, however, in such case is not absolutely void, but it is simply not a binding agreement and may be avoided. If under such voidable contract the school district has accepted and retained benefits, it would still be liable to make just compensation therefor, not because of the contract but upon the principle that one ought to pay for valuable benefits received. . . .

In the case at bar the appellee Dandridge is not endeavoring to recover under a contract made by him with the school district. As a director of the school district, he could not make a binding contract with it in which he was individually interested. . . . His right to receive compensation from the school district is not based on the contract, but it is grounded solely on the principle that he has rendered necessary services from which the school district has received real benefits, and therefore should recover what those services are fairly and reasonably worth.

DEGREE OF INTEREST OF SCHOOL OFFICERS NECESSARY
TO RENDER CONTRACTS UNENFORCIBLE

In a number of states the statutes prohibit school-district officers from entering into contracts with the district, and, even in the absence of such statutes, public policy demands that such contracts be held unenforcible. The question naturally arises, therefore, as to what constitutes self-interest within the contemplation of the law or public policy. A contract between a school district and one of its officers will not be held invalid as violative either of statutory provisions or of public policy unless it can be shown that the officer has some official duty to perform in connection with the contract. If the contract lies wholly and completely outside the line of his official duties and there is no conflict between his interests in the contract and his official duties, the contract is valid.[98]

Where, on the other hand, an officer has any official duty to perform in connection with a contract, the courts are quick to declare it invalid if any appreciable self-interest on his part appears. "The courts are astute to impeach and invalidate any transaction where an official has any personal interest whatever in the matter decided by

98. NOTE: 34 L.R.A. (N.S.) 129; 24 R.C.L. 581.

him. The very 'appearance of evil' must be avoided."[99] Thus it has
been held that a member of a school board cannot enter into a valid
contract to furnish materials to be used by a contractor in constructing
a schoolhouse for the district. In a Wisconsin case, the clerk of a school
board was manager of and a stockholder in a lumber company. A contract was let to build a schoolhouse. The lumber company sold to the
contractor a large part of the material used. Before the building was
finished, the contractor failed, and the company sued the contractor's
surety, which had given bond guaranteeing payment of materials furnished the contractor. The court held that the contract between the
lumber company and the contractor was void and denied recovery
against the surety. The contract was void because, as a result of it, the
clerk had a pecuniary interest in the contract between the school district and the contractor, an interest which was expressly forbidden by
statute.[100] To the same effect is the case of *Northport* v. *Northport
Townsite Company*.[101] In that case a member of a city council was
also a stockholder in a lumber company. The company contracted to
furnish a certain party with lumber to build sidewalks for the city in
case he secured the contract to build the sidewalks, the company to be
paid for the lumber by warrants issued by the city. The court held
that the member of the council was sufficiently interested in the contract with the city to bring him within the operation of a statute which
made it unlawful for any municipal officer to be interested directly
or indirectly in municipal contracts. The court said:

Long experience has taught law makers and courts the innumerable and
insidious evasions of this salutary principle that can be made, and therefore
the statute denounces such a contract if a city officer shall be interested not
only directly, but indirectly. However devious and winding the chain may be
which connects the officer with the forbidden contract, if it can be followed
and the connection made, the contract is void. It would seem that the
interest of a stockholder of a corporation brings such stockholder within the
reason of the rule prohibiting an officer from being interested in the city's
business.

It has been held, however, that a school trustee who has no pecuniary interest or understanding with a contractor at the time his bid is
accepted to build a schoolhouse may lawfully contract thereafter to

99. *Venable* v. *School Committee of Pilot Mountain*, 149 N.C. 120, 62 S.E. 902.

100. *Bissell Lumber Company* v. *Northwestern Casualty and Surety Company*,
189 Wis. 343, 207 N.W. 697. Accord, *Douglas* v. *Pittman*, 239 Ky. 548, 39 S.W.
(2d) 979.

101. *Northport* v. *Northport Townsite Company*, 27 Wash. 543, 68 Pac. 204.

furnish materials to be used in building the house.[102] Nor will the courts issue an injunction to restrain a school board from building a schoolhouse on property donated by one of its members who owns property adjoining the school site. In the case of *Territory* v. *Board of Trustees for High School of Logan County*[103] a school-board member owned a subdivision of land, part of which he donated as a high-school site. An effort was made to enjoin the erection of a high-school building on the site, the allegation being that the donor was interested in the action of the board because of the possible increase in the value of his adjoining property. Said the court:

> We think this conclusion too far-fetched to justify a court in applying to this transaction the doctrine of fraud, which is the underlying principle upon which is rested all the decisions setting aside the acts of agents or trustees.
>
> Public policy undoubtedly forbids that a trustee shall be permitted, as such, to deal with himself as an individual. . . . But the law does not prohibit him from making a donation to his *cestui que trust;* and the mere fact that in this instance he owns adjoining property which may be rendered more or less valuable by reason of the location of the high school building in its near vicinity, cannot be received by the courts as a badge of fraud in the transaction, because the results to follow are purely speculative and hypothetical.

As a general rule, the mere fact that a school officer is related either by affinity or consanguinity to a person contracting with the district does not render the contract void or voidable as violative of public policy or of statutory provisions which forbid contracts between the district and its officers.[104] Thus it has been held that a school board may legally employ a teacher, even though he be a near relative of two of the three members of the board and even though other qualified teachers might have been employed at a much lower salary.[105] In Tennessee, action was brought to remove a director from office because of misconduct, the charge being that he had employed his minor daughter to teach and that he would be entitled to her earnings. The court refused to remove the director, pointing out that there was no express statutory inhibition against his employing his daughter. Moreover, it was said that the father would be estopped to claim the wages he had contracted to pay.[106] In the case of *Lewick* v. *Glazier*, it was

102. *Worrell* v. *Jurden,* 36 Nev. 85, 132 Pac. 1158; *Escondido Lumber, Hay & Grain Company* v. *Baldwin,* 2 Calif. App. 606, 84 Pac. 284.

103. *Territory* v. *Board of Trustees for High School of Logan County,* 13 Okla. 605, 76 Pac. 165.

104. Note: 34 L.R.A. (N.S.) 141.

105. *Dolan* v. *Joint School District No. 13,* 80 Wis. 155, 49 N.W. 960.

106. *State* v. *Burchfield,* 80 Lea (Tenn.) 30.

held that the fact that a trustee of the village was the father of one who contracted to render service to the village did not render the contract invalid.[107] But where the statutes prohibited a school trustee from having any pecuniary interest in any contract made by the board of which he was a member, the board could not legally employ the wife of one of its members to teach in the school of the district. The husband, it was said, had a pecuniary interest in the contract because under the laws of the state the earnings of the wife constituted a part of their common property.[108] "The husband has the control and management of the community property, and he may use it and is part owner in it, and hence is pecuniarily interested in it." Where, however, under the laws of the state, the husband has no financial interest in the earnings of his wife, it is permissible to employ as a teacher the wife of one of the officers of the district.[109] Nor will the courts enforce a contract between the son of a school-board member and the board, where the father is, in fact, interested in the contract. In a New Jersey case, controversy arose among the patrons of the school and among the members of the board as to whether the school property should be sold and a new site selected. The board voted to sell the property, whereupon one of the board members had his son purchase it under an agreement with the father, whereby the son was to hold it for two years, subject to condemnation by the school board at a price named in the agreement. The father belonged to the faction that opposed the sale of the property and was attempting to defeat the purchase of the property by others, hoping that within two years the board would be willing to repurchase the old site, if it could do so at a reasonable price. The son was a young man, twenty-two years old, with no means of his own. The father supplied the funds necessary for the purchase. When the majority faction of the board discovered that it was about to be outwitted, it refused to execute the contract. The court sustained their action on the ground that a school-board member was sufficiently interested in the contract to render it invalid and unenforcible.[110]

107. *Lewick* v. *Glazier,* 116 Mich. 493, 74 N.W. 717.

108. *Nuckols* v. *Lyle,* 8 Idaho 589, 70 Pac. 401.

109. *Thompson* v. *District Board of School District No. 1,* 252 Mich. 629, 233 N.W. 439; *Board of Education* v. *Boal,* 104 Ohio 482, 135 N.E. 540. The Supreme Court of West Virginia takes the opposite view, holding that either a husband or a wife has a pecuniary interest in the employment of the other: *Haislip* v. *White,* 124 W. Va. 633, 22 S.E. (2d) 361.

110. *Ames* v. *Board of Education,* 97 N.J. Eq. 60, 127 Atl. 95.

RATIFICATION OF CONTRACTS

Frequently, contracts which are neither *ultra vires* the powers of the corporation nor prohibited by statute are, nevertheless, invalid, because made in an irregular manner or by parties who acted without authority. That is, some agent of a school district or board of education may undertake to bind the district in excess of the authority granted. A superintendent of schools, for example, may attempt to employ a teacher, or a majority of a board of education may attempt to enter a contract without a formal meeting of the board. Or it may be that a board of trustees undertakes to purchase supplies or build a schoolhouse without first having been authorized to do so by the district meeting as required by statute. After such contracts have been partially or fully performed by the other party acting in good faith, the question naturally arises as to whether the district or the board of education may be regarded as having ratified the invalid contract.

"Ratification, as it relates to the law of agency, is the express or implied adoption of the acts of another by one for whom the other assumes to be acting, but without authority."[111] The rule governing ratification is that a principal may ratify any unauthorized act of an agent which might have been authorized in the first instance.[112] "It is a rule," says the Supreme Court of Nebraska, "subject to few, if any, exceptions, that a corporate authority may ratify and confirm any act or contract in its behalf or for its benefit which it might have lawfully done or made originally."[113] Where, therefore, a school district or board of education enters into a contract invalid because of some irregularity in its execution, the contract may be later ratified, provided that it be one which the district or board might have lawfully made in the first instance.[114] According to the great weight of authority, a

111. *Ryan v. Humphries*, 50 Okla. 343, 150 Pac. 1106, L.R.A. 1915F 1047.

112. *Ryan v. Humphries*, 50 Okla. 343, 150 Pac. 1106, L.R.A. 1915F 1047; *School District No. 47 v. Goodwin*, 81 Ark. 143, 98 S.W. 696; *Saline County v. Gage County*, 66 Neb. 839, 92 N.W. 1050; *Frank v. Board of Education*, 90 N.J. Law 273, 100 Atl. 211, L.R.A. 1917D 206; *Frederick v. Douglas County*, 96 Wis. 411, 71 N.W. 798.

113. *Saline County v. Gage County*, 66 Neb. 839, 92 N.W. 1050.

114. *Boydstun v. Rockwall County*, 86 Tex. 234, 24 S.W. 272; *Glidden State Bank v. School District No. 2*, 143 Wis. 617, 128 N.W. 285; *Hill v. Indianapolis*, 92 Fed. 467; *Ryan v. Humphries*, 50 Okla. 343, 150 Pac. 1106, L.R.A. 1915F 1047; *Frank v. Board of Education*, 90 N.J. Law 273, 100 Atl. 211, L.R.A. 1917D 206; *Frederick v. Douglas County*, 96 Wis. 411, 71 N.W. 798; *Blount v. Baker*, 177 Ark. 1162, 9 S.W. (2d) 802.

contract which is *ultra vires* or prohibited by statute is not susceptible of ratification.

The principle governing ratification has been well expressed by the Supreme Court of Wisconsin:

A municipal corporation may undoubtedly ratify an unauthorized contract made by its agents, which is within the general scope of its corporate powers; but it is equally certain that it cannot ratify such unauthorized acts of its agents as are beyond its scope, or such contracts as it had no power to make originally. . . . Ratification and estoppel are of very much the same nature, and the principles which apply to ratification substantially apply also to estoppel. As said by Mr. Dillon in the passage quoted by the chief justice: "The general doctrine is undoubted that there is ordinarily no estoppel in respect to acts which are in violation of the constitution or of an act of the legislature, or which are obviously, and in the strict and proper sense of the term, *ultra vires*. . . . We mean by it, as here used, the want of legislative power, under any circumstances or conditions, to do the particular act in question." This passage, we believe, expresses the law with clearness.[115]

Applying the rule as stated in the foregoing case, it has been held that a board of education may ratify a contract entered into by members of the board acting individually,[116] or at a meeting of which one or more of the members had no legal notice;[117] a contract with a teacher made by the superintendent or president of the board;[118] or a contract made by an unauthorized agent, such as a school principal or superintendent of buildings.[119] Similarly, a school district may ratify the unauthorized acts of its trustees, such as the purchase of furniture or the construction of a school building.[120] On the other hand, such

115. *Frederick v. Douglas County*, 96 Wis. 411, 71 N.W. 798.

116. *Parrick v. School District No. 1*, 100 Kan. 569, 164 Pac. 1172; *Union School Furniture Company v. School District No. 60*, 50 Kan. 727, 32 Pac. 368, 20 L.R.A. 136; *Crane v. Bennington School District*, 61 Mich. 299, 28 N.W. 105; *Springfield Furniture Company v. School District No. 4*, 67 Ark. 236, 54 S.W. 217; *Board of Education v. News Dispatch Printing & Audit Company*, 117 Okla. 226, 245 Pac. 884; *Johnson v. School Corporation of Cedar*, 117 Iowa 319, 90 N.W. 713; *Bellows v. District Township of West Fork*, 70 Iowa 320, 30 N.W. 582; *Richards v. School Township of Jackson*, 132 Iowa 612, 109 N.W. 1093; *Kreatz v. St. Cloud School District*, 79 Minn. 14, 81 N.W. 533.

117. *Board of Education v. News Dispatch Printing & Audit Company*, 117 Okla. 226, 245 Pac. 884; *School District No. 47 v. Goodwin*, 81 Ark. 143, 98 S.W. 696.

118. *Stewart v. Board of Education*, 104 Okla. 141, 230 Pac. 504; *Hull v. Independent School District of Aplington*, 82 Iowa 686, 46 N.W. 1053, 48 N.W. 82, 10 L.R.A. 273.

119. *Frank v. Board of Education*, 90 N.J. Law 273, 100 Atl. 211, L.R.A. 1917D 206.

120. *Everts v. District Township of Rose Grove*, 77 Iowa 37, 41 N.W. 478, 14 Am. St. Rep. 264; *Haney School Furniture Company v. School District No. 1*, 133 Mich. 241, 94 N.W. 726.

contracts as the following cannot be ratified: a contract in excess of a constitutional or statutory debt limit;[121] a contract to purchase school furniture which has not been approved as to price and quality by the state superintendent, as required by statute;[122] a contract to employ a teacher who has not been recommended by the county superintendent where the law makes employment conditional upon such recommendation;[123] the personal contract of individual board members;[124] or a contract made outside the scope of corporate powers.[125]

While a school board or district may have power to ratify a contract, it is often very difficult to determine whether ratification has, in fact, taken place. Granted that the power to ratify exists, ratification may be said to take place when the acts of the principal, after a knowledge of all material facts, are such as to be inconsistent with any other supposition.[126] "Performance of a contract, permission to the party with whom the corporation contracts to perform, the acceptance of the performance or the fruits of the performance by the corporation, acquiescence in the contract, payment to the other party and the like, all operate as acts of ratification."[127]

The two most common forms of ratification are (1) payment for services rendered and (2) acceptance and use of services and goods furnished under the contract. Where officers of a school district, acting at a regular meeting with knowledge of all the material facts, vote to pay for services received or properly delivered, their act will ordinarily be construed as a ratification. Where, for example, a teacher is permitted to teach and is paid at least her first month's salary, the courts

121. *Riesen v. School District No. 4*, 189 Wis. 607, 208 N.W. 472; *Grady v. Pruit*, 111 Ky. 100, 63 S.W. 283.

122. *First National Bank of Waldron v. Whisenhunt*, 94 Ark. 583, 127 S.W. 968.

123. *Board of Education v. Watts*, 19 Ala. App. 7, 95 So. 498.

124. *Western Publishing House v. District Township of Rock*, 84 Iowa 101, 50 N.W. 551.

125. *Boydstun v. Rockwall County*, 86 Tex. 234, 24 S.W. 272; *Glidden State Bank v. School District No. 2*, 143 Wis. 617, 128 N.W. 285; *Hill v. Indianapolis*, 92 Fed. 467; *Ryan v. Humphries*, 50 Okla. 343, 150 Pac. 1106, L.R.A. 1915F 1047; *Frank v. Board of Education*, 90 N.J. Law 273, 100 Atl. 211, L.R.A. 1917D 206.

126. *Boydstun v. Rockwall County*, 86 Tex. 234, 24 S.W. 272; *Frank v. Board of Education*, 90 N.J. Law 273, 100 Atl. 211, L.R.A. 1917D 206; *Crane v. Bennington School District*, 61 Mich. 299, 28 N.W. 105.

127. *Athearn v. Independent District of Millersburg*, 33 Iowa 105.

almost invariably hold that the contract has been ratified, provided, of course, that it be susceptible of ratification.[128]

As a general rule, acceptance of services or use of property constitutes ratification, without any formal act of ratification on the part of the school authorities. Acceptance of services or use of property by a school board with a knowledge of all material facts is sufficient within itself to constitute ratification, and no formal act on the part of the board is required.[129] In some cases, however, it is held that ratification should be a formal corporate act.[130]

Speaking of the ratification of a contract entered into by school-district officers acting individually, the Supreme Court of Michigan has said: "It was not necessary that there should be a direct proceeding with an express intent to ratify. 'It may be done indirectly, and by acts of recognition or acquiescence, or acts inconsistent with repudiation or disapproval.' "[131]

In the case of *Board of Education* v. *News Dispatch Printing & Audit Company*,[132] two of the three members of a board acting informally employed the plaintiff to audit the books and records of the district. The court held that acceptance of the services constituted a ratification of the contract:

128. *Hermance* v. *Public School District No. 2,* 20 Ariz. 314, 180 Pac. 442; *Athearn* v. *Independent District of Millersburg,* 33 Iowa 105; *Fennell* v. *Lannom,* 46 Okla. 519, 149 Pac. 144; *Ryan* v. *Humphries,* 50 Okla. 343, 150 Pac. 1106, L.R.A. 1915F 1047; *Stewart* v. *Board of Education,* 104 Okla. 141, 230 Pac. 504; *School District No. 47* v. *Goodwin,* 81 Ark. 143, 98 S.W. 696; *Jones* v. *School District No. 144,* 7 Kan. App. 372, 51 Pac. 927; *Parrick* v. *School District No. 1,* 100 Kan. 569, 164 Pac. 1172; *Crane* v. *Bennington School District,* 61 Mich. 299, 28 N.W. 105.

129. *Doyle* v. *School District No. 38,* 30 Okla. 81, 118 Pac. 386; *Board of Education* v. *News Dispatch Printing & Audit Company,* 117 Okla. 226, 245 Pac. 884; *Blount* v. *Baker,* 177 Ark. 1162, 9 S.W. (2d) 802; *Springfield Furniture Company* v. *School District No. 4,* 67 Ark. 236, 54 S.W. 217; *Union School Furniture Company* v. *School District No. 60,* 50 Kan. 727, 32 Pac. 368; *Bellows* v. *District Township of West Fork,* 70 Iowa 320, 30 N.W. 582; *Richards* v. *School Township of Jackson,* 132 Iowa 612, 109 N.W. 1093; *Hull* v. *Independent School District of Aplington,* 82 Iowa 686, 46 N.W. 1053; *Jones* v. *School District No. 3,* 110 Mich. 363, 68 N.W. 222; *Crane* v. *Bennington School District,* 61 Mich. 299, 28 N.W. 105; *Kreatz* v. *St. Cloud School District,* 79 Minn. 14, 81 N.W. 533.

130. *Taylor* v. *District Township of Wayne,* 25 Iowa 447; *Mulhall* v. *Pfannkuch,* 206 Iowa 1139, 221 N.W. 833.

131. *Crane* v. *Bennington School District,* 61 Mich. 299, 28 N.W. 105.

132. *Board of Education* v. *News Dispatch Printing & Audit Company,* 117 Okla. 226, 245 Pac. 884.

The fact that the members of the board permitted the plaintiff to perform services under a contract which they knew had been executed and was in existence, and receiving and enjoying the benefits of the services rendered by the plaintiff, under the contract, completely ratified said contract. The following rule, announced by the court in the case of *Doyle, et al.* v. *School Dist. No. 38*, 118 Pac. 386, 30 Okl. 81, is applicable here:

"The act of the two members of the school district board is employing plaintiffs in error has been fully and completely ratified by the school district by the acceptance of their services, and the enjoyment of the benefits secured to the district by their efforts. . . . When a quasi public corporation receives and retains the benefits of an irregular contract, made by the members of the school district board, acting separately, without any board meeting, it shall be deemed to have ratified the same, and must pay for the services, or other property, so obtained for its use."

The principle that acceptance of services or use of property in and of itself constitutes ratification is subject to an important limitation. Ratification will not be inferred from the retention of benefits which the district had no option to reject.[133] Where, for example, a school district uses a schoolhouse built on land owned by the district, such use will not, as a rule, constitute ratification of the invalid contract under which the building was constructed.[134] In a Connecticut case,[135] the town of Bridgeport voted in town meeting to build a schoolhouse at a cost not to exceed $55,000. A building committee was appointed and authorized to contract for the erection of the house. Contracts were entered into for the construction of a house in excess of the amount authorized, and it was claimed that the town, by taking possession of and using the house had thereby ratified the acts of its committee. The court denied this claim:

Again, it is said that the committee on building and the school committee, on behalf of the town, took possession of the building after it was finished, furnished it, and used it for school purposes, and that the town has in this way the benefit of the plaintiff's labor and materials to the amount claimed in the complaint wholly unpaid for.

133. *Turney* v. *Town of Bridgeport*, 55 Conn. 412, 12 Atl. 520; *Arkansas National Bank* v. *School District No. 99*, 152 Ark. 507, 238 S.W. 630; *Young* v. *Board of Education*, 54 Minn. 385, 55 N.W. 1112, 40 Am. St. Rep. 340; *Wilson* v. *School District No. 4*, 32 N.H. 118.

134. *Turney* v. *Town of Bridgeport*, 55 Conn. 412, 12 Atl. 520; *Allen County Board of Education* v. *Scottsville Builders' Supply Company*, 202 Ky. 185, 259 S.W. 39; *Arkansas National Bank* v. *School District No. 99*, 152 Ark. 507, 238 S.W. 630; *Wilson* v. *School District No. 4*, 32 N.H. 118; *School Directors* v. *Fogleman*, 76 Ill. 189; *Young* v. *Board of Education*, 54 Minn. 385, 55 N.W. 1112, 40 Am. St. Rep. 340.

135. *Turney* v. *Town of Bridgeport*, 55 Conn. 412, 12 Atl. 520. Accord, *Allen County Board of Education* v. *Scottsville Builders' Supply Company*, 202 Ky. 185, 259, S.W. 39.

It is admitted that the building was erected upon a lot owned by the town. The plaintiff knew this fact when he built the structure. The plaintiff made no sort of claim upon the town for any payment beyond the amount appropriated until long after the building was accepted and in use as a school building and the town had paid the plaintiff his contract price and something for extras. There is nothing to show that the committee recognized the plaintiff's right to recover beyond that sum.

Even if the town had received notice that the plaintiff claimed beyond the appropriation before the building was used as a school building, we think it plain that the town had a right to take and continue the possession of the building without incurring liability by that act. The town had no election in the premises. The building had been erected upon a lot owned by the town for the specific purpose of a school-house lot and building. The town had instructed its committee to make a contract, with a certain definite limitation as to the amount of the cost of the building, and the plaintiff knew perfectly well that the committee, neither directly nor indirectly, had any power to contract beyond the letter of that vote.

The town had paid a large sum for the lot and a large sum to the plaintiff. Under the circumstances it is impossible for us to say that this public, political corporation could not use this building for a public school-house because the plaintiff claimed that he had entered into an agreement with the building committee in conscious disregard of the restraints and limitations of their power. There is no authority for the plaintiff's position. . . .

We have touched only generally upon one controlling feature of this case. The rules of law, declaring that an agent of a town must pursue his authority strictly; that if he goes beyond his written authority his act is not valid; that persons dealing with such agents must look to the corporate act of the town as the source and limit of the powers of the agent; that any claimed ratification of previously unauthorized acts of such agent must be done by the town in a lawful manner, and, as a rule, directly, and not by implication, and must be made with full knowledge of all material facts; and that no *estoppel in pais* can be created, except by conduct on the part of the town which the person claiming the estoppel has the right to and does in fact rely on—these are essential to the due and orderly administration of our local public affairs, and should be applied in a spirit of fair respect to the rights of the individual tax-payer.

In the case of *Young* v. *Board of Education*,[136] additional funds were needed to complete a school building. The treasurer of the district borrowed the necessary funds from a bank and completed the building under the direction of the board, although the board never authorized the loan. The court held that no ratification could be inferred from the fact that the district retained and enjoyed the benefits of the expenditure. The case was unlike an unauthorized purchase of chattels which could be restored. The district had no option to reject the improvement. "It would be a very unsafe rule to establish to hold that

136. *Young* v. *Board of Education*, 54 Minn. 385, 55 N.W. 1112, 40 Am. St. Rep. 340.

school officers might borrow money at their pleasure, and bind the district because the same is expended by them in improving the property of the district."

The principles of law governing ratification discussed in the preceding paragraphs are subject to one material qualification. Where the statutes prescribe the mode of making a contract with such definiteness as to exclude all other modes, ratification must follow the procedure prescribed in making the contract in the first instance.[137] Thus it was said in a Texas case: "When there is a mode of contracting prescribed which operates as a limitation upon the power to contract, then the mode prescribed becomes the measure of power, and there can be no ratification inferred from acts recognizing the legality of a contract made in violation of the prescribed mode."[138]

In Wisconsin, as an illustration, a statute provided that "no act authorized to be done by the board shall be valid unless voted at its meeting." And it was provided further that the purchase of maps and certain other supplies should "be approved at a regular meeting of the board at which all the members are present." A map was purchased by two of the members of the board without authority from the board and without the knowledge of the third member. Use of the map, the court held, did not constitute ratification:

The competency of the school district officers to ratify an absolutely void act, giving it original validity, by mere silence, is ruled against appellant by the elementary principle that under no circumstances can an official act, not performed in the manner required by law, and expressly prohibited unless so done, be ratified by those guilty of nonfeasance or misfeasance in the matter, by any less formal action than should have been originally had.[139]

In the case of *First National Bank of Waldron v. Whisenhunt*,[140] the school directors had no authority to purchase charts unless authorized to do so by the electors of the district at the annual election previous thereto. Nevertheless, the directors purchased charts and used them in the schools of the district. In holding that there had been no ratification, the court said:

137. *Boydstun v. Rockwall County*, 23 S.W. (Tex.) 541; *Miller v. Alsbaugh*, 2 S.W. (2d) (Mo.) 208.

138. *Boydstun v. Rockwall County*, 23 S.W. (Tex.) 541.

139. *Caxton Company v. School District No. 5*, 120 Wis. 374, 98 N.W. 231.

140. *First National Bank of Waldron v. Whisenhunt*, 94 Ark. 583, 127 S.W. 968.

The statute expressly provides that such contract can only be authorized by the electors at a meeting regularly called and by a vote cast at an election. This was a necessary condition to be observed before there could be any power to make such a contract, and it could not therefore be ratified except by the observance of those conditions that were essential to the making of a valid contract in the beginning, if it could be ratified in any event.

It should be pointed out, however, that in Arkansas, Oklahoma, and Arizona it has been held that, even though the statutes require a written contract, the contract may be ratified by the acceptance of services,[141] the ratification extending only to the period of performance.[142]

Ratification of acts of unauthorized agents.—Thus far, the discussion has had to do with the ratification of unauthorized acts of authorized agents. It may be, however, that an unauthorized agent, such as a school superintendent or principal, may undertake to bind the district without any authority whatsoever. Thus the question arises as to whether there may be an implied agency and, if so, under what circumstances the acts of such an agent may be ratified. It seems that the rule governing implied agency as it affects private corporations or persons is applicable to municipal corporations and school districts. That is, an agency may be implied from prior conduct where the course of action on the part of the alleged principal and agent has been such as to lead any reasonable person to suppose that the alleged agent is in fact what he represents himself to be. In the case of *Frank v. Board of Education,*[143] Rowland, the supervising architect, and Wilson, vice-principal of the high school of Jersey City, had for a number of years employed one Frank to perform certain labor and to furnish materials needed in keeping the school buildings in repair. Although Rowland and Wilson were acting without authority, the board regularly paid the bills as presented. To meet an emergency, Frank was employed by Rowland and Wilson to repair damages to the heating plant of the high-school building occasioned by excessively cold weather. The work done and materials furnished by Frank were done and furnished in reliance upon the past practice of the board in

141. *Davis* v. *White,* 171 Ark. 385, 284 S.W. 764. Accord, *Hermance* v. *Public School District No. 2,* 20 Ariz. 314, 180 Pac. 442.

142. *Bald Knob Special School District* v. *McDonald,* 171 Ark. 72, 283 S.W. 22; *Williamson* v. *Board of Education of City of Woodward,* 189 Okla. 342, 117 Pac. (2d) 120; *School District No. 6* v. *Whiting,* 52 Ariz. 207, 79 Pac. (2) 959.

143. *Frank* v. *Board of Education,* 90 N.J. Law 273, 100 Atl. 211, L.R.A. 1917D 206. Accord, *Grant* v. *Board of Education,* 136 Atl. (N.J.) 713; *Sebastian* v. *School Directors of School District No. 103,* 317 Ill. App. 524, 47 N.E. (2d) 121. See also *Everett* v. *Board of Public Instruction of Volusia County,* 136 Fla. 17, 186 So. 209.

paying for such materials and labor. The board of education knew the work had been done about the time it was done, but made no attempt to prevent it. Frank presented a bill for $684, which the board refused to pay. Judge Black spoke for the court as follows:

There is but a single question presented by the record in this case to be answered, viz., whether a municipal corporation is liable to pay for work done and materials furnished it, by an unauthorized agent, when the municipality had the power to make a contract for such purchases. If so, whether an agency to purchase such supplies in fact can be implied, from the acts and conduct of the parties, and a ratification of the contract for such supplies be also implied, from like acts and conduct. The application of elemental and well-recognized principles in the law of agency, to the facts, as disclosed by the record in this case, leads us to answer these questions in the affirmative. . . .

The literature of the law of agency is rich in adjudged cases. The principles pertinent to the subject under discussion are these: An agency, as between individuals or business corporations, may be implied from prior habit, or from a course of dealings of a similar nature between the parties. . . . The agency may be implied from the recognition or acquiescence of the alleged principal, as to acts done in his behalf, by the alleged agent, especially if the agent has repeatedly been permitted to perform acts like the one in question. . . . But when it is implied . . . the power of the agent must be determined from no one fact alone . . . but from all the facts and circumstances for which the principal is responsible. . . . So ratification may be implied from any acts, words or conduct on the part of the principal, which reasonably tend to show an intention on the part of the principal to ratify the unauthorized acts or transactions of the alleged agent . . . provided, the principal in doing the acts relied on as a ratification acted with knowledge of the material facts. . . .

The same rules apply to municipal corporations acting within the limits of the powers conferred upon them by the Legislature as to other corporations or private persons. . . .

We think, as the board of education had the power, under the statute, to contract for the work done and material supplied in this case, there was created by conduct an implied agency, an agency, in fact, on the part of Messrs. Rowland and Wilson; and further, that by implication the contracts of these unauthorized agents have been ratified by the acts and conduct of the school board.

Effect of ratification.—A contract once ratified becomes binding *ab initio*[144] and is as valid as though it had been legally made in the first instance.[145] If the invalid contract was entire when made, it

144. *Ryan* v. *Humphries,* 50 Okla. 343, 150 Pac. 1106, L.R.A. 1915F 1047; *Hill* v. *Indianapolis,* 92 Fed. 467.

145. *Jones* v. *School District No. 144,* 7 Kan. App. 372, 51 Pac. 927; *Athearn* v. *Independent District of Millersburg,* 33 Iowa 105; *Ryan* v. *Humphries,* 50 Okla. 343, 150 Pac. 1106, L.R.A. 1915F 1047. See, however, *Boyd* v. *Black School Township,* 123 Ind. 1, 23 N.E. 862; *Kane* v. *School District No. 3,* 52 Wis. 502, 9 N.W. 459.

becomes entire when ratified; one cannot ratify in part and reject in part.[146] Thus, where a contract with a teacher is ratified by permitting him to teach and paying him for the time taught, the district becomes liable for the whole amount stipulated in the contract.[147] In the case of *Hill* v. *Indianapolis*,[148] the board of public works entered into a contract which it had no authority to make without previous authorization of the city council. The council, however, ratified the contract. Speaking of the effect of the ratification, the court said:

> By the very nature of the act of ratification, the party ratifying becomes a party to the original contract. He that was not bound becomes bound by it, and entitled to all the proper benefits of it. He accepts the consideration of the contract as a sufficient consideration for adopting it, and this is quite enough to support a ratification. It follows that the contract, having been ratified by the common council of the city, becomes binding upon it from the date that it was improvidently entered into by the board of public works, and is just as conclusive and binding upon it as though it had been made by the previous authorization of the board of public works.

RECOVERY OF FUNDS ILLEGALLY PAID OUT

In the chapter on the liability of school officers, consideration is given to the liability of such officers to reimburse the district for money paid out on illegal or unenforcible contracts. The question here considered is the right of the school district or taxpayers in the name of the district to recover from the parties to whom the money has been paid. It is a well-established rule that, where private parties deal with one another, money paid out voluntarily with a knowledge of all the material facts, and in the absence of fraud, cannot be recovered because of ignorance of the law or because of a mistake of law. But where third parties deal with the officers of a school district, the situation is different. Such officers are not free to do with the funds of the district what they please; they are agents of the state possessing very limited powers. Moreover, since their powers are expressly or impliedly granted by statute, all who deal with them are charged with a knowledge of their powers. The decisions dealing with the recovery of funds illegally paid out cannot be harmonized. It has been frequently held, however, that where money has been paid out in violation of

146. See, however, *Bald Knob Special School District* v. *McDonald*, 171 Ark. 72, 283 S.W. 22.

147. *Athearn* v. *Independent District of Millersburg*, 33 Iowa 105; *Jones* v. *School District No. 144*, 7 Kan. App. 372, 51 Pac. 927.

148. *Hill* v. *Indianapolis*, 92 Fed. 467.

an express constitutional or statutory prohibition[149] or for a purpose entirely outside the powers of the school district,[150] it may be recovered from the parties to whom it has been paid in an action brought by taxpayers on behalf of the district. Speaking for the Supreme Court of Wisconsin,[151] Judge Winslow well expressed the reasons upon which this line of decisions is based:

There are many cases which hold that, as between man and man, money paid voluntarily, with knowledge of all the facts, and without fraud or duress, cannot be recovered merely on account of ignorance or mistake of the law. . . . This is simply the doctrine of voluntary payment. It is frequently applied to the payment of illegal taxes. It is founded upon the general principle that a man may do what he will with his own. He may give it away, or buy his peace; and, if he does so with knowledge of the facts, he is generally remediless. But the public officials do not stand upon the same basis. They are not dealing with their own. They are trustees for the taxpayers, and, in dealing with public funds, they are dealing with trust funds. All who deal with them know also that the public officials are acting in this trust capacity. To hold that, when public officers have paid out money in pursuance of an illegal and unwarranted contract, such moneys cannot be recovered in a proper action brought upon behalf of the public, merely because the payment has been voluntarily made for services actually rendered, would be to introduce a vicious principle into municipal law, and a principle which would necessarily sweep away many of the safeguards now surrounding the administration of public affairs. Were this, in fact, the law, it can readily be seen that public officials could at all times, with a little ingenuity, subvert and nullify that wholesome principle of the law which prohibits their spending the pubic funds for illegal purposes. All that would be necessary to be done would be to make the contract, have the labor performed, pay out the money, and the public would be remediless. We cannot approve of such a doctrine.

Thus it has been held that where contracts between a school board and one of its members are prohibited by statute, money paid out on such a contract may be recovered.[152] In the case of *Independent School*

149. *Directors of School District No. 302 v. Libby*, 135 Wash. 233, 237 Pac. 505; *School Directors v. Parks*, 85 Ill. 338; *Weitz v. Independent District of Des Moines*, 87 Iowa 81, 54 N.W. 70; *Independent School District No. 5 v. Collins*, 15 Idaho 535, 98 Pac. 857, 128 Am. St. Rep. 76; *Frederick v. Douglas County*, 96 Wis. 411, 71 N.W. 798; *Ridge v. Miller*, 185 Ark. 461, 47 S.W. (2d) 587; *School District No. 9 v. McLintock*, 255 Mich. 197, 237 N.W. 1539; *Vick Consolidated School District No. 21 v. New*, 208 Ark. 874, 187 S.W. (2d) 948.

150. *Milquet v. Van Straten*, 186 Wis. 303, 202 N.W. 670; *Dodge County v. Kaiser*, 243 Wis. 551, 11 N.W. (2d) 348; *Burke v. Wheeler County*, 54 Ga. App. 81, 187 S.E. 246.

151. *Frederick v. Douglas County*, 96 Wis. 411, 71 N.W. 798. Accord, *Egaard v. Dahike*, 109 Wis. 366, 85 N.W. 369.

152. *School Directors v. Parks*, 85 Ill. 338; *Independent School District No. 5 v. Collins*, 15 Idaho 535, 98 Pac. 857, 128 Am. St. Rep. 76. See also *McNay v. Lowell*, 41 Ind. App. 627, 84 N.E. 778; *Weitz v. Independent District of Des*

District No. 5 v. Collins,[153] the statutes made it unlawful for any school-board member to be financially interested in contracts with the board. While Collins was serving on the board, a company in which he was a large stockholder sold goods to the district. The goods were paid for. The court permitted a recovery of the money:

> If money is illegally paid on such void contract, the district may recover it back, and in case the district refuses to do so, any taxpayer of the district may, for and on behalf of the district, maintain an action for the recovery of money so illegally paid. . . .
> The rule contended for by appellant to the effect that neither party to a transaction will be permitted to take advantage of its invalidity while retaining the benefits, applies only to voidable contracts and not to a transaction that is absolutely void.

To the same effect is the case of *Vick Consolidated School District No. 21 v. New,*[154] where it was held that recovery could be had of money paid to a teacher who had taught without a certificate. Here the statutes expressly provided that a teacher who taught without a certificate should receive no compensation.

Similarly, it has been held that money paid out on a contract which the district under no circumstances had authority to make, i.e., *ultra vires* the charter powers of the corporation, could be recovered from the district at the suit of a taxpayer. In Wisconsin, as an illustration, a school board contracted with one Van Straten to transport to and from the public school such pupils as might desire to attend. The contract also provided that he should furnish transportation for those pupils of the district who might desire to attend a private school located in the vicinity of the public school. As a matter of fact, only two or three of the pupils transported attended the public school, whereas twenty-seven attended the private school. The court required Van Straten to pay back the money paid him. The contract was essentially one for the transportation of pupils to a private school and, therefore, entirely without the scope of the powers of the school district. This was not a case, said the court, where the district had received something of value

---

Moines, 87 Iowa 81, 54 N.W. 70; *Directors of School District No. 302 v. Libby,* 135 Wash. 233, 237 Pac. 505; *Vick Consolidated District No. 21 v. New,* 208 Ark. 874, 187 S.W. (2d) 948; *Smith v. Hendricks,* 136 S.W. (2d) (Mo.) 449.

153. *Independent School District No. 5 v. Collins,* 15 Idaho 535, 98 Pac. 857, 128 Am. St. Rep. 76. Accord, *School Directors v. Parks,* 85 Ill. 338.

154. *Vick Consolidated School District No. 21 v. New,* 208 Ark. 874, 187 S.W. (2d) 948.

for which it ought equitably to account.[155] In Wisconsin, too, a county superintendent was required to pay back to the county all sums of money paid to him to defray his expenses to conventions of the National Education Association. This was an expenditure beyond the powers of the county to make.[156] Again, in Georgia, a contract was made to have the books of the county audited, the county board of education to pay half the costs. The court held that this was a contract which the county board had no authority to make and permitted a recovery of the funds paid out under it.[157] Said the court:

> A wrongful payment made by a public officer is not a voluntary payment in so far as the public is concerned. . . . If the thing done is illegal or not warranted by law, however beneficial it may be, the public is not estopped to deny its validity. . . . Where public funds are illegally paid out by county officials or by some agency of the county, it is proper for the county to bring suit for the recovery of the same.

It has been held, too, that money paid out under mistake of fact may be recovered by a school board. In California, where the paymaster of the board of education misinterpreted the salary schedule adopted by the school board, gave teachers erroneous salary ratings, and overpaid them, the court ruled that the board could recover the overpayments. The court pointed out that money paid out by such a governmental agency as a board of education, under either mistake of law or of fact, could be recovered. The reason for this is that school funds are trust funds.[158]

In some jurisdictions, on the other hand, it is held that money paid out on contracts made in violation of some statutory provision or of public policy cannot be recovered where the facts show that the contract was made in good faith and the district retains and enjoys the benefits of its performance. In a New York case,[159] the court refused to require repayment to the district of money paid out on a contract in which board members were personally interested. Said the court:

155. *Milquet* v. *Van Straten*, 186 Wis. 303, 202 N.W. 670.

156. *Dodge* v. *Kaiser*, 243 Wis. 551, 11 N.W. (2d) 348.

157. *Burke* v. *Wheeler County*, 54 Ga. App. 81, 187 S.E. 246.

158. *Aebli* v. *Board of Education*, 62 Calif. App. 706, 145 Pac. (2d) 601. See also *Morgan Park* v. *Knopf*, 199 Ill. 444, 65 N.E. 322; *Ohio National Life Insurance Company* v. *Board of Education*, 387 Ill. 159, 55 N.E. (2d) 163.

159. *Ryszka* v. *Board of Education*, 214 N.Y.S. 264. Accord, *City of Tacoma* v. *Lillis*, 4 Wash. 797, 31 Pac. 321, 18 L.R.A. 372; *Frick* v. *Town of Brinkley*, 61 Ark. 397, 33 S.W. 527; *Witmer* v. *Nichols*, 320 Mo. 665, 8 S.W. (2d) 63; *Johnson* v. *Gibson*, 240 Mich. 515, 215, N.W. 333; *Culver* ex rel. *Longyear* v. *Brown*, 259 Mich. 294, 243 N.W. 10.

In my opinion the arrangement made in reference to the employment of Bromley was one that should not have been made, as it violated the law that a public servant, while in the discharge of his public duty, may not assume a private duty in conflict with his duty to the public. . . . And if this were an action on the contract for payment of the contract price, I would feel compelled to dismiss the complaint.

However, this is an action brought in equity to obtain a judgment restraining the payment of such unpaid balance, and requiring the repayment back of the sums already paid. I am satisfied from proof that the labor and work was all done in a workmanlike manner, that the materials furnished were of the proper quality and quantity. . . . I am further of the opinion that all the acts and transactions were done in the utmost of good faith, and in no way resulted in any injury or loss to the board of education, or to the property in its charge and under its control, to the school fund, or to the city of Lackawanna. In view of this, I cannot see my way clear to grant the relief asked for in the complaint. I feel to do so would be unjust and inequitable.

Similarly, it has been held that money paid out on a contract void because it created an indebtedness in excess of the statutory debt limit could not be recovered.[160] And in Illinois the court refused to permit the recovery of interest paid on bonds which created an indebtedness in excess of the debt limit.[161] Money paid out on a contract entered into at a called meeting of the board of which some of the members had no notice could not be recovered.[162] In Michigan the statutes expressly prohibited school-board members from being interested in contracts let by the board. Even so, the court refused to permit recovery from a board member of money paid to him for the purchase of supplies for the district. The court stressed the fact that the supplies were needed by the district and that there was no evidence of fraud or bad faith in the making or execution of the contract.[163] In other instances, the courts have refused to permit recovery from a school-board member funds paid to him under an illegally executed contract with the board.[164] So, too, money paid a teacher for services rendered while not in possession of a certificate as required by statute could not be recovered from her on behalf of the district. The court rested its opinion upon the fact that both parties to the contract were

160. *Moe* v. *Millard County School District*, 54 Utah 144, 179 Pac. 980.

161. *Ohio National Life Insurance Company* v. *Board of Education*, 387 Ill. 159, 55 N.E. (2d) 163.

162. *Shackleford* v. *Thomas*, 182 Ark. 797, 32 S.W. (2d) 810.

163. *Culver* ex rel. *Longyear* v. *Brown*, 259 Mich. 294, 243 N.W. 10.

164. *Witmer* v. *Nichols*, 320 Mo. 665, 8 S.W. (2d) 63; *Kagy* v. *Independent District*, 117 Iowa 694, 89 N.W. 972.

equally at fault. "Money paid under an agreement which is executed, whether paid as the consideration or in performance of the promise, cannot be recovered back, while the parties are *in pari delicto.*"[165]

Whatever the facts may be in any particular case, the courts will not require money to be paid back to the district if thereby principles of fair dealing and common honesty be violated. Taxpayers may become guilty of laches and thereby lose their right of action. That is, by failure to exercise their rights seasonably they may lose them altogether.[166] He who seeks equity must do equity. Where, therefore, taxpayers, with a knowledge of the facts, permit funds to be paid out without objection and without an attempt to secure injunctional relief, they may be estopped by their own acquiescence and neglect when they come into a court of equity demanding that the money be returned to the treasury of the district. In the case of *Frederick* v. *Douglas County,*[167] for example, a Mr. Grace had been employed by the county to serve as an attorney in important tax cases, the district attorney being young and inexperienced in tax litigation. Action was brought to recover from Grace the amount which had been paid him for his services. The court held that the county board had no authority to employ Grace because the statute made it the duty of the district attorney to represent the county in such matters, but it refused to require Grace to return to the county the money which had been paid him. Said the court:

But while we believe it to be salutary and a correct principle of law to hold that moneys paid out by municipal officials in violation of law may be recovered from the recipient in an action seasonably brought, especially when the transaction is marked by haste, fraud, collusion, or concealment, we believe there are cases in which the circumstances are such that a court of equity ought not to decree the return of money merely because the appropriation thereof was unauthorized, and such a case we believe to be before us now.

The evidence and findings show that *Mr. Grace's* employment began in January, 1895, and it was a matter of public notoriety, and the plaintiff himself and presumably all taxpayers who kept track of the public proceedings knew that he was employed as early as the spring of 1895; that he performed large and valuable services, for which he was from time to time paid; and that not only he, but the county board, acted in entire good faith in the

---

165. *School District No. 46* v. *Johnson,* 26 Colo. App. 433, 143 Pac. 264.

166. *Conners* v. *City of Lowell,* 246 Mass. 279, 140 N.E. 742; *Oliver Iron Mining Company* v. *Independent School District No. 35,* 155 Minn. 400, 193 N.W. 949.

167. *Frederick* v. *Douglas County,* 96 Wis. 411, 71 N.W. 798.

matter. There was no haste and no evidence of collusion or concealment. *Mr. Grace's* services ran through a number of months, and he undoubtedly has fairly earned all the money which has been paid him. During all this time the plaintiff and his fellow taxpayers remained silent, and allowed the services to be rendered and the money to be paid. They took no action until the latter part of November, 1895. . . . Could it, under any view of the circumstances, be said to be equitable to compel *Mr. Grace* to pay back the money which he received for long and valuable labors, rendered honestly and in good faith, the benefit of which the corporation has received, and concerning which the taxpayers of Superior were, or ought to have been, fully informed during their entire progress? Were a court of equity to make this judgment under the circumstances, we should regard it as having become an engine of oppression, rather than an instrument of justice. We do not rest this decision entirely upon the ground that the remedy has been lost by laches, or that the county has become estopped, but upon the ground that under all the circumstances, the plaintiff having invoked the relief of a court of equity, that court, in granting the relief, will not take away the fruit of honest labor.

Similarly, in the case of *Dorner* v. *School District No. 5*,[168] where a school board had for twenty years rented rooms from a Roman Catholic corporation and had allowed sectarian instruction to be given in the public school conducted therein, in violation of a provision of the constitution, taxpayers in behalf of the district could not recover from the church corporation money paid to it as rent.

In case school officers are paid for their services in excess of what is legally due or where they are paid when nothing is due, the excess or illegal payment can be recovered.[169] In such cases the doctrine of acquiescence and voluntary payment does not apply, and the money may be recovered as money wrongfully had and received. Where, for example, a county board of education without authority paid the expenses of a county superintendent while attending a meeting of the state education association, the money could be recovered.[170] Similarly, where a clerk of a school district was paid for his services, even though the statutes made no provision for paying him, the court ordered the money restored to the treasury of the district.[171]

168. *Dorner* v. *School District No. 5*, 137 Wis. 147, 118 N.W. 353, 19 L.R.A. (N.S.) 171.

169. *Leslie County* v. *Hoskins*, 175 Ky. 821, 195 S.W. 142; *Beauchamp* v. *Snider*, 170 Ky. 220, 185 S.W. 868; *Anderson* v. *Burton*, 174 Ky. 456, 192 S.W. 519; *Clarke* v. *School District No. 16*, 84 Ark. 516, 106 S.W. 677; *Wiles* v. *McIntosh County*, 10 N.D. 594, 88 N.W. 710; *Demarest* v. *New Barbadoes*, 40 N.J. Law 604.

170. *Beauchamp* v. *Snider*, 170 Ky. 220, 185 S.W. 868.

171. *Clarke* v. *School District No. 16*, 84 Ark. 516, 106 S.W. 677.

AUTHORITY OF SCHOOL BOARDS TO MAKE CONTRACTS
EXTENDING BEYOND THEIR TERM OF OFFICE

A school board is a corporate entity and, unless restrained by statute, may enter into contracts extending beyond the official life of any or all its present members.[172] The courts reason that a school board is a continuing corporate body, independent of the coming and going of its individual members. It would be against public policy to limit the contractual powers of a board to the official life of its individual members. As was said by the Supreme Court of Mississippi, in upholding a teacher's contract, "the board in power at the time it was alleged the plaintiff was employed had the right to make a contract with her, which, if made by them, could not be set aside or abrogated by their successors in office, except for legal cause in appropriate proceedings."[173] A board may not enter into a contract for an unreasonable period of time or in bad faith.

It should be pointed out, however, that where a contract of employment of a teacher is for a period of performance wholly within the term of a succeeding board, a number of courts hold the contract invalid as being against public policy.[174]

172. *Taylor* v. *School District No. 7*, 16 Wash. 365, 47 Pac. 758; *State* v. *Board of Education*, 94 W. Va. 408, 118 S.E. 877; *Reubelt* v. *School Town of Noblesville*, 106 Ind. 478, 7 N.E. 206; *Gardner* v. *North Little Rock Special School District*, 161 Ark. 466, 257 S.W. 73; *Davis* v. *Public School of City of Escanaba*, 175 Mich. 105, 180 N.W. 1001; *Cleveland* v. *Amy*, 88 Mich. 374, 50 N.W. 293; *Wheeler* v. *Burke*, 162 Ky. 143, 172 S.W. 91; *Wilson* v. *East Bridgeport School District*, 36 Conn. 280; *V. L. Dodds Company* v. *Consolidated School District of Lamont*, 220 Iowa, 812, 263 N.W. 522; *State* ex rel. *Rees* v. *Winchell*, 136 Ohio St. 62, 23 N.E. (2d) 843; *King City High School District* v. *Waibel*, 2 Calif. App. (2d) 65; 37 Pac. (2d) 861; *Stokes* v. *Newell*, 174 Miss. 629, 165 So. 542; *Horvat* v. *Jenkins*, 337 Pa. 193, 10 Atl. 337; *Tate* v. *School District*, 324 Mo. 477, 23 S.W. (2d) 1013, 70 A.L.R. 794.

173. *Stokes* v. *Newell*, 174 Miss. 629, 165 So. 542.

174. See note, 70 A.L.R. 799; *Maynard* v. *Gilbert*, 283 Ky. 227, 140 S.W. 1064; *Shores* v. *Elmore County Board of Education*, 241 Ala. 464, 3 So. (2d) 14. Contra, *King City Union High School District* v. *Waibel*, 2 Calif. App. (2d) 65, 37 Pac. (2d) 861.

CHAPTER X

The School Money

AUTHORITY TO TAX FOR SCHOOL PURPOSES

SPEAKING of the power of a state to tax, the Supreme Court of the United States has said: "Unless restrained by provisions of the Federal Constitution, the power of the State as to the mode, form, and extent of taxation is unlimited, where the subjects to which it applies are within her jurisdiction."[1] The power of the state to tax is exercised by the legislative branch of government. Unless restrained by the state or federal constitution, the state legislature has plenary power over taxation and may tax to such an extent and in such manner and through such agencies as in its judgment will best serve the purposes of government.[2] It may, in its discretion, constitute the state a unit for purposes of state taxation, or it may create quasi-corporations and municipal corporations and confer upon them the power to tax.[3]

It follows, therefore, that the power to tax is never inherent in school districts. Such powers of taxation as they possess are derived exclusively from the constitution and the statutes. Speaking for the Supreme Court of Kansas, Justice Cunningham has said in this connection:

The authority to levy taxes is an extraordinary one. It is never left to implication, unless it is a *necessary* implication. Its warrant must be clearly found in the act of the legislature. Any other rule might lead to great wrong

1. *Shaffer* v. *Carter*, 252 U.S. 37, 40 S. Ct. 221, 64 L. Ed. 445.

2. *Shaffer* v. *Carter*, 252 U.S. 37, 40 S. Ct. 221, 64 L. Ed. 445; *Miller* v. *Childers*, 107 Okla. 57, 238 Pac. 204.

3. *Smith* v. *Board of Trustees of Robersonville Graded School*, 141 N.C. 143, 53 S.E. 524, 8 Ann. Cas 529; *Minsinger* v. *Rau*, 236 Pa. St. 327, 84 Atl. 902, Ann. Cas. 1913E 1324; *City of Louisville* v. *Commonwealth*, 134 Ky. 488, 121 S.W. 411; *Stuart* v. *School District No. 1*, 30 Mich. 69; *Merrick* v. *Inhabitants of Amherst*, 12 Allen (Mass.) 500.

and oppression, and when there is a reasonable doubt as to its existence the right must be denied. Therefore, to say that the right is in doubt is to deny its existence.[4]

It is clear, therefore, that school districts or municipal corporations proper cannot levy taxes for school purposes unless they have express or implied power to do so. It has been held, for example, that, in the absence of specific statutory authority, a board of education cannot spend funds raised by taxation to maintain a clinic for the free medical treatment of pupils,[5] to employ a football coach,[6] or to provide facilities for the transportation of children to and from school. And in Illinois it has been held that a school board cannot build up, year by year, a building fund to be used at some indefinite time in the future.[7] Taxes cannot be levied, moreover, to pay a debt in excess of the constitutional limit of indebtedness.[8] In some jurisdictions the statutes require that taxes be levied for specific purposes, as, for example, educational purposes and building purposes. Where such is the case, taxes cannot be levied for one purpose and be applied to another.[9] If a bonded indebtedness, for example, has been incurred for educational purposes, the tax to meet it must be levied as an educational tax; and if the debt has been incurred for building purposes, it must be met

4. *Marion and McPherson Railway Company* v. *Alexander*, 63 Kan. 72, 64 Pac. 978. Accord, *Missouri, Kansas and Texas Railroad Company* v. *People*, 245 Pac. (Okla.) 617; *Board of Commissioners* v. *Hanchett Bond Company*, 194 N.C. 137, 138 S.E. 614; *Geffert* v. *Yorktown Independent School District*, 290 S.W. (Tex.) 1083.

5. *McGilvra* v. *Seattle School District No. 1*, 113 Wash. 619, 194 Pac. 817, 12 A.L.R. 913.

6. *Rockwell* v. *School District No. 1*, 109 Ore. 480, 220 Pac. 142.

7. *Cleveland, Cincinnati, Chicago & St. Louis Railway Company* v. *People*, 208 Ill. 423, 69 N.E. 832; *Chicago and Alton Railroad Company* v. *People*, 205 Ill. 625, 69 N.E. 72.

8. *People* v. *Toledo, Peoria & Western Railway Company*, 229 Ill. 327, 82 N.E. 420; *Baltimore & Ohio Southwestern Railway Company* v. *People*, 195 Ill. 423, 63 N.E. 262; *Flanders* v. *Board of Trustees of Little Rock Graded School District*, 170 Ky. 627, 186 S.W. 506.

9. *People* v. *Bell*, 309 Ill. 387, 141 N.E. 187; *Chicago and Alton Railway Company* v. *People*, 205 Ill. 625, 69 N.E. 72; *Wabash Railroad Company* v. *People*, 187 Ill. 289, 58 N.E. 254; *People ex rel. Harding* v. *Chicago & Northwestern Railway Company*, 413 Ill. 93, 108 N.E. (2d) 22; *San Benito Independent School District* v. *Farmer's State Bank*, 78 S.W. (2d) (Tex.) 741; *Wilds* v. *School District of City of McKeesport*, 336 Pa. 275, 9 Atl. (2d) 338; *Russell* v. *Frank*, 348 Mo. 533, 154 S.W. (2d) 63.

by taxes levied for such purposes.[10] And where school-district electors approved a bond issue for purposes of erecting and furnishing buildings for high schools, the board of education was not authorized to use part of the money for the erection of a vocational high school.[11] Similarly, where the statutes require contracts to be paid out of revenues accruing during the fiscal year, contracts to be paid out of funds of a later fiscal year are void.[12]

School taxes are state taxes[13] even though they may have been levied by the local district or municipal authorities:

When a municipal body, or a county, or a school district levies taxes for school purposes, the tax so levied is a State and not a municipal, county or district tax, although it may be levied and collected by municipal or county or district officers. The fact that the tax is levied and collected for the State by the agencies of the State appointed for that purpose does not deprive it of its character as a State tax.[14]

It follows, therefore, that school districts or municipalities may be required against their consent to levy taxes for public school purposes.[15] A Kansas case[16] illustrates the reasoning of the courts. County commissioners refused to carry into effect a statute requiring the establishment of a high school, on the ground that the county could not "be compelled to build and maintain a high school without the consent of those who are required to pay for it, and that the legislature exceeded its powers when it attempted to impose such a task and burden upon them." The court, however, held a contrary opinion. It said in part:

10. *People* v. *Chicago & Eastern Illinois Railroad Company*, 300 Ill. 258, 133 N.E. 339; *Chicago & Alton Railway Company* v. *People*, 205 Ill. 625, 69 N.E. 72.

11. *Wilds* v. *School District of City of McKeesport*, 336 Pa. 275, 9 Atl. (2d) 338.

12. *Consolidated School District No. 6* v. *Panther*, 197 Okla. 66, 168 Pac. (2d) 613.

13. *Ramsey* v. *County Board of Education*, 159 Ky. 827, 169 S.W. 521; *City of Louisville* v. *Board of Education*, 154 Ky. 316, 157 S.W. 379; *Ford* v. *Kendall Borough School District*, 121 Pa. St. 543; *People* v. *Bartlett*, 304 Ill. 283, 136 N.E. 654; *Kennedy* v. *Miller*, 97 Calif. 429, 32 Pac. 558; *Garner* v. *Scales*, 183 Tenn. 577, 194 S.W. (2d) 452; *City Board of Education of Athens* v. *Williams*, 231 Ala. 137, 163 So. 802.

14. *City of Louisville* v. *Board of Education*, 154 Ky. 316, 157 S.W. 379.

15. *State* v. *Freeman*, 61 Kan. 90, 58 Pac. 959, 47 L.R.A. 67; *Revell* v. *City of Annapolis*, 81 Md. 1, 31 Atl. 695.

16. *State* v. *Freeman*, 61 Kan. 90, 58 Pac. 959, 47 L.R.A. 67.

The matter of education is one of public interest which concerns all the people of the state, and is, therefore, subject to the control of the legislature. . . . While education is a matter of state interest and public concern, the high school being especially beneficial to the people of the community in which it is established, the burden of maintaining it may be rightfully cast upon them. It is conceded that the legislature has full power to compel local organizations of the state to maintain common schools, and as schools of a higher grade are authorized by the constitution, no reason is seen why such organizations may not be compelled to maintain high schools.

Similarly, in the case of *Revell* v. *City of Annapolis*,[17] it was held that the legislature had the power to require the city of Annapolis to issue bonds for the purpose of raising funds for the erection of a schoolhouse, even though the voters had never given their consent to the issuance of such bonds. The court conceded that there might be some doubt with respect to the power of the legislature to require a city to create a debt for a local purpose in which the state had no concern, but it said that it was unable to find a single case which denied to the legislature the power to compel a municipality to incur a debt for the purpose of erecting a public school building.

It is a general rule that the courts will not control the discretion of school boards except in cases where discretion is abused. Where, therefore, school boards have authority to tax for school purposes, they will be permitted to exercise that authority in such manner as they deem best. In a Pennsylvania case,[18] for example, action was brought by taxpayers to enjoin the collection of school taxes, on the ground that the tax was oppressive and greatly in excess of what was necessary. The court stated the rule governing such cases as follows:

The power of taxation, altogether legislative and in no degree judicial, is committed by the legislature in the matter of schools, to the directors of school districts. If the directors refuse to perform their duties the court can compel them. If they transcend their powers, the courts can restrain them. If they misjudge their pcwer the court can correct them. But if they exercise their unquestionable powers unwisely, there is no judicial remedy.

In harmony with the rule, the courts have repeatedly held that a school board may levy such taxes as it deems necessary to accomplish its purposes, so long as the tax limit is not exceeded.[19] Thus in an

17. *Revell* v. *City of Annapolis*, 81 Md. 1, 31 Atl. 695.

18. *Wharton* v. *School Directors of Cass Township*, 42 Pa. St. 358.

19. *People* v. *Scott*, 300 Ill. 290, 133 N.E. 299; *People* v. *Chicago & Texas Railroad Company*, 223 Ill. 448, 79 N.E. 151; *Laswell* v. *Seaton*, 107 Kan. 439, 191 Pac. 266; *Wright* v. *Board of Education*, 106 Kan. 469, 188 Pac. 439.

Illinois case[20] the board estimated that it would cost forty thousand dollars to construct a school building. Bonds were issued to that amount. Later it was discovered that an additional amount would be necessary to construct the kind of building desired. Consequently, the board levied a tax for building purposes. Taxpayers sought to enjoin the collection of the tax. The injunction was denied:

> It is well established by the decisions of this court that unless the school board has been limited by the vote of the people it has the right to use its own discretion as to the character of the building to be built, and that in its levy for building purposes it has a right to levy sums in addition to the amount voted to pay for the building if such additional sums should be required to build the character of building that it has determined the needs of the district demand. . . .
> It has been many times held by this court, that although a school district has issued bonds for an amount near its constitutional limit of indebtedness the school board may afterwards levy a tax for building purposes to raise money to complete the building if the constitutional limitation is not exceeded.

Similarly, in a Kansas case,[21] it was discovered that funds raised by a bond issue were insufficient to construct the kind of building desired. A proposition to issue additional bonds was defeated by the electors. Thereupon, the board caused a tax to be levied for building purposes, and its action was sustained by the court. A board cannot, however, levy a tax largely in excess of the amount required for a particular purpose with the intent of creating a surplus to be used for another purpose, even though the rate is within the limit fixed by the statute.[22]

EFFECT OF IRREGULARITY IN THE LEVYING OF TAXES

Statutes authorizing school boards to levy and collect taxes usually prescribe in some detail the steps to be taken in order to render the tax legal. Since the power of taxation is an extraordinary power, the procedure prescribed by statute should be followed with particular care. It often happens, nevertheless, that taxes are levied in disregard of some of the statutory requirements. In such cases it is difficult to determine the effect of the irregularity upon the validity of the tax. Some provisions of the statutes are mandatory and must be substantially carried into effect, or the tax will be illegal; other provisions are directory only and may or may not be complied with. It is difficult to

20. *People* v. *Scott,* 300 Ill. 290, 133 N.E. 299.

21. *Laswell* v. *Seaton,* 107 Kan. 439, 191 Pac. 266.

22. *People* v. *Illinois Central Railroad Company,* 266 Ill. 636, 107 N.E. 803.

establish a principle by which a directory statute may be distinguished from a mandatory statute. As a rule, however, the courts will seek to discover and carry into effect the intent of the legislature in enacting the statute. If it is apparent that the legislature intended that the statutory mode of levying taxes should be the exclusive mode, the statute will be regarded as mandatory. But unless a fair consideration of the statute shows the legislature intended compliance with its provisions to be essential to the validity of the proceedings, the statute will be regarded as directory only.

Where the statutes require that notice be given of a special election to determine whether taxes shall be levied, in most jurisdictions the giving of the notice is held to be mandatory.[23] Moreover, in some jurisdictions there must be strict compliance with the statutory mode of publishing the notice.[24] The rule governing the giving of notice has been well stated by Justice Evans, speaking for the Supreme Court of Georgia:

There is a vital distinction between the necessity of a proclamation or publication of notice of a general election, the time and place of which is fixed by law, and that of a special election, which is only to be called and held at the time and place fixed by some authority named in the statute. In the former instance the provision for notice has been considered as directory, inasmuch as the time and place are fixed by law, and the electors are bound to take notice of the same. In such a case a failure to strictly comply with the law as to notice of the election may be treated as an irregularity, as the purpose of the prescribed notice is to give greater publicity to the election, the authority to hold which comes directly from the statute. 15 Cyc. 321. But where the election is only to be called, and the time and place of holding it are to be fixed by some authority named in the statute, after the publication of the prescribed notice, the giving of the statutory notice in the statutory manner is a condition precedent to the holding of a valid election. The giving of the notice in the way prescribed by the statute is mandatory, and a failure to comply with the statute in this respect vitiates the election.[25]

Accordingly, it has been held that failure to give notice the required number of days before an election is held renders the election illegal and the tax voted thereat void.[26] Failure to designate in the notice a

23. *Roberts v. Murphy*, 144 Ga. 177, 86 S.E. 545; *Shanks v. Winkler*, 210 Ala. 101, 97 So. 142; *Bramwell v. Guheen*, 3 Idaho 347, 29 Pac. 110.

24. *Roberts v. Murphy*, 144 Ga. 177, 86 S.E. 545; *Shanks v. Winkler*, 210 Ala. 101, 97 So. 142; *Bramwell v. Guheen*, 3 Idaho 347, 29 Pac. 110; *Canda Manufacturing Company v. Inhabitants of Township of Woodbridge*, 58 N.J. Law 134, 32 Atl. 66.

25. *Roberts v. Murphy*, 144 Ga. 177, 86 S.E. 545.

26. *Shanks v. Winkler*, 210 Ala. 101, 97 So. 142; *Canda Manufacturing Company v. Inhabitants of Township of Woodbridge*, 58 N.J. Law 134, 32 Atl. 66.

definite polling place has likewise been held to vitiate a tax election.[27]

As a general rule, however, substantial compliance with statutory provisions with respect to notice is all that will be required. That is, if the electors have actual notice of the election and an opportunity to express their will freely, the courts will not, as a rule, set the election aside because of some irregularity in the publication of the notice.[28] In a case which came before the Court of Appeals of Kentucky, for example, the order of a board of education calling an election did not specify where the election was to be held or the hours during which it was to be held. There was, however, a full and free vote. The court refused to set aside the will of the people as expressed in the election because of mere irregularities not affecting the result:

> The whole purpose of these school elections is to get a full, free and fair expression of the will of the people voting and entitled to vote at the election. They are not attended with the formality of other elections or surrounded by the safeguards devised to secure fairness in ordinary political elections. When, therefore, there has been a full, free and fair school election and the voters understand the question to be voted on and have ample notice of the time and place when and where the election is to be held, there seems little reason for disturbing the election on mere technical grounds.[29]

In general, irregularities in conducting an election will not render the election void where it can be shown that the irregularities did not affect the results.[30] Rules and regulations governing elections aim primarily to secure a free and untrammeled vote and a correct record and return of the vote. But these regulations are merely means; the end is the freedom and purity of the election. To hold all regulations governing elections to be mandatory and essential to a valid election would, in many cases, be to subordinate substance to form, the end to the means. Thus it has been held that failure to purge the registration lists of the names of persons not qualified to vote is an irregularity which does not render an election void in the absence of proof that

27. *Capps* v. *Parish Board of School Directors*, 138 La. 348, 70 So. 322; *Wallace* v. *Excise Board of Bryan County*, 91 Okla. 101, 216 Pac. 654.

28. *Travelstead* v. *Ray*, 169 Ky. 706, 185 S.W. 91; *Howard* v. *Oliver*, 170 S.W. (Tex.) 261; *Younts* v. *Commissioners of Union County*, 151 N.C. 582, 66 S.E. 575; *Cochran* v. *Kennon*, 161 S.W. (Tex.) 67.

29. *Travelstead* v. *Ray*, 169 Ky. 706, 185 S.W. 91.

30. *Younts* v. *Commissioners of Union County*, 151 N.C. 582, 66 S.E. 575; *Lamb* v. *Palmer*, 79 Okla. 68, 191 Pac. 184; *Shelton* v. *School District No. 22*, 43 Okla. 239, 142 Pac. 1034; *Travelstead* v. *Ray*, 169 Ky. 706, 185 S.W. 91; *Coleman* v. *Board of Education*, 131 Ga. 643, 63 S.E. 41; *Gilleland* v. *Schuyler*, 9 Kan. 569; *Pickett* v. *Russell*, 42 Fla. 116, 28 So. 764.

such irregularity has changed the result of the election.[31] Similarly, it has been held that ballots should not be rejected because of a slight variation in phraseology from the form prescribed by statute, if, from the ballots cast, the voters' intentions were clear with respect to the issue submitted.[32] So, too, failure to keep the registration books open the full time prescribed by statute has been held to be immaterial where every voter was given a fair and ample opportunity to register.[33]

Statutes usually require that school taxes be levied on or before a specified date. Failure to levy the tax by the date prescribed in some jurisdictions is fatal.[34] In Idaho, for example, a statute provided that the annual meeting should be held in each district the third Monday in April and that the electors should decide at such meeting whether a special school tax should be levied. The court ruled that a tax voted at an annual meeting held in September was illegal:

The authorities generally hold that where the statutes authorize the electors of a district to hold an annual meeting at a certain time of the year for the election of officers or levying of taxes, a meeting held and action taken at a different time are invalid. . . . The principle underlying these decisions is the elementary one that the powers of such subdivisions as school districts proceed entirely from statutes and cannot be exercised unless the statutory requirements are substantially complied with. We are constrained to hold that the electors of the district had no power to hold an annual meeting and levy a tax in September.[35]

The reasoning in the Idaho case is supported by a case[36] decided by the Supreme Court of Illinois:

The provisions of section 190 of the School law are controlling in the matter of the levying of the school taxes and the filing of the certificate with the county clerk. That section specifically provides that the board of directors or board of education of each district shall ascertain, as near as practicable, annually, how much money must be raised by special tax for educational and for building purposes for the next ensuing year, and that such amount shall be certified and returned to the township treasurer on or before the first Tuesday in August, annually, and that the certificate shall be signed by the

31. *Coleman* v. *Board of Education*, 131 Ga. 643, 63 S.E. 41.

32. *Du Pre* v. *Cotton*, 134 Ga. 316, 67 S.E. 876.

33. *Younts* v. *Commissioners of Union County*, 151 N.C. 582, 66 S.E. 575.

34. *Smith* v. *Canyon County*, 39 Idaho 222, 226 Pac. 1070; *People* v. *Chicago, Milwaukee & St. Paul Railway Company*, 321 Ill. 499, 152 N.E. 560; *People* v. *Chicago & Alton Railway Company*, 306 Ill. 525, 138 N.E. 105; *Howard* v. *Jensen*, 117 Neb. 102, 219 N.W. 811.

35. *Smith* v. *Canyon County*, 39 Idaho 222, 226 Pac. 1070.

36. *People* v. *Chicago & Alton Railway Company*, 306 Ill. 525, 138 N.E. 105.

president and clerk or secretary and be in the form which is in said section given. The certificates in this case were all in due form, but the levies were not made within the time required and the certificates thereof were not signed within such time. The foregoing provisions of the statute are mandatory, and the failure of the several districts to comply with the several provisions thereof rendered the tax levies void.

Other decisions, however—and they seem to be the better ones—hold that failure to levy a tax within the prescribed time does not render the tax void.[37] The courts taking this position reason that the duty to levy the tax is mandatory but that the time of making the levy is directory only. Provisions with respect to time are considered merely as a direction, with a view simply to orderly and prompt conduct of official business. Moreover, serious inconvenience would often result to the public if tax levies were held invalid merely because of neglect of duty on the part of school officers. It has been held, too, that an abortive attempt to make an assessment does not exhaust the power to make the assessment.[38]

In a number of instances the question has arisen as to the effect of the failure of the taxing authorities to levy taxes upon some of the taxable property of the district. Even though the constitution may require that taxes be uniform in respect to persons and property within the jurisdiction of the body imposing the tax, failure to levy a tax on some of the property of the district will not vitiate the tax on other property.[39]

Authorities whose duty it is to levy taxes should keep a written record of their proceedings, for, as a rule, parol evidence is inadmissible to prove that a tax has been properly levied.[40] Thus it was said by the Supreme Court of Arkansas:

> The testimony by deposition of members of the levying court to the effect that such school taxes were levied in the manner required by statute was clearly incompetent. The statutes regulating the levying of taxes require that the vote shall be taken, and that the clerk shall keep in the county court record a fair written record of the proceedings of said court, and the names

37. *Pond* v. *Negus,* 3 Mass. 230, 3 Am. Dec. 131; *Rural High School District No. 93* v. *Raub,* 103 Kan. 757, 176 Pac. 110.

38. *Pond* v. *Negus,* 3 Mass. 230, 3 Am. Dec. 131.

39. *Merritt* v. *Farris,* 22 Ill. 303; *Williams* v. *The Inhabitants of School District No. 1,* 38 Mass. 75, 32 Am. Dec. 243; *Sam Bassett Lumber Company* v. *City of Houston,* 145 Tex. 492, 198 S.W. (2d) 879.

40. *Great Southern Lumber Company* v. *Jefferson Davis Company,* 133 Miss. 229, 97 So. 545; *Alexander* v. *Capps,* 100 Ark. 488, 140 S.W. 722; *Moser* v. *White,* 29 Mich. 59.

of those members of the court voting in the affirmative and of those voting in the negative on all propositions or motions to levy the tax.

If the school tax of five mills had been levied, that fact could only be shown by the record. As was said by this court in *Hodgkin* v. *Fry,* 33 Ark. 716–721, quoting from the Supreme Court of Michigan: "Every essential proceeding in the course of the levy of taxes must appear in some written and permanent form in the record of the bodies authorized to act upon them."[41]

SITUS OF PROPERTY FOR PURPOSES OF TAXATION

Frequently boards of education may be in doubt as to what property they have authority to tax. For purposes of taxation property may be classified as (1) real property, (2) tangible personal property, and (3) intangible personal property. In the case of real property the rule is a simple one: such property is taxable in the state or taxing district in which it is located, whether the owner be a resident or a nonresident of the state[42] or of the district.[43] In some states, however, it is provided by statute that real estate owned by residents of the state shall be taxed, not in the district where located, but in the district which is the domicile of the owner. Such statutes have been held constitutional with respect to property within the state,[44] although the authority of the legislature to fix the situs of real property in a taxing district of a state other than the one in which it is located is still doubtful. Where a single tract of property lies in more than one taxing district and there is no statute governing such cases, the several parts of the tract are taxable in the districts in which they lie, respectively.[45] In a number of states it is expressly provided by statute that the whole tract be taxed in one of the districts, and such statutes have been invariably upheld.[46]

The situs of personal property for purposes of taxation is so largely determined by the domicile of the owner that it is necessary to have a clear conception of what constitutes domicile. One's domicile is the

41. *Alexander* v. *Capps,* 100 Ark. 488, 140 S.W. 722.

42. *Union Refrigerator Transit Company* v. *Kentucky,* 199 U.S. 194, 26 S. Ct. 36, 50 L. Ed. 140, 4 Ann. Cas. 493; *Savary* v. *Georgetown Fourth School District,* 12 Metc. (Mass.) 178. NOTE: 56 Am. Dec. 524.

43. *Hughes* v. *Ewing,* 93 Calif. 414, 28 Pac. 1067; *Chicago B. & I. Railway Company* v. *Cass County,* 51 Neb. 369, 70 N.W. 955; *Myer* v. *Crispell,* 28 Barb. (N.Y.) 54.

44. NOTE: 56 Am. Dec. 524; 26 R.C.L. 236.

45. *Barker's Lessee* v. *Jackson,* 9 Ham. (Ohio) 163.

46. *Blackstone Manufacturing Company* v. *Blackstone,* 200 Mass. 82, 85 N.E. 880, 18 L.R.A. (N.S.) 755.

place where one actually resides with the intent of living there for an indefinite time.[47] Intent is the important factor, although actual residence for a certain period of time is also necessary. That is, one cannot fix his domicile at a place at which he does not reside and never has resided. In order to have a domicile in a particular place, it is not necessary, however, for one to reside there at all times. One may live elsewhere for a long period of time, or for a great part of the time, without affecting his domicile, provided that he intendeds ultimately to return. Thus it has been held that one who moves into a school district for the purpose of educating his children does not lose his domicile in the original district if it is his intention to return there after the education of his children has been completed.[48] In the case of a corporation, the domicile is the state in which the corporation is incorporated, and within the state the domicile is the place where the corporation maintains its main offices.

The ancient maxim *mobilia sequuntur personam* ("movables follow the person") still obtains with respect to the situs of tangible personal property for purposes of taxation. That is, such property is taxable at the domicile of the owner, even though it may be located in another state.[49] The general rule, however, today is subject to a number of exceptions. In the first place, the legislature may, if it sees fit, make such property located within the state taxable in the district in which it is located rather than in the domicile of the owner. The second exception is this: tangible personal property which is definitely and more or less permanently located outside the state of the owner's domicile may be taxed in the state of its location.[50] And the fact that the property may already have been taxed in the state of the owner's domicile is immaterial.[51] It has been held, however, that authority to

47. *Holt* v. *Hendee*, 248 Ill. 288, 93 N.E. 749.

48. *Montgomery* v. *Lebanon*, 111 Ky. 646, 23 Ky. Law Rep. 891, 64 S.W. 509, 54 L.R.A. 914.

49. *Hawley* v. *Malden*, 232 U.S. 1, 34 S. Ct. 201, 58 L. Ed. 477, Ann. Cas. 1916C 842; *State* v. *Shepherd*, 218 Mo. 656, 117 S.W. 1169, 131 Am. St. Rep. 568; *Commonwealth* v. *American Dredging Company*, 122 Pa. St. 386, 15 Atl. 443, 1 L.R.A. 237.

50. *Pullman's Palace Car Company* v. *Pennsylvania*, 141 U.S. 18, 11 S. Ct. 876, 35 L. Ed. 613; *Marye* v. *Baltimore & Ohio Railroad Company*, 127 U.S. 117, 32 L. Ed. 94, 8 S. Ct. 1037; *Scripps* v. *Fulton County*, 183 Ill. 278, 55 N.E. 700; *Baldwin* v. *Shine*, 84 Ky. 502, 2 S.W. 164; *Rieman* v. *Shepard*, 27 Ind. 288; *Standard Oil Company* v. *Combs*, 96 Ind. 179, 49 Am. Rep. 156.

51. *State* v. *William Deering & Company*, 56 Minn. 24, 57 N.W. 313; *Stevens* v. *Carroll*, 130 Iowa 463, 104 N.W. 433; *Spaulding* v. *Adams County*, 79 Wash. 193, 140 Pac. 367.

tax the property where it is located must be plainly and unequivocally written into the statutes.[52] In particular cases, difficulty arises in determining whether the location of property of a nonresident of a state is, or is not, accompanied with that degree of permanency necessary to make it taxable where located. It is well settled that the mere temporary or transient presence of property of a nonresident does not render it taxable.[53] The following examples illustrate what constitutes sufficient permanency of location. In Connecticut it was held that machinery in a mill was taxable where located, although the owner resided in another state.[54] Hogs slaughtered in Indiana to be shipped to the home of the owner who resided in another state were taxable in Indiana.[55] Agricultural machinery shipped into Minnesota by a nonresident and stored in a warehouse while awaiting sale and distribution was subject to taxation in Minnesota.[56] Cash is taxable where it is located, even though it may belong to a nonresident.[57] In holding that the rolling stock of the Baltimore and Ohio Railroad Company could be taxed where it had an actual situs, the Supreme Court of the United States said: "It is quite true, as the *situs* of the Baltimore and Ohio Railroad Company is in the State of Maryland, that also, upon general principles, is the *situs* of all its personal property; but for purposes of taxation, as well as for other purposes, that *situs* may be fixed in whatever locality the property may be brought and used by its owner by the law of the place where it is found."[58]

The courts have been called upon frequently to determine whether tangible personal property may be taxed in the state of the domicile of the owner as well as in the state of its location and use. For a number of years it was the rule that such property could be taxed in both places.[59] The Supreme Court of the United States has definitely settled

52. *Graham* v. *St. Joseph Township*, 67 Mich. 652, 35 N.W. 808; *Tobey* v. *Kipp*, 214 Mass. 477, 101 N.E. 998.

53. *Fennell* v. *Pauley*, 112 Iowa 94, 83 N.E. 799; *Irvin* v. *New Orleans, etc., Railway Company*, 94 Ill. 105, 34 Am. Rep. 208; *Commonwealth* v. *Dun and Company*, 126 Ky. 108, 102 S.W. 859.

54. *Shaw* v. *Hartford*, 56 Conn. 351, 15 Atl. 742.

55. *Rieman* v. *Shepard*, 27 Ind. 288.

56. *State* v. *William Deering & Company*, 56 Minn. 24, 57 N.W. 313.

57. *Liverpool & L. & G. Insurance Company* v. *Board of Assessors*, 44 La. Ann. 760, 11 So. 91, 16 L.R.A. 56.

58. *Marye* v. *Baltimore & Ohio Railroad Company*, 127 U.S. 117, 32 L. Ed. 94, 8 S. Ct. 1037.

59. *Battle* v. *Mobile*, 9 Ala. 234, 44 Am. Dec. 438.

the issue, however, by holding that tangible personal property cannot be taxed in the state of the owner's domicile where such property is permanently located in another state.[60] An excerpt from the opinion of the court follows:

In this case the question is directly presented whether a corporation organized under the laws of Kentucky is subject to taxation upon its tangible personal property, permanently located in other States, and employed there in the prosecution of its business. Such taxation is charged to be a violation of the due process of law clause of the Fourteenth Amendment. . . .

The power of taxation, indispensable to the existence of every civilized government, is exercised upon the assumption of an equivalent rendered to the taxpayer in the protection of his person and property, in adding to the value of such property, or in the creation and maintenance of public conveniences in which he shares, such, for instance, as roads, bridges, sidewalks, pavements, and schools for the education of his children. If the taxing power be in no position to render these services, or otherwise to benefit the person or property taxed, and such property be wholly within the taxing power of another State, to which it may be said to owe an allegiance and to which it looks for protection, the taxation of such property within the domicil of the owner partakes rather of the nature of an extortion than a tax, and has been repeatedly held by this court to be beyond the power of the legislature and a taking of property without due process of law. . . .

The adoption of a general rule that tangible personal property in other States may be taxed at the domicil of the owner involves possibilities of an entirely serious character. Not only would it authorize the taxation of furniture and other property kept at country houses in other States or even in foreign countries, of stocks of goods and merchandise kept at branch establishments when already taxed at the State of their *situs*, but of that enormous mass of personal property belonging to railways and other corporations which might be taxed in the State where they are incorporated, though their charters contemplated the construction and operation of roads wholly outside the State, and sometimes across the continent, and when in no other particular they are subject to its laws and entitled to its protection.

With respect to intangible personal property, such as bonds, stocks, mortgages, and the like, the general rule is that such property is taxable at the domicile of the owner.[61] There are certain well-established exceptions to the rule, however. Where property is located within the

60. *Union Refrigerator Transit Company* v. *Kentucky*, 199 U.S. 194, 26 S. Ct. 36, 50 L. Ed. 140, 4 Ann. Cas. 493. See also *Culbert* v. *Leake County*, 60 Miss. 142, where it was held that cotton belonging to a resident of Mississippi, but located in another state, could not be taxed in Mississippi.

61. *Kirtland* v. *Hotchkiss*, 100 U.S. 491, 25 L. Ed. 558; *State Tax on Foreign Held Bonds*, 15 Wall. (U.S.) 300, 21 L. Ed. 179; *Commonwealth* v. *Williams*, 102 Va. 778, 47 S.E. 867; *Scripps* v. *Fulton County*, 183 Ill. 278, 55 N.E. 700; *Wright* v. *Southwestern Railway Company*, 64 Ga. 783; *Worthington* v. *Sebastian*, 25 Ohio St. 8.

state, the legislature may provide that it be taxed where it is located, unless prohibited from doing so by some constitutional provision. Again, property located in a state other than that of the owner's domicile may be taxed where it is located, provided that it has acquired a business situs.[62] To acquire a business situs, property must, as a general rule, be used as the basis of business operations, as the subject matter of stock in trade of a business. The rule has been well expressed by the Supreme Court of Minnesota:

A credit, which cannot be regarded as situated in a place merely because the debtor resides there, must usually be considered as having its situs where it is owned,—at the domicile of the creditor. The creditor, however, may give it a business *situs* elsewhere; as where he places it in the hands of an agent for collection or renewal, with a view to reloaning the money and keeping it invested as a permanent business.[63]

As a general rule, intangible personal property which has not acquired a business situs is taxable only in the state of the owner's domicile.[64] Where it has acquired a business situs in another jurisdiction, however, the general rule seems to be that it is subject to taxation in the state in which it is located and in the state of the owner's domicile.[65] The reasons for the rule have been formulated as follows by the Supreme Court of the United States:

There is an obvious distinction between tangible and intangible property, in the fact that the latter is held secretly; that there is no method by which its existence or ownership can be ascertained in the State of its *situs* except perhaps in the case of mortgages or shares of stock. So if the owner be discovered, there is no way by which he can be reached by process in a State other than that of his domicil, or the collection of the tax otherwise enforced. In this class of cases the tendency of modern authorities is to apply the maxim *mobilia sequuntur personam,* and to hold that the property may be taxed at the domicil of the owner as the real *situs* of the debt, and also, more particularly in the case of mortgages, in the State where the property is retained. Such have been the repeated rulings of this court. . . .

62. *Matzenbaugh* v. *People,* 194 Ill. 108, 62 N.E. 546; *In re Jefferson,* 35 Minn. 215, 28 N.W. 256; *Adams* v. *Colonial & U.S. Mortgage Company,* 82 Miss. 263, 34 So. 482, 17 L.R.A. (N.S.) 138.

63. *In re Jefferson,* 35 Minn. 215, 28 N.W. 256.

64. *Kirtland* v. *Hotchkiss,* 100 U.S. 491, 25 L. Ed. 558; *Hurt* v. *Bristol,* 104 Va. 213, 51 S.E. 223; *State* v. *Clement National Bank,* 84 Vt. 167, 78 Atl. 944. See, however, *Commonwealth* v. *Northwestern Mutual Life Insurance Company,* 32 Ky. Law Rep. 796, 107 S.W. 233.

65. *Union Refrigerator Transit Company* v. *Kentucky,* 199 U.S. 194, 26 S. Ct. 36, 50 L. Ed. 140, 4 Ann. Cas. 493; *Fidelity and Columbia Trust Company, etc.,* v. *Louisville,* 245 U.S. 54, 38 S. Ct. 40, L.R.A. 1918C 124.

If this occasionally results in double taxation, it much oftener happens that this class of property escapes altogether. In the case of intangible property, the law does not look for absolute equality, but to the much more practical consideration of collecting the tax upon such property, either in the State of the domicil or the *situs*.[66]

There is some authority, however, to the effect that intangible property which has acquired a business situs is taxable only in the state in which it is located,[67] and there is a noticeable tendency on the part of the courts to extend the rule of exception to such property in the same way as it has been extended to tangible property.

AUTHORITY TO TAX INCOME OF A CITIZEN
OF ANOTHER STATE

It is well settled that a state may tax the income derived from local property and business owned and managed from without by a citizen and resident of another state. The matter has been settled by the Supreme Court of the United States in a case which came before it from the state of Oklahoma. That state enacted a statute making taxable "the entire net income from all property owned, and of every business, trade or profession carried on in this State by persons residing elsewhere." A citizen of Illinois who was engaged in the production of oil in Oklahoma challenged the constitutionality of the act, on the ground that it violated provisions of the federal Constitution. In a decision[68] handed down by the Supreme Court of the United States, the right of a state to tax the income of nonresidents where the income is derived from business carried on within the state was unqualifiedly affirmed:

In our system of government the States have general dominion, and, saving as restricted by particular provisions of the Federal Constitution, complete dominion over all persons, property, and business transactions within their borders; they assume and perform the duty of preserving and protecting all such persons, property, and business, and, in consequence, have the power normally pertaining to governments to resort to all reasonable forms of taxation in order to defray the governmental expenses. Certainly they are not restricted to property taxation, nor to any particular form of excises. . . . That the State, from whose laws property and business and industry derive the protection and security without which production and

66. *Union Refrigerator Transit Company* v. *Kentucky*, 199 U.S. 194, 26 S. Ct. 36, 50 L. Ed. 140, 4 Ann. Cas. 493.

67. *Commonwealth* v. *B. F. Avery & Sons*, 163 Ky. 828, 174 S.W. 518; 26 R.C.L. 282. NOTE: 36 L.R.A. (N.S.) 295.

68. *Shaffer* v. *Carter*, 252 U.S. 37, 40 S. Ct. 221, 64 L. Ed. 445.

gainful occupation would be impossible, is debarred from exacting a share of those gains in the form of income taxes for the support of the government, is a proposition so wholly inconsistent with fundamental principles as to be refuted by its mere statement. That it may tax the land but not the crop, the tree but not the fruit, the mine or well but not the product, the business but not the profit derived from it, is wholly inadmissible.

RECOVERY OF TAXES ILLEGALLY COLLECTED

Occasionally, taxes are illegally collected because of some mistake of the tax authorities or some mistake of law. In such cases the taxpayer, according to the weight of authority, has no recourse if the tax was paid voluntarily or merely under protest.[69] If, on the other hand, a person is compelled by duress to pay an illegal tax, he may recover it.[70] The rule has been clearly expressed by the Supreme Judicial Court of Massachusetts:

A party who has paid voluntarily, under a claim of right, shall not afterwards recover back the money, although he protested at the time against his liability. . . . But it is otherwise when a party is compelled, by duress of his person or goods, to pay money for which he is not liable. It is not voluntary, but compulsory, and he may rescue himself from such duress by payment of the money, and afterwards, on proof of the fact, recover it back. The warrant to collect . . . is in the nature of an execution. . . . When, therefore, a party not liable to taxation is called on, peremptorily, to pay upon such warrant, and he can save himself and his property in no other way than by paying the illegal demand, he may give notice that he so pays it by duress, and not voluntarily, and by showing that he is not liable, recover it back as money had and received.[71]

It has been held that if payment of an illegal tax is made under duress, it need not be paid under protest in order to enable the payer to recover it.[72]

In harmony with the principle expressed by the Massachusetts

69. *Preston* v. *Boston*, 12 Pick. (Mass.) 7; *Conkling* v. *City of Springfield*, 132 Ill. 420, 24 N.E. 67; *Davis* v. *Board of Education*, 323 Ill. 281, 154 N.E. 127; *Walser* v. *Board of Education*, 160 Ill. 272, 43 N.E. 346, 31 L.R.A. 329; *San Diego Land and Town Company* v. *La Presa School District*, 122 Calif. 98, 54 Pac. 528; *Fox* v. *Kountze*, 58 Neb. 439, 78 N.W. 712; *School District No. 30* v. *Cuming County*, 81 Neb. 606, 116 N.W. 522; *Philadelphia & Reading C. and I. Company* v. *Tamaqua Borough School District*, 304 Pa. 489, 156 Atl. 75, 76 A.L.R. 1007; *Wilson* v. *School District of Philadelphia*, 328 Pa. 225, 195 Atl. 90, 113 A.L.R. 1401.

70. *Joyner* v. *Inhabitants of School District No. 3*, 57 Mass. (3 Cush.) 567; *Preston* v. *Boston*, 12 Pick. (Mass.) 7; *Harding* v. *Wiley*, 219 Ill. App. 1.

71. *Preston* v. *Boston*, 12 Pick. (Mass.) 7.

72. *Board of Education of Kenton County* v. *Louisville and Nashville Railroad Company*, 280 Ky. 650, 134 S.W. (2d) 219.

court, it was held in Nebraska that taxes voluntarily paid under authority of a statute later declared unconstitutional became a part of the public fund and were beyond the recall of the taxpayers.[73] And, according to the weight of authority, property owners cannot recover taxes paid on property which was assessed and taxed in the wrong district.[74]

It sometimes happens that property situated near boundary lines is, by mistake, taxed in a district in which it is not located. In such cases the courts are divided with respect to the right of the district in which the property should have been taxed to recover from the district in which the property actually was taxed. In Iowa, land was taxed for a number of years in a district in which it did not lie. The court held that the district in which the land was located could recover from the district which had collected the tax. It said: "This is not a case where one has paid, voluntarily and without protest, taxes wrongfully assessed and collected, but a case where one has received money belonging to another through mistake."[75]

In Arkansas, Illinois, and Pennsylvania, on the other hand, cases involving the same issue have been decided against the district in which the property was actually located.[76] The courts seem to be agreed, however, that under no circumstances should a district be permitted to recover from another district an amount greater than the amount which would have been received if the property had been taxed in the proper district.[77]

---

73. *School District No. 30* v. *Cuming County,* 81 Neb. 606, 116 N.W. 522; *City National Bank of Lincoln* v. *School District of City of Lincoln,* 121 Neb. 213, 236 N.W. 616.

74. *Connell* v. *Board of Education,* 268 Ill. App. 398, 3 N.E. (2d) 717; *Walser* v. *Board of Education,* 160 Ill. 272, 43 N.E. 346, 31 A.L.R. 329; *San Diego Land and Town Company* v. *La Presa School District,* 122 Calif. 98, 54 Pac. 528; *Frost* v. *Fowlerton Consolidated School District No. 1,* 111 S.W. (2d) (Tex.) 754; *Edwards* v. *Board of Commissioners of Oklahoma County,* 169 Okla. 87, 36 Pac. (2d) 6, 94 A.L.R. 1220. Contra, *Churchill* v. *Board of Trustees of Highland Park Graded School,* 28 Ky. Law Rep. 162, 89 S.W. 122.

75. *Independent School District of Town of Kelly* v. *School Township of Washington,* 162 Iowa 42, 143 N.W. 837. See also *School District No. 8* v. *Board of Education,* 115 Kan. 806, 224 Pac. 892; *School District No. 6* v. *School District No. 5,* 255 Mich. 428, 238 N.W. 214.

76. *Walser* v. *Board of Education,* 160 Ill. 272, 43 N.E. 346, 31 L.R.A. 329; *School District No. 153* v. *School District No. 154,* 232 Ill. 322; *Arthur* v. *School District of Polk Borough,* 164 Pa. St. 410, 30 Atl. 299; *Carter Special School District* v. *Hollis Special School District,* 173 Ark. 781, 293 S.W. 722.

77. *Walser* v. *Board of Education,* 160 Ill. 272, 43 N.E. 346, 31 L.R.A. 329.

RIGHT OF SCHOOL DISTRICT TO RECOVER FUNDS
MISAPPROPRIATED TO ANOTHER DISTRICT

Where funds rightfully belonging to one school district are misappropriated to another, the courts will, as a rule, require restitution of the funds to the proper district.[78] The rule followed by many courts has been well expressed by the Supreme Court of Idaho:

Since every school district within the state is a public corporation and an arm of the state, charged with these duties, it seems clear that one district may maintain an action against another, where by either mistake, fraud or inefficiency of public servants, the one district has received and expended for educational purposes, in its territory, more than its share of the public fund; and the other district by reason thereof has received less than its share; and we have not been able to discover any valid reason why such an action may not be maintained. Indeed, if a district cannot prosecute such an action, then clearly there is no way in which the wrong or misapplication of funds may be corrected or redressed. Nor is it a sufficient answer to say that, since the one district has received more money than it was entitled to, and has in fact expended it for school purposes within its district during the year for which collected and apportioned, it cannot be required to withhold from a future apportionment or future taxes enough money to reimburse the district which suffered by loss of the portion to which it was legally entitled.[79]

It has been held, it may be pointed out in this connection, that the title to the sixteenth-section lands granted to the states by the United States vests absolutely in the states and that each state, therefore, is free to dispose of the funds derived from the sale of these lands as it may see fit. In *Sloan* v. *Blytheville* it was said by the Supreme Court of Arkansas:

This court and the Supreme Court of the United States have uniformly held that the title to these sixteenth section lands is vested absolutely in the States, and that the Legislature has exclusive control over the funds. . . . The result of our views is that the grant of the sixteenth section lands submitted to the State by the act of Congress and accepted by the State was of the fee to the lands without limitation upon the power of the State.[80]

78. *Independent School District etc.* v. *Common School District No. 1,* 56 Idaho 426, 55 Pac. (2d) 144, 105 A.L.R. 1267; *School Board* v. *School Board,* 36 La. Ann. 806; *School District* v. *School District,* 255 Mich. 428, 238 N.W. 214; *State ex rel. Wyman* v. *Williams,* 139 Kan. 599, 32 Pac. (2d) 481; *Independent School District* v. *School Township,* 162 Iowa 42, 143 N.W. 837.

79. *Independent School District etc.* v. *Common School District No. 1,* 56 Idaho 426, 55 Pac. (2d) 144, 105 A.L.R. 1267.

80. *Sloan* v. *Blytheville, Special School District No. 5,* 169 Ark. 77, 273 S.W. 387. See also *State ex rel. Holt* v. *State Board of Education,* 195 Ark. 222, 112 S.W. (2d) 18; *Brooks* v. *Koonce,* 275 U.S. 486, 48 S. Ct. 27, 72 L. Ed. 387.

DISPOSITION OF FUNDS DERIVED FROM ATHLETIC
OR OTHER SCHOOL ACTIVITIES

Few cases have come into the courts concerning the management and expenditure of money derived from athletic or other school activities. In a Pennsylvania case, however, it was held that funds derived from such extracurricular activities as athletics or dramatic or musical entertainments must go into the official account of the treasurer and be subject to audit the same as other funds. In this case the school principal had kept a ledger of the various accounts and had spent them much as he saw fit, without specific authority from the board. Under a statute requiring that all funds belonging to the district be audited, the court ruled that monies of this kind were public property and must be paid to the district treasurer and be handled exactly as tax monies.[81]

RIGHT OF TAXPAYER TO ENJOIN COLLECTION
OF ILLEGAL TAX

An injunction will not be issued where the aggrieved party has an adequate remedy at law. It seems well settled, however, that an injunction will lie at the instance of a taxpayer to prevent the collection of an illegal tax.[82] In a case[83] decided by the Supreme Court of Georgia, for example, it was sought to enjoin the collection of a school tax on the ground that the election at which the tax was voted had been irregularly held. The court said:

> When, therefore, it is sought to assess and enforce such a tax against the property, the owner thereof has a right to call in question the authority under which the local officers are proceeding and to say that the law is void or the election is invalid. We do not mean to say that every irregularity or failure to comply strictly with directory provisions of the law will invalidate such an election and render its result of no force as an authority to the officers to proceed; but we do mean that if the election or attempted election

81. *Petition of Auditors of Hatfield Township School District,* 161 Pa. Super. Ct. 388, 54 Atl. (2d) 833.

82. *Shaffer v. Carter,* 252 U.S. 37, 40 S. Ct. 221, 64 L. Ed. 445; *Coleman v. Board of Education,* 131 Ga. 643, 63 S.E. 41; *Howard v. Trustees of School District No. 27,* 31 Ky. Law Rep. 399, 102 S.W. 318; *Cochran v. Kennon,* 161 S.W. (Tex.) 67; *Pickett v. Russell,* 42 Fla. 116, 28 So. 764; *Bramwell v. Guheen,* 3 Idaho 347, 29 Pac. 110; *Carlton v. Newman,* 77 Me. 408, 1 Atl. 194; *State* ex rel. *Gebhardt v. Superior Court for King County,* 15 Wash. (2d) 673, 131 Pac. (2) 943.

83. *Coleman v. Board of Education,* 131 Ga. 643, 63 S.E. 41. Accord, *Cochran v. Kennon,* 161 S.W. (Tex.) 67.

was such as to be unlawful and to confer no valid authority upon the local officials to proceed to assess and collect the tax, the property owner could set up and establish that fact and could prevent the title to his property from being beclouded with an unlawful assessment and seizure.

Moreover, a taxpayer does not lose his right to challenge the legality of a tax merely because he has already voluntarily paid a portion of it. A school district in Kentucky levied a tax to pay an indebtedness in excess of the constitutional debt limit. Certain taxpayers paid the tax for two years and then sought to enjoin further collection. In the course of a decision sustaining the right of the taxpayers to the injunction, it was said: "The taxpayer may at any time when it is sought to exact from him a void tax oppose its collection without reference to the fact that he has theretofore submitted to the illegal burden, and will not be denied the right to assert his legal rights."[84]

In Missouri, however, it has been held that an injunction does not lie to prevent the collection of a tax, on the ground that it was irregularly and fraudulently levied. Equitable relief was denied because, it was said, the owner had an adequate remedy at law and would suffer no irreparable injury. The owner would have a legal remedy against the officer who collected the illegal tax and would not be divested of his property, even though it was sold.[85]

An injunction does not lie to prevent the collection of a tax on the ground that the board of education will use the proceeds for a purpose other than that for which the tax was levied or for an illegal purpose.[86] The time for an injunction in such cases is not when it is sought to collect the tax but when it is sought to spend the funds illegally.

A taxpayer may become guilty of laches and thereby lose his right to secure an injunction to prevent the collection of an illegal tax. One becomes guilty of laches when one fails to exercise one's rights seasonably and thereby prejudices the rights of others. It is elementary that he who seeks equity must do equity. The case of *Loesche* v. *Goerdt*[87] illustrates exceptionally well how a taxpayer may, through inaction, lost his right to enjoin an illegal tax. A tax was voted for the purpose

84. *Howard* v. *Trustees of School District No. 27*, 31 Ky. Law Rep. 399, 102 S.W. 318.

85. *Barrow* v. *Davis*, 46 Mo. 394. See also *Sayre* v. *Tompkins*, 23 Mo. 443.

86. *People* v. *Bates*, 266 Ill. 55; *People* v. *Scott*, 300 Ill. 290, 133 N.E. 299.

87. *Loesche* v. *Goerdt*, 123 Iowa 55, 98 N.W. 571.

of building schoolhouses, but proper notice of the election was not given. Nevertheless, the tax was levied, the houses built, and school conducted therein for a period of three months before the injunction to restrain the collection of the tax was sought. In denying the relief prayed for, the court said in part:

> According to their own statements, they were fully and currently advised of every step taken towards securing the two new schoolhouses, yet they stood by and permitted the houses to be built, the indebtedness to be incurred, and the tax to be levied, and not until after three months of school had been maintained in the new houses did they take any action to test the validity of any of the steps taken in the matter. He who asks a court of equity to give him relief must present a case which appeals to the conscience of the chancellor. He must show that he has been without fault, that no affirmative act of his stands in the way of the relief he prays, and that he has not been guilty of sleeping on his rights to the prejudice of his opponent. The appellants do not come before us with such a showing, and we think they are now estopped from questioning any of the matters they complain of.

DISTRIBUTION OF THE TAX MONEY

The right of the state to require that taxes collected in one school district be expended in another has been challenged in a number of cases, on the ground that such distribution of the school funds violates the constitutional guaranty of uniformity of taxation and constitutes the taking of property without due process of law. It is a well-recognized principle of law that the taxpayers of one municipal corporation cannot be compelled to contribute to the local and municipal purposes of another; and if public education were a local or municipal purpose, funds raised in one school district could not be employed to support schools in another district. But the courts are agreed that public education is in no sense a local or municipal function.[88] It is a state function and school taxes are state taxes, even though they may have been levied and collected by the local district.[89]

It is clear, then, that the legislature, in order to equalize educational opportunities, may provide for a state-wide school tax and distribute the proceeds therefrom to the various districts of the state upon such

88. *City of Louisville* v. *Commonwealth*, 134 Ky. 488, 121 S.W. 411; *Nelson* v. *Mayor, etc., of Town of Homer*, 48 La. Ann. 258, 19 So. 271; *School District No. 76* v. *Ryker*, 64 Kan. 612, 68 Pac. 34; *Board of Education* v. *Alton Water Company*, 314 Ill. 466, 145 N.E. 683.

89. *City of Louisville* v. *Board of Education*, 154 Ky. 316, 157 S.W. 379; *De Vere Ford* v. *Kendall Borough School District*, 121 Pa. St. 543.

bases as may seem wise, provided only that the mode of distribution adopted be made to apply to all districts in the same class or category.[90] A case[91] decided by the Supreme Court of Maine illustrates the reasoning of the courts in cases of this kind. A statute provided that all property in the state be taxed 1.50 mills for common-school purposes. The proceeds were to be distributed to the various cities, towns, and plantations, one-third according to persons of school age and two-thirds according to valuation of property. Unorganized townships, although subject to the tax, were to receive no direct benefit from it. The constitutionality of the statute was called into question on the ground that the statute imposed an unequal burden of taxation upon the unorganized townships. To require four subdivisions of the state to contribute to the fund and to permit only three to share in the benefits was, it was contended, a violation of constitutional rights. Moreover, the statute was challenged on the ground that the mode of distribution adopted benefited the cities and richer towns more than the poorer ones. The court, however, sustained the statute in a decision which is quoted in part:

The Legislature has the right under the constitution to impose an equal rate of taxation upon all the property in the State, including the property in unorganized townships, for the purpose of distributing the proceeds thereof among the cities, towns and plantations for common school purposes, and the mere fact that the tax is assessed upon the property in four municipal subdivisions and distributed among three, is not in itself fatal. . . .

The fundamental question is this, is the purpose for which the tax is assessed a public purpose, not whether any portion of it may find its way back again to the pocket of the tax payer or to the direct advantage of himself or family. . . . In order that taxation may be equal and uniform in the constitutional sense, it is not necessary that the benefits arising therefrom should be enjoyed by all the people in equal degree nor that each one of the people should participate in each particular benefit. . . .

Inequality of assessment is necessarily fatal, inequality of distribution is not, provided the purpose be the public welfare. The method of distributing the proceeds of such a tax rests in the wise discretion and sound judgment of the Legislature. If this discretion is unwisely exercised, the remedy is with the people and not with the court. Such distribution might be according to population, or according to the number of scholars of school age, or according to school attendance, or according to valuation, or partly on one basis and partly on another. The Constitution prescribes no regulation in regard to this matter and it is not for the court to say that one method should

90. *Sawyer* v. *Gilmore*, 109 Me. 169, 83 Atl. 673; *Miller* v. *Childers*, 107 Okla. 57, 238 Pac. 204.

91. *Sawyer* v. *Gilmore*, 109 Me. 169, 83 Atl. 673.

be adopted in preference to another. . . . The distribution of the school mill fund of 1872 has resulted in inequality. That distribution has been, and continues to be, based on the number of scholars, thereby benefiting the poorer towns more than the richer, because they receive more than they pay, and in the opinion of the Justices before cited, that method is deemed constitutional. The act under consideration apportions the newly created common school fund one-third according to the number of scholars and two-thirds according to the valuation as fixed by the State Assessors, thereby benefiting the richer towns more than the poorer, producing inequality in the other direction, but we are unable to see why this method is not equally constitutional with the other. Both taxes are assessed for the same admittedly public purpose, both promote the common welfare, and the fact that the Legislature has seen fit to distribute the two on different bases is not fatal to the validity of either.

The same line of reasoning was followed by the Supreme Court of Ohio in a more recent decision. A statute provided that a tax of 2.65 mills should be levied annually upon all the taxable property of the state. The proceeds of this tax were to be retained in the several counties for the support of schools. Each city school district and each exempted village district was to receive the full amount raised within its own corporate limits. The proceeds of the tax upon property in the territory of the county outside city and exempted village districts were to be apportioned to each district in the county other than city and exempted village districts on the basis of the number of teachers employed, the expense of transporting pupils, daily attendance, and the like. The court refused to hold the law unconstitutional. "The fact that this money is appropriated, not for a local purpose, but for a legitimate state purpose, disposes of the plaintiff's contention that the law takes property without due process, and also disposes of his contention that because the tax is spent outside of his district he is denied the equal protection of the laws."[92]

The legislature may, moreover, require a school district which does not provide adequate school facilities to pay the tuition of its pupils while in attendance at the school of another district.[93] Such a statute, the Supreme Court of Illinois has held, does not deprive a district or its taxpayers of property without due process of law.[94]

It is sometimes provided in state constitutions that the legislature

92. *Miller* v. *Korns,* 107 Ohio St. 287, 140 N.E. 773.
93. *Boggs* v. *School Township of Cass,* 128 Iowa 15, 102 N.W. 796.
94. *Board of Education* v. *Board of Education,* 314 Ill. 83, 145 N.E. 169.

may not impose taxes for the purpose of any county, city, town, or other municipal corporation, but may by general laws confer upon local authorities power to levy taxes for such purposes. Such a provision does not prohibit the legislature from imposing a state-wide school tax upon all the taxable property of the state for the simple reason that education is a state and not a local or municipal purpose;[95] neither does it prevent the legislature from requiring city school districts to levy a minimum school tax.[96]

95. *Atchison, Topeka & Santa Fe Railway Company* v. *State,* 28 Okla. 94, 113 Pac. 921, 40 L.R.A. (N.S.) 1; *State* v. *Board of Education,* 141 Mo. 45, 41 S.W. 924; *State* v. *Owsley,* 122 Mo. 68, 26 S.W. 659; *City of Louisville* v. *Commonwealth,* 134 Ky. 488, 121 S.W. 411.

96. *City of Louisville* v. *Commonwealth,* 134 Ky. 488, 121 S.W. 411.

CHAPTER XI

The School Debt

AUTHORITY TO ISSUE BONDS

THE general rule is that a school district can exercise only such authority as has been expressly or impliedly conferred upon it by statute, or such authority as necessarily grows out of the purposes for which the district was created. With respect to the authority of a school district to incur indebtedness through the issuance of negotiable instruments, the courts apply a stricter rule. In some of the older cases an implied power to borrow money was recognized,[1] but more recently the courts seem to be agreed that power to issue bonds does not exist unless it is granted in clear and unnmistakable terms.[2] The rule has been clearly and forcibly expressed by the Supreme Court of Illinois:

> Where a corporation is created for business purposes, all persons may presume such bodies, when issuing their paper, are acting within the scope of their power. Not so with municipalities. Being created for governmental purposes, the borrowing of money, the purchase of property on time, and the giving of commercial paper, are not inherent, or even powers usually conferred; and unless endowed with such power in their charters, they have no authority to make and place on the market such paper, and persons dealing in it must see that the power exists.[3]

1. *Wallis* v. *Johnson School Township*, 75 Ind. 368; *Bicknell* v. *Widner School Township*, 73 Ind. 501; *State* v. *Babcock*, 22 Neb. 614, 35 N.W. 941; *Bank of Chillicothe* v. *Town of Chillicothe*, 7 Ohio St. 31, 30 Am. Dec. 185. See the more recent case of *Logan* v. *Board of Public Instruction for Polk County*, 118 Fla. 184, 158 So. 720, in which the Supreme Court of Florida held that a county board of public instruction had implied power to borrow money for the operation of the schools.

2. *Brenham* v. *German-American Bank*, 144 U.S. 173, 12 S. Ct. 559; *Hewitt* v. *Board of Education*, 94 Ill. 528; *Coffin* v. *Board of Commissioners of Kearney County*, 57 Fed. 137; *Ashuelot National Bank of Keene* v. *School District No. 7*, 56 Fed. 197. See, however, *Watkins* v. *Ouachita Parish School Board*, 173 La. 259, 136 So. 591.

3. *Hewitt* v. *Board of Education*, 94 Ill. 528.

Authority to issue bonds, moreover, cannot be implied from an express grant of authority to borrow money.[4] Where, for example, a school district had statutory authority to borrow money to pay for schoolhouses, it was held that the district had no authority to issue bonds. It was said by the court:

We think, however, that we may fairly affirm that the two authorities heretofore cited do establish the following propositions: First, that an express power conferred upon a municipal corporation to borrow money for corporate purposes does not in itself carry with it an authority to issue negotiable securities; second, that the latter power will never be implied, in favor of a municipal corporation, unless such implication is necessary to prevent some express corporate power from becoming utterly nugatory; and, third, that in every case where a doubt arises as to the right of a municipal corporation to execute negotiable securities the doubt should be resolved against the existence of any such right.[5]

The case of *School District No. 6* v. *Robb*[6] illustrates the strictness with which the courts interpret statutory authority to issue bonds. The statutes authorized school districts to issue bonds for the purpose of erecting and equipping a schoolhouse or houses in the district. After pointing out that if there was any reasonable doubt as to the existence of power to issue bonds, the doubt would be resolved against the district, the court went on to hold that the district had no power to issue bonds for the purpose of repairing existing buildings.

Since the power of a school district to issue bonds is derived wholly from statutory enactment, the legislature may prescribe the conditions upon which the power may be exercised, and it may prescribe the terms to be embodied in the bonds. And unless the statutory conditions and terms are complied with, the bonds are invalid. To illustrate, a statute in Delaware read: "Any or all said Bonds may be redeemed at the option of the Board of School Trustees at par and accrued interest at any interest period after the expiration of five (5) years from the date of said Bonds." The court held that a board of education had no authority to issue bonds which were not to be re-

4. *Merrill* v. *Monticello*, 138 U.S. 673, 11 S. Ct. 441, 34 L. Ed. 1069; *Brenham* v. *German-American Bank*, 144 U.S. 173, 12 S. Ct. 559; *Ashuelot National Bank of Keene* v. *School District No. 7*, 56 Fed. 197; *Folsom* v. *School Directors of District No. 5*, 91 Ill. 402.

5. *Ashuelot National Bank of Keene* v. *School District No. 7*, 56 Fed. 197.

6. *School District No. 6* v. *Robb*, 150 Kan. 402, 93 Pac. (2d) 905, 124 A.L.R. 879.

deemed before maturity. The provisions of the statute were permissive in form but mandatory in the sense that a duty was imposed upon the board to reserve the right to redeem the bonds after the expiration of five years.[7] And where the statutes provided that bonds "may be made payable in not less than ten nor more than twenty years," bonds payable eleven days less than ten years were void.[8] But where the statutes authorize the issuance of bonds but are silent on such matters as the time that shall elapse between elections approving them or when they shall be payable, much is left to the board's discretion. Thus where the statutes do not stipulate the time that should elapse between bond elections, a school board could call a second election almost immediately after the first.[9]

The proceeds derived from the sale of school bonds must be spent strictly for the purpose or purposes for which the bonds were issued. Thus in North Carolina bonds were voted for the purpose of "erecting and equipping new school buildings and purchasing sites therefor." Later the county commissioners proposed to spend about 70 per cent of the proceeds for enlarging elementary-school buildings, erecting a new elementary school for Negroes, and making additions to another elementary school for Negroes. The court denied the authority. It said:

> While the defendants have a limited authority, under certain conditions, to transfer or allocate funds from one project to another, included within the general purpose for which bonds are authorized, the transfer must be to a project included in the general purpose as stated in the bond resolution and notice of election. . . .
> The law is founded on the principle of fair play, and fair play demands that defendants keep faith with the electors of the district and use the proceeds for the purpose for which the bonds were authorized—the erection and equipment of new buildings and the purchase of sites therefor.[10]

Although a school district may have the general authority to issue bonds, the question of authority may arise with respect to a particular bond issue. Where the electors of a school district vote to issue bonds for an amount greater than the law permits, a board of education will not be restrained from issuing any bonds at all, but may issue them in

7. *Dupont* v. *Mills*, 9 W.W. Harr. 42, 196 Atl. 168, 119 A.L.R. 174.

8. *People's Bank* v. *School District*, 3 N.D. 496, 57 N.W. 787, 28 L.R.A. 642.

9. *Chapel* v. *Allen*, 334 Mich. 176, 54 N.W. (2d) 209; *Tedder* v. *Board of Education of Bolivar County*, 214 Miss. 717, 59 So. (2d) 329.

10. *Waldrop* v. *Hodges*, 230 N.C. 370, 53 S.E. (2d) 263.

the maximum sum authorized by statute.[11] And an injunction will not be granted to restrain the issuance of bonds in an amount less than the amount voted.[12] Unless restrained by constitutional or statutory provision, a school board may exercise its discretion in designating the place at which bonds will be paid, either the principal, or interest, or both.[13] Where the statutes authorize a school board to call elections to determine whether bonds shall be issued, the board may call elections as often as it sees fit.[14] And where bonds have been legally authorized by a vote of the district, they will not be held invalid because of a delay of two or three years in issuing and selling them.[15] In Kentucky the court went so far as to hold that it was permissible for a board to issue bonds eight years after they were voted.[16] It has been held, too, that failure to provide a sinking fund will not invalidate a bond-issue.[17] But a school district has no authority to issue bonds to be bargained away and delivered to a contractor for the erection and furnishing of a schoolhouse for the district.[18] The objection to such a transaction is based upon considerations of public policy. If the bonds are sold and the proceeds received into the treasury, the district may then let the contract at a reasonable price after fair competitive bidding; but where the building is to be paid for in bonds, the competition is confined to those persons who combine the character of contractor and stock broker. It is generally held, too, that

11. *Board of Education v. Davis*, 120 Kan. 768, 245 Pac. 112; *Shover v. Buford*, 17 Colo. 562, 208 Pac. 470; *Stockdale v. School District No. 2*, 47 Mich. 226, 10 N.W. 349; *McPherson v. Foster Brothers*, 43 Iowa 48, 22 Am. Rep. 215; *Vaughn v. School District No. 31*, 27 Ore. 57, 39 Pac. 393. See also *Bauer v. School District No. 127*, 78 Mo. App. 442.

12. *State* ex rel. *Berthot v. Gallatin County High School District*, 102 Mont. 356, 58 Pac. (2d) 264.

13. *Board of Trustees v. Spitzer*, 255 Fed. 136; *Kunz v. School District No. 28*, 11 S.D. 578, 79 N.W. 844.

14. *McKinney v. Cadiz Graded Common School District*, 144 Ky. 85, 137 S.W. 839.

15. *City of Dayton v. Board of Education*, 201 Ky. 566, 257 S.W. 1021; *Gregg v. Board of Commissioners of Randolph County*, 162 N.C. 479, 78 S.E. 301; *Miller v. School District No. 3*, 5 Wyo. 217, 39 Pac. 879; *Covington v. McInnis*, 144 S.C. 391, 142 S.E. 650.

16. *Runyon v. Simpson*, 270 Ky. 646, 110 S.W. (2d) 440. See also *Hager v. Board of Education*, 254 Ky. 791, 72 S.W. (2d) 475.

17. *Bauer v. School District No. 127*, 78 Mo. App. 442; *Wilson v. Board of Education*, 12 S.D. 535, 81 N.W. 952.

18. *State v. School District No. 4*, 16 Neb. 182, 20 N.W. 209.

school boards have no authority to sell bonds at less than par,[19] unless authorized to do so by statute. It has been held, however, that a commission for the sale of bonds is allowable from the proceeds, where the bonds are sold at a price not less than the minimum stipulated by statute.[20]

Right of taxpayer to injunction restraining issuance or sale of illegal bonds.—The general rule is that the taxpayers of a school district may sue to enjoin the issuance or sale of illegal bonds. Thus issuance of bonds will be enjoined if their sale will increase the debt of the district beyond the constitutional or statutory debt limit[21] or if they were authorized at an illegal election.[22]

VALIDITY OF SCHOOL BONDS

School districts must not only have authority to issue bonds; they must exercise their authority in the manner prescribed by statute. The statutes commonly provide for the calling of an election to determine whether the voters of a district are willing to authorize the board of education to issue bonds. When such is the case, the election must be called by the proper authorities, for otherwise the bonds authorized thereat will not be valid.[23] Thus, in the case of *Barry* v. *Board of Education*,[24] bonds authorized at a special election called and conducted by the board of education instead of by the city council and mayor, as provided by statute, were held invalid, and their issuance and sale were enjoined. The court quoted with approval the rule as stated in *Ruling Case Law:*

It is in any event essential to the validity of such elections that they be called, and the time and place thereof fixed by the very agency designated by law and by none other. For example, where a mayor and city council are

19. *Adams* v. *State*, 82 Ill. 132.

20. *Park* v. *Rural Special School District No. 26*, 173 Ark. 892, 293 S.W. 1035; *Franklin Avenue German Savings Institution* v. *Board of Education*, 75 Mo. 408. See also *Davis* v. *White*, 171 Ark. 385, 284 S.W. 764.

21. *Morgan* v. *Board of Supervisors*, 67 Ariz. 133, 192 Pac. (2d) 236.

22. *Morgan* v. *Board of Supervisors*, 67 Ariz. 133, 192 Pac. (2d) 236; *Koch* v. *Harris*, 117 Okla. 172, 245 Pac. 848; *Patton* v. *Independent School District*, 242 Iowa 941, 48 N.W. (2d) 803; *Abrahams* v. *School District No. 33*, 97 Kan. 325, 155 Pac. 16. Contra, *Repsold* v. *Independent School District*, 205 Minn. 316, 285 N.W. 827.

23. *Barry* v. *Board of Education*, 23 N.M. 465, 169 Pac. 314; 9 R.C.L. Sec. 20. NOTE: 90 Am. St. Rep. 61.

24. *Barry* v. *Board of Education*, 23 N.M. 465, 169 Pac. 314.

authorized to call a special election, the mayor has no power to act alone, or where the governor and the board of supervisors are given the authority an election called by the sheriff will be invalid. An election not called by the proper officers is without authority of law and void.

School authorities must follow the statutory provisions with respect to the giving of notice of bond elections. The courts are reluctant, however, to declare an election void and will not do so because of mere irregularities in the giving of notice, unless the statutes expressly declare that the election shall be void if the statutory requirements are not strictly observed. That is, if there has been a substantial compliance with the provisions of the statute and it can be shown that the results of the election were not affected by the irregularities, the courts will hold the election valid.[25] Thus failure to post notices the required number of days[26] or to publish notices in all the places required[27] is immaterial where the electors had actual notice and the results of the election were not affected by failure to follow the statutes literally. In a Nebraska case,[28] for example, the statutes required that notice of the election for the issuance of bonds be published in the newspapers for twenty days prior to the election. This was not done. A majority of the qualified electors of the district, however, voted to issue the bonds. The court refused to hold the election void. It said:

As we construe the statute (section 6801, as amended), the provision for publication of notice is directory. We do not gather from the provisions of the act that it was the intention of the Legislature that the election should be void, where the notice given was not published or was defective. Where the statutory provision for notice is directory, failure to give the notice in compliance with the statute will not necessarily invalidate the election. If it is apparent that the electors generally had actual notice of the time, place and object of the election and participated generally at the polls, and if the

25. *Lee v. Bellingham School District No. 301*, 107 Wash. 482, 182 Pac. 580; *Welborn v. Board of Supervisors*, 130 Miss. 321, 94 So. 224; *Connine v. Smith,* 190 Mich. 631, 157 N.W. 450; *Hicks v. Krigbaum*, 13 Ariz. 237, 108 Pac. 482; *Phillips Investment Company v. School District No. 5*, 26 Colo. App. 362, 144 Pac. 1129; *State v. March*, 108 Neb. 749, 189 N.W. 283; *Miller v. Duke School District No. 1*, 184 N.C. 197, 113 S.E. 786; *Waters v. Gunn*, 218 S.W. (2d) (Tex.) 235; *Sacramento County v. Stephens*, 11 Calif. App. (2d) 110, 53 Pac. (2d) 197; *State ex rel. Board of Education v. Maxwell*, 144 Ohio St. 565, 60 N.E. (2d) 183.

26. *Lee v. Bellingham School District No. 301*, 107 Wash. 482, 182 Pac. 580; *State v. March*, 108 Neb. 749, 189 N.W. 283; *Phillips Investment Company v. School District No. 5*, 26 Colo. App. 362, 144 Pac. 1129.

27. *Hicks v. Krigbaum*, 13 Ariz. 237, 108 Pac. 482.

28. *State v. March*, 108 Neb. 749, 189 N.W. 283.

result of the election is supported by such a vote that it is manifest no other result could have been possible, even though every elector had voted, the election will not be held void on the ground that the notice given was not in accordance with the statute.

Similarly, it was held that a notice containing an erroneous description of the territory of the district did not render an election void where no electors were misled by the error.[29]

Where school bonds are to be issued for more than one purpose, care should be taken by those who conduct the election to submit to the electors each proposition separately. The rule is universal that unrelated and diverse propositions cannot be submitted as one.[30] "The vice of 'doubleness,'" says Mr. Justice Ragland, speaking for the Supreme Court of Missouri,[31] "in submissions at elections is universally condemned. It is regarded as a species of legal fraud because it may compel the voter, in order to get what he earnestly wants, to vote for something which he does not want." It is often difficult, however, to determine just what is a single or a double proposition. There is, indeed, a good deal of conflict among the courts themselves. Mr. Justice Ragland, in the opinion quoted above, stated the rule about as definitely as it can be stated: "If it can be said that the proposed improvements are not naturally related or connected, then it is clear that separate submissions are required; if, on the other hand, the several parts of the project are plainly so related that, united, they form in fact but one rounded whole, it is equally clear that they may be grouped together and submitted as one proposition."

In conformity with the rule as stated, the Supreme Court of Missouri has held that a proposition to issue bonds to purchase schoolhouse sites, to erect schoolhouses and furnish the same, and to build additions to and to repair old buildings was a single proposition.[32] In Kansas the following proposition was submitted to the electors: "Shall the board of education of the city of Pittsburg, Kan., issue its bonds in the sum of $450,000 for the purpose of purchasing sites for school buildings, and for the purpose of constructing additions to school buildings,

29. *Welborn* v. *Board of Supervisors*, 130 Miss. 321, 94 So. 224.

30. *Hart* v. *Board of Education*, 299 Mo. 36, 252 S.W. 441; *Clark* v. *Los Angeles*, 160 Calif. 317, 116 Pac. 966; *In re Validation of Bonds*, 170 Miss. 886, 156 So. 516; *State ex rel. Becker* v. *Smith*, 335 Mo. 1046, 75 S.W. (2d) 574; *People ex rel. Toman* v. *Chicago Great Western, etc.*, 379 Ill. 594, 41 N.E. (2d) 960.

31. *Hart* v. *Board of Education*, 299 Mo. 36, 252 S.W. 441.

32. *Willis* v. *School District of Sedalia*, 299 Mo. 446, 253 S.W. 741.

and for the purpose of constructing new school buildings in the city of Pittsburg?" When called upon to decide whether this was a double or single proposition, the supreme court of that state said: "Here was a question of providing proper school facilities—one proposition, and it was properly submitted as such."[33] It has been held, too, that where bonds are approved for a number of purposes in a single aggregate sum and one of the purposes is illegal, the whole bond issue must fail because it is impossible to separate the good from the bad.[34]

The validity of school bonds is frequently attacked on the ground that the election at which they were authorized was irregularly held. As a rule, however, the courts will not declare an election void because of some irregularity if the electors have had a full and free opportunity to express their will. Unless it can be shown that the irregularity affected the results of the election, the irregularity is immaterial, and the election will be sustained.[35] The purpose of all elections is to ascertain the will of those who are qualified to vote, and, where that will has been ascertained, it would be substituting form for substance to declare the election void because of some error or mistake on the part of election officials. Irregularities which do not affect the results will render an election void only in those cases where the statutes show that it was the intent of the legislature that the election should be void unless conducted in the exact manner prescribed. The rule was clearly expressed in the case of *Horsefall* v. *School District of the City of Salem*.[36] Said the court:

We think it may now be said to be the established rule in this state, as it is generally in other jurisdictions, that where a statute expressly declares any particular act to be essential to the validity of an election, then the act

33. *Board of Education* v. *Davis*, 120 Kan. 768, 245 Pac. 112.

34. *Board of Supervisors of Merced County* v. *Cothran*, 84 Calif. App. (2d) 679, 191 Pac. (2d) 506.

35. *Liddell* v. *Municipality of Noxapater*, 129 Miss. 513, 92 So. 631; *Dye* v. *Brewton*, 119 Miss. 359, 80 So. 761; *Shelton* v. *School Board District No. 22*, 43 Okla. 239, 142 Pac. 1034; *Chambers* v. *Independent School District of Knoxville*, 172 Iowa 340, 154 N.W. 581; *Strawn* v. *Independent School District of Indianola*, 199 Iowa 1078, 203 N.W. 12; *Mack* v. *Independent School District of Corning*, 200 Iowa 1190, 206 N.W. 145; *Casey* v. *Dare County*, 168 N.C. 285, 84 S.E. 268; *Plott* v. *Board of Commissioners of Haywood County*, 187 N.C. 125, 121 S.E. 190; *Stephens* v. *School District No. 3*, 154 Ga. 275, 114 S.E. 197; *Howard* v. *Luke*, 18 Ariz. 563, 164 Pac. 439; *Taylor* v. *Sparks*, 118 S.W. (Ky.) 970; *Bullitt* v. *City of Louisville*, 213 Ky. 756, 281 S.W. 1031; *McKinnon* v. *Union High School District No. 1*, 116 Ore. 543, 241 Pac. 386.

36. *Horsefall* v. *School District of the City of Salem*, 143 Mo. App. 541, 128 S.W. 33.

must be performed in the manner provided, or the election will be void. . . . But if the statute merely provides that certain things shall be done, and does not prescribe what results shall follow if these things are not done, then the provision is directory merely, and the final test as to the legality of either the election or the ballot is whether or not the voters have been given an opportunity to express, and have fairly expressed, their will.

In the following cases irregularities which did not affect the result of the election were held to be immaterial: where ballots were cast by persons not qualified to vote;[37] where ballots did not conform exactly with the phraseology prescribed by statute;[38] where the polls were kept open for a longer time than the statutes prescribed;[39] where improper registration books were used and the proper oath was not administered;[40] and where more than one ballot was delivered to some voters.[41] It has been held, too, that a bond election is not rendered invalid because members of the board of education take an active part in securing an affirmative vote. By becoming board members they surrender none of their rights as citizens.[42] It is legitimate, too, for a board of education to modify the district boundaries so as to secure the approval of a bond issue.[43] It has been held, on the other hand, that failure to hold an election at the place designated by statute is not a mere irregularity, notwithstanding the fact that all electors had due notice.[44]

EFFECT OF RECITALS IN SCHOOL BONDS

School-district bonds commonly contain recitals to the effect that the bonds have been issued according to law, that all acts required by statute to authorize the issuance of the bonds have been done, and that all conditions precedent have been complied with. Recitals may

37. *Strawn* v. *Independent School District of Indianola*, 199 Iowa 1078, 203 N.W. 12; *Shelton* v. *School Board District No. 22*, 43 Okla. 239, 142 Pac. 1034.

38. *Stephens* v. *School District No. 3*, 154 Ga. 275, 114 S.E. 197.

39. *Chambers* v. *Independent School District of Knoxville*, 172 Iowa 340, 154 N.W. 581.

40. *Dye* v. *Brewton*, 119 Miss. 359, 80 So. 761.

41. *McKinnon* v. *Union High School District No. 1*, 116 Ore. 543, 241 Pac. 386.

42. *Chambers* v. *Independent School District of Knoxville*, 172 Iowa 340, 154 N.W. 581.

43. *Stephens* v. *School District No. 3*, 154 Ga. 275, 114 S.E. 197.

44. *Edwards* v. *Board of Supervisors of Bolivar County*, 124 Miss. 165, 87 So. 8.

even state that the bonds have been issued under authority conferred by law and that the constitutional or statutory debt limit has not been exceeded. The question naturally arises as to what effect such recitals have upon the validity of the bonds. Do the recitals, even though they are false, estop the district from denying the validity of the bonds, or must an innocent purchaser for value look beyond the recitals and determine for himself the facts and the law?

The cases dealing with the effect of recitals are numerous and difficult to reconcile and harmonize. It is well settled, however, that, where the statutes authorize the issuance of school bonds upon certain conditions precedent, as, for example, the securing of the consent of a majority of the electors or the levying of a tax sufficient to pay the principal and interest of the bonds, and authorize the board of education or certain officers thereof to determine whether all things required to be done have been done, a recital in the bonds made by those authorized by statute to make the determination that all things required to be done have been done is conclusive when the bonds are in the hands of bona fide purchasers, and the district is estopped to deny the truth of the recital even though it may in fact be false.[45] It should be pointed out, however, that if the statutes require a public record to be kept and this record contradicts the recitals in the bond, the district will not be estopped to contradict the recitals in the bonds by the official record.[46]

Mr. Justice Henry, speaking for the Supreme Court of Texas, has expressed the rule clearly in the following words:

45. *Town of Coloma* v. *Eaves*, 92 U.S. 484, 23 L. Ed. 579; *Chaffee County* v. *Potter*, 142 U.S. 355, 12 S. Ct. 216, 35 L. Ed. 1040; *Dixon County* v. *Field*, 111 U.S. 83, 4 S. Ct. 315, 28 L. Ed. 360; *Spitzer* v. *Village of Blanchard*, 82 Mich. 234, 46 N.W. 400; *Gibbs* v. *School District No. 10*, 88 Mich. 334, 50 N.W. 294, 26 Am. St. Rep. 295; *State* v. *School District No. 50*, 18 N.D. 616, 120 N.W. 555, 138 Am. St. Rep. 787; *Flagg* v. *School District No. 70*, 4 N.D. 30, 58 N.W. 499, 25 L.R.A. 363; *Coler* v. *Dwight School Township*, 3 N.D. 249, 55 N.W. 587, 28 L.R.A. 649; *Bolton* v. *Board of Education*, 1 Ill. App. 193; *State* v. *School District No. 9*, 10 Neb. 544, 7 N.W. 315; *Citizens' Bank* v. *City of Terrell*, 78 Tex. 45, 14 S.W. 1003; *National Life Insurance Company* v. *Board of Education*, 62 Fed. 778; *Independent School District of Sioux City* v. *Rew*, 111 Fed. 1, 55 L.R.A. 364; *Southwest Securities Company* v. *Board of Education*, 40 N.M. 59, 54 Pac. (2d) 412; *Landrum* v. *Centennial Rural High School District*, Tex. Civ. App. 146 S.W. (2d) 799; *Board of Instruction of Dade County* v. *State*, 121 Fla. 703, 164 So. 697. Contra, *Heard* v. *Calhoun School District*, 45 Mo. App. 660; *Thornburgh* v. *School District No. 3*, 175 Mo. 12, 75 S.W. 81.

46. *Southeast Securities Company* v. *Board of Education*, 40 N.M. 59, 54 Pac. (2d) 412.

When the law makes the existence of the power to issue bonds depend upon the existence of a given state of facts, which depend for proof of their existence upon parol evidence, and appoints a tribunal to ascertain the facts and to create the debt and issue negotiable bonds, if it finds that the required facts exist, and the bonds are issued and contain recitals that the facts existed that conferred authority to issue them, and such negotiable bonds go into the hands of *bona fide* holders, they are collectable, notwithstanding the non-existence of the facts required to confer the authority to issue them. In such cases, the validity of the bonds does not exist in disregard or violation of law, but because the ascertainment of the facts that confer the power has been delegated to the body that issues them, and its ascertainment of the facts is held to be conclusive in favor of the innocent holders of the negotiable securities, against which no evidence will be heard.[47]

The case of *Gibbs* v. *School District No. 10*[48] illustrates the application of the rule. In that case, bonds issued by the school district contained a recital to the effect that the bonds had been authorized by a two-thirds vote of the qualified voters in accordance with a certain designated statute. The recital was signed by the director and moderator of the district by order of the district board. An attempt was made to avoid payment of the bonds on the ground that the records of the district failed to show that the required election had been held. The court, however, held that the district was estopped to deny that the bonds had been authorized by the proper vote of the electors. It said in part:

Purchasers of such securities have a right to rely upon all facts asserted or appearing upon the face of the bonds made by any person or body authorized by law to pass upon and determine the facts. . . . The recitals in this bond are made by the director and moderator, who compose a majority of the school board. Neither the school board nor the moderator and director is authorized to issue the bonds unless voted by the district at a lawful meeting; and, under section 5104, before the board can act, they have a function to perform, in its nature somewhat judicial, and that is as to their own authority to issue the bonds. The statute limits that authority to bonds voted by the school district, and consequently the question whether the proceedings to vote such bonds are such as will authorize the board to issue them must be passed upon by the board. A purchaser of the bonds, therefore, need look no further back than the face of the bonds for the facts which show a compliance with the law. . . .

The law under which these bonds were issued authorized the school board to issue them, and made that board the body to determine when such facts existed; and hence when the bonds were issued by their orders, that fact appearing upon the face of the bond, a *bona fide* holder is entitled to recover,

47. *Citizens' Bank* v. *City of Terrell*, 78 Tex. 45, 14 S.W. 1003.

48. *Gibbs* v. *School District No. 10*, 88 Mich. 334, 50 N.W. 294, 26 Am. St. Rep. 295.

and, as against him, the district is not allowed to defend upon the ground that the law was not complied with previous to their determination to issue the bonds. The law having placed that responsibility with the district board, the school district, if defrauded, must seek their remedy against such board.[49]

Similarly, in the case of *Coler* v. *Dwight School Township*,[50] it was held that a recital estopped the school district to deny that the school board had been petitioned as required by statute; and in the case of *Flagg* v. *School District No. 70*,[51] in the face of a recital to the contrary, the district could not contend that the schoolhouse site was not owned by the district.

The theory of the doctrine of estoppel by recital, it will be noted, is based upon the consideration that the legislature having authorized certain individuals or officers to determine whether the facts existed which conferred authority to issue bonds, the determination by those so authorized is final and conclusive. It follows, therefore, and has been so held in numerous cases, that a district is not bound by recitals which were made by persons not authorized to determine whether the required facts existed.[52] That is, a district will not be estopped to deny the existence of a fact or a condition, regardless of what the recital may contain, where the persons making the recital were not authorized to determine the existence of the fact or condition in question. In such a case, the public has no more right to rely upon the recital of the board than upon a certificate by an utter stranger.[53] In this connection, it was said by Mr. Justice Matthews, speaking for the Supreme Court of the United States:

If the officers authorized to issue bonds, upon a condition, are not the appointed tribunal to decide the fact, which constitutes the condition, their recital will not be accepted as a substitute for proof. In other words, where the validity of the bonds depends upon an estoppel, claimed to arise upon the recitals of the instrument, the question being as to the existence of power to issue them, it is necessary to establish that the officers executing the bonds

49. Accord, *Bolton* v. *Board of Education*, 1 Ill. App. 193; *Anderson* v. *Independent School District of Angus*, 78 Fed. 750.

50. *Coler* v. *Dwight School Township*, 3 N.D. 249, 55 N.W. 587, 28 L.R.A. 649.

51. *Flagg* v. *School District No. 70*, 4 N.D. 30, 58 N.W. 499, 25 L.R.A. 363.

52. *Dixon County* v. *Field*, 111 U.S. 83, 4 S. Ct. 315, 28 L. Ed. 360; *Coler* v. *Dwight School Township*, 3 N.D. 249, 55 N.W. 587, 28 L.R.A. 649; *National Life Insurance Company* v. *Board of Education*, 62 Fed. 778; *Independent School District of Sioux City* v. *Rew*, 111 Fed. 1, 55 L.R.A. 364; *Bolton* v. *Board of Education*, 1 Ill. App. 193; *Coffin* v. *Board of Commissioners of Kearney County*, 57 Fed. 137; *Spitzer* v. *Village of Blanchard*, 82 Mich. 234, 46 N.W. 400.

53. *Coler* v. *Dwight School Township*, 3 N.D. 249, 55 N.W. 587, 28 L.R.A. 649.

had lawful authority to make the recitals and to make them conclusive. The very ground of the estoppel is that the recitals are the official statements of those to whom the law refers the public for authentic and final information on the subject.[54]

It is important, in any particular case, to ascertain whether the legislature has conferred authority upon those making recitals to determine the existence of the facts which they assert existed. Such authority is not always, very seldom indeed, conferred in express terms. It is not necessary, however, that it be so conferred. The courts in all cases seek to discover the intent of the legislature, and consequently it has frequently been held that from the general language of the statutes, or from the very nature of the question involved, power to determine the facts contained in recitals may be inferred.[55] "It is not necessary," said the Supreme Court of North Dakota in the case of *Coler* v. *Dwight School Township*,[56] "that the power to determine these facts should have been expressly conferred upon the district officers by the statute." And the Supreme Court of the United States has said in this connection: "While it is true that the act does not in terms say that these commissioners are to decide that all preliminary conditions have been complied with, yet such express direction and authority is seldom found in acts providing for the issuing of bonds. It is enough that full control in the matter is given to the officers named."[57]

The case of *Town of Coloma* v. *Eaves*[58] illustrates the application of the rule. The statutes of Illinois authorized towns to subscribe for stock in a railroad company and to issue bonds in payment, provided the subscription be approved by a majority of the electors of the town. In holding that the town clerk and supervisor had implied power to determine whether the conditions precedent had been complied with, the court said:

54. *Dixon County* v. *Field,* 111 U.S. 83, 4 S. Ct. 315, 28 L. Ed. 360.

55. *Township of Bernards* v. *Morrison,* 133 U.S. 523, 10 S. Ct. 333, 33 L. Ed. 766; *Knox County* v. *Aspinwall,* 24 How. (U.S.) 539, 16 L. Ed. 208; *Town of Coloma* v. *Eaves,* 92 U.S. 484, 23 L. Ed. 579; *Coler* v. *Dwight School Township,* 3 N.D. 249, 55 N.W. 587, 28 L.R.A. 649; *Flagg* v. *School District No. 70,* 4 N.D. 30, 58 N.W. 499, 25 L.R.A. 363; *Fulton* v. *Town of Riverton,* 42 Minn. 395, 44 N.W. 257.

56. *Coler* v. *Dwight School Township,* 3 N.D. 249, 55 N.W. 587, 28 L.R.A. 649.

57. *Township of Bernards* v. *Morrison,* 133 U.S. 523, 10 S. Ct. 333, 33 L. Ed. 766.

58. *Town of Coloma* v. *Eaves,* 92 U.S. 484, 23 L. Ed. 579.

At some time or other, it is to be ascertained whether the directions of the act have been followed; whether there was any popular vote; or whether a majority of the legal voters present at the election did, in fact, vote in favor of the subscription. The duty of ascertaining was plainly intended to be vested somewhere, and once for all; and the only persons spoken of who have any duties to perform respecting the election, and action consequent upon it, are the town clerk and the supervisor or other executive officer of the city or town. It is a fair presumption, therefore, that the legislature intended that those officers, or one of them at least, should determine whether the requirements of the act prior to a subscription to the stock of a railroad company had been met.

Where it is clear that school-district authorities have statutory power to determine whether the facts necessary to authorize the issuance of bonds exist, the question may still arise as to whether the recitals in the bonds are sufficiently broad or detailed to cover all the facts. The general rule is that the recital need not make an exhaustive enumeration of all the acts that have been done or of all the conditions that have been met; it is sufficient if the recital states that all things required by law have been done.[59] And where the recital states that the bonds have been issued in conformity with a certain statute, naming the statute, the recital will, as a rule, be interpreted to mean that all the terms of the statute have been complied with, so far as the officer making the statement had power to pass upon such questions.[60] The Supreme Court of North Dakota has expressed the rule in the following words:

Nor is it essential that the statement should set forth in detail that all of the various conditions precedent have been complied with. It is sufficient if it is stated that the bond was issued in pursuance of the statute, designating it in such a manner as to identify it. This is in legal effect a statement that each and all of the necessary preliminary steps were taken to authorize the issue of the bonds.[61]

The discussion thus far has related to recitals which state that certain conditions precedent have been complied with; it remains to consider the effect of recitals which state that the school district had au-

59. *Dixon County* v. *Field*, 111 U.S. 83, 4 S. Ct. 315, 28 L. Ed. 360; *National Life Insurance Company* v. *Board of Education*, 62 Fed. 778; 19 R.C.L. 1012. NOTE: L.R.A. 1915A 967.

60. *Dixon County* v. *Field*, 111 U.S. 83, 4 S. Ct. 315, 28 L. Ed. 360; *Coler* v. *Dwight School Township*, 3 N.D. 249, 55 N.W. 587, 28 L.R.A. 649; *Flagg* v. *School District No. 70*, 4 N.D. 30, 58 N.W. 499, 25 L.R.A. 363. But see *State* v. *School District No. 50*, 18 N.D. 616, 120 N.W. 555, 138 Am. St. Rep. 787. NOTE: L.R.A. 1915A 951.

61. *Coler* v. *Dwight School Township*, 3 N.D. 249, 55 N.W. 587, 28 L.R.A. 649.

thority to issue the bonds in question. The doctrine of estoppel by recital applies only where powers have been irregularly exercised; it never applies where there is a total lack of power to issue bonds under any circumstances.[62] Purchasers of bonds are charged with a knowledge of the authority of the corporation to issue them, for such authority is a matter of law and not a matter of fact. Obviously, school officials cannot by their recitals create a power to issue bonds where no such power exists. In this connection it has been said by the Supreme Court of the United States:

All parties are equally bound to know the law; and a certificate reciting the actual facts, and that thereby the bonds were conformable to the law, when, judicially speaking, they are not, will not make them so, nor can it work an estoppel upon the county to claim the protection of the law. Otherwise it would always be in the power of a municipal body, to which power was denied, to usurp the forbidden authority, by declaring that its assumption was within the law. This would be the clear exercise of legislative power, and would suppose such corporate bodies to be superior to the law itself.[63]

In the case of *Coffin* v. *Board of Commissioners of Kearney County*,[64] for example, the statutes provided that no county should issue bonds within one year after its organization. A county which had been organized less than six months issued bonds containing a recital "that all acts, conditions, and things required to be done precedent to and in the issuing of this bond have been properly done, happened, and performed, in regular and due form as required by law." The bonds were held invalid regardless of the recital, because the purchaser was bound to know that the county had no authority to issue bonds under any circumstances. Similarly, in a South Dakota case,[65] bonds were issued in a denomination greater than the law allowed. The bonds were void because of a lack of authority to issue them. "Every man," said the court, "is charged with notice of that which the law requires

---

62. *Dixon County* v. *Field*, 111 U.S. 83, 4 S. Ct. 315, 28 L. Ed. 360; *Nesbit* v. *Riverside Independent District*, 144 U.S. 610, 12 S. Ct. 746, 36 L. Ed. 562; *Livingston* v. *School District No. 7*, 9 S.D. 345, 69 N.W. 15; *Spitzer* v. *Village of Blanchard*, 82 Mich. 234, 46 N.W. 400; *Gibbs* v. *School District No. 10*, 88 Mich. 334, 50 N.W. 294, 26 Am. St. Rep. 295; *State* v. *School District No. 50*, 18 N.D. 616, 120 N.W. 555, 138 Am. St. Rep. 787; *Decorah First National Bank* v. *Doon District Township*, 86 Iowa 330, 53 N.W. 301, 41 Am. St. Rep. 489; *Board of Education* v. *Blodgett*, 155 Ill. 441, 40 N.E. 1025, 31 L.R.A. 70, 46 Am. St. Rep. 348.

63. *Dixon County* v. *Field*, 111 U.S. 83, 4 S. Ct. 315, 28 L. Ed. 360.

64. *Coffin* v. *Board of Commissioners of Kearney County*, 57 Fed. 137.

65. *Livingston* v. *School District No. 7*, 9 S.D. 345, 69 N.W. 15.

him to know, and that which, after being put upon inquiry, he might have ascertained by the exercise of reasonable diligence."

Bonds issued in excess of a constitutional or statutory debt limit are void, and their issuance may, of course, be enjoined by taxpayers. But after the bonds have been sold, recitals contained in them may estop the district to deny their validity. The cases in point cannot be harmonized, but the general rule is that recitals expressly stating that the bonds have not been issued in excess of the debt limit are binding upon the district where the bonds do not show on their face the total indebtedness or the total issue in question, and where the purchaser is not charged by law with a knowledge of facts contained in some public record.[66] Such is the case almost without exception where those making the recitals were authorized by law to determine whether the debt limit had been exceeded or not.[67] Where, on the other hand, the recital merely states that the bonds were issued in conformity to law or by virtue of some designated statute, the purchaser will be required to determine for himself whether the debt limit has been exceeded.[68] It has been held, however, that the amount of indebtedness is a matter of public record and that purchasers of bonds are not entitled to rely upon recitals.[69] This is especially true where the bonds show on their face the total amount of the bond issue. Thus, it was said in the case of *Dixon County* v. *Field:*

> In the present case there was no power at all conferred to issue bonds in excess of an amount equal to 10 per cent upon the assessed valuation of the taxable property in the county. In determining the limit of power there were necessarily two factors: the amount of the bonds to be issued, and the amount of the assessed value of the property for purposes of taxation. The amount of the bonds issued was known. It is stated in the recital itself. It was $87,000. The holder of each bond was apprised of that fact. The amount of the assessed value of the taxable property in the county is not stated, but, *ex vi termini*, it was ascertainable in one way only, and that was by reference to the assessment itself, a public record equally accessible to all intending

66. *Chaffee County* v. *Potter,* 142 U.S. 355, 12 S. Ct. 216, 35 L. Ed. 1040; *Sutliff* v. *Lake County,* 147 U.S. 230, 13 S. Ct. 318, 37 L. Ed. 145. But see *Fairfield* v. *Rural Independent School District,* 111 Fed. 453; *Evans* v. *McFarland,* 186 Mo. 703, 85 S.W. 873.

67. *Chaffee County* v. *Potter,* 142 U.S. 355, 12 S. Ct. 216, 35 L. Ed. 1040.

68. *Independent School District* v. *Stone,* 106 U.S. 183, 1 S. Ct. 84, 27 L. Ed. 90; *Doon Township* v. *Cummins,* 142 U.S. 366, 12 S. Ct. 220, 35 L. Ed. 1044; *Dixon County* v. *Field,* 111 U.S. 83, 4 S. Ct. 315, 28 L. Ed. 360; *Buchanan* v. *Litchfield,* 102 U.S. 278, 26 L. Ed. 138; *Decorah First National Bank* v. *Doon District Township,* 86 Iowa 330, 53 N.W. 301, 41 Am. St. Rep. 489.

69. *Citizens' Bank* v. *City of Terrell,* 78 Tex. 45, 14 S.W. 1003.

purchasers of bonds, as well as to the county officers. This being known, the ratio between the two amounts was fixed by an arithmetical calculation. No recital involving the amount of the assessed taxable valuation of the property to be taxed for the payment of the bonds can take the place of the assessment itself, for it is the amount, as fixed by reference to that record, that is made by the constitution the standard for measuring the limit of the municipal power. Nothing in the way of inquiry, ascertainment, or determination as to that fact is submitted to the county officers. They are bound, it is true, to learn from the assessment what the limit upon their authority is, as a necessary preliminary in the exercise of their functions and the performance of their duty, but the information is for themselves alone. All the world besides must have it from the same source, and for themselves. The fact, as it is recorded in the assessment itself, is extrinsic, and proves itself by inspection, and concludes all determinations that contradict it.[70]

RIGHT OF HOLDER OF ILLEGAL BONDS TO
RECOVER FROM DISTRICT

It is well established that bonds which were issued without authority,[71] or for a purpose unauthorized,[72] or in excess of the debt limit,[73] or in violation of the law[74] do not bind the district, and no recovery can be had on the bonds even though they may be in the hands of innocent purchasers. But where the bonds have been sold and the district enjoys the benefits derived therefrom, the question may arise as to whether an innocent purchaser for value may recover on an implied contract in law in a court of equity. The general rule is that where bonds issued by a school district are invalid and unenforcible, the holder may recover the money if it has not been spent or lost and if it can be identified.[75] Moreover, the holder of a bond is entitled to the property purchased with the proceeds derived from the bond, provided that such property can be identified and returned to him with-

---

70. *Dixon County* v. *Field,* 111 U.S. 83, 4 S. Ct. 315, 28 L. Ed. 360.

71. *Hewitt* v. *Board of Education,* 94 Ill. 528.

72. *Board of Education* v. *Blodgett,* 155 Ill. 441, 40 N.E. 1025, 31 L.R.A. 70, 46 Am. St. Rep. 348.

73. *Read* v. *Plattsmouth,* 107 U.S. 568, 2 S. Ct. 208, 27 L. Ed. 414; *Decorah First National Bank* v. *Doon District Township,* 86 Iowa 330, 53 N.W. 301, 41 Am. St. Rep. 489; *Farmers' & Merchants' National Bank of Valley City* v. *School District No. 53,* 6 Dak. 255, 42 N.W. 767.

74. *School District No. 56* v. *St. Joseph, etc., Insurance Company,* 103 U.S. 707, 26 L. Ed. 601; *Doon Township* v. *Cummins,* 142 U.S. 366, 12 S. Ct. 220, 35 L. Ed. 1044; *Decorah First National Bank* v. *Doon District Township,* 86 Iowa 330, 53 N.W. 301, 41 Am. St. Rep. 489; *State* v. *School District No. 50,* 18 N.D. 616, 120 N.W. 555, 138 Am. St. Rep. 787.

75. *Board of Trustees of Fordsville* v. *Postel,* 121 Ky. 67, 88 S.W. 1065, 28 Ky. Law Rep. 37, 123 Am. St. Rep. 184; *Appeal of Luburg,* 1 Monaghan (Pa.) 329, 17 Atl. 245.

out injury to the property of the district or without prejudice to the rights of the district.[76] But if the money has been lost or spent or if the property purchased with the money has been so attached to other property of the district that it cannot be recovered or restored to the holder of the bond without prejudice to the rights of the district, the bondholder is without recourse and without remedy.[77] In some cases, it is true, where one of the parties has performed his part of the contract and the other party retains and enjoys the benefits thereof, the courts will imply a contract and permit a recovery on *quantum meruit.* That is, in order to do justice, a court of equity will permit a recovery, not of the contract price, but of the actual value of the goods furnished. But the doctrine of implied contracts has not been extended, as a rule, to void or *ultra vires* contracts, or to contracts made in direct violation of law.[78] If the district was without authority to make the contract in the first instance, no contract will be implied, for, as has been said, the law will not imply a contract which could not have been made expressly.

The case of *Board of Trustees of Fordsville* v. *Postel*[79] illustrates the rule followed by most courts. In that case, bonds were void because no vote of the legal voters of the district was taken before the bonds were issued. The holders of the bonds brought an action in a court of equity asking that the lot, house, and furniture which were purchased with the proceeds of the bonds be transferred to them. The court said in part:

> The money which the plaintiffs paid is distinctly traced into the schoolhouse, the lot, and furniture, and no other money went into them. This property can be reclaimed, without taking any other property with it or injuring any other person or interfering with his rights. . . .
> No liability, direct or indirect, may be imposed upon the school district under the bonds in question. It is not liable on the bonds, nor can it be made liable by indirection in any way. But, if we ignore the bond transaction

76. *Parkersburg* v. *Brown,* 106 U.S. 487, 1 S. Ct. 442, 27 L. Ed. 238; *Board of Trustees of Fordsville* v. *Postel,* 121 Ky. 67, 88 S.W. 1065, 28 Ky. Law Rep. 37, 123 Am. St. Rep. 184.

77. *City of Litchfield* v. *Ballou,* 114 U.S. 190, 5 S. Ct. 820, 29 L. Ed. 132; *Board of Trustees of Fordsville* v. *Postel,* 121 Ky. 67, 88 S.W. 1065, 28 Ky. Law Rep. 37, 123 Am. St. Rep. 184; *Strickler* v. *Consolidated School District No. 1,* 29 Mo. 136, 291 S.W. 136, 50 A.L.R. 1287; *Powell* v. *Bainbridge State Bank,* 161 Ga. 855, 132 S.E. 60; *Arkansas National Bank* v. *School District No. 99,* 152 Ark. 507, 238 S.W. 630.

78. For a more detailed discussion see chap. ix.

79. *Board of Trustees of Fordsville* v. *Postel,* 121 Ky. 67, 88 S.W. 1065, 28 Ky. Law Rep. 37, 123 Am. St. Rep. 184.

altogether, what have we? The district received $4,000 from the bond-holders. The bonds being void, the district should have returned the money to the bondholders. If the bondholders had learned of the invalidity of the bonds while the district still had the $4,000 in its treasury which they had paid to it, manifestly a court of equity would have required the district to pay back their money to them. It was money obtained by a mutual mistake. While under the Constitution no liability would attach to the district for the money if it had lost it, or if it had spent it and the fund could not be identified and followed, where it may be followed and identified, there is no more reason why property which represents the fund should not be returned than there would be for not returning the money, if it had been placed in a bag and the district had the bag locked up in its safe. The purpose of the Constitution is not to enrich municipalities at the expense of innocent people who deal with them, and when they repudiate their bonds they must act honestly. A loss must not be placed upon the district; but, when justice may be done without inflicting any loss upon the district, equity will lay hold of the conscience of the parties and make them do what is just and right.

A decision of the Supreme Court of the United States is likewise in point. The city of Litchfield issued bonds for a legal purpose but in excess of the constitutional limitation of indebtedness. Although the bonds were invalid, it was contended that a recovery could be had on the ground of an implied contract to repay the money. The court said, in denying the contention:

But there is no more reason for a recovery on the *implied* contract to repay the money than on the *express* contract found in the bonds.

The language of the constitution is that no city, etc., "shall be allowed to become *indebted in any manner or for any purpose* to an amount, including existing indebtedness, in the aggregate exceeding five per centum on the value of its taxable property." It shall not *become indebted.* Shall not incur any pecuniary liability. It shall not do this in *any manner;* neither by bonds, nor notes, nor by express or implied promises. Nor shall it be done for any *purpose;* no matter how urgent, how useful, how unanimous the wish. There stands the existing indebtedness to a given amount in relation to the sources of payment as an impassable obstacle to the creation of any further debt, in any manner, or for any purpose whatever. If this prohibition is worth anything it is as effectual against the implied as the express promise, and is as binding in a court of chancery as a court of law.[80]

Two other cases, although not dealing specifically with bonds, may be cited in this connection. In the case of *Strickler* v. *Consolidated School District No. 1,*[81] bonds issued for the purpose of erecting a

80. *City of Litchfield* v. *Ballou,* 114 U.S. 190, 5 S. Ct. 820, 29 L. Ed. 132. Accord, *Ohio National Life Insurance Company* v. *Board of Education,* 387 Ill. 159, 55 N.E. (2d) 163.

81. *Strickler* v. *Consolidated School District No. 1,* 29 Mo. 136, 291 S.W. 136, 50 A.L.R. 1287.

schoolhouse increased the indebtedness of the district to the legal limit. Owing, however, to the increased cost of materials and labor, the board of directors could not complete the building with the funds in hand. They borrowed money on their personal credit and completed the second story and installed a heating plant. Action was brought for reimbursement, or, if that could not be had, the court was asked to award the second story and heating plant to the directors personally. They proposed to rent the second story and heating plant to the district until the district could legally pay for them. The court denied the relief sought. It held that the directors knew, or should have known, that the district, after the constitutional debt limit had been reached, could not expressly or impliedly undertake to reimburse them for the money advanced to complete the building. Moreover, title to the second story and heating plant could not be vested in the directors, because they could not make use of such property without injury to the building or without prejudice to the rights of the district. Similarly, in the case of *Powell* v. *Bainbridge State Bank*,[82] school trustees had no statutory authority to borrow money. Nevertheless, they borrowed money from a bank to pay the current expenses of the district. The bank, it was held, could not recover from the district the amount loaned.[83]

There are, however, cases which hold that where void bonds are sold and the proceeds arising from such sale are applied to the purposes of the district, the bondholders may recover on *quantum meruit*. That is, under such circumstances, the law will imply a contract, and the bondholders may recover in a court of equity for money had and received.[84] A distinction, however, must be drawn between bonds which are void because *ultra vires* the charter powers of the corporation and bonds which are void because not issued in the manner prescribed. The distinction is between an absolute lack of power and the misuse of a power granted. It is doubtful if any court would hold a district liable even on *quantum meruit* where there was a total lack of power under any circumstance to issue the bonds. But where the

82. *Powell* v. *Bainbridge State Bank*, 161 Ga. 855, 132 S.E. 60.

83. For a contrary decision see *White River School Township* v. *Dorrell*, 26 Ind. App. 538, 59 N.E. 867.

84. *Davis* v. *White*, 171 Ark. 385, 284 S.W. 764; *Geer* v. *School District No. 11*, 111 Fed. 682; *Livingston* v. *School District No. 7*, 11 S.D. 150, 76 N.W. 301. See also *White River School Township* v. *Caxton County*, 34 Ind. App. 8, 72 N.E. 185; *Hoag* v. *Greenwich*, 133 N.Y. 152, 30 N.E. 842; *Bicknell* v. *Widner School Township*, 73 Ind. 501.

invalidity of the bonds grows out of a mere misuse of power, in some jurisdictions a recovery may be had on *quantum meruit.* Thus, in the case of *Geer* v. *School District No. 11,*[85] it was said:

Can the school district, which had ample power to create a general indebtedness for the purpose of erecting school houses, which exercised the power, by voting at an election duly called, to create such indebtedness in the sum of $10,000, which borrowed the money for the purpose of erecting, and with the money so borrowed actually erected, the school house, which it has ever since used and enjoyed, escape payment of the same because, forsooth, it persuaded the lender to unwittingly accept void bonds therefor? In our opinion, it cannot. Any other conclusion would be a sad commentary on the efficiency of courts of justice to do justice.

Similarly, in the case of *Livingston* v. *School District No. 7,*[86] recovery was allowed on *quantum meruit* where a bond was void because issued in excess of the denomination allowed by statute. The court said:

While the doctrine denying relief to all who contract with reference to a subject matter *malum in se* is well recognized, the rule that, where a contract is merely *malum prohibitum,* courts will take notice of circumstances, and in the interest of common honesty grant such relief as justice and equity may require, rests as securely upon principle, and is equally sustained by authority. . . . It would violate the plainest rules of good faith to permit appellant, without any consideration, to retain everything of value received in exchange for a bond executed by itself in a denomination unauthorized; and, while respondent cannot recover upon the instrument, he is entitled to relief against it.

In a case decided by the Supreme Court of Arkansas,[87] the statutes provided that the sale of the bonds should be advertised for twenty days and that bonds should not be sold for less than par. In holding that recovery could be had on bonds sold in disregard of these statutory provisions, the court said:

But these provisions, although mandatory, do not relate to the power of the board of directors to issue the bonds, and if bonds are issued (without collusion or fraud) without compliance with these provisions, the district is estopped, after receiving the proceeds of the bonds and using them, from asserting its own default. . . .
So, here, appellants, had they proceeded before the sale was made, would have been entitled to enjoin the sale of the bonds if they were offered for sale without advertisement or at a price less than par and a reasonable

85. *Geer* v. *School District No. 11,* 111 Fed. 682.

86. *Livingston* v. *School District No. 7,* 11 S.D. 150, 76 N.W. 301.

87. *Davis* v. *White,* 171 Ark. 385, 284 S.W. 764.

brokerage fee. However, they did not do so, and it is now inequitable to grant the relief prayed, that of the cancellation of the bonds, after the district has received and expended their proceeds.

In the federal courts and in Missouri it has been held that bonds issued in excess of the statutory debt limit are wholly void and that no recovery can be had for an amount within the limit of indebtedness.[88] In other jurisdictions, however, the rule is that bonds issued in excess of an amount allowed by law are void as to the excess only.[89] The latter rule seems to be the better one, inasmuch as it has been often held that ordinary contracts in excess of the debt limit are enforcible up to the limit.[90]

SCHOOL-DISTRICT WARRANTS

Warrants are radically different from negotiable bonds. As a rule, they are drawn against some specified fund in actual existence or against funds which will become available at some time during the current fiscal year. They are necessary instruments for carrying on the machinery of school-district administration, but they are not designed as instruments whereby the district may increase its general indebtedness for a period of years. It follows, therefore, that a school district cannot evade the necessity of issuing bonds by issuing long-term interest-bearing warrants.[91] In Nebraska, for example, a school district purchased heating apparatus and in part payment issued an order on September 2, 1889, payable on the first day of March, 1891, with interest at 7 per cent. The court said, in denying a writ of mandamus to pay the order:

88. *Hedges* v. *Dixon County,* 150 U.S. 182, 14 S. Ct. 71, 37 L. Ed. 1044; *Shaw* v. *Independent School District,* 77 Fed. 277; *Thornburgh* v. *School District No. 3,* 175 Mo. 12, 75 S.W. 81.

89. *McKinney* v. *Cadiz Graded Common School District,* 144 Ky. 85, 137 S.W. 839; *Citizens' Bank* v. *City of Terrell,* 78 Tex. 450, 14 S.W. 1003; *Stockdale* v. *School District No. 2,* 47 Mich. 226, 10 N.W. 349.

90. *Anderson* v. *International School District No. 5,* 32 N.D. 413, 156 N.W. 54, L.R.A. 1917E 428, Ann. Cas. 1918A 506; *McGillivray* v. *Joint School District,* 112 Wis. 354, 88 N.W. 310, 58 L.R.A. 100, 88 Am. St. Rep. 969.

91. *Farned* v. *Bolding,* 221 Ala. 217, 128 So. 435; *State* v. *Sabin,* 39 Neb. 570, 58 N.W. 178; *Andrews* v. *School District of City of McCook,* 49 Neb. 420, 68 N.W. 631; *Pomerene* v. *School District No. 56,* 56 Neb. 126, 76 N.W. 414; *Newell* v. *School Directors of District No. 1,* 68 Ill. 514; *Kellogg* v. *School District No. 10,* 13 Okal. 285, 74 Pac. 110; *Board of Public Instruction* v. *Union School Furnishing Company,* 100 Fla. 326, 129 So. 824.

This was, therefore, not a mere order drawn against some fund specified and in existence; it was rather an order payable out of a fund entirely to be provided for in the future. In *School District No. 2, Dixon County* v. *Stough,* 4 Neb. 357, Lake, J., delivering the opinion of this court, said: "Contracts for the erection of a school house should be made with reference to the funds in the treasury for that purpose. The district board have no authority to draw orders in payment thereof on a fund which has been proposed but not raised by taxation." The rule stated is as applicable to orders of the class under consideration as to those referred to in the above opinion; i.e., those for the erection of a school house. . . . If evidences of indebtedness of the nature of that sought to be enforced in this action are to be held valid and binding, it will render wholly inoperative and useless the provisions of the statute regulating and restricting the issuance of bonds by school districts.[92]

School-district warrants, moreover, are not negotiable instruments,[93] nor do they carry with them any of the privileges of negotiable paper except to pass by delivery upon indorsement. The purchaser of such warrants takes them subject to all legal and equitable defenses which existed as to them in the hands of the original payee.[94] There can be no innocent purchaser for value. The courts agree that warrants are mere *prima facie,* and not conclusive, evidence of the validity of the claims against the district by which they were issued. Thus, it has been said by the Supreme Court of Oklahoma:

School warrants are not negotiable paper, and the purchaser or assignee of such paper takes it subject to all defects and defenses. The law prescribes the mode of issuing warrants, and how the school funds shall be appropri-

92. *State* v. *Sabin,* 39 Neb. 570, 58 N.W. 178.

93. *Wright* v. *Kinney,* 123 N.C. 618, 31 S.E. 874; *Goose River Bank* v. *Willow Lake School Township,* 1 N.D. 26, 44 N.W. 1002, 26 Am. St. Rep. 605; *Davis* v. *Steuben School Township,* 19 Ind. App. 694, 50 N.E. 1; *School Directors of District No. 3* v. *Fogleman,* 76 Ill. 189.

94. *Goose River Bank* v. *Willow Lake School Township,* 1 N.D. 26, 44 N.W. 1002, 26 Am. St. Rep. 605; *Crane & Ordway Company* v. *Sykeston School District No. 11,* 36 N.D. 254, 162 N.W. 413; *Kellogg* v. *School District No. 10,* 13 Okla. 285, 74 Pac. 110; *Davis* v. *Steuben School Township,* 19 Ind. App. 694, 50 N.E. 1; *Wright* v. *Kinney,* 123 N.C. 618, 31 S.E. 874; *School Directors of District No. 3* v. *Fogleman,* 76 Ill. 189; *National State Bank* v. *Independent District of Marshall,* 39 Iowa 490; *Boardman* v. *Hayne,* 29 Iowa 339; *State* v. *Melcher,* 87 Neb. 359, 127 N.W. 241; *State* v. *Treasurer of Liberty Township,* 22 Ohio St., 144; *Loan & Exchange Bank* v. *Shealey,* 62 S.C. 337, 40 S.E. 674; *Fine* v. *Stuart,* 48 S.W. (Tenn.) 371; *School District No. 9* v. *First National Bank of Holbrook,* 58 Ariz. 86, 118 Pac. (2d) 78; *Woodward* v. *School District No. 73,* 163 Ore. 63, 94 Pac. (2d) 136; *Lincoln National Bank and Trust Company* v. *School District No. 79,* 124 Neb. 538, 247 N.W. 433; *Velvit Ridge School District No. 91* v. *Bank of Searcy,* 200 Ark. 85, 137 S.W. (2d) 907; *First National Bank of Athens* v. *Murchison Independent School District,* 114 S.W. (2d) (Tex.) 382.

ated, and one who takes a school warrant, for value or otherwise, is required to take notice of all the proceedings of the board leading up to its issue; and, if the warrant has been illegally issued, a taxpayer may enjoin its payment.[95]

In the case of *Goose River Bank* v. *Willow Lake Township*,[96] as an illustration of the rule, a warrant was issued to pay a teacher who had taught without a certificate required by law. In holding that a bank which had purchased the warrant could not recover from the district, the court said in part:

The plaintiff cannot claim protection as an innocent purchaser for value. That such instruments are not negotiable in the sense that their negotiation will cut off defenses is the voice of all the decisions. . . . The purchaser buys at his peril. Nor is the doctrine of estoppel applicable. Could town officers in this manner estop a municipal corporation, void acts—acts void because expressly forbidden by the sovereign—would have validity, and the will of the legislature would be nullified by the conduct or statement of mere municipal agents. . . . No decision can be found holding that a void warrant receives life from the false statement of such an agent, under the circumstances existing in this case. Unless we were willing to leave such corporations to the mercy of dishonest agents, we would not follow such a case could one be found. If an agent can estop the township by a false statement that the teacher has received the certificate, he can estop it also by a false statement that the person to whom the warrant was issued has rendered services in teaching, when in fact such person has not rendered any services at all.

An Illinois case is likewise in point.[97] A statute of that state provided that a schoolhouse could not be built except as authorized by a vote of the people of the district. Directors built a schoolhouse without such vote and issued orders in part payment. The orders were void in the hands of a third party. The purchaser was duty bound to ascertain whether the required vote had been taken.

It has been held, moreover, that school officers are not personally liable on illegal warrants on the ground of legal or constructive fraud. The purchaser of such warrants must safeguard his own interests to the extent of determining whether warrants have been legally issued.[98]

In some jurisdictions it is held that tax anticipation warrants do not create a new debt; they merely change the form of an existing debt.[99] And in Illinois it has been held that tax anticipation warrants do not

95. *Kellogg* v. *School District No. 10*, 13 Okla. 285, 74 Pac. 110.

96. *Goose River Bank* v. *Willow Lake Township*, 1 N.D. 26, 44 N.W. 1002, 26 Am. St. Rep. 605.

97. *School Directors of District No. 3* v. *Foglean*, 76 Ill. 189.

98. *Boardman* v. *Hayne*, 29 Iowa 339.

99. *Jones* v. *Brightwood Independent School District*, 63 N.D. 275, 247 N.W. 884; *Berkeley High School District* v. *Coit*, 55 Pac. (2d) (Calif.) 209.

create an obligation between the school district and the purchaser of the warrants. "The legal effect of the transaction is that the person receiving such warrant discharges the corporation from all liability on account of the services or obligation for which it was drawn." The purchaser of such warrants "must rely solely upon the ability and fidelity of the revenue officers in the collection and payment of the money mentioned in the warrants." Thus a statute authorizing the Board of Education of the City of Chicago to issue bonds in the amount of ten million dollars to pay tax anticipation warrants was declared void, since the bonds would necessitate taxation for a noncorporate purpose. The statute violated the constitutional requirement of due process of law. Moreover, it would impose an unjust burden of double taxation upon those who had already paid their taxes.[100]

In Montana, on the other hand, the court denied the right of a school board to issue bonds to retire tax anticipation warrants for another reason. The warrants, the court reasoned, constituted a debt, and the new bonds, added to the existing debt of the district, would create a debt in excess of the constitutional limit.[101]

DETERMINATION OF THE LIMIT OF INDEBTEDNESS

Since in many states a limit of school-district indebtedness is prescribed by constitution or statute, it is important to know what constitutes indebtedness within the meaning of the law. While there is some conflict among the courts, the general rule is that the restriction is not upon the gross, but upon the net, indebtedness. Gross indebtedness includes the aggregate of all liabilities of whatever nature which may become a legal obligation upon the district, such as bonds,[102] contracts,[103] promissory notes,[104] and interest accrued.[105] From the

100. *Berman v. Board of Education of Chicago,* 360 Ill. 535, 196 N.E. 464, 99 A.L.R. 1029; *Leviton v. Board of Education of City of Chicago,* 374 Ill. 594, 30 N.E. (2d) 497.

101. *Farbo v. School District No. 1,* 95 Mont. 531, 28 Pac. (2d) 455.

102. *School District No. 3 v. Western Tube Company,* 13 Wyo. 304, 80 Pac. 155.

103. *Rettinger v. School Board of City of Pittsburgh,* 266 Pa. St. 67, 109 Atl. 782; *School District No. 3 v. Western Tube Company,* 13 Wyo. 304, 80 Pac. 155; *Anderson v. International School District No. 5,* 32 N.D. 413, 156 N.W. 54, L.R.A. 1917E 428, Ann. Cas. 1918A 506; *Baltimore & Ohio Southwestern Railway Company v. People,* 195 Ill. 423, 63 N.E. 262; *Hampton v. Board of Education,* 195 N.C. 213, 141 S.E. 744.

104. *Rettinger v. School Board of City of Pittsburgh,* 266 Pa. St. 67, 109 Atl. 782; *State v. School Board of Tecumseh Rural High School District No. 4,* 110 Kan. 779, 204 Pac. 742.

105. 24 R.C.L. 611.

gross indebtedness thus arrived at may be deducted cash on hand[106] or in a sinking fund,[107] taxes levied but not collected,[108] property of the district not being used for school purposes,[109] or any other assets available to pay indebtedness. Some courts apply a different rule, but the results are much the same. In determining the indebtedness, they do not include ordinary contracts for current expenses, nor do they deduct cash on hand unless it be in a sinking fund or set aside for the payment of indebtedness, nor do they deduct taxes levied to meet the ordinary expenses for the current year. That is, cash on hand not in a sinking fund and taxes levied to meet current expenses counterbalance contracts for current expenses, neither of which need be considered in determining net indebtedness.[110] Thus contracts with teachers or for rental of a schoolhouse would not be illegal, even though at the time the contracts were entered into the district had reached its limit of indebtedness.[111] Such contracts would be offset by cash on hand and taxes levied to defray current expenses. And some courts have held that contracts for legitimate current expenses do not create an indebtedness, even though taxes have not been levied, the assumption being that they will be levied.[112]

106. *Edwards v. City of Clarkesville,* 35 Ga. App. 306, 133 S.E. 45; *School District No. 3 v. Western Tube Company,* 13 Wyo. 304, 80 Pac. 155; *Anderson v. International School District No. 5,* 32 N.D. 413, 156 N.W. 54, L.R.A. 1917E 428, Ann. Cas. 1918A 506; *Lollich v. Hot Springs Independent School District No. 10,* 47 S.D. 624, 201 N.W. 354; *Dively v. City of Cedar Falls,* 27 Iowa 227.

107. *Reynolds v. Stark,* 90 Okla. 261, 217 Pac. 166; *Rettinger v. School Board of City of Pittsburgh,* 266 Pa. St. 67, 109 Atl. 782; *Cutler v. Board of Education,* 57 Utah 73, 192 Pac. 621; *Farrar v. Britton Independent School District,* 32 N.W. (2d) (Wis.) 627.

108. *Lollich v. Hot Springs Independent School District No. 10,* 47 S.D. 624, 201 N.W. 354; *Rettinger v. School Board of City of Pittsburgh,* 266 Pa. St. 67, 109 Atl. 782; *Edwards v. City of Clarkesville,* 35 Ga. App. 306, 133 S.E. 45; *School District No. 3 v. Western Tube Company,* 13 Wyo. 304, 80 Pac. 155; *Anderson v. International School District No. 5,* 32 N.D. 413, 156 N.W. 54, L.R.A. 1917E 428, Ann. Cas. 1918A 506; *Jones v. Brightwood Independent School District,* 63 N.D. 275, 247 N.W. 884.

109. *School District No. 3 v. Western Tube Company,* 13 Wyo. 304, 80 Pac. 155; *National State Bank v. Independent District of Marshall,* 39 Iowa 490. But see *Threadgill v. Board of Education,* 85 Okla. 121, 204 Pac. 1100.

110. *Cutler v. Board of Education,* 57 Utah 73, 192 Pac. 621; *Little v. Portland,* 26 Ore. 235, 37 Pac. 911. See also *Trepp v. Independent School District of Pocahontas,* 240 N.W. (Iowa) 247.

111. *Edwards v. City of Clarkesville,* 35 Ga. App. 306, 133 S.E. 45; *Grant v. City of Davenport,* 36 Iowa 396; *Little v. Portland,* 26 Ore. 235, 37 Pac. 911.

112. *Edwards v. City of Clarkesville,* 35 Ga. App. 306, 133 S.E. 45; *Grant v. City of Davenport,* 36 Iowa 396; *Wyckoff v. Force,* 61 Calif. App. 246, 214 Pac. 489.

The courts are divided as to whether delinquent taxes may be regarded as assets which may be deducted from gross indebtedness. In some instances it is held that delinquent taxes cannot be regarded as equivalent to cash on hand and therefore are not assets which may be deducted from the gross debt.[113] In other instances they are regarded as deductible assets,[114] at least for a reasonable number of years.

The methods of determining indebtedness may be illustrated by a few concrete examples. In the case of *Rettinger* v. *School Board of the City of Pittsburgh,*[115] the school board contracted for the erection of a schoolhouse for the sum of $4,300. After the house was completed, a warrant was issued for the amount, but it was refused payment on the ground that the contract was in excess of the debt limit. Mr. Justice Frazer, speaking for the Supreme Court of Pennsylvania, said:

> It is further argued that if the $134,000 bond issue is eliminated the school district had nevertheless contracted indebtedness beyond its constitutional limit. The remaining indebtedness is $156,000, to which must be added $3,800, debt represented by an outstanding note for that amount, making a total of $159,800 existing at the time the $4,300 contract in controversy was let, aggregating in all $164,100 of indebtedness, from which must be deducted the sinking fund of $1,583.76, leaving a balance of $162,516.24; deducting from this the borrowing capacity of the board, $150,969.50, there remains $11,546.74 of excess indebtedness to be provided for out of current funds. The rate of school tax for the year 1911 was 6½ mills, which should realize a total school tax of $49,065.12. To this amount should be added the sum of $12,295.67, representing taxes assessed in previous years and collected during 1911, making a total available income of $61,360.79, out of which current running expenses and the additional debt of $11,564.74 must be provided for. We find nothing in the record from which we can accurately determine to what extent this fund was needed for current expenses, and, hence, are unable to state whether the available income at the time the contract in question was made seemed reasonably adequate to take care of the additional obligation. . . . In so far as disclosed by the record the contract when made was within the limit of the current revenues of the school district and so long as the board did not exceed such revenues and such income as may be derived from special taxation, no objection can be made to the creation of the indebtedness. . . . The defendant failed to produce evidence showing current revenues were insufficient to meet the indebtdness and, so far as the record shows, the school board did not violate the constitutional provision requiring it to pay as it goes when certain limits have been overstepped.

113. *Farbo* v. *School District No. 1,* 95 Mont. 531, 28 Pac. (2d) 455; *Mannsville Consolidated School District No. 7* v. *Williamson,* 174 Okla. 18, 49 Pac. (2d) 749.

114. *Ridgeland School District No. 14* v. *Biesmann,* 21 N.W. (2d) (S.D.) 324; *Raynor* v. *King County,* 2 Wash. (2d) 199, 97 Pac. (2d) 696.

115. *Rettinger* v. *School Board of the City of Pittsburgh,* 266 Pa. St. 67, 109 Atl. 782.

The case of *Edwards* v. *City of Clarkesville*[116] illustrates the reasoning of those courts which hold that contracts to meet current expenses do not create an indebtedness. The court said:

A liability of a municipality for a legitimate current expense, where there is at the time of incurring the liability a sufficient sum in the treasury which may be lawfully used to pay the same, or where a sum sufficient to discharge the liability can be raised by taxation during the current year, is not a debt within the meaning of the constitutional provision against the creation of debts by municipalities and other political divisions without due assent of the voters.

To the same effect is the case of *Grant* v. *City of Davenport*,[117] wherein it was said by the Supreme Court of Iowa:

Where the contract made by the municipal corporation pertains to its ordinary expenses, and is, together with other like expenses, within the limit of its current revenues and such special taxes as it may legally, and in good faith intend to levy therefor, such contract does not constitute "the incurring of indebtedness" within the meaning of the constitutional provisions.

Taxes levied for general school purposes cannot be deducted from gross indebtedness unless such indebtedness be made to include all obligations for current expenses. On this point the Supreme Court of Utah has clearly expressed the rule:

The special levy of $39,166.37 for general school purposes for the year 1920, claimed by defendant as an offset to the existing indebtedness of the district, however, presents much greater difficulties. While the levy has been legally made and the collection of the tax may be regarded as a certainty, it is difficult to conceive any theory upon which these taxes may be legally applied for the reduction of the bonded indebtedness complained of by petitioner. Presumably the district, if not already, will be, during the year 1920, under contractual obligations to the amount of this tax for the proper support and maintenance of its public schools. If in theory these taxes may be legally applied in the reduction of the existing bonded indebtedness of the district, then necessarily, to that extent, the district, when said item is so applied, instantaneously becomes indebted in the same amount for general school purposes.[118]

Some courts, however, will not deduct from the gross indebtedness cash in the treasury and uncollected taxes applicable to the payment of indebtedness. Thus it was said by the Supreme Court of Illinois in a leading case:

116. *Edwards* v. *City of Clarkesville*, 35 Ga. App. 306, 133 S.E. 45.
117. *Grant* v. *City of Davenport*, 36 Iowa 396.
118. *Cutler* v. *Board of Education*, 57 Utah 73, 192 Pac. 621.

Upon what principle it is contended that an outstanding debt is not a debt by reason of some cash in the public treasury it is difficult to perceive. As long as the cash is not applied to the payment of the debt the debt must remain. Nor can it be perceived upon what principle uncollected taxes in course of collection can be held to reduce the floating debt until they are actually collected and applied to its reduction.[119]

Similarly, it has been said by the Appellate Court of Indiana: "The law is well settled that money on hand, with which to retire bonds, does not operate to reduce the indebtedness represented by such bonds, and that such bonded indebtedness can only be considered as reduced when the bonds have actually been retired."[120] And in Illinois contracts for ordinary current expenses constitute a debt against which cash on hand and taxes uncollected cannot be set off.[121] Apparently, too, the courts in Montana take the position that current expenses are debts and that uncollected taxes are not deductible assets.[122]

Where contracts are entered into for services to be rendered or goods to be delivered over a period of years, the question arises as to the effect of such contracts upon the indebtedness of the district. If, for example, a district desires to enter into a long-term contract on which the aggregate payments will exceed the amount available from current expenses for the year, does such a contract violate a statutory provision prohibiting the district from incurring an indebtedness in excess of the current revenues? In other words, is the indebtedness increased by an amount equal to the aggregate payments to be spread over a number of years or only by the amount which will fall due annually or at stated intervals? The weight of authority is to the effect that contracts of the kind here under consideration do not create a debt[123] equal to the amount to be paid in the aggregate. The debt in-

119. *City of Chicago* v. *McDonald,* 176 Ill. 404. 52 N.E. 982. Accord, *Wabash Railroad Company* v. *People,* 202 Ill. 9, 66 N.E. 824.

120. *Angola Brick & Tile Company* v. *Millgrove School Township,* 73 Ind. App. 557, 127 N.E. 855.

121. *Springfield* v. *Edwards,* 84 Ill. 626.

122. *Farbo* v. *School District No. 1,* 95 Mont. 531, 28 Pac. (2d) 455.

123. *Walla Walla* v. *Walla Walla Water Company,* 172 U.S. 1, 19 S. Ct. 77, 43 L. Ed. 341; *Wyckoff* v. *Force,* 61 Calif. App. 246, 214 Pac. 489; *Smilie* v. *Fresno,* 112 Calif. 311, 44 Pac. 556; *Posz* v. *Taylor,* 61 Calif. App. 523, 215 Pac. 107; *Toomey* v. *The City of Bridgeport,* 79 Conn. 229, 64 Atl. 215; *Allison* v. *City of Chester,* 69 W. Va. 533, 72 S.E. 472, 37 L.R.A. (N.S.) 1042, Ann. Cas. 1913B 1174; *Crowder* v. *Sullivan,* 128 Ind. 486, 28 N.E. 94, 13 L.R.A. 647; *Laporte* v. *Gamewell Fire Alarm Telegraph Company,* 146 Ind. 466, 45 N.E. 588, 35 L.R.A. 686, 58 Am. St. Rep. 359; *Giles* v. *Dennison,* 15 Okla. 55, 78 Pac. 174; *Protsman* v. *Jefferson-Craig Consolidated School Corporation,* 109 N.E. (2d) (Ind.) 889; *Jefferson School Township* v. *Jefferson Township School Building Company,* 212 Ind. 542, 10 N.E. (2d) 608.

creases as each instalment becomes due and only to that extent,[124] or, as is held by some courts, by the amount to be paid annually or at stated intervals.[125] Thus it was said by the Supreme Court of Errors of Connecticut:

> There is a clear distinction between the expenditure of a sum or the making of a contract creating a present indebtedness for a sum, during any one year, in excess of the revenues or appropriations for that year, and a contract stipulating for the payment of annual sums creating an annual indebtedness for several years, the aggregate amount of which payments or debts would exceed the revenue or appropriation for any one year; but no one of which annual payments or debts would exceed the revenue or appropriation for the year in which it was to be made or incurred. Such restrictions in municipal charters upon the expenditures of each year as those contained in the one before us, are not to be construed as prohibiting municipalities from making contracts for a reasonable term of years for usual and necessary things and stipulating therein for annual payments which will be within the revenue and appropriations for the several years in which they are to be made, and when it is for the best interests of the municipalities that such contracts should be made.[126]

In Kentucky, however, it has been held that a contract for services to be rendered over a period of years creates an indebtedness equal to the total aggregate payment. Thus, where a county board of education agreed to pay $3,000 annually for a period of five years for the privilege of sending pupils in the county district to a city high school, it incurred an indebtedness of $15,000.[127]

A school district cannot, of course, contract for the construction of a schoolhouse and issue warrants therefor, payable annually, where the aggregate amount of the warrants is greater than the indebtedness permitted by law.[128] The fact that the debt is to be paid in instalments does not lessen it. Nor may a school district rent a schoolhouse for a number of years at a stipulated price on the condition that the title to

124. *Wyckoff* v. *Force*, 61 Calif. App. 246, 214 Pac. 489; *Smilie* v. *Fresno*, 112 Calif. 311, 44 Pac. 556; *Allison* v. *City of Chester*, 69 W. Va. 533, 72 S.E. 472, 37 L.R.A. (N.S.) 1042, Ann. Cas. 1913B 1174; *Laporte* v. *Gamewell Fire Alarm Telegraph Company*, 146 Ind. 466, 45 N.E. 588, 35 L.R.A. 686, 58 Am. St. Rep. 359. Note: 37 L.R.A. (N.S.) 1066.

125. *McBean* v. *City of Fresno*, 112 Calif. 159, 44 Pac. 358, 31 L.R.A. 794, 53 Am. St. Rep. 191.

126. *Toomey* v. *The City of Bridgeport*, 79 Conn. 229, 64 Atl. 215.

127. *Board of Education of Hopkinsville Public Schools* v. *Board of Trustees*, 154 Ky. 309, 157 S.W. 697; *Davis* v. *Board of Education*, 260 Ky. 294, 83 S.W. (2d) 34; *Fiscal Court of Jackson County* v. *Board of Education of Jackson County*, 268 Ky. 336, 104 S.W. (2d) 1103.

128. *Territory of Oklahoma* v. *Board of Trustees*, 13 Okla. 605.

the house be transferred to the district at the end of the rental period, where the aggregate of the so-called rents exceeds the indebtedness incurrable at the date of the making of the contract.[129]

There is some conflict among the courts as to whether refunding bonds increase the debt of a school district. Some courts, among them the Supreme Court of the United States, hold that such bonds do increase the indebtedness.[130] According to the weight of authority, however, refunding bonds do not create an indebtedness; they merely change the form of the debt.[131] All the courts hold that there is no increase of indebtedness by an exchange of new obligations for old.[132] Those courts which hold that refunding bonds increase the debt of the district reason that for a short interval between the sale of the new bonds and the retirement of the old the debt is necessarily increased. Such a position seems untenable, because, during the interval between sale and retirement of bonds, the district has in its treasury cash equal to the value of the refunding bonds. A district can scarcely be said to be indebted in the legal sense when it has in its treasury cash with which to meet its obligations. Instead of the debt's being doubled, as is held by the Supreme Court of the United States, it has only changed its form, the cash derived from the sale of the refunding bonds being an asset to offset the liability of either the old or the new bonds.[133]

129. *Billings* v. *Bankers' Bond Company*, 199 Ky. 490, 251 S.W. 643.

130. *Doon Township* v. *Cummins*, 142 U.S. 366, 12 S. Ct. 220, 35 L. Ed. 1044; *Holliday* v. *Hildebrandt*, 97 Iowa 177, 66 N.W. 89; *State* v. *Ross*, 43 Wash. 290, 86 Pac. 575.

131. *Ewert* v. *Mallery*, 16 S.D. 151, 91 N.W. 479; *National Life Insurance Company* v. *Mead*, 13 S.D. 37, 82 N.W. 78, 48 L.R.A. 785, 79 Am. St. Rep. 876; *Everett* v. *Independent School District of Rock Rapids*, 109 Fed. 697; *City of Hogansville* v. *Farrell Heating & Plumbing Company*, 161 Ga. 780, 132 S.E. 436; *Miller* v. *School District No. 3*, 5 Wyo. 217, 39 Pac. 879; *Fairfield* v. *Rural Independent School District*, 116 Fed. 838; *Lancaster City School District* v. *Lamprecht Brothers Company*, 198 Pa. St. 504, 48 Atl. 434; *Jamison* v. *Independent School District of Rock Rapids*, 90 Fed. 387; *Wilson* v. *Board of Education*, 226 Ky. 476, 11 S.W. (2d) 143; *Abbott* v. *Oldham County Board of Education*, 272 Ky. 654, 114 S.W. (2d) 1128; *Southeast Securities Company* v. *Board of Education*, 40 N.M. 59, 54 Pac. (2d) 412; *Kansas City Life Insurance Company* v. *Evangeline Parish School Board*, 58 F. (2d) 39; *State* v. *Smith*, 343 Mo. 288, 121 S.W. (2d) 160.

132. *Taylor* v. *School District of Garfield*, 97 Fed. 753. NOTE: 37 L.R.A. (N.S.) 1099.

133. For an able discussion of this question see *National Life Insurance Company* v. *Mead*, 13 S.D. 37, 82 N.W. 78, 48 L.R.A. 785, 79 Am. St. Rep. 876. See also NOTE: 37 L.R.A. (N.S.) 1099.

Constitutional and statutory provisions restricting the power of school districts to incur indebtedness apply only to indebtedness created by voluntary acts or contracts of the district; they do not apply to involuntary obligations or to obligations imposed by law.[134] In California, for example, the statutes provided that certain common-school districts might be annexed to high-school districts. In the case of *People* v. *San Bernardino High School District*[135] it was contended that such an annexation could not take place because it would operate to increase the debt of the common-school district beyond the limit of legal indebtedness. The court, however, held that the restrictive provisions of the constitution did not apply to debts imposed by law. It said:

In order that one may "incur" a debt or a liability one must necessarily perform some act or take some action—in other words, one must do something that will have the effect of bringing upon one's self the debt or liability. In the instant case it cannot be said that the Highland school district did anything by which any indebtedness or liability was incurred against it. If any debt or liability was created as against the Highland school district, it was one which was not of its own choosing or making, but was thrust upon it primarily by the board of supervisors of San Bernardino county, and secondarily by operation of law. The cases are numerous which announce the principle that in such circumstances there is no infraction of the constitutional provision to which reference has been made.

It follows, of course, that judgments against a school district are not void on the ground that they create a debt in excess of the legal limit of indebtedness.[136] The judgment is not itself a debt, but merely a recognition of a pre-existing debt. Thus it was said by Mr. Justice Deemer, speaking for the Supreme Court of Iowa:

It is contended that the judgment in favor of Edmundson is void, because it creates an indebtedness against the school district in excess of the limitation fixed by the constitution (section 3, art. 11) upon the indebtedness of municipal and political corporations. This contention is based upon the

134. *People* v. *San Bernadino High School District*, 62 Calif. App. 67, 216 Pac. 959; *School District of Pittson Township* v. *School District of Borough of Dupont*, 275 Pa. St. 183, 118 Atl. 308; *Independent School District No. 12* v. *Manning*, 32 Idaho 512, 185 Pac. 723; *Thompson* v. *Independent School District of Allison*, 102 Iowa 94, 70 N.W. 1093; *Edmundson* v. *Independent School District of Jackson*, 98 Iowa 639, 67 N.W. 671, 60 Am. St. Rep. 224; *City of Houston* v. *Tod*, 258 S.W. (Tex.) 839.

135. *People* v. *San Bernardino High School District*, 62 Calif. App. 67, 216 Pac. 959.

136. *Edmundson* v. *Independent School District of Jackson*, 98 Iowa 639, 67 N.W. 671, 60 Am. St. Rep. 224; *Thompson* v. *Independent School District of Allison*, 102 Iowa 94, 70 N.W. 1093.

thought that the obtaining of the judgment was the creation of the debt. Manifestly, this is not true. The judgment is simply evidence—conclusive evidence—of a pre-existing debt, which had been created prior to the time the court rendering it was called upon to act. If the indebtedness which had previously been created was in excess of the constitutional limit, this was a matter which the defendants should have pleaded in defense to the action brought to recover the amount due.[137]

In order to determine whether a debt limit has been exceeded, one must know the exact date when the indebtedness was incurred. It has been held that bonds in excess of the constitutional debt limit at the time of the election authorizing them were void, even though they did not exceed the debt limit at the time of sale.[138] As a general rule, however, the indebtedness is not incurred until the bonds are issued and sold.[139] The financial status of the district at the time the bonds are voted is of no consequence in this connection, for the amount of indebtedness which may be incurred is controlled, not by the assessment next before the election at which the bonds were authorized, but by the assessment next before the issuance and sale of the bonds.[140] Thus it was said by the Supreme Court of Oklahoma:

When is the indebtedness incurred? Obviously, when the obligations by which the district is bound are issued and value received for them. There is no indebtedness until the money is received by the district. The money is not received until the bonds are issued, approved as required by law, and delivered to the purchasers.

Where a vote is required, the validity of bonds issued pursuant to such vote is to be determined by the last assessment of the property before the bonds are issued, not the last assessment before they are voted or directed to be issued.[141]

In the case of *Sutherland* v. *Board of Education*,[142] for example, bonds were voted greatly in excess of the debt limit, but, before all the bonds were issued and sold some two years later, the assessed valuation of the district had so increased as to bring the bonds within

137. *Edmundson* v. *Independent School District of Jackson*, 98 Iowa 639, 67 N.W. 671, 60 Am. St. Rep. 224.

138. *State* ex rel. *Consolidated District* v. *Holmes*, 362 Mo. 1018, 245 S.W. (2d) 882.

139. *Sutherland* v. *Board of Education*, 209 Ky. 351, 272 S.W. 887; *Mistler* v. *Eye*, 107 Okla. 289, 231 Pac. 1045.

140. *Sutherland* v. *Board of Education*, 209 Ky. 351, 272 S.W. 887; *Mistler* v. *Eye*, 107 Okla. 289, 231 Pac. 1045; *Board of Education* v. *National Life Insurance Company*, 94 Fed. 324.

141. *Mistler* v. *Eye*, 107 Okla. 289, 231 Pac. 1045.

142. *Sutherland* v. *Board of Education*, 209 Ky. 351, 272 S.W. 887.

the limit of indebtedness. The court held that the bonds had been legally issued.

At times school districts with different functions occupy the same or overlapping boundaries. In such cases the general rule is that, in determining the debt limit, only the indebtedness of the unit in question can be considered. The debts of the other units should be excluded. Thus if an elementary district lies wholly within the territory of a high-school district, the debt of the latter would not be considered in determining the debt of the former.[143] So, too, debt limits apply to corporate entities and not the specific property. Thus where districts are consolidated and bonds are voted to pay the outstanding debts of the old districts, the bonds will not be declared void, even though the property in one of the old districts would be subject to debt in excess of the statutory debt limit.[144] It has been held, however, that debt-limit restrictions apply to specific territory as well as to corporate entities. Thus in Wyoming a school district embraced all the territory of another district and some additional territory as well. The court held that the total indebtedness of the two districts could not exceed the constitutional debt limit. It should be pointed out, however, that the statute in this case authorizing school districts to issue bonds provided that the bonds should not increase the indebtedness of the territory of the districts affected.[145]

143. *House* v. *School District No. 4,* 120 Mont. 319, 184 Pac. (2d) 285. Accord, *Board of Education* v. *Upham,* 357 Ill. 263, 191 N.E. 876; *Fall* v. *Read,* 194 Ky. 135, 238 S.W. 177; *Straw* v. *Harris,* 54 Ore. 424, 103 Pac. 777.

144. *Huffman* v. *School Board of Independent Consolidated School District,* 230 Minn. 289, 41 N.W. (2d) 455.

145. *Ericksen* v. *School District No. 2,* 67 Wyo. 216, 217 Pac. (2d) 887.

CHAPTER XII

Acquisition and Use of School Property

AUTHORITY TO ACQUIRE SCHOOL SITES

As a rule, the statutes specifically authorize school boards to acquire building sites. Such specific grant of authority is not essential, however, for authority to construct buildings necessarily carries with it authority to buy sites.[1] As an illustration, in West Virginia, bonds were voted to build a number of schoolhouses. The board did not own ground suitable for sites and was of the opinion that it could not use proceeds from the bonds to purchase sites. Hence it delayed action. A writ of mandamus was sought to compel the board to purchase lots and proceed with the buildings. The court issued the writ.

When the statute says that money may be used to build houses, it means it may be used to acquire land for school houses. Necessarily so. It is a necessary implication, if the words do not *per se* mean land, as here used. Commanded to build school houses, it is an incidental power because indispensable to attain the end. You cannot build a school house without land on which to build it.[2]

Moreover, authority to purchase a school site carries with it authority to purchase the necessary playgrounds and athletic fields,[3] and these do not necessarily have to be adjacent to the lot upon which the school building is located.[4]

In the case of *Reiger* v. *Board of Education*,[5] a statute authorized the board of education to "buy or lease sites for school houses with the necessary grounds." The board purchased land for an athletic

1. *Board of Directors* v. *Ruston State Bank*, 133 La. 109, 62 So. 492; *State* v. *Board of Education*, 71 W. Va. 52, 76 S.E. 127, Ann. Cas. 1914B 1238; *Sorenson* v. *Christiansen*, 72 Wash. 16, 129 Pac. 577.

2. *State* v. *Board of Education*, 71 W. Va. 52, 76 S.E. 127, Ann. Cas. 1914B 1238.

3. *Board of Education* v. *Woodworth*, 89 Okla. 192, 214 Pac. 1077; *State* v. *Superior Court*, 69 Wash. 189, 124 Pac. 484; *Reiger* v. *Board of Education*, 287 Ill. 590, 122 N.E. 838.

4. *Reiger* v. *Board of Education*, 287 Ill. 590, 122 N.E. 838.

5. *Reiger* v. *Board of Education*, 287 Ill. 590, 122 N.E. 838.

field two blocks away from the school building. Its authority to do so was challenged. It was contended that the authority to purchase necessary grounds could be exercised only in connection with the buying of sites for schoolhouses and that the necessary grounds must be a part of a school site and contiguous to it. The court held that the board had authority to purchase the athletic field, notwithstanding the fact that it was not contiguous to the school site.

It has been held, however, that a school board cannot, without specific statutory authority, issue bonds for the purchase of land for an agricultural farm to be used for demonstration purposes.[6] The court based its opinion upon the familiar principle that laws authorizing taxation are construed strictly. The counsel for the board argued that inasmuch as the teaching of the principles of agriculture was required by law, the board had the implied power to provide a farm for laboratory purposes. This the court was not willing to concede:

> At first blush this argument appears to be strong, if not conclusive; but upon consideration it is found to be misleading, and to have the fatal defect of proving too much. For if authority to teach the principles of agriculture carried with it authority to establish and operate an agricultural farm, by the same token the authority which is given in the said same act 306 of 1910 to teach "horticulture and home and farm economy" would carry with it authority to establish and operate a farm for instruction in horticulture and a model home for instruction in home economy. Nay, zoology is taught in the high school, and therefore a zoo might be provided and maintained. The time may come when these extensions will be included in our public school system, but it has not yet arrived.

ACCEPTANCE OF DONATIONS

It is familiar doctrine that a school district or a municipality may accept and hold in trust property to be used for public school purposes.[7] In order for a dedication to be valid, it is not necessary that it be reduced to written form. "An express dedication may be made orally, when the use is inaugurated or while it is being enjoyed."[8] Moreover, property may be dedicated for public school purposes, even though there may not be in existence a corporation in which to vest the title or trust.[9] "The public is an ever-existing grantee, capable of

6. *Hemler* v. *Richland Parish School Board,* 142 La. 133, 76 So. 585.

7. *Vestal* v. *Pickering,* 125 Ore. 553, 267 Pac. 821.

8. *Hill* v. *Houk,* 155 Ala. 448, 46 So. 562. See also 13 Cyc. 453.

9. *Normal School-District No. 3* v. *Painter,* 102 Mo. 464, 14 S.W. 938, 10 L.R.A. 493; *Potter* v. *Chapin,* 6 Paige (N.Y.) 639.

taking a dedication for public uses."[10] Thus a dedication may consist of declarations made directly to the public.[11] Where property has been accepted for the use of a public corporation such as a school district, it is the general rule that it must be perpetually administered in accordance with the express wish of the testator. If a diversion is attempted, a court of equity may be called upon to intervene and, if necessary, to name a new trustee to carry out the objects and purposes of the trust.[12]

ACQUISITION OF PROPERTY BY EMINENT DOMAIN

The right to take private property for a public use is an attribute of sovereignty.[13] Such right lies dormant in the state, however, "until legislative action points out the occasions, the modes, and the agencies for its exercise."[14] A board of education cannot, therefore, exercise the right of eminent domain unless expressly authorized to do so by statute.[15]

It would be unconstitutional for the legislature to authorize the taking of property for any but a public use. The courts all seem agreed, however, that the taking of land for a schoolhouse site constitutes the taking of it for such a public use as the law requires.[16] Moreover, authority to acquire land for a schoolhouse site carries with it, by implication, authority to acquire land to be used as playgrounds,[17] as an athletic field,[18] or as a site for a gymnasium.[19]

10. *Normal School-District No. 3* v. *Painter,* 102 Mo. 464, 14 S.W. 938, 10 L.R.A. 493.

11. *Hill* v. *Houk,* 155 Ala. 448, 46 So. 562.

12. *Maxcy* v. *City of Oshkosh,* 144 Wis. 238, 128 N.W. 899, 31 L.R.A. (N.S.) 787.

13. *Lazarus* v. *Morris,* 212 Pa. St. 128, 61 Atl. 815.

14. *Lazarus* v. *Morris,* 212 Pa. St. 128, 61 Atl. 815.

15. *Lazarus* v. *Morris,* 212 Pa. St. 128, 61 Atl. 815; *Dean* v. *County Board of Education,* 210 Ala. 256, 97 So. 741; *Thompson* v. *Trustees of Schools,* 218 Ill. 540; *School District of Columbia* v. *Jones,* 229 Mo. 510, 129 S.W. 705.

16. *Long* v. *Fuller,* 68 Pa. St. 170; *Board of Education* v. *Hackman,* 48 Mo. 243; *Williams* v. *School District No. 6,* 33 Vt. 271; *Richland School Township* v. *Overmyer,* 164 Ind. 382, 73 N.E. 811.

17. *Independent School District of Oakland* v. *Hewitt,* 105 Iowa 663, 75 N.W. 497; *Cousens* v. *School District No. 4,* 67 Me. 280; *State* v. *Superior Court,* 69 Wash. 189, 124 Pac. 484; *City of Binghamton* v. *Buono,* 208 N.Y.S. 60, 124 Misc. Rep. 203.

18. *State* v. *Superior Court,* 69 Wash. 189, 124 Pac. 484.

19. *Sorenson* v. *Christiansen,* 72 Wash. 16, 129 Pac. 577.

The determination of just what land shall be taken and of the amount necessary to be taken is usually vested by statute in the school authorities. Their determination of the matter constitutes an exercise of discretion which will not be controlled by the courts unless abused. That is, the expediency or necessity of taking a particular piece of land is not a matter to be reviewed by a commission or jury.[20] Thus it was said by the Supreme Court of Colorado:

School districts are empowered to take and hold so much real estate as may be necessary for the location and construction of a schoolhouse and convenient use of the school, not in excess of one acre. . . . The question of the location of a school site, and the necessity of taking land therefor, not in excess of one acre, is vested entirely in the school authorities of a district, and the necessities of the district in this respect are not questions for a commission or a jury to determine.[21]

Where property is acquired by eminent domain, it is necessary, of course, that the owner be justly compensated; the taking of property without just compensation would be unconstitutional, in that it would be taking property without due process of law. The fair market value of the land is the measure of compensation to be awarded to the owner.[22] In determining the fair market value, consideration should be given to all the uses to which the land could profitably be put, and the awards should be based upon the most profitable use.[23] Where only a part of the owner's land is taken, the award of compensation should include the depreciation of the value of the land not taken.[24] In other words, the owner is entitled to compensation for such loss as he sustains, whether the loss be the result of the taking of property or of depreciation of the value of property not taken.

Where a school board has taken land by the exercise of the right of eminent domain and later ceases to use the land for school purposes, the question may arise as to the proper disposition of the land. May the board sell the land and apply the proceeds to school purposes, or does the land revert to the original owner? Since the right to take property by eminent domain rests upon considerations of public necessity, it follows that no more land should be taken than public necessity

20. *Richland School Township* v. *Overmyer*, 164 Ind. 382, 73 N.E. 811; *Kirkwood* v. *School District No. 7*, 45 Colo. 368, 101 Pac. 343.

21. *Kirkwood* v. *School District No. 7*, 45 Colo. 368, 101 Pac. 343.

22. *Sargent* v. *Town of Merrimac*, 196 Mass. 171, 81 N.E. 970; 10 R.C.L. 128.

23. 10 R.C.L. 130. Note: 12 L.R.A. 611.

24. Note: 48 L.R.A. (N.S.) 488.

requires. Such is the case with respect to the amount of land to be taken and with respect to the fee to be taken. Where an easement is sufficient, the fee remains in the original owner. As a rule, therefore, where land is taken for school purposes, the fee remains in the owner; the school district may use the land for school purposes, but when it ceases to do so the land reverts to the original owner or to his heirs.[25] Certainly the district does not take fee-simple title to the land unless authorized to do so by statute.[26] On this point, it has been said by the Supreme Court of Pennsylvania:

> The grantee takes what the act gives, and no more. If the act gives an absolute estate, and compensation is provided on this basis the whole title may be acquired. If it only gives the right to use and occupy, the grantee only takes a conditional fee or easement, terminable on the abandonment of the use for which the land was appropriated. The appropriation of land under power of eminent domain does not give a fee simple estate therein, in the absence of express statutory language to that effect, but only a right to use and occupy the land for the purpose for which it is taken.[27]

As a rule, a school board cannot appropriate to its uses land already being used for other public purposes. Thus it has been held that school authorities cannot take by eminent domain a public square,[28] or a part of a county poorhouse farm.[29] On the other hand, it has been held in a number of cases that school lands may be taken for public highways.[30] Where land is needed for two or more public uses, it would seem that the use for which there is the greatest public necessity should prevail. No doubt this is the position the courts would take in any particular case.

AUTHORITY TO SELECT SITES

In some jurisdictions the statutes vest in the electors of the district the authority to select the schoolhouse site. Where this is the case, the procedure prescribed by statute must be followed strictly. Failure, for example, to post the notices required by statute will render void an

25. *Lazarus* v. *Morris*, 212 Pa. St. 128, 61 Atl. 815; *Mulligan* v. *School District of Hanover Township*, 241 Pa. St. 204, 88 Atl. 362.

26. *Mulligan* v. *School District of Hanover Township*, 241 Pa. St. 204, 88 Atl. 362; *Superior Oil Company* v. *Harsh*, 39 F. Supp. 467.

27. *Lazarus* v. *Morris*, 212 Pa. St. 128, 61 Atl. 815.

28. *McCullough* v. *Board of Education*, 51 Calif. 418.

29. *Tyrone Township School District's Appeal*, 1 Monag. (Pa.) 20, 15 Atl. 667.

30. *Rominger* v. *Simmons*, 88 Ind. 453.

election held to select a schoolhouse site.[31] If the authority to designate the site is vested by statute in the electors, they cannot delegate that duty to the trustees or school board.[32]

In most states authority to select the schoolhouse site is vested in the board of education. Frequently, the selection made by the board is not satisfactory to a portion of the electors, and an attempt is made to enjoin the erection of a schoolhouse on the site selected. Where a school board, in the selection of a site, exercises in good faith the discretion vested in it by statute, the courts will not overrule that discretion unless it has been abused.[33] If, on the other hand, the discretion has been abused, if the board has not acted in good faith or for the public good, the courts will interfere and enjoin the act undertaken.[34]

The rule has been well stated by the Supreme Court of Pennsylvania in the case of *Gemmell* v. *Fox*,[35] which was an action to enjoin the selection of a new site:

It is to be presumed, however, in the absence of anything to the contrary, that the school directors are acting within the limits of the discretion with which they are entrusted. The power of the courts to interfere with school directors in the performance of their duties is exceedingly limited; and they are permitted to interfere only where it is made apparent that it is not discretion that is being exercised but arbitrary will or caprice. Discretion involves the exercise of judgment incidental to the proper performance of the duty delegated. When the contention is that the proposed action is unwise, no matter by what consensus of opinion it is shown, the law will refer it to

31. *Bierbaum* v. *Smith*, 317 Ill. 147, 147 N.E. 796; *Roberts* v. *Eyman*, 304 Ill. 413, 136 N.E. 736.

32. *Benjamin* v. *Hull*, 17 Wend. (N.Y.) 437; *Farmers' and Merchants' National Bank of Valley City* v. *School District No. 53*, 6 Dak. 255, 42 N.W. 767.

33. *Roth* v. *Marshall*, 158 Pa. St. 272, 27 Atl. 945; *Gemmell* v. *Fox*, 241 Pa. St. 146, 88 Atl. 426; *Lamb* v. *Redding*, 234 Pa. St. 481, 83 Atl. 362; *Reams* v. *McMinnville*, 153 Tenn. 408, 284 S.W. 382; *State* v. *Watson*, 39 S.W. (Tenn.) 536; *State* v. *Board of Education*, 11 Ohio App. 146; *Venable* v. *School Committee*, 149 N.C. 120, 62 S.E. 902; *Crist* v. *Brownsville Township*, 10 Ind. 461; *Hufford* v. *Herrold*, 189 Iowa 853, 179 N.W. 53; *Chipstead* v. *Oliver*, 137 Ga. 483, 73 S.E. 576; *McInnish* v. *Board of Education*, 187 N.C. 494, 122 S.E. 182; *Sarratt* v. *Cash*, 103 S.C. 531, 88 S.E. 256; *Jennings* v. *Clearwater School District*, 65 Calif. App. 102, 223 Pac. 84; *Vaughn* v. *McCartney*, 217 Ala. 103, 115 So. 30; *Spaulding* v. *Campbell County Board of Education*, 239 Ky. 277, 39 S.W. (2d) 490; *State* v. *Spokane*, 147 Wash. 467, 266 Pac. 189.

34. *Roth* v. *Marshall*, 158 Pa. St. 272, 27 Atl. 945; *Gemmell* v. *Fox*, 241 Pa. St. 146; 88 Atl. 426; *Lamb* v. *Redding*, 234 Pa. St. 481, 83 Atl. 362; *Iverson* v. *Union Free High School District*, 186 Wis. 342, 202 N.W. 788; *Phelps* v. *Witt*, 304 Ky. 473, 201 S.W. (2d) 4.

35. *Gemmell* v. *Fox*, 241 Pa. St. 146, 88 Atl. 426.

mistaken judgment over which it has no supervision. But if it cannot be so referred, if the facts admit of no other conclusion than that the determination of the board has been influenced by other considerations than the public interests, no matter what these may have been, the law will regard it as an abuse of power, and disregard of duty, and it becomes the duty of the courts to interfere for the protection of the public.

The following cases are illustrations of what constitutes abuse of discretion. In the case of *Gemmell* v. *Fox*,[36] the evidence showed that one additional room would take care of the needs of the district for a number of years. A taxpayer offered to donate to the district a lot adjoining the school property. There was no valid reason why the old site should be abandoned. The board, however, undertook to purchase a site some 800 feet distant from the old site. There were coal beds underneath the lot proposed to be acquired, and the corporation owning the coal was without responsibility to support the surface. To purchase this site and to protect the surface would have required from $5,000 to $7,000. In view of the facts, the court held that the determination of the board to acquire the new site was influenced by other considerations than the public interest. Hence, to acquire it would have been an abuse of discretion.

In the case of *Lamb* v. *Redding*,[37] a school board had purchased a school site at a cost of $17,500. In erecting a building to the height of the first floor, they spent an additional $52,000. A new board was elected and proposed to abandon the site so chosen and improved, to purchase another at a cost of $27,000, and to erect thereon a building estimated to cost, when completed, $125,000. All that could be realized from the sale of the old site and the unfinished building was $10,000. The new board sought to justify its action on the following considerations: it was doubtful if the foundations constructed on the old site were sufficient to support the contemplated structure; to complete the building upon which work had been begun would open the door to claims for work done or materials furnished which in equity and good conscience ought not to be paid; and, finally, it rested wholly in the discretion of the board to say whether the change should be made. After pointing out that the evidence showed conclusively that the foundations were entirely adequate and that whatever rights

36. *Gemmell* v. *Fox*, 241 Pa. St. 146, 88 Atl. 426.

37. *Lamb* v. *Redding*, 234 Pa. St. 481, 83 Atl. 362.

might have existed at the time the work was stopped continued to exist, the court took up the question of the right of the board to exercise its discretion. While not disposed to interfere with the exercise of discretion on the part of a school board, the court felt that in this case discretion had been abused. School boards, it was said, cannot exercise arbitrary will or caprice in the name of discretion:

If it appeared that the proposed abandonment of the present site was demanded because of its inadequacy, or because of considerations affecting the public health, or because the adoption of a new site would result in advantages bearing some reasonable proportion to the expenditure required, or that there was reasonable ground for difference of opinion with respect to these matters, the court would be without jurisdiction to interfere with the determination of the board as to its line of action. . . . We should sustain the school board in the present contention if the evidence left us at all in doubt, not as to the wisdom of their policy, for that is no concern of ours, but as to whether that policy was determined upon by public considerations alone. Unfortunately it does not, but is convincing that public interests have been subordinated if not wholly ignored.

The Supreme Court of North Carolina, on the other hand, refused to enjoin the erection of a schoolhouse on a new site, even though it was shown that a railroad track adjoined the lot, that an electric power line had been constructed over part of the lot, and a cotton gin was situated near the proposed site. The board had not abused its discretion. "In our jurisprudence," said the court, "the principle is established that in the absence of gross abuse the courts will not undertake to direct or control the discretion conferred by law upon a public officer."[38] Similarly, the Supreme Court of Pennsylvania held that directors had not abused their discretion in selecting a site on which the right to enter and mine coal was reserved. Moreover, the site was bounded on three sides by much-traveled roads and was subject to an easement for maintaining gas mains across it.[39]

According to the weight of authority, a school board does not exhaust its discretion by a single exercise of it. Even though a site may have been selected, the board, acting in good faith, may change its mind and select another. Where, for instance, a board had selected a site but later decided to build upon another site which had been donated, the court held that it had a right to rescind its former ac-

38. *McInnish* v. *Board of Education,* 187 N.C. 494, 122 S.E. 182.
39. *Gilfillan* v. *Fife,* 266 Pa. St. 171, 109 Atl. 785.

tion, since no rights to third parties had intervened.[40] In a Tennessee case,[41] the board had authority to select a site but, inasmuch as there was some division of opinion in the district, submitted the matter to the voters. A majority of the voters expressed a preference for the so-called Reams lot and it was purchased at a cost of $75,000. Thereafter the lot which had received the second highest number of votes was donated to the district as a school site, and the board decided to build upon it. Action was brought for an injunction to restrain the board from erecting the building, it being claimed that the board, having once exercised its discretion by selecting the Reams lot, was without power or discretion to change the location to some other lot. The court held otherwise and denied the injunction. Moreover, a board cannot limit its freedom to exercise discretion by entering into formal or informal understandings with the public. If a board is to exercise discretion, it must, in the very nature of things, be free to act as it honestly thinks best at the time when final action is taken. Where, for example, bonds are voted on the understanding that the school building is to be erected on a particular site, the board may build on another site if it seems desirable to do so.[42] In the case of *Sarratt* v. *Cash*[43] the facts were as follows. There was a demand for a new building to accommodate the children attending school in the west end of the town of Gaffeney; a committee, appointed to secure the necessary petition for a bond election, represented to the electors that the new building would be erected in the west end of the town; the bond issue was carried, it was alleged, because of these representations; after the bonds were sold, the board decided to erect the building near the center of the town. The court held that the board was not bound by any representations which might have been made. The law vested in the board the duty to exercise discretion and judgment as to the best place to locate the school. This duty was continuing and inalienable; the board could not divest themselves by promises and understandings of the right to a free and untrammeled exercise of their judgment and discretion for the best interest of the district at the time they were required to act as a

40. *Hasbrouck* v. *School Committee*, 46 R.I. 466, 128 Atl. 449. Accord, *Vaughn* v. *McCartney*, 217 Ala. 103, 115 So. 30.

41. *Reams* v. *McMinnville*, 153 Tenn. 408, 284 S.W. (Tenn.) 382.

42. *Jennings* v. *Clearwater School District*, 65 Calif. App. 102, 223 Pac. 84; *Sarratt* v. *Cash*, 103 S.C. 531, 88 S.E. 256; *State* v. *Board of Education*, 88 Kan. 199, 127 Pac. 623; *State* v. *Board of Education*, 11 Ohio App. 146.

43. *Sarratt* v. *Cash*, 103 S.C. 531, 88 S.E. 256.

body. This the voters knew, or should have known. They had no legal right to rely upon the representations made. To the same effect is the opinion rendered in the case of *Jennings* v. *Clearwater School District:*

> The contention which appellant urges most strongly is that prior to the election an understanding was entered into between the electors of the school district and the trustees that the proceeds of the bonds, if voted, would be used to purchase a site adjoining that of the school owned by the district. This proposition is not worthy of serious consideration. The law makes no provision for informal understandings of this character. . . . But there is no place in the entire procedure for understandings, except such as are expressed in the submission upon which the electors vote.[44]

An Ohio case[45] is even stronger. A board of education passed a resolution that a certain village was the most suitable location for a school site, and, pending an election, the board made statements to the effect that the school would be located in the village named. After the election, new territory was added to the district, and the board located the school in another village. The court sustained their action. "Neither the resolution that it was the sense of the board that the most suitable location was at Westboro, nor representations made at the time the bond issue was authorized, can limit the power of that body to exercise its discretion."

There is, however, some authority to the effect that where bonds have been issued upon the definite understanding that the school-house is to be erected on a particular site, the board has no authority to erect the building on another site. Thus, in an Iowa case[46] a proposition to issue bonds not to exceed $15,000 for the erection of a school building on a new site was voted down. Thereafter, a proposition to issue bonds not to exceed $12,500 to erect a building on the old site was approved. The board undertook to erect the building on the new site. The court issued an injunction restraining them from doing so. It was conceded that the board had authority to select the site, but the court reasoned that the site having once been located and the taxpayers having voted bonds to erect the building on the designated place, the board had exercised its discretion and its action could not be revoked unless for some controlling reason.

44. *Jennings* v. *Clearwater School District,* 65 Calif. App. 102, 223 Pac. 84. Accord, *Modesto Investment Company* v. *Modesto City School District,* 213 Calif. 410, 2 Pac. (2d) 387.

45. *State* v. *Board of Education,* 11 Ohio App. 146.

46. *Rodgers* v. *Independent School District,* 100 Iowa 317, 69 N.W. 544.

EMPLOYMENT OF ARCHITECTS

Authority to construct school buildings carries with it, by implication, authority to employ an architect.[47] According to some decisions, which seem to be the more reasonable, a contract between a school board and an architect to prepare general drawings and specifications for a school building is valid, even though the board may not at the time have at its disposal the funds necessary to construct the building,[48] and even though the building may never be erected.[49] In these cases it is reasoned that such plans and specifications are necessary as a preliminary step to enable the board to determine what a building of the kind desired would cost. In case the building is not erected, the architect's fee is chargeable to the general fund.[50] The Supreme Court of Nebraska has said in this connection:

A board of education has power to contract with an architect to prepare general drawings and specifications for a school-house, as a preliminary to determining whether a building, and, if so, what kind, shall be constructed, although, for want of funds devoted to building purposes, it may at that time have no power to erect the building. Such preliminary steps are not a part of the work of construction. . . .

The projected buildings were never erected, the preliminary plans and drawings could not be said to be a part of any construction of buildings, and if not, the expense of them was not any part of a building, or necessarily to be paid from a building fund. They were ordered for the use of the district and were necessary, as much so as many other articles or services which come within the general expenses of a school district, and must be paid for, and from the general fund.[51]

In the case of *People v. Board of Education*,[52] architects were employed to draw up plans and specifications, but the bids were higher than were expected, and the project was abandoned. It was contended

47. *Wyckoff* v. *Force*, 61 Calif. App. 246, 214 Pac. 489; *Fiske* v. *School District of the City of Lincoln*, 59 Neb. 51, 80 N.W. 265; *People* v. *Board of Education*, 190 N.Y.S. 798.

48. *Fiske* v. *School District of the City of Lincoln*, 59 Neb. 51, 80 N.W. 265; *Page* v. *Harlinger Independent School District*, 23 S.W. (2d) (Tex.) 829; *Bonsack & Pearce* v. *School District of Marceline*, 49 S.W. (2d) (Mo.) 1085.

49. *People* v. *Board of Education*, 190 N.Y.S. 798; *Fiske* v. *School District of the City of Lincoln*, 59 Neb. 51, 80 N.W. 265.

50. *Wyckoff* v. *Force*, 61 Calif. App. 246, 214 Pac. 489; *Fiske* v. *School District of the City of Lincoln*, 59 Neb. 51, 80 N.W. 265; *People* v. *Board of Education*, 190 N.Y.S. 798.

51. *Fiske* v. *School District of the City of Lincoln*, 59 Neb. 51, 80 N.W. 265.

52. *People* v. *Board of Education*, 190 N.Y.S. 798.

that the architects could not recover for their services because the board had not stipulated the amount the building should cost as was required by statute. It was said by the court:

> There are two answers to such contention. . . . Second, the services rendered by the relators were in their nature necessary, in part at least, to enable the board to pass the resolution provided for in subdivision 3 in section 875, aforesaid. It requires the services of an architect or of a skilled builder to make an estimate of the funds necessary to build a new school building.

It was further contended that the contract was unenforcible because made in violation of a statute which prohibited the board from incurring any liability "in excess of the amount appropriated or available therefor or otherwise authorized by law." The statute, said the court, was not applicable to the situation involved in the case at bar:

> In the case in question the board was acting under a statute which, in the first instance, required it to prepare an estimate of the cost of the proposed building. To do that it was necessary to have the services of an expert. The board could not comply with the law and advertise for bids until it had had such expert services, and no appropriation could be made for such services until the cost of the building was ascertained, and the cost of such services was based upon the cost of the building.

It has been held, too, that an architect may recover for services rendered on a contract providing that he should have as compensation an amount equal to 5 per cent of the entire cost of the building, even though the contract to construct the building was void because in excess of the constitutional debt limit.[53] But the contract with the architect, it should be noted, did not stipulate the cost of the building, it being provided merely that the building should be "suitable." Under such circumstances the architect had the right to assume that the school board would provide the funds and in doing so keep within the requirements of the constitution.

Some courts, however, hold that a contract between a school board and an architect for plans and specifications is not valid where the plans and specifications call for a building which would cost more than the board could legally spend for that purpose.[54] Inasmuch as the board would have no authority to construct the building, it has no authority to contract for the plans and specifications. In the case of

---

53. *Sauer v. School District of McKees Rocks,* 243 Pa. St. 294, 90 Atl. 150; *Altman v. School District of Uniontown,* 334 Pa. 336, 5 Atl. (2d) 896.

54. *Perkins v. Board of Education,* 161 Fed. 767; *Bair v. School District No. 141,* 94 Kan. 144, 146 Pac. 347. See also *Ritter v. School District of City of Harrisburg,* 291 Pa. St. 439, 140 Atl. 439.

Perkins v. *Board of Education*,[55] the board of education contracted with an architect to prepare plans for a building to cost $400,000. At the time the contract was made, only $200,000 were available for the purpose, although future appropriations were expected. The architect could not recover for his services. Similarly, in Kansas the statutes provided that no school board should incur a debt in excess of the amount appropriated by the district meeting. A district meeting authorized the expenditure of a certain amount for a school building. A contract with an architect to furnish plans and specifications for a building which would cost in excess of the amount authorized was unenforcible. The court held that the limitation contained in the resolution of the district meeting as to costs was binding on both the architect and the school board and that the limitations upon the authority of the board to deal with the architect must be read into, and be made a part of, the contract.[56]

Where an architect agrees to furnish specifications on condition that the building can be erected at a cost reasonably near the estimated cost, or where plans are required for a building not to cost more than a certain sum, it is well settled that there can be no recovery by the architect unless the building can be erected for the sum named or unless the increased cost is due to some special circumstance.[57] Thus where an architect estimated that a building could be erected according to his plans at a cost of $95,000, but the lowest bid was $140,000, the board was justified in abandoning the plans and refusing to pay the architect.[58] The architect had simply failed to perform his part of the contract.

The rule governing damages recoverable by an architect for breach of contract has been clearly expressed in the case of *Page* v. *Harlinger Independent School District*.[59] "An architect wrongfully dismissed is entitled to recover his contract price, less whatever payments have been made, and what it would cost him to perform his contract."

55. *Perkins* v. *Board of Education*, 161 Fed. 767.

56. *Bair* v. *School District No. 141*, 94 Kan. 144, 146 Pac. 347.

57. *Pierce* v. *Board of Education*, 125 Misc. Rep. 589, 211 N.Y.S. 788; 5 C.J. 262.

58. *Pierce* v. *Board of Education*, 125 Misc. Rep. 589, 211 N.Y.S. 788.

59. *Page* v. *Harlinger Independent School District*, 23 S.W. (2d) (Tex.) 829.

BIDS ON BUILDING CONTRACTS

Competitive bidding.—Where the statutes do not require school boards to invite proposals for building contracts and award the contract to the lowest bidder, the board may, or may not, at its discretion, advertise for bids.[60] If it does invite bids under such circumstances, the question may arise as to what extent its discretion in awarding the contract is limited by the terms of the advertisement. Where the advertisement is so worded as merely to invite or induce offers to contract, the board is, of course, in no manner bound.[61] It may ignore the bids altogether and contract with other parties who did not bid at all, or it may enter into a contract based upon entirely different plans and specifications. Where, on the other hand, the advertisement is so worded as to constitute a definite offer to contract and not a mere invitation for offers, the board will be bound when its offer is accepted. That is, if the board in its advertisement offers to award the contract to the lowest bidder, it will be required to do so.

As an illustration, the St. Louis Board of Education had a rule that all contracts be let to the lowest and best bidder. But in advertising for bids for the erection of a school building, it was expressly stated that the board reserved the right to reject any and all bids. The contract was awarded to one who was not the lowest bidder. In holding that the lowest bidder had no cause of action, the Supreme Court of Missouri expressed the rule as follows:

That binding obligations can originate in advertisements addressed to the general public, may be assumed as settled law to-day.

But the effect to be given to such an advertisement as the basis of a contract depends entirely on the intent manifested by its terms.

A public proposal of that nature may be so expressed as to need but an acceptance, or the performance of some act by a person, otherwise undesignated, to constitute an enforceable legal agreement.

While on the other hand, the proposal may amount to nothing more than a suggestion to induce offers of a contract by others.[62]

60. *Smith* v. *Board of Education,* 405 Ill. 143, 89 N.E. (2d) 893.

61. *Kraft* v. *Board of Education,* 67 N.J. Law 512, 51 Atl. 483; *Coward* v. *Mayor of City of Bayonne,* 67 N.J. Law 470, 51 Atl. 490; *Anderson* v. *Board, etc., of St. Louis Public Schools,* 122 Mo. 61, 27 S.W. 610, 26 L.R.A. 707; *Chandler* v. *Board of Education,* 104 Mich. 292, 62 N.W. 370.

62. *Anderson* v. *Board, etc., of St. Louis Public Schools,* 122 Mo. 61, 27 S.W. 610, 26 L.R.A. 707.

Applying these principles to the case before it, the court held that the board had merely invited offers for a contract, had merely opened negotiations.[63]

In many states the statutes require that boards of education advertise for bids on school-building contracts and that the contract be awarded to the lowest responsible bidder. Where such is the case, contracts made in disregard of the statutory requirement are, as a rule, unenforcible.[64] The statutory mode of making the contract is the measure of power of the corporation to make it. The law presumes that those who deal with a school district are informed with respect to the powers it may exercise. Consequently, one who contracts with a school district to erect a school building in disregard of a statute requiring competitive bidding cannot recover on the express contract, nor, as a rule, upon *quantum meruit*.[65] In the case of *Conners* v. *City of Lowell*,[66] a contract was let in disregard of a special act requiring competitive bidding. In holding that the contract was a nullity, the Supreme Judicial Court of Massachusetts said:

> The power of the commission to bind the city by contract depends wholly upon the authority conferred by the special act. The commission has no inherent powers. It must follow exactly the path pointed out by the special act or its conduct is ineffectual to bind the city. A contract made by it in any other way than in strict compliance with all the prerequisites, conditions and forms prescribed in the special act is illegal and does not become an obligation of the city. It is a contract *ultra vires* the statutory power of the city.
>
> The defendant Walker is bound by the limitations imposed by the special act. Those having business relations with a city are charged with notice of the scope of authority of those professing to act as its agents. Benefit to the city is irrelevant in this connection. Walker gains no advantage from an instrument in form a contract but in truth a nullity under the law because not made in conformity with what the Legislature has prescribed as essential to the making of an obligation of the city.

63. Accord, *Chandler* v. *Board of Education*, 104 Mich. 292, 62 N.W. 370.

64. *School District No. 2* v. *Richards*, 62 Mont. 141, 205 Pac. 206; *Conners* v. *City of Lowell*, 246 Mass. 279, 140 N.E. 742; *In re Summit Hill School Directors*, 258 Pa. St. 575, 102 Atl. 278; *Hibbs* v. *Arensberg*, 276 Pa. St. 24, 119 Atl. 727; *St. Paul Foundry Company* v. *Burnstad*, 67 N.D. 61, 269 N.W. 738; *State ex rel. Butler* v. *Dugger*, 172 Tenn. 281, 111 S.W. (2d) 1032.

65. *Reams* v. *Cooley*, 171 Calif. 150, 152 Pac. 293, Ann. Cas. 1917A 1260; *Brady* v. *Mayor, etc., of City of New York*, 16 How. (N.Y.) 432; *Conners* v. *City of Lowell*, 246 Mass. 279, 140 N.E. 742. Contra, *Williams* v. *National Contracting Company*, 160 Minn. 293, 199 N.W. 919; *Fargo Foundry Company* v. *Village of Calloway*, 148 Minn. 273, 181 N.W. 584. See also *McCormick Lumber Company* v. *Highland School District*, 26 Calif. App. 641, 147 Pac. 1183.

66. *Conners* v. *City of Lowell*, 246 Mass. 279, 140 N.E. 742.

In some instances, however, it has been held that a school district will be held for benefits received under a building contract executed in violation of a statute requiring competitive bidding.[67]

Definiteness of specifications.—Where it is required that contracts be awarded on the basis of competitive bidding, it is necessary that the plans and specifications be sufficiently definite to enable all bidders to make a definite bid for definite work to be done.[68] Bids must be made on a common basis, for otherwise there is no competition. The rule has been well expressed by Mr. Justice Brown, speaking for the Supreme Court of Pennsylvania:

When bids are thus invited through due public notice, it goes without saying that bidders ought to be asked to make their bids from "a common standard.". . . All ought to bid upon exactly the same basis. Competitive bidding necessarily implies this. However far apart the bids may be, all bidders propose to do the thing called for. Each proposes to do the same thing, though they may differ as to the compensation to be paid them, and all ought to bid upon exactly the same basis, if there is to be fair competitive bidding.[69]

Thus, where no date for the completion of a building is specified and each bidder designates his own date for the completion, there is not that competitive bidding which the law requires.[70] Time may or may not be an important consideration to the board, but it usually is an important consideration to the contractor. Moreover, if the element of time were omitted in the proposals for contracts, the door would be opened to fraud and collusion.[71]

Other examples of what constitutes definite or indefinite specifications follow. In a New York case the specifications called for "wrought-iron" or "steel" pipes to be used in certain parts of the building. The specification was held to be indefinite, inasmuch as it was not clear whether the use of wrought-iron or steel pipes was left to the option

67. *Burk* v. *Livingston Parish School Board,* 190 La. 504, 182 So. 656; *Hatch* v. *Maple Valley Township Unit School,* 310 Mich. 516, 17 N.W. (2d) 735.

68. *Edmundson* v. *Board of Education,* 248 Pa. St. 559, 94 Atl. 248; *Homan* v. *Board of Education,* 127 Atl. (N.J.) 824; *Hibbs* v. *Arensberg,* 276 Pa. St. 24, 119 Atl. 727; *Warnock* v. *Wray,* 194 N.Y.S. 396; *Hannan* v. *Board of Education,* 25 Okla. 372, 107 Pac. 646, 30 L.R.A. (N.S.) 214.

69. *Edmundson* v. *Board of Education,* 248 Pa. St. 559, 94 Atl. 248.

70. *Edmundson* v. *Board of Education,* 248 Pa. St. 559, 94 Atl. 248; *Homan* v. *Board of Education,* 127 Atl. (N.J.) 824; *Hibbs* v. *Arensberg,* 276 Pa. St. 24, 119 Atl. 727.

71. *Edmundson* v. *Board of Education,* 248 Pa. St. 559, 94 Atl. 248.

of the bidder or the board.[72] In Oklahoma a school board advertised for bids on a heating system in the following terms: "They will further receive bids accompanied by plans and specifications in form of proposal for a steam force blast system of heating and ventilation controlled by automatic heat regulation in all rooms other than halls and toilets, board and supt. room, wall radiation. Each pupil in each room is to receive 1,800 cubic feet of air per hour." In certain rooms a heat of 70° was to be guaranteed in the coldest weather. Bids were received, but each bidder submitted his own plans and specifications together with a description of the materials he proposed to use. All the specifications were substantially different. The court held that this mode of bidding did not constitute competitive bidding.[73] The steam force blast system to be installed might use various types of boilers; in the matter of power, either gasoline, steam, electric, or water motor power might be used; in providing radiation there might be used either the cast-iron or pipe-oil radiation; and, with respect to automatic regulation, there might be used any one of three different systems. Finally, competitive bidding does not result where the architect does not supply a sufficient number of copies of the plans and specifications and thereby deprives a reputable contractor of the opportunity of bidding.[74]

Bids on alternate plans.—Although specifications must be sufficiently definite to constitute a definite basis for bids, a board may ask for bids on various alternate propositions.[75] It may, for example, ask for bids on a building to be constructed of brick, stone, or wood, or it may stipulate that the building be completed within six, nine, or twelve months. That is, instead of submitting merely one proposition to be bid on, a number of alternate propositions may be submitted with discretion in the board with respect to the one it will accept. But each proposition must be definite and separate in order to provide an opportunity for competitive bidding. Thus each contractor may bid upon one or all of the propositions to suit his pleasure. "Specifications other-

72. *Warnock* v. *Wray*, 194 N.Y.S. 396.

73. *Hannan* v. *Board of Education*, 25 Okla. 372, 107 Pac. 646, 30 L.R.A. (N.S.) 214.

74. *Hibbs* v. *Arensberg*, 276 Pa. St. 24, 119 Atl. 727.

75. *Hannan* v. *Board of Education*, 25 Okla. 372, 107 Pac. 646, 30 L.R.A. (N.S.) 214; *Schwitzer* v. *Board of Education*, 79 N.J. Law 342, 75 Atl. 447; *Mayor of City of Baltimore* v. *Flack*, 104 Md. 107, 64 Atl. 702; *Katterjohn & Son* v. *Board of Education*, 202 Ky. 690, 261 S.W. 257.

wise sufficient," says the Supreme Court of New Jersey, "are not objectionable in requiring estimates on certain alternatives therein named. Every bidder in such case has the same opportunity to submit bids on the same alternatives."[76]

The lowest bidder.—Where the statutes require that building contracts be let to the lowest responsible bidder, two questions are likely to arise: who is the lowest bidder within the meaning of the statute, and how is this fact to be determined? In determining the lowest responsible bidder, other things than mere cost should be taken into consideration. The board should take into consideration the ability of bidders to discharge all the obligations which may be expected or required under the terms of the contract.[77] The Supreme Court of Pennsylvania has well expressed the rule thus:

> The term "lowest responsible bidder" does not mean the lowest bidder in dollars; nor does it mean the board may capriciously select a higher bidder regardless of responsibility or cost. What the law requires is the exercise of a sound discretion by the directors; they should call to their assistance the means of information at hand to form an intelligent judgment. They should investigate the bidders to learn their financial standing, reputation, experience, resources, facilities, judgment and efficiency as builders.[78]

In determining who is the lowest responsible bidder, boards of education exercise a discretion vested in them by law. It is a well-recognized legal principle that courts will not interfere with the exercise of discretion on the part of school officers unless discretion has been abused.[79] It follows, therefore, that where a board, acting in good faith, informs itself with respect to the responsibility and reliability of all bidders and reaches a decision, the courts will not overrule the discretion of the board and enjoin the execution of the contract.[80] The finding of the board is conclusive and will not be disturbed by the

76. *Schwitzer* v. *Board of Education,* 79 N.J. Law 342, 75 Atl. 447.

77. *Hudson* v. *Board of Education,* 179 N.E. (Ohio) 701; *Hannan* v. *Board of Education,* 25 Okla. 372, 107 Pac. 646, 30 L.R.A. (N.S.) 214; *Hibbs* v. *Arensberg,* 276 Pa. St. 24, 119 Atl. 727; *Zimmerman* v. *Miller,* 237 Pa. St. 616, 85 Atl. 871; *Schwitzer* v. *Board of Education,* 79 N.J. Law 342, 75 Atl. 447; *Ellingson* v. *Cherry Lake School District,* 55 N.D. 141, 212 N.W. 773.

78. *Hibbs* v. *Arensberg,* 276 Pa. St. 24, 119 Atl. 727.

79. *Hibbs* v. *Arensberg,* 276 Pa. St. 24, 119 Atl. 727; *Gemmell* v. *Fox,* 241 Pa. St. 146, 88 Atl. 426; *Dahl* v. *Independent School District No. 2,* 45 S.D. 366, 187 N.W. 638; *Tufts* v. *State,* 119 Ind. 232, 21 N.E. 892; *Sarratt* v. *Cash,* 103 S.C. 531, 88 S.E. 256.

80. *Schwitzer* v. *Board of Education,* 79 N.J. Law 342, 75 Atl. 447; *Hibbs* v. *Arensberg,* 276 Pa. St. 24, 119 Atl. 727.

courts unless it can be shown that the board acted in bad faith, or unless the proofs are of such a character as to satisfy reasonable men that another lower bidder was responsible.[81] Boards must, however, inquire into the facts sufficiently to form intelligent judgment. They cannot reject the lowest bid unless there is some substantial reason therefor.[82] In a Pennsylvania case, for example, a building contract was awarded to the fourth lowest bidder without investigating the responsibility of the three lowest bidders. This action, the court held, was not the exercise of discretion, and the execution of the contract was enjoined. The board was bound to investigate, and if the bidder measured up to the law's requirement of a responsible bidder, the board could not capriciously award the contract to another.[83] And in New Jersey it was held that the fact that the lowest bidder had delayed the completion of former contracts was not legal ground for rejecting his bid.[84] Moreover, it has been held that the lowest bid cannot be rejected without giving notice to the bidder and affording him an opportunity to be heard. "A determination against the responsibility of a bidder is a judicial matter requiring notice to him."[85] According to the weight of authority, however, notice and hearing are not required.[86]

The question may arise as to whether a school board, under a statute requiring that contracts be let to the lowest responsible bidder, may reject all bids in case none proves satisfactory. No doubt boards may reject all bids, but there must be some satisfactory reason therefor.[87] Statutes requiring that contracts be let to the lowest bidder are enacted to protect the public, and if a board may reject all bids arbitrarily it would open the way to favoritism and corruption. "It

---

81. *Schwitzer v. Board of Education,* 79 N.J. Law 342, 75 Atl. 447; *Culpepper v. Moore,* 40 So. (2d) (Fla.) 366; *Gunnip v. Lautenklos,* 94 Atl. (2d) (Del.) 712.

82. *Hibbs v. Arensberg,* 276 Pa. St. 24, 119 Atl. 727; *Arensmeyer-Warnock-Zarndt, Inc. v. Wray,* 118 Misc. Rep. 619, 194 N.Y.S. 398.

83. *Hibbs v. Arensberg,* 276 Pa. St. 24, 119 Atl. 727.

84. *Homan v. Board of Education,* 127 Atl. (N.J.) 824.

85. *Jacobson v. Board of Education,* 64 Atl. (Vt.) 609. See also *Kelly v. Board of Chosen Freeholders of Essex County,* 90 N.J. Law 411, 101 Atl. 422.

86. *Hudson v. Board of Education,* 179 N.E. (Ohio) 701.

87. *Arensmeyer-Warnock-Zarndt, Inc. v. Wray,* 194 N.Y.S. 398, 118 Misc. Rep. 619.

would afford an easy way to keep on bidding until a favorite contractor was the lowest bidder."[88]

Where a contract is awarded to the lowest bidder but he refuses to execute the contract, the board, it has been held, cannot go back to the old bids and award the contract to the next lowest bidder. The failure to execute the contract makes new bids necessary.[89]

Acceptance of bids.—Not infrequently, misunderstandings arise with respect to what constitutes acceptance of a bid. As in all other cases of contracts, there must be a definite offer and an unqualified acceptance. The mere passage of a resolution by a board that the bid of a certain party has been accepted and that the contract is awarded to him does not complete the contract. The contract is not completed until the bidder has been officially notified that his bid has been accepted.[90] At any time prior to such notification the board may rescind its resolution awarding the contract.[91] And in Pennsylvania it has been held that a building contract does not arise until a written contract embodying all the essential terms of the agreement has been signed. For example, a board of education passed a resolution awarding a plumbing and heating contract to the lowest bidder. The school board, through its secretary, verbally notified the contractor to proceed to execute the written contracts prepared and secure materialmen and performance bonds. The plumber's union notified the board that if it persisted in the award of the contract, labor difficulties would be experienced. The contractor's representative consulted with the union but could arrive at no agreement. Thereupon, the school board rescinded its resolution on the ground that the contractor was not the lowest responsible bidder and awarded the contract to the next lowest bidder. In holding that the original bidder could not recover for breach of contract, the court said:

When a municipal body advertises for bids for public work and receives what appears to be a satisfactory bid, it is within the contemplation of both bidder and acceptor that no contractual relation shall arise therefrom until a

88. *Arensmeyer-Warnock-Zarndt, Inc.* v. *Wray,* 194 N.Y.S. 398, 118 Misc. Rep. 619.

89. *Kutsche* v. *Ford,* 222 Mich. 442, 192 N.W. 714.

90. *Cedar Rapids Lumber Company* v. *Fisher,* 129 Iowa 332, 105 N.W. 595, 4 L.R.A. (N.S.) 177; *Johnston Heating Company* v. *Board of Education,* 161 N.Y.S. 867; *Moody Engineering Company* v. *Board of Education,* 199 N.Y.S. 689; *Kutsche* v. *Ford,* 222 Mich. 442, 192 N.W. 714.

91. *Moody Engineering Company* v. *Board of Education,* 199 N.Y.S. 689; *Johnston Heating Company* v. *Board of Education,* 161 N.Y.S. 867.

written contract embodying all material terms of the offer and acceptance has been formally entered into. The motion whose adoption is evidenced by the minutes of the school district in the instant case meant merely that the proposal was accepted subject to the preparation and execution of a formal contract or subject to the motion being rescinded before the contract was executed. A preliminary declaration of intention to enter a formal contract, which was all the motion amounted to, did not in any way limit the school director's freedom of future action.[92]

Rescission of bids.—Occasionally a contractor, after his bid has been accepted, discovers that he has made a mistake in his calculations or that some item has been omitted which he intended to include. The question then arises as to whether he may rescind his bid or whether he will be required to perform the contract and stand the loss. Where the mistake is not due to gross negligence and goes to the essence of the contract, and no intervening rights have accrued, a court of equity will annul the contract and put the parties *in statu quo*.[93] The mistake, it should be kept in mind, must be fundamental, must affect the substance of the whole consideration and not merely some particular part, even though the part be a material one. The determining consideration in such cases is that the minds of the parties have never in fact met; he who errs is not considered as consenting. Moreover, it is inequitable to permit one of the parties to the contract to take advantage of and profit by the mistake of the other.

Some difficulty may be encountered in determining what constitutes putting the parties *in statu quo*. A contractor who seeks to have his contract with a school board annulled because of a mistake will be held to compensate the board for any loss which it may have suffered as a result of its having relied upon the performance of the contract. But this must not be taken to mean that a contractor who wishes to have his contract annulled because of a mistake must pay a school board the difference between his bid and what it ultimately costs to build the building. To place the parties *in statu quo* does not mean that one shall profit by the mistake of another. The loss to the district must be real and must grow out of its reliance upon the performance of the contract. Unless the district sustain such a loss, the mere annulment of the contract will put the parties *in statu quo*.

92. *Wayne Crouse, Inc.* v. *School District Borough of Braddock*, 341 Pa. 497, 19 Atl. (2d) 843.

93. *Board of School Commissioners* v. *Bender*, 36 Ind. App. 164, 72 N.E. 154; *Kutsche* v. *Ford*, 222 Mich. 442, 192 N.W. 714; *Barlow* v. *Jones*, 87 Atl. (N.J.) 649; *Harran* v. *Foley*, 62 Wis. 584, 22 N.W. 837; *Board of Regents of Murray State Normal School* v. *Cole*, 209 Ky. 761, 273 S.W. 508.

The case of *Kutsche* v. *Ford*[94] illustrates the principles governing the rescission of bids because of mistakes. A contractor omitted in his estimate the cost of plastering and after the bid had been accepted refused to execute the contract. Action was brought to recover from the board the deposit he had made guaranteeing his execution of the contract in case his bid were accepted. In granting the relief sought, the court said:

> In the instant case it may be thought that the school district cannot be said to be placed *in statu quo* when it is considered that the building cost nearly six thousand dollars more than plaintiff's bid. To place *in statu quo* does not mean that one shall profit out of the mistake of another. It does not appear that plaintiff's mistake has made the school building cost more than it otherwise would have cost. The school district, if placed back where it was before the bid, loses nothing except what it seeks to gain out of plaintiff's mistake. To compel plaintiff to forfeit his deposit, because of his mistake, would permit the school district to lessen the proper cost of the school building at the expense of plaintiff, and that, in equity, is no reason at all for refusing plaintiff relief.

To the same general effect was the holding of the court in the case of *Board of School Commissioners* v. *Bender*,[95] where the contractor placed his estimates upon different portions of the work on separate pages in his "estimate book" and in making up his aggregate bid turned two pages instead of one, thus failing to include a material portion of his estimate. Similarly, in a Kentucky case,[96] in which the contractor failed to include in his final estimate the cost of stone work, the court annulled the contract and placed the parties *in statu quo* by requiring the contractor to pay two hundred dollars, the cost of the second advertisement for bids.

Changes in specifications.—After bids have been advertised for and a bid accepted, either before the contract is formally entered into or later while the house is being constructed, it may become desirable to modify somewhat the original specifications. A different type of brick, or roof, or certain modifications in the dimensions of the building may be desired. The question arises, then, as to how far the board may depart from the original specifications. Generally, contracts and the construction of the building must conform to the specifications upon

94. *Kutsche* v. *Ford*, 222 Mich. 442, 192 N.W. 714.

95. *Board of School Commissioners* v. *Bender*, 36 Ind. App. 164, 72 N.E. 154.

96. *Board of Regents of Murray State Normal School* v. *Cole*, 209 Ky. 761, 273 S.W. 508.

which bids were invited.[97] To permit any substantial departure from the specifications might defeat the purpose of the law in requiring competitive bidding and open the door to fraud and favoritism. On the other hand, the courts will permit minor changes made in good faith which do not change substantially the character of the building or unreasonably increase the cost.[98] And this is especially true where there is a clause in the contract providing for such change.[99] Such a clause is permissible, even though the statute may require competitive bidding on the basis of "complete" plans and specifications.

The case of *Criswell* v. *Everett School District No. 24*[100] is a good illustration of how far the courts will go in permitting variations in the final contract from the specifications which formed the basis of the bidding. After a bid had been accepted, the board discovered that they could reduce the cost of the building some thousands of dollars by certain modifications of the plans. They decided to eliminate certain ornamental columns and to change the site of the building from a hillside to more level ground and thereby reduce the cost of the basement. The court held that these were mere changes in detail and did not render the contract illegal:

> Where the plan remains substantially the same and the parties act in good faith, detail features, which are not necessary to the building and which do not change the substantial character of it may be eliminated upon terms agreeable to the board and the bidder entitled to the contract upon the plans as advertised. Where a proper deduction from his bid is made on account thereof, such a change in the specifications would not be *ultra vires* of the board. This, we think, is all that was done in this case.

It has been held, too, that after a contract has been entered into, the specifications may be so altered, with the consent of the contracting parties, as to provide for a different kind of roofing,[101] and a somewhat more expensive kind of brick.[102] But where a board of education found it necessary, after a bid had been accepted, to reduce the cost of the building by about $300,000, the court held new bids were necessary.[103]

97. *Scola* v. *Board of Education*, 77 N.J. Law 73, 71 Atl. 299.

98. *Hibbs* v. *Arensberg*, 276 Pa. St. 24, 119 Atl. 727.

99. *Mueller* v. *Eau Claire County*, 108 Wis. 304, 84 N.W. 430.

100. *Criswell* v. *Everett School District No. 24*, 34 Wash. 420, 75 Pac. 984.

101. *Pung* v. *Derse*, 165 Wis. 342, 162 N.W. 177.

102. *Hibbs* v. *Arensberg*, 276 Pa. St. 24, 119 Atl. 727.

103. *Hanna* v. *Board of Education*, 87 Atl. (2d) (Md.) 846.

ILLEGAL AND VOID BUILDING CONTRACTS

In the chapter on the contractual power and liability of school districts the principles of law and equity governing illegal and void contracts were discussed in some detail. It will be necessary here only to point out some of the general principles governing capital-outlay contracts of this class.

Boards of education have such contractual powers as are conferred upon them by statute expressly or by implication. If, in purchasing school property or equipment, they enter into a contract in excess of the powers thus conferred, the district will not be bound by their act.[104] As has been said by the Supreme Court of New Jersey: "The duties and powers of the public agents of a corporation being prescribed by statute, or charter, all persons are bound to know the limitations thereof; and it results from this doctrine that unauthorized contracts are void, and in actions thereon the corporation may successfully defend on the ground that they are *ultra vires*."[105] And in most jurisdictions a school district is not bound by an *ultra vires* contract, even though the contract has been executed and the district retains and enjoys the use of the property obtained thereby.[106] In some jurisdictions, on the other hand, it has been held that where an *ultra vires* contract has been fully executed and the corporation retains and enjoys the benefits thereof, the corporation is estopped to deny the lack of power to make the contract.[107]

Moreover, where the statutes provide a definite mode of contracting, the mode prescribed is the measure of the district's power, and contracts made in any other manner do not bind the district, nor is the

104. *Fluty* v. *School District No. 11*, 49 Ark. 94, 4 S.W. 278; *A. H. Andrews Company* v. *Delight Special School District*, 95 Ark. 26, 128 S.W. 361; *Anderson* v. *Prairie School Township*, 1 Ind. App. 543, 27 N.E. 439; *Honey Creek School Township* v. *Barnes*, 119 Ind. 213, 21 N.E. 747; *Fletcher* v. *Board of Education*, 85 N.J. Law 1, 88 Atl. 834; *Keeler Brothers* v. *School District No. 3*, 62 Mont. 356, 205 Pac. 217; *Thompson & Company* v. *Lamar County Agricultural High School*, 117 Miss. 621, 78 So. 547; *Charleroi Lumber Company* v. *District of Borough of Bentleyville*, 334 Pa. 424, 6 Atl. (2d) 88.

105. *Fletcher* v. *Board of Education*, 85 N.J. Law 1, 88 Atl. 834.

106. *First National Bank* v. *Adams School Township*, 17 Ind. App. 375, 46 N.E. 832; *Honey Creek School Township* v. *Barnes*, 119 Ind. 213, 21 N.E. 747; *Reams* v. *Cooley*, 171 Calif. 150, 152 Pac. 293, Ann. Cas. 1917A 1260; *McCormick Lumber Company* v. *Highland School District*, 26 Calif. App. 641, 147 Pac. 1183; *First National Bank of Waldron* v. *Whisenhunt*, 94 Ark. 583, 127 S.W. 968.

107. 21 C.J. 1214; 19 R.C.L. 1041.

district liable on such a contract, even though it retains and uses the property obtained thereby.[108] This is true, for example, where the statutes require that the contract be in writing,[109] or that contracts shall be let only after competitive bidding.[110]

Contracts made in violation of a statute are void. Such a contract cannot be enforced, nor can the district be held to pay for benefits received under such a contract.[111] Thus a contract in violation of a constitutional or statutory debt limit under no circumstances binds the district,[112] although it may be enforced up to the limit of indebtedness.

Where a school district purchases property which it had no authority to purchase,[113] or which under the circumstances it was prohibited by statute from purchasing,[114] it will not be held to pay on *quantum meruit* what the property was actually worth. The only remedy which the one who has furnished the property has is to recover it. This can be done where the property can be identified and recovered without injury to the property of the district.[115] Otherwise it cannot be recovered.

108. *Reams* v. *Cooley*, 171 Calif. 150, 152 Pac. 293, Ann. Cas. 1917A 1260; *Leland* v. *School District No. 28*, 77 Minn. 469, 80 N.W. 354; *County Board of Education of Hopkins County* v. *Dudley*, 154 Ky. 426, 157 S.W. 927; *Hutchins* v. *School District No. 1*, 128 Mich. 177, 87 N.W. 80.

109. *Perkins* v. *Independent School District of Ridgeway*, 99 Mo. App. 483, 74 S.W. 122; *Leland* v. *School District No. 28*, 77 Minn. 469, 80 N.W. 354.

110. *Reams* v. *Cooley*, 171 Calif. 150, 152 Pac. 293, Ann. Cas. 1917A 1260; *Brady* v. *Mayor, etc., of City of New York*, 16 How. (N.Y.) 432.

111. *First National Bank of Waldron* v. *Whisenhunt*, 94 Ark. 583, 127 S.W. 968.

112. *McGillivray* v. *Joint School District*, 112 Wis. 354, 88 N.W. 310, 58 L.R.A. 100, 88 Am. St. Rep. 969; *Superior Manufacturing Company* v. *School District No. 63*, 28 Okla. 293, 114 Pac. 328, 37 L.R.A. (N.S.) 1054; *Shonk Land Company* v. *Joachim*, 96 W. Va. 708, 123 S.E. 444.

113. *A. H. Andrews & Company* v. *Curtis*, 2 Tex. Civ. App. 678, 22 S.W. 72; *First National Bank* v. *Adams School Township*, 17 Ind. App. 375, 46 N.E. 832. NOTE: 27 L.R.A. (N.S.) 1117.

114. *McGillivray* v. *Joint School District*, 112 Wis. 354, 88 N.W. 310, 58 L.R.A. 100, 88 Am. St. Rep. 969; *Superior Manufacturing Company* v. *School District No. 63*, 28 Okla. 293, 114 Pac. 328, 37 L.R.A. (N.S.) 1054; *City of Hogansville* v. *Farrell Heating & Plumbing Company*, 161 Ga. 780, 132 S.E. 436; *Shonk Land Company* v. *Joachim*, 96 W. Va. 708, 123 S.E. 444.

115. *School District No. 89* v. *Van Arsdale*, 63 Okla. 82, 162 Pac. 741; *Superior Manufacturing Company* v. *School District No. 63*, 28 Okla. 293, 114 Pac. 328, 37 L.R.A. (N.S.) 1054; *Clark* v. *School Directors of District No. 1*, 78 Ill. 474; *McGillivray* v. *Joint School District*, 112 Wis. 354, 88 N.W. 310, 58 L.R.A. 100, 88 Am. St. Rep. 969; *Moe* v. *Millard County School District*, 54 Utah 144, 179 Pac. 980.

RATIFICATION OF CAPITAL-OUTLAY CONTRACTS

It is elementary that a school board or district cannot ratify a contract which it did not have authority to make in the first instance. If a board makes a building contract which it had no authority to make, it can by no act of its own ratify the contract so as to make it binding on the district.[116] In the case of *School Directors of District No. 3 v. Fogleman*,[117] as an illustration, a statute provided that it should not be lawful for a board of school directors to purchase a schoolhouse site or build a schoolhouse without a vote of the electors of the district. Disregarding this provision of the statutes, a board of directors contracted for the construction of a school building and issued orders in payment therefor. Although the orders had been purchased by a third party, the court held that they were not binding upon the district:

It is also urged by appellee that the school house was accepted by the directors who incurred the debt, and that school was kept in it. That does not legalize the act, or bind the tax-payers. The question here presented is a question of power, and no act of the kind set up can make it valid for any purpose. Nor can the beneficiary in this case resort to such acts in support of his claim.

Similarly, in New Hampshire, a district had no authority to erect a schoolhouse on any site which had not been approved by the county commissioners. In holding that no recovery could be had against the district for a building erected on a site which had not been approved by the commissioners, the court said: "If the district had no power to authorize the building of the school-house, they had no power to bind themselves by a subsequent acceptance."[118] So, too, in Arkansas school directors had no authority to build a schoolhouse or to borrow money for such a purpose unless authorized by the district meeting called after due notice. Without authority from the district meeting, the board of directors borrowed one thousand dollars from a bank and

116. *Brown v. School District No. 6*, 64 N.H. 303, 10 Atl. 119; *School Directors of District No. 3 v. Fogleman*, 76 Ill. 189; *First National Bank of Waldron v. Whisenhunt*, 94 Ark. 583, 127 S.W. 968; *Arkansas National Bank v. School District No. 99*, 152 Ark. 507, 238 S.W. 630; *Turney v. Town of Bridgeport*, 55 Conn. 412, 12 Atl. 520; *Young v. Board of Education*, 54 Minn. 385, 55 N.W. 112, 40 Am. St. Rep. 340; *Frank v. Board of Education*, 90 N.J. Law 273, 100 Atl. 211, L.R.A. 1917D 206; *Ryan v. Humphries*, 50 Okla. 343, 150 Pac. 1106, L.R.A. 1915F 1047.

117. *School Directors of District No. 3 v. Fogleman*, 76 Ill. 189.

118. *Brown v. School District No. 6*, 64 N.H. 303, 10 Atl. 119.

built and occupied a schoolhouse. The court held that the use of the building did not render the district liable to pay for it. "The district being without power to construct the schoolhouse so far as the record discloses, there could be no ratification of an act done in violation of the statute, and such act was a nullity so far as the liability of the district was concerned."[119] Again, where a school board contracts for the construction of a school building at a cost greater than that authorized by the district or town meeting, the mere acceptance and use of the building do not ratify the contract. The contractor can recover, in such a case, the amount authorized by the town meeting and no more.[120] And, of course, contracts *ultra vires* the corporate powers of the school district or in excess of a constitutional or statutory debt limit being void, are not subject to ratification.[121]

Where, on the other hand, a school board or district has authority to purchase property in the first instance, but the contract is unenforcible because of some irregularity in the mode of making it, or because made by some unauthorized agent of the board, the contract may be subsequently ratified.[122] Acceptance and use of property by a school board, with full knowledge of all the facts, usually constitutes ratification, provided that the board had authority to purchase the property in the first instance.[123] Formal action by a school board is not, as a rule, necessary to ratify a contract;[124] ratification takes place where the acts of the board are such as to be inconsistent with any other

119. *Arkansas National Bank* v. *School District No. 99*, 152 Ark. 507, 238 S.W. 630.

120. *Turney* v. *Town of Bridgeport*, 55 Conn. 412, 12 Atl. 520.

121. *Grady* v. *Pruit*, 111 Ky. 100, 63 S.W. 283; *Riesen* v. *School District No. 4*, 189 Wis. 607, 208 N.W. 472; *Frederick* v. *Douglas County*, 96 Wis. 411, 71 N.W. 798; *First National Bank of Waldron* v. *Whisenhunt*, 94 Ark. 583, 127 S.W. 968.

122. *Everts* v. *District Township of Rose Grove*, 77 Iowa 37, 41 N.W. 478, 14 Am. St. Rep. 264; *Haney School Furniture Company* v. *School District No. 1*, 133 Mich. 241, 94 N.W. 726; *Sullivan* v. *School District No. 39*, 39 Kan. 347, 18 Pac. 287; *Saline County* v. *Gage County*, 66 Neb. 839, 92 N.W. 1050; *Frederick* v. *Douglas County*, 96 Wis. 411, 71 N.W. 798.

123. *Union School Furniture Company* v. *School District No. 60*, 50 Kan. 727, 32 Pac. 368, 20 L.R.A. 136; *Sullivan* v. *School District No. 39*, 39 Kan. 347, 18 Pac. 287.

124. *Crane* v. *Bennington School District*, 61 Mich. 299, 28 N.W. 105; *Springfield Furniture Company* v. *School District No. 4*, 67 Ark. 236, 54 S.W. 217; *Jones* v. *School District No. 3*, 110 Mich. 363, 68 N.W. 222.

supposition.[125] Thus, in the case of *School District No. 39 v. Sullivan,*[126] one of the members of a school board made a contract for the construction of a schoolhouse. The court held that use of the property constituted a ratification of the contract.

Use of a school building may not, however, constitute a ratification of the contract under which it was constructed. Ratification will not be inferred from the retention of benefits which the district had no option to reject. Thus, where a house is built upon land owned by the district[127] or is built at a cost greater than the amount authorized by the district,[128] mere use will not of itself constitute ratification.

DEFECTIVE PEFORMANCE OF BUILDING CONTRACTS

Not infrequently, contractors fail to construct school buildings in strict conformance with the terms of the contract. In such a case the right of the board to refuse to accept the building depends upon the extent of the failure to comply with the contract and upon the contractor's having acted in good faith. The commonly accepted rule is that where the contractor acted in good faith, substantial performance is all that is required.[129] Where there is substantial performance, the board will be required to pay the contract price less deductions to cover omissions in performance.[130] The rule has been well expressed by Mr. Justice Knowlton, speaking for the Supreme Judicial Court of Massachusetts:

125. *Frank v. Board of Education,* 90 N.J. Law 273, 100 Atl. 211, L.R.A. 1917D 206; *Boydstun v. Rockwall County,* 23 S.W. (Tex.) 541. Some courts hold, however, that the ratification must be a corporate act. See *Thomas Kane & Company v. School District of Calhoun,* 48 Mo. App. 408; *Dierks Special School District v. Van Dyke,* 152 Ark. 27, 237 S.W. 428.

126. *School District No. 39 v. Sullivan,* 48 Kan. 624, 29 Pac. 141.

127. *Turney v. Town of Bridgeport,* 55 Conn. 412, 12 Atl. 520; *County Board of Education v. Durham,* 198 Ky. 733, 249 S.W. 1028; *Allen County Board of Education v. Scottsville Builders' Supply Company,* 202 Ky. 185, 259 S.W. 39; *Arkansas National Bank v. School District No. 99,* 152 Ark. 507, 238 S.W. 630; *Wilson v. School District No. 4,* 32 N.H. 118; *School Directors of District No. 3 v. Fogleman,* 76 Ill. 189.

128. *Turney v. Town of Bridgeport,* 55 Conn. 412, 12 Atl. 520; *Young v. Board of Education,* 54 Minn. 385, 55 N.W. 1112, 40 Am. St. Rep. 340.

129. *Kasbo Construction Company v. Minto School District,* 48 N.D. 423, 184 N.W. 1029; *Bowen v. Kimbell,* 203 Mass. 364, 89 N.E. 542, 133 Am. St. Rep. 302; *Hollingsworth & Company v. Leachville Special School District,* 157 Ark. 430, 249 S.W. 24; 9 C.J. 110.

130. *Kasbo Construction Company v. Minto School District,* 48 N.D. 423, 184 N.W. 1029; *Bowen v. Kimbell,* 203 Mass. 364, 89 N.E. 542, 133 Am. St. Rep. 302; *Hollingsworth & Company v. Leachville Special School District,* 157 Ark. 430, 249 S.W. 24; 9 C.J. 110.

Formerly it was generally held in this country, as it is held in England, that a contractor could not recover under a building contract, unless there was a full and complete performance of it, or a waiver as to the parts not performed, and that he could not recover on a *quantum meruit* after a partial performance. . . . But in most of the American States a more liberal doctrine has been established in favor of contractors for the construction of buildings, and it is generally held that if a contractor has attempted in good faith to perform his contract and has substantially performed it—although by inadvertence he has failed to perform it literally according to its terms—he may recover under the contract, with a proper deduction to the owner for the imperfections or omissions in the performance.[131]

Similarly, it has been said by the Supreme Court of Arkansas: "A substantial compliance by the contractor is all that is required under the law, he being charged (where there is a substantial compliance) with the difference in value between the work as done and as contracted to be done."[132]

It is a rather difficult matter to lay down a rule as to what constitutes substantial performance. In any particular case individuals and even the courts might disagree. The courts are agreed, however, in principle that there is no substantial performance unless the building is such as to accomplish fully the purposes for which it was erected.

It has been held that when a contractor agrees to produce certain results by the use of certain specified materials, he will be held to produce those results, even though the materials were specified by the board itself. Thus in a Texas case the contract called for the use of certain materials in the plaster of a school building, with the additional stipulation that the contractor would produce a "hard smooth finish free from defects." The contractor used the prescribed materials, but they did not produce the required surface, and he was put to extra expense to produce good plastered surfaces. The court would not allow him to recover for this extra expense. Said the court:

The owner has the right to submit to prospective bidders any character of plans and specifications for the erection of his building. The bidder himself must know the nature of the plans and specifications, and must decide for himself whether or not, by the due execution of the plans and specifications, he can erect and deliver to the owner the character of building called

131. *Bowen* v. *Kimbell*, 203 Mass. 364, 89 N.E. 542, 133 Am. St. Rep. 302.

132. *Hollingsworth & Company* v. *Leachville Special School District*, 157 Ark. 430, 249 S.W. 24.

for by the contract. . . . The owner does not warrant that the materials and plans and specifications will produce the building; that fact the bidder must decide for himself and at his peril.[133]

In New York, on the other hand, where a school building in process of construction collapsed because of faulty design, the contractor was entitled to recover the reasonable value of loss through delay as well as for the extra expense in constructing the building.[134]

Even though a building may not conform to the specifications of the contract, the board of education may choose to accept it unconditionally and thereby waive all claim to damages. Mere occupation and use of a building do not, however, constitute such a waiver of the defects of construction.[135] This is true because it often happens that the board must use the building, such as it is, or else close the school. In a North Dakota case[136] it was contended that use of the building constituted a waiver of defects. In denying the validity of this argument, the court said:

The plaintiff contends that after the completion of the schoolhouse the defendant accepted it by taking possession of it and using it. There is no merit in this contention, as there was no other proper place where a school could be held, and of necessity defendants were compelled to use the building in its defective condition, and in doing so it waived none of its claims or causes of action, if any, against plantiff.

Even where a building has been accepted and paid for, a school district, it has been held, may recover damages for faulty construction. Thus in a Minnesota case it was claimed that the contractor, through fraud and collusion with the inspectors, had failed to lay the brick in the manner specified. As a result, the walls leaked. The court pointed out that since the building had been paid for, the simplest remedy of the school district was a suit for damages. And the measure of damages, if the jury should find on a retrial of the case that the defects were such as to prevent substantial performance, should be the difference between the market value of the building constructed according to plans and its market value as actually constructed.[137]

133. *McDaniel* v. *City of Beaumont*, 92 S.W. (2d) (Tex.) 552.

134. *Kirkpatrick* v. *City of Binghamton*, 9 N.Y.S. (2d) 713, 256 App. Div. 19.

135. *Kasbo Construction Company* v. *Minto School District*, 48 N.D. 423, 184 N.W. 1029; *Lyon-Gray Lumber Company* v. *Wichita Falls Brick & Tile Company*, 194 S.W. (Tex.) 1167.

136. *Kasbo Construction Company* v. *Minto School District*, 48 N.D. 423, 184 N.W. 1029.

137. *Independent School District No. 35* v. *A. Hendenberg and Company*, 214 Minn. 82, 7 N.W. (2d) 511.

LACHES AS APPLIED TO BUILDING CONTRACTS

Where school-building contracts are entered into illegally, taxpayers may enjoin their execution and thus prevent the illegal expenditure of public funds. But it is elementary that he who seeks equity must do equity. Taxpayers may, therefore, become guilty of laches and thereby lose their right of action. That is, by failure to exercise their rights seasonably, they may lose them altogether.[138] Where, therefore, taxpayers with a full knowledge of the facts permit an unenforcible building contract to be executed, they may be denied injunctional relief.[139] The leading case of *Conners* v. *City of Lowell*[140] well illustrates the principle. The city of Lowell entered into a contract for the erection of a school building at a cost of more than one million five hundred thousand dollars. The contract was entered into without inviting public bids as required by law. After the building was completed and paid for with the exception of about one hundred thousand dollars, action was brought to restrain further payments. The building was paid for in monthly instalments, and the injunction was sought two years and seven months after the contract was let. The court held that the plaintiffs had not used due diligence in bringing the suit and were guilty of laches. Consequently, the injunction was denied. The court quoted with approval the following passage from an earlier opinion:

It is a well-established rule in equity that if a party is guilty of laches or unreasonable delay in the enforcement of his rights, he thereby forfeits his claim to equitable relief. This rule is more especially applicable to cases, where a party, being cognizant of his rights, does not take those steps to assert them which are open to him, but lies by, and suffers other parties to incur expenses and enter into engagements and contracts of a burdensome character.

Similarly, in Minnesota, action was brought to have certain building contracts declared invalid because in excess of a statutory debt limit. The court held that the contracts did not exceed the debt limit but that, even if they did, the plaintiffs were guilty of laches:

138. *Greenfield School District* v. *Hannaford Special School District*, 20 N.D. 393, 127 N.W. 499; *State* v. *Miller*, 113 Mo. App. 665, 88 S.W. 637; *Gibson* v. *Searcy*, 192 Ind. 515, 137 N.E. 182.

139. *Conners* v. *City of Lowell*, 246 Mass. 279, 140 N.E. 742; *Oliver Iron Mining Company* v. *Independent School District No. 35*, 155 Minn. 400, 193 N.W. 949; *Lerew* v. *Cresbard Independent School District No. 2*, 46 S.D. 331, 192 N.W. 747.

140. *Conners* v. *City of Lowell*, 246 Mass. 279, 104 N.E. 742.

The evidence is that from the very first plaintiffs knew of the progress of the work. . . . Notwithstanding this, the suit was not begun until the work was nearly completed as to all contracts. No contract remains wholly unperformed. There is not the slightest imputation of bad faith on the part of any of the contractors or subcontractors. So far as completed the district makes use of the buildings, and undoubtedly will continue to claim and use all labor and material that has been incorporated therein. We think plaintiffs waited too long before invoking the equitable powers of the court. To now grant the relief asked would work great harm and injustice to the contractors.

Taxpayers may not stand by and see others put labor and material in public improvements and when these are nearing completion have the contracts therefor adjudged void and payments thereon enjoined. . . . The delay to institute the suit until the defendant contractors had to a great extent, or nearly entirely, performed estops plaintiffs from attacking the contracts.[141]

Some courts hold, however, that taxpayers are not guilty of laches where they fail seasonably to enjoin the execution of a contract creating an indebtedness in excess of a constitutional debt limit.[142]

REVERTER OF SCHOOL PROPERTY TO GRANTOR

Frequently the deed whereby property is conveyed to a school district provides that the property shall be used for school purposes, or for school purposes only; or property may be deeded to the district, provided that it be used for school purposes or so long as it is used for school purposes. In case the school district ceases to use for school purposes property deeded to it subject to such conditions, the question may arise as to whether the property reverts to the original grantor.

The courts are in accord in holding that property deeded to a school district for a consideration will not revert to the original grantor or his heirs unless the deed definitely and clearly provides for such reversion.[143] Clauses in a deed providing for reversion are said to create an estate upon condition subsequent or upon conditional limitation. The law does not look with favor upon the creation of estates upon condition subsequent or upon conditional limitation, and courts will con-

141. *Oliver Iron Mining Company* v. *Independent School District No. 35,* 155 Minn. 400, 193 N.W. 949.

142. *Howard* v. *Trustees of School District No. 27,* 31 Ky. Law Rep. 399, 102 S.W. 318; *Riggs* v. *Stevens,* 92 Ky. 393, 13 Ky. Law Rep. 631, 17 S.W. 1016.

143. *Board of Education* v. *Brophy,* 90 N.J. Eq. 57, 106 Atl. 32; *Raley* v. *County of Umitilla,* 15 Ore. 172, 13 Pac. 890, 3 Am. St. Rep. 142; *McElroy* v. *Pope,* 153 Ky. 108, 154 S.W. 903; *Rawson* v. *School District No. 5,* 7 Allen (Mass.) 125, 83 Am. Dec. 670; *Faith* v. *Bowles,* 86 Md. 13, 37 Atl. 711, 63 Am. St. Rep. 489; *Hollomon* v. *Board of Education,* 168 Ga. 359, 147 S.E. 882.

strue the deed most strictly against the grantor:[144] "The authorities are uniform that estates upon condition subsequent, which, after having been fully vested, may be defeated by a breach of the condition, are never favored in law, and that no deed will be construed to create such an estate unless the language to that effect is so clear that no room is left for any other construction."[145] Again it has been said:

It is no less the dictate of reason and justice than of sound law that courts should require the violation of a condition which involves a forfeiture to be clearly established. Conditions, when they tend to defeat estates, are stricti juris and to be construed strictly. . . .

Conditions subsequent, especially when relied upon to work a forfeiture, must be created by express terms or clear implication, and are strictly construed. . . . If it be doubtful whether a clause in a deed be a covenant or a condition, the courts will incline against the latter construction.[146]

Similarly, it was said by the Court of Appeals of Kentucky: "It is a rule of law that conditions subsequent are not favored, because they tend to destroy estates; and, if it be doubtful whether a clause in a deed be a condition or a covenant, courts will incline to the latter construction."[147]

Where property is deeded to a school district to be used for school purposes,[148] or for school purposes only,[149] or to be used for school

144. *Raley v. County of Umitilla,* 15 Ore. 172, 13 Pac. 890, 3 Am. St. Rep. 142; *McElroy v. Pope,* 153 Ky. 108, 154 S.W. 903; *Higbee v. Rodeman,* 129 Ind. 244, 28 N.E. 442; *Crane v. Hyde Park,* 135 Mass. 147; *Fitzgerald v. County of Modoc,* 164 Calif. 493, 129 Pac. 794, 44 L.R.A. (N.S.) 1229; *Roadcap v. County School Board of Rockingham County,* 194 Va. 201, 72 S.E. (2d) 250; *Shuster v. Board of Education of Hardwick Township,* 17 N.J. Super. 357, 86 Atl. (2d) 16; *Rose v. Board of Directors of School District No. 94,* 162 Kan. 720, 179 Pac. (2d) 181.

145. *Curtis v. Board of Education,* 43 Kan. 138, 23 Pac. 98.

146. *Board of Education v. Brophy,* 90 N.J. Eq. 57, 106 Atl. 32.

147. *Carroll County Academy v. Gallatin Academy,* 104 Ky. 621, 20 Ky. Law Rep. 824, 47 S.W. 617.

148. *Hanna v. Washington School Township,* 73 Ind. App. 382, 127 N.E. 583; *Garrett v. Board of Education,* 109 W. Va. 714, 156 S.E. 115; *Higbee v. Rodeman,* 129 Ind. 244, 28 N.E. 442; *Walker v. Shelby County School Board,* 150 Tenn. 202, 263 S.W. 792; *Hunter v. Murfee,* 126 Ala. 123, 28 So. 7; *Taylor v. County School Trustees,* 229 S.W. (Tex.) 670; *Hodges v. Edmonson County Board of Education,* 256 S.W. (2d) (Ky.) 514; *Fuchs v. Reorganized School District,* 251 S.W. (2d) (Mo.) 677.

149. *Phillips Gas & Oil Company v. Lingenfelter,* 262 Pa. St. 500, 105 Atl. 888, 5 A.L.R. 1495; *Raley v. County of Umitilla,* 15 Ore. 172, 13 Pac. 890, 3 Am. St. Rep. 142; *Taylor v. Binford,* 37 Ohio St. 262; *Brown v. Caldwell,* 23 W. Va. 187, 48 Am. Rep. 376; *Faith v. Bowles,* 86 Md. 13, 37 Atl. 711, 63 Am. St. Rep. 489; *Board of Education v. Brophy,* 90 N.J. Eq. 57, 106 Atl. 32; *Barker v. Barrows,* 138 Mass. 578; *Boone Biblical College v. L. S. Forrist,* 223 Iowa 1260, 275 N.W. 132,

purposes in perpetuity,[150] the courts usually hold that the district holds the property in fee simple and that the property does not revert to the grantor when no longer used for school purposes. The district may sell the property or dispose of it in any way in which it has a right to dispose of any property to which it holds title in fee simple.[151]

The application of the rule as stated in the preceding paragraph is well illustrated by a Pennsylvania case.[152] The deed conveying a lot to a board of school directors provided that the land should be used "for school purposes only." A schoolhouse was erected on the lot and a school conducted therein. Some thirty-seven years later the board executed a lease on the lot for the extraction of oil and gas. It was contended that the board had no right to the oil and gas under the school site, because an absolute fee had not passed to it. The words in the deed restricting the use of the land "for school purposes only," it was claimed, prevented an absolute estate from vesting in the school board. In holding otherwise, the court said:

> Those words are neither preceded nor followed by any condition, restraint upon alienation, or clause of forfeiture for any cause, and, but for their appearance in the deed, the validity of the lease under which Wearing claims would not be questioned; for the right expressly given by the statute to the school district was not only to purchase the lot, but to sell the whole or any part of it and reinvest the proceeds for school purposes. The words upon which the appellant relies as debasing the fee are merely superfluous, and not expressive of any intention of the parties to the conveyance as to the effect to be given to it. The directors of the school district could not have purchased the lot for any other purposes than that named in the deed, and their acceptance of it with the insertion in it of the words "for school purposes only" was a needless admission by them that they were acting within

116 A.L.R. 67; *Board of Education* v. *Long,* 52 N.Y.S. (2d) 323, 268 App. Div. 1053; *Hughes* v. *Gladewater County Line Independent School District,* 124 Tex. 190, 76 S.W. (2d) 471; *Brophy* v. *Board of Education,* 12 N.J. Misc. 460, 172 Atl. 910.

150. *McElroy* v. *Pope,* 153 Ky. 108, 154 S.W. 903; *Rawson* v. *School District No. 5,* 7 Allen (Mass.) 125, 83 Am. Dec. 670; *Heaston* v. *Randolph County,* 20 Ind. 398; *Board of Education of Taylor County* v. *Board of Education of Campbellsville,* 292 Ky. 261, 166 S.W. (2d) 295.

151. *Phillips Gas & Oil Company* v. *Lingenfelter,* 262 Pa. St. 500, 105 Atl. 888, 5 A.L.R. 1495; *McElroy* v. *Pope,* 153 Ky. 108, 154 S.W. 903; *Rawson* v. *School District No. 5,* 7 Allen (Mass.) 125, 83 Am. Dec. 670; *Barker* v. *Barrows,* 138 Mass. 578; *Walker* v. *Shelby County School Board,* 150 Tenn. 202, 263 S.W. 792; *Taylor* v. *County School Trustees,* 229 S.W. (Tex.) 670; *Heaston* v. *Randolph County,* 20 Ind. 398.

152. *Phillips Gas & Oil Company* v. *Lingenfelter,* 262 Pa. St. 500, 105 Atl. 888, 5 A.L.R. 1495.

the powers conferred upon them by the act of assembly. It was simply that, and nothing more, and the deed, in all other respects admittedly conveying an absolute estate, is not affected by them.

In the case of *McElroy* v. *Pope*,[153] a board of education sold land which had been conveyed to it by a deed containing the following words: "The aforesaid three-quarters of an acre is hereby sold and conveyed to the aforesaid trustees and their successors in office of trustees to remain in common school grounds forever for the community hereabout. . . . The receipt of fifty dollars of the aforesaid Thomas Cregor for and in consideration of the said school ground is hereby acknowledged." After the board had ceased to use the ground for school purposes and had sold it, the original grantor sought to recover it. Denying a recovery, the court said:

> It will be observed that there is no provision in the deed that the property shall revert to the grantors, if it ceases to be used as a common school ground, and that the deed is made in consideration of $50 paid by Thomas Cregor. We have held in a number of cases that, if property is donated to a certain charity, it reverts, when the charitable use to which it is dedicated ceases. . . . But we have not applied the same rule where land was conveyed for a valuable consideration, and there was no clause in the deed providing for a reversion to the grantor. . . .
>
> The law favors the vesting of estates. The grantor makes the deed. He chooses his own language. It is therefore just and right that the language of the deed should be construed against him; for, if he wishes to protect himself against the use of the property for other purposes, he can so declare in the deed, and, when he fails to do this, a forfeiture of the title should not be declared where the property has been conveyed for a valuable consideration.

Where, on the other hand, the grantor clearly provides in the deed for reversion of the property when no longer used for school purposes, the grantee does not hold the property in fee simple. The title taken under such a deed is what is known as a qualified, base, or determinable fee. The title of the grantee terminates when the property is no longer devoted to the uses stipulated, and the property reverts. Such language as the following has been held to provide for reversion to the original owner: "So long as used for a school";[154] "So long as said lands shall be used by said district for school purposes";[155] "For the length

---

153. *McElroy* v. *Pope*, 153 Ky. 108, 154 S.W. 903.

154. *Fayette County Board of Education* v. *Bryan*, 263 Ky. 61, 91 S.W. (2d) 990.

155. *Green* v. *Gresham*, 21 Tex. Civ. App. 601, 53 S.W. 382.

of time only which it shall be occupied for that purpose";[156] "So long as same shall be occupied as site for school house and no longer."[157]

In an Ohio case,[158] by way of illustration, property was conveyed to a board of education by a deed, the habendum clause reading, "to have and to hold said premises . . . as long as the same is used for school purposes." In holding that the property reverted to the grantor when abandoned for school uses, the court said:

> We think the form of the Phillips deed is a conditional limitation and that the title taken under the deed is what is called by Blackstone "a base or qualified fee," or what has been generally denominated in modern judicial literature as "a determinable fee." . . . We are, therefore, of opinion that the title ended when the Board of Education abandoned the use of the site for schoolhouse and school purposes, and that the heirs of the grantor then acquired the right to enter and possess the property.

Where the deed provides that property shall revert when no longer used for school purposes, the question may arise as to what in fact constitutes abandonment. Since the law does not regard with favor provisions in deeds providing for forfeiture, the courts will "not hasten to seize upon mistake or neglect, or even misuser of property, to adjudge a forfeiture."[159] It must be very clear that the property has been abandoned for school purposes before the courts will declare a forfeiture, and in order to show abandonment it must be shown that the school authorities intended an abandonment.[160] A temporary neglect to use property for school purposes does not of itself constitute abandonment,[161] and, indeed, neglect for a number of years may not do so.[162] Thus it has been said by the Supreme Court of Minnesota:

> Abandonment, in law, is a question of intention, and, as applied to this case, is the surrender or relinquishment or disclaimer of property rights. . . . Temporarily ceasing to use and occupy the building for a school would be competent evidence of a design to abandon and abandonment; but the fal-

156. *Application of Gladstone,* 15 N.Y.S. (2d) 301, 257 App. Div. 696.

157. *Board of Education* v. *Hollingsworth,* 56 Ohio App. 95, 10 N.E. (2d) 25. See also *Lynch* v. *Bunting,* 3 Terry 171, 29 Atl. (2d) 155; *North Hampton School District* v. *North Hampton Congregational Society,* 97 N.H. 219, 84 Atl. (2d) 833; *Coffelt* v. *Decatur School District,* 212 Ark. 743, 208 S.W. (2d) 1; *Clark* v. *Jones,* 173 Ore. 106, 144 Pac. (2d) 498.

158. *Phillips* v. *Board of Education,* 12 Ohio App. 456.

159. *Mills* v. *Evansville Seminary,* 58 Wis. 135, 15 N.W. 133.

160. *Rowe* v. *City of Minneapolis,* 49 Minn. 148, 51 N.W. 907.

161. *Ritter* v. *Board of Education,* 150 Ky. 847, 151 S.W. 5.

162. *Mills* v. *Evansville Seminary,* 58 Wis. 135, 15 N.W. 133; *Carroll County Academy* v. *Gallatin Academy,* 104 Ky. 621, 20 Ky. Law Rep. 824, 47 S.W. 617; *Osgood* v. *Abbott,* 58 Me. 73.

lacy of appellants' position on this appeal lies in assuming that a failure to use and occupy for a certain period of time conclusively established the design to abandon, as well as a complete abandonment.[163]

Mere intention to abandon may not of itself constitute abandonment if the board changes its mind before the property is in fact abandoned. Thus is the case of *Ritter* v. *Board of Education*,[164] the board decided to change the site of a school and let a contract to build on the new site. Later the board changed its mind and decided to build on the old site. School never ceased to be taught in the building on the old site. The court held that there was no abandonment of the old site within the meaning of a deed providing that on abandonment for school purposes the site should revert to the grantors.

Where land is conveyed to a school board upon condition that it will revert to the grantor when no longer used for school purposes, the board may use it for other than school purposes so long as a school is conducted upon it. The board has the unlimited right to use and control the property until the happening of the event stipulated in the deed. Thus where land is conveyed upon condition that it will revert to the grantor when no longer used for school purposes the land does not revert when leased for development of oil and gas.[165] In a case of this kind it was said by the Supreme Court of Oklahoma:

> The deed provides for forfeiture, if the property should be abandoned as a school site, but does not provide for a forfeiture by the additional use of the property. If the additional use of the property for the production of oil constitutes a wrong, the courts of equity of the state have been open at all times for enjoining the wrong complained about, and as equity affords a remedy, the law will not imply a forfeiture for an act for which the parties did not express a forfeiture in the grant.[166]

Similarly, in a Kentucky case it was contended that the lease of a schoolhouse site for the production of oil and gas worked a forfeiture within the provision of a deed that the land should revert when no longer used for school purposes. In denying the contention, the court pointed out that the grantor had parted with all present interest in the property, that the school board had been vested with unlimited and unrestricted use of the property until the happening of the event

163. *Rowe* v. *City of Minneapolis*, 49 Minn. 148, 51 N.W. 907.

164. *Ritter* v. *Board of Education*, 150 Ky. 847, 151 S.W. 5.

165. *Williams* v. *McKenzie*, 203 Ky. 376, 262 S.W. 598; *Priddy* v. *School District No. 78*, 92 Okla. 254, 219 Pac. 141, 39 A.L.R. 1334.

166. *Priddy* v. *School District No. 78*, 92 Okla. 254, 219 Pac. 141, 39 A.L.R. 1334.

which would end the estate, and that until that event happened the board had all the rights of a fee-simple title holder. Moreover, the use of the land for the extraction of oil and gas did not constitute a use for other than school purposes.[167]

Land conveyed to a school district upon condition does not revert when the district goes out of existence by becoming a part of another district.[168] The subsisting district succeeds to the rights and obligations of the old district. Similarly, there is no reversion where the property is abandoned for school use by mandate of law, as, for example, a provision of law prohibiting the maintenance of a school in a district with a certain school population. Where, however, the abandonment is a voluntary act authorized by law, there is a reversion.[169]

Where land is conveyed upon condition that it shall revert when no longer used for school purposes, does the lease or sale of the land and the application of the funds thus realized to the maintenance of the school constitute a forfeiture? In a Pennsylvania case it was held that a school board could not rent land conveyed for "the use of a public school" and apply the proceeds to school purposes;[170] and in Illinois it was held that land conveyed under a similar limitation could not be sold and the proceeds applied to the support of the school.[171]

There is some division among the courts as to whether the school district or the grantor is entitled to the buildings upon land when the land reverts to the grantor. Thus it was said in an Ohio case:

> The right of the Board of Education to remove the trade fixtures, to-wit, the buildings, is not free from doubt. There is a conflict of decisions in other states. We think, however, the sounder reasoning is in favor of the proposition that the Board of Education may at the time of the abandonment of the premises for the purposes specified, or within a reasonable time thereafter, remove the trade fixtures.[172]

167. *Williams* v. *McKenzie*, 203 Ky. 376, 262 S.W. 598.

168. *Rowe* v. *City of Minneapolis*, 49 Minn. 148, 51 N.W. 907; *Breathett County Board of Education* v. *Bock*, 214 Ky. 284, 283 S.W. 99; *Crane* v. *Hyde Park*, 135 Mass. 147; *Curtis* v. *Board of Education*, 43 Kan. 138, 23 Pac. 98; *Locke* v. *Union Graded School District No. 6*, 185 Okla. 471, 94 Pac. (2d) 547.

169. *Crouse* v. *Board of Education*, 12 Ohio App. 481.

170. *Courtney* v. *Keller*, 4 Penny. (Pa.) 38.

171. *Trustees of Schools of Town No. 16* v. *Braner*, 71 Ill. 546.

172. *May* v. *Board of Education*, 12 Ohio App. 456. Accord, *Phillips* v. *Board of Education*, 12 Ohio App. 459. For other cases holding that the schoolhouse does not revert to the original owner see *Rose* v. *Board of Directors of School District No. 94*, 162 Kan. 720, 179 Pac. (2d) 181; *Brown* v. *Trustees of Schools of Township No. 5*, 403 Ill. 154, 85 N.E. (2d) 747; *Low* v. *Blakeney*, 403 Ill. 156, 83 N.E. (2d) 741.

In other jurisdictions, however, the courts take the opposite view.[173] Thus the Court of Appeals of Indiana has said: "The land having been conveyed to be used by the grantee for a public school, with reversion upon the grantee ceasing to use the land for such purpose, the permanent school building erected on the land became a part of the realty, and could not be removed by the grantee."[174]

As a general rule, where land is conveyed to a school district with a reverter clause in the deed, the grantor retains a vested right which he may transmit to his heirs or assigns. And this is true, even though there be no express provision in the deed that the property shall revert to the grantor's heirs or assigns.[175]

THE USE OF SCHOOL PROPERTY FOR OTHER THAN SCHOOL PURPOSES

It may be said in general that public school property is merely held in trust for the state by the local authorities[176] and that the legislature may therefore authorize the use of such property for any purpose not prohibited by the constitution.[177] There are few cases testing the constitutionality of statutes which authorize collateral use of school property, but it seems that there are not many constitutional restrictions on legislative discretion with regard to the uses to which school property may be put. As an illustration, a statute permitting the use of schoolhouses for literary, religious, and other meetings was held constitutional by the Supreme Court of Illinois.[178] Notwithstanding the fact that the constitution prohibited the appropriation of any public fund for any church or sectarian purpose, the court declared that "religion and religious worship are not so placed under the ban of the constitution that they may not be allowed to become the recipient

---

173. *New Hebron Consolidated School District* v. *Sutton,* 151 Miss. 475, 118 So. 303; *Webster County Board of Education* v. *Gentry,* 233 Ky. 35, 24 S.W. (2d) 910; *North Hampton School District* v. *North Hampton Congregational Society,* 97 N.H. 219, 84 Atl. (2d) 833.

174. *Malone* v. *Kitchen,* 79 Ind. App. 119, 137 N.E. 562.

175. *Fayette County Board of Education* v. *Bryan,* 263 Ky. 61, 91 S.W. (2d) 990; *Cookman* v. *Silliman,* 22 Del. Ch. 303, 2 Atl. (2d) 166; *Moss* v. *Crabtree,* 245 Ala. 610, 18 So. (2d) 467; *Shell Petroleum Corporation* v. *Hollow,* 70 Fed. (2d) 811.

176. *Attorney General* v. *Lowrey,* 199 U.S. 233, 26 S. Ct. 27, 50 L. Ed. 167; *Pass School District* v. *Hollywood City School District,* 156 Calif. 416, 105 Pac. 122, 20 Ann. Cas. 87, 26 L.R.A. (N.S.) 485.

177. *Brooks* v. *Elder,* 108 Neb. 761, 189 N.W. 284.

178. *Nichols* v. *School Directors,* 93 Ill. 61, 34 Am. Rep. 160.

of any incidental benefit whatsoever from the public bodies or authorities of the state." Similarly, in California,[179] Indiana,[180] Iowa,[181] Montana,[182] New York,[183] and Utah,[184] statutes authorizing wide use of schoolhouses have been sustained.

A state is free to permit or withhold the use of school property for nonschool community purposes; but if it makes its school buildings available for public meetings generally, it cannot arbitrarily withhold this privilege from any particular group of citizens. Thus in California a statute prohibited the use of school buildings by "subversive elements"—by any person who was affiliated with an organization advocating the overthrow of the government of the United States by force. Acting under authority of this statute, the board of education of San Diego refused permission to the San Diego Civil Liberties Committee to use the school building for a meeting unless they signed the following oath: "I do not advocate and I am not affiliated with any organization which advocates or has as its object or one of its objects, the overthrow of the present Government of the United States or of any State by force, or other unlawful means." Those seeking the use of the building refused to sign the oath and brought action in mandamus to compel the board of education to permit them to use the building, their contention being that the statute and the board rule violated their constitutional rights. Said the court:

Freedom of speech and of peaceable assembly are protected by the First Amendment of the Constitution of the United States against infringement by Congress. They are likewise protected by the Fourteenth Amendment against infringement by state Legislatures. . . . However reprehensible a Legislature may regard certain convictions or affiliations, it cannot forbid them if they present no "clear and present danger that they will bring about the substantive evils" that the Legislature has a right to prevent. . . . Since the state cannot compel "subversive elements" directly to renounce their convictions and affiliations, it cannot make such a renunciation a condition of receiving the privilege of free assembly in a school building.[185]

179. *Goodman* v. *Board of Education,* 48 Calif. App. (2d) 731, 120 Pac. (2d) 665.

180. *Hurd* v. *Walters,* 48 Ind. 148.

181. *Townsend* v. *Hagan,* 35 Iowa, 194.

182. *Young* v. *Board of Trustees of Broadwater County High School,* 90 Mont. 576, 4 Pac. (2d) 725.

183. *Lewis* v. *Board of Education,* 285 N.Y.S. 164, 157 Misc. 520.

184. *Beard* v. *Board of Education,* 81 Utah 51, 16 Pac. (2d) 900.

185. *Danskin et al.* v. *San Diego Unified School District,* 28 Calif. (2d) 536, 171 Pac. (2d) 885.

Other than school purposes in general.—In the absence of specific statutory authority, boards of education in some states are not permitted by the courts to grant the use of school buildings for other than strictly school purposes.[186] The reasoning on which the decisions are based is well illustrated by an excerpt from an opinion of the Supreme Court of Kansas:

> May the majority of the taxpayers and electors in a school district, for other than school purposes, use or permit the use of the schoolhouse built with funds raised by taxation? . . . We are fully aware of the fact that all over the state the schoolhouse is, by general consent, or at least without active opposition, used for a variety of purposes other than the holding of public schools. Sabbath schools of separate religious denominations, church assemblies, sometimes political meetings, social gatherings, etc., are held there. Now none of these can be strictly considered among the purposes for which a public building can be erected, or taxation employed. . . . The argument is a short one. Taxation is invoked to raise funds to erect the building; but taxation is illegitimate to provide for any private purpose. Taxation will not lie to raise funds to build a place for a religious society, a political society, or a social club. What cannot be done directly cannot be done indirectly. . . . Nor is it an answer to say that its use for school purposes is not interfered with and that the use for other purposes works little, perhaps no, immediately perceptible injury to the building and results in the receipt of immediate pecuniary benefit. The extent of the injury or benefit is something into which courts will not inquire. The character of the use is the only legitimate question.[187]

Other courts take a more liberal view with respect to the implied powers of a school board to permit community use of school buildings. Thus it was said by the Supreme Court of Rhode Island: "Our school system, with all the intellectual and material means for instruction provided by it, was designed to promote public education; and any use of the school property tending to this end, and which does not interfere with the regular schools, may be permitted by the trustees of a school district, as within the spirit of their trust."[188] Similarly, in Wyoming, under a statute merely authorizing the board of education "to direct the sale or other disposition" of schoolhouses, the court held that a board of education had authority to permit the parent-teacher association to use the school building for staging a carnival or show, to rent it to the Knights of Pythias for the purpose of giving a dance,

186. *Spencer* v. *Joint School District*, 15 Kan. 259; *Bender* v. *Streabich*, 182 Pa. St. 251, 37 Atl. 853; *School District No. 8* v. *Arnold*, 21 Wis. 665.

187. *Spencer* v. *Joint School District*, 15 Kan. 259.

188. *Appeal of John W. Barnes*, 6 R.I. 591. Accord, *Greenbanks* v. *Boutwell*, 43 Vt. 207.

and to permit athletic contests to be held in it at which admission fees were charged.[189]

Religious exercises.—The authority of boards of education to permit the use of schoolhouses for religious meetings of one kind or another has been frequently challenged in the courts. According to one line of decisions, such uses are permitted provided there is no interference with the regular work of the school.[190] "Courts in a Christian land," said the Supreme Court of South Carolina, "cannot be supposed to take judicial notice that holding a preaching service in a schoolhouse when not required for a public-school purpose is a breach of the condition" in the deed that the site shall be used for a public schoolhouse.[191] In a Nebraska case[192] it was the opinion of the court that holding Sunday school or religious meetings so infrequently as not to exceed four times a year does not make the schoolhouse a place of worship within the meaning of a constitutional provision that no person shall be compelled to support a place of worship against his consent. In Indiana[193] and Illinois[194] the courts have sustained statutes authorizing the use of school property for religious exercises. While school boards in some states may permit the use of schoolhouses for religious meetings, even in the absence of any specific statutory authority, it should be kept in mind that this is a matter clearly within their discretion,[195] and they cannot be required to permit such use.

In some states, on the other hand, no kind of religious service may be held in a public schoolhouse unless specifically authorized by statute.[196] The courts reason that school districts have only such powers as are delegated by statute or such as are necessary to effectuate the purposes of their creation. Holding religious exercises, it is said, is altogether foreign to the functions of a public school board. Funds raised by taxation, moreover, may not be put to any private use.

189. *Merryman* v. *School District No. 16,* 43 Wyo. 376, 5 Pac. (2d) 267.

190. *Greenbanks* v. *Boutwell,* 43 Vt. 207; *Townsend* v. *Hagan,* 35 Iowa 194; *Davis* v. *Boget,* 50 Iowa 11; *Harmon* v. *Driggers,* 116 S.C. 238, 107 S.E. 923; *State* v. *Dilley,* 95 Neb. 527.

191. *Harmon* v. *Driggers,* 116 S.C. 238, 107 S.E. 923.

192. *State* v. *Dilley,* 95 Neb. 527.

193. *Hurd* v. *Walters,* 48 Ind. 148.

194. *Nichols* v. *School Directors,* 93 Ill. 61, 34 Am. Rep. 160.

195. *Boyd* v. *Mitchell,* 69 Ark. 202, 62 S.W. 61.

196. *Spencer* v. *Joint School District,* 15 Kan. 259; *Bender* v. *Streabich,* 182 Pa. St. 251, 37 Atl. 853; *Dorton* v. *Hearn,* 67 Mo. 301; *Scofield* v. *Eighth School District,* 27 Conn. 498; *School District No. 8* v. *Arnold,* 21 Wis. 665.

Social, fraternal, and political meetings.—In a number of states, under varying statutory provisions, the courts have permitted social
dancing in public school buildings.[197] There is, however, a marked
conflict of judicial opinion with regard to the authority of school
boards to permit the use of school buildings for political meetings and
social gatherings. For example, the Supreme Court of Kansas has ruled
that a schoolhouse may not be used for any purpose other than the
conduct of a public school, the reason being that taxation may not be
invoked for any private purpose.[198] Township trustees in Indiana, on
the other hand, may permit the use of schoolhouses for elections and
other township meetings.[199] Municipal authorities, it has been held,
may not lease the auditorium of a high-school building for use as a
public theater.[200] The court, however, did not wish to be understood
as taking the extreme position that a municipality may not make
casual and incidental use of a school building not inconsistent with
the main purpose for which it was erected. The Supreme Court of
Arkansas sustained a contract by which the upper story of a school
building was leased to the Odd Fellows for use as a lodge.[201] The
Sons of Temperance, on the other hand, were denied the use of a
schoolhouse in Wisconsin, notwithstanding the fact that a majority of
the electors of the district had given their consent.[202] In Illinois, where
a statute authorizes boards of directors to permit such meetings as
they may deem proper, an upper room of a schoolhouse may be leased
to fraternal organizations.[203]

*Authority of school board to lease school property to be used for
private purposes.*—The Supreme Court of Idaho has said: "It is the
almost universal rule that the leasing of school buildings and parks for
private purposes which are not inconsistent with the conduct of the

197. *McClure* v. *Board of Education,* 38 Calif. App. 500, 176 Pac. 711; *Young*
v. *Board of Trustees of Broadwater County High School,* 90 Mont. 576, 4 Pac.
(2d) 725; *Brooks* v. *Elder,* 108 Neb. 761, 189 N.W. 284; *Merryman* v. *School
District No. 16,* 43 Wyo. 376, 5 Pac. (2d) 267; *Beard* v. *Board of Education of
North Summit School District,* 81 Utah 51, 16 Pac. (2d) 900.

198. *Spencer* v. *Joint School District,* 15 Kan. 259.

199. *Trustees of Harmony Township* v. *Osborne,* 9 Ind. 458.

200. *Sugar* v. *Monroe,* 108 La. 677, 32 So. 961.

201. *Cost* v. *Shinault,* 113 Ark. 19, 166 S.W. 740.

202. *School District No. 8* v. *Arnold,* 21 Wis. 665.

203. *Lagow* v. *Hill,* 238 Ill. 428.

school, is not an unconstitutional use of such property."[204] While the rule as thus stated is too broad, a number of courts have applied it. In Vermont it has been held that a private school may be conducted in a public schoolhouse, because such a school is "for the furtherance of the general object and design" for which the building was erected.[205] So, too, in Arkansas, a school board could lease the school building and equipment to teachers for the purpose of operating a tuition school after the public schools had been closed because of a lack of funds.[206] In Texas, Idaho, and North Carolina boards of education have authority to lease the school grounds for the playing of baseball during the summer or at night.[207]

In some jurisdictions, however, the courts deny to school boards the authority to rent school property. Thus in Ohio, the court held that the lease of a public schoolhouse for the conduct of a private school was a violation of the trust to which the building had been dedicated.[208] Moreover, the court refused to draw any distinction between uses which were definitely educational in character and those which were not. Similarly, it has been held in Pennsylvania that a public school building may not be used for a private school or for the giving of private music lessons.[209]

It has been held, too, that a school board has no authority to lease its property under terms that virtually constitute a gift to the other party or for a period of years unless it can be shown that the board will not need the property during the term of the lease. In Arizona a school board leased a school building to the community hospital at a rental of one dollar a year, the hospital to keep the building in repair and the lessee to have the option of renewal every five years. The court held the lease *ultra vires* and void because the board held the property in trust for the educational advancement of youth and could use it for

204. *Hansen v. Independent School District No. 1*, 61 Idaho 109, 98 Pac. (2d) 959.

205. *Russell v. Dodds*, 37 Vt. 497; *Chaplin v. Hill*, 24 Vt. 528.

206. *Burrow v. Pocahontas School District*, 190 Ark. 563, 79 S.W. (2d) 1010.

207. *Royse Independent School District v. Reinhardt*, 159 S.W. (Tex.) 1010; *Hansen v. Independent School District No. 1*, 61 Idaho 109, 98 Pac. (2d) 959; *Smith v. Hefner*, 235 N.C. 1, 68 S.E. (2d) 783.

208. *Weir v. Day*, 35 Ohio St. Rep. 143.

209. *Hysong v. Gallitzin*, 164 Pa. St. 629, 30 Atl. 482, 26 L.R.A. 203. See also *Sherlock v. Village of Winnetka*, 68 Ill. 530.

no other purpose, no matter how worthy.[210] Nor could a board of education in Ohio lease a wing of one of its buildings to be used as a receiving home for neglected children, the lease to run for a period of five years, with an option in the lessee to renew it for another five years. The board, said the court, could not make such a lease "where a present or probable future need therefor exists or is likely to arise."[211]

Commercial purposes.—As a general rule, the courts will not permit the use of school property primarily for purposes of commercial gain.[212] "No authority is given to a school district to acquire real property and hold it for any other purpose than a site for a schoolhouse; nor can the board bind the district to pay for property acquired and held for any other purpose."[213] School boards, it is said, derive their funds from taxation and other sources of public revenue and are not, therefore, free to venture into commercial enterprises. Moreover, school corporations, being mere instrumentalities of the state, exercise only delegated authority. For whatever action it may wish to take, a board of education must find statutory authority, either expressed or implied, or the action must grow out of the general purposes for which the board was created—out of the law of its own being. Obviously, then, the right of a school board to enter into commercial enterprises can be acquired only as the result of a statutory enactment.

A case in point is that of *Tyre* v. *Krug*.[214] The Board of Education of Milwaukee authorized the principals of certain high schools to sell books and supplies in the school buildings. This was done to accommodate the pupils and to enable them to purchase their books at a lower price. It was conceded that the supplies were sold at a profit, though the testimony was conflicting as to whether they were sold for personal profit. The statutes of Wisconsin authorized the board of education to adopt such measures as would promote the good order and

210. *Prescott Community Hospital Commission* v. *Prescott School District No. 1*, 57 Ariz. 492, 115 Pac. (2d) 160.

211. *State ex rel. Baciak* v. *Board of Education*, 88 N.E. (2d) (Ohio) 808.

212. *Presley* v. *Vernon Parish School Board*, 19 La. App. 217, 139 So. 692.

213. *School District* v. *McClure*, 136 Iowa 122, 113 N.W. 554.

214. *Tyre* v. *Krug*, 159 Wis. 39, 149 N.W. 718, L.R.A. 1915C 624. In a more recent case, however, it has been held that books and supplies may be sold in school buildings where they are not sold for a profit (*Cook* v. *Chamberlain*, 199 Wis. 42, 225 N.W. 141). It has been held, too, that a school principal and the parent-teacher association may operate a cafeteria in a school building, provided that they do it without profit (*Bozeman* v. *Morrow*, 34 S.W. [2d] [Tex.] 654).

public usefulness of the schools. This broad grant of powers, however, was not considered sufficient to warrant the action taken, and the supreme court of the state issued an injunction restraining the further sale of books at a profit.

A board of education in West Virginia discovered oil on school property and attempted to execute a lease for the production of oil and gas. The supreme court of appeals found that there was no specific statutory authority for executing such a lease and held that it could not be done.[215] A school board, it was reasoned, is not a business corporation; it cannot "mine, manufacture, produce, barter," because these activities are "utterly foreign to the object of its formation. It cannot lease land held by it though it has the fee-simple legal title. . . . It cannot lease it for money-making, because the statute provides for the accomplishment of its object by taxation, not by negotiation in the business world." The court could scarcely imagine a use to which the property could be put more foreign to the purpose for which the board had been vested with title.

In a more recent case,[216] however, the Court of Appeals of Kentucky ruled that, where trustees have authority by statute to hold and dispose of school property for the use and benefit of the district, they may execute an oil lease on school lands. It was said that the mere leasing of property to others for purposes of development is not engaging in a commercial venture but is only an effort to dispose of the property in such a way as to secure the largest possible returns:

> There can be no sound or practical reason given that will deprive school authorities who own property under which there are valuable minerals from entering into contracts for its development, and particularly would this seem to be true when the character of the mineral is such that adjoining land owners may profit at the expense of the school property by the failure of the school authorities to enter into such contracts.

The court referred to the earlier West Virginia case but declined to follow it as a precedent. Similarly, it has been held in Pennsylvania that land deeded to a school district "for school purposes only" may be leased for the production of oil and gas.[217]

In those states where school property may be used for nonschool

215. *Herald* v. *Board of Education,* 65 W. Va. 765, 65 S.E. 102.

216. *Williams* v. *McKenzie,* 203 Ky. 376, 262 S.W. 598.

217. *Phillips Gas & Oil Company* v. *Lingenfelter,* 262 Pa. St. 500, 105 Atl. 888, 5 A.L.R. 1495.

purposes, it seems that boards of education will be permitted to charge for such uses. For example, in Vermont, where school property may be used for a variety of purposes, even in the absence of any definite statutory authorization, the following decision was rendered:

While it would not be lawful for the district to make lofts, or rooms, for the mere purpose of realizing profit by renting for pay, it would not be unlawful for the district to receive pay and profit for the use of rooms legitimately made for school purposes, when not in use for those purposes, and when they may be used for other purposes without detriment to the district in respect to its schools.[218]

In Arkansas a school district was permitted to lease an unoccupied room in the schoolhouse to the Odd Fellows for a consideration of fifty dollars annually.[219]

Right of taxpayer to enjoin use of school property in competition with his business.—The courts commonly hold that a taxpayer is not entitled to an injunction restraining a legitimate use of school property, even though that use is in competition with, and injurious to, his business.[220] In a Utah case the school authorities permitted the high-school building and grounds to be used for a course in lyceum lectures, musical entertainment, dances, motion-picture shows, football and basketball games, and other entertainment and activities, for many of which an admission fee was charged and to which the general public was invited to attend by various schemes of advertising. The owner of a local theater sought an injunction to prevent the school building to be used for entertainment purposes, claiming that such use was injurious to his business. The court said, in denying the injunction: "If the use made of the school building and grounds is lawful, it matters not that such use is competitive with plaintiff's opera house, or that plaintiff's income has been impaired by such competitive use."[221] Similarly, in Washington the court refused a merchant an injunction to prevent the

218. *Greenbanks v. Boutwell,* 43 Vt. 207. Accord, *Merryman v. School District No. 16,* 43 Wyo. 376, 5 Pac. (2d) 267.

219. *Cost v. Shinault,* 113 Ark. 19, 166 S.W. 740.

220. *Beard v. Board of Education of North Summit School District,* 81 Utah 51, 16 Pac. (2d) 900; *Merryman v. School District No. 16,* 43 Wyo. 376, 5 Pac. (2d) 267; *Hempel v. School District No. 329,* 186 Wash. 684, 59 Pac. (2d) 729.

221. *Beard v. Board of Education of North Summit School District,* 81 Utah 51, 16 Pac. (2d) 900.

students in a school building from operating a cafeteria and candy counter during noon intermission.[222]

Discretion of school board in permitting community uses of school property.—With the growing awareness of the interrelations that should exist between school and community, many states have enacted statutes which expressly authorize the use of school buildings for a variety of nonschool purposes and by community groups. Such statutes should and usually do vest in the board of education a very considerable discretion in permitting or denying the use of school property upon request. And, as pointed out in other connections, the courts will not control the exercise of board discretion unless it is abused or arbitrarily exercised.

A number of cases coming before the courts of New York, Pennsylvania, and California illustrate the reasoning of the courts. A statute in New York authorized boards of education to adopt reasonable rules governing the use of schoolhouses for certain enumerated nonschool purposes. In sustaining a board's refusal to permit the use of a schoolhouse, the court pointed out that its act was discretionary and that, in reaching its decision, many factors might be taken into consideration. The board might properly refuse a request, even though the proposed use was in itself legitimate, if sentiment in the community was divided as to the propriety of the use and if granting the request would result in dissatisfaction and criticism.[223] Similarly, in Pennsylvania the statutes authorized a board of school directors to permit the use of school facilities for "social, recreational, and other proper purposes" under such rules and regulations as the board might adopt. In sustaining a rule made by the Board of Public Education of Pittsburgh denying the use of school facilities for any religious or sectarian purpose, the court said:

Whether the school property shall be used by any group at all is a matter resting within the discretion of each board of school directors. This court is not a superboard of school directors in performance of an official duty. The legislature has delegated this power to the school boards, not to the courts. In the absence of any proof of unreasonableness or an arbitrary or capricious exercise of the power, the judgment of the board must stand.[224]

222. *Hempel* v. *School District No. 329,* 186 Wash. 684, 59 Pac. (2d) 729.

223. *Ellis* v. *Dixon,* 118 N.Y.S. (2d) 815.

224. *McKnight* v. *Board of Public Education,* 365 Pa. 422, 76 Atl. (2d) 207.

So, too, in California, a school board was sustained in its refusal to permit the use of a school auditorium for a mass meeting. The board had reason to suppose that the particular speaker at the proposed meeting would arouse enough organized opposition and demonstration to interfere with the work of the school. Said the court: "It is for the board to determine, not who would motivate a disturbance, but how serious is the risk of disturbance. . . . In passing on an application for an extraneous use of a school auditorium the board must consider the probable effect of the proposed use on the regular school program and must deny one that would lead to an interference with that program."[225]

Where a board of education has exercised its discretion and granted permission to use school facilities and vested interests have accrued to the other party, the courts will not permit a withdrawal of the permission. In Albany, New York, for example, the school board had granted permission to a church organization to use a school auditorium for a concert. The organization went to considerable expense in securing a singer and advertising the meeting. When the board discovered that the singer was to be Paul Robeson, it attempted to revoke the permission on the ground that he was a Communist. The court denied the board the right to cancel the permission to use the school facilities. If the board had had a rule reserving the right to cancel, or if such a right had been stipulated in this particular permit, the case would have been different.[226]

SPECIAL ASSESSMENT FOR LOCAL IMPROVEMENTS

There are in most, if not all, of the states constitutional or statutory provisions which exempt public property from taxation. Very frequently, too, property used for school purposes is expressly exempt from taxation by constitutional or statutory provision. In a great many cases the courts have been called upon to decide whether, under such constitutional and statutory provisions, property being used for school purposes is subject to special assessment for local improvements. The

225. *Payroll Guarantee Association* v. *Board of Education of San Francisco Unified School District*, 27 Calif. (2d) 197, 163 Pac. (2d) 433, 161 A.L.R. 1300. See also *Goodman* v. *Board of Education of San Francisco Unified School District*, 48 Calif. App. (2d) 731, 120 Pac. (2d) 665; *Danskin* v. *San Diego Unified School District*, 28 Calif. (2d) 536, 171 Pac. (2d) 885.

226. *Cannon* v. *Towner*, 188 Misc. 955, 70 N.Y.S. (2d) 303.

decisions are so conflicting that it is entirely impossible to reconcile them. According to the weight of authority, however, property which is being used for school purposes is not subject to special assessment unless expressly made so by statute.[227]

The courts which take this position concede that constitutional provisions which exempt school property from taxation have no application to special assessments. "The rule established by a consensus of authorities—text writers and adjudged cases—is that the constitutional exemption refers alone to taxes for general purposes of revenue, and has no reference to special taxes or assessments for local improvements."[228] The exemption of school property from special assessment is based primarily on the common-law presumption that if the legislature had intended to subject such property to special assessment, it would have so provided in the statutes.

An Arkansas case[229] affords an excellent example of the reasoning followed by a majority of the courts. A statute provided that "all the real property situated" in special tax districts should be assessed for special improvements. The court, nevertheless, held that, under the statute, school property was not subject to special assessment:

The argument in favor of the exemption is that as the statute in defining the property to be assessed does not expressly mention public property, or include it by any necessary implication, the presumption is that it was not intended to be assessed. . . . Although a special tax or assessment is not

227. *City of Louisville* v. *Leatherman*, 99 Ky. 213, 35 S.W. 625; *City of Butte* v. *School District No. 1*, 29 Mont. 336, 74 Pac. 869; *Witter* v. *Mission School District*, 121 Calif. 350, 53 Pac. 905, 66 Am. St. Rep. 33; *City of Hartford* v. *West Middle District*, 45 Conn. 462, 29 Am. St. Rep. 687; *City of Edina* v. *School District of City of Edina*, 305 Mo. 452, 267 S.W. 112, 36 A.L.R. 1532; *Thogmartin* v. *Nevada School District*, 189 Mo. App. 10, 176 S.W. 473; *City of Pittsburgh* v. *Sterrett Subdistrict School*, 204 Pa. St. 635, 54 Atl. 463, 61 L.R.A. 183; *Wilkinsburg Borough* v. *School District of Borough of Wilkinsburg*, 298 Pa. St. 193, 148 Atl. 77; *City of Toledo* v. *Board of Education*, 48 Ohio St. 83, 26 N.E. 403; *Board of Improvement* v. *School District of Little Rock*, 56 Ark. 354, 19 S.W. 969, 16 L.R.A. 418, 35 Am. St. Rep. 108; *Sutton* v. *School City of Montpelier*, 28 Ind. App. 315, 62 N.E. 710; *City of Duluth* v. *Board of Education*, 133 Minn. 386, 158 N.W. 635, L.R.A. 1916F 861; *The Trustees for the Support of the Public Schools* v. *The Inhabitants of the City of Trenton*, 30 N.J. Eq. 667; *Von Steen* v. *City of Beatrice*, 36 Neb. 421, 54 N.W. 677; *Blake* v. *Consolidated Special Tax School District*, 115 Fla. 348, 156 So. 97.

228. *Board of Improvement* v. *School District of Little Rock*, 56 Ark. 354, 19 S.W. 969, 16 L.R.A. 418, 35 Am. St. Rep. 108. Accord, *City of Duluth* v. *Board of Education*, 133 Minn. 386, 158 N.W. 635, L.R.A. 1916F 861.

229. *Board of Improvement* v. *School District of Little Rock*, 56 Ark. 354, 19 S.W. 969, 16 L.R.A. 418, 35 Am. St. Rep. 108.

usually embraced within the meaning of the general term "tax," the rule under which public property is presumed to be exempt from one justifies the presumption as to the other. In speaking of the latter, Judge Cooley says: "Some things are always presumptively exempted from the operation of general tax laws, because it is reasonable to suppose they were not within the intent of the legislature in adopting them. Such is the case with property belonging to the state and its municipalities, and which is held by them for public purposes. All such property is taxable, if the state shall see fit to tax it; but to levy a tax upon it would render necessary new taxes to meet the demand of this tax, and thus the public would be taxing itself in order to raise money to pay over to itself, and no one would be benefited but the officers employed, whose compensation would go to increase the useless levy. It cannot be supposed that the legislature would ever purposely lay such a burden upon public property, and it is therefore a reasonable conclusion that, however general may be the enumeration of property for taxation, the property held by the state and by all its municipalities for governmental purposes was intended to be excluded and the law will be administered as excluding it in fact."

Frequently, however, the courts base their reasoning upon other grounds than the presumption that school property is exempt from special assessment. It is sometimes said, for example, that the special benefit which accrues to school property as a result of local improvements is of a nonpecuniary nature, inasmuch as school property is held and used for educational purposes, is not held for speculation, and is not subject to barter and sale.[230] Sometimes, too, it is held that appropriation of school funds to the payment of special assessments violates constitutional provisions which require that such funds be used for the maintenance of schools and for no other purpose.[231] In a few cases it is reasoned that since school property cannot be sold to pay the assessment, there is no legal method of enforcing it.[232] This reasoning is based, of course, upon the assumption that the sale of the property is the only statutory mode of enforcing the assessment.

There are other courts, however, and they are relatively numerous, which hold that, under constitutional and statutory provisions exempting school property from taxation, such property is not exempt from

230. *City of Butte* v. *School District No. 1*, 29 Mont. 336, 74 Pac. 869; *City of Hartford* v. *West Middle District*, 45 Conn. 462, 29 Am. Rep. 687.

231. *Wilson* v. *Board of Education*, 226 Ky. 476, 11 S.W. (2d) 143; *City of Louisville* v. *Leatherman*, 99 Ky. 213, 35 S.W. 625; *City of Butte* v. *School District No. 1*, 29 Mont. 336, 74 Pac. 869.

232. *City of Pittsburgh* v. *Sterrett Subdistrict School*, 204 Pa. St. 635, 54 Atl. 463, 61 L.R.A. 183; *City of Duluth* v. *Board of Education*, 133 Minn. 386, 158 N.W. 635, L.R.A. 1916F 861.

special assessments for local improvements.[233] According to these courts, taxation is the rule, and no presumption of exemption will be indulged in either with respect to taxes for purposes of general revenue or for assessments for local improvements.

A case decided by the Supreme Court of Illinois is an excellent illustration of the reasoning employed in arriving at the conclusion that school property is subject to special assessment unless expressly exempt. It was said by the court:

> The right of taxation is essential to the very existence of the government, and all property, of every description, in the state, is subject to taxation, unless it has been specifically exempt. All laws exempting property must be subjected by the courts to a strict construction, and hence nothing will be held to be within the exemption which does not clearly appear so to be. . . .
>
> It is also insisted by appellant that the payment of this special assessment out of the school funds would be a diverting of said funds from the object for which they were created. We do not see how that position can be maintained. A special assessment may be levied for the purpose of paving streets, putting down sidewalks, putting in curbing, or for sewer purposes, all of which are, in theory, for the benefit of the property abutting on the line of the improvement. Undeniably all of these improvements are of great benefit, if not of actual necessity, to a public school, and from the most of them no property derives more benefit than does that of the board of education. They are as necessary to the practical use of the property as the furnishing of heat, light, and air. Special assessment for such improvements is but a method of applying the funds of the school district for the benefit of its schools, and is legal and proper.
>
> It is also insisted that there is no method under the law by means of which the property in question can be sold to enforce the collection of this assessment. It may be conceded the property can not be sold to pay the assessment, but there are other methods provided by law by which the payment can be enforced in case the board of education refuses to pay the same.[234]

It is well settled that property in use for a public purpose cannot be sold on execution or other legal process, and the rule is applicable to the sale of public school property to pay local assessments for pub-

233. *Dinn* v. *Board of Education,* 202 N.Y.S. 62, 121 Misc. Rep. 633; *City of Chicago, to Use of Schools* v. *City of Chicago,* 207 Ill. 37, 69 N.E. 580; *Troutman* v. *City of Zeigler,* 327 Ill. 251, 158 N.E. 355; *City of Sioux City* v. *Independent School District of Sioux City,* 55 Iowa 150, 7 N.E. 488; *School District No. 1* v. *City of Helena,* 87 Mont. 300, 287 Pac. 164; *City of Kalispell* v. *School District No. 5,* 45 Mont. 221, 122 Pac. 742; *In re Howard Avenue North,* 44 Wash. 62, 86 Pac. 1117; *City of Spokane* v. *Fonnell,* 75 Wash. 417, 135 Pac. 211; *City of Wichita* v. *Board of Education,* 92 Kan. 967, 142 Pac. 946; *Whittaker* v. *City of Deadwood,* 23 S.D. 538, 122 N.W. 500; *School District No. 1* v. *City of Cheyenne,* 57 Wyo. 121, 113 Pac. (2d) 958; *Bensberg* v. *Parker,* 192 Ark. 908, 95 S.W. (2d) 892.

234. *City of Chicago, to Use of Schools* v. *City of Chicago,* 207 Ill. 37, 69 N.E. 580.

lic improvements. But a judgment may be had against the district for the amount it is due to pay for a local improvement, and this judgment may be paid out of the district's funds as other judgments are paid.[235]

The courts seem to be in agreement that property owned by a school district but not used actually and exclusively for school purposes is subject to special assessments for local improvement.[236] Similarly, it seems to be the commonly accepted rule that lands donated to a state by Congress are not subject to special assessments.[237]

235. *Blake* v. *Consolidated Special Tax School District,* 115 Fla. 348, 156 So. 97; *Wilson* v. *City of Hollis,* 193 Okla. 241, 142 (Pac.) (2d) 633, 150 A.L.R. 1385.

236. *School District* v. *Board of Improvement,* 65 Ark. 343, 46 S.W. 418; *Witter* v. *Mission School District,* 121 Calif. 350, 53 Pac. 905, 66 Am. St. Rep. 33.

237. *Poock* v. *Ely,* 2 Ohio C.D. 408; *People* v. *Trustees of Schools,* 118 Ill. 52, 7 N.E. 262; *Edgerton* v. *Huntington School Township,* 126 Ind. 261, 26 N.E. 156.

CHAPTER XIII

The Contractor's Bond

AUTHORITY TO REQUIRE BONDS

IN MANY states the statutes make it the duty of boards of education to require of a contractor to whom a building contract is awarded a bond conditioned that the contractor will faithfully perform his contract and that he will pay for all labor and materials employed in the construction of the building. But even in the absence of express statutory authority, a board may require such a bond.[1] It is sometimes contended that school districts do not have the power, unless authorized by statute, to require a bond for the protection of third parties, but the courts are not impressed by such a contention. Authority to contract for the erection of a schoolhouse carries with it, by implication, authority to enter into agreements necessary to protect the interests of the district. Obviously, the interests of the district imperatively demand that a bond be given to insure the district against loss growing out of failure to perform the contract on the part of the contractor. To a lesser degree the interests of the district are protected by requiring a bond conditioned that the contractor will pay for all labor and materials going into the construction of the building. The objects of such bonds are the same as the objects secured by lien laws to private parties. The law will not permit liens against school buildings,[2] because

1. *American Surety Company* v. *Lauber*, 22 Ind. App. 326, 53 N.E. 793; *Williams* v. *Markland*, 15 Ind. App. 669, 44 N.E. 562; *Jefferson County Board of Education* v. *Union Indemnity Company*, 218 Ala. 632, 119 So. 837; *Baker* v. *Bryan*, 64 Iowa 561, 21 N.W. 83; *R. Connor Company* v. *Olson*, 136 Wis. 13, 115 N.W. 811; *Board of President and Directors of St. Louis Public Schools* v. *Woods*, 77 Mo. 197; *Nelson Company* v. *Stephenson*, 168 S.W. (Tex.) 61; *Board of Education* v. *Aetna Indemnity Company*, 159 Ill. App. 319; *Union Sheet Metal Works* v. *Dodge*, 129 Calif. 390, 62 Pac. 41.

2. *R. Connor Company* v. *Olson*, 136 Wis. 13, 115 N.W. 811; *Board of President and Directors of St. Louis Public Schools* v. *Woods*, 77 Mo. 197; *Nelson Company* v. *Stephenson*, 168 S.W. (Tex.) 61; *Page Trust Company* v. *Carolina Construction Company*, 191 N.C. 664, 132 S.E. 804; *Morganton Hardware Company*

to do so would be violative of public policy. In the absence of a bond, therefore, those who furnish labor and materials have to rely solely upon the personal responsibility of the contractor. Obviously, bonds conditioned for the payment of labor and materials not only afford protection to persons furnishing such but operate to the interest of the school district by enabling it to secure better and cheaper materials due to the absence of risk and loss. Such bonds greatly increase the credit of the contractor, thus enabling him to secure labor and materials on better terms. Moreover, they strengthen the position of the small contractor and thus promote competition.

EFFECT UPON CONTRACT OF REFUSAL TO
ACCEPT BOND TENDERED

Where a building contract provides that the contractor shall give a bond with such sureties as the board may approve, the question may arise as to the effect upon the contract of the board's refusal to accept the bond tendered. In such a case, a board's action in refusing to accept the bond will be upheld unless the board acts capriciously, unreasonably, or in bad faith.[3]

Where one party agrees to deliver to another party a bond satisfactory to the latter for the performance of the contract the expression of dissatisfaction by the latter with the bond tendered is sufficient, without more, to excuse the latter from the performance of the condition of his contract, if there is no evidence that the rejection of the bond was due to an unreasonable or capricious motive.[4]

Thus, where a board is sued for breach of contract because it refuses to accept the bond tendered, it is not enough to show that the bond was in fact sufficient; it must be shown that the board acted in bad faith, that it was not honestly dissatisfied.[5]

v. *Morganton Graded School*, 150 N.C. 680, 64 S.E. 764, 134 Am. St. Rep. 953, 17 Ann. Cas. 130; *Dalzell v. Bourbon County Board of Education*, 193 Ky. 171, 235 S.W. 360; *Fatout v. Board of School Commissioners*, 102 Ind. 223, 1 N.E. 389; *Green Bay Lumber Company v. Independent School District of Odebolt*, 121 Iowa 663, 97 N.W. 72; *Tennessee Supply Company v. Bina Young & Son*, 142 Tenn. 142, 218 S.W. 225; *Special Tax School District No. 1 v. Smith*, 61 Fla. 782, 54 So. 376, Ann. Cas. 1913A 757.

3. *Vandenberg v. Board of Education*, 117 Kan. 48, 230 Pac. 321; 13 C.J. 675, 676, 678.

4. *Smith v. Weaver*, 41 Pa. Super. Ct. 253.

5. *Vandenberg v. Board of Education*, 117 Kan. 48, 230 Pac. 321; 13 C.J. 678.

CONTRACT AND BOND TO BE CONSTRUED TOGETHER

Where a bond is given to insure the performance of a contract, ordinarily the obligation of the bond is to be read in the light of the contract it is given to secure. That is, the extent of the engagement entered into by the surety is to be measured by the terms of the principal's agreement.[6] The rule has been clearly expressed in the case of *Fuller & Company* v. *Alturas School District:*

But it is also elementary that a bond given to guarantee the execution of a contract according to its terms becomes a part of such contract, and to that contract the sureties become parties the same as though they had actually made and executed the contract itself. Therefore, in interpreting the language of the undertaking for the purpose of gathering its scope or the measure of the liability of the sureties, we must do so by treating or viewing the contract and the undertaking as a whole or as constituting an indivisible contract. In other words, we must, in order to ascertain the nature and extent of the liability to which the sureties have bound themselves, examine the undertaking by the light of the agreement of whose terms it guarantees the faithful performance.[7]

Where, however, the liability as fixed in the contract is broader in its scope than the liability fixed in the bond, it has been held that the terms of the bond determine the surety's liability.[8] The courts reason in such cases that there has been a waiver in the bond of some of the conditions in the contract. Thus it was said in a Wisconsin case: "The fact that the city expressly contracted that the bond given should be for the payment of materialmen and laborers, and then accepted a bond without such a condition, is clearly a waiver of that condition of the contract, and indicates an intention to abandon or relinquish its

6. *Robinson Manufacturing Company* v. *Blaylock*, 192 N.C. 407, 135 S.E. 136; *Ideal Brick Company* v. *Gentry*, 191 N.C. 636, 132 S.E. 800; *Fuller & Company* v. *Alturas School District*, 28 Calif. App. 609, 153 Pac. 743; *Baumann* v. *City of West Allis*, 187 Wis. 506, 204 N.W. 907; *City National Bank of Mason City* v. *Independent School District of Mason City*, 190 Iowa 25, 179 N.W. 947; *Board of Education* v. *U.S. Fidelity & Guaranty Company*, 155 Mo. App. 109, 134 S.W. 18; *Tug River Lumber Company* v. *Smithey*, 107 W. Va. 482, 148 S.E. 850; *Fodge* v. *Board of Education of Oak Park*, 309 Ill. App. 109, 32 N.E. (2d) 650.

7. *Fuller & Company* v. *Alturas School District*, 28 Calif. App. 609, 153 Pac. 743.

8. *Electric Appliance Company* v. *U.S. Fidelity & Guaranty Company*, 110 Wis. 434, 85 N.W. 648, 53 L.R.A. 609; *Ideal Brick Company* v. *Gentry*, 191 N.C. 636, 132 S.E. 800; *Builders' Material & Supply Company* v. *J. B. Evans Construction Company*, 204 Mo. App. 76, 221 S.W. 142; *Dunlap* v. *Eden*, 15 Ind. App. 575, 44 N.E. 560; *Town of Windsor, etc.* v. *Standard Accident Insurance Company*, 112 Vt. 426, 26 Atl. (2d) 83; *Massachusetts Bonding and Insurance Company* v. *United States Radiator Corporation*, 265 Ky. 661, 97 S.W. (2d) 586.

scheme in that respect."[9] Similarly, in Missouri, a contract provided for a bond conditioned for the payment of labor and materials, but the bond was given to indemnify the school board against loss, damage, or liens. The court held that the board in accepting the bond had waived the condition in the contract calling for a bond to protect laborers and materialmen.[10]

INTERPRETATION OF SURETY BONDS

It is a well-established rule that a voluntary or accommodation surety, one who from purely disinterested motives gives bond for another without pay, is a favorite of the law. In such a case the rule of *strictissimi juris* applies, and all doubt is resolved in favor of the surety.[11] But the rule is otherwise in the case of sureties engaged in the business of making bonds for hire. "The old-time accommodation surety has the benefit of the rule, whilst the hireling has not."[12] The courts, almost without exception, hold that in the case of a surety company, acting for compensation, the bond must be construed strictly.[13] Such contracts are to be construed as are other contracts and according to the intention of the contracting parties.[14] Where the terms are definite, the courts will not extend or enlarge upon them. But where the contract is ambiguous, where there is room for construction, the con-

9. *Electric Appliance Company* v. *U.S. Fidelity & Guaranty Company*, 110 Wis. 434, 85 N.W. 648, 53 L.R.A. 609.

10. *Builders' Material & Supply Company* v. *J. B. Evans Construction Company*, 204 Mo. App. 76, 221 S.W. 142.

11. *School District No. 18* v. *McClure*, 224 S.W. (Mo.) 831; *Maryland Casualty Company* v. *Eagle River Union Free High School District*, 188 Wis. 520, 205 N.W. 926.

12. *School District No. 18* v. *McClure*, 224 S.W. (Mo.) 831.

13. *Royal Indemnity Company* v. *Northern Ohio Granite & Stone Company*, 100 Ohio St. 373, 126 N.E. 405, 12 A.L.R. 378; *Joint School District No. 4* v. *Bailey-Marsh Company*, 181 Wis. 202, 194 N.W. 171; *Maryland Casualty Company* v. *Eagle River Union Free High School District*, 188 Wis. 520, 205 N.W. 926; *School District No. 18* v. *McClure*, 224 S.W. (Mo.) 831. NOTE: 12 A.L.R. 382; *Town of Windsor* v. *Standard Accident Insurance Company*, 112 Vt. 426, 26 Atl. (2d) 83.

14. *School District No. 18* v. *McClure*, 224 S.W. (Mo.) 831; *Joint School District No. 4* v. *Bailey-Marsh Company*, 181 Wis. 202, 194 N.W. 171; *Topeka* v. *Federal Union Surety Company*, 213 Fed. 958; *Blyth-Fargo Company* v. *Free*, 46 Utah, 233, 148 Pac. 427.

tract will be construed strongly against the surety and in favor of the indemnity which the obligee had reasonable ground to expect.[15] Such contracts, it is commonly said, have all the features of an insurance contract and must be construed accordingly.[16] The rule and the reason for it have been stated as follows by the Supreme Court of Wisconsin:

> Due to the fact that modern corporations have undertaken the business of becoming sureties and indemnitors, that under such circumstances the applications and bonds are usually prepared by the surety, the same rule of law is applied to those contracts that is applied to other contracts which are prepared by and for the benefit of a party. While it is stated in many opinions that the rules of interpretation applicable to contracts of a gratuitous surety are not to be applied in a case of a surety for compensation, it is meant that a different rule of law is applicable because the changed situation makes it applicable. This court has held that where a bond is given for a money consideration it has all the essential features of an insurance contract and is therefore not to be construed according to the rules of law applicable to the contract of an ordinary accommodation surety. . . .
>
> Such contracts are to be interpreted as are other contracts, with a view to ascertaining and giving effect to the true meaning and intention of the parties.[17]

With respect to the interpretation to be given to a surety contract which is uncertain in its terms, the Supreme Court of Ohio has said:

> Unlike an ordinary private surety, a surety of the character here involved, which accepts money consideration, has the power to and does fix the amount of its premium so as to cover its financial responsibility. This class of suretyships, therefore, is not regarded as "a favorite of the law." . . . And if the terms of the surety contract are susceptible of two constructions, that one should be adopted, if consistent with the purpose to be accomplished, which is most favorable to the beneficiary. . . . Especially is this so when the contract of suretyship employs ambiguous terms relating to those furnishing labor and material which enter into the structure.[18]

15. *Blyth-Fargo Company* v. *Free,* 46 Utah 233, 148 Pac. 427; *Royal Indemnity Company* v. *Northern Ohio Granite & Stone Company,* 100 Ohio St. 373, 126 N.E. 405, 12 A.L.R. 378; *Maryland Casualty Company* v. *Eagle River Union Free High School District,* 188 Wis. 520, 205 N.W. 926; *Topeka* v. *Federal Union Surety Company,* 213 Fed. 958; *United States Fidelity & Guaranty Company* v. *Poetker,* 180 Ind. 255, 102 N.E. 372, L.R.A. 1917B 984.

16. *Joint School District No. 4* v. *Bailey-Marsh Company,* 181 Wis. 202, 194 N.W. 171; *Maryland Casualty Company* v. *Eagle River Union Free High School District,* 188 Wis. 520, 205 N.W. 926; *Rule* v. *Anderson,* 160 Mo. App. 347, 142 S.W. 358.

17. *Joint School District No. 4* v. *Bailey-Marsh Company,* 181 Wis. 202, 194 N.W. 171.

18. *Royal Indemnity Company* v. *Northern Ohio Granite & Stone Company,* 100 Ohio St. 373, 126 N.E. 405, 12 A.L.R. 378.

RELEASE OF SURETY BECAUSE OF VARIANCE IN
PERFORMANCE OF CONTRACT

The principles of the common law declaring the rights and liabilities of sureties were developed in an atmosphere surcharged with sympathy for the surety. Consequently, it was held that any act on the part of the obligee prejudicial to the interests of the surety resulted in a total release of the surety from any liability.[19] And in most jurisdictions it was held that any change in the principal contract, whether it increased the risk of the surety or not, discharged the surety from his obligations.[20] In the case of *Independent District of Mason City* v. *Reichard*,[21] for example, a bond was given to insure the performance of a building contract. Later the terms of the contract were changed. The court held that the surety was entirely relieved of responsibility:

"Any alteration, however *bona fide*, by the creditor and the principal, without the assent of the surety, of the terms of the original agreement, so far as they relate to the subject-matter in respect of which the surety became responsible for the principal, will exonerate the surety" (Chitty on *Contracts* [11th ed.], 776). "And this doctrine seems to hold, although the new terms thus substituted vary only in a slight degree from those of the original agreement" (*idem* 777). In regard to this principle, in *Miller* v. *Stewart,* 9 Wheat. 680, it is said: "It is not sufficient that he [a surety] may sustain no injury by a change in the contract, or that it may even be for his benefit. He has a right to stand upon the very terms of his contract, and if he does not assent to any variation of it, and a variation is made, it is fatal."

Similarly, Mr. Justice Field, speaking for the Supreme Court of the United States, has said with respect to the liability of sureties:

Any change in the contract, on which they are sureties, made by the principal parties to it without their assent, discharges them, and for obvious reasons. When the change is made they are not bound by the contract in its original form, for that has ceased to exist. They are not bound by the contract in its altered form, for to that they have never assented. Nor does it matter how trivial the change, or even that it may be of advantage to the sureties. They have a right to stand upon the very terms of their undertaking.[22]

19. *Miller* v. *Stewart,* 9 Wheat. 680, 6 L. Ed. 189; *Reese* v. *United States,* 9 Wall. 13, 19 L. Ed. 541; *Prairie State Bank* v. *United States,* 164 U.S. 227, 17 S. Ct. 142, 41 L. Ed. 412; *Independent District of Mason City* v. *Reichard,* 50 Iowa 98.

20. *Reese* v. *United States,* 9 Wall. 13, 19 L. Ed. 541; *Miller* v. *Stewart,* 9 Wheat. 680, 6 L. Ed. 189; *Beers* v. *Wolf,* 116 Mo. 179, 22 S.W. 620; *Woodruff* v. *Schultz,* 155 Mich. 11, 118 N.W. 579, 16 Ann. Cas. 346; *Wolf* v. *Aetna Indemnity Company,* 163 Calif. 597, 126 Pac. 470.

21. *Independent District of Mason City* v. *Reichard,* 50 Iowa 98.

22. *Reese* v. *United States,* 9 Wall. 13, 19 L. Ed. 541.

But the rise of bonding companies has created new conditions and a new rule. In the case of a surety for hire, variance in the performance of the contract will not release the surety from his liabilities unless the variance substantially increases the chances of loss insured against.[23] Thus, in the case of *Rule v. Anderson*,[24] it was said:

The deep solicitude of the law for the welfare of voluntary parties who bound themselves from purely disinterested motives never comprehended the protection of pecuniary enterprises organized for the express purpose of engaging in the business of suretyship for profit. To allow such companies to collect and retain premiums for their services, graded according to the nature and extent of the risk, and then to repudiate their obligations on slight pretexts that have no relation to the risk, would be most unjust and immoral and would be a perversion of the wise and just rules designed for the protection of voluntary sureties. The contracts of surety companies are contracts of indemnity and, as such, fall under the rules of construction applicable to contracts of insurance. Since they are prepared by the companies and generally abound with conditions and stipulations devised for the restriction of the obligation assumed by the company, such stipulations must not be extended to favor limitations providing for forfeiture of the contract. They must be strictly construed and no unreasonable right of forfeiture should be allowed.

Paid sureties understand that they are not given the same consideration as are voluntary sureties under the common law, but they seem to be left more or less in doubt as to what extent that consideration has been withdrawn. If there is variation in the performance of the contract from the terms of the contract and the surety thereby suffers loss, is the surety entirely relieved of responsibility, or relieved only *pro tanto?* Perhaps in most jurisdictions the surety would be released entirely where the change in the principal contract materially increased the liability of the surety. The Supreme Court of Wisconsin lays down a rule governing the liability of sureties which seems entirely reasonable. The facts of the case were as follows: a contract for the construction of a school building provided that at the end of each month the district should pay, on certificate of the architect, 90 per cent of the value of the work done and materials provided in the construction of the house. The contractor ran out of funds and was unable

23. *School District v. McCurley*, 92 Kan. 53, 142 Pac. 1077, Ann. Cas. 1916B 238; *Chicago Lumber Company v. Douglas*, 89 Kan. 308, 131 Pac. 563, 44 L.R.A. (N.S.) 843; *Rule v. Anderson*, 160 Mo. App. 347, 142 S.W. 358; *Hileman & Gindt v. Faus*, 178 Iowa 644, 158 N.W. 597; *Cooke v. White Common School District No. 7*, 33 Ky. Law Rep. 926, 111 S.W. 686; *Maryland Casualty Company v. Eagle River Union Free High School District*, 188 Wis. 520, 205 N.W. 926. Note: 12 A.L.R. 382.

24. *Rule v. Anderson*, 160 Mo. App. 347, 142 S.W. 358.

to prosecute the work. Arrangements were made by which the school board advanced money, without the certificate of the architect, to be used by the contractor in carrying the work forward. Money was deposited in a bank to the credit of the contractor, against which deposit he drew checks in payment for labor and materials actually entering into the construction of the building. Finally, the contractor abandoned the work and the school board completed the building, but in doing so it expended a sum in excess of the contract price. Action was brought to recover such excess from the surety, but the surety contended that by the action of the board it had been released. The court refused to relieve the surety entirely, laying down the rule that in such cases the surety should be compensated for such damage as it had suffered by acts prejudicial to its interests:

> It would seem, too, that not every circumstance prejudicial to the interests of the surety should work a total discharge of the surety without any reference or consideration to the extent to which the interests of the surety were in fact prejudiced by such circumstance. In other words, a paid surety should not suffer damage, by breach of any duty or obligation resting upon the indemnified, but neither should the surety be permitted to profit thereby. If the breach on the part of the indemnified results in damage to the surety, the surety should be compensated for such damage, but no further. . . .
>
> There can be no injustice in requiring a paid surety, when in the business for profit, to prove that alleged delinquencies or misconduct on the part of the indemnified resulted not only in damage to the surety, but the extent of such damage. That is nothing more nor less than a rule applied with reference to contracts generally, except perhaps cases where the breach of a contract is so material as to justify the other party in rescinding the contract. We must not be understood as saying that there can be no conduct on the part of the indemnified which will result in the absolute discharge of the paid surety, but we say that, as a general proposition, considerations of justice are fully met when the surety is recouped to the extent of the losses actually sustained by reason of misconduct on the part of the indemnified.[25]

Where the original contract specially provides for changes and alterations, such changes and alterations will not work a release of the surety.[26] Such changes are assumed to have been in the contemplation of the surety when he executed the bond. The alteration in the terms

25. *Maryland Casualty Company* v. *Eagle River Union Free High School District,* 188 Wis. 520, 205 N.W. 926. Accord, *Joint School District No. 4* v. *Bailey-Marsh Company,* 181 Wis. 202, 194 N.W. 171.

26. *Young* v. *Young,* 21 Ind. App. 509, 52 N.E. 776; *Cass* v. *Smith,* 146 Tenn. 218, 240 S.W. 778; *Drumheller* v. *American Surety Company,* 30 Wash. 530, 71 Pac. 25; *Hayden* v. *Cook,* 34 Neb. 670, 52 N.W. 165; *American Surety Company* v. *Lauber,* 22 Ind. App. 326, 53 N.E. 793.

of the original contract must not, however, be so great as to destroy the original contract and create a new one. For example, in the case of *Cass* v. *Smith*,[27] the original contract provided that alterations might be made. The board of education decided to have the basement made four feet deeper than originally planned. The extra expense was two thousand dollars. The court held that this was not, under the circumstances, such an alteration of the original contract as to relieve the surety of responsibility.

Whatever may be the effect of an alteration of the original contract upon the rights of the board as against the surety, there is no change in the obligation of the surety to laborers and materialmen who were not parties to the alteration.[28] That is, where a surety gives a bond guaranteeing the performance of the building contract and also conditioned to pay for all labor and material employed in the construction of the building, a change in the terms of the contract agreed to by the board and the contractor will not release the surety from his obligations to laborers and materialmen. Such a bond has a double obligatory aspect, one for the protection of the school board and one for the protection of laborers and materialmen. The rights of the latter cannot be prejudiced by any acts of either of the other stipulating parties.[29] Where, for example, there was a change in the location of the building from the location called for in the contract, and the change involved a certain amount of grading but in no way affected the general character of the building, the obligation of the surety to materialmen remained unaffected.[30] Of course, if the changes in the original contract were so great as to amount to an abandonment, so that persons furnishing labor and material would necessarily be charged with notice of such abandonment, it might very well, and probably would, be held that the surety was relieved of all liability.

27. *Cass* v. *Smith*, 146 Tenn. 218, 240 S.W. 778.

28. *Equitable Surety Company* v. *United States*, 234 U.S. 448, 34 S. Ct. 803, 58 L. Ed. 1394; *Cass* v. *Smith*, 146 Tenn. 218, 240 S.W. 778; *School District No. 30* v. *Alameda Construction Company*, 87 Ore. 132, 169 Pac. 507; *United States* v. *National Surety Company*, 92 Fed. 549; *U.S. Fidelity and Guaranty Company* v. *Cicero Smith Lumber Company*, 290 S.W. (Tex.) 307.

29. *School District No. 30* v. *Alameda Construction Company*, 87 Ore. 132, 169 Pac. 507.

30. *Equitable Surety Company* v. *United States*, 234 U.S. 448, 34 S. Ct. 803, 58 L. Ed. 1394.

EFFECT OF VOID CONTRACT UPON LIABILITY
OF SURETY

Where a bond is given to insure the performance of a contract which is void, the weight of authority seems to be that the surety is relieved of responsibility to the school board,[31] but that the invalidity of the building contract in no way affects the liability of the surety to those who furnish labor and materials used in the construction of the building.[32] In the case of *Metz* v. *Warrick*,[33] for example, the building contract was not in writing, as the law required. The contract was held to be void, and the surety relieved of all liability. The surety, it was said, could not be bound to guarantee the performance of a contract which did not exist. In this case the bond was not conditioned for the payment of laborers and materialmen, and that issue was not before the court. But where a contract was conditioned to indemnify the obligee for failure to complete the building properly and to pay for the labor and materials used in the construction of the building, the court said:

Although the contract, in our opinion, as heretofore stated, is void, it does not follow that the obligation resting upon the sureties in the contractor's bond is discharged; on the contrary, the weight of authority is that the invalidity of the building contract in no way affects the liability of the sureties upon the contractor's bond for the value of materials and labor furnished the contractor in the prosecution of the public work (4 Elliot on *Contracts* § 3543; 27 L.R.A. [N.S.] 597, n. 13; 13 L.R.A. [N.S.] 793 and note).[34]

LIABILITY OF SURETY AS AFFECTED BY
STATUTORY REQUIREMENTS

Since public policy will not permit those who furnish labor and materials employed in the construction of a school building to file a lien against the building, many states require by statute that a bond be given by the contractor, conditioned to pay for labor and materials. Frequently the bond given does not, in specific terms, provide for payment of labor and materials, or it may even expressly or by necessary

31. *Metz* v. *Warrick*, 217 Mo. App. 504, 269 S.W. 626; *Southern Surety Company* v. *Moores-Coney Company*, 29 Ohio App. 310, 163 N.E. 575.

32. *Kerbow* v. *Wooldridge*, 184 S.W. (Tex.) 746; *Mississippi Fire Insurance Company* v. *Evans*, 153 Miss. 635, 120 So. 738. See also 27 L.R.A. (N.S.) 597 and note; 13 L.R.A. (N.S.) 793 and note.

33. *Metz* v. *Warrick*, 217 Mo. App. 504, 269 S.W. 626.

34. *Kerbow* v. *Wooldridge*, 184 S.W. (Tex.) 746.

implication exclude any liability to pay for labor and materials. The question then arises as to whether the provisions of the statute are to be read into the bond or whether the bond shall be interpreted strictly according to its terms. On this point the decisions are in sharp conflict. It is well established that where it is clear from the surrounding circumstances or certain provisions in the bond that the parties intended to execute a statutory bond, the terms of the statute will be read into the bond, even though in many particulars it does not conform to the statute.[35] But where the bond as given evidently was not intended to conform to the statute or is contradictory to it, the courts are in conflict in their interpretations of it. According to one line of decisions, such a bond is to be regarded as a statutory bond and the terms of the statute are to be read into it.[36] It is assumed in such cases that the parties contracted in contemplation of the statute and that the terms of the statute became a part of the contract. Moreover, to hold otherwise would permit contractors to defeat public policy as expressed in the statutes. But another line of decisions holds that the bond should be interpreted strictly, that whether or not laborers and materialmen are protected depends upon the wording of the bond. In other words, the terms of the statute will not be read into the bond.[37]

35. *Reiff* v. *Redfield School Board*, 126 Ark. 474, 191 S.W. 16; *Acme Brick Company* v. *Taylor*, 223 S.W. (Tex.) 248; *Philip Carey Company* v. *Maryland Casualty Company*, 201 Iowa 1167, 206 N.W. 808; *Fogarty* v. *Davis*, 305 Mo. 288, 264 S.W. 879; *Board of Education* v. *United States Fidelity & Guaranty Company*, 155 Mo. App. 109, 134 S.W. 18; *Tug River Lumber Company* v. *Smithey*, 107 W. Va. 482, 148 N.E. 850; *Maryland Casualty Company* v. *Fowler*, 27 Fed. (2d) 421; *School District* v. *Alameda Construction Company*, 87 Ore. 132, 169 Pac. 507.

36. *Baumann* v. *City of West Allis*, 187 Wis. 506, 204 N.W. 907; *Philip Carey Company* v. *Maryland Casualty Company*, 201 Iowa 1167, 206 N.W. 808; *Globe Indemnity Company* v. *Barnes*, 288 S.W. (Tex.) 121; *Nye-Schneider-Fowler Company* v. *Roeser*, 103 Neb. 614, 173 N.W. 605; *Board of Education* v. *U.S. Fidelity & Guaranty Company*, 155 Mo. App. 109, 134 S.W. 18; *Fogarty* v. *Davis*, 305 Mo. 288, 264 S.W. 879; *School District No. 30* v. *Alameda Construction Company*, 87 Ore. 132, 169 Pac. 507; *Tug River Lumber Company* v. *Smithey*, 107 W. Va. 482, 148 S.E. 850; *Union Indemnity Company* v. *Acme Blow Pipe & Sheet Metal Works*, 150 Miss. 332, 117 So. 251; *Southern Surety Company* v. *Chambers*, 115 Ohio St. 434, 154 N.E. 786; *United States Fidelity and Guaranty Company* v. *Tafel Electric Company*, 262 Ky. 792, 91 S.W. (2d) 42; *Ceco Steel Products Corporation* v. *Tapager*, 208 Minn. 367, 294 N.W. 210; *Camdenton Consolidated School District No. 6* v. *New York Casualty Company*, 340 Mo. 1070, 104 S.W. (2d) 319; *MacDonald* v. *Calumet Supply Company*, 215 Ind. 536, 19 N.E. (2d) 567, 122 A.L.R. 502; *Petition of Leon Keyser, Incorporated*, 89 Atl. (2d) (N.H.) 917; *Metz* v. *Warrick*, 217 Mo. App. 504, 269 S.W. 626; *Fodge* v. *Board of Education of Village of Oak Park*, 309 Ill. App. 109, 32 N.E. (2d) 650.

37. *McCausland & Company* v. *R. A. Brown Construction Company*, 172 N.C. 708, 90 S.E. 1010; *Ideal Brick Company* v. *Gentry*, 191 N.C. 636, 132 S.E. 800;

The case of *Baumann* v. *City of West Allis*[38] is an excellent illustration of the reasoning underlying the decisions which hold that the statute should be read into the bond. The statute provided that in all contracts for the construction of public works a clause be inserted providing for the payment of labor performed and materials used, and that no such contract be made unless the contractor give a bond conditioned for the faithful performance of the contract and for the payment of labor performed and materials furnished in or about the contract. A contract was let for the construction of a building and a bond taken to insure its performance, but neither the contract nor the bond provided for the payment of laborers and materialmen. Nevertheless, the court held that it was a statutory bond and that the surety was liable to subcontractors for the amount of the material and labor furnished by them in the construction of the building.

It is the contention of appellants that the liability sought to be imposed by the statute does not arise unless the provision required by the statute is actually inserted in the contract. If this construction is correct, then the relief which the legislature attempted to afford subcontractors and materialmen is very much like sounding brass. The remedy which the legislature intended to extend may under such a construction be defeated if the parties to the contract do not insert the prescribed provision, and whether the remedy is available to subcontractors and materialmen depends not upon the law but upon the parties to the contract. If this be the proper construction of the law, then the statute might just as well not have been passed, because such was the law before. Such a statute will be construed in the light of the conditions and circumstances which gave rise to the law and to effectuate the purpose which the legislature sought to accomplish. Having discovered that purpose, the law should be construed to give effect thereto. We entertain no doubt that it was the purpose of the legislature to afford a remedy, in the nature of an action against the surety, to all subcontractors furnishing labor or material entering into the construction of public buildings and public works mentioned in the section of the statutes. This purpose may not be defeated by the voluntary act or by the oversight of the parties in failing to insert such a provision in the contract. The law imputes such provision to the contract whether written therein or not. The liability is one arising by virtue of the law independent of the contract. Like the law providing for a standard fire insurance policy, it is both a law and a contract.

Page Trust Company v. *Carolina Construction Company*, 191 N.C. 664, 132 S.E. 804; *United Supply Company* v. *U.S. Fidelity & Guaranty Company*, 32 Ga. App. 472, 123 S.E. 907; *Aetna Casualty & Surety Company* v. *Leathers*, 33 Ga. App. 444, 126 S.E. 881; *Massachusetts Bonding & Insurance Company* v. *Hoffman*, 34 Ga. App. 565, 130 S.E. 375; *Tennessee Supply Company* v. *Bina Young & Son*, 142 Tenn. 142, 218 S.W. 225; *Hardison & Company* v. *Yeaman*, 115 Tenn. 639, 91 S.W. 1111; *Puget Sound Brick, Tile & Terra Cotta Company* v. *School District No. 73*, 12 Wash. 118, 40 Pac. 608; *Dillard* v. *Berry*, 126 Okla. 1, 257 Pac. 772.

38. *Baumann* v. *City of West Allis*, 187 Wis. 506, 204 N.W. 907.

Similarly, in the case of *School District No. 30* v. *Alameda Construc-struction Company*,[39] the statutes provided that any person or firm contracting with a school board for the construction of a schoolhouse should give a bond conditioned to pay for materials and labor. The terms of the statute were read into the bond. "It is true," said the court, "the answer denies that the Surety Company agreed to pay anyone except the School District, but the statute above named must be read as part of the undertaking because the latter instrument was made to fulfill the requirements of that law."

A few cases will serve to illustrate the reasoning of those courts which refuse to read the terms of the statute into a contractor's bond. In the case of *Acme Brick Company* v. *Taylor*,[40] the statute provided that a contractor erecting a public building should execute a bond conditioned to pay for labor and materials used in the construction of the building. Such a bond was not taken, but the court refused to read the terms of the statute into the bond:

> The bond here involved contains no such stipulation, and therefore is not the bond required by the statute with reference to public buildings. It may be good as a common-law bond, but does not bind the surety further than therein specifically stated, which is that the principal shall faithfully perform his contract with the obligees. This it appears he did, for the building was completed and received by the school trustees, and the full price paid therefor. It is true that a statutory bond will be construed in the light of the statute, and will impose upon the bondsman all of the liabilities required by the statute, where it appears that it was the intention to execute such statutory bond; but no such intention appears from the bond in this case. The trustees failed to discharge their duty in not taking a bond as required by statute, but that cannot make the bondsman liable for something that he did not guarantee.

In a Tennessee case[41] it was required by statute that school officers take a bond conditioned to pay for labor and materials. No such stipulation was contained in the bond taken. The court gave the following reason for its refusal to read the statute into the bond:

> It is axiomatic and fundamental that the obligation of a surety is *strictissimi juris*, and cannot be extended beyond the limits of his engagement. It has been held that, where a city takes the usual form of fidelity bond from a surety company in the place of the form of official bond prescribed by statute, the statute cannot be read into it, and the state must abide by the terms and limitations of the bond as given.

39. *School District No. 30* v. *Alameda Construction Company*, 87 Ore. 132, 169 Pac. 507.

40. *Acme Brick Company* v. *Taylor*, 223 S.W. (Tex.) 248.

41. *Hardison & Company* v. *Yeaman*, 115 Tenn. 639, 91 S.W. 1111.

Again, in the case of *Tennessee Supply Company* v. *Bina Young &
Son*[42] the statute required that a bond be taken conditioned to pay
for all labor and materials, but such a bond was not taken. The court
refused to read the statute into the bond and thus make the surety
liable, because it was apparent that the bond had been executed
for the exclusive benefit of the owner (school board). Inasmuch as
laborers and materialmen were not named as beneficiaries in the bond,
they had no cause of action against the surety. Similarly, in North
Carolina a statute made it the duty of school boards to take a bond
conditioned for the payment of laborers and materials. The bond actually given was conditioned to protect the board only. The court refused to read the statute into the bond but said: "And, in reference
to our own statute requiring that a bond to protect such claimants
shall be taken . . . if the statute had provided that any bond taken in
such cases should inure to the benefit of laborers and material men,
this might be construed as constituting a part of contracts to which
the statute applied."[43]

LIABILITY OF SURETY FOR LABOR AND MATERIALS
FURNISHED SUBCONTRACTOR

Where the statutes require that a bond be given conditioned for
the payment of labor and materials used in the construction of a building, the question may arise as to whether such a bond is broad enough
to protect those who furnish labor and materials to a subcontractor.
According to the weight of authority, the surety is not relieved when
the contractor pays the subcontractor; the surety is bound until the
subcontractor pays for labor and materials used.[44] In a North Carolina
case,[45] for example, L. B. Flora and Company contracted to construct

42. *Tennessee Supply Company* v. *Bina Young & Son*, 142 Tenn. 142, 218 S.W.
225.

43. *McCausland & Company* v. *R. A. Brown Construction Company*, 172 N.C.
708, 90 S.E. 1010.

44. *United States* v. *American Surety Company*, 200 U.S. 197, 26 S. Ct. 168,
50 L. Ed. 437; *Standard Electric Time Company* v. *Fidelity & Deposit Company
of Maryland*, 191 N.C. 653, 132 S.E. 808; *Columbia County* v. *Consolidated Contract Company*, 83 Ore. 251, 163 Pac. 438; *School District No. 45* v. *Hallock*, 86
Ore. 687, 169 Pac. 130; *Oliver Construction Company* v. *Williams*, 152 Ark. 414,
238 S.W. 615; *Lower Merion Township School District* v. *Evans*, 295 Pa. St. 280,
145 Atl. 288; *Board of Education* v. *Aetna Casualty & Surety Company*, 305 Ill.
App. 246, 27 N.E. (2d) 337.

45. *Standard Electric Time Company* v. *Fidelity & Deposit Company of Maryland*, 191 N.C. 653, 132 S.E. 808.

a schoolhouse and gave bond, as the statutes required, conditioned to pay for all supplies and "materials furnished for said work." The Flora Company sublet to the Wells Electric Company that portion of the work which had to do with installation of the electric time-equipment and fire-alarm systems. The Wells Electric Company purchased certain fixtures from the Standard Electric Company. The Flora Company, the general contractor, made a complete settlement with the Wells Company, but the Wells Company failed and never paid the Standard Electric Company. The court held that the Standard Electric Company had a right of action against the surety on the bond. To hold that those who furnish labor and materials to a subcontractor are not protected by such a bond would defeat the purpose for which the bond was taken. Moreover, the general contractor may protect himself and his surety against loss by requiring those with whom he deals to give a surety bond for the payment of such persons as furnish work or materials for the building

In Maryland, however, where the bond did not specifically cover subcontractors, the court held that the surety was not liable to subcontractors on a bond conditioned to pay for labor and materials. Said the court: "It seems axiomatic that persons are only bound by the contracts they make, and are not bound by contracts they do not make; that in interpreting contracts effect must be given to the intention of the parties, and that when a contract is written that intention must be found in the language employed where it is clear and unambiguous."[46]

LIABILITY OF SURETY WHERE CONTRACTOR AGREES TO FURNISH LABOR AND MATERIALS

Frequently a contractor agrees to furnish or provide all the labor and materials used in the construction of a building and gives a bond to insure the performance of his contract. The question may then arise as to whether those who furnish labor and materials have a right of action against the surety where the contractor fails to pay for labor and materials used. According to the weight of authority, there is no right of action in such cases because the contractor has not definitely agreed to pay laborers and materialmen.[47] This is true because the

46. *Mayor and City Council of Baltimore, etc.* v. *Maryland Casualty Company,* 171 Md. 667, 190 Atl. 250. See also *Indiana Limestone Company* v. *Cuthbert,* 126 Kan. 262, 267 Pac. 983. NOTE: 111 A.L.R. 305.

47. *Gill* v. *Paysee,* 48 Nev. 12, 226 Pac. 302; *Hardison & Company* v. *Yeaman,*

right to sue on the bond depends entirely upon the terms of the bond and the contract, and the promise to furnish or provide labor and materials cannot be construed as a promise to pay for them. In the case of *Hardison & Company* v. *Yeaman*,[48] both the contract and the bond stipulated that the contractor should "provide good, proper, and efficient materials of all kinds whatsoever for the proper and efficient finishing and completing of all work arising under the contract, and to furnish all materials, labor, etc., of every description." In interpreting this provision of the contract and bond, the court said: "It is very plain that this language does not bind the contractor to pay materialmen and laborers for the material furnished and work done by them, but is simply a stipulation that the contractor will furnish all material and labor necessary in the construction of the building without cost to the owner."

Similarly, in the case of *Petrea* v. *Board of Directors of School District No. 134*[49] the contract merely provided that the contractor should provide all materials and perform all labor. The president of the board of education furnished some lumber to the contractor. There was a disagreement about the amount due for the lumber, and the board, assuming that the contract bound the contractor to pay for materials, paid the president the amount he claimed. The court, however, held that neither the contractor nor his surety was liable for breach of contract, for there was no promise to pay materialmen. The contractor was allowed, therefore, to recover from the board what was due him under the contract. So, too, in a case decided by the Supreme Court of North Carolina,[50] a construction company agreed to construct a school building and to provide all the materials therefor at their own expense. The court held that this agreement did not constitute a contract to pay for all materials but that it was merely an agreement to complete satisfactorily a turnkey job.

---

115 Tenn. 639, 91 S.W. 1111; *Morganton Manufacturing & Trading Company* v. *Anderson*, 165 N.C. 285, 81 S.E. 418, Ann. Cas. 1916A 763; *Warner* v. *Hallyburton*, 187 N.C. 414, 121 S.E. 756; *Petrea* v. *Board of Directors of School District No. 134*, 226 Ill. App. 145; *Green Bay Lumber Company* v. *Independent School District of Odebolt*, 121 Iowa 663, 97 N.W. 72; *Eau Claire–St. Louis Lumber Company* v. *Banks*, 136 Mo. App. 44, 117 S.W. 611; *Puget Sound Brick, Tile & Terra Cotta Company* v. *School District No. 73*, 12 Wash. 118, 40 Pac. 608. Note: Ann. Cas. 1916A 754; *Tremblay* v. *Soucy*, 32 Me. 251, 169 Atl. 737; *Fodge* v. *Board of Education of Village of Oak Park*, 309 Ill. App. 109, 32 N.E. (2d) 650.

48. *Hardison & Company* v. *Yeaman*, 115 Tenn. 639, 91 S.W. 1111.

49. *Petrea* v. *Board of Directors of School District No. 134*, 226 Ill. App. 145.

50. *Warner* v. *Hallyburton*, 187 N.C. 414, 121 S.E. 756.

MEANING OF TERM "LABOR AND MATERIALS" AS USED
IN CONTRACTOR'S BOND

In construing a contractor's bond with respect to the obligations assumed, the courts will not enlarge upon the terms used but will seek merely to discover the intent of the contracting parties. Thus, where a contractor gives a bond conditioned to pay all indebtedness incurred for labor and material furnished in the construction of a school building, the surety on the bond is not liable to a party who has loaned money to the contractor for the purpose of paying for such labor and material, and this is true, even though the money has actually gone into the construction of the building.[51] Nor will the courts hold a surety liable to those who furnish equipment or materials which are used in the construction of the building but which do not go into the construction of the building.[52] The contractor is presumed to be equipped with the necessary tools, machinery, and equipment. Thus it has been held that a surety is not liable for an engine used in hoisting materials,[53] for the rental of a concrete mixer,[54] or for horse feed for teams used in transporting materials.[55]

LIABILITY OF SURETY WHERE BOND IS CONDITIONED TO PROTECT
SCHOOL BOARD AGAINST ALL LIENS AND CLAIMS

A provision in a bond whereby the surety promises to protect the district from all liens on the school building or to pay the claims of laborers and materialmen who may be entitled to liens against the property does not constitute a promise to pay for labor and materials.[56] Such a provision is practically meaningless. This is true because

51. *Rockwell Brothers & Company* v. *Keatley*, 51 Okla. 783, 152 Pac. 449; *United States* v. *Rundle*, 107 Fed. 227, 52 L.R.A. 505. Note: 127 A.L.R. 974.

52. *Nye-Schneider-Fowler Company* v. *Bridges, Hoye & Company*, 98 Neb. 27, 151 N.W. 942; *Royal Indemnity Company* v. *Day & Maddock Company*, 114 Ohio St. 58, 150 N.E. 426.

53. *Nye-Schneider-Fowler Company* v. *Bridges, Hoye & Company*, 98 Neb. 27, 151 N.W. 942.

54. *Royal Indemnity Company* v. *Day & Maddock Company*, 114 Ohio St. 58, 150 N.E. 426.

55. *Cass* v. *Smith*, 146 Tenn. 218, 240 S.W. 778.

56. *Green Bay Lumber Company* v. *Independent School District of Odebolt*, 121 Iowa 663, 97 N.W. 72; *Hunt* v. *King*, 97 Iowa 88, 66 N.W. 71; *Spalding Lumber Company* v. *Brown*, 171 Ill. 487, 49 N.E. 725; *Kerbow* v. *Wooldridge*, 184 S.W. (Tex.) 746. Note: Ann. Cas. 1916A 754.

no one can acquire a lien upon a public building.[57] Thus in an Iowa case[58] the bond was conditioned that the contractor should deliver to the district "said schoolhouse free from liens or claims of any kind," and that he should pay any sum of money that the district might be compelled to pay "to remove any liens, incumbrances or claims of any kind against the building, which may be claimed against the district." The court held that the surety was not liable to materialmen for labor and materials used in the building. "As no liens or claims," said the court, "might be asserted against the building, the sureties were safe in pledging that it should be without them."

DISPOSITION OF FUNDS WHERE CONTRACTOR DEFAULTS

Building contracts commonly provide that the school board shall retain in its own hands until the building is completed a certain percentage of the amount due the contractor each month. When a contractor defaults, it is often a perplexing problem as to what disposition should be made of the funds thus retained. It may be that the contractor has borrowed money from a bank and assigned to the bank as security his rights to the retained percentage. At the same time, he may not have paid for the labor and materials used in the construction of the building. In such a case the bank, the surety on the contractor's bond, and those who have furnished labor and materials may all lay claim to the funds in the hands of the board. In order to prevent loss to the district, the board must determine the proper party to whom the funds are due.

It is elementary that the board may apply the funds in its hands to complete the building according to the terms stipulated in the contract. If the contract provides that the surety of the contractor shall complete the building, it is the duty of the surety, of course, to complete the building as it has agreed to do. Should the surety fail or refuse to complete the building, however, the board may proceed to complete the building itself and apply to that purpose such funds as

57. *R. Connor Company* v. *Olson*, 136 Wis. 13, 115 N.W. 811; *Page Trust Company* v. *Carolina Construction Company*, 191 N.C. 664, 132 S.E. 804; *Dalzell* v. *Bourbon County Board of Education*, 193 Ky. 171, 235 S.W. 360; *Green Bay Lumber Company* v. *Independent School District of Odebolt*, 121 Iowa 663, 97 N.W. 72.

58. *Green Bay Lumber Company* v. *Independent School District of Odebolt*, 121 Iowa 663, 97 N.W. 72.

it may have retained under the terms of the contract. An Iowa case[59] well illustrates the rule. A contractor defaulted, and the surety on his bond refused to complete the building. The board applied the retained percentage due the contractor to the completion of the building, but its right to do so was challenged by one who had furnished material to the original contractor. It was contended that the funds in the board's hands should have been applied to the payment of materials already furnished, and that it was the duty of the surety of the contractor to bear the total cost of completion of the building. The court, however, sustained the right of the board to apply the funds as it had done:

> The right to complete the building under such conditions cannot be made to depend upon a provision of the contract authorizing such to be done, but rests upon the elemental ground that a party to a contract not broken through his fault is entitled to its benefits; and when an expenditure of money is necessary to protect and complete that which is already in his possession, as a result of part performance, such expenditure may be made and recovery had for it.

Where neither the principal contract nor the bond provides that the contractor shall pay for the labor or materials used in the construction of a building, laborers and materialmen have no claim upon the retained percentage in the board's possession.[60] This is true because laborers and materialmen have no lien upon a school building or upon the balance due the contractor. Unless protected in the contract or bond, they stand in the same category as general contract creditors of the contractor.[61] Under such circumstances, moreover, an assignee of the contractor has a claim upon the retained percentage prior to that of laborers and materialmen. In a North Carolina case,[62] the contract to build a schoolhouse did not require the contractor to pay for labor and materials. The contractor borrowed money from a bank, assigning as security his rights in the amount to come due on the building contract. Later he defaulted, and the board completed

59. *Ludowici Caladon Company* v. *Independent School District of Independence,* 169 Iowa 669, 149 N.W. 845.

60. *Page Trust Company* v. *Carolina Construction Company,* 191 N.C. 664, 132 S.E. 804; *Robinson Manufacturing Company* v. *Blaylock,* 192 N.C 407, 135 S.E. 136.

61. *Cass* v. *Smith,* 146 Tenn. 218, 240 S.W. 778.

62. *Page Trust Company* v. *Carolina Construction Company,* 191 N.C. 664, 132 S.E. 804.

the building. It still had in its hands about four thousand dollars due the contractor. The laborers and materialmen and the bank laid claim to this surplus. The court, however, permitted the bank to recover since it was the assignee of the contractor, and the laborers and materialmen had no lien upon the fund.

Where a contractor has borrowed money from a bank and assigned to it as security his rights in the retained percentage in the hands of the school board, it is somewhat difficult to determine whether the bank or the surety on the contractor's bond is entitled to the retained percentage in case the contractor defaults. In order to understand clearly the rights of these parties, one must be familiar with the equitable doctrine of subrogation. In its broadest sense, subrogation is merely the substitution of one person in the place of another with respect to a lawful claim or right.[63] Where equity and good conscience demand that one person be substituted to the legal claims and rights of another, a court of equity will permit substitution. More strictly speaking, where one is required by law, or for the protection of his own interests, to pay the debt of another, he is entitled to be subrogated to all the rights and remedies of the creditor against the person whose debt has been paid.[64]

The right of a surety to subrogation, moreover, begins as of the date of signing the contract of suretyship and not as of the date of paying the debt.[65] It should be kept in mind, however, that the relief afforded by subrogation is never extended to one who voluntarily pays the debt of another, to a mere volunteer.[66] There must always exist the compulsion to pay. It is also true that the right of subrogation does not arise unless the whole debt involved is paid; a *pro tanto* subrogation is never permitted.[67]

Applying the principle of subrogation as thus defined, the courts

63. 25 R.C.L. 311.

64. *Prairie State Bank* v. *United States,* 164 U.S. 227, 17 S. Ct. 142, 41 L. Ed. 412.

65. *Prairie State Bank* v. *United States,* 164 U.S. 227, 17 S. Ct. 142, 41 L. Ed. 412; *Fidelity & Deposit Company of Maryland* v. *Claiborne Parish School Board,* 11 Fed. (2d) 404; *Wasco County* v. *New England Equitable Insurance Company,* 88 Ore. 465, 172 Pac. 126, L.R.A. 1918D 732, Ann. Cas. 1918E 656.

66. *Aetna Life Insurance Company* v. *Middleport,* 124 U.S. 534, 8 S. Ct. 625, 31 L. Ed. 537; *Prairie State Bank* v. *United States,* 164 U.S. 227, 17 S. Ct. 142, 41 L. Ed. 412.

67. *Robinson Manufacturing Company* v. *Blaylock,* 192 N.C. 407, 135 S.E. 136; *Maryland Casualty Company* v. *Fouts,* 11 Fed. (2d) 71.

as a rule hold that where a contractor fails to perform his contract, with respect either to the completion of the building[68] or to the payment for labor and materials,[69] the surety on the contractor's bond has an equity in the retained percentage in the board's hands superior to that of a bank from which the contractor has borrowed money and to which he has assigned as security his rights in the retained percentage. That is, the surety has an equity in the retained percentage superior to that of an assignee of the defaulting contractor. The retained percentage of the consideration, it has been frequently held, is as much for the benefit of the surety as for the party for whom the building is being constructed.[70] Thus it has been said by the Supreme Court of the United States:

> That a stipulation in a building contract for the retention, until the completion of the work, of a certain portion of the consideration, is as much for the indemnity of him who may be guarantor of the performance of the work as for him for whom the work is to be performed; that it raises an equity in the surety in the fund to be created; and that a disregard of such stipulation by the voluntary act of the creditor operates to release the sureties, is amply sustained by authority.[71]

In a Wisconsin case[72] a contractor had borrowed money from a bank and had used the money to pay laborers and materialmen. After the contractor defaulted, the school board paid to the bank five thousand dollars by order of the contractor. The court held that the surety was entitled to the building funds in the board's hands and that the payment to the bank released the surety *pro tanto:*

68. *Prairie State Bank* v. *United States,* 164 U.S. 227, 17 S. Ct. 142, 41 L. Ed. 412; *Joint School District No. 4* v. *Bailey-Marsh Company,* 181 Wis. 202, 194 N.W. 171.

69. *Henningsen* v. *United States Fidelity & Guaranty Company of Baltimore,* 208 U.S. 404, 28 S. Ct. 389, 52 L. Ed. 547; *City National Bank of Mason City* v. *Independent School District of Mason City,* 190 Iowa 25, 179 N.W. 947; *Fidelity & Deposit Company of Maryland* v. *Claiborne Parish School Board,* 11 Fed. (2d) 404; *Wasco County* v. *New England Equitable Insurance Company,* 88 Ore. 465, 172 Pac. 126, L.R.A. 1918D 732, Ann. Cas. 1918E 656; *Southern Surety Company* v. *Sealy Independent School District,* 10 S.W. (2d) (Tex.) 786; *Northwestern Casualty & Surety Company* v. *First National Bank of Madisonville,* 36 S.W. (2d) (Tex.) 535.

70. *Prairie State Bank* v. *United States,* 164 U.S. 227, 17 S. Ct. 142, 41 L. Ed. 412; *Wasco County* v. *New England Equitable Insurance Company,* 88 Ore. 465, 172 Pac. 126, L.R.A. 1918D 732, Ann. Cas. 1918E 656.

71. *Prairie State Bank* v. *United States,* 164 U.S. 227, 17 S. Ct. 142, 41 L. Ed. 412.

72. *Joint School District No. 4* v. *Bailey-Marsh Company,* 181 Wis. 202, 194 N.W. 171.

It is well settled that whenever a creditor has a right and opportunity to apply property of the principal to the satisfaction or security of his debt, he owes to the surety a duty to do so, and release or waiver of that right to the prejudice of the surety and without his consent will discharge the surety, at least *pro tanto*. . . .

The surety, under the principle of law stated, had a right to require the plaintiff to apply the remainder of the building fund to the completion of the building, and the plaintiff had no right, by the acceptance and payment of the order of April 8, 1918, to divert any part of the contract fund to the payment of a general obligation of the company without the consent of the surety. It is immaterial that all or some part of the money loaned by the bank to the company upon its note was used by the company for paying off the claims of laborers or materialmen. The bank having accepted the note of the company, its relation to the company was that of a general creditor. . . .

So long as the company was not in default and continued to perform its contract, the plaintiff was under no obligation to see that the amounts paid to the company were applied to the extinguishment of claims for which the surety might thereafter become liable; but when the company defaulted and refused to further perform, the surety had a right to have the remainder of the building fund applied to the completion of the building and to the discharge of claims for which it might thereafter become liable. The indebtedness due to the bank upon the company's note was not such a claim. By the payment of the note the sum of $5,000 was diverted from the building fund to the prejudice of the surety, and the surety was thereby released *pro tanto*.

In the case of *Wasco County v. New England Equitable Insurance Company*,[73] one Cramer contracted to build a road for a county. Cramer borrowed money from a bank, assigning as security his right in the percentage retained by the county. Cramer defaulted and his surety paid for the labor and materials used in the construction of the road. Both the bank and the surety claimed the retained percentage held by the county. The bank contended that, since the money which it had loaned Cramer was used to pay for labor and materials, the surety had already received the benefit of the bank's money and that therefore it would be inequitable to permit the surety to be subrogated to the rights of the county and thus permit the surety to reap where the bank had sown. The court, however, held otherwise:

The rule established by this court in *Derby v. U.S. Fidelity and Guaranty Co.*, 87 Ore. 34 (169 Pac. 500), and approved by the overwhelming weight of authority entitles the surety to assert the benefits of subrogation as against all moneys which the person named as obligee in the bond owes the contractor at the time the latter abandons performance of his contract; but the right of subrogation is particularly applicable to such funds as by the terms of the contract are reserved and retained until complete performance and

73. *Wasco County v. New England Equitable Insurance Company*, 88 Ore. 465, 172 Pac. 126, L.R.A. 1918D 732, Ann. Cas. 1918E 656.

acceptance of the work. The reserved fund is as much for the indemnity of the surety as it is for the security of the owner for whom the work is to be performed and an equity in such reserved fund is raised in behalf of the surety. . . . The equity . . . under the agreement with the contractor, has its inception at the time when the surety enters into the contract of suretyship, and hence the contractor can neither supplant this equity nor strip it of its priority by borrowing money from some person not obliged to lend and assigning the funds to secure the loan.

It has been held, however, that where money borrowed from a bank has been applied to pay for labor and material, the bank has a claim on the retained percentage in the hands of the board superior to the claim of the surety on the contractor's bond.[74]

In a number of cases where money has been loaned to a contractor and used by him to pay for labor and materials going into the construction of a school building and later the contractor defaults and is unable to repay the loans, an attempt has been made by those making the loan to the contractor to recover from his surety. It is contended in such cases that the creditors of the contractor are entitled to be subrogated to the rights of the laborers and materialmen to whom the money loaned has been paid. The courts, however, commonly deny such claims.[75] It is generally held, however, that the liens and claims of laborers and materialmen are assignable and that, when properly assigned, the assignee becomes vested with all the interests of the assignor.[76] Where, for example, a contractor could not meet payments for labor and materials and the laborers assigned their rights to a bank which paid them, the court held the contractor's surety liable to the bank.[77] The surety had, of course, given a bond conditioned to pay for labor and materials.

Where a contractor defaults, the question may also arise as to the disposition of the funds already due him exclusive of the retained percentage. In such a case, it has been held that the contractor, or an assignee, is entitled to whatever portion of the consideration may have

74. *New Amsterdam Casualty Company* v. *Wurtz*, 145 Minn. 438, 177 N.W. 664.

75. *Union School District* v. *Cloepfil*, 112 Kan. 188, 210 Pac. 192; *Neodesha National Bank* v. *Russell*, 109 Kan. 562, 200 Pac. 281. Note: 127 A.L.R. 974.

76. *Lawson* v. *Board of Instruction of Franklin County*, 118 Fla. 246, 159 So. 14; *Indemnity Insurance Company of North America* v. *W. L. Macatee and Sons*, 129 Tex. 166, 101 S.W. (2d) 553; *Globe Indemnity Company* v. *Hanify*, 217 Calif. 721, 20 Pac. (2d) 689. See also, Note, 118 A.L.R. 57.

77. *Lawson* v. *Board of Public Instruction of Franklin County*, 118 Fla. 246, 159 So. 14.

become due under the terms of the contract.[78] In the case of *American Surety Company of New York* v. *Board of Commissioners of Waseca County*,[79] according to the terms of the contract, the contractor was to be paid on monthly estimates 85 per cent of the cost of labor and materials furnished. The contractor also agreed to pay for labor and materials. While the building was in the process of construction, the surety notified the board that the contractor was not paying for labor and materials and requested that the board refuse to pay the contractor or his assignee an amount due on an estimate theretofore made. The request was denied, and the surety claimed that it was relieved *pro tanto*. The court held otherwise. It said:

> The board had agreed with the contractor, and it was its duty, to pay 85 per cent. of the estimates each month; and this agreement the contractor could enforce. . . . The defendant board had no authority under the statute to enforce the contractor's duty towards the laborers and materialmen by withholding payment on the estimates, and consequently it neglected no duty it owed to plaintiff.

DISTRICT LIABILITY FOR FAILURE TO TAKE CONTRACTOR'S BOND TO PROTECT LABORERS AND MATERIALMEN

Where a statute makes it the duty of school-district officers to take, or of the contractor to give, a bond conditioned to pay for all the labor and materials used in the construction of a building, the question may arise as to the liability of the district in case such a bond is not required or given. While the courts are not in entire accord, the weight of authority is to the effect that a school district is not liable to laborers and materialmen for failure to require such a bond unless made liable by statute.[80] Thus it was said by the Supreme Court of

---

78. *New Amsterdam Casualty Company* v. *Wurtz*, 145 Minn. 438, 177 N.W. 664; *American Surety Company of New York* v. *Board of Commissioners of Waseca County*, 77 Minn. 92, 79 N.W. 649.

79. *American Surety Company of New York* v. *Board of Commissioners of Waseca County*, 77 Minn. 92, 79 N.W. 649.

80. *Freeman* v. *City of Chanute*, 63 Kan. 573, 66 Pac. 647; *Rock Island Lumber and Manufacturing Company* v. *Elliott*, 59 Kan. 42, 51 Pac. 894; *Hannah* v. *Lovelace-Young Lumber Company*, 159 Ga. 856, 127 S.E. 225; *Ink* v. *City of Duluth*, 58 Minn. 182, 59 N.W. 960; *Joseph Nelson Supply Company* v. *Leary*, 49 Utah 493, 164 Pac. 1047; *New York Blower Company* v. *Carbon County High School*, 50 Utah 342, 167 Pac. 670; *Warner* v. *Hallyburton*, 187 N.C. 414, 121 S.E. 756; *Noland* v. *Board of Trustees of Southern Pines School*, 190 N.C. 250, 129 S.E. 577; *Newt Olson Lumber Company* v. *School District No. 8*, 83 Colo. 272, 263 Pac. 723; *I. W. Phillips & Company* v. *Board of Public Instruction of Pasco County*, 98 Fla. 1, 122 So. 793.

Kansas in interpreting a statute which required public officers to take a bond from the contractor conditioned to pay for labor and materials furnished:

> While the statute specifically requires a public officer to take the bond, it does not provide that the neglect of an officer to perform the duty so enjoined raises a liability against the public corporation for which he acts. A quasi-municipal corporation, like a school board, is never liable for the consequences of a breach of public duty or the neglect or wrong of its officers unless there is an express statute imposing the liability. . . . No language in the statute imposes such liability or indicates a legislative purpose that public corporations should suffer a penalty for the neglect of their officers. Whatever liability may be incurred by the officers themselves for a breach of public duty, it is certain that in the absence of an express statute imposing such liability the municipalities cannot be held liable for their neglect.[81]

The chief reason why school districts are not held liable for failure to take the bond required is that they are quasi-corporations representing the state itself; they are arms of the state and, like the state, are not liable unless made so by statute.[82] Moreover, the matter of taking the bond is a public, as distinguished from a corporate or private, duty, and where the duty is public, a municipality is not liable for nonfeasance.[83] In holding that the city of Chanute was not liable to materialmen who had sustained loss by reason of the neglect of the officers of the city to require the bond demanded by statute, the Supreme Court of Kansas expressed the rule as follows:

> There are two kinds of duties which are imposed on a municipal corporation—one arising from the grant of a special power, in the exercise of which the municipality is a legal individual; the other arising from the use of political rights under the general law, in the exercise of which it is a sovereign. The former power is *quasi*-private and is used for private purposes; the latter is public and used for public purposes. . . . In the exercise of its *quasi*-private or corporate power a municipality is like a private corporation, and is liable for a failure to use its power well or for an injury caused by using it negligently. In building its water-works, gas, electric-light plants, sewers, and other internal improvements which are for the exclusive benefit of the corporation, it is in the exercise of its *quasi*-private power and is liable to the same extent as are private corporations. . . . But in the exercise of the

81. *Rock Island Lumber Manufacturing Company* v. *Elliott,* 59 Kan. 42, 51 Pac. 894.

82. *Joseph Nelson Supply Company* v. *Leary,* 49 Utah 493, 164 Pac. 1047; *Freeman* v. *City of Chanute,* 63 Kan. 573, 66 Pac. 647.

83. *Ink* v. *City of Duluth,* 58 Minn. 182, 59 N.W. 960; *Freeman* v. *City of Chanute,* 63 Kan. 573, 66 Pac. 647.

political or public power conferred on it as an arm of the state for the benefit of all the people, its officers, although appointed or elected by the city, paid and subject to be discharged by it, are not the agents of the municipality, but of the state, and the corporation is not liable either for their misfeasance or nonfeasance. . . .

The duty of taking the bond provided for in the statute quoted is not imposed on the corporation. It is not taken for the benefit of the corporation or its inhabitants, but is for the benefit of any person who shall perform labor or furnish material to the person or persons who contract with a public officer to construct any public improvements, whether such persons be residents of the city or elsewhere. The duty is a public one, in the interest of the public, imposed by statute on public officers, and with which the corporation, in its private capacity, has no concern.[84]

Again, it is sometimes said that those who furnish labor and materials are presumed to know the law and that it is their duty to see that the bond has been given before furnishing the labor or materials.[85] If the required bond has not been given, they may resort to mandamus proceedings to require that it be given.[86] In this connection the Supreme Court of Georgia has said: "It was the duty of this materialman to have looked first to his own safety. If, in the exercise of ordinary care, he had not furnished the material until he had examined the bond given by the contractor and had not supplied this material unless or until a proper bond had been given, he would have sustained no loss. Negligence is not one of the rights protected by law."[87]

In a few cases, however, it has been held that failure to take the required bond renders the school district liable to laborers and materialmen for any losses they may have sustained because of the failure to take the bond.[88] It is held in such cases that the duty to take the bond is not a public duty, but a duty to an individual. Being such, failure to take the bond is an individual wrong for which the district will be held to respond in damages.

84. *Freeman* v. *City of Chanute*, 63 Kan. 573, 66 Pac. 647.

85. *Hannah* v. *Lovelace-Young Lumber Company*, 159 Ga. 856, 127 S.E. 225; *Joseph Nelson Supply Company* v. *Leary*, 49 Utah 493, 164 Pac. 1047.

86. *New York Blower Company* v. *Carbon County High School*, 50 Utah 342, 167 Pac. 670.

87. *Hannah* v. *Lovelace-Young Lumber Company*, 159 Ga. 856, 127 S.E. 225.

88. *Northwest Steel Company* v. *School District No. 16*, 76 Ore. 321, 148 Pac. 1134, L.R.A. 1915F 629, Ann. Cas. 1917B 1086. See also *Puget Sound Brick, Tile & Terra Cotta Company* v. *School District No. 73*, 12 Wash. 118, 40 Pac. 608.

PERSONAL LIABILITY OF SCHOOL OFFICERS FOR FAILURE TO TAKE BOND CONDITIONED TO PAY FOR LABOR AND MATERIALS

Where a statute makes it the duty of a school board or district to take a contractor's bond conditioned to pay for the labor and materials used in the construction of a school building, failure to take the required bond does not, as a rule, render the board members personally liable to those who have sustained a loss growing out of the failure to take the bond.[89] In such cases the overwhelming weight of authority is to the effect that there is no personal liability unless such liability be imposed by statute. Various reasons are assigned to support the rule of nonliability. In the first place, it is said that school-district officers represent the state in the performance of a public or governmental duty and therefore, like the state itself, are not subject to suit unless made so by statute. To illustrate, a statute of South Dakota made it the duty of all public corporations, when contracting for the construction of a public building, to require of the contractor a bond conditioned for the payment of all labor and materials used in the construction of the building. In holding that school board members were not personally liable for failure to take the required bond, the court stated the rule as follows:

School districts are state agencies exercising and wielding a distributive portion of the sovereign power of the state, and the officers of school districts are the living agencies through whom the sovereign state act is carried into effect. A school district officer in the performance of his duties acts in a political capacity, as much so as the Governor of a state, and is not liable for negligent acts of omission occurring in the performance of such political or public duties, unless the sovereign power of the state has authorized and consented to a suit for such negligence. Now, in the matter of letting building contracts for the repair or construction of a public school building, and the taking of a contractor's bond, we are of the opinion that the members of a board of education act in a public and political capacity, as an agent of the state, in the carrying out of a portion of the distributed functions of state government, and are not liable to suit for negligent acts of omission, unless the state has by express statute consented to such suit.[90]

89. *Blanchard v. Burns*, 110 Ark. 515, 162 S.W. 63, 49 L.R.A. (N.S.) 1199; *Noland v. Board of Trustees of Southern Pines School*, 190 N.C. 250, 129 S.E. 577; *Plumbing Supply Company v. Board of Education*, 32 S.D. 270, 142 N.W. 1131; *Hydraulic Press Brick Company v. School District of Kirkwood*, 79 Mo. App. 665; *Sailing v. Morrell*, 97 Neb. 454, 150 N.W. 195.

90. *Plumbing Supply Company v. Board of Education*, 32 S.D. 270, 142 N.W. 1131.

Another reason supporting the nonliability rule is that the duty imposed upon school officers to take a bond is imposed upon them in their official, and not in their individual, capacity. Individual members of a corporate body cannot be held individually liable for neglect of duty by the corporation.[91] If there is a neglect of duty, it is the neglect of the body and not of the individuals composing it. Thus it has been said: "In the letting of the contract and in their failure to take the bond of the contractors, the directors did not act as individuals engaged in the enterprise of erecting a building but as a board of directors through which the school district manifested its will.[92]

Moreover, those dealing with a contractor are chargeable with notice whether the bond has been given and have no right to impose liability upon the school officers when they knew or could have known that the bond had not been given.[93] In other words, those dealing with a contractor will not be permitted to require others to bear the consequences of their own carelessness or negligence.

In a few jurisdictions, however, where the statutes require school officers to take a bond, the statutes have been construed as imposing upon the officers a ministerial duty, and failure to take the bond renders the officers personally liable to laborers and materialmen who suffer loss thereby.[94]

91. *Blanchard* v. *Burns,* 110 Ark. 515, 162 S.W. 63, 49 L.R.A. (N.S.) 1199; *Monnier* v. *Godbold,* 116 La. 165, 40 So. 604, 5 L.R.A. (N.S.) 463, 7 Ann. Cas. 768; *Bassett* v. *Fish,* 75 N.Y. 303; *Hydraulic Press Brick Company* v. *School District of Kirkwood,* 79 Mo. App. 665.

92. *Hydraulic Press Brick Company* v. *School District of Kirkwood,* 79 Mo. App. 665. See, however, *Austin* v. *Ransdell,* 207 Mo. App. 74, 230 S.W. 334.

93. *Blanchard* v. *Burns,* 110 Ark. 515, 162 S.W. 63, 49 L.R.A. (N.S.) 1199; *Noland Company* v. *Board. of Trustees of Southern Pines School,* 190 N.C. 250, 129 S.E. 577.

94. *Owen* v. *Hill,* 67 Mich. 43, 34 N.W. 649; *Burton Machinery Company* v. *Ruth,* 196 Mo. App. 459, 194 S.W. 526; *Austin* v. *Ransdell,* 207 Mo. App. 74, 230 S.W. 334.

CHAPTER XIV

Tort Liability of School Districts

LIABILITY OF SCHOOL DISTRICTS FOR NEGLIGENCE

THE common-law principle, almost universally applied by American courts, is that school districts and municipalities are not liable to pupils for injuries resulting from the negligence of the officers, agents, or employees of the district or the municipality.[1] Nor does it matter that the injury was sustained while the pupil was off the school premises[2] or while being transported to or from school.[3] In order to hold a school board liable in such cases, there must be a statute expressly

1. *Krutili* v. *Board of Education*, 99 W. Va. 466, 129 S.E. 486; *Boice* v. *Board of Education*, 160 S.E. (W. Va.) 566; *Hughes* v. *Hartford Accident & Indemnity Company*, 223 Ala. 59, 134 So. 461; *Gold* v. *Mayor & City Council of Baltimore*, 137 Md. 335, 14 A.L.R. 1389; *Sullivan* v. *School District No. 1*, 179 Wis. 502, 191 N.W. 1020; *Nabell* v. *City of Atlanta*, 33 Ga. App. 545, 126 S.E. 905; *Cochran* v. *Wilson*, 287 Mo. 210, 229 S.W. 1050; *McVey* v. *City of Houston*, 273 S.W. (Tex.) 313; *Ernst* v. *City of West Covington*, 116 Ky. 850, 76 S.W. 1089, 3 Ann. Cas. 882, 63 L.R.A. 652; *Freel* v. *School City of Crawfordsville*, 142 Ind. 27, 41 N.E. 312, 37 L.R.A. 301; *Finch* v. *Board of Education*, 30 Ohio St. 37, 27 Am. Rep. 414; *Daniels* v. *Board of Education*, 191 Mich. 339, 158 N.W. 23, L.R.A. 1916F 468; *Hill* v. *Boston*, 122 Mass. 344, 23 Am. Rep. 332; *Howard* v. *Tacoma School District No. 10*, 88 Wash. 167, 152 Pac. 1004, Ann. Cas. 1917D 792; *Wixon* v. *Newport*, 13 R.I. 454, 43 Am. Rep. 35; *Harris* v. *Salem School District*, 72 N.H. 424, 57 Atl. 332; *Bang* v. *Independent School District No. 27*, 177 Minn. 454, 225 N.W. 449; *Mokovich* v. *Independent School District of Virginia*, 177 Minn. 446, 225 N.W. 292; *Spencer* v. *School District No. 1*, 121 Ore. 511, 254 Pac. 357; *Antin* v. *Union High School District No. 2*, 130 Ore. 461, 280 Pac. 664; *Benton* v. *Board of Education*, 201 N.C. 653, 161 S.E. 96; *Consolidated School District No. 1* v. *Wright*, 128 Okla. 193, 261 Pac. 953; *Johnson City Board of Education* v. *Ray*, 154 Tenn. 179, 289 S.W. 502; *Perkins* v. *Trask*, 95 Mont. 1, 23 Pac. (2d) 982; *Cullor* v. *Jackson Township*, 249 S.W. (2d) (Mo.) 393; *Meyer* v. *Board of Education*, 9 N.J. 46, 86 Atl. (2d) 761; *Lawver* v. *Joint School District No. 1*, 232 Wis. 608, 288 N.W. 192; *Lovell* v. *School District No. 13*, 172 Ore. 500, 143 Pac. (2d) 236; *Bartell* v. *School District No. 28*, 114 Mont. 451, 137 Pac. (2d) 422; *Bingham* v. *Board of Education of Ogden City*, 223 Pac. (2d) (Utah) 432; *Tripus* v. *Peterson*, 11 N.J. Super. 282, 78 Atl. (2d) 149; *Reed* v. *Rhea County et al.*, 225 S.W. (2d) (Tenn.) 49.

2. *Whitfield* v. *East Baton Rouge Parish School Board*, 43 So. (2d) (La.) 47.

3. *Roberts* v. *Baker*, 57 Ga. App. 733, 196 S.E. 104; *Wright* v. *Consolidated School District*, 162 Okla. 110, 19 Pac. (2d) 369; *Brooks* v. *One Motor Bus, etc.*, 190 S.C. 379, 3 S.E. (2d) 42.

making it liable, and a statute providing that a school district may sue and be sued does not overcome the common-law immunity. A state legislature may, of course, abrogate the common-law immunity of school districts for accidents growing out of the negligence of their officers or employees, but it must do so in clear and express terms.[4]

Many reasons have been assigned in support of the common-law rule of nonliability of school districts for the negligent acts of their officers and employees. Of these, the most fundamental is that school districts are agents of the state in the performance of public or governmental functions. There has grown up in the United States a commonly accepted doctrine that there is no liability for negligence in the performance of public or governmental duties unless such liability is provided for by statute. The doctrine is, indeed, of very ancient origin. It grew out of the theory of sovereignty. It is based on what was supposed to be the medieval dogma that the king could do no wrong.[5] In America there was no king, but the state was assumed to be sovereign, and the theory took the form that the state could not be sued without its consent. Moreover, immunity from liability has been extended to such quasi-corporations as the state has created for the execution of its policies. These subordinate agencies of the state are emanations of sovereignty and are no more liable than is the sovereign itself. The doctrine is exceedingly difficult to apply because of the great difficulty in distinguishing public or governmental functions from municipal or corporate functions. The courts, however, are agreed that education is a function of government and do not hesitate to apply the rule of nonliability to school districts.

Injuries to pupils.—A few cases will serve to illustrate the reasoning of the courts. In a West Virginia case,[6] a pupil was injured while operating a planer in the manual-training department of a high school. The planer, it seems, was not properly protected by a mantle or guard. In refusing to hold the school district liable, the court stated the rule as follows:

4. *Brooks* v. *One Motor Bus, etc.*, 190 S.C. 379, 3 S.E. (2d) 42; *Thompson* v. *Board of Education*, 20 N.J. Super. 419, 90 Atl. (2d) 63.

5. For a discussion of the development and soundness of the doctrine see Edwin M. Borchard, "Government Liability in Tort," *Yale Law Journal*, XXXIV (November and December, 1924, and January, 1925), 1–45, 129–43, 229–57; "Governmental Responsibility in Tort," *Yale Law Journal*, XXXVI (November, 1926, and April, 1927), 1–41, 757–807.

6. *Krutili* v. *Board of Education*, 99 W. Va. 466, 129 S.E. 486.

The general rule in this country is that a school district, municipal corporation, or school board is not, in the absence of a statute imposing it, subject to liability for injuries to pupils of public schools suffered in connection with their attendance thereat, since such district, corporation, or board, in maintaining schools, acts as an agent for the state and performs a purely public or governmental duty imposed upon it by law for the benefit of the public, for the performance of which it receives no profit or advantage.

In the case of *Anderson* v. *Board of Education,*[7] a pupil was struck on the head by a swing and killed while legally present on the playground of a school. It was claimed that the board negligently permitted a dangerous situation to exist and that the death of the child resulted from the negligence. The court, nevertheless, refused to allow damages:

The theory of the demurrer, if we correctly understand its import, is that the schools of the city of Fargo are a part of the educational system of the state of North Dakota and, as such, are a governmental agency of the state and that, like the state, they are not subject to be sued for a wrongful, tortious act occuring in connection with the exercise of their governmental functions. . . .
All such apparatus is considered approximately as much a part of the needful supplies of schools as are the desks or other needful furniture. It constitutes a necessary part and portion of the school system. The schools would not be kept in needful supplies unless such were a part of them. Hence, when the board of education provides them, it is acting in a purely governmental capacity. In reality, it is a part of the principal duties of the board to provide such needful and necessary apparatus. If it be conceded that the board in furnishing and installing such apparatus and needful supplies in a school or on the school grounds is acting in a governmental capacity—and we think this must be conceded—it cannot be charged with the establishing and maintaining of a nuisance in that respect in the absence of a permissive statute to that effect, and there is no such statute in this state. Neither is it liable in an action of negligence if the act of negligence grew out of some act or acts of the board while acting in a governmental capacity.
Before concluding this opinion, it may be well to observe that the complaint, after setting out the allegations with reference to negligence and the construction and the maintenance of a nuisance, which we have largely above set forth, also alleged the following: "All of which was well known to defendant, its officers, agents, and servants, or, in the exercise of ordinary diligence, should have been known to it and them."
This is an attempt to plead knowledge on the part of the board of education. It states, however, no facts showing that the board had any such knowledge and amounts to nothing more than a mere legal conclusion; but, if facts were stated which showed knowledge, we still do not think the board of education would be liable if it acted in a governmental capacity

7. *Anderson* v. *Board of Education,* 49 N.D. 181, 190 N.W. 807.

in constructing the apparatus in question, and we have concluded it did. . . .
The board, in providing the apparatus, as we have held, was acting within
its governmental capacity and for that reason is protected from liability.

In the case of *Harris* v. *Salem School District*,[8] a pupil was taken ill
from exposure while being transported to and from school. No damages were allowed. The court said:

If it was the duty of the defendants to provide the plaintiff with transportation to and from school . . . it was a public duty, from which the district derived no benefit or advantage . . . and the right of the plaintiff to be
transported was one he enjoyed in common with other scholars in the district, and was also public. . . . But it has long been the recognized law of
this state that an action cannot be maintained against a municipality for the
infringement of such a right in the absence of a statute making it responsible.

Other instances of the application of the doctrine of nonliability in
the performance of a governmental function are: A school board was
not liable for injuries where a pupil was injured as a result of the
negligence of the driver of the school bus,[9] where a flagpole erected
on school grounds fell and injured a pupil,[10] where a pupil was injured
by a jigsaw,[11] and where a pupil was drowned in a swimming pool
operated by the school.[12]

While exemption or immunity of school districts from liability for
negligence usually rests on the theory that school districts are agents
of the state in the performance of a governmental function, various
other reasons are assigned. It is sometimes pointed out that the relation
of master and servant does not exist between a municipality and the
agents it appoints or employs in the execution of its governmental
powers.[13] Some courts hold that school corporations have no funds out
of which damages can be paid, "nor have they any power, expressed
or implied, to raise a fund for such purpose, by taxation or otherwise."[14] In this connection the Court of Appeals of Kentucky has said:

8. *Harris* v. *Salem School District*, 72 N.H. 424, 57 Atl. 332.

9. *Wright* v. *Consolidated School District No. 1*, 162 Okla. 110, 19 Pac. (2d)
369; *Roberts* v. *Baker*, 57 Ga. App. 733, 196 S.E. 104.

10. *Lawver* v. *Joint School District No. 1*, 232 Wis. 608, 288 N.W. 192.

11. *Meyer* v. *Board of Education*, 9 N.J. 46, 86 Atl. (2d) 761.

12. *Perkins* v. *Trask*, 95 Mont. 1, 23 Pac. (2d) 982.

13. *Smith* v. *Seattle School District No. 1*, 112 Wash. 64, 191 Pac. 858.

14. *Freel* v. *School City of Crawfordsville*, 142 Ind. 27, 41 N.E. 312, 37 L.R.A.
301. Accord, *Finch* v. *Board of Education*, 30 Ohio St. 37, 27 Am. Rep. 414;
Wiest v. *School District No. 24*, 68 Ore. 474, 137 Pac. 749, 49 L.R.A. (N.S.)
1026; *State* v. *Board of School Commissioners*, 94 Md. 334, 51 Atl. 289; *Ernst* v.
City of West Covington, 116 Ky. 850, 76 S.W. 1089, 3 Ann. Cas. 882, 63 L.R.A.
652.

The state regards it as her duty to establish and maintain a system of public education. When sums have been collected for that purpose, they cannot be diverted to any other use or purposes. If it could be done, the system would be injured and the public suffer incalculable injury. If someone is injured by the faulty construction of a public-school building or the maintenance of the grounds, no action can be maintained against the district for such injury. The law provides no funds to meet such claims.[15]

School funds, it is said, are trust funds set aside for the sole purpose of maintaining schools, and, like funds held for charitable purposes, they cannot be diverted from the use imposed on them.[16] Such was the reasoning of the Court of Appeals of Maryland in holding that no damages were recoverable where a pupil was fatally injured by falling over a wire strung across a school yard.[17] Similarly, it was said by the Supreme Court of Missouri:

Another equally cogent reason why the board of education cannot be required to respond to an action of the character of that at bar is the nature of the fund intrusted to its care and distribution. School funds are collected from the public to be held in trust by boards of education for a specific purpose. That purpose is education. An attempt, therefore, otherwise to apply or expend these funds is without legislative sanction and finds no favor with the courts. Cases in which hospitals have been held exempt from actions for damages for negligence on account of their character as charitable institutions may not inappropriately be cited in this connection. . . . If it is against public policy as ruled in the foregoing cases to divert charitable funds, so called, from other than the purpose for which they have been collected, how much stronger is the case where the funds are the fruit of taxation, belong to the people, and are to be used for the beneficent purpose of free education.[18]

Still other authorities justify the exemption in part on the ground that school districts "are involuntary corporations, organized, not for profit or gain, but solely for the public benefit."[19] In other words, school districts are the agents of government.

In a number of cases an attempt has been made to draw a distinction between acts imposed by law on a school district and voluntary

15. *Ernst* v. *City of West Covington,* 116 Ky. 850, 76 S.W. 1089, 3 Ann. Cas. 882, 63 L.R.A. 652.

16. *State* v. *Board of School Commissioners,* 94 Md. 334, 51 Atl. 289; *Cochran* v. *Wilson,* 287 Mo. 210, 229 S.W. 1050; *Krutili* v. *Board of Education,* 99 W. Va. 466, 129 S.E. 486.

17. *State* v. *Board of School Commissioners,* 94 Md. 334, 51 Atl. 289.

18. *Cochran* v. *Wilson,* 287 Mo. 210, 229 S.W. 1050.

19. *Redfield* v. *School District No. 3,* 48 Wash. 85, 92 Pac. 770; *Krueger* v. *Board of Education,* 310 Mo. 239, 274 S.W. 811; *Krutili* v. *Board of Education,* 99 W. Va. 466, 129 S.E. 486; *Harris* v. *Salem School District,* 72 N.H. 424, 57 Atl. 332; *Bank* v. *Brainerd School District,* 49 Minn. 106, 51 N.W. 814.

acts, the contention being that in the performance of voluntary acts a school district is liable for the negligence of its officers and agents. The courts, however, have refused to draw such a distinction.[20] "The rule of non-liability at common law applies even in case of duties not imposed *nolens volens,* but also as to those voluntarily assumed by permission of the state, the ground of immunity being, not that the duty is compulsory, but that it is public."[21] A case decided by the Supreme Court of Missouri illustrates the rule. The Board of Education of St. Louis maintained a cafeteria in one of its high-school buildings. An employee in the cafeteria was injured by a food-chopping machine which was set in motion while she was cleaning it. In the suit for damages which followed, the plaintiff contended that the operation of a cafeteria in the school, being merely authorized or permitted by law, "was in the nature of a special, voluntary, and self-imposed duty, and, not being a duty enjoined upon defendant by the law, such operation of it was not the exercise of a governmental function, and for that reason the rule of non-liability" was not applicable.[22] The court, however, refused to draw a distinction between duties imposed and duties voluntarily assumed under the authority of a general statute. The court said:

> There is reason as well as authority for holding that the duty undertaken in this case was the exercise of a governmental function and that its voluntary but authorized assumption did not take from the defendant that immunity from liability which attends the performance of duties imposed. . . . The true ground of distinction to be observed is not so much that the duty is mandatory rather than self-imposed pursuant to authority of a general law but that the duty assumed is public in character and not for profit but for the public good and is directly related to, and in aid of, the general and beneficient purposes of the state.

School districts, in the absence of a statute making them liable, are not liable for injuries to pupils growing out of the negligence of employees.[23] In such cases the rule of *respondeat superior* does not apply.

20. *Howard* v. *Tacoma District No. 10,* 88 Wash. 167, 152 Pac. 1004; *Krueger* v. *Board of Education,* 310 Mo. 239, 274 S.W. 811; *Wixon* v. *Newport,* 13 R.I. 454; *Ernst* v. *City of West Covington,* 116 Ky. 850, 76 S.W. 1089, 63 L.R.A. 652.

21. *Howard* v. *Tacoma School District No. 10,* 88 Wash. 167, 152 Pac. 1004.

22. *Krueger* v. *Board of Education,* 310 Mo. 239, 274 S.W. 811.

23. *Board of Education* v. *McHenry,* 106 Ohio St. 357, 140 N.E. 169; *Dick* v. *Board of Education,* 238 S.W. (Mo.) 1073; *Juul* v. *School District of Manitowoc,* 168 Wis. 111, 169 N.W. 309.

Obviously, if a school district is not liable for the negligent acts of its officers, it is not liable for the negligence of its employees. The principles applicable in the first case are equally applicable in the second case. In an Ohio case, for example, a principal required a pupil, without the consent of his parents, to submit to examination and treatment by a dentist employed by the board of education. In extracting a tooth, the dentist fractured the pupil's jawbone, but the court refused to allow damages against the school district, notwithstanding the charge that the dentist was negligent and incompetent.[24] Similarly, it has been held that the school district was not liable in the following cases: where a pupil was injured on school grounds by a motor truck negligently driven by an employee of the board of education;[25] where a pupil was injured by falling into a pail containing hot water, caustic acid, and chemical compounds, which had been placed in a passageway to be used in scrubbing the floor;[26] where a pupil was injured while operating a buzz saw, the injury growing out of the failure of the teacher to require the pupil to use the safeguards provided by the board of education;[27] and where a pupil sustained injuries because of negligence of the teacher in charge of athletic exercises conducted in a school yard.[28]

Injuries to employees.—The same principles of law which exempt a school district from liability for injuries sustained by pupils exempt it from liability for injuries sustained by employees.[29] Construction and repair of a school building constitute a governmental function just as much as does the conduct of the school itself. Thus a workman who is injured while constructing or repairing a school building has no re-

24. *Board of Education* v. *McHenry,* 106 Ohio St. 357, 140 N.E. 169.

25. *Dick* v. *Board of Education,* 238 S.W. (Mo.) 1073.

26. *Juul* v. *School District of Manitowoc,* 168 Wis. 111, 169 N.W. 309.

27. *Johnson* v. *Board of Education,* 206 N.Y.S. 610.

28. *Katterschinsky* v. *Board of Education,* 212 N.Y.S. 424.

29. *Whitehead* v. *Detroit Board of Education,* 139 Mich. 490; *Freel* v. *School City of Crawfordsville,* 142 Ind. 27, 41 N.E. 312, 37 L.R.A. 301; *McGraw* v. *Rural High School District No. 1,* 120 Kan. 413, 243 Pac. 1038; *Horton* v. *Bienville Parish School Board,* 4 La. App. 123; *Farmer* v. *Poultney School District,* 113 Vt. 147, 30 Atl. (2d) 89; *Thacker* v. *Pike County Board of Education,* 301 Ky. 781, 193 S.W. (2d) 409; *Ford* v. *Independent School District of Shenandoah,* 223 Iowa 795, 273 N.W. 870; *Mayor and Council of Baltimore* v. *Schwind,* 175 Md. 60, 199 Atl. 853.

course against the school district.[30] In a Kansas case,[31] where a workman who had been injured while constructing a school building was seeking damages from the board of education, it was contended that the law of master and servant was applicable. To this contention the court replied:

> The contract of employment contained no express covenant to return plaintiff to a status of good condition at expiration of his employment, and no implied covenant not to injure him. . . . While the contract of employment created the relation of master and servant, the relationship was created not for the private advantage of the incorporators of the school district but to promote the general welfare through education of the young—a sovereign function, to be exercised under immunity of the sovereign from tort liability.

Similarly, in a Michigan case[32] a workman was unable to recover damages from a board of education for injuries sustained while painting a school building. "The affairs of the board of education," said the court, "are as purely a state function as those of the board of health." In the case of *Krueger* v. *Board of Education*,[33] the Supreme Court of Missouri held that the Board of Education of St. Louis was not liable for injuries sustained by an employee in a cafeteria operated by the board in one of the school buildings. The same reasoning that sustains the nonliability of a school board with respect to workmen applies to other school employees, such as teachers, janitors, and the like. Of course, any or all of the employees of a school board may be covered by workmen's compensation insurance.

Injuries to members of the public.—The doctrine of nonliability for negligence applies to the use of school buildings as social centers, civic meetings, and the like. There seems to be no ground for distinction between pupils, employees, and the general public so far as district liability for negligence is concerned, provided that the board of education is performing a public or governmental function. In Massachusetts, for example, a school committee ordered a tree on school grounds to be cut. When the tree was cut, it fell on and injured a man who was at work on a public highway. The court refused damages because

30. *Freel* v. *School City of Crawfordsville*, 142 Ind. 27, 41 N.E. 312, 37 L.R.A. 301; *Whitehead* v. *Detroit Board of Education*, 139 Mich. 490; *Kinnare* v. *City of Chicago*, 171 Ill. 332, 49 N.E. 536; *McGraw* v. *Rural High School District No. 1*, 120 Kan. 413, 243 Pac. 1038. See, however, *Lumpke* v. *School District No. 1*, 130 Ore. 409, 275 Pac. 686.

31. *McGraw* v. *Rural High School District No. 1*, 120 Kan. 413, 243 Pac. 1038.

32. *Whitehead* v. *Detroit Board of Education*, 139 Mich. 490.

33. *Krueger* v. *Board of Education*, 310 Mo. 239, 274 S.W. 811.

the act of cutting the tree was an act of government.[34] Similarly, the city of Worcester, Massachusetts, was not held liable for injuries sustained by a woman whose horse became frightened on a public highway by a blast set off in excavating for the foundations of a public schoolhouse.[35] So, too, the Court of Appeals of Illinois has held that a board of education is not liable for injuries growing out of a social use of a schoolhouse, notwithstanding the fact that entrance fees were charged. The statutes of Illinois permitted the use of schoolhouses for social, civic, and recreational purposes under such conditions and provisions of control as the board might see fit to impose. A board of education let the use of a schoolhouse to a church society for twenty-five dollars. A woman paid the society the admission fee demanded. As she was entering the building, she slipped on ice and was injured. She sued the board for damages, claiming that the board was acting in a proprietary capacity. The court took the position that if the board were acting in a governmental capacity, it was not liable in tort; if it were acting in a proprietary capacity, its acts was *ultra vires* and there was no liability:

It matters not whether the charge of $25 was for the use of the auditorium and a mere incidental charge to reimburse the Board of Education for light, heat, etc., or whether it was purely for profit. If it was the former, we think it was within the power of the Board in connection with its governmental function. If it was for the latter, then it was beyond the power of the School Board. In either case no liability would attach to the Board of Education on account of the injury to plaintiff in error. Where governing bodies of municipal corporations engage in unauthorized enterprises, the corporation cannot be made liable for resulting damages.

To much the same effect is a Massachusetts case,[36] in which it was held that a citizen who was injured while descending defective steps in a schoolhouse for the purpose of voting could not recover damages from the city of Boston, the owner of the schoolhouse.

LIABILITY OF MUNICIPALITIES FOR NEGLIGENCE

In some instances the duty of maintaining the public schools of a community is imposed, not on an independent school district, but on the municipality proper. The question may arise, therefore, as to the

34. *McKenna* v. *Kimball*, 145 Mass. 555, 14 N.E. 789.

35. *Howard* v. *City of Worcester*, 153 Mass. 426, 27 N.E. 11.

36. *McNeil* v. *City of Boston*, 178 Mass. 326, 59 N.E. 810. See also *Boyce* v. *San Diego Union High School District*, 1 Pac. (2d) (Calif.) 1037.

liability of the city for the negligent acts of its officers, agents, and employees in the conduct of the public schools. Some confusion may arise in this connection because of certain fundamental differences in the character of quasi-corporations, such as school districts, and municipal corporations proper. The former are purely political and civil divisions of the state; they perform purely public or governmental functions. The latter are not essentially agents of the state; they are created, in the main, to enable the locality better to administer its affairs. Their duties are essentially local, private, and corporate. Yet they may be utilized by the state for the performance of purely governmental functions with respect to public health, charities, schools, protection of property against fire, maintenance of the peace, and the like. According to the great weight of authority, a municipal corporation is liable for injuries growing out of the negligent performance of its municipal, corporate, or private functions but is exempt from liability for the negligent performance of its purely governmental duties. Efforts to distinguish between the two types of duties have led to great confusion in the law, but the courts are all agreed, it seems, that education is a public or governmental duty. Therefore, a city charged with the duty of administering the public schools enjoys the same exemption as does the school district and for the same reasons.[37] It is not the nature of the corporation that determines the extent of the liability; it is the nature of the duty performed. When the state employs cities to perform functions of government, the cities enjoy the same immunity from liability for actions *ex delicto* as does the state itself.[38] In the case of *Gold* v. *Mayor & City Council of Baltimore*,[39] for instance, action was brought against the mayor and the City Council of Baltimore to recover damages for injuries sustained by a pupil when a door fell in one of the public schools of the city. The court said: "The immunity or exemption from liability in such cases rests upon the

37. *Gold* v. *Mayor & City Council of Baltimore*, 137 Md. 335, 14 A.L.R. 1389; *Finch* v. *Board of Education*, 30 Ohio St. 37, 27 Am. Rep. 414; *Nabell* v. *City of Atlanta*, 33 Ga. App. 545, 126 S.E. 905; *Hill* v. *Boston*, 122 Mass. 344, 23 Am. Rep. 332; *Aiken* v. *City of Columbus*, 167 Ind. 139; *McVey*, v. *City of Houston*, 273 S.W. (Tex.) 313; *Ernst* v. *City of West Covington*, 116 Ky. 850, 76 S.W. 1089, 3 Ann. Cas. 882, 63 L.R.A. 652; *Farmer* v. *Poultney School District*, 113 Vt. 147, 30 Atl. (2d) 89.

38. *Aiken* v. *City of Columbus*, 167 Ind. 139.

39. *Gold* v. *Mayor & City Council of Baltimore*, 137 Md. 335, 14 A.L.R. 1389.

theory that the municipality is in the performance of a public or a governmental duty and is the instrumentality of the state, exercising a governmental function. In the absence of statute expressly or by necessary implication giving the right of action, the municipality is not liable."

LIABILITY OF SCHOOL DISTRICTS IN THE PERFORMANCE OF PROPRIETARY FUNCTIONS

Recognizing that a school district cannot, under the common law, be held liable for the negligence of its agents or employees in the performance of a governmental function, plaintiffs in numerous cases have claimed liability on the ground that the school district was engaged in the performance of a proprietary or private function. In most of these cases the school authorities had charged a fee for admission to some function on the school premises or had derived some financial gain from the activity at which the complaining party was injured.

The courts are not agreed in drawing a distinction between a governmental and a proprietary function with respect to the liability of school districts. Some courts take the position that school districts are created for the purpose of performing a governmental function and that, while acting within the scope of their authority, they cannot engage in a proprietary function. In Tennessee, for example, at a football game at which admission fees were charged, the bleachers collapsed. One of the spectators was injured, and he sued the county board of education on the ground that the bleachers had been negligently constructed and that the county board was engaged in a proprietary function. In refusing damages, the court reasoned: "The mere fact that an admission fee was charged by the High School does not make the transaction an enterprise for profit. . . . The duties of a County Board of Education are limited to the operation of the schools. This is a governmental function. Therefore, in legal contemplation there is no such thing as such a Board acting in a proprietary capacity for private gain."[40]

Other courts, however, recognize the distinction between a govern-

40. *Reed* v. *Rhea County et al.*, 225 S.W. (2d) (Tenn.) 49. See also *Holzworth* v. *State*, 238 Wis. 63, 298 N.W. 163; *Riddoch* v. *State*, 68 Wash. 329, 123 Pac. 450, 42 L.R.A. (N.S.) 251; *Treadway* v *Whitney Independent School District*, 205 S.W. (2d) (Tex.) 97; *Dick* v. *Board of Education*, 238 S.W. (Mo.) 1073; 21 A.L.R. 1327; *Lindstrom* v. *Chicago*, 331 Ill. 144, 162 N.E. 128; *School District* v. *Rivera*, 30 Ariz. 1, 243 Pac. 609, 45 A.L.R. 762.

mental and a proprietary function and intimate or expressly declare that a school board may be held liable in the performance of a proprietary function. Thus it was said by the Court of Civil Appeals of Texas: "There can be no question but that an independent school district is an agency of the state, and, while exercising governmental functions, is not answerable for its negligence in a suit sounding in tort. . . . However, if such a district may properly exercise proprietary acts, and while exercising such proprietary acts is guilty of a tort, the district may be required to answer in damages for such tort."[41]

The Supreme Court of Oregon has taken a stronger position: "The principal question is whether, in the operation of this bus, the school district was acting in a governmental capacity. If it was so acting, it is clear there is no liability against it. . . . If, however, the school district was functioning in a proprietary capacity, it is equally well established in this jurisdiction that it must respond in damages for its negligence."[42]

A number of courts have indicated the test that should be applied in determining whether a particular activity engaged in by a school district is a purely governmental or a proprietary function. In the words of the Supreme Court of Michigan: "The underlying test is whether the act is for the common good of all without the element of special corporate benefit or pecuniary profit."[43]

The courts have uniformly held that a function carried on by a board of education does not lose its governmental nature and become a proprietary function merely because it yields some pecuniary profit or produces revenue to help finance the function in general.[44] Thus it

41. *Braun* v. *Trustees of Victoria Independent School District,* 114 S.W. (2d) (Tex.) 947.

42. *Rankin* v. *School District,* 143 Ore. 449, 23 Pac. (2d) 132. See also *Farmer* v. *Poultney School District,* 113 Vt. 147, 30 Atl. (2d) 89; *Wallace* v. *Laurel County Board of Education,* 287 Ky. 454, 153 S.W. (2d) 915; *Krutili* v. *Board of Education,* 99 W. Va. 466, 129 S.E. 486.

43. *Gunther* v. *Board of Road Commissioners of Cheboygan County,* 225 Mich. 619, 196 N.W. 386. Accord, *Rankin* v. *School District,* 143 Ore. 449, 23 Pac. (2d) 132.

44. *Daszkiewicz* v. *Board of Education of the City of Detroit,* 301 Mich. 212, 3 N.W. (2d) 71; *Thompson* v. *Board of Education,* 12 N.J. Super. 92, 79 Atl. (2d) 100; *Reed* v. *Rhea County et al.,* 225 S.W. (2d) (Tenn.) 49; *Smith* v. *Hefner,* 235 N.C. 1, 68 S.E. (2d) 783; *Kirchoff* v. *City of Janesville,* 255 Wis. 202, 38 N.W. (2d) 698; *Watson* v. *School District of Bay City,* 324 Mich. 1, 36 N.W. (2d) 195.

has been held that a school board does not lose its immunity from tort liability by engaging in a proprietary function where it charges admission fees to athletic contests,[45] charges tuition fees to attend a medical school owned and operated by it,[46] leases an athletic field for playing baseball,[47] sells some of the articles made by students in a vocational high school,[48] or charges pupils living outside the district fees for transportation.[49]

Other instances of a court's refusal to hold a board liable because it was engaged in a proprietary function are: where a teacher took the school bus used for the transportation of pupils before school began in the autumn and drove with some of the school trustees to a place outside the district to get school supplies and had an accident, injuring a third party;[50] and where a school board had a tree planted and trimmed near a buttress to the entrance of a school building and a pupil fell off the buttress and was injured.[51] In a New Hampshire case, however, it was held that where a town rented the third floor of a school building to a lodge and kept the rest of the building for its own use as a schoolhouse, the town was under obligation to keep the premises reasonably safe for lodge members, and, failing this, it would be held liable in tort.[52]

LIABILITY OF SCHOOL DISTRICTS FOR TRESPASS OR MAINTENANCE OF A NUISANCE

The courts are rather sharply divided with respect to the liability of school districts for wilful or positive misconduct of school officers while acting in their corporate capacity. According to one line of

45. *Reed* v. *Rhea County et al.*, 225 S.W. (2d) (Tenn.) 49; *Mokovich* v. *Independent School District*, 177 Minn. 446, 225 N.W. 292; *Thompson* v. *Board of Education*, 12 N.J. Super. 92, 79 Atl. (2d) 100; *Watson* v. *School District of Bay City*, 324 Mich. 1, 36 N.W. (2d) .195.

46. *Daszkiewicz* v. *Board of Education of the City of Detroit*, 301 Mich. 212, 3 N.W. (2d) 71. Accord, *Nabell* v. *Atlanta*, 33 Ga. App. 545, 126 S.E. 905.

47. *Smith* v. *Hefner*, 235 N.C. 1, 68 S.E. (2d) 783.

48. *Kirchoff* v. *City of Janesville*, 255 Wis. 202, 38 N.W. (2d) 698.

49. *Campbell* v. *Hillsboro Independent School District*, 203 S.W. (2d) (Tex.) 663.

50. *Treadway* v. *Whitney Independent School District*, 205 S.W. (2d) (Tex.) 97.

51. *Braun* v. *Trustees of Victoria Independent School District*, 114 S.W. (2d) (Tex.) 947.

52. *Douglas* v. *Hollis*, 86 N.H. 578, 172 Atl. 433.

decisions, a school district is liable for the maintenance of a nuisance[53] or for acts of trespass committed by the board of education representing the district;[54] that is, in some jurisdictions the exemption from responsibility which applies to government agencies in the case of negligence does not extend to cases of active misconduct.

The Supreme Court of Michigan has held that boards of education are liable for trespass.[55] In the case of *Ferris* v. *Board of Education*,[56] the plaintiff owned and occupied a house on a lot adjoining school property. The roof of the schoolhouse had no guards or projections to prevent the falling of snow and ice. During the winter months large quantities of snow and ice slid from the roof of the schoolhouse onto the plaintiff's house and lot and on the sidewalk leading to the back part of the plaintiff's house. The plaintiff notified different members of the board of education of the injury being done to his property, and his wife did likewise. Nothing, however, was done about the matter. One evening, after the plaintiff had returned from work, he was told by his wife that during the afternoon large quantities of snow and ice had fallen from the schoolhouse roof onto his back porch and steps. He went out to investigate, slipped on the ice, and was injured. In awarding damages, the court said:

> The trial court was of the opinion that the defendant, being a municipal corporation, could not be held liable for negligent injuries under the common law, and, there being no liability created by statute, the plaintiff could not recover. It is conceded by counsel for plaintiff that municipal corporations are not generally held liable, under the common law, for negligent injuries to individuals arising from defective plans of construction of public works or failure to keep the same in repair; but it is contended that, where the injury is the result of the direct act or trespass of the municipality, it is liable, no matter whether acting in a public or private capacity. We are

53. *Briegel* v. *City of Philadelphia*, 135 Pa. St. 451; *McCarton* v. *City of New York*, 133 N.Y.S. 939, 24 R.C.L. 606. Note: 37 L.R.A. 301; *Ness* v. *Independent School District of Sioux City*, 230 Iowa 771, 298 N.W. 855; *Bush* v. *City of Norwalk*, 122 Conn. 426, 189 Atl. 608; *Estelle* v. *Board of Education of Borough of Red Bank*, 26 N.J. Super. 9, 97 Atl. (2d) 1; *Neiman* v. *Common School District No. 95*, 171 Kan. 237, 232 Pac. (2d) 422.

54. *Griswold* v. *Town School District of Town of Weathersfield*, 88 Atl. (2d) (Vt.) 829; *Ferris* v. *Board of Education*, 122 Mich. 315, 81 N.W. 98; *Daniels* v. *Board of Education*, 191 Mich. 339, 158 N.W. 23, L.R.A. 1916F 468. See also *Babcock* v. *Seattle School District No. 1*, 12 Pac. (2d) (Wash.) 752.

55. *Ferris* v. *Board of Education*, 122 Mich. 315, 81 N.W. 98; *Daniels* v. *Board of Education*, 191 Mich. 339, 158 N.W. 23, L.R.A. 1916F 468.

56. *Ferris* v. *Board of Education*, 122 Mich. 315, 81 N.W. 98.

satisfied that counsel for plaintiff are right in this contention. The plaintiff had the right to the exclusive use and enjoyment of his property, and the defendant had no more right to erect a building in such a manner that the ice and snow would inevitably slide from the roof and be precipitated upon the plaintiff's premises than it would have to accumulate water upon its own premises and then permit it to flow in a body upon his premises. It has been many times held in this court that a city has no more right to invade, or cause the invasion of, private property than an individual.

It is often difficult to draw a sharp line between mere negligence and a nuisance, but running through all the cases defining a nuisance is "the element of a wrongful, continuing, impending danger to the lives, limbs, or health of the public, or to the legitimate property or personal rights of private persons peculiarly subject to the danger."[57]

In the case of *Bush* v. *City of Norwalk*[58] the plaintiff, an eight-year-old boy, brought action to recover for injuries he received from a fall from a narrow beam—a "balance beam"—he was walking along in the course of his training and instruction in physical education. It was claimed that the beam, from the manner of its construction and use on a slippery floor, constituted a nuisance. The beam was standard equipment used throughout the schools of the city and had been purchased from one of the leading manufacturers of such equipment. Nevertheless, a jury held that the beam constituted a nuisance and awarded damages. Upon appeal, the court sustained the verdict, saying: "In this case the jury might have found that the negligence of the defendant's employees in placing the beam upon the slippery floor had resulted in a continuing condition the natural tendency of which was to create danger and to inflict injury upon all children using it and that, as a matter of fact, a nuisance was created by the use of the beam upon the floor."

So, too, in an Iowa case, damages were awarded to the owner of property adjacent to the school premises because the playground was so used as to constitute a nuisance. Baseballs and soft balls were batted upon his property, and pupils injured his property in seeking to recover them. The plaintiff had been compelled to abandon his garden and flower beds; screens and windows were broken by balls batted by students; the slate roof on his house had been broken into pieces, some of which lodged in the spouting, causing water to leak through

57. *Kilts* v. *Board of Supervisors of Kent County,* 162 Mich. 646, 127 N.W. 821.
58. *Bush* v. *City of Norwalk,* 122 Conn. 426, 189 Atl. 608.

the roof and injure several rooms.[59] And in New York City damages were recovered from the board of education by a pedestrian who was injured when a flagpole fell from a school building to the sidewalk. The board, the court reasoned, was guilty of the maintenance of a nuisance or of negligence in the performance of the statutory duty of keeping the school property in repair.[60] So, too, a school board was liable to a janitor who developed a lung ailment by inhaling excessive coal dust while operating the board's boiler-room, where it could be shown that the board maintained a dangerous condition by its failure to provide ventilating apparatus or to treat the coal in such manner as to prevent dust.[61] And finally, the city of Philadelphia has been held liable in damages for maintaining a defectively constructed privy-well on its property used for school purposes. The city, it was said, was guilty of maintaining a nuisance to the injury of adjoining owners.[62]

In a number of cases the courts, while apparently assuming that a school board could be held liable for the maintenance of a nuisance, have held that the facts did not support such a claim. Such was the case where high-school pupils were permitted to run a hundred-yard dash on a city sidewalk to the injury of a pedestrian,[63] where a pupil drowned in a small bayou which bordered the school grounds,[64] and where a pupil was injured by a falling flagpole which had not been kept in a proper condition.[65]

In some jurisdictions, on the other hand, it is held that a school district cannot be held liable for any kind of tort committed by its officers. It is argued that a board of education is never authorized to commit a tort, and, when it does so, it does not represent the district; that is, its acts *ultra vires*, and the district is not bound. It is commonly argued, too, in this line of decisions, that funds raised for school purposes should and must be applied to those purposes exclusively. Moneys raised to provide educational facilities should not be used to pay damages growing out of tortious acts of school officers.

59. *Ness* v. *Independent School District of Sioux City*, 230 Iowa 771, 298 N.W. 855.

60. *McCarton* v. *City of New York*, 133 N.Y.S. 939.

61. *Estelle* v. *Board of Education of Borough of Red Bank*, 26 N.J. Super. 9, 97 Atl. (2d) 1.

62. *Briegel* v. *City of Philadelphia*, 135 Pa. St. 451.

63. *McDonell* v. *Brozo*, 285 Mich. 38, 280 N.W. 100.

64. *Whitfield* v. *East Baton Rouge Parish School Board*, 23 So. (2d) (La.) 708.

65. *Carlo* v. *School District of Scranton*, 319 Pa. 417, 179 Atl. 561.

A Utah case illustrates the position of those courts which hold that the doctrine of nonliability applies to all torts whether arising from negligence, nuisance, or trespass. The school board of Ogden maintained an incinerator for the disposition of paper and rubbish near a play area for school pupils. Hot ashes were permitted to be spread near this play area, and a small child fell into them and was seriously burned. Action was brought for damages on the claim that the school board had maintained a nuisance. The court refused damages, because, it said, the board of education was performing a governmental function and in doing so was no more liable for damages for the maintenance of a nuisance than for negligence. The rule of immunity applied "even though the firing of the incinerator was performed in such a negligent manner as may be characterized as maintaining a nuisance."[66]

The opinion of the court in the case of *Board of Education v. Volk*[67] is also an excellent illustration of the reasoning on which this line of decisions rests. In excavating on its own lot for the erection of a school building, the Board of Education of Cincinnati wrongfully and negligently, it was alleged, carried the excavation below the statutory depth of nine feet. There was a landslide, as a result of which the foundation and the walls of a building on adjoining property were injured. The court held that the school board was not liable in its corporate capacity:

> The board is not authorized to commit a tort—to be careless or negligent —and, when it commits a wrong or tort, it does not in that respect represent the district, and for its negligence or tort in any form the board cannot make the district liable. It is without power to levy taxes except for school and schoolhouse purposes, and therefore no levy could be legally made to pay a judgment against it if one should be recovered for its torts. The property belonging to the board and to which it holds title in its trust capacity cannot be seized or held to satisfy a judgment for damages. . . . The board is a mere instrumentality of the state to accomplish its purpose in establishing and carrying forward a system of common schools throughout the state. As heretofore stated, these boards are but arms of the sovereign, the state, and the latter has neither authorized nor permitted, by any law, its agents to be sued for tort to either person or property. As the citizen cannot sue the state without its consent, expressed by legislation, its agents, the boards of education, cannot be sued and made liable for damages without consent of the sovereign. . . . Such legislation exists as to contracts made within the scope defined, but it does not extend to official misconduct, negligence, or want of care.

66. *Bingham* v. *Board of Education of Ogden City*, 223 Pac. (2d) (Utah) 432.
67. *Board of Education* v. *Volk*, 72 Ohio St. 469, 74 N.E. 640.

To the same effect is a case decided by the Supreme Court of Illinois.[68] Owners of property adjoining a high-school site commenced the construction of a building on their premises in February. On the first of the following March, the board of education instituted condemnation proceedings to take this property by eminent domain. The petition for condemnation was finally dismissed on the seventeenth of the following July. Action was brought against the board of education on the ground that the condemnation proceedings had not been dismissed within a reasonable time. The court refused damages:

The rule adopted by this state, and generally followed throughout the country, is that corporations of the character of school districts are created *nolens volens* by the general law, to aid in the administration of state government, and are charged as such with duties purely governmental in character. They are therefore not liable for the torts or negligence of their agents, unless such liability is expressly provided by statute. . . . The reason for this rule lies in the fact that a school district of the character here considered is created merely to aid in the administration of the state government. It owns no property, has no private corporate interests, and derives no special benefits from its corporate acts. It is simply an agency of the state, having existence for the sole purpose of performing certain duties deemed necessary to the maintenance of "an efficient system of free schools" within its jurisdiction. In creating such district the state acts in a sovereign capacity, for the more efficient exercise of governmental functions resting in the state, and such district is exempted from the obligation to respond in damages, as master, for the negligent acts of its servants, to the same extent as is the state itself, unless liability is expressly provided by the statute.

The Supreme Court of Arizona has taken the same position. In a case[69] which came before it in 1926, an attempt was made to hold a school board liable in its corporate capacity for the destruction of a building belonging to another. The owner had leased the building to one Serna, who subleased it to the board. Without the knowledge of the owner, the board took possession of the building, cut a hole in the wall for a stovepipe, put in a stove, and employed a janitor. It was alleged that, through the negligence of the janitor, the building was set on fire and destroyed. The court considered but refused to follow the reasoning of the court in the case of *Ferris* v. *Board of Education*[70] because, in its opinion, the court in that case had been "led astray by overlooking the distinction between the ordinary municipal corporation and a school district." It then cited with approval the

68. *Lindstrom* v. *City of Chicago,* 331 Ill. 144, 162 N.E. 128.
69. *School District No. 48* v. *Rivera,* 30 Ariz. 1, 243 Pac. 609, 45 A.L.R. 762.
70. *Ferris* v. *Board of Education,* 122 Mich. 315, 81 N.W. 98.

case of *Board of Education* v. *Volk*,[71] and added: "We see no distinction in principle between the liability of the district or the acts of its officers in one class of torts as against another." Much the same, if not precisely the same, position was taken by the Supreme Court of Oregon. In that state a teacher was given a hearing and was found guilty of immoral conduct. The report of the meeting was written into the record by the clerk of the district. The teacher thereupon sued the board for libel. The court quoted with approval the case of *Board of Education* v. *Volk* and added:

> The district is not liable for tort committed by the directors or clerk in entering upon the district records the reason for the dismissal of the teacher; nor can any unlawful act of the directors or clerk be imputed to the district. . . . We do not believe that it was the intent or is the policy of our law to take the fund intended for the education of the young and apply it to payment for any malicious acts of its officers. It is carrying the doctrine of imputed tort too far to hold that, because the directors or clerk of the district have published a libel or spread it upon the record of the district, the district itself is a malicious libeler.[72]

MODIFICATION OF THE DOCTRINE OF NONLIABILITY

The doctrine of nonliability for tort which is applicable to any agency of the state in the performance of a governmental function has been subjected to criticism as being illogical and unjust. A number of courts have expressed dissatisfaction with it on grounds of social policy. But it is a long- and well-established principle, and the courts take the position that if it is to be changed, the legislature should do it. The Supreme Court of Kansas has expressed the view apparently entertained by most courts: "If the doctrine of state immunity in tort survives by virtue of antiquity alone, it is an historical anachronism . . . and works injustice to everybody concerned . . . the Legislature should abrogate it. But the Legislature must make the change in policy, not the courts."[73]

The courts of New York are the only ones to depart, in some degree, from the common-law immunity from tort. In this state the courts have, in the absence of a statute providing for liability, re-

71. *Board of Education* v. *Volk*, 72 Ohio St. 469, 74 N.E. 640.

72. *Wiest* v. *School District No. 24*, 68 Ore. 474, 137 Pac. 749, 49 L.R.A. (N.S.) 1026.

73. *McGraw* v. *Rural School District No. 1*, 120 Kan. 413, 243 Pac. 1038. Accord, *Sullivan* v. *School District No. 1*, 179 Wis. 502, 191 N.W. 1020; *Thompson* v. *Board of Education*, 20 N.J. Super. 419, 90 Atl. (2d) 63.

peatedly held a school board liable in its corporate capacity for the negligent performance of duties imposed by law on the board itself. More recently, the state has waived, in the Court of Claims Act, its immunity from liability for the negligence of its agents in its charitable and other institutions,[74] and by statute has made boards of education in some classes of school districts liable for damage arising out of the negligence of their employees. In many New York cases, therefore, boards of education have been held liable for the negligence of their teachers or other employees.[75] Similarly, in California and Washington the common-law immunity from tort has been repealed by statute, and in many cases boards of education have been held liable for injuries growing out of the negligence of their employees.[76]

74. *Weber* v. *State*, 53 N.Y.S. (2d) 598.

75. *Weber* v. *State*, 53 N.Y.S. (2d) 598; *Lee* v. *Board of Education of City of New York*, 31 N.Y.S. (2d) 113, 263 App. Div. 23; *Armlin* v. *Spickerman*, 250 App. Div. 810, 294 N.Y.S. 159; *Howell* v. *Union Free School District No. 1*, 250 App. Div. 810, 294 N.Y.S. 333; *Hovey* v. *State*, 287 N.Y. 636, 39 N.E. (2d) 287.

76. *Shannon* v. *Central-Gaither Union School District*, 133 Calif. App. 124, 23 Pac. (2d) 769; *Charonnat* v. *San Francisco Unified School District*, 56 Calif. App. (2d) 840, 133 Pac. (2d) 643; *Eckerson* v. *Ford's Prairie School District No. 11*, 3 Wash. (2d) 475, 101 Pac. (2d) 345.

CHAPTER XV

Personal Liability of School Officers

LIABILITY IN THE EXERCISE OF DISCRETION

WHENEVER a public officer is authorized or required by law to look into the facts and to act upon them in such a manner as to necessitate the exercise of discretion, his acts are quasi-judicial in character.[1] School officers, of course, are not judicial officers, but the performance of most of their duties requires the exercise of judgment and discretion. When such is the case, their acts are quasi-judicial, and as long as they act honestly and in good faith within their jurisdiction, they will not be held liable to an individual for injuries growing out of error of judgment, however great it may be.[2] The rule is based upon sound public policy and is especially applicable to school officers, who, as a rule, serve the public gratuitously. If such officers were held to respond in damages for mere mistakes in judgment, it would be extremely difficult to secure the services of upright men and women to perform the duties of an office which neither pays remuneration nor affords great public honor. The Supreme Court of Maine has well expressed the rule governing the personal liability of school officers:

1. *Sweeney* v. *Young*, 82 N.H. 159, 131 Atl. 155, 42, A.L.R. 757; *Donahoe* v. *Richards*, 38 Me. 379, 61 Am. Dec. 256.

2. *Fertich* v. *Michener*, 111 Ind. 472, 11 N.E. 605, 60 Am. Rep. 709; *Elmore* v. *Overton*, 104 Ind. 548, 4 N.E. 197, 54 Am. Rep. 343; *Danenhoffer* v. *State*, 69 Ind. 295, 35 Am. Rep. 216; *Cooper* v. *McJunkin*, 4 Ind. 290; *Gardner* v. *State*, 4 Ind. 632; *Morrison* v. *McFarland*, 51 Ind. 206; *Adams* v. *Schneider*, 71 Ind. App. 249, 124 N.E. 718; *Dritt* v. *Snodgrass*, 66 Mo. 286, 27 Am. Rep. 343; *McCormick* v. *Burt*, 95 Ill. 263, 35 Am. Rep. 163; *Stewart* v. *Southard*, 17 Ohio 402, 49 Am. Dec. 463; *Gregory* v. *Small*, 39 Ohio St. 346; *Burton* v. *Fulton*, 49 Pa. St. 151; *Donahoe* v. *Richards*, 38 Me. 379, 61 Am. Dec. 256; *Sweeney* v. *Young*, 82 N.H. 159, 131 Atl. 155, 42 A.L.R. 757; *State* v. *Green*, 111 Miss. 32, 71 So. 171; *Hendrix* v. *Morris*, 134 Ark. 358, 203 S.W. 1008; *Kenmare School District No. 28* v. *Cole*, 36 N.D. 32, 161 N.W. 542, L.R.A. 1917D 516; *Spear* v. *Cummings*, 23 Pick. (Mass.) 224, 34 Am. Dec. 53; *Chireno Independent School District* v. *Wedgeworth*, 15 S.W. (2d) (Tex.) 679; *Lemon* v. *Girardot*, 100 Colo. 45, 65 Pac. (2d) 1427; *Dickey* v. *Cordell*, 176 Okla. 205, 55 Pac. (2d) 126; *Board of Education of Oklahoma City* v. *Cloudman*, 185 Okla. 400, 92 Pac. (2d) 837; *Trantham* v. *Russell*, 171 Miss. 481, 158 So. 143; *Medsker* v. *Etchison*, 101 Ind. App. 369, 199 N.E. 429; *Smith* v. *Hefner*, 235 N.C. 1, 68 S.E. (2d) 783.

If in the discharge of their duty in good faith and integrity they err, it is only what is incident to all tribunals. To hold them legally responsible, in such a case, would be to punish them for the honest convictions of the understanding in the decision of a matter submitted to them, and upon which, having assumed jurisdiction, they could not rightfully withhold a decision. The general principle is established by an almost uniform course of decisions, that a public officer, when acting in good faith, is never to be held liable for an erroneous judgment in a matter submitted to his determination. All he undertakes to do, is to discharge his duty to the best of his ability, and with integrity. That he may never err in his judgments, or that he may never decide differently from what some other person may think would be just, is no part of his official undertaking.[3]

It should be noted, however, that the exemption applies only when officers act in good faith and within the scope of their corporate powers.[4] Even a judicial officer proper is not exempt from liability when he acts outside his jurisdiction.[5] Moreover, as will be pointed out later, the rule does not apply to the performance of ministerial duties where the duty is that of an individual officer.

In the case of *McCormick* v. *Burt*,[6] a pupil was excluded from school for disobedience of a rule made by the board of directors. Action for damage was brought against the board members personally. After pointing out that the act was within the jurisdiction of the board and was an act involving the exercise of discretion, the court expressed the rule of law as follows:

In such cases the law seems to be well settled there can be no action maintained against school officers where they act without malice.

The rule is certainly a reasonable one. A mere mistake in judgment, either as to their duties under the law or as to facts submitted to them, ought not to subject such officers to an action. They may judge wrongly, and so may a court or other tribunal, but the party complaining can have no action when such officers act in good faith and in the line of what they think is honestly their duty. Any other rule might work great hardship to honest men who, with the best of motives, have faithfully endeavored to perform the duties of these inferior offices. Although of the utmost importance to the public, no considerable emoluments are attached to these minor offices, and the duties are usually performed by persons sincerely desiring to do good for their neighbors, without any expectation of personal gains, and it would be a very harsh rule that would subject such officers to an action for damages for every mistake they may make in the honest and faithful dis-

3. *Donahoe* v. *Richards*, 38 Me. 379, 61 Am. Dec. 256.

4. *McCutchen* v. *Windsor*, 55 Mo. 149; *Burton* v. *Fulton*, 49 Pa. St. 151.

5. *Burnham* v. *Stevens*, 33 N.H. 247; *Sweeney* v. *Young*, 82 N.H. 159, 131 Atl. 155, 42 A.L.R. 757.

6. *McCormick* v. *Burt*, 95 Ill. 263, 35 Am. Rep. 163.

charge of their official duties as they understand them. It is not enough to aver the action of such officers was erroneous, but it must be averred and proved that such action was taken in bad faith, either wantonly or maliciously. If, in the discharge of their official duties, such officers simply err, it is what other tribunals invested with discretionary powers are liable to do.

Similarly, in a New Hampshire case,[7] a pupil was implicated in having intoxicating cider at a school function. When the board undertook an investigation of the matter, the pupil refused to make any statement and was dismissed for "misconduct." Under the statutes the board was authorized to dismiss pupils for "gross misconduct" or for the violation of reasonable rules. The court held that the dismissal had not been warranted, but refused to hold the board members personally liable in damages:

> Whatever may be the precise line of distinction between judicial and ministerial acts, when the duty of public officers is to "pass upon evidence and decide," the performance of the duty is clearly a judicial act. . . . Under this test the dismissal of the plaintiff was a judicial act. . . .
> The school board had general jurisdiction to dismiss. The general right and authority of dismissal was vested in them, and their exercise of it was not an unwarranted act of assumed power, but merely an erroneous exercise of actual power, for which liability does not attach. . . . Entire independence of school boards in their judicial action is as desirable and important in the public interest as the independence of judges of courts.

So, too, in dismissing a teacher a school board acts judicially, and the individual members thereof will not be answerable in damages for the consequences of their acts, unless actuated by malice or intent to injure.[8] Nor will a school trustee be held personally liable in the absence of corrupt motive for wrongfully excluding a child from school.[9] A county superintendent who exercises in good faith the discretion vested in him by law will likewise be exempt from liability. Thus, in the case of *Elmore* v. *Overton*,[10] the statutes authorized a county superintendent to issue certificates to teachers who passed examinations and who gave satisfactory evidence of good moral character. A superintendent refused to issue a certificate on the ground that the applicant did not have a good moral character. The court held

7. *Sweeney* v. *Young*, 82 N.H. 159, 131 Atl. 155, 42 A.L.R. 757.

8. *Burton* v. *Fulton*, 49 Pa. St. 151; *Morrison* v. *McFarland*, 51 Ind. 206; *Gregory* v. *Small*, 39 Ohio St. 346; *Chamberlain* v. *Clayton*, 56 Iowa 331, 41 Am. Rep. 101; *Roschen* v. *Packard*, 116 Md. 42, 81 Atl. 174; *Christensen* v. *Plummer*, 130 Minn. 440, 153 N.W. 862.

9. *Stewart* v. *Southard*, 17 Ohio 402, 49 Am. Dec. 463.

10. *Elmore* v. *Overton*, 104 Ind. 548, 4 N.E. 197, 54 Am. Rep. 343.

that damages would not be allowed unless it could be shown that the superintendent had acted in bad faith and with malice.

It will be noted that in the case cited in the foregoing paragraph nonliability was conditioned upon the existence of good faith on the part of the officer involved. Some courts, however, go so far as to hold that so long as the act is judicial in nature and within the jurisdiction of the officer, the presence or absence of good faith is immaterial. Thus it was said in the case of *Sweeney v. Young:*

> The public interest that public officers shall be "free and fearless" in the exercise of their judicial duties makes it of immaterial bearing on their liability for their judicial acts whether or not they act from good motives. Their obligation to do justice being owed to the state rather than to the parties coming before them, malice gives the parties no more right to sue than an honest error subjecting the act to reversal. Judicial acts do not lose their character as such because malice induces them.[11]

LIABILITY FOR NEGLIGENCE

Where the law imposes upon a public officer the performance of a duty which involves no exercise of judgment or discretion, the duty is ministerial as distinguished from quasi-judicial. It is well settled that a school officer, like all other public officers, is liable to third persons for injuries sustained because of the failure of such officer to perform ministerial acts or to perform them properly.[12] The officer is liable for nonfeasance—for failure to perform the act at all—or for misfeasance—failure to perform it properly. The rule as stated is undoubtedly applicable to a school officer, such as a county superintendent, who is not a member of any corporate board or body.[13] Thus in Indiana, a township trustee who was required by statute to provide transportation for pupils was held liable to a father who had been put to expense by failure of the trustee to provide the transportation.[14] But where the duty is imposed upon a corporate board or body, the courts are divided with respect to the personal liability of the individuals composing the board. In a number of jurisdictions, board members are held personally liable for failure to perform, or for performing

11. *Sweeney v. Young,* 82 N.H. 159, 131 Atl. 155, 42 A.L.R. 757.

12. *Burton Machinery Company v. Ruth,* 194 Mo. App. 194, 186 S.W. 737; *State v. Lane,* 184 Ind. 523, 111 N.E. 616.

13. *State v. Lane,* 184 Ind. 523, 111 N.E. 616.

14. *State v. Lane,* 184 Ind. 523, 111 N.E. 616.

negligently, a ministerial duty imposed upon the board.[15] As an illustration, in the case of *Owen* v. *Hill*[16] the statutes made it the duty of boards of education, whenever they contracted for the construction of a school building, to require a bond from the contractor conditioned to pay for labor and material used in the erection of the building. A board neglected to require the bond. In holding the board members personally liable, it was said by the court: "In neglecting to require a bond at all, the board neglected the performance of a plain ministerial duty imposed by statute, and it is well settled that when the law casts any duty upon a person which he refuses or fails to perform, he is answerable in damages to those whom his refusal or failure injures."

The case of *Bronaugh* v. *Murray* is also in point.[17] A statute made it the duty of county boards of education in Kentucky to require private bus drivers conveying school children to carry liability insurance. A county board failed to perform this ministerial duty, and its members were held personally liable in a suit for damages by a party injured by one of its bus drivers. Similarly, in Florida, members of a county board of public instruction executed notes in the name of the board in payment for a school site, without having first made a request to the county commissioner to contract such a debt and without having obtained an affirmative vote of the qualified voters, as required by statute. The notes came into the hands of a bank. The court held the board members who had participated in issuing the notes personally liable to the bank. Said the court:

Public officers cannot rightfully dispense with any essential forms of proceedings which the Legislature has prescribed for the purpose of investing them with the power to act in the matter of contracting debts and issuing evidence thereof. . . .

The duty to comply with the indispensable legal formalities required to be observed in the issuance of public securities and evidences of indebtedness, in order to make them valid and bind the corporate body or board so issuing them, is ministerial and non-discretionary in character. A neglect of that duty by proceeding in a manner in disregard of the law and to the special damage of another not a contributor to the default therefore renders the participants in such illegal conduct liable in damages to the person specially injured by such omission or neglect. . . .

15. *Adams* v. *Schneider*, 71 Ind. App. 249, 124 N.E. 718. See also *Burton Machinery Company* v. *Ruth*, 194 Mo. App. 194, 186 S.W. 737; *Austin* v. *Ransdell*, 207 Mo. App. 74; 230 S.W. 334; *Owen* v. *Hill*, 67 Mich. 43, 34 N.W. 649; *Bronaugh* v. *Murray*, 294 Ky. 715, 172 S.W. (2d) 591; *Commonwealth* v. *Fahey*, 156 Pa. Super. 254, 40 Atl. (2d) 167.

16. *Owen* v. *Hill*, 67 Mich. 43, 34 N.W. 649.

17. *Bronaugh* v. *Murray*, 294 Ky. 715, 172 S.W. (2d) 591.

The illegal act or omission of a public corporation or board of which the officer sued was a member, becomes the act of those members who actually participate in its consummation, and such officer members so participating in the illegal act or neglect may be sued and held liable personally for the resulting damage that may have been sustained by a person specially injured by the default of duty.[18]

Both reason and the weight of authority, however, support the rule that school officers are not personally liable for failure to perform a duty, or for its negligent performance, where the duty is imposed upon such officers in their corporate capacity.[19] When the law imposes a duty upon a school board, it addresses itself to the board as a legal entity, and not to the members of the board as individuals. The duty is imposed upon the corporation, and negligence in its performance must be imputed to the corporation.[20] Moreover, school officers perform governmental functions, wield a portion of the sovereign power of the state and, like the state itself, are, while acting in good faith, exempt from liability unless expressly made liable by statute.[21] Thus it has been said by the Supreme Court of South Dakota:

We are of the opinion that there is not now and never was any common-law liability against officers of this class, individually, for neglect to perform official duties. At common law the king could not be sued without his consent. Neither could any officer who represented the king. The same principle has been applied to the sovereign power of the state in this country. Members of a board of education fall within this class of officers who repre-

18. *First National Bank of Key West* v. *Filer*, 107 Fla. 526, 145 So. 204, 87 A.L.R. 267. Accord, *Tritchler* v. *Bergeson*, 185 Minn. 414, 241 N.W. 578. See also *Commonwealth* v. *Zang*, 142 Pa. Super. 566, 16 Atl. (2d) 741, where school officers who let a contract in violation of a statute requiring competitive bidding were convicted of wilful misbehavior in office and sentenced.

19. *Consolidated School District No. 1* v. *Wright*, 128 Okla. 193, 261 Pac. 953, 56 A.L.R. 152; *Bassett* v. *Fish*, 75 N.Y. 303; *Herman* v. *Board of Education*, 234 N.Y. 196, 137 N.E. 24, 24 A.L.R. 1065; *Monnier* v. *Godbold*, 116 La. 165, 40 So. 604, 5 L.R.A. (N.S.) 463, 7 Ann. Cas. 768; *Reese* v. *Isola State Bank*, 140 Miss. 355, 105 So. 636; *Blanchard* v. *Burns*, 110 Ark. 515, 162 S.W. 63, 49 L.R.A. (N.S.) 1199; *Noland Company* v. *Board of Trustees of Southern Pines School*, 190 N.C. 250, 129 S.E. 577; *Fidelity & Deposit Company of Maryland* v. *Board of Education of Pender County*, 202 N.C. 354, 162 S.E. 763; *Plumbing Supply Company* v. *Board of Education*, 32 S.D. 270, 142 N.W. 1131; *Daniels* v. *Board of Education*, 191 Mich. 339, 158 N.W. 23, L.R.A. 1916F 468; *Board of Education* v. *Ray*, 154 Tenn. 179, 289 S.W. 502; *Lemon* v. *Girardot*, 100 Colo. 45, 65 Pac. (2d) 1427; *Medsker* v. *Etchison*, 101 Ind. App. 369, 199 N.E. 429; *Perkins* v. *Trask*, 95 Mont. 1, 23 Pac. (2d) 982.

20. *Monnier* v. *Godbold*, 116 La. 165, 40 So. 604, 5 L.R.A. (N.S.) 463, 7 Ann. Cas. 768.

21. *Plumbing Supply Company* v. *Board of Education*, 32 S.D. 270, 142 N.W. 1131; *Consolidated School District No. 1* v. *Wright*, 128 Okla. 193, 261 Pac. 953, 56 A.L.R. 152; *Lovell* v. *School District No. 13*, 172 Ore. 500, 143 Pac. 236.

sent the king or who represent the sovereign power of the state in a public official capacity. Liability for negligence and suit therefor against the individual officer can only exist by virtue of an express statute creating the individual duty of such officer, and also authorizing the maintenance of a suit for failure to perform such duty.[22]

The case of *Bassett* v. *Fish*[23] is also in point. A teacher brought suit against school trustees personally for injuries sustained in stepping through a hole in the floor of the schoolroom. In refusing to hold the members of the board personally liable, the court pointed out that they were members of a corporate body and that this was the only relation they sustained with respect to the property and teachers of the district. Had any one of the defendants done a wrongful act upon the school premises, thereby causing an injury to a teacher or pupil, he would have been personally liable:

> But it is not seen how a member of a corporate body, upon which body a duty rests, can be held individually liable for the neglect of its duty by that body. There is no duty upon him to act individually. His duty is as a corporator, and it is to act in the corporation in the way prescribed for its action, and by the use of its powers and meanings. And if there is neglect to exert its powers or all its means, it is the neglect of the body and not of the individuals composing it.

Similarly in a Colorado case, a school board, acting under statutory authority, delivered refunding bonds to a bonding company, which was to exchange them for outstanding bonds. Some months later the company became bankrupt and went out of business. Some of the refunding bonds were not exchanged for old bonds but passed into the hands of an innocent purchaser, thereby increasing the bonded debt of the district. The court refused to hold the school-board members personally liable:

> It is not suggested that any member of the board was called upon to, or did, act in his individual capacity, but the entire unfortunate transaction was the act of the duly constituted board. According to all authority, it was a governmental agency functioning for a purely public purpose limited in scope only to educational advancement. As such agency, the sovereign spoke and acted. Whatever intervener claims was a statutory duty, namely "to exchange the bonds," it could only be a board duty; there being no personal or individual duty involved. The board was call upon to act, not the individuals. If we have not said specifically that members of a school board are not liable individually for the improvident, but good-faith actions of the board when they lend their time and sincere efforts for a public purpose

22. *Plumbing Supply Company* v. *Board of Education*, 32 S.D. 270, 142 N.W. 1131.

23. *Bassett* v. *Fish*, 75 N.Y. 303.

without compensation, we should and now do make that pronouncement. If it were otherwise, fear of personal liability would so paralyze such governmental agencies as to make their procurement impossible or their actions lethargic.[24]

In Oklahoma school-board members were not held personally liable for injuries sustained by a pupil while being transported to school in a bus operated by an employee of the board.[25] Nor are board members personlly liable for injuries sustained by a pupil while operating an unguarded buzz saw as a part of his school work. "Their corporate character protects them from individual liability, where their official character is the opportunity or occasion of the neglect. If they neglect to discharge the duties immediately imposed upon them by law, the neglect is that of the corporate body and not of the individuals composing it."[26] So, too, an innocent purchaser of school-district warrants negligently issued has no recourse against the individual members of the board responsible for their issuance. The act of issuing the warrants is the act of the district.[27] In Tennessee board members were not personally liable for injury sustained by a fourteen-year-old girl while playing on a defectively installed ladder in the gymnasium.[28] The members of a school board in California were not held personally liable for injuries to a high-school pupil resulting from the fall of a piano during the physical exercise period.[29] It has been held frequently that board members are not personally liable for failure of the board to require a bond conditioned to pay for labor and materials used in the construction of a school building, even though the duty to take the bond was imposed upon the board by statute.[30]

24. *Lemon* v. *Girardot,* 100 Colo. 45, 65 Pac. (2d) 1427.

25. *Consolidated School District No. 1* v. *Wright,* 128 Okla. 193, 261 Pac. 953, 56 A.L.R. 152.

26. *Herman* v. *Board of Education,* 234 N.Y. 196, 137 N.E. 24, 24 A.L.R. 1065.

27. *Reese* v. *Isola State Bank,* 140 Miss. 355, 105 So. 636.

28. *Board of Education* v. *Ray,* 154 Tenn. 179, 289 S.W. 502.

29. *Dawson* v. *Tulare Union High School District,* 98 Calif. App. 138, 276 Pac. 424.

30. *Antin* v. *Union High School District No. 2,* 130 Ore. 461, 280 Pac. 664; *Blanchard* v. *Burns,* 110 Ark. 515, 162 S.W. 63, 49 L.R.A. (N.S.) 1199; *Hydraulic Press Brick Company* v. *School District of Kirkwood,* 79 Mo. App. 665; *Noland Company* v. *Board of Trustees of Southern Pines School,* 190 N.C. 250, 129 S.E. 577; *Plumbing Supply Company* v. *Board of Education,* 32 S.D. 270, 142 N.W. 1131. Contra, *Owen* v. *Hill,* 67 Mich. 43, 34 N.W. 649; *Burton Machinery Company* v. *Ruth,* 194 Mo. App. 194, 186 S.W. 737; *Austin* v. *Ransdell,* 207 Mo. App. 74, 230 S.W. 334.

School-board members, moreover, are not liable as individuals for injuries growing out of the negligence of their employees.[31] In such cases the doctrine of *respondeat superior* has no application. For example, in a New York case a pupil was injured by falling into an excavation carelessly left open in the school yard by workmen employed in repairing the school building. The court refused to hold the trustees personally liable:

> The employment of workmen for this purpose was necessary, and if they employed competent men, and exercised reasonable supervision over the work, their whole duty as public officers was discharged. They were acting as gratuitous agents of the public, and it could not be expected that they should be personally present at all times during the progress of the work, to supervise the conduct of the workmen.
> In this case it must be assumed, that the defendants were not chargeable with personal negligence, and they omitted no duty imposed upon them by law. It would be equally opposed to justice, and sound public policy, to make them answerable for the negligence of the workmen. They were acting as public officers, and in respect to the acts of persons necessarily employed by them, the doctrine of *respondeat superior* has no application.[32]

PERSONAL LIABILITY ON CONTRACTS

The question frequently arises as to whether school officers can be held personally liable on contracts which they had no authority to make. Where one acting as the agent of a private person enters into a contract beyond the scope of his authority and thereby fails to bind his principal, it is frequently held that he binds himself. In such a case the agent is supposed to know the extent of his authority, whereas the party with whom he contracts is not presumed to know anything concerning it. But in the case of school officers the rule is different. They derive all their powers from the statutes either expressly or by implication. The measure of their authority is, or should be, as well known to those who deal with them as to themselves. Both parties contract with an equal knowledge of the law and with an equal knowledge of the corporate powers of the school district. This being true, the rule is well established that school officers acting in good faith and without fraud will not be held personally liable on contracts, even though it should be discovered that through mistake of the law they

31. *Donovan* v. *McAlpin*, 85 N.Y. 185, 39 Am. Rep. 649; *Consolidated School District No. 1* v. *Wright*, 128 Okla. 193, 261 Pac. 953, 56 A.L.R. 152.

32. *Donovan* v. *McAlpin*, 85 N.Y. 185, 39 Am. Rep. 649. Accord, *Smith* v. *Hefner*, 235 N.C. 1, 68 S.E. (2d) 783.

have exceeded the authority conferred upon them by statute.[33] "Were the rule otherwise," said the Supreme Court of Minnesota,[34] "few persons of responsibility would be found willing to serve the public in that large class of offices, which requires the sacrifice of time and perhaps money, but affords neither honor nor profit to the incumbent." In the case of *Lawrence* v. *Toothaker*,[35] the Board of Education of Berlin contracted, in behalf of the city of Berlin, with an architect to prepare plans for a school building. Soon afterward they notified the architect to cease working on the plans, as they did not wish to use them. He replied he should hold them to the contract and charged his services to the city of Berlin. In a suit against the city he was unsuccessful, because the board had no authority to bind the city. Thereupon, he sued the board members personally. An excerpt from the opinion of the court follows:

It may be conceded that the defendants, as the board of education, had no authority to contract with the plaintiff for and in behalf of the city, and that the attempted exercise of such authority was futile. But it does not follow that the defendants bound themselves to pay for the plaintiff's services. . . . The board's want of statutory power to do what it attempted to do was as much within the cognizance of the plaintiff as that of the defendants. . . . The plaintiff was chargeable with knowledge of their official limitations; and having voluntarily contracted with them in their official capacity . . . he is in no position to claim that the defendants are personally responsible on the contract, in the absence of an express promise by them to incur that responsibility, unless the law would imply a promise of guaranty that they had the requisite power. But "where all the facts and circumstances surrounding the case are known to both the agent and third party, but there is a mutual mistake as to a matter of law,—as the principal's liability, or the legal effect of the agent's written authority,—the agent cannot be held personally responsible by reason of the mere fact that the principal cannot be held, unless the agent by some apt expression guarantees the contract or assumes it himself" (2 Cl. & Sk. Ag. S. 582 b; *Jefts* v. *York*, 10 Cush. 392). And this principle of law is equally applicable when officers, like the defendants, assume to bind the public by their contracts with third parties. Their authority is statutory; and whether their attempted exercise of it in a particular case is authorized is ordinarily a question of law, which

33. *Sanborn* v. *Neal*, 4 Minn. 126, 77 Am. Dec. 502; *Lawrence* v. *Toothaker*, 75 N.H. 148, 71 Atl. 534, 23 L.R.A. (N.S.) 428; *Ogden* v. *Raymond*, 22 Conn. 379, 58 Am. Dec. 429; *First National Bank of Waldron* v. *Whisenhunt*, 94 Ark. 583, 127 S.W. 968; *Coberly* v. *Gainer*, 69 W. Va. 699, 72 S.E. 790; *Watson* v. *Rickard*, 25 Kan. 662; *Humphrey* v. *Jones*, 71 Mo. 62; *Oppenheimer* v. *Greencastle School Township*, 164 Ind. 99, 72 N.E. 1100.

34. *Sanborn* v. *Neal*, 4 Minn. 126, 77 Am. Dec. 502.

35. *Lawrence* v. *Toothaker*, 75 N.H. 148, 71 Atl. 534, 23 L.R.A. (N.S.) 428.

the other contracting party has ample opportunity to investigate and decide for himself. If for any reason he is unwilling to incur that risk, an express guaranty by the other that he acts within the scope of his authority would be necessary to render the latter liable on the contract.

The question has also arisen as to whether school officers are personally liable for official misconduct in issuing warrants or orders without authority. In the case of *Boardman* v. *Hayne*[36] a purchaser of a warrant issued without authority abandoned the warrant as worthless and brought action against the board members personally, on the ground that they had deliberately put into circulation a warrant which was liable to deceive innocent third parties. No actual fraud was imputed, but it was contended that the officers were guilty of constructive or legal fraud. The contention, however, was denied by the court:

> But the rule is that a party is as much bound to protect himself and guard against this, as against actual fraud. The law does not interfere to protect the negligent in such cases any more than in any other. If a party can, by the use of ordinary care and diligence—by the employment of that activity which the law demands at the hands of all—protect himself against injury, he is bound to do so, else he cannot say that he relied upon the acts or representations of others, was deceived thereby to his injury, and hence must be compensated.

The warrant was assignable but not negotiable according to the rules of the law merchant. Hence the assignee acquired no greater rights than the party to whom the warrant was issued. Both alike were bound at their peril to ascertain the extent of powers of the officers issuing the warrant, for their powers were defined by statute. Hence the presumption that the purchaser of the warrant received it "with a full knowledge of the power or want of power to issue it, and of its validity or the want thereof."[37] It has been held, moreover, that school-board members are not personally liable for the negligent issuance of warrants. In the case of *Reese* v. *Isola State Bank*,[38] school trustees caused warrants to be issued in payment for lumber which was never delivered. The county treasurer refused to pay the warrants at the request of the trustees, and an innocent purchaser for value sued the trustees personally. The court refused to allow damages, on the ground that the issuance of the warrants was the act of the district and not of the trustees individually.

36. *Boardman* v. *Hayne*, 29 Iowa 339.
37. Accord, *Bailey* v. *Tompkins*, 127 Mich. 74, 86 N.W. 400.
38. *Reese* v. *Isola State Bank*, 140 Miss. 355, 105 So. 636.

When school officers contract with respect to matters committed to their charge, it is always presumed that they intended to bind the district and not themselves and that parties dealing with them did not rely upon their individual responsibility.[39] This presumption can be rebutted only by circumstances which clearly establish an intention to the contrary.[40] Hence the rule is well established that school officers will not be held personally liable on contracts made on behalf of the district unless there is some apt expression in the contract which shows their intent to be bound.[41] "The intent of the officer to bind himself personally," said Chief Justice Marshall, "must be very apparent indeed to induce such construction of the contract."[42]

When the question arises, therefore, whether a contract binds the district or the board members personally, the fundamental thing to be determined is the intent of the contracting parties. However much courts may differ as to what constitutes evidence of intent, they are all agreed that the contract should be so construed as to give force to the intent of the contracting parties.[43] A written contract is *prima facie* evidence of the intent of the parties who sign it. Where the language of the contract is couched in terms which unmistakably show the intent of the school officers to be bound personally, then they are so bound, and parol and extrinsic evidence to show otherwise will be excluded.[44] Where, on the other hand, the contract is clearly the contract of the district, the district is bound and parol and extrinsic evidence cannot be resorted to in order to charge the school officers.[45] That is, if the contract is clear and unambiguous, the courts will construe it as they find it; neither party to it will be permitted to introduce extrinsic evidence to add to, subtract from, or in any manner vary its terms.[46] But if it is not entirely clear that the contract binds the officers personally,

39. *Sanborn* v. *Neal,* 4 Minn. 126, 77 Am. Dec. 502; *Hodges* v. *Runyan,* 30 Mo. 491; *Monticello School Township* v. *Kendall,* 72 Ind. 91, 37 Am. Rep. 139; *Ogden* v. *Raymond,* 22 Conn. 379, 58 Am. Dec. 429.

40. *Hodges* v. *Runyan,* 30 Mo. 491.

41. *Wing* v. *Glick,* 56 Iowa 473, 9 N.W. 384, 41 Am. Rep. 118; *Sanborn* v. *Neal,* 4 Minn. 126, 77 Am. Dec. 502.

42. *Hodgson* v. *Dexter,* 1 Cranch 345, 2 L. Ed. 130.

43. *Sanborn* v. *Neal,* 4 Minn. 126, 77 Am. Dec. 502.

44. *Western Publishing House* v. *Murdick,* 4 S.D. 207, 56 N.W. 120, 21 L.R.A. 671; *Wing* v. *Glick,* 56 Iowa 473, 9 N.W. 384, 41 Am. Rep. 118.

45. *Andrews* v. *Estes,* 11 Me. 267, 26 Am. Dec. 521.

46. *Andrews* v. *Estes,* 11 Me. 267, 26 Am. Dec. 521.

the law presumes that they intended to bind the district, and extrinsic evidence may be introduced to clear up the ambiguity by showing the actual intention.[47] In such cases the courts will give consideration to the object sought to be accomplished by the contract, to the declaration of the parties at the time the contract was entered into, or to any other evidence of the intent of the contracting parties.[48]

The courts are in substantial agreement, it is believed, upon the principles just stated, but there is much confusion with respect to what constitutes evidence that school officers intended to be bound personally. If, in the body of the note or contract, there is expressed the clear intent to bind the district, according to the weight of authority it is immaterial whether the officers sign in their official or individual capacity.[49] In all such cases, the courts will at least permit the introduction of extrinsic or parol evidence to show that it was intended to contract for the district.[50] As an illustration, in the case of *Sanborn* v. *Neal*[51] a note was given in the following form: "One year from date, we, as trustees of School District No. 10, in Rice County, and Territory of Minnesota, promise to pay John Sanborn or bearer the sum of one thousand one hundred and forty-six and 66/100 dollars. . . . Signed, William Neal, William Sanborn, John Bailor." In construing the contract, the court said:

> This language, if it does not show conclusively that the makers did not intend to promise in their individual capacity, at least renders it doubtful as to the nature of their promise; and in such a case, it appears to us, that the doubt could best be solved by ascertaining the actual intention from the surrounding circumstances,—the debt for which the note was given, the object sought to be attained by the arrangement, the declarations of the parties at the time in the presence of each other, and the disposition made of the money for which the note was given.

After pointing out that the extrinsic evidence showed conclusively that neither party to the contract at the time it was made intended that it should bind the officers personally, the court continued:

47. *Sanborn* v. *Neal*, 4 Minn. 126, 77 Am. Dec. 502; *Wabash Railroad Company* v. *People*, 202 Ill. 9, 66 N.E. 824.

48. *Wabash Railroad Company* v. *People*, 202 Ill. 9, 66 N.E. 824; *Sanborn* v. *Neal*, 4 Minn. 126, 77 Am. Dec. 502.

49. *Sanborn* v. *Neal*, 4 Minn. 126, 77 Am. Dec. 502; *Lyon* v. *Adamson*, 7 Iowa 509; *MacKenzie* v. *Board of School Trustees of Edinburg*, 72 Ind. 189; *Coberly* v. *Gainer*, 69 W. Va. 699, 72 S.E. 790.

50. *Sanborn* v. *Neal*, 4 Minn. 126, 77 Am. Dec. 502; *Wabash Railroad Company* v. *People*, 202 Ill. 9, 66 N.E. 824.

51. *Sanborn* v. *Neal*, 4 Minn. 126, 77 Am. Dec. 502.

The defendants, however, expressly say, in the body of the note, that they promise as trustees of the district. Could they have used language more explicit? Is it at all inconsistent with the intention alleged and proved? Would it have made their intention any more apparent had the defendants added to their signatures the words "trustees," or "as trustees" of the district? The plaintiff's counsel virtually admitted by the argument, that had these words been appended to their signatures, the intention of the defendants to be held in their official capacity only, would have been manifest, even though the note itself was silent on the subject. But we do not think it would have so plainly indicated this intention as the language actually used in the body of the note. To write out at length the legal effect of such a signature would be but to repeat the very language of the note itself; and as the primary object, in all cases, is to ascertain what the parties really intended to declare by the language used, it should make no material difference whether this intention appears in the signature or the body of the instrument.

Similarly, where school officers promise in the body of the note or contract as individuals, but sign in the name of the district, in most jurisdictions they will not be held personally liable.[52] But where there is nothing in the body of the contract or note to indicate that the trustees are acting officially, the form of the signature must be such as to show clearly that they are acting as agents of the district, for otherwise in most jurisdictions they will be bound personally. In such cases it is not enough, according to the weight of authority, to add after the signatures terms descriptive of official status, such as "trustees," "school board," "president," and the like. Such terms, it is said, do not reveal the corporation for which the officers are contracting. By many courts such terms standing alone after the signature of an individual are regarded as merely *descriptio personae*.[53] In a number of jurisdictions it is even held that officers incur personal obligations where, in describing themselves, they set out fully the corporation of which they are officers.

The case of *Wing* v. *Glick*[54] is a good illustration of how school-board members may become personally liable by failing to reveal clearly the corporation for which they are contracting. In that case action was brought to recover from school officers personally on the following contract:

State of Iowa, County of Jones, Township of Hale. Mr. S. J. Wing, 132 South Clark Street, Chicago, Ill. Dear Sir: Please deliver to W. H. Glick at his residence nine sets of national business and primary charts at $36.00

52. *Atkins* v. *Brown*, 59 Me. 90; *Miller* v. *Roach*, 150 Mass. 140.

53. *Trustees of Schools* v. *Rautenberg*, 88 Ill. 219; *Wing* v. *Glick*, 56 Iowa 473, 9 N.W. 384, 41 Am. Rep. 118; *Sharp* v. *Smith*, 32 Ill. App. 336; 35 Cyc. 911.

54. *Wing* v. *Glick*, 56 Iowa 473, 9 N.W. 384, 41 Am. Rep. 118.

per set, $324.00, and we promise to pay for said goods on the first day of March, 1879. . . . I. B. Southwick, Sec'y School Board, W. H. Glick, Pres. School Board.

In the lower court, parol evidence was allowed to show that the contract was executed as the contract of the district township of Hale. The supreme court held that the contract was that of Southwick and Glick and that the parol evidence should have been excluded, because its effect was to add to the terms of a written instrument. Said the court:

It will be observed that the District Township of Hale is not mentioned in the contract, nor are any words, letters or abbreviations used with the design of indicating such district township. Most clearly such district township cannot be said to be a party to the contract so far as its terms are concerned. . . .

If the defendants had not appended to their signatures a description of themselves it would be abundantly evident that they intended to assume a a personal obligation. The language of the contract is "we agree to pay," etc. But the description alone will not enable them to evade the obligation. It is well settled that where a person in executing a contract describes himself as agent without disclosing his principal the contract becomes the personal obligation of the maker and no one else. . . . The defendants describe themselves as officers, but the contract neither shows nor indicates the corporation of which they are officers. Some authorities have gone so far as to hold that the officer incurs a personal obligation, even where in the description of himself he fully sets out the corporation of which he is an officer. In *Honesholl Mutual Fire Insurance Company* v. *Newhall*, 1 Allen 130, the note upon which the action was brought was signed, "Cheever Newhall, President of the Dorchester Avenue R. R. Co." As the note contained no words in the body thereof purporting to bind the Dorchester Avenue R. R. Co., it was held to be the personal obligation of the maker. The same rule was held in *Fiske* v. *Eldridge*, 12 Gray 476, where the note was signed "John S. Eldridge, Trustee of Sullivan R. R."; and in *Sturdivant* v. *Hall*, 59 Me. 172, where the maker described himself as "Treasurer of St. Paul Parish"; and in *Barker* v. *Mechanics' Fire Insurance Co.*, 3 Wend. 94, where the maker described himself as "President of the Mechanics' Fire Insurance Co."; and in *Powers* v. *Briggs*, 79 Ill. 493, where the makers described themselves as "Trustees of" a specified church.

In Indiana, however, it has been held that a contract or note does not impose liability upon school officers where the signature discloses the corporation of which they are officers, even though the body of the instrument contains nothing to indicate that they are acting in a representative capacity.[55] The trustees of a school district signed promissory notes which in no way intimated that the district was to be bound except that after the signatures of the trustees was written "Trustees of

---

55. *Monticello School Township* v. *Kendall*, 72 Ind. 91, 37 Am. Rep. 139.

Monticello School." The court held the notes to be obligations of the school town because of the presumption that school officers do not intend to bind themselves in acting in matters committed to their charge. While this case is contrary to the weight of authority, it seems that in such cases, or in cases where the words "trustees," "school trustees," and the like are added after signatures, parol evidence should be admissible to show the real intent of the contracting parties. That is, in view of the legal presumption against personal obligation, parol evidence should be admissible where the instrument bears on its face some evidence of a representative capacity.

School officers may personally guarantee the payment of a debt contracted for the benefit of the district. If they do so, they will not be heard to complain later that the debt was in excess of the constitutional debt limit or *ultra vires* the powers of the corporation. In such cases the contract of guaranty is that the principal has both capacity to contract to pay and ability to pay.[56]

If school officers wish to avoid personal liability on contracts made officially, it is well to state on the face of the instrument in unmistakable terms that they promise on behalf of the district, and to sign officially in the name of the district. To avoid all possible misunderstanding, it is well to include a statement in the body of the instrument to the effect that they are not acting personally. Where it is discovered that through mistake a personal obligation has been incurred, application may be made to a court of equity to reform the instrument so as to make it conform to the intent of the contracting parties. As a rule, courts of equity will grant such relief.[57]

TORT LIABILITY OF SCHOOL OFFICERS

While school officers are not as a rule individually liable for acts of negligence on the part of the board or its employees, they may be held personally liable for intentional torts committed while administering the affairs of the district.[58] As the Supreme Court of Mississippi

56. *Perry* v. *Brown*, 21 Ky. Law Rep. 344, 51 S.W. 457.

57. *Hanna* v. *Wright*, 116 Iowa 275, 89 N.W. 1108; *Lee* v. *Percival*, 85 Iowa 639, 52 N.W. 543; 23 R.C.L. 333.

58. *Thompson* v. *Shifflett*, 267 S.W. (Tex.) 1030; *Baker* v. *Freeman*, 9 Wend. (N.Y.) 36, 24 Am. Dec. 117; *Betts* v. *Jones*, 208 N.C. 410, 181 S.E. 334; *Stokes* v. *Newell*, 174 Miss. 629, 165 So. 542; *Campbell* v. *Jones*, 257 S.W. (2d) (Tex.) 871; *Whitt* v. *Reed*, 239 S.W. (2d) (Ky.) 489; *Smith* v. *Beverly*, 236 S.W. (2d) (Ky.) 914.

has aptly put it: "It is true that officers are not liable for the honest exercise of discretionary powers confided to them, but when they go outside those powers and commit wrongs under the color of office, there is liability. They are not given immunity from willful wrongs or malicious acts."[59] For example, in North Carolina, school committeemen knowingly practiced nepotism in employing a bus driver. Moreover, they employed him against the protest of patrons that he was reckless and incompetent. While this driver was driving the school bus, it was overturned and a schoolgirl was killed. In an action for damages against the committeemen personally, the court held that it was a matter for the jury to decide whether the committeemen had been actuated by malice or corruption. The court pointed out that "malice in law," as distinguished from "malice in fact," "is presumed from tortious acts, deliberately done without just cause, excuse or justification, which are reasonably calculated to injure another or others."[60] Similarly, where school trustees assess an illegal tax and issue a warrant for its collection, the taxpayer whose property is sold may hold the trustees personally liable in an action for trespass.[61]

LIABILITY FOR MONEY PAID OUT IRREGULARLY OR ILLEGALLY

School officers acting in good faith frequently pay out funds of the district upon irregular or unenforcible contracts. For example, a contract for the construction of a schoolhouse may create an indebtedness in excess of the legal debt limit, and the house may be built, accepted, paid for, and used. Or it may be that a school board pays out funds for the performance of a contract which it had no authority to make. A school board may contract with one of its own members and pay him for the services rendered, or it may pay a teacher for services rendered under an oral contract when the law requires all such contracts to be in writing. In such cases the question may arise as to whether a taxpayer on behalf of the district may recover from the officers the funds thus irregularly or illegally paid out.

According to the weight of authority, school officers will be required to reimburse the district for funds paid out on contracts the subject matter of which is expressly prohibited by the constitution or by

59. *Stokes* v. *Newell,* 174 Miss. 629, 165 So. 542.

60. *Betts* v. *Jones,* 208 N.C. 410, 181 S.E. 334.

61. *Baker* v. *Freeman,* 9 Wend. (N.Y.) 36, 24 Am. Dec. 117.

statute, or *ultra vires* the charter powers of the corporation. That is, if under no circumstances a board has authority to do the thing undertaken, the members of the board will be held to reimburse the district for funds paid out in accomplishing the unauthorized act.[62] If, on the other hand, the subject matter of the contract is not itself prohibited or *ultra vires* the charter powers of the corporation, but the mode of making the contract is irregular or prohibited, the officers will not be held personally liable, provided that they act in good faith and the district retains and enjoys the benefits accruing from the performance of the contract.[63] Perhaps the Court of Appeals of Kentucky has expressed the general rule as well as any other court:

> If the thing done had been illegal, or not warranted by law, however beneficial it might have been, the public ought not be estopped to deny the validity of the expenditure; or, where the thing is authorized, but it is proposed to do it in any unauthorized manner, upon seasonable complaint those charged with doing the thing will be compelled to execute it as the law directs, and prohibited from doing it otherwise. But where the thing is authorized to be done, and is done by the party charged with doing it, but done in a manner contrary to that directed by the statute, the court will not compel the officer to pay back the money and let the public continue to enjoy the benefits of its expenditure. If it is made to appear that the expenditure was in good faith, and the public has got that which it was entitled to, good conscience forbids the recovery. The law, therefore, denies it.[64]

Even though public policy or a statute may prohibit a board member from having pecuniary interest in contracts with the board, where funds have been paid out in good faith on such a contract and the district retains the benefits thereof, the courts will not, as a rule, require the individual members of the board to reimburse the district.[65] The statutes of Kentucky, for example, made it illegal for any school-board member or county superintendent to be financially interested in school contracts. Despite the statute, certain school

62. *Flowers* v. *Logan County,* 138 Ky. 59, 127 S.W. 512, 137 Am. St. Rep. 347; *Keenon* v. *Adams,* 176 Ky. 618, 196 S.W. 173; *Dickinson* v. *Linn,* 36 Pa. St. 431.

63. *Keenon* v. *Adams,* 176 Ky. 618, 196 S.W. 173; *Cagy* v. *Independent District of West Des Moines,* 117 Iowa 694, 89 N.W. 972; *Ryszka* v. *Board of Education,* 214 N.Y.S. 264; *Kenmare School District* v. *Cole,* 36 N.D. 32, 161 N.W. 542, L.R.A. 1917D 516; *State* v. *Farris,* 197 Ind. 128, 150 N.E. 18; *State* v. *Green,* 111 Miss. 32, 71 So. 171; *Miller* v. *Tucker,* 142 Miss. 146, 105 So. 774; *People* v. *Rea,* 185 Ill. 633, 57 N.E. 778.

64. *Flowers* v. *Logan County,* 138 Ky. 59, 127 S.W. 512, 137 Am. St. Rep. 347.

65. *Keenon* v. *Adams,* 176 Ky. 618, 196 S.W. 173; *Ryszka* v. *Board of Education,* 214 N.Y.S. 264; *Cagy* v. *Independent District of West Des Moines,* 117 Iowa 694. 89 N.W. 972.

officers performed labor and furnished supplies and equipment in repairing schoolhouses and were paid therefor. Action was brought against the county superintendent and the members of the county board of education to recover the amount paid out on these contracts. After pointing out that the contracts in question were clearly unlawful and within the prohibition of the statutes, the court continued:

These expenditures, without enumeration, were all for things which were authorized by law, and the amounts paid were not in excess of what the services were fairly worth, and the funds expended, in each instance, were applied to the purposes for which the fund was raised and held. The things, for which they were paid, were not illegal nor unauthorized, and no criticism could be made of the payments, nor the contracts under which they were made, if made upon contracts, to persons, other than sub-district trustees. The vice of the matter consists in the persons to whom the expenditures were made, for the performance of services which the law prohibits a trustee to charge or receive compensation for from the school fund. If the Board of Education had refused to make the payments, as it should have done, it could not have been compelled to do so, and it could have been restrained from doing so, at the suit of any citizen. . . .

Under the above authority [*Flowers* v. *Logan County*, 138 Ky. 59], a recovery cannot be had for the described expenditures against the superintendent nor the members of the Board of Education, if the payments were made in good faith, and the public got that which it was entitled to, and the purpose for which the expenditure was made was for a thing which was lawful to be done, and a thing for which the funds were raised and held. The evidence seems to warrant these conclusions.[66]

Where a school board misjudges its powers and pays out money on a contract which it had no authority to make, the contract being one not expressly prohibited by statute, it has been held that the school-board members are not personally liable. Thus in Oklahoma a board of education spent district funds to pay the expenses of some of its professional personnel to attend a meeting of the National Education Association and to pay the salary of a dentist and nurses. After a court had held that these expenditures were unauthorized and illegal, action was brought to recover the amount paid out from the individual board members. The court refused to hold the board members personally liable:

Every official act of a public officer is accompanied with the presumption of legality. Usually, nothing short of willful misconduct will subject an officer to liability for acts done in the exercise of his official discretion. This is especially true, where he has violated no positive law. This court has heretofore expressed itself in this regard. In *Dickey* v. *Cordell*, 176 Okla.

66. *Keenon* v. *Adams*, 176 Ky. 618, 196 S.W. 173.

205, 55 Pac. (2d) 126, the rule is stated as follows: "In the absence of malice, oppression in office, or willful misconduct, public officers cannot ordinarily be held liable for mistaken exercise of discretion, or error in judgment, in the performance of official duties." This is an expression of the common law, and applies to every discretionary act of all public officers in this state, in the absence of positive legislative enactment to the contrary.[67]

Relatively few cases have come into the courts involving the personal liability of school officers for funds paid out on contracts exceeding the legal limit of indebtedness. Such authority as there is points to the conclusion that a school district cannot accept without objection the benefits of such a contract and thereafter recover from its officers the amount paid out in the execution of the contract.[68] In the leading case of *Kenmare School District* v. *Cole,*[69] action was brought to recover from former members of a school board money paid out on a contract which created an indebtedness in excess of the debt limit. The contract was for the construction of a schoolhouse. The court denied recovery:

It cannot be doubted that by reason of this statute the school district was not placed under any legal obligation to perform the contracts entered into by the school board in so far as their performance involved the necessity of levying taxes in excess of the maximum rate; neither can it be doubted that they were equally void to the extent that they created indebtedness in excess of the limitations prescribed by law; but in our opinion the test of the personal liability of the officers who acted in behalf of the corporation in entering into such contracts is not measured by the binding force of the contracts or the absence thereof. The school district in its corporate capacity can only act through its individual officers, and in so far as the officers of the corporation in good faith and without fraud exercised the powers vested in the corporation by law, they are not personally liable for their action. The defendants while acting in their official capacity did not purport to act individually, and could not, in the absence of statute, be held liable to those who dealt with the corporation. Neither could they, in our opinion, be held liable individually to the corporation on whose behalf they had purported to act, unless their actions were *ultra vires* the charter powers of the corporation, or unless they were guilty of fraud. The plaintiff claims neither in this case. . . .

67. *Board of Education of Oklahoma City* v. *Cloudman,* 185 Okla. 400, 92 Pac. (2d) 837. In Nebraska, however, school-board members who participated in the purchase of a residence for a superintendent when they had no authority to make the purchase were held personally liable (*Fulk* v. *School District No. 8,* 155 Neb. 630, 53 N.W. [2d] 56).

68. *Kenmare School District* v. *Cole,* 36 N.D. 32, 161 N.W. 542, L.R.A. 1917D 516.

69. *Kenmare School District* v. *Cole,* 36 N.D. 32, 161 N.W. 542, L.R.A. 1917D 516.

The building belongs to the district and cannot be taken from it. Thus, while enjoying the fruits of the alleged breach of trust, the plaintiff contends for the right to recover moneys necessarily expended to procure these advantages, and claims that it must be returned to the treasury so that the district may have both the property and the money with which it was acquired. No authority with which we are familiar has gone far enough to sanction this method of enabling a municipal corporation to both have its cake and eat it.

It has been held that school officers are not personally liable for money paid out on contracts let without advertising for bids, as required by law. For example, in Indiana a township trustee in letting a contract for the construction of a school building failed to follow the provisions of the statute requiring competitive bidding. Nevertheless, the court reasoned that the money had been spent for a lawful purpose, the trustee had acted in the belief that he had authority to spend the money, and the township had received full value for funds expended. Since "the only illegality in what was done consisted in the failure to observe certain formalities in the matter of preparing plans and giving notice and letting contracts, neither the township nor the taxpayers on its behalf" could recover from the trustee.[70] Similarly, where two of the three directors of a school district contracted and paid for the digging of a well without any formal meeting of the board, they were not personally liable for the money spent, notwithstanding the fact that a statute required all official action to be taken at a formal meeting of the board. The act was not *ultra vires* the powers of the corporation, the sum paid was reasonable, and there was no loss to the district.[71]

As a rule, taxpayers may enjoin the execution of illegal or unenforcible contracts. Where, therefore, with full knowledge of all the facts, they remain silent while public officers pay out public funds upon such contracts, they may later be estopped to complain. Under the principle of laches, one who fails to assert his legal rights within a reasonable time loses them. Thus, in the case of *Dorner* v. *School District No. 5*[72] a school board had rented part of a parochial school building and conducted the public school therein for a period of

70. *State* v. *Farris,* 197 Ind. 128, 150 N.E. 18.

71. *People* v. *Rea,* 185 Ill. 633, 57 N.E. 778.

72. *Dorner* v. *School District No. 5,* 137 Wis. 147, 118 N.W. 353, 19 L.R.A. (N.S.) 171.

about twenty years. Moreover, they permitted such sectarian instruction in the public school as was prohibited by the state constitution. Action was brought to recover from the board members personally the sums of money paid out in maintaining the school. In denying recovery, the court said:

But, since the application must be to a court of equity, equitable considerations will guide and control in granting or withholding relief. The court will not coerce the enforcement of a strict legal right, however clear, if thereby injustice and inequity will be done. In development of this rule it is well settled that a court of equity may and should refuse to upset consummated and completed transactions to the hurt of those who have acted in good faith at the suit of plaintiffs who, by laches or failure to protest upon opportunity before the acts were done, have induced or justified belief that they acquiesced in and approved such acts. . . . On the faith of such acquiescence, believing that all taxpayers approved, the defendant officers have parted with the money, and, quite obviously, must lose it if compelled to reimburse the district. These plaintiffs at least cannot equitably ask that the defendants so suffer for acts induced and invited by plaintiff's own conduct.

Similarly, in the case of *Kenmare School District* v. *Cole*,[73] where a contract to construct a schoolhouse had created an indebtedness in excess of the debt limit, it was held that taxpayers, who had sought no injunctional relief while the building was being constructed, were guilty of laches and would not, after the building had been completed and paid for, be permitted to recover from the officers personally the moneys paid out for the construction of the building:

It can not be successfully contended that a remedy similar to that contended for in this case is necessary to protect a municipal corporation from the extravagant acts of its officers. The law is very prone to remedy excesses of official action when the interests of taxpayers are involved, but it does not place a premium upon the quiescent indulgence of interested taxpayers by encouraging them to stand by and watch the expenditure of large sums in their behalf in the assurance that they can come into court later and secure the assistance of the law to make a public improvement an unintended private donation.

In refusing to hold school officers liable for moneys paid out on illegal contracts, some courts apply the doctrine that a public officer acting within the scope of his authority in matters requiring the exercise of discretion will not be liable for errors of judgment. In a Mississippi case,[74] for example, action was brought on the official bond

73. *Kenmare School District* v. *Cole,* 36 N.D. 32, 161 N.W. 542, L.R.A. 1917D 516.

74. *Lincoln County* v. *Green,* 111 Miss. 32, 71 So. 171.

of a county superintendent to recover moneys alleged to have been paid out to teachers in excess of the amount called for by their contracts, to teachers with whom no contracts had been made, and on reports alleged to have been signed by some party other than the trustees. It was conceded, however, that the superintendent had acted honestly and in good faith. The court refused to hold the superintendent personally liable:

> While the officer whose acts are here brought in question may have acted indiscreetly in some instances and while there may have been many irregularities in the conduct of the business of his office, it yet remains that he was a public officer charged with the duty of exercising his best judgment and discretion in the performance of his official work, and in this action instituted on his official bond he is protected by the well-recognized principle of law that the officer is not liable for any errors or omissions done or suffered in the exercise of his judicial judgment or discretion. . . .
>
> It will be borne in mind that the several matters complained of in the instant case were items of business within the jurisdiction of the county superintendent, and the services charged to have been illegally paid for were services inuring to the benefit of the county.

And in Arkansas the supreme court has held that school directors are not liable personally for moneys paid out on contracts which they had no authority to make.[75] The money in question had been spent in purchasing and operating a motor truck for conveying children to and from school. While it was conceded that the directors had no authority to spend the funds of the district for such a purpose, so long as they acted in good faith, they incurred no personal liability.

In Minnesota a stricter rule is applied with respect to the personal liability of school officers for money illegally paid out.[76] In that state, school-board members have no authority to spend funds for the purchase of real estate unless authorized to do so by the electors of the district. It is also provided by statute that certain contracts shall not be let except on the basis of competitive bidding. In a leading case[77] the supreme court held that individual members of a school board are personally liable where they purchase real estate without having been authorized to do so by the voters. It was held, too, that board members are personally liable for whatever loss the district may have sustained on contracts let without competitive bidding.

75. *Hendrix* v. *Morris*, 134 Ark. 358, 203 S.W. 1008.

76. *Tritchler* v. *Bergeson*, 241 N.W. (Minn.) 578; *Burns* v. *Essling*, 163 Minn. 57, 203 N.W. 605.

77. *Tritchler* v. *Bergeson*, 241 N.W. (Minn.) 578.

LIABILITY FOR FUNDS LOST IN BANK FAILURE

According to the weight of authority, a school officer is an insurer of the funds committed to his custody, and where, in the exercise of his own discretion, he deposits them in a bank, he, or his surety, is liable if the bank fails or if the money in any way is lost. The rule has been stated as follows. "In effect, according to the weight of authority, a public officer is an insurer of public funds lawfully in his possession, and therefore liable for losses which occur without his fault. He is answerable in all events. The liability is absolute, admitting no excuse, except perhaps the act of God or the public enemy. This standard of responsibility is based upon public policy."[78]

78. *American Surety Company of New York* v. *Ne Smith,* 49 Ga. App. 40, 174 S.E. 262. See also *Thurston County to Use of Vesley et al.* v. *Chemelka,* 135 Neb. 342, 281 N.W. 628. NOTE: 38 A.L.R. 1512.

CHAPTER XVI

Employment of Teachers

THE TEACHER'S CERTIFICATE

Pᴜʙʟɪᴄ education being exclusively a state function, the state may prescribe such qualifications for teachers as public policy may demand. Usually the state prescribes the qualifications which the prospective teacher must meet and delegates to some board or official the duty of determining in any particular case whether the standards have been met. Such determination by the designated officers necessarily involves the exercise of discretion, and it is well settled that the exercise of discretion by such officers will not be controlled by the courts unless it can be shown that the officers have acted arbitrarily and unreasonably.[1] But the officer or agency having authority to issue a certificate may not refuse to grant it arbitrarily and without reasonable cause.[2] For example, in a New York case,[3] a board of examiners refused to grant the petitioner a license to teach on three counts: (1) the college from which she had graduated refused her a recommendation, that being one of the requirements for the issuance of a license; (2) while an undergraduate, the petitioner had been one of the editors of the college paper, and as such, it was alleged, she had caused to be published articles attacking the faculty and advocating communism in general; (3) she had falsely, it was claimed, answered under oath a questionnaire submitted to her by the board of examiners. With respect to the first count, the court reasoned that the refusal of the college to recommend her was immaterial, inasmuch as it had already granted her a diploma. Graduation itself was a stamp of approval, an expression of confidence in the mental and moral qualities

1. *Crawford* v. *Lewis,* 170 Ky. 589, 186 S.W. 492; *Flynn* v. *Barnes,* 156 Ky. 498, 161 S.W. 523; *Keller* v. *Hewitt,* 109 Calif. 146, 41 Pac. 871; *Clay* v. *Independent School District of Cedar Falls,* 187 Iowa 89, 174 N.W. 47.

2. *Keller* v. *Hewitt,* 109 Calif. 146, 41 Pac. 871; *Epstein* v. *Board of Examiners of Board of Education of City of New York,* 295 N.Y.S. 796, 162 Misc. 718.

3. *Epstein* v. *Board of Examiners of Board of Education of New York City,* 295 N.Y.S. 796, 162 Misc. 718.

of the student. No further affirmative action by the college was necessary. The court went on to point out that the second charge against the petitioner was not supported by extracts from the articles she allegedly had published and therefore the charges on this count were "bare conclusions without any facts to support them." One may, the court pointed out, be guilty of utterances of a kind that would disqualify for teaching, but the record here did not disclose such evidence. The third charge the court regarded as a more serious matter. The young woman seeking the license had left blank a question on a sworn questionnaire about her work experience, implying, according to the board of examiners, that she had not been engaged in any trade or in any clerical work or profession other than education for five years prior thereto. Actually, the board of examiners had ascertained that she had been working on the *Daily Worker,* a Communist newspaper. The fact that she had been working on the paper might not itself be ground for refusal to issue the license, but the failure to reveal this information might well indicate an unfitness to teach. The court ruled that the petitioner exhaust her remedies by appeal to the State Commissioner of Education, and, if need be, it would review the case on appeal from his decision.

Since the issuance of certificates involves the exercise of discretion in most instances, an official who refuses to issue a certificate is not personally liable for a mistake in judgment.[4] Liability arises only in those cases where the certificate has been withheld maliciously and without cause.

The principle is well established that a teacher's certificate cannot be attacked collaterally.[5] A certificate is in the nature of a commission. The officer issuing it is assumed to have done his duty. While a direct action may be brought to show that a certificate was not issued in conformity with the law, school authorities may not dismiss a teacher and thereafter set up the defense that the teacher's certificate, valid on its face, was illegally issued. In an Illinois case,[6] as an illustration, in a suit for breach of contract, the defense was that a teacher had been

4. *Elmore* v. *Overton,* 104 Ind. 548, 4 N.E. 197, 54 Am. Rep. 343.

5. *Doyle* v. *School Directors,* 36 Ill. App. 653; *Union School District No. 6* v. *Sterricker,* 86 Ill. 595; *School District No. 25* v. *Stone,* 14 Colo. App. 211, 59 Pac. 885; *Kimball* v. *School District No. 122,* 23 Wash. 520, 63 Pac. 213; *State* ex rel. *Pape* v. *Hockett,* 61 Wyo. 145, 156 Pac. (2d) 299.

6. *Union School District No. 6* v. *Sterricker,* 86 Ill. 595.

granted a certificate without having passed an examination, as the law required. The court held that the defense was not a valid one. It said: "Nor is it conceived that such certificate can be invalidated in this proceeding by proof that no personal examination of the teacher was had. The certificate is in the nature of a commission, and cannot be attacked collaterally."

The state has plenary power with respect to teachers' certificates. A teacher's certificate is not a property right, and it has none of the elements of a contract between the teacher and the state. The state may therefore impose new and additional burdens upon the holders of certificates, even though such holders may have expended money in reliance thereon.[7] A certificate is a mere privilege conferred by the state and is held subject to any law in force at the time of its issuance or any future law providing for its forfeiture.[8] Speaking of licenses, the Supreme Court of the United States has said: "The correlative power to revoke or recall a permission is a necessary consequence of the main power. A mere license by a State is always revocable."[9] Again, it has been said:

A certificate to teach in the public schools is merely a license granted by the state, and is revocable by the state at its pleasure. . . . It is not a contract protected by the due process provisions of either the state or federal Constitution. Such a license is, presumably, accepted and held subject to the then existing and any future law providing for its forfeiture. The Legislature had authority to make the law as it is, and if the applicant did not wish to submit to the conditions affixed for its forfeiture he should not have accepted the certificate. One who accepts a license impliedly agrees to submit to the tribunals which the state has created for determining his fitness to continue in the enjoyment of the privilege granted. This is not a situation where the law attacked is thrust upon the complainant, nor is it one where an inherent right has been invaded, but is one in which the complainant has voluntarily sought and secured a statutory privilege to be enjoyed subject to statutory conditions.[10]

The principle is generally accepted, however, that where a statute authorizes revocation of certificates for certain enumerated causes, a certificate cannot be revoked for any causes other than those specified.[11]

7. *Hodge* v. *Stegall*, 242 Pac. (2d) 720.

8. *Marrs* v. *Matthews*, 270 S.W. (Tex.) 576; *Stone* v. *Fritts*, 169 Ind. 361, 82 N.E. 792, 15 L.R.A. (N.S.) 1147, 14 Ann. Cas. 295.

9. *Doyle* v. *Continental Insurance Company*, 94 U.S. 535, 24 L. Ed. 148.

10. *Marrs* v. *Matthews*, 270 S.W. (Tex.) 586.

11. *Stone* v. *Fritts*, 169 Ind. 361, 82 N.E. 792, 15 L.R.A. (N.S.) 1147, 14 Ann. Cas. 295.

THE TEACHER'S CONTRACT

Necessity of having certificate.—Before a teacher can enter into a valid contract to teach, she must possess such certificate of qualification as is required by law. A contract entered into by a teacher without the certificate required by statute is void,[12] and even though the teacher may actually render the services required of him, he cannot recover either on the contract[13] or on *quantum meruit*.[14] The law regards him as a mere volunteer. Nor does the willingness of the board of education to employ him without a certificate change the rule; the board has no discretion in the matter.[15] It has been held, however, that a board of education may accept free of charge the services of an unlicensed teacher, the prohibition of the law seemingly being against the payment of funds to unqualified teachers and not against incompetent teaching.[16]

The case of *Goose River Bank* v. *Willow Lake School Township* is an excellent illustration of the reasoning of the courts in holding that a teacher who teaches without a certificate can recover nothing on the contract or on *quantum meruit*. In the words of the court:

There is no force in the position that the defendant, having received the benefit of the teacher's services, is liable. Such a doctrine would defeat the policy of the law, which is to give the people of the state the benefit of trained and competent teachers. The law recognizes only one evidence that that policy has been regarded,—the certificate of qualification. If the defendant could be made liable by the mere receipt of the benefit of the services rendered, the law prohibiting the employment of teachers without certificates, and declaring void all contracts made in contravention of that provision, would be, in effect, repealed, and the protection of the people against incompetent and unfit teachers, which such statute was enacted to accomplish, would be destroyed. Where a contract is void because of the express

12. *Goose River Bank* v. *Willow Lake School Township*, 1 N.D. 26, 44 N.W. 1002, 26 Am. St. Rep. 605; *Hosmer* v. *Sheldon School District No. 2*, 4 N.D. 197, 59 N.W. 1035, 25 L.R.A. 383; *Catlin* v. *Christie*, 15 Colo. App. 291, 63 Pac. 328; *Zevin* v. *School District No. 11*, 144 Neb. 100, 12 N.W. (2d) 634; *Buchanan* v. *School District No. 134*, 143 Kan. 417, 54 Pac. (2d) 930.

13. *Board of School Commissioners of Washington County* v. *Wagaman*, 84 Md. 151, 35 Atl. 85; *Barr* v. *Deniston*, 19 N.H. 170; *Flannary* v. *Barrett*, 146 Ky. 712, 14 S.E. 38, Ann. Cas. 1913C 370; *Jenness* v. *School District No. 31*, 12 Minn. 448; *Jackson School Township* v. *Farlow*, 75 Ind. 118. But see *School Directors* v. *Brown*, 58 Vt. 61.

14. *Goose River Bank* v. *Willow Lake School Township*, 1 N.D. 26, 44 N.W. 1002, 26 Am. St. Rep. 605; *Wayne County* v. *Hopper*, 114 Miss. 755, 75 So. 766; *Jackson School Township* v. *Farlow*, 75 Ind. 118.

15. *Barr* v. *Deniston*, 19 N.H. 170; *Harrison Township* v. *Conrad*, 26 Ind. 337.

16. *McDonald* v. *Parker*, 130 Ky. 501, 110 S.W. 810, 33 Ky. Law Rep. 805.

declaration of a statute, or because prohibited in terms, the retention by a municipality of the fruits of such a contract will not subject it to liability, either under the contract or upon a *quantum meruit*.[17]

Where a teacher under the law is entitled to a certificate but has not secured it, the courts are divided with respect to his right to enter into a legal contract. Failure to hold the certificate, according to some courts, is conclusive.[18] Thus it was said by the Supreme Court of Washington:

It seems to us too plain to admit of argument that a mere letter from a county school superintendent stating that an applicant's papers are sufficient to entitle him to a temporary certificate, and that such certificate will be granted on application as provided by statute, is not the equivalent of a temporary certificate. Where a certificate is required as a condition precedent to the right to enter upon an employment or exercise a privilege, a promise to grant the certificate on application will not satisfy the requirements of the law.[19]

Other courts hold that a teacher who is entitled to a certificate may make a valid contract, although he does not at the time actually possess a certificate.[20] It has been held, too, that where a teacher has fulfilled all the requirements for a certificate but there has been some delay in its issuance due to no fault of his own, the certificate, when subsequently issued, should relate back to the date when it should have been issued.[21]

Effect of acquiring certificate after signing contract but before beginning to teach.—Frequently teachers enter into contracts without possessing a certificate but secure a certificate before entering upon the performance of their duties under the contract. Under such circumstances the validity of the contract frequently depends upon the wording of the statute. If the statutes provide that no contract shall be entered into with a teacher who does not possess a certificate, thus indicating the intent of the legislature that the teacher have the cer-

17. *Goose River Bank* v. *Willow Lake School Township*, 1 N.D. 26, 44 N.W. 1002, 26 Am. St. Rep. 605.

18. *Kester* v. *School District No. 34*, 48 Wash. 486, 93 Pac. 907; *Cramer* v. *Board of Education*, 245 Ill. App. 172; *Zevin* v. *School District No. 1*, 144 Neb. 100, 12 N.W. (2d) 634; *Seamonds* v. *School District No. 14*, 51 Wyo. 477, 68 Pac. (2d) 149. Note: 42 L.R.A. (N.S.) 415.

19. *Kester* v. *School District No. 34*, 48 Wash. 486, 93 Pac. 907.

20. *Crabb* v. *School District No. 1*, 93 Mo. App. 254; *School District No. 9* v. *Brown*, 55 Vt. 61; *Libby* v. *Inhabitants of Douglas*, 175 Mass. 128, 55 N.E. 808; *School District No. 1* v. *Ross*, 4 Colo. App. 493, 36 Pac. 560.

21. *Bradfield* v. *Avery*, 16 Idaho 769, 102 Pac. 687, 23 L.R.A. (N.S.) 1228.

tificate as of the date of making the contract, a contract with a teacher who does not possess a certificate at the time of signing the contract will not be enforcible, even though a certificate may have been secured before the date of the opening of the schools.[22] If, on the other hand, the statutes provide that no teacher who does not possess a certificate shall be employed, the courts are divided, some holding that it is sufficient if the teacher secure a certificate before beginning to teach,[23] others holding that the certificate must be in the possession of the teacher at the time of making the contract.[24] In many cases the decision turns upon the meaning given to the term "employment." In a number of cases it is held that a teacher is "employed" when he begins teaching, a distinction being drawn between the contract of employment and employment proper.[25] These cases seem to be the better-reasoned ones, for the evil to be guarded against is not the making of contracts with unqualified teachers but the teaching in the schools by unqualified teachers.

The following cases will serve to illustrate the general principles stated in the preceding paragraph. In a case decided by the Supreme Court of Minnesota[26] the statutes provided: "The board of trustees shall hire for and in the name of the district such teachers as have procured a certificate of qualification, and make a contract with such teachers." A board of trustees entered into a contract with a teacher who had no certificate but who secured one the day he began teaching. Although the teacher taught the school, in accordance with the contract, for the term agreed upon, he was not permitted to recover for his services. It was said by the judge who rendered the decision:

22. *O'Connor* v. *Francis*, 59 N.Y.S. 28; *Jenness* v. *School District No. 31*, 12 Minn. 448.

23. *Lee* v. *Mitchell*, 108 Ark. 1, 156 S.W. 450; *Board of Education* v. *Akers*, 243 Ky. 177, 47 S.W. (2d) 1046; *Crowe* v. *Yates*, 219 Ky. 49, 292 S.W. 483; *Crabb* v. *School District No. 1*, 93 Mo. App. 254; *School District No. 2* v. *Dilman*, 22 Ohio St. 194. See also *Pollard* v. *School District No. 9*, 65 Ill. App. 104; *Schaefer* v. *Jones*, 23 N.D. 593; *Swinford* v. *Chasteen*, 261 Ky. 249, 87 S.W. (2d) 373; *Martin* v. *Knott County Board of Education*, 275 Ky. 483, 122 S.W. (2d) 98.

24. *Hosmer* v. *Sheldon School District No. 2*, 4 N.D. 197, 59 N.W. 1035, 25 L.R.A. 383; *Stanhope* v. *School Directors*, 42 Ill. App. 570; *Stevenson* v. *School Directors*, 87 Ill. 255; *Putnam* v. *School Town of Irvington*, 69 Ind. 80; *Butler* v. *Haines*, 79 Ind. 575; *School District No. 46* v. *Johnson*, 26 Colo. App. 433, 143 Pac. 264.

25. *Lee* v. *Mitchell*, 108 Ark. 1, 156 S.W. 450; *School District No. 2* v. *Dilman*, 22 Ohio St. 194; *Crabb* v. *School District No. 1*, 93 Mo. App. 254.

26. *Jenness* v. *School District No. 31*, 12 Minn. 337.

It seems to me that the sections of the statute above quoted confer no power or authority on the board of trustees to contract with or hire a teacher before he has obtained the requisite certificate of qualification, and that the contract sued upon in this case is therefore void. The statute confers and measures the power of the board, and its affirmative language, that the board shall hire "such teachers as have procured a certificate," implies a negative,—that it shall not hire any other. Every person is presumed to know the law and is bound at his peril to take notice of the public statutes. It must be supposed, therefore, the plaintiff knew that the board had power only to contract with a class of persons to which he did not belong,—those having certificates of qualification to teach.

The case of *Putnam* v. *School Town of Irvington*[27] is a good illustration of the reasoning underlying the decisions which hold that a teacher is employed as of the date of making the contract rather than as of the date of beginning teaching. A statute of Indiana provided:

Trustees shall employ no persons to teach in any of the common schools of the State, unless such persons shall have a license to teach, . . . and in full force at the date of employment; and any teacher who shall commence teaching any such school without a license shall forfeit all claim to compensation out of the school revenue for tuition, for the time he or she teaches without such license.

A teacher had no legal certificate at the date of entering into a contract, but secured one before the beginning of the school term. She was not permitted to teach. In denying her damages for breach of contract, the court said:

To sustain the sufficiency of the complaint, it is contended that the employment referred to in section 28, *supra,* has relation to the time when the school begins, and not to the date of the contract of employment, and that, hence, if the teacher has a license to teach at the time the school is to begin, that is sufficient, notwithstanding the contract of employment may have been entered into previous to the issuing of the license. In our opinion this latter construction can not be maintained. The employment thus referred to evidently means a commission or authorization to teach, and has reference to the contract which confers upon the teacher such a commission or authorization, and not to the future services to be performed under the contract. As we construe this section 28, a contract for the employment of an unlicensed teacher in a common school is void by reason of the statutory inhibition against it, and is not ratified by the subsequent issuance of a license to the teacher. . . .

Any other construction would give great uncertainty to the employment of teachers, as persons contracting in advance to teach might never be able to obtain a license authorizing them to take charge of a school.

27. *Putnam* v. *School Town of Irvington*, 69 Ind. 80.

A number of cases do hold, however, that the term "employ," as used in the statutes, should be construed as relating to the time of beginning teaching and not as relating to the time the contract was made. Thus in an Ohio case,[28] it was said:

The law forbids the *employment* of a teacher who has not a certificate. The teacher is not "employed," within the meaning and intent of this provision, until he engages in the discharge of his duties as teacher. The mischief intended to be guarded against, was the *teaching of a school* by an incompetent person, and not the making of the contract by an incompetent person.

Similarly, in Missouri a statute prohibited the employment of a teacher who did not hold a certificate. In construing the statute, the court said in part:

We do not think, taking sections 8021 and 8022 to be read together, they mean that the teacher must have a certificate at the time of making a contract to teach school in the future. The object of the statute is that the qualification may exist during the term of the employment. The language of the statute is that "no teacher shall be employed," and has reference to the employment and not to the contract of employment. It means that he shall not be engaged in teaching without the required certificate.[29]

Effect of securing certificate subsequent to beginning teaching.—As has been pointed out already, a contract made by a teacher who does not possess the certificate required by law is void and not subject to ratification. If the law requires that a teacher hold a certificate at the date of making the contract or at the time of beginning teaching, failure to have the certificate at the time required is fatal to the contract, and a subsequent procurement of the certificate will not validate the contract.[30] In a case directly in point, it was said:

The original contract was void, because repugnant to the statute, and it could not have been ratified and certainly can not be vitalized by obtaining a certificate and endeavoring to have it read as though of date anterior to the execution of the contract. It would not matter how competent and well fitted he was to teach, nor that he may have been entitled to a first-class certificate; he did not have it when he entered into the contract; and that instrument, being null and void at its inception, could not be vitalized and purified by any subsequent events, but it is so nugatory and infected that nothing can cure it.[31]

28. *School District No. 2* v. *Dilman*, 22 Ohio St. 194.

29. *Crabb* v. *School District No. 1*, 93 Mo. App. 254.

30. *Butler* v. *Haines*, 79 Ind. 575; *Richards* v. *Richardson*, 168 S.W. (Tex.) 50; *School Directors* v. *Jennings*, 10 Ill. App. 643; *Jenness* v. *School District No. 31*, 12 Minn. 337.

31. *Richards* v. *Richardson*, 168 S.W. (Tex.) 50.

Where, on the other hand, a teacher is permitted to teach after he has secured the proper certificate, an implied contract will arise even though the original contract was void, and the teacher will be permitted to recover for his services. In some jurisdictions, it is held that under such circumstances the teacher may recover not only for the services he has rendered but for the amount due him under the original contract from the time he secured his certificate.[32] That is, if he is permitted to teach after he secures a certificate, an implied contract arises, the terms of which may be ascertained by reference to the terms of the original void contract. In an early Vermont case, for example, a teacher began teaching without a certificate. Later she went with the prudential committeeman to the town superintendent and secured a certificate. With the consent and approbation of the committeeman she taught for a week thereafter. In determining the rights of the teacher under such circumstances, the court said:

The continuing of the school by the teacher with the consent and approbation of the prudential committee, after she had obtained a certificate of qualification, was equivalent to making a new contract to commence then, upon the same terms as the original contract. The fact that she had kept the school one week under an express contract which the law avoided, would not make void this implied contract, although the express contract had to be looked at, to ascertain the terms of the implied contract.[33]

Similarly, it was said in a Colorado case[34] where a teacher had entered into a contract without the required certificate:

Should it be contended that the board entered into a contract in August which was void under the statute and unenforceable by the teacher, it may well be held that a valid implied contract arose, as between the board and Miss Hotz, when, as a duly qualified teacher, she entered upon the discharge of her duties on the 6th of September, and continued therein for the ensuing five months. If it be said that it is impossible to ascertain what the terms of this implied contract are, it is replied that the express contract may be looked at to ascertain the terms of the implied one, which the teacher performed until she was discharged. The commencement of the school by the teacher, with the knowledge and consent of the board, after she had secured a certificate of qualification, was equivalent to the making of a new contract upon the terms of the one into which they attempted to enter at their meeting held in August.

32. *Scott* v. *School District No. 2*, 46 Vt. 452; *Hotz* v. *School District No. 9*, 1 Colo. App. 40, 27 Pac. 15.

33. *Scott* v. *School District No. 2*, 46 Vt. 452.

34. *Hotz* v. *School District No. 9*, 1 Colo. App. 40, 27 Pac. 15.

Necessity of holding certificate for the whole term of employment.—
Whether or not it is necessary for a teacher to hold at the time of his
employment a certificate valid for the whole term of his employment
is a matter somewhat difficult to determine in the absence of statutory regulation, for there are few decisions on the subject and such as
there are cannot be harmonized. The weight of authority, however,
seems to be that it is sufficient if the teacher has a legal certificate at
the date of his employment,[35] the assumption being that he will be
able to renew it. Some courts, however, hold that a teacher at the
time of making a contract must possess a certificate valid for the
whole term of employment.[36]

*Authority of school boards to require of teachers qualifications other
than those prescribed by statute.*—While local school authorities cannot legally employ teachers who do not possess the qualifications required by statute, they may exercise a broad discretion in requiring
additional qualifications of teachers whom they employ. Stating the
rule broadly, it may be said that a board of education may refuse to
contract with teachers who fail to meet the requirements set up by
the board itself, provided that such requirements are not unreasonable.[37] In Illinois, Ohio, and Washington, for example, it has been held
that a school board may refuse to employ teachers who are members
of, or affiliated with, a labor union.[38] In this connection the Supreme
Court of Illinois in a majority opinion went so far as to say:

The board has the absolute right to decline to employ or to re-employ any
applicant for any reason whatever or for no reason at all. The board is
responsible for its action only to the people of the city, from whom, through

35. *School District No. 1* v. *Edmonston,* 50 Mo. App. 65; *Barnhardt* v. *Bodenhamer,* 31 Mo. 319; *School District No. 8* v. *Estes,* 13 Neb. 52, 13 N.W. 16.

36. *McCloskey* v. *School District No. 5,* 134 Mich. 235, 96 N.W. 18; *O'Leary*
v. *School District No. 4,* 118 Mich. 469, 76 N.W. 1038. See also *Kimball* v. *School
District No. 122,* 23 Wash. 520, 63 Pac. 213; *De Voe* v. *School District No. 3,*
77 Mich. 610, 43 N.W. 1062.

37. *Daviess County Board of Education* v. *Vanover,* 219 Ky. 565, 293 S.W.
1063; *People* v. *City of Chicago,* 278 Ill. 318, 116 N.E. 158, L.R.A. 1917E 1069;
Crabb v. *School District No. 1,* 93 Mo. 254; *Commonwealth* v. *Board of Education,* 187 Pa. St. 70, 40 Atl. 806, 40 L.R.A. 498; *Commonwealth* v. *Jenks,* 154
Pa. St. 368, 26 Atl. 371; *Fitzpatrick* v. *Board of Education,* 125 N.Y.S. 954, 69
Misc. Rep. 78; *People* v. *Maxwell,* 80 N.Y.S. 726, 80 App. Div. 313; *Simpson
County Board of Education* v. *Bradley,* 246 Ky. 822, 56 S.W. (2d) 528; *Lena* v.
Raftery, 50 N.Y.S. 565, 183 Misc. Rep. 759.

38. *People* v. *City of Chicago,* 278 Ill. 318, 116 N.E. 158, L.R.A. 1917E 1069;
Frederick v. *Owens,* 35 Ohio Cir. Ct. 538; *Seattle High School Chapter No. 200
of the American Federation of Teachers* v. *Sharples,* 159 Wash. 424, 293 Pac. 994.

the mayor, the members have received their appointments. It is no infringement upon the constitutional rights of any one for the board to decline to employ him as a teacher in the schools, and it is immaterial whether the reason for the refusal to employ him is because the applicant is married or unmarried, is of fair complexion or dark, is or is not a member of a trades union, or whether no reason is given for such refusal. The board is not bound to give any reason for its action. It is free to contract with whomsoever it chooses.[39]

In a later case[40] the Supreme Court of Illinois reaffirmed its position that a board may refuse to re-employ an applicant for any reason whatsoever. The same position has been taken by the Court of Appeals of Louisiana.[41] In a case before that court, a board of education had passed a rule "not to employ among the schools of Catahoula Parish during the school session of 1933 and 1934 those teachers . . . or others who, or whose parents voted against the special school tax on August 29th." The court refused a writ of mandamus to compel the board to execute contracts with teachers who had violated the rule. The court refused to grant it, because, it said, the reason of a board for not employing a teacher is not subject to legal inquiry.

It has been held, too, that a board of education may take into consideration the sex of the teachers whom it employs and may refuse to employ teachers for certain positions on the basis of sex alone.[42] A Pennsylvania case is in point.[43] The Board of Education of Philadelphia adopted the following regulation:

And provided further, that male teachers only shall be eligible to the principalship of a grammar school for boys, a mixed grammar school or a consolidated school having three or more full grammar divisions, and to the position of supervising principal of a combined school containing a grammar school for boys or a mixed grammar school.

In sustaining the regulation, the court said in part:

To set men over kindergartens of children from four to six years of age, or to teaching small girls to sew or larger ones to cook, would in the present state of the world's social organization seem incongruous, although there are men cooks and men tailors. So on the other hand women in charge of a

39. *People* v. *City of Chicago*, 278 Ill. 318, 116 N.E. 158, L.R.A. 1917E 1069.

40. *Anderson* v. *Board of Education*, 390 Ill. 412, 61 N.E. (2d) 562.

41. *Lanier* v. *Catahoula Parish*, 154 So. (La.) 469.

42. *Commonwealth* v. *Board of Education*, 187 Pa. St. 70, 40 Atl. 806, 40 L.R.A. 498; *Commonwealth* v. *Jenks*, 154 Pa. St. 368, 26 Atl. 371; *Fitzpatrick* v. *Board of Education*, 125 N.Y.S. 954, 69 Misc. Rep. 78.

43. *Commonwealth* v. *Board of Education*, 187 Pa. St. 70, 40 Atl. 806, 40 L.R.A. 498.

night school of mechanics, or of a school of half-grown and intractable youths, could hardly be expected to have a successful administration. Unless, therefore, some positive mandate of law prevents, it would seem that the question of sex in relation to the qualifications of teachers for different kinds of schools was one peculiarly within the discretionary control of the board of education.

It is permissible, moreover, for a board of education to require of its teachers that they possess certain scholastic or professional fitness in addition to that required by the state as a basis of the issuance of certificates. Thus it was said in a Missouri case in which the right of a school board to require special examinations of teachers was sustained: "It must be admitted that in the interest of a higher educational qualification the defendant's board of directors had the right, in addition to having a statutory certificate, to require her to take an examination in which she should maintain a certain standard of fitness as a teacher."[44]

Effect of failure to make contract definite in its terms.—From the very nature of contracts they must be sufficiently definite to be enforcible. The courts will not undertake to enforce the obligations of a contract where such obligations cannot be discovered. Moreover, sound public policy demands that contracts made by public officers be definite and certain in their terms. It follows, therefore, that "a teacher can not recover from a school corporation for the breach of an executory contract unless it is so full and definite as to be capable of specific enforcement."[45] In the case of *Taylor* v. *School Town of Petersburgh*,[46] for example, it was held that a teacher could not recover on a contract which did not specify the time when the school was to begin, or the grade she was to teach, or the compensation she was to receive. In other cases it has been held that contracts are not enforcible where no definite salary is stipulated or where the matter of salary is left to future agreement.[47] It is to be kept in mind in this connection, however, that teachers contract in contemplation of the law and that every provision of the statutes which relates to the sub-

44. *Crabb* v. *School District No. 1*, 93 Mo. App. 254.

45. *Taylor* v. *School Town of Petersburgh*, 33 Ind. App. 675, 72 N.E. 159. Accord, *Mingo* v. *Trustees of Colored Common School District No. A*, 113 Ky. 475, 24 Ky. Law Rep. 288, 68 S.W. 483; *Atkins* v. *Van Buren School Township*, 77 Ind. 447; *Fairplay School Township* v. *O'Neal*, 127 Ind. 95, 26 N.E. 686.

46. *Taylor* v. *School Town of Petersburgh*, 33 Ind. App. 675, 72 N.E. 159.

47. *Mingo* v. *Trustees of Colored Common School District No. A*, 113 Ky. 475, 24 Ky. Law Rep. 288, 68 S.W. 483; *Atkins* v. *Van Buren School Township*, 77 Ind. 447.

ject matter of the contract will be read into the contract by implication.[48]

Necessity of corporate action in the employment of teachers.—It is well settled that, in order to enter into a valid contract with teachers, a board of education must act in its corporate capacity. The law contemplates that a board of education, in the exercise of the discretion vested in it, should meet and counsel together. Action taken by school-board members acting separately is not the action of the board, though all may agree, and the district will not be bound thereby.[49] The Superior Court of Delaware has expressed the rule clearly:

> The statute contemplates the school committee as a body, acting together as such, in an official capacity; and not as acting separate from each other individually. In the employment of teachers, therefore, the contract to be valid, should either be made at a meeting of the committee in the first instance, or else be ratified at such a meeting of the committee, of which meeting all the committee should have notice, and the opportunity to attend; and at which a majority must be present and act. Such contract may not rest in agreements made upon solicitation or otherwise, with the individual members of the committee apart from each other; but only upon united action at a meeting duly convened.[50]

The reasoning of the courts in sustaining the rule as stated in the preceding paragraph is well illustrated by an excerpt from a decision rendered by the Supreme Court of Arkansas. The court said:

> The different members of a board, scattered in the pursuit of their several avocations are not the board. Duties are cast upon boards composed of a number of persons, in order that they may be discharged with efficiency and wisdom, arising from a multitude of counsel. This purpose can not be

48. *Crabb* v. *School District No. 1,* 93 Mo. App. 254; *Boswell* v. *Consolidated School District No. 8,* 10 S.W. (2d) (Mo.) 665; *Alexander* v. *School District No. 1,* 84 Ore. 172, 164 Pac. 711; *Everett* v. *Fractional School District No. 2,* 30 Mich. 249.

49. *Cloverdale Union High School District* v. *Peters,* 88 Calif. App. 731, 264 Pac. 273; *Smith* v. *School District No. 57,* 1 Penn. Del. 401, 42 Atl. 368; *School District No. 39* v. *Shelton,* 26 Okla. 229, 109 Pac. 67, 138 Am. St. Rep. 962; *School District No. 42* v. *Bennett,* 52 Ark. 511, 13 S.W. 132; *Mitchell* v. *Williams,* 46 S.W. (Tenn.) 325; *Pugh* v. *School District No. 5,* 114 Mo. App. 688, 91 S.W. 471; *School Town of Milford* v. *Powner,* 126 Ind. 528; *Aikman* v. *School District No. 16,* 27 Kan. 129; *Mincer* v. *School District No. 31,* 27 Kan. 253; *McNolty* v. *Board of School Directors,* 102 Wis. 261, 78 N.W. 439; *Third School District in Stoughton* v. *Atherton,* 12 Metc. (Mass.) 105; *Honaker* v. *Board of Education,* 42 W. Va. 170, 24 S.E. 544, 32 L.R.A. 413; *Herrington* v. *District Township of Liston,* 47 Iowa 11; *State* v. *Treasurer of Liberty Township,* 22 Ohio St. 144; *Russell* v. *State,* 13 Neb. 68, 12 N.W. 829; *Scott* v. *Pendley,* 114 Ky. 606, 71 S.W. 647; *Barnhardt* v. *Gray,* 15 Calif. App. (2d) 307, 59 Pac. (2d) 454; *Landers* v. *Board of Education of Town of Hot Springs,* 45 N.M. 446, 116 Pac. (2d) 690.

50. *Smith* v. *School District No. 57,* 1 Penn. Del. 401, 42 Atl. 368.

realized without conference between the members of the board with reference to the matters entrusted to them before they take action thereon. After conference, the board will often escape unwise measures, to which each of the members acting separately would have committed themselves, either from haste, immature consideration, the demands of private engagement, or an unwillingness to shorten the allotted span of life under the entreaties of an importunate agent or teacher.[51]

Necessity of notice of board meetings.—It is well settled that a board of education cannot enter in a valid contract with a teacher unless all the members of the board have had notice of the meeting and an opportunity to attend.[52] In this connection, it was said by the court in the case of *School District No. 42* v. *Bennett:*

> The public selects each member of the board of directors and is entitled to his services; this it cannot enjoy, if two members can bind it without receiving or even suffering the counsel of the other. Two could, if they differed with the third, overrule his judgment and act without regarding it; but he might by his knowledge and reason change the bent of their minds, and the opportunity must be given him.
>
> We conclude that two directors may bind the district by a contract made at a meeting at which the third was present, or of which he had notice; but no contract can be made except at a meeting, and no meeting can be held unless all are present, or unless the absent member had notice.[53]

It is not necessary, however, to give notice of regular meetings which are provided for by statute or by the by-laws of the board. Of such meetings all members have constructive notice, and no further notification is necessary.[54] And if all members of a board are present and all consent to act, lack of notice is immaterial.[55] The mere fact, however, that all are present is not the determining factor; all must give their consent to a meeting of the board.

51. *School District No. 42* v. *Bennett,* 52 Ark. 511, 13 S.W. 132.

52. *School District No. 39* v. *Shelton,* 26 Okla. 229, 109 Pac. 67, 138 Am. St. Rep. 962; *School District No. 42* v. *Bennett,* 52 Ark. 511, 13 S.W. 132; *Burns* v. *Thompson,* 64 Ark. 489, 43 S.W. 499; *Johnson* v. *Dye,* 142 Mo. App. 424, 127 S.W. 413; *Shepherd* v. *Gambill,* 25 Ky. Law Rep. 333, 75 S.W. 223; *Scott* v. *Pendley,* 114 Ky. 606, 71 S.W. 647; *School District No. 76* v. *Kirby,* 27 Colo. App. 300, 149 Pac. 260; *Aikman* v. *School District No. 16,* 27 Kan. 129; *McNolty* v. *Board of School Directors,* 102 Wis. 261, 78 N.W. 439.

53. *School District No. 42* v. *Bennett,* 52 Ark. 511, 13 S.W. 132.

54. *Board of Education* v. *Carolan,* 182 Ill. 119, 55 N.E. 58; *School District No. 42* v. *Bennett,* 52 Ark. 511, 13 S.W. 132.

55. *School District No. 68* v. *Allen,* 83 Ark. 491, 104 S.W. 172; *Lee* v. *Mitchell,* 108 Ark. 1, 156 S.W. 450; *Wysong* v. *Board of Education,* 86 W. Va. 57, 102 S.E. 733; *Hibbard* v. *Smith,* 135 Mo. App. 721, 116 S.W. 487.

Validity of oral contracts.—In the absence of a statutory requirement that contracts be reduced to written form, an oral contract is
valid and enforcible.[56] The rule has been clearly stated by the Supreme
Court of Wisconsin as follows:

> But the statute does not say that the contract must be in writing, and the
> court can not read into the statute provisions not found there for the pur-
> pose of rendering an oral contract, otherwise unobjectionable, void because
> not in writing, in the absence of express statutory requirement. An oral
> contract by a school teacher with a municipality or school district is valid,
> in the absence of requirement that it be in writing.[57]

Where, on the other hand, the statutes specifically require that contracts with teachers shall be in written form, oral contracts are invalid, and no recovery can be had in an action for breach of contract.[58]
Not only that, no recovery can be had on *quantum meruit* for services
actually rendered.[59] In the case of *Taylor v. School District No. 3*,[60]
for example, action was brought to recover for services rendered under

56. *Pearson v. School District No. 8*, 144 Wis. 620, 129 N.W. 940; *Jackson
School Township v. Shera*, 8 Ind. App. 330, 35 N.E. 842; *School Town of Prince-
ton v. Gebhart*, 61 Ind. 187; *Robinson v. Board of Education*, 70 W. Va. 66, 73
S.E. 337; *Jameson v. Board of Education*, 74 W. Va. 389, 81 S.E. 1126.

57. *Pearson v. School District No. 8*, 144 Wis. 620, 129 N.W. 940.

58. *County Board of Education of Hopkins County v. Dudley*, 154 Ky. 426,
157 S.W. 927; *Board of Trustees of Hartford Graded Schools v. Ohio County
Board of Education*, 172 Ky. 424, 189 S.W. 433; *Hutchins v. School District No. 1*,
128 Mich. 177, 87 N.W. 80; *Lewis v. Hayden*, 18 Ky. Law Rep. 980, 38 S.W.
1054; *Leland v. School District No. 28*, 77 Minn. 469, 80 N.W. 354; *Michaelsohn
v. Norway School District*, 63 N.D. 683, 249 N.W. 776; *Krutsinger v. School
Township of Liberty*, 219 Iowa 291, 257 N.W. 797; *Leslie County Board of Education v. Melton*, 277 Ky. 772, 127 S.W. (2d) 846; *Walters v. Topper*, 139 Pa.
Super. 292, 11 Atl. (2d) 649; *Wenders v. White Mills Independent School District*, 171 Pa. Super. 39, 90 Atl. (2d) 318; *Williamson v. Board of Education
of City of Woodward*, 189 Okla. 342, 117 Pac. (2d) 120; *Board of School Commissioners of City of Indianapolis v. State* ex rel. *Wolfolk*, 209 Ind. 498, 199 N.E.
569; *Gordon v. Trustees of Tuscumbia School District*, 191 Miss. 203, 1 So. (2d)
234; *Bankston v. Tangipahoa Parish School Board*, 190 So. (La.) 177. It has
been held, however, that a statute requiring a written contract to create
teachers' employment does not apply to teachers entitled to benefit of tenure act
(*Oxman v. Independent School District of Duluth*, 178 Minn. 422, 227 N.W.
351).

59. *Leland v. School District No. 28*, 77 Minn. 469, 80 N.W. 354; *Metz v.
Warwick*, 217 Mo. App. 504, 269 S.W. 626; *Taylor v. School District No. 3*, 60
Mo. App. 372; *Perkins v. Independent School District of Ridgeway*, 99 Mo. App.
483, 74 S.W. 122; *Lee v. York School Township*, 163 Ind. 339, 71 N.E. 956;
Crane v. Bennington School District, 61 Mich. 299, 28 N.W. 105; *Denison v. Inhabitants of Vinalhaven*, 100 Me. 136, 60 Atl. 798; *Fennell v. Lannom*, 46 Okla.
519, 149 Pac. 144; *Dodd v. Board of Education of Forsyth County*, 46 Ga. App.
235, 167 S.E. 319; *Riche v. Ascension Parish School Board*, 200 So. (La.) 681.

60. *Taylor v. School District No. 3*, 60 Mo. App. 372.

an oral contract where a statute required that contracts of the kind involved should be in written form. The court denied recovery, saying in part:

But the exercise of this power is confined to the mode prescribed by the terms of the statute. It is exclusive of every other mode. Such contract is no contract which the board of directors are authorized to make, unless made in the manner and under the conditions required by the terms of the statute. . . . The undoubted purpose of these requirements is that the terms of the contract shall in no essential particular be left in doubt or to be determined at some future time but shall be fixed when it is entered into. If a person can without such contract in the first instance go and bind the school district as on an implied contract for the value of his services, it would defeat the purpose the legislature had in enacting the statute. . . . The law will not make that valid without writing which the law requires should be in writing. And as said in *Keating* v. *Kansas City*, 84 Mo. 419, "From a void contract no cause of action can arise whether of *quantum meruit* or sounding in damages."

In some jurisdictions, however, it has been held that a teacher may recover for services actually rendered under an oral contract, even though the statutes may require that the contract be reduced to written form.[61] Recovery is allowed upon the theory that acceptance of the services constitutes a ratification of the contract, or upon the theory that the school district has been guilty of laches. In some instances the teacher has been able to recover on *quantum meruit*.[62] Thus it was said in a West Virginia case: "After the service has been rendered in a satisfactory manner to the patrons of the school, and the board has recognized and approved it by receiving her monthly reports, and paying her five months' salary, it is too late for them to object that her appointment was not in writing, as required by law."[63] And in a Kansas case[64] the board had an oral agreement with teachers that if some of them were drafted into the armed services and the remaining teachers took over the work of the drafted teachers, those remaining would be paid a reasonable amount for their services. The

61. *Davis* v. *White*, 171 Ark. 385, 284 S.W. 764; *Bald Knob Special School District* v. *McDonald*, 171 Ark. 72, 283 S.W. 22; *Cook* v. *Independent School District of North McGregor*, 40 Iowa 444; *Williams* v. *Board of Education*, 45 W. Va. 199, 31 S.E. 985; *Joint Consolidated School District No. 2* v. *Johnson*, 166 Kan. 636, 203 Pac. (2d) 242; *Williamson* v. *Board of Education of City of Woodward*, 189 Okla. 342, 117 Pac. (2d) 120; *Day* v. *School District No. 21*, 98 Mont. 207, 38 Pac. (2d) 595.

62. *Jones* v. *School District*, 8 Kan. 263.

63. *Williams* v. *Board of Education*, 45 W. Va. 199, 31 S.E. 985.

64. *Joint Consolidated School District No. 2* v. *Johnson*, 166 Kan. 636, 203 Pac. (2d) 242.

court permitted extra pay for their services, even though the contract had not been reduced to written form.

Necessary formalities in the execution of written contracts.—In order that a contract may meet the legal requirement that it be reduced to written form, it is not necessary that all the provisions of the contract be contained in any single document. The terms of the contract may be gathered from a number of documents, such as letters, telegrams, and resolutions of the school board, provided the documents taken together constitute an entire agreement.[65] Thus where a school board had agreed to employ a certain teacher, had recorded the action in their records, had notified her of their action, and she had accepted by letter, there existed a valid written contract. Moreover, an oral contract which is entered into at a legal meeting of the board and which is definite in all its terms may later be reduced to writing.[66] And where all the terms of a contract have been agreed upon, it is not necessary that the contract be signed at a legal meeting of the board[67] or that those signing the contract sign it at the same time.[68] It has been held, however, that the record of the clerk of a school district disclosing employment of a teacher is insufficient as a written contract where the teacher accepted the employment orally.[69] And even where a board voted to employ a teacher and the supervising principal prepared a contract for her to sign and she signed it and returned it to the board, it was not an executed contract. The board could reconsider the matter and rescind its action under a statute requiring that the contract be signed by both the teacher and the president and secretary of the board.[70]

65. *Taylor* v. *School Town of Petersburgh,* 33 Ind. App. 675, 72 N.E. 159; *Edwards* v. *School District No. 73,* 221 Mo. App. 47, 297 S.W. 1001; *Bailey* v. *Jamestown School District,* 77 S.W. (2d) (Mo.) 1017; *Hall* v. *Delhi–Deer Creek Township Corporation,* 98 Ind. App. 409, 189 N.E. 527.

66. *Faulk* v. *McCartney,* 42 Kan. 695, 22 Pac. 712; *School District No. 68* v. *Allen,* 83 Ark. 491, 104 S.W. 172; *Corum* v. *Common School District No. 21,* 55 Idaho 725, 47 Pac. (2d) 889; *Hugunin* v. *Madison Township of Daviess County,* 108 Ind. App. 573, 27 N.E. (2d) 926.

67. *Faulk* v. *McCartney,* 42 Kan. 695, 22 Pac. 712; *Cloverdale Union High School District* v. *Peters,* 88 Calif. App. 731, 264 Pac. 273.

68. *School District No. 16* v. *Barnes,* 44 Okla. 489, 144 Pac. 1046; *School Town of Milford* v. *Zeigler,* 1 Ind. App. 138, 27 N.E. 303; *Holloway* v. *Ogden School District No. 9,* 62 Mich. 153, 28 N.W. 764.

69. *Petrie* v. *Sherman County Community High School,* 134 Kan. 464, 7 Pac. (2d) 104.

70. *Potts* v. *School District of Penn Township,* 127 Pa. Super. 173, 193 Atl. 290.

With respect to the legality of an oral contract which was later reduced to writing, the Supreme Court of Kansas said:

There was a contract entered into between the plaintiff and the district board, not by a part of the members thereof, but by the district board; that contract, being in parol, was afterwards reduced to writing. It may have been done immediately after the adjournment of the board; in any event, the contract is embodied in writing made and authorized by it. It was the contract of the board, and was reduced to writing. Probably a majority of the contracts for teachers' wages in the state are made in parol, and afterwards reduced to writing; it may be done at a meeting of the district board —that is the better way; it may, however, be directed to be done at that time and immediately afterwards reduced to writing and signed by the parties.[71]

Similarly, in the case of *School District No. 68* v. *Allen*,[72] a board of school directors agreed with a teacher as to the terms of her employment, but, inasmuch as there were no blank contract forms at hand, the contract was not reduced to written form or signed until a later date. The court held the contract met the statutory requirement that contracts with teachers be in writing.

In a case which came before the Supreme Court of Oklahoma an attempt was made to have a contract declared invalid because it had been signed by the various members of the board at different times. The opinion of the court was in part as follows:

If the board had met in regular session and verbally agreed with the teacher to employ her for a term of nine months at sixty dollars per month, and reduced such agreement to writing, it is immaterial, so far as the effect thereof is concerned, whether all parties signed such written agreement at the same time and place or not. The actual agreement between the parties was the meeting of the minds of the teacher as one party and the board, acting for the district, as the other, as to the length of the school term and the amount per month to be paid, and as to other conditions agreed upon. Hence it is immaterial whether all parties to such contract or all the members of the board attached their names to the written memorandum of such agreement at the same time or not.[73]

It should be pointed out that some statutes prescribe a particular contract form or that the contract be signed by the teacher and certain designated members of the board of education. Since the statutory mode of making a contract is usually regarded as the measure of power, such statutes are commonly regarded as mandatory and must

71. *Faulk* v. *McCartney*, 42 Kan. 695, 22 Pac. 712.
72. *School District No. 68* v. *Allen*, 83 Ark. 491, 104 S.W. 172.
73. *School District No. 16* v. *Barnes*, 44 Okla. 489, 144 Pac. 1046.

be followed strictly if contracts are to be valid.[74] For example, in a Pennsylvania case,[75] a board of education elected the plaintiff as high-school principal, the minutes of the board recording this action were duly approved, and the plaintiff accepted the position. At a later date the board refused to execute a contract with the plaintiff and employed another person as principal. The court refused to issue a writ of mandamus requiring the board to execute a written contract with the plaintiff. It reasoned:

It must be recognized that the appointment or election of a teacher or principal in the manner required by statute is a prerequisite to the validity of a written contract. But a valid and enforceable contract between the appellant and the school district required (a) his appointment or election as principal of the high school in the manner specified by the School Code . . . and (b) the execution of a contract in writing on behalf of the board by the president and secretary of the board and signed by the appellant. . . . Both elements are equally vital and essential. No such valid contract having been executed by the parties, the board could rescind or revoke its previous action in electing appellant. . . . Until there was a contract in writing, the board was not without power to rescind or revoke its prior action in appointing or electing appellant.[76]

Delegation of authority to employ teachers.—Where a corporate body, such as a school board, is charged with the performance of a duty which involves the exercise of discretion, the performance of that duty cannot be delegated to others. Authority to contract with teachers cannot, therefore, be delegated to the city superintendent of schools or to some officer or committee of the board itself.[77] In the case of *Taggart* v. *School District No. 1*,[78] speaking of the validity of a contract entered into by a superintendent and a teacher, the court said:

The manifest purpose and spirit of the statute, and the only reasonable construction that can be given it, is that the relation of teacher can not be created except by a written contract embodying the terms prescribed by

74. *Commonwealth* ex rel. *Ricapito* v. *School District of City of Bethlehem*, 148 Pa. Super. 426, 25 Atl. (2d) 786; *Board of School Commissioners of City of Indianapolis*, 209 Ind. 498, 199 N.E. 569; *Ickes* v. *Costlow*, 127 Pa. Super. 180, 193 Atl. 287.

75. *Ickes* v. *Costlow*, 127 Pa. Super. 180, 193 Atl. 287.

76. *Ickes* v. *Costlow*, 127 Pa. Super. 180, 193 Atl. 287.

77. *Taggart* v. *School District No. 1*, 96 Ore. 422, 188 Pac. 908; *Coleman* v. *District of Columbia*, 279 Fed. 990; *State* v. *Jones*, 143 Tenn. 575, 224 S.W. 1041. *Andrews* v. *Union Parish School Board*, 191 La. 90, 184 So. 552; *State* ex rel. *Golson* v. *Winn Parish School Board*, 9 So. (2d) (La.) 342. See also *Hermann* v. *Independent School District*, 24 Idaho 554, 135 Pac. 1159.

78. *Taggart* v. *School District No. 1*, 96 Ore. 422, 188 Pac. 908.

the statute. The duty thus imposed upon the board is not delegable. The directors have been elected by the people to perform a duty requiring their judgment. It is not a ministerial function which can be performed by another.

The Court of Appeals of the District of Columbia has said in the same connection: "This power of appointment requires an exercise of judgment, and could not be delegated to the secretary or anybody else."[79] A board of education may, however, delegate to the superintendent, or to a committee, authority to ascertain proper parties to be employed and even to draw tentative contracts, but such contracts must be confirmed or ratified by the board itself. Where, on the other hand, the terms of a contract have been agreed upon by the board and the teacher, the ministerial duty of executing the contract and of reducing it to the proper form may be delegated to an agent.

Limitations on authority of school boards with respect to term of employment of teachers and superintendents.—A board of education may often find it highly desirable to enter contracts with teachers whereby they shall be employed for a number of years. The question may arise under such circumstances as to the authority of the board to execute a contract of employment covering a number of years and extending beyond the official life of the board as then constituted. The courts, as a rule, hold that, unless restricted by statute and in the absence of fraud or collusion, a school board may employ superintendents and teachers for a period extending beyond the term of office of some of the members of the board,[80] or even beyond the term of office of all the members of the board.[81] Moreover, the great weight

79. *Coleman* v. *District of Columbia*, 279 Fed. 990.

80. *Taylor* v. *School District No. 7*, 16 Wash. 365, 47 Pac. 758; *Splaine* v. *School District No. 122*, 20 Wash. 74, 54 Pac. 766; *State* v. *Board of Education*, 94 W. Va. 408, 118 S.E. 877; *Reubelt* v. *School Town of Noblesville*, 106 Ind. 478, 7 N.E. 206; *Gardner* v. *North Little Rock Special School District*, 161 Ark. 466, 257 S.W. 73; *Gates* v. *School District*, 53 Ark. 468, 14 S.W. 656, 10 L.R.A. 186; *Davis* v. *Public Schools of City of Escanaba*, 175 Mich. 105, 140 N.W. 1001; *Cleveland* v. *Amy*, 88 Mich. 374, 50 N.W. 293; *State* v. *Board of Education*, 95 W. Va. 57, 120 S.E. 183; *Wheeler* v. *Burke*, 162 Ky. 143, 172 S.W. 91; *Wilson* v. *East Bridgeport School District*, 36 Conn. 280; *King City Union High School District* v. *Waibel*, 2 Calif. App. (2d) 65, 37 Pac. (2d) 861; *State ex rel. Ries* v. *Winchell*, 136 Ohio St. 62, 23 N.E. (2d) 843; *V. L. Dodds Company* v. *Consolidated School District of Lamont*, 220 Iowa 812, 263 N.W. 522.

81. *Town of Pearsall* v. *Woolls*, 50 S.W. (Tex.) 959; *Wait* v. *Ray*, 67 N.Y. 36; *School Town of Milford* v. *Zeigler*, 1 Ind. App. 138, 27 N.E. 303; *Sparta School Township* v. *Mendell*, 138 Ind. 188, 37 N.E. 604; *Webster* v. *School District No. 4*, 16 Wis. 316; *Caldwell* v. *School District No. 7*, 55 Fed. 372; *Tate* v. *School*

of authority is to the effect that school boards, acting in good faith, may employ superintendents and teachers for any term of years that is reasonable.[82] What is reasonable is a matter to be determined by the circumstances of each particular case, although employment for an unusual number of years would be strong evidence of fraud. The courts reason that if it were the legislative intent to limit the authority of school boards with respect to the term of employment of teachers, such limitations would be expressed in the statutes. A school board, moreover, is a continuous corporate entity, and the legality of its contracts, therefore, is not conditioned by the official life of its members.

The case of *State* v. *Board of Education*[83] illustrates the reasoning of the courts. In that case a school board employed a school principal in June. In the following July two new board members were elected, and the new board refused to carry out the contract. The court held the contract was binding upon the district. It said in part:

They claim it is unfair to the new president and the new member that they should be required to carry out contracts which they did not help make; but the contracts made are corporate in character, not the contracts of the individuals who then constituted the board. The board by statute is a corporation; it is a continuing corporate body. Its members may change, but the corporation does not change. The corporation in July is the same corporation that it was in the preceding June.

In holding that a school committee could not repudiate a contract made by its predecessor, the Supreme Court of Errors of Connecticut said: "It would be a novel and most mischievous doctrine that the officers who manage the governmental corporations of the state could have no power to make a contract which was not to be performed within the time for which they were elected to office."[84]

In some jurisdictions, on the other hand, it has been held that a board of education cannot make a contract with a teacher to be per-

---

District No. 11, 324 Mo. 477, 23 S.W. (2d) 1013; *Corum* v. *Common School District No. 21*, 55 Idaho 725, 47 Pac. (2d) 889; *Horvat* v. *Jenkins Township School District*, 337 Pa. 193, 10 Atl. (2d) 390.

82. *Wait* v. *Ray*, 67 N.Y. 36; *Caldwell* v. *School District No. 7*, 55 Fed. 372; *Gardner* v. *North Little Rock Special School District*, 161 Ark. 466, 257 S.W. 73; *Davis* v. *Public Schools of the City of Escanaba*, 175 Mich. 105, 140 N.W. 1001; *Moon* v. *School City of South Bend*, 50 Ind. App. 251, 98 N.E. 153; *Sugg* v. *Board of Trustees of Glasgow Graded Common School District*, 225 Ky. 356, 74 S.W. (2d) 198; *Stokes* v. *Newell*, 174 Miss. 629, 165 So. 542.

83. *State* v. *Board of Education*, 94 W. Va. 408, 118 S.E. 877.

84. *Wilson* v. *East Bridgeport School District*, 36 Conn. 280. Accord, *People ex rel. Davidson* v. *Bradley*, 382 Ill. 383, 47 N.E. (2d) 93.

formed after the expiration of the official life of the board.[85] In practically all such cases, however, the decision of the court has turned upon the wording of the statutes. But a Delaware case seems to announce a doctrine contrary to that of other cases. It was said by the court:

Again, while we do not lay down any inflexible rule in every case that outgoing commissioners may not make contracts with teachers extending beyond the current school year and into the terms of the incoming commissioners, yet we do most emphatically say that our free-school system and public policy both plainly demand that the school committee for any year should engage teachers only for that year, and should not make contracts commencing in the year of their successors; that the new commissioners elected for the succeeding year should have a voice in the employment of teachers for that year, and thereby have an opportunity to express the views of the school voters indicated in their election, the very purpose of which may have been to effect a change of teachers.[86]

With respect to the number of years for which a teacher may be employed, the rule is well establishéd that, in the absence of any statutory restriction, a school board acting in good faith may employ a teacher for any number of years that is reasonable, the reasonableness of the term of employment to be determined by the circumstances of each particular case.[87] In sustaining the authority of a board of education to employ a superintendent for a period of three years, the Supreme Court of Michigan reasoned as follows:

The legislature has made the board of education a continuing body, and has confided to it the matter of selecting and employing a superintendent of schools. Why should this court say that the power of the board in this behalf does not extend so far as to permit it to hire a superintendent for more than two years? The court can not extend or diminish the legislative grant of power; what it may do, in a particular case, is to determine whether the action of the board which is questioned is within the power conferred.

I am of the opinion that the limits, and only limits, to the exercise of the power of the board to employ a superintendent of schools are those fixed by reasonableness and good faith. The board of education does not derive its

85. *Chittenden* v. *School District No. 1,* 56 Vt. 551; *Burkhead* v. *Independent School District of Independence,* 107 Iowa 29, 77 N.W. 491; *Independent School District of Liberty* v. *Pennington,* 181 Iowa 933, 165 N.W. 209; *Stevenson* v. *School Directors,* 87 Ill. 255; *Smith* v. *School District No. 57,* 1 Penn. Del. 401, 42 Atl. 368. See also *Calloway* v. *Atlanta Rural High School District No. 2,* 129 Kan. 659, 284 Pac. 377; *Shores* v. *Elmore County Board of Education,* 241 Ala. 464, 3 So. (2d) 14.

86. *Smith* v. *School District No. 57,* 1 Penn. Del. 401, 42 Atl. 368.

87. *Davis* v. *Public Schools of City of Escanaba,* 175 Mich. 105, 140 N.W. 1001; *Gardner* v. *North Little Rock Special School District,* 161 Ark. 466, 257 S.W. 73; *Wait* v. *Ray,* 67 N.Y. 36; *Caldwell* v. *School District No. 7,* 55 Fed. 372.

powers from the district but from the statute. That courts or juries might differ concerning the effect of particular action, as indicating good faith or the contrary, is no reason for refusing the rule. If the board should make a contract for the services of a superintendent for fifty years, or for a year at a salary of fifty thousand dollars, a court, without the intervention of a jury, would promptly set the contract aside as fraudulent. In cases like the one at bar, the question of good faith is one for a jury, which should be instructed that in considering the question all facts bearing upon the propriety and reasonableness of the contract, as well as the actual motives and purposes of the board, may be considered.[88]

Similarly, it has been said by the Supreme Court of Arkansas: "The proper rule seems to be that, unless the statute prescribes a time limit upon the duration of such a contract, the board may make a contract for a reasonable length of time, and the reasonableness of the contract is to be determined by all the circumstances."[89] And in a New York case it was said: "The power to employ teachers is, therefore, very widely made general; and a contract for one year or more, if made in good faith, and without fraudulent collusion, must be held binding."[90]

Ratification of teachers' contracts.—Where a teacher is permitted to teach under an invalid contract and is paid for his services for a month or more, the question may arise as to whether the contract has been ratified. The rule with respect to ratification is that a school board may ratify any contract which it had authority to make in the first instance.[91] "It is a rule," says the Supreme Court of Nebraska,[92] "subject to few, if any, exceptions, that a corporate authority may ratify and confirm any act or contract in its behalf or for its benefit which it might have lawfully done or made originally." It has been held in many cases, for example, that acceptance of a teacher's service constitutes the ratification of a contract made at a meeting of which some members of the board did not have notice,[93] or made by board

88. *Davis* v. *Public Schools of City of Escanaba*, 175 Mich. 105, 140 N.W. 1001.

89. *Garner* v. *North Little Rock Special School District*, 161 Ark. 466, 257 S.W. 73.

90. *Wait* v. *Ray*, 67 N.Y. 36.

91. *Watkins* v. *Special School District of Lepanto*, 122 Ark. 611, 183 S.W. 168; *School District No. 47* v. *Goodwin*, 81 Ark. 143, 98 S.W. 696; *Bishop* v. *Fuller*, 78 Neb. 259, 110 N.W. 715; *Saline County* v. *Gage County*, 66 Neb. 839, 92 N.W. 1050; *Ryan* v. *Humphries*, 50 Okla. 343, 150 Pac. 1106, L.R.A. 1915F 1047.

92. *Saline County* v. *Gage County*, 66 Neb. 839, 92 N.W. 1050.

93. *Watkins* v. *Special School District of Lepanto*, 122 Ark. 611, 183 S.W. 168; *School District No. 47* v. *Goodwin*, 81 Ark. 143, 98 S.W. 696; *Ryan* v. *Humphries*, 50 Okla. 343, 150 Pac. 1106, L.R.A. 1915F 1047; *Elsemore* v. *Inhabitants of Town of Hancock*, 137 Me. 243, 18 Atl. (2d) 692.

members acting separately.[94] The case of *Crane* v. *Bennington School District*[95] is an illustration. In that case, a teacher had been employed by school-district officers acting individually. After teaching ten weeks, the teacher was discharged. In holding that the contract had been ratified in its entirety, the court said:

> When it was admitted without any dispute that the plaintiff taught under this contract for ten weeks, with the sanction and consent of the officers, and that orders were drawn by the proper officers for his pay as such teacher, and cashed by the assessor, who did not sign the contract, without any objection, it becomes entirely immaterial what the book of record showed, or whether there was any corporate action in hiring him or authorizing the contract. The defendant must be held not only estopped by the action of its officers from questioning the validity of the contract, but treated as having fully ratified and confirmed it.
>
> School-district officers can not be permitted by the law to enter into a written contract with a teacher, none of them denying its validity for ten weeks, or half the term, but recognizing it by making payments upon it, in which payments all join, and then, after the teacher, in the utmost good faith and reliance upon the contract, has taught that length of time, discharge him without cause, and plead in bar of his payment under the contract that they never met and consulted, nor took corporate action in hiring him, or made any record in a book of the execution of the contract.

The doctrine of ratification does not apply, however, to contracts which a board of education had no authority to make in the first instance. Obviously, that which cannot be done directly cannot be done indirectly. Thus the following classes of contracts with teachers cannot, as a rule, be ratified: contracts in excess of a constitutional or statutory debt limit;[96] contracts with teachers who do not possess certificates as required by law;[97] oral contracts where the law requires

---

94. *Crane* v. *Bennington School District*, 61 Mich. 299, 28 N.W. 105; *School District No. 56* v. *Jackson*, 110 Ark. 262, 161 S.W. 153; *School District No. 36* v. *Gardner*, 142 Ark. 557, 219 S.W. 11; *Hermance* v. *Public School District No. 2*, 20 Ariz. 314, 180 Pac. 442; *Athearn* v. *Independent School District of Millersburg*, 33 Iowa 105; *Parrick* v. *School District No. 1*, 100 Kan. 569, 164 Pac. 1172; *Graham* v. *School District No. 69*, 33 Ore. 263, 54 Pac. 185; *Landers* v. *Board of Education of Town of Hot Springs*, 45 N.M. 446, 116 Pac. (2d) 690.

95. *Crane* v. *Bennington School District*, 61 Mich. 299, 28 N.W. 105.

96. *Boydstun* v. *Rockwall County*, 23 S.W. (Tex.) 541; *Riesen* v. *School District No. 4*, 189 Wis. 607, 208 N.W. 472; *Grady* v. *Pruit*, 111 Ky. 100, 23 Ky. Law Rep. 506, 63 S.W. 283.

97. *Goose River Bank* v. *Willow Lake School Township*, 1 N.D. 26, 44 N.W. 1002, 26 Am. St. Rep. 605; *Perkins* v. *Inhabitants of Town of Standish*, 62 Atl. (2d) 321. Note: 42 L.R.A. (N.S.) 412.

that the contracts in question be reduced to written form;[98] and contracts between a school board and one of its own members.[99]

Although a school district may have authority to ratify a contract, there may be some difficulty under a given state of facts in determining whether ratification has actually taken place. Ratification may be inferred from acts inconsistent with any other supposition. It is not necessary, as a rule, that a board take formal action, such as ratifying the contract by resolution. The mere acceptance of the services of a teacher, after a knowledge of all the material facts, is sufficient.[100] Thus it was said by the Supreme Court of Iowa: "Performance of a contract, permission to the party with whom the corporation contracts to perform, the acceptance of the performance by the corporation, acquiescence in the contract, payment to the other party and the like, all operate as acts of ratification."[101] The case of *Crane* v. *Bennington School District*[102] illustrates the application of the rule. A teacher was employed by school-district officers acting individually. He taught ten weeks and was paid his salary for the first two months. In the opinion of the court, the contract had been ratified:

It was not necessary that there should be a direct proceeding with an express intent to ratify. "It may be done indirectly, and by acts of recognition or acquiescence, or acts inconsistent with repudiation or disapproval." . . . It was not necessary that these three officers should formally meet together, pass a resolution confirming the contract, and record it, in order to ratify the

98. *Leland* v. *School District No. 28*, 77 Minn. 469, 80 N.W. 354; *Metz* v. *Warwick*, 217 Mo. App. 504, 269 S.W. 626; *Taylor* v. *School District No. 3*, 60 Mo. App. 372; *Bankston* v. *Tangipahoa Parish School Board*, 190 So. (La.) 177; *Dodd* v. *Board of Education*, 46 Ga. App. 235, 167 S.E. 319; *Riche* v. *Ascension Parish School Board*, 200 So. (La.) 681; *Commonwealth* ex rel. *Ricapito* v. *School District of City of Bethlehem*, 25 Atl. (2d) (Pa.) 786. Contra, *Bald Knob Special School District* v. *McDonald*, 171 Ark. 72, 283 S.W. 22; *Cook* v. *Independent School District of North McGregor*, 40 Iowa 444; *Joint Consolidated School District No. 2* v. *Johnson*, 166 Kan. 636, 203 Pac. (2d) 242.

99. *Western Publishing House* v. *District Township of Rock*, 84 Iowa 101, 50 N.W. 551. Contra, *Scott* v. *School District No. 9*, 67 Vt. 150, 31 Atl. 145, 27 L.R.A. 588.

100. *Ryan* v. *Humphries*, 50 Okla. 343, 150 Pac. 1106, L.R.A. 1915F 1047; *Crane* v. *Bennington School District*, 61 Mich. 299, 28 N.W. 105; *Watkins* v. *Special School District of Lepanto*, 122 Ark. 611, 183 S.W. 168; *Chalmers* v. *School District No. 1*, 170 Mich. 250, 136 N.W. 386; *Graham* v. *School District No. 69*, 33 Ore. 263, 54 Pac. 185; *Athearn* v. *Independent District of Millersburg*, 33 Iowa 105.

101. *Athearn* v. *Independent District of Millersburg*, 33 Iowa 105.

102. *Crane* v. *Bennington School District*, 61 Mich. 299, 28 N.W. 105.

action of the moderator and director in hiring the plaintiff, and executing the contract sued upon. Their acts, in drawing and paying the orders without any demur [*sic*] or protest, was a sufficient recognition and approval of the contract. . . . But here the agreement was acted upon by everybody until other controversies arose, and then it was too late to take exception to the want of formalities in engaging the teacher or executing the contract.

Under certain circumstances, however, ratification cannot be inferred from acts of acquiescence. Where the statutes prescribe a mode of contracting to the exclusion of all other modes, the mode prescribed becomes a measure of power, and there can be no ratification inferred from acts recognizing the legality of the contract. That is, the contract cannot be ratified by any less formal action than that required by statute in the making of the contract in the first instance.[103]

Some question may arise with respect to the effect of ratification of a contract. Where an invalid contract with a teacher is ratified, it becomes valid from its inception and in its entirety.[104] That is, a teacher whose contract has been ratified can recover not only for the time he has taught but for the full time stipulated in the contract. A board of education cannot accept in part and reject in part the services of a teacher.

Right of teacher to recover on quantum meruit.—In case a teacher renders services under a contract which is not enforcible, the question may arise as to whether he can recover on *quantum meruit* the actual value of his services. The doctrine has grown up, based upon equitable considerations, that where one of the parties to a contract performs his part of the contract wholly or in part, and the other party receives and retains the benefit of the performance, the party thus benefited will be held to pay the actual value of the benefits received. Th basis of the recovery is not the original contract, but a new contract which the law implies in order that justice and equity may be done. It is well settled, however, that the law will not imply a contract where there was a total lack of authority to make it in the first instance. In other words, the law will not imply a contract which could not have been made expressly.

103. *Martin* v. *Common School District No. 3*, 163 Minn. 427, 204 N.W. 320; *Caxton Company* v. *School District No. 5*, 120 Wis. 374, 98 N.W. 231.

104. *Ryan* v. *Humphries*, 50 Okla. 343, 150 Pac. 1106, L.R.A. 1915F 1047; *Stewart* v. *Board of Education*, 104 Okla. 141, 230 Pac. 504; *School District No. 56* v. *Jackson*, 110 Ark. 262, 161 S.W. 153; *Watkins* v. *Special School District of Lepanto*, 122 Ark. 611, 183 S.W. 168; *Board of Education* v. *Watts*, 19 Ala. App. 7, 95 So. 498.

The rule is clearly illustrated in a case decided by the Court of Appeals of Alabama.[105] The statutes prohibited a county board of education from employing anyone as school principal who had not been recommended by the county superintendent of education. A principal who had been employed in disregard of the statutes sought to recover reasonable compensation for his services. The relief prayed for was denied. The court said: "An implied contract can never arise unless the party sought to be charged is legally authorized to contract, and an implied obligation to pay for services rendered can never exist unless the party for whom the services were rendered was at the time legally authorized to contract for them."

Applying the principle as stated in the preceding paragraphs, the courts have held repeatedly that a teacher who teaches without the certificate required by law cannot recover on an implied contract.[106] It is well settled, too, that one who renders services under an oral contract, where the law requires that it be in writing, is unable to recover on any theory of *quantum meruit*.[107] Contracts in excess of a constitutional or statutory debt limit are wholly void, and one who teaches under such a contract is entirely without recourse.[108] The Supreme Court of Oklahoma said, quoting Gray's *Limitation of the Taxing Power*: "A debt which is in excess of the constitutional or statutory debt limit is void; and in no form can such debt be held valid upon any theory of quantum meruit, or equitable obligation. The absolute lack of power to contract the indebtedness bars every form of action and every legal device by which recovery is sought."[109]

Right of teachers to recover salary while school is closed.—Occasionally it becomes expedient or necessary to close the schools because of an epidemic of some contagious disease, or because the schoolhouse

105. *Board of Education* v. *Watts,* 19 Ala. App. 7, 95 So. 498. Accord, *Rateliff* v. *Buna Independent School District,* 46 S.W. (2d) (Tex.) 459.

106. *Goose River Bank* v. *Willow Lake School Township,* 1 N.D. 26, 44 N.W. 1002, 26 Am. St. Rep. 605; *Wayne County* v. *Hopper,* 114 Miss. 755, 75 So. 766; *Jackson School Township* v. *Farlow,* 75 Ind. 118.

107. *Leland* v. *School District No. 28,* 77 Minn. 469, 80 N.W. 354; *Metz* v. *Warwick,* 217 Mo. App. 504, 269 S.W. 626; *Taylor* v. *School District No. 3,* 60 Mo. App. 372; *Perkins* v. *Independent School District of Ridgeway,* 99 Mo. App. 483, 74 S.W. 122. Contra, *Williams* v. *Board of Education,* 45 W. Va. 199, 31 S.E. 985.

108. *Edwards* v. *School District No. 222,* 117 Okla. 269, 235 Pac. 611; *Clark* v. *School Directors of District No. 1,* 78 Ill. 474; *McGillivray* v. *Joint School District,* 112 Wis. 354, 88 N.W. 310, 58 L.R.A. 100, 88 Am. St. Rep. 969.

109. *Fairbanks-Morse Company* v. *City of Geary,* 59 Okla. 22, 157 Pac. 720.

has been destroyed, or for some other cause which renders the performance of the contract impossible. It is well settled that mere impossibility to perform a contract does not release the contracting parties from their contractual obligations. Certain classes of impossibility do, however, excuse performance. Impossibility to perform excuses performance in the following cases: where the impossibility is due to an act of God, or to an act of a public enemy, or to a change in the law which renders the performance of the contract illegal, or to the death of one of the contracting parties where the contract was for personal service, or to the destruction of the subject matter of the contract where the contract called for a specific subject matter as distinguished from a general subject matter.

Applying the rule as stated in the preceding paragraph, the courts uniformly hold that where the schools are closed by the school authorities because of an epidemic of some contagious disease, the teachers are entitled to their salaries for the time the schools are closed, unless it is specifically provided otherwise in the contract.[110] The courts reason in such cases that as one contracts, so is he bound. If the school authorities had desired to be relieved of the duty of paying teachers while the schools were closed, they could and should have so provided in the contract. Having failed to do so, they cannot plead impossibility of performance. In Michigan, for example, a school board closed the schools because of the prevalence of smallpox in the community. In holding that a teacher could recover his salary for the time the school was closed, the court said in part:

Admitting that the circumstances justify the officers, and yet there is no rule of justice which will entitle the district to visit its own misfortune upon the plaintiff. He was not at fault. He had no agency in bringing about the state of things which rendered it eminently prudent to dismiss the schools. It was the misfortune of the district, and the district and not the plaintiff ought to bear it.[111]

And in a similar case decided by the Supreme Court of Utah, it was said: "Where the contract is to do acts which can be performed, nothing but the act of God or of a public enemy, or the interdiction of

110. *Dewey* v. *Union School District*, 43 Mich. 480, 5 N.W. 646; *Libby* v. *Inhabitants of Douglas*, 175 Mass. 128, 55 N.E. 808; *McKay* v. *Barnett*, 21 Utah 239, 60 Pac. 1100, 50 L.R.A. 371; *Smith* v. *School District No. 64*, 89 Kan. 225, 131 Pac. 557, Ann. Cas. 1914D 139; *Crane* v. *School District No. 14*, 95 Ore. 644, 188 Pac. 712.

111. *Dewey* v. *Union School District*, 43 Mich. 480, 5 N.W. 646.

the law as a direct and sole cause of the failure, will excuse the performance."[112]

Where the schools are closed by order of a board of health acting under statutory authority, the courts are divided with respect to the right of a teacher to recover salary for the time the schools are closed. According to one line of decisions the teacher cannot recover, because, it is said, the school authorities are prevented from carrying out their part of the contract by operation of law.[113] The case of *School District No. 16* v. *Howard*[114] illustrates the reasoning of those courts which deny recovery. Mr. Justice Duffie, speaking for the Supreme Court of Nebraska, said in part:

> Plaintiff in error insists that full performance of the contract on the part of the district was rendered impossible by law, and asserts that under such circumstances it is not liable. It is clearly settled by innumerable authorities that whenever a contract which was possible and legal at the time it was made becomes impossible by act of God, or illegal by an ordinance of the state, the obligation to perform it is discharged. . . . No contract can be carried into effect which was originally made contrary to the provisions of law, or which, being made consistently with the rule of law at the time, has become illegal by virtue of some subsequent law. This is so well settled and so thoroughly understood by the profession that a citation of authorities is unnecessary. It is not claimed that the board of health did not have authority to close the school, or that the order was illegal in any respect. This being so, that order, so long as it remained in force, was a valid legal prohibition against the continuance of the school, and the district, by the force of law, was unable to complete its contract. . . . But the action of the district in closing the school was not voluntary. It was the act of the law, which the district and all others were compelled to obey.

According to another line of decisions, however, the teacher is entitled to recover for the time the school is closed, even though it may have been closed by order of a board of health in the exercise of police power.[115] In a leading case[116] the Supreme Court of Illinois has held that it makes no difference whether the school is closed by the school authorities or by a board of health, so far as the teacher's right

112. *McKay* v. *Barnett*, 21 Utah 239, 60 Pac. 1100, 50 L.R.A. 371.

113. *School District No. 16* v. *Howard*, 5 Neb. (Unof.) 340, 98 N.W. 666; *Gregg School Township* v. *Hinshaw*, 76 Ind. App. 503, 132 N.E. 586, 17 A.L.R. 1222.

114. *School District No. 16* v. *Howard*, 5 Neb. (Unof.) 340, 98 N.W. 666.

115. *Phelps* v. *School District No. 109*, 302 Ill. 193, 134 N.E. 312, 21 A.L.R. 737; *Montgomery* v. *Board of Education*, 102 Ohio St. 189, 131 N.E. 497, 15 A.L.R. 715; *Cashdollar* v. *Board of Education*, 12 Ohio App. 298.

116. *Phelps* v. *School District No. 109*, 302 Ill. 193, 134 N.E. 312, 21 A.L.R. 737.

to recover is concerned. The court reasoned that at the time of making the contract both parties knew that the board of health had statutory authority to close the schools if an epidemic of a contagious disease occurred. Knowing this, the board of education, if it desired to be relieved of liability in case the school was closed, should have inserted in the contract a provision to that effect. In the words of the court:

It was no fault of appellee that the school was closed a portion of the time she was employed to teach, neither was it the fault of appellant. Some one was required to suffer loss resulting from an unforeseen contingency which caused the school to be closed, and the rule is that the loss will rest on the party who has contracted to bear it, for if he did not intend to bear it he should have stipulated against it. If the performance of the contract had been legally impossible it would have been unenforceable, but its performance was not legally impossible. When made, the contract was lawful and valid. Its performance was rendered impossible by the subsequent happening of a contingency which could not be foreseen or known when the contract was made, and the rule is that if one of the parties desires not to be bound in the event of the happening of such a contingency he must so provide in the contract.

All the courts seem agreed that where a teacher is instructed by the school board to hold himself in readiness, the teacher is entitled to his salary for the period during which the school is not in session, even though the school is closed by a board of health in the exercise of its legal authority.[117]

The rule is well established that where a school building is destroyed by fire or storm, or in some other way rendered unfit for use, a teacher may recover for the time during which the school is closed unless the board of education has protected itself from liability by the terms of the contract.[118] In such cases it is held that the impossibility to perform the contract is not the result of an act of God. It is well established, too, that a teacher may recover compensation for the time school is not in session during holidays.[119]

117. *Board of Education* v. *Couch*, 63 Okla. 65, 162 Pac. 485, 6 A.L.R. 740; *Randolph* v. *Sanders*, 22 Tex. Civ. App. 331, 54 S.W. 621.

118. *Clune* v. *School District No. 3*, 166 Wis. 452, 166 N.W. 11, 76 A.L.R. 736; *Charlestown School Township* v. *Hay*, 74 Ind. 127; *School Directors* v. *Crews*, 23 Ill. App. 367; *Corn* v. *Board of Education*, 39 Ill. App. 446. Contra, *Hall* v. *School District No. 10*, 24 Mo. App. 213.

119. *School District No. 4* v. *Gage*, 39 Mich. 484, 33 Am. Rep. 421; *Board of Education* v. *State*, 7 Kan. App. 620, 52 Pac. 466.

CHAPTER XVII

Administration of the Teaching Personnel

TEACHER TENURE

MANY states now have legislation giving teachers permanent tenure. These statutes determine the conditions under which a teacher may require tenure, define the teacher's rights and obligations, state the causes for which a teacher may be dismissed, and prescribe the procedure by which a teacher's contract may be terminated. Subsequent legislatures may feel that public policy and the best interests of the public school system require a modification or even a repeal of the tenure statute. In a number of cases where the legislature has amended or modified a tenure statute, action has been brought to have the act declared void as being in violation of that provision of the federal constitution which makes it unlawful for a state to impair the obligation of a contract. The great weight of authority is that a tenure statute is not in the nature of a contract between the state and the teachers affected by it.[1] The presumption is that an act of a legislature is only an expression of current legislative policy; one legislature should not be regarded as having bound the hands of future legislatures unless the intent to do so is very clear indeed.

A case decided by the Supreme Court of Wisconsin will serve to illustrate the reasoning of the courts. The issue involved was the authority to amend a teacher-tenure statute. The court said:

> If a tenure statute grants gratuities, involves no agreement of the parties as to tenure, requires nothing of the teacher as requisite to acquiring the right of tenure, it creates no vested right to tenure and the right can be

1. *Phelps* v. *Prussia*, 60 Calif. App. (2d) 732, 141 Pac. (2d) 440; *Morrison* v. *Board of Education*, 237 Wis. 483, 297 N.W. 383; *Lapolla* v. *Board of Education*, 15 N.Y.S. (2d) 149; *Phelps* v. *State Board of Education*, 115 N.J. Law 310, 180 Atl. 220; *Taylor* v. *Board of Education*, 31 Calif. App. (2d) 734; *State* ex rel. *McKenna* v. *School District No. 8*, 243 Wis. 324, 10 N.W. (2d) 155, 147 A.L.R. 290; *Groves* v. *Board of Education*, 367 Ill. 91, 10 N.E. (2d) 403; *Morgan* v. *Potter*, 238 Wis. 246, 298 N.W. 763; *Malone* v. *Hayden*, 329 Pa. 213, 197 Atl. 344; *Crawford* v. *Sadler*, 34 So. (2d) (Fla.) 38; *Walsh* v. *School District of Philadelphia*, 343 Pa. 178, 22 Atl. (2d) 909.

taken away. . . . The state by enacting the tenure provision did not surrender its right to redetermine, in the future, the qualifications of its teachers, or its public policy in relation to tenure.[2]

It is possible, however, for a tenure statute to be so worded as to create a contract between the state and the teachers affected by the statute, and in that case a later legislature cannot repeal or amend the statute. The Supreme Court of the United States has clearly described the conditions under which a statute must be regarded as a contract.

In determining whether a law tenders a contract to a citizen it is of first importance to examine the language of the statute. If it provides for the execution of a written contract on behalf of the state the case for an obligation binding upon the state is clear. . . . On the other hand, an act merely fixing salaries of officers creates no contract in their favor and the compensation named may be altered at will by the legislature. This is true also of an act fixing the term or tenure of a public officer or an employee of a state agency. The presumption is that such a law is not intended to create private contractual or vested rights but merely declares a policy to be pursued until the legislature shall ordain otherwise. He who asserts the creation of a contract with the state in such a case has the burden of overcoming the presumption.[3]

In two states, Indiana and Alabama, it has been held that the tenure statutes were so worded as to create a contractual relation between teachers and the state.[4]

RIGHTS OF TEACHERS UNDER TENURE STATUTES

Right of continued employment.—In enacting teacher-tenure legislation it is not the intent, of course, to guarantee teachers employment regardless of changing conditions and changing educational policies. That is to say, it is not the intent of such legislation to limit in any way the right of the school authorities to determine what shall be taught or to determine the positions which efficient administration of the school system may demand. Statutes providing for permanent tenure are to be interpreted as "intending only a regulation of dismissal for causes personal to the employee."[5] Where, therefore, it becomes desirable to abolish positions in the interest of economy or for any other good reason, a school board may do so and discontinue the employ-

2. *Morgan* v. *Potter,* 238 Wis. 246, 298 N.W. 763.

3. *Dodge* v. *Board of Education,* 302 U.S. 74, 58 S. Ct. 98.

4. *State* ex rel. *Anderson* v. *Brand,* 303 U.S. 95, 113 A.L.R. 1482; *Faircloth* v. *Folmar,* 40 So. (2d) (Ala.) 697.

5. *Funston* v. *District School Board for District No. 1,* 130 Ore. 82, 278 Pac. 1075.

ment of teachers, even though they be on tenure.[6] The position commonly taken by the courts was well stated by the Supreme Court of Pennsylvania:

As we have stated before, the purpose of the Tenure Act was to maintain an adequate and competent teaching staff, free from political and personal arbitrary influence, whereby capable and competent teachers might feel secure and more efficiently perform their duty of instruction, but it was not the intention of the legislature to confer any special privileges or immunities upon professional employees to retain permanently their position and pay regardless of a place to work and pupils to be taught; nor was it the intention of the legislature to have the Tenure Act interfere with the control of school policy and the courses of study selected by the administrative bodies; nor was it the intention of the legislature to disrupt a school district's financial scheme. . . . If the teacher must be retained in the circumstances before us, the discretion of the board over its educational policies would be largely eliminated.[7]

School boards, in abolishing positions held by tenure teachers, must, of course, act in good faith. It seems to be the general rule, too, that where the number of teachers has to be reduced in the interest of economy, teachers having tenure have a preference in reappointment when vacancies occur.[8]

Reassignment of teachers.—Teacher-tenure statutes are not intended to guarantee teachers the right to hold any particular positions in any particular schools; they do not prevent a school board from assigning teachers to the various positions in the school system. That is to say, a board may make any reasonable reassignment, but the work assigned must be of the same grade and rank as that the teacher had when he acquired the tenure status.[9] That is to say, a board of edu-

---

6. *Ehret* v. *School District Borough of Kulpmont,* 333 Pa. 518, 5 Atl. (2d) 188; *Werlock* v. *Board of Education,* 5 N.J. Super. 140, 68 Atl. (2d) 547; *Funston* v. *School Board for District No. 1,* 130 Ore. 82, 278 Pac. 1075, 63 A.L.R. 1410; *Bates* v. *Board of Education,* 139 Calif. 145, 72 Pac. 907; *Fidler* v. *Board of Education,* 112 Calif. App. 296, 296 Pac. 912; *State* ex rel. *Ging* v. *Board of Education of Duluth,* 213 Minn. 550, 7 N.W. (2d) 544; *Weider* v. *Board of Education,* 112 N.J. Law 289, 170 Atl. 631; *State* ex rel. *Frank* v. *Meigs County Board of Education,* 140 Ohio St. 381, 44 N.E. (2d) 455; *Bragg* v. *School District of Swarthmore,* 337 Pa. 363, 11 Atl. (2d) 152.

7. *Ehret* v. *School District Borough of Kulpmont,* 333 Pa. 518, 5 Atl. (2d) 188.

8. *Downs* v. *Board of Education,* 13 N.J. Misc. 853, 118 Atl. 688.

9. *Kacsur* v. *Board of Trustees of South Whittier Elementary School District,* 18 Calif. (2d) 586, 116 Pac. (2d) 593; *Hodge* v. *Board of Education,* 22 Calif. App. 341, 70 Pac. (2d) 1009; *State* ex rel. *McNeal* v. *Avoyelles Parish School Board,* 199 La. 859, 7 So. (2d) 165; *Smith* v. *School District No. 18,* 115 Mont. 102, 139 Pac. (2d) 518; *State* ex rel. *Bass* v. *Vernon Parish School Board,* 194 So. (La.) 74.

cation may not exercise its authority to reassign to bring about what are, in fact, demotions.

In a Montana case a teacher was teaching the sixth, seventh, and eighth grades in a town school when he attained tenure. Later he was assigned to an ungraded rural school about ten miles from the town. Most of the pupils were in the lower grades. There was no place he could live in the rural community. The court ruled that he had in effect been dismissed and permitted him to recover damages.[10] Similarly, in West Virginia it was held that a county board of education could not transfer a teacher from a position as principal to a position as teacher in another school.[11] So, too, in Louisiana, a parish school board had no authority to transfer a high-school principal to a teaching position in an elementary school.[12] But in Minnesota the transfer of a member of the teaching corps of the department of education in St. Paul from a position of supervisor of special classes to the principalship of two schools in the system did not constitute a demotion in rank in violation of the tenure statute.[13] And in Indiana a local school authority was upheld in transferring a city school superintendent to a position as school principal. The court ruled that the Indiana statute did not specify that a teacher must hold the same position, but only that he be a permanent teacher in the school corporation.[14] Nor was the transfer of a teacher from a position in a high school to a position in a junior high with no reduction in salary violative of the tenure statute.[15]

Reduction in salary.—Tenure statutes do not prevent boards of education from making any reasonable changes in teachers' salaries. There must be no discrimination as between individual teachers, but a board can change its salary schedules as policy may from time to time dictate.[16] In the words of the Supreme Court of Indiana:

10. *Smith* v. *School District No. 18*, 115 Mont. 102, 139 Pac. (2d) 518.

11. *Pond* v. *Parsons*, 117 W. Va. 777, 188 S.E. 232.

12. *State* ex rel. *Bass* v. *Vernon Parish School Board*, 194 So. (La.) 74.

13. *Henderson* v. *City of St. Paul*, 53 N.W. (2d) (Minn.) 21.

14. *School City of Peru* v. *State*, 212 Ind. 255, 7 N.E. (2d) 176.

15. *Greenway* v. *Board of Education*, 129 N.J.L. 461, 29 Atl. (2d) 890, 145 A.L.R. 404.

16. *Greenway* v. *Board of Education*, 129 N.J.L. 46, 28 Atl. (2d) 99; *Abraham* v. *Sims*, 2 Calif. (2d) 698, 42 Pac. (2d) 1029; *Fidler* v. *Board of Trustees*, 112 Calif. App. 296, 296 Pac. 912; *Doyle* v. *City of St. Paul*, 206 Minn. 649, 289 N.W. 784; *Smith* v. *School District of Philadelphia*, 334 Pa. 197, 5 Atl. (2d) 535.

By the great weight of authority, the rule seems to be that a tenure act does not preclude the employing agency from reducing the teacher's compensation below what it was before the breach occurred, so long as the salary to be paid equals or exceeds the minimum fixed by law and the teacher's classification for that purpose is not arbitrary nor unreasonable. This is necessary in order that administrative officers may be free to exercise the sound discretion with which they are charged; so that the fiscal affairs of the school corporations may be adjusted in accordance with the ability of taxpayers to bear the burdens of the educational system; and to the end that the tenure law may not itself be ultilized to defeat the broad public policy of the commonwealth.[17]

A school board may not, however, single out an individual teacher and materially reduce his salary. In a Georgia case the statutes gave school boards "the right to assign principals and teachers to such positions as, in its judgment, are best for the school system." A school principal on tenure was transferred to a teaching position with a reduction in salary of eight hundred dollars. The court ruled that the board, under the statute, had the authority to transfer her from her position as principal to that of a teacher, provided that the board did not act arbitrarily. However, the court held that in this case the demotion, accompanied by such a substantial reduction in salary, was in effect "a removal from the original position." It ruled that, although she could not by mandamus be restored to her original position, she was entitled to have her original salary restored. Moreover, she was entitled to the salary she would have earned if she had not been demoted.[18]

Dismissal of teachers for marriage.—Tenure statutes commonly state the causes for which teachers may be dismissed, and they usually require the teacher be given notice of the charges against him and an opportunity to defend. Statutes of this kind must be strictly followed, or the dismissal of a teacher will be illegal.

During recent years the courts have frequently been called upon to decide whether the marriage of a woman teacher on tenure constitutes a valid cause for dismissal. It frequently happens that a statute will enumerate the causes for dismissal, such as incompetency, immorality, and insubordination, and then add "for any other good cause." In some instances boards have passed rules to the effect that married teachers will be dismissed, and it is claimed that the violation of this

17. *Haas* v. *Holder*, 218 Ind. 263, 32 N.E. (2d) 590.

18. *Board of Education of Richmond County* v. *Young*, 187 Ga. 644, 1 S.E. (2d) 739.

rule is insubordination. Or again, it may be contended that marriage comes under the statutory provision "other good cause."

Many courts have held that marriage of a woman teacher under tenure does not constitute a legal cause for her dismissal.[19] The courts which take this position reason that marriage does not bear any direct relation to a teacher's fitness or capacity to do her work capably. Therefore, a board rule to the effect that the marriage of a woman teacher will terminate her employment is an unreasonable rule and one beyond the authority of a board to make.

Other courts, however, take a contrary position, holding that a board has authority to enforce a rule providing for the dismissal of married woman teachers or that marriage constitutes "a good cause" for dismissal where such a provision is contained in a statute providing for dismissal.[20] Two excerpts from court decisions, one by the Supreme Judicial Court of Massachusetts and one by the Supreme Court of Ohio, will illustrate the reasoning of the courts that take this position. In the Massachusetts case, the board of education had adopted a rule that "there shall be inserted in the contract of every woman teacher elected a provision that the marriage of the teacher who signs the contract shall terminate the contract and that this provision of the contract shall be in force even after said teacher goes on tenure." The board also had a rule in force: "The marriage of a woman teacher . . . shall operate as an automatic resignation of said teacher, and this regulation shall apply to teachers on tenure." In sustaining the rule, the court said:

The primary question to be decided is whether if a school committee has adopted a policy forbidding the employment of married teachers, the marriage of a woman teacher can be found to be "good cause" for dismissal under [a statute which] provides that a teacher employed at discretion "shall not be dismissed except for inefficiency, incapacity, conduct unbecoming a teacher . . . insubordination or other good cause." . . .

19. *Kostanzer* v. *State*, 205 Ind. 536, 187 N.E. 337; *School District of Wildwood* v. *State Board of Education*, 116 N.J.L. 572, 185 Atl. 664; *Goff* v. *School District of Borough of Shenandoah*, 154 Pa. Super. 239, 35 Atl. (2d) 900; *State ex rel. Schmidtkunz* v. *Webb*, 230 Wis. 390, 284 N.W. 6; *Cardinal* v. *Dimit*, 69 N.E. (2d) (Ohio) 65; *Knox County* v. *State* ex rel. *Nighbert*, 177 Tenn. 171, 147 S.W. (2d) 100; *McKay* v. *State* ex rel. *Young*, 212 Ind. 338, 7 N.E. (2d) 954; *State* ex rel. *Kundert* v. *Jefferson Parish School Board*, 191 La. 102, 184 So. 555.

20. *Greco* v. *Roper*, 145 Ohio St. 243, 61 N.E. (2d) 307; *McQuaid* v. *State*, 211 Ind. 595, 6 N.E. (2d) 547, 118 A.L.R. 1079; *Houghton* v. *School Committee of Somerville*, 306 Mass. 542, 28 N.E. (2d) 1001; *Rinaldo* v. *Dreyer*, 294 Mass. 167, 1 N.E. (2d) 37; *People* ex rel. *Templeton* v. *Board of Education*, 345 Ill. App. 295, 102 N.E. (2d) 751.

"Good cause" for dismissal in a statute of this kind is by no means limited to some form of inefficiency or of misconduct on the part of the person dismissed. Such matters are amply covered by the words which precede "good cause." Good cause includes any ground which is put forward by the committee in good faith and which is not arbitrary, irrational, unreasonable, or irrelevant to the committee's task of building and maintaining an efficient school system.[21]

In the Ohio case the statutes provided that a teacher on tenure might have her contract terminated "for gross inefficiency or immorality; for willful and persistent violations of reasonable regulations of the board of education; or for other good and just cause." The court held that where a contract was entered into with reference to and knowledge of a rule that marriage would terminate a woman's contract, the rule was valid and could be enforced. Said the court:

Under our statutes, a board of education is elected by vote of the people. As already indicated, it is charged with the management and control of the public schools and is authorized to employ and fix the salaries of those operating the schools. Moreover, it may "make such reasonable rules and regulations as it deems necessary for its government and the government of its employees."

It will thus be seen that the General Assembly has granted boards of education wide latitude and discretion in the particulars mentioned and if, as a matter of policy, a board adopts a rule that upon the marriage of a woman teacher her contract will terminate, can it properly be said that the deliberate violation of such a rule does not constitute "good and just cause" for the cancellation of the contract?

A rule of the kind described may have a sound basis in the particular school district and may bear a reasonable relationship to the responsibility of a board of education to build up and maintain an efficient and harmonious school system. Within the discretion conferred, a board may act on the theory that married women as a class will be absorbed with home duties and cares to the detriment of their school work, or on the theory that married women generally have husbands who can support them and that such women should give way to unmarried women qualified to teach and who must support themselves.[22]

AUTHORITY OF TEACHERS TO STRIKE AND OF BOARDS OF EDUCATION TO ENGAGE IN COLLECTIVE BARGAINING WITH TEACHERS

The law governing the right of teachers to strike or the authority of school boards to negotiate with teachers' unions is still in the process of development. In 1951 a significant case dealing with these issues came before the Supreme Court of Errors of Connecticut. In an action

21. *Rinaldo v. Dreyer,* 294 Mass. 167, 1 N.E. (2d) 37.
22. *Greco v. Roper,* 145 Ohio St. 243, 61 N.E. (2d) 307.

for a declaratory judgment, certain questions were addressed to the court. One of these was: "May the plaintiff [the Norwalk Teachers' Association] engage in concerted action such as a strike, work stoppage, or collective refusal to enter upon duties?" The court answered this question in the negative, saying in part:

Under our system, the government is established by and run for all of the people, not for the benefit of any person or group. The profit motive inherent in the principle of free enterprise, is absent. It should be the aim of every employee of the government to do his or her part to make it function as efficiently and economically as possible. The drastic remedy of the organized strike to enfore the demands of unions of government employees is in direct contravention of this principle. It has been so regarded by the heads of the executive departments of the states and the nation. . . .

Few cases involving the right of unions of government employees to strike to enforce their demands have reached the courts of last resort. That right has usually been tested by an application for an injunction forbidding the strike. The right of the governmental body to this relief has been uniformly upheld. . . . The following cases do not necessarily turn on the specific right to strike, but the reasoning indicates that, if faced with that question, the court would be compelled to deny the right to public employees. Seattle High School Chapter No. 200 v. Sharples, 159 Wash. 424, 293 Pac. 994, 72 A.L.R. 1215. . . .

The court was also asked to give an opinion on this question: "Is it permitted to the plaintiff under our laws to organize itself as a labor union for the purpose of demanding and receiving recognition and collective bargaining?" Its answer was a qualified "Yes":

The statutes and private acts give broad powers to the defendent with reference to educational matters and school management in Norwalk. If it chooses to negotiate with the plaintiff with regard to the employment, salaries, grievance procedure and working conditions of its members, there is no statute, public or private, which forbids such negotiations. . . . If the strike threat is absent and the defendant prefers to handle the matter through negotiations with the plaintiff, no reason exists why it should not do so.[23]

LIABILITY OF TEACHERS FOR INJURIES TO PUPILS

According to the great weight of authority, a teacher is not a public officer, is not immune from liability because employed by a governmental agency, and is personally liable for acts of negligence while performing his duties as a teacher.[24] A teacher stands in the relationship of *in loco parentis* to his pupils and must so act as not negligent-

23. *Norwalk Teachers' Association* v. *Board of Education of City of Norwalk,* 138 Conn. 269, 83 Atl. (2d) 482.

24. See, however, *Gray* v. *Hanley,* 64 Atl. (2d) (R.I.) 191; *Fulgoni* v. *Johnston,* 302 Mass. 421, 19 N.E. (2d) 542.

ly to injure them, whether the act is one of misfeasance or nonfeasance. And the teacher is also governed by the common-law obligation that every person must so act or use that which he controls as not to injure another.[25] What the law requires of the teacher is that, in any particular relation to a pupil, he exercise the care and prudence any reasonably prudent person would have exercised in that situation.[26] The courts place emphasis upon the principle of foreseeability; that is, a teacher will be held guilty of negligence if he pursues a course of action which any reasonably prudent person would have regarded as dangerous to the pupil's safety. And it is not necessary that a teacher be able to foresee the exact nature of the injury; it is enough if any reasonably prudent person would have foreseen that some kind of injury might well result from the action being taken. In short, the standard of care of a public school teacher is that which a person of ordinary prudence would exercise under the same circumstances.

COMMON-LAW RIGHT TO DISMISS TEACHERS

It is well settled that school teachers are not public officers; they are employees.[27] Such rights as they have to compensation grow out of the contractual relationship. If, therefore, the statutes make no provision for the dismissal of teachers, there exists in the employing agency an implied power to dismiss a teacher for good and sufficient cause.[28] Thus it was said by the Supreme Court of Indiana: "It does

25. *Brooks* v. *Jacobs*, 139 Me. 371, 31 Atl. (2d) 414.

26. *Brooks* v. *Jacobs*, 139 Me. 371, 31 Atl. (2d) 414; *Woodman* v. *Hemet Union High School District*, 136 Calif. App. 544, 29 Pac. (2d) 257; *Kerby* v. *Elk Grove Union High School District*, 1 Calif. App. 246, 36 Pac. (2d) 431; *Hale* v. *Davies*, 86 Ga. App. 126, 70 S.E. (2d) 923; *Sayers* v. *Ranger*, 16 N.J. Super. 22, 83 Atl. (2d) 775; *Perumean* v. *Wills*, 57 Pac. (2d) (Calif.) 554; *Duda* v. *Gaines*, 12 N.J. Super. 326, 79 Atl. (2d) 695; *Taylor* v. *Kelvin*, 121 N.J.L. 142, 1 Atl. (2d) 433; *Thompson* v. *Board of Education*, 280 N.Y. 92, 19 N.E. (2d) 796; *Gaincott* v. *Davis*, 281 Mich. 515, 275 N.W. 229; *DeGooyer* v. *Harkness*, 70 S.D. 26, 13 N.W. (2d) 815; *Guerrieri* v. *Tyson*, 147 Pa. Super. 239, 24 Atl. (2d) 468.

27. *Board of Education* v. *Bacon*, 22 Ga. App. 72, 95 S.E. 753; *People* v. *Board of Education*, 3 Hun. (N.Y.) 177; *Swartwood* v. *Walbridge*, 10 N.Y.S. 862, 31 N.Y. St. Rep. 757; *School District No. 23* v. *McCoy*, 30 Kan. 268, 1 Pac. 97, 46 Am. St. Rep. 92; *State* v. *Blied*, 188 Wis. 442, 206 N.W. 213; *State* v. *Smith*, 49 Neb. 755, 69 N.W. 114. Contra, *Morley* v. *Power*, 5 Lea (73 Tenn.) 691.

28. *Tadlock* v. *School District No. 29*, 27 N.M. 250, 199 Pac. 1007; *Freeman* v. *Town of Bourne*, 170 Mass. 289, 49 N.E. 435, 39 L.R.A. 510; *Crawfordsville* v. *Hays*, 42 Ind. 200; *Wallace* v. *School District No. 27*, 50 Neb. 171, 69 N.W. 772; *Bays* v. *State*, 6 Neb. 167; *Curkett* v. *Joint School District No. 2*, 159 Wis. 149, 149 N.W. 708; *Foreman* v. *School District No. 25*, 81 Ore. 587, 159 Pac. 1155; *School District of Fort Smith* v. *Maury*, 53 Ark. 471, 14 S.W. 669.

not follow that, because the school trustees in incorporated towns and cities are not authorized by statute to dismiss teachers, they have no power or authority to do so, when there is a valid reason for such dismissal."[29]

STATUTORY RIGHT OF DISMISSAL AT DISCRETION
OF THE SCHOOL BOARD

School authorities may, of course, dismiss teachers for such causes and in such manner as prescribed by statute. It is a well-established rule, of which teachers should be cognizant, that all pertinent provisions of the statutes are, by implication, read into contracts of employment.[30] Thus, it was said by Mr. Justice Harris, speaking for the Supreme Court of Oregon:

> The contract of teaching is made with reference to the provisions of the statute, so that the contractual obligations of the teacher are not necessarily limited to the words found in the written contract, and therefore the contract of teaching includes not only the duties enumerated by the written paper, which for convenience is called the contract, but it also embraces those duties which are imposed under a then-existing statute; and if the teacher breaches this contract of teaching, one of the ordinary legal remedies available to the school board, unless some statute declares to the contrary, would be found in the right summarily to discharge the teacher.[31]

Where, therefore, the employing agency is authorized by statute to dismiss a teacher at pleasure, a teacher may be dismissed without cause and without an opportunity to be heard in his defense.[32] Not only that, the employing agency cannot by contract divest itself of the statutory right to dismiss a teacher at pleasure.[33]

29. *Crawfordsville* v. *Hays*, 42 Ind. 200.

30. *Gillan* v. *Board of Regents*, 88 Wis. 7, 58 N.W. 1042, 24 L.R.A. 336; *Jones* v. *Nebraska City*, 1 Neb. 176, *Maxey* v. *Board of Trustees*, 187 Ky. 729, 220 S.W. 732; *Weidman* v. *Board of Education*, 7 N.Y.S. 309, 54 Hun. 634; *Everett* v. *Fractional School District No. 2*, 30 Mich. 249.

31. *Foreman* v. *School District No. 25*, 81 Ore. 587, 159 Pac. 1155.

32. *Gillan* v. *Board of Regents*, 88 Wis. 7, 58 N.W. 1042, 24 L.R.A. 336; *The Queen* v. *Governors of Darlington School*, 6 Q.B. (Adolphus and Ellis, N.S.) 682; *Jensen* v. *Independent Consolidated District No. 85*, 160 Minn. 233, 199 N.W. 911; *Jones* v. *Nebraska City*, 1 Neb. 176; *Weidman* v. *Board of Education*, 7 N.Y.S. 309, 54 Hun. 634; *Dunavon* v. *Board of Education*, 47 Hun. (N.Y.) 13; *People* v. *Board of Education*, 142 N.Y. 627, 37 N.E. 565.

33. *Gillan* v. *Board of Regents*, 88 Wis. 7, 58 N.W. 1042, 24 L.R.A. 336; *The Queen* v. *Governors of Darlington School*, 6 Q.B. (Adolphus and Ellis, N.S.) 682; *Jensen* v. *Independent Consolidated School District No. 85*, 160 Minn. 233, 199 N.W. 911; *Weidman* v. *Board of Education*, 7 N.Y.S. 309, 54 Hun. 634; *Collins* v. *City of Lewiston*, 107 Me. 220.

AUTHORITY OF SCHOOL BOARDS TO RESERVE IN CONTRACTS
THE RIGHT TO DISMISS TEACHERS AT PLEASURE

In a number of jurisdictions courts have been called on to determine whether a school board, in the absence of statutory authority, may reserve in a contract with a teacher the right to dismiss the teacher at pleasure or upon specified notice. A board may attempt to reserve this right either in the express contract or in the rules and regulations of the board, for it is well settled that all reasonable rules and regulations of a school board defining the relation of the board to its teachers become by implication a part of a teacher's contract.[34]

Some courts hold that school authorities may reserve by contract the right to dismiss teachers at pleasure or upon such notice as the parties may stipulate in the agreement.[35] In a Missouri case,[36] for example, the Board of Education of St. Louis dismissed a teacher because his wife, against whom he had brought action for divorce, accused him of adultery. A by-law of the school board provided that teachers should hold their positions for a year "unless sooner removed by a vote of the majority of the board." The by-law, the court reasoned, became a part of the teacher's contract. Therefore, the board could dismiss the teacher whenever in their opinion the best interests of the schools demanded that he be dismissed. Similarly, in a Tennessee case[37] the Board of Education of Chattanooga adopted a rule that teachers should hold their positions "during the pleasure of the board." A teacher was discharged because the board lacked funds to carry on the work for which he was engaged. When he sued for his salary, the board relied in its defense upon the rule authorizing it to dismiss teachers at pleasure. The court held that the rule of the board became incorporated into the contract. Consequently, the teacher was

---

34. *McLellan v. Board, etc., of St. Louis Public Schools*, 15 Mo. App. 362; *Weatherly v. Chattanooga*, 48 S.W. (Tenn.) 136; *Board of Education v. Cook*, 3 Kan. App. 269, 45 Pac. 119.

35. *Dees v. Board of Education*, 146 Mich. 64, 109 N.W. 39; *Derry v. Board of Education*, 102 Mich. 631, 61 N.W. 61; *Richardson v. School District No. 10*, 38 Vt. 602; *McLellan v. Board, etc., of St. Louis Public Schools*, 15 Mo. App. 362; *Weatherly v. Chattanooga*, 48 S.W. (Tenn.) 136; *Armstrong v. Union School District No. 1*, 28 Kan. 345; *Brown v. School District No. 41*, 1 Kan App. 530, 40 Pac. 826; *School District No. 5 v. Colvin*, 10 Kan. 283; *School District No. 94 v. Gautier*, 13 Okla. 194, 73 Pac. 954; *Argenta Special School District v. Strickland*, 152 Ark. 215, 238 S.W. 9; *Olney School District v. Christy*, 81 Ill. App. 304; *Miner v. Lovilia Independent School District*, 234 N.W. (Iowa) 817.

36. *McLellan v. Board, etc., of St. Louis Public Schools*, 15 Mo. App. 362.

37. *Weatherly v. Chattanooga*, 48 S.W. (Tenn.) 136.

"subject to be discharged at the discretion of the board whenever in the exercise of its judgment, public necessity or convenience required it."

It seems clear, however, that a board of education cannot act arbitrarily even though the right to dismiss a teacher at will is reserved in the contract. Under all circumstances a board, in dismissing a teacher, must act in good faith and not from mere passion, prejudice, or caprice.[38] In fact, some authority exists for the statement that a board of education cannot dismiss a teacher except for cause even though the right to dismiss at will is reserved in the contract. In the case of *Board of Education* v. *Cook*,[39] for example, a teacher's contract provided that she should hold her position for one year "unless sooner removed by vote of the board." The court said, in interpreting the contract:

What, then, is the construction to be given to the words, "unless sooner removed by vote of the board"? Do they mean that the board may arbitrarily remove the teacher by vote, without any fault upon her part, and for no other reason than because it is the pleasure of the members of the board to do so? Or, do they mean that it may remove her for good cause? There is no statute which prescribes the causes for which the board of education of a city of the second class may remove a teacher; neither is there any rule or regulation prescribed by this board in which such causes are enumerated. The contract was for the ensuing school year, "unless sooner removed by vote of the board." This does not specify the causes for which she may be removed. The board could not, therefore, legally remove Miss Cook, by a vote, except for sufficient cause; and the question was properly submitted to the jury as to whether there was sufficient cause for removal.

While some courts hold that a school board may reserve in a contract with a teacher the right to dismiss the teacher at pleasure or in case the teacher fails to give satisfaction, there are other decisions to the effect that school authorities cannot legally write into a teacher's contract a provision reserving the right to dismiss the teacher at pleasure.[40] These latter decisions, in the opinion of the writer, express the correct rule of law. A school district, it should be remembered, is a corporation of very limited powers. Such powers as it possesses are derived from the statutes. If the statutes do not confer the right to

38. *School Directors* v. *Ewington*, 26 Ill. App. 379.

39. *Board of Education* v. *Cook*, 3 Kan. App. 269, 45 Pac. 119; Accord, *Hartmann* v. *Board of Education*, 356 Ill. 577, 191 N.E. 279.

40. *Tripp* v. *School District No. 3*, 50 Wis. 651, 7 N.W. 840; *Henry School Township* v. *Meredith*, 32 Ind. App. 607, 70 N.E. 393; *Sarle* v. *School District No. 27*, 255 Pac. (Ariz.) 994; *Public School District No. 11* v. *Holson*, 31 Ariz. 291, 252 Pac. 509.

make contracts with teachers which are terminable at the pleasure of the board, no such right should be inferred. The interests of the district are adequately protected by the common-law right to dismiss a teacher for sufficient cause. Moreover, teacher tenure is an important matter of public policy. That the best interests of the schools will not be served by permitting local school authorities to employ teachers subject to dismissal at pleasure seems perfectly clear.

The case of *Tripp v. School District No. 3*[41] illustrates the reasoning of those courts which hold that local school authorities cannot by contract reserve the right to dismiss teachers arbitrarily. In that case the school-district board had written into a teacher's contract the following words: "We reserve the right to close the school at any time if not satisfactory to us." The board became dissatisfied with the school, closed it, and dismissed the teacher. The court, however, permitted the teacher to recover her salary for the whole term of the contract. It said:

> The judgment [of the lower court] clearly proceeds upon the ground that under the contract the board could close the school and lawfully discharge the teacher before her term of hiring expired, if they were dissatisfied with her management of the school. . . . Certainly no such power is expressly conferred upon district school boards by the statutes, and we do not think that the good order, efficiency, or usefulness of the common schools of the state would be promoted by holding that such power was conferred upon them by implication or by a liberal construction of the statutes in their favor.

Where the statutes prohibit the dismissal of teachers except for cause, a school board cannot, of course, reserve in a contract for a definite term the right to dismiss at pleasure.[42] Where the statutes provide that teachers may be dismissed for certain specified causes, some courts hold that the school authorities cannot reserve in a teacher's contract the right to dismiss the teacher at will or the right to dismiss him if his services are unsatisfactory.[43] The case of *Thompson v. Gibbs*[44] illustrates the reasoning of these courts. In that case a contract containing the usual stipulations had stamped across its face the following words: "The directors reserve the right to annul all

41. *Tripp v. School District No. 3,* 50 Wis. 651, 7 N.W. 840.

42. *School District No. 3 v. Hale,* 15 Colo. 367, 25 Pac. 308; *Kennedy v. Board of Education,* 82 Calif. 483, 22 Pac. 1042.

43. *Thompson v. Gibbs,* 97 Tenn. 489, 37 S.W. 277, 34 L.R.A. 548; *Frazier v. School District No. 1,* 24 Mo. App. 250; *Sarle v. School District No. 27,* 255 Pac. (Ariz.) 994; *Public School District No. 11 v. Holson,* 31 Ariz. 291, 252 Pac. 509.

44. *Thompson v. Gibbs,* 97 Tenn. 489, 37 S.W. 277, 34 L.R.A. 548.

contracts every fourth month." At the end of four months, without giving any excuse for their action, the directors notified the teacher that his services were no longer required. The statute governing the case provided that teachers might be dismissed for incompetency, improper conduct, or inattention to duty. The court held that the right of dismissal was limited to the causes specified in the statutes and said in part:

If public directors can legally import into their contracts of employment of public teachers a clause such as the one in question, this case illustrates the wrong and injustice which may be done under cover of law. . . . But, independently of the injury that may be done to the individual, public policy would forbid the recognition of such a power unless it is distinctly conferred by the statutes. As has been well urged, if school directors can provide, as in this case, for annulling contracts at the end of four months, they can also reserve the right to terminate them at the end of one month, or at their own pleasure. . . . A system which gave such arbitrary authority to school directors could not result otherwise than in lowering the character of teachers and in demoralizing the public schools. . . . To permit school directors, under the cover of a reservation, such as the one in question, to dismiss a teacher without charges or notice or testimony, would be to approve an evasion of this statute . . . and to tolerate a practice that would be, in the end, extremely hurtful to our common-school system.

In some jurisdictions, on the other hand, it has been held that school authorities may by contract reserve the right to dismiss teachers for other causes than those stipulated in the statutes.[45] In the case of *School District No. 5 v. Colvin*[46] a contract with a teacher provided that he might be dismissed at any time if he failed to give satisfaction to the board. The statute governing the case provided that teachers might be dismissed for "incompetency, cruelty, negligence, or immorality." The teacher failed to give satisfaction and was discharged. The court sustained the action of the school board, saying in part:

The law was made for the benefit of the district. It does not prevent the board from making any other contract with the teacher. In this case they have made one which is not prohibited either by law or public policy. No one doubts that a contract hiring a teacher might be abrogated by mutual consent. So they may stipulate in advance, as in this case, what shall put an end to the contract. That contingency arose, and the board, with the previous consent of the teacher, put an end to the contract. There seems to be no doubt but what that part of the contract was valid.

45. *School Directors* v. *Ewington*, 26 Ill. App. 379; *Armstrong* v. *Union School District No. 1*, 28 Kan. 345; *School District No. 5* v. *Colvin*, 10 Kan. 283; *School District No. 94* v. *Gautier*, 13 Okla. 194, 73 Pac. 954.

46. *School District No. 5* v. *Colvin*, 10 Kan. 283.

LEGAL CAUSE FOR DISMISSAL OF TEACHERS

Under the common law and under statutes generally, teachers can be dismissed only for cause. Where the statutes expressly state the causes for which teachers may be dismissed, a teacher, as a rule, can be dismissed for no other cause.[47] The assumption is that the enumeration of causes in the statutes was intended to be exhaustive. If the legislature had intended that teachers might be dismissed for causes other than those specified, it would have expressed its intent in the statutes. Thus in a New York case[48] the charter of New York City provided for the dismissal of teachers for certain enumerated causes. In holding that the board of education could not, by adopting a rule, establish any other causes of dismissal, the court said:

We think that these statutory provisions are also necessarily exclusive. It is unreasonable to believe that the draftsmen of the Greater New York charter or the legislators who enacted it . . . having . . . provided in the charter for dismissal for specified causes, should have intended by the grant of any general power to the board of education to authorize the removal of teachers from their employment on any other grounds or in any other manner than those stated in the statute.

Some courts hold, however, that a school board may by contract reserve the right to dismiss a teacher for other than statutory causes,[49] while other courts hold to the contrary.[50]

DISMISSAL FOR FAILURE TO OBSERVE SCHOOL-BOARD REGULATIONS

A public school teacher is bound to obey all reasonable rules and regulations of the board which employs him,[51] and it makes no dif-

47. *People* v. *Maxwell*, 177 N.Y. 494, 69 N.E. 1092; *Jameson* v. *Board of Education*, 74 W. Va. 389, 81 S.E. 1126; *Thompson* v. *Gibbs*, 97 Tenn. 489, 37 S.W. 277, 34 L.R.A. 548; *City of Knoxville* v. *State* ex rel. *Hayward*, 175 Tenn. 159, 133 S.W. (2d) 465; *School City of Elwood* v. *State* ex rel. *Griffin*, 203 Ind. 626, 180 N.E. 471, 81 A.L.R. 1027.

48. *People* v. *Maxwell*, 177 N.Y. 494, 69 N.E. 1092.

49. *School Directors* v. *Ewington*, 26 Ill. App. 379; *Armstrong* v. *Union School District No. 1*, 28 Kan. 345; *School District No. 5* v. *Colvin*, 10 Kan. 283; *School District No. 94* v. *Gautier*, 13 Okla. 194, 73 Pac. 954; *Consolidated School District No. 4* v. *Millis*, 192 Okla. 687, 139 Pac. (2d) 183.

50. *Thompson* v. *Gibbs*, 97 Tenn. 489, 37 S.W. 277, 34 L.R.A. 548; *Frazier* v. *School District No. 1*, 24 Mo. App. 250.

51. *Parker* v. *School District No. 38*, 5 Lea (Tenn.) 525; *Farrell* v. *Board of Education*, 122 N.Y.S. 289; *Stuart* v. *Board of Education*, 161 Calif. 210, 118 Pac. 712; *Leddy* v. *Board of Education*, 160 Ill. App. 187; *Board of Education* v. *Swan*, 250 Pac. (2d) (Calif.) 306; *Reed* v. *Orleans Parish School Board*, 21 So. (2d) (La.) 895.

ference whether the rules were in force at the date of his employment or were promulgated at a later date.[52] Rules governing the relations of a board with its teachers in force at the time of employment are, by implication, read into the contract.[53] Moreover, a teacher impliedly consents to obey all reasonable rules and regulations which a board may find it necessary to adopt from time to time in the administration of the school system.[54] All contracts are made in contemplation of the law, and a teacher impliedly consents to obey all rules which a board may legally make.

An illustration of the authority of school boards to enforce reasonable rules and regulations is found in a California case.[55] The Board of Education of San Francisco adopted a resolution requiring teachers to reside within the city and county during the term of their employment. A teacher who resided across the bay in Berkeley brought action to enjoin the enforcement of the rule. The injunction was denied, the court saying in part:

> In contemplation of the fact that the teacher stands *in loco parentis*, that it may become her duty to devote her time to the welfare of individual pupils even outside of school hours, that the hurrying for boats or trains cannot be regarded as conducive to the highest efficiency on the part of the teacher, that tardiness may result from delays or obstructions in the transportation which a non-resident teacher must use, and finally, as has been said, that the "benefit of pupils and resulting benefits to their parents and to the community at large, and not the benefit of teachers, is the reason for the creation and support of the public schools" (*Bates* v. *Board of Education,* 139 Cal. 145, 72 Pac. 907), all these, and many more considerations not necessary to detail, certainly make the resolution in question a reasonable exercise of the power of the board of education. . . .
>
> Nor can we agree with respondent that the resolution in question is the imposition of an additional "qualification" which a teacher must possess, which qualification is not within the power of the board of education to exact. True, section 1793 of the Political Code, in conjunction with 1791 thereof, does prescribe certain qualifications and give a list of causes and reasons for which teachers may be dismissed or removed, but a regulation concerning residence is not an added "qualification," within the contemplation of this law, any more than would be a resolution that a teacher should

52. *Farrell* v. *Board of Education,* 122 N.Y.S. 289.

53. *McLellan* v. *Board, etc., of St. Louis Public Schools,* 15 Mo. App. 362; *Weatherly* v. *Chattanooga,* 48 S.W. (Tenn.) 136; *Board of Education* v. *Cook,* 3 Kan. App. 269, 45 Pac. 119; *Underwood* v. *Board of Public Education,* 25 Ga. App. 634, 104 S.E. 90.

54. *Farrell* v. *Board of Education,* 122 N.Y.S. 289; *Whitehead* v. *School District of North Huntingdon Township,* 145 Pa. St. 418, 22 Atl. 991; *School District of Dennison Township* v. *Padden,* 89 Pa. St. 395.

55. *Stuart* v. *Board of Education,* 161 Calif. 210, 118 Pac. 712.

be free from contagious disease; and it would scarcely be said that, if the board of education passed a resolution to that effect, it would add another and an unlawful "qualification" to those prescribed by the Political Code. Nor does it matter in this case, as respondent argues, that the board of education has no power to dismiss a teacher except for the reasons prescribed by section 1793 of the Political Code. That section itself contemplates dismissal for insubordination and clearly a refusal of a teacher to comply with a reasonable regulation of the board would be such insubordination.

It has been held, too, that a teacher may be dismissed for refusal to comply with a regulation that teachers be vaccinated,[56] for refusal to obey a rule prohibiting the reading of the Bible in the schools,[57] and for refusal to readmit to the school a pupil whom he had expelled against the wishes of the board.[58]

On the other hand, if a board makes an unreasonable rule or a rule in excess of its authority, the teacher is not bound thereby. In the case of *Horne* v. *School District of Chester*[59] the school board made it a condition of employment that a teacher board at a designated place. The teacher boarded at the place designated for five weeks and then informed the board that circumstances had arisen which made her unwilling to board there any longer. She asked to be permitted to board elsewhere but was told that she must board at the home selected if she was to remain in charge of the school. She refused to carry out the board's wishes in the matter and was discharged. In permitting the teacher to recover for breach of contract, the court said: "The rule of the board as to the teacher's boarding-place related to a matter as to which they were given no authority by existing law. . . . Their refusal, therefore, to permit the plaintiff to continue the school with a different boarding-place was unwarranted, and the plaintiff's determination to change her boarding-place did not authorize them to terminate her employment as teacher."

DISMISSAL FOR INCOMPETENCY

Under the common law and under the statutes generally, incompetency constitutes a valid cause for dismissal of a teacher. The rule governing the dismissal of teachers for incompetency has been clearly expressed by the Supreme Court of Indiana:

56. *Lyndall* v. *High School Committee*, 19 Pa. Super. Ct. 232.

57. *New Antioch Board of Education* v. *Pulse*, 7 Ohio N.P. 58.

58. *Parker* v. *School District No. 38*, 5 Lea (Tenn.) 525; *Leddy* v. *Board of Education*, 160 Ill. App. 187.

59. *Horne* v. *School District of Chester*, 75 N.H. 411, 75 Atl. 431.

A teacher, doubtless, like a lawyer, surgeon, or physician, when he undertakes an employment, impliedly agrees that he will bestow upon that service a reasonable degree of learning, skill, and care. When he accepts an employment as teacher in any given school, he agrees, by implication, that he has the learning necessary to enable him to teach the branches that are to be taught therein, as well as that he has the capacity, in a reasonable degree, of imparting that learning to others. He agrees, also, that he will exercise a reasonable degree of care and diligence in the advancement of his pupils in their studies, in preserving harmony, order, and discipline in the school; and that he will himself conform, as near as may be, to such reasonable rules and regulations as may be established by competent authority for the government of the school. . . .

Now, if a teacher, although he has been employed for a definite length of time, proves to be incompetent, and unable to teach the branches of instruction he has been employed to teach, either from a lack of learning, or from an utter want of capacity to impart his learning to others; or if, in any other respect, he fails to perform the obligations resting upon him as such teacher, whether arising from the express terms of his contract or by necessary implication, he has broken the agreement on his part, and the trustees are clearly authorized to dismiss him from such employment.[60]

By the application of the principle stated in the foregoing opinion, it has been held that a teacher may be dismissed because he does not possess the requisite qualities of temper and discretion[61] or because he is unable to maintain proper order and discipline.[62] A teacher, it has been held, is guilty of incompetency when she so conducts herself as to forfeit the good will and respect of the community. In a Pennsylvania case a teacher acted as waitress, and on occasion as bartender, in her husband's beer garden after school hours and during the summer. In the presence of pupils she took a drink of beer, shook dice with customers for drinks, and played and showed customers how to play a pinball machine. The court sustained her dismissal for incompetency.[63] A teacher cannot, however, be dismissed because of general dissatisfaction on the part of parents and pupils. Such evidence is not conclusive of incompetency.[64]

When a teacher is dismissed for incompetency, the burden of proof is upon the board of education. The teacher's certificate is prima facie evidence of qualification and must be overcome by positive evidence

60. *Crawfordsville* v. *Hays,* 42 Ind. 200.

61. *Robinson* v. *School Directors,* 96 Ill. App. 604.

62. *Eastman* v. *District Township of Rapids,* 21 Iowa 590; *Biggs* v. *School of Mt. Vernon,* 45 Ind. App. 572, 90 N.E. 105.

63. *Horosko* v. *School District of Mt. Pleasant,* 335 Pa. 369, 6 Atl. (2d) 866.

64. *Paul* v. *School District No. 2,* 28 Vt. 575.

to the contrary.[65] It has even been held that, where the statutes authorize the board of examiners to revoke certificates for incompetency, district trustees have no right to discharge a teacher for that cause.[66] Moreover, a teacher cannot be dismissed for incompetency before rendering any service under the contract. He has a right to enter the service and have his competency determined by the service rendered.[67] As was said by the Supreme Court of Arkansas: "Matters which occurred under a previous contract would not be ground for the avoidance of a subsequent contract."[68] When a decision as to the competency of a teacher is to be made, the whole course of his conduct must be taken into consideration. Occasional mistakes are not conclusive.[69] It should be kept in mind, too, that the highest qualifications are not demanded of a teacher.[70] In this connection it was said by the Supreme Court of Illinois: "It may be that the evidence fails to show the highest possible qualifications, or a talent for his profession equal to the most eminent and successful teachers. But the law requires no such qualifications; it only requires average qualification and ability, and the usual application to the discharge of the duties of a teacher to fulfil his contract."[71]

DISMISSAL FOR NEGLECT OF DUTY

Under the common law and under statutes providing for the dismissal of teachers for neglect of duty, the courts have been called upon in a number of cases to determine what constitutes neglect within the contemplation of the law. Frequent tardiness has been held a justifiable ground for dismissal.[72] Temporary absence from school without sufficient cause likewise constitutes that degree of neglect

65. *School Directors* v. *Reddick,* 77 Ill. 628; *Neville* v. *School Directors of District No. 1,* 36 Ill. 71.

66. *Carver* v. *School District No. 6,* 113 Mich. 524, 71 N.W. 859. See, however, *School District of Ft. Smith* v. *Maury,* 53 Ark. 471, 14 S.W. 669.

67. *Farrell* v. *School District No. 2,* 98 Mich. 43, 56 N.W. 1053; *Argenta Special School District* v. *Strickland,* 152 Ark. 215, 238 S.W. 9; *Laney* v. *Holbrook,* 150 Fla. 622, 8 So. (2d) 465, 146 A.L.R. 202. But see *Powell* v. *Young,* 148 Ohio St. 342, 74 N.E. (2d) 261; *Roller* v. *Young,* 67 N.E. (2d) (Ohio) 710.

68. *Ottinger* v. *School District No. 25,* 157 Ark. 82, 247 S.W. 789.

69. *Holden* v. *Shrewsbury School District No. 10,* 38 Vt. 529.

70. *Neville* v. *School Directors of District No. 1,* 36 Ill. 71; *School District No. 30* v. *Rath,* 115 Ark. 606, 170 S.W. 561.

71. *Neville* v. *School Directors of District No. 1,* 36 Ill. 71.

72. *School Directors of District No. 1* v. *Birch,* 93 Ill. App. 499.

which justifies a school board in dismissing a teacher. In an Illinois case[73] a teacher employed a substitute to take her place from Wednesday noon until Friday noon, when the school was to be dismissed for a vacation of several days. The teacher had no excuse for her action. She relied solely upon her right to employ a substitute teacher to do her work. In holding that the teacher had broken her contract, the court pointed out that the contract was for personal services and could not be fulfilled by employing a substitute. The court said, however:

A temporary absence of a short time, with the temporary substitution of another competent teacher, might not, under certain circumstances, constitute such a breach of contract as would authorize the employers to consider the contract at an end. The circumstances might be such that the teacher would be warranted in assuming the approval thereof, or the consent thereto by the employers, without any express consent.

It has been held, however, that delay in reporting to duty at the beginning of the school year is not such neglect of duty as to warrant the dismissal of a teacher. Thus, in a Colorado case[74] it was held that a delay in reporting from September 6 to September 28 did not terminate the teacher's contract. In a Kentucky case[75] a teacher was prevented by an interruption in railway traffic caused by floods from reporting for work until three days after the date specified in her contract. The court held that the school trustees had no legal cause to terminate the contract.

DISMISSAL BECAUSE OF LACK OF FUNDS WITH WHICH TO PAY SALARIES

There is not a great deal of judicial authority with respect to the right of school officials to dismiss teachers because of lack of funds with which to pay salaries. The rule supported both by reason and by the weight of authority may be stated as follows: A school board may not dismiss a teacher for lack of funds if it is legally possible to provide the necessary funds either out of the revenue for the current year or out of the income for subsequent years. Even the state legislature cannot by legislative act impair the obligations of a contract, and certainly a school district cannot do so. However, teachers make

73. *School Directors* v. *Hudson*, 88 Ill. 563. Accord, *Auran* v. *Mentor School District No. 1*, 233 N.W. (N.D.) 644. See also *Parrick* v. *School District No. 1*, 100 Kan. 569, 164 Pac. 1172; *Hong* v. *Independent School District No. 245*, 181 Minn. 309, 232 N.W. 329.

74. *School District No. 1* v. *Parker*, 260 Pac. (Colo.) 521.

75. *Turner* v. *Hampton*, 30 Ky Law Rep. 179, 97 S.W. 761.

contracts in contemplation of the law, and a contract which increases the indebtedness of the district beyond the legal debt limit is void. If the statutes provide that a school district must confine its expenditures to the revenue of the current year, contracts creating an indebtedness in excess of that revenue cannot be enforced. A school board cannot, however, dismiss a teacher merely because it does not have on hand the funds with which to pay him.[76] It must show that it had no legal authority to make the contract under the law existing at the time the contract was made. It should be kept in mind in this connection that different principles of law govern where teachers hold their positions on permanent tenure.

A few cases will serve to illustrate the principles stated in the preceding paragraph. In the case of *Myers* v. *Independent School District*[77] a statute prohibited school-district boards from incurring an indebtedness in excess of the revenue appropriated for school purposes during any fiscal year. In making contracts with teachers, the board of education kept within the current revenue but limited itself to $749 for all other current expenses. Nevertheless, it spent for other purposes a good portion of the funds which should have been set aside for teachers. When the school year was about half expired, all funds were exhausted. The court held that the teachers could recover the amounts unpaid on their contracts.

In the case of *Rudy* v. *Poplar Bluff School District*[78] the school was closed and the teacher discharged because of lack of funds. The tax levy provided sufficient funds to pay the teacher, but some of the taxes were not collected. The court permitted the teacher to recover, saying in part:

But the defense here set up fails to show that the revenue "provided for" the school year in question was not sufficient to pay all the teachers; it merely shows that there was a failure to pay into the school-district treasury enough for that purpose. If this is the sound view, then the rights of the teacher, under his contract with the district, may be displaced by the negligence or fraud of the tax collector. If the collector negligently fails to collect the school taxes which are levied, or collects them and fails to turn them over, the directors for this reason may, even upon the brief notice of five

76. *La Rue* v. *Board of Trustees of Baldwin Park School District*, 40 Calif. App. (2d) 287, 104 Pac. (2d) 689; *Board of Public Instruction* v. *Arnold*, 142 Fla. 163, 194 So. 334; *Little* v. *Carter County Board of Education*, 24 Tenn. App. 465, 146 S.W. (2d) 144.

77. *Myers* v. *Independent School District*, 104 Okla. 51, 230 Pac. 498. Accord, *Gentis* v. *Hunt*, 247 Pac. (Okla.) 358.

78. *Rudy* v. *Poplar Bluff School District*, 30 Mo. App. 113.

days, cancel the contract with the teacher. We are of opinion that this is not the law. . . . But, in order to make it appear that the contract with the teacher was *ultra vires* on the part of the directors, it must appear that not enough revenue was "provided" longer to continue the school, and not merely that not enough was collected and turned over to the treasurer of the school board.

If a teacher cannot be paid out of the revenue of the fiscal year for which he is employed, there is no good reason why he cannot be paid from the revenue of some subsequent year unless the statutes provide otherwise. In this connection it was said by the Supreme Court of Rhode Island:

The fixing of the fiscal year is purely a matter of convenience in the handling of the financial and business transactions of the city, and exerts no force or influence upon a contract made with a teacher for her services. The school committee had authority to engage teachers, fix their compensation, and determine their term of service. The obligation thus arising to the city to pay the salaries of teachers is not released or varied by the fixing of the fiscal year, nor does the right to collect the salary covered by the order expire with the close of the fiscal year. It is a contract which the city has entered into through its properly authorized committee, and as such it must be recognized and carried out.[79]

Conditions may arise, however, under which teachers may be dismissed because of lack of funds. Where the statutes limit the expenditure of the district to the revenues provided for the fiscal year, contracts creating an indebtedness in excess of the amount which the district may spend are *ultra vires* and void. Therefore, a teacher who is employed under such a contract may be dismissed when the funds which the district may legally spend are exhausted.[80] A Texas case[81] illustrates the point. A statute provided that "trustees of districts, in making contracts with teachers, shall not create a deficiency debt against the district." The court said:

The trustees were not authorized to contract any debt which would cause a deficiency in the school fund of the district. In other words, they could not contract debts in the employment of teachers to an amount greater than the school fund apportioned to that district for that scholastic year. . . . Any debt contracted greater than that would be a violation of the law, and constitute no claim against the district. . . . The trustees were authorized to expend the sum set apart to the district, but not empowered to contract a debt against the funds of future years.

79. *Hardy* v. *Lee*, 36 R.I. 302, 90 Atl. 383.

80. *Wolfe* v. *School District No. 2*, 58 Wash. 212, 108 Pac. 442; *Collier* v. *Peacock*, 93 Tex. 255, 54 S.W. 1025; *Morley* v. *Power*, 10 Lea (78 Tenn.) 219.

81. *Collier* v. *Peacock*, 93 Tex. 255, 54 S.W. 1025.

ABOLITION OF POSITION

If a teacher has been employed for a definite term, a school board cannot annul the contract by closing school[82] or by abolishing the department or position in which the teacher was engaged to teach.[83] If, on the other hand, a teacher has a permanent tenure unless removed for cause shown, the rule seems to be otherwise. Obviously, the legislature, in giving teachers permanent tenure, did not intend to limit in any way the right of school authorities to determine what should be taught or to determine the positions which efficient administration of the school system might demand.[84] Statutes providing for permanent tenure are to be interpreted as "intending only a regulation of dismissal for causes personal to the employee."[85]

REASSIGNMENT OF TEACHERS

The rule is well established that a teacher cannot be required to perform service of a kind other than that provided for in his contract. Assignment of a teacher to perform work substantially different from that which he has agreed to perform constitutes dismissal.[86] Thus it was said by the Supreme Court of Wisconsin: "The primary department of a public school does not include the sixth, seventh, and eighth grades, and one who contracts to teach the primary department cannot be required to teach said grades in their grade work, even though the classes be sent to the primary room."[87] In Arkansas the court ruled that a teacher who had agreed to teach the first eight grades could not be required to teach the ninth grade as well.[88] In an Indiana case[89]

82. *Hornbeck v. State,* 33 Ind. App. 609, 71 N.E. 916.

83. *School Town of Milford v. Zeigler,* 1 Ind. App. 138, 27 N.E. 303.

84. *Funston v. District School Board for District No. 1,* 130 Ore. 82, 278 Pac. 1075, 63 A.L.R. 1410; *Bates v. Board of Education,* 139 Calif. 145, 72 Pac. 907; *Fidler v. Board of Trustees,* 112 Calif. App. 296, 296 Pac. 912. See also *Cusack v. New York Board of Education,* 174 N.Y. 136, 66 N.E. 677.

85. *Funston v. District School Board for District No. 1,* 130 Ore. 82, 278 Pac. 1075, 63 A.L.R. 1410.

86. *School District No. 21 v. Hudson,* 277 S.W. (Ark.) 18; *Russellville Special School District No. 14 v. Tinsley,* 156 Ark. 283, 245 S.W. 831; *Butler v. Joint School District No. 4,* 155 Wis. 626, 145 N.W. 180; *Jefferson School Township v. Graves,* 150 N.E. (Ind.) 61; *People v. Board of Education,* 174 N.Y. 169; *Jackson v. Independent School District of Steamboat Rock,* 110 Iowa 313, 81 N.W. 596; *Kennedy v. Board of Education,* 82 Calif. 483, 22 Pac. 1042.

87. *Butler v. Joint School District No. 4,* 155 Wis. 626, 145 N.W. 180.

88. *School District No. 21 v. Hudson,* 277 S.W. (Ark.) 18.

89. *Jefferson School Township v. Graves,* 150 N.E. (Ind.) 61.

a teacher holding a certificate authorizing her to teach domestic science, history, civics, and zoölogy entered into a contract to teach "in the public schools of said township, in such building, grade, and room as said trustee may designate." The trustee required that she teach English and German, subjects not included in her certificate. She took an examination in these subjects but failed to make a passing grade, and the trustee dismissed her. In holding that the trustee had violated the contract, the court said:

> We must presume that he intended to keep entirely within the law; that he intended, when he entered into the contract with appellee that she would teach the subjects, and only those subjects, covered by her license. . . . If it should be declared to be the law that a trustee, after entering into such a contract with a teacher, could demand of such teacher that she teach some particular subject not covered by the license of such teacher, and that a failure of such teacher to procure a license covering the subject so demanded of her to be taught constitutes a breach of her contract, then is the way open to any trustee to render of no effect any contract he may have made with any teacher.

Where the statute or the rules of the school board provide for the assignment of teachers to such work or to such positions as the board may determine, a teacher, of course, is bound thereby and may be assigned work in the system at the discretion of the board.[89a] Such is the case because the statutes and the rules of the board are, by implication, read into the contract of employment.

DISMISSAL FOR POLITICAL ACTIVITY

The limitations placed on teachers and superintendents in expressing their political opinions while performing their official duties and the extent to which they may actively engage in politics are matters with regard to which there is not a great deal of judicial authority. However, a California court has held that a teacher may not in the classroom actively espouse the candidacy of a particular candidate. A teacher in the Sacramento High School made the following remarks to one of his classes regarding a candidate for the office of superintendent of schools of Sacramento County: "Many of you know Mr. Golway, what a fine man he is, and that his hopes are to be elected soon. I think he would be more helpful to our department than a lady, and we need more men in our schools. Sometimes your parents do not know one candidate from another; so they might be glad to be in-

89a. *Alexander* v. *School District No. 1,* 84 Ore. 172, 164 Pac. 711; *Underwood* v. *Board of Public Education,* 25 Ga. App. 634, 104 S.E. 90.

formed. Of course, if any of you have relatives or friends trying for the same office, be sure and vote for them." The superintendent of schools filed a complaint with the board of education, charging the teacher who had made the statement with unprofessional conduct. After notice and hearing, the board suspended the offending teacher for a period of ten weeks without pay and authorized the president of the board to reprimand him publicly. The teacher sought a writ of mandamus to compel the board to reinstate him, but the court refused to grant it for the reasons stated in the following excerpt:

It is to be observed that the advocacy before the scholars of a public school by a teacher of the election of a particular candidate for a public office—the attempt thus to influence support of such candidate by the pupils and through them by their parents—introduces into the school questions wholly foreign to its purposes and objects; that such conduct can have no other effect than to stir up strife among the students over a contest for a political office, and the result of this would inevitably be to disrupt the required discipline of a public school. Such conduct certainly is in contravention not only of the spirit of the laws governing the public-school system, but of that essential policy according to which the public-school system should be maintained in order that it may subserve in the highest degree its purposes.[90]

A schoolteacher or superintendent may, however, engage in political activity outside the schoolroom. By becoming a teacher, one does not lose one's rights as a citizen. In an Arkansas case,[91] for example, it was held that a city superintendent had the legal right to oppose vigorously the election of certain candidates for school-board membership. The superintendent was advocating what was described as an "ambitious" building program, in which he was supported by half the board members and opposed by the other half. The evidence showed that he adhered persistently to his plan and was not at all disposed to treat the decision of the board as final in the sense that he ceased to impress the members with his views. Considerable bitterness and factional spirit developed. In a campaign for the election of two new board members, the superintendent wrote a letter to two of his most bitter opponents on the board, challenging them to resign and stand for re-election. Moreover, he took an active part in the campaign and on one occasion made a political speech. It was conceded, however, that he fought in the open and was not guilty of obstructive tactics

90. *Goldsmith v. Board of Education,* 66 Calif. App. 157, 225 Pac. 783.

91. *Gardner v. North Little Rock Special School District,* 161 Ark. 466, 257 S.W. 73.

and that in his relations with the board members he was neither disrespectful nor personally offensive. After the election the superintendent was discharged. When he sued for his salary, the defense was that he had been guilty of insubordination, had opposed the policies of the board, and had engaged in harmful political activities. In holding that the conduct in question did not constitute legal cause for dismissal, the court discussed at some length the political rights of teachers:

> It is difficult to draw a line of demarcation between the political rights of a school teacher, or others engaged in educational work, with respect to activity in politics. Certainly they are not denied the right of free speech or the right to a reasonable amount of activity in all public affairs. . . . Their zeal in political activity must not carry them to such a degree of offensive partisanship that ther usefulness in educational work is impaired or proves a detriment to the school interests affected by their service. It does not appear to us that the evidence in this case shows any such overzeal or activity on the part of the plaintiff.

MARRIAGE AND ABSENCE FOR CHILDBIRTH AS CAUSES OF DISMISSAL WHERE TEACHER IS NOT ON TENURE

The authority of a school board to dismiss a woman teacher who marries during the term of a contract for a specified term of service is not definitely settled. The rule seems well established that marriage, in and of itself, does not constitute a legal cause for the dismissal of a woman teacher. Marriage, the courts hold, may or may not render a teacher inefficient. The courts hold, therefore, that a woman teacher who marries cannot be dismissed unless she has, in effect, agreed to terminate her employment in case of marriage. If the statutes authorize a school board to terminate a teacher's contract in case she marries, the provisions of the statute are, of course, read into the contract and the teacher may be dismissed. Where no such specific statutory authority exists, the courts are divided with respect to the authority of a board to enforce a rule providing for the dismissal of a woman teacher who marries during the term of her contract. A number of courts hold that, inasmuch as marriage is not a reasonable cause for dismissal, a board of education cannot legally dismiss a woman teacher who marries, even though the board may have adopted a rule reserving to itself the right to dismiss teachers under such circumstances.[92] These courts hold that

---

92. *Richards* v. *District School Board for School District No. 1,* 78 Ore. 621, 153 Pac. 482, L.R.A. 1916C 789, Ann. Cas. 1917D 266; *Byington* v. *School Dis-*

a board has no authority to enforce an unreasonable rule and that such a rule is unreasonable. Other courts take the position that such a rule is not unreasonable and may be enforced.[93] Reasonable rules of a board of education are always read into a teacher's contract. Consequently, the teacher, in effect, agrees to terminate her contract in case of marriage. Where a teacher expressly agrees in her contract not to marry or to terminate her employment in case she marries, there is a great deal of uncertainty with respect to the effect of the agreement. In the cases in which this specific issue has come into the courts, it has been held that the teacher could be dismissed.[94] In a great many nonschool cases, however, it has been held that contracts in restraint of marriage are against public policy and therefore void. Absence from school to give birth to a child, it has been held, constitutes such neglect of duty as to warrant dismissal.[95]

A case decided by the Supreme Court of Oregon[96] illustrates the reasoning of those courts which hold that marriage is an unreasonable cause of dismissal and that a board of education is without authority to enforce a rule providing for the dismissal of woman teachers who marry during the term of their employment. A school board passed a rule which read: "Married women shall not be eligible to positions as teachers in the district. . . . All women teachers who marry during their time of service thereby terminate their contracts with the district." A statute provided that teachers could be dismissed only for reasonable cause. In holding that the board had no authority to make or enforce the rule against marriage, the court reasoned as follows:

We prefer to proceed with the inquiry and determine whether the single fact of marriage can . . . be said to be a reasonable cause for dismissal. If a teacher becomes inefficient or fails to perform a duty, or does some act

---

trict of Joplin, 224 Mo. App. 541, 30 S.W. (2d) 621; *People* v. *Maxwell*, 177 N.Y. 494, 69 N.E. 1092; *Knox County* v. *State* ex rel. *Nighbert*, 177 Tenn. 171, 147 S.W. (2d) 100.

93. *Backie* v. *Cromwell Consolidated School District No. 13*, 242 N.W. (Minn.) 389; *Sheldon* v. *School Committee of Hopedale*, 276 Mass. 230, 177 N.E. 94; *Dukes* v. *Smoak*, 181 S.C. 182, 186 S.E. 790; *People* ex rel. *Christner* v. *Hamilton*, 324 Ill. App. 612; *State* ex rel. *Halvorson* v. *Anderson*, 234 Wis. 619, 291 N.W. 795; *Johnson School District No. 14*, 250 Pac. (2d (Wyo.) 890.

94. *Guilford School Township* v. *Roberts*, 28 Ind. App. 355, 62 N.E. 711; *Ansorge* v. *City of Green Bay*, 198 Wis. 320, 224 N.W. 119.

95. *People* v. *Board of Education*, 212 N.Y. 463, 106 N.E. 307; *Auran* v. *Mentor School District No. 1*, 233 N.W. (N.D.) 644.

96. *Richards* v. *District School Board for School District No. 1*, 78 Ore. 621, 153 Pac. 482, L.R.A. 1916C 789, Ann. Cas. 1917D 266.

which of itself impairs usefulness, then a good or reasonable cause for dismissal would exist. The act of marriage, however, does not, of itself, furnish a reasonable cause. That the marriage status does not necessarily impair the competency of all women teachers is conceded by the school authorities when they employ married women, as they are even now doing, to teach in the schools of this district. The reason advanced for the rule adopted by the board is that after marriage a woman may devote her time and attention to her home rather than to her school work. It would be just as reasonable to adopt a rule that, if a woman teacher joined a church, it would work an automatic dismissal from the schools on an imagined assumption that the church might engross her time, thought, and attention to the detriment of the schools; but such a regulation as the one supposed would not even have the semblance of reason. . . . It is impossible to know in advance whether the efficiency of any person will become impaired because of marriage, and a rule which assumes that all persons do become less competent because of marriage is unreasonable because such a regulation is purely arbitrary. If a teacher is just as competent and efficient after marriage, a dismissal because of marriage would be capricious. If a teacher is neglectful, incompetent, and inefficient, she ought to be discharged whether she is married or whether she is single.

Similarly, in West Virginia a statute authorized the dismissal of teachers for "incompetency, neglect of duty, intemperance, profanity, cruelty, or immorality." In holding that under such a statute a woman teacher could not be dismissed because of having married, the court said: "Marriage is not covered by any of these, and therefore does not constitute in and of itself ground of removal."[97] The charter of New York City authorized the removal of teachers for "gross misconduct, insubordination, neglect of duty, or general inefficiency." The board of education passed a rule that, should a woman teacher marry, her position would thereupon become vacant. The court held that the board had no authority to dismiss a woman teacher merely on the ground of marriage, because it had no authority to enact the rule. The board could dismiss for no other causes than those enumerated in the statute.[98]

Where a teacher expressly agrees in her contract not to marry during the term of her employment or, in case she does marry, to terminate her contract, it has been held that the contract is binding and can be enforced.[99] In an Indiana case[100] a teacher, in applying for a posi-

97. *Jameson v. Board of Education*, 74 W. Va. 389, 81 S.E. 1126.

98. *People v. Maxwell*, 177 N.Y. 494, 69 N.E. 1092.

99. *Guilford School Township v. Roberts*, 28 Ind. App. 355, 62 N.E. 711; *Ansorge v. City of Green Bay*, 198 Wis. 320, 224 N.W. 119. See also *Backie v. Cromwell Consolidated School District No. 13*, 242 N.W. (Minn.) 389.

100. *Guilford School Township v. Roberts*, 28 Ind. App. 355, 62 N.E. 711.

tion, told the township trustee that she was not married and did not expect to marry during the school year. Somewhat later she entered into a contract to teach, signing her maiden name, in spite of the fact that she had been married for four days. When the trustee learned her real status, he discharged her. She sued for her salary. The court held that the contract was void because it was secured through fraud and misrepresentation. Further, it was held that, where a teacher promises in her contract not to marry, such a promise becomes a valid part of the contract and, when violated, constitutes a legal cause for dismissal. The Supreme Court of Wisconsin reached the same conclusion.[101] A contract with a teacher read in part:

It is agreed that the contemplated marriage of the party of the second part shall not be performed before the Christmas holidays. If performed at that time, the party of the second part agrees to give thirty days' notice to that effect. If not performed at that time, the party of the second part agrees that she shall not be married until after the close of the school year.

The teacher was married shortly after the Christmas holidays and was discharged. The court held that the contract was valid and that the teacher had no cause of action.

It is doubtful whether the courts in the foregoing cases applied the correct principle of law. In the first place, it has been held in a number of cases that a board of education does not have the implied authority to adopt and enforce a regulation that marriage on the part of a woman teacher shall terminate her contract.[102] If a board has no authority to adopt and enforce such a resolution, it would seem that it has no authority to write into a teacher's contract a provision to the effect that marriage on her part will terminate the contract. In the second place, the great weight of authority is to the effect that contracts in restraint of marriage are void because they are contrary to public policy.[103] In one case it was said: "Courts refuse to enforce or recognize certain classes of acts because against public policy on the ground that

101. *Ansorge* v. *City of Green Bay*, 198 Wis. 320, 224 N.W. 119.

102. *Richards* v. *District School Board for School District No. 1*, 78 Ore. 621, 153 Pac. 482, L.R.A. 1916C 789, Ann. Cas. 1917D 266; *People* v. *Maxwell*, 177 N.Y. 494, 69 N.E. 1092; *Byington* v. *School District of Joplin*, 224 Mo. App. 541, 30 S.W. (2d) 621.

103. *White* v. *Equitable Nuptial Benefit Union*, 76 Ala. 251, 52 Am. Rep. 325; *King* v. *King*, 63 Ohio St. 363, 59 N.E. 111, 52 L.R.A. 157, 81 Am. St. Rep. 635; *Fletcher* v. *Osborn*, 282 Ill. 143, 118 N.E. 446, L.R.A. 1918C 331; *Lowe* v. *Doremus*, 84 N.J. Law 658, 87 Atl. 459, 49 L.R.A. (N.S.) 632.

they have a mischievous tendency, and are thus injurious to the interests of the state, apart from illegality or immorality. A contract in restraint of marriage is of this nature."[104]

There is some tendency to modify the broad rule that contracts in restraint of marriage are void. If the restraint upon marriage is a mere incident to the main purpose and object of the contract, some courts hold that the contract is not void in all its terms but void only with respect to the promise not to marry.[105] It would seem, therefore, that some authority exists for holding that a provision in a teacher's contract restricting her right of marriage is void and without effect, although the contract as a whole may be enforcible.

The Court of Appeals of New York has held that a married teacher who absents herself from school for the purpose of giving birth to a child may be dismissed for neglect of duty.[106] The teacher in question was absent for approximately three months without being excused by the board. The court expressed its opinion as follows:

> The legislature could have provided that the relator might be dismissed for no cause whatever. She had no vested right in the position of teacher. Section 1093 of the city charter has made neglect of duty ground for dismissal without any qualifying words. Absence on account of serious illness or for any other reason, high or low, leaves the duties of the position unperformed, and therefore neglected by the absentee. The statute has lodged with the board of education the power of deciding cases that thus fall within section 1093, and the board is required to pass upon the excuses offered in any case of absence. In the proceeding under review, the board of education discharged its duties fairly, and the courts cannot by mandamus reverse the conclusion reached.

The Supreme Court of North Dakota took the same position as the New York court.[107.]

104. *King* v. *King*, 63 Ohio St. 363, 59 N.E. 111, 52 L.R.A. 157, 81 Am. St. Rep. 635.

105. *Fletcher* v. *Osborn*, 282 Ill. 143, 118 N.E. 446, L.R.A. 1918C 331; *King* v. *King*, 63 Ohio St. 363, 59 N.E. 111, 52 L.R.A. 157, 81 Am. St. Rep. 635; *Crowder-Jones* v. *Sullivan*, 9 Ont. L.R. 27. Contra, *Lowe* v. *Doremus*, 84 N.J. Law 658, 87 Atl. 459, 49 L.R.A. (N.S.) 632.

106. *People* v. *Board of Education*, 212 N.Y. 463, 106 N.E. 307. Accord, *Appeal of School District of City of Bethlehem*, 347 Pa. 418, 32 Atl. (2d) 565; *West Mahaony Township School District* v. *Kelly*, 156 Pa. Super. Ct. 601, 41 Atl. (2d) 344.

107. *Auran* v. *Mentor School District No. 1*, 233 N.W. (N.D.) 644.

RIGHT OF TEACHER TO NOTICE AND HEARING

Where the statutes vest in the employing agency the right to dismiss teachers at discretion and without cause, it is not necessary that a teacher be given notice of the charges against him and an opportunity to explain his conduct.[108] Where, on the other hand, the statutes require that a teacher be given notice and an opportunity to be heard in his defense, the procedure established by statute must be closely followed. If a teacher is dismissed without a hearing under such circumstances, the board will be estopped from pleading the grounds for dismissal, whatever these may be, in an action by the teacher for breach of contract. In other words, the grounds for dismissal cannot be shown unless they have been ascertained and acted on in the manner prescribed by statute.[109] In case the statutes provide that teachers can be dismissed for cause only, a teacher, according to the great weight of authority, cannot be legally dismissed without having been given notice of the charges preferred and an opportunity to be heard in his defense.[110] As a rule, it is not necessary that the statutes expressly provide for notice and hearing; it is sufficient if they provide that a teacher be dismissed for cause only. Thus it was said by the Supreme Judicial Court of Massachusetts:

Where the power is given to remove "for cause," removal is not authorized without notice and hearing even though the statute does not so provide in terms. . . . The term removal "for cause" means removal "for cause sufficient in law." That can only be determined after an opportunity to be heard and a finding so that the sufficiency of the cause may be determined in court.[111]

108. *Gillan* v. *Board of Regents,* 88 Wis. 7, 58 N.W. 1042, 24 L.R.A. 336; *The Queen* v. *Governors of Darlington School,* 6 Q.B. (Adolphus and Ellis, N.S.) 682.

109. *School District No. 26* v. *McComb,* 18 Colo. 240, 32 Pac. 424; *School District No. 1* v. *Parker,* 260 Pac. (Colo.) 521.

110. *Trustees of State Normal School* v. *Cooper,* 150 Pa. St. 78, 24 Atl. 348; *Corrigan* v. *School Committee,* 250 Mass. 334, 145 N.E. 530; *Clark* v. *Wild Rose Special School District No. 90,* 47 N.D. 297, 182 N.W. 307; *Taylor* v. *School District No. 1,* 15 Ariz. 262, 138 Pac. 13; *Morley* v. *Power,* 5 Lea (73 Tenn.) 691; *School District No. 2* v. *Shuck,* 49 Colo. 526, 113 Pac. 511; *School District No. 3* v. *Hale,* 15 Colo. 367, 25 Pac. 308; *School District No. 25* v. *Youberg,* 77 Colo. 202, 235 Pac. 351; *Kellison* v. *School District No. 1,* 20 Mont. 153, 50 Pac. 421; *State* v. *Wunderlich,* 144 Minn. 368, 175 N.W. 677; *Kuehn* v. *School District No. 70,* 221 Minn. 443, 22 N.W. (2d) 220; *Keenan* v. *San Francisco Unified School District,* 214 Pac. (2d) (Calif.) 382; *School District No. 2* v. *Shuck,* 49 Colo. 526, 113 Pac. (2d) 511; *State ex rel. Howard* v. *Ireland,* 114 Mont. 488, 138 Pac. (2d) 569; *In re Swink,* 132 Pa. Super. Ct. 259, 200 Atl. 200.

111. *Corrigan* v. *School Committee,* 250 Mass. 334, 145 N.E. 530.

In a case which came before the Supreme Court of Pennsylvania,[112] the principal of a state normal school was dismissed without notice or hearing on the ground of immoral conduct. In holding that the dismissal was illegal, the court said:

> When he asked for a reason for such treatment, he was pointed to his conviction upon four distinct charges of immoral conduct spread upon the minutes of the board of trustees. When he denied the regularity of such action, a court of equity was appealed to by the trustees to close his mouth and tie his hands. He comes into this court by appeal, and asks whether he may be lawfully tried, convicted, and sentenced without so much as notice that he is accused?
>
> A good character is a necessary part of the equipment of a teacher. Take this away, or blacken it, and the doors of professional employment are practically closed against him. Before this is done there should be at least a hearing, at which the accused may show that the things alleged are not true, or if true are susceptible of an explanation consistent with good morals and his own professional fidelity. We think it is plain, too plain for serious discussion, that the action of the trustees was irregular and unjust to the appellant.

Similarly, in a North Dakota case[113] a teacher was dismissed for neglect of duty without notice and opportunity to be heard. The statutes authorized the dismissal of teachers for cause but made no mention of the right of a teacher to a hearing. Nevertheless, the court held that notice and a hearing were essential:

> We are of the opinion that the statute authorizes removal only for cause as distinguished from removal at the pleasure of the school board, and that the cause must be a real cause affecting the interests of the school. It is elementary that where the power to dismiss an employee of a public corporation is conditioned upon the existence of cause therefor, the employee has a right to know the nature of the charge or charges which it is claimed constitute cause, and the further right to a reasonable opportunity to appear and defend against the charge or charges.

Some courts hold, however, that a teacher is not entitled to notice and hearing unless such right is expressly conferred by statute.[114] These courts reason that the relation between a school board and a teacher is simply that of employer and employee. An employer, it is said, may

112. *Trustees of State Normal School* v. *Cooper*, 150 Pa. St. 78, 24 Atl. 348.

113. *Clark* v. *Wild Rose Special School District No. 90*, 47 N.D. 297, 182 N.W. 307.

114. *State* v. *Preston*, 120 Wash. 569, 208 Pac. 47; *Foreman* v. *School District No. 25*, 81 Ore. 587, 159 Pac. 1155; *Ridenour* v. *Board of Education*, 15 Misc. Rep. 418, 37 N.Y.S. 109, 72 N.Y. St. Rep. 155; *Ewin* v. *Independent School District No. 8*, 10 Idaho 102, 77 Pac. 222; *Maxey* v. *Board of Trustees*, 187 Ky. 729, 220 S.W. 732; *Bump* v. *Union High School District No. 3*, 144 Ore. 390, 24 Pac. (2d) 330.

dismiss an employee without giving notice of charges or an opportunity to be heard. If the dismissal is without legal cause, the employer is liable in an action for breach of contract. In a case decided by the Supreme Court of Washington,[115] for example, a statute authorized the dismissal of teachers "for sufficient cause." In holding that no notice or hearing was required, the court said:

A teacher is an employee, and not a public officer. . . . They are employed in this state by contracts for definite periods with the teacher as one party and the board of directors of the school district as the other. In the absence of express legislation we do not think it can be successfully maintained that one party to a contract must sit as a tribunal before exercising its privilege of terminating it.

Of course, if the contract is terminated wrongfully, the district is liable for the damages suffered, but we hold that the use of the words "for sufficient cause" is simply a limitation upon the power to discharge given by the same section. The investigation which the board may see fit to make is within its own discretion. It should, and probably will, where practicable, discuss matters with the teacher before acting.

Although a teacher may be entitled to a hearing, it is not, as a rule, necessary that the board of education adopt the formal procedure of a court of law. All that is required is that the teacher be notified of the charges against him and be given an opportunity to explain or justify his course of action. The board may adopt whatever procedure it sees fit so long as justice be done.[116] Failure to take evidence under oath or to keep a record of proceedings is immaterial.[117] In determining whether a school board had adopted the proper procedure in dismissing a teacher for incompetence, a New York court said:

This supervisory power is not necessarily in the nature of a judicial trial of issues of fact. The substantial duty of the board is, to see that injustice has not been done to the teacher by the trustees [ward trustees], and that the removal has not been made upon improper or inadequate grounds. The delicate nature of the duty devolved upon the trustees, to see to it that unfit or incompetent persons are not put or kept in charge of the children who attend the common schools, forbids the idea of a trial with the formality and

115. *State* v. *Preston,* 120 Wash. 569, 208 Pac. 47.

116. *People* v. *Board of Education,* 3 Hun. (N.Y.) 177; *School District No. 23* v. *McCoy,* 30 Kan. 268, 1 Pac. 97, 46 Am. Rep. 92; *School District No. 25* v. *Youberg,* 77 Colo. 202, 235 Pac. 351; *Kirkpatrick* v. *Independent School District of Liberty,* 53 Iowa 585, 5 N.W. 750; *Board of Education* v. *Ballou,* 21 Calif. App. (2d) 52, 68 Pac. (2d) 389; *School District No. 1* v. *Thompson,* 214 Pac. (2d) (Colo.) 1020.

117. *School District No. 23* v. *McCoy,* 30 Kan. 268, 1 Pac. 97, 46 Am. Rep. 92; *Anthony* v. *Phoenix Union High School District,* 55 Ariz. 265, 100 Pac. (2d) 988.

strictness that belong to courts. It is only necessary to suggest that they must often act upon moral convictions, rather than established facts, and upon evidences of unfitness, physical, mental, or moral, that would not, in courts, be such proof as would justify a verdict of guilt of specific offenses or immoralities.[118]

A teacher, however, has a right to a fair hearing by those who sit in judgment of his ability or conduct.[119] A member of a school board who is prejudiced against a teacher may be restrained from sitting as a member of the tribunal to hear and determine charges against him. A case decided by the Supreme Court of Washington[120] illustrates the application of the rule. The superintendent of schools of Seattle was charged with malfeasance in office, with conduct unbecoming a superintendent of schools, and with disobedience to the rules of the board of directors. One of the members of the board of directors, who was a personal enemy of the superintendent, publicly announced his intention of finding the superintendent guilty, no matter what the evidence might be. The supreme court issued an injunction restraining this member of the board from sitting at the trial.

The same principle of law is illustrated by other cases. In Massachusetts[121] a teacher was dismissed as a result of votes cast by two members of the school committee who were actuated by feelings of political resentment and ill will against the teacher, more or less openly expressed and exhibited. The court issued a writ of mandamus reinstating the teacher in his position. In the state of Washington a statute provided that a teacher who had been dismissed might appeal to the county superintendent of schools to review the action of the school board. Where, however, the superintendent had been the moving force in dismissing a teacher and had prejudged her case, the court held that the appeal was unnecessary. The teacher might carry her case directly to the courts.[122]

118. *People* v. *Board of Education*, 3 Hun. (N.Y.) 177.

119. *School District No. 23* v. *McCoy*, 30 Kan. 268, 1 Pac. 97, 46 Am. Rep. 92; *State* v. *Board of Education*, 19 Wash. 8, 52 Pac. 317, 40 L.R.A. 317, 67 Am. St. Rep. 706; *Sweeney* v. *School Committee*, 249 Mass. 525, 144 N.E. 377; *Christensen* v. *Plummer*, 130 Minn. 440, 153 N.W. 862; *State* v. *Board of Education*, 40 So. (2d) (Ala.) 689; *Stapleton* v. *Huff*, 173 Pac. (2d) (N.M.) 612.

120. *State* v. *Board of Education*, 19 Wash. 8, 52 Pac. 317, 40 L.R.A. 317, 67 Am. St. Rep. 706.

121. *Sweeney* v. *School Committee*, 249 Mass. 525, 144 N.E. 377.

122. *Caffrey* v. *Superior Court*, 72 Wash. 444, 130 Pac. 747.

DAMAGES RECOVERABLE FOR BREACH OF CONTRACT

A teacher who is illegally dismissed should not assume as a matter of course that he can recover the wages accruing for the remainder of his term of employment. The amount due under the contract is prima facie the measure of recovery, but the board of education is entitled to deduct from that amount as mitigated damages whatever it can show the plaintiff has earned in other employment or could have earned by reasonable diligence in seeking other employment of the same general kind.[123] The burden of showing what the teacher could have earned in other employment, however, is upon the board and not upon the teacher.[124] The rule governing damages recoverable for the breach of a teacher's contract has been clearly expressed by the Supreme Court of Iowa as follows:

When such contract is disregarded by the school district and the teacher is denied the right to perform, it is her duty to find other employment, and, when sued, the school district may show that she has found other employment, or that by the use of reasonable diligence she might have found other employment for the purpose of mitigating the damages; but, if the discharged teacher did not accept other employment, her damages should not be diminished for failure to secure it, unless it be shown that by reasonable diligence she might have secured employment of the same grade in the same locality where she was employed to teach. She was not required to accept employment in another locality or of a different or lower grade. The law is very clear on this proposition.[125]

While a teacher who has been discharged without legal cause must be reasonably diligent in seeking other employment in order to mitigate the damages which the board may be required to pay, he is not

123. *Shill* v. *School Township of Rock Creek,* 209 Iowa 1020, 227 N.W. 412; *Byrne* v. *Independent School District of Strubee,* 139 Iowa 618, 117 N.W. 983; *School Directors* v. *Kimmel,* 31 Ill. App. 537; *School Directors of District No. 1* v. *Birch,* 93 Ill. App. 499; *School Directors of District No. 2* v. *Orr,* 88 Ill. 648; *School Directors* v. *Crews,* 23 Ill. App. 367; *Ottinger* v. *School District No. 25,* 157 Ark. 82, 247 S.W. 789; *School District No. 21* v. *Hudson,* 277 S.W. (Ark.) 18; *Gardner* v. *North Little Rock Special School District,* 161 Ark. 466, 257 S.W. 73; *School District No. 65* v. *Wright,* 42 S.W. (Ark.) 555; *Edwards* v. *School District No. 73,* 297 S.W. (Mo.) 1001; *Haddon School Township of Sullivan County* v. *Willis,* 209 Ind. 356, 199 N.E. 251; *State* ex rel. *Schmidt* v. *School District No. 2,* 237 Wis. 186, 295 N.W. 36.

124. *School Directors of District No. 2* v. *Orr,* 88 Ill. 648; *Doyle* v. *School Directors,* 36 Ill. App. 653; *School Directors* v. *Crews,* 23 Ill. App. 367; *Edwards* v. *School District No. 73,* 297 S.W. (Mo.) 1001.

125. *Byrne* v. *Independent School District of Strubee,* 139 Iowa 618, 117 N.W. 983.

bound to accept work of a nature fundamentally different from that which he agreed to perform in his contract nor in a place inconvenient to him. In the case of *Jackson* v. *Independent School District of Steamboat Rock*,[126] for example, a teacher had been employed to teach in the intermediate department. In January the board offered her a contract to teach in the high-school department at the same salary. When she refused to accept the offer, she was dismissed. In holding that the teacher was not bound to accept the offer in order to mitigate damages, the court said:

> When a servant is wrongfully discharged, he is not bound to accept new employment from the same master, unless (1) the work is in the same general line as that of the first employment, and (2) the offer is made in such a manner as that its acceptance will not amount to a modification of the original agreement. If we were prepared to say that the higher grade of teaching offered was of such a character as that plaintiff was in duty bound to accept it, yet it does not appear that the offer was so made that plaintiff could have accepted it without modifying her original agreement. It was defendant's duty to make this showing. . . . The law would not thus compel plaintiff either to make a new agreement with defendant or lose all her rights under the old one. If plaintiff had accepted the offer as alleged to have been made, and found herself incompetent for the new work, she would have been liable to discharge under the new agreement, and her rights under the other would have been lost. The offer, as set up, does not constitute a defense in whole or part.

Similarly, it has been held that a person who is employed as a school principal need not accept a position as a teacher.[127] If a teacher is dismissed during the summer vacation, it is not necessary, according to the Supreme Court of Michigan, that he seek other employment before the school opens.[128] In such a case the teacher is not presumed to be out of employment until the proffered services have been rejected. If a teacher holds a contract to teach a common school for a definite term, he cannot be transferred at the option of the board to the position of truant officer.[129] It has been held, however, that one who holds a contract of employment as a high-school principal is bound to accept at

126. *Jackson* v. *Independent School District of Steamboat Rock*, 110 Iowa 313, 81 N.W. 596. Accord, *State* ex rel. *Freeman* v. *Sierra County Board of Education*, 49 N.M. 54, 157 Pac. (2d) 234; *Martin* v. *Board of Education*, 120 W. Va. 621, 199 S.E. 887.

127. *Williams* v. *School District No. 189*, 104 Wash. 659, 177 Pac. 635.

128. *Farrell* v. *School District No. 2*, 98 Mich. 43, 56 N.W. 1053.

129. *Russellville Special School District No. 14* v. *Tinsley*, 156 Ark. 283, 245 S.W. 831.

the same salary an elementary-school principalship in order to mitigate the damages due him by the board.[130]

In an unusual case decided by the Supreme Court of Arkansas,[131] it was shown that a teacher was ill for some time after dismissal and during the life of the contract. The lower court refused to instruct the jury that she was not entitled to pay for the time she was ill. The supreme court held that there was no error in the instructions to the jury. The teacher might or might not have been ill if she had not been forced to change her position.

A teacher dismissed without legal cause and securing other employment is entitled, when the amount of damages due him is determined, to have deducted from the amount earned in the new position the expenses necessarily incurred in securing it and the necessary additional cost occasioned by the changed conditions of living.[132] A Colorado case[133] illustrates the rule. A teacher employed to teach in Georgetown was dismissed without legal cause. Later she obtained employment in Cripple Creek but found that the cost of living was twenty dollars a month more in Cripple Creek than it would have been in Georgetown. From the amount the teacher earned in Cripple Creek during the term of her original contract, the court allowed a deduction to cover the cost of railroad fare from Georgetown to Cripple Creek and to cover the extra cost of living. The net earnings at Cripple Creek thus arrived at were deducted from the amount due the teacher under her contract, and the amount so determined was the measure of the teacher's damages.

Where a teacher who has been illegally dismissed secures other employment for a longer term than that covered in the original contract, it has been held that no deduction should be allowed to cover the expenses incurred in securing the new employment. In an Arkansas case[133a] a superintendent of schools was illegally dismissed, but after

130. *Ryan* v. *Mineral County High School District,* 27 Colo. App. 63, 146 Pac. 792.

131. *School District No. 21* v. *Hudson,* 277 S.W. (Ark.) 18.

132. *School District No. 3* v. *Nash,* 27 Colo. App. 551, 140 Pac. 473. See also *Development Company of America* v. *King,* 170 Fed. 923; *Tufts* v. *Plymouth Gold Mining Company,* 14 Allen (96 Mass.) 407; *Dickinson* v. *Talmage,* 138 Mass. 249; *Van Winkle* v. *Satterfield,* 58 Ark. 617, 25 S.W. 1113, 23 L.R.A. 853; *Ray* v. *Board of Education,* 194 Okla. 472, 153 Pac. (2d) 233.

133. *School District No. 3* v. *Nash,* 27 Colo. App. 551, 140 Pac. 473.

133a. *Garder* v. *North Little Rock Special School District,* 161 Ark. 466, 257 S.W. 73.

dismissal he was elected mayor of the city for a term of two years. The court held that he was not entitled to deduct from the amount he had earned as mayor the expenses he had incurred in securing the office. The court said:

Plaintiff's election expenses were incurred in securing the office of mayor for a full term of two years, and should not be deducted from the salary earned during the first part of the term. The expenses are referable to the full term and could not be apportioned to different periods. Whether election expenses should be deducted under any circumstances we need not now decide.

CONCLUSIVENESS OF BOARDS' ACTION IN DISMISSAL OF TEACHERS

It is well established that the dismissal of a teacher by a board of education is not final and conclusive—an appeal may be carried to the courts. In such matters the constitutional division of powers prevents complete jurisdiction by the courts, but a limited jurisdiction is conferred upon the courts by way of certiorari or, in some cases, by statutory appeal.

When an appeal is taken to the court by an aggrieved teacher, the court will, as a rule, make a determination of three things: (1) Did the board of education have jurisdiction, that is, did it act within the scope of authority? (2) Did the board follow the procedures prescribed by statute? and (3) Did the board have some reasonable basis for its action? The courts will not permit a board to dismiss a teacher for some illegal cause. They will require a board to follow the statutory mode of dismissal, as, for example, the giving of notice and the holding of a hearing. What the court will not do is to reweigh evidence in order to determine its credibleness or where the preponderance lies. It will examine the evidence only to determine whether the board acted reasonably or arbitrarily. And if the evidence is such that reasonable men might disagree with respect to the conclusion to be drawn from it, the action of the board will be sustained. The board's finding will be overruled only when it has acted arbitrarily, unreasonably, and without any substantial basis of fact.[134]

134. *State* ex rel. *Rockwell* v. *State Board of Education,* 213 Minn. 184, 6 N.W. (2d) 251, 143 A.L.R. 503; *State* ex rel. *Ging* v. *Board of Education of Duluth,* 213 Minn. 550, 7 N.W. (2d) 544; *Blair* v. *Board of Trustees,* 161 S.W. (2d) (Tex.) 1030; *Laney* v. *Board of Instruction of Orange County,* 153 Fla. 728, 15 So. (2d) 748; *Midway School District of Kern County* v. *Griffeath,* 166 Pac. (2d) (Calif.) 331; *Stiver* v. *State* ex rel. *Kent,* 211 Ind. 380, 1 N.E. (2d) 1006; *Gragg* v. *Hill,* 58 S.W. (2d) (Tex.) 150.

The law governing judicial review of administrative discretion has been clearly expressed by the Supreme Court of Minnesota:

> Complete jurisdiction cannot, either directly or indirectly, be conferred upon the courts in view of the constitutional division of powers of government . . . yet a limited jurisdiction by way of certiorari, and in some cases by statutory appeal, is conferred upon the courts. This is necessarily confined to questions affecting the jurisdiction of the board, the regularity of its proceedings, and, as to merits of the controversy, whether the order or determination in a particular case was arbitrary, oppressive, unreasonable, fraudulant, under an erroneous theory of the law, or without any evidence to support it. A court cannot place itself in the place of the board, try the matter de novo, and substitute its findings for those of the board.[135]

It must not be assumed, however, that boards of education may act arbitrarily or unreasonably in the dismissal of a teacher. The courts will examine the evidence to determine whether the board has abused its discretion, to determine whether there is any reasonable basis for their action. A Florida case illustrates the reasoning the courts usually follow. A school principal had been dismissed on charges of having been intoxicated and of having attempted to seduce a high-school girl. The court overruled the finding of the board, saying:

> The general rule is that administrative findings, in order to be upheld by the courts, must be supported by substantial evidence. This means that there must be evidence which supports a substantial basis of fact from which the fact at issue can be reasonably inferred. It must do more than create a suspicion of the fact to be established, and must be such relevant evidence as a reasonable mind would accept as adequate to support a conclusion. . . . The evidence in this case, tested by this rule, was insufficient to prove any of the charges.[136]

REMEDIES OPEN TO DISMISSED TEACHERS

A teacher who has been illegally dismissed has a right of action against the school board in its corporate capacity for breach of contract;[137] there is no right of action against the school-board members personally unless they have acted maliciously or in bad faith.[138] A

---

135. *State* ex rel. *Ging* v. *Board of Education of Duluth*, 213 Minn. 550, 7 N.W. (2d) 544.

136. *Laney* v. *Board of Education*, 153 Fla. 728, 15 So. (2d) 748.

137. *Burkhead* v. *Independent School District*, 107 Iowa 29, 77 N.W. 491; *Underwood* v. *Board of County School Commissioners*, 103 Md. 181, 63 Atl. 221; *Jackson School Township* v. *Shera*, 8 Ind. App. 330, 35 N.E. 842.

138. *Sprowl* v. *Smith*, 40 N.J. Law 314; *Gregory* v. *Small*, 39 Ohio St. 346; *Adams* v. *Thomas*, 11 Ky. Law Rep. 701, 12 S.W. 940; *Burton* v. *Fulton*, 49 Pa. St. 151.

teacher who is wrongfully discharged may immediately thereafter bring action for damages.[139]

A teacher who has secured judgment against a school district for breach of contract may, in case the district refuses to pay his claim, bring action for a writ of mandamus to compel payment. If the district has no funds with which to pay, a writ of mandamus will issue to compel the proper authorities to raise the required amount by taxation.[140]

Since the teacher is an employee and not a public officer, he cannot, if employed for a definite term, secure a writ of injunction restraining the school authorities from dismissing him. A court of equity will not issue an injunction in such a case because the teacher has an adequate remedy for breach of contract in a court of law.[141] Neither may the patrons of the school, even though they be taxpayers, enjoin the board from dismissing a teacher.[142] In the case of *Jensen* v. *Independent Consolidated School District No. 85*,[143] for example, a taxpayer sought to enjoin the dismissal of a teacher. In denying the injunction, the court used the following language:

> The plaintiff cannot by the extraordinary remedy of injunction compel the school board to keep one employee and enjoin it from employing another employee. Neither can the board be enjoined from violating its contract with a person for his personal services as a teacher. . . . All that plaintiff can require is that the school be open under competent teachers as provided by law and that all children be afforded equal educational facilities. He has no authority to prevent the employment of a particular competent teacher. . . .

139. *Sarle* v. *School District No. 27*, 255 Pac. (Ariz.) 994; *Edwards* v. *School District No. 73*, 297 S.W. (Mo.) 1001; *Boswell* v. *Consolidated School District No. 8*, 10 S.W. (2d) (Mo.) 665; *Robinson* v. *Cabin Creek Board of Education*, 70 W. Va. 66, 73 S.E. 337; *Cheyenne County High School District No. 1* v. *Graves*, 87 Colo. 52, 284 Pac. 1026; 56 C.J. 410.

140. *Bear* v. *Commissioners*, 124 N.C. 204, 70 Am. St. Rep. 586.

141. *School District No. 13* v. *Ward*, 40 Okla. 97, 136 Pac. 588; *School District No. 1* v. *Carson*, 9 Colo. App. 6, 46 Pac. 846. The Supreme Court of Mississippi has, however, held otherwise in *Campbell* v. *Warwick*, 142 Miss. 510, 107 So. 657.

142. *Donald* v. *Stauffer*, 140 Miss. 752, 106 So. 357; *Jensen* v. *Independent Consolidated School District No. 85*, 160 Minn. 233, 199 N.W. 911; *Greer* v. *Austin*, 40 Okla. 113, 136 Pac. 590, 51 L.R.A. (N.S.) 336; *School District No. 1* v. *Carson*, 9 Colo. App. 6, 46 Pac. 846; *Schwier* v. *Zitike*, 136 Ind. 210, 36 N.E. 30.

143. *Jensen* v. *Independent Consolidated School District No. 85*, 160 Minn. 233, 199 N.W. 911.

Contracts for personal service or personal skill will not be enforced, nor will the putting an end to such contracts be restrained. This is especially true when the employment involves public interest and relates, as it does here, to matters which are purely administrative in character.

Similarly, it is well settled that, when a teacher is under employment for a definite term, a writ of mandamus will not be issued to reinstate him in a position from which he has been wrongfully dismissed.[144] The relation existing between the teacher and the school board is purely contractual, and the teacher, therefore, has adequate remedy at law for breach of contract. Thus it was said by the Supreme Court of Nebraska:

> The contract to teach in the common or free schools . . . is one of employment, and the relative positions occupied by the district represented by the board and the teacher are those of employer and employee. A teacher in the schools of the ordinary district is not a public officer, nor is his position an office. . . . This being true, for any violation of the rights of a teacher under an existing contract, there would be an adequate remedy in an action to recover damages for a breach of the contract, and mandamus would not lie.[145]

It follows that a teacher who has been dismissed has no right to retain possession of the school property,[146] even though the dismissal may have been illegal.[147] In a New York case[148] a teacher who had been dismissed attempted to enter the schoolhouse and continue the school but was prevented from doing so by force. She brought action against the trustee for assault and battery. The court ruled against the teacher because she had no right to enforce specific performance of her contract. Similarly, in Arkansas it was held that a superintendent of schools who had been illegally removed had no right to continue in possession of school property.[149] The court said:

144. *Taylor* v. *Marshall,* 12 Calif. App. 549, 107 Pac. 1012; *State* v. *Smith,* 49 Neb. 755, 69 N.W. 114; *Bays* v. *State,* 6 Neb. 167. In Tennessee a contrary rule obtains. A teacher who has been illegally dismissed will be restored to his position by mandamus. In that state, however, a teacher is held to be an officer and not a mere employee (*Morley* v. *Power,* 5 Lea [73 Tenn.] 691).

145. *State* v. *Smith,* 49 Neb. 755, 69 N.W. 114.

146. *Swartwood* v. *Walbridge,* 10 N.Y.S. 862, 31 N.Y. St. Rep. 757.

147. *Gardner* v. *Goss,* 147 Ark. 178, 227 S.W. 25.

148. *Swartwood* v. *Walbridge,* 10 N.Y.S. 862, 31 N.Y. St. Rep. 757.

149. *Gardner* v. *Goss,* 147 Ark. 178, 227 S.W. 25.

If Gardner was wrongfully discharged, a fact which may be conceded for the purposes of the present case, he has his remedy at law for the breach of the contract of employment. But the right to recover damages for the broken contract, if that right exists, does not justify him in refusing to surrender possession of the property and affairs of the school district.

In Tennessee, however, it has been held that a court of equity will not aid school authorities in dispossessing a teacher of school property where the teacher has been illegally dismissed,[150] but in that state a teacher is held to be an officer and not a mere employee.

A teacher who holds his position under a permanent-tenure act, subject to dismissal for cause shown, may, when illegally dismissed, be restored to his position by mandamus.[151] Under such circumstances the teacher has no adequate remedy at law because, the term of his employment being an indefinite time, it is impossible to determine the measure of his damages.

150. *Thompson* v. *Gibbs*, 97 Tenn. 489, 37 S.W. 277, 34 L.R.A. 548.

151. *State* v. *Board of School Directors of City of Milwaukee*, 179 Wis. 284, 191 N.W. 746; *Kennedy* v. *Board of Education*, 82 Calif. 483, 22 Pac. 1042; *People* v. *Board of Education*, 174 N.Y. 169; *State* v. *Board of Education*, 18 N.M. 183, 135 Pac. 96, 49 L.R.A. (N.S.) 62.

CHAPTER XVIII

Teacher Pensions and Retirement Systems

PENSIONS

IN CONSIDERING the law governing teacher-retirement systems, it is important to keep in mind the meaning of the term "pension." It is commonly held that a pension is a gratuity granted by the state in recognition of some service that was not fully or adequately paid for at the time it was rendered. As the Supreme Court of Illinois has put it, a "pension is in the nature of a bounty springing from the appreciation and graciousness of the sovereign."[1] It follows, therefore, that when a state establishes a pension system it in no way creates a contractual relation with those persons who are its beneficiaries.[2] The bounties which the state confers upon pensioners may be given, withheld, distributed, or recalled as the sovereign may desire. The pensioner has no vested right in the pension fund.[3] Where a state's teacher-retirement system falls under the classification of a pension, it is subject to change as the legislature, from time to time, may deem desirable, and teachers may not claim that their contractual rights are being violated.[4]

CONSTITUTIONALITY OF TEACHER-PENSION AND RETIREMENT LEGISLATION

In a number of states, teacher-pension and retirement legislation has been attacked on the ground that it violates either the state or the federal constitution. The most common objection has been that such legis-

1. *Raines v. Board of Trustees of Illinois State Teachers' Pension and Retirement Fund*, 365 Ill. 610, 7 N.E. (2d) 489.

2. *Raines v. Board of Trustees of Illinois State Teachers' Pension and Retirement Fund*, 365 Ill. 610, 7 N.E. (2d) 489; *People v. Retirement Board*, 326 Ill. 579, 158 N.E. 220, 54 A.L.R. 940; *State* ex rel. *Parker v. Board of Education*, 155 Kan. 754, 129 Pac. (2d) 265.

3. *Driggs v. Utah State Teachers' Retirement Board*, 105 Utah 417, 142 Pac. (2d) 657; *Walton v. Cotton*, 60 U.S. 355; *State v. Board of Trustees of Policemen's Pension Fund*, 121 Wis. 44, 98 N.W. 954; *Clarke v. Ireland*, 199 Pac. (2d) (Mont.) 965.

4. *Dodge v. Board of Education of Chicago*, 302 U.S. 74, 58 S. Ct. 98.

lation violates that provision of the Fourteenth Amendment which declares that no state shall deprive any person of liberty or property without due process of law. It has been contended, too, that laws of this kind are class legislation; that they result in the expenditure of public money for private purposes; and that they are local or special laws for the management of public schools. The courts have commonly denied all these contentions.[5] With respect to the contention that the contributions which teachers are required to make to the retirement fund constitute the taking of property without due process of law, it is said by the courts that the relationship existing between the teacher and the state is purely a contractual relationship. The state has the right to say upon what terms it will employ teachers to teach in its schools. The teacher may accept or reject the terms at his pleasure. He knows that the law is a part of his contract. There is, under such circumstances, no taking of property without due process of law and no unreasonable restriction upon freedom of contract. In fact, there is no taking of property at all. The teacher's real salary is the net amount after the required deductions or contributions have been made. Teacher-retirement legislation is not class legislation, because teachers are, in fact, a class set apart by their vocation. Where classifications are based upon real differences and distinctions and operate alike upon all in the same category, there is no local, special, or class legislation. Finally, contributions on the part of the state to a teachers' retirement system do not constitute the expenditure of public funds for private purposes because education is a public purpose and the object to be attained by a pension or teacher-retirement policy is the promotion of the efficiency of the schools.

A few leading cases will serve to illustrate in more detail the reasoning of the courts. In New Jersey all public school teachers employed in the future were required to contribute to the retirement fund. In holding the act constitutional, the court said:

> The argument is that this procedure established by the act constitutes a taking of property of one person and giving it to another, or if the use be considered a public use, then there is a taking of private property without

5. *Trumper* v. *School District No. 55,* 55 Mont. 90, 173 Pac. 946; *State* v. *Levitan,* 181 Wis. 326, 193 N.W. 499; *State* v. *Hauge,* 37 N.D. 583, 164 N.W. 289, L.R.A. 1918A 522; *Allen* v. *Board of Education,* 81 N.J. Law 135, 79 Atl. 101; *Fellows* v. *Connolly,* 193 Mich. 499, 160 N.W. 581.

just compensation. This argument loses sight of the fact that by the terms of the agreement of employment embodying the statutory terms, the salary to be paid was a net amount, and not a gross amount, and that there was in fact no taking.[6]

The act was also attacked upon the ground that it was special legislation, in that teachers employed before its enactment did not have to come under its operation. The court held otherwise. "Where all objects, which can constitutionally be included in a class, are by legislation recognized by inclusion therein, such legislation will be general in the constitutional sense."

The Teachers' Pension Act of Montana provided for monthly deductions from the teachers' salaries, and all teachers employed after the act was passed were required to come under the operation of the act. In holding the act constitutional, the court said in part:

The objections urged to this legislation, so far as they are cognizable by this court, are constitutional in character. They are not very clearly stated, but from the arguments of the appellants' brief we infer the contentions to be that it violates the state Constitution as well as the Fifth and Fourteenth Amendments to the national Constitution. In substance, the provisions thus invoked are: the declaration that all persons possess the inalienable right of acquiring, possessing, and protecting property; the guaranties that no person shall be deprived of life, liberty, or property without due process of law, or be denied the equal protection of the laws; the prohibition against the passage of local or special laws for the management of the common schools; the requirement that taxes shall be uniform and laid by general laws for public purposes. The most cursory examination of the statute thus assailed will disclose that the constitutional propositions insisted upon are inapplicable.

There is no question of taxation involved. The legal relation of the state through its several boards of school trustees with the teachers employed by it is one of contract. It has the right to say upon what terms it will hire or authorize the hiring of persons to teach in its schools. It may, if it sees fit to do so, discriminate in the terms of its contracts upon any basis it chooses to adopt or upon no basis at all. Here it has said to all teachers employed after the approval of the Act:

"Your contract shall have read into it the provisions of this Act; the salary you receive shall in all cases be one dollar per month less than the amount expressed in your contract, that dollar to go into the teachers' pension fund for your benefit when you become entitled to it; you may engage or not upon these terms, just as you like." . . .

Neither, assuming the appellant can raise the question, is there any taking of property from the teachers, with or without due process of law, or any invasion of their right to acquire, possess, and protect property. The

6. *Allen* v. *Board of Education*, 81 N.J. Law 135, 79 Atl. 101.

effect of the Act being as above stated, it results that the salary to be paid is a net amount after the "contributions" or "deductions" prescribed. It is not a gross amount, and thus in fact there is no taking.[7]

A statute may, moreover, provide retirement allowances for teachers already in service, the amount of the allowance to be computed with reference to the entire service of the teacher, before and after enactment of the law. Such a law was enacted by Wisconsin, both the state and the teacher making a contribution to the retirement fund. It was contended that the law, in so far as it affected teachers already in service, appropriated public funds for a private purpose. It was contended, too, that the act granted extra compensation for services already rendered, in violation of the following provisions of the state constitution: "The legislature shall never grant any extra compensation to any public officer, agent, servant or contractor, after the services shall have been rendered or the contract entered into." In denying the validity of both these contentions, the court used the following language:

> Such a contention misconceives the purpose of the law, which is to promote a higher efficiency in the educational system of the state by retaining in service seasoned and experienced teachers. . . .
> If in its judgment the pension system will induce experienced and competent teachers to remain in the service, and that thereby the cause of education will be promoted, the money or funds appropriated for the payment of pensions is appropriated for a public purpose unless the court can say that the pension system will have no such result. This the court cannot do. . . . Whether, so far as teachers in service at the time of the enactment of the law are concerned, it amounts to the granting of extra compensation for service already rendered, in contravention of . . . the Constitution, is a question upon which seemingly few courts have expressly ruled. The only cases cited to our attention in which the question was expressly discussed are *Pennie* v. *Reis*, 80 Cal. 266, 22 Pac. 176; *State* v. *Love*, 89 Neb. 149, 131 N. W. 196, 34 L.R.A. (N. S.) 607, Ann. Cas. 1912C 542. Those cases dealt with laws granting pensions to policemen and firemen, and in both cases it was held that a similar provision did not constitute the granting of extra compensation. . . .
> We do not think it necessarily follows that because the legislature, in its attempts to construct an enduring and efficient pension system, saw fit to base the annuity which teachers already in service are to be awarded in part upon the service rendered prior to the enactment of the law, it was its dominant purpose or intent to award such teachers extra compensation for service already rendered. If the legislature deemed such a provision essential, or even helpful, in winning the cordial cooperation of the most valuable members of the instructional force to the promotion of the suc-

7. *Trumper* v. *School District No. 55*, 55 Mont. 90, 173 Pac. 946.

cessful operation of the scheme by holding out to them an inducement for their continued and devoted service, is it not apparent that the dominant purpose of the provision was to promote the public rather than individual or private welfare, not to grant compensation for prior service but to raise educational standards? . . .

As we view it, the annuity based on past service is not intended to be, or operate as, compensation for past service. It was rather intended to be, and in fact is, an inducement to the seasoned and experienced teacher to remain in the service and give the public the benefit of his experience. We think there was plenty of room for the legislature to determine that the ultimate success of the pension system itself required special consideration of those constituting the educational forces of the state at the time of the enactment of the law, not as compensation for prior service but rather as an inducement to them to remain in the service, to the great benefit of our educational institutions.[8]

In providing funds for teachers' pensions or retirement systems, the legislature may appropriate funds directly from the state treasury, or it may require local districts to make contributions to the state pension fund, or it may apply any fund obtainable for general educational purposes.[9] Such was the position taken by the Supreme Court of North Dakota in a well-reasoned case.[10] A statute of that state provided that the county treasurer should annually set aside from the county tuition fund a sum equal to ten cents for each child of school age in his county and should transmit this sum to the state treasurer to be credited to the state teachers' retirement fund. The act was challenged on the ground that it violated the following provision of the state constitution: "No tax shall be levied except in pursuance of law, and every law imposing a tax shall state distinctly the object of the same, to which only it shall be applied." It was contended that the act in question did not attempt to create a teachers' insurance fund by levying a tax directly for that purpose, but attempted "to reach into a fund created for another purpose to carry out its object." It was contended, too, that the county tuition fund was a local fund, provided for a local purpose, and that when a portion of it was taken for a general purpose, such as the state teachers' insurance and retirement fund, and distributed among teachers throughout the state, such monies were unlawfully diverted. The court overruled all of these contentions:

8. *State v. Levitan,* 181 Wis. 326, 193 N.W. 499.

9. *State v. Kurtz,* 110 Ohio St. 332, 144 N.E. 120; *State v. Hauge,* 37 N.D. 583, 164 N.W. 289.

10. *State v. Hauge,* 37 N.D. 583, 164 N.W. 289, L.R.A. 1918A 522.

It is very clear from a perusal of the whole act that it was not local in its nature nor was education deemed to be local in its nature, but an affair and concern of the whole state. It is also clear that in maintaining the schools and in levying the taxes therefor, the counties and localities are merely acting as agencies of the sovereign state. . . . The statute, in short, is an act of the legislature and not of the locality. It is an exercise of the state taxing power. It furnishes a donation to the respective schools and a fund for common school purposes. Such being the case, there is no reason whatever why a portion of the fund may not be used in the payment of the teachers' pensions, provided that purpose is a general public school purpose; and that the purpose is a public school purpose we have no doubt. . . .

Surely, the providing of a permanent teachers' insurance fund which shall give dignity to the profession, encourage persons to enter it, and provide for old age, is a "provision for the establishment and maintenance of a system of public schools." . . .

It is merely in the nature of an added salary allowance to public servants. If all of the people of the state may be taxed to pay the salaries of the state superintendent of public instruction and the state high school inspector, whose duties are largely to supervise the schools and their teachers, if they may be taxed to support the normal schools and the state universities, which train teachers, they may certainly also be taxed in order to provide a fund which shall increase the efficiency of the teachers themselves, and aid and encourage them to devote their lives to a profession which, though essential to our civilization, has been but poorly encouraged, and has too often been merely looked upon as a stepping stone to other employments.

Nor does the act in any manner violate Section 175 of the Constitution, which provides that "no tax shall be levied except in pursuance to law, and every law imposing a tax shall state distinctly the object of the same, to which only it shall be applied."

The use of a portion of the county-tuition fund for the promotion of the teachers' retirement fund is germane to the general purposes for which the county tuition fund was raised. It was for school purposes. . . . All that the act creating the pension fund does is to state how some of this money shall be used. The granting of pensions is germane to the general purpose of the general act. An exact enumeration of all the items of expenditure to which the revenue of the state may be applied is neither practical nor required by the constitutional provision cited. . . .

Nor, as we have said before, is there any merit in the contention that the residents of one district will be compelled to pay taxes for the support of teachers in another. As was said by Judge Christianson:[11] "We are aware of no constitutional requirement that taxes levied for a general public purpose must be expended and disbursed in the taxing district in which they are collected. If this were true, every department, not only of the state, but also of county government, would soon cease to operate."[12]

In Ohio, on the other hand, a law setting up a fund for the benefit of retired teachers has been held unconstitutional. A statute provided that a certain percentage of teachers' salaries be deducted and credited

11. *State* v. *Taylor*, 33 N.D. 76, 156 N.W. 561.
12. *State* v. *Hauge*, 37 N.D. 583, 164 N.W. 289, L.R.A. 1918A 522.

to the retirement fund. In the opinion of the court this deduction from teachers' salaries constituted the taking of property without due process of law. The court reasoned that money taken from the teachers by virtue of the statute was either taxation for the public good or the taking of money from one person for the benefit of another. If the money raised by deductions from the teachers' salaries be regarded as taxation, the law imposed the burden of taxation upon one class of citizens and thus violated a provision of the constitution which required that taxes be uniform. "A teacher's salary," said the court, "is his property. He has a right, under the Constitution, to use that salary for his own benefit or for the benefit of others, as he sees fit. If he thinks it best to provide for old age, he may do so; but, if he prefers to spend his money as he earns it, it is his right, under the Constitution, to do that."[13]

AUTHORITY OF SCHOOL DISTRICTS TO ESTABLISH RETIREMENT SYSTEMS

School districts may not, it seems, in the absence of statutory authority, deduct portions of teachers' salaries for the purpose of creating a retirement fund. The Board of Education of Minneapolis adopted a rule which required all teachers when employed to enter into a contract whereby they consented to have the board deduct 1 per cent of the monthly salary for the purpose of establishing a pension fund. The court held that the board had no authority to make the rule in the absence of a statute granting such authority. The court reasoned that the effect of the rule would be to compel some teachers to enter into the arrangement without any expectation of receiving any personal benefit therefrom.[14]

VESTED RIGHTS UNDER PENSION AND RETIREMENT LEGISLATION

The authority of the legislature to change a pension or retirement system in so far as it affects teachers who have rendered or are rendering service under it is a question upon which there is a very considerable judicial conflict. The federal constitution prohibits any state from passing legislation which impairs the obligation of contracts. The question is, then, does pension or retirement legislation create a contract between the teacher and the state which the legislature may not subsquently modify without the consent of the teacher?

13. *State* v. *Hibbard*, 22 Ohio Cir. Ct. 252. Affirmed and adopted by the Supreme Court, 65 Ohio St. 574, 58 L.R.A. 654, 64 N.E. 109.

14. *State* v. *Rogers*, 87 Minn. 130, 91 N.W. 430.

Some courts hold that retirement funds for teachers are in the nature of a pension or gratuity which may be modified or abolished at any time; they apply the law governing pensions to teacher-retirement funds. Other courts hold the relation between the teacher and the fund to be contractual in nature and apply to it, as far as possible, the principles of law governing contracts. Whether a teacher-retirement system will be regarded as establishing a pensionary or contractual relationship will depend in part on the wording of the statute; it will depend, too, upon the position taken on such matters by the particular court hearing the case.

Where a statute makes it compulsory upon teachers to have a part of their salary paid into a retirement fund, the courts are divided as to whether a pensionary or a contractual relationship is created between the state and the teacher. A number of courts hold that where teachers are required by law to contribute part of their salary to a retirement fund, a contractual relationship is not established;[15] the teacher in such cases is regarded as having the status of a pensioner. That is to say, the character of a pension fund is not changed by compulsory contributions by way of exactions from the salaries of teachers. The courts which take this position reason that the contributions of teachers to the retirement fund are really not voluntary; that the money contributed to the fund was, in fact, never segregated from other public moneys and paid to individual teachers; that the money said to be contributed by teachers was never theirs to contribute; that, although these contributions are said to be a part of their compensation, the teachers never, in fact, received the money involved or exercised any control over it. What really takes place in such instances, it is said, is that public moneys are merely transferred from one public fund to another. Under such conditions a contractual relationship could not arise.[16]

In some cases it is held that although teachers are required by

15. *Raines* v. *Board of Trustees of Illinois State Teachers' Pension and Retirement Fund*, 365 Ill. 610, 7 N.E. (2d) 489; *Pecoy* v. *City of Chicago*, 265 Ill. 78, 106 N.E. 435; *Pennie* v. *Reis*, 132 U.S. 464, 10 S. Ct. 149; *Clarke* v. *Ireland*, 199 Pac. (2d) (Mont.) 965; *Board of Education of Louisville* v. *City of Louisville*, 288 Ky. 636, 157 S.W. (2d) 737; *Talbott* v. *Independent School District of Des Moines*, 230 Iowa 949, 299 N.W. 536; *State* ex rel. *Parker* v. *Board of Education*, 155 Kan. 754. See annotations 54 A.L.R. 943, 98 A.L.R. 505, 112 A.L.R. 1009, 137 A.L.R. 249.

16. See, however, *Mattson* v. *Flynn*, 216 Minn. 354, which apparently holds that compulsory contributions on the part of teachers create a contractual relationship.

statute to contribute to a retirement fund, a contractual relationship is established between the state and those teachers who elect to come under the operation of the statute. Thus it was said by the Supreme Court of North Dakota:

> When a person becomes a teacher the law makes him a member of the fund and provides for his consent to the assessments and other provisions of the law. His teaching is a compliance therewith. The annuities are in the nature of additional compensation. . . . The relation thus established is in the nature of a contract, the terms of which are contained in the law so accepted by the teacher.[17]

Some courts have ruled, however, that although prior to a teacher's retirement his rights in the retirement fund are inchoate and subject to changes for the improvement and better administration of the fund, after he has completed his payments and retired, a contractual relationship becomes established.[18] And this seems to be true even where the teacher's contribution to the retirement fund is mandatory. Thus it was said by the Supreme Court of Pennsylvania: "Until an employee has earned his retirement pay, or until the time arrives when he may retire, his retirement pay is but an inchoate right; but when the conditions are satisfied, at that time retired pay becomes a vested right of which the person entitled thereto cannot be deprived; it has ripened into a full contractual obligation."[19]

Where a statute sets up a retirement fund for teachers and makes it optional for teachers to come under it and a teacher voluntarily contributes part of her salary to the fund, the statute becomes a contract between the teacher and the state which no subsequent legislature may change.[20] The Supreme Court of Illinois has clearly indicated the distinction which some courts draw between compulsory and voluntary contributions to retirement funds in so far as the rights of teachers are affected:

17. *Payne* v. *Board of Trustees of the Teachers' Insurance and Retirement Fund,* 35 N.W. (2d) 553. See also *State* v. *Blied,* 188 Wis. 442, 206 N.W. 213, in which it was held that pension legislation for teachers constituted a contract.

18. *Crawford* v. *Teachers Retirement Fund,* 164 Ore. 77, 99 Pac. (2d) 729; *Driggs* v. *Utah State Teachers Retirement Board,* 105 Utah 417; *McBride* v. *Retirement Board of Allegheny County,* 330 Pa. 402, 199 Atl. 130; *Board of Education of Louisville* v. *City of Louisville,* 288 Ky. 656, 157 S.W. (2d) 337.

19. *Retirement Board of Allegheny County* v. *McGovern,* 316 Pa. 161, 174 Atl. 400.

20. *Raines* v. *Board of Trustees of Illinois State Teachers' Pension and Retirement Fund,* 365 Ill. 610, 7 N.E. (2d) 489; *Clarke* v. *Ireland,* 199 Pac. (2d) (Mont.) 965; *Ball* v. *Board of Trustees of Teachers' Retirement Fund,* 71 N.J. Law 64, 58 Atl. 111.

There is a wide difference between voluntary contributions to a fund under a statutory elective right and being compelled to suffer deductions without any such right. In the latter case the officer or employee has no voice in determining whether or not he will suffer such exactions. They are imposed by the statute and deducted even if against his will. In the other case it is wholly a matter of choice with him. He may elect to come within the terms of the act and receive its benefits, or he may forego that privilege at his option, with no other effect than to deprive him of participating in the fund. If he does not elect to contribute, he receives and retains the full amount of his salary or wages. If he elects to contribute, the amounts are deducted by his direction. The effect is the same as if his full salary were paid to him and after it became his private means he in turn contributed to the retirement fund. In such case there is neither reason nor authority to hold that the fund remains public money in which he has no right or interest.

Under statutes creating teachers' retirement funds by which it is optional with the teachers to come under their provisions by having a certain sum deducted from their salaries, it is held that the election to participate in the fund raises a contractual relation, the terms of which are ascertained by reference to the statute.[21]

21. *Raines v. Board of Trustees of Illinois State Teachers' Pension and Retirement Fund,* 365 Ill. 610, 7 N.E. (2d) 489.

CHAPTER XIX

School Attendance

COMPULSORY ATTENDANCE

U NDER the English common law a father had almost unlimited control over the education of his child,[1] and in the American colonies the same principle applied until modified by statute.[2] This common-law rule has been superseded, however, in all the states, by compulsory-attendance legislation. The authority of the legislature to pass such legislation has been challenged in a number of cases but has been uniformly sustained.[3] In requiring attendance upon the state schools or others substantially equivalent, the legislature does not confer a benefit upon the parent, or primarily upon the child; it is only doing that which the well-being and safety of the state itself requires.[4]

There are limits, however, to the authority of the state to require attendance at public schools. The Supreme Court of the United States has held that no state has authority to require that children attend public schools exclusively. Such a requirement is a violation of the due-process clause of the Fourteenth Amendment.[5] Whether there is any age limit beyond which school attendance may not be required at any kind of school has not been determined. Conceivably, however, such age limit may exist, for, under the Fourteenth Amendment as interpreted by the Supreme Court of the United States, no state may deprive any person of liberty without due process of law. Should a

1. *Hodges* v. *Hodges,* Peake Add. Cas. 79.

2. *School Board District No. 18* v. *Thompson,* 24 Okla. 1, 103 Pac. 578, 138 Am. St. Rep. 861.

3. *State* v. *Bailey,* 157 Ind. 324, 61 N.E. 730, 59 L.R.A. 435; *State* v. *Jackson,* 71 N.H. 552, 53 Atl. 1021, 60 L.R.A. 739; *Commonwealth* v. *Bey,* 166 Pa. Super. Ct. 136, 70 Atl. (2d) 693.

4. *Bissell* v. *Davison,* 65 Conn. 183, 32 Atl. 348, 29 L.R.A. 251; *State* v. *Bailey,* 157 Ind. 324, 61 N.E. 730, 59 L.R.A. 435; *Fogg* v. *Board of Education,* 76 N.H. 296, 82 Atl. 173, Ann. Cas. 1912C 758, 37 L.R.A. (N.S.) 1110.

5. *Pierce* v. *Society of the Sisters of the Holy Names of Jesus and Mary,* 268 U.S. 510, 45 S. Ct. 571, 69 L. Ed. 1070, 39 A.L.R. 468.

state, therefore, require school attendance for a number of years greater than is reasonably necessary to promote the public welfare, it might be held to have deprived a person of liberty in violation of the Fourteenth Amendment.

The law requiring compulsory attendance must be reasonably enforced. Parents can always set up the defense that their child was kept out of school for sufficient reasons, the sufficiency of the reason being a matter to be determined in court.[6] Thus illness on the part of a child is always a perfect defense. In New Hampshire, as an illustration, a statute provided that children between certain ages should attend school all the time that school was in session unless excused by the school board. The court held that a parent whose child was ill was not required to apply to the board for an excuse.[7] Similarly, it has been held that where a child lives such a distance from school as to make it unreasonable to require that the child walk to school, attendance cannot be required unless transportation is provided.[8] And where a child could not attend a particular school without crossing railroad tracks under such conditions as to endanger its life, attendance could not be required at that particular school.[9]

Some cases have come into the courts involving the authority of school boards to require married girls still within the compulsory school age to attend school. The courts commonly hold that the marriage relationship, regardless of the age of the persons involved, creates conditions and imposes obligations inconsistent with compulsory school attendance.[10]

Occasionally parents prefer not to send their children to a school in the popular sense of the term. It may be that a tutor is employed, or the mother or father may undertake to teach the child at home. Under such circumstances, the question may arise: Does home instruction of this kind meet the requirements of a statute making attendance at a public, private, or parochial school compulsory? As a rule, a parent

6. *Directors of School District No. 302* v. *Libby*, 135 Wash. 233, 237 Pac. 505; *In re Richards*, 7 N.Y.S. (2d) 722, 255 App. Div. 922.

7. *State* v. *Jackson*, 71 N.H. 552, 53 Atl. 1021, 60 L.R.A. 739.

8. *State* v. *Hall*, 74 N.H. 61, 64 Atl. 1102; *In re Richards*, 7 N.Y.S. (2d) 722, 255 App. Div. 922.

9. *Williams* v. *Board of Education*, 79 Kan. 202, 99 Pac. 216, 22 L.R.A. (N.S.) 584.

10. *State* v. *Priest*, 210 La. 389, 27 So. (2d) 173; *In re State in Interest of Goodwin*, 214 La. 1062, 39 So. (2d) 731.

who gives his child substantially the same education he would be able to get in the public schools fulfils the requirements of the compulsory-attendance law.[11] It is the policy of the state that children be educated, not that they be educated in any particular way or in any particular place. The character of the endeavor, it is said, is the determining factor, for numbers do not make a place any more or less a school. A case in point is that of *State* v. *Peterman*.[12] A parent, who had some difficulty with the school authorities, took his child out of the public schools and had a woman teach the child at the regular school hours all the branches taught in the public schools. The woman who undertook to do the teaching had been a public school teacher. She did not have any other children in her "school," did not hold herself out as conducting a private school, had no fixed tuition fees and no school equipment. The statutes provided that children should attend either a public, private, or parochial school. In the opinion of the court the parent had obeyed the law:

> A school, in the ordinary acceptation of its meaning, is a place where instruction is imparted to the young. If a parent employs and brings into his residence a teacher for the purpose of instructing his child or children, and such instruction is given as the law contemplates, the meaning and spirit of the law have been fully complied with. This would be the school of the child or children so educated, and would be as much a private school as if advertised and conducted as such. We do not think that the number of persons, whether one or many, makes a place where instruction is imparted any less or more a school. . . .
>
> The result to be obtained, and not the means or manner of attaining it, was the goal which the lawmakers were attempting to reach. The law was made for the parent who does not educate his child, and not for the parent who employs a teacher and pays him out of his private purse, and so places within the reach of the child the opportunity and means of acquiring an education equal to that obtainable in the public schools of the state.

A parent who assumes the responsibility of providing his child with educational facilities outside a regularly organized school may be called upon to show that those facilities are substantially equivalent to the facilities afforded by the state.[13] "Whether such independent facilities for education, outside of the public schools, are supplied in

11. *State* v. *Peterman*, 32 Ind. App. 655, 70 N.E. 550; *Commonwealth* v. *Roberts*, 159 Mass. 372, 34 N.E. 402; *Wright* v. *State*, 21 Okla. Cr. 430, 209 Pac. 179; *People* v. *Levisen*, 404 Ill. 574, 90 N.E. (2d) 213.

12. *State* v. *Peterman*, 32 Ind. App. 655, 70 N.E. 550.

13. *Wright* v. *State*, 21 Okla. Cr. 430, 209 Pac. 179; *People* v. *Levisen*, 404 Ill. 574, 90 N.E. (2d) 213.

good faith, and whether they are equivalent to those afforded by the state, is a question of fact for the jury, and not a question of law for the court."[14] In view of the fact that association with other children is such a vital part of the education of a child, it might be plausibly argued that no form of purely individual instruction is equivalent to the education afforded in the public schools. Such, indeed, is the position taken by the courts in New Jersey and Washington. In the New Jersey case the court found that parents who were attempting to teach their children at home were inadequately qualified and were not, in fact, properly teaching their children. Then the judge who wrote the opinion went on to say:

I incline to the opinion that education is no longer concerned merely with the acquisition of facts, that the instilling of worthy habits, attitudes, appreciations, and skills is far more important than mere imparting of subject-matter. . . . Education must impart to the child the way to live. This brings me to the belief that, in a cosmopolitan area such as we live in, with all the complexities of life, and our reliance upon others to carry out the functions of education, it is almost impossible for a child to be adequately taught in his home. I cannot conceive how a child can receive in the home instruction and experiences in group activity and social outlook in any manner or form comparable to that provided in the public school.

Similarly, in a case decided by the Supreme Court of Washington, a parent kept his children out of school and undertook to teach them himself. It seems that he made no serious effort to give the children substantially the same instruction which they would have received in the public schools, for at all hours of the day they could be seen playing around the house and yard. The court held that the children were not attending a private school within the meaning of the law:

We have no doubt many parents are capable of instructing their own children, but to permit such parents to withdraw their children from the public schools without permission from the superintendent of schools, and to instruct them at home, would be to disrupt our common school system and destroy its value to the state. . . . We do not think that the giving of instruction by a parent to a child, conceding the competency of the parent to fully instruct the child in all that is taught in the public schools, is within the meaning of the law "to attend a private school." Such a requirement means more than home instruction; it means the same character of school as the public school, a regular, organized and existing institution making a business of instructing children of school age in the required studies and for the full time required by the laws of this state. . . . The parent who teaches his children at home, whatever be his reason for desiring to do so, does not maintain such a school.[15]

14. *Wright* v. *State*, 21 Okla. Cr. 430, 209 Pac. 179.
15. *State* v. *Counort*, 69 Wash. 361, 124 Pac. 910, 41 L.R.A. (N.S.) 95.

It is well settled that a parent may send his child to a private school,[16] but in such case the parent may be called upon to show that the child has been properly and sufficiently instructed. In a Massachusetts case,[17] for example, the law provided that all children between certain ages should attend a public or private school approved by the school committee. A father insisted upon sending his child to a school which the committee would not approve. The court held that the father was acting within his rights, provided that he could show that the private school in question was, in fact, an efficient school. The object of the compulsory-attendance law, it was said, was that children be educated, not that they be educated in any particular way. If it could be shown that the child already knew, or was being sufficiently taught, the branches of learning required by law, the requirements of the compulsory-attendance act had been met.

Where the statutes provide that attendance shall begin with the beginning of the school year and continue for a designated number of weeks, a parent who does not send his child to school may not set up the defense that he intends later to send the child to a private school for a term during the year sufficient to meet the requirements of the law.[18] In order for the parent to escape the penalty of the law, the child must be in attendance at some school at the opening of the school year.

Where the law requires that a child attend school until he has attained a certain age, the child will be required to attend school until that age is reached, regardless of scholastic achievement. Moreover, the child must attend a school, if one is provided, where instruction is given suitable to his attainments. That is, age, and not attainment, is the test to apply in determining whether a child is required to attend school. In Indiana, for example, a statute required that children between the ages of fourteen and sixteen who were not regularly employed should attend either a public or a private school. The question arose as to whether an unemployed eighth-grade graduate under the age of fourteen could be required to attend the high school. The court held that the child could be required to attend the high school, inasmuch as the high school was merely a part of the common-school sys-

16. *Pierce* v. *Society of the Sisters of the Holy Names of Jesus and Mary,* 268 U.S. 510, 45 S. Ct. 571, 69 L. Ed. 1070, 39 A.L.R. 468.

17. *Commonwealth* v. *Roberts,* 159 Mass. 372, 34 N.E. 402.

18. *State* v. *McCaffrey,* 69 Vt. 85, 37 Atl. 234.

tem.[19] Similarly, in the case of *Miller* v. *State*,[20] a statute provided that children should attend school between the ages of seven and sixteen. A child under sixteen who had finished the eighth grade was sent by her father to an elementary school in an adjoining township. She was refused admission. Action was brought against the father for a violation of the compulsory-attendance law. An excerpt from the opinion of the court follows:

The course of study to be pursued in the public schools of our state is prescribed either by statute or by the school authorities in pursuance thereof. These schools include not only elementary schools, but high schools as well. . . . A parent, therefore, is not at liberty to exercise a choice in that regard, but, where not exempt for some lawful reason, must send his child to the school where instruction is provided suitable to its attainments as the school authorities may determine, which under the facts found in the instant case is the township high school.

AUTHORITY OF LEGISLATURE TO PRESCRIBE
AGE OF SCHOOL ATTENDANCE

Many state constitutions make it the duty of the legislature to establish a school system free and open to all the children of the state between certain ages. Whether such constitutional provisions are a limitation upon the authority of the legislature to provide educational facilities for kindergarten and preschool children or for adults is a question of no little practical importance. As has been pointed out previously, it is well established that a state legislature may enact any legislation which is not prohibited by the state or federal constitution. As a rule, a constitutional mandate to establish a school system is not interpreted to be a limitation upon the authority of the legislature. The legislature should do at least as much as the constitution requires; it may do more.[21] Thus it was said by the Supreme Court of New Jersey:

The objection that the school law provides for the education of children between the ages of five and twenty years, while the Constitution requires the Legislature to provide for the instruction of children between five and eighteen only, does not appeal to me with any force. There is nothing in the

19. *State* v. *O'Dell*, 187 Ind. 84, 118 N.E. 529.

20. *Miller* v. *State*, 77 Ind. App. 611, 134 N.E. 209.

21. *In re Newark School Board*, 70 Atl. (N.J.) 881; *In re Kindergarten Schools*, 18 Colo. 234, 32 Pac. 422, 19 L.R.A. 469; *Commonwealth* v. *Hartman*, 17 Pa. St. 118; *State Female Normal School* v. *Auditors*, 79 Va. 233. See, however, *Roach* v. *Board of President and Directors of St. Louis Public Schools*, 77 Mo. 484.

Constitution to forbid the Legislature from providing for better school facilities than the Constitution itself requires.[22]

Similarly, in a Colorado case,[23] the constitution made it the duty of the legislature to establish a system of schools "wherein all residents of the state, between the ages of six and twenty-one years, may be educated gratuitously." In holding that the legislature might authorize the establishment of kindergartens as a part of the public school system, the court said:

And we understand that such doubt is as to whether the language of this section limits the power of the legislature to establish any free schools other than therein specifically mentioned. The rule of construction to be applied to our constitution is announced in *Alexander* v. *People,* 7 Colo. 155, as follows: "The legislature being invested with complete power for all the purposes of civil government, and the state constitution being merely a limitation upon that power, the court will look into it, not to see if the act in question is authorized, but only to see if it is prohibited."

Unless, therefore, the constitution, in express terms or by necessary implication limits it, the legislature may exercise its sovereign power in any way that, in its judgment, will best serve the general welfare. Read in the light of this rule of interpretation, and the wise and liberal policy of the state in educational matters, the section is clearly mandatory, and requires affirmative action on the part of the legislature to the extent and in the manner specified, and is in no measure prohibitory or a limitation of its power to provide free schools for children under six years of age, whenever it deems it wise and beneficial to do so.

RIGHT OF ATTENDANCE AS AFFECTED BY RESIDENCE

It is often difficult to determine what constitutes residence within the meaning of statutes which confer the right to attend school upon all children of certain ages who are residents of a district. Much depends, of course, upon the wording of the statutes in each particular case. But where the statutes do not clearly show the legislative intent, the court may follow a strict interpretation and hold that the child must have a legal domicile in the district; on the other hand, the court may take a more liberal position and hold that a legal domicile is not necessary, that "residence" in the statutory sense means living in or residing in the district in the popular sense. All courts are agreed, however, that the domicile of the child is the domicile of the parent.

Right of attendance of children who are separated from their parents. —According to one line of decisions, a child who lives in a school dis-

22. *In re Newark School Board,* 70 Atl. (N.J.) 881.
23. *In re Kindergarten Schools,* 18 Colo. 234, 32 Pac. 422, 19 L.R.A. 469.

trict other than that in which the parent has a domicile is not entitled to attend the public schools without the payment of tuition.[24] In an Indiana case,[25] for example, the statutes provided that the trustee of the township should establish "a sufficient number of schools for the education of the children therein." In commenting upon the meaning of the statute, the court said:

> This [the statute], literally construed, would embrace all children who might be within the township at the time such schools were established, or such enumeration was made. We are not, however, inclined to adopt that construction. The whole enactment plainly intends that the children who reside, or are domiciled in the township in which such enumeration is made, are alone entitled to participate in the benefit of the common schools therein established.

Consequently, it was held that a child whose parents resided in Tennessee could not attend the public schools of the Indiana township free of tuition, notwithstanding the fact that she lived in Indiana under the control of her brother.

In a case decided by the Court of Appeals of Kentucky, a statute provided that no child whose parents resided beyond the city limits of the city of Winchester should be permitted to attend the public schools except on payment of such tuition fees as the board of education might require. Another section of the statute restricted free school attendance to such children as were bona fide residents of the city. A child whose parents resided in Virginia made her home with her uncle in Winchester. The uncle had agreed with the child's parents to board, clothe, and educate her and to treat her in every way as a member of his family as long as she desired. Notwithstanding this agreement, the court held that the child was not a bona fide resident of the Winchester school district, and could not, therefore, attend the public schools free of tuition.[26]

Most courts, however, and the more recent decisions, hold that, for the purpose of school attendance, it is not necessary that a child be able to establish a legal domicile in the district. Ordinarily, a child is entitled to attend the schools of the district in which he is living, pro-

24. *Wheeler v. Burrow*, 18 Ind. 14; *Board of Education v. Foster*, 116 Ky. 484, 3 Ann. Cas. 692; *Mansfield Township Board of Education v. State Board of Education*, 101 N.J. Law 474, 129 Atl. 765; *Binde v. Klinge*, 30 Mo. App. 285; *Smith v. Binford*, 44 Idaho 244, 256 Pac. 366.

25. *Wheeler v. Burrow*, 18 Ind. 14.

26. *Board of Education v. Foster*, 116 Ky. 484, 3 Ann. Cas. 692.

vided that he is living there for some other purpose than to take advantage of the schools.[27] The older decisions seemed to give special consideration to the rights of the taxpayer; the more recent decisions take into consideration the rights of the child and the policy of the state that all children be educated. Under modern social conditions, children are often inevitably separated from their parents; to deny them the right to attend the public schools free of tuition would often mean that this class of children would be denied the schooling which the state deems it necessary that all should have.

A New York case is illustrative of the reasoning of the courts which take the more liberal view. A child was placed by a charitable institution in a home, where it was treated as a member of the family. The institution paid for the child's board and clothes. At the time of the death of the child's parents, they were not residents of the district in which the child's home was later situated, nor was the charitable institution domiciled there. The statutes provided that the common schools should be free to certain designated children "residing in the district." The court held that the child had a right to attend the public schools free of tuition:

It is probably true that Wisbauer did not have a domicile in the Huntington Union school district in the technical meaning of that term. Domicile in that sense is the actual or constructive presence of a person in a given place, coupled with the intention to remain there permanently. A minor can not exercise an independent intent in this matter. A minor can have no domicile other than that of a parent or guardian, and, where both parents are dead, the domicile of the minor continues to be that of the last surviving parent. To construe the word "residence," as used in the school law, as synonymous with the word "domicile," and to give it the narrow and technical meaning of the latter word, would seriously impair the usefulness of that law, and would defeat various provisions of the statute.[28]

27. *People* v. *Hendrickson*, 104 N.Y.S. 122 (affirmed, 196 N.Y. 551, 90 N.E. 1163); *Mt. Hope School District* v. *Hendrickson*, 197 Iowa 191, 197 N.W. 47; *State* v. *Thayer*, 74 Wis. 48, 41 N.W. 1014; *Public Schols of City of Muskegon* v. *Wright*, 176 Mich. 6, 141 N.W. 866; *Morrison* v. *Smith-Pocahontas Coal Company*, 88 W. Va. 158, 106 S.E. 448; *Board of Education* v. *Lease*, 64 Ill. App. 60; *Mizner* v. *School District No. 11*, 2 Neb. (Unoff.) 238, 96 N.W. 128; *McNish* v. *State*, 74 Neb. 261, 104 N.W. 186, 12 Ann. Cas. 896; *State* v. *Clymer*, 164 Mo. App. 671, 147 S.W. 1119; *Yale* v. *West Middle School District*, 59 Conn. 489, 22 Atl. 295, 13 L.R.A. 161; *Board of Trustees* v. *Powell*, 145 Ky. 93, 140 S.W. 67; *Fangman* v. *Moyers*, 90 Colo. 308, 8 Pac. (2d) 762; *Anderson* v. *Breithbarth*, 62 N.D. 709, 245 N.W. 483; *City of New Haven* v. *Town of Torrington*, 132 Conn. 194, 43 Atl. (2d) 455; *Cline* v. *Knight*, 111 Colo. 8, 137 Pac. (2d) 680, 146 A.L.R. 1281.

28. *People* v. *Hendrickson*, 104 N.Y.S. 122 (affirmed, 196 N.Y. 551, 90 N.E. 1163).

A well-reasoned and frequently cited case decided by the Supreme Court of Wisconsin is to the same general effect. A wife was deserted by her husband, who left her a number of children to support. She secured a position as a teacher in Milwaukee but was unable to establish a permanent home for all her children. For one of the children a home was secured with a doctor, a resident of the village of Waukesha, Wisconsin. The school board of that village refused the child admission to the schools free of tuition. On appeal to the state superintendent of public instruction, it was held that the child had the right to attend the school of the district free of charge. In the course of his opinion, the superintendent said:

> In the incidents of human life families are broken up and must be scattered by the necessities of obtaining a livelihood, by death of one or both parties, or by abandonment of offspring, as in this case. Such children, as all others, are the wards of the state to the extent of providing for their education to that degree that they can care for themselves and act the part of intelligent citizens. To secure these ends, laws relating to public schools must be interpreted to accord with this dominant, controlling spirit and purpose of their enactment, rather than in the narrower spirit of their possible relations to questions of pauperism and administration of estates.

The foregoing opinion of the superintendent was sustained by the court in the following words:

> The contention of the learned counsel is that a minor child who has a father or mother, or both, living, can have no residence for the purpose of the privileges of a public school different from the residence of the father, if living, and of the mother after the death of the father. While this may be the general rule, we think it clear that the statute above referred to . . . clearly contemplated exceptions to the general rule. . . . When the minor has poor parents, the poverty of the parents renders it absolutely necessary, in many cases, that a home for the minor children should be found in a place different from that of the parents; and under the construction insisted upon by the learned counsel of the relator, such unfortunate children, for whose benefit our free schools were especially instituted, would be deprived of all benefit of them. Such construction of the law would be against its beneficent spirit and should not prevail unless the language is so clear that no other can be given to it.[29]

It is clear from the cases cited and discussed in the preceding paragraphs that the great weight of authority is to the effect that a child who is living in a district with some friend, relative, or guardian has the right to attend free of charge the public schools of the district. It is not essential, in most jurisdictions, that the child have a legal domicile

29. *State* v. *Thayer*, 74 Wis. 48, 41 N.W. 1014.

in the district. The rule is different, however, where a child is sent into a school district for the primary purpose of having him attend the schools of the district. In such cases, the courts are agreed that the child has no right to attend the public schools without the payment of tuition.[30]

A New Jersey case[31] illustrates the rule. A girl whose home in New York had been broken up by the separation of her parents was sent by her father to a finishing school maintained by a Miss Towner in New Jersey. After finishing Miss Towner's school, the girl attempted to enter the local high school, but admission was denied unless she paid tuition. On appeal, the court held that the school board was acting within its rights. The child was not a domiciliary resident of the school district, which, in the opinion of the court, was necessary to entitle her to attend the public schools:

> The term "a resident," in a broad sense, includes any person who comes into this state and remains here with the intention to make it his permanent abode. But this legal status is not applicable to a child who is brought or sent into this state by a parent or guardian who is a non-resident, for the purpose of receiving an education in the public schools of this state. The permanent residence of the father is that of the child, until the latter is emancipated and chooses a place of residence of its own.

Much the same conclusion was reached in a case decided by the Supreme Court of Kansas.[32] The father of a family lived on a farm outside the school district of the town of Lecompton. His wife owned two lots and a home in the town of Lecompton. She spent the summer on the farm with her husband and children, but just before school opened in Lecompton she went with her children to live in her home there. She lived in Lecompton most of the time but usually spent the week ends with her husband on the farm. The court held the children were not residents for school purposes of the school district of Lecompton. The residence of the wife and the children was that of the father on the farm.

30. *Mansfield Township Board of Education* v. *State Board of Education*, 101 N.J. Law 474, 129 Atl. 765; *Milton School District No. 1* v. *Bragdon*, 23 N.H. 507; *Horowitz* v. *Board of Education*, 216 N.Y.S. 646; *People* v. *Board of Education*, 26 Ill. App. 476; *State* ex rel. *School District No. 1* v. *School District No. 12*, 45 Wyo. 365, 18 Pac. (2d) 1010; *Sulzen* v. *School District No. 36*, 144 Kan. 648, 62 Pac. (2d) 880.

31. *Mansfield Township Board of Education* v. *State Board of Education*, 101 N.J. Law 474, 129 Atl. 765.

32. *Sulzen* v. *School District No. 36*, 144 Kan. 648, 62 Pac. (2d) 880.

Right of inmates of orphanages and charitable institutions to attend the public schools.—There is some conflict of authority with respect to the right of inmates of orphanages and charitable institutions to attend the public schools of the district in which the institution is located. In some states, notably Michigan, Ohio, Pennsylvania, and Vermont, it has been held that inmates of such institutions are residents of the district in which they have their legal domicile, that is, the domicile of their parents, or last surviving parent. Accordingly, a child living in an orphanage or charitable institution does not have the right to attend the public schools of the district free of charge.[33] If the child attends such a school, his tuition must be paid by the institution or by the district in which he has his domicile.

In Vermont the statutes provided that a town might unite with other towns for the maintenance of a poorhouse. The school law provided that a town might arrange to have its school children attend the schools of another town. The various towns of Sheldon County supported their pauper children in a poorhouse located in the town of Sheldon. In a case decided in 1900 by the Supreme Court of Vermont,[34] it was held that the children living in the poorhouse whose domicile was outside the town of Sheldon had no right to attend the schools of the town of Sheldon without the payment of tuition. The children were still residents of the towns which supported them: "The atmosphere of the latter town, in legal effect, envelops the pauper as fully and thoroughly as if the pauper was kept in the town liable for its support." Consequently, the town of Sheldon was under no legal obligation to provide educational opportunities for children supported by other towns.

The charter of a charitable association in Pennsylvania provided that the object of the association was to be "the care, support, education, and spiritual good of poor and needy children." A statute required the directors of public schools to establish "a sufficient number of public schools for the education of every individual between the ages of six and twenty-one years, in their respective districts." In the

33. *Lake Farm* v. *District Board of School District No. 2*, 179 Mich. 171, 146 N.W. 115, 51 L.R.A. (N.S.) 234; *Commonwealth* v. *Directors of Upper Swatara Township School District*, 164 Pa. St. 603, 30 Atl. 507, 26 L.R.A. 581; *Commonwealth* v. *Brookville Borough School District*, 164 Pa. St. 607, 30 Atl. 509, 26 L.R.A. 584; *Sheldon Poor House Association* v. *Sheldon*, 72 Vt. 126, 47 Atl. 542; *State* v. *Sherman*, 104 Ohio St. 317, 135 N.E. 625; *State* v. *Eveland*, 117 Ohio St. 59, 158 N.E. 169.

34. *Sheldon Poor House Association* v. *Sheldon*, 72 Vt. 126, 47 Atl. 542.

opinion of the court,[35] the inmates of the institution maintained by the association had no right to attend the schools of the district in which the institution was located. The court pointed out that a child under the care and custody of the association could not acquire common-school privileges distinct from those which belonged to him in the place of his residence when he was taken from it. Moreover, the association had taken children into its custody with the avowed purpose of caring for them and giving them an education. Its inability to perform its charter duties with respect to the children under its control could not have the effect of placing any responsibility upon the local school district:

> There is no warrant in our common school system for the contention that an institution like the Children's Industrial Association of Harrisburg may bring into any district it pleases the poor and needy children of other districts for the purpose of maintenance and education in conformity with its charter and thereby impose on the district to which it has brought them a duty it assumed in the acceptance of them. . . . Such a construction would result, in some cases, in a denial to the children of the district of the school facilities it was intended they should have therein. It would impose on some districts burdens they could not maintain.

The reasoning of the court in the case discussed in the preceding paragraph finds support in a case decided by the Supreme Court of Michigan.[36] The facts in the two cases were very much the same, and the two courts reached the same conclusion.

In most cases, on the other hand, it has been held that children who are inmates of an orphanage or charitable institution may attend the public schools of the district in which the orphanage or institution is located.[37] In West Virginia, for example, the Independent Order of

35. *Commonwealth* v. *Upper Swatara Township School District,* 164 Pa. St. 603, 30 Atl. 507, 26 L.R.A. 581.

36. *Lake Farm* v. *District Board of School District No. 2,* 179 Mich. 171, 146 N.W. 115, 51 L.R.A. (N.S.) 234.

37. *Ashley* v. *Board of Education,* 275 Ill. 274, 114 N.E. 20; *Logsdon* v. *Jones,* 311 Ill. 425, 143 N.E. 56; *Grand Lodge, etc.* v. *Board of Education,* 90 W. Va. 8, 110 S.E. 440; *School District No. 2* v. *Pollard,* 55 N.H. 503; *Crain* v. *Walker,* 222 Ky. 828, 2 S.W. (2d) 654; *Salem Independent School District* v. *Kiel,* 206 Iowa 967, 221 N.W. 519; *State ex rel. Board of Christian Service of Lutheran Minnesota Conference* v. *School Board of Consolidated School District No. 3,* 206 Minn. 63, 287 N.W. 625; *Dean* v. *Board of Education of School District No. 89,* 386 Ill. 156, 53 N.E. (2d) 875; *School Township 76 of Muscatine County* v. *Nicholson,* 227 Iowa 290, 288 N.W. 123; *State ex rel. Johnson* v. *Cotton,* 67 S.D. 63, 289 N.W. 71; *Mariadahl Children's Home* v. *Bellegrade School District,* 163 Kan. 49, 180 Pac. (2d) 612; *Wirth* v. *Board of Education for Jefferson County,* 262 Ky. 291, 90 S.W. (2d) 62; *Board of Education of Louisville* v. *Board of Education for Jefferson County,* 265 Ky. 447, 97 S.W. (2d) 11.

Odd Fellows maintained a home near Elkins for the care and support of the orphans of its deceased members. The statutes provided that the public schools should "be open to all youths between the ages of six and twenty-one for the full length of the school term provided in their district." In granting a writ of mandamus requiring the school board of Elkins to admit to the schools of the district the children living in the orphanage, the court used the following language:

> The residence required under our school law is not such as would be required to establish a right to vote, or which would fix liability of a city or county for the support of a pauper, or for the purpose of determining the rights of administration of his estate. The right to attend school is not limited to the place of the legal domicile. A residence, even for a temporary purpose, in a school district, is sufficient to entitle children to attend school there. . . . The only requirement, so far as residence is concerned, is dwelling in the school district. Every child of school age in this state is entitled to attend the public schools in the district in which it actually resides for the time being, whether that be the place of its legal domicile, or the legal domicile of the parents or guardian, or not.[38]

Under an Illinois statute which provided that the public schools should be free to all "persons in the district over the age of six and under twenty-one years," it was held on two occasions that the inmates of an orphans' home had the right to attend free of tuition the public schools of the district in which the home was located.[39] Similarly, in New Hampshire, children who are inmates of a poorhouse are entitled to admission to the schools of the district in which the poorhouse is located.[40]

Right of children to attend school while residing with their parents temporarily in a school district.—Under most statutes, a child whose parents are residing temporarily in a school district has the right to attend the public schools. That is, as a rule, in order that a child may have the right to attend school, it is not necessary that his parents should have established a domicile in the district.[41] It is sufficient if

---

38. *Grand Lodge, etc. v. Board of Education,* 90 W. Va. 8. 110 S.E. 440.

39. *Ashley v. Board of Education,* 275 Ill. 274, 114 N.E. 20; *Logsdon v. Jones,* 311 Ill. 425, 143 N.E. 56.

40. *School District No. 2 v. Pollard,* 55 N.H. 503.

41. *Lisbon School District No. 1 v. Landaff Town School District,* 75 N.H. 324; *School District No. 1 Fractional of Mancelona Township v. School District No. 1 of Custer Township,* 236 Mich. 677, 211 N.W. 60; *State v. Selleck,* 76 Neb. 747, 107 N.W. 1022. *State ex rel. Board of Christian Service of Lutheran Minnesota Conference v. School Board of Consolidated School District No. 3,* 206 Minn. 63, 287 N.W. 625. See, however, *Smith v. Binford,* 256 Pac. (Idaho) 366.

they are living in the district for other purposes than to take advantage of the public schools. In the case of *State* v. *Selleck*,[42] as an illustration, the children of the governor of Nebraska were excluded from the public schools of Lincoln until their tuition should be paid. The governor was living in Lincoln during his term of office, but he retained his domicile in the district of his former residence. The statutes provided that the public schools should be open to all children of certain ages whose parents "lived" within the limits of the school district. The court held that the father of the children in question was living in the Lincoln school district in the statutory sense and that the children should be admitted to school free of tuition.

One other case may be cited in this connection. A farmer in New Hampshire sold his farm and moved his family to the town of Lisbon. He was undecided as to his future residence, but he lived in Lisbon from the autumn of 1905 until the spring of 1907. While living in Lisbon, he maintained his domicile in the place of his former residence. The court held, nevertheless, that his children had the right to attend the public schools in Lisbon. The court pointed out that under the statutes every person "residing in a school district" in which a public school was annually taught was subject to a fine for failure to send to school the children under his custody and control. "If the legal domicile of the child," said the court, "in some town other than that in which it was actually living were an answer to a prosecution under this section, the purpose of the statute would be defeated."[43]

It is well settled, on the other hand, that a parent who moves into a school district primarily for the purpose of putting his children in the public schools will be required to pay tuition for the instruction of his children.[44] In a New York case,[45] by way of illustration, a farmer rented a house in a town near his farm and moved his family into it, taking along sufficient household goods to keep house but leaving the rest of his furniture in the house on the farm. The children attended

42. *State* v. *Selleck*, 76 Neb. 747, 107 N.W. 1022.

43. *Lisbon School District No. 1* v. *Landaff Town School District*, 75 N.H. 324.

44. *Barnard School District* v. *Matherly*, 84 Mo. App. 140; *Board of Education* v. *Crill*, 134 N.Y.S. 311; *Gardner* v. *Board of Education*, 5 Dak. 259, 38 N.W. 433; *State* v. *Board of Education*, 96 Wis. 95, 71 N.W. 123. See also *Mt. Hope School District* v. *Hendrickson*, 197 Iowa 191, 197 N.W. 47; *Grand Lodge, etc.* v. *Board of Education*, 90 W. Va. 8, 110 S.E. 440; *State* v. *Selleck*, 76 Neb. 747, 107 N.W. 1022.

45. *Board of Education* v. *Crill*, 134 N.Y.S. 311.

school in the town during the winter term, but, when the school closed in the spring or early summer, the furniture in town was stored and the family moved back to the farm for the summer. In the following autumn the family returned to the town and the children re-entered school. Action was brought to require the father to pay tuition for the two years his children were in school. The court said, in holding that the father was liable for the payment of the tuition demanded: "It is very clear that his only purpose in living in Holland Patent was to send his children to school there, intending to return to the farm when that object had been attained. . . . Here, I think, the children, as well as the father, were not residents of the Holland Patent school district, and I think we should so hold as a matter of law."

Right of attendance of nonresident pupils.—In many states the statutes provide that, under certain conditions, pupils living in one school district may attend school in another. Such statutes usually apply to pupils in whose home district no high school is maintained or to pupils who can be accommodated more conveniently in some neighboring district. The right to attend school in a district other than that of the pupil's residence may be made to depend upon the consent of the board of education of the home district and of the district to which the child seeks to be transferred. Or it may be that the pupil can be transferred only upon the consent of some other school officer, such as the county superintendent of schools. The right of a pupil to attend school in some district other than that in which he resides being purely statutory, the pupil can have no greater or lesser rights than those conferred by statute. The fact that parents of children own property in a school district or conduct a business in the district is immaterial in determining the right of the children to attend school in the district.[46]

Where the statutes provide for the transfer of pupils from one district to another for purposes of school attendance, the home district is usually required to pay the tuition of pupils thus transferred. Under some statutes, the tuition is a fixed charge; under others, it is the per pupil cost of school maintenance in the district to which the pupil is transferred.

The constitutionality of legislation providing for the transfer of

46. *Cape Girardeau School District No. 63* v. *Frye*, 225 S.W. (2d) (Mo.) 484; *Logan City School District* v. *Kowallis*, 94 Utah 342, 77 Pac. (2d) 348.

pupils from one district to another has been attacked in a number of cases. In general, the contention has been that such legislation requires the taxpayers of one district to bear the burden of educating the children of another district, thus violating the principle of uniformity of taxation. The law on this question is not well established. Where the home district is required to bear its full share of the burden, no more and no less, of educating its pupils in the district to which they are transferred, neither district has any right to complain. But where the burden is unequally distributed between the two districts, the courts are in disagreement as to the legality of the procedure. According to one line of decisions, a statute is constitutional, even though it may require the district to which pupils are transferred to bear a disproportionate part of the burden of their education.[47] The reasoning underlying these decisions is that, education being a public and not a local function, a school district may be required to contribute to the education of children who live without its corporate limits. In order to maintain an efficient state school system, it may be necessary, it is said, to apply funds raised in one district to the schooling of children who live in another.

The reasoning of the courts which take this position is well illustrated in a case decided by the Supreme Court of Indiana. A statute of that state provided that under certain conditions pupils should be entitled to attend the schools of a district other than that in which they resided. The school tax upon the property of parents whose children were transferred was to be paid to the school district in which the children attended school. The state school tax was to be distributed upon the basis of enumeration. Childern were to be enumerated in the district where they attended. The city of Peru refused to receive children transferred to it from other districts because the per pupil cost of the public schools in Peru, including interest on bonds and a sinking fund for their liquidation, was fifteen dollars greater per pupil than the amount which would have been received per pupil by reason of transfers. In issuing a writ of mandamus compelling the admission of the pupils sought to be transferred, the court said:

47. *Edwards v. State,* 143 Ind. 84, 42 N.E. 525; *Edmondson v. Board of Education,* 108 Tenn. 557, 58 L.R.A. 170. See also *City of Columbus v. Town of Fountain Prairie,* 134 Wis. 593, 115 N.W. 111; *Butler v. Compton Junior College District of Los Angeles County,* 176 Pac. (2d) (Calif.) 417; *Independent School District No. 6 v. Common School District No. 38,* 64 Idaho 303, 131 Pac. (2d) 786.

The school system is a State system, established in compliance with the requirements of . . . the constitution, . . . which makes it the duty of the Legislature "to provide for a general and uniform system of common schools, where tuition shall be without charge and equally open to all." . . .

It is not material, therefore, whether or not the school city received as much or more money on account of said transfers from Pike Creek township than the expenses *per capita* of the pupils transferred from that township. The question of profit or loss has nothing whatever to do with the question, or its determination by the school officers or the courts.[48]

The Supreme Court of Tennesse has taken even a stronger position. It has held that a school district may be required to admit nonresident pupils entirely free of tuition. In 1899 the corporate limits of the city of Memphis were greatly extended. At the same time, a statute was enacted which provided that children living within one-half mile of the city limits should have the right to attend the schools of the city free of charge. The act was attacked on the ground that it deprived the Board of Education of Memphis of property contrary to the law of the land, and that its effect was to appropriate municipal funds to other than a corporate purpose. In denying both contentions, the court pointed out that the board of education was a public corporation subject to legislative control. Being such, its powers and responsibilities might be added to or taken away at the pleasure of the legislature. Moreover, the board depended largely for the maintenance of its schools upon sources of income found outside the limits of the school district. Finally, the court rested its opinion upon the consideration that a local purpose might be accomplished outside local corporate limits. In reaching its conclusions, the court said:

Even if the city of Memphis alone furnished the funds for the maintenance of its public schools, it would not necessarily follow that there was a violation of the implied inhibition of this clause of the Constitution [prohibiting the appropriation of municipal funds to other than a corporate purpose] in granting without pay, the privileges of these schools to children living just outside its limits, but located conveniently thereto. In the words of the Constitution, "knowledge, learning, and virtue being essential to the preservation of republican institutions," it might very well be held that it was as conducive to good order and public morals of the community of Memphis that the opportunities and advantages of education afforded by these municipal schools should be availed of by children just beyond, as well as those within, the municipal borders. For it has been held that there may be a corporate purpose, within the provision of this clause, though accomplished outside of local limits.[49]

48. *Edwards* v. *State*, 143 Ind. 84, 42 N.E. 525.

49. *Edmonson* v. *Board of Education*, 108 Tenn. 557, 58 L.R.A. 170.

There are other decisions, however, and they seem to represent the weight of authority, which hold that a school district cannot be required to admit nonresident pupils to its schools unless the home district bears a proportionate share of the cost of school maintenance.[50] To hold otherwise, it is said, would work a violation of the principle of uniformity of taxation. In Nebraska, for example, a statute provided that the high schools of the state should be open to all pupils whose education could not profitably be carried further in the district of their residence. It was further provided that the county board of education of the county in which nonresident pupils lived should pay to the high-school district in which the pupils attended school seventy-five cents per week for each pupil attending. The court held that the statute violated a clause in the constitution which provided for uniformity of taxation. It said:

> For the purposes of this case, assume that the seventy-five cents per week allowed to be collected by the act, from the county generally, be insufficient to meet the expenses of educating the non-resident pupils in a given high school district, it is plain this difference must be made good by levying and collecting taxes on the property of the tax payers resident in the school district, and this difference can not be collected from tax payers of the whole county. Then the tax payers within the school district will pay a greater proportion of these taxes than would those residing within the county, but outside the school district, and while the valuation of the property of those within the school district and those without it might be uniform, yet the rate of taxation, for the same purpose, would be higher on the property within, than upon that without the school district. Again, assume that the seventy-five cents per week exceeds the cost of tuition of such non-resident pupils, then the excess would accrue to the high school districts, and the tax payers thereof would profit at the expense of those outside of the limits of the high school district, and, in either case, the rule of uniformity prescribed in section 6 of said article of the constitution would be violated.[51]

The Court of Civil Appeals of Texas has taken much the same position. A statute provided that pupils in whose district there was no high school might attend some high school outside the district. The home district was to pay the tuition of the nonresident pupil. On this point the statute read: "The rate of tuition charged said pupil shall

50. *City of Dallas* v. *Love*, 23 S.W. (2d) (Tex.) 431; *Todd* v. *Board of Education*, 54 N.D. 235, 209 N.W. 369; *High School District No. 137* v. *Lancaster County*, 60 Neb. 147; *Town of Belle Point* v. *Pence*, 17 S.W. (Ky.) 197. See also *Irvin* v. *Gregory*, 86 Ga. 605, 13 S.E. 120; *Wilkinson* v. *Lord*, 85 Neb. 136, 122 N.W. 699, 24 L.R.A. (N.S.) 1104; *Board of Education* v. *Haworth*, 274 Ill. 538, 113 N.E. 939; *Proviso Township High School District No. 209* v. *Oak Park & River Forest Township High School District No. 200*, 322 Ill. 217, 153 N.E. 369.

51. *High School District No. 137* v. *Lancaster County*, 60 Neb. 147.

be the actual cost of teaching service, based upon the average monthly enrollment in the high school attended, exclusive of all other current or fixed charges, not to exceed $7.50 per month." The cost of high-school instruction in the Dallas high schools was between twelve and thirteen dollars per month for each pupil in attendance. The court held that the statute violated a provision in the state constitution which required uniformity of taxation. Moreover, it violated the Fourteenth Amendment, in that it deprived the taxpayers of the Dallas school district of property without due process of law:

We do not think it can be correctly said that the Legislature has the authority to impose taxes on property within an independent school district for the express purpose of furnishing high school facilities and instructional service to students of other districts, and yet that result is precisely what the provisions of this statute would accomplish, if executed. This result can neither be attained directly, nor accomplished indirectly. . . .

We are of opinion, therefore, that the necessary effect of the objectional provisions of the statute is to impose local tax burdens, and to deprive taxpayers of said districts of property without due process of law to furnish education to students of other districts. Therefore we hold that the statute, in so far as it attempts to coerce high school districts by forcing them without voice or hearing to furnish, at local expense, educational facilities and service to nonresident high school students at less than actual costs, is in contravention of the constitutional provision . . . that guarantees equality and uniformity in taxation, and section 19, art. 1, that prohibits any citizen from being deprived of property except by due course of the law of the land.[52]

A later case decided by the Supreme Court of Oregon is squarely in point with the Texas case.[53]

Right of attendance of pupils living on federally owned or partially owned projects.—Pupils living in territory under the exclusive jurisdiction of the United States government do not, it has been held, have the right to attend the public schools of the community free of tuition.[54] The Court of Appeals of Ohio denied a writ of mandamus to compel a board of education to admit to its schools pupils living on a federally owned project. It said:

The Federal government is without authority to colonize a portion of the territory within a school district for the duration (which we must assume) in furtherance of the war effort and then the government and the residents

52. *City of Dallas* v. *Love*, 23 S.W. (2d) (Tex.) 431. Confirmed by the Supreme Court in *Love* v. *City of Dallas*, 120 Tex. 351, 40 S.W. (2d) 20.

53. *Smith* v. *Barnard*, 142 Ore. 567, 21 Pac. (2d) 204.

54. *Opinion of Justices*, 42 Mass. 580; *State* ex rel. *Moore* v. *Board of Education of Euclid City School District*, 57 N.E. (2d) (Ohio) 118.

of this project, or either, expect to compel free school service or school service for a contribution in amount much less than the cost to others.

The Board is not obliged to furnish school service to residents of this project, known as "Lake Shore Village," except such as were residents of Euclid prior to the establishment of this "village." School service should be furnished upon receipt of tuition for them in an amount comparable to the cost of such service to other resident pupils, measured by the standard of uniform taxation, as fixed by Ohio laws for all residents.[55]

The federal government may, however, acquire the use of land for some federal purpose, such as slum clearance and low-cost housing projects, without acquiring exclusive jurisdiction. As the Supreme Court of the United States put it:

> We know of no constitutional principle which compels acceptance by the United States of an exclusive jurisdiction contrary to its own conception of its interests. The mere fact that the Government needs title to property within the boundaries of a State, which may be acquired irrespective of the consent of the state (*Kohl* v. *United States*, 91 U.S. 367, 23 Law Ed. 449), does not necessitate the assumption by the Government of the burdens incident to an exclusive jurisdiction. . . . In acquiring property the Federal function in view may be performed without disturbing the local administration in matters which may still appropriately pertain to state authority.[56]

In an Ohio case it was held that the acquisition by the federal government of land, on which were located slum-clearance projects for low-income families and war housing projects did not result in the ouster of state jurisdiction and loss of territorial control under state law. Consequently, the court refused to issue an injunction restraining the Board of Education of the City of Cleveland from permitting children residing in the federal housing projects to attend schools of the city free of tuition.[57] It should be pointed out that, under the Lanham Act, payments were made to the city in lieu of taxes. Similarly, in Nebraska, where the federal government had not obtained exclusive jurisdiction over land purchased with federal funds for a farmstead project over which both the state and federal governments had some

55. *State* ex rel. *Moore* v. *Board of Education of Euclid City School District,* 57 N.E. (2d) (Ohio) 118.

56. *Silas Mason Company* v. *Tax Commission,* 302 U.S. 186, 58 S. Ct. 233, 82 L. Ed. 187. See also *James* v. *Dravo Construction Company,* 302 U.S. 134, 58 S. Ct. 208, 82 L. Ed. 155.

57. *McGwinn* v. *Board of Education of Cleveland City School District,* 69 N.E. (2d) (Ohio) 381.

measure of control, children living on the project were entitled to attend the public schools free of tuition.[58]

Authority of school board to require attendance at a particular school.—As a rule, the statutes authorize boards of education to determine what particular school a pupil shall attend. So long as the board acts reasonably and does not abuse its discretion, a pupil must attend the school to which he is assigned.[59] Where a school board in good faith assigns a pupil to a school in the promotion of the best interests of education as it conceives it, its discretion will not be overruled by the courts.[60] It is not necessary that a child be assigned to the school most conveniently located for his attendance,[61] but a child cannot be required to attend a school so situated as to jeopardize the life of the child in approaching it[62] or so far removed from the residence of the child as to make the distance an unreasonable one to walk.[63]

AUTHORITY OF SCHOOL BOARD TO REJECT APPLICANTS FOR ADMISSION TO SCHOOL

School attendance is a privilege which the state confers upon its youth; the only right a child has to school attendance is the right which the state confers upon all other children similarly situated. Since attendance at the state schools is essentially a privilege and not a right, the state may authorize its agents to exclude all children who do not meet the requirements established by the state. Consequently, a school board usually has the implied power to reject applicants for admission who do not conform to the reasonable and necessary requirements established by the board. Thus it has been said by the Supreme Judicial Court of Massachusetts:

58. *Tagge* v. *Gulzow,* 132 Neb. 276, 271 N.W. 803.

59. *Freeman* v. *Franklin Township,* 37 Pa. St. 385; *People* v. *Board of Education,* 26 Ill. App. 476; *State* ex rel. *Lewis* v. *Board of Education of Wilmington School District,* 137 Ohio St. 145, 28 N.E. (2d) 496.

60. *State* ex rel. *Lewis* v. *Board of Education of Wilmington School District,* 137 Ohio St. 145, 28 N.E. (2d) 496.

61. *Williams* v. *Board of Education,* 79 Kan. 202, 99 Pac. 216, 22 L.R.A. (N.S.) 584.

62. *Williams* v. *Board of Education,* 79 Kan. 202, 99 Pac. 216, 22 L.R.A. (N.S.) 584.

63. NOTE: Ann. Cas. 1912A 375.

The law provides that every town shall choose a school committee, who shall have the general charge and superintendence of all the public schools in such town. . . . The general charge and superintendence, in the absence of express legal provisions, includes the power of determining what pupils shall be received and what pupils rejected. The committee may, for good cause, determine that some shall not be received, as, for instance, if infected with any contagious disease, or if the pupil or parent shall refuse to comply with regulations necessary to the discipline and good management of the school.[64]

In a later case the same court ruled that a school committee might refuse to admit to the public schools a girl who had been guilty of immoral conduct.[65] Similarly, school authorities may deny admission to pupils who are so physically unclean as to render them unfit for association in decent society. And in South Dakota, it has been held that a board of education has the implied authority to require a physical examination of all pupils as a condition of admission to school.[66]

The Supreme Court of Kansas has ruled that a board of education has the authority to require graduates of private and parochial elementary schools to pass an examination as a condition of entrance to the public high schools. The court reasoned that it was necessary for the board of education to determine in some way whether a pupil was qualified to do the work of the high school. In the case of pupils coming from the public elementary schools of the state, the board could assume without an examination that the pupils were properly qualified. Such schools are under state control and supervision and are reasonably well standardized. But the case is different with respect to private and parochial schools. Over these the state exercises no right of control or supervision. Consequently, the school board had the right to require an examination of pupils coming from private and parochial schools in order to determine the grade of work for which they were qualified.[67] The court, moreover, went so far as to say, by way of dicta, that the school board had authority to require graduates of public schools other than its own to pass an examination of admission to the high school.

64. *Spear* v. *Cummings*, 23 Pick. (Mass.) 224, 34 Am. Dec. 53.

65. *Sherman* v. *Charlestown*, 8 Cush. (Mass.) 160.

66. *Streich* v. *Board of Education*, 34 S.D. 169, 147 N.W. 779, L.R.A. 1915A 632, Ann. Cas. 1917A 760.

67. *Creyhon* v. *Board of Education*, 99 Kan. 824, 163 Pac. 145, L.R.A. 1917C 993. See also *Kayser* v. *Board of Education*, 273 Mo. 643, 201 S.W. 531.

AUTHORITY TO CLASSIFY PUPILS ON BASIS
OF SCHOLARSHIP

Under its general authority of school management, a board of education may assign a pupil to such grade in the public schools as the previous scholastic record of the pupil warrants. Moreover, the determination of the work which a pupil is prepared to do is an educational matter over which the board has final jurisdiction unless it acts arbitrarily and unreasonably. The case of *Barnard* v. *Shelburne*[68] is an excellent illustration of the principle. The school board of the village of Shelburne adopted a rule that any pupil in the high school standing below 60 per cent in two or more subjects should be demoted one grade. In the case of Freshmen, the deficient pupil was to be dropped from the roll of the school. A pupil in the Freshman class fell below the required standard and was suspended from school with the suggestion that he enter the eighth grade of the public school of the same village. In an action for damages for illegal exclusion from school, the court sustained the action of the board. The court said in part:

The care and management of schools, vested in the school committee, includes the establishment and maintenance of standards for the promotion of pupils from one grade to another and for their continuance as members of any particular class. So long as the school committee act in good faith their conduct in formulating and applying standards and making decisions touching this matter is not subject to review by any other tribunal. It is obvious that efficiency of instruction depends in no small degree upon this feature of our school system. It is an educational question, the final determination of which rests by law in the public officers charged with the performance of that important duty. . . .

When the real ground for exclusion from a particular school or grade is failure to maintain a proper standard of scholarship and there is opportunity afforded to the pupil to attend another school adapted to his ability and accomplishments, there is no illegal exclusion from school within the meaning of the statute.

Much the same position has been taken by the Supreme Court of Ohio.[69] The Board of Education of Sycamore adopted a rule that promotions should be made upon the approval of the board and with the recommendation of the teacher and the superintendent. A pupil completed the work of the fifth grade when eight years of age and was

68. *Barnard* v. *Shelburne*, 216 Mass. 19, 102 N.E. 1095, Ann. Cas. 1915A 751.

69. *Board of Education* v. *Wickham*, 80 Ohio St. 137, 88 N.E. 412.

given a certificate of promotion to the sixth grade. During the summer vacation the pupil studied under a competent tutor. When the school opened in the autumn, the pupil entered the room of the seventh grade without the knowledge of the superintendent or the board. When the superintendent discovered that the pupil was in the seventh grade, he directed him to go to the sixth-grade room. This the pupil refused to do but left school instead. The father of the pupil in question brought action for a writ of mandamus to compel the board to admit the child to the seventh grade. There was considerable conflict in the evidence concerning the ability of the child to do the work of the seventh grade. The circuit court ordered the superintendent of schools in another place to examine the child to determine the nature of the work he was prepared to do. This superintendent found the child competent to do the work of the seventh grade. Certain other teachers were of the same opinion. The superintendent of schools of Sycamore, however, maintained that the child was not competent to do the work of the seventh grade, and the teacher who had the child in the fifth grade testified that he was not competent to enter the seventh grade at the time school closed in the spring. On the evidence disclosed, the circuit court ordered that the child be admitted to the seventh grade. On appeal, the supreme court reversed the opinion of the circuit court. The case turned upon the fact that no application had been made to the board to promote the child to the seventh grade. The court intimated, however, that it is not the function of the courts to control the discretion of school boards in such matters:

The complaint in the present case is that the application of some of these rules to this pupil worked an injustice, in that it denied him the right secured by Section 4013, Revised Statutes, to freely enter the school of the district, and thereby deprived him of a right of promotion which because of his advanced proficiency he was entitled to enjoy, viz.: to be promoted from the fifth to the seventh grade on the ground of merit. But who is empowered to judge of the merit and the proficiency? Is it the father of the child or the school authorities? The trial court seems to have assumed that, in the first instance it is the father, and finally the court. If the father in the first instance had not the right to determine the matter and direct his boy to refuse to go to the sixth grade room to which the school authorities had promoted him, but go to the seventh grade room and insist on remaining there, it is difficult to see how the court could have any power to interfere when asked to deal with a situation in which a parent undertook to do as in this case, viz.: override the school authorities in the management of the school. . . . The boy may have been qualified. Indeed it appears from the whole case that the pupil was mentally a precocious boy. Whether it was best for the boy that he be thus crowded we need not inquire, though that consideration is sought to be impressed upon us pro and con. People, including educators, differ respecting the comparative harm likely to come to a child by untoward cramming and crowding on one hand, or, on the other hand, being kept back in his studies, with the probable resulting opportunity to acquire a habit of idling and wasting time, and will probably continue to differ to the end of time. As yet no better solution of the problem seems to have been made than to leave its determination to the parents, who presumably have more than any others the good of the child at heart. But though this conclusion be accepted it would not justify the claim on the part of the parent to insist upon his way in the face of contrary opinion and decision on the part of the school authorities.

AUTHORITY TO EXCLUDE PUPILS FOR REFUSING TO PAY TUITION AND INCIDENTAL FEES

Where the constitution of a state requires the legislature to establish a system of free public or common schools, a statute authorizing boards of education to charge tuition of resident pupils is, of course, unconstitutional.[70] In an Arkansas case,[71] for example, a statute authorized a special school district to charge tuition fees. The board of education established free elementary schools but attempted to charge tuition of high-school pupils. The court held the statute unconstitutional:

If they did not have sufficient funds, the directors had the authority to limit the common schools to the lower grades; but the Legislature, under our Constitution, could not vest the directors with the power to establish a high school and charge tuition therefor. It could only vest the directors with power to control and manage the common schools, and could vest them with authority to establish schools of lower grades and also high schools, which might be free to all persons between the ages of six and twenty-one years; but it could not give the directors power to charge tuition either in the lower grades or the high school to persons who were entitled to tuition free.

A matriculation fee is essentially a tuition fee and cannot be charged where either the constitution or the statutes require the maintenance

70. *Special School District No. 65* v. *Bangs,* 144 Ark. 34, 221 S.W. 1060; *Irvin* v. *Gregory,* 86 Ga. 605, 13 S.E. 120. See also *State* v. *Wilson,* 221 Mo. App. 9, 297 S.W. 419. And, of course, under such constitutional requirements local boards of education cannot charge tuition fees of resident pupils. See also *Dowell* v. *School District No. 1,* 250 S.W. (2d) (Ark.) 127; *Batty* v. *Board of Education,* 67 N.D. 6, 269 N.W. 49; *Morris* v. *Vandiver,* 164 Miss. 476, 145 So. 228.

71. *Special School District No. 65* v. *Bangs,* 144 Ark. 34, 221 S.W. 1060. See also *Young* v. *Fountain Inn Graded School,* 64 S.C. 131, 41 S.E. 824.

of a free school system.[72] A writ of mandamus will issue to require the school authorities to admit a pupil without the payment of the required fee. In a school district in Georgia, for example, the school funds were exhausted, but in order to keep the school open for a period of nine months, it was decided to charge a matriculation fee of three dollars. In the opinion of the court the school continued to be a public school. The school authorities, therefore, had no right to require a matriculation fee in violation of a constitutional provision that the schools should be free.[73]

It is well established that school authorities may not, under statutes providing for the maintenance of a free school system, require pupils to pay incidental fees to be used in paying teachers' salaries, in extending the school term, or in supporting the school in general.[74] Fees of this kind are essentially tuition fees. Thus in Alabama a writ of mandamus was issued requiring a board of education to readmit a pupil who had been excluded from school for refusing to pay a monthly fee required of all pupils in attendance. A part of the income from the fees was to be employed in paying the teacher's salary and in extending the school term. The court said: "Of course, a rule fixing a reasonable incidental fee and requiring it to be paid on the first day of each month will be upheld by the courts. This discretion as to incidental fees which is lodged in school boards must be reasonably exercised, and a school board will not be permitted to exact tuition from a pupil of a public school under the guise of a mere incidental fee."[75]

In another case decided by the same court, a pupil was expelled for refusing a pay a fee of one dollar a month, the fee to be used, in part at least, in supplementing the teacher's salary. The court held that the teacher was answerable in damages to the pupil, notwithstanding the fact that in expelling the pupil he had been acting under the direction of the school board.[76]

A school board may, on the other hand, impose a reasonable incidental fee to be used in providing water, light, heat, and such neces-

72. *Wilson* v. *Stanford,* 133 Ga. 483, 6 S.E. 528; *Claxton* v. *Stanford,* 160 Ga. 752, 128 S.E. 887; *Brewer* v. *Ray,* 149 Ga. 596, 101 S.E. 667; *Brinson* v. *Jackson,* 168 Ga. 353, 148 S.E. 96.

73. *Claxton* v. *Stanford,* 160 Ga. 752, 128 S.E. 887.

74. *Roberson* v. *Oliver,* 189 Ala. 82, 66 So. 645; *Williams* v. *Smith,* 192 Ala. 428, 68 So. 323.

75. *Roberson* v. *Oliver,* 189 Ala. 82, 66 So. 645.

76. *Williams* v. *Smith,* 192 Ala. 428, 68 So. 323.

sary supplies as brooms and pails.[77] Thus in an Alabama case school trustees exacted of each pupil an incidental fee of thirty-five cents to be used in providing wood and water for the school. A pupil who had been expelled for refusing to pay the fee brought action for damages against the trustees. Although the court conceded that, under the statutes, tuition should be absolutely free, it sustained the action of the trustees in exacting the fee. It was said by the court:

> We think, however, there is a well-defined distinction between tuition and a reasonable incidental fee for heating and lighting the schoolroom. And when the statute makes no provision for a fund for this purpose, the county boards have the right to prescribe a reasonable method for the raising and collection of this fund, and to delegate the authority to the district boards and teachers to enforce said rules.[78]

AUTHORITY TO EXCLUDE PUPILS FROM SCHOOL BECAUSE OF MENTAL OR PHYSICAL DEFECTS

The right to attend the public schools is not absolute. No pupil has the right to attend if his presence in the school impairs its efficiency or interferes with the rights of other pupils. Consequently, it has been held that a pupil who is mentally or physically defective may be excluded from school.[79] A case decided by the Supreme Court of Wisconsin illustrates the reasoning of the courts. A pupil in attendance at a public school was afflicted with a form of paralysis which affected his whole physical and nervous system. He did not have the normal use of his voice, hands, feet, or body. He was slow and hesitating in speech. It was difficult for him to make himself understood. His speech was accompanied with uncontrollable facial contortions. He had an uncontrollable flow of saliva, which drooled from his mouth on to his clothing and books, causing him to present an unclean appearance. It was claimed that his condition produced a depressing and nauseating effect upon both teacher and pupils, that by reason of his physical condition he took up an undue portion of the teacher's time and attention, distracted the attention of the other pupils, and interfered generally with the discipline and progress of the school. The child seemed

77. *Kennedy* v. *County Board of Education*, 214 Ala. 349, 107 So. 907; *Ryan* v. *Sawyer*, 195 Ala. 69, 70 So. 652; *Bryant* v. *Whisenant*, 167 Ala. 325, 52 So. 525; *State* v. *Regents of University*, 54 Wis. 159, 11 N.W. 472.

78. *Bryant* v. *Whisenant*, 167 Ala. 325, 52 So. 525.

79. *Watson* v. *City of Cambridge*, 157 Mass. 561, 32 N.E. 864; *State* v. *Board of Education*, 169 Wis. 231, 172 N.W. 153. See also *West* v. *Board of Trustees of Miami University and Miami Normal School*, 41 Ohio App. 367, 181 N.E. 144.

to be normal mentally and made fair progress in his studies. The board of education transferred him from the regular day school to a school "for the instruction of deaf persons or persons defective in speech." Action was brought to require the school board to reinstate the boy in the regular day school. The court refused to require the child's reinstatement, saying in part:

The right of a child of school age to attend the public schools of this state cannot be insisted upon when its presence therein is harmful to the best interests of the school. This, like other individual rights, must be subordinated to the general welfare. . . .

The duty confronting the school board was a delicate one. It was charged with the responsibility of saying whether this boy should be denied a constitutional right because the exercise of that right would be harmful to the school and to the pupils attending the same. He should not be excluded from the schools except for considerations affecting the general welfare. But if his presence in school was detrimental to the best interests of the school, then the board could not, with due regard to their official oaths, refrain from excluding him, even though such action be displeasing and painful to them. The record convinces us that the board took this view of the situation and considered the question with the highest motives and with a full appreciation of its responsibility. There is no suggestion that any of the members were prompted by bad faith or considerations of ill will. The action of the board in refusing to reinstate the boy seems to have been the result of its best judgment exercised in good faith and the record discloses no grounds for the interference of courts with its action.[80]

The reasoning in the foregoing case finds support in a case decided by the Supreme Judicial Court of Massachusetts.[81] A pupil was excluded from school "because he was too weak-minded to derive profit from instruction." Moreover, the child was unable to take decent physical care of himself. Further, he annoyed other children by pinching them and by making uncouth noises. The court not only sustained the authority of the board to exclude the pupil under the existing state of facts but refused to submit to a jury the determination of the existence of the facts. The court said:

Whether certain acts of disorder so seriously interfere with the school that one who persists in them, either voluntarily or by reason of imbecility, should not be permitted to continue in the school, is a question which the statute makes it their duty to answer, and if they answer honestly in an effort to do their duty, a jury composed of men of no special fitness to decide educational questions should not be permitted to say that their answer is wrong.

80. *State* v. *Board of Education*, 169 Wis. 231, 172 N.W. 153.

81. *Watson* v. *City of Cambridge*, 157 Mass. 561, 32 N.E. 864.

RACE SEGREGATION IN THE PUBLIC SCHOOLS

In the very early case of *Roberts* v. *City of Boston*[82] the court ruled that it was constitutional to segregate Negro pupils for purposes of school attendance, provided that they were afforded substantially the same educational opportunities extended to white pupils. Apparently, this was the beginning of the doctrine of "separate but equal." This doctrine came to be widely accepted and applied by state courts, both North and South. It made its first appearance in the Supreme Court of the United States in the famous case of *Plessy* v. *Ferguson*.[83] In that case, the court applied the doctrine, not to education but to transportation. Later, a number of cases involving racial segregation in schools and colleges came before the Supreme Court of the United States, but it was able to decide them without resolving the issue whether segregation of Negro pupils in and of itself was a violation of the Fourteenth Amendment. That issue came squarely before the court in the case of *Brown et al.* v. *Board of Education of Topeka*.[84]

In reaching its decision, the court considered the circumstances surrounding the adoption of the Fourteenth Amendment in 1868 with the purpose of finding the intent of those who adopted the amendment. It found the evidence inconclusive. Moreover, the court was profoundly influenced by what it regarded as the necessity of keeping the law abreast with the changing conditions of American life. It appeared to be more influenced by what it regarded as changing social fact than by the intent of those who adopted the amendment or by previous judicial precedent. It said:

In approaching this problem, we cannot turn the clock back to 1868 when the Amendment was adopted, or even to 1896 when *Plessey* v. *Ferguson* was written. We must consider public education in the light of its full development and its present place in American life throughout the Nation. Only in this way can it be determined if segregation in public schools deprives these plaintiffs of the equal protection of the laws.

Today, education is perhaps the most important function of state and local governments. Compulsory school attendance laws and the great expenditures for education both demonstrate our recognition of the importance of education to our democratic society. It is required in the performance of our most basic public responsibilities, even service in the armed forces. It is the very foundation of good citizenship. Today it is a principal instrument in awakening the child to cultural values, in preparing him for later professional training, and in helping him to adjust normally to his environment.

82. 59 Mass. 198.

83. 163 U.S. 537.   84. 347 U.S. 483.

In these days, it is doubtful that any child may reasonably be expected to succeed in life if he is denied the opportunity of an education. Such an opportunity, where the state has undertaken to provide it, is a right which must be made available to all on equal terms.

We come then to the question presented: Does segregation of children in public schools solely on the basis of race, even though the physical facilities and other "tangible" factors may be equal, deprive the children of the minority group of equal educational opportunities? We believe that it does. . . .

To separate them [Negro children] from others of similar age and qualifications solely because of their race generates a feeling of inferiority as to their status in the community that may affect their hearts and minds in a way unlikely ever to be undone. . . .

We conclude that in the field of public education the doctrine of "separate but equal" has no place. Separate educational facilities are inherently unequal. Therefore, we hold that the plaintiffs and others similarly situated for whom the actions have been brought are, by reason of the segregation complained of, deprived of the equal protection of the laws guaranteed by the Fourteenth Amendment. This disposition makes unnecessary any discussion whether such segregation also violates the Due Process clause of the Fourteenth Amendment.[85]

In view of the complex problems presented by the formulation of the decrees, the cases were restored to the docket for argument of the parties. The court will formulate its decrees after hearing of further arguments. The policies the court will adopt to carry its decision into practical operation remain to be seen.

85. In *Bolling et al.* v. *Sharpe et al.*, 347 U.S. 497, decided the same day, the court held that the due process-of-law clause of the Fourteenth Amendment was violated by segregation in the District of Columbia.

CHAPTER XX

Transportation of Pupils to and from School

LEGISLATIVE AUTHORITY TO PROVIDE TRANSPORTATION

LEGISLATION authorizing school officers to provide facilities for the transportation of pupils to and from school has been attacked on the ground that it is class legislation, in that it confers special rights and privileges on some and withholds the same rights and privileges from others. The courts, however, have uniformly sustained the authority of the legislature to enact such legislation.[1]

In Tennessee a statute authorized county boards of education to provide transportation for pupils whenever a sufficient number lived too far from school to attend without transportation. The county boards were authorized to exercise their discretion in determining whether transportation should be provided for children living in isolated communities. That is, a board could provide transportation for pupils living in compact communities and deny transportation to pupils in cases where isolated families resided so far away from school that it would be impracticable to furnish transportation. The court held that the act in question was not special or class legislation, because any citizen might bring himself within the operation of the law. The law operated equally upon all in the same category or class. Those parents who lived in out-of-the-way places could secure transportation for their children by moving into more compact communities.[2] Similarly, in Mississippi, it has been held that an act providing for the consolidation of schools and the transportation of pupils is not violative of the uniformity of the educational system.[3]

1. *Cross* v. *Fisher*, 132 Tenn. 31, 177 S.W. 43, Ann. Cas. 1916E 1092; *Bufkin* v. *Mitchell*, 106 Miss. 253, 63 So. 458, 50 L.R.A. (N.S.) 428; *Pasadena City High School District* v. *Upjohn*, 206 Calif. 775, 276 Pac. 341.

2. *Cross* v. *Fisher*, 132 Tenn. 31, 177 S.W. 43, 43 Ann. Cas. 1916E 1092.

3. *Bufkin* v. *Mitchell*, 106 Miss. 253, 63 So. 458, 50 L.R.A. (N.S.) 428.

AUTHORITY OF BOARDS OF EDUCATION TO
PROVIDE TRANSPORTATION

According to the weight of authority, a school board may not spend public funds to provide transportation for pupils unless authorized to do so by specific statutory enactment.[4] A case decided by the Supreme Court of Arkansas illustrates the reasoning of the courts:

While the directions of the statute are in general terms, we find no language authorizing the expenditures of the school funds which is susceptible of a construction which would authorize the purchase or operation of automobiles for the purpose of conveying the pupils to the school, and, so far as we are advised, no statute similar to ours has been so construed. . . .

The Legislature has enumerated the purposes for which revenues may be spent, and as no authority is given to expend money in the transportation of children, we must hold that no such authority exists.[5]

Similarly, in Michigan a statute authorized school boards "To do all things needful and necessary for the maintenance, prosperity, and success of the schools of the district and the promotion of the thorough education of the children thereof." In holding that the statute did not authorize school boards to provide transportation, the court said:

In our opinion "the promotion of the thorough education of the children" as found in the statutes does not authorize the expenditure of money to taxi children to and from school. An examination of the statute involved does not expressly make such a grant, nor is it essential to the purposes of education. It must then follow that, when these expenditures were made by the school districts in 1933, 1934, and 1935, the school boards exceeded their authority.[6]

In a number of jurisdictions, on the other hand, the courts have held that, under broad statutory powers, boards of education have implied authority to provide transportation.[7]

Thus the Supreme Court of Florida reasoned that "the employment of persons to transport pupils to and from the central public schools

4. *Mills* v. *School Directors of Consolidated District No. 552*, 154 Ill. App. 119; *Hendrix* v. *Morris*, 127 Ark. 222, 191 S.W. 499; *State* ex rel. *Beard* v. *Jackson*, 168 Ind. 384, 81 N.E. 62; *State* v. *Cruzan*, 20 Kan. 316, 243 Pac. 329; *Shanklin* v. *Boyd*, 146 Ky. 460, 142 S.W. 1041, 38 L.R.A. (N.S.) 710; *Township School District of Bates* v. *Elliott*, 276 Mich. 575, 268 N.W. 744; *Costigan* v. *Hall*, 249 Wis. 94, 23 N.W. (2d) 495.

5. *Hendrix* v. *Morris*, 127 Ark. 222, 191 S.W. 949.

6. *Township School District of Bates* v. *Elliott*, 276 Mich. 575, 268 N.W. 744.

7. *People* v. *Graves*, 153 N.E. (N.Y.) 49; *Foster* v. *Board of Education*, 131 Kan. 160, 289 Pac. 959; *Williams* v. *Board of Public Instruction for Holmes County*, 133 Fla. 624, 182 So. 837; *Homestead Bank* v. *Best*, 174 S.C. 522, 178 S.E. 143. See also *Sherbert* v. *School District*, 169 S.C. 191, 168 S.E. 391.

is an implied power vested in the County Board of Public Instruction by reason of the necessity which the centralization of schools imposed."[8]

Likewise, in New York, it has been held that authority to consolidate school districts carries with it, by implication, authority to provide transportation. In holding that the commissioner of education might require union free school districts to provide transportation, the court said:

> The Education Law permits the formation of small school districts into a union free school district, and, once the formation of such a district has taken place, the board of education therein is given broad powers to the end that "all of the children" of the district may "be educated." If a board of education is derelict in its duty in this respect, or refuses or neglects to carry out the object for which the district has been formed, the commissioner, under the Education Law, is clothed with power to compel action.[9]

Similarly, it has been held by the Supreme Court of Kansas that a board of education has the implied authority to expend tax moneys for transportation of undernourished children to special schools.[10]

Where school officers have authority to provide transportation of pupils, they must do so in strict conformity with the statutes. The school busses may not be used for other purposes. Thus it has been held that school busses could not be used legally to transport pupils to athletic contests between schools, to moving picture shows, and to picnics. Neither could they be used to transport teachers to teachers' institutes and conventions.[11]

CONTRACTS FOR THE TRANSPORTATION OF PUPILS

In some instances the statutes authorize local boards of education to enter contracts for the transportation of pupils to and from school. And in such instances, as a rule, the contract must be let to the lowest responsible bidder. In determining the responsibility of a bidder, the official discretion of a board will not be controlled by the courts, unless it is abused. In letting contracts of this kind, boards may and should take into consideration many elements other than pecuniary

8. *Williams* v. *Board of Public Instruction for Holmes County,* 133 Fla. 624, 182 So. 837.

9. *People* v. *Graves,* 153 N.E. (N.Y.) 49.

10. *Foster* v. *Board of Education,* 131 Kan. 160, 289 Pac. 959.

11. *Schmidt* v. *Blair,* 203 Iowa 1016, 213 N.W. 593.

ability.[12] Where, however, a board abuses its discretion, the courts will interfere. In a Mississippi case, for example, a contract to convey pupils to and from school was let to an eighteen-year-old boy whose right leg had been cut off near his body. Although the boy's bond was signed by two solvent securities, the court held the contract void. In an action to have the contract canceled, the court pointed out that, in the first place, a minor could not be held to the performance of his contract. In the second place, the words "responsible bidder" conveyed the idea of a responsible person in the sense that such a person would be capable of looking after the children committed to his care. In the instant case, the lowest bidder was not so qualified.[13]

Where the statutes require competitive bidding in the letting of contracts for the transportation of pupils, the specifications must be clear and precise, or else there will be no real competition. Nor may a board lay down specifications that are not relevant to the purpose to be accomplished in order that the bid be given to a favorite bidder. Thus in a New Jersey case a local board twice rejected all bids and then drew up specifications, in excess of those prescribed by the State Board of Education, which made competition difficult, if not impossible. The specifications were such that only the sister-in-law of one of the board members could meet them. The contract was declared illegal by the State Board of Education, and the Court of Errors and Appeals sustained its action.[14]

Where a school board illegally awards a contract for transportation of pupils to one who is not, in fact, the lowest responsible bidder, the remedy open to the lowest bidder is an action to enjoin the execution of the contract. This action he can bring as a taxpayer and possibly in his own private capacity. But unless his bid was accepted and then rejected, he cannot sue the board for damages because there is no basis for such an action in law.[15]

12. *Cooper* v. *Townsend*, 143 Miss. 108, 108 So. 273.

13. *Bright* v. *Ball*, 138 Miss. 508, 103 So. 236. It has been held, however, that one who makes a contract to convey pupils to school may employ a minor to do the work, provided that the minor is capable (*Dear* v. *Bullock*, 141 Miss. 643, 107 So. 197.)

14. *Rankin* v. *Board of Education of Egg Harbor*, 135 N.J.L. 299, 51 Atl. (2d) 194.

15. *Boro-wide School Transportation Company* v. *Board of Education of City of New York*, 293 N.Y.S. 553, 162 Misc. 1.

DISCRETION OF BOARD WITH RESPECT TO TRANSPORTATION
ROUTES AND PUPILS TO BE TRANSPORTED

Where school officers have authority to provide transportation, they may exercise a broad discretion in establishing routes over which the transportation vehicles shall pass, and their discretion will not be controlled by the courts unless it is abused. It is not necessary that the conveyance be sent to the home of each particular child. Children may be required to walk any reasonable distance to meet the bus or other conveyance employed by the school board.[16] On this point the law is well established.

In Indiana a township trustee established a route for the school wagon along a road running east and west. A public highway ran north from this road for three-quarters of a mile, ending at the house of one Young. One-half mile from the route, on the north road, lived one Stuart. Near Stuart's home was a railroad track which children were required to cross in going to and from school. Over this track four passenger trains and six freight trains passed daily, one about the time children would cross the track in going to school. Young had two boys, seven and nine years of age, and Stuart had two girls, eight and nine, respectively. Young and Stuart brought action to compel the trustee to convey their children to and from their homes. In refusing to issue the writ of mandamus prayed for, the court said:

The facts alleged in the complaint, together with any other pertinent facts, might properly be considered by the township trustee and the county superintendent in determining where the school wagon shall be driven. But so long as those officers are not shown to have abused the discretion vested in them by law the courts cannot interfere to control their action. Whether it was better for four small children to cross the railroad twice each day on foot, or for a school wagon with children in it to be driven across four times each day, was a question for the officers to decide in laying out a route for the school wagon.[17]

Similarly, in Ohio a father, in seeking a writ of mandamus to compel the board of education to send the school wagon to his door, alleged that his thirteen-year-old daughter was required to meet the

16. *Lyle* v. *State*, 172 Ind. 502, 88 N.E. 850; *State* v. *Mostad*, 28 N.D. 244, 148 N.W. 831; *State* v. *Board of Education*, 102 Ohio St. 446, 132 N.E. 16; *Commonwealth* v. *Benton Township School District*, 277 Pa. St. 13, 120 Atl. 661; *Woodlawn School District No. 6* v. *Brown*, 223 S.W. (2d) (Ark.) 818; *Proctor* v. *Hufnail*, 111 Vt. 365, 16 Atl. (2d) 518; *Walters* v. *State*, 212 Wis. 132, 248 N.W. 777; *Flowers* v. *Independent School District of Tama*, 235 Iowa 332, 16 N.W. (2d) 570; *State ex rel. Rice* v. *Tompkins*, 203 S.W. (2d) 881.

17. *State* v. *Miller*, 193 Ind. 492, 141 N.E. 60.

wagon one-half mile from his residence at a point where no shelter from cold and storms was provided. The court held that the matters complained of were within the administrative discretion of the school board and that its discretion could not be controlled by mandamus.[18] Other instances in which the courts refused to overrule the discretion of a board in establishing transportation routes are: where a twelve-year-old boy had to walk a mile and a half to meet the bus;[19] where children, under a statute providing that children living two and one-half miles or more from school should be transported, were required to walk nine-tenths of a mile to meet the bus;[20] and where children, under a similar statute, were required to walk one-half mile to the bus route.[21]

The courts will, however, overrule a board's discretion if it appears to be abused. In a Kentucky case the statutes required school boards to furnish transportation to elementary pupils who did not live within a reasonable walking distance of their respective schools. In granting a writ of mandamus to compel the board of education to provide transportation for certain children, the court said:

Appellants are correct in this later contention [that the board has a broad discretion in deciding whether or not appellee's children actually live within a reasonable walking distance of the school]. Nevertheless, this court has the right and duty to review any such discretion, when it has been exercised, in order to determine whether or not it may have been abused in any particular instance. . . . So, now looking to the conditions of this specific case, we find that these young children were walking distances of 2 to 3 miles to their school in Shelbyville. We find that there was and is a tortuous road presenting a possible peril upon its pedestrians, particularly little children, in almost every furlong of its length. This road has neither sidewalks nor graveled berm. This route is one of heavy travel, both by trucks and other vehicles. This route crosses a narrow bridge, a railroad, a federal highway where fast-moving traffic continually chants a funeral dirge for the unwary. Now it does seem entirely possible to consider that one school route of 2 miles might constitute a reasonable walking distance while another and different school route of only 1 mile might constitute an unreasonable walking distance. The hazards and highway conditions of any particular route should certainly enter into a proper determination of what constitutes a reasonable walking distance.[22]

18. *State* v. *Board of Education*, 102 Ohio St. 446, 132 N.E. 16.

19. *Proctor* v. *Hufnail*, 111 Vt. 365, 16 Atl. (2d) 518.

20. *Flowers* v. *Independent School District of Tama*, 235 Iowa 332, 16 N.W. (2d) 570.

21. *Walters* v. *State*, 212 Wis. 132, 248 N.W. 777.

22. *Schmidt* v. *Payne*, 304 Ky. 58, 199 S.W. (2d) 990.

Where the statutes confer authority upon school boards to provide transportation, the courts, as a rule, will not control the discretion of the board with respect to the pupils to be transported. That is, the board may refuse to provide transportation for a pupil who lives in some isolated or inaccessible place.[23] In a Vermont case, for example, the statutes provided that the schools should be located so as to serve the best interests of education and give all the pupils as nearly equal advantages as practicable. The statutes further provided that the school directors might use 25 per cent of the school money for purposes of transportation. Action was brought by a parent to compel the school directors to provide transportation for his children. The court refused the relief sought:

> The end sought here is equality of school privileges, but the statute clearly recognizes the fact that entire equality is impossible of attainment, and that much must be left to the discretion of those in whose hands the administration of the law is placed. The differences in the number of scholars to be provided for, in the means available for the various demands of the work, in the proximity of schools and the condition of roads, and in the ages and strength of scholars, are such as to induce a belief that absolute rules would be more likely to work injustice than the exercise of official discretion.[24]

Similarly, in New Hampshire a statute authorized school boards to provide schools at such places within the district as would subserve the best interests of education and to use "a portion of the school money, not exceeding twenty-five per cent., for the purpose of conveying scholars to and from school." A parent who lived four and one-half miles from the nearest school sought to require the board to provide transportation for his nine-year-old boy. There was one one other child living in that locality, and she lived on a different road. The court refused to issue a writ of mandamus requiring the board to provide transportation for the pupil in question:

> If, for instance, the money required to pay for the transportation of one pupil from a remote part of the district might be used to substantially increase the educational advantages of a hundred other pupils in the town, as by adding a week or two to the length of the school year, it is evident that the aggregate educational advantages derived from the public-school system in the district would be enhanced by expending the money in that way. It might appear that it was not practicable to furnish transportation for one scholar, when it would occasion a substantial curtailment of school

23. *Carey* v. *Thompson*, 66 Vt. 665, 30 Atl. 5; *Fogg* v. *Board of Education*, 76 N.H. 296, 82 Atl. 173, 37 L.R.A. (N.S.) 1110, Ann. Cas. 1912C 758.

24. *Carey* v. *Thompson*, 66 Vt. 665, 30 Atl. 5.

advantages to all the other scholars in the town, because the interest of the public in the intelligence of the people generally is paramount to the special interest or desire of a single individual. The expense of transporting one scholar might be so much in excess of the average expense of educating all other scholars in the district as to result in a gross and unreasonable inequality of expense and a consequent lowering of the degree of efficiency in all the schools of the town. Such a result would not "best subserve the interests of education," in its public governmental aspect, and for that reason it might be deemed impracticable to expend the money in that way. The pupils' equality of privilege under the statute is limited or modified by its practicability, which involves a consideration of its effect upon the success of the school system in the district as a whole. . . .

If a pupil's home is located several miles from a school, in a rough, mountainous, and uninhabited part of the town, it is not probable that the Legislature intended that a considerable part of the public school money should be expended in providing daily conveyance for him to attend school. The inconvenient location of his home is his misfortune, which the state does not attempt to overcome for his benefit by substantially reducing the efficiency of all the schools in the town. The rule of equality of advantage in his case prescribed by the Legislature would be impracticable, unless the interest of the public in the education of its youth is to be subordinated to the interest of a single individual.[25]

LIABILITY OF SCHOOL DISTRICT AND SCHOOL-DISTRICT OFFICERS FOR INJURIES TO PUPILS

The principle of nonliability in tort of school districts and school officers while in the performance of a governmental function applies in cases where school children suffer injuries while being transported to and from school.[26] The rule commonly applied by the courts has been well expressed in a Georgia case where a child was killed as a result of the alleged negligence of a bus driver. Said the court:

The transportation by the authorities of a local school district, or the trustees of a local school district, of children to and from school by motorbus, makes accessible to the school children the facilities of education authorized and provided for them by law, and is therefore a part of the operation of the school system, and such school authorities when engaged in such transportation are in the operation of a governmental function, and are therefore not liable in tort, either in their official capacity, or as individuals, for any negligence, through themselves or their agents, in the operation by them of a motorbus, causing injuries to one of the school children, while being transported to and from school.[27]

25. *Fogg v. Board of Education,* 76 N.H. 296, 82 Atl. 173, 37 A.L.R. (N.S.) 1110.

26. *Ayers v. Board of Education of Hart County,* 56 Ga. App. 146, 192 S.E. 256; *Roberts v. Baker et al.,* 57 Ga. App. 733, 196 S.E. 104; *Wright v. Consolidated School District No. 1,* 162 Okla. 110, 19 Pac. (2d) 369; *Schornack v. School District No. 17,* 64 N.D. 215, 266 N.W. 141.

27. *Roberts v. Baker,* 57 Ga. App. 733, 196 S.E. 104.

Similarly, it was said by the Supreme Court of South Dakota in applying the principle of immunity from tort in a case where a child had been injured while being transported to school:

> It is sufficient to state, that if the respondent districts did not exceed the authority granted them, then they were performing a governmental function as an agent of the state, and in the absence of a statute imposing liability for negligence, they are not liable for negligence in the performance of such governmental function. . . . On the other hand, if the respondent school districts did exceed the authority granted them, then the acts of the school district officers in so exceeding their authority were ultra vires, and the districts cannot be held liable for negligence in the performance of such acts which were ultra vires and beyond the officers' scope of authority.[28]

PERSONAL LIABILITY OF BUS DRIVER

Immunity from liability for injuries to school children while being transported to and from school does not apply to drivers of school busses. The driver of a school bus will be held personally liable for injuries growing out of his own negligence, and this is true whether he be the operator of his own bus under contract with the district or whether he is employed by the district to operate one of its own busses.[29] The driver of a school bus cannot escape liability for injuries to pupils resulting from his negligent operation of the bus, on the ground that he is performing a governmental function.[30]

The degree of care which the driver of a school bus must exercise in order to escape liability for negligence in case a child is injured is not always easy to determine. In some instances the courts have ruled that the driver must exercise "extraordinary care" or the "highest degree of

28. *Schornack* v. *School District No. 17*, 64 S.D. 215, 266 N.W. 141. See, however, *McDonald* v. *Central School District No. 3*, 39 N.Y.S. 103, 179 Misc. 333.

29. *Sheffield*, v. *Lovering*, 51 Ga. App. 353, 180 S.E. 523; *Cartwright* v. *Graves*, 182 Tenn. 114, 184 S.W. (2d) 373; *Tipton* v. *Willey*, 47 Ohio App. 236, 191 N.E. 804; *Olson* v. *Cushman*, 224 Iowa 974, 276 N.W. 777; *Lempke* v. *Cummings*, 253 Wis. 570, 34 N.W. (2d) 673; *Burnett* v. *Allen*, 114 Fla. 489, 154 So. 515; *Garrett* v. *Bee Line, Inc.*, 13 N.Y.S. (2d) 154; *Reeves* v. *Tittle*, 129 S.W. (2d) (Tex.) 364; *Hunter* v. *Boyd*, 203 S.C. 518, 28 S.E. (2d) 412; *Leach* v. *School District No. 322*, 197 Wash. 384, 85 Pac. (2d) 666; *Gaudette* v. *McLaughlin*, 88 N.H. 368, 189 Atl. 872; *Shannon* v. *Central-Gaither Union School District*, 133 Calif. App. 124, 23 Pac. (2d) 769; *Archuleta* v. *Jacobs*, 43 N.M. 425, 94 Pac. (2d) 706.

30. *Wynn* v. *Gandy*, 170 Va. 590, 197 S.E. 527. See, however, *Hibbs* v. *Independent School District of Green Mountain*, 218 Iowa 841, 251 N.W. 606, in which the court held that the principle of immunity from tort in the performance of a governmental function applies to the employees of a school district, including a bus driver.

care."[31] Other courts hold that "ordinary" or "reasonable" care is all that is required.[32] However, the distinction between the highest degree of care and ordinary care turns out to have no great importance in the cases decided. The courts universally hold that a bus driver must exercise the degree of care any reasonably prudent person would exercise in the given situation. This rule of reasonable prudence and care governs the bus driver in all the relations he has with pupils whom he transports to and from school. It governs the condition of the bus, the speed at which it is driven, the discipline of pupils while on the bus, and the circumstances under which they are permitted to leave it. A bus driver will not escape liability by pleading that he did not foresee the precise injury that the pupil sustained; he will be held liable if a reasonably prudent person, under the circumstances, would have anticipated *some* injury.

The Supreme Court of Tennessee, after an examination of cases from many states, makes an excellent summary of the principles of law governing the personal liability of bus drivers:

Through all these cases recognizing liability for neglect of care of the safety of child passengers after alighting from the vehicle run recognition of these controlling principles:

1. That the age of the child and his consequent ability or lack of ability to look after his own safety after alighting from the bus is . . . the "dominant factor." . . .

2. That a peculiar and special obligation arises out of the nature of the relationship of the driver of a school bus to the children entrusted to his care. Whether or not this be termed a "high degree of care," in the technical sense, it is generally held that this relationship demands a special care proportionate to the age of the child and its ability, or lack of it, to care for itself.

3. That the zone or area of legal responsibility for care of immature school children extends beyond the mere landing of the child from the bus in a place safe in itself, and includes the known pathway the child must immediately pursue.

4. That the duty to warn is an imperative incident of the general obligation to exercise care proportionate to the age of the child and the attendant conditions in discharging a school child from a bus.

5. That the question in this class of cases is one for the determination by the jury, on the particular facts of the case under consideration.[33]

31. *Davidson* v. *Horne*, 86 Ga. App. 220, 71 S.E. (2d) 464; *Jordan* v. *Wiggins*, 66 Ga. App. 534, 18 S.E. (2d) 512; *Leach* v. *School District No. 322*, 197 Wash. 384, 85 Pac. (2d) 666.

32. *Gaudette* v. *McLaughlin*, 88 N.H. 368, 189 Atl. 872; *Foster* v. *Einer*, 69 Calif. App. (2d) 341, 158 Pac. (2d) 978; *Burnett* v. *Allen*, 114 Fla. 489, 154 So. 515.

33. *Cartwright* v. *Graves*, 182 Tenn. 114, 184 S.W. (2d) 373.

A Florida case will also serve to illustrate the degree of care a bus driver must exercise with respect to the children he transports. The facts were that the wire screening inside the bus had fallen into disrepair, thus enabling a pupil to reach through the screening and open the door of the bus while it was still in motion. One pupil opened the door while the bus was still in motion and a seven-year-old boy got off, went around behind the bus, started across the road and was struck by another car. In the words of the court:

> By assuming to perform the contract [with the school board] . . . the defendant, by necessary implication, assumed to perform every act, reasonably necessary for the safety of the children entrusted to his care while in transportation, which would include the operation of safely receiving the children into the bus and in superintending and directing their safe exit from the bus and their safe departure from the bus.
>
> The bus driver who contracts to furnish transportation and to transport school children . . . becomes a special contractor for hire. . . . As the contract contemplated the transportation of children who are incompetent to be charged with the assumption of risk because of their tender years and inexperience, it likewise contemplates and, by implication at least, binds the person contracting to furnish and conduct the means of transportation to use every reasonable precaution and care for the safety of such children and to prevent any harm or damage coming to them, either in approaching the bus, or while riding in the bus or when alighting from and leaving the immediate proximity of the bus at the completion of their journey, or at any time during the journey. Whether a person contracting and performing such a contract has used all such reasonable care and caution is a question for the determination of a jury in each case.[34]

It frequently happens that a bus driver is negligent in permitting a child to depart from the bus and the child is struck by the negligent driver of another car. In such cases the negligence of the driver of the car that actually struck the child will not exonerate the driver of the bus.[35] The sequence of cause and effect is not broken by the intervening negligence of the third party if the driver of the bus might have reasonably foreseen that some injury to the child in question was a probability. In such cases the test is foreseeability. As the Supreme Court of South Carolina has well expressed it: "The intervening negligence of a third person will not excuse the first wrongdoer, if such intervention ought to have been foreseen in the exercise of due care.

34. *Burnett* v. *Allen,* 114 Fla. 489, 154 So. 515.

35. *Hunter* v. *Boyd,* 203 S.C. 518, 28 S.E. (2d) 412; *Reeves* v. *Tittle,* 129 S.W. (2d) (Tex.) 364; *Cartwright* v. *Graves,* 182 Tenn. 114, 184 S.W. (2d) 373; *McDonald* v. *Central School District No. 3,* 39 N.Y.S. (2d) 103, 179, Misc. 333.

In such case, the original negligence still remains active, and a contributing cause of the injury. The test is to be found in the probable consequences reasonably anticipated, and not in the number or exact character of the events subsequently arising."[36]

Whether or not a bus driver has exercised, in any particular case, the reasonable care and diligence required of him is ordinarily a matter of fact to be determined by a jury.[37] A court, as a rule, will not take the case from the jury, or direct a verdict, if the established facts are such that reasonable men would not disagree on the conclusions to be drawn. Moreover, it is not the court's prerogative to substitute its judgment for the jury's; the verdict of the jury must stand unless it is a plain deviation from the evidence, that is, unless it is against the manifest weight of the evidence or contrary to law.[38]

SCHOOL-DISTRICT TRANSPORTATION INSURANCE

A school district in transporting children to and from school is in the performance of a governmental function and is, therefore, immune from liability for injuries to pupils resulting from the negligent acts of its officers or employees, unless made liable by statutory enactment. Where a school board is immune from liability because of the operation of the common law and no statute makes it liable, it probably does not have the implied authority to carry insurance to protect itself against loss or to protect others against the negligence of its employees. On this point, however, there is as yet little judicial authority. In Tenessee, statutes authorizing county school boards to require of bus drivers a bond for the faithful performance of the duties imposed upon them were held to confer upon county boards power to take out liability insurance covering the operation of the school busses.[39] And where a county board carried such a policy and a pupil

36. *Locklear* v. *Southeastern Stages, Inc.,* 193 S.C. 309, 8 S.E. (2d) 321.

37. *McDonald* v. *Central School District No. 3,* 39 N.Y.S. (2d) 103, 179 Misc. 333; *Kawaguchi* v. *Bennett,* 189 Pac. (2d) (Utah) 109; *Haase et al.* v. *Central Union High School District,* 27 Calif. App. (2d) 319; *Cartwright* v. *Graves,* 182 Tenn. 114, 184 S.W. (2d) 373; *Jordan* v. *Wiggins,* 66 Ga. App. 534, 18 S.E. (2d) 512; *Wynn* v. *Gandy,* 170 Va. 590, 197 S.E. 527; *Archuleta* v. *Jacobs,* 43 N.M. 425, 94 Pac. (2d) 706.

38. *Wynn* v. *Gandy,* 170 Va. 590, 197 S.E. 527; *In re estate of Baldwin,* 162 Calif. 471, 123 Pac. 267; *Dickerhoof* v. *Bair,* 54 Ohio App. 320, 6 N.E. (2d) 990; *Pendarvis* v. *Pfeifer,* 132 Fla. 724, 182 So. 307.

39. *Rogers* v. *Butler,* 170 Tenn. 125, 92 S.W. (2d) 414. See also *Taylor* v. *Cobble,* 28 Tenn. App. 167, 187 S.W. (2d) 648.

was injured because of the negligence of one of its bus drivers, judgment for damages was allowed against the county, but for not more than could be collected from the insurance company.

In a number of cases in West Virginia, however, the court has taken the position—and it seems the better law—that a board of education has no authority, unless given it by statute, to take out indemnity or liability insurance. Thus it was held that authority to take out liability insurance could not be implied from authority to transport pupils. The reasoning underlying the West Virginia decisions is that, since a school board cannot be held liable for the negligence of its employees, there is nothing against which an insurance policy could operate. Such a policy would be "without basis or justification."[40]

The governmental immunity of a school board from liability for injuries to pupils riding on school busses is not affected or waived by the fact that the board has been authorized by statute to carry liability insurance.[41] And such is the case, even though the insurance policy covers the school board as well as its employees.[42] It follows, therefore, that a school board will not be held liable, even under a statute that makes it a party to a suit, in an amount greater than the coverage of the insurance policy.

Since school boards are not liable under the common law for injuries to pupils, there is no reason why a board should take out indemnity insurance, that is, insurance merely to protect itself against damages. Under such a policy it has been held that no action could be brought against the insurance company for damages resulting from the negligent operation of a school bus.[43]

Where a school district takes out liability insurance without statutory authority to do so, its act is *ultra vires*. Even so, the insurance

40. See *Boire* v. *Board of Education of Rock District*, 160 S.E. (W. Va.) 566; *Board of Education of Raleigh County* v. *Commercial Casualty Insurance Co.*, 116 W. Va. 503, 182 S.E. 87; *Adkins* v. *Western and Southern Indemnity Company*, 186 S.E. (W. Va.) 302; *Bradfield* v. *Board of Education of Pleasants County*, 36 S.E. (2d) (W. Va.) 512.

41. *Wallace* v. *Laurel County Board of Education*, 287 Ky. 454, 153 S.W. (2d) 915; *Kesman* v. *School District of Fallowfield*, 345 Pa. 457; *Rittmiller* v. *School District No. 84*, 104 Fed. Supp. 187; *Taylor* v. *Knox County Board of Education*, 292 Ky. 767, 167 S.W. (2d) 700, 145 A.L.R. 1333; *Utz* v. *Board of Education of Brooke County*, 126 W. Va. 823, 30 S.E. (2d) 342.

42. *Rittmiller* v. *School District No. 84*, 104 Fed. Supp. 187.

43. *Brooks* v. *Clark County*, 297 Ky. 549, 180 S.W. (2d) 300; *Simons* v. *Gregory*, 120 Ky. 116, 85 S.W. 751.

company will, as a rule, be held liable under its contract. The doctrine of *ultra vires* is intended to protect taxpayers and the public from the unauthorized acts of public officers; it may not, as a rule, be invoked by third parties who deal with public corporations. In an Illinois case, for example, a school board, without statutory authority to do so, carried liability insurance covering injuries to pupils on the school grounds. A pupil lost an eye from injuries sustained while playing on the school grounds. The court permitted the school district to be sued, refusing to permit it to plead in defense its own illegal act in taking out the insurance. The court reasoned that the protection of public funds is the only justification for nonliability in tort in cases of this kind. And since the school district was covered by an insurance policy, it could be held liable in an amount not exceeding the coverage of the policy.

CHAPTER XXI

Rules and Regulations of Boards of Education

GENERAL AUTHORITY TO REGULATE THE CONDUCT OF PUPILS

IN DETERMINING whether school officers or teachers have authority to enforce a particular rule or regulation governing the conduct of pupils, the courts universally apply the test of reasonableness. It is well established by a great number of cases that school officers may enforce any rule which is reasonable and necessary to promote the best interests of the schools.[1] The courts are, indeed, very reluctant to declare a board regulation unreasonable. They will never substitute their own discretion for that of the school authorities; the enforcement of a rule will never be enjoined, because, in the opinion of the court, the rule is unwise or inexpedient; a rule will not be set aside unless it clearly appears to be unreasonable.[2] A board regulation is not reasonable or unreasonable per se; its reasonableness is determined by the circumstances of each particular case. A rule which is reasonable in a warm climate may be unreasonable in a cold climate; a rule may be reasonable when applied to a boy of sixteen but unreasonable when applied to a girl of six.

1. *Fertich* v. *Michener,* 111 Ind. 472, 11 N.E. 605, 60 Am. Rep. 709; *Flory* v. *Smith,* 145 Va. 164, 134 S.E. 360; *State* v. *District Board of School District No. 1,* 135 Wis. 619, 116 N.W. 232, 16 L.R.A. (N.S.) 730; *Pugsley* v. *Sellmeyer,* 158 Ark. 247, 250 S.W. 583, 30 A.L.R. 1212; *Wilson* v. *Board of Education,* 233 Ill. 464, 15 L.R.A. (N.S.) 1136, 84 N.E. 697, 13 Ann. Cas. 330; *Thompson* v. *Beaver,* 63 Ill. 353; *Spiller* v. *Woburn,* 12 Allen (Mass.) 127; *Stromberg* v. *French,* 60 N.D. 750, 236 N.W. 477; *Bozeman* v. *Morrow,* 34 S.W. (2d) (Tex.) 654; *Richardson* v. *Braham,* 125 Neb. 142, 249 N.W. 557; *Byrd* v. *Begley,* 262 Ky. 422, 90 S.W. (2d) 370.

2. *Pugsley* v. *Sellmeyer,* 158 Ark. 247, 250 S.W. 538, 30 A.L.R. 1212; *State* v. *District Board of School District No. 1,* 135 Wis. 619, 116 N.W. 232, 16 L.R.A. (N.S.) 730; *State* v. *Burton,* 45 Wis. 150, 30 Am. Rep. 706; *Wilson* v. *Board of Education,* 233 Ill. 464, 15 L.R.A. (N.S.) 1136, 84 N.E. 697, 13 Ann. Cas. 330; *King* v. *Jefferson City School Board,* 71 Mo. 628, 36 Am. Rep. 499.

In case boards of education fail to formulate rules and regulations, superintendents, principals, and teachers may make and enforce such reasonable rules and regulations as may be necessary in the administration of the schools.[3] Inasmuch as the teacher stands *in loco parentis*, he may enforce obedience to any reasonable and lawful commands.[4]

Neither school boards nor teachers, however, may enforce rules governing the conduct of pupils with respect to matters over which the board has no jurisdiction. That is, the conduct which the board undertakes to regulate must have some direct relation to the management and well-being of the school. In Wisconsin, for example, a pupil was expelled from school for refusing to obey a rule which required each pupil of sufficient bodily strength, upon returning from the playground at recess, to bring in a stick of wood fitted for use in the stove. In holding that the rule could not be enforced, the court pointed out that the school board must confine its rules to matters which concern the education of pupils or discipline in the school and that it could not, according to its fancy or humor, enforce rules on all manner of subjects. In the words of the court:

Any rule or regulation which has for its object anything outside of the instruction of the pupil—the order requisite for instruction—is beyond the province of the board of education to adopt. The requirement that school children should bring up wood, when not by way of punishment, has nothing to do with the education of the child. It is nothing but manual labor, pure and simple, and has no relation to mental development.[5]

Where an attempt is made to enforce an unreasonable rule or one which is *ultra vires*, recourse may be had to the courts on the part of the parties aggrieved. The school officers are not themselves the final judges of what constitutes a reasonable regulation.[6] Moreover, whether a rule is or is not reasonable is a matter of law, to be determined by the court, and not a matter of fact, to be determined by the jury. Thus it was said by the Supreme Court of Iowa: "It was certainly never the intention of the legislature to confer upon school boards, superintend-

3. *State* v. *Randall,* 79 Mo. App. 226;   *Deskins* v. *Gose,* 85 Mo. 485, 55 Am. Rep. 387; *Patterson* v. *Nutter,* 78 Me. 509, 7 Atl. 273, 57 Am. Rep. 818; *Sheehan* v. *Sturges,* 53 Conn. 481, 2 Alt. 841.

4. *State* v. *Burton,* 45 Wis. 150, 30 Am. Rep. 706.

5. *State* v. *Board of Education,* 63 Wis. 234, 23 N.W. 102, 53 Am. Rep. 282.

6. *Pugsley* v. *Sellmeyer,* 158 Ark. 247, 250 S.W. 538, 30 A.L.R. 1212; *Thompson* v. *Beaver,* 63 Ill. 353; *School City of Evansville* v. *Culver,* 182 N.E. (Ind.) 270.

ents of schools, or other officers discharging quasi-judicial functions, exclusive authority to decide questions pertaining to their jurisdiction and the extent of their power. All such questions may be determined by the courts of the state."[7] A court will therefore enjoin the enforcement of an unreasonable rule, or, if a pupil has been excluded from school because of disobedience of an unreasonable rule, a court will issue a writ of mandamus requiring reinstatement of the pupil.

The courts will determine whether a rule governing pupil conduct is reasonable; they will not, however, review the findings of a school board with respect to facts. That is, whether a pupil has or has not been guilty of certain conduct is a matter of fact to be determined by the school authorities and will not be reviewed by the courts unless it can be shown that the school authorities have acted maliciously or in bad faith.[8] In an Illinois case[9] as an illustration, a pupil was expelled from school because he had joined a secret society in violation of a rule of the board. The pupil contended that he was not a member of the society and had not, therefore, violated the rule. The court refused to review the finding of the board as to the facts. It said:

> The power to determine what constitutes disobedience or misconduct lies within the Board of Education, and under no circumstances, except where fraud, corruption, oppression or gross injustice is palpably shown, is a court of law authorized to review the decision of the Board of Education, and to substitute its judgment for that of the Board. . . .
> The power of the Board to exercise its honest and reasonable discretion in such cases without the interference of the courts is well settled.

Similarly, in a Kentucky case[10] a pupil was expelled for writing an insulting composition. The court refused to review the facts with the view of determining the guilt or innocence of the pupil. An excerpt from the opinion of the court follows:

> It necessarily follows that those in charge of said school must be allowed to judge of and determine as to the propriety of expelling scholars therefrom, and it is manifest that those in charge of the school are better qualified to judge of and determine as to what offenses justify expulsion than the

7. *Perkins* v. *Independent School District of West Des Moines*, 56 Iowa 476, 9 N.W. 356.

8. *Watson* v. *City of Cambridge*, 157 Mass. 561, 32 N.E. 864; *Hodgkins* v. *Rockport*, 105 Mass. 475; *Board of Education* v. *Booth*, 110 Ky. 807, 23 Ky. Law Rep. 288, 62 S.W. 872, 53 L.R.A. 787; *Smith* v. *Board of Education*, 182 Ill. App. 342.

9. *Smith* v. *Board of Education*, 182 Ill. App. 342.

10. *Board of Education* v. *Booth*, 110 Ky. 807, 23 Ky. Law Rep. 288, 62 S.W. 872, 53 L.R.A. 787.

courts can ordinarily be. . . . Our conclusion is that those in charge of such schools have a right to formulate such necessary rules as, in their judgment, will best promote the public good; and, if such rules are violated by any pupil, the right to expel such pupil exists, and may be exercised by the proper school authorities; and the question as to the guilt or innocence of the accused can not be reviewed by the courts unless it appears that such pupil was expelled arbitrarily or maliciously. We do not feel called upon to determine in this case whether the plaintiff was guilty of the offense for which it seems she was expelled from school. It may be that she did not mean to insult her teacher. That question was determined by the superintendent, and his action ratified by the board of education, and we do not think we have the authority to weigh and determine the evidence in respect thereto. We are not of the opinion that the evidence in this case tends to show that the teacher, superintendent or board of education acted maliciously or unfairly in the matter under consideration.

RULES RESTRICTING ADMISSION TO SCHOOL

Although the law may provide that all the children of the state have the right to attend the public schools, it is not intended that this right should be unrestricted. A board of education may enforce reasonable regulations governing the time pupils may enter the public schools. In Illinois, for example, an attempt was made to enforce a regulation to the effect that pupils arriving at school age during the school year would be admitted, to school only during the first month of the autumn and spring terms, beginning on about the first of September and April, respectively. The court held that the board of education had the authority "to adopt reasonable rules and regulations, in regard to the admission of persons over six years of age, which may operate to prevent such persons from entering school immediately after arriving at the age of six years." However, the court regarded the rule in question as unreasonable:

We are of opinion that the rule which caused appellee's child, who arrived at school age only thirty-one days after the fall term commenced, to lose the benefits of the free school, not only during the remaining months of that term, but also during the whole of the following winter term, was not a reasonable one or calculated to promote the objects of the law.[11]

In a somewhat similar case decided by the Supreme Judicial Court of Massachusetts,[12] a rule provided that pupils under seven years of age who desired to attend should enter school within three or four weeks after the beginning of the autumn term. Pupils under seven

11. *Board of Education* v. *Bolton*, 85 Ill. App. 92.
12. *Alvord* v. *Inhabitants of Chester*, 180 Mass. 20, 61 N.E. 263.

years of age seeking to enter school thereafter would be denied admission unless they were qualified to enter classes already in existence. In holding that the rule was reasonable, the court used the following language:

Children under seven years of age, although allowed to attend the public schools, are not required to attend. Grading is a permitted if not an essential feature of the public school system. The introduction late in the school year of a very young scholar not qualified to enter the existing classes, would tend to impair the efficiency of the school, and so to prevent the other scholars from attaining such advancement in learning and in training as would enable them to proceed with their education in due course. The right given to every child . . . to attend the public schools is not unqualified, but is "subject to such reasonable regulations as to the numbers and qualifications of pupils to be admitted to the respective schools, and as to other school matters, as the school committee shall from time to time prescribe."

The Supreme Court of Kansas has held to be reasonable a rule which required all persons not graduates of a public elementary school to pass an entrance examination as a condition of admission to high school.[13] In South Dakota a school board has authority to enforce a rule which excludes from school pupils who refuse to submit to a physical examination by a licensed physician.[14]

REGULATION OF DRESS AND PERSONAL APPEARANCE OF PUPILS

Relatively few cases have come into the courts testing the authority of school boards to regulate the dress and personal appearance of pupils. A novel case of this kind, however, has been decided by the Supreme Court of Arkansas.[15] A board of education adopted the following rule: "The wearing of transparent hosiery, low-necked dresses, or any style of clothing tending towards immodesty of dress, or the use of face paint or cosmetics, is prohibited." A high-school girl insisted upon using talcum powder and was suspended from school until she consented to abide by the rule of the board. She sued for writ of mandamus requiring the board to readmit her. In refusing the writ, the court reasoned as follows:

13. *Creyhon* v. *Board of Education,* 99 Kan. 824, 163 Pac. 145, L.R.A. 1917C 993.

14. *Streich* v. *Board of Education,* 34 S.D. 169, 147 N.W. 779, Ann. Cas. 1917A 760, L.R.A. 1915A 632.

15. *Pugsley* v. *Sellmeyer,* 158 Ark. 247, 250 S.W. 538, 30 A.L.R. 1212.

The question, therefore, is not whether we approve this rule as one we would have made as directors of the district, nor are we required to find whether it was essential to the maintenance of discipline. On the contrary, we must uphold the rule unless we find that the directors have clearly abused their discretion, and that the rule is not one reasonably calculated to effect the purpose intended, that is, of promoting discipline in the school, and we do not so find. . . . The courts have this right of review, for the reasonableness of such rule is a judicial question, and the courts will not refuse to perform their functions in determining the reasonableness of such rules, when the question is presented. But, in so doing, it will be kept in mind that the directors are elected by the patrons of the schools over which they preside, and the election occurs annually. These directors are in close and intimate touch with the affairs of their respective districts, and know the conditions with which they have to deal. . . .

We are unwilling to say, as a matter of law, that a local condition might not exist which would make a rule of this character desirable in aid of the discipline of the school, and we therefore decline to annul it, for we will not annual a rule of the kind unless a valid reason for doing so is made to appear; whereas, to uphold it, we are not required to find a valid reason for its promulgation.

One of the justices, however, wrote a dissenting opinion. He said: "I think that a rule forbidding a girl pupil of her age [eighteen] from putting talcum powder on her face is so far unreasonable and beyond the exercise of discretion that the court should say that the board of directors acted without authority in making and enforcing it."

In only one case, it seems, has a court passed upon the authority of school officers to require pupils in the public schools to wear uniforms. The trustees of a county agricultural high school in Mississippi adopted a rule requiring pupils to wear a prescribed uniform, not only while in attendance at school, but "when visiting public places within five miles of the school, even on Saturdays and Sundays." Action was brought to enjoin the enforcement of the rule as being *ultra vires*. In defense it was claimed that, because of local conditions, such a regulation was necessary for the maintenance of discipline. The court sustained the rule with respect to students living in dormitories but held that it was not applicable to day students except while in attendance at the school and while going to and from school.[16]

The Supreme Court of Iowa has passed upon the reasonableness of a rule which required pupils participating in graduating exercises to wear caps and gowns. The caps and gowns were furnished free by the board of education. A number of pupils, however, refused to wear

16. *Jones* v. *Day*, 127 Miss. 136, 89 So. 906, 18 A.L.R. 645.

them. Such pupils as refused were not allowed to take part in the graduating exercises and were not granted diplomas. A writ of mandamus was sought by one of the pupils to compel the board to grant her a diploma as well as a certified copy of her grades. In granting the writ prayed for, the court said:

Conceding appellant's contention that there was a rule formerly adopted, and effective at the time in question, we hold that such a rule is unreasonable and a nullity as a condition precedent to receive a diploma. The wearing of a cap and gown on commencement night has no relation to educational values, the discipline of the school, scholastic grades, or intellectual advancement. Such a rule may be justified, in some instances, from the viewpoint of economy; but from a legal viewpoint, the board might as well attempt to direct the wearing of overalls by the boys and gingham dresses by the girls. The enforcement of such a rule is purely arbitrary, and especially so when the offending pupil has been passed for graduation, after the performance on her part of all prescribed educational requirements. We are not questioning the propriety of wearing caps and gowns. It is a custom we approve. The board may deny the right of a graduate to participate in the public ceremony of graduation unless a cap and gown is worn.[17]

In what appears to be the only other case dealing with the authority of school boards to regulate the dress and personal appearance of pupils, it was held that pupils may be forbidden to wear metal heel-plates when it appears that the use of such plates injures the floors and causes noise and confusion.[18]

AUTHORITY TO REQUIRE PUPILS TO PAY FOR INJURY TO SCHOOL PROPERTY

The courts are in agreement in holding that boards of education may not require pupils to pay for injury to school property where the injury grows out of acts of neglect or carelessness. A school board in Michigan,[19] for example, attempted to enforce a rule to the effect that any pupil who should deface or injure school property should be suspended from school until full satisfaction was made. While playing, a pupil negligently and carelessly broke a window in the schoolhouse. The father of the pupil refused to pay for the window, and the child

17. *Valentine* v. *Independent School District of Casey*, 191 Iowa 1100, 183 N.W. 434.

18. *Stromberg* v. *French*, 60 N.D. 750, 236 N.W. 477.

19. *Holman* v. *Trustees of School District No. 5*, 77 Mich. 605, 43 N.W. 996, 6 L.R.A. 534.

was suspended from school. In holding that the rule was unreasonable, the court pointed out that a pupil can be expelled only for wilful or malicious acts. Moreover, the practical operation of such a rule might, in some instances, have the effect of depriving poor children of the right of a common-school education.

Speaking of a similar rule, the Supreme Court of Indiana has said:

Carelessness on the part of children is one of the most common, and yet one of the least blameworthy of their faults. In simple carelessness there is no purpose to do wrong. To punish a child for carelessness in any case is to punish it where it has no purpose or intent to do wrong or violate rules.

But beyond this, no rule is reasonable which requires of the pupils what they cannot do. The vast majority of pupils, whether small or large, have no money at their command with which to pay for school property which they injure or destroy by carelessness or otherwise. If required to pay for such property, they would have to look to their parents or guardians for the money. If the parent or guardian should not have the money, or if they should refuse to give it to the child, the child would be left subject to punishment for not having done what it had no power to do.[20]

The Supreme Court of Iowa places the unreasonableness of such a rule upon even broader considerations. It says:

The State does not deprive its citizens of their property or their liberty, or of any rights, except as a punishment for a crime. It would be very harsh and obviously unjust to deprive a child of education for the reason that through accident and without intention of wrong he destroyed property of the school district. Doubtless a child can be expelled from school as a punishment for breach of discipline or for offences against good morals, but not for innocent acts.

In this case the plaintiff was expelled not because he broke the glass, but because he did not pay the damage sustained by the breaking. His default in this respect was no breach of good order or good morals. The rule requiring him to make payment is not intended to secure good order but to enforce an obligation to pay a sum of money. We are clearly of the opinion that the directors have no authority to promulgate or enforce such a rule.[21]

HEALTH REGULATIONS OF SCHOOL BOARDS

Since attendance at the public schools is a privilege extended by the state, the state may, through properly constituted authorities, exclude from school all pupils whose presence in the schools would jeopardize the health of other pupils.[22] Thus pupils who are merely suspected of

20. *State* v. *Vanderbilt*, 116 Ind. 11, 18 N.E. 266.

21. *Perkins* v. *Independent School District of West Des Moines*, 56 Iowa 476, 9 N.W. 356.

22. *Stone* v. *Probst*, 165 Minn. 361, 206 N.W. 642; *Martin* v. *Craig*, 42 N.D. 213, 173 N.W. 787; *Carr* v. *Inhabitants of Dighton*, 229 Mass. 304, 118 N.E. 525.

being affected with a contagious disease may be excluded from school. In North Dakota, for example, a survey made by the public health service of the federal government revealed that in a certain county there were 120 positive cases and 350 suspected cases of trachoma. The county board of health issued an order excluding the suspected cases from school. It was said by the court, in sustaining the action of the health authorities:

> The order of exclusion in the instant case can not be said to be unreasonable. It only excludes those whose cases are positive and suspected, who are not at the time under treatment. The seriousness of the disease and its communicable character afford ample foundation for such an order; and, even conceding that it may be doubted in the instant case whether the children in question are affected, the doubt is one that must be resolved in favor of the authorities charged with the serious responsibility of preventing the spread of the disease. This is a case where mandamus does not issue as a matter of right, but where it will only issue in the exercise of a judicial discretion, and this discretion should not be exercised in a way that might result in needlessly exposing healthful children to a disease as serious as trachoma.[23]

As a general rule, boards of education, under their general powers, have authority to enforce regulations whereby pupils who are a menace to the health of their associates may be excluded from school. A case in point is that of *Stone* v. *Probst*.[24] The charter of the city of Minneapolis provided that the board of education should have "the entire control and management of all the common schools within the city . . . and make rules and regulations for the government of schools." Pursuant to authority thus conferred, the board of education enacted rules whereby principals and teachers were required to "be on the alert to discover suspected contagious diseases, filth, or vermin, and physical and mental defects." A child suspected of being infected with a contagious disease was to be excluded from school until an examination revealed the absence of infection. A pupil who was ill with a throat infection was excluded from school until she should furnish the school authorities with a negative report from a throat culture submitted to the division of public health of the city. "In addition thereto she was also required to present a certificate from a physician as to the condition of her throat, or submit to a physical examination by the regularly employed school physician or nurses." The pupil, who was a

23. *Martin* v. *Craig*, 42 N.D. 213, 173 N.W. 787.
24. *Stone* v. *Probst*, 165 Minn. 361, 206 N.W. 642.

member of the Christian Science church, refused to comply with the demand of the board. She contended that the rules of the board were illegal in that they violated a constitutional provision which prohibited the legislature from delegating legislative powers. In other words, the rules of the board were not merely administrative regulations but a legislative enactment. It was further contended that the board of education had no authority to make the rules in question, because the matter of public health had been delegated to the board of public welfare. Finally, the rules were attacked as being arbitrary and unreasonable. The court overruled all these contentions and sustained the rules in an opinion from which the following quotation is taken:

To have the entire control and management, with power to make rules and regulations, means almost every power necessary or essential for the proper administration of such schools. It must be conceded by all that one of the primary duties of the board is to protect the health of the many children in their charge. Persons differ only in how this is to be accomplished. Efforts for prevention do much to avoid an epidemic. The demand upon the board for vigilance in this respect is imperative. All authority exercised in the protection of the public health is to be liberally construed. We hold that the language of the charter by fair implication confers upon the board of education the power to make and enforce the rules involved. In fact it could not effectually carry out the purposes for which it exists without such power. . . .

It is contended here that the school board by its rules has assumed to enact a law, and that it is without legislative authority. Of course the legislative body can not be permitted to relieve itself of this power by delegating it to another body. But the constitutional inhibition can not be extended so as to prevent the grant of legislative authority to administrative boards to adopt rules to carry out a particular purpose. It can not be claimed that every grant of power to administrative boards involving the exercise of discretion in judgment must be considered as a delegation of legislative authority. There are many matters relating to methods or details which may be by the legislative body referred to a particular administrative board. Such matters fall within the domain of the right of the legislative body to authorize an administrative board to make rules or regulations in aid of the successful execution of some general statutory provision or to enable it to carry out the purpose of its existence. These rules come within this class and are administrative provisions. They are also the result of the valid exercise of the police power invested in the board of education by virtue of the language of the charter.

The court concluded its opinion by pointing out that the rules of the board were reasonable and should not be disturbed by the courts.

As has been pointed out in another connection, a school board may refuse to admit to school pupils who will not submit to a physical examination by a licensed physician.[25] It has already been pointed out, too, that a school board may spend public funds for purposes of health inspection,[26] although it may not spend such funds for purposes of remedial treatment.[27]

AUTHORITY OF SCHOOL BOARDS WITH RESPECT
TO VACCINATION

In the exercise of its police power a state may require that all persons be vaccinated. A statute of Massachusetts, for example, required the inhabitants of a city or town to be vaccinated whenever, in the opinion of the board of health, vaccination was necessary to safeguard the public health and the public safety. The constitutionality of the statute was challenged before the Supreme Court of the United States. In the opinion of that court, the act in question was not unreasonable, arbitrary, or oppressive. Neither did it deprive any person of liberty guaranteed by the federal constitution.[28] Similarly, the state may authorize or require boards of education to make vaccination a condition of school attendance, regardless of the existence or nonexistence of smallpox in the school district. The constitutionality of statutes which authorize or require the exclusion from public schools of all unvaccinated pupils has been tested in a great number of cases, but the courts have, without exception, sustained such legislation as a valid exercise of the police power of the state.[29] Such legislation is not an

25. *Streich* v. *Board of Education*, 34 S.D. 169, 147 N.W. 779, L.R.A. 1915A 632, Ann. Cas. 1917A 760.

26. *City of Dallas* v. *Mosely*, 286 S.W. (Tex.) 497; *State* v. *Brown*, 112 Minn. 370, 128 N.W. 294; *Hallett* v. *Post Printing & Publishing Company*, 68 Colo. 573, 192 Pac. 658, 12 A.L.R. 919.

27. *McGilvra* v. *Seattle School District No. 1*, 113 Wash. 619, 194 Pac. 817, 12 A.L.R. 913.

28. *Jacobson* v. *Commonwealth of Massachusetts*, 197 U.S. 11, 25 S. Ct. 358, 49 L. Ed. 643, 3 Ann. Cas. 765.

29. *Zucht* v. *King*, 260 U.S. 174, 43 S. Ct. 24, 67 L. Ed. 194; *Bissell* v. *Davison*, 65 Conn. 183, 32 Atl. 348, 29 L.R.A. 251; *Viemeister* v. *White*, 179 N.Y. 235, 72 N.E. 97, 70 L.R.A. 796, 103 Am. St. Rep. 859; *People* v. *Ekerold*, 211 N.Y. 386, 105 N.E. 670, L.R.A. 1915D 223; *French* v. *Davidson*, 143 Calif. 658, 77 Pac. 663; *Abeel* v. *Clark*, 84 Calif. 226, 24 Pac. 383; *State Board of Health* v. *Watsonville School District*, 13 Calif. App. 514, 110 Pac. 137; *Stull* v. *Reber*, 215 Pa. St. 156, 64 Atl. 419; *Field* v. *Robinson*, 198 Pa. St. 638, 48 Atl. 873; *State* v. *Shorrock*, 55 Wash. 208, 104 Pac. 214; *State* v. *Board of Education*, 76 Ohio St. 297, 81 N.E. 568, 10 Ann. Cas. 879; *Barber* v. *School Board of Rochester*, 82 N.H. 426, 135 Atl. 159; *Zucht* v. *King*, 225 S.W. (Tex.) 267.

arbitrary and unreasonable restraint upon personal liberty;[30] it does not constitute the delegation of legislative authority;[31] it does not interfere with rights of conscience;[32] and it is not special or class legislation, in that it affects only one class of persons, namely, school pupils.[33]

In the absence of statutory authority, the right of a school board to exclude from school pupils who have not been vaccinated depends, as a rule, upon the existence or nonexistence of smallpox in the community. The courts all agree that where an epidemic of smallpox exists or is threatened, boards of education may, under the general authority conferred upon them to govern the schools, make vaccination a condition of school attendance.[34] The rule has been stated as follows by the Court of Civil Appeals of Texas:

> The power of local bodies to require the vaccination of school children as a condition to their admission to public schools, in the absence of express authority, is dependent upon the conditions existing in the community with reference to smallpox. When an epidemic exists or is imminent there can be no doubt that the power may be exercised. It has also been held that such regulations may be adopted and enforced when smallpox exists in a community, and by some courts the expression is used that such regulations may be adopted when an epidemic is reasonably apprehended. In this case it was found that no epidemic existed or was imminent, but that the existing conditions with reference to smallpox constituted a menace to the public health. We conclude from our investigation of the authorities that it is not necessary for an epidemic to exist or be imminent in order for the school board to be justified in adopting and enforcing the regulation complained of, because, if the conditions are such that they constitute a menace to the public health, it can not be said that the board's action was unreasonable and that the want of necessity for the measures has been shown to be "clear,

30. *Viemeister* v. *White,* 179 N.Y. 235, 72 N.E. 97, 70 L.R.A. 796, 103 Am. St. Rep. 859; *Abeel* v. *Clark,* 84 Calif. 226, 24 Pac. 383; *Cram* v. *School Board of Manchester,* 82 N.H. 495, 136 Atl. 263.

31. *Zucht* v. *King,* 225 S.W. (Tex.) 267; *Blue* v. *Beach,* 155 Ind. 121, 56 N.E. 89, 50 L.R.A. 64, 80 Am. St. Rep. 195; *State* v. *Board of Education,* 21 Utah 401, 60 Pac. 1013; *Hagler* v. *Larner,* 284 Ill. 547, 120 N.E. 575.

32. *Staffel* v. *San Antonio School Board,* 201 S.W. (Tex.) 413; *Commonwealth* v. *Green,* 268 Mass. 585, 168 N.E. 101.

33. *French* v. *Davidson,* 143 Calif. 658, 77 Pac. 663.

34. *Auten* v. *Board of Directors,* 83 Ark. 431, 104 S.W. 130; *Duffield* v. *School District of City of Williamsport,* 162 Pa. St. 476, 29 Atl. 742, 25 L.R.A. 152; *Staffel* v. *San Antonio School Board,* 201 S.W. (Tex.) 413; *Zucht* v. *San Antonio School Board,* 170 S.W. (Tex.) 840; *Hagler* v. *Larner,* 284 Ill. 547, 120 N.E. 575; *Glover* v. *Board of Education,* 14 S.D. 139, 84 N.W. 761.

manifest, and undoubted." If existing conditions constitute a menace to the public health, an epidemic is threatened and it can not be said that it did not reasonably appear to the board to be necessary to adopt the regulation.[35]

While the courts will not hold that vaccination is a preventive of smallpox, they will hold that a board of education has the right to act upon the common belief that it is such a preventive.[36] In a Pennsylvania case,[37] for example, the court refused to issue a writ of mandamus to compel the school board to admit unvaccinated pupils at a time when smallpox existed in the district and in a number of nearby towns. An excerpt from the opinion of the court follows:

Is the regulation now under consideration a reasonable one? That is to be judged of in the first instance by the city authorities and the school board. It is only in the case of an abuse of discretionary powers that the court will undertake to supervise official discretion. Vaccination may be, or may not be, a preventive of smallpox. That is a question about which medical men differ and which the law affords no means of determining in a summary manner. A decided majority of the medical profession believe in its efficacy. . . . In the present state of medical knowledge and public opinion upon this subject it would be impossible for a court to deny that there is reason for believing in the importance of vaccination as a means of protection from the scourge of smallpox. The question is not one of science in a case like the present. We are not required to determine judicially whether the public belief in the efficacy of vaccination is absolutely right or not. We are to consider what is reasonable in view of the present state of medical knowledge and the concurring opinions of the various boards and offices charged with the care of the public health. The answers of the city and the school board show the belief of the proper authorities to be that a proper regard for the public health and for the children of the public schools requires the adoption of the regulation complained of. They are doing, in the utmost good faith, what they believe it is their duty to do; and though the plaintiff might be able to demonstrate by the highest scientific tests that they are mistaken in this respect, that would not be enough. It is not an error in judgment, or a mistake upon some abstruse question of medical science, but an abuse of discretionary power, that justifies the courts in interfering with the conduct of the school board or setting aside its action.

A pupil cannot defeat the operation of a rule requiring vaccination on the ground that it violates rights of conscience. In so holding, the court in a Texas case[38] pointed out that the control of the schools in San Antonio was given by law to the San Antonio board of education,

35. *Zucht* v. *San Antonio School Board*, 170 S.W. (Tex.) 840.

36. *Auten* v. *Board of Directors*, 83 Ark. 431, 104 S.W. 130.

37. *Duffield* v. *School District of City of Williamsport*, 162 Pa. St. 476, 29 Atl. 742, 25 L.R.A. 152.

38. *Staffel* v. *San Antonio School Board*, 201 S.W. (Tex.) 413.

"and not to individual parents, no matter how correct their consciences, convictions, faith, and religious beliefs may be."

According to the great weight of authority, a school board cannot, unless authorized to do so by statute, make vaccination a condition of school attendance in the absence of an actual or imminent epidemic of smallpox.[39] The courts reason that boards of education, being creatures of the legislature, can exercise only such powers as are expressly or impliedly granted. Authority to enforce a general, continuing rule requiring vaccination as a condition of school attendance, regardless of the existence or nonexistence of smallpox, is a power which cannot be implied or inferred. Thus it was said by the Supreme Court of Michigan:

> It is not a question as to what the legislature might do, under the police power, about requiring vaccination as a prerequisite to attending school; nor is it a question of whether the legislature could confer this power upon the school board. The board of education is a creature of the statute. It possesses only such powers as the statute gives it. The legislature has said who may and should attend the public schools. It nowhere undertakes to confer the power upon the school board to change these conditions by passing a general, continuing rule excluding children from the public schools until they comply with conditions not imposed upon them by the legislative branch of the government. In what I have said I do not mean to intimate that during the prevalence of diphtheria or smallpox, or any other epidemic of contagious disease, in a school district, the board may not, under its general powers, temporarily close the schools, or temporarily say who shall be excluded from the schools until the epidemic has passed; but what I do say is that the legislature has not undertaken to give them the power, when no epidemic of contagious disease exists or is imminent in the district, to pass a general, continuing rule which would have the effect of a general law excluding all pupils who will not submit to vaccination.[40]

It seems that some courts hold, however, that a school board may, without specific statutory authority and in the absence of smallpox, exclude from the public schools pupils who do not present a certificate of vaccination.[41] In a North Carolina case,[42] during an epidemic of

39. *Mathews* v. *Kalamazoo Board of Education,* 127 Mich. 530, 86 N.W. 1036, 54 L.R.A. 736; *Potts* v. *Breen,* 167 Ill. 67, 47 N.E. 81, 39 L.R.A. 152; *People* v. *Board of Education,* 234 Ill. 422, 84 N.E. 1046, 17 L.R.A. (N.S.) 709, 14 Ann. Cas. 943; *Burroughs* v. *Mortenson,* 312 Ill. 163, 143 N.E. 457.

40. *Mathews* v. *Kalamazoo Board of Education,* 127 Mich. 530, 86 N.W. 1036, 54 L.R.A. 736.

41. *Hutchins* v. *School Committee of the Town of Durham,* 137 N.C. 68, 49 S.E. 46; *In the Matter of Rebenack,* 62 Mo. App. 8.

42. *Hutchins* v. *School Committee of the Town of Durham,* 137 N.C. 68, 49 S.E. 46.

smallpox in the town of Durham, the school board passed a rule excluding from school pupils who had not been vaccinated. Action was brought to require the admission of an unvaccinated child. At the time the court rendered its decision there was, it seems, no danger of the spread of smallpox. Nevertheless, the court sustained the rule in language that intimates the rule would have been upheld even in the absence of smallpox. The court said:

> The plaintiff relies upon *Potts* v. *Breen,* 167 Ill. 67, . . . that, in the absence of express legislative power, a resolution requiring vaccination as a prerequisite to attending schools is unreasonable, when smallpox does not exist in the community, and there is no reasonable ground to apprehend its appearance. We are not inclined to follow that authority. With the present rapid means of intercommunication, smallpox may make its appearance in any community at any moment without any notice given beforehand, and incalculable havoc be made, especially among the school children, which can not be remedied by a subsequent order excluding the nonvaccinated. "An ounce of prevention is worth a pound of cure."

AUTHORITY OF BOARDS OF HEALTH TO MAKE VACCINATION A CONDITION OF SCHOOL ATTENDANCE

In the exercise of the police power of the state, the legislature may authorize boards of health to exclude from school all unvaccinated pupils, even though no smallpox may exist in the community at the time. A Texas case[43] is in point. Acting upon authority granted it by the city council, the local board of health of San Antonio passed a rule that all children attending either a public or private school should be vaccinated. In sustaining the authority of the city council to confer upon the board of health authority to enforce the rule in question, the court said:

> When we reach the conclusion, as we do, that these ordinances were enacted in pursuance of a grant of wise and valid power, which the Legislature expressly delegated to the city council through its charter, "to enforce vaccination," we pronounce its validity without reference to the actual existence of smallpox or not, though appellant concedes it exists among certain Mexicans all the time. . . . The board of health is the public agency through which the city council acts to determine the necessity arising to put the ordinance in effect as to its provisions, and that is no delegation of legislative power. It lays down the event in which the necessity to the public health requires the action, and is valid. It is a valid exercise of power. . . .
> We hold that the ordinance is valid; not unreasonable on the claimed ground that it operates without reference to the actual existence of a smallpox epidemic in the city; that there is no unlawful discrimination against

43. *Zucht* v. *King,* 225 S.W. (Tex.) 267.

persons attending schools, and it is not unreasonable and arbitrary, in view of the conditions in the Mexican quarter of the city and the crowding together of people in street cars, jitneys, theaters, churches, passenger depots, factories, laundries, parks, etc. Nor does it deny to appellant, or any pupil, rights and privileges without due course of the law of the land.

An appeal was taken to the Supreme Court of the United States.[44] In sustaining the ordinance in question, that court pointed out that its own decisions had already established the rule that it is within the police power of the state to provide for compulsory vaccination;[45] that a state may, consistent with the federal constitution, delegate to a municipality authority to determine under what conditions health regulations shall become operative;[46] and that a municipality may vest in its officials broad discretion in matters affecting the application and enforcement of health laws.[47]

According to the weight of authority, a board of health, in the absence of an actual or threatened epidemic of smallpox, cannot make vaccination a condition of school attendance unless expressly authorized to do so by statute.[48] In a case decided by the Supreme Court of Wisconsin,[49] for example, the state board of health was authorized by statute "to make such rules and regulations and to take such measures as may, in its judgment, be necessary for the protection of the people of the state from Asiatic cholera, or other dangerous contagious diseases." Acting under this grant of authority, the board of health passed a rule that no pupil should be permitted to attend a public or private school without a certificate of vaccination. The rule was held to be invalid for two reasons. In the first place, the rule was an attempt to exercise legislative power on the part of the board of health. "Our conclusion," said the court, "is that the rule under consideration could be made operative only as an act of legislative power, and it does not come within the domain of the power to make rules and regulations in

44. *Zucht* v. *King*, 260 U.S. 174, 43 S. Ct. 24, 67 L. Ed. 194.

45. *Jacobson* v. *Massachusetts*, 197 U.S. 11, 25 S. Ct. 358, 49 L. Ed. 643, 3 Ann. Cas. 765.

46. *Laurel Hill Cemetery* v. *San Francisco*, 216 U.S. 358, 30 S. Ct. 301, 54 L. Ed. 515.

47. *Lieberman* v. *Van De Carr*, 199 U.S. 552, 26 S. Ct. 144, 50 L. Ed. 305.

48. *Rhea* v. *Board of Education*, 41 N.D. 449, 171 N.W. 103; *State* v. *Burdge*, 95 Wis. 390, 70 N.W. 347; *Osborn* v. *Russell*, 64 Kan. 507, 68 Pac. 60; *Burroughs* v. *Mortenson*, 312 Ill. 163, 143 N.E. 457.

49. *State* v. *Burdge*, 95 Wis. 390, 70 N.W. 347.

aid or execution of some general statutory provision." In the second place, the rule was regarded as unreasonable and arbitrary because there was very little danger of smallpox at any place in the state.

Similarly, in North Dakota a statute authorized the state board of health "to make and enforce all needful rules and regulations for the prevention and cure, and to prevent the spread of any contagious disease." In holding that the board of health did not have authority to make vaccination a condition of school attendance at all times, the court said: "The authorities uniformly hold that a board of health, constituted as our board of health is, possessing requisite general powers for the prevention and spread of contagious diseases, cannot formulate and enforce rules which merely have a tendency in that direction, but which are not founded upon any existing condition or upon a danger not reasonably to be apprehended."[50]

In Arkansas, on the other hand, it was held[51] that a board of health, having general control and supervision of all matters pertaining to the health of the citizens of the state and having authority to suppress contagious diseases and to prevent their spread, might require vaccination as a condition of school attendance. The court pointed out, however, that smallpox was prevalent in the state and that the rule had been adopted at a time when soldiers were being transported in and out of the state in great numbers. In view of the fact that an epidemic of smallpox might result unless preventive measures were adopted, the court held that the rule was a reasonable one and was one within the authority of the board to enforce.

It is well established, however, that, where an epidemic of smallpox exists or is imminent, a board of health may, under its general and implied authority, exclude from school all unvaccinated pupils[52] or even order the schools to be closed.[53] In a number of cases the exercise of such authority on the part of boards of health has been challenged on the ground that it constitutes the exercise of legislative

50. *Rhea* v. *Board of Education*, 41 N.D. 449, 171 N.W. 103.

51. *State* v. *Martin*, 134 Ark. 420, 204 S.W. 622.

52. *State* v. *Board of Education*, 21 Utah 401, 60 Pac. 1013; *State* v. *Zimmerman*, 86 Minn. 353, 90 N.W. 783, 58 L.R.A. 78, 91 Am. St. Rep. 351; *Hagler* v. *Larner*, 284 Ill. 547, 120 N.E. 575; *People* v. *Board of Education*, 224 Mich. 388, 195 N.W. 95; *Blue* v. *Beach*, 155 Ind. 121, 56 N.E. 89, 50 L.R.A. 64, 80 Am. St. Rep. 195; *State* v. *Partlow*, 119 Wash. 316, 205 Pac. 420.

53. *State* v. *Zimmerman*, 86 Minn. 353, 90 N.W. 783, 58 L.R.A. 78, 91 Am. St. Rep. 351.

power. The courts concede that the legislature cannot delegate legislative power to a board of health, but they all agree, it seems, that a board of health is merely exercising administrative discretion when it excludes unvaccinated pupils from school in the presence of a threatened or actual epidemic of smallpox.[54]

In a case decided by the Supreme Court of Illinois[55] the statute authorized the city council of Granite City "to appoint a board of health, and prescribe its powers and duties." The council was further authorized "to do all acts, make all regulations which may be necessary or expedient for the promotion of health or the suppression of disease." The city council passed an ordinance conferring upon the board of health authority, upon the appearance of an epidemic of smallpox, to make all regulations necessary or expedient for the suppression of the disease. The board of health passed a regulation, in the face of an epidemic of smallpox, requiring that, while the epidemic existed, all children who had not been vaccinated should be excluded from the public schools. In refusing to enjoin the enforcement of the regulation, the court said:

The courts are practically a unit in holding that in the event of a present or threatened epidemic such rules and regulations as are now under consideration are reasonable and should be upheld—and such has been the rule in States where there has been no express authority requiring vaccination. Where small-pox is epidemic it is not a necessary prerequisite to require vaccination that pupils have been personally exposed. . . .

The resolution of the board of health was reasonable in view of the fact that small-pox was epidemic and the disease likely to spread from the many cases then existing in the city. . . .

The foregoing clauses of the statute and the ordinance of Granite City conferred upon the board of health of said city ample authority to pass said resolution under the existing facts. The passing of the resolution by the board was the mere exercise of an administrative function and not the exercise of a legislative power, as contended by the appellants. The delegation of power to make a law would, if conferred upon the board of health, be a legislative power, and such a delegation would be void. However, the conferring of authority or discretion upon the board of health to execute a law or ordinance is not a delegation of legislative authority, and the rule is well established that such may be done.

In some instances the authority of a board of health to close the schools because of the existence of an epidemic of smallpox or to re-

54. *Blue* v. *Beach*, 155 Ind. 121, 56 N.E. 89, 50 L.R.A. 64, 80 Am. St. Rep. 195; *State* v. *Martin*, 134 Ark. 420, 204 S.W. 622; *Hagler* v. *Larner*, 284 Ill. 547, 120 N.E. 575; *State* v. *Board of Education*, 21 Utah 401, 60 Pac. 1013.

55. *Hagler* v. *Larner*, 284 Ill. 547, 120 N.E. 575.

quire vaccination as a condition of school attendance has been challenged by the local board of education. As a rule, where an epidemic of smallpox exists or is threatened, a board of health may, in the exercise of its general powers to protect the public health, require a board of education to exclude from school all unvaccinated pupils.[56] In Lansing, Michigan, for example, there was an outbreak of smallpox. For a time the board of health and the board of education worked in harmony. The board of health adopted a resolution excluding from the public schools all pupils and teachers who had not been vaccinated. The board acted under authority of a statute which read in part as follows: "When the smallpox, or any other disease dangerous to the public health, is found to exist in any township, the board of health shall use all possible care to prevent the spreading of the infection . . . by such means as in their judgment shall be most effectual for the common safety." The board of education also adopted a resolution reciting that there were only seventeen cases of smallpox existing in the city and directing the readmission to school of pupils who had not been vaccinated. Mandamus proceedings were brought against the school board to require the enforcement of the resolution of the board of health. The court held that the board of health had not exceeded its authority nor abused its discretion. Consequently, the writ prayed for was issued.[57] Similarly, in Kentucky, the state board of health was authorized to enforce rules and regulations to prevent the spread of contagious diseases. County boards of health were authorized to enforce the rules and regulations of the state board of health. Moreover, county boards themselves were authorized "to inaugurate and execute and to require the heads of families and other persons to execute such sanitary regulations as the local board may consider expedient to prevent the outbreak and spread of cholera, smallpox," and other contagious diseases. The state board of health passed a regulation that no person could become a member of any public school without furnishing a certificate of vaccination. The county board of education of Jefferson County adopted a resolution requiring the county health officer to enforce the rule of the state board of health. A local

56. *People* v. *Board of Education*, 224 Mich. 388, 195 N.W. 95; *Board of Trustees of Highland Park Graded Common School District No. 46* v. *McMurtry*, 169 Ky. 457, 184 S.W. 390; *Hill* v. *Bickers*, 171 Ky. 703, 188 S.W. 766; *State* v. *Beil*, 157 Ind. 25, 60 N.E. 672.

57. *People* v. *Board of Education*, 224 Mich. 388, 195 N.W. 95.

school board sought to enjoin the enforcement of the rule. The court refused to grant the injunction because in its opinion the language of the statute was broad enough to confer upon boards of health authority to issue the order in question.[58]

It has been held, however, that a board of health cannot close the schools unless specifically authorized to do so by statute. Thus, it was said by the Supreme Court of Oregon:

> Although the state board is given "general supervision of the interests of the health and life of the citizens of the state," that provision should not be construed to mean that it alone has power to close the public schools of the state. Such authority would be very broad and far-reaching, and would have to be read into the statute by construction. If it had been the intent of the Legislature to confer such a vast power upon the state board of health, it should have used language far more specific and certain than that appearing in the section quoted.[59]

A contrary position has been taken by the Supreme Court of Arizona.[60] The board of health of Globe, Arizona, ordered the schools closed because of an epidemic of influenza. The board of education brought action to test the authority of the board of health to close the schools. Although the board of health had no express statutory authority to close the schools, the court sustained its action:

> While school trustees and educational administrative officers are invested with power to establish, provide for, govern, and regulate public schools within their respective jurisdictions, they are in these respects no wise subject to the discretion or control of the state or county or city boards of health, yet when the necessity arises to close the schools for the protection of the public health such emergency, while it exists, is a superior power to that given the school administrative officers, and the law of necessity controls the situation during the existence of the emergency giving rise to the power.

Although a board of health may have authority to exclude unvaccinated pupils from school, it does not alone possess such authority. A board of education may always act independently whenever conditions are such as to require vaccination. The very act of creating a board of education vests in it by implication that degree of police power necessary for the board to accomplish the objects of its creation.[61] Thus it was said in the case of *Stone* v. *Probst:*

58. *Board of Trustees of Highland Park Graded Common School District No. 46* v. *McMurtry,* 169 Ky. 457, 184 S.W. 390.

59. *Crane* v. *School District No. 14,* 95 Ore. 644, 188 Pac. 712.

60. *Globe School District No. 1* v. *Board of Health of City of Globe,* 20 Ariz. 208, 179 Pac. 55.

61. *McSween* v. *Board of School Trustees,* 60 Tex. Civ. App. 270, 129 S.W. 206.

It is claimed that the matter of health is delegated to the board of public welfare by chapter 14 of the city charter. It is. It does not follow, however, that, because the people through their charter have delegated such power to that board, the board of education is denied the exercise of the same powers to such an extent as may be reasonably necessary to carry out the purposes for which it was created.[62]

In some jurisdictions the courts have been called upon to decide whether a school board may prescribe the form of vaccination. Wherever the issue has been raised, the courts have held that boards of education may, when authorized to require vaccination at all, require evidence of scarification and injection of the virus of cowpox into the human system.[63] Evidence of vaccination through the taking of medicine internally may be rejected. The statutes of Pennsylvania, for example, required all pupils attending a public school to present a certificate of successful vaccination. A child was vaccinated by a method recognized by the International School of Homeopathy, that is, by taking medicine in powder form through the mouth. The board of health, however, had prescribed a form of certificate which showed that the child had been vaccinated by scarification. In sustaining the authority of the board of health to require vaccination by scarification, the court said: "The ordinary and usual means of 'vaccination' and the sense in which it must be supposed to have been used by the legislature, is inoculation with the virus of cowpox for the purpose of communicating that disease as a prophylactic against smallpox. It indicates an operation, and not a result."[64]

To the same effect was a case[65] decided by the Court of Civil Appeals of Texas. A board of education refused to accept a certificate of vaccination issued by a homeopathic physician to a child who, it was claimed, had been rendered immune by the taking of medicine internally. The court sustained the position of the board.

Where the law makes school attendance compulsory and at the same time requires or authorizes boards of education to require vaccination as a condition of school attendance, the courts are in disagreement as to whether a parent who refuses to have his child vac-

62. *Stone* v. *Probst*, 165 Minn. 361, 206 N.W. 642.

63. *State* v. *Cole*, 220 Mo. 697, 119 S.W. 424, 22 L.R.A. (N.S.) 986; *Lee* v. *Marsh*, 230 Pa. St. 351, 79 Atl. 564; *Abney* v. *Fox*, 250 S.W. (Tex.) 210; *Allen* v. *Ingalls*, 182 Ark. 991, 33 S.W. (2d) 1099.

64. *Lee* v. *Marsh*, 230 Pa. St. 351, 79 Atl. 564.

65. *Abney* v. *Fox*, 250 S.W. (Tex.) 210.

cinated may be prosecuted under the compulsory-attendance statute. In a New York case[66] it has been held that, when a parent is prosecuted under the compulsory-attendance act, it is no defense that the child was sent to school but excluded because it had not been vaccinated. In that state a statute provided that no person who had not been vaccinated should be admitted to the public schools. The following year a statute was enacted requiring all children to attend school. A pupil who refused to be vaccinated was excluded from school. Action was brought against his father for violation of the compulsory-attendance act. It was contended that the exclusion from school was a valid defense to the action. The court held otherwise:

If indifferent or selfish parents for ulterior purposes, such as the desire to place young children at labor instead of school, or from capricious or recalcitrant motives, may be allowed to manufacture easy excuses for not sending their children to school, a ready method will have been developed for evading the statute compelling such attendance, and if the statute which requires parents to see to it that their children attend and take advantage of this school system may be lightly and easily evaded, the purposes of the state in providing and insisting on education will be frustrated and impaired. Failure to comply with the statute ought not to be excused except for some good reason.

It is perfectly evident that in a great city like New York with its complex and varying conditions, regulations must be adopted for the purposes of preserving discipline, order and health in the public schools. Some of these regulations would be so plain and essential that no reasonable person would think of disputing their validity or of making unwillingness to comply therewith a basis for not sending his children to school. The question which within certain limits is presented here is whether the statute and the by-laws of the board of education in that city adopted under and in accordance with the statute requiring vaccination as a condition of attending the public schools, are under ordinary conditions so unusual or oppressive that a parent should be allowed to make his unwillingness to comply therewith a basis for not sending his children to school, for that is what the present position of the defendant amounts to. I do not think they are of such a character. . . .

It does not require much spirit of prophecy to foresee what will follow a contrary construction of the statutes. If a parent may escape all obligations under the statute requiring him to send his children to school by simply alleging that he does not believe in vaccination, the policy of the state to give some education to all children, if necessary by compelling measures, will become more or less a farce under existing legislation.

Other courts, however, take a contrary position.[67] They reason that a penal statute must be strictly construed. If, they hold, the compul-

66. *People* v. *Ekerold,* 211 N.Y. 386, 105 N.E. 670, L.R.A. 1915D 223.

67. *Commonwealth* v. *Smith,* 9 Pa. Dist. Rep. 625; *State* v. *Cole,* 220 Mo. 697, 119 S.W. 424, 22 L.R.A. (N.S.) 986; *State* v. *Turney,* 31 Ohio Cir. Ct. Rep. 222.

sory-attendance statute does not itself make vaccination a condition of attendance, exclusion from school of an unvaccinated pupil is a perfect defense in an action against a parent for violation of the attendance act. It is reasoned, moreover, that if the statute requiring vaccination and the statute requiring attendance be construed together, the result would be compulsory vaccination.[68]

A Pennsylvania case[69] is in point. An act of the legislature required school attendance; another act made it the duty of school officers to exclude from school all children who had not had smallpox or who did not submit a certificate of successful vaccination. A parent refused to have his child vaccinated and was proceeded against under the compulsory-attendance act. The court held that the parent had a perfect defense:

> It must be remembered in construing this statute that it does not make it the duty of the persons covered by it to obtain a certificate for presentation to the teacher that the child has been successfully vaccinated or had previously had smallpox; and unless you can read that into the statute, we are at a loss to see how this judgment can be sustained. The defendant discharged all the duties expressly enjoined by the statute by sending his son to school; and while another statute required the teacher to refuse him admission, in default of the certificate, the discharge of that duty by the teacher added nothing to the duties prescribed by the statute under which this judgment was entered.
>
> This is a penal statute and must be construed strictly and according to its letter. The meaning of this rule of construction is that penal statutes, such as the one under consideration, are not to be regarded as including anything which is not within their letter as well as their spirit, which is clearly and intelligently described in the very words of the statute as well as manifestly intended by the legislature. . . .
>
> We must conclude from the foregoing that the compulsory-education Act, by its terms, did not make it obligatory upon the defendant to obtain a certificate. His sole duty prescribed by it was to send his son to school. He did this. . . . The defendant made a complete answer to the case of the Commonwealth when he showed that he had sent his son to school until he was denied admission by the teacher.

RESTRICTION UPON MEMBERSHIP IN HIGH-SCHOOL FRATERNITIES

The authority of the legislature to prohibit membership in high-school fraternities has been tested in a number of jurisdictions. Without exception, the courts have held that the legislature may prohibit fraternities and secret societies in the public schools of the state and

68. *State* v. *Turney,* 31 Ohio Cir. Ct. Rep. 222.
69. *Commonwealth* v. *Smith,* 9 Pa. Dist. Rep. 625.

may authorize or require boards of education to expel any pupil maintaining membership in such fraternities or societies.[70] The statutes of Iowa, for example, provided that it should be unlawful for any pupil attending a public school to become a member of any fraternity or society except such as might be sanctioned by the board of school directors. The statute was challenged as being unconstitutional, on the ground that it delegated arbitrary and unregulated powers; that it was class legislation; that it worked "an arbitrary and capricious destruction of personal rights secured by fundamental law by means of exercising an utterly unjustified paternalism"; and that it violated the due-process-of-law clause of the Fourteenth Amendment. In the opinion of the court, however, the statute was a valid exercise of the legislative authority of the state.[71] A similar statute was challenged in California, on the ground that it was special and class legislation inasmuch as it applied to public school pupils but did not apply to students in normal schools. In sustaining the statute, the court held that the classification in question was based upon real distinctions and therefore legal. It was further held by the court that the statute did not abridge the privileges and immunities of citizens of the United States in violation of the Fourteenth Amendment. The right to attend the public schools is a right growing out of state, and not out of federal, citizenship. Therefore, the privileges and immunities involved did not come under the inhibitions of the federal constitution.[72] The same general conclusion was reached by the Supreme Court of Mississippi in the case of *Board of Trustees* v. *Waugh*.[73] And in Illinois, the supreme court has held that a statute making it the duty of school boards to expel pupils maintaining membership in fraternities or sororities does not discriminate between pupils similarly situated.[74]

It seems that no case has yet come into the courts involving the authority of school boards, in the absence of specific statutory authority, to suspend or expel pupils on the ground of membership in frater-

70. *Sutton* v. *Board of Education*, 306 Ill. 507, 138 N.E. 131; *Lee* v. *Hoffman*, 182 Iowa 216, 166 N.W. 565, L.R.A. 1918C 933; *Bradford* v. *Board of Education*, 18 Calif. App. 19, 121 Pac. 929; *Steele* v. *Sexton*, 253 Mich. 32, 234 N.W. 436; *Satan Fraternity et al.* v. *Board of Public Instruction for Dade County*, 156 Fla. 222, 22 So. (2d) 892; *Hughes* v. *Caddo Parish School Board*, 65 S. Ct. 562, 323 U.S. 685; *Antell* v. *Stokes*, 287 Mass. 103, 191 N.E. 407.

71. *Lee* v. *Hoffman*, 182 Iowa 216, 166 N.W. 565, L.R.A. 1918C 933.

72. *Bradford* v. *Board of Education*, 18 Calif. App. 19, 121 Pac. 929.

73. *Board of Trustees* v. *Waugh*, 105 Miss. 623, 62 So. 827.

74. *Sutton* v. *Board of Education*, 306 Ill. 507, 138 N.E. 131.

nities. In a number of cases, however, it has been held that a board of education, under its general authority to manage the schools, may limit the privileges of pupils who maintain membership in fraternities.[75] Perhaps the leading case in point is that of *Wilson* v. *Board of Education*.[76] The Board of Education of Chicago adopted a rule whereby all pupils who were members of a secret society should be denied the privilege of representing the school in any literary or athletic contest or in any other public capacity. Action was brought to enjoin the enforcement of the rule on the ground that it was unreasonable, that it was a violation of the natural rights of the pupils, and that it was an unlawful discrimination against those pupils who belonged to secret societies. In denying the injunction, the court said in part:

The power of the board of education to control and manage the schools and to adopt rules and regulations necessary for that purpose is ample and full. The rules and by-laws necessary to a proper conduct and management of the schools are, and must necessarily be, left to the discretion of the board, and its acts will not be interfered with nor set aside by the courts, unless there is a clear abuse of the power and discretion conferred. Acting reasonably within the powers conferred, it is the province of the board of education to determine what things are detrimental to the succesful management, good order, and discipline of the schools and the rules required to produce these conditions. It was the judgment of the superintendent of schools of Chicago, as well as of the board of education, that membership in secret societies, known as Greek letter fraternities or sororities, was detrimental to the best interests of the schools. Whether this judgment was sound and well founded is not subject to review by the courts. The only question for determination is whether the rule adopted to prevent or remedy the supposed evil was a reasonable exercise of the power and discretion of the board. . . .

Assuming, as we must, that the adoption of the rule was not an abuse of power or discretion conferred by law upon the board, the courts can not, and should not, interfere with its enforcement. Pupils attending the schools may decide for themselves whether they prefer membership in the secret societies, with the disqualification from representing their schools in literary or athletic contests or other public capacities, or whether they prefer these latter privileges to membership in said societies. It is for the board of education, within the reasonable exercise of its power and discretion, to say what is best for the successful management and conduct of the schools, and not for the courts.

75. *Wilson* v. *Board of Education*, 233 Ill. 464, 84 N.E. 697, 15 L.R.A. (N.S.) 1136, 13 Ann. Cas. 330; *Wayland* v. *Board of School Directors*, 43 Wash. 441, 86 Pac. 642, 7 L.R.A. (N.S.) 352; *Coggins* v. *Board of Education*, 223 N.C. 763, 28 S.E. (2d) 527; *Isgrig* v. *Srygley*, 197 S.W. (2d) (Ark.) 39; *Burkitt* v. *School District No. 1*, 246 Pac. (2d) (Ore.) 566; *Wilson* v. *Abilene Independent School District*, 190 S.W. (2d) (Tex.) 406.

76. *Wilson* v. *Board of Education*, 233 Ill. 464, 84 N.E. 697, 15 L.R.A. (N.S.) 1136, 13 Ann. Cas. 330.

The Supreme Court of Washington has sustained substantially the same kind of rule.[77] In Missouri, on the other hand, a rule of the Board of Education of St. Louis prohibiting fraternity members from representing the school in any capacity or from participating in graduating exercises was held to be unreasonable. The court based its opinion upon the absence of evidence to support the conclusion that fraternity membership was detrimental to the operation and control of the school.[78]

AUTHORITY OF SCHOOL BOARDS TO ENFORCE REGULATIONS GOVERNING PUPIL CONDUCT OFF THE SCHOOL GROUNDS AND OUT OF SCHOOL HOURS

The rule is well established by many cases that school authorities may govern the conduct of pupils while off the school grounds and out of school hours. A board of education may discipline a pupil for any act, no matter where or when committed, provided that the act tends immediately and directly to destroy the discipline and to impair the efficiency of the school.[79]

In an early Vermont case[80] a pupil, upon his return home from school, was sent to drive home a cow. While passing the teacher's house, in the presence of another pupil, he contemptuously called the teacher "old Jack Seaver." The next morning after school opened the teacher gave the offending pupil a sound whipping with a rawhide. In upholding the teacher in an action brought against him for assault and battery, the court rendered an opinion which has frequently been cited and quoted with approval. It said:

> Where the offense has a direct and immediate tendency to injure the school and bring the master's authority into contempt, as in this case, when done in the presence of other scholars and of the master, and with a design to insult

77. *Wayland* v. *Board of School Directors*, 43 Wash. 441, 86 Pac. 642, 7 L.R.A. (N.S.) 352.

78. *Wright* v. *Board of Education*, 295 Mo. 466, 246 S.W. 43.

79. *Lander* v. *Seaver*, 32 Vt. 114, 76 Am. Dec. 156; *Burdick* v. *Babcock*, 31 Iowa 562; *Kinzer* v. *Independent School District of Marion*, 129 Iowa 441, 105 N.W. 686, 3 L.R.A. (N.S.) 496; *State* v. *District Board of District No. 1*, 135 Wis. 619, 116 N.W. 232, 16 L.R.A. (N.S.) 730; *Sherman* v *Charlestown*, 8 Cush. (Mass.) 160; *O'Rourke* v. *Walker*, 102 Conn. 130, 128 Atl. 25, 41 A.L.R. 1308; *Mangum* v. *Keith*, 147 Ga. 603, 95 S.E. 1; *Deskins* v. *Gose*, 85 Mo. 485, 55 Am. Rep. 387; *Douglas* v. *Campbell*, 89 Ark. 254, 116 S.W. 211, 20 L.R.A. (N.S.) 205; *Jones* v. *Cody*, 132 Mich. 13, 92 N.W. 495, 62 L.R.A. 160; *Sweeney* v. *Young*, 82 N.H. 159, 131 Atl. 155, 142 L.R.A. 757; *Guethler* v. *Altman*, 26 Ind. App. 587, 60 N.E. 355; *Balding* v. *State*, 23 Tex. App. 172, 4 S.W. 579.

80. *Lander* v. *Seaver*, 32 Vt. 114, 76 Am. Dec. 156.

him, we think he has the right to punish the scholar for such acts if he comes again to school. The misbehavior must not have merely a remote and indirect tendency to injure the school. All improper conduct or language may perhaps have, by influence and example, a remote tendency of that kind. But the tendency of the acts so done out of the teacher's supervision for which he may punish, must be direct and immediate in their bearing upon the welfare of the school, or the authority of the master and the respect due to him. Cases may readily be supposed which lie very near the line, and it will often be difficult to distinguish between the acts which have such an immediate and those which have such a remote tendency. Hence, each case must be determined by its peculiar circumstances.

In the same connection, it has been said by the Supreme Court of Iowa:

If the effects of acts done out of school hours reach within the school-room during school hours and are detrimental to good order and the best interests of the pupils, it is evident that such acts may be forbidden. Truancy is a fault committed away from school. Can it be pretended that it cannot be reached for correction by the school board and teachers? A pupil may engage in sports beyond school that will render him unfit to study during school hours. Cannot these sports be forbidden? The view that acts, to be within the authority of the school board and teachers for discipline and correction, must be done within school hours, is narrow, and without regard to the spirit of the law and the best interests of our common schools. It is in conflict, too, with authority.[81]

The following cases will serve to illustrate still further the extent to which the courts will permit school authorities to control out-of-school conduct of pupils. In Massachusetts a girl pupil was guilty of immoral conduct off the school grounds. The court sustained the right of the board to exclude her from school.[82] In a Connecticut case[83] a pupil was guilty of annoying small girls while on their way home from school. The court sustained the authority of the teacher to punish the pupil, notwithstanding the fact that the offense was committed after he had reached his home and on the premises of his parents. A rule prohibiting pupils from attending any show, moving-picture show, or social function except on Friday nights and on Saturdays was sustained by the Supreme Court of Georgia.[84] In a Texas case,[85] it was held that a teacher could legally punish a pupil for refusing to work arithmetic examples at home. In the case of *Douglas* v. *Camp-*

81. *Burdick* v. *Babcock,* 31 Iowa 562.
82. *Sherman* v. *Charlestown,* 8 Cush. (Mass.) 160.
83. *O'Rourke* v. *Walker,* 102 Conn. 130, 128 Atl. 25, 41 A.L.R. 1308.
84. *Mangum* v. *Keith,* 147 Ga. 603, 95 S.E. 1.
85. *Balding* v. *State,* 23 Tex. App. 172, 4 S.W. 579.

bell[86] the Supreme Court of Arkansas held that a board of education had authority to suspend from school a pupil who was drunk and disorderly upon the streets of the village on Christmas Day. In a Michigan case[87] it was held that the Board of Education of Detroit had authority to enforce a rule requiring that pupils go directly home at the close of school. Rules prohibiting pupils from fighting and using profane language while going to and from school have been sustained in a number of cases.[88]

There are limits, however, beyond which school authorities may not go in controlling the conduct of pupils while off the school grounds. The act which is sought to be regulated must directly and immediately impair the discipline and well-being of the school. In Mississippi, for example, a school board adopted a rule which required all pupils to remain in their homes and study from seven to nine in the evening. Any pupil who violated the rule was subject to corporal punishment at the discretion of the teacher. The court enjoined the enforcement of the rule upon the following grounds:

Certainly a rule of the school, which invades the home and wrests from the parent his right to control his child around his own hearthstone, is inconsistent with any law that has yet governed the parent in this state. . . . In the home the parental authority is and should be supreme, and it is a misguided zeal that attempts to wrest it from them. . . .
It may be that the school authorities would have a right to make certain regulations and rules for the good government of the school which would extend and control the child even when it has reached its home; but, if that power exists, it can only be done in matters which would per se have a direct and pernicious effect on the moral tone of the school, or have a tendency to subvert and destroy the proper administration of school affairs.[89]

The reasoning in the foregoing case is supported by the case of *State* v. *Osborne*.[90] The faculty of a state normal school adopted a rule prohibiting students from attending parties, entertainments, or places of public amusement except by permission. The court held that such a rule could not be enforced against a student who lived with her parents and who attended a party with their consent. Similarly, in

86. *Douglas* v. *Campbell*, 89 Ark. 254, 116 S.W. 211, 20 L.R.A. (N.S.) 205. Accord, *Sweeney* v. *Young*, 82 N.H. 159, 131 Atl. 155.

87. *Jones* v. *Cody*, 132 Mich. 13, 92 N.W. 495, 62 L.R.A. 160.

88. *Hutton* v. *State*, 23 Tex. App. 386, 5 S.W. 122, 59 Am. Rep. 776; *Deskins* v. *Gose*, 85 Mo. 485, 55 Am. Rep. 387.

89. *Hobbs* v. *Germany*, 94 Miss. 469, 49 So. 515, 22 L.R.A. (N.S.) 983.

90. *State* v. *Osborne*, 24 Mo. App. 309.

a Missouri case[91] it was held that a school board had no authority to enforce a rule prohibiting pupils from attending social parties during the school term. In the words of the court:

> It certainly could not have been the design of the Legislature to take from the parent the control of his child while not at school, and invest it in a board of directors or teacher of a school. If they can prescribe a rule which denies to the parent the right to allow his child to attend a social gathering, except upon pain of expulsion from a school which the law gives him the right to attend, may they not prescribe a rule which would forbid the parent from allowing the child to attend a particular church, or any church at all, and then step *in loco parentis* and supersede entirely parental authority? For offenses committed by the scholar while at school, he is amenable to the laws of the school; when not at school, but under charge of the parent or guardian, he is answerable alone to him.

AUTHORITY OF SCHOOL BOARDS TO REQUIRE PUPILS TO PURSUE PARTICULAR SUBJECTS

The authority of the state to require all pupils to pursue a particular study has been tested in the courts in only a few cases. There seems to be little doubt, however, that the state possesses such authority. Since the public schools exist primarily for the purpose of training pupils for citizenship, the state, through its legally constituted agents, may undoubtedly require all pupils to pursue those studies essential to good citizenship.[92] If the state can compel a child to go to school, it can unquestionably prescribe what studies the child shall pursue in the interests of good citizenship.

In a case[93] decided by the Supreme Court of Maine a statute authorized the school committee "to direct the general course of instruction, and what books shall be used in the respective schools." A school committee required all pupils to read the Bible in the schools. A Catholic pupil was expelled for disobeying the regulation of the board. In sustaining the board in the action which it had taken, the court said in part:

> The right to prescribe the general course of instruction and to direct what books shall be used must exist somewhere. The Legislature have seen fit to repose the authority to determine this in the several superintending school committees. They may therefore rightly exercise it. . . .
> So, in this case, the same general and extensive power over the subject

91. *Dritt* v. *Snodgrass,* 66 Mo. 286, 27 Am. Rep. 343.

92. *People* v. *Stanley,* 255 Pac. (Colo.) 610.

93. *Donahoe* v. *Richards,* 38 Me. 379, 61 Am. Dec. 256.

matter is granted; and the course of studies, and the books prescribed by the superintending school committee are to be regarded as if established and prescribed by the act of the Legislature.

In the absence of express statutory authority, however, there is some conflict among the courts as to whether a school board may require a pupil to pursue a particular subject against the wishes of his parents. It is conceded that a board of education may prescribe the course of study and may include in it other subjects than those prescribed by law. It is also conceded that a pupil may be denied a diploma unless he has pursued satisfactorily the prescribed studies. However, according to the weight of authority, a parent may make a reasonable selection of studies for his child to pursue from such studies as are taught in the school.[94] No selection is reasonable, however, which interferes with the discipline or well-being of the school or which interferes with the rights of other pupils.

A Nebraska case[95] illustrates the reasoning of those courts which accord the parent the right to select his child's studies. A pupil was expelled from school because her father refused to permit her to study grammar. The father's objection to the study was that it was not being taught as it was when he went to school. The court required the school board to readmit the pupil. It said in part:

Now who is to determine what studies she shall pursue in school: a teacher, who has a mere temporary interest in her welfare, or her father, who may reasonably be supposed to be desirous of pursuing such course as will best promote the happiness of his child?

The father certainly possesses superior opportunities of knowing the physical and mental capabilities of his child. It may be apparent that all the prescribed course of studies is more than the strength of the child can undergo; or he may be desirous, as is frequently the case, that his child while attending school, should also take lessons in music, painting, etc., from private teachers. This he has a right to do. The right of the parent, therefore, to determine what studies his child shall pursue, is paramount to that of the trustees or teacher.

Schools are provided by the public in which prescribed branches are taught, which are free to all within the district between certain ages. But no pupil attending the school can be compelled to study any prescribed branch

94. *State* v. *Ferguson,* 95 Neb. 63, 144 N.W. 1039, 50 L.R.A. (N.S.) 266; *State* v. *School District No. 1,* 31 Neb. 552, 48 N.W. 393; *Trustees of Schools* v. *People,* 87 Ill. 303, 29 Am. Rep. 55; *Rulison* v. *Post,* 79 Ill. 567; *School Board District No. 18* v. *Thompson,* 24 Okla. 1, 103 Pac. 578, 24 L.R.A. (N.S.) 221, 138 Am. St. Rep. 861, 19 Ann. Cas. 1188; *Morrow* v. *Wood,* 35 Wis. 59, 17 Am. Rep. 471.

95. *State* v. *School District No. 1,* 31 Neb. 552, 48 N.W. 393.

against the protest of the parent that the child shall not study such branch, and any rule or regulation that requires the pupil to continue such studies is arbitrary and unreasonable. There is no good reason why the failure of one or more pupils to study one or more prescribed branches should result disastrously to the proper discipline, efficiency, and well-being of the school.

Such pupils are not idle, but merely devoting their attention to other branches; and so long as the failure of the students, thus excepted, to study all the branches of the prescribed course does not prejudice the equal rights of other students, there is no cause for complaint.

An Illinois case[96] is likewise in point. A pupil passed all the required subjects for admission to high school except grammar. He was refused admission because of that deficiency. His father did not wish him to study grammar. In issuing a writ of mandamus requiring admission, the court expressed the following opinion with respect to the right of parents to select the studies of their children:

No parent has the right to demand that the interests of the children of others shall be sacrificed for the interests of his child; and he cannot, consequently, insist that his child shall be placed or kept in particular classes, when by so doing others will be retarded in the advancement they would otherwise make; or that his child shall be taught studies not in the prescribed course of the school, or be allowed to use a textbook different from that decided to be used in the school. . . . The rights of each are to be enjoyed and exercised only with reference to the equal rights of all others. . . .

The policy of the school law is only to withdraw from the parent the right to select the branches to be studied by the child, to the extent that the exercise of that right would interfere with the system of instruction prescribed for the school, and its efficiency in imparting education to all entitled to share in its benefits. No particular branch of study is compulsory upon those who attend school, but schools are simply provided by the public in which prescribed branches are taught, which are free to all within the district between certain ages. . . .

It is not claimed that every pupil attending the high school must pursue every study taught therein, and manifestly, in the absence of legislation expressly requiring this, a regulation to that effect would be regarded as arbitrary and unreasonable, and could not, therefore, receive the sanction of the courts. Conceding that all the branches of study decided to be taught in the school shall not necessarily be pursued by every pupil, we are unable to perceive how it can, in any wise, prejudice the school, if one branch rather than another be omitted from the course of study of a particular pupil.

A case[97] decided by the Supreme Court of Colorado holds that a school board cannot require a pupil to receive instruction not essential to good citizenship. Consequently, the board could not require all pupils to attend the reading of the Bible. The court held that the

96. *Trustees of Schools* v. *People,* 87 Ill. 303, 29 Am. Rep. 55.

97. *People* v. *Stanley,* 81 Colo. 276, 255 Pac. 610.

liberty of the parent to select for his child all studies which are not essential to good citizenship is a liberty guaranteed by the Fourteenth Amendment.

The District Court of Appeals of California has held, in a novel case,[98] that a school board may not expel a pupil for refusing to participate in social dancing. The statutes authorized boards of education to provide courses in physical education. Dancing was made a part of the required course of study in a certain school district. The dances taught were the "waltz," the "polka," the "two-step," and the "fox trot." The dancing was performed in couples, male and female. The father of two children objected to their dancing, on religious and moral grounds. The children refused to dance and were expelled from school. In granting a writ of mandamus requiring the readmission of the pupils to school, the court pointed out that neither the state nor any of its agents had authority to deprive parents of their natural and constitutional right to govern the moral and ethical conduct of their children. To hold that any such overreaching power existed in the state "would be distinctly revolutionary and possibly subversive of that home life so essential to the safety and security of society and the government which regulates it."

In some jurisdictions, on the other hand, it has been held that a board of education may, even in the absence of express statutory authority, require a pupil to pursue a particular study, regardless of the wishes of the pupil's parents. Thus in Indiana the school authorities of the city of La Porte adopted a regulation requiring all high-school pupils to devote some time to the study and practice of music. The father of one of the pupils, without assigning any reason for his action, refused to permit his son to study music. The pupil was expelled from school for disobeying the rule. The court refused to issue a writ of mandamus requiring the reinstatement of the pupil, on the ground that the rule in question was a reasonable one. "The arbitrary wishes of the relator in the premises," the court said, "must yield and be subordinated to the governing authorities of the school city of La Porte, and their reasonable rules and regulations for the government of the pupils of its high school."[99] Similarly, in New Hampshire, a

98. *Hardwick v. Board of School Trustees*, 54 Calif. App. 696, 205 Pac. 49.

99. *State v. Webber*, 108 Ind. 31, 8 N.E. 708, 58 Am. Rep. 30. See also *W. P. Myers Publishing Company v. White River School Township*, 28 Ind. App. 91, 62 N.E. 66.

pupil was excluded from school for refusing to prepare assigned written exercises and declamations. Action was brought to recover damages for unlawful suspension. In holding that there had been no unlawful suspension, the court said:

The power of each parent to decide what studies the scholars should pursue, or what exercises they should perform, would be a power of disorganizing the school and practically rendering it substantially useless. However judicious it may be to consult the wishes of the parents, the disintegrating principle of parental authority to prevent all classification and all system in any school, public or private, is unknown to the law.[100]

Much the same position has been taken by the courts of Ohio, Georgia, and Kentucky. In the Ohio case[101] rhetoric was prescribed as a part of the curriculum, and a rule was adopted to the effect that any pupil who failed, without reasonable excuse, to prepare such rhetorical exercise as might be required should be suspended from school. A pupil was suspended for violating the rule. In an action for damages for unlawful suspension, the court held that the rule was a reasonable one. In the Georgia case[102] the court held that the school authorities had power to require all pupils to write compositions and to enter into debates, notwithstanding the contention of a parent that he had the right to select the course of study his child should pursue. In the Kentucky case[103] the court sustained the authority of the school board to expel a pupil for refusing to take the part of an Irish character in commencement exercises.

The school authorities have the unquestioned right to prescribe the mode of instruction in any particular subject. Consequently, it has been held in Massachusetts and Vermont that a pupil who refuses to take a subject because his parents object to the mode of instruction may be excluded from school. In the Massachusetts case[104] a teacher of bookkeeping detailed to one of the pupils the duty of correcting problems by use of a "key book," which contained the answers. A pupil submitted a problem which was marked wrong. She worked on it another week and a half, and it was again marked wrong. After working still another week, she submitted the same result to the

100. *Kidder* v. *Chellis,* 59 N.H. 473.

101. *Sewell* v. *Board of Education,* 29 Ohio St. 89.

102. *Samuel Benedict Memorial School* v. *Bradford,* 111 Ga. 801, 36 S.E. 920.

103. *Cross* v. *Board of Trustees,* 129 Ky. 35, 33 Ky. Law Rep. 472, 110 S.W. 346.

104. *Wulff* v. *Inhabitants of Wakefield,* 221 Mass. 427, 109 N.E. 358.

teacher, who marked the work correct. In the meantime the pupil became nervous, lost her appetite, and was unable to sleep. Her stepfather protested to the board of education the manner of marking the papers in the course. The board, however, refused to require any change. Thereupon, a request was made that the pupil be excused from taking the course. Again the board of education refused the request. The pupil refused to do the work of the course any longer and was expelled from school. In sustaining the authority of the board in the action which it took, the court said:

> The real and vital question is not whether the plaintiff was guilty of misconduct in refusing to attend her class, but whether a parent has the right to say a certain method of teaching any given course of study shall be pursued. The question answers itself. Were it otherwise, should several parents hold diverse opinions all must yield to one or confusion and failure inevitably follow. The determination of the procedure and the management and direction of pupils and studies in this Commonwealth rests in the wise discretion and sound judgment of teachers and school committee, whose action in these respects is not subject to the supervision of this court. . . .
>
> The case at bar is one purely of administrative detail and its exercise violates no legal right of pupil or parent. The plaintiff was without right in requiring that the principal personally should attend to the supervision of her individual work, perhaps to the neglect of more important duties.

The court in the foregoing case, it should be pointed out, seems to have lost sight entirely of the fundamental issue of the right of the parent to select the studies of his child.

In an early Vermont case,[105] it was held that school trustees had authority to expel a pupil for refusing to write an English composition. The court reasoned that English composition was an allowable mode of teaching the various subjects of the curriculum.

Attention should be called to the fact that the cases holding that the school authorities may suspend from school a pupil who refuses to pursue a particular study or to perform some exercise, such as the writing of a composition, give little consideration to the question of the right of parents to select their children's studies. Indeed, in a number of cases that question seems scarcely to have been raised. The courts seem to have been thinking rather in terms of the disciplinary power of school boards. However that may be, the weight of authority is clearly to the effect that a parent may make any reasonable selection of studies from those which the school offers.

105. *Guernsey* v. *Pitkin*, 32 Vt. 224, 76 Am. Dec. 171.

BIBLE READING AND RELIGIOUS INSTRUCTION

Whether a board of education has the legal authority to permit or require Bible reading in the schools, to authorize the use of the Bible as a reading book, or to give credit for religious instruction carried on outside the schools depends very largely upon the wording of the constitution of the state and upon the interpretation which the supreme court gives to the constitution. In many of the state constitutions there are provisions which possibly may be so interpreted as to prevent Bible reading or religious instruction of any kind in the public schools. Some of these provisions are: no one shall be compelled to attend any place of worship or be compelled to pay taxes to support any place of worship; neither the state nor any subdivision thereof may aid any sectarian school; civil rights and privileges shall not be affected by religious opinion; no money shall be appropriated to aid any church or sectarian school; no sectarian instruction shall be given in the public schools. In general, it has been held that such provisions are not violated by statutes or board regulations permitting the reading of the Bible,[106] the repeating of the Lord's Prayer,[107] the saying of prayers,[108] or the singing of hymns,[109] although on this point the courts are in irreconcilable conflict.

The following case[110] will serve to illustrate the reasoning of those courts which permit Bible reading, the saying of prayers, and other forms of religious instruction in the public schols. It was the habit of

106. *People* v. *Stanley,* 81 Colo. 276, 255 Pac. 610; *Wilkerson* v. *Rome,* 152 Ga. 762, 110 S.E. 895, 20 A.L.R. 1334; *Moore* v. *Monroe,* 64 Iowa 367, 20 N.W. 475, 52 Am. Rep. 444; *Knowlton* v. *Baumhover,* 182 Iowa 691, 166 N.W. 202, 5 A.L.R. 841; *Billard* v. *Board of Education,* 69 Kan. 53, 76 Pac. 422, 105 Am. St. Rep. 148, 66 L.R.A. 166; *Hackett* v. *Brooksville Graded School District,* 120 Ky. 608, 87 S.W. 792, 117 Am. St. Rep. 599, 69 L.R.A. 592; *Donahoe* v. *Richards,* 38 Me. 379, 61 Am. Dec. 256; *Spiller* v. *Woburn,* 12 Allen (Mass.) 127; *Pfeiffer* v. *Board of Education,* 118 Mich. 560, 77 N.W. 250, 42 L.R.A. 536; *State* v. *Scheve,* 65 Neb. 853, 91 N.W. 846, 59 L.R.A. 927; *Nessle* v. *Hum,* Ohio Nisi Prius, 140; *Stevenson* v. *Hanyon,* 7 Pa. Dist. Rep. 585; *Church* v. *Bullock,* 104 Tex. 1, 109 S.W. 115 (affirming, 100 S.W. 1025); *Lewis* v. *Board of Education,* 285 N.Y. 164; *Kaplan* v. *Independent School District,* 171 Minn. 142, 214 N.W. 18.

107. *Moore* v. *Monroe,* 64 Iowa 367, 20 N.W. 475, 52 Am. Rep. 444; *Billard* v. *Board of Education,* 69 Kan. 53, 76 Pac. 422, 105 Am. St. Rep. 148, 66 L.R.A. 166.

108. *Wilkerson* v. *Rome,* 152 Ga. 762, 110 S.E. 895, 20 A.L.R. 1334; *Hackett* v. *Brooksville Graded School District,* 120 Ky. 608, 87 S.W. 792, 117 Am. St. Rep. 599, 69 L.R.A. 592; *Spiller* v. *Woburn,* 12 Allen (Mass.) 127.

109. *Moore* v. *Monroe,* 64 Iowa 367, 20 N.W. 475, 52 Am. Rep. 444.

110. *Hackett* v. *Brooksville Graded School District,* 120 Ky. 608, 87 S.W. 792, 117 Am. St. Rep. 599, 69 L.R.A. 952.

the teacher to open school in the morning by reading a passage from the King James version of the Bible and by offering a particular prayer which was thought to be nonsectarian. The court held that such practices did not make the school a "place of worship" or a "sectarian school." The court held, too, that the Bible is not a sectarian book and that mere reading of the Bible is not sectarian instruction. The court said:

As neither the form nor substance of the prayer complained of seems to represent any peculiar view or dogma of any sect or denomination, or to teach them, or to detract from those of any other, it is not sectarian in the sense that the word is commonly used and understood, and as it was evidently intended in the section [of the Constitution] quoted. . . .

Though it be conceded that any prayer is worship, and that public prayer is public worship, still appellant's children were not compelled to attend the place where the worshipping was done during the prayer. The school was not a "place of worship," nor are its teachers "ministers of religion," within the contemplation of section 5 of the Constitution, although a prayer may be offered incidentally at the opening of the school by a teacher. . . .

That the Bible, or any particular edition, has been adopted by one or more denominations as authentic, or by them asserted to be inspired, cannot make it a sectarian book. The book itself, to be sectarian, must show that it teaches the peculiar dogmas of a sect as such, and not alone that it is so comprehensive as to include them by partial interpretation of its adherents. Nor is a book sectarian merely because it was edited or compiled by those of a particular sect. It is not the authorship nor mechanical composition of the book, nor the use of it, but its contents, that give it its character. . . .

We believe the reason and weight of authorities support the view that the Bible is not of itself a sectarian book, and, when used merely for reading in common schools, without note or comment by teachers, is not sectarian instruction; nor does such use of the Bible make the schoolhouse a house of religious worship.

In some jurisdictions, on the other hand, it has been held that Bible reading is sectarian instruction or violative of constitutional guaranties of religious liberty.[111] Thus it was said by the Supreme Court of Illinois:

The reading of the Bible in school is instruction. Religious instruction is the object of such reading, but whether it is so or not, religious instruction is accomplished by it. . . .

The only means of preventing sectarian instruction in the schools is to exclude altogether religious instruction, by means of the reading of the Bible or otherwise. The Bible is not read in the public schools as mere literature

111. *People* v. *Board of Education,* 245 Ill. 334, 92 N.E. 251, 29 L.R.A. (N.S.) 442, 19 Ann. Cas. 220; *Herold* v. *Parish Board,* 136 La. 1034, 68 So. 116, L.R.A. 1915D 941, Ann. Cas. 1916A 806; *State* v. *Edgerton School District No. 8,* 76 Wis. 177, 44 N.W. 967, 20 Am. St. Rep. 41, 7 L.R.A. 330. See also *State* v. *Scheve,* 65 Neb. 853, 91 N.W. 846, 93 N.W. 169, 59 L.R.A. 927.

or mere history. It cannot be separated from its character as an inspired book of religion. It is not adapted for use as a text book for the teaching, alone of reading, of history, of literature, without regard to its religious character.[112]

In the absence of any constitutional or statutory provisions making it mandatory that the Bible be read in the public schools, a board of education may enforce a rule prohibiting Bible reading or morning devotional exercises.[113] The management of the schools is placed under the control of the board of education, and the courts have no authority to interfere with the discretion of the board by directing what instruction shall be given or what books shall be taught.

In California it has been held[114] that a board of education may purchase copies of the King James version of the Bible to be used in the library of a public high school, notwithstanding the fact that a statute explicitly provided that "no publication of a sectarian, partisan, or denominational character may be used or distributed in any school, or be made a part of any library." The court reasoned that neither the King James translation nor the Douai version of the Bible is a sectarian book.

According to the weight of authority, the wearing of a religious garb does not in and of itself constitute sectarian instruction.[115] In New Mexico and New York, however, the courts have held to the contrary.[116] And in two cases it has been held that it is not unconstitutional for members of a religious order, who teach in the public schools, to give their earnings to their order.[117]

112. *People* v. *Board of Education,* 245 Ill. 334, 92 N.E. 251, 29 L.R.A. (N.S.) 442, 19 Ann. Cas. 220.

113. *Board of Education* v. *Minor,* 23 Ohio St. 211, 13 Am. Rep. 223.

114. *Evans* v. *Selma High School District,* 193 Calif. 54, 222 Pac. 801, 31 A.L.R. 1121.

115. *Hysong* v. *Gallitzin School District,* 164 Pa. St. 629, 30 Atl. 482, 26 L.R.H. 203; *Commonwealth* v. *Herr,* 229 Pa. St. 132, 78 Atl. 68; *City of New Haven* v. *Town of Torrington,* 132 Conn. 194, 43 Atl. (2d) 455; *State* ex rel. *Johnson* v. *Boyd,* 217 Ind. 348, 28 N.E. (2d) 256; *Gerhardt* v. *Heid,* 66 N.D. 444, 267 N.W. 127.

116. *Zellers* v. *Huff,* 55 N.M. 501, 236 Pac. (2d) 949; *O'Connor* v. *Hendrick,* 184 N.Y. Ct. App. 421, 77 N.E. 612.

117. *Gerhardt* v. *Heid,* 66 N.D. 444, 267 N.W. 127; *Zellers* v. *Huff,* 55 N.M. 501, 236 Pac. (2d) 949.

CHAPTER XXII

Discipline and Punishment of Pupils

SUSPENSION AND EXPULSION

THE principle is well established that a board of education may suspend or expel from school any pupil who disobeys a reasonable rule of the board.[1] The rule, however, must be reasonable, and it must be one within the jurisdiction of the board to make. Whether or not a rule has been violated is ordinarily a matter of fact to be determined by the school authorities, and unless they abuse their discretion and act arbitrarily and unreasonably, a court will not review their finding of fact.[2]

Some idea of what the courts will regard as reasonable rules may be had from a consideration of the instances in which the authority of school boards to suspend or expel pupils has been upheld. Boards have been sustained in suspending or expelling pupils for violation of the following rules: a rule prohibiting pupils from leaving the school grounds during the noon recess without permission;[3] a rule prohibiting pupils from taking lunch during recess except at the school cafeteria or lunch brought from home;[4] a rule prohibiting the playing of football on the school grounds or under the auspices of the high school;[5] a rule prohibiting pupils from attending moving-picture shows except on Friday night and on Saturday;[6] a rule requiring pupils to prepare

1. *Kinzer* v. *Independent School District of Marion,* 129 Iowa 441, 105 N.W. 686, 3 L.R.A. (N.S.) 496; *Flory* v. *Smith,* 145 Va. 164, 134 S.E. 360; *Mangum* v. *Keith,* 147 Ga. 603, 95 S.E. 1; *Pugsley* v. *Sellmeyer,* 158 Ark. 247, 250 S.W. 538, 30 A.L.R. 1212; *Donahoe* v. *Richards,* 38 Me. 379, 61 Am. Dec. 256.

2. *Board of Education* v. *Booth,* 110 Ky. 807, 23 Ky. Law Rep. 288, 62 S.W. 872, 53 L.R.A. 787; *Smith* v. *Board of Education,* 182 Ill. App. 342.

3. *Flory* v. *Smith,* 145 Va. 164, 134 S.E. 360.

4. *Bishop* v. *Independent School District,* 119 Tex. 403, 29 S.W. (2d) 312.

5. *Kinzer* v. *Independent School District of Marion,* 129 Iowa 441, 105 N.W. 686, 3 L.R.A. (N.S.) 496.

6. *Mangum* v. *Keith,* 147 Ga. 603, 95 S.E. 1.

a rhetorical exercise;[7] a rule requiring all pupils to study music;[8] a rule prohibiting the use of face paint and cosmetics;[9] a rule providing for expulsion for absence or tardiness without sufficient excuse;[10] a rule requiring pupils to write compositions and to enter into debates;[11] and a rule requiring all pupils to read the Bible in the school.[12]

The following rules, on the other hand, have been held to be unreasonable: a rule requiring pupils to pay for school property which they have accidentally or carelessly destroyed;[13] a rule requiring a pupil to bring in firewood;[14] a rule making it obligatory upon a pupil to pursue a particular subject against the wishes of his parents;[15] a rule requiring pupils to remain in their homes and study between seven and nine o'clock in the evening;[16] a rule requiring pupils to participate in social dancing as a part of the curriculum;[17] and a rule prohibiting married persons otherwise eligible from attending school.[18]

It is well established that a board of education may expel or suspend a pupil from school, even though the pupil may not have violated any rule whatever. School relationships are inherently such that no set of rules, however exhaustive, can cover every offense against good order and deportment. It follows, therefore, that school authorities may dismiss a pupil for any offense which interferes with the orderly conduct of the school or which impairs the usefulness and well-being of the

7. *Sewell* v. *Board of Education*, 29 Ohio St. 89.

8. *State* v. *Webber*, 108 Ind. 31, 8 N.E. 708, 58 Am. Rep. 30.

9. *Pugsley* v. *Sellmeyer*, 158 Ark. 247, 250 S.W. 538, 30 A.L.R. 1212.

10. *King* v. *Jefferson City School Board*, 71 Mo. 628, 36 Am. Rep. 499; *Ferriter* v. *Tyler*, 48 Vt. 444, 21 Am. Rep. 133; *Burdick* v. *Babcock*, 31 Iowa 562; *Churchill* v. *Fewkes*, 13 Ill. App. 520.

11. *Samuel Benedict Memorial School* v. *Bradford*, 111 Ga. 801, 36 S.E. 920; *Guernsey* v. *Pitkin*, 32 Vt. 224, 76 Am. Dec. 171.

12. *Donahoe* v. *Richards*, 38 Me. 379, 61 Am. Dec. 256.

13. *Holman* v. *Trustees of School District No. 5*, 77 Mich. 605, 43 N.W. 996, 6 L.R.A. 534; *Perkins* v. *Board of Directors*, 56 Iowa 476, 9 N.W. 356.

14. *State* v. *Board of Education*, 63 Wis. 234, 23 N.W. 102, 53 Am. Rep. 282.

15. *School Board District No. 18* v. *Thompson*, 24 Okla. 1, 103 Pac. 578, 138 Am. St. Rep. 861; *Trustees of Schools* v. *People*, 87 Ill. 303, 29 Am. Rep. 55; *Morrow* v. *Wood*, 35 Wis. 59, 17 Am. Rep. 471; *State* v. *School District No. 1*, 31 Neb. 552, 48 N.W. 393; *State* v. *Ferguson*, 95 Neb. 63, 144 N.W. 1039, 50 L.R.A. (N.S.) 266.

16. *Hobbs* v. *Germany*, 94 Miss. 469, 49 So. 515, 22 L.R.A. (N.S.) 983.

17. *Hardwick* v. *Board of School Trustees*, 54 Calif. App. 696, 205 Pac. 49.

18. *McLeod* v. *State*, 154 Miss. 468, 122 So. 737, 63 A.L.R. 1161; *Nutt* v. *Board of Education*, 128 Kan. 507, 278 Pac. 1065.

school. Such is the case, regardless of the existence or nonexistence of a rule covering the offense.[19]

In the case of *State* v. *Hamilton*,[20] for example, a pupil was guilty of general misbehavior. In holding that the board of education was not without power to expel the pupil, even though it had adopted no rules whatever in regard to the conduct of the school, the court said: "It matters not whether rules have been announced by either directors or teachers. If the conduct of the pupil is such as reasonably to satisfy such school officers that the presence of that pupil is detrimental to the interests of the school, then the power of expulsion is conferred."

To the same effect is a decision rendered by the Supreme Court of Wisconsin.[21] Two high-school pupils published in the local newspaper a poem which was a "take-off" on the rules of the school board. Upon refusing to make an apology, the pupils were suspended from school. In seeking a writ of mandamus to compel their reinstatement, the pupils contended that they had violated no rules of the board and that the board was, therefore, without authority to suspend them. The court, however, took a contrary view:

> It is clear, therefore, that a rule might have been adopted by the school authorities to meet the situation here presented. This court in the quotation already made from the opinion in the *Burpee Case*[22] recognizes certain obligations on the part of the pupil which are inherent in any proper school system, which constitute the common law of the school, and which may be enforced without the adoption in advance of any rules upon the subject.

In a number of other cases, the courts have sustained the authority of school boards to exclude pupils from school for offenses with respect to which no rules existed. The right of a board to expel pupils for the following offenses has been upheld: for denouncing the policies of the board of education at a meeting of the student body for the avowed purpose of creating in the minds of the students a spirit of insubordina-

---

19. *State* v. *District Board of School District No. 1*, 135 Wis. 619, 116 N.W. 232, 16 L.R.A. (N.S.) 730; *State* v. *Hamilton*, 42 Mo. App. 24; *Wooster* v. *Sunderland*, 27 Calif. App. 51, 148 Pac. 959; *Vermillion* v. *State*, 78 Neb. 107, 110 N.W. 736, 15 Ann. Cas. 401; *Board of Education* v. *Helston*, 32 Ill. App. 300; *Douglas* v. *Campbell*, 89 Ark. 254, 116 S.W. 211, 20 L.R.A. (N.S.) 205; *Sherman* v. *Charlestown*, 8 Cush. (Mass.) 160; *Wulff* v. *Inhabitants of Wakefield*, 221 Mass. 427, 109 N.E. 358.

20. *State* v. *Hamilton*, 42 Mo. App. 24.

21. *State* v. *District Board of School District No. 1*, 135 Wis. 619, 116 N.W. 232, 16 L.R.A. (N.S.) 730.

22. *State* v. *Burton*, 45 Wis. 150, 20 Am. Rep. 706.

tion;[23] for refusing to tell who had written obscene language on the school building;[24] for persistent disobedience to the teacher;[25] for being drunk and disorderly on the streets on Christmas Day;[26] for immoral conduct;[27] for refusing to take a subject because of objection to the method of teaching it;[28] and, for refusing to take a part in commencement exercises.[29] It has been held, moreover, that the school authorities may exclude from school pupils who are mentally or physically defective.[30]

In Iowa, however, under a statute authorizing a board of directors to dismiss pupils for gross immorality or for persistent violation of the regulations of the board, it was held that a board had no authority to expel a pupil for publishing in a local newspaper an article which held the board up to ridicule. The court based its decision upon the fact that the pupil had not violated any rule of the board.[31]

It is well established, moreover, that a teacher may temporarily suspend a pupil from school for any offense which impairs the discipline and interferes with the orderly conduct of the school.[32] While a teacher may not exclude a pupil in opposition to the rules or wishes of the school board,[33] all his authority over his pupils is not derived from the board. There is inherent in his position the authority to govern the school in a reasonable and humane way, and this authority includes the right to suspend pupils until the board of education has an opportunity to pass final judgment. Thus it was said by the Supreme Court of Wisconsin in a case which has often been cited with approval:

23. *Wooster* v. *Sunderland*, 27 Calif. App. 51, 148 Pac. 959.

24. *Board of Education* v. *Helston*, 32 Ill. App. 300.

25. *Vermillion* v. *State*, 78 Neb. 107, 110 N.W. 736, 15 Ann. Cas. 401.

26. *Douglas* v. *Campbell*, 89 Ark. 254, 116 S.W. 211, 20 L.R.A. (N.S.) 205.

27. *Sherman* v. *Charlestown*, 8 Cush. (Mass.) 160.

28. *Wulff* v. *Inhabitants of Wakefield*, 221 Mass. 427, 109 N.E. 358.

29. *Cross* v. *Board of Trustees of Walton Graded Common Schools*, 129 Ky. 35, 33 Ky. Law Rep. 472, 110 S.W. 346.

30. *Watson* v. *City of Cambridge*, 157 Mass. 561, 32 N.E. 864; *State* v. *Board of Education*, 169 Wis. 231, 172 N.W. 153.

31. *Murphy* v. *Independent District of Marengo*, 30 Iowa 429.

32. *State* v. *Randall*, 79 Mo. App. 226; *State* v. *Burton*, 45 Wis. 150, 30 Am. Rep. 706.

33. *State* v. *Burton*, 45 Wis. 150, 30 Am. Rep. 706; *Parker* v. *School District No. 38*, 5 Lea (Tenn.) 525.

While the principal or teacher in charge of a public school is subordinate to the school board or board of education of his district or city, and must enforce rules and regulations adopted by the board for the government of the school, and execute all its lawful orders in that behalf, he does not derive all his power and authority in the school and over his pupils from the affirmative action of the board. He stands for the time being *in loco parentis* to his pupils, and because of that relation he must necessarily exercise authority over them in many things concerning which the board may have remained silent. In the school, as in the family, there exist on the part of the pupils the obligations of obedience to lawful commands, subordination, civil deportment, respect for the rights of other pupils and fidelity to duty. These obligations are inherent in any proper school system, and constitute, so to speak, the common law of the school. Every pupil is presumed to know the law, and is subject to it, whether it has or has not been reënacted by the district board in the form of written rules and regulations. Indeed it would seem impossible to frame rules which would cover all cases of insubordination and all acts of vicious tendency which the teacher is liable to encounter daily and hourly.[34]

A Missouri case illustrates the application of the principle. A pupil during the recess period purposely ran against another pupil younger than himself and wounded him in the face. The teacher requested the pupil who had committed the offense to accompany the injured pupil to his home. The offending pupil refused to obey the teacher, whereupon he was told to take his books and go home. The board of education investigated the affair. The older pupil confessed that he had purposely run against the other pupil and that he refused to make an apology or to accompany him home. The offending pupil was expelled from school. Thereupon, his parents brought action for a writ of mandamus to enforce his reinstatement. It was contended that the request or order of the teacher to accompany the wounded pupil home was beyond his authority to make and that the order was oppressive and humiliating. In sustaining the authority of the teacher to make the request in question, the court said:

In the absence of a rule or rules prescribing the names and methods of punishment, the teacher is authorized to inflict such humane and reasonable punishment to enforce the rules of the board and good discipline and order, as he may deem most conducive to these ends; and the jurisdiction of the school board to make needful rules for the conduct of the pupils and of the teacher to enforce such rules, is not confined to the school room and school premises, but extends over the pupil on his road from his home to school and return. . . . The teacher of a school as to the children of his school, while under his care, occupies for the time being the position of parent or guardian, and it is his right and duty not only to enforce discipline to preserve order and to teach, but also to look after the morals, the health and

34. *State* v. *Burton,* 45 Wis. 150, 30 Am. Rep. 706.

the safety of his pupils; to do and to require his pupils to do whatever is reasonably necessary to preserve and conserve all these interests, when not in conflict with the primary purposes of the school or opposed to law or a rule of the school board. Neither the law nor a rule of the board was transgressed by the teacher in this instance; the order or request to Warren Beaty was reasonable, not unlawful, and he should have obeyed it.[35]

In a Vermont case[36] the court even went so far as to hold that a teacher had the right to demand that a certain pupil be expelled and that when the school committee refused to expel the pupil, the teacher might refuse to teach without losing her right of recovery under the contract. It was said by the court:

The teacher could not perform the duties of her employment without maintaining proper and necessary discipline in the school, and when all her other means for doing so failed in respect to the boy, it was her right, and might be her duty, to expel him, to save the rest of the school from being injured by his presence. It was not the duty of the teacher, under the contract, to teach the school without maintaining proper and necessary discipline in it; and if the committee insisted that she should have the boy there, when she could not have him there and have the discipline too, it was equivalent to insisting that she should teach the school without the discipline; which she was not bound to do.

In some jurisdictions it is provided by statute that a pupil cannot be expelled from school without notice of the charges against him and without an opportunity to be heard in his defense. Where such is the case, a pupil cannot be legally expelled without the required notice and hearing.[37] The hearing, however, need not be conducted with all the formalities of a regular court of law. It is enough if the pupil is given a full and free opportunity to present such evidence as he may care to present.[38]

There is not a great deal of judicial authority with respect to the right of a pupil to be heard before dismissal from school where no such right is guaranteed by statute. Such authority as there is points to the conclusion that no such right exists.[39] In a Nebraska case the statute authorizing school boards to expel pupils read: "The school board may authorize or order the suspension or expulsion from the school, whenever in their judgment the interests of the school demand it, of any

35. *State* v. *Randall*, 79 Mo. App. 226.

36. *Scott* v. *School District No. 2*, 46 Vt. 452.

37. *Jones* v. *City of Fitchburg*, 211 Mass. 66, 97 N.E. 612; *Morrison* v. *City of Lawrence*, 186 Mass. 456, 72 N.E. 91.

38. *Morrison* v. *City of Lawrence*, 186 Mass. 456, 72 N.E. 91.

39. *Vermillion* v. *State*, 78 Neb. 107, 110 N.W. 736, 15 Ann. Cas. 401; *Flory* v. *Smith*, 145 Va. 164, 134 S.E. 360. See also *State* v. *Hamilton*, 42 Mo. App. 24.

pupil guilty of gross misdemeanors or persistent disobedience." The district court issued a writ of mandamus requiring the reinstatement of a pupil on the ground that she had not been given a notice and hearing. In reversing the opinion of the district court, the supreme court rendered the following opinion:

The statute under which the board is authorized to expel a pupil does not, in terms, provide for any notice, either to the pupil or to the parents, that a hearing is to be had or action taken. It is probably true that in such proceedings the board acts in a quasi judicial manner, but that no trial in the sense of a judicial inquiry is contemplated by the statute is evident. . . . The proceeding, in our judgment, is more like the action of an administrative board in making inquiry as to existing facts upon which they are required to act. In doing this they may use their own judgment and pursue any course which, in their opinion, will fully inform them of the facts attending the subject matter of the inquiry. In case of the suspension or expulsion of a pupil, the necessities of the case may often require immediate action on the part of the teacher or of the board. To require notice and a formal trial would in many cases defeat the object of the statute. Where the pupil is guilty of "gross misdemeanors and persistent disobedience," summary action may be required, and this was undoubtedly the view of the legislature in not providing for notice and a formal trial. . . .

Our examination of the authorities and the necessities requiring it lead us to believe that the rule is this: That the teacher, when occasion demands, may suspend or expel a pupil; that the board, upon such inquiry as their own judgment may suggest and approve, may, without notice to the pupil or to the parents, suspend or expel a pupil who, in the language of the statute, is guilty of "gross misdemeanors or persistent disobedience," and that the welfare of our common school system requires that they be invested with this authority.[40]

A board of education does not have authority to expel a pupil for an indefinite period. Ordinarily, the period of exclusion will not be construed to continue beyond the current school year.[41] Moreover, a board of education may not discipline a pupil for an act committed while attending school in another district. In an Arkansas case a pupil refused to take punishment for an offense against the good order of the school. His father had him transferred to another district. The authorities of the district to which he was transferred refused to admit him until he returned to the school which he had been attending and took his punishment. In granting a writ of mandamus requiring the board of the district to which the pupil had been transferred to admit him to school, the court pointed out that *ex post facto* rules and regulations are in violation of the Constitution.[42]

40. *Vermillion* v. *State,* 78 Neb. 107, 110 N.W. 736, 15 Ann. Cas. 401.
41. *Board of Education* v. *Helston,* 32 Ill. App. 300.
42. *Stephens* v. *Humphrey,* 145 Ark. 172, 224 S.W. 442.

REMEDY FOR WRONGFUL EXCLUSION FROM SCHOOL

Where a pupil has been illegally excluded from school, a writ of mandamus will lie to compel the proper authorities to admit the pupil to school;[43] where an attempt is being made to enforce an unreasonable rule, the enforcement of the rule may be restrained by injunction.[44] A pupil who has been arbitrarily and maliciously excluded from school has a right of action for damages against the school-board members personally.[45] There can be no recovery, however, unless it can be shown that the school-board members acted maliciously; for mere mistakes in judgment in expelling pupils there is no liability.[46] Similarly, a teacher who expels a pupil for violating an unreasonable rule will not be held liable in damages in the absence of a showing of malice.[47]

The case of *Dritt* v. *Snodgrass*[48] illustrates the reasoning of the courts. A pupil was expelled from school for violating a rule which prohibited pupils from attending social parties. The court held that neither the teacher nor the school directors could be held to respond in damages. In the words of the court:

School directors are elected by the people, receive no compensation for their services, are not always, or frequently, men who are thoroughly informed as to the best methods of conducting schools. They are authorized, and it is their duty to adopt reasonable rules for the government and management of the school, and it would deter responsible and suitable men from accepting the position, if held liable for damages to a pupil expelled under a rule adopted by them, under the impression that the welfare of the school demanded it, if the courts should deem it improper. They are to determine what rules are proper, and who shall say that the rule adopted in this case was harsh and oppressive? I might think it was; wiser men would maintain that it was proper and right, that pupils attending social parties are liable to have their minds drawn off from their studies, and thus to be retarded in their progress; but whether the rule was a wise one or not, the directors and teachers are not liable to an action for damages for enforcing it—even to the expulsion of a pupil who violated it.

43. *Holman* v. *Trustees of School District No. 5*, 77 Mich. 605, 43 N.W. 996, 6 L.R.A. 534.

44. *Hobbs* v. *Germany*, 94 Miss. 469, 49 So. 515, 22 L.R.A. (N.S.) 983.

45. *Board of Education* v. *Purse*, 101 Ga. 422, 28 S.E. 896, 41 L.R.A. 593.

46. *Dritt* v. *Snodgrass*, 66 Mo. 286, 27 Am. Rep. 343; *McCormick* v. *Burt*, 95 Ill. 263, 35 Am. Rep. 163; *Donahoe* v. *Richards*, 38 Me. 379, 61 Am. Dec. 256; *Stephenson* v. *Hall*, 14 Barb. (N.Y.) 222; *Churchill* v. *Fewkes*, 13 Ill. App. 520; *Sweeney* v. *Young*, 82 N.H. 159, 131 Atl. 155, 42 A.L.R. 757; *Stewart* v. *Southard*, 17 Ohio St. 402, 49 Am. Dec. 463; *Spear* v. *Cummings*, 23 Pick. (Mass.) 224, 34 Am. Dec. 53.

47. *Churchill* v. *Fewkes*, 13 Ill. App. 520; *Dritt* v. *Snodgrass*, 66 Mo. 286, 27 Am. Rep. 343. See, however, *Williams* v. *Smith*, 192 Ala. 428, 68 So. 323.

48. *Dritt* v. *Snodgrass*, 66 Mo. 286, 27 Am. Rep. 343.

Similarly, in the case of *Churchill* v. *Fewkes*[49] it was held that a teacher and school directors were not liable for suspending a pupil from school in the absence of proof of malice. "If appellants were acting in good faith," said the court, "however much they may have been mistaken as to their power under the law, this action cannot be maintained against them."

Where, however, a pupil is excluded from school in palpable violation of a statute conferring the right of attendance, both the board members and the teacher may be held answerable in damages. Where the law is plain and mandatory, there can be no exercise of discretion. Thus, in an Alabama case,[50] the statutes provided that all pupils might attend school free of charge. In holding that a pupil who had been expelled for refusing to pay a tuition fee could recover from the teacher, the court said:

Appellant acted under the direction of the school board; but he must be charged in law with a knowledge of the unlawful character of his act. As a joint tort-feasor with the school board, he is liable, notwithstanding their direction in the premises. There can be no innocent agency in the commission of an act upon its face unlawful and tortious.

In matters of discipline, teachers and masters of schools exercise a discretion for which, in the absence of abuse, they cannot be held to answer. . . . But that principle is of no avail to appellant, for the reason that he was not exercising his right of discipline, but rather, in a case where there was no appearance of an occasion or excuse for discipline, for the sole purpose of enforcing an unlawful demand, he deprived appellee of a valuable right or privilege which by law and without price is extended to all the children of the state.

Where the act of exclusion is that of the teacher alone, it has been held that there is no right of action against the teacher because there is no privity of contract between teacher and parent. That is, a teacher is not an independent public officer exercising his own judgment with respect to the admission and exclusion of pupils. A pupil is not denied his legal right to attend school unless excluded by the school committee or board.[51] In an Illinois case, on the other hand, the superintendent of schools of Chicago was held personally liable for excluding unvaccinated pupils from school without authority to exclude the pupils having been conferred by either the board of education or the board of health.[52] In the words of the court:

49. *Churchill* v. *Fewkes*, 13 Ill. App. 520.
50. *Williams* v. *Smith*, 192 Ala. 428, 68 So. 323.
51. *Spear* v. *Cummings*, 23 Pick. (Mass.) 224, 34 Am. Dec. 53.
52. *Burroughs* v. *Mortenson*, 312 Ill. 163, 143 N.E. 457.

The superintendent and his assistants had no right to exclude him [the pupil] except pursuant to regulations established by the board of education or board of health. There were no such regulations. There was no matter submitted to the superintendent which he was required to determine. He could act only in accordance with the established rules. Since there were no rules he could not act. The absence of rules would not justify him in taking the matter into his own hands and acting arbitrarily, without regard to any rules but his own discretion.

CORPORAL PUNISHMENT OF PUPILS

The courts all agree that a teacher to a certain extent stands *in loco parentis* with respect to corporal punishment of pupils. By the act of sending a child to school, the parent delegates to the teacher authority to discipline the pupil for all offenses against the good order and effective conduct of the school. It is not to be understood, however, that a teacher has the same general right to punish for all offenses as does the parent. The teacher's right to administer corporal punishment is restricted to the limits of his jurisdiction and responsibility as a teacher.[53] The courts are in accord in holding that teachers, acting in good faith, may inflict reasonable corporal punishment upon pupils for all offenses within the jurisdiction of the school authorities.[54] The jurisdiction of the teacher extends to acts committed off the school grounds, as well as to those committed on the school premises.[55] The nature of the act, not the place where it was done, determines the right of the teacher to punish. Nor is a pupil twenty-one years of age or older exempt from discipline. He stands in the same relation to the school as do all the other pupils.[56] There are limits, however, beyond which a teacher may not legally go in inflicting corporal punishment. A teacher who transcends these limits may be held liable in either a civil or a criminal action.

53. *Vanvactor* v. *State*, 113 Ind. 276, 15 N.E. 341, 3 Am. St. Rep. 645; *Stevens* v. *Fassett*, 27 Me. 266; *Lander* v. *Seaver*, 32 Vt. 114, 76 Am. Dec. 156.

54. *Lander* v. *Seaver*, 32 Vt. 114, 76 Am. Dec. 156; *Sheehan* v. *Sturges*, 53 Conn. 481, 2 Atl. 841; *Boyd* v. *State*, 88 Ala. 169, 7 So. 268, 16 Am. St. Rep. 31; *Vanvactor* v. *State*, 113 Ind. 276, 15 N.E. 341, 3 Am. St. Rep. 645; *State* v. *Mizner*, 50 Iowa 248, 24 Am. Rep. 769; *State* v. *Pendergrass*, 19 N.C. 365, 31 Am. Dec. 416; *Patterson* v. *Nutter*, 78 Me. 509, 7 Atl. 273, 57 Am. Rep. 818; *Stevens* v. *Fassett*, 27 Me. 266; *Hutton* v. *State*, 23 Tex. App. 386, 5 S.W. 122, 59 Am. Rep. 776; *Balding* v. *State*, 23 Tex. App. 172, 4 S.W. 579; *Marlar* v. *Bill*, 181 Tenn. 100, 178 S.W. (2d) 634; *People* v. *Mummert*, 50 N.Y.S. (2d) 699.

55. *Balding* v. *State*, 23 Tex. App. 172, 4 S.W. 579; *Lander* v. *Seaver*, 32 Vt. 114, 76 Am. Dec. 156; *O'Rourke* v. *Walker*, 102 Conn. 130, 128 Atl. 25, 41 A.L.R. 1308.

56. *Stevens* v. *Fassett*, 27 Me. 266; *State* v. *Mizner*, 50 Iowa 248, 24 Am. Rep. 769.

It is difficult to draw a precise distinction between legal and illegal corporal punishment. Indeed, there is disagreement among the courts themselves. According to one line of decisions, a teacher will not be held liable for assault and battery, or for damages in a civil action, unless it can be shown that he inflicted a permanent or lasting injury upon the pupil, or that he punished the pupil with malicious intent.[57] That is, if no lasting injury is inflicted upon the pupil, the teacher will not be held liable for excessive punishment administered in good faith. The teacher exercises judicial discretion in determining the gravity of the offense and the punishment that it merits. But where the teacher is actuated by malice, the punishment is illegal, no matter how moderate, for there is no such thing as legal punishment from improper motives.[58]

The leading case of *State v. Pendergrass*,[59] decided by the Supreme Court of North Carolina in 1837, illustrates the reasoning of the courts in those cases which support the principles stated in the preceding paragraph. A woman teacher whipped one of her young pupils with a switch, leaving marks upon the body of the pupil for a number of days after the chastisement. In rendering a decision in an action for assault and battery, the court expressed what it considered the proper rule of law, as follows:

The line which separates moderate correction from immoderate punishment, can only be ascertained by reference to general principles. The welfare of the child is the main purpose for which pain is permitted to be inflicted. Any punishment, therefore, which may seriously endanger life, limbs or health, or shall disfigure the child, or cause any other permanent injury, may be pronounced in itself immoderate, as not only being unnecessary for, but inconsistent with, the purpose for which correction is authorized. But any correction, however severe, which produces temporary pain only, and no permanent ill, cannot be so pronounced, since it may have been necessary for the reformation of the child, and does not injuriously affect its future welfare. We hold, therefore, that it may be laid down as a general rule, that teachers exceed the limits of their authority when they cause lasting mischief; but act within the limits of it, when they inflict temporary pain.

When the correction administered is not in itself immoderate, and therefore beyond the authority of the teacher, its legality or illegality must depend entirely, we think, on the *quo animo* with which it was administered. Within

57. *State v. Thornton*, 136 N.C. 610, 48 S.E. 602; *State v. Pendergrass*, 19 N.C. 365, 31 Am. Dec. 416; *Heritage v. Dodge*, 64 N.H. 297, 9 Atl. 722; *Commonwealth v. Seed*, 5 Pa. L.J. Rep. 78; *Boyd v. State*, 88 Ala. 169, 7 So. 268, 16 Am. St. Rep. 31.

58. *Dill v. State*, 87 Tex. Cr. Rep. 49, 219 S.W. 481; *Haycraft v. Grigsby*, 88 Mo. App. 354; *Boyd v. State*, 88 Ala. 169, 7 So. 268, 16 Am. St. Rep. 31; *Cooper v. McJunkin*, 4 Ind. 290; *State v. Pendergrass*, 19 N.C. 365, 31 Am. Dec. 416.

59. *State v. Pendergrass*, 19 N.C. 365, 31 Am. Dec. 416.

the sphere of his authority, the master is the judge when correction is required, and of the degree of correction necessary; and like all others intrusted with a discretion, he cannot be made penally responsible for error of judgment, but only for wickedness of purpose. The best and wisest of mortals are weak and erring creatures, and in the exercise of functions in which their judgment is to be the guide, cannot be rightfully required to engage for more than honesty of purpose, and diligence of exertion. His judgment must be *presumed* correct, because he is *the judge,* and also because of the difficulty of proving the offense, or accumulation of offenses, that call for correction; of showing the peculiar temperament, disposition, and habits, of the individual corrected; and of exhibiting the various milder means, that may have been ineffectually used, before correction was resorted to.

But the master may be punishable when he does not transcend the powers granted, if he grossly abuse them. If he use his authority as a cover for malice, and under pretense of administering correction, gratify his own bad passions, the mask of the judge shall be taken off, and he will stand amenable to justice, as an individual not invested with judicial power.

Whether or not a teacher was actuated by malice in punishing a pupil is a matter of fact to be determined by the jury.[60] Unreasonable, cruel, and excessive punishment may, however, of itself be convincing evidence of the existence of malice.[61] Thus it was said by the Supreme Court of Alabama:

The more correct view, however, and the one better sustained by authority, seems to be that when, in the judgment of reasonable men, the punishment inflicted is immoderate or excessive, and a jury would be authorized, from the facts of the case, to infer that it was induced by legal malice, or wickedness of motive, the limit of lawful authority may be adjudged to be passed. In determining this question, the nature of the instrument of correction used may have a strong bearing on the inquiry as to motive or intention.[62]

Again, it was said by the Supreme Court of Indiana:

To support a charge of assault and battery it is necessary to show that the act complained of was *intentionally* committed. But in the case of the chastisement of a pupil, the *intent* may be inferred from the unreasonableness of the method adopted or the excess of force employed, but the burden of proving such unreasonableness or such excess rests upon the State.[63]

According to other decisions which support the better rule of law, a teacher must exercise reasonable judgment and discretion in administering discipline and must graduate the punishment to the nature of

60. *Boyd* v. *State,* 88 Ala. 169, 7 So. 268, 16 Am. St. Rep. 31.
61. *Boyd* v. *State,* 88 Ala. 169, 7 So. 268, 16 Am. St. Rep. 31.
62. *Boyd* v. *State,* 88 Ala. 169, 7 So. 268, 16 Am. St. Rep. 31.
63. *Vanvactor* v. *State,* 113 Ind. 276, 15 N.E. 341, 3 Am. St. Rep. 645.

the offense, as well as to the size and age of the offender.[64] It is not enough to show that the teacher acted honestly and in good faith. If, in the opinion of reasonable men, the punishment was unreasonable and excessive, the teacher is guilty of assault. The assumption, however, is always in favor of the teacher, and it must be affirmatively shown that the punishment was clearly excessive and unreasonable.[65] In case there is any reasonable doubt as to the reasonableness of the punishment, the teacher should have the benefit of the doubt.

The reasoning underlying this second line of decisions is well expressed in an opinion rendered by the Supreme Court of Vermont:

> The law, as we deem it to exist, is this: A schoolmaster has the right to inflict reasonable corporal punishment. He must exercise reasonable judgment and discretion in determining when to punish and to what extent. In determining upon what is a reasonable punishment, various considerations must be regarded—the nature of the offense, the apparent motive and disposition of the offender, the influence of his example and conduct upon others, and th sex, age, size and strength of the pupil to be punished. Among reasonable persons much difference prevails as to the circumstances which will justify the infliction of punishment, and the extent to which it may properly be administered. On account of this difference of opinion, and the difficulty which exists in determining what is a reasonable punishment, and the advantage which the master has by being on the spot to know all the circumstances—the manner, looks, tone, gestures, and language of the offender (which are not always easily described)—and thus to form a correct opinion as to the necessity and extent of the punishment, considerable allowance should be made to the teacher by way of protecting him in the exercise of his discretion. Especially should he have this indulgence when he appears to have acted from good motives and not from anger or malice. Hence the teacher is not to be held liable on the ground of excessive punishment, unless the punishment is clearly excessive and would be held so in the general judgment of reasonable men. If the punishment be thus *clearly* excessive, then the master should be held liable for such excess, though he acted from good motives in inflicting the punishment, and in his own judgment considered it necessary and not excessive. But if there is any reasonable doubt whether the punishment was excessive, the master should have the benefit of the doubt.[66]

64. *Hathaway* v. *Rice*, 19 Vt. 102; *Lander* v. *Seaver*, 32 Vt. 114, 76 Am. Dec. 156; *Sheehan* v. *Sturges*, 53 Conn. 481, 2 Atl. 841; *Patterson* v. *Nutter*, 78 Me. 509, 7 Atl. 273, 57 Am. Rep. 818; *Cooper* v. *McJunkin*, 4 Ind. 290; *Gardner* v. *State*, 4 Ind. 632; *Vanvactor* v. *State*, 113 Ind. 276, 15 N.E. 341, 3 Am. St. Rep. 645; *Commonwealth* v. *Randall*, 4 Gray (Mass.) 36; *Anderson* v. *State*, 3 Head (Tenn.) 455; *Berry* v. *Arnold School District*, 199 Ark. 1118, 137 S.W. (2d) 256.

65. *Lander* v. *Seaver*, 32 Vt. 114, 76 Am. Dec. 156; *Vanvactor* v. *State*, 113 Ind. 276, 15 N.E. 341, 3 Am. St. Rep. 645; *Patterson* v. *Nutter*, 78 Me. 509, 7 Atl. 273, 57 Am. Rep. 818; *Anderson* v. *State*, 3 Head (Tenn.) 455; *State* v. *Mizner*, 50 Iowa 248, 24 Am. Rep. 769.

66. *Lander* v. *Seaver*, 32 Vt. 114, 76 Am. Dec. 156.

Where a teacher punishes a pupil moderately but injuries result which could not have been foreseen by a reasonably prudent person, the teacher will not be held liable in an action for damages. If, on the other hand, a reasonably prudent person would have foreseen that the act would naturally or probably cause an injury, even though the exact form of the injury might not have been foreseen, the teacher will be held liable. In a North Carolina case,[67] for example, a teacher threw a pencil at a pupil who was not paying attention to the recitation. The pupil turned his head unexpectedly, and the pencil struck him in the eye, causing partial, if not total, blindness. In passing upon the liability of a teacher under such circumstances, it was said by the court:

It is undoubtedly true that a teacher is liable if, in correcting or disciplining a pupil, he acts maliciously or inflicts a permanent injury, but he has the authority to correct his pupil when he is disobedient or inattentive to his duties, and any act done in the exercise of this authority and not prompted by malice is not actionable, though it may cause permanent injury, unless a person of ordinary prudence could reasonably foresee that a permanent injury of some kind would naturally or probably result from the act. There is a distinction, we think, between the case of an injury inflicted in the performance of a lawful act and one in which the act causing the injury is in itself unlawful or is, at least, a wilful wrong. In the latter case the defendant is liable for any consequence that may flow from his act as the proximate cause thereof, whether he could foresee or anticipate it or not; but when the act is lawful, the liability depends, not upon the particular consequence or result that may flow from it, but upon the ability of a prudent man, in the exercise of ordinary care, to foresee that injury or damage will naturally or probably be the result of his act.

There is some disagreement among the courts with respect to the liability of a teacher for the reasonable punishment of a pupil for the violation of an unreasonable rule. In some jurisdictions the teacher is held liable.[68] In the case of *Morrow* v. *Wood*[69] a teacher whipped a pupil for refusing to study geography against the wish of his father. The teacher was guilty of assault. In the case of *Rulison* v. *Post*[70] force was used in expelling a pupil who refused to study bookkeeping. The pupil was able to recover damages for trespass. It was trespass to expel with force where there was no right to expel at all.

67. *Drum* v. *Miller*, 135 N.C. 204, 47 S.E. 421.

68. *Morrow* v. *Wood*, 35 Wis. 59, 17 Am. Rep. 471; *Rulison* v. *Post*, 79 Ill. 567; *State* v. *Vanderbilt*, 116 Ind. 11, 18 N.E. 266. See also *Williams* v. *Smith*, 192 Ala. 428, 68 So. 323.

69. *Morrow* v. *Wood*, 35 Wis. 59, 17 Am. Rep. 471.

70. *Rulison* v. *Post*, 79 Ill. 567.

The better reason, however, supports the view that a teacher should not be held personally liable for mistakes in judgment in enforcing unreasonable rules. Where a teacher honestly believes that a rule is reasonable and necessary and employs moderate punishment in its enforcement, he should not be held liable in damages, even though a court may regard the rule as unreasonable. In such cases the teacher, like the board of education, exercises a quasi-judicial discretion. The law imposes upon the teacher a duty involving the exercise of discretion and holds the teacher liable if he fails to act honestly and in good faith. But neither reason nor public policy demands that the teacher be held liable for honest mistakes in judgment. It is well established that school-board members are not liable for erroneous judgments in matters submitted to their determination,[71] and there seems to be no good reason why the same rule should not apply to teachers. This view is, in fact, supported by judicial authority.[72] In the case of *Fertich* v. *Michener*,[73] the board of education had a rule that pupils should be excused from the schoolroom upon request. A teacher detained a pupil for ten or fifteen minutes after the class was dismissed as a penalty for having asked to retire and having retired without permission. It was alleged that the pupil was detained under the authority of the superintendent. Action was brought against the superintendent for damages. In denying damages, the court applied to teachers the same rule of nonliability as applies to school officers.

71. *Stephenson* v. *Hall*, 14 Barb. (N.Y.) 222; *McCormick* v. *Burt*, 95 Ill. 263, 35 Am. Rep. 163; *Churchill* v. *Fewkes*, 13 Ill. App. 520; *Dritt* v. *Snodgrass*, 66 Mo. 286, 27 Am. Rep. 343; *Branaman* v. *Hinkle*, 137 Ind. 496, 37 N.E. 546; *Donahoe* v. *Richards*, 38 Me. 379, 61 Am. Dec. 256; *Sweeney* v. *Young*, 82 N.H. 159, 131 Atl. 155, 42 A.L.R. 75; *Stewart* v. *Southard*, 17 Ohio 402, 49 Am. Dec. 463.

72. *McCormick* v. *Burt*, 95 Ill. 263, 35 Am. Rep. 163; *Churchill* v. *Fewkes*, 13 Ill. App. 520; *Fertich* v. *Michener*, 111 Ind. 472, 11 N.E. 605, 60 Am. Rep. 709; *Dritt* v. *Snodgrass*, 66 Mo. 286, 27 Am. Rep. 343.

73. *Fertich* v. *Michener*, 111 Ind. 472, 11 N.E. 605.

CHAPTER XXIII

Recent Changes in School Law

INTRODUCTION

L AW is not static; nor should it be. Like all aspects of the social milieu, it is constantly changing. This is readily recognized and universally accepted in statutory law. Almost daily, newspapers carry stories about statutes that have been newly enacted by some state legislature or by the Congress of the United States, or concerning some statute that is being considered for adoption or that should be or has been amended or repealed. Although the voters are not necessarily in full agreement as to needed changes, they are in agreement that it is within the province of the legislative department of government to enact new statutes and to amend or even repeal existing legislation.

With respect to judge-made or court-made law—often referred to as common law—the situation is quite different. Many are not aware that law, which is considered an expression of public policy, is made by the judicial as well as the legislative branch of government. When a state court rules that, in the absence of a statute concerning the subject, school districts have the same immunity from liability as does the state itself, it is expressing public policy; and this expression of policy becomes the law just as surely as though the legislature had enacted it in the form of a statute.

Changes in judge-made law occur in several ways. When a question that has never been before the courts is the subject of litigation, the principle of law announced by the court may be thought of as a new law. Many of these cases of first impression result from the court's interpretations of new statutes. It may thus be said that the law changes as the result of accretion. But change also results from alteration. This happens when the courts change their thinking. Many who are aware of the fact that court rulings are law insist that, in the interest of maintaining the principle of separation of powers, courts should refrain whenever possible from ruling on matters that have the effect of becoming statements of public policy. Many argue that once

616

a rule has become recognized as the law courts should thereafter never change it. They reason that if a ruling of the courts needs to be changed only the legislature, which is presumed to know of the need, should change it. They also reason that if the courts are permitted to change their rulings, as time passes the law is left so uncertain that one can never be sure just what it is. Those who oppose this view argue that the law should be flexible—that courts should be in a position to change their rulings as social conditions change—that this is the essence of equity. They argue that to do otherwise would put the law in a straitjacket. In this connection a New York court has said: "The law is not merely a composition of cold type; it is a living organism which moulds itself to meet the needs of an ever changing civilization."[1]

An Iowa court, pursuing this matter in more detail, said:

It is true that the law should not be, and is not, static; it should grow and develop with economic, political, and cultural conditions which surround it. This, however, does not mean that it should not generally be definite and settled. The rule of stare decisis [the doctrine that legal principles embodied in judicial decisions should be accepted as authoritative in cases with factual backgrounds similar to those in which they were enunciated] has its basis in something stronger than the thought that courts should follow hide-bound precedent without regard to justice or equity. It derives from the consideration that when the courts have fully and fairly considered a proposition and have decided it, only the most pressing reasons should require, or in fact even permit, an opposite holding. Lawyers and clients have a right to know what the law is, and to order their affairs accordingly.[2]

Possibly even more significant is the following statement taken from a decision by a higher court in New Jersey:

It is to the credit and the glory of the common law that it has always had within itself the seed of change, keeping pace with the march of the years and the advance of thought. Wherever it has lagged it has been because of the conservatism which was hesitant to recognize the changing times and the need to revise the law's precedents. But always and eventually the common law caught up with the times and molded itself to the newer needs for the public good. . . .

. . . Emancipation from earlier constricting attitudes and holdings is part of the process of judicial growth and public service.[3]

From what has been said it is evident that the law does, and must, change. Although the courts may be reluctant to abandon old ways of

1. *Application of Fallon*, 178 N.Y.S. (2d) 459.

2. *Swan Lake Consolidated School District* v. *Consolidated School District of Dolliver*, 58 N.W. (2d) 349 (Iowa).

3. *A. P. Smith Mfg. Co.* v. *Barlow*, 26 N.J.S. 106, 97A. (2d) 186.

thinking and accept new ones, they do not hesitate to do so when the law is no longer in tune with the times—when it is out of line with current economic, political, social, and cultural conditions. "School Law," a discrete field of law, is no exception. It is constantly changing, and it is with these changes that this chapter deals.

THE NATURE OF CHANGES IN SCHOOL LAW

Although recent changes in school law are fairly numerous, those of greater significance can conveniently be grouped into a very few categories. In the first place there are significant changes in the application of the common-law rule of school-district immunity from tort liability. Then there are changes in the law as it relates to the pupil, both directly and indirectly. And finally there are changes relating to the teacher. Although there are other more or less minor changes, most important of recent changes may be so classified.

TORT LIABILITY OF SCHOOL DISTRICTS

The general rule "almost universally applied by American courts, is that school districts and municipalities are not liable . . . for injuries resulting from the negligence of the officers, agents, or employees of the district or the municipality" in the absence of statute making them liable (p. 393). In New York the courts, unlike those of other states, departed somewhat from this rule. They early took the position that a school board might be held liable in its corporate capacity for negligent performance of duties imposed upon it by statute.

Until recently only a few states, notably California, New York, and Washington, have had statutes making school districts answerable in damages for the torts of their officers, agents, and employees; and in Washington the law was not comprehensive. It provided that the immunity rule would still apply to certain types of torts—for example, those growing out of the use of athletic and shop equipment. Just recently the legislature has seen fit to amend the law so as to remove these exceptions, with the result that the immunity rule is now, practically or entirely, nonexistent. In some other states the legislatures have recently made districts liable by statute. In some states the statutes make districts liable for certain types of injuries only—generally those growing out of the transportation of pupils. In these cases, it is not unusual for the legislature to limit the amount of damages that can be recovered from the district. A few states, without specifically mentioning the doctrine of immunity, have enacted laws permitting school districts to carry liability insurance. A few other states, particularly New York, New Jersey, Connecticut, Massachusetts, and just recently Illinois, have enacted "save harmless" laws. These laws, although they do not specifically make school districts liable in damages for torts, provide that if a judgment is rendered against an employee because of injuries growing out of his negligence, the district must reimburse the employee in the amount of the judgment. Such laws, it is generally held, do not authorize an injured party to bring suit against the school district or school board. In Connecticut, however it was recently held that, under a "save harmless" statute, the board may be made a party to an action in tort.[4]

Although the tort-immunity rule has been the object of much criticism, the courts have been reluctant to abandon or overthrow it. They feel that if the rule is to be changed it should be done by the legislature, not the courts. In 1959 the Supreme Court of Illinois, in a landmark decision, became the first state higher court to actually abrogate this common-law rule by judicial fiat.[5] Before considering this case it might be well to consider a case decided some seven years earlier (1952) by the Appellate Court of Illinois.[6] Although the court did not abrogate the common-law rule of sovereign immunity in this case, it did provide evidence that the rule was in the process of erosion. This was an action for damages against a school district, brought by a pupil who had lost an eye as the result of alleged negligence on the part of the defendant district's agent. The complaint alleged that the district carried liability insurance in an amount sufficient to pay any damages that might be assessed against it and offered to limit the collection of any judgment the court might render to the amount of the insurance coverage. The defendant school district pleaded governmental immunity. The court, recognizing the rule of immunity but taking its cue from an earlier decision rendered by the Supreme Court of Illinois (*Moore* v. *Moyle*, 405 Ill. 555) in which it was held that a charitable organization would be held liable to the extent of its insurance coverage, held for the plaintiff. It took the

4. *Pastor* v. *City of Bridgeport*, 238 A. (2d) 43 (Conn.).

5. *Molitor* v. *Kaneland Community Unit District*, 18 Ill. (2d) 11, 163 N.E. (2d) 89.

6. *Thomas* v. *Broadlands Community Consolidated School District*, 348 Ill. App. 567, 109 N.E. (2d) 636.

position that the immunity rule was not absolute and might be waived. It reasoned that the only defensible reason for the rule is that it is in the public interest to protect public funds and to prevent their dissipation by paying damage claims. Here, because there was no reason for applying the rule, since the funds were protected by insurance, the court had no reluctance to assessing damages against the district. In so doing, it said:

> Defendant asserts in its brief that the basis for governmental immunity is that a State or subdivision thereof cannot be sued without its consent. In this defendant is only partially correct, for it has stated the rule and not the reason for the rule. . . .
> Immunity of a municipal corporation cannot be justified upon the theory that the King can do no wrong, or any paraphrase thereof. Such a justification does not lend itself to the age in which we live, and its harsh consequences to society condemn it.

Although this case gives some evidence of dissatisfaction with the rule by Illinois courts, it was not, as indicated previously, until seven years later that the rule was completely abrogated in Illinois.[7] In this case the plaintiff, who was injured when a school bus in which he was riding hit a culvert, exploded, and burned, brought an action against the district that operated the bus, on the ground that the district's employee—the driver—was negligent. There was no allegation of the existence of insurance, although the district did carry insurance with limits of $20,000 per person and $100,000 per accident. Instead, the plaintiff recognized the existence of the immunity rule and frankly asked the court to abrogate it in its entirety. This the court did, saying:

> We are of the opinion that none of the reasons advanced in support of school district immunity have any true validity today. Further we believe that abolition of such immunity may tend to decrease the frequency of school bus accidents by coupling the power to transport pupils with the responsibility of exercising care in the selection and supervision of the drivers. . . .
> We conclude that the rule of school district tort immunity is unjust, unsupported by any valid reason, and has no rightful place in modern day society.

In abrogating the tort immunity doctrine, the court was not unmindful of the comment so frequently made by other courts when asked to take this position—even though the doctrine may be outmoded, it is the task of the legislature, not the courts, to change the

---

7. *Molitor* v. *Kaneland Community Unit District,* 18 Ill. (2d) 11, 163 N.E. (2d) 89.

law. It recognized this argument but, rejecting it, disposed of it as follows:

Defendant strongly urges that if said immunity is to be abolished, it should be done by the legislature, not by this court. With this contention we must disagree. The doctrine of school district immunity was created by this court alone. Having found that doctrine to be unsound and unjust under present conditions, we consider that we have not only the power, but the duty, to abolish that immunity. "We closed our courtroom doors without legislative help, and we can likewise open them." Pierce v. Yakima Valley Memorial Hospital Ass'n., 43 Wash. 2d 162, 260 P.2d 765, 774.

In light of the growing criticism of the immunity doctrine found in both majority and dissenting opinions, it was generally expected that this decision would be accepted as precedent and that many other higher state courts would soon follow Illinois's leadership and abrogate the doctrine as it applies in their respective states. This has not been true, however. Now, ten years later, the doctrine has been repudiated by judicial fiat in only three other states—Wisconsin,[8] Minnesota,[9] and Arizona.[10] The Minnesota decision is somewhat different, since here the court abrogated the common-law rule of immunity prospectively.[11] In this case an action for damages was brought against a school district, a principal, and a teacher when a five-year-old child was injured while playing on a slide that allegedly was defective. Although the court denied recovery against the district on the ground that it was immune from liability under the common-law rule, it served notice that following the adjournment of the next session of the legislature it would abrogate the rule. Apparently preferring that the legislature change the law, the court gave it a chance to do so before abrogating it itself. It said:

The court is unanimous in expressing its intention to overrule the doctrine of sovereign tort immunity as a defense with respect to tort claims against school districts . . . arising after the next Minnesota legislature adjourns, subject to any statutes which now or hereafter limit or regulate the prosecution of such claims.

It is at this point that the law relating to the liability of school districts now stands. Although there has been no great rush by other state courts to follow the example set by the Supreme Court of Illinois

8. *Holytz* v. *City of Milwaukee*, 17 Wis. (2d) 26, 115 N.W. (2d) 618.
9. *Spanel* v. *Mounds View School District*, 264 Minn. 279, 118 N.W. (2d) 795.
10. *Stone* v. *Arizona State Highway Commission*, 93 Ariz. 384, 381 P. (2d) 107.
11. *Spanel* v. *Mounds View School District*, 264 Minn. 279, 118 N.W. (2d) 795

in abrogating the common-law rule of immunity, that the courts of three other states have done so, that dissatisfaction with the rule by some courts that continue to follow it appears to be more widespread, and that some state legislatures are becoming concerned with certain aspects of the problem leads to the conclusion that the law with respect to tort liability is gradually changing and the rule of immunity is being eroded.

THE LAW AND THE PUPIL

Introduction.—As was indicated earlier, numerous changes of comparatively recent date are to be noted in school law as it relates to pupils. One reason for this may be a newly aroused interest in individual rights. This awareness of individual rights appears to be at the root of changes not only in judicial thinking but in the types of cases being litigated. In the past, many cases involving pupils were "fought out" on the question of a board's authority to enact a specific rule and the reasonableness of the rule in question. Today many similar cases, instead of simply questioning the reasonableness of a particular rule, concern themselves with whether the rule under consideration violates certain rights guaranteed to the individual by the federal consititution. In the past it appears to have been generally conceded that constitutional safeguards erected to protect the rights of individuals were applicable to adults only and not to minors. With the increasing awareness of individual rights all this is changing, and the law is changing as the result of accretion and the alteration of judicial thinking.

Segregation on the basis of race.—Although it is impossible to isolate the point at which changes in the law relating to the rights of pupils began to be noted, these changes were dramatized by the decision of the United States Supreme Court in the famous *Brown* case,[12] (1954), which held that the segregation of pupils on the basis of race was unconstitutional (pp. 548–49).[13]

In its decision in this case, the Court subordinated the question of appropriate remedy to the primary question of the constitutionality of segregating pupils by race. Consequently it announced in the decision proper that it was restoring the cases to the docket for future argu-

12. *Brown* v. *Board of Education of Topeka,* 347 U.S. 483, 74 S. Ct. 686.

13. Although it was the *Brown* case that focused public attention on this trend, it is to be noted in such earlier cases as the flag-salute case (1943)—*Board of Education of West Virginia* v. *Barnette,* 319 U.S. 624, 63 S. Ct. 1178.

ment before considering how the decision announced would be implemented. On May 31, 1955, almost exactly one year after its first decision in 1954, the Court handed down a second decision, which has been referred to as the "implementation decree."[14] In this decision the Court remanded the four cases which on appeal to the Supreme Court were joined, argued together, and reported under the title *Brown v. Board of Education of Topeka*. In counseling fair play, the Court said:

> In fashioning and effectuating the decrees, the courts will be guided by equitable principles. Traditionally, equity has been characterized by a practical flexibility in shaping its remedies and by a facility for adjusting and reconciling public and private needs. These cases call for the exercise of these traditional attributes of equity power.

Although appearing to counsel patience, the Court left no doubt that it disapproved of delaying tactics, saying:

> Courts of equity may properly take into account the public interest in the elimination of . . . [any] obstacles in a systematic and effective manner. But it should go without saying that the vitality of these constitutional principles cannot be allowed to yield simply because of disagreement with them.

Finally, by way of further guidance to the courts to whom it remanded these cases, the Court instructed them to take such proceedings and enter such orders as were necessary to admit the parties concerned to racially integrated schools "with all deliberate speed."

Although the first *Brown* case made it clear that the practice of segregating public-school pupils on the basis of race was unconstitutional, and the second *Brown* case provided some guidelines for implementing the Court's holding in the first case, these two cases have raised many new questions and have spawned hundreds of cases in this field. In this connection a federal district court has said that the more questions that are answered regarding constitutionality, the more appear to be raised.[15] Many of these cases, however, involve judicial evaluations of implementation plans adopted to meet the requirements mentioned in the two *Brown* cases and in the increasing number of decisions handed down by the federal courts of appeals as they have attempted to interpret *Brown*. Some of these plans, as was to be expected, were deliberate attempts to skirt the law and obviously were not good-faith attempts to eliminate segregation as a

14. *Brown* v. *Board of Education of Topeka*, 349 U.S. 294, 75 S. Ct. 753.
15. *Blocker* v. *Board of Education*, 226 F. Supp. 208.

practice. Since many cases concerned specific sets of facts, comparatively few are of general interest or application.

Some cases, however, are of major importance, since they represent attempts to interpret what the Court said in the *Brown* cases. For example, the meaning of the Court's order to proceed "with all deliberate speed" in the desegregation of individual schools is subject to various interpretations. In the earliest cases the courts interpreted this liberally and were generous in granting time to achieve the ultimate goal—desegregation. They gave their approval to implementation plans that provided for desegregation at the rate of one grade per year. As time passed and some boards made little or no progress, the courts began to become impatient. A federal district court, in 1965, gave evidence of its impatience when it said, "The later the start, the shorter the time allowed for transition."[16] One year earlier, ten years after the decision in the first *Brown* case, the United States Supreme Court expressed its impatience when it said. "There has been entirely too much deliberation and not enough speed."[17] Now it appears that time has run out. Recently the Supreme Court said, "The burden on a school board today is to come forward with a plan . . . that promises realistically to work now."[18]

One of the early attempts at interpreting the *Brown* decisions was made by the United States District Court in South Carolina—a court that originally decided one of the cases that was appealed and ruled on in *Brown I*.[19] It illustrates the opportunities for interpretation that occur in the Supreme Court's decision. It said:

It is important that we point out exactly what the Supreme Court has decided and what it has not decided in this case. It has not decided that the federal courts are to take over or regulate the public schools of the state. It has not decided that the states must mix persons of different races in the schools or must require them to attend schools or must deprive them of the right of choosing the schools they attend. What it has decided, and all that it has decided, is that a state may not deny to any person on account of race the right to attend any school that it maintains. This, under the decision of the Supreme Court, the state may not do directly or indirectly; but if the schools which it maintains are open to children of all races, no violation of the Constitution is involved even though the children of different races voluntarily attend different schools, as they attend differ-

16. *Lockett* v. *Board of Education*, 342 F. (2d) 225.

17. *Griffin* v. *School Board of Prince Edward County*, 377 U.S. 218, 84 S. Ct. 1226.

18. *Green* v. *County School Board*, 88 S.Ct. 1689.

19. *Briggs* v. *Elliott*, 132 F. Supp. 766.

ent churches. Nothing in the Constitution or in the decision of the Supreme Court takes away from the people freedom to choose the schools they attend.

It does not forbid such segregation as occurs as the result of voluntary action. It merely forbids the use of governmental power to enforce segregation. The Fourteenth Amendment is a limitation upon the exercise of power by the state or state agencies, not a limitation upon the freedom of individuals.

As stated, this decision is cited here not so much because of its holding as because it furnishes a prime example of the fact that the *Brown* case is subject to various interpretations. Although it has been cited with approval by some courts, it has been criticized by others, especially by those who take the view that the Supreme Court not only condemned segregation but required integration. This is at the root of the question of the constitutionality of *de facto* segregation—a subject that will be considered in some detail later. The United States Court of Appeals, Eighth Circuit, in criticizing the point made in this case—that the Constitution does not require integration, but only forbids segregation—said:

The dictum in Briggs has not been followed or adopted by this Circuit and it is logically inconsistent with Brown and subsequent decisional law on this subject. This well-known dictum may be applicable in some logical areas where geographic zones permit of themselves without discrimination a segregated school system, but must be equally inapplicable if applied to school systems where the geographic or attendance zones are biracially populated.[20]

An examination of some of the most recent decisions handed down by the highest court in the land—the United States Supreme Court—gives a concise view of the law as it relates to segregation, since they provide evidence of the kind of implementation that meets with the Court's approval.[21] A reading of these three cases, all of which were decided the same day, makes it clear that the Court will approve geographic zoning of a school district for attendance purposes if the boundaries of the zones are not gerrymandered. Likewise, it is clear that the Court will approve plans that provide freedom of choice by the pupils in selecting the schools they wish to attend, but only where the application of the plan gives evidence of achieving the desired end result and where the choice is not between a segregated school and a desegregated school.

20. *Kemp* v. *Beasley*, 352 F. (2d) 14.

21. *Green* v. *County School Board*, 88 S. Ct. 1689; *Monroe* v. *Board of Commissioners*, 88 S. Ct. 1700; *Raney* v. *Board of Education*, 88 S. Ct. 1697.

In one of these cases[22] the Court, in ruling on the constitutionality of a freedom-of-choice plan in a school district in Virginia which operated two schools—a combined elementary and high school for Negroes and a similar school for whites—and which permitted students assigned to either school to transfer to the other if they chose to do so, said:

> The question for decision is whether, under all the circumstances here, respondent School Board's adoption of a "freedom-of-choice" plan which allows a pupil to choose his own public school constitutes adequate compliance with the Board's responsibility "to achieve a system of determining admission to the public schools on a non-racial basis. . . ." Brown v. Board of Education of Topeka, Kan., 349 U.S. 294, 300–301, 75 S. Ct. 753, 756, 99 L.Ed. 1083 (*Brown II*).

In light of the fact that after three years of operation under a freedom-of-choice plan not a single white child had expressed a desire to enter the Negro school and 85 percent of Negro children were still enrolled in the all-Negro school, the Court expressed its disapproval of the plan as it operated, saying:

> The school system remains a dual system. Rather than further the dismantling of the dual system, the plan has operated simply to burden children and their parents with a responsibility which *Brown II* placed squarely on the School Board. The Board must be required to formulate a new plan and, in light of other courses which appear open to the Board, such as zoning, fashion steps which promise realistically to convert promptly to a system without a "white" school and a "Negro" school, but just schools.

The Court made it clear that, in ruling as it did, it was not condemning freedom-of-choice as a school-board practice. It did, however, point out that such plans had not, as a rule, proved very successful, saying:

> Although the general experience under "freedom of choice" to date has been such as to indicate its ineffectiveness as a tool of desegregation, there may well be instances in which it can serve as an effective device. Where it offers real promise of aiding a desegregation program to effectuate conversion of a state-imposed dual system to a unitary, nonracial system there might be no objection to allowing such a device to prove itself in operation. On the other hand, if there are reasonably available other ways, such for illustration as zoning, promising speedier and more effective conversion to a unitary, nonracial school system, "freedom of choice" must be held unacceptable.

From this it seems clear that the constitutionality of a freedom-of-choice plan will be determined by the way it operates. Finally, the

22. *Green v. County School Board*, 88 S. Ct. 1689.

Court gave guidance to school boards in districts that have previously been characterized by segregation when it said, "The burden on a school board today is to come forward with a plan that promises realistically to work, and promises realistically to work *now*."

The second case, decided May 27, 1968, had a factual background very similar to that of the *Green* case just commented upon.[23] This was an action brought to prohibit a board of education from continuing to maintain a school system that, allegedly, was segregated. In the school district in question there was no residential segregation, both races residing throughout the district. The plan complained of—a freedom-of-choice plan—required pupils to choose annually between enrolling in one of two schools—the Field School, which until 1965 had been all Negro, and the Gould School, which had been all white. Those not exercising a choice were automatically assigned to the school they had attended the preceding year. After the plan had been in operation for three years, the results mirrored those in *Green*. Not a single white child had transferred to the Field School, and over 85 percent of the Negro children were still enrolled in the Field School. Relying on its decision in *Green*, the Court refused to approve the plan.

The third case involved a variant of the freedom-of-choice plan known as the "free-transfer" plan.[24] This plan provided for the automatic assignment of pupils living in attendance zones set up by the board according to geographic and natural boundaries and "according to the capacity and facilities of the [school] buildings" located in the zones. It also included a "free-transfer" provision. Any pupil, after registering in the school in his zone, could transfer freely to a school in another zone if space permitted. As late as 1964, the board had maintained three junior high schools—one all Negro and two all white. When after trying the plan for three years the board refused to change it, this action was brought. The plaintiffs asked that the board be required to set up a "feeder system" under which each junior high school would draw its pupils from certain specified elementary schools. They contended that the free-transfer plan did not work, since after three years the former Negro junior high school was still all black and not a single white pupil in that school's attendance area was enrolled in the Negro school, but a little over 80 percent of all Negro pupils in the entire district were enrolled there. Relying on its decision in *Green*, the Court held that the plan was inadequate and said:

23. *Raney v. Board of Education*, 88 S. Ct. 1697.
24. *Monroe v. Board of Commissioners*, 88 S.Ct. 1700.

Plainly, the plan does not meet respondent's "affirmative duty to take whatever steps might be necessary to convert to a unitary system in which racial discrimination would be eliminated root and branch." Green v. County School Board. . . . Only by dismantling the state-imposed dual system can that end be achieved. And manifestly, that end has not been achieved here nor does the plan approved by the lower courts for the junior high schools promise meaningful progress toward doing so. . . . That the Board has chosen to adopt a method of achieving minimal disruption of the old pattern is evident from its long delay in making any effort whatsoever to desegregate, and the deliberately discriminatory manner in which the Board administered the plan until checked by the District Court.

Finally, the Court made this significant statement:

We do not hold that "free transfer" can have no place in a desegregation plan. But like "freedom of choice," if it cannot be shown that such a plan will further rather than delay conversion to a unitary, nonracial, nondiscriminatory school system, it must be held unacceptable.

As was indicated earlier, when the United States Supreme Court rendered its memorable decision dealing with segregation in the public schools in the *Brown* case it answered one question, but that answer raised many more. Not the least of these is the constitutionality of what has come to be known as *de facto* segregation. By *de facto* segregation is meant segregation that is not imposed by law or board rule but which exists by virtue of some fact such as housing patterns. It is present when there is racial imbalance of pupils in individual schools. Although the imbalance is not intentional or deliberate, it is still looked upon by some as a form of segregation. Two main types of questions have arisen with respect to *de facto* segregation. First, there is the question whether the practice is subject to the same constitutional strictures as *de jure* segregation. In other words, whether a school board *must* mix the races in individual schools where racial imbalance occurs because of the creation of school attendance-area boundaries that are drawn on a geographical basis and not in an arbitrary manner. The second question concerns the authority of a school board to take race into consideration as it redraws attendance-area boundaries in such manner as to reduce racial imbalance in individual schools. Needless to say, the answers to these questions are to be found in the interpretations of the two *Brown* cases.

With respect to the first question—whether a board *must* correct racial imbalance—there appears to be little division among the courts. Although the United States Supreme Court has never ruled on this question specifically, it is significant that on the several occasions when this question has been before United States courts of appeals, they have ruled that *de facto* segregation is not unconstitutional—that the *Brown* decisions do not require affirmative action on the part of the board to mix the races where there is no *de jure* segregation.[25]

In one case decided by the United States Court of Appeals, Tenth Circuit, in which attendance-zone boundaries were complained of simply because they resulted in racial imbalance in individual schools, although there was no evidence that they had been drawn and pupil assignments had been made so as to insure the continuation of a dual system of schools, the court upheld the legality of the board's action.[26] With respect to the practice of zoning and the maintenance of neighborhood schools, the court pointed out that "in the absence of a showing that such school systems are being used to deprive a student of his constitutional rights . . . [they] are not objectionable on constitutional grounds," even if there is an imbalance of races in particular schools. Then, with respect to the authority of a school board to zone a district for attendance purposes, the court said: "The drawing of school zone lines is a discretionary function of a school board and will be reviewed only to determine whether the school board acted arbitrarily. . . . There is no showing that the Board acted arbitrarily in this case." Finally, with respect to the contention that the board was in reality maintaining a segregated system in spite of its "positive and affirmative duty to eliminate segregation in fact as well as segregation by intention," the court noted that "although the Fourteenth Amendment prohibits segregation, it does not command integration of the races in the public school and Negro children have no constitutional right to have white children attend school with them."

In another case, the United States Court of Appeals, Seventh Circuit, held that the *Brown* case did not mandate racial balance, nor did it prohibit racial imbalance in the schools.[27] It said:

We approve . . . of the statement in the District Court's opinion [213 F. Supp. 819], "Nevertheless, I have seen nothing in the many cases dealing with the segregation problem which leads me to believe that the law requires that a school system developed on the neighborhood school plan, honestly and conscientiously constructed with no intention or purpose to

25. *Bell* v. *School City of Gary*, 324 F. (2d) 209; *Gilliam* v. *School Board*, 345 F. (2d) 325; *Downs* v. *Board of Education*, 336 F. (2d) 988; *Springfield School Committee* v. *Barksdale*, 348 F. (2d) 261; *Deal* v. *Cincinnati Board of Education*, 369 F. (2d) 55; *Offerman* v. *Nitkowski*, 378 F. (2d) 22.

26. *Downs* v. *Board of Education*, 336 F. (2d) 988.

27. *Bell* v. *School City of Gary*, 324 F. (2d) 209.

segregate the races, must be destroyed or abandoned because the resulting effect is to have a racial imbalance in certain schools where the district is populated almost entirely by Negroes or whites."

And the United States Court of Appeals, Sixth Circuit, holding similarly, had this to say regarding *de facto* segregation:

> If the separation in imbalanced schools is the result of racial discrimination, the officials must take steps to remedy the situation. However, the Constitution does not prescribe any single particular cure, and the mere fact of imbalance alone is not a deprivation of equality in the absence of discrimination.[28]

It is significant that a bit of dictum in a decision of a federal district court in Washington, D.C., is interpreted by some as disapproving of *de facto* segregation.[29] Others differ. Since this is dictum, at best, it does not carry the weight of those decisions that have ruled on the substantive issue. These decisions shed additional light on the meaning of *Brown*. They appear to indicate that the intent of the Supreme Court was to abolish the use of governmental power to enforce segregation but not to command integration; that is, that the Court did not demand the mixing of races in the public schools where imbalance is not the result of affirmative action.

With respect to the second of the two main legal questions growing out of *de facto* segregation—whether a school board may take race into consideration when it changes boundaries of attendance areas so as to achieve racial balance without infringing on the constitutional rights of white children, particularly, the weight of authority is to the effect that there is nothing unconstitutional about such action. Most of the cases involving this question, oddly enough, have been decided in state and not federal courts. In one federal case, brought by taxpayers and parents of white children, challenging the constitutionality of a plan drawn up by the Montclair, New Jersey, school board, which had as its purpose the changing of boundaries of attendance areas to eliminate racial imbalance in the public schools, the court upheld the board's action.[30] Taking note of decisions by state courts in both New Jersey and New York, the court, in agreement with them, said that "a local board of education is not constitutionally prohibited from taking race into account in drawing or redrawing school attendance lines for the purpose of reducing or eliminating *de facto* segregation in its

28. *Deal* v. *Cincinnati Board of Education*, 369 F. (2d) 55.
29. *Hobson* v. *Hansen*, 269 F. Supp. 401.
30. *Fuller* v. *Volk*, 230 F. Supp. 25.

schools." To the same effect is a statement by the United States Court of Appeals, Second Circuit, approving the action taken by the Buffalo, New York, school board in correcting racial imbalance.[31]

> Consideration of race is necessary to carry out the mandate in *Brown*, and has been used . . . in cases following *Brown*. Where its use is to insure against, rather than to promote deprivation of equal educational opportunity, we cannot conceive that our courts would find that the state denied equal protection to either race by requiring its school boards to act with awareness of the problem.

One other question regarding *de facto* segregation was recently answered by the Supreme Judicial Court of Massachusetts.[32] This case was brought to question the constitutionality of a Massachusetts statute requiring school committees to take appropriate action to reduce racial imbalance, which it defined as existing "when the per cent of non-white students in any public school is in excess of fifty per cent of the total number of students in such school." The court, ruling that the act was not unconstitutional, said: "It would be the height of irony if the racial imbalance act, enacted as it was with the laudable purpose of achieving equal educational opportunities, should, by prescribing school pupil allocations based on race, founder on unsuspected shoals in the Fourteenth Amendment."

Another source of questions regarding segregation is the "Guidelines" set up early in 1965 by the United States Office of Education, Department of Health, Education, and Welfare. The purpose of the "Guidelines" is to emphasize certain policies, under Title VI of the Civil Rights Act of 1964, respecting segregation and to fix minimum standards to be used in determining the eligibility of elementary and secondary schools for receiving federal assistance. Here the question is largely one of conflict between two separate branches of government —the executive branch and the judicial branch. The "Guidelines" have been accepted by the courts as minimum standards for desegregation. In the first case in which they received judicial attention—a case decided by the United States Court of Appeals for the Fifth Circuit—the court, taking judicial cognizance of them, said that the judiciary has "functions and duties distinct from those of the executive department, but in carrying out a national policy the three departments of government are united by a common objective."[33] Then it

31. *Offerman v. Nitkowski*, 378 F. (2d) 22.
32. *School Committee v. Board of Education*, 227 N.E. (2d) 729 (Mass.)
33. *Singleton v. Jackson Municipal Separate School District*, 348 F. (2d) 729.

added that, in the absence of any legal questions, "the United States Office of Education is better qualified than the courts and is the more appropriate federal body to weigh administrative difficulties inherent in school desegregation plans." As a result, the court said that it welcomed the HEW—Health, Education, and Welfare—Guidelines. Six months later the same court, in another decision involving the same school district, stated that although it attached great significance to the Guidelines and accepted them as minimum standards for desegregation, it did not thereby abdicate its "judicial responsibility for determining whether a school desegregation plan violates federally guaranteed rights."[34]

In a third case decided by the same court (1966), pointing out that it was not binding itself to the HEW Guidelines or abdicating its judicial responsibility, it said that "HEW's standards are substantially the same as this Court's standards."[35] Then, in its decree, which embodied most of the HEW Guidelines, it said:

> We summarize the Court's policy as one of encouraging the maximum legally permissible correlation between judicial standards for school desegregation and HEW Guidelines. This policy may be applied without federal courts abdicating their proper judicial function. The policy complies with the Supreme Court's increasing emphasis on more speed and less deliberation in school desegregation. It is consistent with the judiciary's duty to the Nation to cooperate with the two other coordinate branches of government in carrying out the national policy expressed in the Civil Rights Act of 1964.

Religion and education.—Among the rights guaranteed to the people in the Bill of Rights is freedom of religion. The First Amendment to the Constitution of the United States provides that "Congress shall make no law respecting an establishment of religion or prohibiting the free exercise thereof." This has been held applicable to the states as well as to Congress by virtue of the Fourteenth Amendment. It is under this amendment that one who feels that his rights are being violated because of certain religious practices followed in some schools may seek redress.

Although Bible reading is one of the oldest and most common of school practices that have religious implications, strangely enough its constitutionality appears not to have been questioned in the federal courts until recently (1963), although it had been the subject of

---

34. *Singleton* v. *Jackson Municipal Separate School District,* 355 F. (2d) 865.
35. *United States* v. *Jefferson County Board of Education,* 372 F. (2d) 836.

litigation on numerous occasions in state courts (pp. 598–600). In general, the state courts have held that statutes or board rules permitting or requiring Bible reading and the recitation of the Lord's Prayer do not violate state constitutional provisions, although a few—for example, state courts in Illinois, Wisconsin, and Nebraska—have held differently.

In 1963, however, in a case of first impression as far as that court was concerned, the United States Supreme Court held that a statute requiring Bible reading in the public schools violates the establishment clause of the First Amendment and that a board rule, adopted pursuant to statutory authority, requiring Bible reading and the saying of the Lord's Prayer is also unconstitutional.[36]

This decision was the result of hearing two cases together on appeal. One case—*Schempp* v. *School District of Abington Township*, 177 F. Supp. 398—questioned the constitutionality of a Pennsylvania statute that required public schools to open school each morning with the reading, without comment, of ten verses from the Holy Bible. The second case—*Murray* v. *Curlett*, 228 Md. 239, 179 A. (2d) 698—questioned the constitutionality of a school-board rule, enacted pursuant to a statute permitting the board to do so, requiring the reading of a chapter from the Bible without comment, and the recitation of the Lord's Prayer in unison at the opening of each school day. The first-mentioned case was an appeal from a decision of the United States District Court, Eastern District, of Pennsylvania, which had held the statute in question to be unconstitutional. The second case was an appeal from a decision of the Maryland Court of Appeals, which upheld the constitutionality of the board rule.

The Supreme Court considered both the "free exercise" and the "establishment" clauses of the First Amendment but relied heavily upon the latter when, for example, it said:

Applying the Establishment Clause principles to the cases at bar we find that the States are requiring the selection and reading at the opening of the school day of verses from the Holy Bible and the recitation of the Lord's Prayer by the students in unison. These exercises are prescribed as part of the curricular activities of the students who are required by law to attend school. They are held in the school building under the supervision and with the participation of teachers employed in those schools. The trial court in . . . [*Schempp*] has found that such an opening exercise is a

36. *School District of Abington Township* v. *Schempp*, 374 U.S. 203, 83 S. Ct. 1560.

religious ceremony and was intended by the State to be so. We agree with the trial court's findings as to the religious character of the exercises. Given that finding, the exercises and the law requiring them are in violation of the Establishment Clause.

This case is especially important for the rule it laid down to be followed in determining whether a particular law or practice comes within the ban imposed by the First Amendment. Regarding this rule, the Court said:

> The test may be stated as follows: what are the purpose and primary effect of the enactment? If either is the advancement or inhibition of religion then the enactment exceeds the scope of legislative power as circumscribed by the Constitution. That is to say that to withstand the strictures of the Establishment Clause there must be a secular legislative purpose and a primary effect that neither advances nor inhibits religion.

Not only are Bible reading and the recitation of the Lord's Prayer in public schools forbidden by the First Amendment, but the Supreme Court of the United States has also held that the recitation of an official prayer, even though it may be nondenominational, is also unconstitutional.[37] This case was brought to test the constitutionality of the practice of reciting a prayer composed by the Board of Regents in New York and recommended for use in the public schools. The prayer in question was nondenominational and read as follows: "Almighty God, we acknowledge our dependence upon Thee, and we beg Thy blessing upon us, our parents, our teachers and our country." Holding that the use of the prayer was in violation of the establishment clause of the First Amendment, the Court stated that "the constitutional prohibition against laws respecting an establishment of religion must at least mean that . . . it is no part of the business of government to impose official prayers for any group of the American people to recite as a part of a religious program carried on by government." Although one cannot be certain how the Court would have ruled had the prayer been composed by someone other than a government agency, from the following quotation it seems clear that the answer would have been the same:

> We think that by using its public school system to encourage recitation of the Regent's prayer, the State of New York has adopted a practice wholly inconsistent with the Establishment Clause. There can, of course, be no doubt that New York's program of daily classroom invocation of God's blessing as prescribed in the Regent's prayer is a religious activity. It is a

37. *Engel v. Vitale,* 370 U.S. 421, 82 S. Ct. 1261.

solemn avowal of divine faith and supplication for the blessings of the Almighty.

Although the *Schempp*[38] and *Engel* cases are authority for the conclusion that Bible reading with prayer is unconstitutional, they are not to be interpreted as barring the Bible from the public schools entirely. In the *Schempp* case the Court, by way of dictum, gave its approval to the practice of studying the Bible and religion in the public schools, provided the instruction is purely objective. Although this matter was not before the Court directly, it said:

It might well be said that one's education is not complete without a study of comparative religion or the history of religion and its relationship to the advancement of civilization. It certainly may be said that the Bible is worthy of study for its literary and historic qualities. Nothing we have said here indicates that such study of the Bible or religion, when presented objectively as part of a secular program of education, may not be effected consistently with the First Amendment.

Although the United States Supreme Court has to date ruled on the constitutionality of no other school practices that have religious implications, other federal and higher state courts have done so. Their holdings do not carry the same weight as do those of the United States Supreme Court, but they serve as guidelines for evaluating such practices. The United States Court of Appeals, Seventh Circuit, was faced with the question of the constitutionality of one such practice in a kindergarten class in Illinois.[39] In this case children recited the following verse before eating: "We thank you for the flowers so sweet; we thank you for the food we eat; we thank you for the birds that sing; we thank you for everything." In holding that the practice was unconstitutional, the court refused to accept the argument that the use of the verse was secular, and it said that the First Amendment was designed to provide a bulwark against those who wish to impose their religious beliefs upon others through government action.

Likewise, the Court of Appeals, First Circuit, has held that the practice of saying a voluntary prayer could be prohibited by school authorities.[40] When parents of various religious faiths requested school officials to permit kindergarten children to recite a prayer in which they expressed their love for God, and the board of education denied

38. *School District of Abington Township* v. *Schempp*, 374 U.S. 203, 83 S. Ct. 1560.
39. *DeSpain* v. *DeKalb County Community School District*, 384 F. (2d) 836.
40. *Stein* v. *Oshinsky*, 348 F. (2d) 999.

their request, this action was brought to compel the board to accede to their request. The court, without ruling on the constitutionality of the practice, held that there was no duty imposed upon the school officials to permit the public prayer, and their refusal to approve the request was no violation of either the "free exercise" or the "freedom of speech" clause of the First Amendment.

In Michigan a United States district court, in applying the principles laid down in *Engel* and *Schempp*, has held that pupils who wish to pray or read the Bible in school may do so in the morning before school opens or in the afternoon after school closes, provided there are intervals of at least five minutes between such exercises in the morning and the time school officially opens and between the close of school in the afternoon and the time such exercises commence, and provided no bells are rung to call the pupils to worship.[41]

Again, in New Hampshire the Supreme Court has ruled on the constitutionality of two other practices that have religious overtones.[42] Under an arrangement whereby the Senate of New Hampshire may request the opinion of the Supreme Court of that state with regard to the constitutionality of pending legislation, the court found that a bill requiring a period of silence for the purpose of meditation during the first classes of each day was not a violation of the constitution. Likewise, it saw nothing unconstitutional in a bill that required the display of the motto "In God We Trust" in each classroom in the state. It stated that since this was the national motto, and since it was commonly displayed on coins, currency, and federal buildings, and since the words were to be found in our national anthem, there could be no objection to displaying it in public-school classrooms.

The Supreme Court of New Jersey, in a case involving "Black Muslims," was called upon to interpret the famous *Barnette* case (319 U.S. 624), which held unconstitutional a statute requiring students in public schools to salute the flag and pledge allegiance to it (pp. 10–11).[43] In this case parents of children who were excluded from school for refusal to pledge allegiance to the flag brought this action to have the children reinstated. The parents stated that they "believe in a religion known as Islam, and that followers of this religion known as Muslims, or sometimes 'Black Muslims,' are taught that their sole

41. *Reed* v. *Van Hoven*, 237 F. Supp. 48.
42. *Opinion of the Justices*, 228 A. (2d) 161 (N.H.).
43. *Holden* v. *Board of Education*, 216 A. (2d) 387 (N.J.).

allegiance is to Almighty God Allah." The board, accepting the hold-ing in *Barnette*, argued that it was never intended to be so interpreted as to be applicable to plaintiffs whose beliefs, it claimed, were "as much politically as religiously motivated and were closely intertwined with . . . racial aspirations." The court ruled against the board and in favor of the parents. It took the position that in the *Barnette* case the Court indicated "its feeling that the freedom guaranteed by the First Amendment extends beyond a particular set of religious beliefs to the much broader sphere of intellect and spirit."

Aside from ruling on the constitutionality of school practices that have religious overtones, the constitutionality of statutes granting state funds for the use of students in private and parochial schools has been the subject of litigation comparatively recently. In 1968 the United States Supreme Court was again faced with deciding the constitutionality of a state statute providing for free textbooks for pupils enrolled in other than public schools.[44] This case came from New York, where the statute in question required school boards "to purchase and to loan upon individual request" school books to pupils in grades seven to twelve who are enrolled in private schools. Al-though it held the statute constitutional, as it did a similar Louisiana statute, in the earlier *Cochran* case decided in 1930 (p. 50), the two cases are distinguishable. In *Cochran*, the plaintiff based his case on the ground that the Louisiana statute, which provided for free text-books for all children enrolled in private schools, violated the Four-teenth Amendment since it constituted the taking of property by taxation without "due process of law." In this case, the plaintiff based his objection to the constitutionality of the New York statute primarily on the ground it violated the First Amendment, since it constituted a "law respecting an establishment of religion." For this reason the Court stated that the *Everson* case, which upheld the constitutionality of a law providing free transportation for pupils enrolled in private and parochial schools, was "most nearly in point" for the questions raised in this case. First, the Court noted that in the *Everson* case it had said that the establishment clause of the First Amendment "bars a state from passing 'laws which aid one religion, aid all religions, or prefer one religion over another,' and bars too any 'tax in any amount, large or small . . . levied to support any religious activities or institu-tions. . . .'" In spite of this, the Court stated that the establishment

44. *Board of Education* v. *Allen*, 88 S. Ct. 1923.

clause does not bar a state from extending the benefits of its statutes "to all citizens without regard to their religious affiliation." Neither does it bar a state from paying "the bus fare of parochial school pupils as part of a general program under which it pays the fares of pupils attending public and other schools." The Court also stated that in *Everson* it had held that it was immaterial that the law in question helped children to get to church schools, even though some of the children might not have been able to attend such schools otherwise. Then applying the test laid down in the *Schempp* case and followed in others, that the test of unconstitutionality of an act under the First Amendment is whether the purpose and primary effect of the statute is "the advancement or inhibition of religion," the court said:

The statute upheld in *Everson* would be considered a law having "a secular legislative purpose and a primary effect that neither advances nor inhibits religion." We reach the same result with respect to the New York law requiring school books to be loaned free of charge to all students in specified grades. . . . The law merely makes available to all children the benefits of a general program to lend school books free of charge. Books are furnished at the request of the pupil and ownership remains, at least technically, in the State. Thus no funds or books are furnished to parochial schools, and the financial benefit is to parents and children, not to schools. Perhaps free books make it more likely that some children choose to attend a sectarian school, but that was true of the state-paid bus fares in *Everson* and does not alone demonstrate an unconstitutional degree of support for a religious institution.

Finally, to the plaintiff's contention that books are different from buses, the Court said:

The major reason offered by appellants for distinguishing free textbooks from free bus fares is that books, but not buses, are critical to the teaching process, and in a sectarian school that process is employed to teach religion. However this Court has long recognized that religious schools pursue two goals, religious instruction and secular education. . . . [In] Cochran v. Louisiana State Board of Education [p. 50] . . . appellants said that a statute requiring school books to be furnished without charge to all students, whether they attended public or private schools, did not serve a "public purpose," and so offended the Fourteenth Amendment. Speaking through Chief Justice Hughes, the Court summarized as follows its conclusion that Louisiana's interest in the secular education being provided by private schools made provision of textbooks to students in those schools a properly public concern: "[The State's] interest is education, broadly; its method comprehensive. Individual interests are aided only as the common interest is safeguarded."

In this decision there were three dissenting opinions written by Justices Black, Douglas, and Fortas.

Shortly after handing down its decision in the New York textbook case, just considered, the Supreme Court was asked to rule on another case regarding the application of the First Amendment—a case involving the constitutionality of a statute concerning state control over the curriculum.[45] The statute in question made it unlawful for any teacher in any state institution in Arkansas to "teach the theory or doctrine that mankind ascended or descended from a lower form of animal." It was contended that the statute violated the establishment and free exercise clauses of the First Amendment. The Court agreed and said: "The First Amendment mandates government neutrality." Expanding upon this, it said:

Arkansas' law cannot be defended as an act of religious neutrality. Arkansas did not seek to excise from the curriculum of its schools . . . all discussion of the origin of man. The law's effort was confined to an attempt to blot out a particular theory because of its supposed conflict with the biblical account, literally read. Plainly, the law is contrary to the mandate of the First, and in violation of the Fourteenth Amendment to the Constitution.

When the United States Supreme Court rules that a particular educational practice, such as Bible reading and the recitation of the Lord's Prayer, is prohibited under the United States Constitution, that ruling becomes the law of the land and is binding in each of the fifty states. Where, however, it rules that a particular practice—such as using public funds to pay for the transportation of pupils attending private and parochial schools—is not unconstitutional, it does not mean that the practice may be followed in all fifty states. In some, it may be unconstitutional under some particular provision of the state constitution. For example, in Missouri,[46] Alaska,[47] Oklahoma,[48] Wisconsin,[49] Delaware,[50] and Hawaii[51] it has been held that provisions in the state constitutions prohibit the use of public funds for the transportation of nonpublic school pupils. In Oregon, the same was held regarding the furnishing of free textbooks to nonpublic schools pupils.[52]

45. *Epperson v. State of Arkansas*, 89 S. Ct. 266.
46. *McVey v. Hawkins*, 258 S.W. (2d) 927 (Mo.).
47. *Matthews v. Quinton*, 362 P. (2d) 932 (Alaska).
48. *Board of Education v. Antone*, 384 P. (2d) 911 (Okla.).
49. *State v. Nussbaum*, 115 N.W. (2d) 761 (Wis.).
50. *Opinion of the Justices*, 216 A. (2d) 668 (Del.).
51. *Spears v. Honda*, 449 P. (2d) 130 (Hawaii).
52. *Dickman v. School District*, 366 P. (2d) 533 (Ore.).

No federal courts have ruled on the constitutionality of such other school practices with religious implications as baccalaureate services, Christmas programs, and dual enrollment. The Supreme Court of Missouri, however, has ruled on one aspect of the practice of dual enrollment,[53] sometimes referred to as shared-time. It held that sending public school teaching personnel into parochial schools for instructional purposes was unconstitutional under the Missouri constitution. It failed to rule, however, on the practice of sending parochial school pupils into public schools for part of their instruction, because this was unnecessary since a compulsory school law in Missouri requires that the school day be six hours in length and that pupils be in attendance in no more than one school.

Pupil rights and school-board rules.—The constitutionality of school-board rules relating to pupils and pupil behavior has recently been the subject of considerable litigation. In much of this litigation, the question of pupil rights has been the real issue. At the bottom of much of this litigation is the question of the constitutionality of board rules relating to married students and to pupil dress.

Pupil marriages

With the recent increase in marriages among high-school pupils, litigation involving the constitutionality of board rules relating to the admission and suspension of students who marry has also increased. Most of these cases have questioned the reasonableness of the rules in question. One legal principle that these cases have established is that a school board may not require married girls who are still within the compulsory school-attendance age to attend school (p. 520). Likewise, there is agreement that a board rule permanently prohibiting married pupils, otherwise eligible, from attending public schools is unreasonable and therefore unenforceable (p. 602). On the other hand, it has recently been held that even though a board may not prohibit the attendance of married pupils permanently, it may prohibit their attendance temporarily—that is, for *a limited period of time* immediately following marriage *where it is shown that such marriages are likely to result in confusion and disorder and affect the discipline of the school adversely.*[54] Whether it will be accepted as precedent

53. *Special District for Education and Training of Handicapped Children* v. *Wheeler,* 408 S.W. (2d) 60 (Mo.).

54. *State* v. *Marion County Board of Education,* 302 S.W. (2d) 57 (Tenn.).

remains to be seen. In such cases, the question of legality may revolve around the length of the limited period of time. In the case just cited, the court held that a board rule barring a married pupil from school attendance for the remainder of the school term in which the marriage was solemnized was not unreasonable. On the other hand, a Kentucky court, although not definitely disapproving the principle that a school-board rule prohibiting attendance by married pupils for a limited period of time is legal, did hold that a rule prohibiting such a person from attending school for one full year was unreasonable.[55] How it would have held had the prohibition covered some shorter period of time can only be surmised. The court condemned "the unreasonable and arbitrary effect of the regulation . . . since it imposes the identical result in every case, without regard to the circumstances of any case." In Texas, the court struck down a board rule requiring pupils who marry during a school term to withdraw for the remainder of the term.[56] In so doing it made clear its disagreement with the decision in the Tennessee case previously mentioned—*State v. Marion County Board of Education*—when it held that the board rule's arbitrariness lay in the fact that it "made marriage, ipso facto, the basis for denial of a student's right to obtain an education." It also said, "If a student is entitled to admission, the question of the length of exclusion is not material."

In a still later Texas case,[57] the court of civil appeals held that marriage alone is not sufficient cause for suspending a pupil from attendance at school for a definite period of three weeks. It should be noted that in this case there was no evidence that the marriage resulted in any disturbance of the school. Noting that the girl in question was an honor student who hoped to obtain a college scholarship, and that her husband was having such a difficult time academically that the loss of three weeks' schooling might result in his failing, the court said:

> The great preponderance of the evidence . . . established that the presence and attendance . . . [of the married couple] did not cause turmoil, and unrest and upheaval against education by fellow students. The appellees were not approached by other students regarding the subject of

55. *Board of Education v. Bentley*, 383 S.W. (2d) 677 (Ky.).

56. *Anderson v. Canyon Independent School District*, 412 S.W. (2d) 387 (Tex.).

57. *Carrollton-Farmers Branch Independent School District v. Knight*, 418 S.W. (2d) 535 (Tex.).

married life. The ability of appellees to study was not affected by marriage. The evidence also showed that the resolution suspending students from school for marriage had not been uniformly applied.

Pointing out that the pupils were guilty of no improper conduct, and the suspension was for the simple fact that they were married while pupils in school, the court summarized its holding as follows:

> We think the weight of authority in Texas and in the United States is to the effect that marriage *alone* is not a proper ground for a school district to suspend a student from attending school for scholastical purposes only. [Emphasis supplied.]

In another Texas case, the court held unreasonable a board rule that forbade admission of a married mother.[58] In this case a sixteen-year-old mother, who was married but who had filed for divorce, sought to enter high school but was prevented from so doing by the board rule in question. The court appears to have based its decision on the fact that this rule amounted to an attempt to bar permanently married pupils covered by the rule. In commenting that "this holding does not mean that rules disciplining the children may not be adopted, but any such rule may not result in suspension beyond the current term," the court appears to give approval to the rule laid down in the Tennessee case, and to differ with the rule followed in *Anderson* and *Knight*—the Texas cases just commented upon. Since it was decided before these cases, one can only wonder if the court had later changed its thinking.

In an Ohio case, a slightly different question relating to the marriage of pupils was before the court.[59] Here the question was the authority of the school board to suspend a pregnant married pupil for the period of the pregnancy. The court upheld the board's action, since it contended that the purpose of the rule was to protect the mother and the unborn child from possible injury. In so holding, it is questionable whether the court was establishing a precedent. In this case, the board had provided the prospective mother with home instruction. How the court would have ruled had this not been true is, of course, debatable. Consequently, one is cautioned against generalizing too broadly on the basis of this case.

Another aspect of the married-pupil problem that has spawned considerable litigation recently relates to the authority of a school board to prohibit married pupils from participating in extracurricular

58. *Alvin Independent School District* v. *Cooper*, 404 S.W. (2d) 76 (Tex.).
59. *State* v. *Chamberlain*, 175 N.E. (2d) 539 (Ohio).

activities. In general, the courts have upheld the actions of boards in restricting married students from engaging in such activities.[60] Most of these cases involve the question of the authority of a board to deny to married boys the right to participate in athletics. In the first case of this type to come before the courts, a male pupil who had married before the board enacted a rule prohibiting married students from engaging in athletic activities and from holding class offices or any other such positions brought an action questioning the legality of the rule.[61] He had played football before his marriage and desired to continue to participate in this sport. The main grounds on which he challenged the legality of the rule was that it was arbitrary and also that playing football, coupled with the possibility of his receiving an athletic scholarship in college, was a scholastic right which entitled him to protection under a section of the Texas constitution which forbids the enactment of retroactive laws. The court ruled against him. It held the rule was reasonable, not arbitrary or capricious.

The last of these cases was decided in Iowa.[62] It was an action brought by a married male pupil who, because of a board rule, was prohibited from participating in basketball. He contended that the rule was illegal. The court, commenting on the authority of school boards to regulate the conduct of pupils, said: "It is not within their power to govern or control the individual conduct of students *wholly* outside the school room or playgrounds. However, the conduct of pupils which directly relates to and affects management of the school and its efficiency is a matter within the sphere of regulations by school authorities." Holding that the board did not abuse its authority in enacting the rule in question, the court, quoting with approval from a decision by the Supreme Court of Utah—*Starkey* v. *Board of Education,* 381 P.(2d) 718 (Utah)—which upheld a similar rule, said:

We have no disagreement with the proposition advocated that all students attending school should be accorded equal privileges and advantages. But the participation in extracurricular activities must necessarily be subject to regulations as to eligibility. Engaging in them is a privilege which may be claimed only in accordance with the standards set up for

60. *Kissick* v. *Garland Independent School District,* 330 S.W. (2d) 708 (Tex.); *Cochrane* v. *Board of Education,* 103 N.W. (2d) 569 (Mich.); *State* v. *Stevenson,* 189 N.E. (2d) 181 (Ohio); *Starkey* v. *Board of Education,* 381 P. (2d) 718 (Utah); *Board of Directors* v. *Green,* 147 N.W. (2d) 854 (Iowa); *Carrollton-Farmers Branch Independent School District* v. *Knight,* 418 S.W. (2d) 535 (Tex.).

61. *Kissick* v. *Garland Independent School District,* 330 S.W. (2d) 708 (Tex.).
62. *Board of Directors* v. *Green,* 147 N.W. (2d) 854 (Iowa).

participation. It is conceded, as plaintiff insists, that he has a constitutional right both to attend school and to get married. But he has no "right" to compel the Board of Education to exercise its discretion to his personal advantage so he can participate in the named activities.

Pupil dress

Other board rules—relating to the dress of pupils—have also been the subject of litigation recently. Although courts are not concerned with the wisdom of such rules, they are concerned with their reasonableness and constitutionality (pp. 568–70). In general, they take the position that the right of a pupil and his parents to determine what he shall wear must be subordinated to school-board restrictions based upon the efficient management of the schools. The question of the authority of school boards to prohibit pupils from wearing so-called civil rights or freedom buttons was recently before the United States Court of Appeals, Fifth Circuit, on two occasions. The court, in ruling on the legality of a rule to this effect, took a similar position to that taken by the courts in the "marriage" cases—that the reasonableness of the rule was determined by the extent to which the wearing of the buttons disrupted the efficiency and discipline of the school.[63] In one case, the wearing of the buttons was accompanied by considerable commotion, disorder, and disruption in the school.[64] As a result, the court upheld a regulation of the school board that forbade the wearing of such buttons. To the plaintiffs' contention that the board rule violated the right to freedom of speech guaranteed them by the First Amendment to the Constitution of the United States, the court said:

> Cases of this nature, which involve regulations limiting freedom of expression and communication of an idea which are protected by the First Amendment, present serious constitutional questions. . . . The constitutional guarantee of freedom of speech "does not confer an absolute right to speak" and the law recognizes that there can be an abuse of such freedom.

In the second case, where the wearing of the freedom buttons resulted only in mild curiosity but no commotion, the same court declared that the rule in question was unreasonable and therefore unenforceable.[65] The court, as in the *Blackwell* case, recognized the issue of freedom of speech but pointed out that the constitutional

63. *Blackwell* v. *Issaquena County Board of Education,* 363 F. (2d) 749; *Burnside* v. *Byars,* 363 F. (2d) 744.

64. *Blackwell* v. *Issaquena County Board of Education,* 363 F. (2d) 749.

65. *Burnside* v. *Byars,* 363 F. (2d) 744.

guarantee embodied therein is not absolute, saying: "But the liberty of expression guaranteed by the First Amendment can be abridged by state officials if their protection of legitimate state interests necessitates the invasion of free speech." But in this case there was no commotion and so the court found that there was no need for protecting the state's interest which would justify the rule forbidding the wearing of the buttons. Here the court set the following criterion for judging the reasonableness of a board rule:

Regulations which are essential in maintaining order and discipline on school property are reasonable . . . [A] reasonable regulation is one which measurably contributes to the maintenance of order and decorum within the educational system.

About the same time that the Court of Appeals, Fifth Circuit, was deciding the two cases just commented upon, a federal district court in Iowa was deciding a similar case.[66] Only here the question before the court was the authority of a school board to enact and enforce a rule forbidding the wearing of black armbands as a protest against the war in Vietnam. The court, in upholding the action of the board in suspending pupils who did not abide by the rule, took a slightly different position from that taken by the Court of Appeals, Fifth Circuit. In fact, it may be said to have expanded that rule. It held that the right of freedom of speech or expression is not absolute and that the board need not wait until a commotion arises before infringing on that right—that it was sufficient if the board had reason to believe that the wearing of the armbands *might* disrupt the good order of the school. It said:

It is the view of the Court that actions of school officials in this realm should not be limited to those instances where there is a material or substantial interference with school discipline. School officials must be given a wide discretion and if, under the circumstances, a disturbance in school discipline is reasonably to be anticipated, actions which are reasonably calculated to prevent such a disruption must be upheld by the Court.

This case was appealed to the United States Court of Appeals, Eighth Circuit.[67] Since the court was equally divided, the district court's decision was affirmed without opinion. An appeal was then taken to the United States Supreme Court, which on February 24,

66. *Tinker* v. *Des Moines Independent Community School District*, 258 F. Supp. 971.
67. *Tinker* v. *Des Moines Independent Community School District*, 383 F. (2d) 988.

1969, reversed the decision of the district court,[68] thereby approving the rule laid down in *Burnside*. The Court, accepting the district court's view that the wearing of armbands was "the type of symbolic act that is within the Free Speech Clause of the Fourteenth Amendment," stated that the pupils' First Amendment rights must not be infringed upon unless the action which the board is attempting to prohibit actually interferes or collides with "the school's work or the rights of other students to be secure and let alone." Accordingly, since there was no evidence of disorder or disturbance, the court upheld the right of the pupils to wear the armbands in question, and said:

In our system, undifferentiated fear or apprehension of disturbance is not enough to overcome the right to freedom of expression. . . .
    In order for the State in the person of school officials to justify prohibition of a particular expression of opinion, it must be able to show that its action was caused by something more than a mere desire to avoid the discomfort and unpleasantness that always accompany an unpopular viewpoint. Certainly where there is no finding and no showing that the exercise of the forbidden right would "materially and substantially interfere with the requirements of appropriate discipline in the operation of the school," the prohibition cannot be sustained. *Burnside* v. *Byars*, supra, at 749.

Then, in commenting on the rights of pupils in general, it said:

    In our system, state-operated schools may not be enclaves of totalitarianism. School officials do not possess absolute authority over their students. Students in school as well as out of school are "persons" under our Constitution. They are possessed of fundamental rights which the State must protect, just as they themselves must respect their obligations to the State. In our system, students may not be regarded as closed-circuit recipients of only that which the State chooses to communicate.

Since this decision was rendered by the Supreme Court of the United States, the rule laid down becomes "the law of the land" and is decisive in the matter. Nevertheless, it is appropriate to point out that it was rendered by a divided court. There were two concurring and two dissenting opinions. In one concurring opinion, Justice Stewart, although agreeing with the judgment of the Court and much that it said, saw fit to make one criticism of its reasoning. He said: "I cannot share the Court's uncritical assumption that, school discipline aside, the First Amendment rights of children are co-extensive with those of adults."

Justice Black, in his dissenting opinion, was quite critical of the

68. *Tinker* v. *Des Moines Independent Community School District*, 89 S. Ct. 733.

majority opinion. For example, he said: "The Court's holding in this case ushers in what I deem to be an entirely new era in which the power to control pupils by the elected 'officials of state supported public schools . . .' in the United States is in ultimate effect transferred to the Supreme Court." He summarized the Court's holding as follows:

As I read the Court's opinion it relies upon the following grounds for holding unconstitutional the judgment of the Des Moines school officials and the two Courts below. First the Court concludes that the wearing of armbands is "symbolic speech" which is "akin to pure speech" and therefore protected by the First and Fourteenth Amendments. Secondly, the Court decides that the public schools are an appropriate place to exercise "symbolic speech" as long as normal school functions are not "unreasonably" disrupted. Finally, the Court arrogates to itself, rather than to the State's elected officials charged with running the schools, the decision as to which school disciplinary regulations are reasonable.

Then he commented on it, saying:

Assuming that the Court is correct in holding that the conduct of wearing armbands for the purpose of conveying political ideas is protected by the First Amendment, . . . the crucial remaining questions are whether students and teachers may use the schools at their whim as a platform for the exercise of free speech—"symbolic" or "pure"—and whether the Courts will allocate to themselves the function of deciding how the pupils [sic] school day will be spent. While I have always believed that under the First and Fourteenth Amendments neither the State nor Federal Government has any authority to regulate or censor the content of speech, I have never believed that any person has a right to give speeches or engage in demonstrations where he pleases and when he pleases.

It appears that Justice Black was especially disturbed by two things. First, he was disturbed because as a result of this decision students were permitted "to broadcast political or any other views to educate and inform the public." He took the position that "taxpayers send children to school on the premise that at their age they need to learn, not teach." He was also disturbed because this case was reestablishing "the old reasonableness due process test, the doctrine that judges have the power to hold laws unconstitutional upon the belief of the judges that they are 'unreasonable,' 'arbitrary,' 'shock the conscience,' 'irrational,' 'contrary to fundamental "decency,"'" or some other such flexible term without precise boundaries," which he argued had previously prevailed but had long since been discarded. His reason was that "it gives judges power to strike down any law they do not like." (This case is commented on in much detail here, since, as it will be shown later, it has come to be accepted as precedent in cases where school boards have attempted to suspend pupils for violating rules prohibiting the wearing of long hair, where there was no evidence that the wearing of long hair disrupted the school's activities.)

Pupil grooming

In general the courts take the same position regarding rules prohibiting the wearing of long hair by male students as they do toward rules barring pupils whose dress does not conform to standards determined by the board. There are two main approaches to the question of the authority of the board to enact such rules, as indicated by a federal district court in Texas which was called upon to rule on whether a school board had the right to deny admission to a student "solely because of the length and style of . . . [his] hair."[69] It said:

> There are two ways to approach this problem of authorization. The court could focus on the school administration and attempt to justify the regulation by emphasizing the educational need for an academic atmosphere and the resulting demand that disturbances be kept to a minimum. Or, it can focus more directly on the individual student and evaluate the need for regulation by examining the purpose of public school education in terms of the individual. The regulation must serve both purposes.

In this particular case the court, without ignoring the first approach, chose to focus on the second, saying: "We feel that where the effects of the regulation extend beyond the classroom and bear directly on the student's person and his freedom of expression, the latter approach provides a more reasonable basis for school concern, and it is here that the court should look to justify the regulation."

An analysis of all the cases dealing with this question reveals that although the courts have not ignored the first approach, all except perhaps one of these cases have focused on the second. In this case—the first of the long-hair cases (1965)—no question of the constitutional rights of pupils was raised.[70] The sole question before the court was whether the board rule in question was reasonable. Here a boy who was suspended from school for refusal to conform to a board rule prohibiting boys from wearing "extreme haircuts" brought an action against the school officials to restrain them from preventing him from attending school. He charged that the rule was unreasonable. He

69. *Ferrell* v. *Dallas Independent School District,* 261 F. Supp. 545.
70. *Leonard* v. *School Committee of Attleboro,* 212 N.E. (2d) 468 (Mass.).

was a professional musician, and he contended that long hair was an "essential factor in his professional success." He made no point of the constitutionality of the rule or its vagueness. The court, refusing to rule on the wisdom of the rule, stated that it would confine itself to the question of whether there was a rational basis for it. It stated that it would reverse the board's decision "only if convinced that the regulation of pupils' hair styles and lengths could have no reasonable connection with the successful operation of the school." Finding that there was a rational basis for the rule, the court held that it was reasonable and could be enforced. It said:

The discretionary powers of the [school] committee are broad, and the courts will not reverse its decision unless it can be shown that it acted arbitrarily or capriciously. . . . The committee could have concluded that regardless of the detriment to plaintiff's professional life, only the strictest application of the regulation could ensure its success. We cannot say that its decision was an abuse of power.

In all other cases the approach was in the direction of the constitutional rights of pupils. In these cases the constitutionality of board rules regulating the type and length of haircuts was the main issue before the courts. Because it is difficult to generalize on the basis of these cases, because they grew out of different factual situations—for example, in some the wearing of long hair by male students appeared to be accompanied by classroom or school disruptions, but in others it was not—and because they were argued on different bases, these cases must necessarily be considered in some detail. In these cases the plaintiffs contended that the rules in question violated certain specific amendments to the United States Constitution. Specifically, their constitutionality has been challenged on the ground they violated various rights guaranteed to pupils by the First, Fourth, Fifth, Eighth, Ninth, and Fourteenth Amendments. The reasoning of the courts with respect to the constitutionality of such rules under each of these amendments will now be considered in turn.

In the first place, it has been held that board rules of the type in question do not violate the First Amendment, which guarantees the right of freedom of speech and expression.[71] In the third long-hair case to come before the higher courts (1967), the plaintiff, who had been suspended from school for failure to comply with a board rule prohibiting the wearing of "long, shaggy hair and/or exaggerated side-

71. *Davis* v. *Firment,* 269 F. Supp. 524; *Miller* v. *Gillis,* — F. Supp. —.

burns," brought an action against the school board for damages under the Civil Rights Act.[72] He contended, among other things, that by compelling him to cut his hair the school board was infringing on his First Amendment right of freedom of speech. He contended, further, that the choice of a particular style of wearing his hair constituted symbolic expression. The court, rejecting this, said:

> Symbolic expression has been held to be entitled to First Amendment protection. . . . But a symbol must symbolize a specific idea or viewpoint. A symbol is merely a vehicle by which a concept is transmitted from one person to another; unless it represents a particular idea, a "symbol" becomes meaningless. It is, in effect, not really a symbol at all.
>
> It can be said that saluting a flag is a symbolic method of expressing loyalty to the nation represented by that flag or that the wearing of "freedom buttons" by Negroes is "a means of silently communicating an idea and to encourage the members of their community to exercise their civil rights.". . . But just what does the wearing of long hair symbolize? What is student Davis trying to express? Nothing really.

A federal district court in Illinois, took the same position in a long-hair case decided September 25, 1969.[73] In this case the plaintiff, who was seeking admission to school after being suspended because his hair style did not meet the standards prescribed in a dress code, sought to have the code declared unconstitutional on the ground it was in violation of several constitutional amendments, including the First. Although the court held that it was unconstitutional, it refused to do so on First Amendment grounds. It said:

> I cannot agree with the contention that the plaintiff's rights under the First Amendment have been violated. The plaintiffs have cited numerous cases which show that the freedom of speech has been extended far beyond the use of actual words and that acts themselves can, under certain situations, constitute speech protected by this Amendment. Thus, in *Tinker* v. *Des Moines Independent Community School District,* 393 U.S. 503 (1968) [*sic*], the Supreme Court held that a school board did not have the right to proscribe the wearing of armbands worn as a symbol of students' dislike for the war in Vietnam. Likewise, the wearing of freedom buttons was held to be an act of free speech and therefore protected by the Constitution. *Burnside* v. *Byars,* 363 F. 2d 744 (5 Cir. 1966).
>
> These are the only two cases cited by the plaintiffs which pertain directly to the appearance of the student or to something worn by such students and which involved a violation of the First Amendment. It is clear that these cases may be distinguished on the grounds that they pertain to objects which are symbols of movements or ideas easily expressed and readily identifiable.

72. *Davis* v. *Firment,* 269 F. Supp. 524.
73. *Miller* v. *Gillis,* — F. Supp. —.

David's wearing of his hair at shoulder length has never been contended by him to be part of a movement of hair growers, nor is it a symbol of some easily identifiable idea. It is a mere exercise of the wearer's choice of hair styles.

At this point it is well to note that in two other long-hair cases the plaintiffs contended that a board rule regulating hair style was unconstitutional because it violated the First Amendment.[74] In neither case, however, did the court find it necessary to rule on this point, since it found the rules violative of other constitutional amendments.

It has also been held that board rules regulating hair length and haircut styles are not unconstitutional on the ground that they invade the right of privacy, which, it has been held, is protected by the Fourth Amendment.[75] In the first of the long-hair cases, the Supreme Judicial Court of Massachusetts (1965) had the following to say about the right of privacy, without relating what it said to the federal constitution:

We are mindful that the regulation of haircuts may affect the private and personal lives of students more substantially than do restrictions regarding dress. Whereas the latter need not operate beyond the school premises, the former will inevitably do so. Therefore the plaintiff contends that the challenged ruling is an invasion of family privacy touching matters occurring while he is at home and within the exclusive control of his parents.
. . . the domain of family privacy must give way in so far as a regulation reasonably calculated to maintain school discipline may affect it. The rights of other students, and the interest of teachers, administrators and the community at large in a well run and efficient school system are paramount.[76]

Likewise, a California court has held that a board rule forbidding male pupils to wear beards does not violate the right of privacy.[77] (Although this case concerns the wearing of a beard rather than long hair, the constitutional issues are the same.) It said:

It is next urged that because a beard cannot be donned and doffed for work or play as wearing apparel generally can . . . the Board's ruling has the effect of extending into petitioner's home life, thereby violating his right of privacy. . . .
This argument has been advanced before.

74. *Breen* v. *Kahl*, 296 F. Supp. 702; *Griffin* v. *Tatum*, 300 F. Supp. 60.

75. *Ferrell* v. *Dallas Independent School District*, 392 F. (2d) 697; *Miller* v. *Gillis*,—F. Supp.—; *Akin* v. *Board of Education*, 68 Cal. Rptr. 557; *Leonard* v. *School Committee of Attleboro*, 212 N.E. (2d) 468 (Mass).

76. *Leonard* v. *School Committee of Attleboro*, 212 N.E. (2d) 468 (Mass).

77. *Akin* v. *Board of Education*, 68 Cal. Rptr. 557.

Then, citing the *Leonard* case just commented upon, the court gave
the rule its approval.

Finally, in a long-hair case originating in Illinois, a federal district
court, without mentioning the right of privacy, had the following to
say regarding the application of the Fourth Amendment to this case:

> Plaintiffs also have contended that David's rights under the Fourth
> Amendment have been violated. I cannot agree with this. . . . Plaintiffs
> have cited the case of *Griswold* v. *Connecticut*, 381 U.S. 479 (1965) as a
> source for the doctrine of expansion of the protection of the First and
> Fourth Amendments of the Constitution on the grounds that there is a vast
> "penumbra" of constitutional protection. While it is argued that a person in
> order to be guaranteed personal security against unreasonable seizure must
> be protected against unreasonable seizures of zones of conduct by the
> state, I find that the law does not go that far. Besides, it is unnecessary to
> speculate on such protection in this case. There is no logical relationship
> between the Fourth Amendment protection and the facts of this case.[78]

Likewise, it has been held that a board rule regulating hair styles is
not violative of pupils' Fifth Amendment rights. In a Texas case
certain pupils who were members of a musical combo and played
professionally were denied admission to school because they refused
to have their hair cut and abide by a board rule that prohibited
"Beatle" haircuts. They brought an action to restrain the board from
enforcing the rule in which they charged, among other things, that it
violated their Fifth Amendment right to engage in their chosen
occupation.[79] They based this argument on the fact that they had a
contract with their agent which required that they keep their hair
long. The court, refusing this argument, said: "Further, the terms
upon which a public free education is granted in the high schools of
Texas cannot be fixed or determined by the pupils themselves. Nor is a
contract which is unenforceable against the minor plaintiffs in this
State to be considered determinative of the right." On appeal, the
United States Court of Appeals, Fifth Circuit, affirming the decision of
the district court, had this to say on the matter:

> We recognize that appellants are professional musicians performing as a
> musical combo. Their right to follow this chosen business or occupation free
> from unreasonable governmental interference comes within the liberty and
> property concepts of the Fifth Amendment. . . . The action taken by
> school authorities does not, in our view, interfere with appellants' right to
> continue in their chosen occupation of rock and roll musicians. It is common

78. *Miller* v. *Gillis,* — F. Supp. —.
79. *Ferrell* v. *Dallas Independent School District,* 261 F. Supp. 545.

knowledge that many performers are required to use special attire and makeup, including wigs or hairpieces, for their public appearances. At this stage in appellants' lives school may be more important than their commercial activities. In any event, we do not feel that their business activity is eliminated, as a practical matter because of the school's rules and regulations.[80]

With respect to the Eighth Amendment, it has been held that such board rules as are here considered are not unconstitutional on this ground. In the only case in which violation of the Eighth Amendment was alleged, the court disposed of this issue by saying:

The suggestion that the requirement that student Davis cut his hair in order to attend school is a cruel and inhuman punishment prohibited by the Eighth Amendment is wholly without merit.[81]

Likewise, it has been held that such rules are not violative of rights guaranteed by the Ninth Amendment.[82] In one of the early long-hair cases (1967) a student who had been suspended for failure to comply with a school board rule that stated "Exceptionally long, shaggy hair . . . shall not be worn," brought an action under the Civil Rights Act asking damages due to public embarrassment to the student and his father in the amount of $12,000 for each.[83] He contended that the board's action was in violation of several constitutional amendments, including the Ninth—"The enumeration in the Constitution, of certain rights, shall not be construed to deny or disparage others retained by the people." The court, rejecting this contention, said:

Plaintiff contends that student Davis has a "fundamental personal right of free choice of grooming" and argues that such a right can be found under the reasoning of the *Griswold* case. But if this case is to fall within the ambit of *Griswold*, there must be some specific provision or provisions of the Bill of Rights from which student Davis' right of grooming emanates, or, if it is permissible to follow the approach of Justice Goldberg, the right must at least be "fundamental." The Court is of the opinion that this right is not of such a nature that it can be based on the guarantees provided in the Bill of Rights and, while the right of *privacy* may be so sacred as to be "fundamental," the same certainly cannot be said for the "right of free choice of grooming."

Then, in one of the most recent long-hair cases, one with a background very similar to the *Davis* case just considered, it was also

80. *Ferrell* v. *Dallas Independent School District*, 392 F. (2d) 697.
81. *Davis* v. *Firment*, 269 F. Supp. 524.
82. *Davis* v. *Firment*, 269 F. Supp. 524; *Miller* v. *Gillis*, — F. Supp. —.
83. *Davis* v. *Firment*, 269 F. Supp. 524.

contended that a board rule regulating hair styles constituted a violation of a pupil's rights guaranteed him under the Ninth Amendment.[84] Here the court said:

> I do not agree with plaintiffs' contention that the dress code violates rights under the Ninth Amendment. Justice Goldberg's remarks as to this amendment in the Griswold case were directed to a factual situation concerning the delicate relationship between doctors and their patients in the matter of certain birth control devices. The facts in that case bear no comparison to the one at bar. A similar argument was rejected in the case of *Davis* v. *Firment*, 269 F. Supp. 524 (E.D.La. 1967) in a fact situation very similar to the one here.

With respect to the Fourteenth Amendment the situation is somewhat different. An analysis of all the reported cases dealing with constitutionality of board rules, regulating the style of male pupils' haircuts, indicates that the courts are or have been in disagreement on whether such rules violate Fourteenth Amendment rights. In the earlier cases it was held that such rules were not in violation of the due process clause of the Fourteenth Amendment,[85] and one of the later cases held that where the rule was applied uniformly it did not violate one's rights under the equal protection clause of that same amendment.[86] On the other hand, the later cases, especially those decided after the United States Supreme Court rendered its decision in *Tinker*, have held that such rules are violative of the due process clause[87] or the equal protection clause[88] of the Fourteenth Amendment. The reason for this disagreement seems to be emphasis by the courts; one view places major emphasis upon the rights of pupils, the other, although recognizing the rights of pupils, emphasizes also the rights of school officials. Some courts appear to believe that school officials may exercise any and all powers necessary to control, restrain, and correct pupils that are reasonably necessary for that purpose; and that a rule prohibiting male pupils from wearing long hair is not arbitrary and unreasonable. Others take the view that the authority of school officials must be exercised consistent with constitutional safeguards of the rights of pupils; and the exercise of authority by the

84. *Miller* v. *Gillis*, — F. Supp. —.

85. *Davis* v. *Firment*, 269 F. Supp. 524; *Ferrell* v. *Dallas Independent School District*, 392 F. (2d) 697.

86. *Akin* v. *Board of Education*, 68 Cal. Rptr. 557.

87. *Breen* v. *Kahl*, 296 F. Supp. 702; *Griffin* v. *Tatum*, 300 F. Supp. 60; *Meyers* v. *Arcata Union High School District*, 75 Cal. Rptr. 68.

88. *Miller* v. *Gillis*, — F. Supp. —.

board to regulate hair styles is unconstitutional in the absence of any evidence that the wearing of certain hair styles affects the health of other pupils, violates the rights of other pupils, or disrupts the school to the point of preventing it from realizing the purpose for which it exists. Needless to say, the decision of the United States Supreme Court in *Tinker* has had much to do with framing the prevailing view.

The first case that actually gave attention to the constitutionality of such rules was decided by a federal district court in Louisiana (1967).[89] Here the court said:

> That student Davis was given a constitutionally valid hearing which complied with due process under the Fourteenth Amendment . . . is apparent when we consider the many conferences with school authorities on this hair cut issue which finally culminated in a hearing . . . in the office of the Superintendent . . . with student Davis present and represented by his counsel, before the whole Orleans Parish School Board. . . . Even plaintiffs' counsel does not allege that the hearings surrounding his client's suspension were not fair and impartial. His complaint is that the result . . . is wrong and violates student Davis' right to keep his hair long.

Although there appeared to be evidence that the violation of this rule in the past by other students had caused disruptions and disturbances, there appeared to be none in connection with Davis's actions. The rule appeared to be based on the school officials' belief that disruption would or might occur.

Early the following year (April 1968) the United States Court of Appeals, Fifth Circuit, in a decision in a case with a similar background, cited *Davis,* where it was held the board rule was not unreasonable and arbitrary, and held that here there was no denial of procedural due process, and the rule in question did not violate the Fourteenth Amendment.[90] In a concurring opinion Judge Godbold provides a good example of an attempt to put into proper focus the rights of pupils and those of school officials. He said:

> A school may not stifle dissent because the subject matter is out of favor. Free expression is itself a vital part of the education process. But in measuring the appropriateness and reasonableness of school regulations against the constitutional protections of the First and Fourteenth Amendments the courts must give full credence to the role and purposes of the schools and of the tools with which it is expected that they deal with their problems, and careful recognition to the differences between what are reasonable restraints in the classroom and what are reasonable restraints on the street corner.

89. *Davis* v. *Firment,* 269 F. Supp. 524.
90. *Ferrell* v. *Dallas Independent School District,* 392 F. (2d) 697.

It is well to note that although there had been earlier disturbances in the school resulting from the wearing of long hair, this had ceased. As a result of the board's attempting to apply this rule, there was some disturbance which, the district court pointed out, "could have been deliberately planned by the previously mentioned 'agent' for the boys."[91]

Finally, a state court has held that a board rule of the type under consideration did not violate the equal protection clause of the Fourteenth Amendment where it was shown that it was applied uniformly to all.[92] Here again there appears to have been no disruption of the school, but school officials felt that the wearing of a beard was likely to result in disruption of the educational system.

As was indicated previously, all the later cases—those decided in 1969—have held that board rules regulating hair styles violate the Fourteenth Amendment. Early in 1969 (February 10) a California court ruled that a board rule prohibiting the wearing of "extreme" hair styles was unconstitutional and violated due process because it was so vague that it was unenforceable.[93] It said:

> A "law" violates due process "if it is so vague and standardless that it leaves the public uncertain as to the conducts it prohibits or leaves judges and jurors free to decide, without any legally fixed standards, what is prohibited and what is not in each particular case. . . ." The "dress policy" concerning hair styles in the present case is "vague and standardless." It is not a "law.". . . but a violation means suspension from school. The importance of an education to a child is substantial . . . and the state cannot condition its availability upon compliance with an unconstitutionally vague standard of conduct. . . .
> We recognize that school regulations not unlike the one here involved were upheld in each of the two principal cases which deal with male high school students who were suspended because of the length of their hair . . . [*Ferrell* and *Leonard*]. . . . [A]pparently, none of the students affected . . . challenged the respective regulation upon the ground of vagueness. Therefore, we do not read either decision as constitutional authority for the enforceability of a "policy" which proscribes—but which does not define—"extremes of hair styles."

Then, ten days later, a federal district court in Wisconsin (February 20, 1969) ruled that a board rule regulating hair style violated pupils' rights guaranteed under the due process clause of the Fourteenth

91. *Ferrell* v. *Dallas Independent School District,* 261 F. Supp. 545.
92. *Akin* v. *Board of Education,* 68 Cal. Rptr. 557.
93. *Meyers* v. *Arcata Union High School District,* 75 Cal. Rptr. 68.

Amendment.[94] The court pointed out that the freedom of an adult "to present himself or herself physically to the world in the manner of his or her choice is a highly protected freedom," and if the state were to impair it "in the absence of a subordinating interest in so doing" this would deprive the adult "of liberty without due process of law in violation of the Fourteenth Amendment." It then raised the question whether such an "indignity, intolerable if imposed upon adults," could be imposed on minors, and answered this in the negative. As a result it held that the rule in question violated the Fourteenth Amendment.

In this case defendants justified the rule on two grounds: (1) the wearing of long hair distracts fellow students from their schoolwork, and (2) students who conform to community standards perform better in school than do those who do not. With respect to these two contentions, the court responded that the defendant school officials were relying only on opinion since there was no evidence that long hair acted to distract fellow students, and "no empirical findings" were presented to it regarding the caliber of work performed by those who did and those who did not conform to the norm. Consequently, it ruled that defendants did not meet the criterion of "a substantial burden of justification" to warrant the adoption of the rule which infringed on the pupils' Fourteenth Amendment rights, since it is only when there is "a substantial burden of justification" that a school board may impair the constitutional rights of pupils. From this it seems clear that had the wearing of long hair been shown to be disruptive, the court would have approved the enactment of the rule. This is the first case in which the courts took the position that only the existence of a disruptive effect would warrant the enactment of such a rule. Only four days later, on February 24, the United States Supreme Court, in the *Tinker* case which was considered earlier, ruled that fear of disruption was not sufficient to warrant the enactment of a rule that infringed on one's First Amendment rights.[95] Although this case was concerned with the right of pupils to wear armbands, a form of symbolic expression under the First Amendment, courts were not slow to apply the principles it enunciated to long-hair cases where there was no evidence of disruption of school activities.

Early in May 1969, a federal district court in Alabama, relying

94. *Breen* v. *Kahl*, 296 F. Supp. 702.
95. *Tinker* v. *Des Moines Independent School District*, 89 S. Ct. 733.

heavily on *Breen* and *Tinker,* held that a board rule regulating the hair style of male pupils was unconstitutional under both the equal protection clause and the due process clause of the Fourteenth Amendment.[96] In this case it should be noted that no disruption of the school appeared to result from the wearing of hair in the style forbidden by the rule. "The most that the authorities . . . advanced in support of their regulation is some unidentified fear or apprehension of disturbance if they did not require the boys . . . to keep their hair cut in accordance with their regulation." This, the court said, "is not enough to overcome the constitutional right of this plaintiff and others similarly situated." With respect to the rule's unconstitutionality, the court said:

> This Court recognizes . . . the basic principle that school authorities are possessed with the power and the duty to establish and enforce regulations to deal with activities which may materially and substantially interfere with the requirements of appropriate discipline in the school. However, in this instance the application of this haircut rule to this plaintiff by the State of Alabama—acting through the school authorities . . . constitutes an arbitrary and unreasonable classification; for the reason, the invocation of the rule as a basis for suspending the plaintiff as a student from this public school clearly violates the *equal protection clause* of the Fourteenth Amendment. . . . Furthermore, this Court finds and concludes that the imposition of the rule to this plaintiff to the point of suspension infringes upon fundamental substantive liberties protected by the *due process clause* of the Fourteenth Amendment. . . . Although there is disagreement over the proper analytical framework, there can be little doubt that the constitution protects the freedoms to determine one's hair style and otherwise to govern one's personal appearance. [Emphasis supplied.]

Finally, in the last of the long-hair cases to be reported, a federal district court in Illinois held (September 25, 1969) that a board rule of the type considered violated the equal protection clause of the Fourteenth Amendment.[97] In this case, again, there was no evidence that any disturbance or disruption resulted from wearing the hair in the manner complained of. Although the court here, as in the *Griffin* case just considered, relied heavily on *Breen* and *Tinker,* it should be noted that although it agreed with Judge Doyle in the conclusion reached in the *Breen* case, that the rule violated the Fourteenth Amendment, unlike Judge Doyle it concluded that it violated the equal protection clause rather than the due process clause of the Fourteenth Amend-

---

96. *Griffin* v. *Tatum,* 300 F. Supp. 60.
97. *Miller* v. *Gillis,* — F. Supp. —.

ment. In taking this position, the court pointed out that it was in agreement with Judge Doyle when he said: "I find that to deny a . . . 17 year old twelfth-grade male access to a public high school . . . is to inflict . . . irreparable injury for which no remedy at law is adequate." But, it said later: "While agreeing with the opinion of Judge Doyle . . . I do not consider this issue to be one of denial of due process. Rather, it involves a denial of equal protection of the laws." In arriving at this conclusion, the court reasoned that the rule "creates an arbitrary class of those few people who wish to wear their hair in a manner different from the masses—arbitrary in that the regulation makes the acquisition of all education depend on the length of one's hair." It also pointed out that the rule was arbitrary since it applied to students only and not to teachers, some of whom also wore long hair.

As a result of a study of all the long-hair cases reported, it may be concluded that the courts are in agreement that board rules regulating the length and style of male pupils' hair are not in violation of the First, Fourth, Fifth, Eighth, and Ninth Amendments to the Constitution of the United States. This is relatively unimportant, however, since according to the weight of authority such rules are held to be unconstitutional under the due process and the equal protection clauses of the Fourteenth Amendment, where there is no evidence that disturbance or disruption of school activities resulted from wearing hair in a style prohibited by the rule. Although there is some disagreement on this matter, the later cases are in agreement, and because of the principle laid down by the Supreme Court in *Tinker* to the effect that "undifferentiated fear or apprehension of disturbance is not enough to overcome the right of freedom of expression," it seems clear that these later cases, which rely in part on *Tinker*, constitute the weight of authority on this subject.

From what has been said it must not be concluded that pupil rights in the field of hair style are absolute. Although pupils have the right to wear their hair as they see fit, the board can always step in and control hair styles when this becomes necessary to quell a disturbance resulting therefrom, or when necessary to guarantee the health and rights of other students. In the *Breen* case, in which the court held such a rule violated the Fourteenth Amendment, it implied, at least, that such a rule might be enforced if "the distraction caused by male high school students whose hair length exceeds the Board standard is so aggravated, so frequent, so general, and so persistent that this invasion of their individual freedom by the state is warranted."[98] It also stated that although the freedoms accorded individuals demand a high degree of protection, they may be curtailed or infringed upon if the "attempted justification [for so doing] be in terms of health, physical danger to others, obscenity, or distraction of others from their various pursuits." Likewise, the United States Supreme Court, in speaking of First Amendment rights of pupils, said:

But conduct by the student, in class or out of it, which for any reason— whether it stems from time, place, or type of behavior—materially disrupts classwork or involves substantial disorder or invasion of the rights of others is, of course, not immunized by the constitutional guaranty of freedom of speech.[99]

Although the Court made this comment regarding only one of the freedoms, it would seem that it is equally applicable to all.

One other significant generalization growing out of an analysis of these long-hair cases concerns the extent to which minor pupils possess rights guaranteed them and protected by the United States Constitution. In the past, as will be shown in the section entitled "Pupil rights with respect to procedural due process," it appears that the courts have frequently acted upon the assumption that safeguards against the infringement of individual rights guaranteed by the United States Constitution were placed there solely for the benefit of adults. This is changing and courts are taking the position that the Constitution applies to minors as well as adults.[100] In *Breen,* the federal district court, in a decision rendered February 20, 1969, had this to say regarding the constitutional rights of minors: "It is time to broaden the constitutional community by including within its protections younger people whose sole claim to dignity matches that of their elders."[101] The United States Supreme Court in the *Tinker* case, previously commented upon, took the same position. It said: "Students . . . are 'persons' under our Constitution."[102] Although this was the opinion of the majority of the Court, it is well to remember that

98. *Breen* v. *Kahl,* 296 F. Supp. 702.

99. *Tinker* v. *Des Moines Independent Community School District,* 89 S. Ct. 733.

100. *Breen* v. *Kahl,* 296 F. Supp. 702; *Griffin* v. *Tatum,* 300 F. Supp. 60; *Miller* v. *Gillis,* — F. Supp. —; *Tinker* v. *Des Moines Independent Community School District,* 89 S. Ct. 733.

101. *Breen* v. *Kahl,* 296 F. Supp. 702.

102. *Tinker* v. *Des Moines Independent Community School District,* 89 S. Ct. 733.

Justice Stewart, although concurring in the decision reached, rejected the Court's assumption that "First Amendment rights of children are co-extensive with those of adults," as, of course, did Justice Black in his dissenting opinion. A federal district court in Illinois, in another long-hair case, decided seven months after *Tinker* (September 25, 1969) and relying on it, amplified the Supreme Court's language somewhat when it said:

> Students are persons under the Constitution; they have the same rights and enjoy the same privileges as adults. Children are not second class citizens. The protections of the Constitution are as available to the new-born infant as the most responsible and venerable adult in the nation."[103]

But even before the United States Supreme Court had ruled in *Tinker,* a California court, in a long-hair case, pointed out that the constitution protects the rights of minor pupils as well as those of adult teachers, and said: "Adulthood is not a prerequisite; the state and its educational agencies must heed the rights of all persons, including those of school boys."[104]

Procedural due process and expulsion
As was previously indicated, many courts in the past, as well as many school officials, have appeared to have acted upon the assumption that the safeguards of personal or individual rights guaranteed by the United States Constitution were placed there solely for the benefit of adults; and they have given little attention to the *procedures* they have employed in enforcing rules and regulations against juvenile transgressors. Today this is changing and, as a result of recent court decisions, some legal guidelines appear to be emerging.

Specifically, some of the most significant of these cases concern the meaning of the "due process" clause with respect to the rights of minors who come in conflict with constituted authorities. Although there is a paucity of such cases dealing with the rights of minors as pupils—only one directly in point—there are two cases, both recently decided by the Supreme Court of the United States, dealing with the rights of juveniles when appearing in juvenile courts, from which some deductions or inferences may be drawn regarding pupils.

In one of these cases, decided in 1966, the Court, although basing its decision on a technicality, expressed a philosophy that provides a

103. *Miller* v. *Gillis,* — F. Supp. —.
104. *Meyers* v. *Arcata Union High School District,* 75 Cal. Rptr. 68.

hint as to how it might rule if faced directly with the question of the due-process rights of pupils.[105] In commenting on some juvenile court practices, the Court made some statements that might well be equally applicable to hearings given pupils before suspension or expulsion from school. For example, it stated that "the admonition to function in a 'parental' relationship is not an invitation to procedural arbitrariness." Since schools and teachers function in a "parental" relationship to the pupil, this appears to be pertinent. The Court also noted that "there is no place in our system of law for reaching a result of such tremendous consequences without ceremony—without hearing, without effective assistance of counsel, without a statement of reasons." Since a proceeding to expel a pupil from school can have tremendous consequences, at least as far as the pupil is concerned, this statement appears to be applicable to such a proceeding. Finally, by way of further explanation of its position, the Court said: "We do not mean . . . to indicate that the hearing to be held [by a juvenile court] must conform with all of the requirements of a criminal trial or even of the usual administrative hearing; but we do hold that the hearing must measure up to the essentials of due process and fair treatment."

In the second of the two juvenile-court cases, decided one year later (1967), the Court, noting that "Under our Constitution, the condition of being a boy does not justify a kangaroo court," saw fit to comment on two specific practices that might well have application to proceedings before school boards.[106] Concerning the right of a juvenile to adequate notice of a hearing, it said:

The child and his parents or guardian [are to] be notified in writing, of the specific charge or factual allegations to be considered at the hearing, and such written notice [is to] be given at the earliest practicable time, and in any event sufficiently in advance of the hearing to permit preparation.

With respect to the juvenile's right to be represented by counsel, the Court added:

The juvenile needs the assistance of counsel to cope with problems of law, . . . to insist upon regularity of proceedings, and to ascertain whether he has a defense and to prepare to submit it. The child "requires the guiding hand of counsel at every step in the proceedings against him."

105. *Kent* v. *United States*, 383 U.S. 541, 86 S. Ct. 1045.
106. *Application of Gault*, 87 S. Ct. 1428.

Finally, it should be noted that the Court expressed its concept of due process as follows:

Due process of law is the primary and indispensable foundation of individual freedom. It is the basic and essential term in the compact which defines the rights of the individual and delimits the powers which the State may exercise.

Although the cases just considered do not deal directly with the rights of pupils under the "due process" clause, they have implications therefor. Since the subject has not been ruled on specifically by the United States Supreme Court, these cases are extremely significant, because they come as close to this issue as anything the Court has said. The last case is particularly significant because of one statement: "Neither the Fourteenth Amendment nor the Bill of Rights is for adults alone."[107]

Although, as indicated, the United States Supreme Court has never expressed itself squarely on the question of the general rights of pupils under "due process," a lower federal court—a federal district court in New York—has, in a decision rendered after the Supreme Court's decision in *Kent* but before its decision in *Gault*.[108] This case concerned the constitutionality of a board rule denying to pupils the right to be represented by counsel at a so-called guidance conference. The purpose of the conference was that of "providing an opportunity for parents, teachers, counsellors, supervisors, et al., to plan educationally for the benefit of the child." The court held that the board rule, denying to pupils the right to counsel at a hearing that could result in putting in jeopardy the pupil's liberty and right to attend a public school, and that could place his parents in jeopardy of being proceeded against in a child-neglect action, was unconstitutional. It said:

Fundamental fairness dictates that a student cannot be expelled from a public educational institution without notice and hearing. . . . This principle has been applied to suspension from a state university. . . . Arbitrary explusions and suspensions from the public schools are also constitutionally repugnant on due process grounds. . . . The need for procedural fairness in the state's dealing with college students' rights to public education, where in many instances students are adults and have already attained at least a high school diploma, should be no greater than the need for such fairness when one is dealing with the expulsion or suspension of juveniles

107. *Application of Gault*, 87 S. Ct. 1428.
108. *Madera* v. *Board of Education*, 267 F. Supp. 356.

from the public schools. Such fairness seems especially required when the child involved has yet to acquire even the fundamental educational prerequisites that would allow him to go on to college.

Finally, the court appears to have laid down some guidelines as to what constitutes a legal hearing. It said:

> Defendants have objected that the presence of an attorney would change a "therapeutic" conference into an adversary proceeding, to the great detriment of any children involved. This court does not agree that this is the necessary consequence of having an attorney present. This court does not by this decision say that a full, judicial style hearing with cross-examination of child witnesses and strict application of the rules of evidence is required. There should be latitude for the Board in conducting such a hearing. But this latitude should not be so wide as to preclude the child and parents from exercising their constitutionally protected right to be represented at such a hearing by counsel.

On appeal this decision was reversed, largely on the basis that the trial court misconceived of the nature of the "guidance conference."[109] The court said that the sole authority of such a conference was to decide whether a child should be retained in the school in which he was enrolled or be transferred to another school. It also said that a whole series of conferences, investigations, and hearings must follow before a child is subject to the "serious consequences" which the trial court mentioned. It characterized the conference in question as simply a preliminary investigation and pointed out that no statements made in any preliminary conference, such as this one, could be introduced as evidence in any hearing. In reversing the trial court, the higher court was not critical of the court's reasoning if the conference had been of the type the trial court understood it to be.

The two *Madera* cases must be interpreted to mean that at a preliminary investigation or conference, a pupil cannot complain if he is denied the right to counsel, but that such a denial at a conference that could result in depriving him of his liberty or the right to attend school deprives him of his right to due process.

In any case, these decisions, aside from the two Supreme Court decisions rendered in juvenile court cases—*Kent* and *Gault*—give evidence of judicial concern that school boards accord due process to all pupils whose individual rights are in danger of being impaired. But considered together with *Kent* and *Gault* they raise many questions concerning the nature of hearings that should be accorded pupils by

109. *Madera* v. *Board of Education*, 386 F. (2d) 778.

school boards and school officials, and the legality of all types of disciplinary actions taken against pupils. The main conclusion to which they point is that the Fourteenth Amendment and the Bill of Rights are equally applicable to minor pupils and to adults. Furthermore, whether a pupil's rights are impaired in a particular case must be decided in terms of the facts peculiar to each case. Until such time as the United States Supreme Court has ruled on some of the questions related to the subject of procedural due process as it relates to the minor, the law must remain hazy.

THE LAW AND THE TEACHER

Constitutional rights of the teacher.—Teachers have frequently invoked provisions of the Constitution of the United States—primarily those found in the First, Fifth, and Fourteenth Amendments—in protecting themselves against the consequences of state action. Actions of this type, classified according to subject, usually deal with loyalty oaths, protection against self-incrimination, academic freedom, freedom of speech, freedom of expression, freedom of association, and segregation by race. These will be considered in turn.

Loyalty oaths

In general, the courts are in agreement that there is no constitutional prohibition against board rules or legislative enactments requiring teachers to take oaths of allegiance or loyalty oaths. To the contention of individual teachers and teachers' associations that a statute that singles out teachers and requires them to take an oath is unconstitutional because it degrades teachers and makes them "second-class" citizens, the courts respond negatively. In speaking of the oath as a requirement for employment, the Supreme Court of Oregon, by way of dictum, said:

We . . . hold that the oath required of a teacher is a factor of significance which elevates a teacher's employed status far above that of many lesser state employees. It places the position occupied in close proximity to that of an official of the state, thereby exalting a teachership in terms of professional importance, public respect and legislatively recognized effectiveness.[110]

Likewise, in commenting on the subject of oaths for teachers, the Supreme Court of New Jersey has said:

110. *Monaghan* v. *School District,* 211 Ore. 360, 315 P. (2d) 797.

The aim is not to stifle beliefs as such, but to disqualify for teaching one who, however capacitated otherwise, believes in the objective of overthrow of the government, Federal or state, by force or violence or other unlawful means. . . . One so mentally conditioned is deemed unsuited for the instruction of youth in the schools supported by public funds.[111]

The fact that courts find nothing unconstitutional in the fact that oaths may be required of teachers as a condition of employment does not mean that the constitutionality of all oath laws will be upheld. On several occasions the Supreme Court of the United States has held that the nature or wording of a required oath renders it unacceptable to the Court.[112] Although several of these cases were brought by college professors, the oaths in question were generally applicable to public school teachers as well. Besides, the constitutional issues are identical regardless of the public institution in which the teacher is employed. A number of other cases relating to the constitutionality of teacher oaths have been decided by higher state courts. But because of the position it occupies in the judicial structure or hierarchy, only those cases decided by the United States Supreme Court are considered here.

One of the early oath cases decided by the Supreme Court (1952) concerned the constitutionality of an oath law enacted by the legislature in the State of Oklahoma.[113] Certain faculty members of a state institution of higher education refused to subscribe to the oath affirming they were not presently affiliated with any organization determined to be "subversive" by the United States Attorney General and had not been affiliated with any such organization during the preceding five years. A taxpayer brought this action to enjoin the payment of salaries to the faculty members in question. At issue was the constitutionality of the statute. The Court held that the statute violated the due-process clause of the Fourteenth Amendment, since it was not limited to those who were affiliated with such organizations and who knew them to be subversive. The real significance of this decision is its holding that a state may exclude teachers who refuse to take a statutory oath, but only if, after notice and hearing, the teachers are

111. *Thorp* v. *Board of Trustees*, 79 A. (2d) 462 (N.J.).
112. *Wieman* v. *Updegraff*, 344 U.S. 183, 73 S. Ct. 215; *Crampp* v. *Board of Public Instruction*, 82 S. Ct. 275; *Baggett* v. *Bullitt*, 377 U.S. 360, 84 S. Ct. 1316; *Elfbrandt* v. *Russell*, 384 U.S. 11, 86 S. Ct. 1238; *Keyishian* v. *Board of Regents*, 385 U.S. 589, 87 S. Ct. 675; *Whitehall* v. *Elkins*, 88 S. Ct. 184.
113. *Wieman* v. *Updegraff*, 344 U.S. 183, 73 S. Ct. 215.

shown to have had knowledge that the organizations with which they may be or may have been affiliated are subversive in character.

About the same time (1952) the United States Supreme Court upheld the constitutionality of the much-discussed Feinberg Law in New York.[114] Although not prescribing an oath, this statute made membership in any organization listed by the New York State Board of Regents as subversive—after the organizations were given notice and the opportunity to be heard—*prima facie* evidence of disqualification for employment in public schools. The Court took the position that a teacher's "associates, past and present, as well as . . . [his] conduct may properly be considered in determining fitness and loyalty." Considering the effect of the law on teachers, the Court said:

It is clear that such persons have the right under our law to assemble, speak, think and believe as they will. . . . It is equally clear that they have no right to work for the state in the school system on their own terms. . . . They may work for the school system upon the reasonable terms laid down by the proper authorities. . . . If they do not choose to work on such terms, they are at liberty to retain their beliefs and associations and go elsewhere.

Then, concerning the right of the state to "screen" its teachers, the Court said:

A teacher works in a sensitive area. . . . There he shapes the attitudes of young minds towards the society in which they live. In this, the state has a vital concern. . . . That the school authorities have the right and the duty to screen the officials, teachers, and employees as to their fitness to maintain the integrity of the schools as a part of ordered society, cannot be doubted.

Fifteen years later (1967), when the constitutionality of the Feinberg Law was again the issue before the Supreme Court of the United States, the Court reversed itself.[115] It held that the law was "unconstitutionally vague" and therefore violated the First Amendment. It also based its decision on the fact that it penalized "mere knowing membership without any showing of specific intent to further the unlawful aims" of organizations said to be subversive. With respect to its earlier decisions upholding the law, in the *Adler* case, it said:

To the extent that Adler sustained the provision of the Feinberg Law constituting membership in an organization advocating forceful overthrow of government a ground for disqualification, pertinent constitutional doctrines have since rejected premises upon which that conclusion rested.

114. *Adler* v. *Board of Education*, 342 U.S. 485, 72 S. Ct. 380.
115. *Keyishian* v. *Board of Regents*, 385 U.S. 589, 87 S. Ct. 675.

Adler is therefore not dispositive of the constitutional issues we must decide in this case. . . .

But constitutional doctrine which has emerged since that decision has rejected its major premise. That premise was that public employment, including academic employment, may be conditioned upon the surrender of constitutional rights which could not be abridged by direct government action.

In taking the position it did, the Court was following a position it had taken earlier (1964) in a case coming from the State of Washington,[116] and in (1966) in a case from Arizona.[117] In both of these cases it declared teacher-oath laws unconstitutional. In the *Baggett* case, the Court held two loyalty-oath statutes unconstitutional on the ground that they were vague and violated due process. It arrived at this conclusion because the wording of the statutes was too broad and too uncertain, even though they went into considerable detail in defining "subversive persons." In the *Elfbrandt* case, decided two years later (1966), the Court again held that a statute providing that one who signed a loyalty oath and thereafter became affiliated with the Communist party or any other organization that had for its purpose the overthrow of the state government would be subject to dismissal and criminal prosecution for perjury, was so vague as to be unconstitutional. In so doing, it followed the reasoning in *Baggett.*

The most recent loyalty-oath case decided by the United States Supreme Court (1967) concerned the constitutionality of a Maryland statute.[118] The oath in question required the teacher to swear that he was not "engaged in one way or another in the attempt to overthrow the government of the United States, or the State of Maryland, or any political subdivision of either of them, by force or violence." Another section of the statute defined a subversive as any person who commits or attempts to commit, or advocates, advises, or teaches any person to commit, any act intended to overthrow, destroy, or alter the constitutional form of government of the nation, state, or any of their political subdivisions by revolution, force, or violence. In holding the statute unconstitutional, the Court followed its reasoning in *Baggett, Elfbrandt,* and *Keyishian.* Again, it held the statute was so vague as to be unenforceable, saying:

116. *Baggett* v. *Bullitt,* 377 U.S. 360, 84 S. Ct. 1316.
117. *Elfbrandt* v. *Russell,* 384 U.S. 11, 86 S. Ct. 1238.
118. *Whitehill* v. *Elkins,* 88 S. Ct. 184.

Precision and clarity are not present. Rather we find an overbreadth that makes possible oppressive or capricious application as regimes change. That very threat, as we said in another context . . . may deter the flowering of academic freedom as much as successive suits for perjury.

Like the other oath cases mentioned, we have another classic example of the need for "narrowly drawn" legislation . . . in this sensitive and important First Amendment area.

Without considering loyalty-oath cases decided by higher state courts, the law as laid down by the United States Supreme Court is clear. The legal principle that emerges is that the state may enact teacher-oath laws to protect its public schools and public-school pupils from subversive influences. But if the constitutionality of such laws is to be upheld, they may not exclude from employment those teachers who are known to be members of organizations that have subversive aims unless it can be shown that it was the intent of such persons to assist in the furtherance of the aims of the organizations. In other words, membership in an organization known to be subversive is not alone sufficient grounds for disqualifying a teacher from employment. Then, too, it is well to keep in mind the words of Justice Douglas, who said in the *Keyishian* case, "The oath required must not be so vague and broad as to make men of common intelligence speculate at their peril as to its meaning."[119]

Protection against self-incrimination

Closely related to the question of the rights of teachers with respect to loyalty oaths is that of the right of teachers to plead the Fifth Amendment, which provides that "No person . . . shall be compelled in any criminal case to be a witness against himself." This is because most Fifth-Amendment cases, as well as loyalty-oath cases, have concerned the membership of teachers in certain organizations considered by some to be subversive. In construing the Fifth Amendment, the courts have held that the privilege against self-incrimination applies to hearings before official investigative bodies, both state and federal. Before 1956 courts were divided on the constitutionality of statutes and board rules that provided for the dismissal of teachers who "took" the Fifth Amendment and refused to answer questions asked by investigating committees. That year, the United States Supreme Court

119. *Keyishian v. Board of Regents*, 385 U.S. 589, 87 S. Ct. 675.

appears to have settled the issue.[120] It held that the dismissal of a teacher who refused to testify before a congressional committee, under the authority of a New York City charter provision that provided for the dismissal of public employees under such conditions, was illegal on the ground that it violated the teacher's rights under the "due process" clause of the Fourteenth Amendment. Concerning the teacher's rights under the Fifth Amendment, the court said:

> At the outset we must condemn the practice of imputing a sinister meaning to the exercise of a person's constitutional right under the Fifth Amendment. The right of an accused person to testify . . . was so important to our forefathers that they raised it to the dignity of a constitutional enactment, and it has been recognized as "one of the most valuable prerogatives of the citizen.". . . We have affirmed our faith in this principle [and] . . . we scored the assumption that those who claim this privilege are either criminals or perjurers. The privilege against self-incrimination would be reduced to a hollow mockery if its exercise could be taken as equivalent either to a confession of guilt or conclusive presumption of perjury. . . . [A] witness may have a reasonable fear of prosecution and yet be innocent of any wrongdoing. The privilege serves to protect the innocent who otherwise might be ensnared by ambiguous circumstances.

Two years later, the United States Supreme Court was again faced with a somewhat similar case.[121] Only this time the real issue was not the right of a teacher to refuse to answer questions before an investigating committee but his refusal to answer questions put to him by his superintendent of schools regarding his connections with so-called subversive organizations. The teacher, a tenure teacher in Philadelphia, was called before the superintendent on several occasions and asked about his associations with subversive organizations. On each occasion he refused to answer the superintendent's questions. As a result, the board dismissed him on the ground of "incompetency." The board's proceedings for dismissal were initiated several days after the teacher had refused to testify before a federal investigative committee. The Supreme Court identified the issue as "whether the Federal Constitution prohibits . . . [a teacher's] discharge for statutory 'incompetency' based on his refusal to answer the Superintendent's questions." Here, the Court held against the teacher and in favor of the board. It reasoned that the questions asked by the superintendent were relevant to the question of the teacher's competence or fitness and

120. *Slochower* v. *Board of Higher Education,* 350 U.S. 551, 76 S. Ct. 637.
121. *Beilan* v. *Board of Public Education,* 357 U.S. 399, 78 S. Ct. 1317.

that he had the duty to provide the answers. In arriving at its conclusion, the Court reasoned as follows:

> By engaging in teaching in the public schools, petitioner did not give up his right to freedom of belief, speech or association. He did, however, undertake obligations of frankness, candor and cooperation in answering inquiries made of him by his employing Board examining into his fitness to serve it as a public school teacher.

Some find it difficult to recognize a distinction between the *Slochower* and *Beilan* cases, since in both cases the Court was divided. It is only fair to note that in the *Slochower* case the teacher's competency was not an issue, whereas it was in *Beilan*. From these two cases it may be concluded that a teacher's action in refusing to testify before a federal or state investigative committee inquiring into his association with subversive organizations will be upheld, but his refusal to answer similar questions asked him by school authorities may be considered grounds for dismissal.

Freedom of speech

Another freedom guaranteed to teachers that has inspired litigation is freedom of speech. Although most cases involving freedom of speech have concerned college rather than public-school teachers, the principles of law identified by the courts are equally applicable to both groups. Much of what the United States Supreme Court has had to say on this subject has been said by way of dicta in the cases involving the constitutionality of loyalty oaths and the right of teachers to "take" the Fifth Amendment, which have already been considered. In *Wieman* v. *Updegraff*, [122] in which the Court held an Oklahoma loyalty-oath law unconstitutional, Justice Frankfurter, in a concurring opinion, had the following to say regarding freedom of speech for teachers:

> To regard teachers—in our entire educational system, from the primary grades to the university—as the priests of our democracy is therefore not to indulge in hyperbole. . . . Teachers must fulfill their function by precept and practice, by the very atmosphere which they generate; they must be exemplars of open-mindedness and free inquiry. They cannot carry out their great and noble task if the conditions for the practice of a responsible and critical mind are denied to them. They must have the freedom of responsible inquiry, by thought and action, into the meaning of social and economic ideas, into the checkered history of social and economic dogma. They must be free to sift evanescent doctrine, qualified by time and circumstance, from that restless, enduring process of extending the bounds

122. 344 U.S. 183, 73 S. Ct. 215.

of understanding and wisdom, to assure which the freedoms of thought, of speech, of inquiry, of worship are guaranteed by the Constitution of the United States against infraction by national or State government.

Then the same Court, in 1959, in a case involving the right of a college teacher to refuse to answer questions put to him by a subcommittee of the House Un-American Activities Committee, made the following comments regarding freedom of speech:

Broadly viewed, inquiries cannot be made into the teaching that is pursued in any of our educational institutions. When academic teaching-freedom and its corollary learning-freedom, so essential to the well-being of the Nation, are claimed, this Court will always be on the alert against intrusion by Congress into this constitutionally protected domain. But this does not mean that the Congress is precluded from interrogating a witness merely because he is a teacher. An educational institution is not a constitutional sanctuary from inquiry into matters that may otherwise be within the constitutional legislative domain merely for the reason that inquiry is made of someone within its walls.[123]

From these cases it may be concluded that the courts recognize the importance of freedom of speech for teachers and will "be on the alert against intrusion" by government into this field. But they give little in the nature of guidelines covering specific situations. A few courts have done this, however. In at least two decisions by lower federal courts it has been held that freedom of speech serves to protect teachers engaged in civil rights activities outside school hours. They have held that participation in such activities is no ground for the dismissal of a teacher.[124] Likewise, in California it has been held that the right of freedom of speech extends to the action of a teacher in criticizing the school board that employed him.[125] In this case the teacher, who was also a parent, wrote several letters to the newspapers criticizing the schools and their administration. The question before the court was whether the teacher's conduct constituted unprofessional conduct justifying dismissal. In holding that it did not, the court reasoned that employment as a teacher does not prevent one from criticizing as a parent. In other words, it granted the teacher the right of freedom of speech under the existing circumstances.

In a similar case, the United States Supreme Court (1968) reversed the decision of the Illinois Supreme Court which had upheld the

123. *Barenblatt* v. *United States,* 360 U.S. 109, 79 S. Ct. 1081.
124. *Rackley* v. *School District,* 258 F. Supp. 676; *Williams* v. *Sumter School District,* 255 F. Supp. 397.
125. *Board of Trustees* v. *Owens,* 23 Cal. Rptr. 710.

action of a school board in dismissing a teacher who had written a letter to a newspaper regarding a proposed school tax increase.[126] The letter was critical of the board and the superintendent for the way they had handled past proposals for raising and using school funds. In addition, it contained certain inaccurate statements. With respect to the teacher's right to freedom of speech guaranteed him by the First Amendment, the Court said:

> To the extent that the Illinois Supreme Court's opinion may be read to suggest that teachers may constitutionally be compelled to relinquish the First Amendment rights they would otherwise enjoy as citizens to comment on matters of public interest in connection with the operation of the public schools in which they work, it proceeds on a premise that has been unequivocally rejected in numerous prior decisions of this Court.

In an Ohio case, it has been held that the writings and speech of a teacher, when of a purely private nature, and when not to the detriment of a school system, are of no concern to the school board.[127] In this case a teacher who had been dismissed on the grounds of immorality after it was discovered that he had written two letters to a former student that contained "language which many adults would find gross, vulgar and offensive and which some 18-year-old males would find unsurprising and fairly routine," brought an action for reinstatement. The court, ruling in favor of the teacher and against the board, had the following to say, which has implications for freedom of speech on the part of teachers:

> The private conduct of a man, who is also a teacher, is a proper concern to those who employ him only to the extent it mars him as a teacher, who is also a man. Where his professional achievement is unaffected, where the school community is placed in no jeopardy, his private acts are his own business and may not be the basis of discipline.
> The freedom of action of a public school teacher, like that of all contracting parties, is partly hedged in by the terms of his contract. But there is no term which waives his right to privacy, his right to private communication, free from unwarranted intrusion. That is not to say there may be no intrusion. The limit of a private right is reached where public injury begins.

Although the cases just considered concern themselves with the rights of teachers to freedom of speech in situations outside the classroom, it must not be inferred that teachers do not have the same

---

126. *Pickering v. Board of Education*, 88 S. Ct. 1731.

127. *Jarvella v. Willoughby-Eastlake City School District*, 233 N.E. (2d) 143 (Ohio).

rights with respect to actions taken in the classroom. The same rule applies to both cases. The right of freedom of speech, as already indicated, is not absolute, and a school board may curtail a teacher's actions if they tend to disturb the school, or if they result in public injury. This point was emphasized in a recent case that had its origin in Maryland.[128] In this case, a school board refused to reemploy a nontenure teacher because he allegedly continued to place the book *Brave New World* on a reading list for one of his classes after the parent of a student had complaind and the teacher's principal had notified him of the complaint, in which the parent argued that the book was "assertedly atheistic, obscene, and immoral." The board, in refusing to reemploy the teacher, acted under a statute that provided that a board could refuse to reemploy a nontenure teacher with or without cause and without a hearing, by giving him written notice in June or July. In spite of the statute, the teacher brought this action to compel the board to rehire him. He contended that the action taken by the board violated his constitutional rights since it denied him the right of freedom of speech. The court rejected this, noting that since the board was under no legal obligation to reemploy him, there was no evidence that the teacher's "personal right to free expression was in any way inhibited by the school authorities." With respect to the matter of freedom of speech, it then said:

The right of free speech or expression, like other First Amendment guarantees, is not absolute. Where the abridgement of the abstract right of free speech results from government action taken for the protection of other substantial public rights, no constitutional deprivation will be found to exist. . . . No unconstitutionality results where the right of free speech is reasonably curtailed as a prerequisite to continued government employment.

With respect to a teacher's right to freedom of speech in the classroom, a Wisconsin court has pointed out one limitation.[129] The right appears to exist only where the utterances of the teacher are confined to the field of his specialty. In this case, a tenure teacher who was dismissed by a school board on the statutory ground of "ineffiency and lack of good behavior" brought an action for reinstatement. Primarily, the charges against the teacher grew out of an investigation by the superintendent of the teacher's use of "class time

128. *Parker* v. *Board of Education,* 237 F. Supp. 222.
129. *State* v. *Board of School Directors,* 111 N.W. (2d) 198 (Wis.).

scheduled for instruction in public speaking" for discussing sex matters. Among other things, it was alleged that the teacher discussed "prostitution, sexual activity, pre-marital relations and abortion" with his students during class periods. The court stated the issue as follows: "May a teacher . . . be discharged for his conduct in discussing matters of sex in his classes, which is alleged to transgress 'good behavior' when the teacher has violated no rule promulgated by the superintendent or the board, and has received no advance warning that such conduct was disapproved by the school authorities?" Apparently concluding that the teacher had exceeded the bounds of propriety by discussing a subject foreign to the subject he was employed to teach, the court ruled in favor of the board and approved its dismissal of the teacher. In so doing, the court did not appear to frown upon the teaching of sex by one qualified and certified to teach it. From this it may be concluded that the right of free speech does not give the teacher the right to teach anything and everything he desires. It protects him only when he teaches within the field of his specialty. When he wanders outside his specialty, his actions may well be considered injurious to the school and, therefore, to the public.

From the cases just considered it seems clear that a teacher has the same right to freedom of speech as does any citizen, and he loses no individual rights by becoming a teacher. In this connection it should be remembered that one's right to freedom of speech is not absolute. As indicated in the quotations just cited, the limit of the "right is reached where public injury begins."[130] So long as a teacher does not exercise his right to freedom of speech in such a manner as to injure the school that employs him, the board may not curtail it. Needless to say, this balance between rights of the individual and rights of the public is delicate at best. Each case, therefore, must be considered separately in light of the facts that surround it. Consequently, generalization is difficult.

Freedom of expression

Closely allied to the question of a teacher's right to freedom of speech is his right to freedom of expression. As with freedom of speech, a teacher has the right to freedom of expression regardless of what form it takes, but only so long as his actions are not inimical to the interests

130. *Jarvella* v. *Willoughby-Eastlake City School District*, 233 N.E. (2d) 143 (Ohio).

of his employer—the school district—and not injurious to the public. This was the holding of a California court in a case involving the constitutionality of a school-board rule forbidding the wearing of beards by teachers.[131] The court ruled that the right to wear a beard, although an unnamed right, was still a constitutionally protected "liberty" within the breadth of meaning of the First Amendment. Consequently, it took the position that the board rule was unenforceable in the absence of evidence that wearing beards had an adverse effect on the school—that is, in the absence of evidence that it disrupted or impaired school discipline or the teaching process. Noting that a beard cannot be changed, as can wearing apparel, the court said:

> This is not to say that all male teachers at all high schools, regardless of circumstances may wear beards while teaching in classrooms and that the practice may not be prohibited or otherwise restrained under appropriate circumstances. What we hold is simply that, on the record before us, *with the complete absence of any actual experience at the high school involved as to what the actual adverse effect of the wearing of a beard by a male teacher would be upon the conduct of the educational processes there,* beards as such, on male teachers without regard to their general appearance, their neatness and their cleanliness, cannot constitutionally be banned from the classroom and from the campus.

Finally, speaking more directly to the issue of what is involved in the First Amendment, the court said:

> Personal liberties protected by the due process clause of the 14th Amendment include both fundamental political rights, closely allied with the 1st Amendment right of free speech, such as the right to engage in political activities . . . and the right to associate for the advancement of beliefs and ideas, whether they be political, economic, religious or cultural . . . and fundamental rights of a more private and individual nature, such as the . . . right to marry the person of one's choice.

Freedom of association

The right of freedom of association, mentioned by the court in the quotation just cited, as applied to teachers, has also been the subject of litigation. The rights of teachers with respect to membership in so-called subversive organizations have previously been considered in connection with the discussion regarding loyalty oaths, and the "taking" of the Fifth Amendment. It must be remembered that all these cases were concerned with was the constitutionality of specific stat-

131. *Finot v. Pasadena City Board of Education,* 58 Cal. Rptr. 520.

utes requiring teachers to take oaths or to testify relating to their associations with subversive organizations. These cases were concerned with due process largely and not with the right of teachers to hold membership in organizations they knew to be subversive. In most cases, it appears to be conceded that teachers have no such right. For example, in the *Slochower* case commented on earlier the Supreme Court said:

The State has broad powers in the selection and discharge of its employees, and it may be that proper inquiry would show Slochower's continued employment to be inconsistent with a real interest of the State. But there has been no such inquiry here. We hold that the summary dismissal of appellant violates due process of law.[132]

The rights of teachers to membership in other types of organizations —those not labeled subversive—is different. A few such cases have attracted the attention of the courts. For example, as early as 1917 it was held that teachers did not have the right to join labor unions.[133] Cases of this sort simply illustrate that the question of teacher membership in proscribed organizations is not a new one. (It should be noted that these decisions relating to the right of teachers to join labor unions have been overruled, as will be shown in the section on collective negotiations which follows.)

In general the courts, in considering the question of teachers' freedom of association, take a position similar to that which they take on the question of freedom of speech. They hold that a teacher is free to maintain membership in any group of a political, social, religious, or racial nature he chooses, as long as his membership therein has no adverse effect on the schools and is not injurious to the public. For example, it has been held that a teacher has a right to associate himself with civil-rights organizations and to participate in such civil-rights activities as peaceful picketing and demonstrations outside school hours,[134] and that such action on the part of a teacher is not sufficient grounds for a board to fail to reemploy him or to dismiss him. Furthermore, the Supreme Court of the United States has held that a state law requiring an organization to furnish a list of its members, under penalty, was unconstitutional because it deprived

132. *Slochower* v. *Board of Higher Education,* 350 U.S. 551, 76 S. Ct. 637.

133. *People* v. *City of Chicago,* 116 N.E. 158 (Ill.). See also: *Seattle High School Chapter No. 200 of A.F.T.* v. *Sharples,* 293 P. 994 (Wash.).

134. *Rackley* v. *School District,* 258 F. Supp. 676; *Williams* v. *Sumter School District,* 255 F. Supp. 397; *Johnson* v. *Branch,* 364 F. (2d) 177.

members of their right of freedom of association.[135] And in another decision the same Court held unconstitutional a statute requiring teachers to file yearly a list of organizations in which they held membership.[136]

Segregation by race

Following the Brown decision (1954) declaring that the segregation of pupils by race was unconstitutional, there were sporadic cases that questioned the constitutionality of segregating faculties (teachers). Most of these cases concerned the constitutionality of particular desegregation plans. The main thrust of the problem of segregation of faculties came about ten years after *Brown*. In 1965 the United Sates Court of Appeals, Fourth Circuit, affirmed a decision by a district court which had held that a desegregation plan that omitted any plan for desegregating the faculty did not give sufficient reason for rejecting the plan.[137] The main significance of this case is that, on hearing the appeal, the United States Supreme Court for the first time considered the question of desegregation of faculties.[138] It reversed the decision of the Court of Appeals, and in so doing said: "There is no merit to the suggestion that the relation between faculty allocation on an alleged racial basis and the adequacy of the desegregation plans is entirely speculative."

Less than one month later the Supreme Court discussed in some detail another aspect of segregation of faculty.[139] In this case it considered the right of pupils to sue in cases of staff segregation, saying:

Two theories would give students not yet in desegregated grades sufficient interest to challenge racial allocation of faculty: (1) that racial allocation of faculty denies them equality of educational opportunity without regard to segregation of pupils; and (2) that it renders inadequate an otherwise constitutional pupil desegregation plan soon to be applied to their grades. . . . Petitioners [students] plainly had standing to challenge racial allocation of faculty under the first theory and thus they were improperly denied a hearing on this issue.

In one of the most recent pronouncements on the question of segregation of faculty, made in 1968, the United States Supreme

135. *NAACP* v. *Alabama,* 357 U.S. 449, 78 S. Ct. 1163.
136. *Shelton* v. *Tucker,* 364 U.S. 479, 81 S. Ct. 247.
137. *Bradley* v. *School Board,* 345 F. (2d) 310.
138. *Bradley* v. *School Board,* 86 S. Ct. 224.
139. *Rogers* v. *Paul,* 86 S. Ct. 358.

Court, in a footnote to a decision in which it remanded a case to a district court for further proceedings, directed that court to "take into account [in addition to pupil assignment] . . . any other proposed alternatives . . . in light of considerations respecting other aspects of the school system such as the matter of *faculty* and *staff desegregation* [Emphasis added]."[140]

The United States Court of Appeals, Sixth Circuit, after considering many cases in which the courts have commented upon faculty desegregation, summarized the law as it relates to this problem as follows:

It is inescapably clear . . . that segregation in faculty and staff for some time now has not been, and certainly no longer is, constitutionally permissible and that this fact has been repeatedly stressed in several integration cases which in recent years have come to this court. . . .

. . . Again we repeat . . . : (1) a school board may not continue to operate a segregated teaching staff; (2) such desegregation should have been begun many years ago; (3) the board must take accelerated and positive action to end discriminatory practices in assignment and recruitment; (4) employment, assignment, transfer and discharge of teachers must be free from racial consideration; (5) whenever possible, requests of faculty and staff to transfer into minority situations should be honored; (6) a board should make "all additional positive commitments necessary to bring about some measure of racial balance in the staffs of the individual schools in the very near future"; (7) we are not content at this late date with a plan which contains only a statement of general good intention; and (8) a positive commitment to a reasonable program is necessary. . . . We do not encourage and we may not countenance delay.[141]

Although this is a rather detailed statement of the law, it does not provide many definite guidelines to assist school boards in solving what "may well be the most difficult problem in the desegregation process."[142] The need for such guidelines is made clear in a decision of the United Sates Court of Appeals, Sixth Circuit, where the court said:

No Supreme Court decision, however, has as yet provided a blue print that will achieve faculty desegregation. The United States Office of Education has indicated that, in some affirmative way, school boards must act to correct past discriminatory practices in the assignment of teachers. But its recommendations do not have the force of law; neither does it provide clear guidelines to make easy the job of school boards in dealing with this problem. It will be difficult to eliminate the forcing of people into places and positions because of race and at the same time compulsorily assign a school teacher on the basis of his or her race.[143]

140. *Green* v. *County School Board*, 88 S. Ct. 1689.
141. *Yarbrough* v. *Hulbert-West Memphis School District*, 380 F. (2d) 962.
142. *Kelley* v. *Altheimer, Arkansas Public School District*, 378 F. (2d) 483.
143. *Monroe* v. *Board of Commissioners*, 380 F. (2d) 955.

In the absence of such a blueprint of a faculty desegregation plan by the United States Supreme Court, litigation is bound to continue. Only after the Court speaks can it be known what the law really demands.

Collective negotiations.—The problem of "collective negotiation," sometimes referred to as "collective bargaining" or "professional nego-tiations," as it relates to teachers and the teaching profession, is of such recent date that little is as yet known regarding its legal aspects. Legislation in this field is limited at best. Although it is on the increase, less than one-half of the fifty states have at this time enacted statutes dealing directly with this subject; and of course the National Labor Relations Act, since it exempts employees of the United States, the states, and their political subdivisions, is not pertinent. Likewise, litigation regarding this subject is still limited, and many questions for which answers are being sought have never been the subject of litigation. It is only when a particular subject has been before the courts on numerous occasions and the decisions are in agreement that precedent, which can be relied upon in isolating principles of law, is established; and so generalization is difficult. In spite of this, an analysis of those decisions which are available points to the emer-gence of certain general principles of law that appear to be sound and will, it is believed, be accepted as establishing precedent.

One such principle is that labor legislation applicable to the private sector of the economy is not necessarily applicable to school districts. School districts are agencies of the state, created by the state to carry out a specific function, and therefore have only those powers specifi-cally granted to them and those necessarily implied from those granted. This point was recently made by the Supreme Court of Kansas.[144] This case, which involved school employees other than teachers—maintenance and custodial employees—is without doubt equally applicable to teachers. It raised the question whether a gen-eral statute providing for election of "collective bargaining units" was applicable solely to industry or whether it was equally applicable to school districts. The court, holding that because it did not specifically mention that it was applicable to the state and its various subdivisions it was applicable to industry solely, said: "The general rule . . . that statutes limiting rights or interests will not be interpreted to include the sovereign power [the state] unless it be expressly named or

---

144. *Wichita Public School Employees Union* v. *Smith,* 397 P. (2d) 357 (Kan.).

intended by necessary implication . . . applies to statutes limiting the power to control compensation, terms and conditions of employment." Then, by way of justifying its position, the court said:

> The objects of a political subdivision are governmental—not commercial. It is created for public purposes and has none of the peculiar characteristics of enterprises maintained for private gain. It has no authority to enter into negotiations with labor unions concerning wages, and make such negotiations the basis for final appropriations.

The court was not as adamant as this might sound, since in saying that the statutes relating to collective bargaining must be interpreted as applying to private industry it added these significant words—"at least until such time as the legislature shows a definite intent to include political subdivisions." From this it is evident that the rule is applicable only in the absence of statute and that the statute may change the rule whenever the legislature sees fit to do so.

Then, too, it appears that in the absence of statute forbidding them to do so there is little or no reason to believe that teachers are not free to organize and join professional associations or labor unions or any other such organizations of their own choosing. Although this question appears not to have been litigated recently, authorities seem to agree that in light of current judicial thinking a board rule denying teachers this right would in all probability be held unconstitutional on the ground that it denied teachers the right of freedom of assembly and freedom of association guaranteed them by the First Amendment of the Constitution of the United States. (See the earlier section dealing with freedom of association as it relates to teachers.)

This right of freedom of assembly and freedom of association has one basic limitation. It does *not* confer on teachers the right to strike. At this point labor law as it relates to the private sector of the economy is different from that which relates to public employment. Concerning the right of a union of custodial employees of a school district to use the strike as a weapon for bargaining purposes, the Supreme Court of Illinois said:

> Although this is a case of first impression in a reviewing court of this jurisdiction, it is, so far as we can ascertain, the universal rule that there is no inherent right in municipal employees to strike against their governmental employer, whether Federal, State, or a political subdivision thereof, and that a strike of municipal employees for any purpose is illegal. . . . The underlying basis for the policy against strikes by public employees is the sound and demanding notion that governmental functions may not be

impeded or obstructed, as well as the concept that the profit motive, inherent in the principle of free enterprise, is absent in the governmental function.[145]

Although this case concerned school-district employees other than teachers, the decision would have been the same had teachers been involved. If additional evidence in support of this principle that teachers may not strike is necessary, a decision from Connecticut's highest court in an earlier case (see pp. 473–74) is apropos. Concerning this subject, the court there said:

The government . . . must employ people [teachers] to carry on its tasks. They exercise some part of the sovereignty entrusted to it. They occupy a status entirely different from those who carry on a private enterprise. They serve the public welfare and not a private purpose. To say they can strike is the equivalent of saying that they can deny the authority of government and contravene the public welfare.[146]

Whether the state, acting through the legislative department of government, may change this common-law rule and vest teachers with the right to strike appears never to have been the subject of litigation. Nevertheless the courts have commented on this subject, and although their comments may be considered to be dicta they are worth noting. The Supreme Court of New Hampshire, in holding a teachers' strike illegal, said: "There is no doubt the Legislature is free to provide by statute that public employees may enforce their right to collective bargaining by arbitration or strike."[147] When it is recalled that the authority of the legislature with respect to education is plenary, there seems little doubt that other courts will accept this bit of dictum as law if the question comes before them for decision.

With respect to the legislature's authority in matter related to teachers' strikes, it seems clear that it may implement the common-law rule and provide a penalty for teachers who refuse to obey it and do go out on strike. In New York the legislature did this, and the legality of its action was questioned in the courts.[148] The act in question, known as the Condon-Wadlin Act, prohibited strikes and, for its violation, provided for termination of employment. In this case its constitutionality was questioned on the ground that it provided that

145. *Board of Education* v. *Redding,* 207 N.E. (2d) 427 (Ill.).

146. *Norwalk Teachers Association* v. *Board of Education,* 138 Conn. 269, 83 A. (2d) 482.

147. *City of Manchester* v. *Manchester Teachers Guild,* 131 A. (2d) 59 (N.H.).

148. *Pruzan* v. *Board of Education,* 209 N.Y. S (2d) 966.

one could lose his position without a full hearing, thereby depriving him of due process, and that it also deprived teachers of their constitutional right to free speech, free assembly, and the right to petition the legislature. The court rejected these contentions and upheld the constitutionality of the law.

Closely related to the right to strike is the right to picket. The law in this respect is not as clear as it is with respect to the right to strike. In general, however, it appears that if strikes by teachers are barred, so also is picketing, since the one is practically concomitant with the other. The right to picket was considered in some detail in the Illinois case that also considered the right of school-district employees to strike.[149] In this case, the union contended that picketing is a form of speech and that when conducted in a peaceful manner it is immune from restraint, regulation, and control under the guarantees afforded free speech by the First Amendment. Although not condemning picketing entirely, the court rejected this contention. It said:

However, the premise that peaceful picketing is immune from all regulation and control is a false one. While picketing has an ingredient of communication, the cases make it clear that it cannot be dogmatically equated with constitutionally protected freedom of speech, and that picketing is more than free speech because picket lines are designed to exert, and do exert, influences which produce actions and consequences different from other modes of communication. . . . It is now well established that the latter aspects of picketing may be subject to restrictive regulations . . . and while the specific situation must control decision, it is more than clear that a State may, without abridging the right of free speech, restrain picketing where such curtailment is necessary to protect the public interest and property rights and where the picketing is for a purpose unlawful under State laws or policies, whether such policies have been expressed by the judical organ or the legislature of the state.

This case appears to be authority for the principle of law that peaceful picketing is illegal and may be enjoined if carried out for the purpose of supporting a strike of state employees—teachers—where such a strike is illegal because of either common or decisional law or statutory law.

Another limitation on the right of teachers to join labor unions and professional organizations of their choice should be noted. Membership in such organizations does not carry with it the right to demand recognition by the employing school district or the right to professional negotiation, particularly where such demands are made under

149. *Board of Education* v. *Redding,* 207 N.E. (2d) 427 (Ill.).

threat to strike. On the other hand, there appears to be no good reason why a school board may not recognize such organizations and agree to negotiate with them on such matters as employment, salary, grievances, and working conditions if it wishes to do so, even though there is no statute covering the subject. This, of course, follows from the general principle of law that in the exercise of its discretionary authority a board is the sole judge of how it may act as long as it does not violate any constitutional or statutory provisions. In matters involving discretion, the courts will intervene only if a board acts illegally, fraudulently, arbitrarily, or capriciously. So, in the absence of statute requiring the board to act in a particular manner, it may arrive at its decisions following negotiations if it wishes. A Connecticut court decision made this point. It said:

> If . . . [a board] chooses to negotiate with . . . [a teachers' association or union] with regard to the employment, salaries, grievance procedure and working conditions of its members, there is no statute, public or private, which forbids such negotiations. . . . If the strike threat is absent and the . . . [board] prefers to handle the matter through negotiations with the . . . [association or union] no reason exists why it should not do so.[150]

With respect to negotiations by the board, in Wisconsin, where the statute requires that the board negotiate with teachers' organizations "on questions of wages, hours, and conditions of employment," the Supreme Court has held, by way of dictum, that the content of the curriculum was one subject that the board did not have to negotiate.[151] On the other hand, it held that the board was required to negotiate on the matter of the school calendar.

One other aspect of the problem of "professional negotiations" concerns the authority of the board to include a "closed-shop" or "union-shop" provision in an agreement with a teachers' bargaining group.[152] Litigation on this subject is sparse at best and is not conclusive. A decision by a lower court in Illinois has held that a closed-shop contract between a school board and custodial employees is not

150. *Norwalk Teachers Association* v. *Board of Education,* 138 Conn. 269, 83 A. (2d) 482.

151. *Joint School District* v. *Wisconsin Employment Relations Board,* 155 N.W. (2d) 78 (Wis.).

152. A "closed-shop" agreement provides that the board will employ only those who are members of the union; a "union-shop" agreement provides that all employees must join the union or association within a certain specified time.

legal.[153] (Undoubtedly the court would have held as it did had the contract been with teachers rather than the custodial group.) Not only did it hold the contract illegal, but it went further and denied the right of the legislature to enact a law to the contrary, saying:

> It would not be contended that the legislature of our State could pass a law providing that certain work required by the State or by a board of education should be done only by members of a particular organization. Such a law would be unconstitutional and void on the ground of discrimination. So, a school board, an agency and creature of the State, which could have no more authority in this regard than the State itself, cannot enter into a contract of the nature of the one involved in this case except under the penalty of it being illegal and void for the same reason.

In the Connecticut case, referred to earlier, the court, more by way of dictum, since it was not required to rule on the question, said that "any agreement by the board to hire only union members would clearly be an illegal discrimination."[154] In a Montana case, where the court was faced with the question of the legality of a union-shop provision in a contract between a school board and a teachers' union,[155] the question was whether a contract that provided that all teachers would be required to join the union within a certain specified time and that they would be required to maintain their membership in the union as long as they were employed by the board was legal. Under the agreement, any teacher who failed to maintain his membership in the union would be denied any salary raises to which he might otherwise be entitled. In ruling the contract illegal, the court said:

> We do not pass upon the point whether it would be competent for the Legislature to place such authority in the school trustees. There is respectable authority holding that such action by the Legislature would be unconstitutional. . . .
>
> For the purpose of this case it is sufficient to say that the School Trustees have no authority or power to discriminate between the teachers employed by it as to the amount of salary paid to each because of their membership or lack of membership in a labor union. The School Trustees have no authority to invade that field. As well might it be argued that the Board of School Trustees might provide that the increased salary shall not be allowed to those who do not affiliate with a certain lodge, service club, church or political party.

153. *Chapin* v. *Board of Education,* Circuit Court of Illinois, Peoria County, Case No. 21255.

154. *Norwalk Teachers Association* v. *Board of Education,* 138 Conn. 269, 83 A. (2d) 482.

155. *Benson* v. *School District,* 344 P. (2d) 117 (Mont.).

Because this case was brought by teachers whose status was statutory, since they were on tenure, and since the court used the words "For the purpose of this case" one cannot be absolutely certain whether the court was only denying the legality of the union-shop agreement as it applied here, or whether it was voicing a blanket condemnation.

In Missouri, however, the court has held directly opposite to the decisions of the courts just noted.[156] It took the position that a provision in a local salary schedule to the effect that each teacher must join the "Community Teachers' Association, the National Education Association, the Missouri State Teachers' Association, and the St. Louis Suburban Teachers' Association," and that failure to do so precluded the teacher's receipt of the schedule's benefits and placed him outside the salary schedule, was constitutional. In so holding, the court said: "In the teaching profession, as in all professions, membership in professional organizations tends to increase and improve the interest, knowledge, experience and overall professional competence." As a result, it approved the rule on the ground that it was not only the power but the duty of boards "to adopt rules . . . which seek to elevate the standards of teachers." One can but wonder if the court would have ruled as it did had the rule required membership in local, state, and national teachers' unions. To say the least, the courts do not appear to be in agreement on the question and the law in this respect at least is badly in need of clarification. Therefore one cannot be certain of the legality or illegality of closed-shop and union-shop provisions in agreements between school boards and teacher bargaining groups. The weight of authority, however, seems to indicate that they are illegal.

Again, the law as it relates to the question of whether a school board, in negotiating with a union or professional group, may in the absence of statute recognize it as the exclusive bargaining agent for all teachers is not clear. Although there appears to be no litigation dealing with this point directly, the decision of a New Jersey court in dealing with this matter as it concerns one type of state employee— New Jersey Turnpike Authority employees—may be applicable, since teachers, like Turnpike workers, are state employees.[157] Here the court said:

156. *Magenheim v. Board of Education*, 347 S.W. (2d) 409 (Mo.).
157. *New Jersey Turnpike Authority v. American, etc., Employees*, 83 N.J.S. 389.

It should be emphasized that any one or more representatives may speak only for those employees who chose them. The Turnpike has no right to recognize a representative of only a segment of its employees as agents for all the employees of the Turnpike. Therefore, if five separate groups of Turnpike employees each have a different representative, all five representatives are entitled to recognition.

Whether courts will take this position in cases regarding teachers is yet to be determined. Closely related to this question whether a board may recognize an exclusive bargaining agent for teachers is the question whether, if this is legal, teachers may require a school board to hold an election to determine a majority representative with the right of exclusive representation. Of course, if the matter is covered by statute the statute is decisive, unless its constitutionality is questioned.

Another legal problem growing out of the matter of professional negotiations is the legality of a "dues checkoff" clause in a collective bargaining agreement. Under such a clause, the district would deduct or withhold from teachers' salaries the amount of their dues for membership in unions or professional organizations and pay the sum of such amounts deducted or withheld directly into the organizations' treasuries. In some places this is common practice. In the absence of any statute forbidding it, there appears to be little reason for believing that a district could not do this, provided it is purely voluntary on the part of teachers. If such deductions were made for all teachers, whether they requested it or not, it is believed that it might be questioned, since such a practice would point to the existence of a closed shop, the legality of which is questionable.

Finally, it should be noted that since a board may agree to negotiate with bargaining groups of teachers, it seems clear that if it wished it could agree to arbitrate any differences. But in this connection it is also clear that an agreement to abide by an arbitrator's decision would not be legal, since this would be an example of a board's delegating its discretionary authority—something a board may not do (see pp. 168–71).

One other aspect of the problem of professional negotiations relates to "sanctions." Although sanctions may be considered closely related to strikes, they are different and deserve to be treated separately. In general, sanctions are attempts by local, state, or national associations to discourage teachers from applying for jobs in certain state or local school systems. In New Jersey, when the president of a local teachers' association, whose probationary period was to expire, was not offered a new contract, the resignations of a substantial number of teachers were offered, and the board brought an action seeking an injunction against the local, state, and national teachers' associations which apparently attempted to invoke sanctions.[158] These organizations had sent notices to various teacher-preparation institutions attacking conditions in the school system. These went so far as to threaten teachers who applied and accepted jobs in the system with censure or with expulsion from or denial of membership in the organizations. The teachers' associations defended on the ground of free speech. The court granted the injunction but said it was not restraining the teachers from expressing their opinions regarding the school system, but was barring the "expression and threatening action to accomplish a purpose proscribed by the public policy of the State of New Jersey." The court also noted that the associations were imposing "the extreme sanction of resignation of teachers and the blackballing of the district." It found that "the actions taken . . . constituted a coercive activity designed for the sole purpose of compelling the board to act in accordance with their desires," and that this was a violation of New Jersey's constitution. To the associations' contention that they had the right to discipline their own members, the court retorted that such a procedure was "repugnant to our public policy."

Right of nontenure teachers to reemployment.—In the past it has been held that a school board is entirely free to determine whether or not to renew the yearly contracts of teachers not on tenure and that it need not give a reason for refusing to do so. Since such a teacher's rights are determined by the contract, which covers a particular specified period, the courts have reasoned that his rights do not extend beyond the term of the contract. So he cannot complain that failure to reemploy him is a denial of due process. Recently, however, there have been some court decisions that give cause to reexamine thinking on this matter. It now appears that teachers on yearly contracts do have some rights that may not be violated without infringing upon their right to due process.

The position of courts in earlier times is well illustrated by a decision of the Supreme Court of Illinois rendered in 1917. This resulted from an action brought against the Board of Education of the City of Chicago questioning the legality of a school board's action in

158. *Board of Education* v. *New Jersey Education Association,* 233 A. (2d) 84 (N.J.).

refusing to employ teachers who were members of, or affiliated with, a teachers' union (pp. 446–47). The court said:

The board has the absolute right to decline to employ or to re-employ any applicant for any reason or for no reason at all. . . . It is no infringement upon the constitutional rights of any one for the board to decline to employ him as a teacher in the schools. . . . The board is not bound to give any reason for its action. It is free to contract with whomsoever it chooses.[159]

It is significant that this case was decided on the basis of contract law rather than individual rights.

As was stated, this decision is an old one—1917. Today things are changing. Although the Fourteenth Amendment to the Constitution has, since its passage, stood as a bulwark against violations of due process by the state, it is only recently that teachers and pupils have invoked its protection to any great extent. Currently, many cases which at an earlier date would have questioned the legality of a school board's action on the ground of "reasonableness" are now questioning it on the ground that it violates due process. Needless to say, many of these are federal cases. Before proceeding, it might be well to point out how matters of state action involving teachers sometimes end up in the federal courts. It is because of rights granted by the federal constitution and federal statutes. The Fourteenth Amendment provides that "no State shall make or enforce any law which shall abridge the privileges or immunities of citizens of the United States; nor shall any State deprive any person of life, liberty, or property without due process of law; nor deny to any person within its jurisdiction the equal protection of the laws."

Then, too, some cases are brought pursuant to the provision of a federal statute—the Civil Rights Act of 1871—which reads as follows:

Every person who, under color of any statute, ordinance, regulation, custom or usage, of any State or Territory, subjects, or causes to be subject, any citizen of the United States or other person within the jurisdiction thereof to the deprivation of any rights, privileges, or immunities secured by the Constitution and laws, shall be liable to the party injured in an action at law, suit in equity, or other proper proceeding for redress.

In one of the early cases in which a nontenure teacher sought protection under the Civil Rights Act, complaint was based upon her discharge.[160] A New York teacher who exercised her option to serve on

159. *People v. City of Chicago,* 278 Ill. 318, 116 N.E. 158.
160. *Bomar v. Keyes,* 162 F. (2d) 136.

a federal grand jury, which necessitated her absence from classes for about four weeks, was discharged. She appealed to the Commissioner of Education for reinstatement, and he dismissed her appeal on the ground that since she had not attained tenure her dismissal was not subject to review. She then appealed to a federal district court, alleging a violation of the Civil Rights Act. When it too ruled against her she appealed to a United States Circuit Court of Appeals, which ruled in her favor. Judge Learned Hand, speaking for the majority, stated that if she was discharged solely for the reason alleged, she was entitled to a review on the question she raised regardless of the fact that she was not on tenure. He took the position that she had "an expectancy of continued employment" and could not be discharged in violation of her rights guaranteed by the United States Constitution, and a trial was required.

Just recently a rash of cases have appeared concerning nontenure teachers whose contracts have not been renewed. The most important of these will be considered chronologically and then an attempt will be made to generalize.

The first of these cases was decided by a United States Court of Appeals in 1965.[161] This was an appeal from the decision of a district court in Maryland which upheld a school board's action in failing to renew a contract of a nontenure teacher. The teacher raised a number of issues involving infringement of rights under the First, Fourth, and Fourteenth Amendments. He contended among other things that part of the reason his contract was not renewed was that he had instructed his pupils to read *Brave New World*, which, he said, had been proscribed by the board, thereby violating his right of freedom of speech. The court, without going into the constitutional area, ruled in favor of the board, basing its ruling on the fact "his engagement was simply probationary and that 'either of the parties to this contract may terminate it at the end of the first or second year by giving notice in writing to the other during the month of June or July.'" Nothing was said about any right of expectancy.

Almost exactly two years later, in 1967, in a case brought by a probationary teacher whose contract was not renewed, the Supreme Court of Wisconsin took the opposite view. This case involved the question whether a nontenure teacher could be denied reemployment

161. *Parker* v. *Board of Education*, 348 F. (2d) 464.

because of his activities as chairman of a teachers' association welfare committee without violating his constitutional rights.[162] Although the question was not posed directly, the court saw fit to consider it and answered in the negative, holding that a statute that prohibited school boards from encouraging or discouraging membership in any labor organization or association and which gave teachers the right to refrain from joining such organizations or associations modified an earlier statute which permitted school boards to refuse to rehire teachers "on any ground or for no reason at all." The court said, "A school board may not terminate a teacher's contract because the teacher has been engaging in labor activities."

One year later, in 1968, the Supreme Court of the United States was faced with the question of the right of a school board to dismiss a teacher for writing a letter to a newspaper in which he was critical of the board and which contained certain false statements.[163] In reversing the decision of the Illinois Supreme Court, which had ruled in favor of the board, the court took the position that the interest of school authorities "in limiting teachers' opportunities to contribute to public debate is not significantly greater than its interest in limiting a similar contribution by any member of the general public." Then, getting to the crux of the matter—whether the board's action infringed upon the teacher's rights under the First and Fourteenth Amendments—the Court said:

> To the extent that the Illinois Supreme Court's opinion may be read to suggest that teachers may constitutionally be compelled to relinquish the First Amendment rights they would otherwise enjoy as citizens to comment on matters of public interest in connection with the operation of the public schools in which they work, it proceeds on a premise that has been unequivocally rejected in numerous prior decisions of this Court. . . . "[T]he theory that public employment which may be denied altogether may be subjected to any conditions, regardless of how unreasonable, has been uniformly rejected."

Shortly after this decision by the United States Supreme Court another case involving the constitutional rights of teachers was handed down by the Court of Appeals, Seventh Circuit.[164] This was an action brought by two teachers in a Chicago suburban school district

162. *Muskego-Norway Consolidated Schools* v. *Wisconsin Employment Relations Board,* 151 N.W. (2d) 617 (Wis.).

163. *Pickering* v. *Board of Education,* 88 S. Ct. 1731.

164. *McLaughlin* v. *Tilendis,* 398 F. (2d) 287.

under the Civil Rights Act of 1871 in which they sought damages of $100,000 from the superintendent and the members of the board. One had been discharged before completing his second year of probationary service. The other failed to receive a new contract at the end of two years of service. They contended that this was the result of their having been associated with the American Federation of Teachers, AFL-CIO. This was an appeal of a decision by the federal district court, which dismissed their action on the ground the "plaintiffs had no First Amendment rights to join or form a labor union, so there was no jurisdiction under the Civil Rights Act." The Court of Appeals reversed the district court's decision and remanded the case for trial. It said:

> Illinois has not prohibited membership in a teachers' union, and defendants do not claim that the individual plaintiffs engaged in any illegal strikes or picketing. Moreover, collective bargaining contracts between teachers' unions and school districts are not against the public policy of Illinois. . . . These very defendants have not adopted any rule, regulation or resolution forbidding union membership. Accordingly no paramount public interest of Illinois has warranted the limiting of . . . [these teachers'] right of association.

It also said:

> It is settled that teachers have the right of free association, and unjustified interference with teachers' associational freedom violates the Due Process clause of the Fourteenth Amendment.

It is interesting to note that this court, taking judicial cognizance of the Supreme Court's decision in *Pickering,* handed down earlier that same month, said: "If teachers can engage in scathing and partially inaccurate public criticism of their school board, surely they can form and take part in associations to further what they consider to be their well-being."

This case, it may be noticed, protects associational freedom only and leaves unanswered the question, "What other freedoms do teachers have that are protected by the due-process clause?"

A similar complaint came out of New York.[165] It was alleged that a high-school teacher had been denied tenure solely because he had exercised his constitutional rights by engaging in the activities of a teachers' union. This, according to the court, constituted a cause of action.

165. *Albaum* v. *Carey,* 283 F. Supp. 3.

More recently (1969) a number of cases of the type just considered have been before the courts. The United States Court of Appeals, Tenth Circuit, in a case appealed from the United States District Court, District of Colorado, was faced with the question of the right of a college board of trustees to refuse to renew the contract of a nontenure professor who had served under two annual contracts.[166] Although this case dealt with the rights of a professor in a state-supported college, it appears to be equally applicable to a public-school teacher. Plaintiff contended that the board's action stemmed from his constitutionally protected rights under the First and Fourteenth Amendments. The board defended its action on the basis of a statute that gave it the power to "appoint or employ, discharge and suspend, contract and fail to renew contracts" of employees. The plaintiff averred that he was a pacifist by religious conviction and that it was because of his oral and written expression of his views that his reappointment was denied. He contended that he had an "expectancy of continued employment" and that the board's action constituted "an interest which the law will protect against invasion by acts in violation of the Civil Rights Act." The court, taking cognizance of *Pickering*, said: "The principle stated teaches that public employment may be denied altogether subject, however, to the restriction that unreasonable conditions may not be imposed upon the granting of public employment." The court upheld the action of the board, thereby appearing to rely on contractual status rather than constitutional rights. It said:

> We think . . . [the statute granting authority to the board] precludes Jones from having the relief he seeks in this proceeding. His claimed interest must find its source in his expired appointment which constituted whatever contract existed. The provision . . . acknowledged became a part of any contract that may have existed between him and the college.

This provision, it noted, "specifically denies an expectancy to continued employment; therefore, absent an expectancy there could be no interest." Then it added this: "One has no constitutional right to a 'remedy' against the lawful conduct of another."

In a dissenting opinion, Judge Seth made several significant points. First, he stated that the majority's decision said that in the absence of tenure "the board has unlimited power to discharge teachers." (Perhaps this is the real significance of this case—it applies only where

166. *Jones* v. *Hopper*, 410 F. (2d) 1323.

there is no statutory provision for tenure. Had there been a tenure law the court might have recognized the "right of expectancy" and held differently.) Regarding the statutory authority of the board, Judge Seth said: "No matter how broad their discretion may be by statute or by custom it cannot be used to deprive teachers of their constitutional rights." Finally, in criticism of the majority opinion, he said:

> It would appear that a tenure requirement as a basis for asserting a cause of action has long been abandoned. . . . Teachers of whatever status do not give up First Amendment rights by reason of their employment. Pickering expressly so holds. Non-tenure teachers cannot be held to have more limited constitutional rights than do others. . . . Tenure is not the status which gives rise to the rights to be protected.

This dissenting opinion appears to be more in line with most present cases than does the majority decision.

Just one week after *Jones* was decided, the Court of Appeals of Michigan rendered a similar decision.[167] In this case a probationary teacher, whose work had been rated satisfactory for two years, and who was denied a contract for the succeeding year, sought a writ of mandamus to compel the board to reemploy him. The statute provided that after a probationary teacher had completed two years of work with a satisfactory rating he should be employed continuously. Another statute provided that a probationary teacher should be employed for the following year unless the board notified him in writing at least 60 days before the end of the school year that his services would be discontinued. In this case the defendant had served such notice on time. The court interpreted the law as not imposing a duty on the board to reemploy one who received a satisfactory rating, as contended by plaintiff, and refused to grant the writ of mandamus, saying:

> This case does not involve discharge or demotion. It is a case of not rehiring plaintiff which the board could decide to do, and its action is controlling on the facts of the case. We find it unnecessary to discuss the constitutional issues raised by plaintiff.

Just two days later, the Court of Appeals of New York held that a letter, addressed to administrators and teachers in the school district, which criticized the school administrators was within the free speech protection laid down in *Pickering*.[168] Although the letter may not have been discreet and may have contained some fallacies, the court held

---

167. *Munro* v. *Elk Rapids Schools,* 169 N.W. (2d) 527 (Mich.).
168. *Puentes* v. *Board of Education,* 250 N.E. (2d) 232 (N.Y.).

that the board was without authority to suspend its writer—a teacher and union official—without pay, since it constituted a deprivation of the teacher's rights guaranteed him by the First Amendment.

Another New York case was decided somewhat differently by a trial court.[169] In this case a nontenure teacher who had acted as president of her teachers' association and as such had engaged in collective bargaining was denied reemployment by the board. She lodged a complaint with the Public Employment Relations Board, alleging that the board's refusal to reemploy her was an act of reprisal because of her organizational activities. A hearing was granted by the board (PERB) on the complaint, and it ordered the school board to reemploy her. When the board refused, this action was brought to compel it to carry out PERB's order. The school board contended that the statute permitted it to discontinue the services of a probationary teacher at any time, without giving its reasons for doing so. The plaintiff took the position that the subsequently enacted Taylor Law, which granted teachers the right to organize and which created PERB with the authority to settle disputes, modified the other statute "to the extent that such a denial of tenure must not be in violation of a teacher's right to organize, join, and participate in employee negotiations." The court rejected this on the ground that had the legislature intended such consequences it could have so provided. Since it did not, the court ruled that the board's action in not reemploying the teacher could not be challenged. It also held that the board could not be compelled to state its reasons because of statute. How the court would have held had the question of the teacher's constitutional rights been raised can only be surmised.

Then within the past year the Court of Appeals, Fifth Circuit, had something to say on denying tenure to teachers.[170] This was an action brought by two teachers in Dade County, Florida, who were in the third year of probationary service and were denied a contract for the ensuing year, which would have given them tenure status. They filed a complaint alleging that one was denied tenure because of activity in the local teachers' association, and the other because she advanced demands for campus freedom in her classes. The United States District Court, Southern District of Florida, dismissed the complaint without a trial, and this appeal was taken. The court here remanded

169. *Helsby* v. *Board of Education,* 301 N.Y.S. (2d) 383.
170. *Pred* v. *Board of Public Instruction,* 415 F. (2d) 851.

the case for trial. It quoted extensively from United States Supreme Court decisions in answering the board's argument to the effect that no one had a right to public employment and concluded by saying: "Equally unpersuasive is the argument that since there is no right to public employment, school officials only allowed these teacher contracts to expire—and thus they cannot be liable for a violation of any rights protected by . . . [the Civil Rights Act]." By way of clarifying the issue it said:

The right sought to be vindicated is not a contractual one nor could it be since no right to reemployment existed. What is at stake is the vindication of constitutional rights—the right not to be punished by the state or to suffer retaliation at its hand because a public employee persists in the exercise of first amendment rights.

Then relying on the *Pickering* decision, it stated that the problem is one of balance between the interest of the teacher and the interest of the state. In remanding the case, the court said:

On the facts must rest the determination of whether the denial of a continuing contract was (*a*) a reprisal for these actions in expressions of idea, thoughts, or association rather than permissible non-discriminatory professional evaluation, and, if so, (*b*) whether under the circumstances in relation to the reasonable demands of a system of organized responsible learning these actions were protected. On a finding of (*a*) and (*b*) the remedy (*c*) might well also depend on all of the facts.

Early in 1970 two cases that presented the clear-cut issue of the due-process procedural rights of nontenure teachers were decided by the United States District Court, Western District, of Wisconsin.[171] One case challenged the right of a school district to refuse to retain two public-school teachers.[172] In this case the district contended that the teachers had no right to have their contracts renewed under Wisconsin law, which permits boards to refuse to renew nontenure teachers' contracts "for any cause or no cause at all." In taking this position, the board admitted it could not refuse to renew a contract if it based its action on race, religion, or the exercise of First Amendment rights. But in this case there was no such allegation. With this the court was in agreement, but it expanded on the board's contention and stated that a nontenure teacher's rights are not limited to protection afforded by the First Amendment. Speaking of a teacher's due-

171. *Gouge* v. *Joint School District,* 310 F. Supp. 984; *Roth* v. *Board of Regents of State Colleges,* 310 F. Supp. 972.
172. *Gouge* v. *Joint School District,* 310 F. Supp. 984.

process procedural rights, it said: "A teacher in a public elementary or secondary school is protected by the due process clause of the Fourteenth Amendment against a nonrenewal decision which is wholly unreasonable."

The court then noted that in this case there was the issue of "identifying the reason for dismissal," since otherwise there was no way to determine if there was a factual basis for it. Although the board did not attempt to conceal the reasons for its action, it did not explain all of them completely. As a result the court was unable to determine whether the board had acted arbitrarily. In conclusion, the court made it clear that a basic principle is that a nontenure teacher has the basic due-process right to prove that a board's refusal to renew his contract is arbitrary.

The second case, although involving the right of a college professor to reemployment, is equally applicable to public-school teachers. It was brought by an assistant professor at Wisconsin State University at Oshkosh, who, after teaching for one year, was denied reemployment by the Board of Regents. It gave him no reason for its action and offered him no hearing. He contended that the reason "was to retaliate against him for his expressions of opinion in the exercise of his freedom guaranteed by the First and Fourteenth Amendments."[173] Further, he contended that the board's action "has caused and will cause damage to . . . [his] professional reputation and standing." The court, reasoning as it did in the *Gouge* case, ruled that the board must give him its reasons and a hearing or must reinstate him. In arriving at its decision the court differentiated between the rights of tenure and nontenure professors. Noting that "the concept of tenure enjoys a rational basis," it stated that it is only fair that the employing agency be given a reasonable time in which to observe the employee and that during that time the employer should have considerable latitude in deciding whether he should be retained, and added:

To expose him to non-retention on a basis wholly without reason, whether subtle or otherwise, is unjust. . . .
. . . under the due process clause of the Fourteenth Amendment the decision not to retain a professor employed by a state university may not rest on a basis wholly unsupported in fact, or on a basis wholly without reason. The standard is considered to be less severe than the standard of "cause" as the latter has been applied to professors on tenure.

173. *Roth* v. *Board of Regents of State Colleges,* 310 F. Supp. 972.

Although the rule laid down by the court is both clear and sound, the difficulty in applying it—in determining what is "less severe"—is self-evident.

After having considered the most significant cases pertinent to the retention of nontenure teachers, the following generalizations appear to be warranted. A teacher, like any other citizen, is protected by the Bill of Rights and the Fourteenth Amendment to the Constitution of the United States. The rights of teachers in states that have no tenure statutes appear to be the same as those of probationary teachers— those that have not attained tenure status—in those states that do have tenure statutes. Both generally serve on year-to-year contracts. To this rule there may be one exception. It might be held that only probationary teachers, not teachers on annual contracts, have the "right of expectancy," since they may expect tenure status later. Although in the Colorado case involving the college professor it was held that no "right of expectancy" existed where the plaintiff had no right to tenure, it may be significant that one judge, in a dissenting opinion, said: "A tenure requirement as a basis for asserting a cause of action has long been abandoned. . . . Teachers of whatever status do not give up First Amendment rights."

In spite of some decisions to the contrary, the weight of authority is to the effect that the Fourteenth Amendment due-process clause protects a teacher against a board refusal to rehire him, even if the statute gives the board such right for any reason or for no reason at all.

In light of the most recent cases—the Wisconsin cases—the due-process clause protects a teacher from being refused reemployment by a school board, unless its reason or reasons are given. This follows from the fact that since the teacher may challenge his not being reemployed on the ground that the board's action has no basis in fact or is unreasonable, he cannot take advantage of his rights unless he knows the reason for the board's action.

Although, as stated, courts are in disagreement concerning the right of the nontenure teacher to reemployment under the due-process clause, a noticeable trend favoring the teacher appears to be emerging.

Index

710 *The Courts and the Public Schools*

of expression, 675–76; freedom of speech, 671–75; hair styles of, 659; as *in loco parentis,* 565, 605, 610, 662; liability of, 474–75, 610–15; life insurance for, 166–67; and loyalty oaths, 665–69; marriage of, 471–73, 492–96; negligence of, 399, 474–75; nontenure, 688–98; pensions and retirement systems, 509–18; political activity of, 490–92; probationary, 694–98; protection against self-incrimination, 669–71; qualifications of, 437, 446–48; reassignment of, 469–71, 489–90, 502–3; reemployment of, 447, 688–98; residence of, 96, 110, 482, 483; rights of, 468–74, 665–98; right of collective negotiations, 680–88; right to join unions, 681, 683–84; right to notice and hearing, 497–500; right to picket, 683; right to punish, 610–15; right to strike, 473–74, 681–83; salaries, 108, 448, 463–66, 470–71, 510–18, 687; segregation of, 678–80; sex of, 447–48; tenure of, 6–8, 467–73, 688–98; unions, 446, 473–74

Teachers' colleges, and practice teaching, 157–59

Teachers' associations. *See* Labor unions

Tenure: lack of, 688–98; statutes, 6–8, 467–73

Terms, of school officers, 130–32, 137–39

Textbooks: provision of to parochial and private schools, 50, 637–38, 639; uniformity of, 25, 29

Time limits: on action, 188–89; on building contracts, 327; on suspension, 607; on taxation, 261–62

Tinker v. *Des Moines Independent Community School District,* 650, 654–55, 657–61

Title, to public office, attacks upon, 142–44

Torts, nonliability of school districts for, 393–412, 618–22

Transfer of pupils, 45–46, 534–37, 541, 568

Transportation: authority to provide, 550–52; contracts for, 552–53; free,

34; liability of drivers, 557–61; need for insurance, 561–63; nonliability for accidents, 557–58, 618; provision of to private schools, 47–52, 637–38, 639; routes for, 554–57

Trespass, liability for, 405–10

Tuition fees: for nonresident pupils, 276, 525–38; for resident pupils, 544–46

Tutors, right to hire, 520–21

Ultra vires, doctrine of, 145, 160, 206–9, 215–28, 335, 429–35, 563

Unemployment compensation, 5

Uniformity: of school systems, 32–35; of textbooks, 25, 29

Uniforms, school, 569

Unions. *See* Labor unions

Union-shop contracts, 684–86

Use of property: as ratification of contract, 338–39; as waiver of defects, 341

Vaccination: authority of board of health to require, 578–83; authority of school board to require, 574–78, 583–86; form of, 584; refusal of, 585–86

Vagueness: of school board rules, 656; of statutes, 667, 668–69

Validating legislation, 36–42

Volunteers: school officers as, 123; uncertified teachers as, 440

Votes: creation of school district by, 61; number necessary for passage of measures, 181–82. *See also* Quorum

Warrants: liability for, 300–302, 423, 429; limit on, 307; nature of, 299–302

Welfare, public: education as threat to, 44; importance of education to, 23–26, 42; and police power of states, 12–19, 22

Winslow, Judge (Supreme Court of Wisconsin), 247

Workmen's Compensation Act, 167

Workmen's compensation insurance, 167–68, 400

Zoning, of school districts, 625–31